T0350522

Asset-Liability and Liquidity Management

The Wiley Finance series contains books written specifically for finance and investment professionals as well as sophisticated individual investors and their financial advisors. Book topics range from portfolio management to e-commerce, risk management, financial engineering, valuation and financial instrument analysis, as well as much more. For a list of available titles, visit our Web site at www.WileyFinance.com.

Founded in 1807, John Wiley & Sons is the oldest independent publishing company in the United States. With offices in North America, Europe, Australia and Asia, Wiley is globally committed to developing and marketing print and electronic products and services for our customers' professional and personal knowledge and understanding.

Asset-Liability and Liquidity Management

POOYA FARAHVASH

WILEY

Published by John Wiley & Sons, Inc., Hoboken, New Jersey.

Published simultaneously in Canada.

For general information on our other products and services or for technical support, please contact our Customer Care Department within the United States at (800) 762-2974, outside the United States at (317) 572-3993 or fax (317) 572-4002.

Wiley publishes in a variety of print and electronic formats and by print-on-demand. Some material included with standard print versions of this book may not be included in e-books or in print-on-demand. If this book refers to media such as a CD or DVD that is not included in the version you purchased, you may download this material at http://booksupport.wiley.com. For more information about Wiley products, visit www.wiley.com.

Library of Congress Cataloging-in-Publication Data:

Names: Farahvash, Pooya, author.
Title: Asset-liability and liquidity management / Pooya Farahvash.
Description: First Edition. | Hoboken : Wiley, 2020. | Series: Wiley
    finance series | Includes index.
Identifiers: LCCN 2020005300 (print) | LCCN 2020005301 (ebook) | ISBN
    9781119701880 (hardback) | ISBN 9781119701927 (adobe pdf) | ISBN
    9781119701910 (epub)
Subjects: LCSH: Asset-liability management. | Bank liquidity.
Classification: LCC HG1615.25 .F367 2020 (print) | LCC HG1615.25 (ebook)
    | DDC 332.1068/1—dc23
LC record available at https://lccn.loc.gov/2020005300
LC ebook record available at https://lccn.loc.gov/2020005301

Cover Design: Wiley
Cover Image: © fractal-an / Shutterstock

Printed in the United States of America

SKY10070181_032124

To my parents: Mahin and Ahmad

Contents

CHAPTER 2
Valuation: Fundamentals of Fixed-Income and Non-Maturing
Products   **115**

About the Author

Pooya Farahvash is vice president of Treasury Modeling and Analytics at American Express Company, overseeing the development of models used in ALM, liquidity risk management, stress testing, and deposit products. He previously worked at investment bank Jefferies in liquidity risk management and at CIT Group in asset-liability and capital management. His experience in the banking industry is focused in treasury department activities, specifically in the areas of interest rate risk, liquidity risk, asset-liability management, deposit modeling, and economic capital. Dr. Farahvash is also an adjunct instructor at New York University, teaching analytical courses. He received both his PhD degree in Industrial and Systems Engineering and MS degree in Statistics from Rutgers University, New Jersey. He currently lives in New York City.

Preface

In recent years, use of quantitative methods in asset-liability management (ALM) has increased significantly, particularly among medium- to large-size banks and insurance companies. This partly reflects the importance of effective balance sheet planning and managing related risks in achieving earnings and equity valuation targets. Traditionally and in the past, balance sheet management efforts were mainly focused on funding activities to ensure that the bank's assets are properly funded at the lowest cost possible. Lack of risk awareness, however, was always a major weakness in this approach and recent history has shown that poorly managed balance sheets can lead to catastrophic events for banks. In one view, the failures of several banks and investment banks during the financial crisis of 2007–2009 were partially due to ineffective balance sheet management practices. Newer banking strategies rely on ALM techniques that are based on accurate and precise calculations to evaluate the impact of various risk factors on earnings and value of the firm. These metrics are designed to assess the efficiency of the balance sheet management efforts while taking various risks, such as interest rate risk, into consideration.

This book presents the fundamentals of asset-liability management in banking. During my years of practice as an ALM analyst in various banks, I generally felt that there was a need for a book that provides a comprehensive view of ALM as it is exercised in practice. The goal of this book is to present the fundamentals and methodologies that are commonly used by banks in their ALM analysis. The book is written for professionals who are active in asset-liability management, financial risk management, and treasury analytics. This book can also be used as the main textbook for a graduate-level course in the aforementioned areas.

The main materials in the book are organized in three parts. The first part, consisting of Chapters 1 through 7, is focused on the interest rate concept and related topics, interest rate modeling methods, and valuation of financial instruments. Many ALM analyses require valuation of positions on the balance sheet of a bank, as well as valuation of off-balance-sheet exposures, such as derivative contracts. Materials in this part provide the fundamentals for valuation of common financial instruments, including fixed- and floating-rate loans, fixed-income securities such as bonds, equity securities, mortgage-backed and asset-backed securities, and callable or putable bonds. Valuations of common derivative products such as stock options, future options, interest rate swaps, interest rate forwards, interest rate caps and floors, and swaptions are also discussed. Since some topics reviewed in the interest rate models chapter require knowledge of valuation methods, that chapter is placed after the fundamentals of valuation are explained.

The second part of the book, consisting of Chapters 8, 9, and 10, is focused on two fundamental ALM metrics: economic value of equity and net interest income, and their related scenario analysis. The topics discussed in this part rely on the materials explained in Part One.

The third part of the book, consisting of Chapters 11 and 12, covers two topics that are closely related to ALM: liquidity risk and funds transfer pricing. Liquidity risk is the risk factor behind one of the gap measurements that the ALM process aims to optimize and funds transfer pricing is an internal allocation method of the net interest income. There are some practitioners who view liquidity risk management and funds transfer pricing as separate and independent topics from ALM. Recent trends, however, indicate that banks are moving toward a holistic view in managing the interest rate risk and the liquidity risk by combining the resources and required analysis of the two risk types. Particularly, there are many commonalities between data required for ALM and liquidity risk management. Funds transfer pricing, if done properly, internalizes the interest rate risk and liquidity risk among business units of a bank, and hence plays an important role in balance sheet management.

Asset-liability management studies are part of quantitative finance. In ALM, mathematical modeling and statistical concepts are mixed with high-level business decision making on how to run a bank. For the quantitative techniques discussed and used in this text, the general approach is to focus on applications and outcomes rather than providing deep discussions on supporting theories and proof of equations. For readers who are interested in theoretical background, each chapter provides a list of references for the origins of methods and further discussions. Since several subjects introduced in this book rely on statistical concepts, an appendix is added to cover the basic elements of probability and statistics in a concise form. These materials should help a reader who is not proficient in statistics to gain an understanding of the subjects that are needed in other parts of the book.

Methods discussed in this text when applied to the entire balance sheet of a bank require extensive computations. For the most part, examples provided are simple enough so the reader can follow and understand the topics. In practice, software packages are available that can perform the analysis explained here for balance sheets with a large number of positions. The book is not written with any particular software in mind, however, as the concepts discussed here are applicable to any ALM analysis, regardless of the software used.

In some of the examples and illustrations throughout the book I occasionally use a LIBOR–swap curve for coupon calculation of floating-rate instruments or for discounting. The principles discussed, however, are applicable if any other interest rate, such as SOFR or OIS, was used instead. In some of the examples presented in the book, the reader may notice some minor differences between the results shown here and results if calculations are performed using a spreadsheet software. This is due to rounding errors that may occur at a calculation step and those errors generally make no difference in the final outcomes.

I would like to thank those individuals who commented on the manuscript, and those who were involved in the production process of the book.

Pooya Farahvash
New York
February 2020

Abbreviations

ABCP:	asset-backed commercial paper
ABS:	asset-backed security
ACT:	Actual (used in day count conventions)
ADR:	annual default rate
AFC:	available funds cap
ALLL:	allowance for loan and lease losses
APR:	annual prepayment rate
APS:	absolute prepayment speed
BAU:	business as usual
BBA:	British Bankers' Association
BCBS:	Basel Committee on Banking Supervision
BHC:	bank holding company
BIS:	Bank for International Settlements
bps:	basis points (0.01%)
CB:	coupon-bearing bond
CD:	certificate of deposit
CDF:	cumulative distribution function
CDO:	collateralized debt obligation
CDR:	constant default rate
CDS:	credit default swap
CFP:	contingency funding plan
CMBS:	commercial mortgage-backed security
CME:	Chicago Mercantile Exchange
CMO:	collateralized mortgage obligation
CP:	commercial paper
CPI:	Consumer Price Index
CPR:	constant prepayment rate
CVaR:	conditional value-at-risk

DCF:	discounted cash flow
DF:	discount factor
DR:	default rate (periodic)
DV01:	dollar value of a basis point
DVP:	delivery versus payment
EaR:	earnings-at-risk
EBIT:	earnings before interest and taxes
EBITDA:	earnings before interest, taxes, depreciation, and amortization
ECB:	European Central Bank
EMTN:	Europe medium-term note
EONIA:	Euro Overnight Index Average
EPS:	earnings per share
EVE:	economic value of equity
EWI:	early waning indicator
FASB:	Financial Accounting Standards Board
FCFE:	free cash flow to equity
FCFF:	free cash flow to firm
FDIC:	Federal Deposit Insurance Corporation
Fed:	Federal Reserve System
FOMC:	Federal Open Market Committee
FRA:	forward rate agreement
FRBNY:	Federal Reserve Bank of New York
FSA:	Financial Services Authority
FTP:	funds transfer pricing
FX:	foreign exchange
GDP:	gross domestic product
GMRA:	global master repurchase agreement
HELOC:	home equity line of credit
HIC:	hold in custody
HQLA:	high quality liquid asset
IBF:	international banking facility
IBR:	income-based repayment
ICAAP:	internal capital adequacy assessment process
ICE:	Intercontinental Exchange
IID:	independent and identically distributed
IRRBB:	interest rate risk in the banking book
ISDA:	International Swaps and Derivatives Association
LCR:	liquidity coverage ratio
LGD:	loss given default
LIBOR:	London Interbank Offered Rate

LR:	loss rate
LRNVR:	locally risk-neutral valuation relationship
LTV:	loan to value
MBS:	mortgage-backed security
MDR:	monthly default rate
MMDA:	money market deposit account
MPR:	monthly payment rate
MSRP:	manufacturer's suggested retail price
MTL:	month to liquidation
MTN:	medium-term note
NAS:	non-accelerated senior
NII:	net interest income
NOW:	negotiable order of withdrawal
NSFR:	net stable funding ratio
NWCI:	net working capital investment
OAS:	option-adjusted spread
OIS:	overnight index swap
OTS:	Office of Thrift Supervision
PAC:	planned amortization class
PB:	price-to-book value
PCA:	principal component analysis
PD:	probability of default
PDF:	probability density function
PE:	price-to-earnings
PFE:	potential future exposure
PLUS:	Parent Loan for Undergraduate Students
PMF:	probability mass function
PPC:	prospectus prepayment curve
PR:	prepayment rate (periodic)
PS:	price-to-sales
PSA:	Public Securities Association
PV:	present value
PV01:	present value of a basis point
QRM:	qualified residential mortgage
Repo:	repurchase agreement
Reverse repo:	reverse repurchase agreement
RMBS:	residential mortgage-backed security
ROE:	return on equity
SDA:	standard default assumption
SIV:	structured investment vehicle

SLABS:	student loan asset-backed security
SMM:	single monthly mortality
SOFR:	Secured Overnight Financing Rate
SONIA:	Sterling Overnight Index Average
SPE:	special purpose entity
SPV:	special purpose vehicle
VaR:	value-at-risk
WAC:	weighted average coupon
WACC:	weighted average cost of capital
WAM:	weighted average maturity
ZB:	zero-coupon bond

Introduction

A bank at its core is a financial intermediary institution that collects funds from those individuals or entities who do not have immediate use for them and lends to those who can use the capital to generate economic benefits. Depositors with excess cash can benefit from the interest earned on their deposits while borrowers can benefit from the borrowed funds for their personal needs, such as purchasing real properties, or business needs, such as investing in their small business ventures. As the facilitators of such fund transfers, banks earn the difference between the interest paid to the depositors and the interest earned from the borrowers. A bank with an asset-driven business model seeks to originate assets through lending activities and simultaneously pursue funding methods to fund those assets, whereas a bank with a liability-driven business model primarily focuses on collecting deposits and then attempts to lend or invest the proceeds from the deposits. While traditionally deposits are the main *source of funds* in the banking industry, nowadays banks use a variety of methods to raise funds, including the issuance of short-term and long-term notes, securitization, and collateralized borrowings. *Use of funds* is also evolved from traditional lending in the form of loans to individuals and businesses, in investment in securities, and even in speculation using derivatives. The net revenue a bank makes is the difference between the costs associated with its sources of funds and earnings from the instruments where available funds are invested and used.

A bank manages its sources and uses of funds by trying to match them based on different criteria. One such criterion is based on the principal cash flows. The status of a bank as a financial intermediary, which is often supported by the central bank of the country, allows it to have a lower cost of funds compared to other entities. In particular, the bank's short-term borrowings are usually significantly cheaper compared to long-term alternatives. This allows the bank to fund long-term assets that are more profitable by cheaper short-term liabilities. While economically this seems like a sound business model, it potentially increases the risk for banks of not being able to fulfill their obligations when they are due. When the return of the principal amount borrowed by the bank is due before the principal lent is returned, this may lead to the bank's failure, should it not have any alternative source to replace the needed funds. A prudent banking practice is to align or overlap the terms of asset and liability positions such that there are always available funds to cover short- to medium-term liability maturities. However, in practice this is hard to achieve for individual asset or liability positions. Except in rare cases in which a particular debt position is raised to fund a large asset portfolio or a particular investment project, individual asset positions, such as loans and investment in securities, are not funded by distinct liability positions. Banks raise funds in micro form through deposits or in bulk form by issuing bonds. This makes the principal matching between assets and liability difficult, if not impossible. Due to this, banks may attempt to match the principal cash flows on a portfolio level. But even this approach has its limitations, since non-maturing products such as credit card accounts or savings accounts do not have contractual maturity dates. To overcome this, existing balances of non-maturing products are assumed to follow some modeled *runoff profiles* that act as amortization schedules for them. This allows the bank to estimate principal cash flows related to these products and to create *principal cash flow schedules* at an aggregated level, for example, for the bank as a whole or at a subsidiary level. Such schedules provide an overview of amounts and timings of expected principal cash flows and help in the planning and coordination of asset originations and debt issuances. This approach, however, does not incorporate planned changes in the assets and the liabilities. For example, if the bank is planning to grow a certain asset portfolio or to issue new debt securities in the near future, they are not reflected in a *static cash flow schedule*. Particularly, expected changes in balances of non-maturing products due to macroeconomic factors are not included. A *dynamic cash flow schedule* incorporates planned and expected changes in the asset and liability portfolios. A more sophisticated version of such a schedule considers all principal and interest payments to create a comprehensive view of cash flows a bank can experience in a short- to medium-term time horizon in the future. *Cash flow gap*, sometimes referred to as *maturity gap*, is the net value of cash flows generated by assets and liabilities in a specific time period. Minimizing cash flow gap is one way to reduce the risk of adverse events due to the mismatch between asset and liability cash flows, particularly their principal flows.

A bank may manage its uses of funds based on the reliability and persistency of the sources of funds. Funding sources being unavailable when they are needed may lead to the bank's failure. To assess their readiness, banks often perform scenario analysis to evaluate the impact of unavailability of one or more funding sources on their cash flow schedules and ultimately on their balance sheets. This enables them to obtain a view of the potential *liquidity gap* they may face in the future.

Interest rate is another criterion used by banks for matching their sources and uses of funds. The margin between the interest rate a bank pays on its liabilities and the rate it earns on its assets is a defining factor in the net profit of a bank, and maintaining this margin is crucial for future earnings that grow along with the growth of the balance sheet. In one categorization view, asset and liability positions of a bank can be either fixed-rate or floating-rate. The rate of a fixed-rate instrument is constant and does not change throughout its term, whereas the rate of a floating-rate instrument can change periodically, based on its contractual setting. For example, a conventional mortgage loan is a fixed-rate instrument while a home equity line of credit (HELOC) is an example of a floating-rate product. The effective rates of floating-rate instruments are often set in conjunction with a market interest rate index, such as prime rate index or effective federal funds rate index. As these rate indexes change, so do the rates of the floating-rate positions. However, the change in rates may not be simultaneous, as floating-rate instruments often follow specific rate-setting schedules, for example, every three or six months. Therefore, once a market rate index is changed it may take a few months until the rate of a floating-rate instrument that is pegged to that index changes.

Depending on the business model, a bank may originate both fixed-rate and floating-rate assets and fund them using a combination of fixed-rate and floating-rate liabilities. The mismatch between rate type of asset and liability positions can have an adverse impact on the net interest margin. Consider a bank with a balance sheet where the majority of asset positions are fixed-rate and the majority of liability positions are floating-rate. If the overall market interest rate increases, the interest income from assets would not materially change due to the fixed-rate nature of those positions, but interest expense from the floating-rate liabilities would increase, resulting in an overall decrease in the net interest margin. Conversely, a decline in overall market interest rate would result in an increase in the net interest margin. This volatility eventually impacts the overall net income of the bank.

One approach for maintaining a stable interest margin is to keep the composition of fixed- and floating-rate positions comparable and unchanged through time. This approach, however, is often impractical. Having comparable portfolios with respect to their rate types may not be in line with the business model of a bank. For example, a local or a regional bank that is focused on the mortgage market usually has a large portfolio of fixed-rate mortgages while such bank's main source of funding is often floating-rate savings products. Maintaining a position-level composition of assets and liabilities with respect to rate type is also prohibitive. For example, when a fixed-rate position matures it may not be feasible, or even economically justified, to replace it with another fixed-rate position. As an alternative, banks try to maintain the composition of their assets and liabilities at the portfolio level.

Even if the position-level or portfolio-level fixed- and floating-rate composition is maintained, the bank is still exposed to volatility in the net interest margin due to the timing of changes in the rates of floating-rate instruments. Rate resetting refers to the timing and periodicity that the rate of a floating-rate instrument changes. Consider a bank with a large floating-rate asset portfolio that resets on a monthly basis and a comparably large floating-rate debt note that resets quarterly. In an interest rate declining environment, the interest rate of the asset portfolio changes every month and decreases in line with decreases in the overall market interest rate, leading to a constant decline in the interest income from that portfolio. However, the interest rate of the debt note resets every three months. Hence the decline in the market interest rate does not impact the income from the asset and the expense of the liability at the same time, leading to periodical tightening of the net interest margin.

To assess the impact of changes in the interest rate on the net interest income, banks compare principals of assets and liabilities that are repriced during a period, where *repricing* here refers to changes in the effective rates. *Earning gap* is the net value of repriced principal of assets and liabilities during a specific period (e.g., one year). Minimizing the earning gap is one way to reduce the risk of adverse impact on the net interest margin due to changes in the interest rate level and timing of changes.

Aside from effect on earnings, changes in the interest rate can also impact a bank from a valuation point of view. A bank's management team, as agents of shareholders, are tasked with safeguarding the value of the firm against different risks, most notably the interest rate risk. Changes in the interest rate impact the value of fixed-rate and floating-rate instruments differently, where generally the value of a fixed-rate instrument is more sensitive to change in the interest rate compared to the value of a floating-rate instrument. The term of the instrument also influences the sensitivity of its value to the interest rate, where generally a long-term position is more sensitive compared to a short-term position. *Duration* of a financial instrument reflects the sensitivity of its value to a change in the interest rate level. To protect the value of the firm, banks compare durations of asset and liability portfolios and obtain a *duration gap* for the balance sheet. Minimizing the duration gap is one way to reduce the risk of adverse impact on the value of the firm due to changes in the interest rate.

Asset-liability management (ALM) is the process of optimizing the earning gap, the duration gap, the cash flow gap, and the liquidity gap of a bank in a holistic way and on a risk-aware basis. The close relationships between these notions require a comprehensive approach in managing their absolute impacts on the bank's earnings and the firm's value, as well as their interactions among themselves. A well-defined ALM process takes all aforementioned gaps into account in managing the balance sheet, as actions taken to optimize one gap may have an undesirable effect on another. Normally, the treasury department of a bank is in charge of ALM and in doing so, it coordinates its balance sheet management efforts with other business units that are in charge of asset originations or deposit collections.

ASSET-LIABILITY MANAGEMENT METRICS

ALM analysis is mainly focused on two metrics that have a close relationship to the gap measurements introduced above: *economic value of equity* and *net interest income*.

The economic value of equity (EVE) of a bank is the difference between the economic value of its assets and the economic value of its liabilities, calculated at a specific point in time. One of the main responsibilities of a bank's management team is to preserve the economic value of equity, protect it against various risks, and increase it through business activities. ALM studies that are focused on the EVE aim to identify and analyze scenarios where changes in risk factors such as interest rate would lead to a decrease in the EVE of the bank. Once those scenarios are identified, the bank management team sets limits against the potential decreases in the EVE associated with each scenario and tasks the treasury department, as the entity in charge of the balance sheet management, to coordinate asset originations and funding activities to adhere to those limits.

The net interest income (NII) of a bank is the difference between the interest income from the assets and the interest expense from the liabilities during a specific time period. For traditional banks with significant lending businesses, the net interest income is usually the main component of total earnings. ALM studies that are focused on the NII aim to identify and analyze scenarios where changes in risk factors, specifically the interest rate, would lead to a decrease in the NII of the bank. Similar to the EVE, for identified scenarios the bank has specific limits for a potential decrease in the NII and manages its balance sheet to adhere to those limits. Earnings-based ALM studies are often focused on net interest income but more comprehensive analysis may include other incomes, such as fee-based revenues, to provide a more comprehensive view on scenarios leading to a potential decrease in total earnings.

Both the EVE and the NII are suitable metrics for quantification of the interest rate risk. Changes in the interest rate impact the EVE and NII and expected future interest rate levels are used in the calculation of both. In the EVE analysis, the expected future interest rates are used to estimate future cash flows needed for valuation of the positions on the balance sheet and in the NII analysis they are used to estimate accrued interests in future periods, for example, during quarterly time buckets in the next two years. Interest rate also impacts the EVE through the discounting process where present values of expected future cash flows are obtained using discount factors that depend on the interest rate.

The EVE and the NII metrics are closely related, although the EVE has a broader scope. The value of a firm depends on its earnings and for a bank it specifically depends on the net interest income. Therefore the firm's earnings are reflected in the value of its equity. The main differences between the two metrics are in the time horizon of the analysis and the treatment of changes in the balance sheet during that period:

- The NII analysis is usually focused on a short-to-medium time horizon, for example, one to three years from the analysis date. However, since the EVE metric is based on the economic value of the balance sheet positions, the analysis time horizon is effectively extended to the time of the last expected future cash flow.
- The EVE is based on values of existing positions on the balance sheet at a specific point in time and expected changes in the balance sheet in the future are usually not included in the valuation process. In the NII analysis and depending on the selected treatment, the balance sheet may be assumed to be in a runoff mode, where positions matured during the analysis time horizon are not replaced, or it may be assumed to be constant with no changes during the horizon, or a dynamic balance sheet may be assumed when planned changes in the portfolios are reflected in the interest income and the interest expense calculation.

While the EVE and the NII are appropriate metrics for measuring the interest rate risk at the balance sheet level, neither of them is suitable for quantification of the liquidity risk. Banks often assess their exposures to liquidity risk by performing *liquidity stress test* analysis. In such analysis, several hypothetical stress scenarios are assumed and the impact of each case on (i) cash flows from the assets and liabilities, (ii) funding sources, and (iii) available cash and cash-equivalent assets, are estimated. Using this approach, banks can identify the potential scenarios that lead to a liquidity event and subsequently create contingency plans accordingly.

Funds transfer pricing (FTP) is one of the areas that are closely related to the ALM but often overlooked in practice. FTP is an internal allocation method of the net interest income among business units of banks on a risk-aware basis. Implementation of the FTP system is often based on the ALM platform, since both systems require position-level data as well as market data.

ALM RISK FACTORS

Interest rate is by far the most important risk factor considered in the ALM analysis. Depending on its balance sheet, a bank may be exposed to different types of interest rate risk. *Yield curve risk* is generally referred to as the potential for an adverse impact on NII or EVE of the bank due to inconsistent changes in the interest rates with different terms. If compositions of fixed- and floating-rate instruments on the balance sheet are uneven, or when the timing of floating-rate instrument rate settings are not aligned, the bank may be exposed to *interest rate gap risk*. When floating-rate assets and liabilities of a bank are based on different market rate indexes (e.g., assets are based on the prime index and liabilities are based on LIBOR or SOFR), uneven movement of those indexes may have an adverse impact on the EVE and the NII, exposing the bank to *interest rate basis risk*.

When certain conditions are met, some financial contracts allow one side to terminate the contract prior to its maturity or to significantly alter it. This is usually referred to as the counterparty having an *option* on the contract. In turn, this can materially change the expected cash flows of such instruments, exposing the banks to *option risk*. Particularly, when the borrower of a loan has the option to return the principal amount earlier than scheduled, it may force the bank to re-lend the returned fund in unfavorable conditions (e.g., lending in a low interest rate environment), impacting the EVE and the NII adversely. This is referred to as *prepayment risk*. Prepayment risk is notably present for mortgage loans when borrowers' refinancing activities can change the expected cash flows significantly. Option and prepayment risks usually have a close relationship with the level of the interest rate, and for that reason they are often characterized as interest rate risk.

Interest rate risk is not the only risk factor included in the ALM analysis. For a bank with a multi-currency balance sheet, *exchange rate risk* can be a significant source of uncertainty in the earnings and value of the bank. *Functional currency* of a bank usually is the currency of the country where the bank is incorporated and conducts most of its business. When a bank transfers funds from the functional currency to another currency, the income earned is eventually expected to be returned to the functional currency. The exchange rate at each conversion step can impact the earnings amount and the net income of the bank. The economic value of equities of multi-currency banks also depends on the exchange rates and their volatilities. From a balance sheet management point of view, and depending on the amount of foreign currency exposures, the exchange rate can be a significant source of risk; this makes it essential for banks to include the currency exchange rate risk factor in their ALM analysis based on both EVE and NII metrics.

Changes in securities prices can impact the EVE of banks with significant investment or trading portfolios. While a change in the market interest rate is the main driver behind the change in the securities prices, other factors such as changes in supply and demand forces, the release of new information regarding a security or its issuer, or even the spread of misinformation in the market can lead to unexpected price changes. The risk for a potential adverse impact from this on the EVE of a bank is generally referred to as *price risk*. Practitioners often use *market risk* term to refer to the interest rate risk, the exchange rate risk, and the price risk, collectively.

Credit risk in a financial contract generally refers to the risk of counterparty default. For example, for a commercial loan, credit risk arises from the possibility that the borrower will fail to make required payments at scheduled times. For a bond, since the price depends on the credit rating, credit risk may refer to the potential of an adverse impact on the price of the security due to the change in its rating. Credit risk factor is usually included in the ALM analysis by considering the impact on the position's cash flows, both in the NII and the EVE analysis. An alternative approach in incorporating credit risk in the EVE analysis is to discount cash flows based on a risk-adjusted interest rate curve instead of the risk-free rate.

Liquidity risk is the risk of a bank not being able to fulfill its financial obligation at the required time without incurring excessive costs or suffering extreme losses. Unexpected large cash outflows, inability to roll a maturing debt note, and run on demand deposits are some of the circumstances that can lead to a *liquidity event*. While realization of adverse events due to market risk or credit risk results in financial losses, a liquidity event can be catastrophic to a bank, leading to bank failure and eventual bankruptcy. There is a close relationship between ALM and liquidity risk management and often a single group within the treasury department of a bank is responsible for both. Since ALM systems can produce position-level expected cash flows required for the EVE and the NII analysis of different scenarios, the same cash flows can be used in liquidity risk analysis.

ORGANIZATION OF THIS BOOK

The topics discussed in this book are organized in several chapters and one appendix. A brief overview of each chapter is presented below.

Chapter 1: Interest Rate

The concept of interest rate is at the core of any financial analysis and understanding notations used to represent the interest rate and its market conventions is essential for the topics discussed throughout this book. In this chapter we start our discussion by presenting the interest rate concept, different types of interest rates, and various ways they are quoted and used in financial analysis. In doing so we explain the present and future values of cash flows and discuss how they are related to the interest rate. We also introduce the important concept of compounding and explain the difference between simple interest and compounded interest. Cash flows of financial instruments are derived based on their contractual characteristics. For example, a borrower of a mortgage loan usually makes monthly payments but the contract of a commercial loan may be structured such that the borrowing company pays every three months. There are different market conventions that define these characteristics and understanding them is crucial for cash flow analysis. In this chapter we introduce a few of these market conventions, including payment and accrual periods, day count conventions, and business day adjustments. Quoted interest rates in the market have different terms (e.g., 1-month rate or 1-year rate) and may reflect periodic coupon payments. In this chapter we discuss a technique known as bootstrapping to put rates with different terms and coupon payments on a similar footing. Rates obtained from this process are known as spot rates or zero-coupon rates and play an important role in quantitative finance. In this chapter we also discuss the important concepts of forward rate, implied forward rate, and future rate. These are all indications of interest rates in the future, but derived using different methods and used for different purposes.

An interest rate swap contract is a derivative product widely used in finance for hedging against movement of interest rate. Swap contracts usually have a long term (e.g., 2 years to 10 years). For this reason, interest rates used in swap contracts are often used to extend short-term rates, and together they create an interest rate curve. In this chapter we introduce interest rate swap contracts, discuss their valuation, and explain how a swap rate is derived and is associated with short-term rates. Components of interest rates, namely their risk and term structures, and a few methods for interpolation of rates are also explained in this chapter.

Chapter 2: Valuation: Fundamentals of Fixed-Income and Non-Maturing Products

In this chapter, the discounted cash flow method as the fundamental technique for valuation of financial instruments is introduced. We start our discussion by explaining the most common amortization methods that are used for derivation of principal cash flows. One broad categorization of financial instruments is based on the type of their coupon rate. A fixed-rate instrument has a constant coupon rate that does not change during its term, but the coupon rate of a floating-rate instrument changes based on the value of an interest rate index. In this chapter we discuss the valuation of fixed-rate and floating-rate instruments and in doing so we introduce the important concepts of yield, duration, and convexity. In particular, we explain how duration and convexity can be used to approximately estimate the change in value of a financial instrument due to the change in the interest rate. We then use this method to explain how the value of a fixed-income financial instrument, such as a bond, can be immunized against the change in the interest rate.

Another broad categorization of financial instrument is based on their terms. A maturing product has a contractual term and a specific maturity date. A bond or a mortgage loan are examples of maturing financial instruments. A non-maturing product does not have a contractual maturity date. A savings account or a credit card account are examples of non-maturing products. In this chapter we review a few treatments commonly used in practice to estimate cash flows of non-maturing products that are needed for valuation purposes. In the last topic of this chapter we discuss the issue of prepayment and how it impacts the cash flows of a financial instrument and its valuation.

Chapter 3: Equity Valuation

This chapter covers three equity valuation methods: the dividend discount model, the discounted free cash flow method, and the comparative approach. The dividend discount model and the discounted free cash flow method are both based on discounting expected future cash flows, where in the former they are dividend payments and in the latter they are cash flows generated by the firm that are available to the equity holders. In the comparative valuation approach a measurement of the stock price, often in the form of a ratio, is compared with the firm's peers to estimate if the market price of equity is overvalued or undervalued.

Chapter 4: Option Valuation

An option contract provides its holder the right, but not the obligation, to take an action, such as purchasing an equity security or returning a bond to the issuer, within specific settings defined at the contract. Execution of an option can materially change the cash flows of the contract and therefore the contract value should reflect this. The value of an option contract depends on the value of other products or financial indexes, generally referred to as the *underlying*. In this chapter we introduce the fundamentals of option valuation by first focusing on stock options. Specifically, three option valuation techniques are discussed here: binomial trees, the Black-Scholes-Merton model, and Monte Carlo simulation. The binomial tree method is a discrete-time approach that defines the change in the value of the underlying in a tree-like structure. Black-Scholes-Merton is a continuous-time model that presents evolution of the value of the underlying through time. Monte Carlo simulation is based on creating a large number of simulated paths of the underlying value during a specific time horizon and using them to obtain the expected value of the option.

Volatility of the underlying value plays an important role in option valuation. In this chapter we discuss derivation of the volatility and introduce two methods to model the volatility when it is not constant through time: generalized autoregressive conditional heteroscedasticity (GARCH) and exponentially weighted moving average (EWMA).

In the last section of this chapter we introduce another type of option when the underlying is a futures contract. A futures contract is an agreement between two parties to buy and sell an asset at some time in the future within specific settings defined at the contract initiation. Futures options are options written on futures contracts based on prices of commodities or financial instruments. Here we first introduce futures contracts and then discuss the Black model for valuation of futures options.

Chapter 5: Interest Rate Models

An interest rate model is a mathematical formulation that characterizes the movement of interest rates over a period of time. Interest rate models are used for simulation of the interest rate, which in turn can be used for valuation of financial instruments or simulation of interest earnings in a specific scenario. Interest rate models are also useful for valuation of complex derivative products. In this chapter we introduce a few interest rate models that are commonly used in the ALM analysis. To do so, we first explain the concepts of short rate and instantaneous forward rate and discuss how the spot rate and the short rate are associated. We then present four interest rate models: Vasicek, Hull-White, Ho-Lee, and Black-Karasinski. These four models have a lot in common while some specific features distinguish them from each other. The Hull-White model can be considered an extension of the Vasicek and the Ho-Lee is a special case of the Hull-White model. Short rates produced by these three models can be positive or negative but a short rate produced by the Black-Karasinski model is always positive.

An interest rate tree is a discrete-time representation of a continuous-time interest rate model. In this chapter we introduce construction of a trinomial tree based on the Hull-White model and then extend our discussion to construction of an interest rate tree based on the Black-Karasinski model. These interest rate trees, also known as lattice models, can be used for valuation of complex financial securities, where cash flows and other characteristics of the instruments at a specific time depend on the level of the interest rate at that time.

Parameters of an interest rate model are often estimated using values of liquid market-traded financial products. This process is referred to as model calibration. Interest rate cap and floor and swaption contracts are usually used in calibration of interest rate models. In this chapter we introduce these derivative products and then demonstrate how they are used in the calibration process.

Chapter 6: Valuation of Bonds with Embedded Options

Callable and putable bonds have contractually embedded options that allow the investor (in the case of the putable bond) or the issuer (in the case of the callable bond) to recall or redeem the note. In this chapter we explain how the interest rate tree, discussed in the previous chapter, can be used for valuation of callable and putable bonds. In doing so, we also introduce the important concept of the option-adjusted spread.

Chapter 7: Valuation of Mortgage-Backed and Asset-Backed Securities

For many traditional banks, mortgage loans comprise a large portion of their asset originations. To free up the funding required for these assets, banks often package the mortgage loans into new securities through a process known as securitization. These mortgage-backed securities are then sold to investors who usually could not directly invest in the mortgage sector. Valuation of the mortgage-backed securities is a challenging task as many factors, such as interest rate level, prepayment, and potential default of the borrowers, are involved in the process. In this chapter we first introduce the basic mathematics of mortgage loans and then discuss how the Monte Carlo simulation method can be used to value the mortgage-backed securities. Asset-backed securities are another class of financial products that are created through the securitization process. The most common asset-backed securities are based on pools of auto loans, credit card receivables, student loans, and home equity loans. In the second part of this chapter we briefly introduce these four types of securities and explain their valuation method using Monte Carlo simulation.

Chapter 8: Economic Value of Equity

Economic value of equity (EVE) is the difference between the economic value of the assets of a bank and the economic value of its liabilities at a specific point in time. Management of EVE and its relationship with the structure of assets and liabilities of the bank is an integral part of an effective balance sheet management strategy and consequently it is crucial for the bank to regularly assess the potential change in the EVE in different market conditions. In this chapter we first introduce the concept and calculation of the economic value of equity and then present the duration gap as a basic approach in analyzing the potential change in the EVE when the interest rate level changes. When the discounted cash flow method is used in valuation of asset or liability positions for the EVE analysis, the yield curve used for discount factor generation may need to be adjusted for the riskiness of positions being valued. Here we explain how risk-adjusted yield curves are created and used.

Beyond the basic duration gap method, scenario analysis is the main approach for EVE studies. In this chapter we explain EVE scenario analysis based on the interest rate and the exchange rate risk factors. The last section of this chapter presents an overview of the Basel committee guidelines on managing interest rate risk in the banking book as well as procedures for scenario generation and EVE analysis.

Chapter 9: Net Interest Income

Net interest income (NII) is the difference between the interest income and the interest expense during a specific time period. For traditional banks the net interest income is the main component of their total earnings. Sensitivity of the net interest income to the interest rate level highly depends on the type and rate-setting behavior of positions on the balance sheet. In this chapter we introduce calculation of the net interest income and specifically explain two approaches for calculation of the interest income or expense for a floating-rate instrument. Since the net interest income is evaluated during a time horizon in the future it is important to decide whether expected balance sheet changes in that period are to be incorporated in the NII analysis. In this regard there are three treatments usually considered in practice. In the first treatment the balance sheet is assumed in a runoff mode where matured, amortized, or runoff positions are not replaced while in the second treatment the balance sheet is assumed constant throughout the analysis horizon and matured positions are replaced such that making this assumption holds. The third treatment is the most comprehensive approach where forecasted changes in the balance sheet are considered in the analysis and hence a dynamic view of the NII is obtained.

The earning gap method is a first step in sensitivity analysis of the NII in different interest rate environments. In this chapter we introduce the earning gap and then move to more comprehensive scenario analysis where impacts on the NII of parallel or non-parallel shocks to the current interest rate curves are studied. The scenario analyses discussed in this chapter are focused on the interest rate and the exchange rate risk factors. The last section of this chapter provides an overview of the Basel committee guidelines for the NII analysis.

Chapter 10: Equity and Earnings-at-Risk

EVE and NII scenario analyses focus on a limited number of scenarios. This chapter extends the topics discussed earlier by considering the cases in which a large number of simulated scenarios are generated to study the potential extreme changes in the EVE and the NII. We start this chapter by introducing the value-at-risk (VaR) method. VaR is a popular technique widely used for risk management purposes. We explain three general approaches in obtaining the VaR of a position or a portfolio: historical sampling, Monte Carlo simulation, and the variance-covariance method. We then use the VaR concept in the EVE and the NII analysis.

Equity-at-risk is the near-maximum potential decrease in the economic value of equity due to changes in risk factors and earnings-at-risk is the near-maximum potential decrease in estimated earnings due to changes in risk factors. Both metrics are defined for a specific time horizon and for a given probability confidence level. The first step in the equity-at-risk and the earnings-at-risk analyses is to generate a large number of simulated scenarios for the risk factors considered in the analysis. One method for scenario generation is to sample the historical values of a risk factor and use them to generate simulated paths of the risk factor in the future. The second method is based on the Monte Carlo simulation where a quantitative model, often in the form of a stochastic process, is developed to represent the behavior of a risk factor through time and then the model is used to generate simulated paths of the factor in the future. In this chapter we discuss both methods and introduce a few general models for simulating risk factors such as exchange rates or prices of stocks and commodities. We then follow by explaining how the equity-at-risk and the earnings-at-risk analyses are performed by focusing on the interest rate and the exchange rate risk factors. In this chapter we also introduce the delta-gamma approximation method, which is commonly used in the value-at-risk analysis to reduce the computational burden of a valuation process.

Chapter 11: Liquidity Risk

After the financial crisis of 2007–2009, the importance of liquidity risk management increased considerably and many banks implemented various tools to measure, monitor, and control this risk. We start this chapter by introducing some of the common funding channels and discuss the potential of each channel in producing or contributing to a liquidity event. Particularly, liquidity events related to repurchase agreement (repo) contracts were some of the most impactful during the financial crisis period. In this chapter we introduce repo contracts and discuss the circumstances in which they can cause a liquidity stress event. We then follow by discussing a few methods to manage the liquidity risk of the repo contracts.

Cash flow gap analysis is one of the main tools in liquidity risk measurement. Cash flow gap schedules are often created for at least three scenarios. In a business-as-usual case, the cash inflows and outflows during a specific period based on the normal course of business are estimated and compared. In an idiosyncratic stress case, a stress event particular to the firm is assumed and its impacts on cash flows and their timings are evaluated. In a market-wide stress case, it is assumed that the stress event has impacted the entire market, hence cash flows are reevaluated based on the assumption that the firm's counterparties are also under stress. Multi-currency cash flow gap analysis is applicable to a firm with a multi-currency balance sheet. In this chapter we explain these cash flow gap schedules using several examples.

The last section of this chapter provides an overview of two liquidity risk monitoring tools proposed by the Basel committee. Regulatory entities in many countries have already required the banks in their jurisdictions to implement these tools. They are the liquidity coverage ratio and the net stable funding ratio. Here we introduce both ratios and provide their calculation details using examples.

Chapter 12: Funds Transfer Pricing

Analysis and measurement of net interest income is usually performed at the balance sheet level of a bank or its standalone entities such as its major subsidiaries. In doing so, when sensitivity of the net interest income to risk factors is analyzed the assumption is that the entity as a whole attempts to minimize the risk. Past experiences have shown that this may not be the case for large banks where individual business units aim to maximize their own earnings irrespective of impacts on the total bank's risk level. The association of compensation and year-end rewards to individual business unit performance is one of the main factors in encouraging this behavior. This often has a negative consequence for the bank when business units' risk-taking activities to maximize their own performance measures expose the bank to a level of risk that is beyond its designated tolerance limits. Funds transfer pricing (FTP) is an internal allocation method of distributing the interest margin and the net interest income among relevant units within the bank and to internalize the interest rate and liquidity risks to the business units that are sources of risk-generating activities. There is a close relationship between the net interest income measurements at the aggregated bank level and funds transfer pricing as a distribution method of the net interest income to business units.

In this chapter we first introduce the concept of funds transfer pricing and its benefits. We then explain two FTP techniques commonly used in practice: the pool method and the match maturity method. Particularly, we demonstrate FTP rate assignment based on the matched maturity method for fixed-rate instruments, for floating-rate instruments, and for non-maturing products. In the last section of this chapter characteristics of a good FTP system are discussed.

Appendix: Elements of Probability and Statistics

In the appendix we review a few important topics in probability and statistics that help in understanding the topics discussed in the main body of the book.

CHAPTER 1

Interest Rate

Finance charges, fees, and principal gains are the most common earnings channels in the finance industry. The most traditional revenue source for banks and many non-bank financial institutions is the finance charges associated with lending activities. Commercial and personal loans, student loans, lines of credit, mortgages, and many other financial instruments create revenue for the entities that underwrite and sell these products. Many banks provide fee-based services to their customers as well and charge them accordingly. Various checking, savings, retirement, and investment accounts offered by financial institutions include monthly fees that may vary by account activities and outstanding balances. Investment banks often offer a range of fee-based advisory services, including equity and debt issuances, mergers and acquisitions, and restructuring. Trading, clearing, and bookkeeping services offered by brokerage houses are also fee-based. Financial institutions with trading desks have significant, although volatile, revenue through gains on principal of traded securities. Financial institutions always attempt to diversify their earnings and utilize more than one of these channels. For example, broker-dealer firms rely on fee-based earnings for services offered through their brokerage divisions, as well as principal gain revenues from their trading activities on their own security inventory.

Finance charge as one of the main sources of revenue in finance is based on the well-known economic concept of the *time value of money*, signifying that a sum of money at the present time is worth more than an equal sum in the future, due to its potential earning power. What associates the value of present-time money to future-time money is known as the *interest rate*.

In this chapter we introduce the interest rate and its measurement methods. Concepts of compounding frequency, day count convention, and business day adjustment rules that are closely related to interest rates are explained as well. We introduce the risk-free rate and its proxies as the fundamental component of interest rate. Common interest rate measurements, including Treasury yield, LIBOR, federal funds, prime, swap, and OIS rates, are introduced and their relationships are discussed. We then continue our discussion of interest rates by providing details on construction of various interest rate curves and explain the relationship between spot and forward rates that is critical for many financial analysis. We finish this chapter by introducing some of the interest rate shocks that are commonly used in asset-liability management analysis.

Understanding of the interest rate concept is crucial for comprehension of other finance topics; hence materials presented in this chapter are fundamental to the topics discussed in the remainder of this book.

INTEREST RATE, FUTURE VALUE, AND COMPOUNDING

The interest rate is a method of measuring the cost of borrowing or the return on lending. Consider investor A, who invests in a bank savings account that promises to pay "8% annual interest." Assume the investor put $100 in that account and keeps it there for one full year. At the end of the year he earns 8% of $100, which is $8 interest in addition to his original invested amount of $100, for a total of $108. This can be presented as:

$$100 \times (1 + 0.08) = 108 \tag{1.1}$$

where 0.08 in the above formula is the interest rate for the duration of the investment. Here the original $100 is *principal* and the $8 is *interest*. Assume investor A decides to reinvest the original $100 principal plus the $8 interest from the first year in the same savings account and keep it there for another year, and assume the account interest rate for the second year is "8% annual interest." At the beginning of the second year the invested amount is $108; therefore during the second year the investor earns $108 \times 0.08 = $8.64 interest. Total investment in that savings account at the end of the second year is:

$$108 \times (1 + 0.08) = 116.64$$

The same result is achieved by considering that investor A invested $100 in the savings account that pays 8% annually for two years (two periods); therefore:

$$100 \times (1 + 0.08)^2 = 116.64$$

The $110.64 balance at the end of the second year is known as *future value*. It has two components: the original principal of $100 and the earned interest of $16.64. Since in each year the annual interest rate is 8% the earned interest for two years based on the original principal of $100 is $16, calculated as:

$$2 \times (100 \times 0.08) = 16$$

The extra \$0.64 is the interest earned in the second year over the reinvested interest from the first year:

$$8 \text{ [Interest earned in first year and reinvested]}$$

$$\times \, 0.08 \text{ [Interest rate of second year]} = 0.64$$

The concept of reinvesting interest earned in previous period(s) and earning interest on both principal and reinvested interest is known as *compounding interest*. *Compounding frequency* defines the periodicity of interest calculation and its reinvestment. In contrast to compounding interest, *simple interest* earns interest on principal only.

A bank quote of "8% annual interest" is incomplete without stating the compounding frequency. Compounding frequency indicates how often the interest is calculated and reinvested. In the above example, the bank quote should be "8% annual interest, compounded annually," meaning that the quoted interest rate of 8% is an annual rate and the compounded frequency is also annual. To illustrate the concept of compounding better, now assume that there is a different bank offering a savings account with a quoted interest rate of "8% annual interest, compounded semi-annually." The annual rate is 8% as before, but this product has a semi-annual compounding frequency. This means that the interest is calculated and reinvested every six months. Suppose investor B invests \$100 in the savings account with semi-annual compounding frequency for one year. In the first six months he earns $8\%/2 = 4\%$ on his original principal of \$100 and his total investment at the end of six months is:

$$100 \times \left(1 + \frac{0.08}{2}\right) = 104$$

The \$4 interest earned in the first half of the year is reinvested and for the second half of the year the 4% interest is earned on \$104; therefore, at the end of the first year total investment value is:

$$104 \times \left(1 + \frac{0.08}{2}\right) = 108.16 \tag{1.2}$$

Comparing Equations (1.1) and (1.2), at the end of the first year investor B earned \$0.16 more than investor A by investing in a savings account with semi-annual compounding frequency. The extra \$0.16 is the interest earned in the second half of the year over the reinvested interest earned in the first half. Dividing by 2 in the Equation (1.2) is needed since the quoted interest rate is annual and to convert it to the interest for six months we need to divide it by 2. In this case, every half-year is known as the *period* and there are two periods in each year. The 4% here is known as the *periodic interest rate*.

If investor B keeps the \$108.16 balance at the end of the first year in the same savings account for one more year and the quoted interest rate for the second year is "8% annual interest, compounded semi-annually," the total investment (principal and interest) at the middle of the second year is (rounded to two decimals):

$$108.16 \times \left(1 + \frac{0.08}{2}\right) = 112.49$$

and total investment at the end of the second year is:

$$112.49 \times \left(1 + \frac{0.08}{2}\right) = 116.99$$

An alternative way of obtaining the same result is to note that investor B invested \$100 for four periods of a half-year each while the interest earned on each half-year period is 8%/2. So:

$$100 \times \left(1 + \frac{0.08}{2}\right)^4 = 116.99$$

Generally, if principal (P) is invested for t years, where the annual interest rate is r and the number of periods in a year (compounding frequency) is m, the total future value (FV) at the end of t years is:

$$FV = P\left(1 + \frac{r}{m}\right)^{m \times t} \tag{1.3}$$

In the above equation, r is annual interest rate in decimal, t is measured in years, and $m \times t$ is the number of periods. For semi-annual compounding frequency, m is 2. Other compounding frequencies that are commonly used are quarterly, monthly, and daily. m values for these compounding frequencies are presented in Table 1.1.

For example, an investment of \$100 for two years ($t = 2$) in a savings account that pays 8% ($r = 0.08$) annually with quarterly compounding ($m = 4$) has a future value of:

$$FV = 100 \times \left(1 + \frac{0.08}{4}\right)^{4 \times 2} = 117.17$$

A compounding frequency that is extensively used in quantitative finance is *continuous compounding*. Continuous compounding is achieved when in Equation (1.3) an infinite value of m is considered. It can be shown that in the limiting case of m, the future value of the investment is obtained as:

$$FV = P \times e^{r_c t} \tag{1.4}$$

TABLE 1.1 Compounding frequency

Periodicity	m
Annually	1
Semi-annually	2
Quarterly	4
Monthly	12
Daily	365
Continuous	∞

where t is the length of time in years and r_c is the annual interest rate with continuous compounding. For example, for an investment amount of $100 for two years and an annual interest rate of $r = 8\%$ with continuous compounding, the future value is:

$$FV = 100 \times e^{0.08 \times 2} = 117.35$$

The interest rate presented in a financial contract usually is quoted as an annualized rate. However, it is also important to note the compounding frequency of the quoted interest rate. As observed above, for a given time horizon and principal amount, an 8% annual interest rate compounded semi-annually and an 8% annual interest rate compounded quarterly do not yield to the same future values. An annual interest rate quoted with a compounding frequency can be converted to an annual interest rate with other compounding frequencies. For example, consider a 10% annual interest rate compounded semi-annually. The future value of a $1 investment with this interest rate for one year using Equation (1.3) is:

$$P = \$1, m = 2, t = 1, r = 0.10, FV = ?:$$

$$FV = 1 \times \left(1 + \frac{0.10}{2}\right)^{2 \times 1} = 1.1025$$

The annual rate with annual compounding that produces the same future value is 10.25%, obtained as follows:

$$P = \$1, m = 1, t = 1, FV = \$1.1025, r = ?:$$

$$1.1025 = 1 \times \left(1 + \frac{r}{1}\right)^{1 \times 1} \Rightarrow r = 0.1025$$

Therefore, a 10.25% annual rate compounded annually is equivalent to a 10% annual rate compounded semi-annually. Generally, for a given principal amount P and time t, two quoted annual rates r_1 and r_2 with compounding frequencies of m_1 and m_2 produce the same future value if:

$$P\left(1 + \frac{r_1}{m_1}\right)^{m_1 t} = P\left(1 + \frac{r_2}{m_2}\right)^{m_2 t}$$

Hence:

$$\left(1 + \frac{r_1}{m_1}\right)^{m_1} = \left(1 + \frac{r_2}{m_2}\right)^{m_2} \tag{1.5}$$

Equation (1.5) can be used to convert a quoted annual interest rate from one compounding frequency to another. It is also possible to convert an interest rate with continuous compounding to rates with other compounding frequencies. For a given principal amount P and time t, if annual interest rate r has a compounding frequency of m and r_c is the annual interest rate with continuous compounding, to have the same future value based on these two rates, we have:

$$P\left(1 + \frac{r}{m}\right)^{mt} = Pe^{r_c t}$$

Hence:

$$r = m(e^{(r_c/m)} - 1) \tag{1.6}$$

and:[1]

$$r_c = m \ln\left(1 + \frac{r}{m}\right) \tag{1.7}$$

Equations (1.6) and (1.7) can be used to convert interest rates with continuous compounding to rates with other compounding frequencies and vice versa. For example, a continuous compounding interest rate that is equivalent to a 6% annual rate with semi-annual compounding is 5.91%, obtained as:

$$r_c = 2 \ln\left(1 + \frac{0.06}{2}\right) = 0.0591$$

Use of Time Notation versus Period Notation

Consider a given interest rate with a specific compounding frequency. To determine the future value of a cash flow based on this interest rate we can think of the interest amount as being accumulated for either a certain time (in years) in the future or a certain number of periods. There is an association between time, period, and compounding frequency. Consider an investment of $100 for three years that pays 10% annual interest compounded semi-annually. Using *time notation* and based on Equation (1.3), since $t = 3$ and $m = 2$, we have:

$$FV = 100 \times \left(1 + \frac{0.10}{2}\right)^{2 \times 3} = 134.01$$

The same result can be obtained if we use *period notation*. Since the compounding frequency is semi-annual, we can define a period as having a length of 0.5 year and therefore there are six periods for the duration of this investment. The periodic interest rate is $10\%/2 = 5\%$ for each half-year period and the future value is calculated as:

$$FV = 100 \times (1 + 0.05)^6 = 134.01$$

Generally, in using period notation we have:

$$FV = P(1 + r_{pr})^n \tag{1.8}$$

where r_{pr} is the periodic interest rate and n is the total number of periods. The two approaches are obviously the same but sometimes it is easier to consider period notation in calculating the future value and sometimes the year notation is preferred. A summary of the two approaches is shown here:

Time Notation	**Period Notation**
$FV = P\left(1 + \dfrac{r}{m}\right)^{mt}$	$FV = P(1 + r_{pr})^n$

t = Time (in years)

m = Compounding frequency

r = Annual interest rate (in decimal)

n = Number of periods $n = mt$

r_{pr} = Periodic interest rate $r_{pr} = \dfrac{r}{m}$

Simple Interest

Assume an investor deposits $100 for two years in a savings account that pays 5% annually with simple interest. The earned interest in the first year is $5 ($100 \times 0.05 = \$5$). Since the account pays simple interest (no compounding), the $5 interest earned in the first year is not considered reinvested and hence will not generate interest in the second year. Therefore the interest earned in the second year is also $5 only ($100 \times 0.05 = \$5$). The future value of this investment at the end of two years is:

$$FV = 100 + (100 \times 0.05) + (100 \times 0.05) = 110$$

Generally, future value of investment of principal P with annual simple interest of r for duration of time t (in years) is obtained as:

$$FV = P(1 + rt) \tag{1.9}$$

We can find the equivalent compounding interest of a simple interest rate and vice versa. If r_s is the annual simple interest rate and r is the annual interest rate with compounding frequency m, then for the two to produce the same future value at time t for a given principal P we have:

$$P(1 + tr_s) = P\left(1 + \frac{r}{m}\right)^{mt}$$

Therefore:

$$r = m\left[(1 + tr_s)^{\frac{1}{mt}} - 1\right] \tag{1.10}$$

and

$$r_s = \frac{1}{t}\left[\left(1 + \frac{r}{m}\right)^{mt} - 1\right] \tag{1.11}$$

Similarly, to convert a continuous compounding rate r_c to simple interest rate r_s and vice versa, we can use the following formula:

$$r_s = \frac{1}{t}(e^{r_c t} - 1) \tag{1.12}$$

$$r_c = \frac{1}{t}\ln(1 + tr_s) \tag{1.13}$$

ACCRUAL AND PAYMENT PERIODS

Payment frequency is another important characteristic of a financial instrument. Payment frequency defines how often an interest amount is paid to a counterparty. Common payment frequencies are annually, semi-annually, quarterly, monthly, and at maturity date (at-end). It is important to distinguish between payment and compounding frequencies and the periods associated with each. An *accrual period* is the period over which interest is accumulated. The accrual period is determined using the compounding frequency. A *payment period* is the time between two payment dates. The payment period is determined using the payment frequency.

At the end of an accrual period, the interest amount accumulated during the preceding accrual period is calculated and reinvested by adding it to the principal. The interest amount for the following accrual period is then calculated based on this adjusted principal amount. This is continued until the next payment date. At each payment date, the interest amount accrued since the previous payment date is paid out to the counterparty and the interest amount calculation for the following accrual period is calculated based on the original principal or based on the amortized principal.[2]

Compounding and payment frequencies do not need to be the same. Consider a bank's investment product with the following quote: the account pays "10% annual interest, compounded quarterly, paid semi-annually." The compounding frequency of this financial product is quarterly, the length of each accrual period is 0.25 year, and there are eight accrual periods in two years. The payment frequency is semi-annual and the length of each payment period is 0.5 year. There are four payment periods in two years and payment dates are at $t = 0.5$, $t = 1$, $t = 1.5$, and $t = 2$. Assume an investor invests $100 in this account for two years and at each payment date he receives the interest payment and does not reinvest it back into the account. However, at $t = 0.25$, $t = 0.75$, $t = 1.25$, and $t = 1.75$, which are between payment dates, an accrual period ends and the accrued interest is reinvested until the following payment date. At time $t = 0.25$ the first accrual period ends. Accrued interest in this period is:

$$100 \times \frac{0.10}{4} = 2.5$$

At $t = 0.25$, this interest is reinvested (since the first payment date is not reached yet) and added to the principal ($100 + 2.5 = 102.5$), and in the second accrual period (from $t = 0.25$ to $t = 0.5$) the accrued interest is calculated as:

$$102.5 \times \frac{0.10}{4} = 2.5625$$

Total interest payment for the first half of the first year (from $t = 0$ to $t = 0.5$), that is, the first payment period, is:

$$2.5 + 2.5625 = 5.0625$$

We can get to the same result by using Equation (1.3) and taking the difference between the future value at $t = 0.5$ and the original principal amount:

$$100 \times \left(1 + \frac{0.10}{4}\right)^{4 \times 0.5} - 100 = 5.0625$$

The $5.0625 is the interest accrued in two accrual periods in the first payment period and is paid out to the investor at $t = 0.5$. Immediately after this interest payment at $t = 0.5$, the principal is again $100 and accrued interest during the second half of the first year (from $t = 0.5$ to $t = 1$), that is, the second payment period, is calculated as:

$$100 \times \left(1 + \frac{0.10}{4}\right)^{4 \times 0.5} - 100 = 5.0625$$

This interest amount of $5.0625 is paid out at $t = 1$. The accrued interest for the third and fourth payment periods are similarly calculated as $5.0625 and are paid at $t = 1.5$ and $t = 2$. This calculation is summarized in Table 1.2. In this table, the initial investment amount of $100 is presented with a negative sign to identify it as a cash outflow from the investor's point of view, which occurred at the beginning of the investment. The ending balance in an accrual period is calculated as the beginning balance plus the accrued interest in that period minus the interest paid at the end of that period (if there is any actual interest payment in that period). Also, the ending balance of a period is carried over to the beginning balance of the next period. Figure 1.1 presents a schematic view of cash flows associated with this investment from the investor's point of view. The investor deposits $100 at $t = 0$ and every six months at $t = 0.5$, $t = 1$, $t = 1.5$, and $t = 2$ receives $5.0625 interest payments. At $t = 2$ he also receives the original invested principal of $100 back.

TABLE 1.2 Interest calculation when compounding and payment frequencies are not the same

t (Year)	Accrual Period	Payment Period	Accrued Interest (A)	Interest Cash Flow (C)	Principal Cash Flow (D)	Begin-ning (B)	Ending (E) = (A) + (B) − (C) − (D)
0					−100		
0.25	1		2.5			100	102.5
0.5	2	1	2.5625	5.0625		102.5	100
0.75	3		2.5			100	102.5
1	4	2	2.5625	5.0625		102.5	100
1.25	5		2.5			100	102.5
1.5	6	3	2.5625	5.0625		102.5	100
1.75	7		2.5			100	102.5
2	8	4	2.5625	5.0625	100	102.5	0

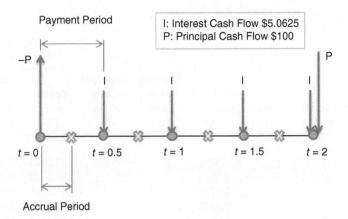

Payment Period

I: Interest Cash Flow $5.0625
P: Principal Cash Flow $100

Accrual Period

FIGURE 1.1   Cash flow schematic for an investment for two years, with quarterly compounding and semi-annual payments

What if the investor had the option to reinvest the interest amount received every six months in the same investment product earning the same interest based on the original quote? In this case, as before, the accrued interest in the first accrual period (from $t = 0$ to $t = 0.25$) is calculated as $2.5 and added to the original principal. The principal of $102.5 is then used to calculate the accrued interest of $2.5625 in the second accrual period (from $t = 0.25$ to $t = 0.5$). In the previous case the total interest of $5.0625 was paid out at $t = 0.5$, but now this amount is being reinvested. Therefore, the principal at the beginning of the third accrual period (from $t = 0.5$ to $t = 0.75$) is now $100 + 5.0625 = 105.0625$ and the accrued interest in this period is:

$$105.0625 \times \frac{0.10}{4} = 2.6266$$

This interest is now added to the principal of $105.0625 and the principal used at the beginning of the fourth accrual period is $105.0625 + 2.6266 = 107.6891$. So the accrued interest in the fourth accrual period is:

$$107.6891 \times \frac{0.10}{4} = 2.6922$$

This process is repeated for eight accrual periods and the calculation is summarized in Table 1.3. At the end of the last accrual period the future value is $121.8403, which consists of $100 original principal and $21.8403 total accrued interest in eight accrual periods. At that point ($t = 2$), both components are paid out to the investor.

TABLE 1.3 Interest calculation with at-end interest payment

						Balance in Accrual Period	
t (Year)	Accrual Period	Payment Period	Accrued Interest (A)	Interest Cash Flow (C)	Principal Cash Flow (D)	Begin-ning (B)	Ending (E) = (A) + (B) - (C) - (D)
0					-100		
0.25	1		2.5000			100.0000	102.5000
0.5	2		2.5625			102.5000	105.0625
0.75	3		2.6266			105.0625	107.6891
1	4		2.6922			107.6891	110.3813
1.25	5		2.7595			110.3813	113.1408
1.5	6		2.8285			113.1408	115.9693
1.75	7		2.8992			115.9693	118.8686
2	8	1	2.9717	21.8403	100	118.8686	0
				FV = 21.8403	+	100 = 121.8403	

In this case, the interest payment has occurred at the end of the investment period (the end of the contract). This is referred to as having an at-end payment frequency. Figure 1.2 presents a schematic view of the cash flows associated with this case from the investor's point of view.

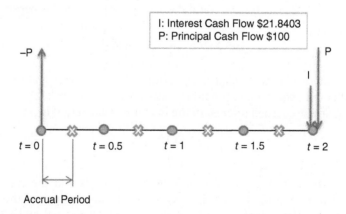

FIGURE 1.2 Cash flow schematic for an investment for two years, with quarterly compounding and at-end payment

In the case of reinvestment, we could directly calculate the future value by realizing that this case is equivalent to investing $100 for two years in an account that pays an annual interest of 10%, compounded quarterly. By indicating that the investment is for two years, we are implying that (i) the interest rate is locked at 10% for the entire two years, (ii) the interest amount earned in each accrual period is not withdrawn and is reinvested, and (iii) there is only one interest payment at the end of the investment life. Using Equation (1.3) we have:

$$P = \$100, m = 4, t = 2, r = 0.10, FV = ?:$$

$$FV = 100 \times \left(1 + \frac{0.10}{4}\right)^{4 \times 2} = 121.8403$$

Or using period notation and Equation (1.8) we have:

$$P = \$100, n = 2 \times 4 = 8, r_{pr} = \frac{0.10}{4} = 0.025, FV = ?:$$

$$FV = 100 \times (1 + 0.025)^8 = 121.8403$$

PRESENT VALUE AND DISCOUNT FACTOR

So far we have discussed how to obtain the future value of a cash flow invested at the present time earning interest over a certain period of time. When investing $100 in an account that pays an annual rate of 10% compounded annually, the future value at one year from now is $110. In other words, $110 is the future value of $100 one year from now, based on a 10% annual interest rate compounded annually. Equivalently, we can say $100 is the *present value* of a future cash flow of $110 occurring one year from now, based on a 10% annual interest rate compounded annually. The present value of a future cash flow tells us how much that cash flow is worth today, based on a given interest rate. The concept of present value is one of the most important notions in finance. It is specifically used in the valuation of a financial instrument where the present value of exact or estimated future cash flows generated by the instrument is considered as its economic value.

Consider a scenario in which an investor is planning to invest in an account that pays 10% annual interest compounded semi-annually. This investment is for a future cash requirement of $100,000 10 years from now. How much should the initial invest amount be? To answer this, consider Equation (1.3) again:

$$FV = P\left(1 + \frac{r}{m}\right)^{mt}$$

The future value is \$100,000 and t is 10 years; r is 10% and, since the compounding frequency is semi-annual, m is 2. By solving for P we have:

$$P = \frac{100{,}000}{\left(1 + \frac{0.10}{2}\right)^{2 \times 10}} = 37{,}688.95$$

Therefore, if \$37,688.95 is invested in that account today, the investor will have \$100,000 10 years from now if all interests earned during this period are reinvested. The \$37,688.95 is the present value of the \$100,000 based on a 10% annual rate compounded semi-annually. Generally, the present value of a future cash flow C occurring t years from now is obtained as:

$$PV = \frac{C}{\left(1 + \frac{r}{m}\right)^{mt}} \tag{1.14}$$

where r is the relevant annual interest rate (in decimal) and m is the compounding frequency as provided in Table 1.1. From this equation it is clear that to find the present value of a future cash flow we reduce that cash flow by multiplying it by a factor that is less than 1. In finance, the process of calculating the present value of a future cash flow is known as *discounting* and the multiplier factor to do this is known as the *discount factor (DF)*. Hence Equation (1.14) can be rewritten as:

$$PV = DF_t C \tag{1.15}$$

$$DF_t = \frac{1}{\left(1 + \frac{r}{m}\right)^{mt}} \tag{1.16}$$

DF_t in this equation can be interpreted as the multiplier factor to discount a cash flow occurring at time t in the future to its equivalent present value at time zero. The discount factor is a function of the relevant interest rate r and its compounding frequency m. Revisiting the investment example above, the discount factor for time $t = 10$ is calculated as:

$$DF_{t=10} = \frac{1}{\left(1 + \frac{0.10}{2}\right)^{2 \times 10}} = 0.3768895$$

We can find the present value of a cash flow occurring at $t = 10$ using this discount factor as long as the relevant interest rate for that cash flow is a 10% annual rate compounded semi-annually. For example, the present value of \$500 occurring at $t = 10$ is (rounded to two decimal points):

$$0.3768895 \times 500 = 453.51$$

We can find discount factors for other times similarly. For example, for a 10% annual rate compounded semi-annually, the discount factor for $t = 2$ is:

$$DF_{t=2} = \frac{1}{\left(1 + \frac{0.10}{2}\right)^{2 \times 2}} = 0.8227024$$

We can also calculate the discount factor for times that are fractions of a year. For example, based on the same interest rate above, the discount factor for $t = 0.5$ is:

$$DF_{t=0.5} = \frac{1}{\left(1 + \frac{0.10}{2}\right)^{2 \times 0.5}} = 0.9523809$$

Table 1.4 presents a few discount factors calculated for different times based on a 10% annual interest rate compounded semi-annually. From this table, it is clear that discount factors for times that are closer to present time ($t = 0$) are larger than discount factors for times that are further away in the future. This is in line with the general expectation that cash flows closer to the present time are worth more than cash flows that are further away in the future. Therefore, closer cash flows are discounted less when their present values are calculated.

TABLE 1.4 Discount factors for 10% annual interest rate compounded semi-annually

t (year)	Discount Factor
0	1
0.5	0.952380952
1	0.907029478
1.5	0.863837599
2	0.822702475
2.5	0.783526166
3	0.746215397
4	0.676839362
5	0.613913254
6	0.556837418
7	0.505067953
8	0.458111522
9	0.415520655
10	0.376889483

For the case of simple interest, the present value of a cash flow C and the discount factor are as follows:

$$PV = \frac{C}{1+rt} \tag{1.17}$$

$$DF_t = \frac{1}{1+rt} \tag{1.18}$$

For example, the discounted value of a future cash flow of $400 occurring 0.5 year from now, based on a 10% annual simple interest rate, is:

$$PV = DF_{t=0.5} \times 400 = \frac{1}{1+0.10 \times 0.5} \times 400 = 0.952381 \times 400 = 380.95$$

For a rate with continuous compounding, the present value and discount factor are calculated as follows:

$$P = Ce^{-r_c t} \tag{1.19}$$

$$DF_t = e^{-r_c t} \tag{1.20}$$

Present Value of Several Cash Flows

A common method in the valuation of a financial instrument is to determine the present values of all cash flows (exact or estimate) generated by the instrument and use the summation of these present values as the current value of the instrument. Assume that a financial instrument produces $80 six months from now, $120 one year from now, $160 one and a half years from now, and $1,200 two years from now. Also assume that the prevailing market interest rate for 0.5 year, 1 year, 1.5 years, and 2 years is an 8% annual rate compounded semi-annually. In practice, interest rates vary for different terms but for now we assume that all terms have the same interest rate. The present value of this cash flow series using Equation (1.14) is calculated as follows:

$$PV = \frac{80}{\left(1+\frac{0.08}{2}\right)^{2\times0.5}} + \frac{120}{\left(1+\frac{0.08}{2}\right)^{2\times1}} + \frac{160}{\left(1+\frac{0.08}{2}\right)^{2\times1.5}} + \frac{1200}{\left(1+\frac{0.08}{2}\right)^{2\times2}}$$

$$= 1{,}355.87$$

The $1,355.87, which is the present value of all cash flows generated by this instrument, is considered the current value of the instrument. In practice, discount factors are calculated separately and reused whenever a cash flow discounting is needed. Table 1.5 repeats the above calculation for this

TABLE 1.5 Calculation of the current value of an instrument based on the present values of its cash flows

Year	Period	DF	Cash Flow	Discounted Cash Flow
0.5	1	0.96153846	80	76.92
1	2	0.92455621	120	110.95
1.5	3	0.88899636	160	142.24
2	4	0.85480419	1200	1,025.77
				1,355.87

instrument where discount factors are first calculated using Equation (1.16) and used to obtain the present values of cash flows.

Generally, for a series of cash flows C_t the present value is calculated as:

$$PV = \sum_{t=1}^{n} DF_t C_t \qquad (1.21)$$

where C_t and DF_t are the cash flow and discount factor at time t, n is the total number of cash flows, and discount factors are calculated based on interest rate type (simple vs. compounding).

Present Value of Annuity and Perpetuity

An *annuity* is a financial instrument with several cash flows with equal amounts. If the level cash flows occur at the end of each period, the instrument is an *ordinary annuity*. Car loans are an example of an ordinary annuity. If the level cash flows occur at the beginning of each period, the instrument is an *annuity due*. Car leases are an example of an annuity due. The present value of an ordinary annuity with equal cash flows C and n periods can be derived using Equation (1.21). If periodic interest rate is r and it is the same for all periods of the annuity, the present value can be obtained using:

$$PV = C \left(\frac{1 - \frac{1}{(1+r)^n}}{r} \right) \qquad (1.22)$$

For example, for an ordinary annuity with equal cash flows of \$10,000 and eight periods, when periodic interest rate is 5% for all periods, the present value is:

$$PV = 10,000 \times \frac{1 - \frac{1}{(1+0.05)^8}}{0.05} = 64,632.13$$

If the instrument is annuity due, the first cash flows occurs at $t = 0$ (present time), so no discounting is needed for the first cash flow. If the instrument in the previous example is an annuity due, the present value is obtained by adding \$10,000 to the present value of an ordinary annuity with $n - 1 = 7$ periods:

$$PV = 10,000 + 10,000 \times \frac{1 - \frac{1}{(1+0.05)^7}}{0.05} = 67,863.73$$

Alternatively, the value of the annuity due can be calculated as:

$$PV \text{ of annuity due} = PV \text{ of ordinary annuity} \times (1 + r) \qquad (1.23)$$

For the annuity due in our example we have:

$$PV \text{ of annuity due} = 64,632.13 \times (1 + 0.05) = 67,863.73$$

Sometimes we need to find the future value of an annuity at some period n in the future. This value is calculated as:

$$FV = C \left(\frac{(1 + r)^n - 1}{r} \right) \qquad (1.24)$$

and similarly the future value of an annuity due is calculated as:

$$FV \text{ of annuity due} = FV \text{ of ordinary annuity} \times (1 + r) \qquad (1.25)$$

A *perpetuity* is an annuity where level cash flows continue forever. The present value of a perpetuity with level cash flows of C when the periodic interest rate is r can be obtained using:

$$PV = \frac{C}{r} \qquad (1.26)$$

For example, the present value of a perpetuity with level cash flows of \$10,000 when the periodic interest rate is 5% is:

$$PV = \frac{10,000}{0.05} = 200,000$$

DAY COUNT AND BUSINESS DAY CONVENTIONS

So far in our discussions we have assumed an accrual period is either a fraction of a year (e.g., $t = 0.5$) or a multiple of a year (e.g., $t = 2$), without considering the number of days in the period. For example, consider a six-month loan with a start date of May 15, 2015, and an end date of November 15, 2015. There are

185 days between the starting and ending dates of this loan. To calculate the interest amount, should we assume the length of lending is 0.5 year or 0.5068 year, obtained by dividing 185 by 365, the total number of days in 2015? In practice, the number of days in a period is important. A *day count convention* defines how days in an accrual period are counted. For example, for a three-month investment, the day count convention defines whether those three months should be considered as having 30 days each or 31 days (if applicable). It also clarifies whether the year should be assumed to have 365 days, 366 days (if it is a leap year), or a shorter version of 360 days. A day count convention is usually included in the contractual agreement between all parties involved in a financial product. For example, when a bank issues a consumer loan, the day count convention used in calculating the interest rate is included in the contract. Also, for a benchmark interest rate index, the day count convention applicable to the quoted rate is known by parties using the index.

The day count convention is sometime referred to as *accrual basis* and is commonly presented in the form of a fraction. The numerator indicates how many days in the accrual period are counted and the denominator indicates how many days are assumed for the reference period, which is typically a full year. Following are the most common day count conventions.

30/360

According to this convention, the number of days in each month is always assumed to be 30 days and a year is considered to have 360 days in total. Some U.S. corporate bonds and interest rate swap contracts use this accrual basis. As an example, consider an investment of $100 for three months, starting August 4, 2015, and ending November 4, 2015. Investment begins at the start of August 4 and ends at the start of November 4, so August 4 should be counted in and November 4 should be excluded. This investment product pays a 10% annual rate, compounded monthly. Since the length of the investment is three months, based on a 30/360 accrual basis, the total number of investment days is $3 \times 30 = 90$ days, even though there are actually 92 days between August 4 and November 4, including the starting date and excluding the ending date.

Let's first calculate the future value of this investment at the end of three months by breaking down the calculation period by period. The first period starts on August 4 and ends on September 3. There are 31 actual days in this period but due to the 30/360 accrual basis we assume this period has the length of 30 days. The accrued interest in period 1 is therefore calculated as (rounded to two decimal points):

$$100 \times \frac{30}{360} \times 0.10 = 0.83$$

Payment occurs at the end of the investment so this accrued interest is reinvested and the beginning balance for period 2 is: $100 + 0.83 = 100.83$. In the second period the accrued interest is calculated as:

$$100.83 \times \frac{30}{360} \times 0.10 = 0.84$$

The ending balance for period 2 (beginning balance for period 3) after reinvestment is: $100.83 + 0.84 = 101.67$. Finally, the accrued interest in period 3 is calculated as:

$$101.67 \times \frac{30}{360} \times 0.10 = 0.85$$

The balance at the end of the third period, the future value, is obtained as: $101.67 + 0.85 = 102.52$. This calculation is summarized in Table 1.6. Note that in this table, the day count for all periods is indicated as 30, based on a 30/360 day count convention.

We could obtain the future value at the end of three months directly by using period notation and Equation (1.8). To do so, first we need to calculate the periodic rate. Here each period is one month and since a 30/360 accrual basis is used, the periodic interest rate is:

$$r_{pr} = \frac{30}{360} \times 10\% = 0.8333\%$$

Based on a 30/360 accrual basis, a year has 12 equal-length months and the number of periods in this example is three. Therefore, the future value is:

$$FV = 100 \times (1 + 0.008333)^3 = 100.52$$

Equivalently, we could get to the same result if year notation and Equation (1.3) are used. Since the compounding frequency is monthly, $m = 12$. The length of investment is three months and based on 30/360 day

TABLE 1.6   Calculation of interest based on a 30/360 day count convention

	Date		Beginning	Day	Periodic Interest	Interest	Ending
Period	From	To	Balance	Count	Rate	Amount	Balance
1	8/4/2015	9/3/2015	$100.00	30	0.8333%	$0.83	$100.83
2	9/4/2015	10/3/2015	$100.83	30	0.8333%	$0.84	$101.67
3	10/4/2015	11/3/2015	$101.67	30	0.8333%	$0.85	$102.52

count convention, each month is exactly $\frac{1}{12}$ of a year, totaling $\frac{3}{12}$. Therefore, the future value is:

$$FV = 100 \times \left(1 + \frac{0.10}{12}\right)^{12 \times \frac{3}{12}} = 100.52$$

In the examples discussed before introducing the day count convention, we implicitly assumed a 30/360 accrual basis. Based on a 30/360 accrual basis, a month is always $\frac{1}{12}$ year, a quarter is always $\frac{3}{12}$ year, and a half-year is always $\frac{6}{12}$ year, no matter how many days are actually included in the accrual or payment period.

Actual/Actual (Act/Act)

Based on this convention, the actual number of days in the accrual period and actual number of days in the year are considered in calculating the accrued interest amount. U.S. Treasury bonds use this accrual basis.[3] Consider again the $100 investment for three months, starting on August 4, 2015, and ending on November 4, 2015. In the first period, between August 4 and September 3, there are 31 actual days (including both August 4 and September 3). Year 2015 has 365 actual days. Therefore, based on the Act/Act day count convention the interest accrued during the first period is $0.85, calculated as:

$$100 \times \frac{31}{365} \times 0.10 = 0.85$$

Since the compounding frequency is monthly and payment happens at the end of investment, this accrued interest is added to the original principal and the starting balance used for calculating the interest of the second period is $100 + 0.85 = 100.85$. This calculation is shown in the first rows of Table 1.7. For the first period, the periodic interest of 0.8493% is calculated as $\frac{31}{365} \times 10\% = 0.8493\%$. The second period starts on September 4 and ends on October 3. There are 30 actual days between (and including) these days. Considering the starting balance of $100.85, the accrued interest based on the Act/Act day count convention is calculated as:

$$100.85 \times \frac{30}{365} \times 0.10 = 0.83$$

The ending balance of the second period is $100.85 + 0.83 = 101.68$. The periodic interest rate for this accrual period is $\frac{30}{365} \times 10\% = 0.8219\%$. This calculation is shown in the second row of Table 1.7.

TABLE 1.7 Calculation of interest based on an Actual/Actual day count convention

Period	Date From	Date To	Beginning Balance	Day Count	Periodic Interest Rate	Interest Amount	Ending Balance
1	8/4/2015	9/3/2015	$100.00	31	0.8493%	$0.85	$100.85
2	9/4/2015	10/3/2015	$100.85	30	0.8219%	$0.83	$101.68
3	10/4/2015	11/3/2015	$101.68	31	0.8493%	$0.86	$102.54

The last period starts on October 4 and ends on November 3. There are 31 actual days between (and including) these days. Therefore, the accrued interest for this accrual period is calculated as:

$$101.68 \times \frac{31}{365} \times 0.10 = 0.86$$

The ending balance, the future value, is obtained as $101.68 + 0.86 = 102.54$ and the periodic interest rate for the third period is $\frac{31}{365} \times 10\% = 0.8493\%$. This calculation is shown in the third row of Table 1.7. Note that in this table, the day count for each period is the actual number of days in that period.

We can obtain the same result if we use period notation and a variation of Equation (1.8). In using period notation, we should keep in mind that the periodic interest rate for a period can be different from other periods. This is due to the use of an Act/Act day count convention and the fact that there could be a different number of days in each period. As noted above, the periodic interest rate is 0.8493% for periods 1 and 3 where each period has 31 days, but for period 2 with 30 days, the periodic interest rate is 0.8219%. To obtain future value using period notation and considering the monthly compounding, we need to consider each period separately, as follows:

$$FV = 100 \times (1 + 0.8493\%) \times (1 + 0.8219\%) \times (1 + 0.8493\%) = 102.54$$

Can we use year notation and Equation (1.3) here? We can, but it produces an approximate result. In using Equation (1.3) we essentially assume that the periodic interest rate for all periods is the same and equal to $\frac{r}{m}$, regardless of the actual portion of a year that a period represents. This means that, for a monthly compounding frequency of a 10% annual rate, the periodic interest rate is $\frac{r}{m} = \frac{10\%}{12} = 0.8333\%$, but, as shown above, due to an Act/Act day count convention, the periodic interest rate varies from period to period. In this case using period notation and calculating the interest amount period by period is the correct approach.

Actual/365 (Act/365)

This day count convention is similar to Act/Act but the number of days in a year is always assumed as 365 days, even for leap years. Many consumer loans use this convention.

Actual/360 (Act/360)

This day count convention is similar to Act/Act but the number of days in a year is always assumed as 360 days. The London Interbank Offered Rate (LIBOR) is based on this convention.[4] We discuss LIBOR in more detail in another section of this chapter.

While a day count convention defines the method of counting days in a period, a *business day convention* outlines adjusting the timing of cash flows in accordance with a given holiday schedule. Business day convention and the associated holiday schedule is a contractual feature and decided at the time of contract inception. When a payment date falls on a weekend or a holiday (non-business days), the business day convention determines when the cash flow should occur. The most common business day conventions are as follows.

No Adjustment: The timing of cash flows is not adjusted for non-business days.

Previous: If a payment date falls on a non-business day, it is adjusted to the preceding business day before that non-business day.

Modified Previous: If a payment date falls on a non-business day, it is adjusted to the preceding business day before that non-business day, unless this causes the payment date to fall into the previous calendar month, in which case the next business day after that non-business day is used.

Following: If a payment date falls on a non-business day, it is adjusted to the next business day after that non-business day.

Modified Following: If a payment date falls on a non-business day, it is adjusted to the next business day after that non-business day, unless this causes the cash flow to fall into the next calendar month, in which case the business day before that non-business day is used.

End of Month – No Adjustment: The cash flow date is set to occur at the end of the month even if it is a non-business day.

For example, if a payment is to occur on September 3, 2016, which is a Saturday, and the "following" business day convention is used, the payment date is adjusted to occur on the next business day, Monday, September 5, 2016.

TREASURY YIELD CURVE AND ZERO-COUPON RATE

We now know enough about the interest rate to introduce the concept of yield curve. We start our discussion by focusing on the *Treasury yield curve*. Later in this chapter we discuss LIBOR-swap and OIS curves.

For financing government activities and public works, governments around the world borrow money by issuing securities. In the United States, the Treasury Department regularly issues securities with different maturities (terms). Some of the new issuances are to roll previously issued notes that are maturing and some are to finance new funding requirements. U.S. Treasury securities with an original term of less than one year are called *Treasury bills* (*T-bills*) and those with an original term of greater than one year are called *Treasury notes* or *Treasury bonds*. A Treasury bill is a *zero-coupon security*, meaning that it does not pay any interest in the form of a coupon payment prior to its maturity. It is sold at a discount and redeemed at the time of maturity at full face value (par value) and hence provides a return to the investor in the form of an increase in the original principal amount invested. Treasury notes and bonds are coupon-paying securities and pay interest every six months. The coupon rate for a Treasury bond is the annual rate of interest it pays. If the coupon rate of a Treasury bond is c (%), it pays $c/2$ (%) every six months. At the maturity date the face or par value is also returned to the investor.

In the previous "Present Value of Several Cash Flows" section we learned how to derive the current value of a financial instrument using the present value of its future cash flows. Depending on market conditions and supply and demand forces, the market value of a Treasury bond changes and may be different from the current value calculated using the present value method. *Bond yield* is the interest rate that if used in discounting future cash flows of a bond provides a present value that is equal to its market value. Consider a Treasury note with $1,000 face value with two years to maturity and a coupon rate of 10% annual rate – that is, it pays 5% interest to the investor every six months. The current market value of this note is $1,020. For simplicity, let's assume a 30/360 day count convention[5] so cash flows occur exactly at 0.5-year, 1-year, 1.5-year, and 2-year points. At each of these points an interest payment of $50 is paid to the investor ($\frac{10\%}{2} \times 1000 = 50$). The face value is also paid back at the maturity date. The yield y of this Treasury bond can be calculated by solving for y in the following equation:

$$\frac{50}{\left(1+\frac{y}{2}\right)^{2\times0.5}} + \frac{50}{\left(1+\frac{y}{2}\right)^{2\times1}} + \frac{50}{\left(1+\frac{y}{2}\right)^{2\times1.5}} + \frac{1,050}{\left(1+\frac{y}{2}\right)^{2\times2}} = 1,020$$

The yield that satisfies this equation is $y = 8.89\%$ annual rate compounded semi-annually.[6] This is the 2-year Treasury yield with semi-annual compounding. This is also referred to as *yield-to-maturity*, since the assumption used in its calculation is that the investor buys the security and holds it until the maturity date. If we use the Act/Act accrual basis, which is the day count convention for Treasury bonds, we still can calculate the yield but it requires some more effort. Assume that today's date is July 15, 2013, and the maturity date of our 2-year bond is July 15, 2015. Payment dates and the number of days between two consecutive payment dates are as follows:

Date	Period	Day Count
7/15/2013	0	
1/15/2014	1	184
7/15/2014	2	181
1/15/2015	3	184
7/15/2015	4	181

There are 184 actual days between January 15, 2014, and the valuation date (now) of July 15, 2013. If y is the annual yield with semi-annual compounding, the discount factor from the first payment date of January 15, 2014, to the valuation date (i.e., the discount factor at the end of the first period) is calculated as:

$$DF_{period\ 1} = \frac{1}{\left(1+\frac{184}{365}y\right)}$$

Discount factor at the end of the second period have two parts: one to discount back a cash flow occurring at the end of the second period to the end of the first period and one to discount back one more period from the end of the first period to the valuation date. There are 181 days in period 2 and 184 days in period 1, so:

$$DF_{period\ 2} = \frac{1}{\left(1+\frac{184}{365}y\right)\left(1+\frac{181}{365}y\right)}$$

Discount factors for dates at the end of the third and fourth periods are calculated similarly by discounting back one period at a time using the exact number of days in each period. Based on these discount factors, the present value of the Treasury bond cash flows is calculated and when set equal to the market value the yield is obtained by solving for y:

$$\frac{50}{\left(1 + \frac{184}{365}y\right)} + \frac{50}{\left(1 + \frac{184}{365}y\right)\left(1 + \frac{181}{365}y\right)} + \frac{50}{\left(1 + \frac{184}{365}y\right)\left(1 + \frac{181}{365}y\right)\left(1 + \frac{184}{365}y\right)}$$
$$+ \frac{1050}{\left(1 + \frac{184}{365}y\right)\left(1 + \frac{181}{365}y\right)\left(1 + \frac{184}{365}y\right)\left(1 + \frac{181}{365}y\right)} = 1020$$

The yield of 8.88% obtained from solving this equation is the annualized 2-year Treasury yield with semi-annual compounding based on an Act/Act day count convention. As can be seen here, the yield obtained using 30/360 and Act/Act are very close and for simplicity many financial publications assume a 30/360 accrual basis for Treasury bonds. Yields for terms longer than two years are obtained using the same technique and based on observed market values of Treasury bonds with corresponding maturities.

To find Treasury yields for terms of up to one year, we can use T-bill market values. T-bills are zero-coupon securities and are issued with original maturities of 4 weeks (almost 1 month), 13 weeks (almost 3 months), 26 weeks (almost 6 months), and 52 weeks (almost 1 year). T-bills are *money market* instruments that have an Act/360 day count convention, and yields are usually presented in the form of a simple interest rate. For a zero-coupon bond maturing in t year with face value N, present value based on annual simple interest r is obtained using Equation (1.17) as:

$$PV = \frac{N}{1 + rt}$$

Yield y is the interest rate used in the denominator of this equation that makes the present value, PV, equal to the current market value, MV. If we replace PV and r with MV and y respectively and solve for y, we have:

$$y = \frac{1}{t}\left(\frac{N - MV}{MV}\right) \tag{1.27}$$

We can use Equation (1.27) to calculate Treasury yields based on T-bill market values.[7] Assume that a T-bill with an original term of 52 weeks and a face value of $1,000 has a current market value of $996 and 90 days to maturity.

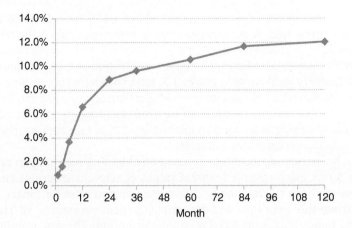

FIGURE 1.3   A sample Treasury yield curve

Using an Act/360 day count convention and Equation (1.27) we can calculate the yield as follows:

$$y = \frac{1}{\frac{90}{360}} \times \frac{1000 - 996}{996} = 0.0161 = 1.61\%$$

This is the Treasury yield for 90 days, or roughly three months, based on simple interest. Note that time t used in the preceding calculation is the remaining time to maturity and not the original term of the T-bill.

If we repeat this procedure, we can calculate the Treasury yields for different terms based on observed market values of Treasury bills and bonds. A graphical representation of yields obtained this way is known as the *Treasury yield curve*. An example for this yield curve is shown in Figure 1.3.

Bootstrapping

A yield curve, such as the one we constructed earlier, is based on observed market values of securities. Such rates are sometimes referred to as *market rates*. In this curve some yields are obtained based on the market value of securities that are zero-coupon and some are based on coupon-paying bonds. Many ALM analyses require yields that are based on zero-coupon bonds. A *t*-year *zero-coupon rate* is the interest rate earned by investing for t years where the investment does not pay any intermediate interest or principal and all cash flows occur at the end of t years. When an investor buys a T-bill for $996 today and after 90 days at the maturity receives the full face amount of \$1,000, the investment yield of 1.61%, as calculated above, is a zero-coupon rate. A zero-coupon rate is sometimes called the *zero rate* or *spot rate*.

Not all rates obtained through market observation are zero-coupon rates. For the Treasury yield curve in Figure 1.3, rates with terms of one year or less are zero-coupon rates but rates for terms longer than one year are not. To calculate discount factors used in valuation we need zero-coupon rates for different terms. *Bootstrapping* is a common method used to obtain zero-coupon rates from available market prices and rates.

The bootstrapping technique is based on obtaining zero-coupon rates for shorter terms using observed market values of relevant securities and successively applying the method to obtain zero-coupon rates for longer terms. To illustrate this technique and for simplicity, here we assume all Treasury bills and bonds have a 30/360 day count convention. The first step in bootstrapping is to select appropriate securities for their market values to be used in the calculation. Assume market values of four different Treasury securities with \$1,000 face values and different remaining times to maturity, are available, as presented in Table 1.8. In this table, the 6-month and 1-year securities are zero-coupon T-bills and the other two are coupon-paying Treasury bonds. All these securities are selected such that the cash flow (interest or principal payments) are occurring at the 0.5-year, 1-year, 1.5-year, and 2-year points from now.

Our goal here is to obtain zero-coupon rates with semi-annual compounding frequency. Starting from the 6-month T-bill, since this security is a zero-coupon note, the yield-to-maturity associated with investing now in this security and holding it until the maturity date is the 6-month zero-coupon rate or 6-month spot rate. We can calculate this yield using Equation (1.27), which provides yield based on simple interest, and then convert it to a rate with semi-annual compounding using Equation (1.10), or we can directly calculate the yield based on semi-annual compounding. From Equation (1.14), if we replace the present value with the market value of the security MV and consider that the only future cash flow of this investment is the face value N

TABLE 1.8 Market values of selected Treasury securities used in bootstrapping

Security Type	Coupon Rate (%)	Time to Maturity	Market Value (\$)
Zero-Coupon	–	6 months	982.00
Zero-Coupon	–	1 year	938.09
Semi-Annual Coupon-Paying	8%	1.5 years	1,016.00
Semi-Annual Coupon-Paying	10%	2 year	1,020.00

occurring at maturity date in t years, the yield y is calculated as follows:

$$MV = \frac{N}{\left(1 + \frac{y}{m}\right)^{mt}}$$

so

$$y = m\left[\left(\frac{N}{MV}\right)^{\frac{1}{mt}} - 1\right] \tag{1.28}$$

For the 6-month T-bill in Table 1.8, the time to maturity is $t = 0.5$ year. So for $m = 2$ we have:

$$y = 2\left[\left(\frac{1,000}{982}\right)^{\frac{1}{2\times0.5}} - 1\right] = 0.0367 = 3.67\%$$

The 3.67% is the 0.5-year zero-coupon rate with semi-annual compounding. Similarly, using the available price of a 1-year zero-coupon T-bill we can obtain the 1-year spot rate with semi-annual compounding as:

$$y = 2\left[\left(\frac{1,000}{938.09}\right)^{\frac{1}{2\times1}} - 1\right] = 0.0649 = 6.49\%$$

The 6.49% is the 1-year zero-coupon rate with semi-annual compounding. The 1.5-year Treasury bill in Table 1.8 is a coupon-paying instrument. Since there is 1.5 year remaining until the maturity date and the bond pays interest every six months, the interest cash flows occur at 0.5-year, 1-year, and 1.5-year points. Each interest payment amount is $\frac{8\%}{2} \times \$1,000 = \$40$. The principal repayment of $1,000 occurs at the maturity data at 1.5 years. From previous steps we already have 0.5-year ($r_{t=0.5}$) and 1-year ($r_{t=1}$) spot rates and in this step of the bootstrapping process we are trying to find the 1.5-year spot rate ($r_{t=1.5}$). By setting the discounted cash flows of this bond equal to its available market value we can obtain this spot rate as follows:

$$\frac{40}{\left(1 + \frac{r_{t=0.5}}{2}\right)^{2\times0.5}} + \frac{40}{\left(1 + \frac{r_{t=1}}{2}\right)^{2\times1}} + \frac{1,040}{\left(1 + \frac{r_{t=1.5}}{2}\right)^{2\times1.5}} = 1,016$$

Since $r_{t=0.5} = 3.67\%$ and $r_{t=0.5} = 6.49\%$, both with semi-annual compounding, we have:

$$\frac{40}{\left(1 + \frac{0.0367}{2}\right)^{2\times0.5}} + \frac{40}{\left(1 + \frac{0.0649}{2}\right)^{2\times1}} + \frac{1,040}{\left(1 + \frac{r_{t=1.5}}{2}\right)^{2\times1.5}} = 1,016$$

Solving the above equation provides us with $r_{t=1.5} = 6.91\%$. This is the 1.5-year zero-coupon rate with semi-annual compounding. This spot rate is consistent with the spot rates with shorter terms obtained before and observed market value of Treasury bond with 1.5 year to maturity.

So far in the bootstrapping process, we have spot rates for 0.5-year, 1-year and 1.5-year. Using these spot rates and market value of the 2-year Treasury bond from Table 1.8 we can find 2-year spot rate as follows:

$$\frac{50}{\left(1 + \frac{r_{t=0.5}}{2}\right)^{2 \times 0.5}} + \frac{50}{\left(1 + \frac{r_{t=1}}{2}\right)^{2 \times 1}} + \frac{50}{\left(1 + \frac{r_{t=1.5}}{2}\right)^{2 \times 1.5}} + \frac{1050}{\left(1 + \frac{r_{t=2}}{2}\right)^{2 \times 2}} = 1{,}020$$

Using $r_{t=0.5} = 3.67\%$, $r_{t=0.5} = 6.49\%$, and $r_{t=1.5} = 6.91\%$ in the above equation and solving for 2-year spot rate provides us with $r_{t=2} = 9.1\%$. This is the 2-year zero-coupon rate with semi-annual compounding. Table 1.9 summarizes Treasury spot rates we obtained here.

The bootstrapping process can be repeated to obtain spot rates for other terms. A graphical representation of obtained zero-coupon rates or spot rates is known as a *Treasury zero curve* or *spot curve*. An example of this curve is shown in Figure 1.4 along with the Treasury yield curve we constructed before. As can be seen from this graph, Treasury yield curve and spot curve are not identical. For example, the 2-year Treasury yield we calculated before was 8.89% with semi-annual compounding, but the 2-year Treasury spot rate calculated here is 9.1% with the same compounding frequency. The 8.89% is the rate of return of buying a Treasury note that pays intermediate coupons every six months and holding it until its maturity date in two years. The 9.1% is the rate of return of investing in a Treasury security (e.g., a Treasury STRIPS) that pays no interest until its maturity in two years when its full face value is paid. In Figure 1.4 we used linear interpolation to obtain rates between two terms with available

TABLE 1.9 Sample Treasury spot rates with a semi-annual compounding frequency and associated discount factors (DF)

Time to Maturity	Spot Rate (%)	DF
0.5 year	3.67%	0.982000
1 year	6.49%	0.938090
1.5 years	6.91%	0.903073
2 years	9.10%	0.836992

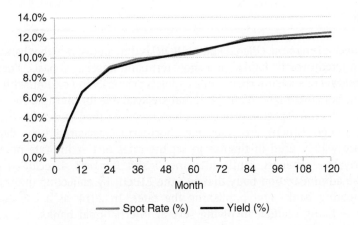

FIGURE 1.4   Sample Treasury spot curve and yield curve

Treasury rates. We discuss rate interpolation methods in more detail later in this chapter.

Spot rates are useful in calculating discount factors. Consider spot rates in Table 1.9 again. Since the rates in that table are presented with a semi-annual compounding frequency, we can use Equation (1.16) to calculate discount factors associated with each term. For example, using the 2-year spot rate of 9.1% compounded semi-annually, the discount factor for the 2-year point is calculated as:

$$DF_{t=2} = \frac{1}{\left(1 + \frac{0.091}{2}\right)^{2\times2}} = 0.836992$$

The last column of Table 1.9 provides discount factors for other terms calculated similarly.

Treasury rates are widely used in quantitative finance as a benchmark for *risk-free rates*. The risk-free rate is the theoretical rate of return in an investment where there is no chance of losing either the original principal or the expected interest payments. Considering the Treasury rate as risk-free stems from the notion that governments cannot default on their financial obligations. This is not entirely true – sovereign debt defaults have occurred in the past, for example, in Russia (1998) and Argentina (2001). Even U.S. Treasury bonds that have been always assumed to be risk-free securities and rated AAA by major rating agencies faced a downgrade by Standard & Poor's in 2011 as a consequence of the failure to raise the debt ceiling due to political reasons.

LIBOR

The *London Interbank Offered Rate (LIBOR)* is the interest rate that banks lend to other creditworthy banks for a short-term and unsecured basis. There is a large market of such interbank time deposits primarily in London, with terms ranging from overnight to one year, that are available for multiple currencies. When such time deposits are in U.S. dollars they are called *Eurodollar* deposits.

Although LIBOR are rates for short-term unsecured time deposits, they are widely used in finance to set the rates of floating-rate notes and in derivative products. Until 2014 the *British Banker's Association (BBA)* was the administration body that sets the LIBOR by collecting quotes from participating banks and publishing the rates. In 2014, as a consequence of a rate-fixing scandal involving several international banks, the administration of LIBOR was transferred to the *Intercontinental Exchange (ICE)*. LIBOR is calculated on a daily basis (except holidays) using the average of the submitted rates by participating banks where the highest and lowest 25% of submitted rates are excluded. The rates are published at 11:45 a.m. London time.

Terms of LIBOR are overnight, 1 week, 1 month, 2 months, 3 months, 6 months, and 12 months and after the reform in 2013 they are published for the U.S. dollar (USD), euro (EUR), British pound sterling (GBP), Japanese yen (JPY), and Swiss franc (CHF) currencies. Published LIBOR are annualized rates. For example, a 3-month USD LIBOR of 0.315% is the annual interest rate for a 3-month U.S. dollar deposit offered by a bank to another bank. Short-term lending products based on LIBOR are considered money market instruments and hence the quoted annual rates are simple interest. The day count convention for USD, EUR, CHF, and JPY LIBOR is Act/360 and for GBP LIBOR is Act/365.

LIBOR is widely used in finance as a benchmark rate for different financial products. Many floating-rate loans are indexed to LIBOR and several derivative contracts use LIBOR in their structures. For example, if a floating-rate loan is based on 3-month USD LIBOR, the effective interest rate of the contract is determined based on the value of 3-month USD LIBOR at the time of rate setting. *Rate setting* or *rate fixing* usually occurs in predetermined intervals (e.g., every six months).[8] For deposits or contracts that are based on USD, EUR, CHF, and JPY LIBOR, the settlement is two days after the rate fixing and for the ones that are based on GBP LIBOR or for any overnight (O/N) LIBOR, the settlement is on the same day. Table 1.10 presents a sample of U.S. dollar LIBOR for different terms as of August 31, 2016.

Many practitioners used to consider LIBOR to be a reliable and market-driven risk-free rate. This practice, however, is changing and other

TABLE 1.10   USD LIBOR as of August 31, 2016

Term	Notation	Rate (%)
1 day	O/N or 1D	0.41944
1 week	1W	0.44383
1 month	1M	0.52489
2 months	2M	0.66300
3 months	3M	0.83933
6 months	6M	1.24450
12 months	12M	1.55711

Source: The Board of Governors of the Federal Reserve System (U.S.); retrieved from FRED, the Federal Reserve Bank of St. Louis (https://fred.stlouisfed.org).

interest rate benchmarks are now being considered as market-driven risk-free interest rates.

Interest for Eurodollar term deposits is an *add-on interest*. Assume a bank borrows $1 million from another bank at a 1-month LIBOR of 0.52489% for 30 days. After 30 days the bank pays back the original $1 million borrowed amount plus the interest of:

$$1,000,000 \times \frac{0.52489}{100} \times \frac{30}{360} = \$437.41$$

Recall for T-bills, which are also money market instruments, the interest is deducted from the notional amount at the initiation time (the time the T-bill is originally issued) and the full notional amount is paid back at the maturity date, but for Eurodollar deposits the interest is added to the notional amount and paid at the end of the deposit term.

There are two rates for term deposits between creditworthy banks in euro currency. One is the Euro LIBOR that is published by ICE and one is the *Euro Interbank Offered Rate (EURIBOR)* published by the European Central Bank in Frankfurt. EURIBOR is more popular and has a wider use than EUR LIBOR. EURIBOR is published for eight different terms: 1 week, 2 weeks, 1 month, 2 months, 3 months, 6 months, 9 months, and 12 months. It has an Act/360 day count convention and two-day settlement period.

FORWARD RATES AND FUTURE RATES

Forward rates and *future rates* are estimates of interest rates in a future time. If the estimation is done using current spot rates with different terms, the estimated interest rates are called *implied forward rates*, and if the estimation is done using prices of traded securities or derivative products, the estimated interest rates are called *forward rates*. Future contracts are standardized exchange-traded derivative contracts that are based on various underlying assets. Certain future contracts use interest rates as the underlying benchmark and hence can be used to obtain estimates of interest rates in the future. Estimated interest rates based on these future contracts are called *future rates*. In this section we discuss forward and future rates in more detail. We start our discussion with implied forward rates and then introduce two derivative products that can be used to obtain forward rates and future rates.

Implied Forward Rates

Implied forward rates are interest rates in the future that are implied from current spot rates. Information carried by spot rates available at the present time provides us with the expected interest rates in the future. Implied forward rates with different terms are calculated using the spot rates.

Assume that today is August 31, 2016, and LIBORs for various terms are as shown in Table 1.10. Rates shown in that table are spot rates in simple interest form and with day count conventions of Act/360. An investor is considering two options for investing $100:

1. Investing for three months until November 30, 2016 (91 days) at a current 3-month spot rate of 0.83933% and then at the end of that time investing the proceeds from the first investment at the future 3-month rate r_f for another three months until February 28, 2017 (90 days).
2. Investing for six months until February 28, 2017 (181 days) at a current 6-month spot rate of 1.24450%.

If these two options provide different returns on investment, then there is an arbitrage opportunity. Market traders always look for such opportunities and when found act to take advantage of those mismatches. Hence, if such an arbitrage opportunity exists, it will be eliminated rather quickly by market participants' actions. Hence, generally we can assume on average that financial markets are *arbitrage-free*. Based on the arbitrage-free principle the two investments should have the same future values, therefore:

$$100 \times \left(1 + \frac{0.83933}{100} \times \frac{91}{360}\right) \times \left(1 + r_f \times \frac{90}{360}\right) = 100 \times \left(1 + \frac{1.24450}{100} \times \frac{181}{360}\right)$$

Solving this equation provides us with $r_f = 1.65067\%$. This is the implied forward rate three months from now (as of November 30, 2016) for the term of 3 months. The rate calculated this way has the same type (here simple interest) as the original spot rates used to derive it and it is a zero-coupon rate.

We use $r_{t,T}$ notation for implied forward rates, where t is the as-of date of the implied forward rate and T is the term of the rate. So r_f calculated above based on this notion is shown as $r_{11/30/2016,90\ days}$ (i.e., the implied forward rate as of November 30, 2016, with a term of 90 days) or sometimes is shown as $r_{90\ days,90\ days}$ (i.e., the implied forward rate 90 days from now, with a term of 90 days).

Figure 1.5 presents a schematic view of the implied forward rate and its relationship with spot rates. We can generalize the calculation of the implied forward rate as follows.

Suppose we are interested in calculating the implied forward at time t with a term of T, i.e., $r_{t,T}$. We need two spot rates: r_{T_1} is the spot rate with term T_1, which is equal to t (the as-of date of the implied forward rate), and r_{T_2} is the spot rate with term T_2, where $T = T_2 - T_1$ and $T_2 > T_1$. Rates are simple interest and annualized. T_1 and T_2 are in years based on the day count convention applicable to associated spot rates. The implied forward rate $r_{t,T}$ is also simple interest and obtained as:

$$r_{t,T} = \frac{1}{T}\left(\frac{1 + r_{T_2}T_2}{1 + r_{T_1}T_1} - 1\right) \tag{1.29}$$

In this example, based on an Act/360 day count convention, $T_1 = \frac{91}{360}$ year, $T_2 = \frac{181}{360}$ year, and $T = \frac{181-91}{360} = \frac{90}{360}$ year. Equation (1.29) is applicable when spot rates and calculated forward rates are simple interest. To illustrate the use

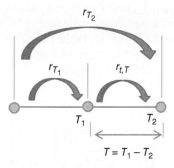

FIGURE 1.5 Schematic view of implied forward rate and its relationship with spot rates

of Equation (1.29) further, assume we are looking for the 1-month implied forward rate as of October 31, 2016. We can use 2-month and 3-month spot rates from Table 1.10 and calculate the implied forward rate as follows:

$r_{T_1} = 0.66300\%$ and $T_1 = \dfrac{61}{360}$ year (61 days between August 31 and October 31)

$r_{T_2} = 0.83933\%$ and $T_2 = \dfrac{91}{360}$ year (91 days between August 31 and November 30)

$T = \dfrac{91-61}{360} = \dfrac{30}{360}$ (30 days between October 31 and November 30)

$$r_{10/31/2016, 30\ days} = \left(\dfrac{1}{\dfrac{30}{360}}\right)\left(\dfrac{1 + \dfrac{0.83933}{100} \times \dfrac{91}{360}}{1 + \dfrac{0.66300}{100} \times \dfrac{61}{360}} - 1\right) = 1.19652\%$$

If the spot rates are compounding interest rate, Equation (1.29) can be modified to produce the implied forward rate with the same compounding frequency as spot rates:

$$r_{t,T} = m\left[\left(\dfrac{\left(1 + \dfrac{r_{T_2}}{m}\right)^{mT_2}}{\left(1 + \dfrac{r_{T_1}}{m}\right)^{mT_1}}\right)^{\frac{1}{mT}} - 1\right] \tag{1.30}$$

In Equation (1.30), T_1, T_2, and $T = T_2 - T_1$ are in years and m is the compounding frequency. For example, assume spot rates with semi-annual compounding as of today are as shown in Table 1.11. The implied forward rate at $t = 2$ for a term of $T = 1$ ($r_{2Y,1Y}$) is calculated using a 2-year spot rate of 1.94% and a 3-year spot rate of 2.12%, as follows:

$$r_{2Y,1Y} = 2 \times \left[\left(\dfrac{\left(1 + \dfrac{0.0212}{2}\right)^{2\times3}}{\left(1 + \dfrac{0.0194}{2}\right)^{2\times2}}\right)^{\frac{1}{2\times1}} - 1\right] = 2.4805\%$$

If the spot rates have continuous compounding, the forward rate with the same compounding frequency can be obtained as follows:

$$e^{r_{T_1} T_1} \times e^{r_{t,T}(T_2 - T_1)} = e^{r_{T_2} T_2}$$

TABLE 1.11 Assumed spot rates with semi-annual compounding

Term	Rate (%)
0.5 year	0.50
1 year	1.20
1.5 years	1.67
2 years	1.94
2.5 years	2.05
3 years	2.12

By taking the natural logarithm of both sides and rearranging we have:

$$r_{t,T} = \frac{r_{T_2} T_2 - r_{T_1} T_1}{T_2 - T_1} = \frac{r_{T_2} T_2 - r_{T_1} T_1}{T} \tag{1.31}$$

Equations (1.29), (1.30), and (1.31) can be combined into one equation using discount factor notation. Assume DF_{T_1} and DF_{T_2} are discount factors using spot rates with terms T_1 and T_2. These are factors to discount a cash flow occurring at T_1 and T_2 back to the current date. $DF_{t,T}$ is the discount factor based on the implied forward rate $r_{t,T}$. It is the factor to discount a cash flow occurring at $t + T$ back to t (or discounting from T_2 back to T_1). Figure 1.6 presents a schematic view of a discount factor based on implied forward rate and its relationship to discount factors based on spot rates. Using these notations and from Equations (1.29), (1.30), or (1.31) we have:

$$DF_{t,T} = \frac{DF_{T_2}}{DF_{T_1}} \tag{1.32}$$

Having a discount factor that discounts back from time $t + T$ to time t, we can calculate the implied forward rate at t for the term of T. If the implied forward rate with compounding interest is required, we can use Equation (1.16) to obtain the implied forward rate:

$$r_{t,T} = m\left(DF_{t,T}^{-\frac{1}{mT}} - 1\right) \tag{1.33}$$

If the implied forward rate with simple interest is required, we can use Equation (1.18) to obtain the implied forward rate:

$$r_{t,T} = \frac{1}{T}(DF_{t,T}^{-1} - 1) \tag{1.34}$$

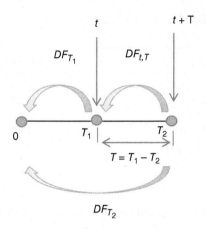

FIGURE 1.6 Discount factor based on implied forward rate and its relationship to discount factors based on spot rates

And finally, if the implied forward rate with continuous compounding is needed, we can use Equation (1.20) to obtain the implied forward rate as:

$$r_{t,T} = -\frac{1}{T}\ln DF_{t,T} \qquad (1.35)$$

Using Equations (1.32), (1.33), (1.34), and (1.35) makes calculating implied forward rates straightforward. First, we need to calculate discount factors for different dates in the future using available or interpolated spot rates, considering interest types of spot rates (simple vs. compounding), and applicable day count conventions. For example, assume using current spot rates we calculated discount factors for 183 days and 273 days from now as $DF_{183\text{ days}} = 0.998958$ and $DF_{273\text{ days}} = 0.987893$. The applicable discount factor to discount a cash flow occurring at 273 days in the future back to 183 days in the future (i.e., discounting back for 90 days) using Equation (1.32) is:

$$DF_{183\text{ days},90\text{ days}} = \frac{DF_{273\text{ days}}}{DF_{183\text{ days}}} = \frac{0.987893}{0.998958} = 0.988923$$

The 3-month implied forward rate at $t = 183$ days from now is calculated using Equation (1.34) as:

$$r_{183\text{ days},90\text{ days}} = \frac{1}{\frac{90}{360}} \times (0.988923^{-1} - 1) = 4.4802\%$$

Forward Rate Agreements

A *forward rate agreement (FRA)* is a derivative product in which the underlying is not an asset but an interest rate. The most common FRAs are based on LIBOR. In an FRA one side of the contract (the *long side*) agrees to an obligation to pay based on the fixed-rate interest on a given notional amount at a future time. The other side of the contract (the *short side*) agrees to an obligation to pay based on a floating interest rate index (e.g., 6-month USD LIBOR), at the same future date and based on the same notional amount. Assume company A and bank B have entered into an FRA in which A is long and B is short. The notional amount is $1 million and the maturity of the contract is in 90 days from now. The agreed-on fixed rate is 4% and the underlying is 6-month USD LIBOR. The common notation for this contract is "3 × 9," where the "3" indicates that the expiration of the contract is three months from contract initiation time and the "9" indicates that nine months from initiation time (or six months from expiration of the contract) the cash flow is supposed to occur.

Based on this FRA, at the maturity date of the contract party A has an obligation to pay 4% interest on the notional amount for 180 days after the maturity date of the contract. The 180 days is based on the term of the underlying (6-month LIBOR). On the other hand, party B has an obligation to pay interest based on the 6-month LIBOR as of the maturity date, whatever the 6-month LIBOR at the maturity date is, and based on the same notional amount, at 180 days after the maturity date. The FRA is settled at the maturity date of the contract and parties do not wait for 180 days to settle. At the maturity date a discounted net amount is paid to one side of the contract by the other side.

For example, assume 90 days has passed and the 6-month LIBOR at the maturity date of the contract is 5%. At that time, party A is obligated to pay 4% × $1 million, 180 days after the maturity date and party B is obligated to pay 5% × $1 million, 180 days after the maturity date. Since FRAs are settled at the maturity date, the net amount that is supposed to be paid 180 days after the maturity date is discounted back to the maturity date using the prevailing market interest rate at that date. Since the 6-month LIBOR at the maturity date was higher than the agreed-on fixed rate, the discounted net amount will be paid to party A (the long side). The cash flow from party B to party A is:

$$1{,}000{,}000 \times \left[\frac{(0.05 - 0.04) \times \frac{180}{360}}{1 + 0.05 \times \frac{180}{360}} \right] = 4{,}878.05$$

Note that to discount the net amount, the interest rate used in the denominator is the 6-month LIBOR at the maturity date (5%) and not the fixed rate of the FRA (4%). Also, the term of the underlying is used (180 days) and not the time to maturity date (90 days). If the 6-month LIBOR at the maturity date was lower than 4%, the net cash flow would become negative, meaning the payment would be from party A to party B. We can generalize the net cash flow to the long side of FRA at the maturity date as follows:

$$\text{FRA payoff} = N \left[\frac{(r - r_f)\left(\frac{T}{360}\right)}{1 + r\left(\frac{T}{360}\right)} \right] \tag{1.36}$$

where:

N = Notional amount

r_f = Agreed-on fixed rate of contract

r = Rate of underlying index at expiration of contract

T = Time to maturity (in days)

In Equation (1.36), 360 is used since FRAs are usually based on LIBOR.[9] If this payoff is negative, it would be a cash flow to the short side of the contract. FRAs are available in the market for different maturities and based on different underlying rates. Common FRA maturities range from 1 month to 12 months. The most common underlying rates for FRAs are 30-day LIBOR, 60-day LIBOR, 90-day LIBOR, and 180-day LIBOR.

While implied forward rates are obtained using spot rates, derivative products such as FRAs, when traded in a liquid market, provide a direct view on expected interest rate levels in the future. *Forward rates* are future interest rates obtained using market-traded securities or derivatives.

The value of an FRA contract at its inception is zero. Fixed rates in FRA contracts are considered as market-presumed forward rates of the underlying interest rate index at the maturity time of contracts. For example, in the above FRA the 4% fixed rate is what market participants expect the 6-month LIBOR to be at 90 days from contract inception. Therefore FRA rates are considered as benchmarks for forward rates. Using these forward rates we can extend the LIBOR spot curve beyond the one-year point (the longest LIBOR term). We will explain this application in a later section of this chapter when we discuss building the LIBOR-swap spot curve.

Interest Rate Futures

Eurodollar futures contracts are a standardized exchange-traded derivative product where the underlying is the 3-month (90-day) Eurodollar interest rate. It is one of the most popular interest rate futures products traded on the *Chicago Mercantile Exchange (CME)*.

Eurodollar futures contracts are used both for hedging purposes and speculation and they have different maturity dates going out to 10 years. In Eurodollar future contracts the underlying is the 90-day LIBOR expressed in quarterly compounding using an Act/360 day count convention, based on a \$1 million notional amount. The contract is traded based on the 90-day LIBOR at the expiration date of the contract; therefore one can use such a contract to lock in an interest rate at a future date. The quoted price of each contract is based on $100 - r_f$ where r_f is the future rate priced into the contract at its inception. The final settlement of the contract is a cash settlement at the expiration date based on the 3-month LIBOR published by ICE for that date.

Eurodollar future contracts are marked-to-market every day and, based on the value of the contract on each day, the margin accounts of the long (purchaser) and short (seller) sides of the contract are credited or debited accordingly. Every 1 basis point change in the underlying interest rate would result in a \$25 gain or loss to the long or short positions of the contract:

$$1,000,000 \times \left(\frac{0.01}{100}\right) \times \frac{90}{360} = 25$$

The long position gains \$25 and short position loses \$25 every time 3-month LIBOR falls by 1 basis point. The opposite is true if 3-month LIBOR increases by 1 basis point.

Assume today a Eurodollar future contract with 1-year term is quoted as 96.5. This means the 3-month LIBOR 1 year from now (at the expiration date) which is priced into the contract is 3.5% ($100 - 3.5 = 96.5$). We call this 3.5% rate the future rate. Eurodollar future contract is settled at the maturity date and the contract settlement value based on contractual rate of 3.5% is:

$$1,000,000 \times \left(\frac{100 - 3.5}{100}\right) \times \frac{90}{360} = 991,250$$

Assume that the 3-month LIBOR at the maturity date of the contract reached 3% and hence the final settlement price is $100 - 3 = 97$. Based on the 3-month LIBOR of 3% at the expiration date, the final contract price is 97 and the final contract value is:

$$1,000,000 \times \left(\frac{100 - 3}{100}\right) \times \frac{90}{360} = 992,500$$

The difference of $992,500 - 991,250 = 1,250$ is what the long side of the contract gains at the expiration date.[10] The short side loses \$1,250 at that date.

While both Eurodollar future contracts and FRAs indicate estimates of interest rate at some time in the future, there are differences between the two derivatives. First, for Eurodollar future contracts the settlement happened at the expiration date (T_1) based on the interest rate at that date and without considering the investment for an extra three months (the term of the underlying) after the contract maturity date. Recall that for FRA, at the expiration date the contract is settled but it is assumed an investment happens for the term of the underlying (T) and the net cash flow at the end of that period $(T_2 = T_1 + T)$ is discounted back to the maturity date of the contract at T_1 to calculate gain or loss. Second, the Eurodollar future contract has a daily mark-to-market, whereas FRA doesn't have such a feature.

Due to these differences, future rates priced into Eurodollar future contracts are higher than forward rates obtained from FRAs for similar terms. To obtain forward rates from future rates an adjustment is required. One such approximate adjustment, commonly referred to as *convexity adjustment*, is as follows (Hull 2005):[11]

$$\text{Forward rate} = \text{Future rate} - 0.5\,\sigma^2 T_1 T_2 \qquad (1.37)$$

where σ is the volatility of a short-term interest rate (also known as *short rate*), expressed annually, and T_1 and T_2 are as defined above, expressed in years. Equation (1.37) assumes that rates are stated with continuous compounding. We discuss short rate in more detail in a later chapter when we discuss interest rate models. After this adjustment is made, forward rates obtained from Eurodollar future contracts can be used to extend the LIBOR spot curve beyond the 1-year point. We use this later in this chapter when we discuss building the LIBOR-swap spot curve.

SWAP RATE

Another popular derivative product that is widely used by both financial and non-financial companies is the *interest rate swap*. In its simplest form, an interest rate swap (*plain-vanilla interest rate swap*) is a bilateral agreement between two parties to exchange cash flows in specific times in the future, where one side's cash flow is based on a fixed rate and the other side's is based on a floating-rate index. Both cash flows are in the same currency and based on the same notional amount. The fixed rate used in an interest rate swap contract is known as the *swap rate*. The floating-rate index used in most interest rate swap contracts is LIBOR for the corresponding currency. Swap contract details and conventions are usually set based on predefined *Master Agreements* by *International Swaps and Derivatives Association (ISDA)*.

The terms of interest rate swap contracts vary, usually from 2 years to 10 years and occasionally longer. In a plain-vanilla interest rate swap contract, one side pays a fixed rate on a given notional amount (*fixed-payer*) and the other side pays a floating rate on the same notional amount (*floating-payer* or *fixed-receiver*). At the inception or expiration date of the contract, notional amounts are not exchanged and during the term of the contract calculated interest amounts of the two sides are netted so payments are net amounts of payment periods, paid by one side to the other. Day count convention, payment frequency of the fixed and floating sides, and reset frequency of the floating side of swap contracts vary in different markets. For example, for British Pound Sterling interest rate swaps, usually the floating side is based on 6-month GBP LIBOR with an Act/365 day count convention and semi-annual payment and reset frequencies, and the fixed side is based on an Act/365 day count convention and semi-annual payments. For U.S. dollar interest rate swaps, the floating side is usually based on 3-month USD LIBOR with an Act/360 day count convention and quarterly payment and reset frequencies, and the fixed side has a 30/360 day count convention and semi-annual payments.

Consider a GBP plain-vanilla interest rate swap with an inception date of December 15, 2016. The contractually agreed fixed rate is 1.1% and the floating rate is based on 6-month GBP LIBOR, which we assume at the time of contract inception ($t = 0$) was 0.70%. The maturity of the contract is two years and the notional amount is £1 million. The fixed payments occur, based on semi-annual frequency, on June 15 and December 15, 2017, and June 15 and December 15, 2018. The floating payments also occur on the same dates and both sides used an Act/365 day count convention. The first fixed payment on June 15, 2017 is calculated as:

$$1,000,000 \times 0.011 \times \frac{182}{365} = 5,484.93$$

where 182 is the number of days between the inception date of December 15, 2016, and the first payment date of June 15, 2017. This is the amount the fixed-payer should pay to the floating-payer side. The rate for the first floating payment is set on December 15, 2016, when the 6-month GBP LIBOR was 0.70%. Therefore, the first floating payment on June 15, 2017, is calculated as:

$$1,000,000 \times 0.007 \times \frac{182}{365} = 3,490.41$$

This is the amount the floating-payer should pay the fixed-payer side. In practice the net of these two cash flows (i.e., 5,484.93 − 3,490.41 = 1,994.52) is paid by the side that has the higher cash outflow (in this case, the fixed-payer pays £1,994.52 to the floating-payer side). The second fixed payment occurs on December 15, 2017. The amount of this payment is calculated as:

$$1,000,000 \times 0.011 \times \frac{183}{365} = 5,515.07$$

where 183 is the number of days between the first payment date of June 15, 2017, and the second payment date of December 15, 2017. The floating rate interest for the second floating payment is set on June 15, 2017. That rate is unknown at the time of contract inception. Assume the 6-month GBP LIBOR as published by ICE at June 15, 2017, is 1.15%. The amount of the second floating payment occurring on December 15, 2017, is calculated as:

$$1,000,000 \times 0.0115 \times \frac{183}{365} = 5,765.75$$

On December 15, 2017, the net amount of $5,765.75 - 5,515.07 = 250.68$ is paid by the floating-payer to the fixed-payer side, since the cash outflow of the floating-payer is larger than the fixed-payer cash outflow. Using the actual 6-month GBP LIBOR at December 15, 2017, and June 15, 2018, net cash flow at the third payment date of June 15, 2018, and the fourth and final payment date of December 15, 2018, are calculated similarly. At the maturity date of December 15, 2018, only the net of the interest payments is exchanged and the notional amount is not swapped.

At the inception of the contract, the first floating payment is known because the interest rate was set at the beginning of the accrual period, but the floating rates for payment dates of December 15, 2017, June 15, 2018, and December 15, 2018, are unknown at that time. Table 1.12 summarizes the cash flow calculation when realized 6-month GBP LIBOR for December 15,

TABLE 1.12 Cash flow of a GBP plain-vanilla interest rate swap based on assumed 6-month GBP LIBOR

	Date	t (Day)	Day Count	Fixed Payment	Floating Payment	Net Payment by Fixed-Payer	6-month GBP LIBOR
Inception	12/15/2016	0					0.70%
	6/15/2017	182	92	5,484.93	3,490.41	1,994.52	1.15%
	12/15/2017	365	91	5,515.07	5,765.75	(250.68)	1.05%
	6/15/2018	547	92	5,484.93	5,235.62	249.32	1.04%
Maturity	12/15/2018	730	91	5,515.07	5,214.25	300.82	

TABLE 1.13 USD Swap rates as of August 31, 2016, end-of-day

Term	Notation	Rate (%)
2 years	2Y	1.04
3 years	3Y	1.09
5 years	5Y	1.19
7 years	7Y	1.30
10 years	10Y	1.43
30 years	30Y	1.70

Source: The Board of Governors of the Federal Reserve System (U.S.); retrieved from FRED, the Federal Reserve Bank of St. Louis (https://fred.stlouisfed.org).

2016, June 15, 2017, December 15, 2017, and June 15, 2018, are assumed as 0.70%, 1.15%, 1.05%, and 1.04%, respectively.

Banks and investment banks are the usual *market-makers* in a swap market. These firms are willing to engage with qualified counterparties as either the fixed-payer or fixed-receiver side of an interest rate swap. The fixed interest rates a market-maker is willing to pay or receive in an interest rate swap contract (bid and offer rates) are actively collected by financial news and data companies and the average of the bid and offer rates are reported as the *swap rate* for different terms. Table 1.13 presents a sample of U.S. dollar swap rates as of the end of August 31, 2016. These are *swap par rates*. We will learn in the next section how to derive *spot rates* from these par rates and use them to extend the LIBOR spot curve.

Determination of the Swap Rate

As mentioned above, the swap rate is the fixed rate used in the fixed leg of the interest rate swap contract. This rate is determined such that the value of the swap contract is zero at its inception date; hence there is no premium paid by either side to enter into a plain-vanilla interest rate swap contract.[12] Cash flows of a plain-vanilla interest rate swap can be replicated by combining a fixed-rate bond and a floating-rate bond with the notional amounts, payment, and reset frequencies that are the same as the swap contract. To have a zero value for the swap contract at the inception date, values of these two bonds should be equal. The fixed rate that makes this equality hold is the swap rate.

In the next chapter we explain the valuation of financial instruments in more detail. Here we briefly discuss the use of bond valuation to demonstrate deriving the swap rate using the replicating bonds method. The value of each replicating bond is the present value of its expected cash flows. The fixed leg of the swap is replicated by a fixed-rate bond. The notional amount of this bond is the same as the swap notional. The fixed-rate bond has several interest payments occurring on the same payment dates as the swap fixed leg. The rate used for deriving these interest payments is the swap rate, which is set at the contract's inception. This is the rate that we are aiming to calculate. The fixed-rate bond also has one principal payment equal to the notional amount, occurring at the maturity date of the swap. Note that for the swap contract itself the notional amount is not exchanged, but for the replicating bond we do consider a principal payment equal to the notional amount at the maturity date. The floating leg of the swap is replicated by a floating-rate bond, with the same notional amount as the swap contract. The floating-rate bond has several interest payments occurring at the same payment dates of the swap floating leg. The rate used for the first interest payment is known at the contract's initiation time but rates for subsequent interest payment are not available at that time but can be estimated. One approach to estimating these unknown rates is to assume they are equal to the implied forward rates calculated from the spot rates as of contract inception time. The floating-rate replicating bond also has a principal payment equal to the notional amount, occurring at the maturity date of the swap contract.

To continue our discussion and in the remainder of this section, we use the following notation. Consider an interest rate swap contract with an original term of n periods and a notional amount of N. τ_i and τ_j are the lengths of payment periods of the fixed and floating legs of the contract for periods i and j, based on corresponding contractual day count conventions (e.g., if the fixed-leg day count convention is Act/365, then τ_i is the actual number of days in period i divided by 365). The swap contract matures after n periods, and n_{fxd} and n_{flt} are the number of periods for the fixed and floating legs respectively ($n_{fxd} \leq n$ and $n_{flt} \leq n$). For ease of notation in the following equations we use n to present the number of periods of either fixed or floating legs of the swap. This is just for simplifying the equations, but the results presented here are applicable whether payment frequencies and hence number of payment periods of the fixed and floating legs are the same or not.

Also assume that r_{j,τ_j} is the implied forward rate at the end of period j for the term τ_j (e.g., for an interest rate swap with a floating leg based on the LIBOR 3-month rate, τ_j is three months). DF_i and DF_j are discount factors from the end of periods i and j to the inception time of the swap contract. Here we make a simplification assumption that rate setting (rate fixing) dates and payment dates are the same. In practice, a rate fixing date is usually two business days before the start of a payment period. To obtain a swap rate $r_{sw,n}$ for an interest rate swap maturing at the end of period n we can use values of the fixed-rate and floating-rate bonds that replicate cash flows of two legs of the swap contract as follows:

$$\text{Value of Fixed-Rate Bond} = N \times DF_n + \sum_{i=1}^{n} Nr_{sw,n}\tau_i DF_i \qquad (1.38)$$

$$\text{Value of Floating-Rate Bond} = N \times DF_n + \sum_{j=1}^{n} Nr_{j-1,\tau_j}\tau_j DF_j \qquad (1.39)$$

By setting the values of these two bonds to be equal and solving for the swap rate $r_{sw,n}$ we have:

$$r_{sw,n} = \frac{\sum_{j=1}^{n} r_{j-1,\tau_j}\,\tau_j DF_j}{\sum_{i=1}^{n} \tau_i DF_i} \qquad (1.40)$$

This formula can be used even if implied forward rates and discount factors are not derived from the same spot rates. However, if they are from the same curve, we can simplify this formula by using Equation (1.34) and replacing the numerator with its equivalent as:

$$\sum_{j=1}^{n} r_{j-1,\tau_j}\tau_j DF_j = \sum_{j=1}^{n} \left[\frac{1}{\tau_j}\left(\left(\frac{DF_j}{DF_{j-1}}\right)^{-1} - 1 \right) \right] \tau_j DF_j = \sum_{j=1}^{n} (DF_{j-1} - DF_j)$$

$$= 1 - DF_n \qquad (1.41)$$

The last part of Equation (1.41) is obtained by expanding the consecutive sum and knowing that $DF_0 = 1$. Using this, the equation for the swap rate can be rewritten as:

$$r_{sw,n} = \frac{1 - DF_n}{\sum_{i=1}^{n} \tau_i DF_i} \qquad (1.42)$$

We could get to Equation (1.42) directly by means of a known concept in bond valuation. When rates used for estimating future interest payments of a floating-rate bond are implied forward rates calculated from the same interest rate curve that discount factors are based on, the bond value is equal to its notional value at each payment date when the rate for the next accrual period is set. This is usually referred to as the bond being *at par* at rate-fixing dates. We discuss the reasoning behind this concept in the next chapter. Based on this, the value of the replicating floating-rate bond is simply equal to the notional amount N at the contract's inception (i.e., at the first fixing date). Hence, we can set the value of the fixed-rate replicating bond equal to the par value N and solve for the swap rate, which gives us the same result as in Equation (1.42). This is also the reason that the rate obtained using this approach is referred to as the swap par rate.

Thus, when implied forward rates and discount factors are obtained from the same spot curve, Equations (1.40) and (1.42) provide the same results for the swap rate, but when two different curves are used, only Equation (1.40) is applicable. We discuss the need for the use of multiple curves in a later section of this chapter.

Example

To demonstrate deriving the swap rate, assume 6-month, 12-month, 18-month, and 24-month spot rates as of September 20, 2017, are 0.89%, 1.23%, 1.41%, and 1.63%. These rates are annualized rates quoted with continuous compounding and an Act/365 convention. Now consider a 2-year interest rate swap contract with a semi-annual payment frequency and an Act/365 day count convention for both fixed and floating legs. The floating leg of the swap is based on the 6-month LIBOR index. To calculate the 2-year swap rate using Equation (1.40), we need discount factors at the end of each payment period as well as implied 6-month forward rates for each period. The discount factor at the end of the first period on March 20, 2018, is calculated using Equation (1.20) and the available 6-month spot rate as:

$$DF_1 = e^{-0.0089 \times \frac{181}{365}} = 0.99559630$$

where 181 is the actual number of days between September 20, 2017, and March 20, 2018, and index 1 in DF_1 indicates the discount factor for the end of the first period. The discount factors at the end of second, third, and fourth periods corresponding to September 20, 2018, March 20, 2019, and September 20, 2019, are calculated similarly and shown in Table 1.14. The 6-month LIBOR implied forward rates with simple interest and an Act/365 convention are calculated using these discount factors and Equations (1.32) and (1.34). For example, the 6-month forward rate as of March 20, 2018, is obtained using discount factors in Table 1.14 as follows:

$$r_{1,6M} = \frac{1}{(184/365)} \times \left(\left(\frac{DF_2}{DF_1} \right)^{-1} - 1 \right)$$

$$= \frac{1}{(184/365)} \times \left(\left(\frac{0.98777534}{0.99559630} \right)^{-1} - 1 \right) = 1.5706\%$$

where 184 is the actual number of days between March 20, 2018, and September 20, 2018. The 6-month LIBOR implied forward rates at the end of the second and third periods are obtained similarly as $r_{2,6M} = 1.7808\%$ and $r_{3,6M} = 2.2960\%$. The 6-month spot rate as of September 20, 2017, is 0.89% with continuous compounding and to be aligned with implied forward rates calculated above, this rate should be stated in simple interest form. This conversion is done using Equation (1.12) as:

$$r_{0,6M} = \left(\frac{365}{181} \right) \left(e^{0.0089 \times \frac{181}{365}} - 1 \right) = 0.8920\%$$

TABLE 1.14 Assumed spot rates and calculated discount factors and 6-month LIBOR implied forward rates used for deriving a 2-year swap rate as of September 20, 2017

Period	Date	Time (Years, Act/365)	Period Length (Years, Act/365)	Spot Rate*	DF	6-month LIBOR Implied Forward**
0	9/20/2017				1	0.8920%
1	3/20/2018	0.49589	0.49589	0.89%	0.99559630	1.5706%
2	9/20/2018	1.00000	0.50411	1.23%	0.98777534	1.7808%
3	3/20/2019	1.49589	0.49589	1.41%	0.97912883	2.2960%
4	9/20/2019	2.00000	0.50411	1.63%	0.96792565	

*Annualized rate – Continuous compounding – Act/365
**Annualized rate – Simple interest – Act/365

Table 1.14 also lists the length of each period in the year, rounded to five decimal points. Having the discount factors, implied forward rates, and

(continued)

(*continued*)

length of periods, we can use Equation (1.40) to calculate the 2-year swap rate with a semi-annual payment frequency as:

$$r_{\text{sw,2Y}} = \frac{\begin{array}{l} 0.008920 \times 0.49589 \times 0.99559630 + 0.015706 \\ \times 0.50411 \times 0.98777534 + 0.017808 \times 0.49589 \\ \times 0.97912883 + 0.022960 \times 0.50411 \times 0.96792565 \end{array}}{\begin{array}{l} 0.49589 \times 0.99559630 + 0.50411 \times 0.98777534 \\ + 0.49589 \times 0.97912883 + 0.50411 \times 0.96792565 \end{array}} = 1.6322\%$$

Alternatively, since here the same spot rates are used for deriving discount factors and implied forward rates, we can use Equation (1.42) and data from Table 1.14 to calculate the 2-year swap rate as:

$$r_{\text{sw,2Y}} = \frac{1 - 0.96792565}{\begin{array}{l} 0.49589 \times 0.99559630 + 0.50411 \times 0.98777534 \\ + 0.49589 \times 0.97912883 + 0.50411 \times 0.96792565 \end{array}} = 1.6322\%$$

As expected, the two methods provide the same result for the swap rate. We can think of the floating leg of this swap as a series of consecutive loans with a 6-month term each, with rates of the 6-month LIBOR implied forward. The swap rate is the effective rate that replicates the return of these rolling loans. We can also verify that, since the implied forward rates and discount factors are obtained using the same spot curve, the replicating floating-rate bond is at par. Assuming a notional amount of $10 million, the value of the replicating floating-rate bond is calculated as:

Discounted Interest Payments
$$\left[\begin{array}{l} \$10\text{MM} \times 0.008920 \times 0.49589 \times 0.99559630 + \$10\text{MM} \times 0.015706 \times 0.50411 \times 0.98777534 \\ + \$10\text{MM} \times 0.017808 \times 0.49589 \times 0.97912883 + \$10\text{MM} \times 0.022960 \times 0.50411 \times 0.96792565 \end{array} \right.$$

Discounted Principal Payment
$$\left[+ \$10\text{MM} \times 0.96792565 = \$10\text{MM} \right.$$

Valuation of Interest Rate Swap Contracts

The replicating bonds approach is useful in interest rate swap valuation. The value of a plain-vanilla interest rate swap at any time during its life is equal to the difference between the values of the replicating floating-rate and fixed-rate bonds. Using the notations introduced earlier, the value of a swap with original term T and swap rate $r_{sw,T}$ from the point of view of the fixed-payer side (floating-receiver side) is obtained as:

$$V_{sw,T} = N \left[\sum_{j=1}^{n} r_{j-1,\tau_j} \tau_j DF_j - r_{sw,T} \sum_{i=1}^{n} \tau_i DF_i \right] \tag{1.43}$$

In this equation, n represents the number of remaining payment periods of the floating and fixed legs of the contract. The value from the point of view of the floating-payer side (fixed-receiver side) is $-V_{sw,T}$. This equation can be used regardless of whether the same spot curve is used for calculating discount factors and implied forward rates. However, if they are from the same spot curve, we can use the result from Equation (1.41) to simplify Equation (1.43) as:

$$V_{sw,T} = N \left[1 - DF_n - r_{sw,T} \sum_{i=1}^{n} \tau_i DF_i \right] \tag{1.44}$$

Example

Consider again the interest rate swap with an inception date of September 20, 2017, discussed in the previous example, with a notional amount of $10 million and a swap rate of 1.6322%. Assume one month has passed and today is October 20, 2017. During this month the interest rate has increased to where the spot rate with a term ending on March 20, 2018, is 1.09%, on September 20, 2018, is 1.43%, on March 20, 2019, is 1.61%, and on September 20, 2019, is 1.83%. These spot rates are presented in Table 1.15. Calculating the discount factors and 6-month LIBOR implied forward rates using these spot rates is done similarly as explained before. For example, discount factors as of March 20, 2018, and September 20, 2018, and the 6-month LIBOR implied forward rate as of March 20, 2018, are calculated as follows:

$$DF_1 = e^{-0.0109 \times \frac{151}{365}} = 0.99550084$$

$$DF_2 = e^{-0.0143 \times \frac{335}{365}} = 0.98696110$$

(continued)

(*continued*)

$$r_{1,6M} = \frac{1}{(184/365)} \times \left(\left(\frac{DF_2}{DF_1}\right)^{-1} - 1\right)$$

$$= \frac{1}{(184/365)} \times \left(\left(\frac{0.98696110}{0.99550084}\right)^{-1} - 1\right) = 1.7164\%$$

In these calculations, 151 and 335 are the actual number of days between the valuation date of October 20, 2017, and the first and second payment dates of March 20, 2018, and September 20, 2018, respectively, and 184 is the actual number of dates between the first and second payment dates. Other discount factors and implied forward rates are calculated similarly and presented in Table 1.15. Having the discount factors, implied forward rates, and lengths of periods, we can use Equation (1.43) and data from Table 1.15 to calculate the value of the swap from the point of view of the fixed-payer side as of October 20, 2017, as follows:[13]

$$V_{sw,2Y} = \$10MM \times \left[\sum_{j=1}^{4} r_{j-1,\tau_j} \tau_j DF_j - 1.6322\% \times \sum_{i=1}^{4} \tau_i DF_i\right]$$

$$= \$10MM \times [0.010925 \times 0.41370 \times 0.99550084 + 0.017164$$

$$\times 0.50411 \times 0.98696110 + 0.019525 \times 0.49589 \times 0.97749652$$

$$+ 0.024621 \times 0.50411 \times 0.96551283 - 0.016322$$

$$\times (0.41370 \times 0.99550084 + 0.50411 \times 0.98696110 + 0.49589$$

$$\times 0.97749652 + 0.50411 \times 0.96551283)] = \$37,888.34$$

In this case, since the interest rate has increased, the value of the contract has moved in favor of the fixed-payer side, with an increase of $37,888.34 from the initial $0 at the inception of the contract. The swap contract from the point of view of the floating-payer is –$37,888.34. Alternatively, we can use Equation (1.44) to calculate the value of the swap as:

$$V_{sw,2Y} = \$10MM \times \left[1 - DF_4 - 1.6322\% \times \sum_{i=1}^{4} \tau_i DF_i\right]$$

$$= \$10MM \times [1 - 0.96551283 - 0.016322 \times (0.41370 \times 0.99550084$$

$$+ 0.50411 \times 0.98696110 + 0.49589 \times 0.97749652 + 0.50411$$

$$\times 0.96551283)] = \$37,888.34$$

TABLE 1.15 Assumed spot rates and calculated discount factors and 6-month LIBOR implied forward rates used for valuation of an interest rate swap contract as of October 20, 2017, with 23 months' remaining life

Period	Date	Time (Years, Act/365)	Period Length (Years, Act/365)	Spot Rate*	DF	6-month LIBOR Implied Forward**
0	10/20/2017				1	1.0925%
1	3/20/2018	0.41370	0.41370	1.09%	0.99550084	1.7164%
2	9/20/2018	0.91781	0.50411	1.43%	0.98696110	1.9525%
3	3/20/2019	1.41370	0.49589	1.61%	0.97749652	2.4621%
4	9/20/2019	1.91781	0.50411	1.83%	0.96551283	

*Annualized rate – Continuous compounding – Act/365
**Annualized rate – Simple interest – Act/365

Another way to obtain the value of this swap contract is to evaluate the impact of the difference between the current 23-month swap rate in the market as of the valuation date (i.e., the swap rate determined using the spot rate as of October 20, 2017) and the swap rate locked in the contract (i.e., 1.6322%). Using the spot rates in Table 1.15 and Equation (1.40), the market-implied 23-month swap rate is:

$$
r_{sw,23M} = \frac{\begin{array}{c} 0.010925 \times 0.41370 \times 0.99550084 + 0.017164 \times 0.50411 \\ \times\, 0.98696110 + 0.019525 \times 0.49589 \times 0.97749652 + 0.024621 \\ \times\, 0.50411 \times 0.96551283 \end{array}}{\begin{array}{c} 0.41370 \times 0.99550084 + 0.50411 \times 0.98696110 \\ +0.49589 \times 0.97749652 + 0.50411 \times 0.96551283 \end{array}}
$$

$$
= 1.8336\%
$$

The market-implied swap rate of 1.8336% is higher than the locked swap rate of 1.6322%. This works to the advantage of the fixed-payer side of the swap contract by paying a rate that is below the prevailing market rate. At each payment date, the payoff to the fixed-payer side due to this deviation is equal to the rate difference multiplied by the swap notional amount and by period length.

Summation of discounted values of these cash flows is the swap value. Using data from Table 1.15, we have:

$$V_{sw,2Y} = \$10\text{MM} \times (0.018336 - 0.016322) \times (0.41370 \times 0.99550084$$
$$+ 0.50411 \times 0.98696110 + 0.49589 \times 0.97749652 + 0.50411$$
$$\times 0.9655128) = 37{,}888.34$$

This is the same value obtained using Equation (1.43) or (1.44).

So far, the interest rate swap contracts we've considered in this section are *spot-starting*, where the swap rate is set at the present time and the first period of contract starts immediately after settlement. There are also *forward-starting* interest rate swap contracts, where the swap rate is set at the present time but the first period starts sometime in the future. Valuation of forward-starting swaps is done using the replicating bonds approach, similar to what is explained above, while using implied forward rates and discount factors that are associated with the timing of future periods.

LIBOR-Swap Spot Curve

Due to the wide use of LIBOR in various financial products and derivative contracts, many banks use the LIBOR curve as the risk-free or close to risk-free spot curve for ALM analysis.[14] However, since the longest term of LIBOR is one year, their usage in a spot curve is limited. To overcome this obstacle, practitioners extend the LIBOR curve beyond one year by using rates obtained from FRAs, interest rate futures, and swap contracts. The spot curve that is constructed using the combination of these products and rates is called the *LIBOR-swap spot curve*. The short end of this curve, up to one year, is constructed using LIBOR. The middle part of the curve is derived using either forward rates from FRAs or future rates based on future contracts. The long end of the curve is based on swap rates obtained from quoted swap rates.[15]

Since LIBORs are inherently zero-coupon rates, they can be used in the spot curve. However, to use these rates in a bootstrapping process of longer-term rates we need to change the compounding frequency and day count convention. LIBORs are simple interest with different day count conventions depending on the currency (e.g., the USD LIBOR uses Act/360 while the GBP LIBOR uses Act/365). The LIBOR-swap spot curve we build here is based on continuous compounding with an Act/365 day count convention, so we need to modify LIBOR accordingly. A unified compounding frequency (here, continuous compounding) is used to make rates at the short end of the curve in line with rates in the middle and long end of the curve.

TABLE 1.16 Spot rates of a hypothetical LIBOR-Swap spot curve with continuous compounding and Act/365 convention

	Term	Notation	Rate (%)
	1 day	1D	0.42526
	1 week	1W	0.44997
	1 month	1M	0.53206
Short end of curve	2 months	2M	0.67184
	3 months	3M	0.85010
	6 months	6M	1.25788
	12 months	12M	1.56657
	15 months	15M	1.65403
Middle section of curve	18 months	18M	1.71812
	21 months	21M	1.80003
	2 years	2Y	1.89538
	3 years	3Y	1.96342
Long end of curve	5 years	5Y	2.43212
	7 years	7Y	2.67543
	10 years	10Y	3.11022

To demonstrate the construction of a LIBOR-swap spot curve, assume 3-month LIBOR as of today is 0.83933%. To convert this annual simple interest rate to an annual continuous compounding rate, we can use Equation (1.7). To do so, first we multiply the rate by $\frac{90}{360}$ (based on an Act/360 day count convention) to get to the periodic rate and when converting it to the continuous compounding using Equation (1.7), we multiply it by $\frac{365}{90}$ to annualize the rate (based on an Act/365 day count convention). So:

$$\frac{365}{90} \ln\left(1 + 0.0083933 \times \frac{90}{360}\right) = 0.0085010$$

0.85010% is the 3-month spot rate with continuous compounding and an Act/365 day count convention. We can convert LIBOR for other terms similarly. The first part of Table 1.16 presents spot rates obtained from a hypothetical LIBOR curve for different terms up to one year, including the 3-month spot rate we obtained earlier, based on continuous compounding and an Act/365 day count convention.

Spot rates for the middle part of the LIBOR-swap spot curve are obtained either from forward rates based on FRAs or from future rates based on traded interest rate future contracts. Since FRAs provide forward rates directly, they are preferred, but FRAs have a less liquid market compared to interest rate future contracts. Future contracts are exchange-traded and more liquid, thus providing better transparency of the data used in the bootstrapping process. However, obtaining the forward rate from the future rate requires the adjustment for the convexity, as explained in the "Interest Rate Futures" section.

Assume today a Eurodollar future contract maturing in one year with underlying 90-day USD LIBOR is priced at 98. This implies the future 90-day rate of 2% at one year from now. To obtain the spot rate for 15 months we can use the spot rate for 12 months from Table 1.16 along with the forward rate obtained from the future rate, after convexity adjustment.

The future rate of 2% per annum is based on quarterly compounding and an Act/360 day count convention. First, we need to convert this rate into continuous compounding and Act/365 to be aligned with conventions of zero rates presented in Table 1.16. This is done as follows:

$$\frac{365}{90} \ln\left(1 + 0.02 \times \frac{90}{360}\right) = 0.0202273$$

The 2.02273% is the 90-day future rate 365 days from today, with continuous compounding. Assuming volatility of 0.015,[16] we can calculate the approximate forward rate using Equation (1.37) to adjust for the convexity, as follows:

$$\text{Forward rate} = \text{Future rate} - 0.5\sigma^2 T_1 T_2 = 0.020227 - 0.5 \times 0.015^2$$

$$\times \frac{365}{365} \times \frac{455}{365} = 0.0200870$$

where 455 days is 365 days plus the 90 days of the underlying LIBOR and 2.00870% is the 90-day forward rate one year from today, with continuous compounding ($r_{12M,3M}$). To calculate the spot rate for 15 months, using Equation (1.31) we have:

$$r_{T_2} = \frac{r_{t,T}(T_2 - T_1) + r_{T_1} T_1}{T_2} \tag{1.45}$$

Here $T_1 = 365$ days, $T_2 = 455$ days, and $r_{T_1} = 1.56657\%$ (1-year spot rate from Table 1.16). Therefore:

$$
\begin{aligned}
r_{15M} &= \frac{r_{12M,3M}(455 - 365) + r_{12M}\, 365}{455} \\
&= \frac{0.0200870 \times (455 - 365) + 0.0156657 \times 365}{455} \\
&= 0.0165403
\end{aligned}
$$

The 1.65403% is the 15-month spot rate as of today, with continuous compounding and an Act/365 day count convention. We can use this spot rate to derive other spot rates in the middle section of the LIBOR-swap curve using the methodology explained earlier. In doing so we recursively calculate longer-term spot rates using shorter-term spot rates and forward rates derived based on either FRAs or interest rate futures contracts. The second part of Table 1.16 shows spot rates obtained in this way for 15-month, 18-month, and 21-month terms for a hypothetical LIBOR-swap spot curve.

Forward rates from FRAs and interest rate futures contracts can be used to derive spot rates for terms of up to two years. Beyond that point, practitioners use swap rates to extend the spot curve to longer terms of up to 10 years, and sometimes as far as 30 years, using a bootstrapping technique similar to the discussion in the "Bootstrapping" section. As discussed earlier, cash flows of a plain-vanilla interest rate swap can be replicated by a fixed-rate bond and a floating-rate bond with the same notional amounts and payment frequencies similar to the fixed and floating legs of the swap contract. At each rate-fixing date, the floating-rate bond value is equal to its par value if implied forward rates used for calculating interest payments are obtained using the same spot curve that discount factors are based on. Therefore, at the inception date of the swap contract: (1) the values of the fixed-rate and floating-rate bonds that replicate the swap cash flows are equal, and (2) the floating-rate bond is at par value. Consequently, this implies that the replicating fixed-rate bond should also be at par value. Using this outcome and since the coupon rate of the replicating fixed-rate bond is the swap rate, we can use the bootstrapping technique to calculate spot rates for longer terms by using shorter-term spot rates and progressing forward recursively.

Assume that today is December 15, 2016, and the 2-year swap rate is 1.9%, stated with semi-annual compounding frequency and a 30/360 day count convention. Payment dates are on June 15 and December 15, 2017, and June 15 and December 15, 2018. Assume spot rates for the first three of these dates are the same as rates with 6-month, 12-month, and 18-month terms we obtained earlier and shown in Table 1.16. Those spot rates may not be exactly aligned with the payment dates of this swap contract but for simplicity we assume they are aligned. When spot rates are not available for a date for which a discount factor is needed, we can use interpolation to estimate the required rate using available spot rates at adjacent term points. We explain the interpolation methods in the next section, so for now we assume that available spot rates obtained in the previous steps are in line with the payment dates of this swap contract. Since the swap rate is 1.9%, assuming a $100 notional amount and based on a 30/360 day count convention each coupon payment is: $100 \times \frac{180}{360} \times \frac{1.9}{100} =$ $0.95. This coupon amount is paid at each payment date. Since spot rates obtained earlier are based on continuous compounding, discount factors are calculated using Equation (1.20). At the contract's inception, the value of the replicating fixed-rate bond, based on four coupon payments of $0.95 each and a principal payment of $100, should be equal to a par value of $100. Thus:

$$0.95\, e^{-\frac{1.25787}{100}\times\frac{182}{365}} + 0.95\, e^{-\frac{1.56657}{100}\times\frac{365}{365}} + 0.95\, e^{-\frac{1.71812}{100}\times\frac{547}{365}}$$

$$+ (100 + 0.95\,)e^{-\frac{r}{100}\times\frac{730}{365}} = 100$$

In this equation, 182, 365, 547, and 730 are actual days between the payment dates and the present date (December 15, 2016) and spot rates are the ones obtained in previous steps from Table 1.16; r is the 2-year spot rate that we are trying to find. Solving the equation for r results in $r = 1.89538\%$. This is the 2-year spot rate with continuous compounding and an Act/365 day count convention. The same methodology can be used recursively to obtain spot rates for longer terms by using swap rates with longer terms and spot rates for shorter terms that are obtained in previous steps. The third part of Table 1.16 shows spot rates obtained in this way for two-year terms and longer for a hypothetical LIBOR-swap spot curve.

Spot rates collected in Table 1.16 are based on continuous compounding and an Act/365 day count convention. If needed, the compounding frequency of these rates can be changed to any other frequency using Equation (1.6). Spot rates presented based on any compounding frequency can be used to calculate the discount factors needed for ALM analysis. A graphical representation of the spot rates is called a *LIBOR-swap spot curve*. The spot curve we constructed here is shown in Figure 1.7. In this curve we have used a linear interpolation to connect available spot rates. In the next section we discuss interpolation methods in more detail.

We can generalize the bootstrapping of spot rates from swap rates using the replicating bonds approach and notation introduced earlier in this section. Since the value of the floating-rate replicating bond at the contract's inception is equal to the par value, by setting the value of the fixed-rate replicating bond in Equation (1.38) equal to N and solving for DF_n we have:

$$DF_n = \frac{1 - r_{sw,n} \sum_{i=1}^{n-1} \tau_i DF_i}{1 + r_{sw,n}\tau_n} \tag{1.46}$$

Once we have the swap par rates, Equation (1.46) can be used recursively to obtain the discount factors and subsequent spot rates of the LIBOR-swap curve. Instead of using LIBOR for a 12-month term, some practitioners prefer to calculate the 12-month spot rate from the forward rate obtained either

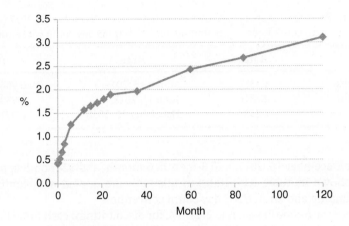

FIGURE 1.7 A hypothetical LIBOR-swap spot curve

from FRAs or future contracts. This approach is based on the idea that using spot rates implied by market-traded contracts is more practical. Sometimes for terms longer than two years and up to five years, spot rates are calculated based on FRAs and futures, and swap rates are used for bootstrapping spot rates for terms longer than five years.

Past experiences during adverse market conditions showed widening spreads between rates of government-issued notes and non-government securities. This reinforces the idea of using a non-Treasury spot curve for the valuation of non-government securities. Before the financial crisis of 2007–2009, LIBOR and the extension of the curve using swap rates were treated as risk-free rates and many commercial and investment banks used a LIBOR-swap spot curve in their ALM analysis. This practice has changed since the crisis, and financial institutions are now inclined to use other curves as the risk-free rates. We discuss one such alternative curve in an upcoming section of this chapter.

INTERPOLATION METHODS

Treasury and LIBOR-swap spot curves discussed in previous sections can be used to obtain discount factors for calculating present value. Spot curves are derived for a limited number of terms, ranging from overnight to 10 or 30 years. Overnight, 1-week, 1-month, 3-month, 6-month, 1-year, 3-year, 5-year, 7-year, and 10-year are the most common terms included in a spot curve. Discount factors for the future dates that correspond to the terms of available spot rates can be calculated using the spot rates directly. For example, assume

TABLE 1.17 A sample spot curve with three terms as of December 15, 2017 (rates are quoted with continuous compounding and an Act/365 day count convention)

Term	Rate	Date	DF
3 months	1.35%	March 15, 2018	0.99667677
6 months	2.23%	June 15, 2018	0.98894214
12 months	2.85%	December 15, 2018	0.97190229

today is December 15, 2017, and 3-month, 6-month, and 12-month spot rates are as shown in Table 1.17. Rates in this table are quoted with continuous compounding and an Act/365 day count convention.

Since the 6-month spot rate is 2.23%, for discounting a cash flow that falls on the future date of June 15, 2018 (i.e., six months from today) we can use that spot rate to calculate the discount factor as follows:

$$DF_{\text{June 15, 2018}} = e^{-\frac{2.23}{100} \frac{182}{365}} = 0.98894214$$

Here we used Equation (1.20) and 182 is the actual number of days between June 15, 2018, and today. We can obtain discount factors for March 15, 2018, or December 15, 2018, similarly, since we have the exact spot rates corresponding to these dates. But what if we need to discount a cash flow that occurs on September 30, 2018, using the above spot curve? The spot rate for that exact date is not available. There are two methods to obtain the discount factor for a target date:

1. Interpolate the available rates at adjacent dates to the target date and then use the interpolated rate to calculate the discount factor.
2. Interpolate the available discount factors for dates that are adjacent to the target date to directly obtain the discount factor.

Next we discuss two popular methods that can be used to interpolate between adjacent spot rates or adjacent discount factors. Our discussion here is focused on interpolating spot rates but the procedures can be applied to discount factors in a similar fashion.

Piecewise Linear Interpolation

In a spot curve such as the one shown in Figure 1.7 each point is represented by a zero rate and its associated term. These points, often referred to as *term points*, are either directly observed in the market or obtained using bootstrapping, as we explained for Treasury and LIBOR-swap spot curves. In interpolation terminology, these points are called *knots*. For example, in the simple spot curve presented in Table 1.17, a point with a term of six months and a rate of 2.23% is a knot. Similarly, a point with a term of 12 months and a rate of 2.85% is another knot. If the spot curve in Table 1.17 is part of the LIBOR-swap curve, rates at these two knots are directly observed in the market, via LIBOR published by ICE. These knots are adjacent since there are no other available knots between them. The area of the curve between two adjacent knots is called an *interval*.

In piecewise linear interpolation, the spot rate for a term between terms of two adjacent knots is obtained based on its position on a straight line that connects two adjacent knots. In Figure 1.7 we used piecewise linear interpolation where knots are connected using straight lines. If r_i and r_{i+1} are spot rates at two adjacent knots with terms t_i and t_{i+1}, the linearly interpolated spot rate r (target rate) with term t (target term) between these two points is calculated using:

$$r = r_i + \frac{(t - t_i)}{(t_{i+1} - t_i)}(r_{i+1} - r_i) \tag{1.47}$$

In this formula, instead of using terms of adjacent rates (in years) and the target term (in years), we can simply use the corresponding dates of those rates. As an example, consider again the spot rates in Table 1.17. The spot rate for September 30, 2018, can be obtained by linearly interpolating between the 6-month and the 12-month spot rates with corresponding dates of June 15, 2018, and December 15, 2018, as follows:

$$r = \frac{2.23}{100} + \frac{(\text{Sep. }30, 2018 - \text{Jun. }15, 2018)}{(\text{Dec. }15, 2018 - \text{Jun. }15, 2018)} \times \left(\frac{2.85}{100} - \frac{2.23}{100}\right)$$

$$= \frac{2.23}{100} + \frac{107}{183} \times \left(\frac{2.85}{100} - \frac{2.23}{100}\right) = 2.5925\%$$

Figure 1.8 presents the linear interpolation of spot rates in Table 1.17, where knots at March 15, 2018, and June 15, 2018, are connected by a straight line and knots at June 15, 2018, and December 15, 2018, are connected by another straight line with a different slope. The second line is what we used to calculate the interpolated rate of 2.5925% for September 30, 2018. Having this spot rate, we can calculate the discount factor for that date for discounting back to December 15, 2017, as:

$$DF_{\text{Sep. }30, 2018} = e^{-\frac{2.5925}{100}\frac{289}{365}} = 0.99979475$$

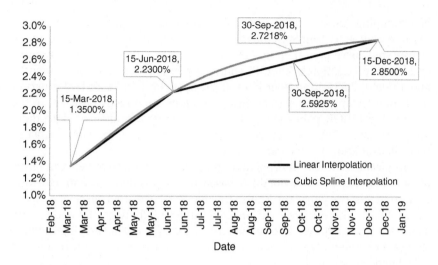

FIGURE 1.8 Piecewise linear and cubic spline interpolations of spot curve in Table 1.17

Piecewise linear interpolation is tractable and easy to implement. However, it may create kinks around points where the slope of the spot curve is changing. This issue in turn results in unrealistic jumps in implied forward rates. Curve-smoothing techniques, such as the cubic spline method, discussed in the next section, solve this problem.

Piecewise Cubic Spline Interpolation

In this interpolation method, two adjacent knots are connected by a curve with a polynomial function. To create a smooth transition from a curve in one interval to the one in the next interval, certain constraints are applied to the polynomial functions of different intervals to ensure the continuity of the spot curve and to prevent the occurrence of kinks in the curve. These constraints are:

1. At each knot, values of polynomial functions in two adjacent intervals that share the knot are equal (to ensure continuity).
2. At each knot, values of the first and second differential of polynomial functions in two adjacent intervals that share the knot are equal (to ensure smoothness).
3. At ending knots (e.g., for overnight and 30-year terms), values of the second differential of the polynomial function for the intervals that contain the ending knots are zero (to be able to solve for unknown coefficients).[17]

To develop a cubic spline interpolation for a spot curve, the term of each known spot rate r_i is shown by t_i. For a curve with terms $t_1, t_2, \cdots, t_{n-1}, t_n$ there are n knots. For example, in the LIBOR-swap spot curve presented in Table 1.16, $t_1 = 1$ day and $t_n = 10$ years. Since there are n knots, there are $n - 1$ intervals between those knots. The cubic polynomial function for interval i, between knots with terms t_i and t_{i+1}, is as follows:

$$S_i(t) = a_i(t - t_i)^3 + b_i(t - t_i)^2 + c_i(t - t_i) + d_i \quad t \in [t_i, t_{i+1}] \tag{1.48}$$

The first and second derivatives of this function are:

$$S_i'(t) = 3a_i(t - t_i)^2 + 2b_i(t - t_i) + c_i \tag{1.49}$$

$$S_i''(t) = 6a_i(t - t_i) + 2b_i \tag{1.50}$$

Considering there are $n - 1$ intervals and the polynomial function of each interval has four parameters, there is a total of $4(n - 1)$ unknown parameters that need to be estimated to completely determine the smoothed spot curve. We can use the constraints described earlier to set up $4(n - 1)$ equations and solve for the unknown parameters. The first constraint ensures that the smoothed curve is continuous by setting the values of polynomial functions in adjacent intervals equal to the spot rate at the knot they share. Therefore:

$$S_i(t_i) = r_i \quad \text{and} \quad S_i(t_{i+1}) = r_{i+1}$$

If we apply these to Equation (1.48) we have:

$$S_i(t_i) = r_i \Rightarrow$$

$$a_i(t_i - t_i)^3 + b_i(t_i - t_i)^2 + c_i(t_i - t_i) + d_i = r_i$$

or

$$d_i = r_i \tag{1.51}$$

$$S_i(t_{i+1}) = r_{i+1} \Rightarrow$$

$$a_i(t_{i+1} - t_i)^3 + b_i(t_{i+1} - t_i)^2 + c_i(t_{i+1} - t_i) + d_i = r_{i+1} \tag{1.52}$$

Equations (1.51) and (1.52) together provide $2(n - 1)$ equations. The second constraint ensures the smooth transition between curves of adjacent intervals by setting values of the first and the second derivative of polynomial functions equal at the knot shared by the adjacent intervals. Therefore:

$$S_{i-1}'(t_i) = S_i'(t_i) \text{ and } S_{i-1}''(t_i) = S_i''(t_i)$$

If we apply these to Equations (1.49) and (1.50) we have:

$$S'_{i-1}(t_i) = S'_i(t_i) \Rightarrow$$

$$3a_{i-1}(t_i - t_{i-1})^2 + 2b_{i-1}(t_i - t_{i-1}) + c_{i-1} = 3a_i(t_i - t_i)^2 + 2b_i(t_i - t_i) + c_i \Rightarrow$$

$$3a_{i-1}(t_i - t_{i-1})^2 + 2b_{i-1}(t_i - t_{i-1}) + c_{i-1} - c_i = 0 \tag{1.53}$$

Equation (1.53) is applicable for all spot rates with term t_i where $i = 2, \cdots, n$. Therefore, it provides $n - 2$ equations. For the second derivative we have:

$$S''_{i-1}(t_i) = S''_i(t_i) \Rightarrow$$

$$6a_{i-1}(t_i - t_{i-1}) + 2b_{i-1} = 6a_i(t_i - t_i) + 2b_i \Rightarrow$$

$$6a_{i-1}(t_i - t_{i-1}) + 2b_{i-1} - 2b_i = 0 \tag{1.54}$$

Equation (1.54) is applicable for all spot rates with term t_i where $i = 2, \cdots, n$. Thus, it provides another $n - 2$ equations. The third constraint provides us with the last two equations we need to solve for the unknown parameters. This constraint sets the second derivative of the polynomial functions at two ending knots t_1 and t_n equal to zero:

$$S''_1(t_1) = 0 \quad \text{and} \quad S''_{n-1}(t_n) = 0$$

If we apply these to Equation (1.50) we have:

$$S''_1(t_1) = 0 \Rightarrow$$

$$6a_1(t_1 - t_1) + 2b_1 = 0 \Rightarrow$$

$$b_1 = 0 \tag{1.55}$$

$$S''_{n-1}(t_n) = 0 \Rightarrow$$

$$6a_{n-1}(t_n - t_{n-1}) + 2b_{n-1} = 0 \tag{1.56}$$

The sets of equations presented in Equations (1.51) through (1.56) together provide us with the $4n - 4$ equations needed to solve for the $4n - 4$ unknown parameters of the cubic spline functions. Table 1.18 summarizes these equations.

Software such as *MATLAB®*, *Mathematica®*, or *SAS®* have built-in algorithms to simultaneously solve the above sets of equations and determine the smoothed curve. ALM software vendors usually include cubic spline as one of the available interpolation methods, either for spot rates or for discount factors.

TABLE 1.18 Equations to obtain cubic spline parameters for n knots

Equation Set	Interval	Number of Equations
$d_i = r_i$	$i = 1, \cdots, n$	$2(n-1)$
$a_i(t_{i+1} - t_i)^3 + b_i(t_{i+1} - t_i)^2 + c_i(t_{i+1} - t_i) + d_i = r_{i+1}$		
$3a_{i-1}(t_i - t_{i-1})^2 + 2b_{i-1}(t_i - t_{i-1}) + c_{i-1} - c_i = 0$	$i = 2, \cdots, n$	$n - 2$
$6a_{i-1}(t_i - t_{i-1}) + 2b_{i-1} - 2b_i = 0$	$i = 2, \cdots, n$	$n - 2$
$b_1 = 0$	$i = 1$	1
$6a_{n-1}(t_n - t_{n-1}) + 2b_{n-1} = 0$	$i = n - 1$	1

In SAS, the *Expand* procedure can be used to perform cubic spline interpolation. List 1.1 shows an SAS code that can be used for interpolating the spot curve in Table 1.17. In this list the input dataset is *ratedata*. It has three records, the same as in Table 1.17. If other records are added to this dataset with specific dates in the *date* field and null values in the *rate* field, the *Expand* procedure produces interpolated rates for those records and includes the results in the output dataset indicated in the *out* option. The estimated parameters (a_i, b_i, and c_i for each interval) are included in the output dataset indicated in the *outest* option. For cubic spline interpolation, the selected method in the *Convert* statement should be *spline*.[18]

Table 1.19 presents the estimated parameters for the two intervals between the three knots in the spot curve in Table 1.17. Figure 1.8 presents the cubic spline interpolation of this spot curve and compares it with linear interpolation. Unlike the linear interpolation, the cubic spline produces a smooth transition from one interval to the next one around each knot. The interpolated spot rate for September 30, 2018, is obtained using the estimated parameters and Equation (1.48) as:

$$
\begin{aligned}
r_{\text{Sep. 30,2018}} &= 0.0000000006 \times (\text{Sep. 30, 2018} - \text{Jun. 15, 2018})^3 - 0.0000003369 \\
&\quad \times (\text{Sep. 30, 2018} - \text{Jun. 30, 2018})^2 + 0.0000749865 \\
&\quad \times (\text{Sep. 30, 2018} - \text{Jun. 15, 2018}) + 0.0223 \\
&= 0.0000000006 \times (107)^3 - 0.0000003369 \times (107)^2 \\
&\quad + 0.0000749865 \times (107) + 0.0223 = 2.7218\%
\end{aligned}
$$

In this equation, 0.0223 is the spot rate at June 15 (in decimals) and similar to the example of linear interpolation method; instead of terms here we used

TABLE 1.19   Estimated parameters of cubic spline interpolation of the spot curve in Table 1.17 obtained using the SAS *Expand* procedure

Interval	a_i	b_i	c_i
March 15–June 15	−0.0000000012	0.0000000000	0.0001059850
June 15–December 15	0.0000000006	−0.0000003369	0.0000749865

dates associated with spot and target rates. The interpolated rate for September 30 using cubic spline is higher than what was obtained using linear interpolation (2.7218% vs. 2.5925%). This is due to the curvature of the polynomial function used in the cubic spline method that is needed to produce a smooth transition around June 15.

LIST 1:   **Cubic spline interpolation in SAS using the *Expand* procedure**

```
libname i "C:\ALLM";
ods graphics on;
proc sort data= i.ratedata;
by date;
run;
/* cubic spline interpolation */
proc expand data= i.ratedata   out= interpolation_result_spl
   outest=estimated_param_spl plots=converted;
id date;
convert rate / method=spline(natural);
run;
```

While the cubic spline method has the advantage of producing smooth interpolated spot curves, which is a desirable feature for implied forward calculation, sometimes it may result in unexpected outcomes. Figure 1.9 presents a case where the cubic spline method is used to interpolate rates of 2.65%, 2.23%, and 2.85% on March 15, June 15, and December 15, 2018. Here the rate decreases from March 15 to June 25 and inclines afterward. Since the rate from June 15 to December 15 increases from 2.23% to 2.85%, interpolated rates for any dates between June 15 and December 15 would normally be expected to be above 2.23% and below 2.85%. However, the fitted polynomial for this interval produces an interpolated rate of 2.2131% for July 20, which is lower than the rate at June 15. This is, again, due to the constraints applied to the adjacent polynomials to enforce a smooth transition around June 15; however, this unexpected result may be considered as counterintuitive. In cases where rates are low, this issue may even result in negative interpolated rates while rates at adjacent knots are positive. Figure 1.10 presents an example of such

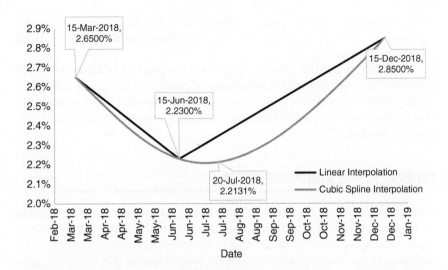

FIGURE 1.9   Interpolation using the cubic spline method may result in interpolated rates that are lower than the rates at adjacent knots

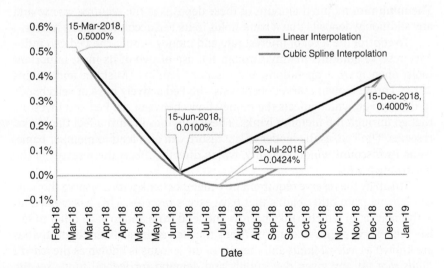

FIGURE 1.10   Interpolation using the cubic spline method may result in negative interpolated rates, whereas rates at adjacent knots are positive

a case where cubic spline is used to interpolate rates of 0.5%, 0.01%, and 0.4% on March 15, June 15, and December 15, 2018, where the interpolated rate for July 20 is –0.0424%.

Cubic spline interpolation does not have the problem of kinks occurring at knots. This method has the advantage of producing a smooth spot curve but as demonstrated above it may also result in unexpected interpolated rates. It is also harder to implement and less tractable compared to the linear interpolation method.

FEDERAL FUNDS AND PRIME RATES

Central banks around the world, as the bodies responsible for implementation of monetary policies, use various tools at their disposal to regulate the supply of money and pursue interest rate targets to achieve their mandates on economic activities. In the United States, the *Federal Reserve System* is in charge of monetary policies. The structure of the Federal Reserve System consists of a Board of Governors, 12 regional Federal Reserve Banks, and the *Federal Open Market Committee* (FOMC). All banks that are members of the Federal Reserve (*Fed*) are required to hold deposits with the Fed. These deposits are called *reserves*. The minimum required amount of these deposits is the *required reserve* and any additional deposits that a bank holds in its Fed account is *excess reserve*.

To control the level of interest rate and money supply, the Fed can influence reserve amounts mainly through the use of two of its most important tools: open market operations and discount lending (Mishkin and Eakins 2012). Through open market operations, the Fed actively buys or sells bonds in the market, which affects the money flows between the Fed and investors that go through the member banks. These activities in turn affect the banks' reserves. The Fed, as the lender of last resort, can also lend to member banks using its discount window facility, which directly affects the reserves of the borrowing banks.

To satisfy the reserve requirement, a member bank with a reserve shortage can borrow from other banks that have excess reserves. This has created an active market in which banks borrow and lend from and to each other to satisfy the reserve requirement. The funds transferred in such lending activities are known as *federal funds* and the rate of those loans is known as the *federal funds rate*. At any given day, supply and demand for federal funds set the federal funds rate and the weighted average rates of the unsecured short-term lending between banks for each date, as reported by *Federal Reserve Bulletin,* is known as the *effective federal funds rate,*[19] which is quoted in Act/360. While the Fed has no direct control on the effective fed funds rate, through its open market operations and discount lending, it can control the level of reserves and hence influence that interest rate. The Federal Open Market Committee sets its goal and expectation of the effective federal funds rate at its periodic meetings, which occur eight times a year, roughly every six weeks. That rate is known as the *federal funds target rate* and the Fed, using the aforementioned tools, attempts to make the effective federal funds rate follow this target rate.

The term of federal funds loans is usually overnight; therefore the effective federal funds rate is an overnight rate, but similar to other interest rates it is quoted in an annualized form. The Federal Reserve System publishes a weekly report, commonly known as H.15, of the selected market interest rates, including the effective federal funds rate.[20] While the effective federal funds rate may not be directly used in setting interest rates for consumer and commercial loans, it has a significant effect on the overall interest rate level and the economy.

The *prime rate* is a reference rate or index that banks use to price short-term business and consumer loans. Banks use the prime rate as their base lending rate and add extra spread to this rate as *commercial margin* to compensate for the additional risks taken by issuing the loan. In the United States, a major portion of commercial loans are priced based on the prime rate. Many consumer lending products, such as home equity loans, personal lines of credit, and credit cards, are also priced based on the prime rate. For example, a credit card may charge the revolving balance based on "prime rate + 15%." When the prime rate is 3.50% the effective annual rate of that credit card loan is 3.50% + 15% = 18.50% . Loans that are priced based on an interest rate index, such as the prime rate, are called *floating-rate or variable-rate loans*.

The Federal Reserve System collects prime rates from banks and deposit institutions and reports the rate posted by a majority of the top 25 banks in its H.15 report as the prime rate. The prime rate is a short-term rate. Although it doesn't have a specific term associated with it, the prime rate is quoted in an annualized form. For example, the annualized prime rate as of November 1, 2016, as reported in H.15 was 3.5%.

Different banks may change their prime rates at any time depending on banks' specific requirements and market conditions, but the prime rate tends to move closely with other market short-term interest rates. Specifically, since the late 1990s the prime rate has been around 3% above the federal funds rate, except for a period of a few months during the financial crisis of 2007–2009. Figure 1.11 shows the prime and the effective federal funds rates from January 2000 to April 2019, along with the difference (spread) between the two rates. This graph clearly shows the co-movement between rates, where the average of the differences is close to 3.07% in this period.[21] The prime rate, however, changes less frequently than the effective federal funds rate. The prime rate often changes discretely by multiples of 25 basis points

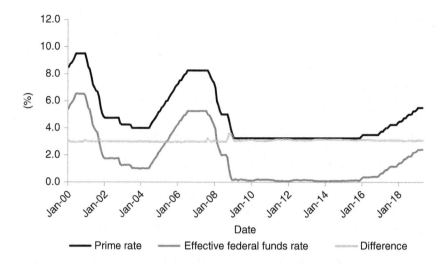

FIGURE 1.11 Prime and effective federal funds rates and spread between them
Data source: The Board of Governors of the Federal Reserve System (U.S.); retrieved from FRED, the Federal Reserve Bank of St. Louis (https://fred.stlouisfed.org).

and for that reason some criticize the use of the prime rate as an index in loan pricing as being slow to respond to changes in market conditions. After the financial crisis of 2007–2009, the Fed followed a low interest rate policy where for a relatively long period of time the fed funds target rate was kept at a range of 0% to 0.25%. Due to this policy the prime rate remained at a steady level of 3.25% from the beginning of 2009 until December 2015, when finally the Fed increased its target by 25 bps. During 2016 to early 2019 the Fed gradually increased the fed funds target rate and the prime rate increased accordingly.

The effective fed funds rate and the prime rate are both widely used in ALM analysis. Since many financial products are floating-rate instruments indexed to the prime rate, for valuation and earning analysis, either future forecasts or implied forward rates of the prime index are needed to estimate future cash flows. As discussed in the section "Implied Forward Rates," to calculate the implied forward rate from a spot curve, rates with different terms are required and for this reason direct calculation of the implied forward for the prime rate is not applicable. As an alternative, the prime rate can be modeled as a constant spread over other short-term rates such as LIBOR or OIS (discussed in the next section). Then implied forward rates from LIBOR or OIS curves plus the additional spread can be used as forecasted prime rates. However, due to assumption of the constant spread, this method of forecasting the prime rate exposes banks to the *basis risk*, which we discuss later in this chapter.

OVERNIGHT INDEX SWAP RATE

The *overnight index swap (OIS)* is similar to the plain-vanilla interest rate swap, where cash flows of fixed and floating legs are exchanged at predefined intervals. In practice, only the net cash flow is paid from one side to the other side. The contract has a notional amount that is used for calculating interest payments, but it is not exchanged. The rate of the fixed leg of the swap is the *OIS rate*. The rate of the floating leg is based on a daily published index of an overnight rate and is compounded on a business day basis during each payment period. U.S. dollar OIS contracts are based on the effective fed funds rate, which is quoted in Act/360. EUR-based OIS contracts use *Euro Overnight Index Average (EONIA)* as the floating-rate index. This index is the volume-weighted average rate of unsecured overnight lending in EUR among banks in European Union and European Free Trade Association countries. The calculation agent of EONIA is the *European Central Bank (ECB)* and is quoted in Act/360. GBP-based OIS contracts use the *Sterling Overnight Index Average (SONIA)*. This index is the volume-weighted average of unsecured overnight lending in GBP among banks in the United Kingdom. The rate is administered by the *Bank of England* and is quoted in Act/365.

Since the rate of the floating leg compounds daily, for USD-based OIS contracts, the effective floating rate would be the geometric average of daily fed funds rates during a payment period. However, for weekends and holidays, the rate is treated as simple interest, set at the last business day before off days. Hence the rate is compounded on a business day basis. This leads to a minor deviation between a geometric average of the federal funds rate during the payment period and the actual effective rate used for calculating floating-leg interest payment. Since the effective fed funds rate is quoted on an Act/360 basis, the annualized effective rate of a floating leg of an OIS contract for payment period i with an Act/360 convention is calculated as:

$$r_i = \frac{360}{n_i} \left[\prod_{j=f_i}^{l_i} \left(1 + \frac{r_{eff_j} \times n_j}{360} \right) - 1 \right] \tag{1.57}$$

where:

r_i = Annualized effective rate for payment period i of OIS floating leg

n_i = Actual number of days in period i

f_i = First day of period i

l_i = Last day of period i

r_{eff_j} = Annualized effective fed funds rate as of day j

n_j = Number of days the effective fed funds rate r_{eff_j} is applicable

(for weekdays one day and for weekends three days).

This effective rate is set at the end of each floating-leg payment period. Assume an OIS contract with a $100 million notional amount and a seven-day term, from Wednesday of one week to Tuesday of the following week. The fixed rate of the contract (1-week OIS rate) is 2.05%. There is only one payment period for fixed and floating legs of this contract. Assume effective federal funds rates are as follows: Wednesday 2.01%, Thursday 2.05%, Friday 2.03%, Monday 2.06%, Tuesday 2.02%.

In this case, the Friday rate is used for Saturday and Sunday as well while treated as simple interest within this three-day window. The annualized effective floating leg rate is calculated as:

$$r_i = \frac{360}{7}\left[\left(1+\frac{0.0201}{360}\right)\left(1+\frac{0.0205}{360}\right)\left(1+\frac{0.0203\times 3}{360}\right)\left(1+\frac{0.0206}{360}\right)\right.$$
$$\left.\left(1+\frac{0.0202}{360}\right)-1\right] = 2.033\%$$

Payments from fixed-payer and floating-payer sides of the contract are:

$$\text{Fixed-payer cash flow} = 100,000,000 \times 0.0205 \times \frac{7}{360} = 39,861.11$$

$$\text{Floating-payer cash flow} = 100,000,000 \times 0.02033 \times \frac{7}{360} = 39,530.56$$

At the payment date, the fixed-payer side pays $39,861.11 − $39,530.56 = $330.55 to the other side of the contract.

When the term of an OIS contract is less than one year, the fixed rate is usually quoted as a simple rate and when the term is longer than one year, the fixed rate is often quoted as a compounding rate. For example, for an OIS contract with a three-year maturity, the fixed rate may be quoted as an annual rate with semi-annual payment and compounding periodicity. For long-term OIS contracts, fixed and floating legs can have different periodicities. OIS contracts have become more liquid and many banks and other financial institutions trade them for hedging and speculation purposes. A combination of short- and long-term OIS rates constitutes the *OIS curve* and a bootstrapping technique, similar to the one discussed earlier in this chapter, can be used to create the *OIS spot curve*.

OIS Discounting

Prior to the financial crisis of 2007–2009, LIBOR-swap curves were widely considered to be risk-free or close to risk-free and were used for cash flow discounting in the valuation of derivative contracts and other financial instruments. Liquidity and the credit crisis that started in 2007 changed the perception of LIBOR as a near-risk-free rate. During this period, dealings with large banks that were traditionally perceived as safe transactions suddenly became high risk and this was reflected in large deviation of LIBOR, as an interbank unsecured lending rate, from the Treasury rate. Figure 1.12 presents the spread between the 3-month LIBOR and 3-month T-Bill rate, usually referred to as *TED spread,* in basis points. An increase in TED spread is often considered to be a sign of stress in financial markets. Before the financial crisis of 2007–2009, TED spread was relatively stable. For example, the average TED spread in 2005 and 2006 was around 50 bps but as can be seen from Figure 1.12, in the second half of 2007 and after investment bank *Bear Stearns* liquidated two hedge funds, the turmoil in LIBOR started and throughout the financial crisis TED spread remained at an elevated and volatile level, peaking close to 450 bps at one point. Events of this period led to an increased awareness of the risk associated with unsecured interbank lending and market participants started to include credit and liquidity risk premiums in interbank lending rates. Moreover, LIBOR with different terms displayed different risk premia depending on lending term. An interest rate curve that has such characteristics is said to exhibit both *term structure* and

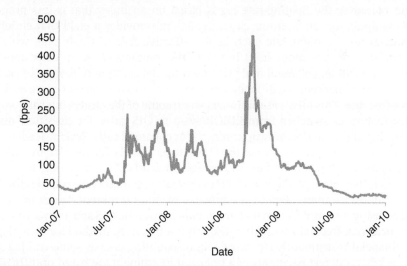

FIGURE 1.12 TED Spread: Spread between 3-month LIBOR and 3-month T-Bill rate in basis points from January 2007 to January 2010
Source: The Board of Governors of the Federal Reserve System (U.S.); retrieved from FRED, the Federal Reserve Bank of St. Louis (https://fred.stlouisfed.org).

risk structure. We discuss components of interest rate later in this chapter. Due to these events, LIBOR is no longer considered a risk-free rate.

Another consequence of the financial crisis of 2007–2009 was that nowadays more banks require their swap counterparties to enter into bilateral collateral posting agreements. As demonstrated earlier in this chapter, the value of a swap contract depends on interest rate level and as the interest rate changes so does the value of the contract. Daily collateral posting protects both sides of the contract when the value of the swap contract moves against the opposite party. For example, if party A and party B are two sides of a bilateral interest rate swap contract and if at the end of a business day the value of the contract from party A's point of view increased by $100,000, party B is required to post the same amount of cash or cash-equivalent (e.g., Treasury bonds) with party A on the next business day as collateral. This way if party B faces a credit event (e.g., bankruptcy), party A is covered by the collateral. Due to a mandate by the *Dodd-Frank Wall Street Reform and Consumer Protection Act of 2010*, many of these bilateral swaps are now standardized and cleared through clearinghouses. Exchange organizations value the swap contracts on a daily basis and require collateral posting from the side that is affected by the value movement.

This collateralization significantly reduced the credit risk of swap contracts, effectively to a non-material level. OIS contracts are collateralized and moreover the floating-rate leg is based on an index that is less prone to manipulation. In addition, posted collateral provides a yield that closely matches an overnight rate such as the effective federal funds rate, which is the floating-rate index used in USD OIS contracts. To keep consistency between yield on collateral and yield used for discounting of derivative cash flows, many market practitioners nowadays prefer to use the OIS curve as the risk-free rate. This idea was reinforced when some of the largest international clearinghouses switched from LIBOR-swap to OIS curve for cash flow discounting and valuation of swap contracts for collateral calls. Several academic works also proposed the use of the OIS rate as a proxy for the risk-free rate. For example, Hull and White (2013) suggest that an OIS curve should be used as a risk-free rate regardless of whether derivative contracts are collateralized.

OIS discounting refers to the practice of finding present values of cash flows using discount factors that are obtained from the OIS spot curve. Due to the near-risk-free nature of OIS rates, this is a preferred method for valuation of financial instruments. However, OIS discounting creates some complications when interest payments of a financial instrument are based on LIBOR. Particularly, the bootstrapping method of the LIBOR-Swap curve needs to be revised. Recall from an earlier section that, to extend LIBOR and obtain longer term spot rates, we used the bootstrapping technique, which was based on the replicating bonds approach. There, we argued that the floating-rate replicating bond is at par at any rate-fixing date. This enabled us to recursively calculate spot rates from the available swap rates and construct the LIBOR-swap spot curve. The notion of floating-rate replicating bonds being at par was based on the fact that LIBOR implied forward rates used for estimation of interest payment cash flows, and discount factors used for discounting those cash flows, were obtained from the same spot curve. When the OIS spot curve is used to calculate discount factors, this condition does not hold any more and therefore we cannot consider the floating-rate replicating bond to be at par. This means:

- We can no longer use Equation (1.46) to recursively bootstrap discount factors and spot rates from shorter-term discount factors and available swap rates.
- The use of OIS discounting also impacts the LIBOR implied forward rates and they should be stripped from swap rates in a different way.

Although when using OIS discounting we can no longer ascertain that the floating-rate replicating bond is at par, the swap contract value at the inception time still must be zero. We can use this knowledge and available swap rates to calculate LIBOR implied forward rates while using OIS discounting. These LIBOR implied forward rates in turn can be used to construct a revised version of the LIBOR-swap spot curve.

We use DF_t^{OIS} notation to represent the discount factor at time t based on the OIS spot curve. Now consider again the value of fixed-rate and floating-rate replicating bonds presented in Equations (1.38) and (1.39). If we use OIS discounting, we need to replace the discount factors in those equations by DF_i^{OIS} and DF_j^{OIS}. When swap rate $r_{sw,n}$ is available, by setting values of these two replicating bonds equal, we have:

$$N \times DF_n^{OIS} + \sum_{i=1}^{n} N r_{sw,n} \tau_i DF_i^{OIS} = N \times DF_n^{OIS} + \sum_{j=1}^{n} N r_{j-1,\tau_j} \tau_j DF_j^{OIS}$$

From this and since OIS discount factors are all available, we can solve for the LIBOR implied forward rate associated with the last floating-leg payment period as follows:

$$r_{n-1,\tau_n}^* = \frac{r_{sw,n} \sum_{i=1}^{n} \tau_i DF_i^{OIS} - \sum_{j=1}^{n-1} r_{j-1,\tau_j} \tau_j DF_j^{OIS}}{\tau_n DF_n^{OIS}} \tag{1.58}$$

This is the LIBOR implied forward rate as of beginning of the last floating leg payment period for a term of τ_n. This approach in calculating the LIBOR implied forward rate is usually referred to as the *dual-curve* method, since two interest rate curves, OIS and LIBOR, are involved in the calculation. Here we used $*$ notation to emphasize that the LIBOR implied forward rate obtained using dual-curve stripping is different from what would be obtained if only one curve, LIBOR, was used.

Equation (1.58) can be used recursively to calculate LIBOR implied forward rates and subsequently constructing a revised LIBOR-swap spot curve. To demonstrate this, assume the current 6-month LIBOR is $r_{0,6M}$ and the market-quoted 1-year swap rate with semi-annual payment frequency is $r_{sw,1Y}$; both are available at the present time. Using available OIS discount factors and Equation (1.58) we can obtain the 6-month LIBOR implied forward rate at $t = 0.5$ year $r^*_{0.5Y,6M}$ as:

$$
r^*_{0.5Y,6M} = \frac{r_{sw,1Y}\left(\tau_1 DF_1^{OIS} + \tau_2 DF_2^{OIS}\right) - r_{0,6M}\tau_1 DF_1^{OIS}}{\tau_2 DF_2^{OIS}}
$$

Having this implied forward rate from $t = 0.5$ to $t = 1$ year, we can use Equation (1.18) to calculate the *periodic* discount factor as:

$$
DF^*_{0.5Y,1Y} = \frac{1}{1 + \tau_2 \times r^*_{0.5Y,6M}}
$$

Here we used $DF^*_{0.5Y,1Y}$ notation to emphasis that (i) this is the periodic factor that discounts a cash flow occurring at $t = 1$ year back to $t = 0.5$ year (not back to $t = 0$), and (ii) this discount factor, although based on a LIBOR-swap curve, is different from the case when only one curve is used. By multiplying this discount factor with the discount factor from $t = 0.5$ year to present time $t = 0$, obtained using the current 6-month LIBOR spot rate, we get to the discount factor from $t = 1$ to $t = 0$:

$$
DF^*_{1Y} = DF_{0.5Y} \times DF^*_{0.5Y,1Y}
$$

Once the discount factor DF^*_{1Y} is obtained we can convert it to a spot rate with the desirable compounding frequency. For example, to present the 1-year spot rate in continuous compounding we can convert DF^*_{1Y} to spot rate r^*_{1Y} as:

$$
r^*_{1Y} = -\frac{1}{365} \ln DF^*_{1Y}
$$

This is the rate at the 1-year term point of the revised LIBOR-swap spot curve. Once $r^*_{0.5Y,6M}$ is obtained, and having quoted swap rate $r_{sw,1.5Y}$ available, this process can be repeated to calculate the 6-month LIBOR implied forward at $t = 1$ year: $r^*_{1Y,6M}$ and 1.5-year spot rate: $r^*_{1.5Y}$, and so on. As noticed, as a consequence of OIS discounting, the LIBOR-swap spot curve constructed using the dual-curve stripping method discussed here is different from the one built using only one curve.

When determining swap rate, we still can use Equation (1.40), providing OIS discount factors and revised LIBOR implied forward rates are used, but Equation (1.42) is no longer applicable, since the floating-rate replicating bond is not at par any more:

$$r_{sw,n} = \frac{\sum_{j=1}^{n} r^*_{j-1,\tau_j} \tau_j DF^{OIS}_j}{\sum_{i=1}^{n} \tau_i DF^{OIS}_i} \tag{1.59}$$

Likewise, Equation (1.43) can be used for the valuation of a plain-vanilla interest rate swap contract when OIS discount factors are used, but Equation (1.44) is no longer applicable with OIS discounting. The following table compares traditional single-curve bootstrapping of the LIBOR-swap curve discussed in an earlier section of this chapter with the dual-curve method explained here.

Traditional Bootstrapping of LIBOR-Swap Curve	**Bootstrapping of LIBOR-Swap Curve with OIS Discounting**
LIBOR and Swap Rate	LIBOR and Swap Rate
$DF_n = \dfrac{1 - r_{sw,n} \sum_{i=1}^{n-1} \tau_i DF_i}{1 + r_{sw,n} \tau_n}$	$r^*_{n-1,\tau_n} = \dfrac{r_{sw,n} \sum_{i=1}^{n} \tau_i DF^{OIS}_i - \sum_{j=1}^{n-1} r_{j-1,\tau_j} \tau_j DF^{OIS}_j}{\tau_n DF^{OIS}_n}$
Discount Factor	LIBOR Implied Forward Rate
$r_{t_n} = -\dfrac{1}{t_n} \ln DF_n$	$DF^*_{n-1,n} = \dfrac{1}{1 + \tau_n \times r^*_{n-1,\tau_n}}$
	$DF^*_n = \prod_{j=1}^{n} DF^*_{j-1,j}$
Spot Rate	Discount Factor
	$r^*_{t_n} = -\dfrac{1}{t_n} \ln DF^*_n$
	Spot Rate

Secured Overnight Financing Rate

Prior to 2012, the *British Bankers' Association (BBA)* administered LIBOR. Member banks were submitting the interest rates that they would pay for borrowing from other banks to the BBA, where the data was compiled and used to publish *BBA LIBOR* daily. In 2012 it was revealed that there had been significant fraud and collusion by some member banks related to submitted rates. This scandal led to an increase in oversight of LIBOR, particularly by the U.K. *Financial Services Authority (FSA),* and member banks are now required to submit actual interest rates that they pay for borrowing from other banks. Administration of LIBOR was also taken from the BBA and in 2014 Intercontinental Exchange became the new administrator and publisher of *ICE LIBOR.*

Extensive use of LIBOR in financial products, especially derivatives, along with concern about LIBOR sustainability and potential for manipulation and misrepresentation of rates, encouraged regulators around the world to look for ways to reduce the dependence of financial markets on LIBOR. This led to studies to find alternatives to LIBOR to represent true short-term interbank lending or borrowing rates, particularly for the overnight term. In the United States, in 2017 the Federal Reserve selected the *secured overnight financing rate (SOFR)* as the benchmark for the overnight borrowing rate and started to publish the rate in 2018. SOFR is the cost of borrowing for an overnight term and on a secured basis.

A *repurchase agreement (repo)* is a financial contract in which one side lends cash to another side while taking a security, such as U.S. Treasury or corporate bonds, as collateral for protection. Hence repo is a *secured* way of borrowing or lending. At the end of the contract's term, which is usually short-term and usually overnight, the lender returns the collateral and the borrower returns the borrowed cash amount plus the applicable interest amount. The rate used in such a contract is known as the *repo rate.* When two sides of a repo contract deal directly with each other, it is known as a *bilateral* repo. If a third party acts as a clearing agent between the two sides of a repo contract, it is known as a *tri-party* repo. We discuss repo contracts in more detail in a later chapter. SOFR is compiled using repo rates with an overnight term and U.S. Treasury securities collateral. It is a volume-weighted median of transaction-level rates of tri-party and bilateral repo contracts while excluding some contracts with special collateral. The New York Federal Reserve Bank is the administrator of SOFR and publishes the rate every day. It is expected that OIS contracts based on SOFR will gain popularity in financial markets, leading to construction and usage of a SOFR-based spot curve.

COMPONENTS OF INTEREST RATE

As the market value or price of a traded bond changes in the market, its yield changes as well. Recall that bond yield is the interest rate that if used in discounting future cash flows of that bond, results in a present value that is equal to the bond's current market value. At issuance time the coupon rate of the bond and its yield are equal and this makes the price of the security to be at par. After the inception supply and demand forces in the market determine the price of the bond and hence its yield.

Generally, we can consider two major components for the yield of a traded security: the risk-free rate and risk spread. Risk spread itself is comprised of several components. Figure 1.13 presents a general view of the components of yield of a traded security. The main components of the yield are:

- **Risk-Free Rate:** The risk-free rate is the theoretical rate of return in an investment where there is no probability of loss of either the original principal or the expected interest payments. For example, in the United States, Treasury yields with different terms are considered to be risk-free rates, since it is generally believed that the U.S. government will not default on its financial obligations. As discussed before, practitioners used to consider LIBOR with different terms as market-driven risk-free rates. As the risk-free rate changes, the yield of the bond changes accordingly. While the risk-free rate is impacted by supply and demand in the market, the level of that rate is highly influenced by the central bank. As discussed before, in the United States the Federal Reserve System, through its open market operations, controls the level of the effective federal funds rate and Treasury yields by actively buying and selling Treasury securities, or by participating in the repo market for those securities.
- **Risk Spread:** For a non-government-issued bond, the yield includes an extra spread that represents the risk involved in investing in a bond that has a chance of default and hence loss of future cash flows, including the original principal. This is the **credit risk spread**. It also includes the premium required to compensate for the uncertainty in the future value of the security or future cash flows generated by the security, as market condition changes. This is the **market risk spread**. As the perception of these risks in the market changes, the risk spread changes accordingly and therefore the yield of the bond varies over time.

For example, consider a case where an investment bank is assisting a manufacturing firm to issue a new 5-year fixed-rate bond. Part of the service

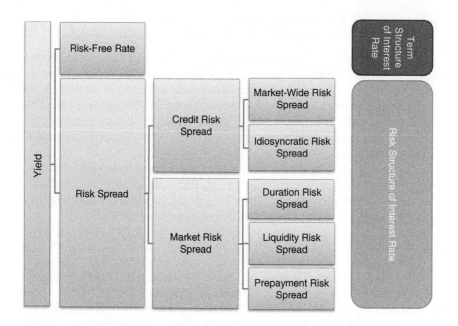

FIGURE 1.13   Components of a financial security's yield

that the investment bank provides is to find investors that are willing to buy the bond at the inception date. The coupon of the bond is determined by considering the risk-free rate and additional risk spread. Assume the 5-year Treasury rate is 2% today and potential investors demand a 75 bps extra spread to compensate for the risk associated with investing in the bond. This 75 bps extra spread includes components of risk spread discussed earlier. The firm then issues a new bond with a coupon rate of 2.75%. At the inception date, the yield of the bond is equal to this coupon rate. After the issuance, as the bond is traded in the secondary market, investors' perception of its riskiness may change or the risk-free rate may change. These can lead to a change in bond price and subsequently its yield.

For loans (such as mortgages and personal loans), components of the rate are similar to those for security yields, but the risk-free rate is replaced by a funding rate plus a funding margin. These two together represent the bank's internal cost of funding the loan, including any administrative costs. Components of risk spread (i.e., credit and market risk spreads), are applicable to loan rates as well. For example, when issuing a new mortgage to a borrower the bank considers the possibility of the default on the loan (a credit risk event) and uncertainty in future cash flows due to prepayment (a market risk event), and includes a premium to compensate for such risks.[22] Hence components of a loan rate can be stated as:

$$\text{Loan Rate} = \text{Funding Rate} + \text{Funding Margin} + \text{Risk Spread} \qquad (1.60)$$

To understand why different bonds with the same term to maturity have different yields, we need to consider components of the risk spread in more detail. The relationship that defines the comparative yields of different bonds with different levels of risk but same terms to maturity is known as the *risk structure of interest rate*. To understand why bonds with similar perceptions of their riskiness (e.g., Treasury bonds) and different terms have different yields, we need to learn about the *term structure of interest rate* and factors that affect the departure of rates at various tenures. The relationship that defines the comparative yields of different bonds with the same level of risk but different terms to maturity is the term structure of interest rate.

Risk Structure of Interest Rate

Bonds with the same term to maturity but different riskiness perceptions may have different yields. Figure 1.14 presents average monthly yields for three

FIGURE 1.14 Long-term Treasury yield and Aaa and Baa corporate bond yields
Source: The Board of Governors of the Federal Reserve System (U.S.), Moody's Seasoned Aaa and Baa Corporate Bond Yield®; retrieved from FRED, the Federal Reserve Bank of St. Louis (https://fred.stlouisfed.org).

classes of securities: long-term Treasury bonds, long-term corporate bonds with Aaa ratings, and long-term corporate bonds with Baa ratings. Treasury yield is considered a risk-free rate. Aaa bonds are assumed to be the closest corporate bonds to risk-free bonds; however, investing in such bonds still carries some risk. The yield of Aaa bonds is slightly higher than Treasury yield. The Baa bonds are generally perceived as the lowest rating bonds that are still considered to be *investment grade*. Yields of Baa bonds are higher than those of Aaa bonds. The difference between yields of corporate bonds with different ratings and Treasury yield is the *risk spread*.

The risk spread, as a component of the yield, consists of two major components: credit risk spread and market risk spread. *Credit risk spread* is to compensate for the possibility of default by the borrower (issuer of the bond) that leads to the loss of future cash flows, both interest and principal payments. *Market-wide risk spread* is part of the credit risk spread that is the premium required by investors to compensate for the general economic condition while *idiosyncratic risk spread* is the premium required based on the assessment of the risk of individual borrower (issuer), or risk associated within a sector (e.g., airline industry).

Market risk spread is to compensate for the uncertainty in potential changes in the value of the security due to changes in market conditions, or uncertainty in the timing and amount of cash flows generated by the security. The value of longer-term securities has higher sensitivity to changes in the market interest rate and *duration risk spread* is the premium to reflect this uncertainty. *Liquidity risk spread* is the premium associated with the willingness of buyers and sellers to participate in the market and trade the security. *Prepayment risk spread* is the premium to reflect the uncertainty in future cash flows when the security has optionality that allows borrower to change the timing of cash flows (e.g,. early repayment of principal).

Figure 1.15 shows the risk spread between a hypothetical risk-free yield curve (e.g., Treasury) and the yield curve of corporate bonds. The relationship between these two yields at different terms defines the risk structure of the yield curve for the risky bond. The risk spreads at different terms depend on the market perception of the level of risk and need not be equal. For example, in Figure 1.15, S_1, S_2, and S_3 are not equal.

Term Structure of Interest Rate

Bonds with the same riskiness perceptions but different terms to maturity may have different yields. The term structure of interest rate defines the relationship between yields at different terms when the riskiness perceptions of considered bonds are alike. A yield curve, as a graphical representation of yields at different terms, may have different shapes. Figure 1.16 presents four

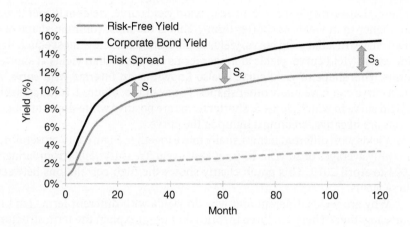

FIGURE 1.15 Risk spread between hypothetical risk-free and corporate bond yield curves

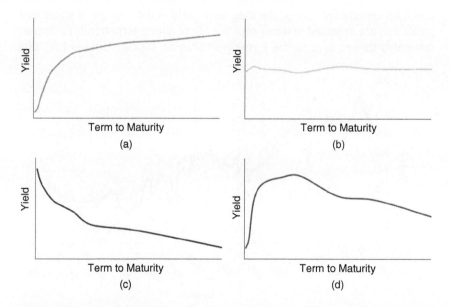

FIGURE 1.16 General shapes of yield curve: (a) upward, (b) flat, (c) downward, and (d) variable direction sloping

general shapes of a yield curve. In an upward yield curve, yields at longer terms are higher than yields at shorter terms. This is the most common shape of a yield curve. In a flat yield curve, yields at different terms are almost equal. In a downward yield curve, yields at longer terms are lower than yields at shorter terms. This shape of yield curve is also known as an *inverted yield curve*. A yield curve can have many other shapes. For example, Figure 1.16(d) presents a yield curve in which slopes at shorter terms are positive while slopes at longer terms are negative, creating a hump in the curve.

Yields with different terms usually move together. Figure 1.17 presents the monthly averages of 20-year, 10-year, and 5-year Treasury yields from January 1994 to April 2019. This graph clearly shows the high correlations between these yields.

Why are yields different and why do yields with different terms tend to move together? There are three theories that try to explain the term structure of the yield curve and why the shape of the yield curve changes over time.

Expectation Theory

Based on *expectation theory*, the long-term yield is the average of short-term yields that are expected to occur over the life of a long-term bond. To demonstrate this theory, assume the 1-year zero coupon Treasury rate is 1.5% now

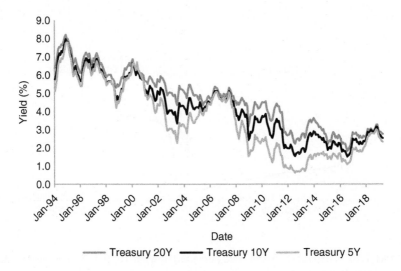

FIGURE 1.17   Treasury yields of different terms
Source: The Board of Governors of the Federal Reserve System (U.S.); retrieved from FRED, the Federal Reserve Bank of St. Louis (https://fred.stlouisfed.org)

and the market expects the same rate one year from now to be 2%. The current 2-year zero-coupon Treasury rate is therefore obtained as:

$$(1 + r_{0,2})^2 = (1 + r_{0,1})(1 + r_{1,1})$$

where $r_{0,2}$ is the current 2-year zero-coupon Treasury rate, $r_{0,1}$ is the current 1-year zero-coupon Treasury rate, and $r_{1,1}$ is the expected 1-year zero-coupon Treasury rate one year from now. So the 2-year zero-coupon Treasure rate is calculated as:

$$r_{0,2} = \sqrt{(1 + r_{0,1})(1 + r_{1,1})} - 1 = \sqrt{(1 + 0.015)(1 + 0.02)} - 1 = 1.75\%$$

So based on the market expectation that the 1-year rate one year from now (2%) will be higher than the current 1-year rate (1.5%), the current 2-year rate is expected to be higher than the current 1-year rate (1.75% > 1.5%). This leads to an upward slope between the 1-year and 2-year points of the curve.[23] The 2-year rate is approximately the arithmetic average of the current 1-year rate and the 1-year rate one year from now:

$$r_{0,2} \cong \frac{1.5\% + 2\%}{2} \cong 1.75\%$$

The exact result obtained earlier is the geometric average of these rates. This clarifies the initial description we provided for the expectation theory that long-term yield is the average of short-term yields during the life of the long-term yield. Expectation theory is based on the assumption that investors have no preference between bonds with a certain maturity over other bonds with other maturities, and bonds with different maturities can be substituted for each other as long as they provide equal or better yields. According to the expectation theory, when the yield curve is upward sloping, the market expects short-term yields to rise in the future. For example, in the example, the market expected the 1-year yield to increase from 1.5% to 2% and that resulted in an upward slope between the 1-year and 2-year term points of the current yield curve. When the yield curve is downward sloping, the expectation theory indicates that the market expects the short-term yields to decrease in the future. This results in an inverted current yield curve. Based on this theory, as the economic and market conditions change, expectations of market participants about future short-term yields also change and that leads to changes in the shape of the yield curve over time. Based on this theory, the close relationship of yields with different terms explains the co-movement of the yields, as shown in Figure 1.17.

Market Segmentation Theory

Market segmentation theory is based on the assumption that yields at each term point are based on supply and demand of market participants for bonds with that term and are independent of yields at other term points. In market segmentation theory, bonds with a certain maturity are not assumed to be substitutes for bonds with other maturities and each term is considered independent of other terms. As opposed to expectation theory, market segmentation theory assumes investors have a preference for bonds with a certain maturity.

Based on market segmentation theory, supply and demand define bond prices at different term points. Hence if there is a higher demand for short-term bonds, it increases prices of short-term bonds, which in turn results in decreases in short-term yields (compared to long-term yields). This leads to the typical upward-sloping yield curve. On the other hand, if there is a higher demand for long-term bonds, it increases prices of long-term bonds, which in turn results in decreases in long-term yields (compared to short-term yields). This leads to an inverted yield curve. Based on this theory, as the economic and market conditions change, supply and demand of bonds with different terms also change and that leads to changes in the shape of the yield curve over time. This theory, however, fails to explain why yields with different maturities tend to move together, as seen in Figure 1.17.

Liquidity Premium Theory

Liquidity premium theory is a combination of the expectation and the market segmentation theories. Based on this theory, the long-term yield is the average of short-term yields that are expected to occur during the life of the long-term yield plus a liquidity premium that represents the supply and demand for the bonds at that term. This theory allows for the preference for different bonds by investors (as was assumed in market segmentation theory) through the inclusion of the liquidity premium while allowing bonds with different terms to be substitutes for each other (as was assumed in expectation theory). Changes in market and economic conditions, and changes in supply and demand of bonds with different terms, all contribute to changes in the shape of the yield curve over time. This theory has the flexibility to explain all shapes of the yield curve and also the co-movement of yields with different terms.

Inflation and Interest Rate

The absolute price level, as an indicator of macroeconomic activity, is a measure of the overall price level in the economy. A sustained increase in the price level over time is known as *inflation,* whereas *deflation* is a sustained decrease in the price level. The *inflation rate* is the measurement of how price levels change over time. One of the common methods used to quantify the inflation rate is to use the *Consumer Price Index* (CPI). CPI is developed by the *Bureau of Labor Statistics* and is the weighted average of prices consumers pay for a fixed basket of goods and services in a given period of time relative to the combined prices of an identical basket of goods and services in a base period.

Interest rate (or yield) has a direct relationship with the inflation rate. The *real interest rate* is the interest rate after adjusting for inflation and the *nominal interest rate* is before adjusting for inflation. Since the ultimate goal of an investor is to increase his or her purchasing power (or at least to maintain it), the inflation rate should be considered in investment decisions. The relationship between real and nominal interest rates and inflation rate, known as the *Fisher* effect,[24] is as follows:

$$1 + r_N = (1 + r_R)(1 + f) \qquad (1.61)$$

where

r_N = Nominal interest rate

r_R = Real interest rate

f = Inflation rate

For example, if the nominal interest rate of an investment is 8% and the inflation rate is 2%, the real interest rate is:

$$r_R = \frac{(1 + 0.08)}{(1 + 0.02)} - 1 = 5.88\%$$

NEGATIVE INTEREST RATE

We started this chapter by introducing the interest rate as the cost of borrowing or return on lending. When a lending institution lends money to a borrower, in return the borrower pays interest on the borrowed amount. Conversely, when a depositor places cash with a deposit-taking entity, such as a bank, in return the depositor receives interest on the deposit amount. This is the core business model of lending and depository institutions. A negative interest rate contradicts this dynamic. If the interest rate is negative, a lender has to pay the borrower for the lent amount, or a depositor has to pay the deposit-taking institution to hold the cash. Generally, the nominal interest rate is expected to be positive. However, depending on the relationship between the nominal interest rate and inflation, the real interest rate can become negative. For example, consider the Fisher effect in Equation (1.61). If the inflation rate is 5% while nominal interest rate is 3%, the real interest rate is –1.9%. It is the nominal interest rate that is expected to be positive.

While it is counterintuitive to have a negative interest rate, it has a precedent in Europe and Japan. Figure 1.18 shows the deposit facility rate of the *European Central Bank (ECB)* from January 1999 to September 2019. This is the overnight rate received by depository institutions within the *European Union (EU)* for overnight deposits with ECB. This rate is set by ECB every six weeks as part of its monetary policy implementation. The rate has been negative since June 2014. Generally, ECB uses the negative benchmark interest rate as a stimulus to economic growth by encouraging the lending institutions to lend more. In the past, other central banks also used the negative interest rate as a monetary policy tool to boost economic growth.

Aside from the negative interest rate occurrence due to monetary policy implementation, *flight to quality* during market turmoil can also lead to negative interest rates. In such circumstances investors may prefer to *park* their cash in government securities that are deemed safe, rather than investing

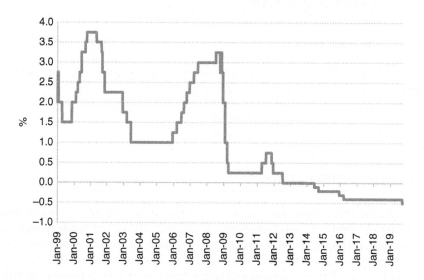

FIGURE 1.18   European Central Bank deposit facility rate
Source: European Central Bank Statistical Data Warehouse (https://sdw.ecb.europa .eu).

in money market funds or even depositing with banks. This leads to a high demand for government securities, which in turn can push their yields into a negative level. In September 2008 and during the height of the financial crisis, the yield of 3-month T-bills fell slightly below zero for a very brief period, before climbing back to a low positive level (Mishkin and Eakins 2012).

When an interest rate is negative, discount factors calculated based on that rate are greater than 1, producing the counterintuitive results that contradict the time value of money concept. Assume a zero-coupon financial instrument with a face value of $100 and a 1-month remaining term. The proceeds from investing in this instrument is its face value at the maturity date. If the current annualized 1-month risk-free rate is 0.05% with continuous compounding, the current value of the instrument, assuming a 30/360 accrual basis, is $100 \times e^{-(0.05/100) \times (1/12)} = 99.9958$. This indicates that a future value of $100 is worth $99.9958 now, underlining the time value of the money. However, when the rate is −0.05%, the current value of the instrument is $100 \times e^{-(-0.05/100) \times (1/12)} = 100.0042$, implying that to receive $100 in the future one has to invest $100.0042 now. In normal circumstances an investor would not proceed with such an investment, as it makes more sense to just hold on to the cash rather than investing in a loss-making deal. Only in extraordinary situations, such as an economic crisis, would one proceed with such an investment and only when investing in the instrument is perceived to be safer than holding the cash.

While a negative benchmark interest rate is possible, it does not necessarily mean that consumer loans are issued with negative coupon rates. Once the credit spreads and profit margins are incorporated, fixed-rate loans such as mortgages, or floating-rate facilities such as credit cards, would still have positive coupon rates, even if the benchmark interest rate used to set them is negative.

INTEREST RATE SHOCK

The impact of an interest rate change on the balance sheet and earnings of a bank can be significant and one of the main purposes of ALM analysis is to assess such impacts. The analysis starts by assuming a series of hypothetical changes in the current yield curve (or current spot curve). Those changes in interest rate, commonly referred to as *interest rate shocks*, can be assumed such that they change only the level of the curve or change both the level and the shape of the curve. Interest rate shocks can be categorized into two general groups: parallel shocks and non-parallel shocks. Next we discuss each in more detail, assuming shocks are applied to spot curves. In future chapters we discuss the impact of different interest rate shocks on the economic value of equity and the net interest income of banks.

Parallel Shock

In a parallel shock, rates at every term point of the curve are shifted upward or downward by an equal amount. For example, in a +100 bps parallel shock 1% is added to rates at every term point of the curve while in a –100 bps parallel shock 1% is deducted from rates at every term point. Depending on current rates and the magnitude of the shock, a downward shock may result in negative rates. While the chances negative rates occurring in the United States is remote, negative rates have occurred in Europe and Japan. When a downward shock results in negative rates, the curve may be floored at zero. An upward parallel shock (e.g., +100 bps, +200 bps, +300 bps, etc.) only changes the level of the yield curve, but a downward parallel shock (e.g., –100 bps, –200 bps, –300 bps, etc.), if rates are floored, can also change the shape of the yield curve. Figure 1.19 depicts upward parallel +100 bps, +200 bps, and +300 bps shocks applied to a hypothetical spot curve, where the shape of the curve is unchanged. Figure 1.20 shows a downward parallel –100 bps shock to this curve with two different treatments of negative rates: (i) when rates are

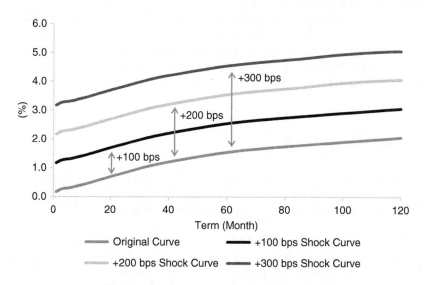

FIGURE 1.19 Upward parallel shocks to spot curve

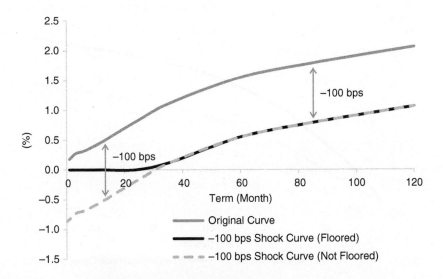

FIGURE 1.20 Downward parallel shocks to spot curve

not floored and allowed to become negative, hence the shape of the curve is unchanged, and (ii) when rates are floored at 0% and hence the shape of the spot curve is changed.

Non-Parallel Shock

Steepening or flattening shock: In a steepening or flattening shock, rates at different term points of the curve are changed such that both the shape and level of the curve are changed. A steepening shock is constructed by increasing rates at longer term points of the curve more than rates at shorter term points, or by decreasing rates at shorter term points of the curve compared to rates at longer term points. Figure 1.21 shows a steepening shock applied to a hypothetical spot curve. A flattening shock is constructed by adjusting rates at different term points to change the shape of the curve so it is flatter compared to the original curve. Figure 1.22 shows a flattening shock applied to a hypothetical spot curve.

   Butterfly shock: In a butterfly shock, rates at different term points are changed so the curvature of the curve is changed. Such a shock changes both the shape and level of the curve. Figure 1.23 shows a butterfly shock applied to a hypothetical spot curve.

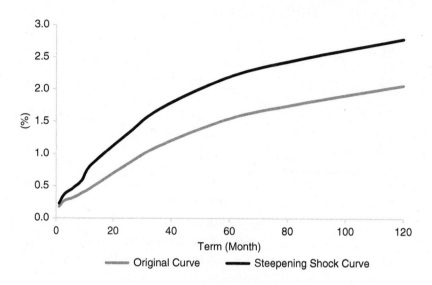

FIGURE 1.21   Steepening shock to spot curve

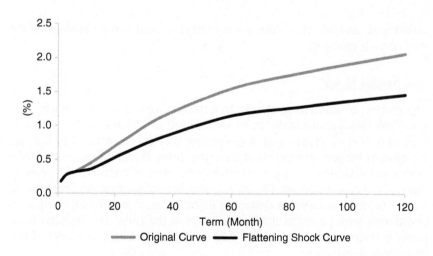

FIGURE 1.22   Flattening shock to spot curve

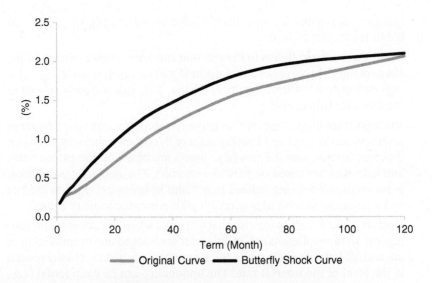

FIGURE 1.23 Butterfly shock to spot curve

INTEREST RATE RISK

Interest rate risk refers to the potential loss from unexpected changes in interest rate, which can have a negative impact on a bank's earnings and the economic value of its equity. If not properly hedged, a change in interest rate can have an adverse impact on the earnings, equity, and capital position of a bank. It may even indirectly impact a bank's liquidity position. A change in interest rate may have the opposite effect on different asset types. For example, an increase in interest rate may lead to an increase in interest income of a floating-rate portfolio while at the same time may reduce the value of an investment portfolio. Generally, interest rate risk is categorized as follows.

Interest Rate Gap Risk: Refers to the risk that can arise when positions on the asset and liability sides of the balance sheet overall have different settings and timing with respect to changes in the interest rate. When the interest rate rises and liabilities reset earlier than assets, or when the interest rate falls and assets reset earlier than liabilities, in both cases banks may face a period of lower (or even possibly negative) net interest income, or may be exposed to adverse change in the economic value of equity. Such cases can occur when the yield curve has a parallel or non-parallel shift. In other words, changes in both level and shape of the yield curve may lead to interest rate gap risk. Another case that leads to the rise of interest rate gap risk is when the amounts of fixed-rate and floating-rate assets and liabilities are not aligned.

Yield Curve Risk: Refers to the risk that can arise when a change in the shape of the yield curve (its curvature or slope) adversely impacts the earnings or economic value of equity of a bank. This risk is closely related to the interest rate gap risk.

Interest Rate Basis Risk: Refers to the risk that can arise when different positions on the asset and liability sides of the balance sheet are based on different interest rate indexes (e.g., assets are based on the prime index and liabilities are based on LIBOR 1-month). The imperfect correlation between the underlying indexes may result in lower net interest income and a potential adverse impact on a bank's economic value of equity.

Option Risk: Refers to the risk that can arise when the amount and timing of cash flows of assets or liabilities can be changed due to optionality of on- and off-balance-sheet items. Such optionality is usually closely related to the level of the interest rate. The optionality can be contractual (e.g., cap and floor of interest rate in a loan, or an interest rate option contract bought or sold), or could be embedded (e.g., callability of Muni securities), or could be behavioral (e.g., prepayment of mortgages or early withdrawal of deposit accounts).

SUMMARY

- The three most common revenue sources of financial companies are finance charges, fees, and principal gains.
- The interest rate is a method of quantifying the cost of borrowing or return on lending.
- Simple interest is earning interest on principal only while compounding interest is earning interest on principal as well as earning interest on reinvested interest from previous periods.
- Interest rates can be presented in simple interest, periodic compounding, and continuous compounding.
- Payment frequency is the periodicity of interest amount payments while accrual period is the period when interest is accumulated. Accrual period is determined using the compounding frequency.
- To find the present value of a cash flow occurring at a future date, the cash flow should be multiplied by the discount factor calculated for that future date.
- An annuity is a financial instrument with several cash flows of equal amounts and a perpetuity is an annuity where level cash flows continue forever.

- Day count convention defines how days in an accrual period are counted. The most common day count conventions are Act/Act, 30/360, Act/365, and Act/360.
- Business day convention defines any adjustment that is needed to align cash flows with business days according to a contractually agreed holiday schedule. The most common business day conventions are no adjustment, following, modified following, modified previous, and end of month with no adjustment.
- A zero-coupon security is a financial instrument that does not pay any interest in the form of a coupon payment prior to its maturity.
- Bond yield or yield-to-maturity is an interest rate that if used in discounting future cash flows of a security produces a present value that is equal to the bond's current market value.
- Zero-coupon rate or zero rate or spot rate is the interest earned on an investment where all interest and principal payment cash flows occur at the end of the investment period, and no cash flows occur before that date.
- Bootstrapping is a technique for constructing a spot curve using available short-term, medium-term, and long-term market rates and relevant securities prices. It involves successively using shorter-term rates to obtain longer-term spot rates.
- LIBOR is the short-term lending interest rate among AA-rated banks, on an unsecured basis. Terms of LIBOR are overnight, 1 week, 1 month, 2 months, 3 months, 6 months, and 12 months.
- Forward and future rates are estimates of interest rate in a future time. Implied forward rate is the future interest rate that is implied by current spot rates.
- A forward rate agreement is a derivative product where underlying is an interest rate index.
- A Eurodollar futures contract is a standardized exchange-traded derivative product where the underlying is the 3-month Eurodollar interest rate.
- A fixed rate used in an interest rate swap contract is known as the swap rate. It is derived such that the value of the swap contract is zero at the inception time.
- The LIBOR-swap spot curve is constructed using three sets of rates: the short-term section of the curve is based on ICE LIBOR, the medium-term section of the curve is bootstrapped from FRAs and futures contracts, and the long-term section of the curve is bootstrapped from swap rates.
- The value of a swap contract can be calculated using the replicating bonds approach, where fixed and floating legs of a swap are replicated by fixed-rate and floating-rate bonds with comparable specifications.
- In the linear interpolation method, two adjacent knots are connected using a line, while in the cubic spline method they are connected by a cubic polynomial function.

- The effective federal funds rate is the weighted average of the rate of unsecured short-term loans between banks to satisfy reserve requirements with the Fed.
- The prime rate is a reference rate that banks use to price short-term commercial or consumer loans. The prime rate is highly correlated to the federal funds rate.
- An overnight index swap is a fixed for floating interest rate swap where the floating leg is based on an overnight index such as the federal funds rate.
- OIS discounting refers to the practice of discounting expected cash flows of a financial instrument using discount factors derived from the OIS spot curve.
- The secured overnight financing rate is the short-term borrowing interest rate for an overnight term and on a secured basis.
- The yield of a security has two main components: the risk-free rate and risk spread. Risk spread itself includes credit risk spread and market risk spread. Components of credit risk spread are market-wide spread and idiosyncratic spread. Components of market risk spreads are duration, prepayment, and liquidity risk spreads.
- The term structure of yield curves explains why bonds with the same riskiness perceptions but different terms to maturity may have different yields.
- The risk structure of yield curves explains why bonds with the same term to maturity but different riskiness perceptions may have different yields.
- The inflation rate is the measurement of how price levels change over time. Notional and real interest rates and inflation rate are connected.
- In ALM analysis, parallel and non-parallel shocks are applied to a spot curve and impacts on net interest income and the economic value of equity of the bank are studied.
- A negative interest rate is a consequence of monetary policies by central banks or flight to quality.

NOTES

1. ln is natural logarithm function.
2. In another chapter we discuss the concept of amortization when the principal amount itself is paid back during the life of the financial instrument and hence the interest amount calculation is based on the outstanding principal amount, which may or may not be equal to the original principal.
3. Treasury bills (T-bills) are based on an Act/360 accrual basis.
4. Except for British pound LIBOR, where an Act/365 convention is used.
5. U.S. Treasury bonds have an Act/Act accrual basis.

6. Microsoft® Excel Solver can be used to solve this nonlinear equation and obtain the yield.

7. Equation (1.27) provides the yield of a zero-coupon security, which should not be confused with a discount rate that is commonly used to quote a T-bill. The discount rate is calculated as: $= \left(\frac{1}{t}\right)\left(\frac{N-MV}{N}\right)$, where the denominator is the face value. For example, if a T-bill currently has a market value of \$996 and 28 days to maturity, the discount rate is calculated as: $d = \frac{360}{28} \times \frac{1000-996}{1000} = 0.051428 = 5.1428\%$. So if a T-bill is quoted with a discount rate of 5.1428%, then you can calculate the current market value (current price) using this equation and get to the market value of \$996.

8. We discuss floating-rate instruments in more detail in a future chapter.

9. GBP LIBOR has an Act/365 day count convention.

10. Since the rate has fallen by 50 basis points and each basis point results in a \$25 change, the long position gain is therefore $50 \times 25 = 1{,}250$.

11. Such a convexity adjustment is model dependent and the equation varies depending on the interest rate model used.

12. Although no premium is paid, depending on bilateral agreements or clearinghouse rules, there still may be initial collateral posting required from one or both parties of a swap contract.

13. Due to rounding error, the results shown in this section may be slightly different if calculations are repeated in a spreadsheet.

14. This practice is changing and nowadays other interest rate curves are considered to be risk-free. In another section of this chapter we discuss one such rate curve.

15. Sometimes the short end of the curve only up to a 6-month term is constructed using LIBOR and the middle part of the curve starts from 6-months and up to 2-years is bootstrapped using FRAs or future rates.

16. Volatility is obtained by calibrating an interest rate model to the data observed in the market. In a later chapter we discuss interest rate models in more detail.

17. A spline built using these end knot conditions is known as a natural spline.

18. In the *Convert* statement, if instead of *spline* we use *join*, SAS performs a linear interpolation.

19. As of March 2016, the effective federal funds rate reported in the Federal Reserve System H.15 report is calculated using the volume-weighted median of transaction-level data collected from depository institutions.

20. https://www.federalreserve.gov/releases/h15/.

21. This average is calculated using the differences of two rates when quoted as monthly averages.

22. In the terminology used here, we separated the funding margin (as an administrative cost) from the risk spread (as a premium due to riskiness of the lending). Some ALM software uses the term *margin* to reference the combination of the administrative cost and the risk spread together.

23. Here we used zero-coupon rates for simplicity but the same concept can be applied to coupon-paying bonds.

24. After American economist Irving Fisher.

BIBLIOGRAPHY

Bartels, Richard H., John C. Beatty, and Brian A. Barsky. *An Introduction to Splines for Use in Computer Graphics and Geometric Modeling*. Morgan Kaufmann, 1995.

Hull, John C. *Options, Futures, and Other Derivatives*. 6th ed. Prentice-Hall, 2005.

Hull, John C., and Alan White. "LIBOR vs. OIS: The Derivatives Discounting Dilemma." *Journal of Investment Management* 11, no. 3 (2013): 14–27.

Hull, John C., and Alan White. "OIS Discounting, Interest Rate Derivatives, and Modeling of Stochastic Interest Rate Spread." *Journal of Investment Management* 13, no. 1 (2015): 64–83.

Mishkin, Frederic S., and Stanley Eakins. *Financial Markets and Institutions*. 7th ed. Prentice Hall, 2012.

CHAPTER 2

Valuation: Fundamentals of Fixed-Income and Non-Maturing Products

*I*ntrinsic, theoretic, or economic value of a financial instrument is the present value of the future cash flows expected from the instrument. *Valuation date* is the date that cash flows are discounted back. The interest rate used in discounting the future cash flows is selected such that it captures the current market condition, as well as expectation of the future interest rate environment. Those rates should be adjusted for the riskiness of the instrument. Theoretical values of two financial instruments with identical contractual future cash flows are not the same; if one is perceived to have higher risk, such as counterparty default risk, compare to the other.

Many financial instruments, such as bonds and stocks, are actively traded in their associated markets. The *market value* of a financial instrument is the price that market participants are willing to trade the instrument. A *bid price* is the maximum price a market participant is willing to pay to buy the instrument and an *ask price* is the minimum price at which a market participant is accepting to sell the instrument. Market prices depend on the supply and demand forces, as well as economy and political environments, and fluctuate from one day to another or even during a trading day. Often news about a company, its customers, or its suppliers affects prices of financial securities associated with that firm. For these reasons, market value and economic value of an instrument are not always equal.

While both market values and economic values of financial instruments are used in asset-liability management (ALM) analysis, economic values play a more important role. First, not all financial instruments on the balance sheet of a firm have an active and liquid market, and hence their market values may not be readily available. Second, for ALM scenario analysis, such as the study of a parallel shift in the spot curve, market values are not usable, since they reflect instrument values based on the current spot curve and not the shifted curve. In this chapter we discuss the fundamentals for derivation of economic value of financial instruments. In our discussion about cash flow

115

generation and valuation, we focus on generic fixed-rate and floating-rate type instruments and explain methodologies for valuation of each type. Valuation of plain-vanilla bonds and important concepts of duration and convexity are discussed in this chapter. Valuation methods of more complex fixed-income securities, such as callable bonds or asset-backed securities, are discussed in a later chapter. In this chapter we also discuss valuation of non-maturing products such as savings accounts or credit card receivables. The possibility of default of a financial instrument or early repayment of its principal amount affect its valuation, and at the end of this chapter we introduce a framework for adjustment of cash flows for possibility of default and prepayment.

In discussions and examples presented in this chapter we do not consider a risk spread for the yield curve, so discount factors are obtained using rates from a risk-free spot curve without any adjustment. We will discuss risk-adjusted curves in another chapter. In examples and illustrations of this chapter we occasionally use the LIBOR-swap curve for calculation of floating-rate instruments coupons or as the risk-free curve for discounting. The principles discussed here, however, are still applicable if any other interest rate curve, such as overnight index swap (OIS), is used.

PRINCIPAL AMORTIZATION

The starting point in the valuation of a financial instrument is to determine its expected cash flows. Generally, for a financial instrument such as a loan or a bond, there are two types of cash flows expected: principal payments and interest payments. Principal payments are cash flows for the repayment of the original borrowed amount that are paid back by the borrower. Interest payments are cash flows for the cost of borrowing, calculated based on the periodic outstanding principal and effective interest rate for each period. The amortization method is a framework that defines the process of principal repayments, including time and amount of principal cash flows. An amortization schedule is a contractual characteristic of a financial instrument. The amortization can start at the first period after the instrument inception, or later on during the life of the instrument. There are several common amortization methods that are used in different financial products, and we will discuss each in the following sections.

Bullet Payment at Maturity

According to this amortization method the principal amount is repaid fully in a single cash flow at the maturity date of the instrument. Assume that a loan issued with a principal amount of \$100,000 at $t = 0$ matures in four periods.

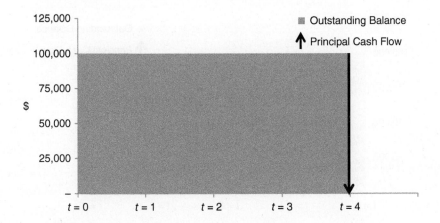

FIGURE 2.1 Example of bullet payment at maturity amortization method

Note: Cash outflow of principal amount at $t = 0$ inception time is not shown in this graph and only principal repayment cash flow is shown.

Figure 2.1 shows a schematic view of the principal payment cash flow and outstanding balance based on this amortization method.

Linear Amortization

In this method of amortization, principal payments are equally distributed over amortization periods during the life of the instrument. Each principal payment amount is:

$$P = \frac{N}{n} \tag{2.1}$$

where

$\quad P$ = Principal payment amount
$\quad N$ = Principal (notional) amount
$\quad n$ = Number of amortization periods (amortization interval)

Consider a $100,000 loan that matures in four periods, where amortization starts at the first period and ends at the last period. Based on linear amortization, the principal payment amount is:

$$P = \frac{100,000}{4} = 25,000$$

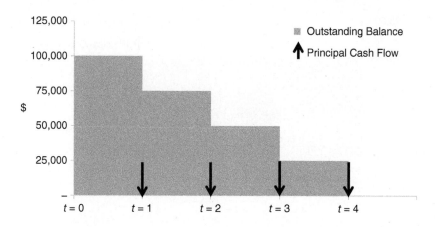

FIGURE 2.2   Example of linear amortization method

Figure 2.2 shows a schematic view of the principal payments and outstanding balance for this loan throughout its life based on the linear amortization method.

Constant Payment Amortization

In this method, the interest payment and the principal payment for each period is calculated such that the sum of them remains constant in all periods. In the constant payment amortization method, the principal payment amount cannot be defined independent of the interest payment amount. To first calculate the constant periodic payment amount, recall from Chapter 1 that the value of an ordinary annuity is calculated as:

$$V = C \left(\frac{1 - \dfrac{1}{(1+r)^n}}{r} \right)$$

where

$V = $ Value of annuity at inception
$C = $ Periodic payment
$r \ = $ Periodic interest rate
$n \ = $ Number of periods

Since at inception the value of the instrument is equal to its initial principal (notional) amount N, we have:

$$N = C \left(\frac{1 - \dfrac{1}{(1+r)^n}}{r} \right)$$

or

$$C = \frac{r\,N}{1 - \dfrac{1}{(1+r)^n}} \qquad (2.2)$$

Each constant payment amount C obtained from Equation (2.2) consists of interest and principal payments. The interest amount in period j is obtained by multiplying the outstanding balance at the end of previous period $j-1$, which is the same as the outstanding balance at the beginning of period j, by the periodic interest rate. Therefore, the principal payment amount for period j is obtained as:

$$P_j = C - I_i = C - B_{j-1} r \qquad (2.3)$$

where B_{j-1} is the outstanding principal balance at the end of period $j-1$. Note that $\sum_{j=1}^{n} P_j = N$. Consider again the $100,000 loan issued at $t = 0$ with a life of four periods and a periodic interest rate of 25%. The periodic payment is calculated as follows:

$$C = \frac{0.25 \times 100,000}{1 - \dfrac{1}{(1+0.25)^4}} = 42,344.17$$

Table 2.1 shows calculated interest and principal payment amounts for this loan. For period 1, the interest payment amount is $I_1 = 100,000 \times 0.25 = 25,000$ and the principal payment amount is $P_1 = 42,344.17 - 25,000 = 17,334.17$. The interest and principal amounts for other periods are calculated similarly. The original principal of $100,000 is fully amortized at the end of the fourth period. Figure 2.3 shows a schematic view of the principal payments, outstanding balance, and breakdown of the interest and principal amounts in each period when constant payment amortization is used.

This is the common amortization method for residential mortgage loans in the United States. Borrowers' early payments mainly consist of interest payments and as the loan vintage increases the portion of the payment that goes toward the principal repayment increases.

TABLE 2.1   Cash flow calculation based on constant payment amortization

Period	Total Payment	Interest Payment	Principal Payment	Outstanding Balance
0				100,000.00
1	42,344.17	25,000.00	17,344.17	82,655.83
2	42,344.17	20,663.96	21,680.22	60,975.61
3	42,344.17	15,243.90	27,100.27	33,875.34
4	42,344.17	8,468.83	33,875.34	0.00

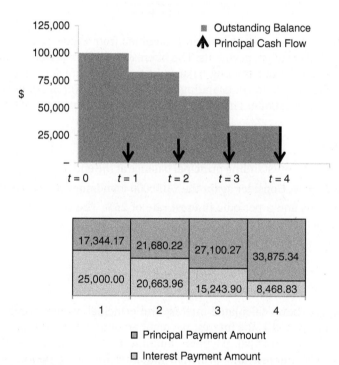

FIGURE 2.3   Example of constant payment amortization method

This amortization method can also be used for floating-rate instruments. At each reset date the payment amount will be recalculated using Equation (2.2) based on the outstanding principal and the new effective rate at that date and amortization schedule is updated accordingly.

Sum-of-Digits Amortization

In this method of amortization, similar to the constant payment method, the periodic principal payment amount cannot be defined independent of the interest payment amount. This amortization method can be used only for fixed-rate instruments. In order to calculate the principal payment amount of each period, the first total interest payment over the life of the instrument should be calculated as follows:

$$I = N \times r \times n \tag{2.4}$$

where I is total interest paid over the life of the instrument. The total principal amount repaid during the life of instrument is equal to the principal N. Therefore, the constant periodic payment is:

$$C = \frac{N + I}{n} \tag{2.5}$$

Each constant payment C consists of interest and principal payments. Thus, for period j, we have:

$$C = I_j + P_j$$

The interest payment amount for period j is obtained using the following equation:

$$I_j = I\left(\frac{n + 1 - j}{S}\right) \tag{2.6}$$

where S is the sum of the period numbers in the amortization interval:

$$S = 1 + 2 + \cdots + n = \frac{n(1 + n)}{2}$$

Finally, the principal payment amount for period j is obtained as:

$$P_j = C - I_j = C - I\left(\frac{n + 1 - j}{\frac{n(1+n)}{2}}\right) \tag{2.7}$$

Note that $\sum_{j=1}^{n} P_j = N$ and $\sum_{j=1}^{n} I_j = I$. Similar to the constant payment method, this amortization method results in a higher portion of interest payments in early periods and, as instrument vintage increases, the portion of principal payment increases. As an example, consider again the $100,000 loan issued at $t = 0$ with a life of four periods and periodic interest rate of 25%. To obtain principal payments based on a sum-of-digits amortization method, as a first step the total interest paid over the life of loan is calculated as:

$$I = 100,000 \times 0.25 \times 4 = 100,000$$

The periodic payment amount is:

$$C = \frac{N + I}{T} = \frac{100,000 + 100,000}{4} = 50,000$$

The sum-of-digits value is:

$$S = \frac{4(4 + 1)}{2} = 10$$

For period 1, the interest payment amount is calculated using Equation (2.6) as:

$$I_1 = 100,000 \times \frac{4 + 1 - 1}{10} = 40,000$$

Hence, the principal payment amount for period 1 is:

$$P_1 = 50,000 - 40,000 = 10,000$$

Interest and principal payment amounts for other periods are calculated similarly. Table 2.2 shows calculated interest and principal payment amounts for all four periods. Figure 2.4 shows a schematic view of the principal payments, outstanding balance, and breakdown of the interest and principal amounts in each period.

TABLE 2.2 Cash flow calculation based on sum-of-digits amortization

Period	Total Payment	Interest Payment	Principal Payment	Outstanding Balance
0				100,000.00
1	50,000.00	40,000.00	10,000.00	90,000.00
2	50,000.00	30,000.00	20,000.00	70,000.00
3	50,000.00	20,000.00	30,000.00	40,000.00
4	50,000.00	10,000.00	40,000.00	0.00

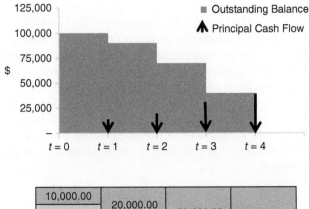

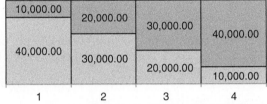

□ Interest Payment Amount □ Principal Payment Amount

FIGURE 2.4 Example of the sum-of-digits amortization method

Custom Amortization Schedule

Principal repayment of a financial instrument can be based on a custom amortization schedule specific to that instrument. Such an amortization schedule can be based on the amortized amount in each period or based on a percentage of the original principal. Table 2.3 shows an example of a custom amortization schedule for a $100,000 loan maturing in four periods, where 30% of the

TABLE 2.3 Custom amortization schedule

Period	Amortization Percentage	Principal Payment	Outstanding Balance
0			100,000.00
1	30%	30,000.00	70,000.00
2	30%	30,000.00	40,000.00
3	20%	20,000.00	20,000.00
4	20%	20,000.00	0.00

original principal is amortized in period 1, 30% in period 2, 20% in period 3, and 20% in period 4. The loan is fully amortized in four periods.

For valuation of non-maturing products (e.g., savings accounts or credit card receivables) a custom amortization schedule known as a *runoff or liquidation profile* is constructed and used to determine the future cash flows. We discuss this in more detail later in this chapter.

In quantitative finance, a common way of representing an amortization schedule is by using an *amortization factor*. The amortization factor for a period i is defined as the ratio of the outstanding balance of a financial instrument at the end of that period B_i to the initial balance at the inception of the instrument B_0:

$$A_i = \frac{B_i}{B_0} \tag{2.8}$$

In this example the amortization factors for the four periods are $A_1 = 0.3$, $A_2 = 0.3, A_3 = 0.2$, and $A_4 = 0.2$. If n is the number of periods in amortization interval, $\sum_{i=1}^{n} A_i = 1$.

FIXED-RATE INSTRUMENT

A fixed-rate instrument is a financial product with an effective rate that is fixed and set at the contract inception. This interest rate is constant and does not change over the life of the product. Many commercial and consumer loans underwritten by U.S. and European banks and non-bank firms are of the fixed-rate type. The known and fixed interest rate is the key to valuation of this type of instrument. In the discussion that follows we assume that the principal payment schedule is known and no prepayment or loss is considered. Later in this chapter we introduce a framework for inclusion of principal loss and prepayment.

Valuation

Determination of cash flows and valuation of a fixed-rate instrument that does not have optionality is straightforward. Using the contractual amortization schedule we can determine the principal payment cash flows and, since the effective rate for all accrual periods is known, interest cash flows are also known at the valuation date. Discounting these known cash flows using appropriate discount factors provides us with the value of the instrument at the valuation date. Assuming that the accrual period i is the period that ends with payment date i, generally the value of a fixed-rate instrument is calculated as:

$$V = \sum_{\substack{i=\text{First interest payment date} \\ \text{after valuation date}}}^{\substack{\text{Last interest} \\ \text{payment date}}} B_{i-1} r_i \tau_i DF_i + \sum_{\substack{j=\text{First principal payment} \\ \text{date after valuation date}}}^{\substack{\text{Last principal} \\ \text{payment date}}} P_j DF_j$$

(2.9)

where

V = Value of instrument at valuation date
r_i = Effective annual interest rate for period i
τ_i = Accrual time for period i (e.g., actual days in period i/365)
B_{i-1} = Outstanding balance at the end of period $i-1$ (or at the beginning of period i)
P_j = Principal payment at payment date j
DF_i and DF_j = Discount factors at interest payment date i and principal payment j

For a fixed-rate instrument, the effective rate r_i is constant and equal for all periods. To demonstrate the valuation of fixed-rate instruments, consider a term loan with the following specifications:

Position F1

Type	Fixed-Rate Loan
Currency	USD
Outstanding balance	75,000.00
Rate	5.5%
Start (inception) date	6/15/2013
Maturity date	6/15/2017
Amortization type	Bullet at maturity date
Payment frequency	Quarterly
Compounding frequency	Quarterly
Accrual basis	Actual/365
Most recent payment date	3/15/2015

The valuation date is March 31, 2015, and assume the spot rate curve is as shown in Figure 2.5 (all rates are annualized) and discount factors for

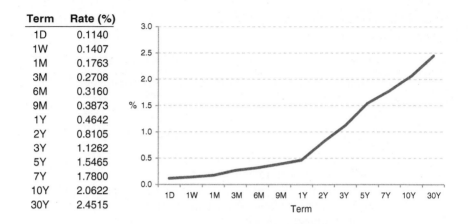

Term	Rate (%)
1D	0.1140
1W	0.1407
1M	0.1763
3M	0.2708
6M	0.3160
9M	0.3873
1Y	0.4642
2Y	0.8105
3Y	1.1262
5Y	1.5465
7Y	1.7800
10Y	2.0622
30Y	2.4515

FIGURE 2.5   Spot rate curve assumed as of March 31, 2015

TABLE 2.4   Discount factors using assumed spot rate curve as of March 31, 2015

Date	DF
6/15/2015	0.999478
9/15/2015	0.998562
12/15/2015	0.997310
3/15/2016	0.995638
6/15/2016	0.993564
9/15/2016	0.990979
12/15/2016	0.987986
3/15/2017	0.984597
6/15/2017	0.980901
9/15/2017	0.976857
12/15/2017	0.972468
3/15/2018	0.967746

selected dates are as shown in Table 2.4. These discount factors are calculated using rates from the spot rate curve in Figure 2.5 without including additional risk spreads. Application of risk-adjusted curves is discussed in another chapter.

The amount of interest cash flow for each period occurring at the payment date can be calculated as follows:

$$I_j = B_{j-1} r_j \tau_j \tag{2.10}$$

where

I_j = Interest amount for period j
τ_j = Accrual period (e.g., actual days in period j /365)
r_j = Effective annual interest rate for period j
B_{j-1} = Outstanding balance at the end of period $j-1$ (or at the beginning of period j)

For the fixed-rate instrument the effective rate r_j is constant and does not change from period to period. For simplicity we assume no business day adjustment here. The first cash flow of this instrument occurs on June 15, 2015, when the first interest payment is due. This cash flow has two parts: one part is the accrued interest from the most recent interest payment of March 15 (in the past of the valuation date) to March 31 (valuation date), a 16-day period, and the second part is for accrued interest from April 1 to June 15 (date of first payment), a 76-day period. The total cash flow occurring on the first payment date is therefore calculated as:

$$75,000 \times \frac{5.5}{100} \times \frac{16}{365} + 75,000 \times \frac{5.5}{100} \times \frac{76}{365} = 1,039.73$$

This cash flow occurs on June 15, 2015. Note that the accrual basis "Actual/365" of the instrument is used in determining the interest amount. The discount factor for June 15, 2015, from Table 1.4 is 0.999478; therefore, the discounted value of this cash flow (discounted to the valuation date) is:

$$0.999478 \times 1,039.73 = 1,039.18$$

The second cash flow of the instrument occurs on the second interest payment date, which is based on quarterly payment frequency and is set for September 15, 2015. There are 92 days between the previous payment date of June 15, 2015, and this payment date and hence the interest amount for this period is calculated using Equation (2.10) as:

$$75,000 \times \frac{5.5}{100} \times \frac{92}{365} = 1,039.73$$

Since this cash flow occurs on September 15, 2015, the discount factor for that date from Table 2.4 is 0.998562. Hence the discounted value of this cash flow is:

$$0.998562 \times 1,039.73 = 1,038.23$$

The cash flows of other interest payments that occur quarterly on the 15th of the months of December 2015, March 2016, June 2016, September 2016, December 2016, March 2017, and June 2017 are calculated similarly and discounted back to the valuation date using discount factors from Table 2.4.

On June 15, 2017, which is the maturity date of the instrument, there are two cash flows occurring. One is the last interest payment and the other is the principal repayment, based on the amortization schedule of the instrument. The interest cash flow amount on this date is calculated as:

$$75,000 \times \frac{5.5}{100} \times \frac{92}{365} = 1,039.73$$

where 92 is the number of days between March 15, 2017, and June 15, 2017. The notional repayment cash flow is equal to $75,000; therefore, total cash flow on June 15, 2017 is:

$$1,039.73 + 75,000 = 76,039.73$$

The discount factor for June 15, 2017, from Table 2.4 is 0.980901; therefore, the discounted value of this last cash flow is:

$$0.980901 \times 76,039.73 = 74,587.42$$

These calculations are summarized in Table 2.5. In this table:

- The "Date" column includes the payment date (except for March 31, 2015, which is the valuation date).
- The "t (Day)" column is the number of days between each payment date and the valuation date.
- The "τ (Day)" column represents the number of actual days between consecutive payment days (number of accrual days).
- The "Outstanding Principal" column represents the balance of the loan at the beginning of each accrual period.
- The "Principal Cash Flow" and "Interest Cash Flow" columns contain the scheduled principal repayment and interest cash flow at each payment date, respectively.
- The "Interest Rate" column includes the effective rate for the accrual period that ends at the associated payment date. For a fixed-rate instrument this rate is the same for all periods.
- The "Total Cash Flow" column is the sum of the principal and interest cash flows at each payment date.
- The "DF" column contains the discount factor for the payment date.
- The "Discounted Value" column is the result of multiplying the "Total Cash Flow" and "DF" columns.

TABLE 2.5 Valuation of position F1, a fixed-rate instrument

Date	t (Day)	τ (Day)	Outstanding Principal	Principal Cash Flow	Interest Rate (%)	Interest Cash Flow	Total Cash Flow	DF	Discounted Value
3/31/2015	0	16	75,000.00		5.5%	180.82			
6/15/2015	76	76	75,000.00		5.5%	858.90	1,039.73	0.999478	1,039.18
9/15/2015	168	92	75,000.00		5.5%	1,039.73	1,039.73	0.998562	1,038.23
12/15/2015	259	91	75,000.00		5.5%	1,028.42	1,028.42	0.997310	1,025.66
3/15/2016	350	91	75,000.00		5.5%	1,028.42	1,028.42	0.995638	1,023.94
6/15/2016	442	92	75,000.00		5.5%	1,039.73	1,039.73	0.993564	1,033.03
9/15/2016	534	92	75,000.00		5.5%	1,039.73	1,039.73	0.990979	1,030.35
12/15/2016	625	91	75,000.00		5.5%	1,028.42	1,028.42	0.987986	1,016.07
3/15/2017	715	90	75,000.00		5.5%	1,017.12	1,017.12	0.984597	1,001.46
6/15/2017	807	92	75,000.00	75,000.00	5.5%	1,039.73	76,039.73	0.980901	74,587.42
									82,795.34

The value of the position on the valuation date of March 31, 2015, is the sum of the discounted values presented in the last column of this table: $82,795.34. Note that the first cash flow in this table is occurring on June 15, 2015, and as discussed before it has two parts: accrued interest from the previous interest payment date to the valuation date: $180.82, and accrued interest from the valuation date to the next interest payment date: $858.90. Although the $180.82 part is shown in the row dated March 31, the cash flow actually occurs on June 15 and is discounted back from that date.

Yield

Yield is the internal rate of return that makes the value of a financial instrument derived based on the discounted cash flow (DCF) method equal to its market value. When the market price is not readily available, yield can be calculated by setting the economic value of the instrument derived using the method explained earlier equal to the discounted value of the cash flows while using yield as the interest rate. In other words, if the economic value of an instrument is V and y is the annual yield, solving the following equation for y provides us with the yield:

$$V = \sum_{\substack{t \text{ for all} \\ \text{cash flows}}} \frac{C_t}{\left(1 + \frac{y}{m}\right)^{mt}} \tag{2.11}$$

where

V = Instrument value
t = Time between valuation date and cash flow date (year), determined based on accrual basis
C_t = Cash flow occurring at time t
m = Numbers of compounding period per year (12 for monthly, 4 for quarterly, 2 for semi-annual, and 1 for annual)
y = Yield (annual)

For example, consider the fixed-rate instrument F1 we studied in the previous section. The economic value of the loan based on the assumed spot rate curve in Figure 2.5 was derived as $82,795.34. To obtain yield of this loan we need to discount the cash flows shown in the "Total Cash Flow" column of Table 2.5, using the yield as the interest rate, and then solve for the yield. This is done by following these steps:

- The compounding frequency of this loan is quarterly, hence $m = 4$.
- There are nine cash flows occurring on a 3-month interval starting from June 15, 2015, to June 15, 2017. The amounts of these cash flows are listed in Table 2.5's "Total Cash Flow" column.

- t in Equation (2.11) is calculated by dividing the number of days between the cash flow date and the valuation date by 365 (since the accrual basis is Actual/365).
- Base on Equation (2.11) and the economic value of $82,795.34, we have:

$$82{,}795.34 = \frac{1{,}039.73}{\left(1+\dfrac{y}{4}\right)^{4\times\frac{76}{365}}} + \frac{1{,}039.73}{\left(1+\dfrac{y}{4}\right)^{4\times\frac{168}{365}}} + \frac{1{,}028.42}{\left(1+\dfrac{y}{4}\right)^{4\times\frac{259}{365}}}$$

$$+ \frac{1{,}028.42}{\left(1+\dfrac{y}{4}\right)^{4\times\frac{350}{365}}} + \frac{1{,}039.73}{\left(1+\dfrac{y}{4}\right)^{4\times\frac{442}{365}}} + \frac{1{,}039.73}{\left(1+\dfrac{y}{4}\right)^{4\times\frac{534}{365}}}$$

$$+ \frac{1{,}028.42}{\left(1+\dfrac{y}{4}\right)^{4\times\frac{625}{365}}} + \frac{1{,}017.12}{\left(1+\dfrac{y}{4}\right)^{4\times\frac{715}{365}}} + \frac{7{,}6039.73}{\left(1+\dfrac{y}{4}\right)^{4\times\frac{807}{365}}}$$

- Solving this equation using a numerical technique such as the *Newton–Raphson method* provides us with an annual yield of 0.8592.[1]

If the discount factors from the spot rate curve are not available but the yield of the instrument is available, Equation (2.11) can be used to value the instrument. For example, if the annual yield for product F1 was available as 0.8592% and we did not have discount factors from the spot rate curve, we can value this loan using Equation (2.11) as shown in Table 2.6. The first eight columns of this table are similar to Table 2.5. Other columns are:

- The "t (Year)" column shows the number of days between the cash flow date and the valuation date divided by 365 to convert it to years (based on an Actual/365 accrual basis).
- The "Discounted Value Using Yield" column includes the cash flows divided by $\left(1+\dfrac{y}{m}\right)^{mt}$, where y is the annual yield, $m = 4$ due to quarterly compounding, and t is from the "t (Year)" column.

Notice that the value of discounted cash flows in the last column of Table 2.6 are different from what is shown in the last column of Table 2.5, but the sum of the discounted cash flows, which is the value of the loan calculated in this method, is equal to what was obtained before. This is not surprising because we calculated the yield in the first place by setting the results of the two methods equal. The point of this exercise was to show that the value of an instrument obtained based on the current market-driven spot rate curve and the value calculated using the current yield of the instrument are the same.

TABLE 2.6 Valuation of position F1, a fixed-rate instrument, using yield

Adjusted Date	t (Day)	Day Count	Outstanding Principal	Principal Cash Flow	Interest Rate (%)	Interest Cash Flow	Total Cash Flow	t (Year)	Discounted Value Using Yield
3/15/2015									
3/31/2015	0	16	75,000.00		5.5%	180.82			
6/15/2015	76	76	75,000.00		5.5%	858.90	1,039.73	0.2082	1,037.87
9/15/2015	168	92	75,000.00		5.5%	1,039.73	1,039.73	0.4603	1,035.63
12/15/2015	259	91	75,000.00		5.5%	1,028.42	1,028.42	0.7096	1,022.18
3/15/2016	350	91	75,000.00		5.5%	1,028.42	1,028.42	0.9589	1,020.00
6/15/2016	442	92	75,000.00		5.5%	1,039.73	1,039.73	1.2110	1,028.98
9/15/2016	534	92	75,000.00		5.5%	1,039.73	1,039.73	1.4630	1,026.75
12/15/2016	625	91	75,000.00		5.5%	1,028.42	1,028.42	1.7123	1,013.42
3/15/2017	715	90	75,000.00		5.5%	1,017.12	1,017.12	1.9589	1,000.17
6/15/2017	807	92	75,000.00	75,000.00	5.5%	1,039.73	76,039.73	2.2110	74,610.35
									82,795.34

TABLE 2.7 Discount factors using +100 bps shifted spot curve as of March 31, 2015

Date	DF
6/15/2015	0.997373
9/15/2015	0.993930
12/15/2015	0.990205
3/15/2016	0.986093
6/15/2016	0.981719
9/15/2016	0.976738
12/15/2016	0.971378
3/15/2017	0.965652
6/15/2017	0.959648
9/15/2017	0.953331
12/15/2017	0.946705
3/15/2018	0.939784

While the values of an instrument obtained from these two methods (using yield vs. using spot rate curve) are the same, an equivalent shift in the spot rate curve and in the yield does not produce an equal change in the value of the instrument. To see this, consider position F1 again. Assume a parallel shift of +100 bps is applied to the spot rate curve and the discount factors are recalculated. The new discount factors are presented in Table 2.7.

If we recalculate the value of loan F1 using the same approach shown in Table 2.5 while replacing the discount factors with the new ones from Table 2.7, we obtain the value of the loan as $81,091.68. This represents a change of –$1,703.66 from the original value of $82,795.34. As expected, an increase in interest rate decreased the value of the loan.

Now consider a +100 bps addition to the yield. The original annual yield was calculated as 0.8592%. An increase of 100 bps set the annual yield at 1.8592%. If we recalculate the value of loan F1 using Equation (2.11) and the same approach shown in Table 2.6 while using the yield of 1.8592%, we obtain the value of the loan as $81,081.81. This represents a change of –$1,713.52 from the original value. This comparison is summarized in Table 2.8 along with results for +200 bps and +300 bps shifts to the spot curve and yield. In each case and in absolute term, the decrease in value due to a positive parallel shift to the spot curve is less than the decrease in value due to the same change in the yield.

Duration and Convexity

From the previous discussions the relationship between interest rate and value of a financial instrument is clear. Estimating the impact of interest rate

TABLE 2.8   Impact of +100 bps, +200 bps, and +300 bps parallel shifts on spot rate curve and similar change in yield on value of fixed-rate loan F1

	Spot Curve + 100 bps	Yield + 100 bps	Spot Curve + 200 bps	Yield + 200 bps	Spot Curve + 300 bps	Yield + 300 bps
Base case value	82,795.34	82,795.34	82,795.34	82,795.34	82,795.34	82,795.34
Value after shift	81,091.68	81,081.82	79,432.42	79,409.05	77,816.21	77,775.96
Change in value	−1,703.66	−1,713.52	−3,362.92	−3,386.29	−4,979.13	−5,019.38

changes on a position or a portfolio helps ALM analysts and risk managers in taking necessary steps to minimize the potential detrimental effect of such changes on the earnings and value of a bank's equity.

One way to estimate the impact of an interest rate change scenario on the value of a financial instrument is to fully revalue the position under the new interest rate regime. For example, in the example in the previous section we showed that a +100 bps change in the yield of a fixed-rate loan resulted in a decrease of $1,713.52 in its value. The full revaluation provides an accurate assessment of the potential change in value. While this is a preferred method, it is also possible to estimate the impact of interest rate change on the value of an instrument approximately but without the need for full revaluation. This can be done by using *duration* and *convexity* measurements. We start our discussion about duration and convexity by first introducing the *Macaulay duration*.

Remaining life (or simply *life*) of a financial instrument is the time from the valuation date to the maturity date of the instrument. *Macaulay duration* (Macaulay 1938) is an alternative measurement of the life of the instrument that incorporates time value of the money. It is the weighted average of time of cash flows, where each weight is a contribution (portion) of the present value of the cash flow in the total value of the instrument. Based on the valuation and using the yield discussed in the previous section, Macaulay duration can be calculated as follows:

$$D_{Mac} = \sum_{\substack{t \text{ for all} \\ \text{cash flows}}} t \frac{\frac{C_t}{\left(1+\frac{y}{m}\right)^{mt}}}{V} \tag{2.12}$$

Since V is the value of the instrument, the second part of this equation can be considered as the contribution of the present value of each cash flow in the total value of the instrument. If we define these contributions as weights (w_t), Equation (2.12) can be rewritten as:

$$D_{Mac} = \sum_{\substack{t \text{ for all} \\ \text{cash flows}}} t \times w_t \qquad (2.13)$$

where

$$w_t = \frac{\dfrac{C_t}{\left(1+\dfrac{y}{m}\right)^{mt}}}{V} \qquad (2.14)$$

To demonstrate the calculation of the Macaulay duration, consider the sample fixed-rate loan F1 from the previous section. Recall that the valuation date is March 31, 2015, and that the loan matures on June 15, 2017; therefore, the remaining life of this loan based on an Actual/365 basis is $807/365 = 2.211$ year, where 807 is the number of days between the valuation date and the maturity date. Calculation of the Macaulay duration using Equation (2.13) is presented in Table 2.9. In this table:

- The "t (Day)" and "t (Year)" columns are times of cash flow in day and year.
- The "Total Cash Flow" column shows the cash flow amount at each payment date.
- The "Discounted Value Using Yield" column is the present value of each cash flow obtained by discounting using the yield.
- The "w_t" column includes calculated weights, using Equation (2.14). Alternatively, the weights are obtained by dividing the "Discounted Value Using Yield" column by the total value of the instrument ($V = \$82,795.34$). The sum of entries in this column is 1.
- The "tw_t" column includes the result of multiplying the time of each cash flow in the "t (Year)" column by the weight in column w_t. The sum of the entries in this column is the Macaulay duration.
- The "$t\left(1 + \dfrac{t}{m}\right)w_t$" column includes the result of multiplying t (in year), $1 + \dfrac{t}{m}$ ($m = 4$ for quarterly compounding), and weight in column w_t. The sum of the entries in this column will be used later when we discuss convexity.

In Table 2.9, the sum of the entries of column tw_t is the Macaulay duration of this loan equal to 2.0991 year:

$$D_{Mac} = \sum_{t} tw_t = 2.0991$$

TABLE 2.9 Calculation of Macaulay duration for fixed-rate loan F1

Date	t (Day)	Total Cash Flow	t (Year)	w_t	tw_t	$t(t+1/m)w_t$	Discounted Value Using Yield
6/15/2015	76	1,039.73	0.2082	0.012535	0.0026	0.0012	1,037.87
9/15/2015	168	1,039.73	0.4603	0.012508	0.0058	0.0041	1,035.63
12/15/2015	259	1,028.42	0.7096	0.012346	0.0088	0.0084	1,022.18
3/15/2016	350	1,028.42	0.9589	0.012319	0.0118	0.0143	1,020.00
6/15/2016	442	1,039.73	1.2110	0.012428	0.0150	0.0220	1,028.98
9/15/2016	534	1,039.73	1.4630	0.012401	0.0181	0.0311	1,026.75
12/15/2016	625	1,028.42	1.7123	0.012240	0.0210	0.0411	1,013.42
3/15/2017	715	1,017.12	1.9589	0.012080	0.0237	0.0523	1,000.17
6/15/2017	807	76,039.73	2.2110	0.901142	1.9924	4.9032	74,610.35
				1.0000	2.0991	5.0776	82,795.34

The Macaulay duration of 2.0991 year for this loan is less than the remaining life of 2.211 years. In general, for a fixed-rate instrument with all positive cash flows the Macaulay duration is between the time of the first cash flow and the maturity date of the instrument.

While the Macaulay duration presents a relationship between the interest rate and value of an instrument, a better measurement of the interest rate sensitivity is *modified duration*. Modified duration is a measurement of the sensitivity of value of an instrument to changes in yield and is defined as follows:

$$D_{Mod} = -\frac{1}{V}\frac{\Delta V}{\Delta y} \tag{2.15}$$

where

D_{Mod} = Modified duration
V = Value of instrument
y = Yield (annual)

When change in yield Δy is small, the fraction $\frac{\Delta V}{\Delta y}$ can be a representative of the first derivative of the value as a function of the yield. Recall from Equation (2.11) that the value of an instrument as a function of its yield can be written as:

$$V = \sum_t \frac{C_t}{\left(1 + \dfrac{y}{m}\right)^{mt}}$$

By taking the first derivative with respect to yield, we have:

$$\frac{dV}{dy} = \frac{d\sum_t C_t(1 + y/m)^{-mt}}{dy} = -\sum_t tC_t\left(1 + \frac{y}{m}\right)^{-mt-1}$$

$$= -\frac{1}{1 + \dfrac{y}{m}}\sum_t t\,\frac{C_t}{\left(1 + \dfrac{y}{m}\right)^{mt}}$$

By replacing $\frac{dV}{dy}$ in the definition of the modified duration in Equation (2.15) by its equivalent from above, we have:

$$D_{Mod} = -\frac{1}{V}\frac{\Delta V}{\Delta y} = -\frac{1}{V}\left(-\frac{1}{1 + \dfrac{y}{m}}\sum_t t\,\frac{C_t}{\left(1 + \dfrac{y}{m}\right)^{mt}}\right) = \frac{1}{1 + \dfrac{y}{m}}\sum_t t\,\frac{\dfrac{C_t}{\left(1 + \dfrac{y}{m}\right)^{mt}}}{V}$$

Finally, from the definition of the Macaulay duration and Equations (2.13) and (2.14), modified duration can be calculated as:

$$D_{Mod} = \frac{1}{1+\frac{y}{m}}\sum_t t\,w_t = \frac{1}{1+\frac{y}{m}}D_{Mac} \tag{2.16}$$

This equation presents the relationship between the Macaulay duration and the modified duration. Modified duration for our sample fixed-rate loan F1 with an annual yield of 0.8592% and quarterly compounding can be calculated using Equation (2.16) as:

$$D_{Mod} = \frac{1}{1+\frac{0.8592/100}{4}} \times 2.0991 = 2.0946$$

Modified duration can be used to approximately estimate the change in the value of the instrument for small changes in the yield. From the definition of the modified duration in Equation (2.15), we have:

$$\Delta V = -D_{Mod}V\Delta y \tag{2.17}$$

To demonstrate the use of Equation (2.17), consider a change of +0.5% in the yield of sample loan F1. Using Equation (2.17), the change in the value of the loan due to this change in the yield is obtained as:

$$\Delta V = -2.0946 \times 82{,}795.34 \times \frac{0.50}{100} = -867.13$$

Thus, using the modified duration we estimated that for an increase of 0.50% in yield, the value of the loan would drop by $867.13 from the base value of $82,795.94 to $81,928.21. If we perform a full revaluation using the method described in the previous section and based on the new yield of 0.8592% + 0.50% = 1.3592%, we obtain the new value of $81,933.41, which reflects a change in value of $861.92. The change in value approximated by the modified duration is very close to what we obtained using the full revaluation. Use of the modified duration for obtaining approximate change-in-value of an instrument performs well as long as the amount of change in yield is small. For large yield changes, however, the modified duration performs poorly. Table 2.10 presents the approximate changes in value of the sample loan F1 obtained using the modified duration for various changes in yield and comparison with change-in-values calculated from full revaluation. From this table we can see that for small Δy's, the ΔV's obtained using the modified duration are very close to the results from the full revaluation, but as the absolute value of Δy increases, the approximation deteriorates. This is due to the fact that since the modified duration is based on the first derivative

TABLE 2.10 Change in value obtained using full revaluation and approximation using modified duration for sample loan F1

Δy	Exact Revaluation		Approx. Using Duration	
	Value	ΔV	Value	ΔV
−0.75%	84,107.89	1,312.55	84,096.04	1,300.70
−0.50%	83,667.73	872.39	83,662.47	867.13
−0.25%	83,230.22	434.88	83,228.91	433.57
−0.10%	82,968.20	172.86	82,968.77	173.43
0.00%	82,795.34	0.00	82,795.34	0 .00
+0.10%	82,622.93	(172.40)	82,621.91	(173.43)
+0.25%	82,363.08	(432.26)	82,361.77	(433.57)
+0.50%	81,933.41	(861.92)	81,928.21	(867.13)
+0.75%	81,506.33	(1,289.01)	81,494.64	(1,300.70)
+1.00%	81,081.82	(1,713.52)	81,061.07	(1,734.27)
+2.00%	79,409.05	(3,386.29)	79,326.80	(3,468.54)
+3.00%	77,775.96	(5,019.38)	77,592.53	(5,202.80)

of the value function, it approximates ΔV based on the assumption that the relationship between an instrument's value and its yield is linear while in reality that relationship is non-linear. Figure 2.6 presents values of the sample fixed-rate loan F1 for different yields, (i) obtained using exact valuation and (ii) derived using approximation with the modified duration. The curvature of the exact (true) value curve is not captured in the approximate value obtained using modified duration, which is the tangent line to the value curve at the current yield.

From Table 2.10 and Figure 2.6 a few observations can be made:

- The tangent line that represents the value approximated using the modified duration is close to the true value for small Δy, but it deviates rather significantly when Δy is large.
- The approximate value obtained using the modified duration is always lower than the true value. This is due to the positive curvature of the value curve for loan F1.
- For a given increase in yield, the absolute value of the ΔV is less than ΔV for the same decrease in yield. Notice in Table 2.10 that when the yield changes by −0.75% (a decrease in yield), the value increases by $1,312.55, but for a +75% increase in yield (a same-size increase in yield), value decreases by $1,289.01. This is due to the asymmetric nature of the value curve around the current yield.

From this discussion it is clear that to better approximate the change in the value of an instrument without the need for full revaluation, we need to

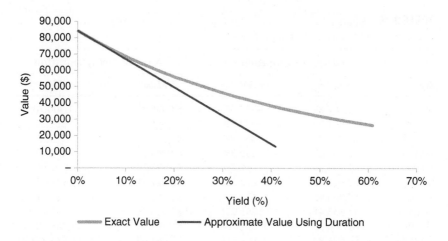

FIGURE 2.6 Sample fixed-rate loan F1; value versus yield; exact valuation versus approximation using modified duration

consider the curvature of the value curve as well. This is done using *convexity*. Convexity is a measurement of the sensitivity of the duration of an instrument to changes in the yield. It captures the curvature of the value curve and is defined as follows:

$$Conv = \frac{1}{V}\frac{\Delta^2 V}{\Delta y^2} \tag{2.18}$$

where

$$Conv = \text{Convexity}$$
$$V = \text{Value of instrument}$$
$$y = \text{Yield (annual)}$$

For small Δy the ratio $\frac{\Delta^2 V}{\Delta y^2}$ can be a representative of the second derivative of the value function with respect to the yield. Consider the value of instrument as a function of yield presented in Equation (2.11). By taking the second derivative of this equation with respect to the yield, we have:

$$\frac{d^2 V}{dy^2} = \frac{d^2 \sum_t C_t (1 + y/m)^{-mt}}{dy^2} = -\sum_t \left(\frac{1}{m}\right)(-mt-1)tC_t\left(1+\frac{y}{m}\right)^{-mt-2}$$

$$= \frac{1}{\left(1+\dfrac{y}{m}\right)^2}\sum_t t\left(t+\frac{1}{m}\right)C_t\left(1+\frac{y}{m}\right)^{-mt}$$

By placing $\frac{d^2V}{dy^2}$ from this equation into the definition of the convexity, we have:

$$Conv = \frac{1}{V}\frac{\Delta^2 V}{\Delta y^2} = \frac{1}{V}\left(\frac{1}{\left(1+\frac{y}{m}\right)^2}\sum_t t\left(t+\frac{1}{m}\right)C_t\left(1+\frac{y}{m}\right)^{-mt}\right)$$

$$= \frac{1}{\left(1+\frac{y}{m}\right)^2}\sum_t t\left(t+\frac{1}{m}\right)\frac{\overbrace{\dfrac{C_t}{\left(1+\dfrac{y}{m}\right)^{mt}}}}{V}$$

Using Equation (2.14) for weights we can simplify the above equation as:

$$Conv = \frac{1}{\left(1+\frac{y}{m}\right)^2}\sum_t t\left(t+\frac{1}{m}\right)w_t \qquad (2.19)$$

To calculate the convexity for the sample fixed-rate loan F1, with an annual yield of 0.8592% and quarterly compounding, in Table 2.9 we calculated the value of $t\left(t+\frac{1}{m}\right)w_t$ for each cash flow date. The sum of entries in that column is 5.0776 and therefore using Equation (2.19) the convexity is:

$$Conv = \frac{1}{\left(1+\frac{0.8592/100}{4}\right)^2} \times 5.0776 = 5.0559$$

Convexity can be used to improve the approximation of change-in-value due to change in yield obtained using the modified duration. To see this, first consider the instrument value as a function of yield:

$$V(y) = \sum_t \frac{C_t}{\left(1+\frac{y}{m}\right)^{mt}}$$

Here $V(y)$ represents value as a function of y and not a multiplication of V and y. Assume yield changes from y to $y + \Delta y$. Using Taylor series for expansion of $V(y)$ function[2] and by only including the first two derivative terms, we can approximate the value of the instrument for $y + \Delta y$ yield as follows:

$$V(y + \Delta y) \cong V(y) + \frac{dV}{dy}\Delta y + \frac{1}{2}\frac{d^2V}{dy^2}(\Delta y)^2$$

Using definitions of modified duration and convexity, we can replace $\frac{dV}{dy}$ and $\frac{d^2V}{dy^2}$ in the previous equation to have:

$$V(y + \Delta y) - V(y) \cong -D_{Mod}V(y)\,\Delta y + \frac{1}{2}Conv\,V(y)(\Delta y)^2$$

which for simplicity can be rewritten as:

$$\Delta V \cong -D_{Mod}V\,\Delta y + \frac{1}{2}Conv\,V\,(\Delta y)^2 \qquad (2.20)$$

The first term on the right-hand side of this equation is a linear approximation of value change. We used this before in Equation (2.17). If we use both terms of the right-hand side of this equation, a more accurate quadratic approximation of value change is obtained. To demonstrate the use of Equation (2.20) consider again the sample fixed-rate loan F1 and assume a 0.50% change in the yield. The change in the value can be approximated as follows:

$$\Delta V \cong -2.0946 \times 82{,}795.43 \times \frac{0.50}{100} + \frac{1}{2} \times 5.0559 \times 82{,}795.43 \times \left(\frac{0.50}{100}\right)^2$$

$$= -861.90$$

Compare this estimated change in value of –$861.90 from this quadratic approximation with the exact figure obtained from the full revaluation: –$861.92, and value change estimated using linear approximation: –$867.13 from Table 2.10. As can be seen, the quadratic approximation, where both modified duration and convexity are utilized, provides a more accurate estimate of the change in value than the linear approximation, which only uses modified duration. Table 2.10 is reproduced in Table 2.11 with the addition of quadric approximation of value changes. For small Δy, quadratic approximated ΔV is very close to the exact ΔV obtained from the full revaluation.

Dollar Duration and Dollar Convexity

Dollar duration is defined as the negative of the change in value per change in the yield, and hence from the definition of the modified duration it is equal to the modified duration multiplied by the current value:

$$D_{Dollar} = -\frac{\Delta V}{\Delta y} = D_{Mod} \times V \qquad (2.21)$$

TABLE 2.11 Change in value obtained using (i) full revaluation, (ii) linear approximation, and (iii) quadratic approximation, for sample loan F1

Δy	Exact Revaluation		Linear Approximation		Quadratic Approximation	
	Value	Change in Value	Value	Change in Value	Value	Change in Value
−0.75%	84,107.89	1,312.55	84,096.04	1,300.70	84,107.81	1,312.47
−0.50%	83,667.73	872.39	83,662.47	867.13	83,667.71	872.37
−0.25%	83,230.22	434.88	83,228.91	433.57	83,230.21	434.88
−0.10%	82,968.20	172.86	82,968.77	173.43	82,968.98	173.64
0.00%	82,795.34	0.00	82,795.34	0.00	82,795.34	0.00
+0.10%	82,622.93	(172.40)	82,621.91	(173.43)	82,622.12	(173.22)
+0.25%	82,363.08	(432.26)	82,361.77	(433.57)	82,363.08	(432.26)
+0.50%	81,933.41	(861.92)	81,928.21	(867.13)	81,933.44	(861.90)
+0.75%	81,506.33	(1,289.01)	81,494.64	(1,300.70)	81,506.41	(1,288.93)
+1.00%	81,081.82	(1,713.52)	81,061.07	(1,734.27)	81,082.00	(1,713.34)
+2.00%	79,409.05	(3,386.29)	79,326.80	(3,468.54)	79,410.52	(3,384.82)
+3.00%	77,775.96	(5,019.38)	77,592.53	(5,202.80)	77,780.91	(5,014.43)

DV01 or *dollar value of a basis point* is the change in value for a 1 bps change in the yield. You can see the dollar duration in the first part of Equation (2.20). Dollar duration is analogous to *delta* for options. Similarly we can define *dollar convexity* as the second derivative of value with respect to the yield, and from the definition of the convexity it is equal to multiplication of the convexity and the current value:

$$Conv_{Dollar} = \frac{\Delta^2 V}{\Delta y^2} = Conv \times V \qquad (2.22)$$

Dollar convexity is analogous to *gamma* for options and you can see the dollar convexity in the second part of Equation (2.20).

Portfolio Duration and Convexity

Modified duration and convexity of a portfolio of instruments are the weighted average of the modified durations and convexities of instruments in the portfolio, where each weight is the proportion of the instrument value to the total portfolio value. This is deduced from the definition of the modified duration and the convexity. Assume a portfolio P consists of n instruments with current values of $V_1, V_2, \cdots, V_n$:

$$V_P = V_1 + V_2 + \ldots + V_n$$

If modified duration and convexity of instrument i are D_{Mod_i} and $Conv_i$, the modified duration and the convexity of the portfolio are obtained as:

$$D_{ModP} = \frac{V_1}{V_p} D_{Mod1} + \frac{V_2}{V_p} D_{Mod2} + \ldots + \frac{V_n}{V_p} D_{Modn} \qquad (2.23)$$

$$Conv_P = \frac{V_1}{V_p} Conv_1 + \frac{V_2}{V_p} Conv_2 + \ldots + \frac{V_n}{V_p} Conv_n \qquad (2.24)$$

These identities are exact if instruments have the same yield; otherwise they are a good approximation of the portfolio's modified duration and convexity.

Effective Duration and Effective Convexity

So far in our discussion about duration we have assumed that the relationship between the value of the instrument, its cash flows, and the interest rate follows a simple and straightforward functional form. For some instruments, however, this relationship does not necessary present itself as simply as what is considered here, especially when the instrument has embedded options. In such cases we can define an *effective duration*, which is an approximation of the modified duration using the true value of the instrument for certain changes in the yield. Assume $V(y)$ is a general functional form for the value of an instrument as a function of its yield, and Δy is a small change in yield. Using the definition of derivative of a function with a central difference approximation, the effective duration is defined as:

$$D_{Eff} = \frac{V(y - \Delta y) - V(y + \Delta y)}{2\,V(y)\Delta y} \qquad (2.25)$$

$V(y)$ is the current value of the instrument and $V(y - \Delta y)$ and $V(y + \Delta y)$ are values of the instrument obtained by decreasing and increasing the yield by Δy respectively and recalculating the value considering all the complexity of the relationship between the instrument value and the interest rate. Since the effective duration can be obtained for instruments with embedded options, it is sometimes referred to as an *option-adjusted duration*.

Consider the sample loan F1 again with a current value of $82,795.34. Assume a change in yield of $\Delta y = 0.50\%$. From Table 2.10 the values of the loan when yield increases by 0.50% and decreases by 0.50% were calculated as $81,933.41 and $83,667.73, respectively. Based on this the effective duration is:

$$D_{Eff} = \frac{83,667.73 - 81,933.41}{2 \times 82,795.34 \times \dfrac{0.50}{100}} = 2.0947$$

Similarly, we can define an *effective convexity* as an approximate measurement of an instrument's convexity with a complex valuation structure. Based on approximation of the second derivative of a function, the effective convexity is defined as:

$$Conv_{Eff} = \frac{V(y - \Delta y) + V(y + \Delta y) - 2V(y)}{V(y)(\Delta y)^2} \tag{2.26}$$

Interest Rate Risk Immunization

The concept of duration as an interest rate sensitivity measurement can be used in interest rate risk management. Consider a bank with a zero-coupon liability with principal amount N_L maturing at time T from now. From an ALM point of view the best way to ensure that this liability is fully covered is to have a zero-coupon asset (or a portfolio of several zero-coupon assets) that matures at the same time T with the total principal amount N_A, which is equal to N_L. In this case, ignoring liquidity and credit risks, no matter the direction of interest rate movement from now to time T, the asset and liability are matched. This method of interest rate risk immunization is known as *cash flow matching*.

While this might be an ideal case, in practice cash flow matching faces several difficulties. It may not be possible to invest in asset positions that have the exact same maturities as the liability positions, or suitable zero-coupon assets to invest in might be hard to find. Also, from a profit-and-loss point of view, full cash flow matching may not be an efficient way to manage the interest rate risk.

Consider a bank that has a zero-coupon liability L with the following specifications. Analysis date is March 31, 2015.

Position L	
Type	**Zero-Coupon Note**
Currency	USD
Principal balance	81,000.00
Maturity date	8/31/2017
Payment frequency	N/A
Compounding frequency	Semi-annual
Accrual basis	30/360

Assume that the current yield curve is flat (i.e., spot rates are the same for all terms) and current yield is at 2%. The value of this position at time $t = 0$ is calculated as follows:

$$V_{L_{t=0}} = \frac{N_L}{\left(1 + \dfrac{y}{m}\right)^{mT}}$$

where

$m =$ Number of compounding period per year ($m = 2$ for semi-annual compounding)
$y =$ Yield ($y = 2\%$)
$N_L =$ Principal amount of liability L
$V_{L_{t=0}} =$ Value of liability L at time $t = 0$
$T =$ Time to maturity

The maturity date of L is at August 31, 2017. There are 29 months between the analysis date and the maturity date. Using a 30/360 accrual basis, the time to maturity is calculated as: $T = 29/12 = 2.4167$ years. Therefore:

$$V_{L_{t=0}} = \frac{81,000}{\left(1 + \dfrac{0.02}{2}\right)^{2 \times 2.4167}} = 77,196.64$$

The Macaulay duration of L is equal to its time to maturity: $D_{Mac_L} = 2.4167$. According to the cash flow matching method, to immunize this liability position with respect to interest rate risk, the bank should invest in a zero-coupon asset with the same maturity date and principal amount. If such an asset exists and investment is economically justified, then the task is easy. In the absence of such investment opportunity the bank decides to invest in coupon-paying note A1 with the following specifications:

Position A1	
Type	**Fixed-Rate Note**
Currency	USD
Principal balance	73,929.65
Coupon rate	3.525%
Maturity date	3/31/2018
Amortization type	Bullet at maturity date
Payment frequency	Semi-annual
Compounding frequency	Semi-annual
Accrual basis	30/360

The bank chooses the principal balance of the asset note such that the value of the asset A1 at time $t = 0$ is the same as the value of liability L at $t = 0$. This is based on the notion that at time $t = 0$ proceeds from the issuance of liability L, which is equal to its value at that time, are used to purchase asset A1. Asset A1 has six coupon payments that are based on a 30/360 accrual basis occurring on $t = 0.5$, $t = 1$, $t = 1.5$, $t = 2$, $t = 2.5$, and $t = 3$ years, and principal repayment occurs on the maturity date of March 31, 2018, which is at $t = 3$. The value of asset A1 at time $t = 0$ is therefore calculated as follows:

$$V_{A1_{t=0}} = \frac{C_1}{\left(1 + \frac{y}{m}\right)^{m \times 0.5}} + \frac{C_2}{\left(1 + \frac{y}{m}\right)^{m \times 1}} + \frac{C_3}{\left(1 + \frac{y}{m}\right)^{m \times 1.5}}$$

$$+ \frac{C_4}{\left(1 + \frac{y}{m}\right)^{m \times 2}} + \frac{C_5}{\left(1 + \frac{y}{m}\right)^{m \times 2.5}} + \frac{C_6 + N_{A1}}{\left(1 + \frac{y}{m}\right)^{m \times 3}}$$

where

N_{A1} = Principal amount of asset A1
C_i = Coupon amount (interest payment) at time i:

$$C_i = N_{A1} \times \frac{Coupon\ Rate}{100} \times \frac{180}{360} = 73{,}929.65 \times 0.03525 \times 0.5 = 1{,}303.01$$

$V_{A1_{t=0}}$ = Value of asset A1 at time $t = 0$

Using a yield of $y = 2\%$ we have:

$$V_{A1_{t=0}} = \frac{1{,}303.01}{\left(1 + \frac{0.02}{2}\right)^{2 \times 0.5}} + \frac{1{,}303.01}{\left(1 + \frac{0.02}{2}\right)^{2 \times 1}} + \frac{1{,}303.01}{\left(1 + \frac{0.02}{2}\right)^{2 \times 1.5}}$$

$$+ \frac{1{,}303.01}{\left(1 + \frac{0.02}{2}\right)^{2 \times 2}} + \frac{1{,}303.01}{\left(1 + \frac{0.02}{2}\right)^{2 \times 2.5}}$$

$$+ \frac{1{,}303.01 + 73{,}929.65}{\left(1 + \frac{0.02}{2}\right)^{2 \times 3}} = 77{,}196.65$$

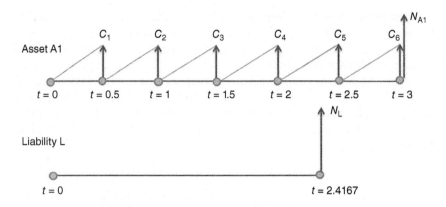

FIGURE 2.7 Cash flow of asset A1 and liability L

Figure 2.7 shows a schematic view of cash flows of asset A1 and liability L. Since the maturity date of asset A1 is after the maturity date of the liability position and it pays four coupons prior to the maturity of L, the bank is planning to invest the cash inflows from the coupon payments at the prevailing market interest rate until the maturity date of liability L. At that time asset A1 should be sold and a combination of proceeds from selling A1 and reinvested coupon proceeds should be used to cover the cash outflow of principal of liability L. Assume first that there is no change in interest rate and yield remains at 2% level until the maturity date of liability L on August 31, 2017 (i.e., at $t = 2.4167$ years). Value of L at that time is simply its principal amount:

$$V_{L t=2.4167} = 81,000$$

The value of asset A1 at $t = 2.4167$ year has two parts:

1. Value of reinvested coupons: The first coupon is received on September 30, 2015. There are 23 months between that date and the maturity date of L. Using the 30/360 accrual basis the investment time is $\frac{23}{12} = 1.9167$ years. There are three other coupons on March 31, 2016, September 30, 2016, and March 31, 2017. These coupons are 17, 11, and 5 months before August 31, 2017, and therefore investment times are $\frac{17}{12} = 1.4167$, $\frac{11}{12} = 0.9167$, and $\frac{5}{12} = 0.4167$ years, respectively. The future value of these reinvested

coupons at $t = 2.4167$, based on investment rate of 2%, is:

$$V_{Reinvestment_{t=2.4167}}$$

$$= 1{,}303.01 \times \left(1 + \frac{0.02}{2}\right)^{2 \times 1.9167} + 1{,}303.01$$

$$\times \left(1 + \frac{0.02}{2}\right)^{2 \times 1.4167} + 1{,}303.01 \times \left(1 + \frac{0.02}{2}\right)^{2 \times 0.9167}$$

$$+ 1{,}303.01 \times \left(1 + \frac{0.02}{2}\right)^{2 \times 0.4167} = 5{,}334.80$$

2. Value of asset A1: The value of the original asset A1 at $t = 2.4167$ is the present value of its remaining cash flows. The first coupon after August 31, 2017, occurs on September 30, 2017, so the accrual time is $\frac{1}{12} = 0.0833$. The last coupon and principal of A1 is received on March 31, 2018, which is seven months from August 31, 2017, and hence the accrual time is $\frac{7}{12} = 0.5833$. Therefore, the value of A1 at $t = 2.4167$ is:

$$V_{A1_{t=2.4167}} = \frac{1{,}303.01}{\left(1 + \frac{0.02}{2}\right)^{2 \times 0.0833}} + \frac{1{,}303.01 + 73{,}929.65}{\left(1 + \frac{0.02}{2}\right)^{2 \times 0.5833}} = 75{,}665.21$$

The total value of the asset and reinvestment is:

$$V_{A_{t=2.4167}} = 5{,}334.80 + 75{,}665.21 = 81{,}000$$

Hence, total proceeds from selling asset A1 and the value of reinvested coupons are equal to the value of liability L at its maturity date and the liability is fully covered. If we define surplus S as the difference between the value of the asset and the value of liability at any given time, based on the previous results the surplus at $t = 2.4167$ years is zero:

$$S_{t=2.4167} = V_{A_{t=2.4167}} - V_{L_{t=2.4167}} = 81{,}000 - 81{,}000 = 0$$

This strategy, however, leads to two risk types: *price risk* and *reinvestment risk*. Reinvestment risk is the risk related to scenarios when future cash inflows are invested at lower interest rates than the expected yields. In the earlier discussion we assumed that received coupons are reinvested at the 2% yield. If yields drop below 2%, then the proceeds from the reinvested coupons at the maturity date of liability may be insufficient. Price risk is the risk related to scenarios when assets are sold at future dates at prices that are lower than expected prices. In the earlier discussion we calculated the value of asset A1 at the maturity date of liability L using the 2% yield. If the yield increases above 2%, it results in a decrease in value of asset A1, and proceeds from selling A1 may be insufficient.

Consider a case where the yield goes up by 1% immediately after $t = 0$. If we repeat the previous calculation for the value of reinvested coupons and asset A1 at $t = 2.4167$ years, total asset-side value is as follows:

For $y = 3\%$:

$$V_{A_{t=2.4167}} = V_{Reinvestment_{t=2.4167}} + V_{A1_{t=2.4167}} = 5{,}397.04 + 75{,}236.93$$
$$= 80{,}633.93$$

The increase in yield increases the value of reinvested coupons and decreases the value of the asset A1 at $t = 2.4167$ years, but the magnitudes of the change are not equal. Surplus in this case is:

$$S_{t=2.4167} = V_{A_{t=2.4167}} - V_{L_{t=2.4167}} = 80{,}633.93 - 81{,}000 = -366.03$$

A negative surplus means the liability is not fully covered. Table 2.12 presents the value of surplus at $t = 2.4167$ years for different changes in yield occurring immediately after $t = 0$. Here possible upward changes in the

TABLE 2.12 Surplus between asset A1 plus reinvested coupons, and liability L at maturity of L for different yields

Yield	Change in Yield	Surplus (S)
0	−2%	747.71
1%	−1%	371.23
2%	0	0.00
3%	1%	(366.03)
4%	2%	(726.95)
5%	3%	(1,082.81)
6%	4%	(1,433.67)
7%	5%	(1,779.61)
8%	6%	(2,120.69)
9%	7%	(2,456.96)
10%	8%	(2,788.48)
11%	9%	(3,115.31)
12%	10%	(3,437.52)

interest rate lead to negative surplus and lack of coverage for the liability. This is a clear indication of interest rate risk for this combination of asset and liability portfolio.

To immunize the liability position the bank should choose an asset to invest in such that change in the value of the asset due to interest rate change is equal (or very close) to the change in the value of the liability. This can be accomplished by choosing an asset that has the same duration as the liability. This method of interest rate risk immunization is known as *duration matching*.

Continuing with our earlier example, since the Macaulay duration of liability L is equal to its time to maturity, $D_{MacL} = 2.4167$, and in order to achieve a duration matching immunization, the bank decides to invest in an asset A2 with the following specifications:

Position A2

Type	Fixed-Rate Note
Currency	USD
Principal balance	74,441.74
Rate	3.525%
Maturity date	9/30/2017
Amortization type	Bullet at maturity date
Payment frequency	Semi-annual
Compounding frequency	Semi-annual
Accrual basis	30/360

As was the case for asset A1, again the bank chooses the principal balance of the asset such that the value of the asset A2 at time $t = 0$ is the same as the value of liability L at $t = 0$. Asset A2 has five coupon payments that are based on a 30/360 accrual basis occurring on $t = 0.5, t = 1, t = 1.5, t = 2$, and $t = 2.5$ years, and principal repayment occurs on the maturity date of September 30, 2017, which is at $t = 2.5$ years. The value of asset A2 is therefore calculated as follows:

$$V_{A2_{t=0}} = \frac{C_1}{\left(1 + \dfrac{y}{m}\right)^{m \times 0.5}} + \frac{C_2}{\left(1 + \dfrac{y}{m}\right)^{m \times 1}} + \frac{C_3}{\left(1 + \dfrac{y}{m}\right)^{m \times 1.5}}$$

$$+ \frac{C_4}{\left(1 + \dfrac{y}{m}\right)^{m \times 2}} + \frac{C_5 + N_{A2}}{\left(1 + \dfrac{y}{m}\right)^{m \times 2.5}}$$

where

N_{A2} = Principal amount of asset A2
C_i = Coupon amount (interest payment) at time i:

$$C_i = N_{A2} \times \frac{Coupon\ Rate}{100} \times \frac{180}{360} = 74{,}441.74 \times 0.03525 \times 0.5 = 1{,}312.04$$

$V_{A2_{t=0}}$ = Value of asset A2 at time $t = 0$

So:

$$V_{A2_{t=0}} = \frac{1{,}312.04}{\left(1 + \dfrac{0.02}{2}\right)^{2 \times 0.5}} + \frac{1{,}312.04}{\left(1 + \dfrac{0.02}{2}\right)^{2 \times 1}} + \frac{1{,}312.04}{\left(1 + \dfrac{0.02}{2}\right)^{2 \times 1.5}}$$

$$+ \frac{1{,}312.04}{\left(1 + \dfrac{0.02}{2}\right)^{2 \times 2}} + \frac{1{,}312.04 + 74{,}441.74}{\left(1 + \dfrac{0.02}{2}\right)^{2 \times 2.5}} = 77{,}196.64$$

Therefore $V_{A2_{t=0}} = 77{,}196.64$, the same value as liability L at $t = 0$. The Macaulay duration of asset A2 is calculated using Equation (2.12) as $D_{Mac A2} = 2.4167$ years. This is the same as the Macaulay duration of liability L. Thus, a duration match is achieved. The bank uses the same strategy as before to cover the liability L at its maturity on $t = 2.4167$ by reinvesting the received coupons at the prevailing market interest rate until the maturity date of L and selling A2 at that time.

First assume no change in interest rate and that yield remains at 2% until the maturity of L. The combination of (i) the value of reinvested coupons and (ii) the value of asset A2 at $t = 2.4167$ is calculated as before, and total value covers liability cash outflow at $t = 2.4167$ (i.e., zero surplus):

For $y = 2\%$:

$$V_{A_{t=2.4167}} = V_{Reinvestment_{t=2.4167}} + V_{A2_{t=2.4167}} = 5{,}371.75 + 75{,}628.25$$

$$= 81{,}000 \tag{2.27}$$

$$S_{t=2.4167} = V_{A_{t=2.4167}} - V_{L_{t=2.4167}} = 81{,}000 - 81{,}000 = 0$$

Now consider a 1% increase in yield immediately after $t = 0$. The combination of (i) the value of reinvested coupons and (ii) the value of asset A2, and surplus at $t = 2.4167$, are as follows:

For $y = 3\%$:

$$V_{A_{t=2.4167}} = V_{Reinvestment_{t=2.4167}} + V_{A2_{t=2.4167}}$$

$$= 5{,}434.42 + 75{,}566.03 = 81{,}000.45 \qquad (2.28)$$

$$S_{t=2.4167} = V_{A_{t=2.4167}} - V_{L_{t=2.4167}} = 81{,}000.45 - 81{,}000 = 0.45$$

By comparing Equations (2.27) and (2.28) it can be seen that an increase of 1% in yield increased the value of reinvested coupons and decreased the value of asset A2 at $t = 2.4167$ year but these two changes are such that the total change in asset value resulted in a surplus of only \$0.45. Table 2.13 presents the value of surplus at $t = 2.4167$ for a different change in yield occurring immediately after $t = 0$. Here any change in interest rate leads to a positive surplus and therefore coverage of the liability. Figure 2.8 shows the values of reinvested coupons, the value of asset A2, and the total asset value at $t = 2.4167$ for different yields.

Instead of investing in a single asset A2, which may be hard to arrange, the bank can invest in a portfolio of assets with different durations. In that case the combination of different assets should be selected such that the total portfolio duration matches the duration of the liability. To ensure that a slight change in interest rate results in an increase in surplus value, the bank should also aim to maximize the portfolio convexity (Redington 1952). When yield curve is flat

TABLE 2.13 Surplus between asset A2 plus reinvested coupons, and liability L at maturity of L for different yields, when duration matching is used

Yield	Change in Yield	Surplus (S)
0	−2%	1.92
1%	−1%	0.49
2%	0	0.00
3%	1%	0.45
4%	2%	1.84
5%	3%	4.18
6%	4%	7.45
7%	5%	11.67
8%	6%	16.82
9%	7%	22.92
10%	8%	29.97
11%	9%	37.96
12%	10%	46.89

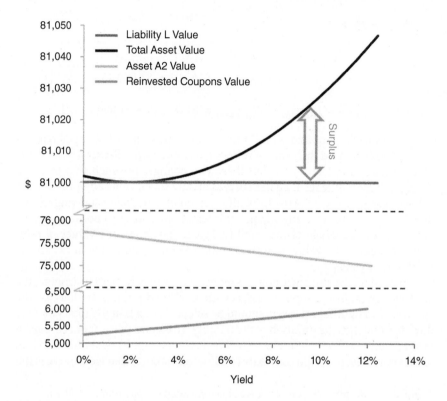

FIGURE 2.8 Values of (a) reinvested coupons, (b) asset A2, (c) total assets, and (d) liability L for different yields when duration matching is used. A different scale is used in different parts of the graph.

and all assets have the same yield, the duration and convexity of the portfolio is the weighted average of the assets' durations and convexities where weights are proportions of assets in the portfolio. Therefore, the appropriate portfolio can be obtained by solving this linear programming set:

$$Maximize \sum_{i=1}^{n} a_i Conv_i$$

$$Subject\ to: \sum_{i=1}^{n} a_i D_{Mac_i} = D_{Mac_L}$$

$$\sum_{i=1}^{n} a_i = 1$$

where

$$a_i = \text{Proportion of asset } i \text{ in asset portfolio}$$
$$Conv_i = \text{Convexity of asset } i$$
$$D_{Mac_i} = \text{Macaulay duration of asset } i$$
$$D_{Mac_L} = \text{Macaulay duration of liability L}$$

The duration matching immunization technique has some limitations. First, the method as described here assumes a flat yield curve and hence only parallel changes in the curve are considered. In practice this is rarely the case. Also as time passes, the asset values change and therefore this method requires continuous rebalancing of the portfolio to keep the duration matching in effect. Maybe the most serious criticism of this method is the violation of the arbitrage-free principle in valuation. To address some of these limitations, other methods have been developed to construct the immunization portfolio (Fong and Vasicek 1983). In practical ALM analysis, banks rely on scenario analysis to study the impact of changes in the yield curve (any shaped curve and not just flat) on the surplus between assets and liabilities of their balance sheets. We discuss this approach in more detail in future chapters.

Key Rate Duration

We are now in a good position to extend the concept of the modified duration introduced in the previous section and to consider (i) full term structure of the yield curve, and (ii) non-parallel shift in the yield curve.

Recall that in the "Yield" section we demonstrated that the current value of an instrument obtained using discount factors based on the instrument yield or using discount factors based on spot curve are the same. However, it was also shown that an equivalent shift to the spot curve and to the yield does not produce equal changes in the value of the instrument. This is due to the fact that a parallel shift in the spot curve is not equivalent to the same change in the instrument yield, unless the spot curve is flat (i.e., spot rates are the same for all maturities).

The modified duration as a measurement of sensitivity of the instrument value to the interest rate is based on the change in instrument yield, therefore it implicitly assumes (i) the spot curve is flat and (ii) change in instrument yield is equivalent to a parallel shift in the spot curve (i.e., all spot rates are changed by an equal amount). To relax these two assumptions and to expand our interest rate sensitivity discussion, here we first introduce *Fisher-Weil duration* and then discuss a generalization of the modified duration. This is followed by introduction of the *key rate duration*.

Fisher-Weil Duration

Fisher-Weil duration (Fisher and Weil 1971) is based on the discount factors using the spot curve and hence considers the full term structure of the yield curve. Fisher-Weil duration can be considered a generalization of the Macaulay duration:

$$D_{FW} = \sum_{\substack{t \text{ for all} \\ \text{cash flows}}} t \frac{\dfrac{C_t}{\left(1 + \dfrac{r_t}{m}\right)^{mt}}}{V} \tag{2.29}$$

where

$$
\begin{aligned}
V &= \text{Current value of instrument} \\
r_t &= \text{Spot rate for time } t \text{ (annual)} \\
C_t &= \text{Cash flow at time } t \\
m &= \text{Numbers of compounding period per year} \\
t &= \text{Time of each cash flow}
\end{aligned}
$$

Or using discount factor notation it can be written as:

$$D_{FW} = \sum_{\substack{t \text{ for all} \\ \text{cash flows}}} t \frac{df_t \, C_t}{V} \tag{2.30}$$

where

$$df_t = \text{Discount factor obtained using spot curve for time } t$$

Similar to the Macaulay duration we can write the Fisher-Weil duration as the weighted-average time of cash flows:

$$D_{FW} = \sum_{\substack{t \text{ for all} \\ \text{cash flows}}} t\omega_t \tag{2.31}$$

where weights are defined as:

$$\omega_t = \frac{\dfrac{C_t}{\left(1 + \dfrac{r_t}{m}\right)^{mt}}}{V} \tag{2.32}$$

Or using discount factor notation:

$$\omega_t = \frac{df_t \, C_t}{V} \tag{2.33}$$

Consider the sample loan F1 introduced earlier in this chapter. In Table 2.9 we calculated the Macaulay duration of 2.0991 year for this loan. Table 2.14 presents calculation of Fisher-Weil duration along with the repeated calculation of Macaulay duration for comparison. In this table:

- The column "Total Cash Flow" is the total cash flow for interest payment and principal payment based on contractual interest rate and amortization schedule.
- The column "DF Based on Spot Curve" contains the discount factors based on the spot curve of Figure 2.5, as presented in Table 2.4.
- The column "Discounted Value Using DF" is the present value of each cash flow using the aforementioned discount factors.
- The column "ω_t" is the weight as defined in Equation (2.33) using current value of $V = 82{,}795.34$.
- Column "$t\omega_t$" is the multiplication of the weight "ω_t" and the "t (year)" columns. Summation of entries in this column is the Fisher-Weil duration.
- The "Discounted Value Using Yield" and "w_t" columns are discounted value and weight using the yield and the sum of the entries in column "tw_t" is the Macaulay duration, the same as in Table 2.9.

In Table 2.14, two weights, w_t (for Macaulay duration) and ω_t (for Fisher-Weil duration), are slightly different, but due to rounding they may seem equal. From Table 2.14 we can see that the Fisher-Weil duration (2.0988) and the Macaulay duration (2.0991) are not exactly equal, although they are very close.

Assume that r_t is the vector of spot rates from the current spot curve: $r_t = (r_1, r_2, \cdots, r_t, \cdots, r_n)$. Elements of this vector are rates from the spot curve for different maturities. To extend the modified duration to consider the full term structure of the yield curve, first assume a parallel shift of Δr to all rates of spot curve. The modified duration can be redefined as:

$$D_{Mod} = -\frac{1}{V}\frac{\Delta V}{\Delta r} \tag{2.34}$$

The current value of instrument V can be presented as:

$$V(r_t) = \sum_{\substack{t \text{ for all} \\ \text{cash flows}}} \frac{C_t}{\left(1 + \dfrac{r_t}{m}\right)^{mt}} \tag{2.35}$$

TABLE 2.14 Calculation of Fisher-Weil duration for fixed-rate loan F1

Date	t (Day)	t (Year)	Total Cash Flow (A)	DF based on Spot Curve (B)	Discounted Value Using DF (C) = (A)×(B)	$\omega_t = (C)/V$	$t\omega_t$	Discounted Value Using Yield (D)	$w_t = (D)/V$	tw_t
6/15/2015	76	0.2082	1,039.73	0.999478	1,039.18	0.0126	0.0026	1,037.87	0.0125	0.0026
9/15/2015	168	0.4603	1,039.73	0.998562	1,038.23	0.0125	0.0058	1,035.63	0.0125	0.0058
12/15/2015	259	0.7096	1,028.42	0.997310	1,025.66	0.0124	0.0088	1,022.18	0.0123	0.0088
3/15/2016	350	0.9589	1,028.42	0.995638	1,023.94	0.0124	0.0119	1,020.00	0.0123	0.0118
6/15/2016	442	1.2110	1,039.73	0.993564	1,033.03	0.0125	0.0151	1,028.98	0.0124	0.0150
9/15/2016	534	1.4630	1,039.73	0.990979	1,030.35	0.0124	0.0182	1,026.75	0.0124	0.0181
12/15/2016	625	1.7123	1,028.42	0.987986	1,016.07	0.0123	0.0210	1,013.42	0.0122	0.0210
3/15/2017	715	1.9589	1,017.12	0.984597	1,001.46	0.0121	0.0237	1,000.17	0.0121	0.0237
6/15/2017	807	2.2110	76,039.73	0.980901	74,587.42	0.9009	1.9918	74,610.35	0.9011	1.9924
					82,795.34	1.0000	2.0988	82,795.34	1.0000	2.0991

The value of the instrument after a parallel shift of Δr to the spot curve is represented by $V(\boldsymbol{r_t} + \Delta r)$, where $\boldsymbol{r_t} + \Delta r$ is the vector of the shifted spot rates. All rates in this vector are shifted equally by the same amount Δr: $\boldsymbol{r_t} + \Delta r = (r_1 + \Delta r, r_2 + \Delta r, \cdots, r_t + \Delta r, \cdots, r_n + \Delta r)$. Therefore:

$$V(\boldsymbol{r_t} + \Delta r) = \sum_t \frac{C_t}{\left(1 + \dfrac{r_t}{m} + \dfrac{\Delta r}{m}\right)^{mt}}$$

Assuming small Δr, using the Taylor series expansion, and considering only the first-order derivative term, we have:

$$V(\boldsymbol{r_t} + \Delta r) = \sum_t C_t \left(\frac{1}{\left(1 + \dfrac{r_t}{m}\right)^{mt}} - \frac{mt\dfrac{\Delta r}{m}}{\left(1 + \dfrac{r_t}{m}\right)^{mt+1}} \right)$$

$$= \sum_t \frac{C_t}{\left(1 + \dfrac{r_t}{m}\right)^{mt}} - \Delta r \sum_t \frac{tC_t}{\left(1 + \dfrac{r_t}{m}\right)^{mt+1}}$$

Using Equation (2.35), we have:

$$V(\boldsymbol{r_t} + \Delta r) = V(\boldsymbol{r_t}) - \Delta r \sum_t \frac{tC_t}{\left(1 + \dfrac{r_t}{m}\right)^{mt+1}}$$

or

$$\frac{V(\boldsymbol{r_t} + \Delta r) - V(\boldsymbol{r_t})}{\Delta r} = -\sum_t \frac{tC_t}{\left(1 + \dfrac{r_t}{m}\right)^{mt+1}}$$

By multiplying both sides by $-\dfrac{1}{V}$ we have:

$$-\frac{1}{V} \times \frac{\Delta V}{\Delta r} = \sum_t \frac{\dfrac{tC_t}{\left(1+\dfrac{r_t}{m}\right)^{mt+1}}}{V}$$

By comparing this equation with the redefined modified duration in Equation (2.34), we have:

$$D_{Mod} = \sum_t \frac{t}{\left(1 + \dfrac{r_t}{m}\right)} \frac{\dfrac{C_t}{\left(1+\dfrac{r_t}{m}\right)^{mt}}}{V} \qquad (2.36)$$

Or using the weight notation in Equation (2.32), we have:

$$D_{Mod} = \sum_t \frac{t}{1 + \frac{r_t}{m}} \omega_t \tag{2.37}$$

Equation (2.37) is a generalization of the modified duration that was first introduced in Equation (2.16). This version considers the full term structure of the yield curve. Both versions of modified duration are listed in the following table for ease of comparison.

Modified duration based on yield (assuming parallel shift in a flat spot curve)	Modified duration based on spot curve (assuming parallel shift in a general spot curve with full term structure)
$D_{Mod} = \dfrac{1}{1 + \frac{y}{m}} \sum_t t w_t$	$D_{Mod} = \sum_t \dfrac{t}{1 + \frac{r_t}{m}} \omega_t$
$w_t = \dfrac{\dfrac{C_t}{\left(1 + \frac{y}{m}\right)^{mt}}}{V}$	$\omega_t = \dfrac{\dfrac{C_t}{\left(1 + \frac{r_t}{m}\right)^{mt}}}{V}$

Key Rate Duration

So far in this section we have expanded our definition of the modified duration to consider the full term structure of the yield curve. However, we are still assuming that an equal shift of Δr is applied to all spot rates (i.e., a parallel shift to the curve). *Key rate duration* (Ho 1992) is a method to measure the sensitivity of instrument value to non-parallel shifts in the yield curve. Figure 2.9 presents the original spot curve that we used so far in this chapter and a new curve, where the rate at the 2-year term is shifted up by 0.5% while keeping other spot rates, including rates at adjacent key terms of 1-year and 3-year, unchanged. Such a rate change creates a triangular shift on the curve around the shocked key term. The purpose of the key rate duration is to find a measurement of the sensitivity of the instrument value to such change in the spot curve.

Assume that r_t is the spot rate for a given maturity on the spot curve.[3] The key rate duration is the equivalent of the redefined modified duration in Equation (2.36), when only one particular rate r_t on spot curve is shifted by Δr_t and spot rates for other key terms are kept unchanged. It can be written as:

$$KRD_t = -\frac{1}{V} \frac{\Delta V}{\Delta r_t} \tag{2.38}$$

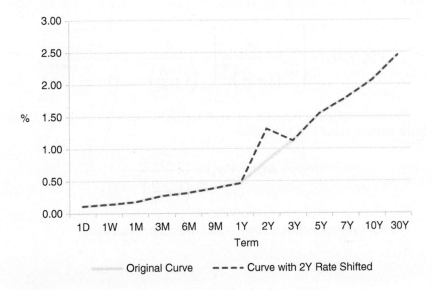

FIGURE 2.9 +0.5% shift in 2-year key term of spot curve while rates on other key terms are unchanged

Assume that the value of the instrument after a shift of Δr_t only to term t of the spot curve is represented by $V(r_t + \Delta r)$, where $r_t + \Delta r$ is the vector of the shifted spot rates as defined below:

$r_t = (r_1, r_2, \cdots, r_t, \cdots, r_n) =$ Vector of spot rates for all key terms (annual)
$\Delta r_t = (0, 0 \cdots, \Delta r_t, \cdots, 0) =$ Vector of shifts (Δr_t for term t and zero for other terms)
$r_t + \Delta r_t = (r_1, r_2, \cdots, r_t + \Delta r_t, \cdots, r_n) =$ Vector of shifted spot rates

We have:

$$V(r_t + \Delta r_t) = \left(\sum_{i \neq t} \frac{C_i}{\left(1 + \dfrac{r_i}{m}\right)^{mi}} \right) + \frac{C_t}{\left(1 + \dfrac{r_t}{m} + \dfrac{\Delta r_t}{m}\right)^{mt}}$$

Assuming small Δr_t and by using the Taylor series expansion and considering only the first-order derivative term, we have:

$$V(r_t + \Delta r_t) = \left(\sum_{i \neq t} \frac{C_i}{\left(1 + \dfrac{r_i}{m}\right)^{mi}} \right) + C_t \left(\frac{1}{\left(1 + \dfrac{r_t}{m}\right)^{mt}} - \frac{mt \dfrac{\Delta r_t}{m}}{\left(1 + \dfrac{r_t}{m}\right)^{mt+1}} \right)$$

or

$$V(r_t + \Delta r_t) = \left(\sum_{i \neq t} \frac{C_i}{\left(1 + \frac{r_i}{m}\right)^{mi}} \right) + \frac{C_t}{\left(1 + \frac{r_t}{m}\right)^{mt}} - \frac{C_t t \Delta r_t}{\left(1 + \frac{r_t}{m}\right)^{mt+1}}$$

Summation of the first two terms on the right-hand side of this equation is the current value $V(r_t)$, therefore:

$$V(r_t + \Delta r_t) = V(r_t) - \frac{C_t t \Delta r_t}{\left(1 + \frac{r_t}{m}\right)^{mt+1}}$$

By multiplying both sides by $-\frac{1}{V}$ and rearranging, we have:

$$-\frac{1}{V} \frac{V(r_t + \Delta r_t) - V(r_t)}{\Delta r_t} = \frac{t}{1 + \frac{r_t}{m}} \frac{\dfrac{C_t}{\left(1 + \frac{r_t}{m}\right)^{mt}}}{V}$$

By comparing this equation with the definition of the key rate duration in Equation (2.38), we have:

$$KRD_t = \frac{t}{1 + \frac{r_t}{m}} \frac{\dfrac{C_t}{\left(1 + \frac{r_t}{m}\right)^{mt}}}{V} \qquad (2.39)$$

By comparing Equations (2.39) and (2.36) it can be seen that redefined modified duration is the summation of the key rate duration over all key terms of the curve.

After the key rate duration for a key term of the spot curve is obtained, we can measure the sensitivity of the instrument value to changes in rate for that particular term. Also, if we obtain key rate durations for multiple key terms we can approximately measure the impact of a non-parallel shift in the spot curve on the instrument value. In practice, key rate durations are obtained in a similar fashion as effective duration discussed in the previous section, using the following equation:

$$KRD_{t\ Eff} = \frac{V(r_t - \Delta r_t) - V(r_t + \Delta r_t)}{2 V(r_t) \Delta r_t} \qquad (2.40)$$

where

$$r_t = (r_1, r_2, \cdots, r_t, \cdots, r_n) = \text{Vector of spot rates for all key terms}$$
$$\text{(annual)}$$
$$r_t + \Delta r_t = (r_1, r_2, \cdots, r_t + \Delta r_t, \cdots, r_n) = \text{Vector of upward shifted spot rates}$$
$$\text{for only term } t$$
$$r_t - \Delta r_t = (r_1, r_2, \cdots, r_t - \Delta r_t, \cdots, r_n) = \text{Vector of downward shifted spot}$$
$$\text{rates for only term } t$$

To demonstrate calculation of the key rate duration, consider sample loan F1 again. To calculate the key rate duration for the 2-year key term, shifts of $\pm 0.10\%$ are applied to the 2-year spot rate while rates at other key terms are kept unchanged. When calculating the discount factors, rates for any date falling between 1-year and 2-year and between 2-year and 3-year term points are interpolated linearly (hence the triangular shape of the shift). For each scenario the value of the instrument is calculated as summarized in the following:

Instrument value using original spot rate curve: $V(r_t) = 82{,}795.34$

Instrument value using spot curve with 2-year term shifted by $+0.10\%$: $V(r_t + \Delta r_t) = 82{,}661.76$

Instrument value using spot curve with 2-year term shifted by -0.10%: $V(r_t - \Delta r_t) = 82{,}929.20$

Using these results, the key rate duration for the 2-year term is calculated as:

$$KRD_{2Y\ Eff} = \frac{V(r_t - \Delta r_t) - V(r_t + \Delta r_t)}{2\,V(r_t)\,\Delta r_t} = \frac{82{,}929.20 - 82{,}661.76}{2 \times 82{,}795.34 \times \dfrac{0.10}{100}} = 1.6151$$

Following the same approach we can calculate the key rate duration for other key terms that are relevant to loan F1, as shown in Table 2.15. If we calculate effective duration based on a parallel shift of $\pm 0.10\%$ for all terms of the curve we have:

Instrument value using original spot rate curve: $V(r_t) = 82{,}795.34$

Instrument value using spot curve shifted by $+0.10\%$ in all terms: $V(r_t + \Delta r) = 82{,}623.93$

Instrument value using spot curve shifted by -0.10% in all terms: $V(r_t - \Delta r) = 82{,}968.20$

TABLE 2.15   Key rate duration for sample fixed-rate loan F1

Term	Base Value	Upward Shift Value	Downward Shift Value	Shift (%)	KRD
1D	82,795.34	82,795.34	82,795.34	0.10%	0.0000
1W	82,795.34	82,795.34	82,795.34	0.10%	0.0000
1M	82,795.34	82,795.39	82,795.29	0.10%	0.0007
3M	82,795.34	82,795.58	82,795.10	0.10%	0.0029
6M	82,795.34	82,795.87	82,794.81	0.10%	0.0064
9M	82,795.34	82,796.12	82,794.56	0.10%	0.0094
1Y	82,795.34	82,798.54	82,792.15	0.10%	0.0386
2Y	82,795.34	82,929.20	82,661.76	0.10%	1.6151
3Y	82,795.34	82,829.45	82,761.24	0.10%	0.4119
					2.0851

Therefore, effective duration based on this parallel shift is:

$$D_{Eff} = \frac{V(r_t - \Delta r) - V(r_t + \Delta r)}{2\,V(r_t)\,\Delta r_t} = \frac{82{,}968.20 - 82{,}623.93}{2 \times 82{,}795.34 \times \dfrac{0.10}{100}} = 2.0851$$

This effective duration that is obtained based on a parallel shift of the spot curve on all key terms is equal to the summation of key rate durations obtained in Table 2.15:

$$D_{Eff} = \sum_{\substack{t \text{ for all} \\ \text{key rates}}} KRD_{t\ Eff} \tag{2.41}$$

Finally, assume that we are interested in approximately estimating the impact of a non-parallel shift in the spot curve on the value of loan F1, where the 3-month rate is increased by +50 bps, the 1-year rate is increased by +80 bps, and rates of other key terms are not changed. Using the key rate durations from Table 2.15 the change in value can be approximated as:

$$\Delta V \cong -KRD_{3M}\,V\Delta r_{3M} - KRD_{1Y}\,V\Delta r_{1Y}$$

$$= -0.0029 \times 82{,}795.34 \times \frac{0.50}{100} - 0.0386 \times 82{,}795.34$$

$$\times \frac{0.80}{100} = -1.22 - 25.55 = -26.78$$

So, the value of the F1 loan would drop approximately by $26.78. If we fully revalue the F1 loan using the altered spot curve, the value of the loan would be $82,768.69, reflecting an exact value decrease of $26.65.

FLOATING-RATE INSTRUMENT

A floating-rate instrument is a financial product with an effective rate that is not constant and can change during the life of the product. The effective rate of such instrument is usually dependent on the value of an interest rate index such as prime rate, 1-month LIBOR, or 3-month EURIBOR. *Reset date* or *rate fixing date* is the date when the new effective rate is determined and used for future interest calculation. *Reset frequency* is the periodicity that the effective rate of a floating-rate instrument is reset. For example, if the reset frequency of a floating-rate loan is quarterly, the effective rate used to calculate the accrued interest is reset every three months.

In the United States many of the commercial loans underwritten by banks are floating-rate loans. Since most banks fund a major portion of their balance sheets using floating-rate bonds, floating-rate assets, such as commercial loans, perform as a natural hedge against the interest rate risk. Many consumer products, such as credit card loans or home-equity lines of credit, are also floating-rate type.

Unlike fixed-rate instruments where all future cash flows are known at the valuation date, cash flows for a floating-rate instrument are only known until the next reset date. On that date a new effective rate is set based on the contractual specification of the instrument (e.g., value of 3-month LIBOR at the reset date plus 50 bps spread) and used for succeeding cash flow calculation. Hence cash flows following the first reset date are not known at the valuation date. As discussed before, the principal of economic valuation of financial products is based on derivation of future cash flows and discounting them back to the valuation date. Not knowing all future cash flows of floating-rate instruments would pose a challenge in valuation of such products.

Generally, there are three methods used in practice to value a floating-rate instrument and we discuss each method in the following sections. In principle, all these methods use the discounted cash flow concept in a similar fashion as explained for the fixed-rate instruments, but the effective rate for each period can be different from the rate of the previous or the following periods.

In the following discussion on valuation of floating-rate instruments we focus on cases where repayment of the principal, both amounts and timings, are known and based on a predetermined schedule; therefore, prepayment is not considered. It is also important to note that here we do not consider a risk spread and discount factors are obtained using rates from the risk-free spot curve without any additional spread. The impact of prepayment on cash flows is discussed in a later section of this chapter, and inclusion of risk spread will be discussed in another chapter.

Before we start our discussion about valuation methods it is necessary to clarify common rate setting (rate fixing) rules for floating-rate instruments.

Pre-Period-Initiation Rate Setting

According to this rule the effective rate of an accrual period is set at the reset date that is before and closest to the beginning day of the period.

Consider a floating-rate loan that has an outstanding balance of $100,000 on January 16, 2015, and the effective rate of the loan is based on a rate index with 40 bps additional contractual spread. The reset and payment frequencies of the loan are monthly. The most recent reset date was January 13, 2015, and based on a monthly reset frequency the next three reset dates occur on February 13, March 13, and April 13. The most recent payment date was January 16, 2015, and based on a monthly payment frequency the next three payment dates are February 16, March 16, and April 16. Assume that the rate index values at January 13, February 13, March 13, and April 13 are 0.17%, 0.19%, 0.21%, and 0.18% respectively. Based on the pre-period-initiation rate setting rule the rate used to calculate the accrued interest from January 16, 2015, to February 16, 2015 (31 days), is the rate set at January 13. Therefore, the effective rate during this accrual period is 0.17% + 0.40% = 0.57% and the accrued interest is calculated as follows (using an Actual/365 accrual basis):

$$100,000 \times \frac{0.1700 + 0.4000}{100} \times \left(\frac{31}{365}\right) = 48.41$$

For the period from February 16, 2015, to March 16, 2015 (28 days), the rate is set at February 13 and the effective rate for this accrual period is 0.19% + 0.40% = 0.59%. The interest cash flow is then calculated as:

$$100,000 \times \frac{0.1900 + 0.4000}{100} \times \left(\frac{28}{365}\right) = 45.26$$

Similarly, for the period from March 16, 2015, to April 16, 2015 (31 days), the rate is set at March 13 and the effective rate is 0.21% + 0.40% = 0.61%, and the interest cash flow for this period is:

$$100,000 \times \frac{0.2100 + 0.4000}{100} \times \left(\frac{31}{365}\right) = 51.81$$

For valuation purpose, these cash flows are assumed to occur on February 16, March 16, and April 16, 2015, respectively, as shown in Figure 2.10.

Post-Period-Initiation Rate Setting

According to this rule the effective rate of an accrual period is set at the reset date that is within the accrual period and is closest to the ending day of the period.

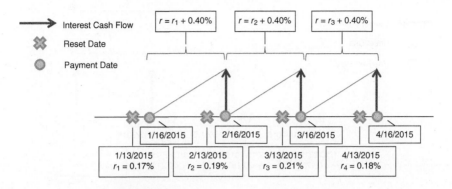

FIGURE 2.10   Pre-period-initiation rate setting

Consider the same floating-rate loan discussed previously. Based on the post-period-initiation rate setting rule, the rate used to calculate the accrued interest from January 16, 2015, to February 16, 2015 (31 days), is set at February 13, and therefore the effective rate is 0.19% + 0.40% = 0.59%. The accrued interest for this period is calculated as:

$$100,000 \times \frac{0.1900 + 0.4000}{100} \times \left(\frac{31}{365}\right) = 50.11$$

For the period from February 16, 2015, to March 16, 2015 (28 days), the rate is set at March 13 and the effective rate is 0.21% + 0.40% = 0.61%. The interest cash flow is calculated as:

$$100,000 \times \frac{0.2100 + 0.4000}{100} \times \left(\frac{28}{365}\right) = 46.79$$

And similarly, for the period from March 16, 2015, to April 16, 2015 (31 days), the rate is set at April 13 and the effective rate is 0.18% + 0.40% = 0.58%. The interest cash flow for this period is:

$$100,000 \times \frac{0.1800 + 0.4000}{100} \times \left(\frac{31}{365}\right) = 49.26$$

For valuation purpose, these cash flows are assumed to occur on February 16, March 16, and April 16, 2015, respectively, as shown in Figure 2.11.

The pre-period-initiation rate setting is more common in practice and in the remainder of our discussion about valuation of floating-rate instruments we assume this rule is applicable in derivation of interest amount. Also, for simplicity here we assume that no business day convention adjustment is applied.

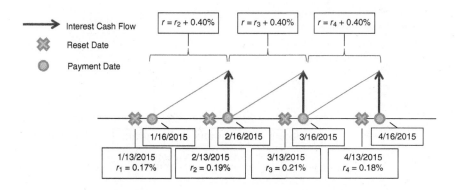

FIGURE 2.11   Post-period-initiation rate setting

Valuation Using Estimated Interest Rates at Future Reset Dates

The common method for valuation of floating-rate instruments is to use estimated interest rates in future reset dates to generate estimated cash flows. Discounted values of the estimated interest cash flows and principal payments provide the economic value of the instrument. The estimated rates can be obtained either based on implied forward rates or by using a forecasting model. It should be noted that discount factors are calculated using the spot curve as of the valuation date. If the valuation is in the past or is the present day, the spot curve at valuation date is fully available and there is no estimation required to derive the discount factors. The estimated rates are then only needed for derivation of the future interest payment cash flows.

Using Implied Forward Rate

As discussed in Chapter 1, implied forward rate is the future rate of a given term determined using the current yield curve. Implied forward rates contain all information available in the current yield curve and reflect the estimation of future interest rates as perceived by overall market as of the current time. To demonstrate the use of implied forward rates in valuation of floating-rate instruments, consider the following position in a floating-rate product:

Position P1

Type	Floating-Rate Loan
Currency	USD
Outstanding balance	125,000.00
Rate base index	3-month LIBOR

Position P1

Type	Floating-Rate Loan
Spread (bps)	200
Start date	6/15/2013
Maturity date	6/15/2017
Amortization type	Bullet at maturity date
Payment frequency	Quarterly
Compounding frequency	Quarterly
Reset frequency	Quarterly
Accrual basis	Actual/360
Most recent payment date	3/15/2015
Most recent reset date	3/15/2015

The valuation date is March 31, 2015, and the pre-period-initiation rate setting rule is used. Assume that the spot curve as of March 31, 2015, is as shown in Figure 2.5. Using this spot curve, the 3-month LIBOR implied forward rates are calculated and shown in Table 2.16 (refer to Chapter 1 for details of calculation of implied forward rates).

Assume that the 3-month LIBOR at the most recent reset date of March 15, 2015, was 0.2690%. Similar to fixed-rate instruments, interest cash flows for

TABLE 2.16 3-month LIBOR implied forward rates using assumed spot curve as of March 31, 2015

Date	Rate (%)
6/15/2015	0.3590
9/15/2015	0.4966
12/15/2015	0.6643
3/15/2016	0.8166
6/15/2016	1.0211
9/15/2016	1.1983
12/15/2016	1.3766
3/15/2017	1.4747
6/15/2017	1.6198
9/15/2017	1.7853
12/15/2017	1.9520
3/15/2018	1.8070

floating-rate instruments are calculated using Equation (2.10), but the effective rate r_j for a period can be different from the previous or the following periods. The first cash flow occurs on June 15, 2015, and is the accrued interest in the period of March 15 to June 15 (92 days). Considering the 2% contractual spread, the effective rate for this accrual period is $0.2690\% + 2.00\% = 2.2690\%$ and the interest cash flow is calculated as follows:

$$125,000 \times \frac{0.2690 + 2.00}{100} \times \frac{92}{360} = 724.82$$

Since this cash flow occurs on June 15, 2015, the appropriate discount factor from Table 2.4 is 0.999478 and the discounted value of this interest cash flow at the valuation date is:

$$724.82 \times 0.999478 = 724.44$$

The next reset date occurs on June 15, 2015, where the 3-month LIBOR implied forward rate from Table 2.16 is 0.3590%. Therefore, the effective rate for the accrual period of June 15 to September 15 (92 days) is $0.3590\% + 2.00\% = 2.3590\%$ and the interest cash flow, occurring on September 15, 2015, is calculated as:

$$125,000 \times \frac{0.3590 + 2.00}{100} \times \frac{92}{360} = 753.56$$

The discounted value of this cash flow using $DF = 0.998562$ from Table 2.4 is:

$$753.56 \times 0.998562 = 752.47$$

The following reset date is on September 15, 2015, where the 3-month LIBOR implied forward is 0.4966% and the effective rate for the next accrual period of September 15 to December 15 (91 days) is $0.4966\% + 2.00\% = 2.4966\%$. The interest cash flow occurs on December 15, 2015, and its discounted values are:

$$125,000 \times \frac{0.4966 + 2.00}{100} \times \frac{91}{360} = 788.85$$

$$788.85 \times 0.997310 = 786.73$$

The other interest cash flows and their discounted values are calculated similarly. These calculations are summarized in Table 2.17. In this table:

- The "Date" column includes the payment date (except for March 31, 2015, which is the valuation date).

- The "t (Day)" column is the number of days between each payment date and the valuation date.
- The "Day Count" column represents the number of actual days between consecutive payment days (number of accrual days).
- The "Outstanding Principal" column represents the balance of the loan at the beginning of each accrual period.
- The "Principal Cash Flow" and "Interest Cash Flow" columns contain the scheduled principal payment and estimated interest cash flow at each payment date, respectively.
- The "Interest Rate" column includes the effective rate for the accrual period that ends at the associated payment date.
- The Total Cash Flow" column is the summation of the principal and interest cash flows at each payment date.
- The "DF" column contains the discount factor for the payment date.
- The "Discounted Value" column is the multiplication of the "Total Cash Flow" and "DF" columns.

In Table 2.17 the calculation of the first cash flow of $724.82 occurring on June 15, 2015, is broken into two parts: the first part of $126.06 associated with the accrued interest from March 15 to the valuation date of March 31 (16 days) and the second part of $598.76 is for interest accrued from April 1 to June 15 (76 days). The effective rate of both parts is 0.2690% + 2.00% = 2.2690% and the sum of these two parts is equivalent to $724.82, as derived previously. Although the $126.06 amount in Table 2.17 is shown in the row dated March 31, the cash flow actually occurs on June 15 and is discounted back from that date.

The last interest cash flow occurs on the maturity date of June 15, 2017. Based on the amortization schedule of this product, the principal of the loan is repaid at this maturity date. The last row in Table 2.17 includes both the last interest cash flow of $1,109.98 and the principal cash flow of $125,000, which are discounted using $DF = 0.980901$ from Table 2.4. The economic value of the position P1 is hence derived by adding up the discounted values of interest and principal cash flows (sum of last column in Table 2.17) as $130,690.88.

Using Forecasted Rate

Historical analysis has shown that the implied forward rates based on spot curve often do not provide reliable forecasts for future rates. When alternative sources of forecasted interest rates are available, they can be used for the estimation of future interest payments (interest cash flows). Banks utilize a variety of tools to forecast the movement of interest rates in the future. In the United States, "Fed watchers" are individuals or teams in financial firms or in

TABLE 2.17 Valuation of position P1, a floating-rate instrument, using implied forward rates

Date	t (Day)	Day Count	Outstanding Principal	Principal Cash Flow	Interest Rate (%)	Interest Cash Flow	Total Cash Flow	DF	Discounted Value
3/31/2015	0	16	125,000.00		2.2690	126.06			
6/15/2015	76	76	125,000.00		2.2690	598.76	724.82	0.999478	724.44
9/15/2015	168	92	125,000.00		2.3590	753.56	753.56	0.998562	752.47
12/15/2015	259	91	125,000.00		2.4966	788.85	788.85	0.997310	786.73
3/15/2016	350	91	125,000.00		2.6643	841.86	841.86	0.995638	838.19
6/15/2016	442	92	125,000.00		2.8166	899.75	899.75	0.993564	893.96
9/15/2016	534	92	125,000.00		3.0211	965.06	965.06	0.990979	956.35
12/15/2016	625	91	125,000.00		3.1983	1,010.57	1,010.57	0.987986	998.43
3/15/2017	715	90	125,000.00		3.3766	1,055.19	1,055.19	0.984597	1,038.93
6/15/2017	807	92	125,000.00	125,000.00	3.4747	1,109.98	126,109.98	0.980901	123,701.37
									130,690.88

academia who observe and interpret Federal Reserve System statements and actions for potential changes in monetary policy that can lead to changes in interest rate. Surveys from financial experts and economists are another source to assess the overall expectation of future interest rate levels.

Use of quantitative econometric models is another method to forecast the interest rate. Some banks have internally developed interest rate forecasting models while others procure such forecasts from external firms. One of the advantages of using quantitative models for forecasting the interest rate is that it enables a bank to study the impact of certain economic condition on the interest rate and eventually on its earnings and capital position.

Similar to the implied forward rate case, here we use an example to demonstrate the use of forecasted interest rates in valuation of a floating-rate instrument. It is a common practice to forecast a future interest rate on a monthly interval and express the forecasted rates for future month-end dates. Thus, when the reset dates of a floating-rate position fall between dates with available forecasted rates, usually an interpolation method is used to obtain the forecasted rates at the required reset dates. Here we use a linear interpolation method, as shown in the following equation:

$$r = r_i + \frac{(t - t_i)}{(t_{i+1} - t_i)} \times (r_{i+1} - r_i) \qquad (2.42)$$

where:

$r =$ Interpolated rate
$t =$ Interpolation date
$t_i =$ Date of previous month-end
$r_i =$ Rate at previous month-end
$t_{i+1} =$ Date of next month-end
$r_{i+1} =$ Rate at next month-end

Consider again floating-rate loan P1 studied in the previous section. The valuation date is March 31, 2015, and the spot curve as of this date is as shown in Figure 2.5. Assume that forecasted 3-month LIBOR obtained from a quantitative model for the next 36 months from the valuation date are as shown in Table 2.18. Rates in this table are simple interest with an Actual/360 day count convention.

As before, assume that the 3-month LIBOR at the most recent reset date of March 15, 2015, was 0.2690%. The first cash flow occurs on June 15, 2015, and is related to the accrued interest of March 15 to June 15 period (92 days).

TABLE 2.18   Forecasted 3-month LIBOR

	Date	Rate (%)	Date	Rate (%)
Actual	3/31/2015	0.2708		
Forecast	4/30/2015	0.3106	10/31/2016	0.8508
	5/31/2015	0.3408	11/30/2016	0.8708
	6/30/2015	0.3773	12/31/2016	0.9206
	7/31/2015	0.4006	1/31/2017	0.9604
	8/31/2015	0.4434	2/28/2017	0.9888
	9/30/2015	0.4771	3/31/2017	1.0108
	10/31/2015	0.4985	4/30/2017	1.0560
	11/30/2015	0.5159	5/31/2017	1.0707
	12/31/2015	0.5508	6/30/2017	1.0905
	1/31/2016	0.6007	7/31/2017	1.1407
	2/29/2016	0.6206	8/31/2017	1.1508
	3/31/2016	0.6568	9/30/2017	1.1566
	4/30/2016	0.6999	10/31/2017	1.1805
	5/31/2016	0.7100	11/30/2017	1.2208
	6/30/2016	0.7411	12/31/2017	1.2714
	7/31/2016	0.7906	1/31/2018	1.2702
	8/31/2016	0.8190	2/28/2018	1.3168
	9/30/2016	0.8312	3/31/2018	1.3732

The effective rate for this accrual period is $0.2690\% + 2.00\% = 2.2690\%$ and the interest cash flow is calculated as:

$$125{,}000 \times \frac{0.2690 + 2.00}{100} \times \frac{92}{360} = 724.82$$

This cash flow occurs on June 15, 2015, and discount factor as of this date can be obtained using spot rates. This discount factor from Table 2.4 is 0.999478, so the discounted value of the interest cash flow is:

$$724.82 \times 0.999478 = 724.44$$

The next interest payment occurs on September 15, 2015. The effective rate of the accrual period from June 15 to September 15 (92 days) is set on June 15. From Table 2.18 we have the forecasted rates for May 31 of 0.3408 and for June 30 of 0.3773. To obtain the forecasted 3-month LIBOR at June 15 we can interpolate rates on May 31 and June 30 using Equation (2.42), as follows:

$$R_{6/15/2015} = \frac{(6/15/2015 - 5/31/2015)}{(6/30/2015 - 5/31/2015)} \times (0.3773 - 0.3408)$$

$$+ 0.3408 = 0.3591$$

Using this interpolated rate, at June 15 the effective rate for the accrual period from June 15 to September 15 is 0.3591% + 2.00% = 2.3591%. The interest cash flow on September 15 is calculated as follows:

$$125{,}000 \times \frac{0.3591 + 2.00}{100} \times \frac{92}{360} = 753.59$$

To discount this cash flow there are two options available. The first approach is to use discount factors obtained using the spot curve as of March 31, 2015, the valuation date. Some commercial ALM softwares use this option even though the forecasted rates in futures dates are different from the implied forward rates based on the spot curve. However, often practitioners believe using the discount factor from the spot curve, when the forecasted future rates and the implied forward rates are different, creates discrepancy in the valuation. The second option is to use the forecasted rates to calculate a periodic discount factor from each payment date to the previous one and then aggregate them to obtain the cumulative discount factor from each payment date to the valuation date. Here we use this second option. Since the interpolated 3-month LIBOR on June 15 is 0.3591% and this rate is in simple interest form, the periodic discount factor using this rate from September 15 to June 15 is:

$$DF_{Sep.15\ to\ Jun.15} = \frac{1}{\left(1 + \dfrac{0.3591}{100} \times \dfrac{92}{360}\right)} = 0.999083$$

where 92 is the number of days between June 15 and September 15, 2015. The discount factor from June 15 to March 31, 2015, the valuation date, is 0.999478 obtained from the current spot curve, so the cumulative discount factor from September 15, 2015, to March 31, 2015, is:

$$DF_{Sep.15\ to\ Mar.31} = 0.999083 \times 0.999478 = 0.998561$$

Thus, the cash flow occurring at September 15, 2015, discounted back to the valuation date, is:

$$753.59 \times 0.998561 = 752.50$$

TABLE 2.19   Periodic and cumulative discount factors obtained using forecasted rates. The discount factor as of June 15, 2015, is calculated using spot curve in Figure 2.5, and discount factors as of other dates are calculated using forecasted 3-month LIBOR from Table 2.18

Date	Periodic DF	Cumulative DF
6/15/2015	0.999478	0.999478
9/15/2015	0.999083	0.998561
12/15/2015	0.998838	0.997401
3/15/2016	0.998655	0.996060
6/15/2016	0.998372	0.994438
9/15/2016	0.998149	0.992598
12/15/2016	0.997919	0.990532
3/15/2017	0.997807	0.988359
6/15/2017	0.997452	0.985841
9/15/2017	0.997246	0.983126
12/15/2017	0.997092	0.980267
3/15/2018	0.996896	0.977225

Table 2.19 presents periodic and cumulative discount factors calculated using a similar method for other payment dates of position P1 using forecasted 3-month LIBOR from Table 2.18.

The next accrual period is from September 15 to December 15 (91 days) and the rate is set on September 15. Using forecasted rates on August 31 and September 30 from Table 2.18, the interpolated 3-month LIBOR as of September 15 is obtained as:

$$R_{9/15/2015} = \frac{(9/15/2015 - 8/31/2015)}{(9/30/2015 - 8/31/2015)} \times (0.4771 - 0.4434) + 0.4434$$

$$= 0.4603$$

The effective rate for this accrual period is $0.4603\% + 2.00\% = 2.4603\%$. The interest cash flow occurring on December 15 is:

$$125,000 \times \frac{0.4603 + 2.00}{100} \times \frac{91}{360} = 777.37$$

Using the forecasted rate as of September 15, the periodic discount factor from December 15 to September 15 is:

$$DF_{Dec.15 \ to \ Sep.15} = \frac{1}{\left(1 + \frac{0.4603}{100} \times \frac{91}{360}\right)} = 0.998838$$

By multiplying this discount factor by the discount factor from September 15 to March 31 obtained earlier, we have the cumulative discount factor from December 15 to March 31, the valuation date, as:

$$DF_{Dec.15 \ to \ Mar.31} = 0.998838 \times 0.998561 = 0.997401$$

We can use this discount factor to discount the cash flow on December 2015 back to the valuation date:

$$777.37 \times 0.997401 = 775.35$$

The other interest cash flows and their discounted values are calculated similarly. The principal payment is $125,000, occurring at the maturity date of June 15, 2017, and is discounted back to the valuation date using cumulate discount factor obtained from periodic forecasted rates. These calculations are summarized in Table 2.20. Similar to the previous example, in this table the calculation of the first interest payment is divided into two parts: the first part is the accrued interest from March 15 to the valuation date and the second part is the accrued interest from the valuation date to the first payment date. The sum of these two amounts constitutes the cash flow of $724.82 occurring at the first payment date of June 15, 2015. The economic value of position P1 is calculated by summing up the discounted values of interest and principal cash flows (the sum of the last column in Table 2.20) for a total of $130,699.91.

The difference between the value of position P1 when implied forward rates are used (Table 2.17) versus when forecasted rates are used (Table 2.20) highlights the fact that the estimation method of the future interest rate makes a difference in calculated present value of a floating-rate instrument. When we use the implied forward rates, we rely on current spot curve to estimate future interest rates. If there is a lack of an alternative forecasting mechanism, this may be an acceptable choice. However, interest rate estimates based on robust forecasting models that incorporate both historical movement of interest rate and future econometric indicators are generally preferred in estimating future interest rates.

Valuation Using Assumption of Par Value at Next Reset Date

This approach is based on the idea that value of a floating-rate instrument is not subject to interest rate risk as long as the effective rate is not fixed. Therefore, the discounted value of future cash flows (interest payments and principal repayments) from the next reset date (i.e., beyond the point that effective rate is set) to the maturity date is equivalent to a single cash flow with the amount equal to outstanding principal occurring at the next reset date.

TABLE 2.20 Valuation of product P1, a floating-rate instrument, using interpolated forecasted rates

Date	t (Day)	Day Count	Outstanding Principal	Principal Cash Flow	Interest Rate (%)	Interest Cash Flow	Total Cash Flow	DF	Discounted Value
3/31/2015	0	16	125,000.00		2.2690	126.06			
6/15/2015	76	76	125,000.00		2.2690	598.76	724.82	0.999478	724.44
9/15/2015	168	92	125,000.00		2.3591	753.59	753.59	0.998561	752.50
12/15/2015	259	91	125,000.00		2.4603	777.37	777.37	0.997401	775.35
3/15/2016	350	91	125,000.00		2.5328	800.29	800.29	0.996060	797.14
6/15/2016	442	92	125,000.00		2.6381	842.73	842.73	0.994438	838.04
9/15/2016	534	92	125,000.00		2.7256	870.66	870.66	0.992598	864.22
12/15/2016	625	91	125,000.00		2.8251	892.65	892.65	0.990532	884.20
3/15/2017	715	90	125,000.00		2.8793	899.77	899.77	0.988359	889.29
6/15/2017	807	92	125,000.00	125,000.00	2.9994	958.16	125,958.16	0.985841	124,174.73
									130,699.91

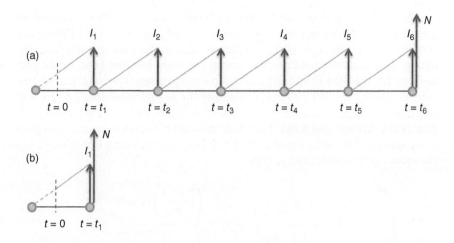

FIGURE 2.12 Cash flows after the next reset date of a floating-rate instrument are replaced by a single cash flow equal to the principal amount at the next reset date.

This means the instrument has par value at the next reset date. Consider a floating-rate instrument shown in Figure 2.12 with principal payment of N at the maturity date of t_6 and six expected interest payments of $I_1, I_2, I_3, I_4, I_5,$ and I_6 occurring at $t_1, t_2, t_3, t_4, t_5,$ and t_6. The valuation date at $t = 0$ is between the most recent reset date and the next reset date of t_1. Since the rate for the first interest cash flow I_1 is set prior to $t = 0$ the cash flow amount is exact and known while other interest cash flows are estimated (since their effective rates are not set yet). Value of this instrument at time $t = 0$ is the present value of the interest and principal cash flows (Figure 2.12 a):

$$V_{t=0} = PV_{t=0}(I_1, I_2, I_3, I_4, I_5, I_6, N_{(at\ t_6)}) \tag{2.43}$$

where $PV_{t=0}$ denotes present value calculation at time $t = 0$. In a valuation method based on the assumption of par value at the next reset date, the discounted value of interest cash flows $I_2, I_3, I_4, I_5,$ and I_6 occurring at $t_2, t_3, t_4, t_5,$ and t_6, and principal payment N occurring at t_6 is equivalent to a single cash flow equal to principal payment N occurring at the next reset date of t_1:

$$N_{(at\ t_1)} = \text{Discounted value at } t_1 \text{ of } I_2, I_3, I_4, I_5, I_6, N_{(at\ t_6)}$$

Hence the value of the floating-rate instrument at the valuation date is simply the present value of (i) interest payments occurring up to, and including, the next reset date, and (ii) the principal amount occurring at the next reset date (Figure 2.12 b):

$$V_{t=0} = PV_{t=0}(I_1, N_{(at\ t_1)}) \tag{2.44}$$

As discussed earlier, rate setting of a floating-rate instrument is based on a benchmark rate index plus a contractual spread (e.g., 3-month LIBOR plus 200 bps). To see the logic of this valuation method, first assume that the valuation date is t_5. At this date an interest payment has just been made and the rate for the next (and last) interest payment is set. This rate will be the then-prevailing market rate at t_5 (assuming the pre-period-initiation rate setting rule is applied). Hence the cash flow I_6 is set and fixed. The principal cash flow is also known and fixed. Therefore the valuation of this instrument at t_5 is the same as the valuation of a fixed-rate instrument. Using Equation (2.11) the value of the instrument at t_5 is:

$$V_{t_5} = \frac{I_6 + N}{\left(1 + \dfrac{y_5}{m}\right)^{m(t_6 - t_5)}} = \frac{\left(\dfrac{r_{t_5} + s}{m}\right)N + N}{\left(1 + \dfrac{y_5}{m}\right)^{m(t_6 - t_5)}}$$

where

m = Number of compounding periods per year
V_{t_5} = Value of instrument at time t_5
N = Principal amount
I_6 = Interest payment amount at time t_6
y_5 = Yield associated with valuation V_{t_5} obtained at t_5 (annual)
t_5 and t_6 = Payment times (year)
r_{t_5} = Benchmark rate index at time t_5
s = Spread over benchmark rate index

First note that, for a floating-rate instrument when the rate is reset to a market rate, the yield of the instrument at that time is also equal to that market rate. Thus, the prevailing market rate would be the most appropriate rate for discounting cash flows to obtain the market value at that time. If a spread is included in rate setting, that spread should be considered in the yield and discounting; therefore, $y_5 = r_{t_5} + s$. Second, note that the value of $m(t_6 - t_5)$ is equal to 1, representing one period. To see this, remember t_5 and t_6 are times of cash flow, in year units. For example, assume the instrument has semi-annual compounding and payment frequency (i.e., $m = 2$), and interest payments happen 0.5 year apart. So time between t_6 and t_5 is 0.5 year and hence $m(t_6 - t_5) = 2 \times 0.5 = 1$. Or assume that the instrument has quarterly compounding and payment frequency (i.e., $m = 4$), and interest payments happen 0.25 year apart. So time between t_6 and t_5 is 0.25 year and hence

$m(t_6 - t_5) = 4 \times 0.25 = 1$. For any periodicity $m(t_6 - t_5) = 1$. Based on these, we have:

$$V_{t_5} = \frac{\left(\dfrac{r_{t_5} + s}{m}\right)N + N}{\left(1 + \dfrac{r_{t_5} + s}{m}\right)^1} = \frac{N\left(1 + \dfrac{r_{t_5} + s}{m}\right)}{\left(1 + \dfrac{r_{t_5} + s}{m}\right)} = N$$

We just showed that the value of the instrument at time t_5, immediately after an interest payment, is equal to the principal amount at t_5. Therefore, value of the instrument at time $t = 0$ changed from what is shown in Equation (2.43) to the following:

$$V_{t=0} = PV_{t=0}(I_1, I_2, I_3, I_4, I_5, N_{(at\ t_5)})$$

Now assume that the valuation date is t_4. Using $V_{t_5} = N$ obtained above and following the same rationale, we have:

$$V_{t_4} = \frac{I_5 + N}{\left(1 + \dfrac{y_4}{m}\right)^{m(t_5 - t_4)}} = \frac{\left(\dfrac{r_{t_4} + s}{m}\right)N + N}{\left(1 + \dfrac{r_{t_4} + s}{m}\right)^1} = \frac{N\left(1 + \dfrac{r_{t_4} + s}{m}\right)}{\left(1 + \dfrac{r_{t_4} + s}{m}\right)} = N$$

And the value of the instrument at time $t = 0$ is:

$$V_{t=0} = PV_{t=0}(I_1, I_2, I_3, I_4, N_{(at\ t_4)})$$

Continuing this process will result in the conclusion that:

$$V_{t=0} = PV_{t=0}(I_1, N_{(at\ t_1)})$$

which is the same as Equation (2.44). To summarize, we just showed:

- The value of the floating-rate instrument immediately after an interest payment is always equal to the par value.
- The value of the floating-rate instrument at the valuation date is the present value of the interest payments occurring up to, and including, the next reset date and principal payment occurring at the next reset date.

Since in this valuation method it is not necessary to generate all future cash flows, the method is less computationally intense, and requires less database capacity. This is important since the number of positions on the balance sheet of larger banks, even after aggregation, is enormous and any reduction in computational time and database capacity requirement is important. At the same time, the main disadvantage of this valuation method is also related to the absence of a full cash flow schedule. Many banks use cash flow schedules generated by ALM models, especially the estimated cash flows that are generated based on either implied forward rates or forecasted rates, in their liquidity risk management models. Lack of full cash flow schedule in this method makes the output of ALM process incomplete and inappropriate for liquidity risk management purposes. It should be emphasized that this method is valid only when rates used for determination of interest payment cash flows and rates used for discount factors calculation are from the same interest rate curve; otherwise the floating-rate instrument is not at its par value at a reset date.

Duration and Convexity

Based on the previous discussion it is easy to see that the Macaulay duration of a floating-rate instrument is the time from the valuation date to the next reset date. With the assumption of the par value at the next reset date, the value of a floating-rate instrument can be written as:[4]

$$V = \frac{C_1 + N}{\left(1 + \dfrac{y}{m}\right)^{mt_1}}$$

(2.45)

where

$V =$ Value of instrument
$N =$ Principal amount
$t_1 =$ Time between valuation date and first reset date (year), determined using accrual basis
$C_1 =$ Interest cash flow occurring at time t_1 (set and known as of valuation date)
$m =$ Numbers of compounding period per year
$y =$ Yield (annual)

From the definition of the Macaulay duration in Equation (2.12) and the valuation of the floating-rate instrument in Equation (2.45), we have:

$$D_{Mac} = \sum_t t \frac{\dfrac{C_t}{\left(1 + \dfrac{y}{m}\right)^{mt}}}{V} = t_1 \frac{\dfrac{C_1 + N}{\left(1 + \dfrac{y}{m}\right)^{mt_1}}}{\dfrac{C_1 + N}{\left(1 + \dfrac{y}{m}\right)^{mt_1}}} = t_1$$

Therefore the Macaulay duration of a floating-rate instrument is the time from the valuation date to the next reset date (in year). To obtain the modified duration and convexity, we take the first and second derivative of value in Equation (2.45) with respect to yield, as follows:

$$\frac{d}{dy}\left(\frac{C_1 + N}{\left(1 + \dfrac{y}{m}\right)^{mt_1}}\right) = -\frac{t_1}{1 + \dfrac{y}{m}} \frac{C_1 + N}{\left(1 + \dfrac{y}{m}\right)^{mt_1}}$$

$$\frac{d^2}{dy^2}\left(\frac{C_1 + N}{\left(1 + \dfrac{y}{m}\right)^{mt_1}}\right) = \frac{t_1\left(t_1 + \dfrac{1}{m}\right)}{\left(1 + \dfrac{y}{m}\right)^2} \frac{C_1 + N}{\left(1 + \dfrac{y}{m}\right)^{mt_1}}$$

Assuming small Δy and using the definitions of the modified duration and convexity, we have:

$$D_{Mod} = -\frac{1}{V}\frac{\Delta V}{\Delta y} = -\frac{1}{\dfrac{C_1 + N}{\left(1 + \dfrac{y}{m}\right)^{mt_1}}} \times \left[-\frac{t_1}{1 + \dfrac{y}{m}} \frac{C_1 + N}{\left(1 + \dfrac{y}{m}\right)^{mt_1}}\right]$$

or

$$D_{Mod} = \frac{t_1}{1 + \dfrac{y}{m}} \qquad\qquad (2.46)$$

and

$$Conv = \frac{1}{V}\frac{\Delta^2 V}{\Delta y^2} = \frac{1}{\frac{C_1 + N}{\left(1 + \frac{y}{m}\right)^{mt_1}}} \times \left[\frac{t_1\left(t_1 + \frac{1}{m}\right)}{\left(1 + \frac{y}{m}\right)^2} \frac{C_1 + N}{\left(1 + \frac{y}{m}\right)^{mt_1}} \right]$$

or

$$Conv = \frac{t_1\left(t_1 + \frac{1}{m}\right)}{\left(1 + \frac{y}{m}\right)^2} \tag{2.47}$$

Valuation Using Simulated Interest Rate Paths

In the *Monte Carlo simulation* method, simulated interest rates in the future are used for valuation of floating-rate instruments. Simulated rates can be used both for determining the interest rates for future cash flows and also for calculation of discount factors. In another chapter we discuss several interest rate models that can be used for generating simulated interest rate paths. To demonstrate valuation of a floating-rate instrument using Monte Carlo simulation, consider position P2, a floating-rate instrument, with the following characteristics. For simplicity here we assume P2 has a 30/360 accrual basis and simulated 3-month rates are already converted to this accrual basis.

Position P2

Type	Floating-Rate Loan
Currency	USD
Outstanding balance	50,000.00
Rate base index	3-month LIBOR
Spread (bps)	25
Start date	12/31/2016
Maturity date	12/31/2018
Amortization type	Bullet at maturity date
Payment frequency	Quarterly
Compounding frequency	Quarterly
Reset frequency	Quarterly
Accrual basis	30/360
Most recent payment date	n/a
Most recent reset date	12/31/2016

TABLE 2.21 Ten simulated interest rate paths (%)

	2016	2017				2018			
As-of Date:	15-Dec	15-Mar	15-Jun	15-Sep	15-Dec	15-Mar	15-Jun	15-Sep	15-Dec
$t\rightarrow$	0	0.25	0.5	0.75	1	1.25	1.5	1.75	2
$i\rightarrow$	0	1	2	3	4	5	6	7	8
Iteration↓	t_0	t_1	t_2	t_3	t_4	t_5	t_6	t_7	t_8
1	0.2900	0.3697	0.4181	0.2942	0.7260	0.7455	1.0027	1.2956	1.3818
2	0.2900	0.2586	0.3281	0.2332	0.3571	1.1262	1.0393	1.0224	1.5674
3	0.2900	0.3030	0.4407	0.3874	0.4478	1.1550	1.0265	1.9694	1.4274
4	0.2900	0.4474	0.4017	0.2855	0.5287	0.9734	1.0753	1.5325	1.6358
5	0.2900	0.3212	0.4775	0.3994	0.5084	1.0171	1.0886	1.4925	1.6467
6	0.2900	0.3717	0.2946	0.3249	0.5618	0.7421	1.0669	1.0970	1.6252
7	0.2900	0.4218	0.4502	0.1835	0.4676	0.8415	1.0007	1.6137	1.6849
8	0.2900	0.4348	0.3294	0.3506	0.5695	0.7597	1.0446	1.6628	1.1218
9	0.2900	0.3271	0.3735	0.3833	0.7636	0.3974	1.2560	1.3054	1.5930
10	0.2900	0.3494	0.2656	0.3451	0.4417	0.7688	1.1545	1.2293	1.1383

Assume that the valuation date is December 31, 2016. Consider 10 simulated interest rate paths, as shown in Table 2.21. Each path provides nine 3-month LIBOR as seen at time t_i, with quarterly compounding and a 30/360 basis. The first rate of 0.2900% is the 3-month rate as of the valuation date, and hence it is the same in all 10 simulation paths. Subsequently eight rates are simulated. Consider the rate of 0.3697% in path (iteration) 1 at time t_1. This is the annualized simulated 3-month rate as seen at time t_1 (i.e., as of March 31, 2017) for a term from t_1 to t_2. Or consider rate 1.0224% in iteration 2 at time t_7. This is the annualized simulated 3-month rate as seen at time t_7 (i.e., as of September 31, 2017) for a term from t_7 to t_8. These simulated rates are produced using an arbitrage-free interest rate model.[5] Figure 2.13 shows the first two paths (first two iterations) of simulated 3-month rates from Table 2.21. We use these simulated rates to value the position P2.

For position P2 reset dates are aligned to t_0, t_1, t_2, t_3, t_4, t_5, t_6, and t_7, and payment dates are at t_1, t_2, t_3, t_4, t_5, t_6, t_7, and t_8. Consider path 1. The rate for determination of the first interest amount is set at t_0. The 3-month rate at t_0 is 0.2900% and, including the 25 bps contractual spread, the total effective rate is: 0.2900% + 0.2500% = 0.5400%. The interest amount that is payable at t_1 is then calculated as:

$$\frac{0.5400}{100} \times 50,000 \times \frac{1}{4} = 67.50$$

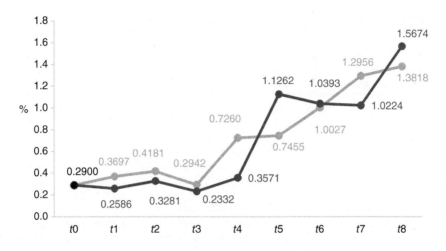

FIGURE 2.13   Paths 1 and 2 of simulated 3-month rates from Table 2.21

For the second interest cash flow, the rate is set at t_1. From Table 2.21, the 3-month rate of path 1 at t_1 is 0.3697% and, considering the spread, the total effective rate is 0.3697% + 0.2500% = 0.6197%. Therefore, the interest amount payable at t_2 is:

$$\frac{0.6197}{100} \times 50{,}000 \times \frac{1}{4} = 77.46$$

This calculation is repeated for the rest of the periods in path 1. The last interest cash flow occurs at t_8, the maturity date of the contract, where the rate of this last interest cash flow is set at t_7. Total effective rate for this cash flow is: 1.2956% + 0.2500% = 1.5456%, and the interest amount payable at t_8 is:

$$\frac{1.5456}{100} \times 50{,}000 \times \frac{1}{4} = 193.20$$

Based on bullet amortization, the principal payment of $50,000 occurs at t_8; therefore, the total cash flow at t_8 is 193.20 + 50,000 = 50,193.20. The effective rates and cash flows for other paths can be calculated similarly. They are presented in Table 2.22 and Table 2.23 for all 10 paths.

To discount the calculated cash flows we follow a two-step approach to obtain discount factors. We introduced this method in an earlier example of this chapter. In the first step we calculate one-period discount factors using rates from Table 2.21. In this table, the term of a rate as seen at time t_i is from t_i to t_{i+1}, with quarterly compounding. Therefore, the discount factor from t_i to t_{i-1} is calculated as:

$$DF_{t_i} = \frac{1}{\left(1 + \dfrac{r_{t_{i-1}}}{4}\right)^{4 \times 0.25}}$$

TABLE 2.22 Total effective rates (%) of position P2 based on 10 simulated interest rate paths from Table 2.21. Position P2 reset dates are t_0, t_1, t_2, t_3, t_4, t_5, t_6 and t_7.

Iteration	t_0	t_1	t_2	t_3	t_4	t_5	t_6	t_7	t_8
1	0.5400	0.6197	0.6681	0.5442	0.9760	0.9955	1.2527	1.5456	
2	0.5400	0.5086	0.5781	0.4832	0.6071	1.3762	1.2893	1.2724	
3	0.5400	0.5530	0.6907	0.6374	0.6978	1.4050	1.2765	2.2194	
4	0.5400	0.6974	0.6517	0.5355	0.7787	1.2234	1.3253	1.7825	
5	0.5400	0.5712	0.7275	0.6494	0.7584	1.2671	1.3386	1.7425	
6	0.5400	0.6217	0.5446	0.5749	0.8118	0.9921	1.3169	1.3470	
7	0.5400	0.6718	0.7002	0.4335	0.7176	1.0915	1.2507	1.8637	
8	0.5400	0.6848	0.5794	0.6006	0.8195	1.0097	1.2946	1.9128	
9	0.5400	0.5771	0.6235	0.6333	1.0136	0.6474	1.5060	1.5554	
10	0.5400	0.5994	0.5156	0.5951	0.6917	1.0188	1.4045	1.4793	

TABLE 2.23 Total cash flow (interest and principal) ($) of position P2 based on 10 simulated interest rate paths from Table 2.21. Position P2 payment dates are t_1, t_2, t_3, t_4, t_5, t_6, t_7 and t_8.

Iteration	t_0	t_1	t_2	t_3	t_4	t_5	t_6	t_7	t_8
1	0	67.50	77.46	83.51	68.02	122.00	124.44	156.59	50,193.20
2	0	67.50	63.57	72.26	60.41	75.89	172.02	161.16	50,159.05
3	0	67.50	69.12	86.34	79.67	87.23	175.62	159.56	50,277.43
4	0	67.50	87.17	81.46	66.94	97.34	152.92	165.67	50,222.81
5	0	67.50	71.40	90.94	81.18	94.80	158.39	167.33	50,217.81
6	0	67.50	77.72	68.07	71.86	101.47	124.01	164.62	50,168.38
7	0	67.50	83.98	87.52	54.19	89.70	136.44	156.34	50,232.96
8	0	67.50	85.59	72.42	75.08	102.44	126.21	161.82	50,239.10
9	0	67.50	72.14	77.94	79.16	126.71	80.93	188.26	50,194.43
10	0	67.50	74.93	64.45	74.38	86.46	127.35	175.57	50,184.92

where 0.25 year is the length of each period based on a 30/360 convention, and 4 is due to the quarterly compounding. Note that to discount a cash flow occurring at time t_i we use the rate set at time t_{i-1}. Consider the first path. The discount factor at t_1 is calculated as:

$$DF_{t_1} = \frac{1}{\left(1 + \frac{r_{t_0}}{4}\right)^{4 \times 0.25}} = \frac{1}{\left(1 + \frac{0.2900/100}{4}\right)^{4 \times 0.25}} = 0.999276$$

This is a one-period discount factor from time t_1 to t_0. The one-period discount factor from t_2 to t_1 is calculated as:

$$DF_{t_2} = \frac{1}{\left(1 + \frac{r_{t_1}}{4}\right)^{4\times0.25}} = \frac{1}{\left(1 + \frac{0.3697/100}{4}\right)^{4\times0.25}} = 0.999077$$

One-period discount factors for other periods of path 1 and for other paths are calculated similarly and are shown in Table 2.24.

In the next step we aggregate one-period discount factors to obtain the cumulative discount factor for each period. For a cash flow that occurs at t_8, using the one-period discount factor at t_8 from Table 2.24 provides us with the discounted value at t_7. The result then must be multiplied by the one-period discount factor at t_7 to obtain discounted value at t_6. We continue this until the discounted value at t_0 is obtained. Therefore, the *cumulative discount factor* at t_8 is:

$$CDF_{t_8} = DF_{t_1} \times DF_{t_2} \times DF_{t_3} \times DF_{t_4} \times DF_{t_5} \times DF_{t_6} \times DF_{t_7} \times DF_{t_8}$$

Generally, the cumulative discount factor for time t_i is obtained as:

$$CDF_{t_i} = \prod_{j=1}^{i} DF_{t_j} \tag{2.48}$$

For example, for path 1 and using one-period discount factors from Table 2.24, the cumulative discount factor for time t_5 is calculated as:

$$CDF_{t_5} = DF_{t_1} \times DF_{t_2} \times DF_{t_3} \times DF_{t_4} \times DF_{t_5}$$
$$= 0.999276 \times 0.999077 \times 0.998956 \times 0.999265 \times 0.998188 = 0.994772$$

Table 2.25 provides the calculated cumulative discount factors for time t_1 to t_8 for all 10 paths in our example.

The last step of valuation of position P2 is to multiply simulated cash flows from Table 2.23 by the cumulative discount factors from Table 2.25 to obtain the discounted value of each cash flow at t_0. For each path, the sum of these discounted cash flows is the simulated value of position P2 at t_0. These values are presented in Table 2.26. Finally, since the simulated interest rate paths in Table 2.21 have equal probabilities, the estimated value of position P2 at t_0 is the average of the simulated values in Table 2.26, obtained as \$50,248.68:

$$V_{t_0} = \frac{\sum_{k=1}^{n} V_{t_0 k}}{n} \tag{2.49}$$

TABLE 2.24 One-period discount factors based on interest rate paths from Table 2.21

Iteration	t_0	t_1	t_2	t_3	t_4	t_5	t_6	t_7	t_8
1	1	0.999276	0.999077	0.998956	0.999265	0.998188	0.998140	0.997499	0.996771
2	1	0.999276	0.999354	0.999180	0.999417	0.999108	0.997192	0.997409	0.997451
3	1	0.999276	0.999243	0.998899	0.999033	0.998882	0.997121	0.997440	0.995101
4	1	0.999276	0.998883	0.998997	0.999287	0.998680	0.997573	0.997319	0.996183
5	1	0.999276	0.999198	0.998808	0.999002	0.998731	0.997464	0.997286	0.996283
6	1	0.999276	0.999072	0.999264	0.999188	0.998597	0.998148	0.997340	0.997265
7	1	0.999276	0.998947	0.998876	0.999541	0.998832	0.997901	0.997504	0.995982
8	1	0.999276	0.998914	0.999177	0.999124	0.998578	0.998104	0.997395	0.995860
9	1	0.999276	0.999183	0.999067	0.999043	0.998095	0.999007	0.996870	0.996747
10	1	0.999276	0.999127	0.999336	0.999138	0.998897	0.998082	0.997122	0.996936

TABLE 2.25 Cumulative discount factors based on interest rate paths from Table 2.21

Iteration	t_0	t_1	t_2	t_3	t_4	t_5	t_6	t_7	t_8
1	1	0.999276	0.998353	0.997310	0.996578	0.994772	0.992921	0.990439	0.987241
2	1	0.999276	0.998630	0.997812	0.997230	0.996341	0.993543	0.990969	0.988442
3	1	0.999276	0.998519	0.997420	0.996455	0.995341	0.992475	0.989935	0.985085
4	1	0.999276	0.998159	0.997158	0.996447	0.995131	0.992716	0.990054	0.986275
5	1	0.999276	0.998474	0.997283	0.996288	0.995024	0.992500	0.989806	0.986127
6	1	0.999276	0.998348	0.997613	0.996803	0.995405	0.993562	0.990919	0.988209
7	1	0.999276	0.998223	0.997101	0.996643	0.995480	0.993390	0.990911	0.986929
8	1	0.999276	0.998191	0.997369	0.996496	0.995079	0.993193	0.990606	0.986505
9	1	0.999276	0.998459	0.997527	0.996573	0.994674	0.993686	0.990576	0.987354
10	1	0.999276	0.998403	0.997741	0.996881	0.995781	0.993871	0.991011	0.987974

TABLE 2.26 The sum of discounted cash flows based on interest rate paths from Table 2.21

Iteration	$V_{t_{0,k}}$
1	50,248.65
2	50,248.82
3	50,248.58
4	50,248.60
5	50,248.59
6	50,248.75
7	50,248.69
8	50,248.65
9	50,248.69
10	50,248.78
Average:	**50,248.68**

where n is the number of simulation paths. In practice a much larger number of simulated interest rate paths should be used to have converging results, leading to a more reliable valuation.

NON-MATURING INSTRUMENT

A *non-maturing* product is a financial instrument with no contractual maturity date. Deposits products, such as checking or savings accounts, credit cards and home equity lines of credit are all non-maturing instruments. The discounted cash flow method can be used to value non-maturing products, once future cash flows are estimated. However, since for such products outstanding balances in future dates are unknown, both interest and principal cash flow types are required to be estimated. For a maturing product, such as a certificate of deposit (CD) or a U.S. Treasury bond, a contractual amortization schedule defines the principal payment amounts and their timings, and therefore at each future period outstanding balance required for interest cash flow calculation is known in advance. However, for a non-maturing product the flexibility given to the counterparty with respect to timing and amount of principal payments or additional drawdowns makes the future outstanding balances unknown. Hence, neither principal nor interest cash flows are exactly known at the valuation date. One approach to overcome this obstacle is to assume that the portfolio or sub-portfolio of a non-maturing product follows an aggregated amortization schedule, usually referred to as *runoff profile* or *runoff curve*. A runoff profile is a schedule that shows how the balance of a portfolio or a segment of a portfolio of a non-maturing product is changed based on an assumed *treatment*.

In valuation of a non-maturing instrument, a runoff profile plays the same role as an amortization schedule for a maturing instrument. Runoff profiles are usually expressed in a percentage form, starting from 100% and gradually decreasing to 0% level. Following are the most common treatments used for development of runoff profiles needed for valuation of non-maturing instruments.

No New Business Treatment

This treatment is based on the assumption that the bank does not acquire any new account or any new customer for the non-maturing instrument. It is also assumed that existing accounts enter into a runoff mode. For credit card products, runoff mode means customers do not use their cards for new purchases and hence do not add new balances at the end of a payment cycle to their existing balances. Customers gradually pay off existing balances and at some point in the future their balances reach zero. For deposit products, runoff mode means customers do not have future credit transactions (deposits) into their accounts and gradually, through debit transactions (withdrawals), deplete their current balances, and at some point in the future their balances reach zero.

Banks use various modeling techniques to construct runoff profiles for different non-maturing instruments and different treatments. Figure 2.14 shows a sample runoff profile constructed for a non-maturing deposit product, based on "no new business" treatment. Here the runoff profile is built using an exponential decay functional form that is often used for this purpose. Exponential decay function has the following form:

$$B_t = B_0 e^{-\lambda t} \tag{2.50}$$

where B_0 is the starting balance at the start of runoff, B_t is the balance at time t, λ is the decay factor, and t is time. The decay factor should be calibrated for each non-maturing instrument portfolio, or for a segment of the portfolio. One method of calibrating λ is as follows:

- Segment the portfolio by grouping accounts into different cohorts based on their vintages. For example, if the vintage is based on account open dates in each month, all accounts that are opened in January 2013 can be treated as one segment.

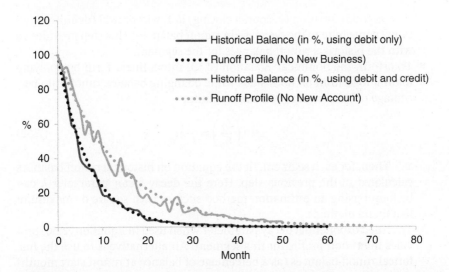

FIGURE 2.14 Sample runoff profiles for a non-maturing deposit product constructed based on two different treatments

- For each segment select a buildup period to allow accounts to reach to a steady status with respect to their balances. For a given segment, this period starts at the month of accounts opening dates (which are the same for all accounts in a segment) and ends at the month when the bank believes the accounts in the segment, collectively, have reached a steady state with respect to balance. The month at the end of this period is the *runoff start month* and subsequent months are *runoff periods*. For example, if a segment is defined for all accounts opened in January 2013 and the bank analysis shows those accounts reach to a steady state after 1 year, the runoff start month for this segment is January 2014 and the runoff period starts from February 2014.
- The aggregated balance of all accounts in the segment at the runoff start month (B_0 in Equation (2.50)) is the starting point of the calculation of the runoff profile. Since here the runoff profile is constructed for "no new business" treatment, using only debit transaction amounts for months in the runoff period, the aggregated runoff balances (B_t in Equation (2.50)) are calculated recursively as:

$$B_t = B_{t-1} - Debit_t \qquad (2.51)$$

In Equation (2.51), $Debit_t$ is entered as a positive number. This recursive calculation is continued until the runoff balance reaches zero or all available historical data are exhausted. In "no new business" treatment both account attrition (accounts closing) and withdrawal (debit transactions) contribute to the decrease in runoff balances. This step provides us with the historical runoff balances for the segment.

■ Transform the nonlinear Equation (2.50) into a linear form by applying natural logarithm on both sides while changing balance runoff into percentage of balance at runoff start month:

$$\ln\left(\frac{B_t}{B_0}\right) = -\lambda t \tag{2.52}$$

Then, for each segment, fit the equation on historical runoff balances calculated in the previous step. Here the decay factor parameter λ can be found using an estimation method such as least square or maximum likelihood methods.

■ The fitted exponential decay parameter when used in Equation (2.50) provides the runoff profile for this segment. An alternative is to use the historical runoff balances (as a percentage of balance at runoff start month) obtained in an earlier step as the runoff profile, and if historical observed runoffs were not enough to completely deplete the starting balance, we can use the fitted exponential decay function to extend the runoff profile to zero.[6]

■ In "no new business" treatment, derivation of runoff profile using either approach mentioned above leads to a runoff profile that is a downward curve for the entire runoff period. This is due to effect of account attrition and consideration of only debit amounts.

■ Other than vintage, a portfolio can be segmented based on other characteristics, such as balance tier, location, or even a combination of these attributes.

Example

To illustrate the use of a runoff profile in valuation of a non-maturing instrument, consider a savings deposit product. A segment of this portfolio has an outstanding balance of $100,000 as of March 31, 2015, and an annual rate of 1.5%. The bank forecasts that the rate of this product remains the same for the next two years. Based on "no new business" treatment and using historical data, the bank has constructed a runoff profile for this segment as presented in first three columns of Table 2.27. This particular segment has a runoff length of 16 months until balance reaches zero. In applying the runoff profile there are three alternatives

TABLE 2.27 Example of valuation of a non-maturing position using runoff profile

Date	t	Runoff Profile	Outstanding Bal. (Period Begin)	Outstanding Bal. (Period End)	Principal Cash Flow	Average Bal.	Days in Month	Interest Cash Flow	Total Cash Flow	DF	PV
3/31/2015	0	100.00		100,000							
4/30/2015	1	63.76282	100,000.00	63,762.82	36,237.18	81881.41	30	100.95	36,338.13	0.999853	36,332.80
5/31/2015	2	40.65697	63,762.82	40,656.97	23,105.85	52209.89	31	66.51	23,172.36	0.99962	23,163.56
6/30/2015	3	25.92403	40,656.97	25,924.03	14,732.94	33290.50	30	41.04	14,773.98	0.999316	14,763.88
7/31/2015	4	16.52989	2,5924.03	16,529.89	9,394.14	21226.96	31	27.04	9,421.18	0.999032	9,412.06
8/31/2015	5	10.53992	16,529.89	10,539.92	5,989.97	13534.91	31	17.24	6,007.21	0.998721	5,999.53
9/30/2015	6	6.72055	10,539.92	6,720.55	3,819.37	8630.24	30	10.64	3,830.01	0.998396	3,823.87
10/31/2015	7	4.28521	6,720.55	4,285.21	2,435.34	5502.88	31	7.01	2,442.35	0.997983	2,437.42
11/30/2015	8	2.73237	4,285.21	2,732.37	1,552.84	3508.79	30	4.33	1,557.17	0.997544	1,553.34
12/31/2015	9	1.74224	2,732.37	1,742.24	990.13	2237.30	31	2.85	992.99	0.99705	990.06
1/31/2016	10	1.11090	1,742.24	1,110.90	631.34	1426.57	31	1.82	633.16	0.996498	630.94
2/29/2016	11	0.70834	1,110.90	708.34	402.56	909.62	29	1.08	403.64	0.995941	402.00
3/31/2016	12	0.45166	708.34	451.66	256.68	580.00	31	0.74	257.42	0.995375	256.23
4/30/2016	13	0.28799	451.66	287.99	163.67	369.82	30	0.46	164.12	0.994698	163.25
5/31/2016	14	0.18363	287.99	183.63	104.36	235.81	31	0.30	104.66	0.993936	104.03
6/30/2016	15	0.11709	183.63	117.09	66.54	150.36	30	0.19	66.73	0.993167	66.27
7/31/2016	16	0.00000	117.09	0.00	117.09	58.54	31	0.07	117.16	0.992309	116.26
					100,000						**100,215.50**

(*continued*)

assumptions available. We can assume outstanding balance at each period is reduced by the relevant runoff percentage (i) at the beginning of the period, or (ii) at the end of the period, or (iii) reduction is distributed equally throughout the period. Here we assume reduction of the balance occurs at the end of the period. For $t = 1$ (i.e., end of April 30, 2015) the runoff balance is at 63.76282% of the starting balance. Hence the end-of-period balance is $100,000 \times 63.76282 = \$63,762.82$. So at the end of the first period (first month), a principal cash flow of $100,000 − \$63,762.82 = \$36,237.18$ occurs.

The principal balance that is used for calculation of interest amount is based on the product offering. Here we assume for this savings product the interest for a month is calculated based on average balance during the period. For period 1, this average balance is ($100,000 + \$63,762.82)/2 = \$81,881.41$. Hence, the interest for period 1 is calculated as:

$$81,881.41 \times \frac{1.5}{100} \times \frac{30}{365} = 100.95$$

30 is the number of days in the first period. The total cash flow occurring at the end of period on April 30, 2015, is $36,237.18 + \$100.95 = \$36,338.13$. Using the discount factor of 0.999853 obtained from Table 2.4 and using linear interpolation of rates, the discounted value of this cash flow is $36,338.13 \times 0.999853 = \$36,332.80$.

This calculation is repeated for other periods until the balance of the segment is fully depleted at the end of the period 16, as shown in Table 2.27. The economic value of this segment of the savings product is summation of discounted cash flows for all periods, a total value of $100,215.50.

No New Account Treatment

This treatment is based on the assumption that the bank does not acquire any new account or any new customer for the non-maturing instrument. Unlike "no new business," in this treatment it is assumed that the existing accounts remain active and customers continue to use their products. For existing accounts, on one hand, customer activities lead to increase or decrease of balances. For example, for credit cards, existing accounts' balances increase when customers use their cards and roll over balances, and decrease when customers pay their bills. Or for deposit accounts, new deposits increase outstanding balances and withdrawals or bill payment activities decrease outstanding balances. On the other hand, account attrition over time decreases the number of existing accounts. While, due to customer activities, it is possible that outstanding balances increase from one month to the next, generally as the effect of account attrition phases in, this dynamic results in a gradual decrease in overall balances over the runoff period. However, this decline is slower compared to the "no new business" treatment, as customer activities of existing accounts lessen the effect of account attrition. Figure 2.14 presents a sample runoff profile based on a "no new account" treatment.

To construct the runoff profile based on "no new account," the same procedure introduced for "no new business" can be used with the following differences:

- In calculation of historical runoff balances, both debit and credit transactions of existing accounts should be considered:

$$B_t = B_{t-1} + Credit_t - Debit_t \qquad (2.53)$$

  In this equation $Credit_t$ and $Debit_t$ are positive numbers.
- In this treatment, the historical runoff balances no longer exhibit a downward curve, and for some months the balances may actually increase due to existing accounts' activities.
- The exponential decay function can be used to fit the data, as the effect of account attrition usually creates an overall downward curve for the runoff profile. As an alternative, a quadratic function may be used to fit the observed historical data.
- Since both credit and debit transactions are used to calculate historical runoff balances, it is more likely that when all historical data are exhausted the balance for the segment is not completely depleted. Similar to "no new business" treatment, either the fitted function (exponential decay or quadratic function) can be used for the entire runoff profile, or observed historical balances (as a percentage of balance at runoff start month) can be used in the runoff profile and extended using the functional form to reach to zero level.
- As shown in Figure 2.14, runoff for "no new account" treatment is generally slower compared to the "no new business" treatment.

Constant Balance Treatment

Another potential treatment for non-maturing products is to assume that their balances remain constant and equal to the balances as of the valuation date. This treatment is based on the assumption that the existing accounts' activities along with the effect of account attrition and impact of new accounts overall result in future balances that are equal to the current balance of the product. Assumption of constant balance has two implications. First, due to a constant and level outstanding balance, there are no principal cash flows and value of the position is derived only based on interest cash flows. Second, to value the position using discounted cash flow method, a *termination date* and a *terminal value* assumption is needed. The terminal date is the date when the last interest cash flow is assumed. The termination date is needed to have a finite number of future interest cash flows that are discounted to obtain the present value of the non-maturing instrument. This assumption allows the incorporation of forecasted or implied forward interest rates in future dates for calculation of interest amounts.

An alternative to termination date is to treat the constant balance non-maturing product as a perpetuity instrument and derive its present value using formula for a perpetuity instrument. This assumption, however, does not allow for incorporation of forecasted or implied forward rates in valuation of the non-maturing product.

INCLUSION OF PREPAYMENT AND DEFAULT: A ROLL FORWARD APPROACH

Default of a financial instrument occurs when the obligor fails to pay the required cash flows to the counterparty based on the contractually agreed schedule. Trigger of a *default event* can be due to the failure of payment of either principal or interest and, depending on the contract, a partial payment that is less than the contractually agreed amount may also trigger the default event. When the borrower of a loan fails to make the required monthly payment, the loan is first designated as *delinquent*. Banks usually categorize the delinquent loans in 30, 60, and 90 days delinquency groups. Often a loan that is delinquent more than 90 days is considered *at default*. When a loan defaults, the lender loses both the remaining principal amount and future interest income from the loan. The risk of this to occur is referred to as *credit risk* of the loan. In a *collateralized* loan, obligor pledges an asset, such as a real property, to back the loan. In case of default of a collateralized loan the lender may recoup part or the entire amount of loss using the collateral.

Prepayment is the early repayment of the principal amount borrowed, in part or in full. A partial prepayment is known as *curtailment*. Prepayment is an option held by the borrower and depending on the contract (i) it may not be allowed, (ii) it may be allowed at any time during the life of the contract, or (iii) it may be allowed but only during certain period of the contract life. Prepayment by the borrower may or may not include a penalty fee. Often the borrower prepays the loan to take advantage of a current low interest rate environment; hence the probability of prepayment increases when the interest rate level decreases. If prepayment occurs due to decrease in interest rate, the lender would be reinvesting the returned principal in a lower interest rate than the rate of the original contract. The risk of this occurring is referred to as *prepayment risk* of a loan.

Prepayment and default change the cash flow of a financial instrument and hence impact its value. If at the valuation date the occurrence and timing of prepayment or default in the future are certain, adjusting the cash flows to reflect their impacts is straightforward. However, in practice often the occurrence or timing of these events are not known in advance. The common approach to incorporate the impacts of prepayment and default in valuation of financial instruments is to assume these events can occur only at discrete times with certain periodicities, for example, with the same frequency as payment frequency. Then using estimated *probability of default (PD)* and *probability of prepayment* in future periods, calculate the *expected values* of the instruments.

This approach can be applied either at the instrument level or at the aggregated (portfolio) level. At the instrument level, Monte Carlo simulation can be used to simulate occurrence and timing of default event and prepayment amounts and obtain the expected instrument value based on a large number of simulated scenarios. At the aggregated level, the impact of default and prepayment on portfolio cash flows and outstanding balances in future periods is estimated and used to obtain the expected value of the portfolio. Here, we describe a *roll forward* methodology applied at the aggregated level to incorporate default and prepayment in cash flow analysis of a loan portfolio.

Assume that the current aggregated outstanding balance of a portfolio of N loans is B_0. In this approach, we assume that the portfolio consists of B_0 number of micro loans, each with an outstanding balance of \$1. This assumption allows us to remove the prepaid or defaulted micro loans in their entirety from the portfolio and estimate the cash flows based on the remaining outstanding balance.

Scheduled outstanding balance is the balance of a loan based on the contractually agreed amortization schedule, without consideration of prepayment or default events. Likewise, *scheduled cash flows* (principal or interest payments) of a loan are the contractually expected cash flows when no default or prepayment is considered. In the following discussion we first develop a series of equations to derive scheduled cash flows and ending balances using the roll forward method. In this method, cash flows and ending balance of one period are derived based on information of the previous period and this is continued recursively one period at a time. Then, these equations are modified to include the impacts of prepayment and default.

Assume that B_{S_i} is the scheduled outstanding balance of the portfolio at the end of period i, obtained by aggregating scheduled outstanding balances of all loans in the portfolio. Earlier in this chapter we introduced the amortization factor as the ratio of the outstanding balance at the end of a period to the initial balance. Therefore, for our aggregated loan portfolio, the amortization factor A_i is defined as:

$$A_i = \frac{B_{s_i}}{B_0} \tag{2.54}$$

The portfolio scheduled balance B_{s_i} is found by adding the scheduled balance of individual loans at the end of period i and by using it in Equation (2.54) we can calculate A_i. From Equation (2.54) we have:

$$B_{s_i} = A_i B_0$$

Also when we use Equation (2.54) for period $i - 1$, we obtain:

$$B_0 = \frac{B_{s_{i-1}}}{A_{i-1}}$$

By combining these two equations, we have:

$$B_{s_i} = B_{s_{i-1}} \frac{A_i}{A_{i-1}} \tag{2.55}$$

The aggregated scheduled principal payment for period i is the difference between the aggregated outstanding balance at the end of period $i - 1$ and period i. Hence:

$$P_{s_i} = B_{s_{i-1}} - B_{s_i}$$

Using Equation (2.55), we have:

$$P_{s_i} = B_{s_{i-1}} - B_{s_{i-1}} \frac{A_i}{A_{i-1}}$$

or

$$P_{s_i} = B_{s_{i-1}} \left(1 - \frac{A_i}{A_{i-1}} \right) \tag{2.56}$$

Assume that r_i is the effective rate for the aggregated portfolio in period i. If the portfolio consisted of fixed-rate loans, r_i is constant for all future periods and is obtained as the weighted average rates of loans, weighted by their current outstanding balances. This rate is assumed for each micro loan and, since in our approach default or prepayment removes some of the micro loans in their entirety, the effective rate r_i is unaffected by prepayment or default. If loans are floating-rate type with the same reference index (e.g., all loans are based on the prime rate but with different spreads), r_i is obtained by adding the weighted average spreads of loans, weighted by their current outstanding balances, to the forecasted reference index at each future period. This weighted average spread is assumed for each micro loan, and since default or prepayment removes micro loans in their entirety, the spread used in calculation of the effective rate is unaffected by prepayment or default. Using r_i, the aggregated scheduled interest payment and total aggregated scheduled cash flow for period i are calculated as:

$$I_{s_i} = B_{s_{i-1}} r_i \tag{2.57}$$

$$C_{s_i} = P_{s_i} + I_{s_i} \tag{2.58}$$

Based on this, the roll forward equation for aggregated scheduled ending balance for period i is:

$$B_{s_i} = B_{s_{i-1}} - P_{s_i} \tag{2.59}$$

Thus far, we developed roll forward equations for the scheduled cash flows and scheduled balance. We can now modify them to incorporate the prepayment and default. Here we assume default and prepayment frequencies are the same as the payment frequency. When a micro loan defaults, it is considered as a *non-performing* position. A non-performing loan no longer pays principal or interest and after a certain time its balance is charged-off or recovered, either partially or fully. Remaining micro loans that are not defaulted comprise the *performing balance* of the portfolio.

Default rate for period i, DR_i, is the estimated percentage of outstanding balance that defaults in period i condition to the micro loans comprising the outstanding balance have survived up to the beginning of the period. Using historical data, banks develop statistical models to estimate the periodic default rates in future periods. If Δt is the length of the period in years, we can convert periodic default rate DR_i to an annual default rate ADR_i, and vice versa using the following equations[7]:

$$ADR_i = 1 - (1 - DR_i)^{\frac{1}{\Delta t}} \tag{2.60}$$

$$DR_i = 1 - (1 - ADR_i)^{\Delta t} \tag{2.61}$$

If $B_{perf,i-1}$ is the aggregated performing balance at the end of period $i-1$, using the periodic default rate we can calculate D_i, the aggregated amount of new default in period i, as:

$$D_i = B_{perf,i-1} DR_i \tag{2.62}$$

Prepayment rate for period i, PR_i, is the estimated percentage of available-to-prepay balance that is prepaid in period i, where the available to prepay is the performing balance minus the expected principal payment in that period. Banks use behavioral modeling techniques and historical data to estimate future prepayment rates. Similar to the default rate, periodic prepayment rate for a period of Δt year length can be converted to an annual prepayment rate of APR_i and vice versa using the following equations:

$$APR_i = 1 - (1 - PR_i)^{\frac{1}{\Delta t}} \tag{2.63}$$

$$PR_i = 1 - (1 - APR_i)^{\Delta t} \tag{2.64}$$

The expected principal payment in period i is the difference between performing balances at the end of period $i-1$ and the end of period i, when no prepayment is considered. Using Equation (2.55) the performing balance at the end of period i with no prepayment is $B_{Perf,i-1} \frac{A_i}{A_{i-1}}$; hence, the aggregated expected payment in period i, $P_{Exp,i}$, is obtained as:

$$P_{Exp,i} = B_{Perf,i-1} - B_{Perf,i-1} \frac{A_i}{A_{i-1}}$$

or

$$P_{Exp,i} = B_{Perf,i-1} \left(1 - \frac{A_i}{A_{i-1}} \right)$$

Since prepayment rate is the ratio of the prepayment amount to the available-to-prepay balance, we have:

$$PR_i = \frac{PP_i}{B_{Perf,i-1} - P_{Exp,i}}$$

or

$$PP_i = (B_{Perf,i-1} - P_{Exp,i}) PR_i = \left(B_{Perf,i-1} - B_{Perf,i-1} \left(1 - \frac{A_i}{A_{i-1}} \right) \right) PR_i$$

So the aggregated prepayment amount for prepayment i is obtained as:

$$PP_i = B_{Perf,i-1}\frac{A_i}{A_{i-1}}PR_i \tag{2.65}$$

In Equation (2.56), we developed the relationship between scheduled outstanding balance and scheduled principal payment amount. We can modify this equation to incorporate the default by decreasing the outstanding performing balance at the beginning of the period by the amount of new default obtained from Equation (2.62). Hence, the aggregated principal payment in period i is obtained as:

$$P_i = (B_{Perf,i-1} - D_i)\left(1 - \frac{A_i}{A_{i-1}}\right) \tag{2.66}$$

We can express this principal payment amount as a function of the scheduled principal payment amount. From Equation (2.56) we have:

$$P_{si} = B_{si-1}\left(1 - \frac{A_i}{A_{i-1}}\right) \Rightarrow \left(1 - \frac{A_i}{A_{i-1}}\right) = \frac{P_{si}}{B_{si-1}}$$

Thus:

$$P_i = P_{si}\frac{B_{Perf,i-1} - D_i}{B_{si-1}} \tag{2.67}$$

Similarly, we can modify Equation (2.57), which shows the relationship between scheduled outstanding balance and scheduled interest payment amount, to incorporate the default. In doing so, the aggregated interest payment in period i is obtained as:

$$I_i = (B_{Perf,i-1} - D_i)r_i \tag{2.68}$$

We can express this interest payment amount as a function of the scheduled interest payment amount. From Equation (2.57), we have:

$$I_{si} = B_{si-1}r_i \Rightarrow r_i = \frac{I_{si}}{B_{si-1}}$$

Thus:

$$I_i = I_{si}\frac{B_{Perf,i-1} - D_i}{B_{si-1}} \tag{2.69}$$

Subsequently, the roll forward equation for aggregated ending performing balance for period i is:

$$B_{Perf,i} = B_{Perf,i-1} - D_i - PP_i - P_i \tag{2.70}$$

When a loan defaults, its outstanding balance at the time of default is considered as *non-performing balance*. After a certain period a non-performing loan is either considered as a loss and its balance is written off, or if the loan is collateralized, the non-performing balance is partially or fully recovered. For new default occurring in a period, assume T is the number of periods until the charge-off or recovery. So, new default occurred in T period before is partially charged-off and partially recovered in a period i. If LR_i is the loss rate and $1 - LR_i$ is the recovery rate in period i, the aggregated charge-off and recovery amounts are obtained as:

$$CO_i = D_{i-T}\, LR_i \tag{2.71}$$

$$RC_i = D_{i-T}\, (1 - LR_i) \tag{2.72}$$

where

CO_i = Aggregated charge-off amount (loss) in period i for new default occurred in period $i - T$

RC_i = Aggregated recovery amount in period i for new default occurred in period $i - T$

LR_i = Loss rate in period i for new default occurred in period $i - T$

Having the principal and interest payments along with the prepayment and recovery amounts for period i, total aggregated cash flows is calculated as:[8]

$$CF_i = P_i + PP_i + I_i + RC_i \tag{2.73}$$

We can also use the following roll forward equation to track the non-performing balance:

$$B_{Non\text{-}Perf,i} = B_{Non\text{-}Perf,i-1} + D_i - CO_i - RC_i \tag{2.74}$$

Firms use the expected future charge-off to estimate *allowance for loan and lease losses (ALLL)*. This reserve amount reflects the credit losses for loans and leases, estimated as of the analysis date, but that have not been written down yet. Since such credit losses are likely to become charged-off in the future, ALLL is established to absorb these future losses. ALLL is presented as a contra-asset on the balance sheet. In near future, current expected credit losses (CECL) standard, which is based on expected losses over the life of the exposures, is replacing ALLL.

Example

To demonstrate the roll forward methodology introduced in this section, consider a portfolio consisting of 32 term loans with a current total outstanding balance of \$450,000 and weighted average remaining term of one year. Payment frequency is monthly, and the portfolio's weighted average monthly rate is 1.35%. The outstanding balance is amortized linearly each month over the remaining 1-year term. Here we assume that the monthly default rate is 0.5% and the monthly prepayment rate is 1%, both constant over the life of the portfolio. We further assume that the loss rate is 70% for any month and the time to recovery or charge-off is three months.

Each month 1/12 portion of the outstanding balance is amortized. Hence, the amortization factor for the first month is $(12 - 1)/12 = 0.916667$ and the amortization factor for the second month is $(12 - 2)/12 = 0.833333$, and so on. At the beginning of period 1 the performing balance is \$450,000. Hence, the aggregated new default for this period is obtained using Equation (2.62) as:

$$D_1 = B_{perf,0} DR_1 = 450,000 \times 0.5\% = 2,250$$

The aggregated prepayment amount in period 1 is obtained using Equation (2.65) as:

$$PP_1 = B_{Perf,0} \frac{A_1}{A_0} PR_1 = 450,000 \times \frac{0.916667}{1} \times 1\% = 4,125$$

Aggregated principal and interest payments for period 1 are calculated using Equations (2.66) and (2.68):

$$P_1 = (B_{Perf,0} - D_1)\left(1 - \frac{A_1}{A_0}\right) = (450,000 - 2,250)\left(1 - \frac{0.916667}{1}\right)$$

$$= 37,312.50$$

$$I_1 = (B_{Perf,0} - D_1)r_1 = (450,000 - 2,250) \times 1.35\% = 6,044.63$$

And the aggregated outstanding performing balance at the end of period 1 is obtained using Equation (2.70):

$$B_{Perf,1} = B_{Perf,0} - D_1 - PP_1 - P_1$$

$$= 450,000 - 2,250 - 4,125 - 37,312.50 = 406,312.50$$

(continued)

TABLE 2.28 Aggregated balance and cash flows of a portfolio, considering prepayment and default, obtained using a roll forward method

Period	Beginning Performing Balance	Amortization Factor	Default	Prepayment	Principal	Interest	Ending Performing Balance
0	450,000.00	1.000000					
1	450,000.00	0.916667	2,250.00	4,125.00	37,312.50	6,044.63	406,312.50
2	406,312.50	0.833333	2,031.56	4,090.91	36,752.81	5,457.79	363,437.22
3	363,437.22	0.750000	1,817.19	4,050.00	36,162.00	4,881.87	
4	321,408.03	0.666667	1,607.04	4,000.00	35,533.44	4,317.31	280,267.54
5	280,267.54	0.583333	1,401.34	3,937.50	34,858.28	3,764.69	240,070.43
6	240,070.43	0.500000	1,200.35	3,857.14	34,124.30	3,224.75	200,888.64
7	200,888.64	0.416667	1,004.44	3,750.00	33,314.03	2,698.44	162,820.16
8	162,820.16	0.333333	814.10	3,600.00	32,401.21	2,187.08	126,004.85
9	126,004.85	0.250000	630.02	3,375.00	31,343.71	1,692.56	90,656.12
10	90,656.12	0.166667	453.28	3,000.00	30,067.61	1,217.74	57,135.23
11	57,135.23	0.083333	285.68	2,250.00	28,424.77	767.47	26,174.77
12	26,174.77	0.000000	130.87	0	26,043.90	351.59	0

The ending performing balance of period 1 is the starting balance of period 2, and by repeating similar calculations we can obtain the cash flows and ending balances of periods 2 to 12. Table 2.28 shows the amortization factors for 12 months, along with the aggregated beginning and ending performing balances and aggregated cash flows of this portfolio, assuming the aforementioned prepayment and default rates.

In this example, since the time to charge-off or recovery is 3 months, there is no charge-off or recovery amounts in periods 1, 2, and 3. Charge-off and recovery amounts in period 4 are calculated using Equations (2.71) and (2.72) based on the default amount of $2,250 from period 1 as:

$$CO_4 = D_1 LR_1 = 2,250 \times 70\% = 1,575$$

$$RC_4 = D_1(1 - LR_1) = 2,250 \times 30\% = 675$$

The charge-off and recovery amounts for other periods are calculated similarly, considering the three months' assumed lag from the default time. Total cash flow of the portfolio in each period is then obtained by adding the principal, interest, prepayment, and recovery cash flows. Discounting these estimated total cash flows for all periods to the current time provides us with the portfolio's estimated value.

SUMMARY

- Intrinsic, theoretic, or economic value of a financial instrument is the present value of its future expected cash flows.
- Valuation date is the date when future cash flows of a financial instrument are discounted back to obtain the instrument value as of that date.
- Market value of a financial instrument is the price at which market participants are willing to buy or sell the instrument.
- Generally, a financial instrument has two types of cash flow: principal payments are cash flows for the repayment of the original borrowed amount. Interest payments are cash flows for the cost of the borrowing, calculated based on the periodic outstanding principal and effective interest rate for each period.

- Amortization method is a framework that defines the process of principal repayments, including time and amount of principal cash flows. Bullet payment at maturity, linear, constant payment, and sum-of-digits are the most common types of amortization method. Some financial instruments are based on custom amortization schedules.

- Discounted cash flow method is the fundamental technique for valuation of financial instruments.

- A fixed-rate instrument is a financial product with an effective rate that is fixed and does not change over the life of the product.

- Yield is the internal rate of return that makes the value of a financial instrument derived using the discounted cash flow method equal to its market value.

- Macaulay duration is the weighted average of times of cash flows of an instrument, where each weight is the contribution of present value of the cash flow in total value of the instrument.

- Modified duration is a measurement of the sensitivity of value of an instrument to change in yield. Modified duration can be used to obtain change in value of a financial instrument for a given change in its yield. However, the result is approximate, since the modified duration is derived assuming the relationship between instrument value and its yield is linear while in reality that relationship is non-linear.

- Convexity is a measurement of the sensitivity of the duration of an instrument to change in its yield.

- Dollar duration is the negative of change in value of an instrument per change in yield. Dollar convexity is the second derivative of value with respect to yield.

- Modified duration and convexity of a portfolio of instruments are the weighted average of the modified durations and convexities of instruments in the portfolio, where each weight is the proportion of the instrument value to the total portfolio value.

- Effective duration is an approximate measurement of modified duration for an instrument with complex valuation function. Effective convexity is an approximate measurement of convexity for an instrument with complex valuation function.

- Price risk is the risk of having assets sold at future dates at prices that are lower than expected prices. Reinvestment risk is the risk of having future cash inflows invested at lower interest rates than the expected rates.

- Duration matching is an interest rate immunization method where assets and liabilities are selected such that their aggregated modified durations are equal. When this condition is met, then a change in interest rate changes the aggregated values of assets and liabilities almost equally. To have an effective duration matching, the portfolio needs to be rebalanced periodically.

- Key rate duration is a sensitivity measure of an instrument value to a change in rate at one term point of the spot curve.

- A floating-rate instrument is a financial product with an effective rate that is not constant and can change during the life of the product. The reset or rate fixing date is a date when the effective rate of an accrual period is determined. Reset frequency is the periodicity of the effective rate setting of a floating-rate instrument.

- In pre-period-initiation rate setting, the effective rate of an accrual period is set at the reset date that is before and closest to the beginning day of the period. In post-period-initiation rate setting the effective rate of an accrual period is set at the reset date that is within the accrual period and is closest to the ending day of the period.

- In valuation of floating-rate instrument, unknown rates of future accrual periods can be estimated using implied forward method or using a rate forecasting model.

- When combined with a runoff profile, a discounted cash flow method can be used to value non-maturing products. A runoff profile or runoff curve is a schedule that shows how balance of a portfolio or a segment of a portfolio of a non-maturing product is changed based on an assumed treatment. In "no new business" treatment, no new account or customer is acquired while existing accounts are paid off gradually and not used for new activities. In "no new account" treatment, no new account is acquired but existing accounts are used as usual. In "constant balance" treatment outstanding balances of non-maturing products are assumed to remain constant.

- A financial instrument is considered performing when the obligor pays principal and interest based on a contractually agreed schedule. The instrument is deemed delinquent if the obligor currently does not pay principal or interest at expected scheduled times, but future payments are still possible. When the obligor does not pay principal or interest and no future payment is expected, the instrument is considered non-performing or in default. Outstanding balance of a defaulted instrument, after a certain period and depending on whether it is collateralized or not, is either charged off or recovered.

■ One approach to incorporate the impact of credit losses (defaults) and pre-payments in valuation is to use a roll forward method at an aggregated level. In a roll forward method, outstanding balance, interest, and principal payments, prepayment, and new default amounts in one period are derived recursively using information from the previous period.

NOTES

1. *Solver* in *Microsoft Excel* can be used to solve this equation and calculate the yield.
2. Taylor series expansion of real function $f(x)$ about point a is $f(x) = f(a) + f'(a)(x - a) + \frac{f''(a)}{2!}(x - a)^2 + \cdots$.
3. Boldface $\boldsymbol{r_t}$ represents the vector of all rates of spot rate curve while r_t is one particular spot rate of that curve for maturity t.
4. For simplicity and to develop a closed form solution, here it is assumed that the next interest cash flow and the next reset date occur at the same time.
5. The LIBOR market model, discussed in another chapter, can be used to produce forward rates with characteristics described here.
6. Exponential decay function does not reach exactly to zero level; therefore, when the level reaches a predetermined low level, for example, below 0.1% of the starting balance, calculation of the runoff profile is stopped.
7. These equations are derived by noting if the length of the period is Δt year; there are $\frac{1}{\Delta t}$ periods in one year. If one minus annual default rate is the annual survival rate, it is equal to the multiplication of $\frac{1}{\Delta t}$ number of periodic survival rates. Hence: $1 - ADR_i = (1 - DR_i)^{\frac{1}{\Delta t}}$ or $ADR_i = 1 - (1 - DR_i)^{\frac{1}{\Delta t}}$. By rearranging this we obtain $DR_i = 1 - (1 - ADR_i)^{\Delta t}$.
8. In portfolio valuation some practitioners do not include the recovery amount in total expected cash flows.

BIBLIOGRAPHY

Finnerty, John D. "Measuring the Duration of a Floating-Rate Bond." *Journal of Portfolio Management* 15, no. 4 (1989): 67–72.

Fisher, Lawrence, and Roman L. Weil. "Coping with the Risk of Interest-Rate Fluctuations, Return to Bondholders from Naive and Optimal Strategies." *Journal of Business* 44, no. 4 (1971): 408–431.

Fong, H. Gifford, and Oldrich Vasicek. "The Tradeoff between Return and Risk in Immunized Portfolios." *Financial Analysts Journal* 39, no. 5 (September and October 1983): 73–78.

Ho, Thomas S.Y. "Key Rate Durations: Measures of Interest Rate Risks." *Journal of Fixed Income 2*, no. 2 (1992): 29–45.

Macaulay, Frederick R. "Some Theoretical Problems Suggested by the Movements of Interest Rates, Bond Yields, and Stock Prices in the United States since 1856." National Bureau of Economic Research, 1938.

Redington, Frank. "Review of the Principles of Life-Office Valuations," *Journal of the Institute of Actuaries* 78, no. 3 (1952): 286–340.

CHAPTER 3

Equity Valuation

The *equity* of a company is the difference between its assets (what it owns) and its liabilities (what it owes). A *common stock* represents an ownership interest in the equity of a company. For example, if company XYZ has 1,000,000 outstanding shares of common stock, a holder of one share has a 1/1,000,000 ownership interest in the equity of the company. A holder of a common stock, or *equity security*, also has the right to a proportion of the earnings of the issuing company. The board of directors of the company may decide to distribute part of the periodic profit to the shareholders, a payment known as a *dividend*. The most common form of the dividend is the *cash dividend,* where shareholders receive cash payments based on the number of shares they own at a certain date. *Retained earnings* is the part of the profits that have not been distributed as dividends. At the *declaration date* the board of directors of a company declares dividend payment for those who own stocks at the *record date* (a day in the future of the declaration date). *Ex-dividend date*, which is usually two business days before the record date, is the cutoff point that defines who receives the dividend and who doesn't. Holders of shares of stock that are purchased at ex-dividend date or after do not receive a dividend payment for that period while those who owned the stock before the ex-dividend date are eligible to receive a dividend for each share they own. *Payment date* is when dividends are actually paid to the shareholders of record.

Equity and investment analysts use a range of methods to estimate the value of a stock. One approach in valuation of equity securities is to use the discounted cash flow method. We introduced this approach in a previous chapter and used it in valuation of fixed income securities and non-maturity products. In an application of this method for equity valuation, the expected cash flows from investment in an equity security are discounted using the required rate of return of the investment and aggregated to obtain the equity value. Value obtained using this approach depends on the nature of the expected cash flows considered in the valuation process, and different expected cash flows may result in different current value for the security. In practice, equity analysts use this approach to obtain a relative value for the equity compared to the current market price of the stock, and based on this comparison they make recommendations to buy, hold, or sell. In this chapter we consider two types of expected future cash flows for valuation: in the first method we consider dividends while the second method is based on free cash flow to equity holders. Later in this chapter we study a different valuation technique that does not use the discounted cash flow method and is based on comparative price ratios.

DIVIDEND DISCOUNT MODEL

Discounted cash flow method assumes the intrinsic value of an equity security is the present value of its expected cash flows in the future. In the *dividend discount model (DDM)*, expected future dividends are used in the valuation of stock. When investing in an equity security the expected cash flows from this investment include dividend payments and cash flow from selling the equity in the future. Assume company XYZ pays dividends on a quarterly basis. D_0 is the dividend just paid, and D_i is the expected dividend to be paid at the end of period i in the future. Many companies pay dividends on a quarterly basis, but here we consider a general periodicity. An investor is planning to buy one share of XYZ stock and hold it for n periods. Assume R is the periodic *required rate of return*. This is the minimum return the investor is willing to accept for investing in a share of XYZ stock for one period. Also assume that the expected cash flow from selling this share (i.e., the market price of one share of XYZ) n periods from now is P_n. Based on this setup the estimated current value of one share of XYZ using discounted cash flow method is:

$$V_0 = \frac{D_1}{(1+R)^1} + \frac{D_2}{(1+R)^2} + \cdots + \frac{D_{n-1}}{(1+R)^{n-1}} + \frac{D_n}{(1+R)^n} + \frac{P_n}{(1+R)^n}$$

In a limiting case where n is sufficiently large, we can ignore the sale cash flow P_n as it happens far in the future and the discounted value of that cash flow is negligible. Therefore, the current equity value V_0 is obtained as:

$$V_0 = \sum_{i=1}^{\infty} \frac{D_i}{(1+R)^i} \tag{3.1}$$

This is known as a dividend discount model, first introduced by John Burr Williams (1938). To overcome the need for aggregation of an infinite number of dividend cash flows required in this model, and to emphasize the importance of growth in equity valuation, Gordon and Shapiro (1956) introduced a method to associate the equity price, rate of return of the investment, dividend yield, and the earnings growth. This method can be used in the estimation of the current value of stock when future dividend growth is assumed constant.

If g is the expected constant periodic growth rate of the dividend in the future, we have:

$$D_i = D_{i-1}(1 + g) \tag{3.2}$$

We can also express the value of a dividend at the end of period i based on D_0, dividend just paid, and the growth rate as:

$$D_i = D_0(1 + g)^i \tag{3.3}$$

By rewriting Equation (3.1) using Equation (3.3), we have:

$$V_0 = \sum_{i=1}^{\infty} \frac{D_0(1 + g)^i}{(1 + R)^i}$$

This is a geometric series and can be expressed as:[1]

$$V_0 = \frac{D_0(1 + g)}{R - g} \tag{3.4}$$

or

$$V_0 = \frac{D_1}{R - g} \tag{3.5}$$

This model, commonly known as the *Gordon growth model*, is only valid when $R > g$, that is, the required rate of return should be greater than the expected growth rate of dividend. By rearranging Equation (3.5) we can illustrate the components of the required rate of return R as dividend yield $\frac{D_1}{V_0}$ and expected growth rate of the dividend g:

$$R = \frac{D_1}{V_0} + g \tag{3.6}$$

Example

Assume that XYZ Company pays a quarterly dividend. It just paid a dividend of $0.30 per share. The expected quarterly growth rate of the dividend is 1.5% and required rate of return for an investor is 3.5%. Using Equation (3.4) the estimated current value of one share of XYZ Company is obtained as:

$$V_0 = \frac{0.30 \times (1 + 0.015)}{0.035 - 0.015} = 15.225$$

As mentioned above, the Gordon growth model is based on the assumption of a constant dividend growth rate. Since this assumption may not be applicable for all future periods, practitioners often use multi-stage models where different growth rates are assumed in different periods. To illustrate this, consider a two-stage model where a high growth rate of g_h is expected for the first n periods in the future, followed by a low or steady growth rate of g_l in the succeeding periods. To derive the estimated current value of stock based on this model, we can break Equation (3.1) into two parts: the first part from period 1 to period n and the second part from period $n + 1$ and after:

$$V_0 = \sum_{i=1}^{n} \frac{D_i}{(1+R)^i} + \sum_{j=n+1}^{\infty} \frac{D_j}{(1+R)^j}$$

The second part of this equation is the present value of all cash flows occurring after the end of period n. This present value is equivalent to the value of all those cash flows discounted first to the end of period n, and then discounted back to period 0. Thus, the previous equation can be restated as:

$$V_0 = \sum_{i=1}^{n} \frac{D_i}{(1+R)^i} + \frac{V_n}{(1+R)^n}$$

where V_n is the value of all cash flows occurring after the end of period n, discounted back to the end of period n. The first part of the previous equation can be restated based on a constant growth rate of g_h and the dividend just paid using $D_i = D_0(1 + g_h)^i$. Also, V_n in the second part of the previous equation can be stated using the Gordon growth model based on constant growth rate of g_l. So:

$$V_0 = \sum_{i=1}^{n} \frac{D_0(1+g_h)^i}{(1+R)^i} + \frac{\dfrac{D_{n+1}}{R-g_l}}{(1+R)^n}$$

The expected dividend at the end of period $n + 1$ can be stated based on the dividend just paid and growth rates of g_h and g_l as:

$$D_{n+1} = D_0(1 + g_h)^n(1 + g_l)$$

Therefore:

$$V_0 = \sum_{i=1}^{n} \frac{D_0(1+g_h)^i}{(1+R)^i} + \frac{D_0(1+g_h)^n(1+g_l)}{(1+R)^n(R-g_l)} \tag{3.7}$$

This equation provides the estimated current value of the equity based on growth rates of two stages, the dividend just paid and the investor's required rate of return.

Example

Consider again XYZ Company with a quarterly dividend payment schedule. The dividend just paid is $0.30 per share. The expected dividend growth for the next eight quarters is 2% and after that it is 1%. As in the previous example the investor's required rate of return is 3.5%. Using the two-stage model in Equation (3.7) we can obtain the estimated current value of one share of XYZ stock as:

$$V_0 = \sum_{i=1}^{8} \frac{0.30 \times (1 + 0.02)^i}{(1 + 0.035)^i} + \frac{0.30 \times (1 + 0.02)^8(1 + 0.01)}{(1 + 0.035)^8(0.035 - 0.01)}$$

$$= 2.2487 + 10.784 = 13.0327$$

DISCOUNTED FREE CASH FLOW METHOD

An alternative method in equity valuation is based on discounting the expected cash flows generated by a firm through its normal operation, after accounting for all relevant expenses and non-cash charges. In this method we aim to obtain true expected cash flows of the firm that are available to all stakeholders and then discount those cash flows using an appropriate discount rate. *Free cash flow to firm (FCFF)* is the cash flow available to all suppliers of capital, including equity and debt holders, after all expenses and taxes are paid and capital expenditure and change in working capital are considered. FCFF is different from *cash flow from operations (CFO)* reported in the statement of cash flows. *Free cash flow to equity (FCFE)* is the cash flow available to equity holders of the company after FCFF is adjusted for cash flows related to the debts. Depending on the source of information and details of data available, practitioners may use different methods to calculate FCFF. Since net income, as presented in income statement, or cash flow from operations, as presented in statement of cash flows, are impacted by some elements that are not true cash flows, the use of FCFF and FCFE in valuation of a company or its equity is preferred. Here we demonstrate derivation of FCFF and FCFE using a simple balance sheet and income statement and explain the application of free cash flows in equity valuation.

Before getting into details of derivation of FCFF and FCFE, first we need to introduce the concept of cost of capital and its components. Firms raise funds usually by selling partial ownership, for example, by selling equity securities or raising debt through directly borrowing or selling debt securities. The cost of capital is the minimum rate of return required by all investors in the company. Assuming the firm raises capital only through equity and debt and no preferred stock is issued, the *weighted average cost of capital (WACC)* is calculated as:

$$WACC = \frac{MV_D}{MV_E + MV_D} R_D(1 - t) + \frac{MV_E}{MV_E + MV_D} R_E \qquad (3.8)$$

where

MV_D = Market value of debt
MV_E = Market value of equity
R_D = Cost of debt
R_E = Cost of equity
t = Effective tax rate

Weighted average cost of capital is the minimum rate of return required by all equity and debt investors. The weighting scheme used in WACC is based on market values of equity and debt, as opposed to the book values, to reflect the current capital structure of the firm. Cost of equity R_E is the required rate of return by equity investors. One method to obtain R_E is to use dividend yield and expected dividend growth rate and using Equation (3.6). Cost of debt R_D is the rate of return required by debt investors. This is the interest rate to be paid if the firm issues new debt securities. If the firm has outstanding debt securities, weighted average of yield to maturity of those securities can be used as the proxy for R_D. Coupon rates of current outstanding debt securities of the firm should not be used for R_D as those rates do not represent current cost of debt.

In calculating FCFF we aim to obtain true cash flows that are available to the providers of capital. FCFF can be calculated from the net income with proper adjustment for non-cash charges and other true cash flow items, as follows:

$$FCFF = NI + DP + IE(1 - t) - CI - NWCI \qquad (3.9)$$

where

NI = Net income
DP = Depreciation (and amortization)
IE = Interest expense
t = Effective tax rate
CI = Capital investment
$NWCI$ = Net working capital investment

In this equation we assumed that depreciation is the only non-cash charge. This equation can be modified to consider adjustments for other non-cash charges. Such non-cash charges are deducted when net income is calculated so they are added back when deriving FCFF. The interest expense, after considering its impact on tax obligation of the firm, is also deducted when net income is calculated. Therefore, after-tax interest expense is added back when deriving FCFF. Since capital spending (e.g., investment in fixed assets and investment in net working capital) impact cash flow, they are deducted in FCFF derivation to adjust for their effect on cash flow of the firm. Generally, net working capital is defined as:

$$Net\ working\ capital = Current\ asset - Current\ liability \qquad (3.10)$$

Cash and cash equivalents, accounts receivable, and inventory are common components of the current assets, and accounts payable, notes payable, and the current portion of long-term debt are common components of the current liability. In FCFF calculation practitioners often do not include cash and cash equivalents as components of the current asset and also do not include notes payable and current portion of long-term debt as components of the current liability. Exclusion of the cash and cash equivalents is based on the idea that by focusing on the change in the net working capital we are trying to find its impact on the cash, and therefore the change in cash itself should not be considered. Exclusion of short-term debts is to stress that interest expenses related to those items are financing costs and not operation expenses.

We can also derive FCFF by starting from *earnings before interest and taxes (EBIT)* or *earnings before interest, taxes, depreciation, and amortization (EBITDA)*. First notice that net income can be stated based on EBIT and EBITDA as follows:

$$NI = EBIT - IE - (EBIT - IE)t = EBIT(1 - t) - IE(1 - t)$$

$$NI = EBITDA - DP - IE - (EBITDA - DP - IE)t$$

$$= EBITDA(1 - t) - IE(1 - t) - DP(1 - t)$$

By replacing net income in Equation (3.9) with these equations, we obtain:

$$FCFF = EBIT(1 - t) + DP - CI - NWCI \qquad (3.11)$$

$$FCFF = EBITDA(1 - t) + DP \times t - CI - NWCI \qquad (3.12)$$

FCFF is the cash available to all capital providers. By excluding the after-tax interest paid to the debt holders and considering the net impact of borrowing during the target period (e.g., one year) we can obtain the cash flow available to the equity holders only. Using FCFF we can calculate FCFE as follows:

$$FCFE = FCFF - IE(1 - t) + NB \qquad (3.13)$$

where NB is the net borrowing, that is, the difference between debt issued and debt repaid during the target period.

FCFE can be directly calculated from the net income as:

$$FCFE = NI + DP - CI - NWCI + NB \qquad (3.14)$$

In valuation of a firm's equity using free cash flow method, we can use either FCFF or FCFE. In this approach forecasted free cash flows for a future period are estimated by forecasting elements of the balance sheet and income statement that are used in calculation of FCFF or FCFE. Subsequently these forecasted free cash flows are discounted using the appropriate discount rates. Since FCFF is the free cash flow available to all capital providers of the firm, the appropriate discount rate is WACC and the estimated preset value of forecasted FCFF is the value of the firm. Hence to obtain the value of the equity we need to deduct the value of debt from the present value result. On the other hand, since FCFE is the free cash flow available only to equity holders, if forecasted FCFE is used in equity valuation, the appropriate discount rate is the required rate of return on equity and the obtained present value is the value of the firm's equity. After the value of the total equity is estimated, it can be divided by the number of outstanding shares to obtain value of one share of stock. If $FCFF_i$ is the estimated free cash flow to the firm at the end of period i, we have:

$$VE_0 = \sum_{i=1}^{\infty} \frac{FCFF_i}{(1 + WACC)^i} - VD_0 \qquad (3.15)$$

where VE_0 is the current value of the firm's equity and VD_0 is the current value of the firm's debt. If the firm's debt is traded in the market, total market value of the firm's debt securities can be used as VD_0; otherwise it can be evaluated using the discounted cash flow method discussed in Chapter 2. Value of one share of the equity V_0, is then obtained by dividing VE_0 by the number of outstanding shares. Equivalently, if $FCFE_i$ is the estimated free cash flow to equity holders at the end of period i, we have:

$$VE_0 = \sum_{i=1}^{\infty} \frac{FCFE_i}{(1 + R_E)^i} \qquad (3.16)$$

Similar to our discussion for dividend discount model, since calculation of present value in the form of an infinite sum as presented in the two previous equations is not practical, analogous to the Gordon growth model, we can assume that FCFF or FCFE grow at a constant rate. In this case the infinite sums in Equations (3.15) and (3.16) change into a geometric series. If g is the constant growth rate assumed for FCFF or FCFEE, we have:

$$VE_0 = \frac{FCFF_0(1+g)}{WACC - g} - VD_0 = \frac{FCFF_1}{WACC - g} - VD_0 \qquad (3.17)$$

$$VE_0 = \frac{FCFE_0(1+g)}{R_E - g} = \frac{FCFE_1}{R_E - g} \qquad (3.18)$$

Use of the two-stage model is also common for equity valuation using FCFF and FCFE. In this approach the FCFF or FCFE for a limited number of periods are estimated directly using forecasted elements of the balance sheet and the income statement, and after that initial period a constant growth rate is assumed for the free cash flows. Assume that n is the number of periods where FCFF or FCFE are directly estimated using their forecasted components and g is the constant growth rate assumed for period $n + 1$ and after. Using a similar method explained for two-stage dividend discount model, we can develop the following equations for the two-stage free cash flow model:

$$VE_0 = \sum_{i=1}^{n} \frac{FCFF_i}{(1 + WACC)^i} + \frac{1}{(1 + WACC)^n} \times \frac{FCFF_{n+1}}{(WACC - g)} - VD_0 \qquad (3.19)$$

$$VE_0 = \sum_{i=1}^{n} \frac{FCFE_i}{(1 + R_E)^i} + \frac{1}{(1 + R_E)^n} \times \frac{FCFE_{n+1}}{(R_E - g)} \qquad (3.20)$$

Example

To demonstrate the use of free cash flows in equity valuation, consider the simplified balance sheet and income statement of XYZ Company for fiscal year ending December 31, 2015, are presented in Tables 3.1 and 3.2, along with the forecasted balance sheets and income statements for fiscal years 2016, 2017, and 2018. Effective tax rates for these years are assumed to be 35% and the earnings retention rate is 40%. The valuation date is at the beginning of 2016 ($t = 0$); therefore, forecasted free cash flows for 2016 and after are needed for valuation of the firm equity. Here we use a two-stage

(continued)

(*continued*)

model where free cash flows for 2016, 2017, and 2018 are calculated using forecasted balance sheets and income statements, and after that a constant growth is assumed. For calculation of capital investment and investment in net working capital, actual balance sheet and income statements of 2015 are needed and included in Tables 3.1 and 3.2. For demonstration purposes, here we have assumed that investment in net working capital, capital investment, and new borrowing during 2015 (i.e., from the end of 2014 to the end of 2015) are zero. This impacts actual FCFF and FCFE for 2015; however, these free cash flows are not used in equity valuation.

TABLE 3.1 Simplified balance sheet of XYZ Company at the end of 2015 (actual), along with forecasted balance sheets for 2016, 2017, and 2018 year-ends (in $ million)

	Actual	*Forecast*		
Asset	*2015*	*2016*	*2017*	*2018*
Cash and Cash Equivalent	710.0	752.9	829.2	883.5
Account Receivable	950.0	970.0	990.0	1020.0
Inventory	1200.0	1215.0	1230.0	1237.0
Current Asset	2860.0	2937.9	3049.2	3140.5
Fixed Asset	2535.0	2542.0	2546.0	2550.0
Accumulated Depreciation (deduction)	50.0	100.0	150.0	200.0
Total Asset	5345.0	5379.9	5445.2	5490.5
Liability				
Account Payable	900.0	910.0	915.0	918.0
Note Payable	160.0	120.0	100.0	60.0
Current Liability	1060.0	1030.0	1015.0	978.0
Long-Term Debt	2490.0	2492.0	2493.0	2490.0
Common Equity	1400.0	1400.0	1400.0	1400.0
Retained Earnings	395.0	457.9	537.2	622.5
Total Equity	1795.0	1857.9	1937.2	2022.5
Total Liability and Equity	5345.0	5379.9	5445.2	5490.5

TABLE 3.2 Simplified income statement of XYZ Company for the 2015 fiscal year (actual), along with forecasted income statements for fiscal years 2016, 2017, and 2018 (in $ million)

	Actual	*Forecast*		
	2015	**2016**	**2017**	**2018**
EBITDA	360.0	425.0	450.0	465.0
Depreciation	50.0	50.0	50.0	50.0
EBIT	310.0	375.0	400.0	415.0
Interest Expense	68.0	70.0	72.0	71.0
Taxable Income	242.0	305.0	328.0	344.0
Tax	84.7	106.8	114.8	120.4
Net Income	157.3	198.3	213.2	223.6
Retained Earnings	62.9	79.3	85.3	89.4
Dividend	94.4	119.0	127.9	134.2

Calculations of the forecasted FCFF from the net income for 2016, 2017, and 2018 are presented in Table 3.3. For 2016, forecasted net income from Table 3.2 is $198.3 million. Forecasted depreciation in 2016 is $50 million and forecasted after-tax interest expense is $70 million × (1 − 0.35) = $45.5 million. Capital investment in 2016 is calculated as the difference

TABLE 3.3 Calculation of free cash flow to firm, starting from net income (in $ million)

	Actual	*Forecast*		
	2015	*2016*	*2017*	*2018*
+ NI	157.3	198.3	213.2	223.6
+ Depreciation	50.0	50.0	50.0	50.0
+ Interest Expense × (1 − t)	44.2	45.5	46.8	46.2
− Capital Investment	0.0	7.0	4.0	4.0
− Investment in Net Working Capital	0.0	25.0	30.0	34.0
FCFF	251.5	261.8	276.0	281.8

(*continued*)

(continued)

between the value of fixed asset at the end of 2015 and at the end of 2016: $2,542 million − $2,535 million = $7 million. Similarly, investment in net working capital is the difference between net working capital at the end of 2015 and at the end of 2016. However, here we do not include cash and notes payable; hence investment in net working capital in 2016 is calculated as:

(Account Receivable + Inventory − Account Payable) for 2016

   − (Account Receivable + Inventory − Account Payable) for 2015

   = ($970 million + $1,215 million − $910 million)

   − ($950 million + $1,200 million − $900 million) = $25 million

By placing these figures in Equation (3.9) we have:

FCFF = $198.3 million + $50 million + $45.5 million − $7 milliom

   − $25 million = $261.8 million

In Table 3.3 forecasted FCFF for 2017 and 2018 are calculated similarly as $276 million and $281.8 million respectively. As mentioned earlier in calculation of FCFF we can also start from EBIT or EBITDA using Equations (3.11) and (3.12). Tables 3.4 and 3.5 show these calculations, which result in the same forecasted FCFF when we started from the net income.

TABLE 3.4   Calculation of free cash flow to firm, starting from EBIT (in $ million)

	Actual	*Forecast*		
	2015	*2016*	*2017*	*2018*
+ EBIT × (1 − t)	201.5	243.8	260.0	269.8
+ Depreciation	50.0	50.0	50.0	50.0
− Capital Investment	0.0	7.0	4.0	4.0
− Investment in Net Working Capital	0.0	25.0	30.0	34.0
FCFF	251.5	261.8	276.0	281.8

TABLE 3.5 Calculation of free cash flow to firm, starting from EBITDA (in $ million)

	Actual	*Forecast*		
	2015	*2016*	*2017*	*2018*
+ EBITDA × (1 − *t*)	234.0	276.3	292.5	302.3
+ Depreciation × *t*	17.5	17.5	17.5	17.5
− Capital Investment	0.0	7.0	4.0	4.0
− Investment in Net Working Capital	0.0	25.0	30.0	34.0
FCFF	251.5	261.8	276.0	281.8

We can calculate forecasted FCFE for 2016, 2017, and 2018 from corresponding forecasted FCFF using Equation (3.13). Table 3.6 presents this calculation. For 2016 we obtained the forecasted FCFF of $261.8 million. The after-tax interest expense for this year is $45.5 million and net borrowing is calculated as the difference between long-term debt at the end of 2015 and at the end of 2016 as: $2,492 million − $2,490 million = $2 million. So forecasted FCFE for 2016 is:

FCFE = $261.8 million − $45.5 million + $2 million = $218.3 million

Forecasted FCFE for 2017 and 2018 are calculated similarly as $230.2 million and $232.6 million, respectively. We can calculate FCFE directly from the net income using Equation (3.14). This calculation is shown in Table 3.7, which results in the same forecasted FCFE obtained in Table 3.6. To value the equity of the company we use a two-stage model based on free cash flow to equity, where FCFE for the first three years in the future

TABLE 3.6 Calculation of free cash flow to equity from free cash flow to firm (in $ million)

	Actual	*Forecast*		
	2015	*2016*	*2017*	*2018*
+ FCFF	251.5	261.8	276.0	281.8
− Interest Expense × (1 − *t*)	44.2	45.5	46.8	46.2
+ New Borrowing	0.0	2.0	1.0	−3.0
FCFE	207.3	218.3	230.2	232.6

(*continued*)

(*continued*)

TABLE 3.7   Calculation of free cash flow to equity, starting from net income (in $ million)

	Actual	Forecast		
	2015	2016	2017	2018
+NI	157.3	198.3	213.2	223.6
+Depreciation	50.0	50.0	50.0	50.0
− Capital Investment	0.0	7.0	4.0	4.0
− Investment in Net Working Capital	0.0	25.0	30.0	34.0
+New Borrowing	0.0	2.0	1.0	−3.0
FCFE	207.3	218.3	230.2	232.6

are forecasted first and then a constant annual growth rate of 1.5% is assumed for the years after. Assuming the annual required rate of return of equity is 8% and using Equation (3.20) when $n = 2$, we have:

$$VE_0 = \frac{FCFE_1}{(1 + R_E)^1} + \frac{FCFE_2}{(1 + R_E)^2} + \frac{1}{(1 + R_E)^2} \times \frac{FCFE_3}{(R_E - g)} = \frac{\$218.3 \text{ million}}{(1 + 0.08)^1}$$

$$+ \frac{\$230.2 \text{ million}}{(1 + 0.08)^2} + \frac{1}{(1 + 0.08)^2} \times \frac{\$232.6 \text{ million}}{(0.08 - 0.015)} = \$3,467.4 \text{ million}$$

Assuming XYZ Company has 25 million outstanding shares, the value of one share is then obtained as $138.70. By comparing this intrinsic value obtained here by the current market price of the stock, an analyst can determine whether the stock is overvalued or undervalued.

COMPARATIVE VALUATION USING PRICE RATIOS

A *price ratio* is the ratio of the price of the equity to another measurement that reflects value of the firm. In comparative valuation method we compute a price ratio for the firm and compare it to a benchmark ratio. The benchmark ratio is either average or median of the same ratio for a peer group of firms, or the intrinsic ratio computed based on the fundamentals of the firm (e.g., using discounted cash flows). Price ratios are often used for understanding whether a stock is relatively undervalued or overvalued in the market compared to its peers or compared to the financial fundamentals of the firm. Price ratios are also very useful for comparison of different stocks in a peer group when making investment decisions. Among many price ratios, price-to-earnings, price-to-book value, and price-to-sales are commonly used in practice and we introduce them in this section.

■ *Price-to-earnings (P/E) ratio* is defined as:

$$P/E = \frac{Price\ of\ Equity\ per\ Share}{Earnings\ per\ Share} \tag{3.21}$$

In this equation *earnings per share (EPS)* is for a given period (e.g., during a year). Based on the time horizon of EPS there are different variations of P/E ratio; however, the following two versions are the most common:

- ■ *Current or trailing P/E ratio* is calculated by dividing the current stock price by earnings per share in the past one year.
- ■ *Forward or leading P/E ratio* is calculated by dividing the current stock price by forecasted earnings per share for the next one year.

When computing and comparing P/E ratios, the EPS should be carefully examined for the following issues to ensure the obtained ratios are comparable:

- ■ Time period used in derivation of EPS: As mentioned earlier, the P/E ratio can be calculated either based on forward or forecasted earnings or based on historical results. For comparative analysis, the EPS of the firm and those included in the benchmark should be based on the same timeframe.
- ■ Impact of accounting practice used in reported EPS: Accounting rules impact the reported earnings and for comparability the earnings of the firm and those included in the benchmark may need to be adjusted to put them on the same footing.
- ■ Impact of share dilution on EPS: Execution of stock options and conversion of convertible bonds can change the number of outstanding shares and therefore results in diluted EPS. When using EPS in P/E ratio calculation, the impact of share dilution should be considered to ensure the results are comparable.
- ■ Impact of one-time items that are not expected to recur: If earnings of the firm or for those that are included in the benchmark are impacted by one-time items, such as unit sales or a large expense, and when such items are not expected to recur in the future, for comparability it is recommended to adjust the EPS for such one-time items.
- ■ Impact of business and economic cycle on EPS: Since EPS often has a positive relationship with the business cycle (i.e., EPS is high at the peak of the business cycle and low at the trough of the cycle), P/E ratio has an opposite relationship with the business cycle. In comparative analysis this

countercyclicality of P/E ratio should be considered. One way to overcome this issue is by normalizing the EPS by taking average of historical earnings over a full business cycle and using that as the denominator when calculating the trailing P/E ratio. An alternative way for normalizing EPS is by taking average of historical return on equity (ROE) over a full business cycle and using current book value of equity per share to transfer the result to a normalized EPS.

- Impact of earnings manipulation: Earnings manipulation by firm management, such as a change in the timing of operating cash flows within allowable accounting rules, can impact the quality of reported earnings. This issue should be considered when calculating EPS for the firm or for those included in the benchmark.

Comparison of P/E ratio of a firm to a benchmark comprised of a group of peers is based on the principle that similar assets should have similar prices. The P/E ratio benchmark can be mean or median of P/E ratios of several companies with similar businesses or companies in the same industry or sector. When using a benchmark in comparative analysis it is important to check whether assets in the benchmark group themselves are correctly priced or not.

Example

Assume that the EPSs of XYZ Company for the past four quarters are $2.31, $2.24, $2.15, and $1.99. The current market price of one share is $126.90. The average of the trailing P/E ratios of a group of six companies that are considered peers of XYZ Company is 15.2. An equity analyst believes that the reported EPS and EPS of those firms in the peer group are comparable. The trailing P/E of XYZ is calculated as:

$$P_0/E_0 = \frac{126.9}{2.31 + 2.24 + 2.15 + 1.99} = 14.6$$

By comparing XYZ's P/E ratio of 14.6 versus 15.2 of the peer group the stock is perceived as undervalued.

Comparison of P/E ratio of a firm to its intrinsic value is based on the principle that intrinsic value is supported by the financial fundamentals of the company. A P/E ratio that is above or below the intrinsic ratio is an indication of the stock being overvalued or undervalued. In calculation of the intrinsic value of P/E ratio, some practitioners rely on some form of discounted cash flow model. One method is to use dividend discount model and the Gordon growth model to derive an equation for intrinsic value of P/E ratio. To do so, first note that the approximate relationship between retention rate b, the growth rate of earnings or dividend g, and return on equity can be expressed as:

$$g = ROE \times b \tag{3.22}$$

This equation assumes the capital structure of the firm remains constant over time and it indicates that the approximate growth in earnings is associated with the rate that the earnings is retained and reinvested in the firm. Assuming a constant retention rate, the relationship between dividend yield and retention rate can be expressed as:

$$b = 1 - \frac{D_i}{P_i} \tag{3.23}$$

where D_i is the dividend paid at the end of period i and P_i is the equity value at that time. By changing the notation of current value V_0 to current price P_0 in the Gordon growth model in Equation (3.4), the intrinsic trailing P/E ratio is calculated by dividing both sides of Equation (3.4) by the past one-period earnings E_0 as:

$$\frac{P_0}{E_0} = \frac{\frac{D_0}{E_0}(1+g)}{R-g}$$

where R in this equation is the required rate of return of equity and is equivalent to R_E used in our discussion on the free cash flow analysis. From Equation (3.23) $\frac{D_0}{E_0}$ is equivalent to $1 - b$, so:

$$\frac{P_0}{E_0} = \frac{(1-b)(1+g)}{R-g} \tag{3.24}$$

The intrinsic leading P/E ratio is derived similarly by dividing both sides of Equation (3.5) by forecasted one-period earnings E_1 and replacing $\frac{D_1}{E_1}$ by $1 - b$:

$$\frac{P_0}{E_1} = \frac{1-b}{R-g} \tag{3.25}$$

Example

Consider XYZ Company in the previous example with a trailing P/E ratio of 14.6. Assume the analyst estimates a sustainable earnings growth rate of 5%. Historically the company has a retention rate of 40% and it is believed

(continued)

> (*continued*)
>
> this rate will remain constant at the same level in the future. The required rate of return of equity is 9%. Using (3.24) the intrinsic trailing P/E ratio is calculated as:
>
> $$\frac{P_0}{E_0} = \frac{(1 - 0.4)(1 + 0.05)}{0.09 - 0.05} = 15.75$$
>
> By comparing XYZ's trailing P/E ratio of 14.6 versus its intrinsic value of 15.75, the stock is perceived as undervalued.

Price-to-book value (P/B) is another price ratio that is popular among equity analysts. This ratio is defined as:

$$P/B = \frac{Price\ of\ Equity\ per\ Share}{Book\ Value\ of\ Equity\ per\ Share} \qquad (3.26)$$

Book value of equity is computed by taking the difference between the book value of total assets and the book value of total liabilities. If the company has preferred stock, the book value of the common shareholder equity is obtained by deducting the book value of the preferred stock from the value obtained by netting assets and liabilities. The book value of equity per share is then obtained by dividing the total book value of equity by number of outstanding shares of common equity. Similar to the P/E ratio, when computing and comparing P/B ratios, the book value of equity should be carefully examined for the following issues to ensure the obtained ratios are comparable:

- Impact of accounting practice used on book value of equity: Use of different accounting rules can lead to differences in book value of equity; therefore, it may be necessary to adjust the results to obtain comparable P/B ratios of the firm and the ones used in the benchmark.
- Difference between book value and market value: Depending on the accounting practice used, balance sheet items often are reported at historical or cost basis. Therefore, book values of those items can be substantially different from their market values and this may impact the suitability of the book value of equity. In certain circumstances, it may

be necessary to adjust book values of some balance sheet items to align to their market values and use the adjusted values in calculation of the book value of equity.

- Impact of off-balance-sheet items: For companies with substantial off-balance-sheet activities, for example, financial firms and banks, the values of off-balance-sheet assets and liabilities may need to be included in calculation of the book value of equity.

Similar to the P/E ratio, the P/B ratio can be compared to the average or median of peer group P/B ratios, or to its intrinsic value calculated using a valuation technique, such as discounted cash flow method. When using the Gordon growth model in finding intrinsic value of the P/B ratio, first note that ROE can be expressed based on leading earnings E_1 and current book value of equity B_0 as:

$$ROE = \frac{E_1}{B_0}$$

or

$$E_1 = ROE \times B_0$$

By replacing E_1 in Equation (3.25) with its equivalent from above we have:

$$\frac{P_0}{ROE \times B_0} = \frac{1 - b}{R - g}$$

or

$$\frac{P_0}{B_0} = \frac{ROE \times (1 - b)}{R - g}$$

Also, since $g = ROE \times b$, we have:

$$\frac{P_0}{B_0} = \frac{ROE \times \left(1 - \frac{g}{ROE}\right)}{R - g}$$

or

$$\frac{P_0}{B_0} = \frac{ROE - g}{R - g} \tag{3.27}$$

Example

Assume that a company has total assets of $860 million and total liabilities of $750 million. It has no preferred stock and 5,000,000 outstanding common shares. The book value of equity per share is calculated as:

$$B_0 = \frac{\$860 \ million - \$750 \ million}{5 \ million} = 22.0$$

If current market price of one share is $86.3, the price-to-book value ratio is:

$$\frac{P_0}{B_0} = \frac{86.3}{22.0} = 3.92$$

A peer group of this company consisted of eight firms with similar business and balance sheet structure. Average P/B ratio of the peer group is 2.8. By comparing the P/B ratio of 3.92 with the benchmark value of 2.8, the stock is perceived as overvalued. Assume that the current ROE of the firm is 18% and estimated future growth rate is 5%. The required rate of return of equity is 8.9%. Using Equation (3.27) the intrinsic P/B ratio is calculated as:

$$\frac{P_0}{B_0} = \frac{0.18 - 0.05}{0.089 - 0.05} = 3.33$$

By comparing the P/B ratio of 3.92 versus its intrinsic value of 3.33 the stock is perceived as overvalued.

Price-to-sales (P/S) ratio is another price ratio used by equity analysts. This ratio is defined as:

$$P/S = \frac{Price \ of \ Equity \ per \ Share}{Sales \ per \ Share} \tag{3.28}$$

Sales per share is the total sales for a given period (e.g., during last year) divided by the number of outstanding shares. Similar to P/E and P/B ratios, P/S ratio can be compared to average or median of peer group P/S ratios, or to its intrinsic value obtained using a valuation technique such as discounted cash flow method. If the Gordon growth model is used as the valuation model, the intrinsic P/S ratio is obtained by noting $D_0 = E_0 \times (1 - b)$. By replacing D_0 in Equation (3.4) we have:

$$P_0 = \frac{E_0(1 - b)(1 + g)}{R - g}$$

Dividing both sides of this equation by current sales per share results in:

$$\frac{P_0}{S_0} = \frac{\frac{E_0}{S_0}(1 - b)(1 + g)}{R - g}$$

Since $m_0 = \frac{E_0}{S_0}$ is the current profit margin, we have:

$$\frac{P_0}{S_0} = \frac{m_0(1 - b)(1 + g)}{R - g} \tag{3.29}$$

To evaluate the relative value of the stock, the P/S ratio of the firm calculated from Equation (3.28) can be compared either to mean or median of its peer group P/S ratios, or its intrinsic value obtained from Equation (3.29).

SUMMARY

- The value of equity of a company is the difference between total value of its assets and total value of its liabilities.
- A common stock represents an ownership interest in the equity of a company.
- Dividend is distribution of part of the periodic profit earned by a company to its shareholders.
- Retained earnings is the part of the periodic profit earned by a company that has not been distributed as dividend.
- If a stock share is purchased on the ex-dividend date or after, the buyer will not receive the next dividend payment and it goes to the seller.
- In the dividend discount model the intrinsic value of equity is obtained by finding the present value of its expected future dividend payments.

- The Gordon growth model is a special implementation of dividend discount model based on assumption of a constant growth rate of future dividend.
- In a multi-stage dividend discount model different growth rates are assumed for different periods.
- The discounted free cash flow method for valuation of equity is based on estimating true expected cash flows generated by the firm that are available to all stakeholders and then discounting them using an appropriate discount rate.
- Free cash flow to firm is the cash flow available to the equity and debt holders. Free cash flow to equity is the cash flow available to the equity holders only.
- Weighted average cost of capital is the minimum rate of return required by all equity and debt investors.
- Cost of equity is the required rate of return by equity investors.
- Cost of debt is the required rate of return by debt investors.
- In derivation of the weighted average cost of capital, market values of equity and debt should be used and not their book values.
- When using free cash flow to firm for valuation of equity, the appropriate discount rate is the weighted average cost of capital and when free cash flow to equity is used, required rate of return on equity is the appropriate discount rate.
- Price-to-earnings ratio is the price of equity per share divided by earnings per share for a specific period. Current or trailing P/E ratio is calculated by dividing the current stock price by earnings per share in the past one year. Forward or leading P/E ratio is calculated by dividing the current stock price by forecasted earnings per share for the next one year.
- Price-to-book value ratio is the price of equity per share divided by the book value of equity per share.
- Price-to-sales ratio is the price of equity per share divided by sales per share for a specific period.

NOTE

1. A simple case of geometric series is when the ratio of two consecutive terms is a constant ratio γ. When $|\gamma| < 1$ the sum of the infinite geometric series is a finite value: $a + a\gamma + a\gamma^2 + a\gamma^3 + \cdots = \sum_{i=0}^{\infty} a\gamma^i = \frac{a}{1-\gamma}$. Setting $a = \frac{D_0(1+g)}{1+R}$ and $\gamma = \frac{1+g}{1+R}$ provides us with Equation (3.4).

BIBLIOGRAPHY

Brealey, Richard A., Stewart C. Myers, and Franklin Allen. *Principles of Corporate Finance*, 12th ed. McGraw-Hill/Irwin, 2016.

Gordon, Myron J., and Eli Shapiro. "Capital Equipment Analysis: The Required Rate of Profit." *Management Science* 3, no. 1 (1956): 102–110.

Ross, Stephen, Randolph Westerfield, and Bradford Jordan. *Essentials of Corporate Finance*, 7th ed. McGraw-Hill/Irwin, 2010.

Williams, John Burr. *The Theory of Investment Value*. Cambridge, MA: Harvard University Press, 1938.

Option Valuation

A n *option* is a class of financial contract whose value depends on the value of another financial instrument. The underlying instrument or element (e.g., interest rate) is usually called the *reference* or *underlying*. An option contract provides its owner with the right, but not the obligation, to take an action within some contractually specified parameters for a specific period of time in the future. For example, the action could be buying an asset at a certain price. Similar to other financial contracts, each option contract has two sides: one side buys the right to take the contractually specified action within a given time, commonly referred to as the *long* side, while the other side sells the right to the buyer and is contractually obligated to abide by the action taken by the buyer. This side is commonly referred to as the *short* side. Depending on the type of option contract, a premium may or may not be paid by the long side to the short side at the contract inception time. Taking the action granted by the option contract is commonly referred to as *exercising the option*. The contractual price in an option is known as the *strike price* or *exercise price*, the period of time that the contract is binding is known as the *term*, and the date when the contract ends is the *maturity* or *expiration date*. In an *American option* the holder may exercise the option at any day or some specific dates during the term of the contract. In the *European option* the holder can exercise the option only at the maturity date.

The most common option contract type grants one side the right to buy the underlying asset and the other side the right to sell the asset. Therefore, depending on the point of view of the side of the contract, there are two types of options. A *call option* provides the holder the right, but not the obligation, to buy the underlying asset at a given price and for a specified time period. A *put option* provides the holder the right, but not the obligation, to sell the underlying asset at a given price and for a specified time period.

Historically, options were over-the-counter contracts and traded bilaterally between counterparties. After the financial crisis of 2007–2009 and the subsequent increase in regulatory oversight, most option types are now traded through exchange organizations with adequate margin requirements. *Margin* is the cash (or high-quality securities like government bonds, if allowed by the

237

exchange) that an option seller or buyer places with the exchange to guarantee the fulfillment of the contract in the future.

Option contracts can be classified based on the type of their underlying asset. The most well-known option contract is probably the stock option, where the underlying asset is the common stock. In the following sections we focus our discussion on the stock option and its valuation. Many fundamentals of the stock option and its valuation methods are applicable to other option types. Later in this chapter we discuss options on futures contracts. Options on interest rate are discussed in a later chapter when we introduce interest rate models. The value of an option contract depends on the volatility of the underlying. In this chapter we introduce a few methods for derivation of volatility and introduce a popular approach in modeling non-constant volatility.

STOCK OPTION

A stock call option provides the buyer of the contract with the right to purchase a certain number of shares of a company's stock at a given price and for a specified time period. Assume that an investor purchases a European call option on 100 shares of XYZ Company at a strike price of $45 per share, for a premium of $100 for the entire contact. Current market price of a share of XYZ is $44.20. The option term is six months. Since the option is European, the option holder can exercise the contract only at the maturity date, that is, six months from the contract inception date. At the maturity date, two cases are possible:

- First, assume that the price of one share of XYZ Company at the option maturity date is $47.30. Since the market price is above the strike price of $45, it is beneficial to the option holder to exercise the contract and buy 100 shares of XYZ at $45. The seller of the call option contract is obligated to sell at a strike price of $45, even though the market price is above $45. After exercising the option, if shares are sold immediately in the market, the option buyer side can earn a payout of $100 \times (47.3 - 45) = \$230$ at the maturity date. To calculate the profit to the buyer of this call option, the premium cost of the contract, adjusted for the time value of the money, as well as the transaction costs should be deducted from this payout.
- Second, assume that the price of one share of XYZ Company at the option maturity date is $41.10. Since the market price is below the strike price, it is not beneficial to the option holder to exercise the contract; therefore, she would let it expire without exercising it. The loss to the buyer of this call option is the premium cost, adjusted for the time value of the money.

The choice held by the buyer of the call option in not exercising the contract is what differentiates an option contract from forward or futures contracts, where execution is required. Generally, the buyer of a call option expects the price of the stock to increase over the term of the contract, reaching a level sufficiently above the strike price to have a positive payoff and a profit.

A stock put option provides the buyer of the contract with the right to sell a certain number of shares of a specific stock at a given price and for a specified time period. Consider again the stock of XYZ Company and assume that an investor purchases a European put option on 100 shares of XYZ Company at a strike price of $43 per share, for a premium of $120 for the entire contract. The option term is six months. At the maturity date, two cases can happen:

- First, assume that the price of one share of XYZ Company at the option maturity date is $47.30. Since the market price is above the strike price of $43, it is not beneficial to the put option holder to exercise the contract and she would let it expire without exercising it. The loss to the buyer of the put option is the premium cost, adjusted for the time value of money.
- Second, assume that the price of one share of XYZ Company at the option maturity date is $41.10. Since the market price is below the strike price of $43, it is beneficial to the option holder to exercise the contract and sell 100 shares of XYZ at $43. The seller of the put option contract is obligated to buy at a strike price of $43, even though the market price is below $43. At the maturity date, the buyer of this put option can buy $100 shares of XYZ at open market at the market price of $41.10 per share and sell them to the seller of the put option at $43 per share, hence earning a payout of $100 \times (43 - 41.1) = \$190$ at the maturity date. To calculate the profit to the buyer of this put option, the premium cost of the contract, adjusted for the time value of the money, as well as the transaction costs should be deducted from this payout.

Generally, the buyer of a put option expects the price of the stock to decrease over the term of the contract, reaching a level sufficiently lower than the strike price to have a positive payoff and a profit. If the call and put options discussed in the previous examples were American instead of European, the holder of the option could exercise it at any time during the six-month term of the contract. This would give more flexibility to the option holder in deciding the timing of the exercise and exiting the contract.

From this discussion it should be clear that the value of an option contract depends on the value of the underlying. To value an option, first we need to define its payoff. The payoff of an option can be determined by noting the condition that makes exercising it profitable to the holder of the contract.

Assuming the underlying stock pays no dividend during the term of option, and ignoring the premium paid at the inception and the transaction cost, the payoff to the buyer of a European call option (the *long* position on the call option) at the maturity date T is:

$$\text{Payoff}_{T:\text{ Long European Call}} = \text{Max}(S_T - X, 0) \tag{4.1}$$

where S_T is the price of underlying stock at the maturity date of the contract and X is the contractual strike price. The payoff to the seller of a European call option (the *short* position on the call option) at the maturity date is:

$$\text{Payoff}_{T:\text{ Short European Call}} = -\text{Payoff}_{T:\text{ Long European Call}} = \text{Min}(X - S_T, 0) \tag{4.2}$$

Similarly, the payoff to the buyer of a European put option (the long position on the put option) at the maturity date T is:

$$\text{Payoff}_{T:\text{ Long European Put}} = \text{Max}(X - S_T, 0) \tag{4.3}$$

And the payoff to the seller of a European put option (the short position on the put option) at the maturity date is obtained as:

$$\text{Payoff}_{T:\text{ Short European Put}} = -\text{Payoff}_{T:\text{ Long European Put}} = \text{Min}(S_T - X, 0) \tag{4.4}$$

Equations (4.1) through (4.4) also provide the payoff of a long or short position on an American call or put option but only at the maturity date. A call option is *in-the-money* when $S_T > X$, *out-of-the-money* when $S_T < X$, and *at-the-money* when $S_T = X$. A put option is in-the-money when $S_T < X$, out-of-the-money when $S_T > X$, and at-the-money when $S_T = X$.

Stock option contracts are usually written on 100 shares of the underlying stock. For simplicity, in this chapter we assume that an option contract is based on one share of the underlying stock. The option value derived based on one share can be adjusted for the total number of underlying shares in the contract by multiplying it by the number of shares.

BOUNDARY VALUES

Before we start our discussion on valuation of stock options, it is helpful to find some limits around the option value. To establish these limits, first we need to discuss the concept of the risk-free rate. The *risk-free rate* is the interest rate that an investor can expect to earn on an investment that carries no risk. While in practice any investment can carry some level of risk, usually an investment in government securities, such as U.S. Treasury bills, is considered a risk-free investment and the yield on such investment is assumed as the risk-free rate. The concept of risk-free rate is widely used in quantitative finance and many analytical techniques, including option valuation models, rely on it.

Developing a closed-form expression for option value limits depends on the option type and whether the underlying stock pays any dividend during the term of the option. First assume that there is no dividend payment during the term of the option. The limits we establish in the following section are for a long position on the option. In this section we also make the following additional assumptions:

- An investor can buy or sell options on stock without any restriction.
- Transaction costs, tax considerations, and the impact of a margin requirement are not included in the analysis.
- An investor can lend or borrow at the risk-free rate without any restriction.
- An investor can buy or sell a whole or a fraction of a share.

In the following sections option values are specified from the point of view of a long position holder, unless otherwise stated.

Call Option

Since a call option provides its holder with the right to buy a stock, logically its current value (V_0) cannot be greater than the current value of the stock itself, regardless of whether it is a European or American option. So:

$$V_{0:European\ Call} \leq S_0 \qquad (4.5)$$

$$V_{0:American\ Call} \leq S_0 \qquad (4.6)$$

To find upper bound for a call option, consider the following two portfolios:

Portfolio (I): A long position on a European call option on one share of a stock, plus a cash amount equal to $Xe^{-r_f T}$, where X is the strike price of the call option contract, r_f is the annualized risk-free rate with continuous compounding, and T is the term of the option, in years.

Portfolio (II): A long position on one share of the stock (the same stock as the underlying of the call option in portfolio (I) above).

At time $t = 0$:

- The cost (current value) of acquiring portfolio (I) includes the value of option $V_{0:European\ Call}$ and the cash amount of $e^{-r_f T}$.
- The cost of portfolio (II) is the price of stock S_0.

At time $t = T$:

- The cash in portfolio (I) is invested at risk-free rate r_f. Therefore, at $t = T$ it has value of X. The value of the option in portfolio (I) depends on whether the call option is in-the-money or out-of-the-money:
  - If $S_T > X$, the option is exercised and one share of stock is acquired for a payment equal to X, which is obtained from the cash investment, so the value of portfolio (I) is equal to the value of stock S_T.
  - If $S_T < X$, the option is not exercised and expires with no value, so the value of portfolio (I) is X.
    Therefore the value of portfolio (I) at $t = T$ is Max(X, S_T).
- The value of portfolio (II) at $t = T$ is the value of stock at time S_T.

From this it is clear that the value at $t = T$ of portfolio (I) is always greater than or equal to the value of portfolio (II). Based on an arbitrage-free argument, the cost or value at $t = 0$ of portfolio (I) should also be greater than or equal to the cost of portfolio (II). So:

$$V_{0:\ European\ Call} + Xe^{-r_f T} \geq S_0$$

By rearranging, and since the value of the long position on an option cannot be negative, we have:

$$V_{0:\ European\ Call} \geq \text{Max}(0, S_0 - Xe^{-r_f T}) \tag{4.7}$$

In an arbitrage-free environment, the value of an American call option cannot be less than Max$(0, S_0 - X)$, since if the value of an in-the-money American call option is less than $S_0 - X$, it can be bought and exercised immediately for a net profit. Hence, for the value of an American call option, a lower bound is Max$(0, S_0 - X)$. At the same time, since an American call option provides the holder with the ability to exercise it earlier than the maturity date, which is an extra feature compared to a European option, its value must be at least equal to a comparable European call option. Therefore, the lower bound obtained in Equation (4.7) for the European call option is also a lower bound for an American call option:

$$V_{0:\ American\ Call} \geq \text{Max}(0, S_0 - Xe^{-r_f T}) \tag{4.8}$$

Put Option

Since a put option provides its holder with the right to sell a stock at the strike price, logically its current value cannot be greater than the strike price. For an American put option, which can be exercised at any time until the maturity date, the strike price is the upper bound, but for a European put option, which can only be exercised at the maturity date and hence the maximum value of the strike price can be achieved only at the maturity date, the upper bound at the current time is the present value of the strike price. So:

$$V_{0:\ European\ Put} \le Xe^{-r_f T} \tag{4.9}$$

$$V_{0:\ American\ Put} \le X \tag{4.10}$$

To find the upper bound for a put option, consider the following two portfolios:

Portfolio (I): A long position on a European put option on one share of a stock, plus a long position on one share of the stock. This combination sometimes is referred to as a *protective put* since the put option acts like an insurance when the stock price declines below the strike price.

Portfolio (II): Cash amount equal to $Xe^{-r_f T}$.

At time $t = 0$:

- The cost (current value) of acquiring portfolio (I) includes the value of option $V_{0:\ European\ Put}$ and the value of stock S_0.
- The cost of portfolio (II) is the cash value of $Xe^{-r_f T}$.

At time $t = T$:

- The value of portfolio (I) at $t = T$ depends on whether the put option is in-the-money or out-of-the-money:
  - If $S_T > X$, the option is not exercised and expires with no value, so the value of portfolio (I) is equal to the value of stock S_T.
  - If $S_T < X$, the option is exercised and one share of stock is sold for X, so the value of portfolio (I) is X.
        Therefore, the value of portfolio (I) at $t = T$ is $Max(X, S_T)$.
- The cash in portfolio (II) is invested at risk-free rate r_f. Therefore, the value of portfolio (II) at $t = T$ is X.

From this, it is clear that the value of portfolio (I) at $t = T$ is always greater than or equal to the value of portfolio (II). Therefore, in an arbitrage-free environment, the cost or value at $t = 0$ of portfolio (I) should also be greater than or equal to the cost of portfolio (II). So:

$$V_{0: European\ Put} + S_0 \geq Xe^{-r_f T}$$

By rearranging, and since the value of a long position on an option cannot be negative, we have:

$$V_{0: European\ Put} \geq Max(0, Xe^{-r_f T} - S_0) \tag{4.11}$$

In an arbitrage-free environment, the value of an American put option cannot be less than $Max(0, X - S_0)$, since if the value of an in-the-money American put option is less than $X - S_0$, it can be bought and exercised immediately for a net profit. Hence, for the value of an American put option, a lower bound is $Max(0, X - S_0)$. Since an American put option provides the holder with the ability to exercise it earlier than the maturity date, which is an extra feature compared to a European option, its value must be greater than or equal to a comparable European put option. Also note that $Max(0, X - S_0)$ is higher than $Max(0, Xe^{-r_f T} - S_0)$. Therefore:

$$V_{0: American\ Put} \geq Max(0, X - S_0) \tag{4.12}$$

To summarize, we have found the following boundaries for the value of a long position on a European or American call or put option when the underlying pays no dividend:

	European		American	
	Lower Bound	**Upper Bound**	**Lower Bound**	**Upper Bound**
Call	$Max(0, S_0 - Xe^{-r_f T})$	S_0	$Max(0, S_0 - Xe^{-r_f T})$	S_0
Put	$Max(0, Xe^{-r_f T} - S_0)$	$Xe^{-r_f T}$	$Max(0, X - S_0)$	X

As mentioned earlier, since the American option provides the extra feature of possible early exercise compared to the European option, it is logical to think that the value of the American option should be greater than or equal to the comparable European option. While this is true, we also have to evaluate whether exercising of an option early is an optimal decision for the option holder. Consider an American call option. If an option holder is planning to hold the stock after the term of the option and the stock does not pay any dividend during the option term, it is not an optimal decision to exercise an American call option earlier than its maturity date. To see the logic behind this, consider the case in which an American call option holder exercises the option earlier than its maturity at time $t = \tau < T$. Note that when the option holder exercises the call option, she should pay strike price X to buy the stock. So as soon as the option is exercised and X is paid out, the option holder has forgone the interest she could have earned by investing X in a risk-free interest-bearing account for the duration of $T - \tau$ while the stock she bought could have been acquired at any time from τ to T at the same price of X. Therefore, from a time value of money perspective, if exercise is beneficial, it is more valuable for an American call option holder to exercise and pay the strike price at the latest time that is possible, that is, at the option maturity.

Another reason for not exercising an American call option earlier than its maturity date is related to the insurance that the call option provides to its holder. A call option can be considered to be insurance against the fall of a stock price below the strike price. Consider an American call option, where the underlying stock price is $50 and the strike price is $40. The option has two months remaining on its term. If the holder exercises the option now and acquires one share of stock for $40 and then the stock price later drops to $30, she suffers a financial loss. However, if she was holding the call option and not exercising it, she would not incur a loss when the stock price drops to $30. Therefore, it is more beneficial to the holder of an American call option to hold the option rather than the stock itself to take advantage of the insurance it provides. Once the option is exercised, this insurance is gone.

Based on this discussion and when the underlying stock pays no dividend during the term of the option, early exercise of an American call option is not optimal. Hence, in this case, the value of an American call option is *equal to* the value of the comparable European call option.

For an American put option, it may be beneficial to its holder to exercise earlier than the option maturity date. If the option is sufficiently in-the-money, exercising the put option prior to its maturity can be an optimal decision. To demonstrate, consider an extreme case for an American put option when the underlying stock price is very close to $0 while the strike price is $8. In such a condition, if the option holder exercises, she can have a gain of close to $8. Since stock price cannot become negative, the gain cannot exceed $8, but it can decrease if stock price increases. Thus, in this case it is optimal for the holder to exercise early. Also, although holding an American put option when combined with holding the stock itself is insurance against the stock price falling below the strike price, it may be optimal to exercise early and forgo this insurance. As an example, consider again the extreme case when the strike price is $8 and the stock price is near $0. In such a case it is beneficial to the holder to exercise the option and gain the $8, since the insurance from the put option is no longer effective.

Based on this discussion and when the underlying stock pays no dividend during the term of the option, early exercise of an American put option can be optimal. Hence, in this case, the value of an American put option is *equal to or greater than* the value of the comparable European put option.

When the underlying stock pays dividends during the term of the option, for both American call and put options, it can be beneficial to exercise them earlier than the maturity date. The holder of an American call option may exercise the option immediately before the ex-dividend date to get the dividend payment by owning the stock. However, the amount of dividend influences the optimality of the decision to exercise the option early. Therefore, when the underlying stock pays dividends during the term of the option, the value of an American call or put option is *equal to or greater than* its comparable European call or put option.

For the case when the underlying stock pays dividends during the term of the option, we can find a closed-form expression for the lower bounds of European call and put options. First, assume that dividend payments are in the form of distinct cash flows that are certain or highly probable, and can be predicted with high accuracy. This is often a valid assumption since stock options usually have a short term (e.g., six months) and the expected dividend during this short term can be predicted based on the most recent dividend payment, the state of the economy, and the company's past and expected future earnings. We can use a similar method to the one explained earlier to obtain these limits, but in this case the current price of a stock should be adjusted for the present value of the expected dividend payments. Assume that $V_{0:\,Dividend}$ is the present value of all expected dividend payments during the term of the option. The lower bounds for a long position on a European call and a European put option are as follows (Hull 2005):

$$V_{0:\,European\ Call} \geq \mathrm{Max}(0, S_0 - V_{0:\,Dividend} - Xe^{-r_f T}) \tag{4.13}$$

$$V_{0:\,European\ Put} \geq \mathrm{Max}(0, Xe^{-r_f T} - S_0 + V_{0:\,Dividend}) \tag{4.14}$$

These two equations are similar to Equations (4.7) and (4.11) but the current value of stock is adjusted for the present value of expected dividends.

If dividend payments are assumed to be in the form of a continuous dividend yield q, where q is presented with continuous compounding, by replacing S_0 with $S_0 e^{-qT}$ and adjusting Equations (4.7) and (4.11) the lower bound for a long position on a European call and a European put option are obtained as (Hull 2005):

$$V_{0:\,European\ Call} \geq \mathrm{Max}(0, S_0 e^{-qT} - Xe^{-r_f T}) \tag{4.15}$$

$$V_{0:\,European\ Put} \geq \mathrm{Max}(0, Xe^{-r_f T} - S_0 e^{-qT}) \tag{4.16}$$

PUT–CALL PARITY

So far in our discussions about options, we have focused on put and call options separately. *Put–call parity* is an identity that defines a relationship between values of comparable call and put options. The strike prices, terms, and underlying stocks of comparable put and call options are the same. To establish this relationship, we consider two cases: when the underlying stock pays no dividend during the term of options, and when it does pay a dividend. Then, for each case we find the relationship between European put and call options and American put and call options separately.

Underlying Stock Does Not Pay Dividends

First consider a non-dividend-paying stock and put and call options that are both European. To establish the put–call parity, consider the following two portfolios:

> *Portfolio (I):* A long position on a European call option on one share of a stock, plus a cash amount equal to $e^{-r_f T}$.
>
> *Portfolio (II):* A long position on a European put option on one share of the stock, plus a long position on one share of the stock (the same stock as in portfolio (I) above).

At time $t = 0$:

- The cost (current value) of portfolio (I) includes the value of the call option $V_{0:\,European\,Call}$ and the cash value of $e^{-r_f T}$.
- Cost of portfolio (II) includes the value of the put option $V_{0:\,European\,Put}$ and value of the stock S_0.

At time $t = T$:

- The cash in portfolio (I) is invested at risk-free rate r_f. Therefore, at $t = T$ it has a value of X. The value of the option in portfolio (I) depends on whether the call option is in-the-money or out-of-the-money:
    - If $S_T > X$, the option is exercised and one share of stock is acquired for a payment equal to X, which is obtained from the cash investment, so the value of portfolio (I) is equal to the value of stock S_T.
    - If $S_T < X$, the option is not exercised and expires with no value, so the value of portfolio (I) is X.
      Therefore, the value of portfolio (I) at $t = T$ is $\text{Max}(X, S_T)$.
- The value of portfolio (II) at $t = T$ depends on whether the put option is in-the-money or out-of-the-money:
    - If $S_T > X$, the option is not exercised and expires with no value, so the value of portfolio (II) is equal to the value of stock S_T.

- If $S_T < X$, the option is exercised and one share of stock is sold for X, so the value of portfolio (II) is X.

    Therefore the value of portfolio (II) at $t = T$ is $\text{Max}(X, S_T)$.

Since the values of portfolios (I) and (II) at $t = T$ are both equal to $\text{Max}(X, S_T)$, based on an arbitrage-free argument, their values at $t = 0$ should also be the same. So:

$$V_{0:\,European\ Call} + Xe^{-r_f T} = V_{0:\,European\ Put} + S_0 \qquad (4.17)$$

This identity is the put–call parity for European options when the underlying pays no dividends during the term of the options. If this relationship does not hold, an arbitrage opportunity exists.

Example

To demonstrate the arbitrage opportunity when put–call parity does not hold, consider a stock with a current price of $44.20. A European call option and a European put option are written on this stock. Both options have a strike price of $45 with terms of six months. Assume that the current price of the put option for one share is $2 and the current price of the call option for one share is $3. Also assume that the continuous compounding annualized risk-free rate is 3%. The left-hand side of the put–call parity in Equation (4.17) is equivalent to:

$$V_{0:\,European\ Call} + Xe^{-r_f T} = 3 + 45 \times e^{-0.03 \times 0.5} = 47.33$$

The right-hand side of the put–call parity in Equation (4.17) is equivalent to:

$$V_{0:\,European\ Put} + S_0 = 2 + 44.2 = 46.2$$

Since the put–call parity does not hold, an arbitrage opportunity exists. Because the right-hand side of the put–call parity is lower than the left-hand side, it is perceived that the portfolio on the left-hand side is overvalued and the one on the right-hand side is undervalued. To take advantage of the arbitrage opportunity, one strategy is to short the overvalued portfolio on the left-hand side and long the undervalued portfolio on the right-hand side:

At time $t = 0$:

- Short (sell) the call option for $3.
- Borrow $43.20 at a risk-free rate of 3%.

- Long (buy) the put option at a cost of $2.
- Long (buy) the stock at the cost of $44.20.

  Total cost at $t = 0$ is $3 + $43.20 − $2 − $44.20 = $0.
  At time $t = 0.5$:

- If $S_T > X$:
  - The call option will be exercised; use one share of stock when the counterparty exercises the option and receive $X = $45.
  - Repay the borrowed amount, which at a rate of 3% is equal to $43.2 \times e^{0.03 \times 0.5} = 43.85 at $t = 0.5$.
  - Let the put option expire without exercising it.

  The net profit at $t = 0.5$ is $45 − $43.85 = $1.15.

- If $S_T < X$:
  - The call option will not be exercised.
  - Repay the borrowed amount, which at a rate of 3% is equal to $43.2 \times e^{0.03 \times 0.5} = 43.85 at $t = 0.5$.
  - Exercise the put option; sell one share of stock through the option for $X = $45.

  The net profit at $t = 0.5$ is $45 − $43.85 = $1.15.
  As noted earlier, no matter what the price of stock at the maturity date is, this strategy provides a positive risk-free return. In practice, trading activities of market participants erode the existence of such arbitrage opportunities and the market returns to an arbitrage-free state quickly.

The put–call parity identity only holds for European options. For American options when the underlying stock pays no dividend, the put–call parity has the form of an inequality (Hull 2005). To establish this inequality, consider the following two portfolios, where all options have the same strike price, term, and underlying stock:

Portfolio (I): A long position on a European call option on one share of a stock, plus a cash amount equal to X.

Portfolio (II): A long position on an American put option on one share of the stock, plus a long position on one share of the stock.

At time $t = 0$:

- The cost (current value) of portfolio (I) includes the value of the European call option $V_{0: European\ Call}$ and a cash value of X.

- The cost of portfolio (II) includes the value of the American put option $V_{0:\ American\ Put}$ and the value of the stock S_0.

At time $0 < t \leq T$:

- The cash in portfolio (I) is invested at risk-free rate r_f and at $t = T$ it has a value of $e^{r_f T}$. Therefore, value of the portfolio at the option maturity date is $\text{Max}(S_T - X, 0) + X e^{r_f T}$. Since stock and strike prices are positive numbers, we can express the value of portfolio (I) at $t = T$ as $\text{Max}(S_T, X) - X + X e^{r_f T}$.
- The value of portfolio (II) depends on whether the American put option is exercised early or not:
  - If the American put option is not exercised early, it is equivalent to a European put option and portfolio (II) is identical to portfolio (II) that was used when the put–call parity for European option is established, so the value of portfolio (II) at $t = T$ is $\text{Max}(S_T, X)$. By a comparison of portfolio (I) and (II) values, it is clear that the value of portfolio (I) is greater than or equal to the value of portfolio (II).
  - If the American put option is exercised early, say at a time $t = \tau < T$, the value of portfolio (II) at that time is X but the value of portfolio (I), even if the call option has no value, is at least $X e^{r_f \tau}$, which is greater than the value of portfolio (II) when $r_f > 0$.

From this, it is clear that, whether the American put option is exercised early or not, the value of portfolio (I) is greater than or equal to the value of portfolio (II). So, based on the arbitrage-free argument, the cost of portfolio (I) should be greater than or equal to the cost of portfolio (II):

$$V_{0:\ European\ Call} + X \geq V_{0:\ American\ Put} + S_0$$

As explained in the previous section, in the absence of dividend payments from the underlying stock, exercising an American call option early is not an optimal decision. Hence, the value of the American and European call options should be the same. So:

$$V_{0:\ American\ Call} + X \geq V_{0:\ American\ Put} + S_0$$

or

$$V_{0:\ American\ Call} - V_{0:\ American\ Put} \geq S_0 - X \qquad (4.18)$$

Also, since exercising an American put option early may be an optimal decision, the value of the American put option is greater than or equal to the value of the comparable European put option:

$$V_{0:\ American\ Put} \geq V_{0:\ European\ Put}$$

By replacing $V_{0:\ European\ Put}$ with its equivalent from the put–call parity in Equation (4.17) we have:

$$V_{0:\ American\ Put} \geq V_{0:\ European\ Call} + Xe^{-r_f T} - S_0$$

And since the values of the American and European call options are the same, we have:

$$V_{0:\ American\ Put} \geq V_{0:\ American\ Call} + Xe^{-r_f T} - S_0$$

or

$$V_{0:\ American\ Call} - V_{0:\ American\ Put} \leq S_0 - Xe^{-r_f T} \qquad (4.19)$$

By combining inequalities (4.18) and (4.19) we have:

$$S_0 - X \leq V_{0:\ American\ Call} - V_{0:\ American\ Put} \leq S_0 - Xe^{-r_f T} \qquad (4.20)$$

This inequality presents the relationship between values of American call and put options when the underlying stock pays no dividend during the term of options.

Underlying Stock Pays Dividends or Provides Yield

To establish put–call parity when the underlying stock pays dividends, consider the case where dividend payments are in the form of distinct cash flows during the term of the options and they can be forecasted with high accuracy. Assume that the present value of all dividends during the term of the options is $V_{0:Div}$. In this case, and using a similar approach discussed earlier, for European options the put–call parity is derived as:

$$V_{0:\ European\ Call} + Xe^{-r_f T} + V_{0:Div} = V_{0:\ European\ Put} + S_0 \qquad (4.21)$$

Also, for this case the inequality that captures the relationship between the values of the American put and call options is:

$$S_0 - X - V_{0:Div} \leq V_{0:\ American\ Call} - V_{0:\ American\ Put} \leq S_0 - Xe^{-r_f T} \qquad (4.22)$$

Generally, if the underlying asset provides a continuous yield q, where q is presented with continuous compounding, the put–call parity for the European options and the corresponding inequality for the American options are as follows:

$$V_{0:\ European\ Call} + Xe^{-r_f T} = V_{0:\ European\ Put} + S_0 e^{-qT} \qquad (4.23)$$

$$S_0 e^{-qT} - X \leq V_{0:\ American\ Call} - V_{0:\ American\ Put} \leq S_0 - Xe^{-r_f T} \qquad (4.24)$$

Annex 1 of this chapter provides the derivation of the above relationships. To summarize, the put–call parity for the European options and the counterparty inequality for the American options are as follows:

	Asset Pays No Dividend	Asset Pays Dividend Cash Flow	Asset Provides Continuous Yield
European Options	$V_{0:\,Call} + Xe^{-r_f T}$ $= V_{0:\,Put} + S_0$	$V_{0:\,Call} + Xe^{-r_f T} +$ $V_{0:\,Div} = V_{0:\,Put} + S_0$	$V_{0:\,Call} + Xe^{-r_f T}$ $= V_{0:\,Put} + S_0 e^{-qT}$
American Options	$S_0 - X \leq$ $V_{0:\,Call} - V_{0:\,Put}$ $\leq S_0 - Xe^{-r_f T}$	$S_0 - X - V_{0:\,Div}$ $\leq V_{0:\,Call} - V_{0:\,Put}$ $\leq S_0 - Xe^{-r_f T}$	$S_0 e^{-qT} - X$ $\leq V_{0:\,Call} - V_{0:\,Put}$ $\leq S_0 - Xe^{-r_f T}$

BINOMIAL TREE

The value of a stock option depends on the value of the underlying stock. Due to this dependency and the conditional nature of the option payoff, the simple discounted cash flow method is not a suitable method for the valuation of options. Generally, there are two approaches for option valuation. One is based on dividing the time to maturity of the option into discrete intervals and estimating the option value at discrete points in time; the other approach is based on modeling the evolution of option value as a continuous-time process. In this section we introduce the *binomial tree*, which is a discrete-time approach for option valuation, and in the following section we study a continuous-time model.

The binomial tree method is based on dividing the term of the option into several equal-size time periods and creating a tree-like structure, consisting of several nodes located at the borders of these time intervals. Then we estimate option value at each of these nodes, considering the relationship between values at adjacent nodes. The binomial tree method can be used for valuation of put and call options, as well as both European and American option types. It can also be used for valuation of options when the underlying stock pays dividends. The binomial tree method finds the value of an option in relationship to the value of the underlying stock, hence movement of the underlying value in the future is important in this method. Fundamentals of the binomial tree method were first introduced by Cox, Ross, and Rubinstein (1979). Here we explain the implementation of this method as outlined by Hull (2005).

To start our discussion, first consider the case where the entire term of the option is one time period and the underlying stock pays no dividend during this period. If we use Δt to indicate the length of this period, and as before T is the term of the option, in a one-period binomial tree $\Delta t = T$. The first step in constructing the tree is to decide how the value of the underlying stock changes between the beginning and ending points of this time period. In the binomial tree method we assume that there are only two possibilities for the stock price to change during a time period: it is either increased by a percentage or decreased by another percentage. For example, if the stock price at the beginning of the period is \$44.20, we may assume that stock over the next six months either increases by 10% or decreases by 10%.[1] Thus, the stock price at the end of six months is either $44.2 \times (1 + 0.10) = 48.62$ or $44.2 \times (1 - 0.10) = 39.78$. For ease of reference, here we use u to indicate the upward movement multiplier (i.e., $1 + 0.10 = 1.10$ in this example) and d to indicate the downward movement multiplier (i.e., $1 - 0.10 = 0.90$ in this example). So if the current stock price is S_0, at the end of the period the stock price is either up to $S_u = S_0 \times u$ or down to $S_d = S_0 \times d$. Assume that the value of an option at the beginning of a period is V_0. At the end of the period when stock is at S_u, the option value is V_u and when the stock price is at S_d, the option value is V_d. Figure 4.1 presents a schematic view of the change in the underlying stock price and option value in a one-period binomial tree. It should be noted that the binomial tree, as a discrete-time model, is only concerned with the stock and option values at the beginning and ending points of the time period and not between these two points.

Values of the option at two nodes at the ending point of the time interval (nodes B and C in Figure 4.1) are available from the payoff of the option, which

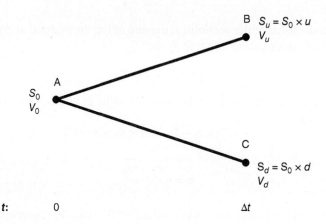

FIGURE 4.1 A one-period binomial tree

depends on the price of the stock at each node and option type. If the strike price is X, the values of a call option at these two nodes are $V_u = \text{Max}(S_u - X, 0)$ and $V_d = \text{Max}(S_d - X, 0)$ and for a put option they are $V_u = \text{Max}(X - S_u, 0)$ and $V_d = \text{Max}(X - S_d, 0)$.

To find the current value of the option V_0 using the one-period binomial tree in Figure 4.1, we base our derivation on the following arguments. First, if a portfolio consisted of a combination of the underlying stock and the option contract is constructed such that the values of the portfolio in both nodes B and C (up and down states) are equal, then the portfolio is riskless, since regardless of whether the stock price increases to node B or decreases to node C the investor has the same return. Second, we consider an arbitrage-free market where any possible arbitrage opportunity is quickly eliminated by actions of market participants. In an arbitrage-free market a riskless portfolio earns the risk-free rate. Therefore, to find the current option value, we first establish the riskless portfolio and find its value at the end of the time period using the known option value at nodes B and C. Then by comparing the discounted value of this portfolio with the cost of establishing the portfolio at $t = 0$ we can find the current value of the option.

Assume that a portfolio consists of a long position on n shares of a stock and a short position on one option on the same underlying stock. The value of the portfolio at $t = 0$ (the cost of establishing the portfolio) is:

$$n \times S_0 - V_0$$

The value of the portfolio at the end of the time period at node B, that is, when the stock moves up to S_u, is:

$$n \times S_0 \times u - V_u$$

And the value of the portfolio at the end of the time period at node C, that is, when the stock moves down to S_d, is:

$$n \times S_0 \times d - V_d$$

To have a riskless portfolio the portfolio value at nodes B and C should be equal, so:

$$n \times S_0 \times u - V_u = n \times S_0 \times d - V_d$$

or

$$n = \frac{V_u - V_d}{S_0(u - d)} \tag{4.25}$$

In Equation (4.25) the option values of V_u and V_u at terminal nodes are known from the payoff functions of the option. Hence a portfolio that includes a long position on n shares of stock, where n is calculated using Equation (4.25), and a short position on the option is riskless and its value is the same whether the stock moves up to node B or moves down to node C. In an arbitrage-free market such a riskless portfolio has a return equal to the risk-free rate. Therefore, we can use the risk-free rate to discount the portfolio value from the end of the period to $t = 0$. By setting the discounted value of the portfolio equal to the cost of establishing portfolio at $t = 0$ we have:

$$n \times S_0 - V_0 = (n \times S_0 \times u - V_u)e^{-r_f \Delta t}$$

By solving this equation for V_0 and replacing n with its equivalent from Equation (4.25), we have:

$$V_0 = \frac{V_u - V_d}{u - d}(1 - ue^{-r_f \Delta t}) + V_u e^{-r_f \Delta t}$$

To simplify this equation, we can define parameter π as:

$$\pi = \frac{e^{r_f \Delta t} - d}{u - d} \tag{4.26}$$

Using this parameter, the equation for the current price of the option is:

$$V_0 = e^{-r_f \Delta t}[\pi V_u + (1 - \pi)V_d] \tag{4.27}$$

Equations (4.26) and (4.27) together provide us with the current price of the option using a one-period binomial tree.

Example

Consider a European call option with a strike price of $41 and a term of six months. The underlying stock pays no dividend during the term of the option. Current stock price is $44.20. Annual risk-free rate with continuous compounding is 3%. Assume that the stock price is expected to either increase by 10% in the next six months or decrease by 10% during this period. Therefore the stock price at six months is either $44.2 \times (1 + 0.1) = 48.62$ or $44.2 \times (1 - 0.10) = 39.78$. The value of the call option at $t = 0.5$ when the stock price is up at $48.62 is $V_u = \text{Max}(48.62 - 41, 0) = 7.62$ and when the stock price is down at $39.78 is $V_d = \text{Max}(39.78 - 41, 0) = 0$. To use the binomial tree to price this option, a riskless portfolio can be

(continued)

(continued)

constructed by taking a long position in n shares of stock and shorting a call option on one share of the same stock where n is calculated using Equation (4.25) as:

$$n = \frac{7.62 - 0}{44.2 \times (1.1 - 0.9)} \cong 0.862$$

The cost of setting up this portfolio at $t = 0$ is:

$$0.862 \times 44.2 - V_0$$

The value of this portfolio when the stock is up at \$48.62 is:

$$0.862 \times 48.62 - 7.62 = 34.29$$

And its value when the stock is down at \$39.78 is:

$$0.862 \times 39.78 - 0 = 34.29$$

Since the value of the portfolio is independent from the stock price in up and down states, the portfolio is considered riskless and hence its value at the termination date can be discounted to $t = 0$ using the risk-free rate. By setting the discounted value of this riskless portfolio equal to the cost of it at $t = 0$ we can find the value of the European call option:

$$34.29 \times e^{-0.03 \times 0.5} = 0.862 \times 44.2 - V_0$$

$$V_0 = 4.32$$

We can get to the same result directly using Equations (4.26) and (4.27):

$$\pi = \frac{e^{0.03 \times 0.5} - 0.9}{1.1 - 0.9} \cong 0.5756$$

$$V_0 = e^{-0.03 \times 0.5}[0.5756 \times 7.62 + (1 - 0.5756) \times 0] = 4.32$$

In the valuation of an option using a binomial tree we make a few assumptions. First, we assume that the market is *complete* and *efficient*. In such a market every asset has a price and all information available about the asset is already reflected in that price. We assume that the market is *frictionless*, where transaction costs are negligible. We assume that buying or selling a partial asset is possible. We also assume that the market is arbitrage-free, where any arbitrage opportunity is quickly eliminated by market participants' actions. The use of the risk-free rate in discounting is not an assumption but rather due to the nature of the constructed portfolio's being riskless. This is a crucial point in option valuation.

When an asset is riskless, a risk-neutral investor expects a risk-free return from investing in that asset. But for a risky asset, a risk-averse or risk-taking investor expects a different return than the risk-free yield. For a risky asset the discounting of future cash flows or payoffs is done by using an adjusted risk-free rate. This adjustment depends on the risk tolerance of the investor and it may be different for different investors.

Going back to option pricing using a binomial tree, if we follow the fundamentals of valuation, we need to find the expected payoff of the option at a time period using the real probability distribution of price movement, and then discount it back to the previous period using a risk-adjusted rate. However, as mentioned above, the risk-adjusted rate may be different for different investors and is not readily available. It turns out that instead of this approach we can adjust the probability distribution of price movement to reflect the riskiness of the underlying asset and obtain the expected payoff of the option at a period using this adjusted probability distribution, and then use the risk-free rate to discount this expected payoff back to the previous period. This is known as *risk-neutral valuation* and it is exactly what we did when we illustrated the construction of the binomial tree method earlier. The parameter π introduced can be seen as the probability of an upward movement in the stock price in a *risk-neutral environment* and $1 - \pi$ is the probability of the downward movement in such an environment. Since the amount of anticipated upward and downward movements of the stock price (u and d) is embedded in the derivation of these probabilities, they already reflect the risk of the underlying asset in option valuation. Hence $\pi V_u + (1 - \pi)V_d$ can be considered as the expectation of the option payoff at a time step and since the valuation is now done in a risk-neutral environment, the risk-free rate can be used to discount back the expected payoff to the previous period by multiplying it by $e^{-r_f \Delta t}$. This way, although we are now valuing the option in a risk-neutral environment, the value obtained is the same value as in the risky environment. Due to this tactic the value of the option found using the binomial tree method is often referred to as the *risk-neutral value*.

A common method for estimating up and down multipliers, u and d, is to associate them with the volatility of the stock. Cox, Ross, and Rubinstein (1979) proposed the following equations to incorporate the market volatility in estimating up and down multipliers:

$$u = e^{\sigma\sqrt{\Delta t}}$$

$$d = \frac{1}{u} = e^{-\sigma\sqrt{\Delta t}}$$

(4.28)

where σ is the standard deviation of change in the price of the underlying stock. In an upcoming section of this chapter we discuss calculation and alternative modeling methods of volatility parameter σ in more detail.

We can generalize the one-period binomial tree introduced earlier to a multi-period one. The general process of valuing an option using a multi-period binomial tree is as follows:

▪ Divide the term of the option into several time periods of equal size Δt. If T is the term of the option, for an N-period binomial tree $\Delta t = \dfrac{T}{N}$.

▪ Create a tree structure in which each node at a time step is branching out to two nodes at the next time step. The tree is recombining, meaning that an upward movement in stock price followed by a downward movement ends in the same node as a downward movement followed by an upward movement. A tree with such structure with six periods is shown in Figure 4.2. Starting from $t = 0$ there is only one node at this time step, followed by two nodes at time $t = \Delta t$, three nodes at time $2\Delta t$, and so on. Generally, if time steps are characterized as $i \times \Delta t$, where $i \in \{0, 1, \cdots, N\}$, each node in the tree can be identified by two indexes i and j, where for each $i, j \in \{0, 1, \cdots, i\}$. For example, since nodes B and C in the tree in Figure 4.2 are at time step $2 \times \Delta t$, node C can be identified using $i = 1$ and $j = 0$ indexes and node B can be identified using $i = 1$ and $j = 1$ indexes.

▪ Derive the stock price at each node of the tree using upward and downward multipliers. The underlying stock price at the first node at $t = 0$ is the current price S_0. Stock prices at nodes in subsequent time steps are obtained by multiplying the price either at the preceding node in the previous time step with the upward multiplier u or by the downward multiplier d, where u and d are from Equation (4.28). Generally stock price at a node identified by i and j indexes as defined above is:

$$S_{i,j} = S_0 u^j d^{i-j} \tag{4.29}$$

For example, for node H in Figure 4.2, which is located at $i = 3, j = 2$ stock price is $S_{i=3,j=2} = S_0 u^2 d$. This means that the current stock price has increased two times by the u multiplier and decreased one time by the d multiplier to reach the level of node H. However, the order that these changes are applied to the current stock price is not relevant. The stock price can move from the level at node A to node H by (i) two consecutive upward moves followed by a downward move, or (ii) one upward move, one downward move, followed by another upward move, or (iii) a downward move, followed by two consecutive upward moves. All three paths get the current stock price at node A to the level at node H.

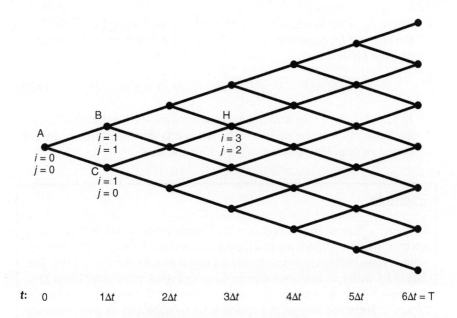

FIGURE 4.2 A six-period binomial tree

■ Calculate the value of the option at nodes located at the end of the tree at the last time step $t = T$ using the payoff function of the option. For a call option, the payoff at ending nodes where $i = N$ is $V_{N,j} = \text{Max}(S_{N,j} - X, 0)$ and for a put option it is $V_{N,j} = \text{Max}(X - S_{N,j}, 0)$, where X is the option strike price.

■ Find the option values at the intermediary nodes by discounting the expected value of the option at succeeding nodes using Equation (4.27). First using Equation (4.26) we can calculate the probability of an upward move. At each intermediary node, the expected value of the option at succeeding nodes is calculated and discounted using the risk-free rate. For an American option, the possibility of an early exercise should also be examined at each intermediary node. Generally, the value of a European option, call or put, at an intermediary node identified by i and j indexes is:

$$V_{i,j} = e^{-r_f \Delta t}[\pi V_{i+1,j+1} + (1 - \pi)V_{i+1,j}] \tag{4.30}$$

For an American option, the evaluation of exercising early should be incorporated in this formula. Hence, the value of an American call option at an intermediary node identified by i and j indexes is:

$$V_{i,j} = \text{Max}(S_{i,j} - X, e^{-r_f \Delta t}[\pi V_{i+1,j+1} + (1 - \pi)V_{i+1,j}]) \tag{4.31}$$

where $S_{i,j}$ is the stock price at that node obtained using (4.29). Similarly, the value of an American put option at an intermediary node identified by i and j indexes is:

$$V_{i,j} = \text{Max}(X - S_{i,j}, e^{-r_f \Delta t}[\pi V_{i+1,j+1} + (1 - \pi)V_{i+1,j}]) \qquad (4.32)$$

▪ Repeat the above step walking backward toward the beginning of the tree until the value at the node located at $t = 0$ is obtained. This is the estimated value of the option using the binomial tree.

Example

Consider a European put option with a strike price of $41 and a term of six months. The underlying stock pays no dividend during the term of the option. Assume that the current stock price is $44.20, the annual risk-free rate is 3% with continuous compounding, and stock price volatility is 25%. Figure 4.3 presents a six-period binomial tree for valuation of this option contract. Since the term of the option is six months and six time steps are used in this binomial tree, each time step is one month or 0.0833 year. Using the given volatility, the upward and downward multipliers are calculated as:

$$u = e^{0.25 \times \sqrt{0.0833}} = 1.074837$$

$$d = \frac{1}{1.0748} = 0.930374$$

The probability of upward movement π is calculated using Equation (4.26) as:

$$\pi = \frac{e^{0.03 \times 0.0833} - 0.9304}{1.0748 - 0.9304} = 0.499293$$

The price at each node of the tree is calculated using Equation (4.29). For example, at node A in Figure 4.3 where $i = 6$ and $j = 0$ the stock price is $44.2 \times 1.074837^0 \times 0.930374^6 = 28.6660$ or at node B where $i = 6$ and $j = 1$ it is $44.2 \times 1.074837^1 \times 0.930374^5 = 33.1171$. The stock prices at other nodes are obtained similarly. There are seven nodes at the end of the tree at $t = 0.5$. The value of the option at each of these nodes is obtained using the payoff function of a put option. For example, at node A the option value is $\text{Max}(0, 41 - 28.6660) = 12.3340$ and at node B it is $\text{Max}(0, 41 - 33.1171) = 7.8829$. The option values at the other terminal nodes of the tree are obtained similarly. Moving one time step back to time $t = 5\Delta t = 0.4167$ year, the value of the option at each node at this time can be calculated as the discounted expected value from the succeeding nodes using Equation (4.30). For example, the value of the option at node C (V_C) in Figure 4.3 is calculated using the option values at nodes A and B (V_A and V_B) as:

$$V_C = e^{-r_f \Delta t}[\pi V_B + (1 - \pi)V_A]$$

$$= e^{-0.03 \times 0.0833}[0.499293 \times 7.8829 + (1 - 0.499293) \times 12.3340]$$

$$= 10.0863$$

t:	0	0.0833	0.1667	0.25	0.3333	0.4167	0.5
							S = 68.1518, V = 0.0000
						S = 63.4066, V = 0.0000	
					S = 58.9919, V = 0.0000		S = 58.9919, V = 0.0000
				S = 54.8845, V = 0.0000		S = 54.8845, V = 0.0000	
			S = 51.0631, V = 0.1705		S = 51.0631, V = 0.0000		S = 51.0631, V = 0.0000
		S = 47.5078, V = 0.6697		S = 47.5078, V = 0.3415		S = 47.5078, V = 0.0000	
	S = 44.2000, V = 1.5582		S = 44.2000, V = 1.1708		S = 44.2000, V = 0.6837		S = 44.2000, V = 0.0000
		S = 41.1225, V = 2.4519		S = 41.1225, V = 2.0037		S = 41.1225, V = 1.3689	
			S = 38.2593, V = 3.7417		S = 38.2593, V = 3.3300		S = 38.2593, V = 2.7407
				S = 35.5955, V = 5.4935		S = 35.5955, V = 5.3022 B	
					S = 33.1171, V = 7.6784 C		S = 33.1171, V = 7.8829
						S = 30.8113, V = 10.0863 A	
							S = 28.6660, V = 12.3340

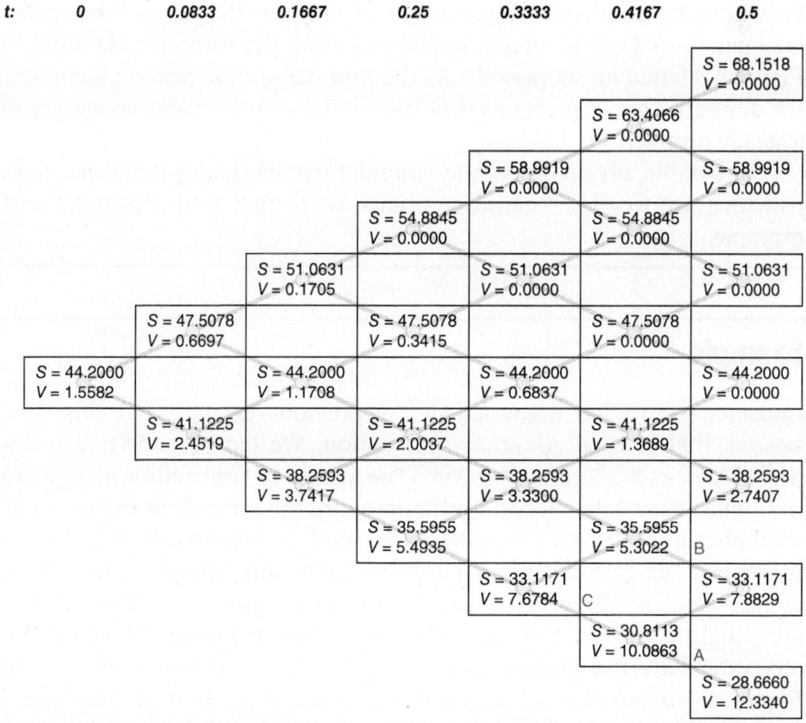

FIGURE 4.3 Valuation of a European put option using a six-period binomial tree

After the option values at all nodes at $t = 0.4167$ are calculated, we move backward one time step and repeat this process for nodes at time

(*continued*)

(*continued*)

$t = 4\Delta t = 0.3333$ year. This is continued until the value of the option at time $t = 0$ is obtained. In our example, the option values at two nodes at time $t = 1\Delta t = 0.0833$ year in Figure 4.3 are 0.6697 and 2.4519. Therefore, the value of the option at $t = 0$ is calculated as:

$$V_0 = e^{-0.03 \times 0.0833}[0.499293 \times 0.6697 + (1 - 0.499293) \times 2.4519] = 1.5582$$

In practice, using only six time periods in the binomial tree method is not sufficient and using a larger number of periods is recommended. The number of periods used in the tree impacts the option value obtained. For instance, in the previous example, if we increase the number of periods to 12, where the length of each period is 1/24 of a year, the value of the option is obtained as \$1.4832, which is different from the value we obtained in Figure 4.3 based on six periods. As the number of time periods increases, the difference between results decreases and the option value converges to a steady number.

One of the advantages of the binomial tree method is that it provides us with a way to value American options. We demonstrate this in the next example.

Example

Consider the option discussed in the previous example but this time assume that it is an American put option. We have $X = \$41$, $T = 0.5$, $S = \$44.20$, $r_f = 3\%$, and $\sigma = 25\%$. The values of probability π, upward multiplier u, and downward multiplier d are the same as in the previous example: $u = 1.074837$, $d = 0.930374$, and $\pi = 0.499293$. Figure 4.4 presents a six-period binomial tree to value this option. Stock prices at each node of this tree are calculated using Equation (4.29) and they are equal to the prices in the nodes of the tree in Figure 4.3, as parameter values are the same in both examples. For example, at node C in Figure 4.4 where $i = 5$ and $j = 0$, the stock price is $44.2 \times 1.074837^0 \times 0.930374^5 = 30.8113$ and at node D where $i = 6$ and $j = 2$, the stock price is $44.2 \times 1.074837^2 \times 0.930374^4 = 38.2593$. The value of the option at the final nodes at time $t = 0.5$ are obtained using the payoff function of a put option and they are identical to the payoff at terminal nodes of the tree in the previous example. For example, at node D the option value is $\text{Max}(0, 41 - 38.2593) = 2.7407$.

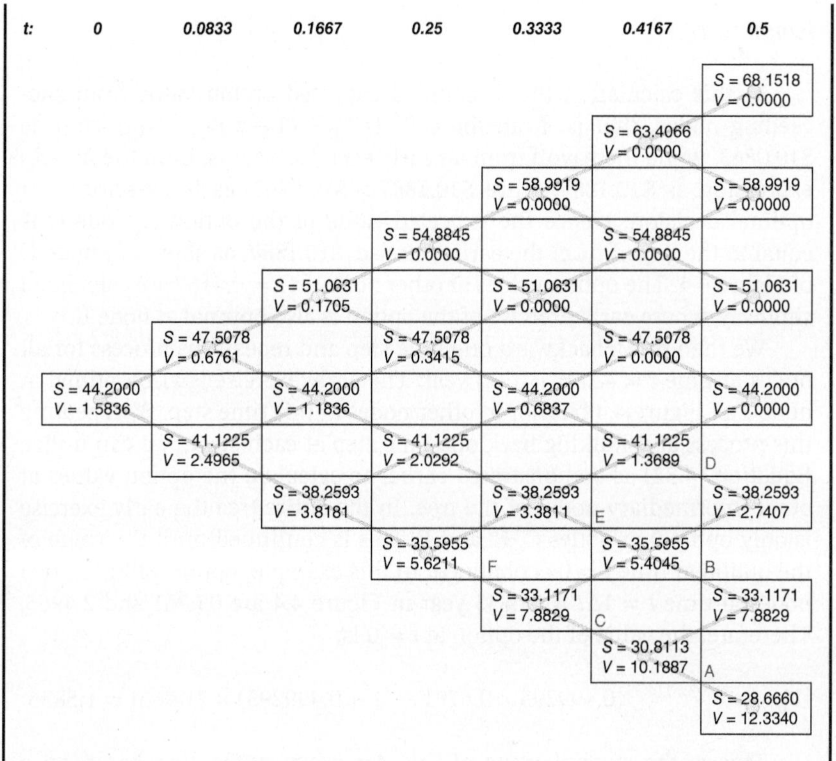

t:	0	0.0833	0.1667	0.25	0.3333	0.4167	0.5
							S = 68.1518 V = 0.0000
						S = 63.4066 V = 0.0000	
					S = 58.9919 V = 0.0000		S = 58.9919 V = 0.0000
				S = 54.8845 V = 0.0000		S = 54.8845 V = 0.0000	
			S = 51.0631 V = 0.1705		S = 51.0631 V = 0.0000		S = 51.0631 V = 0.0000
		S = 47.5078 V = 0.6761		S = 47.5078 V = 0.3415		S = 47.5078 V = 0.0000	
	S = 44.2000 V = 1.5836		S = 44.2000 V = 1.1836		S = 44.2000 V = 0.6837		S = 44.2000 V = 0.0000
		S = 41.1225 V = 2.4965		S = 41.1225 V = 2.0292		S = 41.1225 V = 1.3689 D	
			S = 38.2593 V = 3.8181		S = 38.2593 V = 3.3811 E		S = 38.2593 V = 2.7407
				S = 35.5955 V = 5.6211 F		S = 35.5955 V = 5.4045 B	
					S = 33.1171 V = 7.8829 C		S = 33.1171 V = 7.8829
						S = 30.8113 V = 10.1887 A	
							S = 28.6660 V = 12.3340

FIGURE 4.4 Valuation of an American put option using a six-period binomial tree

Moving one time step back to time $t = 5\Delta t = 0.4167$ year, the value of the option at each node at this time is calculated as the discounted expected value from the succeeding nodes while evaluating the possibility and impact of the early exercise of this American option. Equation (4.32) can be used to calculate the option values at all intermediary nodes. For example, the value of the option at node C (V_C) in Figure 4.4 is calculated using the option values at nodes A and B (V_A and V_B) and evaluating the possibility of early exercise using the price at node C (S_C) as:

$$V_C = \text{Max}(X - S_C, e^{-r_f \Delta t}[\pi V_B + (1 - \pi)V_A])$$

$$= \text{Max}(41 - 30.8113, e^{-0.03 \times 0.0833}[0.499293 \times 7.8829$$

$$+ (1 - 0.499293) \times 12.3340])$$

$$= 10.1887$$

(continued)

(*continued*)

In this calculation the discounted expected option value from succeeding nodes, that is, from the $e^{-r_f \Delta t}[\pi V_B + (1 - \pi)V_A]$ expression, is $10.0863, while the payoff from an early exercise, that is, from the $X - S_C$ expression, is $10.1887. Since $10.1887 > $10.0863, early exercise is an optimal decision. Hence the expected value of the option at node C is equal to the payoff from the early exercise: $10.1887, as shown in node C of Figure 4.4. The option values at other nodes at $t = 0.4167$ are calculated similarly, where early exercise of the option is also optimal at node E.

We then move backward one time step and repeat this process for all nodes at time $t = 4\Delta t = 0.3333$ year. The early exercise is also optimal at node F of Figure 4.4 but not in other nodes at this time step. By repeating this process and walking back one time step at each stage, we can utilize Equation (4.32) as demonstrated earlier to calculate the option values at other intermediary nodes of the tree. In the entire tree the early exercise is only optimal at nodes C, E, and F. This is continued until the value of the option at time $t = 0$ is obtained. In this example, option values at two nodes at time $t = 1\Delta t = 0.0833$ year in Figure 4.4 are 0.6761 and 2.4965. Therefore, the value of the option at $t = 0$ is:

$$V_0 = e^{-0.03 \times 0.0833}[0.499293 \times 0.6761 + (1 - 0.499293) \times 2.4965] = 1.5836$$

This is the current value of this American put option based on a six-period binomial tree. As mentioned earlier, in practice a much larger number of periods is needed to achieve a stable result. By comparing the value of the American put option obtained in this example with the European put option in the previous example, we can see that the value of the American option is larger than the comparable European option. This is expected due to the extra feature of possible early exercise that the American option provides to its holder.

A binomial tree can also be used to value an option when the underlying stock pays dividends. In order to do so, first we need to discuss the impact of a dividend payment on the stock price. Ignoring the tax impact, at the ex-dividend date the price of the stock decreases by the amount of dividend per share. If an investor purchases a share of a stock immediately before the ex-dividend date, she receives the dividend payment, but if she buys the share immediately after that date, she misses that dividend payment. So, stock is less valuable to the investor immediately after a dividend payment by the amount of the dividend. When the tax impact is considered, the drop in the stock price is not exactly equal to the dividend amount and is closer to the after-tax dividend per share. We can use this concept in valuation of an option when the underlying stock pays a dividend during the term of the option. For simplicity, here we ignore the tax impact and also assume that volatility of the stock price is constant during the term of the option and not impacted by the dividend payment.

In using a binomial tree in valuation of an option when the underlying stock pays dividends in the form of one or more cash flows, one approach is based on separating the stock price at each node into two components (Hull 2005). One part of the stock price is the discounted value of dividend payments during the term of option. Assuming such dividend payments can be estimated with high accuracy, this part of the stock price at each node is obtained easily. The other part of the stock price is uncertain and depends on the stock volatility through the up and down multipliers. In the proposed approach a binominal tree is first constructed based on the uncertain part of the stock price and then the tree is adjusted to incorporate the discounted value of dividend payments. This approach has the advantage of keeping the tree recombining. We illustrate this method using the following example.

Example

Consider the American put option from the previous example but this time assume that the current stock price is $S_0 = \$46.80$ and it is expected to pay a dividend of $2.63 at four and a half months from now at $t = 0.375$ (the ex-dividend date). As in the previous example, the option specifications are: $X = \$41$, $T = 0.5$, $r_f = 3\%$, and $\sigma = 25\%$.

The first step in valuation of this option is to separate the portion of the stock price that is due to the expected dividend payment from the uncertain part of the price, which is driven by the assumed volatility. Since there is one dividend payment of $2.63 expected at $t = 0.375$ year, the present value of this dividend at $t = 0$ is:

$$2.63 \times e^{-0.03 \times 0.375} = 2.6$$

The next step is to take this discounted value of $2.60 out of the current stock price and build a six-period binomial tree assuming the current price is $46.80 - \$2.60 = \$44.20$. Based on this stock price, and since all other option specifications are identical to the previous example, the binomial

(continued)

(*continued*)

tree constructed for this step is the same as the one developed in the previous example and shown in Figure 4.4.

Next, we need to adjust the stock prices at some of the nodes of the tree using the discounted value of the expected dividend and reevaluate the options at those nodes. Figure 4.5 presents this adjusted tree. Stock prices at those nodes of the tree that are located after the dividend payment do not need any adjustment. In Figure 4.5 all stock prices and option values at those nodes at time $t = 0.4167$ and $t = 0.5$ that are located after the dividend payment at $t = 0.375$ are not adjusted and they

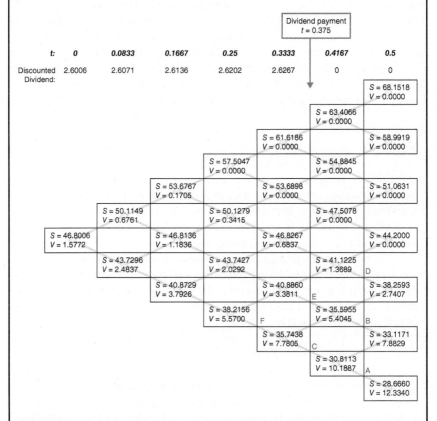

FIGURE 4.5 Valuation of an American put option using a six-period binomial tree when the underlying stock has a single expected dividend payment

are equal to the corresponding values in the tree in Figure 4.4. As before, at nodes C and E early exercise is optimal. Stock prices at all nodes located at time steps that are before the dividend payment should be adjusted by adding the expected dividend amount, discounted to the time where the node is located. For example, for all nodes that are located at $t = 0.3333$ the discounted value of the expected dividend payment is $2.63 \times e^{-0.03 \times (0.375 - 0.3333)} = 2.6267$ or for those nodes located at $t = 0.25$ the adjustment amount is $2.63 \times e^{-0.03 \times (0.375 - 0.25)} = 2.6202$. The amounts of these adjustments for each time step are also shown in the top section of Figure 4.5. The stock prices are first adjusted and then option values, including the possibility of early exercise, are reevaluated based on the adjusted prices. For example, at node F in Figure 4.5 the stock price before adjustment (from Figure 4.4) is $33.1171 and the discounted expected dividend payment is $2.6267, so the adjusted stock price at this node is $S_F = \$33.1171 + \$2.6267 = \$35.7438$. Using Equation (4.32) and based on this adjusted price, the option value at node F is obtained as:

$$V_F = \text{Max}(X - S_F, e^{-r_f \Delta t}[\pi V_E + (1 - \pi)V_C])$$

$$= \text{Max}(41 - 35.7438, e^{-0.03 \times 0.0833}[0.499293 \times 5.4045$$

$$+ (1 - 0.499293) \times 10.1887])$$

$$= 7.7805$$

Here early exercise at node F is no longer optimal. This process is continued for all nodes that are located before the dividend payment until the value of the option at time $t = 0$ is obtained. In this example, the option values at the two nodes at time $t = 0.0833$ in Figure 4.5 are 0.6761 and 2.4837. Therefore, the value of this option at $t = 0$ is calculated as:

$$V_0 = e^{-0.03 \times 0.0833}[0.499293 \times 0.6761 + (1 - 0.499293) \times 2.4837] = 1.5772$$

The binomial tree method can also be used for options where underlying assets provide a continuous yield q. In this case the general methodology discussed earlier remains the same and only Equation (4.26) changes to:

$$\pi = \frac{e^{(r_f - q)\Delta t} - d}{u - d} \tag{4.33}$$

THE BLACK–SCHOLES–MERTON MODEL

The binomial tree method for option valuation discussed in the previous section is based on partitioning the time to maturity of an option into discrete time intervals. In such a discrete-time method, time progresses in separate and identifiable steps and the values of the option and the underlying stock at each time step are evaluated while their behavior during the intervals is ignored. Decreasing the length of the time intervals generally leads to improvement in result accuracy. In contrast, in a continuous-time model the values of the option and the underlying asset progress continuously through time and their evolutions are functions of time and modeled as stochastic processes. Stochastic processes are introduced in this book's Appendix, "Elements of Probability and Statistics."

The *Black–Scholes–Merton* model is a continuous-time model for valuation of European options. This model is the result of pioneering work on option pricing by Fischer Black and Myron Scholes (1973). Black and Scholes were assisted by Robert Merton, who later elaborated and enhanced that work in his landmark publication (Merton 1973b). The model is still a popular option valuation tool and is used either directly for valuation purposes or as a benchmark for other valuation techniques.

In the Black–Scholes–Merton model the underlying stock is assumed to follow a geometric Brownian motion stochastic process where the evolution of percentage change in the stock price in a short period of time is modeled as:

$$\frac{dS(t)}{S(t)} = \mu \, dt + \sigma \, dW(t) \tag{4.34}$$

where $S(t)$ is the stock price at time t, μ is the annual expected return, σ is the constant annual volatility of the stock, and $dW(t)$ is the Wiener process, so $W(t)$ has a normal distribution with mean 0 and variance t: $W(t) \sim N(0, t)$. This equation implies that the percentage change in the stock price has a normal distribution with mean $\mu \, dt$ and variance $\sigma^2 dt$:

$$\frac{dS(t)}{S(t)} \sim N(\mu \, dt, \sigma^2 dt) \tag{4.35}$$

Equivalently, we can write this process as:

$$dS(t) = \mu \, S(t) \, dt + \sigma \, S(t) \, dW(t) \tag{4.36}$$

By applying Itô's lemma to the natural logarithm function of $S(t)$ defined by the above process we obtain:[2]

$$d\ln S(t) = \left(\mu - \frac{\sigma^2}{2}\right) dt + \sigma \, dW(t) \tag{4.37}$$

This equation implies that the change in $\ln S(t)$ has a normal distribution with mean $\left(\mu - \dfrac{\sigma^2}{2}\right) dt$ and a variance of $\sigma^2 dt$:

$$d \ln S(t) \sim N\left(\left(\mu - \frac{\sigma^2}{2}\right) dt, \sigma^2 dt\right) \qquad (4.38)$$

The Black–Scholes–Merton model is based on the assumption of an arbitrage-free market, where short selling is allowed and stock is divisible. Transaction costs and tax impacts are ignored, and volatility is assumed constant. We also assume that the underlying stock pays no dividend during the term of the option. We remove this last assumption later and discuss the case when the underlying stock does pay dividends. Derivation of the stochastic differential equation at the foundation of the Black–Scholes–Merton model starts from the process presented in Equation (4.36) and by using a similar argument used for the binomial tree, a riskless portfolio is constructed that earns the risk-free rate. The resulting process can be used to model the value of many derivative products where their underlying asset follows the process in Equation (4.36). Here we do not demonstrate the derivation of this differential equation and focus on the solution obtained for the European stock options when appropriate boundary conditions are applied. Details of derivation of the Black–Scholes–Merton stochastic differential equation can be found in Hull (2005). The Black–Scholes–Merton formulas for valuation of European call and put options when the underlying stock pays no dividend are as follows:

$$V_{0:\,European\ Call} = \Phi(d_1)\, S_0 - \Phi(d_2)\, X e^{-r_f T} \qquad (4.39)$$

$$V_{0:\,European\ Put} = \Phi(-d_2)\, X e^{-r_f T} - \Phi(-d_1)\, S_0 \qquad (4.40)$$

where:

$$d_1 = \frac{\ln\left(\dfrac{S_0}{X}\right) + \left(r_f + \dfrac{\sigma^2}{2}\right) T}{\sigma \sqrt{T}}$$

$$d_2 = d_1 - \sigma\sqrt{T} = \frac{\ln\left(\dfrac{S_0}{X}\right) + \left(r_f - \dfrac{\sigma^2}{2}\right) T}{\sigma \sqrt{T}} \qquad (4.41)$$

$\Phi(.)$ is the cumulative probability distribution function of the standard normal distribution[3] and other notation is the same as in the binomial tree method.

As can be seen from Equations (4.39) and (4.40), the Black–Scholes–Merton valuation formulas are independent of μ, the expected return of the stock. The expected return on an investment depends on the risk preference of investors but since it does not appear in the Black–Scholes–Merton model final formulas, it implies that option values based on this model are valid when investors have any risk preference. Hence, the Black–Scholes–Merton model, similar to the binomial tree method, is a risk-neutral valuation technique, but the value obtained using this model in the risk-neutral environment is the same value as in the risky environment. When we value a derivative product such as stock options in the risk-neutral environment we use the risk-free rate to discount the expected payoff. In the risky environment, the expected return should have been adjusted to reflect the risk preference of the investor, as well as the rate used in discounting the expected payoff. The offsetting impact of these two factors would result in the same option value as in the risk-neutral environment. This is reflected in the independence of the Black–Scholes–Merton model from the expected return of the underlying stock.

Example

Consider a European call option with a $T = 0.5$ term and a strike price of $X = \$41$. Assume that volatility of the underlying stock is $\sigma = 25\%$ and the annual continuous compounding risk-free rate is $r_f = 3\%$. The current stock price is $S_0 = \$44.20$ and it pays no dividend during the term of the option. From Equations (4.39) and (4.41) the value of this option using the Black–Scholes–Merton model is obtained as:

$$d_1 = \frac{\ln\left(\frac{44.2}{41}\right) + \left(0.03 + \frac{0.25^2}{2}\right) \times 0.5}{0.25 \times \sqrt{0.5}} = 0.59836916$$

$$d_2 = 0.598369158 - 0.25 \times \sqrt{0.5} = 0.42159246$$

$$V_{0:\,European\;Call} = \Phi(0.59836916) \times 44.2 - \Phi(0.42159246)$$

$$\times 41 \times e^{-0.03 \times 0.5} = 5.262$$

If this option is a European put, its value is obtained using Equation (4.40) as:

$$V_{0:\,European\;Put} = \Phi(-0.42159246) \times 41 \times e^{-0.03 \times 0.5} - \Phi(-0.59836916)$$

$$\times 44.2 = 1.4516$$

Recall from Figure 4.3 that when we valued this very same option using a six-period binomial tree, its value was obtained as $1.5582. As mentioned, six periods are barely enough in the binomial tree and a larger number of periods is needed for a more accurate result that converges to a steady value. As the number of periods in the binomial tree increases, the resulting option value approaches the value from the Black–Scholes–Merton model. For example, if the number of periods in the binomial tree in Figure 4.3 is increased to 12, the put option value is obtained as $1.4832, which is closer to the $1.4516 obtained using the Black–Scholes–Merton model. In a limiting case, the result from the binomial tree method converges to the option value from the Black–Scholes–Merton model.

It is easy to confirm the put–call parity from the option values obtained from the Black–Scholes–Merton model. In this example, by placing $5.262 for the value of the European call option and $1.4516 for the value of the European put option in Equation (4.17) and rounding the results to four decimal points, we have:

$$V_{0: European\ Call} + Xe^{-r_f T} = V_{0: European\ Put} + S_0$$
$$5.262 + 41 \times e^{-0.03 \times 0.5} = 1.4516 + 44.2$$
$$45.6516 = 45.6516$$

We can use the Black–Scholes–Merton model when the underlying stock pays dividends during the term of the option. This is done by following the same approach explained for the binomial tree where the value of the underlying stock is divided into two components: a certain part due to the discounted value of dividend payments during the term of the option, assuming dividend cash flows can be estimated with high accuracy, and an uncertain part that follows the stochastic process introduced earlier in this section. The Black–Scholes–Merton valuation formulas are then used by first adjusting S_0 by deducting the present value of the expected dividend payments during the term of the option from the current stock price. This approach assumes the volatility of the stock price does not change due to this adjustment.

Example

Consider the European call and put options in the previous example but this time assume that the underlying stock is expected to pay a dividend of $2.63 at four and a half months from now at $t = 0.375$ (the ex-dividend

(continued)

(*continued*)

date). The present value of this dividend payment using the risk-free rate is:

$$2.63 \times e^{-0.03 \times 0.375} = 2.6006$$

So the current stock price should be adjusted downward by this amount:

$$S_0 = 44.2 - 2.6006 = 41.5994$$

The values of the European call and put options are:

$$d_1 = \frac{\ln\left(\frac{41.5994}{41}\right) + \left(0.03 + \frac{0.25^2}{2}\right) \times 0.5}{0.25 \times \sqrt{0.5}} = 0.25534587$$

$$d_2 = 0.25534587 - 0.25 \times \sqrt{0.5} = 0.07856917$$

$$V_{0: European\ Call} = \Phi(0.25534587) \times 41.5994 - \Phi(0.07856917)$$

$$\times 41 \times e^{-0.03 \times 0.5} = 3.5323$$

$$V_{0: European\ Put} = \Phi(-0.07856917) \times 41 \times e^{-0.03 \times 0.5}$$

$$- \Phi(-0.25534587) \times 41.5994 = 2.3224$$

Comparison of the results obtained here with the previous example where underlying stock paid no dividend is in line with the expectation that dividend payment reduces the value of the call option but increases the value of the put option.

As noted earlier, the Black–Scholes–Merton model can be used to value the European options, with or without dividend payments, but it cannot be used to value the American options. A few methodologies are proposed in academia to alter this model for use in approximate valuation of the American options; however, use of the binomial tree method seems to be more practical for this purpose.

Generalization of the Black–Scholes–Merton Model

An alternative approach to incorporating the dividend of the underlying stock in the Black–Scholes–Merton model is to assume that the stock provides a continuous yield. As a dividend payment cash flow reduces the stock price at the ex-dividend date, assumption of a dividend yield also leads to a decrease in the growth rate of the stock by the dividend yield. Consider a stock with a dividend yield of q with continuous compounding, where the price at $t = 0$ is S_0 and at the option maturity is S_T. If this stock has no dividend yield, the growth rate of the stock price would be higher (in absolute terms). This can be achieved either by changing the price at the option maturity to $S_T e^{-qT}$ and keeping the price at $t = 0$ as before, or by changing the price at $t = 0$ to $S_0 e^{-qT}$ and keeping the price at the option maturity as before. Since the Black–Scholes–Merton model formula depends on S_0 we choose the latter. This means that for a stock with dividend yield q, we can use the Black–Scholes–Merton model by replacing S_0 with $S_0 e^{-qT}$ (Merton 1973b; Hull 2005).

We can further generalize the Black–Scholes–Merton model to provide the option value at any time t between the initiation of the contract and its maturity date. Assuming the stock price at time t is S_t and since T is the original term of the contract, the remaining time to maturity is $T - t$. By replacing S_0 with S_t and T with $T - t$ we obtain the Black–Scholes–Merton model for valuation of European options at any time t before contract maturity.

These modifications lead to the following formulas for the Black–Scholes–Merton model to calculate the value of a European option at time t when the underlying asset provides continuous yield q:

$$V_{t:\,European\ Call} = \Phi(d_1)\, S_t e^{-q(T-t)} - \Phi(d_2)\, X e^{-r_f(T-t)} \tag{4.42}$$

$$V_{t:\,European\ Put} = \Phi(-d_2)\, X e^{-r_f(T-t)} - \Phi(-d_1)\, S_t e^{-q(T-t)} \tag{4.43}$$

$$d_1 = \frac{\ln\left(\dfrac{S_t}{X}\right) + \left(r_f - q + \dfrac{\sigma^2}{2}\right)(T - t)}{\sigma\sqrt{T - t}} \tag{4.44}$$

$$d_2 = d_1 - \sigma\sqrt{T - t}$$

These formulas can be used for European options on any underlying asset that provides a continuous yield. They reduce to formulas in Equations (4.39), (4.40), and (4.41) when $t = 0$ and $q = 0$.

OPTION VALUATION USING MONTE CARLO SIMULATION

We used Monte Carlo simulation method in Chapter 2 for valuation of floating-rate instruments. This method can also be used to value options. The underlying model of the Monte Carlo simulation method is a continuous-time model, such as the geometric Brownian motion model introduced earlier in this chapter, but to implement the simulation approach, the model is discretized and hence the Monte Carlo simulation method, similar to the binomial tree, is a discrete-time valuation method. In applying the Monte Carlo simulation method in option valuation, we first use the discrete version of a stochastic process of stock price to generate many paths of simulated stock prices from the valuation time to the maturity date of the option. The average of the discounted values of the option payoffs based on these simulated paths provides the estimated option value.

Valuation of European options using Monte Carlo simulation is a straightforward task since there is no need to evaluate the impact of early exercise and hence there is no need to estimate the value of an option at a point in time if it is not exercised. Valuation of American options using simulation, however, is more involved. We start our discussion by focusing on European options and later in this section we introduce a method that can be used for valuation of American options using simulation.

The first step in this approach is to generate simulated stock prices. The model that is usually used for this purpose is the geometric Brownian motion introduced earlier in this section in Equations (4.36) and (4.37). Use of the model in the form of Equation (4.37), reproduced below, where the evolution of the natural logarithm of the stock price is modeled, is more common in practice:

$$d \ln S(t) = \left(\mu - \frac{\sigma^2}{2} \right) dt + \sigma \, dW(t)$$

Using the Euler scheme the approximate discretized version of this equation for discrete times $0 < t_1 < t_2 < \cdots < t_n$ is:

$$\ln S(t_{i+1}) - \ln S(t_i) = \left(\mu - \frac{\sigma^2}{2} \right)(t_{i+1} - t_i) + \sigma\sqrt{t_{i+1} - t_i}\, \varepsilon_{i+1}$$

or

$$S(t_{i+1}) = S(t_i) \, exp\left[\left(\mu - \frac{\sigma^2}{2} \right)(t_{i+1} - t_i) + \sigma\sqrt{t_{i+1} - t_i}\, \varepsilon_{i+1} \right] \qquad (4.45)$$

where $i = 0, 1, \cdots, n - 1$, and ε_{i+1} is an independent random instance generated from the standard normal distribution.[4] Equation (4.45) can be used to simulate random paths of the stock price. Since for European options the simulated stock prices during the time from the valuation date ($t = 0$) until the maturity date of the option T is not needed, the stock price at time T can be directly simulated using:

$$S_T = S_0 \, exp\left[\left(\mu - \frac{\sigma^2}{2} \right) T + \sigma \sqrt{T}\, \varepsilon \right] \qquad (4.46)$$

where S_T is the stock price at time T, S_0 is the current stock price, and ε is a random instance generated from the standard normal distribution.

The general procedure for valuation of European options using the Monte Carlo simulation method is as follows:

- Using Equation (4.46), generate a large number of the simulated stock prices at the maturity date of the option.
- For each path or iteration, calculate the option payoff using the simulated stock prices. For a European call the payoff is $\text{Max}(S_{T_j} - X, 0)$ and for a European put the payoff is $\text{Max}(X - S_{T_j}, 0)$, where S_{T_j} is the simulated stock price at time T for iteration j and X is the strike price.
- Calculate the average (expectation) of the payoffs at time T obtained in the previous step and discount it back to $t = 0$ using the risk-free rate.

It should be noted that since we value the option in the risk-neutral environment, the expected return of stock μ in Equation (4.46) is the risk-free rate and we discount the expected payoff also using the risk-free rate. Similar to our discussion in the previous section, if μ based on the risk preference of the investor is used in simulating the stock price, then the discounting of the expected payoff should also be done using a risk-adjusted rate. Since the risk-adjusted rate is not readily available, we can perform the valuation in the risk-neutral environment but the option value obtained is the same as in the risky environment.

Example

Consider the European call option introduced in the example of the previous section where, using the Black–Scholes–Merton model, the option value is obtained as $5.262. Recall that the option and underlying stock price have the following specifications: $T = 0.5$, $X = \$41$, $\sigma = 25\%$, $r_f = 3\%$, $S_0 = \$44.2$, and no dividend payment is expected during the term of the option.

At the first iteration of the simulation assume the random draw from the standard normal distribution is 0.408. Using Equation (4.46), the simulated stock price at $t = 0.5$ for iteration $j = 1$ is:

$$S_{T_1} = 44.2 \times exp\left[\left(0.03 - \frac{0.25^2}{2}\right) \times 0.5 + 0.25 \times \sqrt{0.5} \times 0.408\right] = 47.4763$$

The option payoff is then calculated as $\text{Max}(47.4763 - 41, 0) = 6.4763$. Repeating this process provides us with more instances of the simulated

(continued)

(*continued*)

stock price and the corresponding option payoff at $t = 0.5$. Table 4.1 presents 10 of these simulated values for our example. We repeated this process 10,000 times and the average of simulated payoffs was obtained as 5.3314. Discounting this value to $t = 0$ using a risk-free rate of 3% provides us with the option value of $e^{-0.03 \times 0.5} \times 5.3314 = 5.252$.

TABLE 4.1   Ten sample simulated stock prices and payoffs of a European call option obtained using Monte Carlo simulation

Path #	E	Stock Price	Option Payoff
1	0.4080	47.4763	6.4763
2	1.0525	53.0283	12.0283
3	0.9832	47.9633	6.9633
4	0.8228	52.5033	11.5033
5	0.4566	34.2229	0
6	0.5935	37.2814	0
7	0.6724	53.5674	12.5674
8	0.6548	35.1064	0
9	-1.4885	36.6558	0
10	1.1027	40.6549	0

Compared to European options, valuation of American options using Monte Carlo simulation is more involved. Recall from the binomial tree method that, due to the possibility of early exercise in American options, it is required to evaluate the holding value of the option (i.e., the remaining value of the option if it is not exercised at a point in time and continued to the next time step) and compare it to the payoff from the early exercise. In binomial tree this is done easily since the option's holding value at any time step is calculated as $e^{-r_f \Delta t}[\pi V_u + (1 - \pi)V_d]$, where values of the option at the following two nodes are already known and reflect the possibility of early exercise in future time steps. This is not the case for the simulation method. There are a few methods proposed to overcome this issue; here we discuss the method proposed by Andersen (2000). This method is based on a direct search for early exercise boundaries. After boundaries are established for each time step during the simulation period, a new set of simulated stock prices is generated that can be compared to those boundaries for early exercise evaluation. This method can be used for valuation of both American and Bermudan options. A *Bermudan option* is a type of option that the holder has the right, but not the obligation, to exercise on predetermined dates during the term of the contract. It can be thought of as an option type between European and American options since it can be exercised early but only at specific days (e.g., one day of each month during the term of option).

The general procedure of this method is as follows:

- Using a model such as the one presented in Equation (4.45), generate a large number of simulated stock price paths. Due to the possibility of early exercise, the entire path of the simulated stock prices from $t = 0$ to the option maturity is needed. For Bermudan options the simulation time steps can be set to match the allowable exercise dates but for American options a more granular time step is needed. This method is computationally intensive, and this should be taken into account when choosing the simulation time step length and number of paths (sample size).
- Starting from the last time step and walking backward in time, search for a boundary value for stock price S_t^* at each time step such that:
  - For a put option, if the stock price is below S_t^*, the option is exercised, and if it is above S_t^*, the option is not exercised. For a call option, if the stock price is below S_t^*, the option is not exercised, and if it is above S_t^*, the option is exercised.
  - The selected boundary value produces the optimal (maximum) value for the option in a given time step.
- After boundary values for all time steps are determined, generate another set of a large number of simulated stock prices and, using the boundary values from the previous step, evaluate the early exercise at each time step.
- The value of the option is the average of discounted payoffs over all simulated stock price paths. For each path, the discounting is done from the time step in which the option exercise has occurred. If for a simulated path the option is not exercised throughout the entire path, including the maturity date, the payoff for that path is zero.

The following example demonstrates this method for an American put option.

Example

Consider an American put option with three-month term. For simplicity, here we consider a simulation time step with a length of one month. This means that in our example we examine the early exercise every month over

(continued)

(*continued*)

the term of the option. This is to simplify our discussion and in practice the simulation time step length should be shorter to produce more granular paths for the simulated stock price and to enable the evaluation of early exercise more frequently. The strike price is $22 and the current stock price is $21. Option volatility is assumed as 30% and the risk-free rate for all terms is 3%. Assume that simulated stock prices for 10 paths are as presented in Table 4.2. In practice, the number of paths should be much larger.

TABLE 4.2   Ten simulated stock prices for derivation of boundary values for evaluation of early exercise of an American put option

Time	Path									
(Month)	1	2	3	4	5	6	7	8	9	10
0	21.00	21.00	21.00	21.00	21.00	21.00	21.00	21.00	21.00	21.00
1	22.51	20.20	21.22	22.65	18.85	21.68	22.98	22.48	21.20	22.66
2	21.57	17.56	21.40	19.99	21.11	20.79	23.59	23.21	20.74	18.10
3	20.51	19.78	21.40	17.21	20.36	20.27	19.23	23.13	21.71	22.23

Starting from $t = 3$ months, the boundary value at this time step is the same as the strike price. Since this is a put option, if the stock price is below $S^*_{t=3} = X = 22$, the option will be exercised and if stock price is above this boundary value, the option will not be exercised. Based on this, the option is exercised at all paths except 8 and 10. Payoffs at $t = 3$ are as follow, with an average value of 1.5530:

Time:	3	S^*:	22.00								
Path:	1	2	3	4	5	6	7	8	9	10	Average
Option Exercised?	Yes	Yes	Yes	Yes	Yes	Yes	Yes	No	Yes	No	
Payoff:	1.4900	2.2200	0.6000	4.7900	1.6400	1.7300	2.7700	0.0000	0.2900	0.0000	1.5530

Moving backward to $t = 2$, first assume $S^*_{t=2} < 17.56$, where 17.56 is the lowest simulated stock price at this time step. Since no simulated stock price is below this boundary value, no early exercise occurs and the payoff for each path is equal to the holding value, which is the discounted pay-off from $t = 3$. These payoffs are shown below where each is obtained by multiplying the payoff at $t = 3$ from the preceding table by $e^{-0.03 \times \frac{1}{12}}$. The average of these payoffs is 1.5491:

Time:	2	S*:	<17.56								
Path:	1	2	3	4	5	6	7	8	9	10	Average
Option Exercised?	No	No	No	No	No	No	No	No	No	No	
Payoff:		1.4863	2.2145	0.5985	4.7780	1.6359	1.7257	2.7631	0.0000	0.2893	0.0000 1.5491

Continuing at $t = 2$, now assume that $S^*_{t=2} = 17.56$. Based on this boundary value, the option is assumed to be exercised only at path 2. Therefore the payoff of the option for this path, assuming early exercise, is $22 - 17.56 = 4.44$. Payoffs for other paths with no early exercise are, as before, equal to the discounted payoffs from $t = 3$, as shown in the following table, with an average value of 1.7717:

Time:	2	S*:	17.56								
Path:	1	2	3	4	5	6	7	8	9	10	Average
Option Exercised?	No	Yes	No	No	No	No	No	No	No	No	
Payoff:		1.4863	4.4400	0.5985	4.7780	1.6359	1.7257	2.7631	0.0000	0.2893	0.0000 1.7717

Now assume that $S^*_{t=2} = 18.10$, the second-lowest simulated stock price at $t = 2$. Based on this boundary value, the option is assumed to be exercised at paths 2 and 10. Payoffs for these two paths are 4.44 and 3.90 and payoffs for the rest of the paths are discounted payoffs from $t = 3$, as shown in the following table, with an average value of 2.1617:

Time:	2	S*:	18.10								
Path:	1	2	3	4	5	6	7	8	9	10	Average
Option Exercised?	No	Yes	No	No	No	No	No	No	No	Yes	
Payoff:		1.4863	4.4400	0.5985	4.7780	1.6359	1.7257	2.7631	0.0000	0.2893	3.9000 2.1617

Repeating this process for $S^*_{t=2}$ of 19.99, 20.74, 20.79, 21.11, 21.40, 21.57, 23.21, and 23.59 (i.e., other simulated stock prices at $t = 2$), we obtained average payoffs of 1.8849, 1.9819, 1.9304, 1.8558, 1.8559, 1.7503,

(continued)

(continued)

1.7503, and 1.4740 respectively. A comparison of these averages shows the optimal expected option payoff at $t = 2$ is 2.1617 when $S_{t=2}^* = 18.10$. Hence this is the boundary value for a stock price that would be used for evaluation of an early exercise decision at $t = 2$.[5] Also, since the preceding table contains payoffs according to the optimal early exercise decision for $t = 2$, the holding values for $t = 1$ are calculated by discounting payoffs in this table.

Moving backward to $t = 1$, first assume that $S_{t=1}^* < 18.85$, where 18.85 is the lowest simulated stock price at this time step. Since no simulated stock price at this time step is below this boundary value, no early exercise occurs and the payoff for each path is equal to the holding value. Holding values are the discounted payoffs from $t = 2$ based on $S_{t=2}^* = 18.10$. Payoffs for $t = 1$ and $S_{t=1}^* < 18.85$ are shown in the following table, with an average value of 2.1563:

Time:	1	S*:	<18.85								
Path:	1	2	3	4	5	6	7	8	9	10	Average
Option Exercised?	No	No	No	No	No	No	No	No	No	No	
Payoff:	1.4826	4.4289	0.5970	4.7661	1.6318	1.7214	2.7562	0.0000	0.2886	3.8903	2.1563

For example, in the above table, the payoff for path 1 of 1.4826 is obtained as $1.4863 \times e^{-0.03 \times \frac{1}{12}}$ where 1.4863 is the payoff of path 1 at $t = 2$ with an optimal boundary value of $S_{t=2}^* = 18.10$.

Continuing at $t = 1$ and repeating this process for $S_{t=1}^*$ of 18.85, 20.20, 21.20, 21.22, 21.68, 22.48, 22.51, 22.65, 22.66, and 22.98 (i.e., simulated stock prices at $t = 1$), the average payoffs are obtained as 2.3081, 2.0452, 2.0964, 2.1146, 1.9745, 1.9745, 1.8263, 1.3496, 0.9606, and 0.6850, respectively. By comparing these averages, the optimal payoff value of 2.3081 is obtained when $S_{t=1}^* = 18.85$. Payoffs at $t = 1$, based on this optimal boundary value, are shown in the following table:

Time:	1	S*:	18.85								
Path:	1	2	3	4	5	6	7	8	9	10	Average
Option Exercised?	No	No	No	No	Yes	No	No	No	No	No	
Payoff:	1.4826	4.4289	0.5970	4.7661	3.1500	1.7214	2.7562	0.0000	0.2886	3.8903	2.3081

Finally, the early exercise decision at $t = 0$ is based on comparing the holding value and payoff from early exercise. Here the holding value is $2.3081 \times e^{-0.03 \times \frac{1}{12}} = 2.3023$, which is higher than the early exercise payoff of $22 - 21 = 1$.

After early exercise boundary values for all simulation time steps are obtained, they can be used in the next phase when a new and independent set of simulated stock prices is generated to determine the expected option value. To illustrate this, assume that four new simulated stock price paths are generated as shown in Table 4.3.

TABLE 4.3 Four simulated stock prices for valuation of an American put option

Path → ↓Time (Month)	1'	2'	3'	4'
0	21.00	21.00	21.00	21.00
1	21.51	21.51	18.05	19.30
2	22.30	17.57	22.56	21.30
3	21.10	22.51	20.92	23.89

To emphasize that these paths are different and independent from the ones used in derivation of the early exercise boundary values, they are tagged as 1', 2', 3', and 4'. Evaluating the early exercise and the option payoff based on these paths is done as follows:

Path 1': Comparing the simulated stock at time $t = 1$, $t = 2$, and $t = 3$ with boundary values of $S_{t=1}^{*} = 18.85$, $S_{t=2}^{*} = 18.10$, and $S_{t=3}^{*} = 22$ shows that the option is not exercised at $t = 1$ and $t = 2$ but exercised at the maturity date of $t = 3$. Therefore, the discounted value of the payoff of this path at $t = 0$ is $\text{Max}(0, 22-21.1) \times e^{-0.03 \times \frac{3}{12}} = 0.8933$.

Path 2': For this path, the simulated stock price at $t = 1$ is above the boundary value of $S_{t=1}^{*} = 18.85$ so the option is not exercised early at this time step. However, the simulated stock price at $t = 2$ is 17.57, which is below the boundary value of $S_{t=2}^{*} = 18.10$, indicating an early exercise. Therefore, discounting the payoff of the early exercise is done from $t = 2$ to $t = 0$ as $\text{Max}(0, 22-17.57) \times e^{-0.03 \times \frac{2}{12}} = 4.4079$.

(*continued*)

(*continued*)

Path $3'$: Since the simulated stock price at $t = 1$ is 18.05 and this is below the boundary value of $S^*_{t=1} = 18.85$, the option is exercised early at $t = 1$ and the discounted value of the payoff for this path is $\text{Max}(0, 22{-}18.05) \times e^{-0.03 \times \frac{1}{12}} = 3.9401$.

Path $4'$: Comparing the boundary values with simulated stock prices, including at the maturity date, indicates that the option is not exercised at any time. Hence the discounted payoff of this path is zero.

The average of the discounted payoff over all four paths is 2.3103. This is the holding value for $t = 0$. Comparing this average with the payoff from early exercise at $t = 0$ of $22 - 21 = 1$ shows that immediate early exercise is not optimal and hence the option value is 2.3103.

In practice, both for the first phase of simulation when boundary values are determined, and for the second phase when expected payoffs are calculated, a much larger number of paths is needed to obtain a more reliable and converging result. Also, as mentioned earlier, the simulation time step length should be granular enough to better represent the possibility of early exercise in an American option. One final note about this approach is that it tends to underestimate the option price and, rather, provides a lower bound for it, which is generally tight.

SENSITIVITY OF OPTION VALUE

The option valuation methods discussed in this chapter employ different approaches in valuation while using the same set of inputs: strike price, current stock price, time to maturity, volatility, and risk-free rate, and, when the underlying stock pays dividends, dividend yield or cash flow. Since strike price is non-stochastic and assuming dividend yield or cash flow can be estimated with high accuracy, we can focus on the other four inputs and study the sensitivity of option value to those parameters. In this section we introduce these sensitivity measures and their applications in risk management of option exposures.[6]

Sensitivity to Underlying Price

Sensitivity of the option value to the underlying stock price is represented by *delta* δ and defined as:

$$\delta = \frac{\Delta V}{\Delta S} \tag{4.47}$$

where V is the option value and S is the stock price. Delta is the rate of change in option value with respect to the change of the underlying stock price. More precisely, delta is the first derivative of the option value with respect to the stock price:

$$\delta = \frac{\partial V}{\partial S} \qquad (4.48)$$

The delta of an option, once obtained, can be used for hedging a position in an option against the movement of the underlying stock price. This technique is known as *delta hedging*. To illustrate, consider a bank that sold (short) 30 call option contracts, each contract for 100 shares of the underlying stock. The current stock price is $44.20 and assume that delta of this option is 0.72. Later in this section we discuss how to calculate an option delta. Since the total number of underlying shares in this short position is $30 \times 10 = 3,000$, the bank bought (long) $\delta \times 3,000 = 0.72 \times 3,000 = 2,160$ shares to hedge the option exposure. Assume that stock price increases by $1. From Equation (4.47) the change in the value of short options is equal to $-0.72 \times 1 \times 3,000 = -\$2,160$, where the negative sign is due to the short position and 3,000 is the total number of underlying shares. At the same time, a $1 increase in stock price leads to a change of value in long stocks equal to $1 \times 2,160 = \$2,160$. Therefore, the total change in value of the portfolio of short options and long stocks is $-\$2,160 + \$2,160 = 0$. Similarly, a $1 decrease in stock price leads to a $-0.72 \times (-1) \times 3,000 = \$2,160$ increase in the value of short options and a $(-1) \times 2,160 = -\$2,160$ decrease in the value of long stocks, resulting in no change in total value of the portfolio of short options and long stock. Another way to demonstrate this delta hedging mechanism is to note that the delta of the short option is $-0.72 \times 3,000 = -\$2,160$ and the delta of the long stock is $+0.72 \times 3,000 = +\$2,160$, leading to a delta of $0 for the portfolio. A portfolio with a delta of zero is *delta-neutral,* where small changes in the underlying stock price do not change the value of the portfolio materially. Generally, the delta of a portfolio of positions in options that have the same underlying stock and positions in the underlying stocks can be derived using the delta of individual positions as:

$$\delta_{Portfolio} = \sum_{i=1}^{n} \omega_i \delta_i \qquad (4.49)$$

where n is the total number of positions, each with quantity ω_i and an individual delta of δ_i. The delta of a European call option is positive; therefore, to hedge a short position in a European call option, a long position in the underlying stock is needed where the number of shares bought is equal to the option delta multiplied by the number of underlying stocks in the option contract. Conversely, to hedge a long position in a European call option, a short position in the underlying stock is required. The delta of a European put option is negative, so to hedge a short position in a European put option, a short position in the underlying stock is needed, and to hedge a long position in a European put option, a long position in the underlying stock is required.

This approach, however, does not completely hedge the movement of stock price and is only effective if the stock price changes by a small amount. Since the delta of an option itself depends on the underlying stock price, as the stock price changes the delta of the option also changes. This means that to keep a portfolio delta-neutral, the composition of the portfolio should be revised frequently. Consider the call option discussed earlier with a delta of 0.72. Assume that a few days later the delta of the call option changes to 0.80 due to change in the stock price. At that point, a \$1 increase in stock price leads to a decrease of $-0.80 \times 1 \times 3{,}000 = -\$2{,}400$ in the short option position while the increase in the long stock position is still $1 \times 2160 = \$2{,}160$. Hence the portfolio is not fully hedged anymore. To rebalance the portfolio, the bank needs to purchase an additional $0.08 \times 3{,}000 = 240$ shares to hedge the portfolio again.

Another reason for the imperfect hedge using delta is the nonlinear relationship between the option value and the underlying stock price. Considering option value as a function of the underlying stock price, since delta is the first derivative of this function, it represents the slope of a line tangent to the option value curve at a specific stock price. This is shown schematically in Figure 4.6.

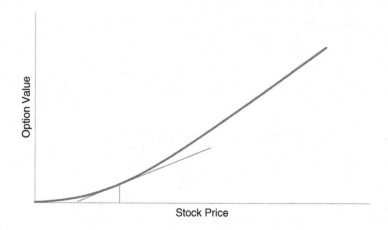

FIGURE 4.6   Option value versus stock price

Hence delta only captures the linear relationship between the change in stock price and option value, and such a linear relationship can be assumed only for a small change in stock price.

To improve the delta hedge we can consider the rate of change in delta with respect to the change in the underlying stock price. This measurement is known as gamma γ and defined as:

$$\gamma = \frac{\Delta\delta}{\Delta S} \tag{4.50}$$

More precisely, gamma is defined as:

$$\gamma = \frac{\partial\delta}{\partial S} = \frac{\partial^2 V}{\partial S^2} \tag{4.51}$$

We can use the Black–Scholes–Merton valuation formulas to obtain equations for the delta and gamma of European options. Using generalized Black–Scholes–Merton valuation formulas presented in Equations (4.42), (4.43), and (4.44), the delta of a European call option is obtained as:

$$\delta_{European\ Call} = \Phi(d_1)\, e^{-q(T-t)} \tag{4.52}$$

And for a European put option delta is:

$$\delta_{European\ Put} = (\Phi(d_1) - 1)\, e^{-q(T-t)} \tag{4.53}$$

These two equations provide us with the delta of European call and put options at a time t between the initiation of the contract and its maturity date, where the stock price at time t is S_t, T is the original term of the contract, $T - t$ is the remaining time to maturity, and q is the dividend yield. Since $\Phi(\ )$ is the cumulative standard normal distribution function, its first derivative, that is, $\varphi(\ ) = \Phi'(\ )$, is the probability density function of the standard normal distribution. Using this notation, the gammas of the European call and put options can be presented as:

$$\gamma_{European\ Call} = \frac{\varphi(d_1)\, e^{-q(T-t)}}{S_t\, \sigma\, \sqrt{T - t}} \tag{4.54}$$

$$\gamma_{European\ Put} = \frac{\varphi(d_1)\, e^{-q(T-t)}}{S_t\, \sigma\, \sqrt{T - t}} \tag{4.55}$$

The gammas of the European call and put options are equal. Derivation of these four equations is presented in Annex 2 of this chapter.

Example

Consider a call option with a strike price of $41 and a time to maturity of six months. The current underlying stock price is $44.20 and the risk-free rate is 3% and dividend yield is 0.5%, both with continuous compounding. Option volatility is assumed as 25%. Using Equations (4.44) and (4.42), d_1, d_2, and option value are calculated as:

$$d_1 = \frac{\ln\left(\frac{44.2}{41}\right) + \left(0.03 - 0.005 + \frac{0.25^2}{2}\right) \times 0.5}{0.25 \times \sqrt{0.5}} = 0.58422702$$

$$d_2 = 0.58422702 - 0.25 \times \sqrt{0.5} = 0.40745033$$

$$V_{European\ Call} = \Phi(0.58422702) \times 44.2 \times e^{-0.005 \times 0.5} - \Phi(0.40745033)$$
$$\times 41 \times e^{-0.03 \times 0.5} = 5.1822$$

Using Equations (4.52) and (4.54) delta and gamma of this call option are obtained as:

$$\delta_{European\ Call} = \Phi(0.58422702)\ e^{-0.005 \times 0.5} = 0.7187$$

$$\gamma_{European\ Call} = \frac{\varphi(0.58422702)\ e^{-0.005 \times 0.5}}{44.2 \times 0.25 \times \sqrt{0.5}} = 0.0429$$

When stock price changes by a small amount, the value of this call option changes by a factor of 0.7187 and the delta itself changes by a factor of 0.0429.

We can obtain a relationship between change in option value, change in stock price, delta, and gamma by applying Taylor series expansion to the option value as a function of the stock price near S_t:

$$V(S) = V(S_t) + \frac{\partial V(S_t)}{\partial S}(S - S_t) + \frac{1}{2!}\frac{\partial^2 V(S_t)}{\partial S^2}(S - S_t)^2$$
$$+ \frac{1}{3!}\frac{\partial^3 V(S_t)}{\partial S^3}(S - S_t)^3 + \cdots$$

By keeping the first three terms of the right-hand side of this equation and ignoring the higher-order terms while replacing the first and second derivatives with delta and gamma we obtain:

$$\Delta V \cong \delta\ \Delta S + \frac{1}{2}\gamma\ \Delta S^2 \tag{4.56}$$

For the call option in previous example, using both delta and gamma to estimate the change in value of the option when stock price increases by \$1 yields the following:

$$\Delta V \cong \delta\ \Delta S + \frac{1}{2}\gamma\ \Delta S^2 = 0.7187 \times 1 + \frac{1}{2} \times 0.0429 \times 1^2 = 0.7401$$

Gamma complements delta in estimating the change in option value by compensating for the nonlinear relationship between option value and the underlying stock price. The relationship between change in option value, change in stock price, delta, and gamma expressed in Equation (4.56) is very similar to the relationship between change in bond value, change in interest rate, modified duration, and convexity introduced in an earlier chapter and reproduced below:

$$\Delta V \cong -Duration\ V\ \Delta y + \frac{1}{2}\ Convexity\ V\ (\Delta y)^2$$

For a fixed-income instrument, $-Duration \times V$ plays the same role as delta for an option and $Convexity \times V$ is similar to gamma.

Similar to delta hedging, a portfolio of options can be made *gamma-neutral*. In the delta hedging process, since a position stock has a delta of 1, we used the position in the underlying stock as the hedging instrument. However, the stock has a gamma of zero and cannot be used as the hedging instrument to make the portfolio gamma-neutral. A position in another option is needed for gamma hedging, since the option has a nonlinear relationship with its underlying stock and hence has a non-zero gamma. Assume that the gamma of a delta-neutral portfolio of options is γ. By adding a position in another option with a gamma of $-\gamma$ we can make this portfolio gamma-neutral but then the portfolio is no longer delta-neutral and it should be rebalanced to make it delta-neutral again. To demonstrate this, consider the bank with a short position of 30 call option contracts written on 3,000 shares discussed earlier to demonstrate delta hedging. Assume that the delta of options in this short position is 0.72 and its gamma is 0.04. Thus the gamma of the short position is $-3,000 \times 0.04 = -120$, where negative is to indicate the short position. As demonstrated before, a long position in 2,160 shares of underlying stock makes the portfolio delta-neutral. Consider another option that is traded in the market with the same underlying stock with a delta of 0.65 and gamma of 0.25. To make the short position in the original option gamma-neutral, we need to take a long position in this new market-traded option for $120/0.25 = 480$ shares. The gamma of the new option is $480 \times 0.25 = 120$, so the gamma of the total portfolio is zero. Adding this long position in the new option, however, increases the delta of the total portfolio to $480 \times 0.65 = 312$. So we need to sell 312 shares of the long position in underlying stock that is held for hedging the original option to make the total portfolio delta-neutral again. Similar to delta hedging, gamma hedging is only effective for a short period of time and the portfolio should be rebalanced frequently to keep it delta-neutral and gamma-neutral.

Sensitivity to Volatility

As volatility rises, the value of a call or put option increases. The volatility parameter used in option valuation can change over time. So far we have assumed that the volatility parameter is constant. Later in this chapter we discuss various techniques for modeling the volatility. Here we study the sensitivity of the option value to the volatility. This sensitivity measure is represented by vega $\mathcal{V}$ and is defined as:

$$\mathcal{V} = \frac{\Delta V}{\Delta \sigma} \tag{4.57}$$

Or more precisely, vega is defined as the first derivative of the option value function with respect to the volatility parameter:

$$\mathcal{V} = \frac{\partial V}{\partial \sigma} \tag{4.58}$$

A high value for vega indicates a high sensitivity of option value to the change in volatility. Using the Black–Scholes–Merton model as the option valuation tool, the vegas of European call and put options are obtained as:

$$\mathcal{V}_{European\ Call} = \varphi(d_1)\, S_t\, \sqrt{T - t}\, e^{-q(T-t)} \tag{4.59}$$

$$\mathcal{V}_{European\ Put} = \varphi(d_1)\, S_t\, \sqrt{T - t}\, e^{-q(T-t)} \tag{4.60}$$

where d_1 is defined in (4.44). Other notations used in these equations are the same used in delta and gamma formulas. The vegas of European call and put options are equal. Derivations of Equations (4.59) and (4.60) are presented in Annex 2 of this chapter.

Example

Consider again the call option introduced in an example earlier in this chapter with the following specifications: $S_t = 44.2, X = 41, \sigma = 25\%, T - t = 0.5, r = 3\%$, and $q = 0.5\%$. d_1 for this option was calculated earlier as 0.58422702. Vega for this option is obtained using Equation (4.59) as:

$$V_{European\ Call} = \varphi(0.58422702) \times 44.2 \times \sqrt{0.5} \times e^{-0.005 \times 0.5} = 10.4861$$

Hence, a 1% change in σ approximately results in a change of $1\% \times 10.4861 = 0.104861$ in the option value. This estimate is approximate since the relationship between the option value and the volatility is nonlinear.

Compared to delta and gamma hedging, making a portfolio *vega-neutral* is more involved. Since the underlying stock has a zero vega and cannot be used as the hedging instrument, to make the portfolio both gamma- and vega-neutral two separate positions in two different options with the same underlying stock are needed. To demonstrate this, again consider the short option position used in the previous delta and gamma hedging examples. Recall that the delta and gamma of this short option are $\delta_S = 0.72$ and $\gamma_S = 0.04$, and the number of underlying stocks of this short option position is $\omega_S = 3,000$. The vega of this option is assumed as $V_S = 10.5$. Also assume that there are two market-traded options with the same underlying stock as the option in the short position, with the following sensitivity measures:

$$\text{Option A: } \delta_A = 0.65, \gamma_A = 0.25, V_A = 8$$
$$\text{Option B: } \delta_B = 0.8, \gamma_B = 0.5, V_A = 6$$

To achieve simultaneous gamma and vega neutrality, we need to determine the positions in options A and B by finding the number of underlying stocks for each (i.e., ω_A and ω_B) such that the total portfolio gamma and vega are zero:

$$\omega_S \gamma_S + \omega_A \gamma_A + \omega_B \gamma_B = 0$$
$$\omega_S V_S + \omega_A V_A + \omega_B V_B = 0$$

or

$$-3,000 \times 0.04 + \omega_A \times 0.25 + \omega_B \times 0.5 = 0$$
$$-3,000 \times 10.5 + \omega_A \times 8 + \omega_B \times 6 = 0$$

Solving these equations provides us with $\omega_A = 6{,}012$ and $\omega_B = -2{,}766$, meaning that a long position in option A based on 6,012 underlying shares and a short position in option B based on 2,766 underlying shares are needed to make the portfolio gamma-neutral and vega-neutral. The portfolio delta is then calculated as:

$$\omega_S \delta_S + \omega_A \delta_A + \omega_B \delta_B = -3{,}000 \times 0.72 + 6{,}012 \times 0.65 - 2{,}766 \times 0.8 = -465$$

Therefore, a long position of 465 shares of the underlying stock is needed to make the portfolio delta-neutral.

Unlike delta hedging, which is relatively straightforward, achieving gamma and vega neutrality requires trading in specific options that may not be available in the market or can lead to excessive hedging cost. Due to this, in practice making a portfolio of options delta-neutral is more common compared to making it gamma- or vega-neutral.

Sensitivity to the Interest Rate

The sensitivity of the option value to the interest rate is represented by *rho* ρ and is the rate of change in option value with respect to a change in the risk-free interest rate:

$$\rho = \frac{\Delta V}{\Delta r_f} \tag{4.61}$$

More precisely, rho is the first derivative of option value function with respect to the risk-free rate:

$$\rho = \frac{\partial V}{\partial r_f} \tag{4.62}$$

A high value for rho indicates a high sensitivity of option value to the interest rate. Using the Black–Scholes–Merton model as the valuation tool, the rho of European call and put options is obtained as:

$$\rho_{European\ Call} = \Phi(d_2)\, X\, (T - t)\, e^{-r_f(T-t)} \tag{4.63}$$

$$\rho_{European\ Put} = -\Phi(-d_2)\, X\, (T - t)\, e^{-r_f(T-t)} \tag{4.64}$$

where d_2 is defined in Equation (4.44). Other notations used in these equations are the same that were used in the delta, gamma, and vega formulas introduced earlier. Derivations of Equations (4.63) and (4.64) are presented in Annex 2 of this chapter.

Example

Consider again the European call option that was used in earlier examples for delta, gamma, and vega. d_2 for this option was calculated as 0.40745033. Using Equation (4.63), rho is calculated as:

$$\rho_{European\ Call} = \Phi(0.40745033) \times 41 \times 0.5 \times e^{-0.03 \times 0.5} = 13.2914$$

Therefore, a 1% change in the risk-free rate results in a change of approximately $1\% \times 13.2914 = 0.132914$ in the option value.

Sensitivity to the Passage of Time

After an option contract's inception, as time passes the value of an option changes. An option value's sensitivity to the passage of time is represented by *theta* θ and defined as:

$$\theta = \frac{\Delta V}{\Delta t} \tag{4.65}$$

If T is the original term of the contract and $T - t$ is the remaining term, theta can be defined as the first derivative of the option value function with respect to t:

$$\theta = \frac{\partial V}{\partial t} \tag{4.66}$$

Using the Black–Scholes–Merton model as the option valuation tool, the thetas of European call and put options are expressed as:

$$\theta_{European\ Call} = \frac{-\varphi(d_1)\, S_t\, \sigma\, e^{-q(T-t)}}{2\sqrt{T-t}} + \Phi(d_1)\, q\, S_t\, e^{-q(T-t)}$$
$$- \Phi(d_2)\, r_f\, X\, e^{-r_f(T-t)} \tag{4.67}$$

$$\theta_{European\ Put} = \frac{-\varphi(d_1)\, S_t\, \sigma\, e^{-q(T-t)}}{2\sqrt{T-t}} - \Phi(-d_1)\, q\, S_t\, e^{-q(T-t)}$$
$$+ \Phi(-d_2)\, r_f\, X\, e^{-r_f(T-t)} \tag{4.68}$$

Derivations of Equations (4.67) and (4.68) are presented in Annex 2 of this chapter.

> ## Example
>
> Consider again the European call option used in earlier examples for delta, gamma, vega, and rho. The parameters used in those examples are: $S_t = 44.2$, $X = 41$, $\sigma = 25\%$, $T - t = 0.5$, $r_f = 3\%$, and $q = 0.5\%$. d_1 and d_2 for this option were calculated earlier as 0.58422702 and 0.40745033, respectively. Using Equation (4.67), the theta of this European call option is calculated as:
>
> $$\theta_{European\ Call} = \frac{-\varphi(0.58422702) \times 44.2 \times 0.25 \times e^{-0.005 \times 0.5}}{2 \times \sqrt{0.5}}$$
> $$+ \Phi(0.58422702) \times 0.005 \times 44.2 \times e^{-0.005 \times 0.5}$$
> $$- \Phi(0.40745033) \times 0.03 \times 41 \times e^{-0.03 \times 0.5} = -3.2602$$
>
> Considering the six-month remaining term of this option, a theta of -3.2602 means that after a month is passed, the price of this call option will decrease by approximately $\frac{1}{12} \times 3.2602 = 0.2717$.

VOLATILITY

So far in our discussion of option valuation, we have considered volatility as a given parameter that is readily available and selected by the analyst. Volatility is the most important factor in option pricing and a great deal of models and methodologies have been developed that focus on the appropriate volatility for use in option valuation. In this section, first we discuss derivation of the volatility parameter using past data of the underlying stock price. Volatility obtained this way is called *historical volatility* and is constant for any given date. Such constant volatility can then be used in option valuation techniques discussed earlier in this chapter. Then we introduce *implied volatility*, which is the volatility derived using an option pricing technique from available option values. In practice, there is plenty of evidence that volatility changes over time. In a following section we introduce a few methods for modeling non-constant volatility.

Historical Volatility

Defining volatility as the standard deviation of change in the price of the underlying stock of an option contract, we can use historical data of the stock price to calculate the volatility. Recall that Equation (4.37) implies that the change in the natural logarithm of stock price in a short time period Δt has a normal distribution with a mean of $\left(\mu - \frac{\sigma^2}{2}\right)\Delta t$ and a variance of $\sigma^2 \Delta t$, where μ and σ are the annual expected return and annual volatility of the stock. So:

$$\ln S_{t+\Delta t} - \ln S_t \sim N\left(\left(\mu - \frac{\sigma^2}{2}\right)\Delta t, \sigma^2 \Delta t\right)$$

or

$$\ln \frac{S_{t+\Delta t}}{S_t} \sim N\left(\left(\mu - \frac{\sigma^2}{2}\right)\Delta t, \sigma^2 \Delta t\right) \tag{4.69}$$

Based on this, if we have a series of daily historical stock prices, we can use them to find an estimator for volatility σ. In this case, $\Delta t = 1$ day. Assume at the end of day $t - 1$ we have $n + 1$ historical stock prices as:

$$S_{t-n-1}, S_{t-n}, \cdots, S_{t-2}, S_{t-1}$$

From this data series we can calculate n logarithm of daily price changes:

$$\ln \frac{S_{t-n}}{S_{t-n-1}}, \cdots, \ln \frac{S_{t-2}}{S_{t-3}}, \ln \frac{S_{t-1}}{S_{t-2}}$$

From Equation (4.69) the standard deviation of this series is an estimate for $\sigma\sqrt{\Delta t}$ where Δt is in years. Historical stock prices are usually obtained for each market trading day and assuming there are 252 trading days in a calendar year, $\Delta t = \frac{1}{252}$ year. Defining r_{t-i} as the logarithm of daily price change for day $t - i$ and $\bar{r}$ as the average of them over n available data points, we have:[7]

$$r_{t-i} = \ln \frac{S_{t-i}}{S_{t-i-1}} \tag{4.70}$$

$$\bar{r} = \sum_{i=1}^{n} \frac{r_{t-i}}{n} \tag{4.71}$$

$$\hat{\sigma}_{t\,(Daily)} = \sqrt{\frac{\sum_{i=1}^{n}(r_{t-i} - \bar{r})^2}{n - 1}} \tag{4.72}$$

$$\hat{\sigma}_{t\,(Annual)} = \sqrt{252}\,\hat{\sigma}_{t\,(Daily)}$$

where hat over $\hat{\sigma}_t$ indicates that this is an estimated value. $\hat{\sigma}_t$ in Equation (4.72) is the historical volatility as of the end of trading day $t - 1$ and can be used as an estimate for the volatility for trading day t. Selecting the number of historical stock prices to use in this calculation often is based on the term of the option that the volatility used for its valuation. For example, for valuing an option with a 90-day term, we can use 90 historical stock prices to calculate the volatility.

Example

Assume that historical prices of a company for 16 trading days from December 26, 2018, to January 17, 2019, are as listed in Table 4.4. This table also shows the calculated value for logarithm of daily price changes r_{t-i}. For example, logarithms of daily price changes for January 17, 2019 ($i = 1$) and for January 16, 2019 ($i = 2$) are calculated as:

$$r_{t-1} = \ln \frac{99.17}{99.41} = -0.00241716$$

$$r_{t-2} = \ln \frac{99.41}{97.99} = 0.01438728$$

TABLE 4.4   Historical prices of a company stock and calculation of historical volatility

Date	As-of Day	i	Price	r_{t-i}
1/17/2019	$t-1$	1	99.17	−0.00241716
1/16/2019	$t-2$	2	99.41	0.01438728
1/15/2019	$t-3$	3	97.99	−0.00458179
1/14/2019	$t-4$	4	98.44	−0.00111681
1/11/2019	$t-5$	5	98.55	0.00294701
1/10/2019	$t-6$	6	98.26	−0.00578418
1/9/2019	$t-7$	7	98.83	0.00182297
1/8/2019	$t-8$	8	98.65	0.00487756
1/7/2019	$t-9$	9	98.17	0.00541342
1/4/2019	$t-10$	10	97.64	0.04407475
1/3/2019	$t-11$	11	93.43	−0.02379680
1/2/2019	$t-12$	12	95.68	0.00376964
12/31/2018	$t-13$	13	95.32	0.00948674
12/28/2018	$t-14$	14	94.42	−0.00274987
12/27/2018	$t-15$	15	94.68	0.00891158
12/26/2018	$t-16$	16	93.84	
			Average:	0.00368296

Since there are 16 historical prices available, we have 15 daily price changes. The average of logarithms of price changes in Table 4.4 is obtained as $\bar{r} = 0.00368296$. Using Equation (4.72) we have:

$$\hat{\sigma}_{t\,(Daily)} = \sqrt{\frac{\sum_{i=1}^{15}(r_{t-i} - \bar{r})^2}{14}}$$

$$= \sqrt{\frac{(-0.00241716 - 0.00368296)^2 + \cdots + (0.00891158 - 0.00368296)^2}{14}}$$

$$\cong 0.014218$$

$$\hat{\sigma}_{t\,(Annual)} = \sqrt{252}\,\hat{\sigma}_{t\,(Daily)} = \sqrt{252} \times 0.014218 \cong 0.225708$$

Hence, based on this data set, daily and annual volatilities of the stock price at the end of January 17, 2019, are approximately 1.42% and 22.57%, which can be used as an estimated volatility for day t, January 18, 2019.

In this method all historical data points used in the estimation process impact the volatility equally. In practice, in estimating volatility it is often desirable to assign higher importance to more recent observations compared to older data points. Therefore, a natural extension of this methodology is to assign different weights to historical price changes. This way we can assign higher weights to more recent data to increase their importance in calculating historical volatility. Assume that ω_{t-i} is the positive weight given to the logarithm of daily change for day $t - i$ where the sum of weights of all n available data points is 1. Based on this, Equations (4.70) and (4.71) can be written as:

$$\bar{r} = \sum_{i=1}^{n}\omega_{t-i}r_{t-i} \tag{4.73}$$

$$\hat{\sigma}_{t\,(Daily)} = \sqrt{\frac{n\sum_{i=1}^{n}\omega_{t-i}(r_{t-i} - \bar{r})^2}{n-1}} \tag{4.74}$$

where for each i, $0 < \omega_{t-i} < 1$ and $\sum_{i=1}^{n}\omega_{t-i} = 1$.

Implied Volatility

For an option contract, *implied volatility* is the volatility of the underlying asset, which when used in an option pricing model will return a value equal to the market price of the option. Implied volatility provides an estimate of what market participants implicitly assume for the volatility of the underlying asset when providing a price quotation for an option contract, or when buying or selling the contract.

For the stock options we have studied so far, any of the three valuation methods explained in this chapter (i.e., binomial tree, Black–Scholes–Merton model, and Monte Carlo simulation) can be used for derivation of the implied volatility. The general procedure for calculation of the implied volatility is as follows:

- Obtain the market value of the option contract.
- Assume an initial volatility value for the underlying stock.
- Perform the valuation of the option using the selected method using the volatility from the previous step as an input and obtain the option value.
- Iteratively change the input volatility until the option value from the selected method is equal to the observed market value of the option contract. In practice, the iterative process is repeated until the difference between two values is lower than a predefined threshold.
- At the end of this process, the input volatility that produces the value equal, or very close, to the observed market value is the implied volatility.

Implied volatilities are often derived and quoted based on the Black–Scholes–Merton model as the valuation method.

Example

Consider a European call option with a three-month term and a strike price of $98. The underlying stock has an expected dividend yield of 1.2% and the risk-free rate is 3.5%, both with continuous compounding. Current stock price is $102 and the market quote for this option contract for a call on one share is 7.0808. To find the implied volatility using the Black–Scholes–Merton model, we first assume that the volatility is 25%. Using Equations (4.42) and (4.44), the option value is calculated as:

$$d_1 = \frac{\ln\left(\frac{102}{98}\right) + \left(0.035 - 0.012 + \frac{0.25^2}{2}\right) \times (3/12)}{0.25 \times \sqrt{3/12}} = 0.428543$$

$$d_2 = 0.428543 - 0.25 \times \sqrt{3/12} = 0.303543$$

$$V_{0:\ European\ Call} = \Phi(0.428543) \times 102 \times e^{-0.012 \times \frac{3}{12}}$$

$$- \Phi(0.303543) \times 98 \times e^{-0.035 \times \frac{3}{12}} = 7.5565$$

Since this value is above the quoted market price, we need to decrease the input volatility in the next trial. By assuming volatility is 22%, the option value is obtained as 7.0063. Since this result is below the quoted market price we need to increase the input volatility in the next trial. By repeating this process the implied volatility is obtained as 22.41%, which makes the option value from the Black–Scholes–Merton model very close to the quoted price of 7.0808.

It can be shown that the implied volatility of the European call and put options with the same strike price and term are the same. Market participants often quote option prices based on their Black–Scholes–Merton implied volatilities. The quoted implied volatilities vary by the strike price and term, forming a *volatility surface*. Table 4.5 shows a sample of such an implied volatility surface for the option contract discussed in our example.

Non-Constant Volatility

The option valuation methods discussed so far in this chapter all assume that the volatility of the underlying stock is constant. In fact, there is plenty of evidence indicating that volatility changes over time. Figure 4.7 presents the 25-day historical volatility of the S&P 500 index from February 1985 to February 2019, calculated using Equation (4.74) and presented on a daily basis. The historical volatility is clearly changing over time. For example, during the 2014–2016 period, volatility is substantially lower than during the financial crisis period of 2007–2009. Another feature of the volatility change that

TABLE 4.5 A sample of implied volatility by option strike and term. Numbers in the body of table are volatilities in percentage

Strike→ Vol↘ ↓Term	...	94	95	96	97	98	99	100	101	102	...	119	120	...
1M	...	23.61	22.73	21.93	21.18	20.50	19.86	19.27	18.73	18.21	...	19.58	19.88	...
2M	...	23.46	22.92	22.41	21.91	21.44	20.97	20.53	20.10	19.68	...	18.13	18.26	...
3M	...	23.94	23.54	23.15	22.77	22.41	22.07	21.74	21.44	21.15	...	18.63	18.63	...
6M	...	23.39	23.12	22.86	22.61	22.36	22.12	21.90	21.68	21.46	...	19.09	19.01	...
9M	...	23.52	23.30	23.09	22.89	22.69	22.50	22.31	22.13	21.95	...	19.72	19.63	...
12M	...	23.62	23.44	23.26	23.08	22.91	22.74	22.58	22.42	22.27	...	20.20	20.11	...
18M	...	23.71	23.55	23.41	23.26	23.12	22.98	22.84	22.71	22.71	...	20.83	20.75	...
24M	...	23.78	24.15	24.12	24.04	23.99	23.67	23.10	23.06	22.95	...	21.32	21.26	...

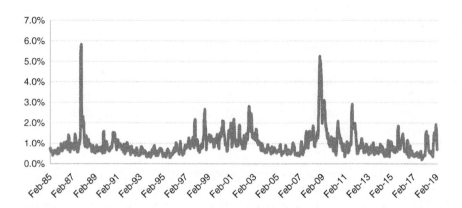

FIGURE 4.7   25-day rolling historical volatility of the S&P 500 index
Source: Original index data from FRED, the Federal Reserve Bank of St. Louis
(https://fred.stlouisfed.org/series/SP500).

can be seen in this graph is volatility clustering, where a high-volatility day
is usually followed by another high-volatility day while a low-volatility day
is often followed by another low-volatility day. Non-constant volatility is also
evidenced from the price of options traded in the market. If the volatility
is constant, it should be independent of the strike price or term of the
option but in practice implied volatility that is driven by option price varies
systematically with both.[8] The Black-Scholes–Merton model assumes that
volatility is constant and this is usually considered as a weakness of option
valuation using this model.

There are a few approaches proposed in academia and used by finance
practitioners to model volatility that changes over time. In this section we
briefly review a few of these techniques and in the following section we
demonstrate how one of them can be used in option valuation.

ARCH and GARCH Models

To start our discussion, assume that the daily rate of return of an asset, such
as stock, has two components: an anticipated part and an unanticipated part.
This can be presented using the following model:

$$r_t = \mu_t + u_t \tag{4.75}$$

where r_t is the daily rate of return, its anticipated part is μ_t, and the unanticipated part is u_t. μ_t can be considered as constant or modeled so it changes
over time. Regression or time series techniques can be used to model μ_t. For
example, it can be a function of the risk-free rate or it can even be assumed

to be zero, if the expected daily rate of return of the asset is very small. The unanticipated part of daily rate of return u_t is assumed to have a random nature, acting like *shock* or *noise* around μ_t. Since u_t has a random nature, it can be represented by a random variable with an assumed probability distribution. The most common approach is to assume that u_t has a normal distribution with mean 0 and a variance that depends on time.[9] To ease the notation of the upcoming formulas and following the common convention used in quantitative finance literature, here we use h_t to represent the variance of u_t. Therefore we can show u_t as follows:

$$u_t = \sqrt{h_t}\varepsilon_t \tag{4.76}$$

where ε_t is a random variable with standard normal distribution $\varepsilon_t \sim N(0,1)$. Based on this notation, and since we use the volatility term to refer to the standard deviation of asset price changes, time-dependent volatility is $\sqrt{h_t}$. If μ_t follows a simple modeling structure, such as the *capital asset pricing model (CAPM)*,[10] where volatility of the daily rate of return r_t is governed only by the volatility of u_t, we can consider μ_t to be the conditional expectation of r_t and h_t as the conditional variance of both u_t and r_t, given all the available information until and including time $t-1$:

$$\mu_t = E[r_t|\mathcal{F}_{t-1}] \tag{4.77}$$
$$\sigma_t^2 = h_t = Var[r_t|\mathcal{F}_{t-1}] = Var[u_t|\mathcal{F}_{t-1}] = E[u_t^2|\mathcal{F}_{t-1}]$$

where $\mathcal{F}_{t-1}$ is the set of all information available until and including time $t-1$. The last part of this equation is obtained by noting that the mean of u_t is zero. In the remainder of this section we refer to r_t as daily rate of return and u_t as daily shock, where both are assumed to have continuous compounding.

The focus of a volatility model is to capture the behavioral variance of u_t and its evolution through time. The *autoregressive conditional heteroscedasticity (ARCH)* model which was first introduced by Engle (1982) is a pioneering work in modeling time-varying variance. In one implementation method of this model we can assume that a variance of u_t at time t, conditional to all information available until and including time $t-1$, is a function of previous daily shocks (lagged shocks). If we use q of such lagged shocks, one way to present an ARCH model of order q, ARCH(q), is as follows:

$$r_t = \mu_t + u_t \quad u_t \mid \mathcal{F}_{t-1} \sim N(0, h_t)$$
$$u_t = \sqrt{h_t}\varepsilon_t \quad \varepsilon_t \sim N(0,1) \tag{4.78}$$

$$h_t = \alpha_0 + \sum_{i=1}^{q} \alpha_i u_{t-i}^2 \tag{4.79}$$

where $\alpha_0 > 0$ and $\alpha_i \geq 0$ for all $i > 0$. Equation (4.78) is the model for the mean of the rate of return and Equation (4.79) is the model for its variance. To ensure that the process is stationary and u_t has a finite long-run variance, we must have $\sum_{i=1}^{q} \alpha_i < 1$. It can be shown that the unconditional variance of u_t or r_t is obtained as (Hamilton 1994):

$$\sigma^2 = \frac{\alpha_0}{1 - \sum_{i=1}^{q} \alpha_i} \tag{4.80}$$

The recursive equation of h_t in (4.79) is the center of the ARCH model. This equation presents the estimate of the variance at time t as a linear function of squares of previous daily shocks. In this recursive process, ε_t is a sequence of *independent and identically distributed (iid)* random instances from a standard normal distribution. In a variation of the ARCH model it is assumed that ε_t has student's t-distribution.

A natural extension of ARCH is to model variance at time t as a function of the square of previous daily shocks, as well as a linear function of previous variances. This extension is known as the *generalized autoregressive conditional heteroscedasticity (GARCH)* model, which was first introduced by Bollerslev (1986) and has since gained popularity both in academia and with practitioners in modeling time-varying variances of return of different asset types. If we use q lagged shocks and p lagged variances, one way to present a GARCH(p,q) model is:

$$h_t = \alpha_0 + \sum_{i=1}^{q} \alpha_i u_{t-i}^2 + \sum_{j=1}^{p} \beta_j h_{t-j} \tag{4.81}$$

where the model for the rate of return is similar to Equation (4.78). In this equation, $\alpha_0 > 0$, $\alpha_i \geq 0$ and $\beta_i \geq 0$ for all i and $j > 0$. Similar to the ARCH model, to have a stationary process and hence to have a finite long-run variance for u_t, in the GARCH model we must have $\sum_{i=1}^{\max(q,p)}(\alpha_i + \beta_i) < 1$. It can be shown that the unconditional variance of u_t or r_t is obtained as (Hamilton 1994):[11]

$$\sigma^2 = \frac{\alpha_0}{1 - \sum_{i=1}^{\max(q,p)}(\alpha_i + \beta_i)} \tag{4.82}$$

The GARCH model provides a recursive method to estimate conditional variance at time t using a linear combination of the square of previous daily shocks and another linear combination of previous estimated variances. The nature of the GARCH model allows us to model the clustering of volatility where one large variance tends to be followed by another large variance. Parameters α_i in the model presented in Equation (4.81) are usually referred to as ARCH parameters and β_i as GARCH parameters. Since ε_t is normally distributed, the maximum likelihood estimation method, introduced in the book's Appendix, can be used to estimate the parameters of the GARCH model. Statistical software packages such as SAS® can fit the GARCH model to time series data and estimate its parameters.

A special case of the GARCH model that is usually used in practice is when $q = 1$ and $p = 1$. In a GARCH(1,1) model the variance at time t, h_t, is a linear function of estimated variance at previous step h_{t-1} and the square of the most recent shock u_{t-1}^2:

$$h_t = \alpha_0 + \alpha_1 u_{t-1}^2 + \beta_1 h_{t-1} \tag{4.83}$$

Example

Consider a time series that consists of daily stock prices of a publicly traded company over a period of two years, from January 18, 2017, to January 17, 2019. A partial view of this series is shown in Table 4.6. We fitted the following GARCH (1,1) to this dataset:

$$r_t = 0.002524 + u_t$$

$$u_t = \sqrt{h_t}\varepsilon_t \quad \varepsilon_t \sim N(0,1)$$

$$h_t = 0.0000071 + 0.1395\, u_{t-1}^2 + 0.8112\, h_{t-1}$$

where $\alpha_0 = 0.0000071$, $\alpha_1 = 0.1395$, and $\beta_1 = 0.8112$. In this model, the expected daily rate of return is a constant: $\mu_t = 0.002524$. Hence:

$$u_{t-1} = r_{t-1} - 0.002524 = \ln \frac{S_{t-1}}{S_{t-2}} - 0.002524$$

Table 4.6 demonstrates the recursive estimation of the conditional variance of u_t, which is the same as the conditional variance of r_t. The stock price at the oldest data point at January 18, 2017, is used to calculate the first rate of return, hence the recursive process starts at January 19, 2017. We can initialize h_t at this date by either assuming a zero value or using the unconditional variance of u_t, or set the h_t equal to the square of the most recent observed shock u_{t-1}^2. Here we used $u_{t-1}^2 = (-0.01290157)^2 = 0.00016645$ to initialize conditional variance at January 19, 2017. This is the estimated variance for the next trading

(continued)

(*continued*)

TABLE 4.6 Estimation of volatility using a GARCH (1,1) model

Date	Price (S)	Rate of Return (r)	Shock (u)	Conditional Variance (h)	Conditional Volatility (σ)
1/17/2019	99.17	−0.00241716	−0.00494116	0.00012853	0.011337
1/16/2019	99.41	0.01438728	0.01186328	0.00014549	0.012062
1/15/2019	97.99	−0.00458179	−0.00710579	0.00014640	0.012100
1/14/2019	98.44	−0.00111681	−0.00364081	0.00016304	0.012769
1/11/2019	98.55	0.00294701	0.00042301	0.00018995	0.013782
1/10/2019	98.26	−0.00578418	−0.00830818	0.00022538	0.015013
1/9/2019	98.83	0.00182297	−0.00070103	0.00025721	0.016038
1/8/2019	98.65	0.00487756	0.00235356	0.00030824	0.017557
1/7/2019	98.17	0.00541342	0.00288942	0.00037028	0.019243
1/4/2019	97.64	0.04407475	0.04155075	0.00044627	0.021125
1/3/2019	93.43	−0.02379680	−0.02632080	0.00024448	0.015636
1/2/2019	95.68	0.00376964	0.00124564	0.00017350	0.013172
12/31/2018	95.32	0.00948674	0.00696274	0.00020486	0.014313
12/28/2018	94.42	−0.00274987	−0.00527387	0.00023544	0.015344
12/27/2018	94.68	0.00891158	0.00638758	0.00027671	0.016635
12/26/2018	93.84	−0.04337627	−0.04590027	0.00032534	0.018037
12/26/2018	93.84	−0.04337627	−0.04590027	0.00032534	0.018037
..	..	..	..	..	..
1/20/2017	76.20	−0.00640986	−0.00893386	0.00015326	0.012380
1/19/2017	76.69	−0.01037757	−0.01290157	0.00016645	0.012902
1/18/2017	77.49				

day of January 20, estimated at the end of January 19. On January 20 the observed daily rate of return and shock amounts are:

$$r_{t-1} = \ln \frac{76.20}{76.69} = -0.00640986$$

$$u_{t-1} = r_{t-1} - 0.002524 = -0.00640986 - 0.002524 = -0.00893386$$

Therefore, the estimated daily variance for the next trading day obtained at the end of January 20 is calculated as:

$$h_t = 0.0000071 + 0.1395 \times (-0.00893386)^2 + 0.8112$$

$$\times 0.00016645 = 0.00015326$$

This recursive process is continued through the available data to obtain the estimated daily volatilities. On January 17, 2019, the last date with available data, the estimated daily volatility for the next trading day is calculated as follows:

The most recent observed daily rate of return is:

$$r_{t-1} = \ln \frac{99.17}{99.41} = -0.00241716$$

The most recent observed daily shock is:

$$u_{t-1} = r_{t-1} - 0.002524 = -0.00241716 - 0.002524 = -0.00494116$$

The estimated daily variance at the end of the previous trading day is 0.00014549, so the estimated daily variance for the next trading day is:

$$h_t = 0.0000071 + 0.1395 \times (-0.00494116)^2 + 0.8112$$

$$\times 0.00014549 = 0.00012853$$

This is the estimated daily variance for the next trading date of January 18, 2019, obtained at the end of January 17, 2019. The volatility is the square root of this value, as shown in the last column of Table 4.6:

$$\sigma_{t(Daily)} = \sqrt{0.00012853} = 1.1337\%$$

Assuming there are 252 trading days in a calendar year, the estimated annual volatility is obtained as:

$$\sigma_{t(Annual)} = \sqrt{252} \times 1.1337\% = 17.9971\%$$

Using Equation (4.82), the unconditional daily variance of the rate of return (long-run variance) based on this GARCH model is obtained as:

$$\sigma^2 = \frac{\alpha_0}{1 - \alpha_1 - \beta_1} = \frac{0.0000071}{1 - 0.1395 - 0.8112} = 0.000144$$

Forecasting Volatility Using the GARCH Model

We can use the GARCH model to forecast volatility at k days ahead. Focusing on the GARCH (1,1) model, assume that we are at the end of day $t - 1$.

Equation (4.83) provides the conditional variance for the next day, day t:

$$h_t = \alpha_0 + \alpha_1 u_{t-1}^2 + \beta_1 h_{t-1}$$

The one-day-ahead forecast using the available data until the end of day $t-1$, $\mathcal{F}_{t-1}$ is (Tsay 2010):

$$h_{t+1} = \alpha_0 + \alpha_1 u_t^2 + \beta_1 h_t$$

From Equation (4.78) we have $u_t = \sqrt{h_t}\varepsilon_t$ or $u_t^2 = h_t \varepsilon_t^2$. By replacing u_t^2 in the preceding formula with $h_t \varepsilon_t^2$, and by simultaneously adding and deducting $\alpha_1 h_t$, we have:

$$h_{t+1} = \alpha_0 + \alpha_1 h_t \varepsilon_t^2 + \beta_1 h_t + \alpha_1 h_t - \alpha_1 h_t$$

or

$$h_{t+1} = \alpha_0 + h_t(\alpha_1 + \beta_1) + \alpha_1 h_t(\varepsilon_t^2 - 1)$$

Similarly for two days ahead, the forecasted conditional variance is:

$$h_{t+2} = \alpha_0 + h_{t+1}(\alpha_1 + \beta_1) + \alpha_1 h_{t+1}(\varepsilon_{t+1}^2 - 1)$$

This is a forecast based on available information until time $t-1$. Since the mean of ε_t is zero and its variance is 1, the conditional expectation of $\varepsilon_{t+1}^2 - 1$ given $\mathcal{F}_{t-1}$ is zero. Hence:

$$\widehat{h}_{t+2}|\mathcal{F}_{t-1} = \alpha_0 + \widehat{h}_{t+1}(\alpha_1 + \beta_1)$$

where $|\mathcal{F}_{t-1}$ is added to this formula to emphasize that the forecasted conditional variance for two days ahead is based on information until and including day $t-1$ and the hat sign is an indication of an estimated or forecasted value. By repeating this process we obtain:

$$\widehat{h}_{t+k}|\mathcal{F}_{t-1} = \alpha_0 + \widehat{h}_{t+k-1}(\alpha_1 + \beta_1) \quad k \geq 1 \tag{4.84}$$

This recursive formula can be used to obtain k-day-ahead forecasted conditional variance, given all information until and including day $t-1$. In a limiting case when $k \to \infty$, the forecasted conditional variance $\widehat{h}_{t+k}$ converges to the unconditional long-run variance of $\alpha_0/1 - \alpha_1 - \beta_1$.

Example

To demonstrate forecasting conditional variance using GARCH, consider the previous example in this section. The daily conditional variance for January 18, 2019, estimated at the end of January 17, 2019, is $h_t = 0.00012853$. To forecast one-day-ahead daily conditional variance for the next trading day at January 21, 2019,[12] based on data available until the end of January 17, 2019, we can use Equation (4.84) as follows:

$$\widehat{h}_{t+1}|\mathcal{F}_{t-1} = 0.0000071 + \widehat{h}_t(0.1395 + 0.8112)$$

$$= 0.0000071 + 0.00012853 \times (0.1395 + 0.8112)$$

$$= 0.00012929$$

Also the forecasted two-days-ahead daily conditional variance for January 22, 2019, based on available data until the end of January 17, 2019, is obtained as:

$$\widehat{h}_{t+2}|\mathcal{F}_{t-1} = 0.0000071 + \widehat{h}_{t+1}(0.1395 + 0.8112)$$

$$= 0.0000071 + 0.00012929 \times (0.1395 + 0.8112)$$

$$= 0.00013002$$

The GARCH-M Model

In a *GARCH-M* or *GARCH-in-mean* model the mean of the rate of return depends on the volatility. Generally a GARCH-M model can be presented as:

$$r_t = \mu(h_t) + u_t \quad u_t|\mathcal{F}_{t-1} \sim N(0, h_t)$$

$$u_t = \sqrt{h_t}\varepsilon_t \quad \varepsilon_t \sim N(0, 1) \tag{4.85}$$

$$h_t = \alpha_0 + \sum_{i=1}^{q} \alpha_i u_{t-i}^2 + \sum_{j=1}^{p} \beta_j h_{t-j}$$

In this equation, expression $\mu(h_t)$ indicates that the mean of daily rate of return itself is a function of h_t. In practice, several functional forms are considered for $\mu(h_t)$, including the following simple form (Tsay 2010):

$$\mu(h_t) = \mu_0 + \gamma h_t \tag{4.86}$$

where μ_0 is a constant and is usually assumed to be equal to the daily risk-free rate. γ is the risk premium, which associates the expected rate of return of the asset with the expected level of its volatility. The model presented in Equation (4.86) combined with the GARCH model of h_t indicates the existence of autocorrelation in r_t. Another functional form proposed for $\mu(h_t)$ is:

$$\mu(h_t) = \mu_0 + \gamma\sqrt{h_t} - \frac{1}{2}h_t \tag{4.87}$$

We use this functional form in the next section when using GARCH for option valuation. Another non-linear functional form for $\mu(h_t)$ proposed in academic work contains the term $\ln h_t$.

The Exponentially Weighted Moving Average Model

Consider the GARCH (1,1) model introduced earlier. If parameters α_1 and β_1 are such that $\alpha_1 + \beta_1 = 1$, the process of h_t is said to have a *unit root*. The GARCH model that results from having $\alpha_1 + \beta_1 = 1$ is known as *integrated GARCH (IGARCH)*. If we define parameter λ such that $\beta_1 = \lambda$ and $\alpha_1 = 1 - \lambda$, we can define an IGARCH(1,1) model as:

$$h_t = \alpha_0 + (1 - \lambda)u_{t-1}^2 + \lambda h_{t-1} \tag{4.88}$$

where $0 < \lambda < 1$. In an IGARCH model, unconditional variance is not defined. A k-day-ahead forecast using IGARCH(1,1) is obtained by repeated substitution in Equation (4.84) and considering $\alpha_1 + \beta_1 = 1$. So:

$$\hat{h}_{t+k}|\mathcal{F}_{t-1} = k\alpha_0 + h_t \quad k \geq 1 \tag{4.89}$$

From this equation it can be seen that the future forecasted conditional volatility, using all information until and including time $t - 1$, is a function of the most immediate estimated volatility h_t. The effect of h_t remains persistent throughout the future days and the forecasted conditional volatility becomes a line with a slope of α_0.

A special case of IGARCH model in which $\alpha_0 = 0$ has gained popularity in practice, especially for risk management purposes. This special case of IGARCH is called the *exponentially weighted moving average (EWMA)*. A common practice in use of EWMA is to assume that the expected daily rate of return is zero (i.e. $\mu_t = 0$). Based on this, one way to present the EWMA model is as follows:

$$r_t = u_t \qquad u_t|\mathcal{F}_{t-1} \sim N(0, h_t)$$

$$u_t = \sqrt{h_t}\varepsilon_t \quad \varepsilon_t \sim N(0, 1) \tag{4.90}$$

$$h_t = (1 - \lambda)u_{t-1}^2 + \lambda h_{t-1} \tag{4.91}$$

In the EWMA model, since $\alpha_0 = 0$, from Equation (4.90) it is clear that the k-day-ahead forecasted volatility is simply h_t and it remains at this level for all future days. The popularity of the EWMA model is largely due to its use in risk management software RiskMetrics®, which uses this model as one of its forecasting tools for volatilities and correlations of different asset types.

Parameter λ of the EMWA model presented in Equation (4.91) is called the *decay factor*. λ is the weight applied to the most recent estimated variance, whereas $1 - \lambda$ is the weight applied to the square of the most recent observed shock. In the recursive form of the EWMA model the weight assigned to the square of shocks u_{t-1}^2 decreases exponentially as we move back through time and the name of the model is due to this feature. To see this, first consider the weighted historical volatility formula in Equation (4.74). This is an unbiased estimator of standard deviation of a random variable with normal distribution. In the Appendix we introduce the maximum likelihood estimation method. The maximum likelihood estimator for the standard deviation of normal distribution (a biased estimator) is similar to the unbiased estimator used in Equation (4.74) but its denominator is n instead of $n - 1$. Many volatility models, including the ones considered in this section, use the maximum likelihood method for parameter estimation. If we modify Equation (4.74) by applying it to shocks u_{t-i} (instead of r_{t-i}) and make it a maximum likelihood estimator by changing the denominator to n, and since $\bar{u} = 0$, we have:

$$h_t = \sum_{i=1}^{n} \omega_{t-i} u_{t-i}^2 \tag{4.92}$$

where $0 < \omega_{t-i} < 1$ and $\sum_{i=1}^{n} \omega_{t-i} = 1$. We now reparametrize weights as $\omega_{t-i} = (1 - \lambda)\lambda^{i-1}$, so:

$$h_t = (1 - \lambda)\sum_{i=1}^{n} \lambda^{i-1} u_{t-i}^2 \tag{4.93}$$

In this weighting scheme, as i increases and we walk back through time, each weight is decreased by multiplying it by λ, decreasing the impact of older u_{t-i}^2 on estimated volatility. By expanding Equation (4.93) we have:

$$h_t = (1 - \lambda)[\lambda^0 u_{t-1}^2 + \lambda^1 u_{t-2}^2 + \lambda^2 u_{t-3}^2 + \lambda^3 u_{t-4}^2 + \cdots]$$
$$= (1 - \lambda)u_{t-1}^2 + \lambda(1 - \lambda)[u_{t-2}^2 + \lambda u_{t-3}^2 + \lambda^2 u_{t-4}^2 + \cdots]$$

Also if we expand h_{t-1} using Equation (4.93) we have: $h_{t-1} = (1 - \lambda)[u_{t-2}^2 + \lambda u_{t-3}^2 + \lambda^2 u_{t-4}^2 + \cdots]$. By substituting this in the previous formula we have:

$$h_t = (1 - \lambda)u_{t-1}^2 + \lambda h_{t-1}$$

This is the same as the model presented in Equation (4.91). In the EWMA model a lower decay factor λ means that greater weights are given to more recent data for estimating volatility. In an original RiskMetrics document released by J.P. Morgan in 1996, λ is estimated as 0.94 when daily time series data are used for estimating daily volatility using EWMA.

The EWMA model in Equation (4.91) can be used to estimate daily conditional volatility using all available information until and including time $t - 1$. At the end of day $t - 1$, the most recent observed shock is u_{t-1} and the estimated volatility for day $t - 1$, which is estimated at the end of day $t - 2$, is h_{t-1}. These two together are sufficient to estimate volatility for day t.

Example

The prices of a stock of a publicly traded company for the last 16 trading days from December 26, 2018, to January 17, 2019, are listed in Table 4.7. Note that in this table the most recent trading day (day $t - 1$) is shown in the first row and previous trading days are listed in subsequent rows. Here we assume that the mean of the daily rate of return is zero, that is, μ_t in Equation (4.78) is zero. Hence:

$$u_{t-1} = r_{t-1} = \ln \frac{S_{t-1}}{S_{t-2}}$$

For example, shock as of December 27, 2018, is calculated as:

$$u_{t-1} = \ln \frac{94.68}{93.84} = 0.00891158$$

We can initialize the conditional variance for the recursive process by setting it equal to zero or equal to the square of observed shock at the first available date. In our example, since the stock price on December 26, 2018, is used to calculate the first shock, the first available shock is at December 27, 2018. Here we used $u_{t-1}^2 = (0.00891158)^2 = 0.00007942$ to initialize conditional variance at December 27. For subsequent days we can recursively use Equation (4.91) to estimate daily variance. Here we use $\lambda = 0.94$. At the end of December 28, the observed shock is −0.00274987. The volatility estimated for this day at the end of the previous trading day is 0.00007942. Hence estimated variance for the next trading day is calculated as:

$$h_t = (1 - 0.94) \times u_{t-1}^2 + 0.94 \times h_{t-1}$$

$$= 0.06 \times (-0.00274987)^2 + 0.94 \times 0.00007942$$

$$= 0.00007510$$

TABLE 4.7 Estimation of volatility using the EWMA model

Date	Price (S)	Shock (u)	Conditional Variance (h)	Conditional Volatility (σ)
1/17/2019	99.17	−0.00241716	0.00013890	0.011786
1/16/2019	99.41	0.01438728	0.00014740	0.012141
1/15/2019	97.99	−0.00458179	0.00014359	0.011983
1/14/2019	98.44	−0.00111681	0.00015142	0.012305
1/11/2019	98.55	0.00294701	0.00016100	0.012689
1/10/2019	98.26	−0.00578418	0.00017072	0.013066
1/9/2019	98.83	0.00182297	0.00017949	0.013397
1/8/2019	98.65	0.00487756	0.00019073	0.013811
1/7/2019	98.17	0.00541342	0.00020139	0.014191
1/4/2019	97.64	0.04407475	0.00021237	0.014573
1/3/2019	93.43	−0.02379680	0.00010193	0.010096
1/2/2019	95.68	0.00376964	0.00007229	0.008502
12/31/2018	95.32	0.00948674	0.00007600	0.008718
12/28/2018	94.42	−0.00274987	0.00007510	0.008666
12/27/2018	94.68	0.00891158	0.00007942	0.008912
12/26/2018	93.84			

This is the estimated volatility for the next trading day of December 31, made at the end of December 28. This process is continued until the last available data point at January 17, 2019. The estimated variance for this day, made at the end of the previous trading day, is 0.00014740 and the observed shock value is −0.00241716. Therefore, estimated variance for the next trading day is calculated as:

$$h_t = (1 - 0.94) \times u_{t-1}^2 + 0.94 \times h_{t-1}$$

$$= 0.06 \times (-0.00241716)^2 + 0.94 \times 0.00014740 = 0.00013890$$

This is the estimated volatility for the next trading day of January 18, 2019. As mentioned before, this is also the forecasted volatility for any future day based on information available until and including day $t - 1$ of January 17 using a EWMA model with λ of 0.94. Forecasted daily and annual conditional volatilities are calculated as:

$$\sigma_{t(Daily)} = \sqrt{0.00013890} = 1.1786\%$$

$$\sigma_{t(Annual)} = \sqrt{252} \times 1.1786\% = 18.7092\%$$

The EWMA Model for Covariance

The EWMA model can be used to forecast the volatility of a portfolio with more than one asset. In this case the covariance of multiple assets follows a model similar to the EWMA model introduced earlier. Consider two assets where the shocks around their expected mean of rate of returns are represented by u_t and v_t. An exponentially weighted moving average model for the covariance of these two can be presented as (MSCI/J.P. Morgan/Reuters 1996):

$$\text{Cov}_{u,v_t} = (1 - \lambda)u_{t-1}v_{t-1} + \lambda\text{Cov}_{u,v_{t-1}} \tag{4.94}$$

where Cov_{u,v_t} is the conditional covariance of the rate of return of two assets at time t and λ is the decay factor. The structure of this model is very similar to the EWMA model for conditional variance in Equation (4.91), where the square of the most recent shock is replaced by multiplication of two observed shocks for two different assets. While in theory it is possible to have different decay factors for modeling variances and covariances of different assets, this significantly increases the complexity of analysis of volatility of a multi-asset portfolio. This is especially important since a variance-covariance matrix built using forecasted values from corresponding models should be internally consistent by being positive semidefinite.[13] Due to this, in practice usually the same decay factor is assumed for all variance and covariance models. Similar to variance, the covariance model in Equation (4.94) can be expressed in an exponentially weighted scheme as:

$$\text{Cov}_{u,v_t} = (1 - \lambda)\sum_{i=1}^{n} \lambda^{i-1}u_{t-1}v_{t-1} \tag{4.95}$$

Once the forecasted variances and covariance are obtained from the corresponding models, the forecasted correlation is calculated as:

$$\rho_{u,v_t} = \frac{\text{Cov}_{u,v_t}}{\sqrt{h_{u_t}h_{v_t}}} \tag{4.96}$$

In this equation, variances, covariance, and correlation are all conditional to $\mathcal{F}_{t-1}$.

Example

To demonstrate the use of the covariance model, consider again the previous example in which an EWMA model is used to estimate variance. In Table 4.8 we applied a EWMA model with $\lambda = 0.94$ to the S&P 500 rate of returns for the same period as the previous example. The S&P 500 index levels as of December 26 and 27, 2018, are used to calculate the first shock as:

$$v_{t-1} = \ln \frac{2488.83}{2467.70} = 0.00852618$$

TABLE 4.8 Estimation of correlation using an EWMA model

Date	Price (S)	u_{t-1}	h_{u_t}	S&P 500	v_{t-1}	h_{v_t}	Covariance
1/17/2019	99.17	−0.00241716	0.00013890	2615.11	−0.00037850	0.00010689	0.00010683
1/16/2019	99.41	0.01438728	0.00014740	2616.1	0.00221950	0.00011370	0.00011359
1/15/2019	97.99	−0.00458179	0.00014359	2610.3	0.01066464	0.00012065	0.00011880
1/14/2019	98.44	−0.00111681	0.00015142	2582.61	−0.00527143	0.00012109	0.00012950
1/11/2019	98.55	0.00294701	0.00016100	2596.26	−0.00014635	0.00012704	0.00013739
1/10/2019	98.26	−0.00578418	0.00017072	2596.64	0.00450827	0.00013515	0.00014619
1/9/2019	98.83	0.00182297	0.00017949	2584.96	0.00408965	0.00014248	0.00015718
1/8/2019	98.65	0.00487756	0.00019073	2574.41	0.00964860	0.00015051	0.00016674
1/7/2019	98.17	0.00541342	0.00020139	2549.69	0.00698598	0.00015417	0.00017438
1/4/2019	97.64	0.04407475	0.00021237	2531.94	0.03375938	0.00016090	0.00018310
1/3/2019	93.43	−0.02379680	0.00010193	2447.89	−0.02506828	0.00009842	0.00009981
1/2/2019	95.68	0.00376964	0.00007229	2510.03	0.00126772	0.00006459	0.00006810
12/31/2018	95.32	0.00948674	0.00007600	2506.85	0.00845658	0.00006861	0.00007214
12/28/2018	94.42	−0.00274987	0.00007510	2485.74	−0.00124232	0.00006843	0.00007163
12/27/2018	94.68	0.00891158	0.00007942	2488.83	0.00852618	0.00007270	0.00007598
12/26/2018	93.84			2467.70			

Similar to the previous example the variance estimation for the S&P 500 index is started at December 27, 2018, by setting h_{v_t} equal to $v_{t-1}^2 = (0.00852618)^2 = 0.00007270$. This process is continued until the most recent day of January 17, 2019, as shown in Table 4.8 in columns "S&P 500," "v_{t-1}," and "h_{v_t}." To demonstrate the calculation of conditional covariance we also included price, shock, and conditional variances of the asset from the previous example in Table 4.8 in columns "Price (S)," "u_{t-1}," and "h_{u_t}." We can now calculate conditional covariance for each trading day using Equation (4.94). For the last day with available data (i.e., $t-1$ day: January 17, 2019), the observed shock to the stock price and S&P 500 are $u_{t-1} = -0.00241716$ and $v_{t-1} = -0.00037850$. Therefore,

(*continued*)

(continued)

estimated daily covariance for the next trading day of January 18, 2019, is:

$$\text{Cov}_{u,v_t} = (1 - 0.94)u_{t-1}v_{t-1} + 0.94 \times \text{Cov}_{u,v_{t-1}}$$

$$= 0.06 \times (-0.00241716) \times (-0.00037850) + 0.94 \times 0.00011359$$

$$= 0.00010683$$

where 0.00011359 is the covariance for January 17, estimated at the end of January 16. Since from Table 4.8 estimated variances for the next trading day of the stock and S&P 500 are 0.00013890 and 0.00010689, we can calculate the forecasted correlation for January 18 as:

$$\rho_{u,v_t} = \frac{\text{Cov}_{u,v_t}}{\sqrt{h_{u_t}h_{v_t}}} = \frac{0.00010683}{\sqrt{0.00013890 \times 0.00010689}} = 0.876707$$

The forecasted daily variance-covariance matrix for day t: January 18, 2019, is:

$$\begin{bmatrix} 0.00013890 & 0.00010683 \\ 0.00010683 & 0.00010689 \end{bmatrix}$$

OPTION VALUATION USING A GARCH MODEL

The option valuation techniques discussed earlier in this chapter all assumed that the volatility of change in the price of the underlying asset is constant. In other words, the volatility of the rate of return of the underlying asset was assumed to remain unchanged from the valuation date to the maturity of the option contract. Most notably, the Black–Scholes–Merton model is based on a constant volatility assumption and this is generally considered to be a weakness of this model. There are several approaches proposed in academic works that focus on option valuation based on non-constant volatility assumption. Here we review the method proposed by Duan (1995). This method models the dynamic of change in underlying stock price using a GARCH model in a risky environment and then uses the estimated parameters in a different model in a risk-neutral environment. Monte Carlo simulation can be used to produce an evolution path of the underlying stock in a risk-neutral environment.

The Black–Scholes–Merton option valuation model can be considered a special case of this approach.

Earlier in this chapter we discussed the risk-neutral valuation concept, which greatly simplifies option valuation. In academic works, valuation in a risk-neutral environment is often referred to as valuation under *Q-measure*, where the probability of an asset price movement is assumed such that it allows the use of the risk-free rate for discounting of payoffs. Contrarily, in a risky environment when investors have a preference for different assets based on their perceived riskiness, they require a risk premium when investing in such assets. In this risky environment the probability of an asset price movement is assumed such that discounting of payoffs should be done using a risk-adjusted rate, and such valuation is referred to as valuation under *P-measure*. One important feature of the model proposed by Duan is that in a risk-neutral environment it is a function of the risk premium of the underlying asset, which is in contrast with the risk-neutral valuation used in the Black–Scholes–Merton and binomial tree methods discussed earlier. Duan introduced a generalized version of risk neutralization and referred to it as the *locally risk-neutral valuation relationship (LRNVR)*. This version of risk neutralization stipulates that one-period-ahead conditional variance of the rate of return of the underlying asset is the same whether a risk-neutral or risky environment is considered.

The model proposed by Duan for a one-period rate of return of an underlying asset in P-measure (risky environment) is as follows:

$$r_t = \ln \frac{S_t}{S_{t-1}}$$

$$r_t = r_f + \gamma \sqrt{h_t} - \frac{1}{2} h_t + u_t$$

$$u_t = \sqrt{h_t} \varepsilon_t \quad u_t | \mathcal{F}_{t-1} \sim N(0, h_t) \quad \varepsilon_t \sim N(0,1) \tag{4.97}$$

$$h_t = \alpha_0 + \sum_{i=1}^{q} \alpha_i u_{t-i}^2 + \sum_{j=1}^{p} \beta_j h_{t-j}$$

where r_f is the one-period risk-free rate[14] and γ is the risk premium; both are assumed constant. Other notations used in this formula are as introduced earlier. This is a GARCH-M model, where the expected rate of return is of the form introduced earlier in Equation (4.87). Common implementation of this model assumes a GARCH(1,1) for the process of h_t and daily period. In the model presented in Equation set (4.97) if $p = 0$ and $q = 0$, the variance becomes a constant and the model reduces to the lognormal process assumed in the Black–Scholes–Merton model.

Following the introduction of this model, Duan argued that under a locally risk-neutral valuation relationship the conditional mean of the rate of return of an asset in a risk-neutral environment, conditioned to all information until and including time $t - 1$, is equal to the risk-free rate while conditional variance of the rate of return is the same in both risk-neutral and risky environments. The importance of this approach is that it allows the estimation of parameters of the aforementioned GARCH-M model in a risky environment based on observed data and then uses them in a different but analogous model that is defined in a risk-neutral environment for option valuation where discounting of payoffs can be carried out using the risk-free rate. Duan's model for a one-period rate of return of an underlying asset in Q-measure (risk-neutral environment) is as follows:

$$r_t = r_f - \frac{1}{2}h_t + w_t$$

$$w_t = \sqrt{h_t}\xi_t \quad w_t|\mathcal{F}_{t-1} \sim N(0, h_t) \quad \xi_t \sim N(0, 1) \tag{4.98}$$

$$h_t = \alpha_0 + \sum_{i=1}^{q} \alpha_i(w_{t-i} - \gamma\sqrt{h_{t-i}})^2 + \sum_{j=1}^{p} \beta_j h_{t-j}$$

In this model, while the conditional mean of the rate of return in a risk-neutral environment is the risk-free rate, the unconditional mean still depends on the risk preference of investors through the risk premium.[15] Also, the model for conditional variance h_t is no longer exactly a GARCH model, although it is very similar to it.

Assuming the asset price at the beginning of the process is S_t, the price at some time $T > t$ is obtained by aggregating the rate of return using the model introduced in Equation (4.98) from time t to T as:

$$S_T = S_t exp\left[(T - t)r_f - \frac{1}{2}\sum_{s=t+1}^{T} h_s + \sum_{s=t+1}^{T} w_t\right] \tag{4.99}$$

The Monte Carlo simulation method can be used to value a European call option using the model described here. First the model outlined in Equation (4.97) is fitted to the observed data of the underlying asset's rate of return to estimate the model parameters. The maximum likelihood estimation method is often used for this purpose. Having the parameters estimated, we can use the model outlined in Equations (4.98) and (4.99) to simulate paths of asset prices to the maturity of the option and obtain the payoffs. Finally, the risk-free rate is used to discount the expected payoffs. The value of a European put option can be found using put–call parity. We demonstrate the use of this option valuation technique in the following example based on a GARCH (1,1) model.

Consider a European call option where the underlying asset is a liquid market index with 10 days to maturity. The current price of the underlying asset is $2,760.17 and the strike price is $2,740. Assume that the daily risk-free rate is 0.006575%. The GARCH-M model in Equation (4.97) with $p = 1$ and $q = 1$ is fitted to the data for daily rate of return of the underlying asset for a period of eight years, from November 1, 2010, to November 30, 2018, and estimated parameters are obtained as: $\alpha_0 = 0.00000344$, $\alpha_1 = 0.169520$, $\beta_1 = 0.788676$, and $\gamma = 0.054206$. SAS® software is used to estimate these parameters using the maximum likelihood method. List 1 provides a sample code that uses the *SAS proc model* to estimate parameters of the model. In this code, variable *&r_f* is the daily risk-free rate and dataset *dailyreturn* has a variable *r* that contains the natural logarithm of the daily rate of return of the underlying asset, that is, r_t in Equation (4.97), for an eight-year period.

LIST 1: **A sample SAS code for estimation of a GARCH-M model**

```
proc model data = dailyreturn;
     parms alpha0 0.1 alpha1 0.1 beta1 0.75 gamma 0.05;
h = alpha0+ alpha1*xlag(resid.r**2,mse.r)+ beta1*xlag(h.r,
     mse.r);
     r = &r_f + gamma*sqrt(h) - 0.5*h;
     h.r = h;
fit r / fiml method = marquardt converge=0.0001 maxiter=10000;
run;
```

Once the parameters of the model are estimated, the model in a risk-neutral environment outlined in Equation (4.98) can be used to simulate the daily conditional variance. In our example, since $p = 1$ and $q = 1$, and using $w_t = \sqrt{h_t}\xi_t$, the process for h_t from Equation (4.98) can be rewritten as:

$$h_t = \alpha_0 + \alpha_1 h_{t-1}(\xi_{t-1} - \gamma)^2 + \beta_1 h_{t-1} \qquad (4.100)$$

where $\xi_{t-1} \sim N(0,1)$. So, based on estimated parameter values, we have:

$$h_t = 0.00000344 + 0.169520 \times h_{t-1} \times (\xi_{t-1} - 0.054206)^2 + 0.788676 \times h_{t-1} \qquad (4.101)$$

This recursive process can be used to simulate the daily conditional variance of the underlying asset from the valuation date $(t = 0)$ to the option maturity date at $t = 10$ day. The simulated asset value at each day can be calculated using Equation (4.99). Here we simulate the asset price on a daily basis; hence $T - t$ in Equation (4.99) is one day and since $p = 1$ and $q = 1$, we can rewrite this equation to simulate asset price on a daily basis as:

$$S_t = S_{t-1} exp \left[r_f - \frac{1}{2} h_t + \sqrt{h_t} \xi_t \right] \qquad (4.102)$$

where r_f is the daily risk-free rate of 0.006575%, h_t is the daily volatility from Equation (4.101), and $\xi_t \sim N(0, 1)$.

Assume that at the start of the process at $t = 0$ the estimated daily volatility for the next day is 0.00010959. This means that when the model in Equation (4.101) is applied to the available eight years of historical data, at the last day the daily conditional variance is 0.00010959, which can be used as the estimated variance for the next day. Table 4.9 presents results of three simulated paths based on this model where daily volatility and asset price are simulated for 10 days, from valuation date at day 0 to option maturity at day 10. Consider path 1. The random instances generated from a standard normal distribution for ξ_t at day 1 is –0.56690707 and the estimated h_t for day 1, made at the end of day 0, is 0.00010959. Therefore, using Equation (4.102) the simulated asset price for day 1 is:

$$S_{Day\ 1} = 2760.17 \times exp \left[0.00006575 - \frac{1}{2} \times 0.00010959 \right.$$

$$\left. + \sqrt{0.00010959} \times (-0.56690707) \right] = 2{,}743.87$$

The simulated daily conditional variance made at the end of day 1, which is the estimate for day 2, is obtained using Equation (4.101) as:

$$h_{Day\ 2} = 0.00000344 + 0.169520 \times 0.00010959 \times (-0.56690707 - 0.054206)^2$$

$$+ 0.788676 \times 0.00010959 = 0.00009703$$

Using this estimated variance for day 2 and based on a standard normal random instance of 0.27725494, the simulated asset price for day 2 is:

$$S_{Day\ 2} = 2743.87 \times exp \left[0.00006575 - \frac{1}{2} \times 0.00009703 \right.$$

$$\left. + \sqrt{0.00009703} \times 0.27725494 \right] = 2{,}751.42$$

TABLE 4.9 Simulation of daily volatility and asset price based on a GARCH-M model

Path→	1			2			3		
Day↓	ξ_t	h_t	S_t	ξ_t	h_t	S_t	ξ_t	h_t	S_t
0			2760.17			2760.17			2760.17
1	−0.56690707	0.00010959	2743.87	1.00046566	0.00010959	2789.26	0.26776219	0.00010959	2767.95
2	0.27725494	0.00009703	2751.42	−0.13267914	0.00010650	2785.48	0.80928454	0.00009071	2789.42
3	−0.95526080	0.00008078	2727.97	−1.38631255	0.00008806	2749.54	−0.52373725	0.00008375	2776.15
4	0.42192742	0.00008110	2738.42	0.48718519	0.00010387	2763.26	1.30483422	0.00007423	2807.62
5	−0.04707566	0.00006926	2737.43	−0.17684863	0.00008865	2758.72	−0.79895185	0.00008166	2787.49
6	0.92006063	0.00005818	2756.81	−0.97866391	0.00007416	2735.65	0.34820021	0.00007791	2796.14
7	0.06816254	0.00005671	2758.33	−0.25635150	0.00007533	2729.65	0.65928088	0.00006603	2811.26
8	−0.91202861	0.00004817	2741.04	−0.55961387	0.00006408	2717.54	−0.16304114	0.00005961	2807.82
9	0.32067393	0.00004905	2747.32	−0.53413501	0.00005807	2706.60	0.42549017	0.00005092	2816.47
10	1.66027657	0.00004271	2777.41	0.21452812	0.00005264	2710.92	−0.45486483	0.00004479	2808.03

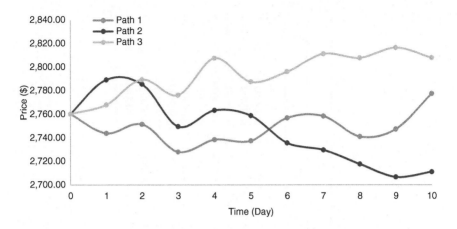

FIGURE 4.8 Three simulated paths of an asset price for 10 days using a GARCH-M
model

The simulated daily conditional variance made at the end of day 2, which
is the estimate for day 3, is calculated as:

$$h_{Day\ 3} = 0.00000344 + 0.169520 \times 0.00009703 \times (0.27725494 - 0.054206)^2$$

$$+ 0.788676 \times 0.00009703 = 0.00008078$$

By continuing this process as shown in Table 4.9 the simulated asset price
for day 10 is obtained as 2,777.41. Therefore the payoff at option maturity for
this path is:

$$\text{Max}(S_{Day\ 10} - X, 0) = \text{Max}(2,777.41 - 2,740.0) = 37.41$$

Following the same method, the simulated asset price at day 10 for paths 2
and 3 are obtained as \$2,710.92 and \$2,808.03; hence option payoffs are \$0 and
\$68.03. Figure 4.8 shows three simulated paths generated using the GARCH-M
model described here. Finally, the value of the option contract is the expected
payoff discounted using risk-free rate. So:

$$V_{Day\ 0} = e^{-10 \times 0.00006575}(37.41 + 0 + 68.03\ ) = 35.13$$

In real application of this model, the number of simulated paths should
be much larger than three (e.g., 50,000 paths).

FUTURES OPTIONS

Stock is not the only asset type used as the underlying for options. Specifically, options with futures contracts as their underlying are very popular instruments and there are active and liquid financial markets for trading such options. In this section we first briefly introduce futures contracts and then discuss options on futures.

Futures Contract

A *futures contract* is an agreement between two parties in which the buyer agrees to purchase the underlying asset from the seller at a future date and at a price specified at the contract's inception. A futures contract has a long side (buyer) and a short side (seller). Since the value of a futures contract depends on the value of the underlying asset, it is considered a derivative financial instrument. Various asset types are used as the underlying for futures contracts. For example, some of the most liquid futures contracts are based on precious metals (e.g., gold) or commodities, such as corn, cotton, or crude oil. Financial instruments such as U.S. Treasury notes, the Eurodollar, the federal funds rate, and the S&P 500 index are also used as underlying assets of futures contracts. Futures contracts are standardized agreements and are bought and sold in exchanges or clearinghouses and are highly regulated. They are subject to a *daily mark-to-market*, where the clearinghouse takes the role of agent of two parties for performing the mark-to-market and *daily settlement* process.

At the inception of the contract, an *initiation margin* is placed by both parties in their corresponding margin accounts with the clearinghouse. The initiation margin is to ensure that both parties can deliver or buy the asset when needed and have enough funds for daily settlement. As the price of the underlying asset changes during a trading day, the value of the bilateral futures contract changes as well and one side gains while the other side incurs losses. At the end of a trading day, the clearinghouse calculates these daily gains and losses and settles the contract by applying the gains and losses to the corresponding margin accounts of the two parties. Each side of the contract is required to keep a *maintenance margin requirement*. If the balance of the margin account falls below this level, the clearinghouse makes a *margin call* where the recipient of the call is required to deposit a *variation margin* amount to bring the account balance back to the initial margin level. Due to this daily mark-to-market and settlement, a holder of a futures contract has little to no credit risk exposure to the other party.

Depending on the contract and its underlying asset, at its maturity date a futures contract is settled either in cash or delivery of the underlying asset.

A position on a futures contract can be closed out by taking an opposite position on the underlying asset. For example, if a trader has a long position on a futures contract with an underlying asset of 100 ounces of gold, to close out he can take a short position on a futures contract with an underlying asset of 100 ounces of gold and effectively exit the contract. Many traders prefer to close out their futures positions in this way and settle in cash rather than taking delivery.

To continue our discussion, we should clarify the notation and meaning of *futures price* vs. *value of futures contract*. Consider a futures contract with maturity date T. We use notation F_0 to represent the futures price of the underlying asset as agreed at inception for delivery at time T. At the inception of a futures contract no premium is exchanged between two parties and the value of the futures contract is zero. Progress of time and trading activities results in a change in the futures price for the maturity at time T. We use notation F_t to represent the futures price at time t for delivery at time T. Due to the daily mark-to-market and settlement process, the value of the futures contract at any time during a trading day is the accumulated gain or loss up to that time of the day from the last settlement. This means that the value of the futures contract at any time prior to daily settlement is the difference between the futures price at that time and the futures price at last settlement (*settlement price*). If the most recent settlement price was F_s and the current futures price at time t before the next daily settlement is F_t, the value of the futures contract is $F_t - F_s$.[16] Immediately after a mark-to-market and settlement, the value of the futures contract is zero. The futures price converges to the spot price at the contract maturity (i.e., $F_T = S_T$).

Using the arbitrage-free approach and when there is no storage cost and the underlying asset does not generate any cash flow, it can be argued that for a futures contract with term T the futures price at $t = 0$ is the compounded spot price S_0 at the risk-free rate r_f:

$$F_0 = S_0 e^{r_f T} \tag{4.103}$$

where r_f has a continuous compounding. To extend this, assume the futures value at option maturity (time T) of all storage costs is $V_{T:\, Storage\, Cost}$ and the futures value of all cash flows generated by the underlying asset is $V_{T:\, Cash\, Flow}$. In this case the futures price at $t = 0$ is:

$$F_0 = S_0 e^{r_f T} + V_{T:\, Storage\, Cost} - V_{T:\, Cash\, Flow} \tag{4.104}$$

Option on Futures Contract

An *option on a futures contract*, or simply a *futures option*, is an option contract in which the underlying is a futures contract. A futures option is a derivative instrument with another derivative as its underlying. The holder of a call option on a future has the right, but not the obligation, to buy a futures contract, with a specific term (maturity) and with a specific future price (strike price), by taking the long side of the underlying futures contract. Conversely, the holder of a put option on a future has the right, but not the obligation, to sell a futures contract by taking the short side of the underlying futures contract. Futures options are often American style, with expiration dates that are usually on or a few days before the earliest delivery date of the underlying futures contract. Futures options are very popular financial instruments and widely traded in various exchanges. Compared to spot options, futures options are more liquid and market prices are readily available via the exchange data systems. Futures options also provide a low-cost trading platform for active market participants.

If a futures option expiration date is prior to the expiration date of the underlying futures contract, upon option exercise, it will settle into the futures contract, which can be immediately closed out and make the settlement of the option into all cash. As before, assume that X is the strike price of the option. When a call futures option is exercised, the holder of the option contract takes the long side of the underlying futures contract with a delivery price equal to the last settlement price F_s and also receives a cash amount equal to the difference between the last settlement price and strike price $F_s - X$. If he immediately closes out the long position on the futures contract where future price is F_t, it provides a cash flow of $F_t - F_s$. Therefore, effective payoff of the call futures option exercised at time t is the sum of the above two cash flows:

$$\text{Payoff}_{t:\,Call\ Futures\ Option} = \text{Max}(F_t - X, 0) \qquad (4.105)$$

Similarly, when a put futures option is exercised, the holder of the option contract takes the short side of the underlying futures contract with a delivery price equal to the last settlement price F_s and in addition he receives a cash amount equal to the difference between the strike price and last settlement price $X - F_s$. If he immediately closes out the short position on the futures contract where the futures price is F_t, it provides a cash flow of $-(F_t - F_s)$. This makes the effective payoff of the put futures option as follows:

$$\text{Payoff}_{t:\,Put\ Futures\ Option} = \text{Max}(X - F_t, 0) \qquad (4.106)$$

For example, consider a call option where the underlying is a futures contract on 100 ounces of gold, with expiration in March 2019 and a strike price of $1,100. The last settlement price on gold futures was $1,288.80 (per ounce) and the current futures price is $1,294.70. If this option is exercised, the holder of the option takes the long side of a gold futures contract with a delivery price of $1,288.80 and a cash amount of ($1,288 − $1,100) × 100 = $18,880. If the long position on the gold futures contract is closed out immediately, it provides an additional cash amount of ($1,294.70 − $1,288.80) × 100 = $590. Total payoff is therefore $18,880 + $590 = $19,470.

Consider a European call option on an asset, such as stock, with a strike price of X and maturity T. This is the type of option we studied in previous sections of this chapter. Since the option underlying is the spot price of the asset, this option sometimes is referred to as a *spot option*. Now consider a comparable European call futures option with the same maturity and strike price, where the underlying futures contract has the same maturity date as the futures option itself. At the option maturity the payoff of the spot option is $\text{Max}(S_T - X, 0)$. Payoff of the futures option is $\text{Max}(F_T - X, 0)$; however, since the maturity dates of the option and futures contracts are the same, as time passes the futures price converges to the spot price and at the maturity date the futures and spot prices are equal. So payoff of the futures option is also $\text{Max}(S_T - X, 0)$. Since both spot and futures options have the same payoffs at T, their values at $t = 0$ should also be the same. The above argument holds for European put futures and spot options as well. Therefore, when futures option and underlying futures contract mature at the same time, the values of the European spot and futures options are equal. This is not true for American options and depending on the relative futures price versus spot price, the value of an American futures option can be greater or less than the comparable American spot option. The relationship between values of comparable spot and futures options is summarized in Table 4.10.

TABLE 4.10   Relationship between values of comparable spot options versus futures options

Option Type	Spot and Future Prices	Option Value
European (when option maturity = futures maturity)	$F_T = S_T$	$V_{Futures,\,Call} = V_{Spot,\,Call}$ $V_{Futures,\,Put} = V_{Spot,\,Put}$
American (when option maturity ≤ futures maturity)	$F_t > S_t$	$V_{Futures,\,Call} \geq V_{Spot,\,Call}$ $V_{Futures,\,Put} \leq V_{Spot,\,Put}$
	$F_t < S_t$	$V_{Futures,\,Call} \leq V_{Spot,\,Call}$ $V_{Futures,\,Put} \geq V_{Spot,\,Put}$

Put–Call Parity for Futures Options

Similar to spot options, we can establish a put–call parity between values of European call and put futures options. To establish this, consider the following two portfolios:

> *Portfolio (I):* A long position on a European call option on a futures contract, plus a cash amount equal to $e^{-r_f T}$.
>
> *Portfolio (II):* A long position on a European put option on the same futures contract in portfolio (I), plus a long position on the futures contract itself, plus a cash amount equal to $F_0 e^{-r_f T}$, where as before F_0 is the futures price at $t = 0$ for delivery at T.

At time $t = 0$:

- The cost (current value) of portfolio (I) includes the value of the call option $V_{0:\ Futures\ European\ Call}$ and the cash value of $e^{-r_f T}$.
- Since the value of the futures contract is zero, the cost of portfolio (II) includes the value of the put option $V_{0:\ Futures\ European\ Put}$ and the cash value of $F_0 e^{-r_f T}$.

At time $t = T$:

- The cash in portfolio (I) is invested at risk-free rate r_f and at $t = T$ has the value of X. The value of the option in portfolio (I) depends on whether the call futures option is in-the-money or out-of-the-money:
  - If $F_T > X$, the option is exercised and the effective payoff of the option is $F_T - X$. This, combined with X from the cash investment, results in a total value of F_T.
  - If $F_T < X$, the option is not exercised. The payoff from the option is zero and the value of portfolio (I) is X from the cash investment.

    Therefore the value of portfolio (I) at $t = T$ is $\text{Max}(X, F_T)$.
- The cash in portfolio (II) is invested at risk-free rate r_f and at $t = T$ it has the value of F_0. The value of portfolio (II) at $t = T$ depends on whether the put futures option is in-the-money or out-of-the-money:
  - If $F_T > X$, the option is not exercised. Hence, the payoff from the option is zero, the payoff from the long position in the futures contract is $F_T - F_0$, and the cash value is F_0. Therefore, the value of portfolio (II) at $t = T$ is F_T.

- If $F_T < X$, the option is exercised. The payoff from the option is $X - F_T$, the payoff from the long position in the futures contract is $F_T - F_0$, and the cash value is F_0. Therefore, the value of portfolio (II) at $t = T$ is X.

Based on this the value of portfolio (II) at $t = T$ is $\text{Max}(X, F_T)$.

Since the values of portfolios (I) and (II) at $t = T$ are both equal to $\text{Max}(X, F_T)$, following an arbitrage-free argument, their values at $t = 0$ should also be the same. So:

$$V_{0:\,Futures\ European\ Call} + Xe^{-r_f T} = V_{0:\,Futures\ European\ Put} + F_0 e^{-r_f T} \qquad (4.107)$$

This is the put–call parity for European futures options. By comparing this identity with the put–call parity for spot options when the underlying pays a continuous dividend as presented in Equation (4.23), it can be seen that if spot price S_0 is replaced by futures price F_0 and asset yield q is set to the risk-free interest rate r_f, the two put–call parities are identical. This leads to the conjecture that futures options can be treated as spot options when underlyings provide continuous yield equal to the risk-free rate. This observation is in line with the way the futures price is obtained from the spot price presented in Equation (4.103). We can use this result to obtain the inequality relating values of American call and put futures options by replacing S_0 with F_0 and q with r_f in Equation (4.24) to obtain:

$$F_0 e^{-r_f T} - X \le V_{0:\,Futures\ American\ Call} - V_{0:\,Futures\ American\ Put} \le F_0 - Xe^{-r_f T}$$
$$(4.108)$$

Black Model

Black (1976) was the first to introduce a model for valuation of European futures options. This model is as follows:

$$V_{t:\,European\ Call\ Futures} = \Phi(d_1)\, F_t e^{-r_f(T-t)} - \Phi(d_2)\, Xe^{-r_f(T-t)} \qquad (4.109)$$

$$V_{t:\,European\ Put\ Futures} = \Phi(-d_2)\, Xe^{-r_f(T-t)} - \Phi(-d_1)\, F_t e^{-r_f(T-t)} \qquad (4.110)$$

$$d_1 = \frac{\ln\left(\frac{F_t}{X}\right) + \left(\frac{\sigma^2}{2}\right)(T-t)}{\sigma\sqrt{T-t}} \qquad (4.111)$$

$$d_2 = d_1 - \sigma\sqrt{T-t}$$

where:

T = Option maturity
F_T = Futures price at time t
σ = Volatility of change in future price
X = Strike price
r_f = Annual risk-free rate

This set of formulas provides values of European put and call futures options at time t before maturity and they are usually referred to as the Black model. This model is very popular among practitioners and is used for valuing a variety of options. The Black model is comparable with the Black–Scholes–Merton model when the underlying pays a continuous yield as presented in Equations (4.42), (4.43), and (4.44), when continuous yield q is set equal to risk-free rate r_f and spot price S_t is replaced with futures price F_t.

Example

Consider a European call futures option with a strike price of $1,100 and a time to maturity of six months ($T - t = 0.5$ year) on a futures contract on 100 ounces of gold. The current futures price is $1,294.70 per ounce of gold. The risk-free interest rate is 3% and the volatility of the futures price is 25%. Using the Black model, the value of this option is derived as:

$$d_1 = \frac{\ln\left(\frac{1294.70}{1,100}\right) + \left(\frac{0.25^2}{2}\right)(0.5)}{0.25 \times \sqrt{0.5}} = 1.010279$$

$$d_2 = 1.010279 - 0.25 \times \sqrt{0.5} = 0.833503$$

$$V_{0:\ European\ Call\ Futures} = \Phi(1.010279) \times 1,294.70 \times e^{-0.03 \times 0.5}$$

$$- \Phi(0.833503) \times 1,100 \times e^{-0.03 \times 0.5} = 211.800561$$

Therefore, for a futures contract on 100 ounces of gold, the value of the European call futures option is $21,180.06.

Using a Binomial Tree for Valuation of Futures Options

The Black model can be used for valuation of European futures options; however, futures options are usually American. As for the spot options, the binomial tree method can be used for valuation of both European and American futures options. The general methodology described earlier for the use of the binomial tree for valuation of spot options is also applicable to futures options. From Equation (4.33) when the underlying asset provides a continuous yield q the probability of up movement in a binomial tee is:

$$\pi = \frac{e^{(r_f-q)\Delta t} - d}{u - d}$$

As discussed previously, the futures price is similar to a spot price when the underlying provides a continuous yield that is equal to the risk-free rate. By setting q equal to the risk-free rate in this equation we have:

$$\pi = \frac{1 - d}{u - d} \tag{4.112}$$

Therefore we can use Equation (4.112) along with Equations (4.28) to (4.32) introduced earlier to construct a binomial tree for valuation of futures options, where values of the underlying at tree nodes are futures prices instead of spot prices.

Example

Consider the call option on a futures contract on 100 ounces of gold introduced in the example of the Black model section but this time assume that the option is American. We have: $T - t = 0.5$ year, $F_t = \$1{,}294.70$, $r_f = 3\%$, $\sigma = 25\%$, and $X = \$1{,}100$. We use a binomial tree with six time steps, each with a length of one month ($\Delta t = 0.0833$ year) to value this option. It should be noted that, due to the daily settlement, the gain and loss of a position in a futures contract is realized at the end of each trading day. Here and as an approximation we assume such a gain or loss is realized at the end of a time step of the tree. We can reduce the effect of this approximation by decreasing the length of each time step of the tree, preferably to daily. Figure 4.9 presents this tree. Using Equation (4.28) and the given volatility, the up and down multipliers are calculated as follows:

$$u = e^{\sigma\sqrt{\Delta t}} = e^{0.25 \times \sqrt{0.0833}} = 1.074837$$

$$d = \frac{1}{u} = \frac{1}{1.0748} = 0.930374$$

Probability of upward movement π is calculated using Equation (4.112) as:

$$\pi = \frac{1 - 0.930374}{1.074837 - 0.930374} = 0.481966$$

The futures price at each node of the tree is calculated using Equation (4.29). For example, at node A in Figure 4.9 the futures price is $1294.70 \times 1.074837^6 \times 0.930374^0 = 1996.2925$, or at node B the futures price is calculated as $1294.70 \times 1.074837^5 \times 0.930374^1 = 1727.9818$. Option values at terminal nodes are payoffs of the call futures option from Equation (4.105). For example, the payoff at node A is $\text{Max}(1996.2925 - 1100, 0) = 896.2925$, or at node B is $\text{Max}(1727.9818 - 1100, 0) = 627.9818$. Futures prices and option values at other terminal nodes are obtained similarly.

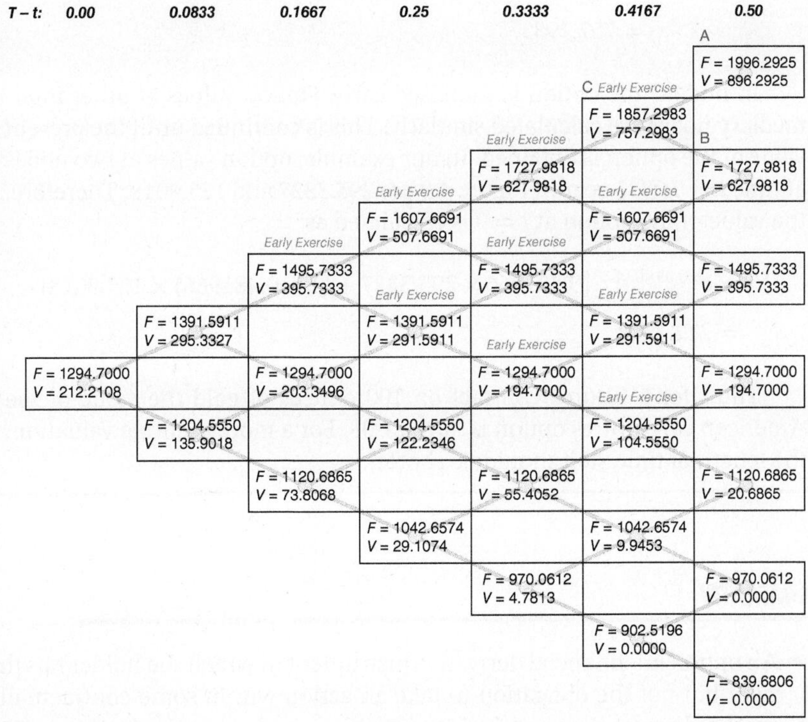

T − t:	0.00	0.0833	0.1667	0.25	0.3333	0.4167	0.50
							A: F = 1996.2925; V = 896.2925
						C *Early Exercise* F = 1857.2983; V = 757.2983	
					Early Exercise F = 1727.9818; V = 627.9818		B: F = 1727.9818; V = 627.9818
				Early Exercise F = 1607.6691; V = 507.6691		*Early Exercise* F = 1607.6691; V = 507.6691	
			Early Exercise F = 1495.7333; V = 395.7333		F = 1495.7333; V = 395.7333	*Early Exercise*	F = 1495.7333; V = 395.7333
		Early Exercise F = 1391.5911; V = 295.3327		F = 1391.5911; V = 291.5911	*Early Exercise*	F = 1391.5911; V = 291.5911	
	F = 1294.7000; V = 212.2108		F = 1294.7000; V = 203.3496		F = 1294.7000; V = 194.7000	*Early Exercise*	F = 1294.7000; V = 194.7000
		F = 1204.5550; V = 135.9018		F = 1204.5550; V = 122.2346		F = 1204.5550; V = 104.5550	
			F = 1120.6865; V = 73.8068		F = 1120.6865; V = 55.4052		F = 1120.6865; V = 20.6865
				F = 1042.6574; V = 29.1074		F = 1042.6574; V = 9.9453	
					F = 970.0612; V = 4.7813		F = 970.0612; V = 0.0000
						F = 902.5196; V = 0.0000	
							F = 839.6806; V = 0.0000

FIGURE 4.9 Valuation of an American call futures option using a six-period binomial tree

(continued)

(*continued*)

Moving one time step back to time $t = 5\Delta t = 0.4167$ year, since the option type is American, the value of the option at each node is calculated as the discounted expected value from the succeeding nodes while evaluating the possibility of early exercise, using Equation (4.31). For example, consider node C in Figure 4.9. The futures price at this node is $F_C = 1294.70 \times 1.074837^5 \times 0.930374^0 = 1857.2983$. The option value at this node V_C is calculated using option values at nodes A and B as follows:

$$V_C = \text{Max}(F_C - X, e^{-r_f \Delta t}[\pi V_A + (1 - \pi)V_B])$$

$$= \text{Max}(1857.2983 - 1100, e^{-0.03 \times 0.0833}[0.481966$$

$$\times 896.2925 + (1 - 0.481966) \times 627.9818])$$

$$= 757.2983$$

In node C the option is exercised early. Option values at other intermediary nodes are calculated similarly. This is continued until the present value of the option is obtained. In our example, option values at two nodes at time $t = 0.0833$ year in Figure 4.9 are 295.3327 and 135.9018. Therefore, the value of the option at $t = 0$ is calculated as:

$$V_0 = e^{-0.03 \times 0.0833}[0.481966 \times 295.3327 + (1 - 0.481966) \times 135.9018]$$

$$= 212.2108$$

Thus, for a futures contract on 100 ounces of gold the value of the American call futures option is $21,221.08. For a more accurate valuation, the length of time step should be shorter.

SUMMARY

■ An option is a financial derivative instrument in which the holder has the right but not the obligation to take an action within some contractually specified parameters and during a specific period of time in the future. The value of an option contract depends on the value of the financial instrument used as the reference or underlying in the contract.
■ Different references are used in option contracts, including stock spot prices, interest rates, and futures prices.

- A call option provides the holder the right but not the obligation to buy the underlying asset at a given price (strike price) and at a specified time period. A put option provides the holder the right but not the obligation to sell the underlying asset at a given price and at a specified time period.
- The holder of an American option may exercise it at any day or some specific dates during the term of the contract. The holder of a European option can exercise it only at the maturity date of the contract.
- The payoff of a long position on a European call option is the stock price at the option maturity date minus the option strike price. If this difference is negative, the payoff is zero. The payoff of a short position on a European call option is equal to the payoff of a long position on the same option but with the opposite sign.
- The payoff of a long position on a European put option is the option strike price minus the stock price at the option maturity date. If this difference is negative, the payoff is zero. The payoff of a short position on a European put option is equal to the payoff of a long position on the same option but with the opposite sign.
- When underlying stock pays no dividend during the term of an option, early exercise of an American call option is not optimal and therefore the value of the American call option is equal to the value of the comparable European call option. However, in such case, early exercise of an American put option can be optimal; hence the value of an American put option is greater than or equal to the value of the comparable European put option.
- When underlying stock pays dividends during the term of an option, it can be optimal for both American call and put options to exercise earlier than the maturity date and hence values of American options are greater than or equal to values of their comparable European options.
- Put–call parity is a relationship between values of European call and put options. Such a relationship can be established whether the underlying pays dividends or not. For American call and put options, an inequality can be established that captures the relative relationship between option values.
- The binomial tree method is a discrete-time option valuation or pricing technique that consists of a tree-like structure, made of several nodes located at distinct time intervals. Option value is estimated at each node, considering values of the option and the underlying at adjacent nodes.
- The binomial tree method can be used for valuation of call and put options for both European and American types. It can be used for valuation of options whether the underlying pays dividends or not.
- In valuing options using the binomial tree method, we assume that the market is arbitrage-free and that all available information in the market is

reflected in the price of the underlying. We also assume that transaction costs are negligible and buying or selling fractions of the underlying is possible.

■ Risk-neutral valuation of stock option refers to the approach when we adjust the probability distribution of underlying asset price movement to reflect its riskiness and obtain the expected payoff of the option at a period, using this adjusted probability distribution while using the risk-free rate to discount the expected payoff back to the previous period. Option value obtained this way in the risk-neutral environment is the same as in the risky environment.

■ The Black–Scholes–Merton model is a continuous-time model for valuation of European options. In the Black–Scholes–Merton model the underlying stock is assumed to follow a geometric Brownian motion stochastic process and valuation formulas are independent of the expected return of the underlying stock.

■ In option valuation using the Black–Scholes–Merton model we assume that the market is arbitrage-free, short selling is allowed, and stock is divisible, meaning we can buy or sell fractions of the underlying stock. We also assume that transaction costs and tax impacts are negligible. The most important assumption of the Black–Scholes–Merton model is the assumption of constant volatility.

■ The Black–Scholes–Merton model can be used for valuation of European options whether the underlying stock pays dividends or not.

■ The Monte Carlo simulation method for option valuation is based on the use of a discretized version of a stochastic process to produce simulated prices of underlying. The average of the discounted values of the option payoffs based on these simulated paths provides the estimated option value.

■ Delta is the sensitivity of option value to the underlying stock price.

■ Gamma is the sensitivity of delta to the underlying stock price.

■ The relationship between change in option value, change in stock price, delta, and gamma can be summarized as $\Delta V \cong \delta \, \Delta S + \frac{1}{2} \gamma \, \Delta S^2$.

■ Vega is the sensitivity of option value to the volatility.

■ Rho is the sensitivity of option value to the interest rate.

■ Theta is the sensitivity of option value to the passage of time.

■ Historical volatility is obtained using past data of the underlying asset price. Implied volatility is the volatility of the underlying asset, which when used in an option pricing model will return a value equal to the market price of the option.

■ Autoregressive conditional heteroscedasticity (ARCH) and generalized autoregressive conditional heteroscedasticity (GARCH) are two methodologies to model time-varying volatility.

- In one version of the ARCH model we assume variance of daily shock at time t, conditional to all information available until and including time $t - 1$, is a function of previous daily shocks. In the GARCH model variance of daily shock at time t is a function of the square of previous daily shocks and a linear function of previous variances.
- In a GARCH-M or GARCH-in-mean model the mean of the rate of return is a function of volatility.
- Integrated GARCH (IGARCH) is a GARCH model with a unit root. Exponentially weighted moving average (EWMA) is a special case of an IGARCH model. It has one parameter λ decay factor, which is the weight applied to the most recent estimated variance while $1 - \lambda$ is the weight applied to the square of the most recent observed shock.
- A futures contract is an agreement between two parties in which one side agrees to purchase the underlying asset from the other side at a future date and at a specific price. Various asset types are used as the underlying for futures contracts, including precious metals, commodities, financial products, and financial indexes. Depending on the contract and its underlying, at its maturity date a futures contract is settled either in cash or delivery of the underlying asset.
- At the inception of a futures contract an initiation margin is placed by both parties in their corresponding margin accounts with a clearinghouse. The futures contract is marked-to-market on a daily basis and depending on the amount and direction of change in contract value, a margin call is placed requiring one side to deposit a variation margin amount.
- An option on a futures contract, or futures option, is an option contract where the underlying is a futures contract. Futures options are often American type.
- The Black model is a popular tool used for valuation of European futures options. It is comparable with the Black–Scholes–Merton model when the underlying pays a continuous yield.

ANNEX 1: DERIVATION OF PUT–CALL PARITY WHEN THE UNDERLYING PAYS DIVIDENDS

Asset with Dividend Cash Flow

Assume that the present value of all expected dividend cash flows from the underlying stock during the term of options is $V_{0:Div}$. To establish the put–call parity for European options, consider the following portfolios:

Portfolio (I): A long position on a European call option on one share of a stock, plus a cash amount equal to $V_{0:Div} + Xe^{-r_f T}$.

Portfolio (II): A long position on a European put option on one share of the stock, plus a long position on one share of the stock.

At time $t = 0$:

- The cost of portfolio (I) includes the value of the call option $V_{0: European\ Call}$ and the cash value of $e^{-r_f T} + V_{0:Div}$.
- The cost of portfolio (II) includes the value of the put option $V_{0: European\ Put}$ and the value of the stock S_0.

At time $t = T$:

- The cash in portfolio (I) is invested at risk-free rate r_f. Thus, at $t = T$ it has the value of $X + V_{0:Div}e^{r_f T}$. The value of the option in portfolio (I) depends on whether the call option is in-the-money or out-of-the-money:
  - If $S_T > X$, the option is exercised; one share of stock is acquired for a payment of X, so the value of portfolio (I) is equal to the value of stock at $t = T$ and the future value of dividend payments expected during the term of the option, which can be derived from the present value $V_{0:Div}$. So the value of portfolio (I) is $S_T + V_{0:Div}e^{r_f T}$.
  - If $S_T < X$, the option is not exercised and expires with no value. So the value of portfolio (I) is $X + V_{0:Div}e^{r_f T}$.

    Therefore the value of portfolio (I) at $t = T$ is $Max(X + V_{0:Div}e^{r_f T}, S_T + V_{0:Div}e^{r_f T})$.
- The value of portfolio (II) at $t = T$ depends on whether the put option is in-the-money or out-of-the-money:
  - If $S_T > X$, the option is not exercised and expires with no value. So the value of portfolio (II) is $S_T + V_{0:Div}e^{r_f T}$.
  - If $S_T < X$, the option is exercised and one share of stock is sold at $t = T$ for X. So the value of portfolio (II) is $X + V_{0:Div}e^{r_f T}$.

    Therefore the value of portfolio (II) at $t = T$ is $Max(X + V_{0:Div}e^{r_f T}, S_T + V_{0:Div}e^{r_f T})$.

Since the values of portfolios (I) and (II) at $t = T$ are equal, based on the arbitrage-free argument, their values at $t = 0$ should also be the same. So:

$$V_{0: European\ Call} + Xe^{-r_f T} + V_{0:Div} = V_{0: European\ Put} + S_0 \qquad (4.113)$$

This identity is the put–call parity for European options when the underlying stock pays dividends in the form of distinct cash flows during the terms of the options. When options are American, we can find an inequality that captures the relationship between the values of call and put options when the underlying stock pays dividends. To establish this inequality, consider the following two portfolios, in which all options have the same strike price, term, and underlying stock:

> *Portfolio (I):* A long position on a European call option on one share of a stock, plus a cash amount equal to $X + V_{0:Div}$.
>
> *Portfolio (II):* A long position on an American put option on one share of the stock, plus a long position on one share of the stock.

At time $t = 0$:

- The cost of portfolio (I) includes the value of the European call option $V_{0:\text{European Call}}$ and a cash value of $X + V_{0:Div}$.
- The cost of portfolio (II) includes the value of the American put option $V_{0:\text{American Put}}$ and the value of the stock S_0.

At time $0 < t \le T$:

- The cash in portfolio (I) is invested at risk-free rate r_f and at $t = T$ it has a value of $e^{r_f T} + V_{0:Div}e^{r_f T}$. Therefore, the value of the portfolio at $t = T$ is $\text{Max}(S_T - X, 0) + Xe^{r_f T} + V_{0:Div}e^{r_f T}$. Since the stock and strike prices are positive numbers, the portfolio value can be expressed as $\text{Max}(S_T, X) - X + Xe^{r_f T} + V_{0:Div}e^{r_f T}$.
- The value of portfolio (II) depends on whether the American put option is exercised early or not:
    - If the American put option is not exercised early, it is equivalent to a European put option and the value of portfolio (II) at $t = T$ consists of value from the combination of the option and stock, and the value from dividends received during the term of option. In the section "Put–Call Parity" we showed that the value from the option and stock combination, whether $S_T > X$ or $S_T < X$, is $\text{Max}(S_T, X)$. The value from dividends at $t = T$ is the future value of dividend payments expected during the term of the option, which can be derived from the present value $V_{0:Div}$. So the value of portfolio (II) at $t = T$ is $\text{Max}(S_T, X) + V_{0:Div}e^{r_f T}$. By comparing the values of portfolios (I) and (II), it is clear that the value of portfolio (I) is greater than or equal to the value of portfolio (II).
    - If the American put option is exercised early, say at a time $t = \tau < T$, the value of the portfolio (II) at that time at most is $X + V_{0:Div}e^{r_f \tau}$. However, the value of portfolio (I), even if the call option has no value at $t = \tau$, is at least $(X + V_{0:Div})e^{r_f \tau}$, which is greater than the value of portfolio (II).

From this, we can conclude that, whether the American put option is exercised early or not, the value of portfolio (I) is greater than or equal to the value of portfolio (II). So, based on the arbitrage-free argument, the cost of portfolio (I) should be greater than or equal to the cost of portfolio (II):

$$V_{0:\, European\ Call} + X + V_{0:\, Div} \geq V_{0:\, American\ Put} + S_0$$

When the underlying stock pays dividends, the value of an American call option is greater than or equal to the value of a comparable European option. So in the previous inequality, we can replace the value of the European call option with the value of an American call option and the inequality still holds. So:

$$V_{0:\, American\ Call} + X + V_{0:\, Div} \geq V_{0:\, American\ Put} + S_0$$

or

$$V_{0:\, American\ Call} - V_{0:\, American\ Put} \geq S_0 - X - V_{0:\, Div}$$

In the "Put–Call Parity" section we showed that when the underlying stock pays no dividends we have:

$$V_{0:\, American\ Call} - V_{0:\, American\ Put} \leq S_0 - X e^{-r_f T}$$

Since a dividend payment reduces the value of the call option and increases the value of the put option, this inequality also holds when the underlying stock pays dividends. Therefore, by combining the previous two inequalities we have:

$$S_0 - X - V_{0:\, Div} \leq V_{0:\, American\ Call} - V_{0:\, American\ Put} \leq S_0 - X e^{-r_f T} \quad (4.114)$$

This inequality captures the relationship between the values of American call and put options when underlying stock pays dividends in the form of distinct cash flows during the term of options.

Asset with Continuous Yield

Assume that the underlying asset provides a continuous yield q, where q is presented with continuous compounding. To establish the put–call parity for European options, consider the following two portfolios:

Portfolio (I): A long position on a European call option on one share of an asset, plus a cash amount equal to $e^{-r_f T}$.

Portfolio (II): A long position on a European put option on one share of an asset, plus a long position on an e^{-qT} share of the asset, where proceeds from asset yield are reinvested in the same underlying asset.

At time $t = 0$:

- The cost of portfolio (I) includes the value of the European call option $V_{0:\ European\ Call}$ and a cash value of $e^{-r_f T}$.
- The cost of portfolio (II) includes the value of the European put option $V_{0:\ European\ Put}$ and a cost of $S_0 e^{-qT}$ for acquiring e^{-qT} shares of the asset.

At time $t = T$:

- The cash in portfolio (I) is invested at risk-free rate r_f and at $t = T$ it has a value of X. The value of the option in portfolio (I) depends on whether the call option is in-the-money or out-of-the-money:
  - If $S_T > X$, the option is exercised; one share of the asset is acquired for a payment of X, so the value of portfolio (I) is equal to value of the asset S_T.
  - If $S_T < X$, the option is not exercised and expires with no value. So the value of portfolio (I) is X.

    Therefore the value of portfolio (I) value at $t = T$ is Max(X, S_T).
- Since proceeds from asset yield received from the initial holding of a e^{-qT} share of asset are reinvested in the same asset, total accumulation is equal to one share at time $t = T$. The value of portfolio (II) at $t = T$ then depends on whether the put option is in-the-money or out-of-the-money:
  - If $S_T > X$, the option is not exercised and expires with no value. So the value of portfolio (II) is S_T.
  - If $S_T < X$, the option is exercised and one share of the asset is exchanged for X. So the value of portfolio (II) is X.

    Thus, the value of portfolio (II) at $t = T$ is Max(X, S_T).

Since the values of portfolio (I) and (II) at $t = T$ are equal, based on the arbitrage-free argument, their values at $t = 0$ should also be equal. So:

$$V_{0:\ European\ Call} + Xe^{-r_f T} = V_{0:\ European\ Put} + S_0 e^{-qT} \qquad (4.115)$$

This identity is the put–call parity for European options when the underlying asset provides a continuous yield. As before, for this case and for American options we can develop an inequality to associate the values of call and put options. To establish this inequality, first consider the following two portfolios:

Portfolio (I): A long position on a European call option on one share of an asset, plus a cash amount equal to X.

Portfolio (II): A long position on an American put option on one share of asset, plus a long position on an e^{-qT} share of the asset, where proceeds from asset yield are reinvested in the same underlying asset.

At time $t = 0$:

- The cost of portfolio (I) includes the value of the European call option $V_{0:\,European\,Call}$ and a cash value of X.
- The cost of portfolio (II) includes the value of the American put option $V_{0:\,American\,Put}$ and a cost of $S_0 e^{-qT}$ for acquiring e^{-qT} shares of asset.

At time $0 < t \leq T$:

- The cash in portfolio (I) is invested at risk-free rate r_f and at $t = T$ it has a value of $Xe^{r_f T}$. The value of portfolio (I) depends on whether the call option is in-the-money or out-of-the-money and at $t = T$ it is equal to $\text{Max}(S_T - X, 0) + Xe^{r_f T}$, or equivalently $\text{Max}(S_T, X) - X + Xe^{r_f T}$.
- The value of portfolio (II) depends on whether the American put option is exercised early or not:
  - If the American put option is not exercised early, it is equivalent to a European put option. The reinvested proceeds from the asset yield accumulate to one share at $t = T$ and hence the value of portfolio (II) at $t = T$ is $\text{Max}(S_T, X)$. By comparing the values of portfolios (I) and (II), it is clear that the value of portfolio (I) is greater than the value of portfolio (II).
  - If the American put option is exercised early, say at time $t = \tau < T$, the reinvested proceeds from the asset yield accumulate to only an $e^{-qT} e^{q\tau}$ share and the remaining portion of one share needed for the option exercise should be purchased from the market at a market price of S_τ. Hence the value of portfolio (II) is $X - S_\tau(1 - e^{-qT} e^{q\tau})$, which is less than or equal to X. However, the value of portfolio (I), even if the call option has no value, is greater than X.

From this argument we can see that, whether the American put option is exercised early or not, the value of portfolio (I) is greater than or equal to the value of portfolio (II). Hence, based on the arbitrage-free argument, the cost of portfolio (I) should be greater than or equal to the cost of portfolio (II):

$$V_{0:\,European\,Call} + X \geq V_{0:\,American\,Put} + S_0 e^{-qT}$$

Since the value of an American call option, when the underlying asset pays a dividend or provides a yield, is greater than or equal to the value of a comparable European call option, we have:

$$V_{0:\,American\ Call} + X \geq V_{0:\,American\ Put} + S_0 e^{-qT}$$

or

$$S_0 e^{-qT} - X \leq V_{0:\,American\ Call} - V_{0:\,American\ Put} \qquad (4.116)$$

Next consider the following two different portfolios:

Portfolio (III): A long position on a European put option on one share of the asset, plus a long position on one share of the asset, where proceeds from the asset yield received are reinvested in the same underlying asset.

Portfolio (IV): A long position on an American call option on one share of the asset, plus a cash amount equal to $Xe^{-r_f T}$.

At time $t = 0$:

- The cost of portfolio (III) includes the value of the European put option $V_{0:\,European\ Put}$ and the price of one share S_0.
- The cost of portfolio (IV) includes the value of the American call option $V_{0:\,American\ Call}$ and the cash value of $Xe^{-r_f T}$.

At time $0 < t \leq T$:

- Since proceeds from asset yield are reinvested in the underlying asset, their accumulated value at $t = T$ is $S_T e^{qT}$. The value of portfolio (III) at $t = T$ depends on whether the European put option is in-the-money or out-of-the-money. Based on similar logic used earlier, the value of portfolio (III) is equal to $Max(X - S_T, 0) + S_T e^{qT}$, or equivalently $Max(S_T, X) - S_T + S_T e^{qT}$.
- The value of portfolio (IV) depends on whether the American call option is exercised early or not:
  - If the American call option is not exercised early, it is equivalent to a European call option. The cash invested at the risk-free rate has the value of X at $t = T$ and the value of portfolio (IV) is $Max(S_T, X)$. By comparing this with the value of portfolio (III), it is clear that the value of portfolio (III) is greater than the value of portfolio (IV).
  - If the American call option is exercised early, say at time $t = \tau < T$, the invested cash is accumulated only to $Xe^{-r_f T} e^{r_f \tau}$ and the rest of the amount needed for the option exercise should be borrowed at the

risk-free rate. Hence the value of portfolio (IV) is $S_\tau - X(1 - e^{-r_f T} q^{r_f \tau})$, which is less than or equal to S_τ. However, the value of portfolio (III), even if the put option has no value, is $S_\tau e^{q(T-\tau)}$, which is greater than or equal to S_τ.

From this argument it is clear that, whether the American call option is exercised early or not, the value of portfolio (III) is greater than or equal to the value of portfolio (IV). Hence, based on the arbitrage-free argument, the cost of portfolio (III) should be greater than or equal to the cost of portfolio (IV):

$$V_{0:\,European\,Put} + S_0 \geq V_{0:\,American\,Call} + Xe^{-r_f T}$$

Since when the underlying asset pays dividends or provides yield the value of an American put option is greater than or equal to the value of a comparable European put option, we have:

$$V_{0:\,American\,Put} + S_0 \geq V_{0:\,American\,Call} + Xe^{-r_f T}$$

or

$$V_{0:\,American\,Call} - V_{0:\,American\,Put} \leq S_0 - Xe^{-r_f T} \tag{4.117}$$

By combining Equations (4.116) and (4.117) we have:

$$S_0 e^{-qT} - X \leq V_{0:\,American\,Call} - V_{0:\,American\,Put} \leq S_0 - Xe^{-r_f T} \tag{4.118}$$

ANNEX 2: DERIVATION OF DELTA, GAMMA, VEGA, RHO, AND THETA

Delta

In Equation (4.44), d_1 and d_2 are defined as:

$$d_1 = \frac{\ln\left(\frac{S_t}{X}\right) + \left(r_f - q + \frac{\sigma^2}{2}\right)(T-t)}{\sigma\sqrt{T-t}}$$

$$d_2 = d_1 - \sigma\sqrt{T-t} = \frac{\ln\left(\frac{S_t}{X}\right) + \left(r_f - q - \frac{\sigma^2}{2}\right)(T-t)}{\sigma\sqrt{T-t}}$$

By taking the first derivative of d_1 and d_2 with respect to S_t we have:

$$\frac{\partial d_1}{\partial S_t} = \frac{\partial d_2}{\partial S_t} = \frac{1}{S_t \sigma \sqrt{T-t}} \tag{4.119}$$

If $\Phi()$ is the cumulative probability distribution of standard normal, $\varphi() = \Phi'()$ is the probability density function of standard normal:

$$\Phi'(a) = \Phi'(-a) = \frac{1}{\sqrt{2\pi}} e^{-\frac{a^2}{2}}$$

Therefore, since $d_1 = d_2 + \sigma\sqrt{T-t}$, we have:

$$\Phi'(d_1) = \Phi'(d_2 + \sigma\sqrt{T-t}) = \frac{1}{\sqrt{2\pi}} e^{-\frac{\left(d_2 + \sigma\sqrt{T-t}\right)^2}{2}}$$

$$= \Phi'(d_2) exp\left(-\frac{1}{2}\sigma^2(T-t) - \sigma d_2\sqrt{T-t}\right)$$

Replacing d_2 in the exponent part of this equation with its definition from Equation (4.44) results in:

$$\Phi'(d_1) = \Phi'(d_2) \exp\left(-\frac{1}{2}\sigma^2(T-t) - \ln\left(\frac{S_t}{X}\right) - \left(r_f - q - \frac{\sigma^2}{2}\right)(T-t)\right)$$

or

$$\Phi'(d_1) = \Phi'(d_2)\frac{X}{S_t}e^{-(r_f - q)(T-t)} \tag{4.120}$$

The value of a European call option based on the Black–Scholes–Merton model is presented in Equation (4.42) as:

$$V_{t:\,European\,Call} = \Phi(d_1)\,S_t\,e^{-q(T-t)} - \Phi(d_2)Xe^{-r_f\,(T-t)}$$

Delta is the first derivative of this function with respect to S_t so:

$$\delta_{European\,Call} = \frac{\partial V_t}{\partial S_t} = \frac{\partial}{\partial S_t}[\Phi(d_1)S_t e^{-q(T-t)} - \Phi(d_2)Xe^{-r_f\,(T-t)}]$$

$$= \Phi'(d_1)\frac{\partial d_1}{\partial S_t}S_t e^{-q(T-t)} + \Phi(d_1)\,e^{-q(T-t)}$$

$$- \Phi'(d_2)\frac{\partial d_2}{\partial S_t}Xe^{-r_f\,(T-t)}$$

In this equation we can replace $\Phi'(d_1)$ with its equivalent from Equation (4.120). Also based on Equation (4.119), we can replace $\frac{\partial d_1}{\partial S_t}$ with $\frac{\partial d_2}{\partial S_t}$ since they are equal. So:

$$\delta_{European\ Call} = \Phi'(d_2)\frac{X}{S_t}e^{-(r_f-q)(T-t)}\frac{\partial d_1}{\partial S_t}S_t e^{-q(T-t)}$$

$$+ \Phi(d_1)\, e^{-q(T-t)} - \Phi'(d_2)\frac{\partial d_1}{\partial S_t}Xe^{-r_f(T-t)}$$

Since the first and third terms of this equation cancel out, we obtain:

$$\delta_{European\ Call} = \Phi(d_1)\, e^{-q(T-t)} \tag{4.121}$$

Noting that since $\Phi(-d_1) = 1 - \Phi(d_1)$, we can use a similar approach explained earlier to obtain the delta of a European put option as:

$$\delta_{European\ Put} = (\Phi(d_1) - 1)\, e^{-q(T-t)} \tag{4.122}$$

Gamma

By taking derivative of delta in Equation (4.121) with respect to S_t we have:

$$\gamma_{European\ Call} = \frac{\partial}{\partial S_t}[\Phi(d_1)\, e^{-q(T-t)}] = \Phi'(d_1)\frac{\partial d_1}{\partial S_t}\, e^{-q(T-t)}$$

Replacing $\frac{\partial d_1}{\partial S_t}$ with its equivalent from Equation (4.119) provides us with the gamma for a European call option as:

$$\gamma_{European\ Call} = \frac{\varphi(d_1)\, e^{-q(T-t)}}{S_t\sigma\sqrt{T-t}} \tag{4.123}$$

Similarly, by taking the derivative of Equation (4.122) with respect to S_t and replacing $\frac{\partial d_2}{\partial S_t}$ with its equivalent from Equation (4.119) we have:

$$\gamma_{European\ Put} = \frac{\varphi(d_1)\, e^{-q(T-t)}}{S_t\, \sigma\, \sqrt{T-t}} \tag{4.124}$$

Vega

To derive the vega, first note that since $d_2 = d_1 - \sigma\sqrt{T-t}$ we have:

$$\frac{\partial d_1}{\partial \sigma} - \frac{\partial d_2}{\partial \sigma} = \sqrt{T-t} \tag{4.125}$$

For a European call option, vega is the first derivative of the option value function from Equation (4.42) with respect to σ, so:

$$\mathcal{V}_{European\ Call} = \frac{\partial}{\partial \sigma}[\Phi(d_1)\, S_t\, e^{-q(T-t)} - \Phi(d_2)Xe^{-r_f(T-t)}]$$

$$= \Phi'(d_1)\frac{\partial d_1}{\partial \sigma}\, S_t\, e^{-q(T-t)} - \Phi'(d_2)\frac{\partial d_2}{\partial \sigma}\, Xe^{-r_f(T-t)}$$

By replacing $\Phi'(d_2)$ with its equivalent from Equation (4.120) we have:

$$\mathcal{V}_{European\ Call} = \Phi'(d_1)\frac{\partial d_1}{\partial \sigma}\, S_t\, e^{-q(T-t)}$$

$$- \left(\Phi'(d_1)\frac{S_t}{X}e^{(r_f-q)(T-t)}\right)\frac{\partial d_2}{\partial \sigma}\, X\, e^{-r_f\ (T-t)}$$

$$= \Phi'(d_1)\frac{\partial d_1}{\partial \sigma}\, S_t\, e^{-q(T-t)} - \Phi'(d_1)\frac{\partial d_2}{\partial \sigma}S_t e^{-q(T-t)}$$

$$= \Phi'(d_1)S_t e^{-q(T-t)}\left[\frac{\partial d_1}{\partial \sigma} - \frac{\partial d_2}{\partial \sigma}\right]$$

Using the result from Equation (4.125) we can simplify this equation as:

$$\mathcal{V}_{European\ Call} = \varphi(d_1)\, S_t\, \sqrt{T-t}\, e^{-q(T-t)} \tag{4.126}$$

Using the same approach, the vega of the European put option is derived as:

$$\mathcal{V}_{European\ Put} = \varphi(d_1)\, S_t\, \sqrt{T-t}\, e^{-q(T-t)} \tag{4.127}$$

Rho

To derive the rho, first note that since $d_2 = d_1 - \sigma\sqrt{T-t}$, taking the derivative with respect to r_f yields:

$$\frac{\partial d_1}{\partial r_f} = \frac{\partial d_2}{\partial r_f} \tag{4.128}$$

For a European call option, rho is the first derivative of the option value function from Equation (4.42) with respect to r_f:

$$\rho_{European\ Call} = \frac{\partial}{\partial r_f}[\Phi(d_1)\, S_t\, e^{-q(T-t)} - \Phi(d_2)Xe^{-r_f(T-t)}]$$

$$= \Phi'(d_1)\frac{\partial d_1}{\partial r_f}\, S_t\, e^{-q(T-t)} - \Phi'(d_2)\frac{\partial d_2}{\partial r_f}\, Xe^{-r_f(T-t)}$$

$$+ \Phi(d_2)X(T-t)e^{-r_f(T-t)}$$

By replacing $\Phi'(d_1)$ with its equivalent from Equation (4.120) we have:

$$\rho_{European\ Call} = \left(\Phi'(d_2)\frac{X}{S_t}e^{-(r_f-q)(T-t)}\right)\frac{\partial d_1}{\partial r_f}\ S_t\ e^{-q(T-t)}$$

$$- \Phi'(d_2)\frac{\partial d_2}{\partial r_f}\ X\ e^{-r_f\ (T-t)} + \Phi(d_2)X(T-t)e^{-r_f(T-t)}$$

$$= \Phi'(d_2)\left(\frac{\partial d_1}{\partial r_f} - \frac{\partial d_2}{\partial r_f}\right)Xe^{-r_f(T-t)}$$

$$+ \Phi(d_2)X(T-t)e^{-r_f(T-t)}$$

By using the result from Equation (4.128) we obtain:

$$\rho_{European\ Call} = \Phi(d_2)X(T-t)e^{-r_f(T-t)} \tag{4.129}$$

Following a similar method, the rho of a European put option is obtained as:

$$\rho_{European\ Put} = -\Phi(-d_2)\ X\ (T-t)\ e^{-r_f(T-t)} \tag{4.130}$$

Theta

To derive the theta, first note that since $d_2 = d_1 - \sigma\sqrt{T-t}$, by taking the derivative with respect to t we have:

$$\frac{\partial d_1}{\partial t} - \frac{\partial d_2}{\partial t} = -\frac{\sigma}{2\sqrt{T-t}} \tag{4.131}$$

Since theta is the sensitivity to the passage of time, the theta of a European call option is derived by taking the derivative of the option value function in Equation (4.42) with respect to t:

$$\theta_{European\ Call} = \frac{\partial}{\partial t}[\Phi(d_1)S_t e^{-q(T-t)} - \Phi(d_2)Xe^{-r_f(T-t)}]$$

$$= \Phi'(d_1)\frac{\partial d_1}{\partial t}S_t e^{-q(T-t)} + \Phi(d_1)qS_t\ e^{-q(T-t)}$$

$$- \Phi'(d_2)\frac{\partial d_2}{\partial t}Xe^{-r_f(T-t)} - \Phi(d_2)r_f\ Xe^{-r_f(T-t)}$$

By replacing $\Phi'(d_2)$ in this equation with its equivalent from Equation (4.120) we have:

$$\theta_{European\ Call} = \Phi'(d_1)\frac{\partial d_1}{\partial t}S_t e^{-q(T-t)} + \Phi(d_1)qS_t e^{-q(T-t)}$$

$$- \left(\Phi'(d_1)\frac{S_t}{X}e^{(r_f-q)(T-t)}\right)\frac{\partial d_2}{\partial t}Xe^{-r_f(T-t)}$$

$$- \Phi(d_2)r_f\,Xe^{-r_f(T-t)}$$

$$= \Phi'(d_1)S_t e^{-q(T-t)}\left(\frac{\partial d_1}{\partial t} - \frac{\partial d_2}{\partial t}\right) + \Phi(d_1)qS_t e^{-q(T-t)}$$

$$- \Phi(d_2)r_f\,Xe^{-r_f(T-t)}$$

By incorporating Equation (4.131) into this equation we obtain:

$$\theta_{European\ Call} = \frac{-\varphi(d_1)S_t\sigma e^{-q(T-t)}}{2\sqrt{T-t}} + \Phi(d_1)qS_t e^{-q(T-t)} - \Phi(d_2)r_f\,Xe^{-r_f(T-t)}$$

$$(4.132)$$

Using a similar method, the theta for a European put option is derived as:

$$\theta_{European\ Put} = \frac{-\varphi(d_1)S_t\sigma e^{-q(T-t)}}{2\sqrt{T-t}} - \Phi(-d_1)qS_t e^{-q(T-t)} + \Phi(-d_2)r_f\,Xe^{-r_f(T-t)}$$

$$(4.133)$$

NOTES

1. Up and down percentages do not need to be equal.
2. For details of derivation of this equation see the Appendix.
3. Microsoft® Excel's NORM.S.DIST(a, TRUE) function can be used to obtain probability from the cumulative distribution function of the standard normal for value a.
4. Microsoft® Excel's NORM.S.INV(RAND()) function can be used to create a random instance from the standard normal probability distribution.
5. Based on 10 simulated paths used here, any stock price in the range of $17.56 < S^*_{t=2} \leq 18.10$ is the boundary value for early exercise at $t = 2$ month. An increase in the number of simulated stock price paths reduces this to a tighter range.
6. These sensitivity measurements are often referred to as *Greeks*.

7. Defining daily price change in this form implies a continuous compounding rate of return.
8. In practice this is often referred to as a *volatility smile*, where the graph of volatility to strike price resembles a smile figure.
9. One alternative is to assume a student's *t*-distribution for u_t.
10. The capital asset pricing model (CAPM) has the following general form:

$$E[\text{rate of return}] = r_f + \beta(r_M - r_f)$$

where r_f is the risk-free rate, r_M is the expected return of market, $r_M - r_f$ is known as the market premium, and β is the sensitivity of the expected asset rate of return to the market premium.
11. This notation implies that $\alpha_i = 0$ when $i > q$ and $\beta_i = 0$ when $i > p$.
12. January 19 and 20, 2019, are not trading days.
13. A matrix A is positive definite when for any non-zero $x \in \mathbb{R}^d$ we have $xAx^T > 0$. A is positive semidefinite when $xAx^T \geq 0$.
14. Earlier in this chapter we used r_f to reference the annual risk-free rate. Here it is used to indicate the one-period risk-free rate and since volatility models discussed in this section are based on daily periodicity, here r_f is the one-day risk-free rate.
15. For example, in the case of $p = 1$ and $q = 1$, unconditional variance is $\frac{\alpha_0}{1-(1+\gamma^2)\alpha_1-\beta_1}$.
16. Here we ignore the impact of the time value of money during the short period within a trading day.

BIBLIOGRAPHY

Anderson, Leif. "A Simple Approach to the Pricing of Bermudan Swaptions in the Multifactor LIBOR Model." *Journal of Computational Finance* 3, no. 2 (January 2000): 5–32.

Björk, Tomas. *Arbitrage Theory in Continuous Time*, 3rd ed. Oxford University Press, 2009,

Black, Fischer. "Fact and Fantasy in the Use of Options." *Financial Analysts Journal* 31, no. 4 (July 1975): 36–72.

Black, Fischer. "The Pricing of Commodity Contracts." *Journal of Financial Economics* 3, nos. 1–2 (March 1976): 167–179.

Black, Fischer, and Myron Scholes. "The Pricing of Options and Corporate Liabilities." *The Journal of Political Economy* 81, no. 3 (1973): 637–654.

Bollersley, Tim. "Generalized Autoregressive Conditional Heteroscedasticity." *Journal of Econometrics* 31, no. 3 (April 1986): 307–327.

Boyle, Phelim P. "Options: A Monte Carlo Approach." *Journal of Financial Economics* 4, no. 3 (May 1977): 323–338.

Cox, John C., Stephen A. Ross, and Mark Rubinstein. "Option Pricing: A Simplified Approach." *Journal of Financial Economics* 7, no. 3 (1979): 229–263.

Duan, Jin-Chuan "The GARCH Option Pricing Model." *Mathematical Finance* 5, no. 1 (January 1995): 13–32.

Engle, Robert T. "Autoregressive Conditional Heteroscedasticity with Estimates of the Variance of United Kingdom Inflation." *Econometrics* 50, no. 4 (July 1982): 987–1008.

Hamilton, James D. *Time Series Analysis*. Princeton University Press, 1994.

Hull, John C. *Options, Futures, and Other Derivatives*, 6th ed. Prentice-Hall, 2005.

Merton, Robert C. "The Relationship between Put and Call Option Prices: Comment." *The Journal of Finance* 28, no. 1 (1973a): 183–184.

Merton, Robert C. "Theory of Rational Option Pricing." *The Bell Journal of Economics and Management Science* 4, no. 1 (1973b): 141–183.

MSCI/J.P. Morgan/Reuters. RiskMetrics Technical Document, 4th ed. December 17, 1996.

Nelson, Daniel B. "Stationarity and Persistence in the GARCH (1,1) Model." *Econometric Theory* 6, no. 3 (September 1990): 318–334.

Tsay, Ruey S. *Analysis of Financial Time Series*, 3rd ed. Wiley, 2010.

CHAPTER 5

Interest Rate Models

Interest rate is the main risk factor examined in ALM analysis. The fundamental business model of a bank as a financial intermediary is based on the difference between interest earned on its assets and interest paid on its liabilities. The existence of this spread exposes the bank to interest rate risk on its earnings. Interest rate scenario analysis and planning for possible adverse cases are integral parts of banks' balance sheet management and to perform these, ALM teams rely on interest rate models. An interest rate model is a mathematical construct that characterizes the movement of interest rate over a period of time. It considers the stochastic nature of rate movement while taking into account the current interest rate environment, as well as historical rate movements.

A change in interest rate also impacts the value of assets and liabilities of banks. We introduced the discounted cash flow method in an earlier chapter as the fundamental tool for valuation of financial instruments. However, for some complicated instruments, such as callable bonds and mortgage-backed securities, we cannot perform valuation based only on the discounted cash flow method. For such instruments, alternative valuation methods are developed that are founded on interest rate models.

In this chapter we introduce a few interest rate models and we will use these models in later chapters for valuation purposes and also in simulation analysis of net interest income. Our focus in this chapter is on the arbitrage-free interest rate models that are commonly used in ALM analysis and implemented in many ALM software packages. These arbitrage-free models fit the current term structure of interest rate and hence are preferred to those models that do not have this feature. In this chapter we also discuss interest rate option contracts and their valuation methods.

INSTANTANEOUS FORWARD RATE AND SHORT RATE

To start our discussion about interest rate models, consider an investment of \$1 in a risk-free savings account. Figure 5.1 presents a schematic view of this investment. Assume that the value of this investment at time $t > 0$ is $B(t)$. In a

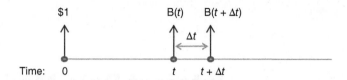

FIGURE 5.1　Schematic view of an investment in a bank savings account

short period of time Δt the investment in this account earns an interest amount based on interest rate $r(t)$. This is the interest rate the bank pays for the balance at time t for a short term of Δt. The value of the investment in the bank account at time $t + \Delta t$ is calculated as:

$$B(t + \Delta t) = B(t)(1 + r(t)\Delta t) \tag{5.1}$$

In the limiting case when $\Delta t \to 0$ the change in value of the investment $dB(t)$ in a short period of time dt is presented as:

$$dB(t) = B(t)r(t)dt$$

Assuming continuous compounding for interest rate, this equation can be written as:

$$B(t) = e^{\int_0^t r(\tau)d\tau} \tag{5.2}$$

where $B(0) = 1$, and where $r(t)$ is the *instantaneous spot rate* at time t, also known as *short rate* at time t. It is the interest rate paid at time t for a very short term. Short rate follows a stochastic process and the interest rate models that we discuss in this chapter analyze the evolution of $r(t)$ through the time.

Assume that $T = t + \Delta t$ and value of investment at time T is $B(T)$. From Equation (5.1) we have:

$$B(T) = B(t)(1 + r(t)(T - t))$$

or

$$\frac{1}{1 + r(t)(T - t)} = \frac{B(t)}{B(T)}$$

The right-hand side of this equation is the discount factor of a cash flow occurring at time T, discounted back to time t:

$$D(t, T) = \frac{B(t)}{B(T)} = e^{-\int_t^T r(\tau)d\tau} \tag{5.3}$$

$D(t, T)$ also follows a stochastic process. Now consider a zero-coupon bond maturing at time T that pays \$1 at the maturity. We use $P(t, T)$ notation to indicate the value of this bond at time t, where $t < T$ and $P(T, T) = 1$. $P(t, T)$ at time t is known and deterministic, but $D(t, T)$ is based on short rate $r(t)$ and hence is stochastic. In a risk-neutral world $P(t, T)$ is the expectation of $D(t, T)$.

We can now use the zero-coupon bond price $P(t, T)$ to explain the short rate. Let's start by assuming that a spot rate at time $t \geq 0$ for the maturity at T is $r(t, T)$. This is a rate for a period with length $T - t$. If time t is now ($t = 0$), then $r(0, T)$ is the current spot rate with maturity at T. $r(t, T)$ is therefore a generalization of the spot rate as seen at any time $t \geq 0$. Assuming continuous compounding, the value of a zero-coupon bond at time t that pays \$1 at the maturity T (i.e., for period with length of $T - t$) is:

$$P(t, T) = 1 \times e^{-r(t,T)(T-t)}$$

or

$$P(t, T) = e^{-r(t,T)(T-t)} \tag{5.4}$$

From this we can write the continuous compounding spot rate at time t with maturity at T as:

$$r(t, T) = -\frac{\ln P(t, T)}{T - t} \tag{5.5}$$

Now consider another zero-coupon bond at time t, paying \$1 at maturity time S where $S > T$. The price of this bond $P(t, S)$ is calculated as:

$$P(t, S) = e^{-r(t,S)(S-t)} \tag{5.6}$$

where $r(t, S)$ is the spot rate at time t with maturity at S. Figure 5.2 shows a schematic view of these two zero-coupon bonds.

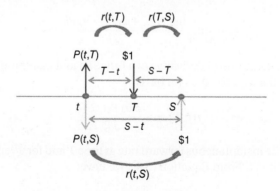

FIGURE 5.2 Schematic view of spot rates and forward rates as seen at time t

Using spot rates $r(t, T)$ and $r(t, S)$, and based on the arbitrage-free pricing principle, an $r(T, S)$ forward rate at time T for a term of $S - T$ can be obtained as:

$$e^{r(t,S)(S-t)} = e^{r(t,T)(T-t)} \times e^{r(T,S)(S-T)}$$

or

$$r(T, S) = \frac{1}{S - T} \ln \frac{e^{r(t,S)(S-t)}}{e^{r(t,T)(T-t)}}$$

Using Equations (5.4) and (5.6) we have:

$$r(T, S) = \frac{1}{S - T} \ln \frac{\dfrac{1}{P(t, S)}}{\dfrac{1}{P(t, T)}}$$

or

$$r(T, S) = -\frac{\ln P(t, S) - \ln P(t, T)}{S - T} \tag{5.7}$$

where $r(T, S)$ is the continuous compounding forward rate at time T for a term of $S - T$, as seen at time t. It is important to note that this forward rate is defined using spot rates at time t (and not time 0); hence the forward rate $r(T, S)$ is the rate for the period from T to S prevailing at time t (Figure 5.2).

The period between T and S is the term of the forward rate and as we let S to move closer to T the term of the forward rate decreases. In a limiting case when $S \to T$ the forward rate is known as the *instantaneous forward rate* and by setting $\Delta T = S - T$, we have:

$$f(t, T) = \lim_{S \to T} r(T, S) = \lim_{S \to T} -\frac{\ln P(t, S) - \ln P(t, T)}{S - T}$$

$$= -\lim_{\Delta T \to 0} \frac{\ln P(t, T + \Delta T) - \ln P(t, T)}{\Delta T}$$

Using the definition of derivative of a function and assuming $P(t, T)$ is the continuous differentiable at T, we have:

$$f(t, T) = -\frac{\partial \ln P(t, T)}{\partial T} \tag{5.8}$$

$f(t, T)$ is the instantaneous forward rate at time T and for a very short term, prevailing at time t. From Equation (5.8), we have:

$$P(t, T) = e^{-\int_t^T f(t,u)\, du} \tag{5.9}$$

By placing the result of Equation (5.9) into Equation (5.5), we obtain:

$$r(t, T) = \frac{1}{T-t} \int_t^T f(t, u) \, du \tag{5.10}$$

Equations (5.9) and (5.10) demonstrate that the price of zero-coupon bond and spot rates at time t can be derived from the instantaneous forward rate. The instantaneous forward rate plays an important role in quantitative finance and we use it throughout this chapter.

From Equation (5.10) we can rewrite the relationship between the instantaneous forward rate and spot rate as follows:

$$f(t, T) = \frac{\partial[(T-t) \, r(t, T)]}{\partial T}$$

or equivalently,

$$f(t, T) = r(t, T) + (T - t)\frac{\partial r(t, T)}{\partial T} \tag{5.11}$$

We are now ready to revisit the instantaneous spot rate, or short rate. The instantaneous spot rate can be defined as the limiting case of the spot rate at time t when $T \to t$:

$$r(t) = \lim_{T \to t} r(t, T) \tag{5.12}$$

In other words, the short rate at time t is the spot rate at time t when the term of the rate is very short. On the other hand, from Equation (5.11) and when $T \to t$, we have:

$$r(t) = f(t, t) \tag{5.13}$$

In other words, the short rate at time t is the instantaneous forward rate at time t prevailing at the same time t.

So far we have defined the spot rate, forward rate, instantaneous forward rate, and instantaneous spot rate (short rate) and derived relationships between them. Using these concepts, we can now redefine the spot curve and introduce the instantaneous forward curve:

- Function $T \to r(t, T)$ is the *spot curve* at time t. It is the curve that shows the zero-coupon rates (spot rates) for different terms (different Ts) as seen at time t (prevailing at time t). Time t is called the *as-of-date* of the curve.
- Function $T \to f(t, T)$ is the *instantaneous forward curve*. It is the curve that shows instantaneous forward rates at different future times (different Ts) as seen at time t (prevailing at time t).[1]

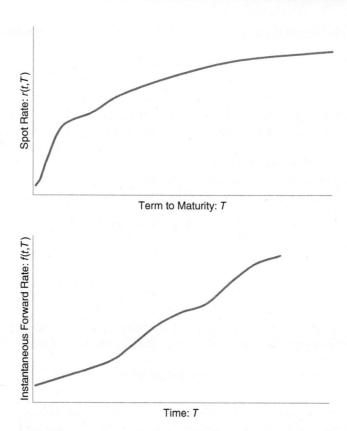

FIGURE 5.3   Sample spot curve and instantaneous forward curve

Figure 5.3 presents a sample spot curve and an instantaneous forward curve prevailing at time t. It is important to note that every spot curve can be represented by an instantaneous forward curve, and vice versa.

Going back to the start of this section when we introduce the short rate and its relationship to the value of an investment in a savings account, it was mentioned that in a risk-neutral world the value of a zero-coupon bond $P(t, T)$ is the expectation of discount factor $D(t, T)$, which is a function of $r(t)$:

$$P(t, T) = E[D(t, T)]$$

where E represents the expectation of a random variable. From Equation (5.3) we have:

$$P(t, T) = E\left[e^{-\int_t^T r(\tau)d\tau}\right] \tag{5.14}$$

Placing this result into Equation (5.5) we have:

$$r(t, T) = -\frac{1}{T-t} \ln \left(E\left[e^{-\int_t^T r(\tau)d\tau} \right] \right) \tag{5.15}$$

This equation indicates that once we define the stochastic process of short rate $r(t)$, then the whole term structure of the spot curve is defined. In the following sections we discuss a few models that analyze the evolution of $r(t)$ through time. In these models the short rate follows an Itô process. The Itô process is discussed in the Appendix. Models introduced here are one-factor models in which only one source of uncertainty is assumed. They are commonly used in practice, especially for ALM analysis. For discussions of other models refer to Hull (1990) and Brigo and Mercurio (2001).

Some of the models developed for evolution of the short rate have the property that the continuous compounding spot rate is an affine function[2] of the short rate in the form of:

$$r(t, T) = \alpha(t, T) + \beta(t, T)\, r(t) \tag{5.16}$$

where α and β are deterministic functions of t and T. Such models are said to have an *affine term structure*. It can be shown that the relationship in Equation (5.16) is satisfied when the price of a zero-coupon bond has the following form (Brigo and Mercurio 2001):

$$P(t, T) = A(t, T)e^{-B(t,T)\, r(t)} \tag{5.17}$$

where A and B are also deterministic functions of t and T. By combining the previous two equations and Equation (5.4), we have:

$$\alpha(t, T) = \frac{-\ln A(t, T)}{T - t} \tag{5.18}$$

$$\beta(t, T) = \frac{B(t, T)}{(T - t)} \tag{5.19}$$

Therefore, using $A(t, T)$ and $B(t, T)$ notations, Equation (5.16) can be written as:

$$r(t, T) = -\frac{1}{T-t} \ln A(t, T) + \frac{1}{T-t} B(t, T)\, r(t) \tag{5.20}$$

A few of the models that we discuss in the following sections provide us with a closed-form solution for a zero-coupon bond in the form presented in Equation (5.17) and hence $A(t, T)$ and $B(t, T)$ are available. Subsequently Equation (5.20) can be used to obtain the relationship between the spot rate $r(t, T)$ and short rate $r(t)$.

VASICEK MODEL

In his pioneering work on modeling the term structure of interest rates, Vasicek (1977) developed a model for evolution of the short rate through time. In this model the stochastic process for the short rate in a risk-neutral world is as follows:

$$dr(t) = k(\theta - r(t))dt + \sigma \, dW(t) \tag{5.21}$$

Here k, θ, and σ are constant, $dW(t)$ represents a Wiener process, and $r(0)$ is equal to the current spot rate for a very small term. The Vasicek model has a *mean reversion* property, where short rates generated by the stochastic model move toward a long-term level. In the model presented in Equation (5.21) the mean reversion level is θ and k is the speed at which the short rate approaches this long-term level. Whenever the short rate is above the long-term level, the drift term of the stochastic process is negative, and when it is below that level the drift is positive. Mean reversion of a short rate model is a desirable feature as there is historical evidence of such a trend for the interest rate. σ is the standard deviation of rate of change in short rate, that is, the standard deviation of $dr(t)/r(t)$. By integrating Equation (5.21) for any $0 \leq s < t$, we have:

$$r(t) = r(s)e^{-k(t-s)} + \theta \left(1 - e^{-k(t-s)}\right) + \sigma \int_s^t e^{-k(t-\tau)}dW(\tau) \tag{5.22}$$

In the Vasicek model the short rate $r(t)$ is normally distributed. For any $0 \leq s < t$ conditional mean and variance of the distribution, conditioned to all available information available, until and including time s: $\mathcal{F}_s$, are:

$$E[r(t)|\mathcal{F}_s] = r(s)e^{-k(t-s)} + \theta \left(1 - e^{-k(t-s)}\right) \tag{5.23}$$

$$Var[r(t)|\mathcal{F}_s] = \frac{\sigma^2}{2k} \left[1 - e^{-2k(t-s)}\right] \tag{5.24}$$

The Vasicek model is an affine term structure model and the price of the zero-coupon bond can be presented as Equation (5.17). It can be shown that the expressions for $A(t, T)$ and $B(t, T)$ functions are as follows (Brigo and Mercurio 2001):

$$P(t, T) = A(t, T)e^{-B(t,T) \, r(t)}$$

$$A(t, T) = \exp\left[(B(t, T) - T + t)\left(\theta - \frac{\sigma^2}{2k^2}\right) - \frac{\sigma^2 B(t, T)^2}{4k}\right] \tag{5.25}$$

$$B(t, T) = \frac{1 - e^{-k(T-t)}}{k} \tag{5.26}$$

For $k = 0$, $B(t, T) = T - t$ and $A(t, T) = \exp\left[\frac{\sigma^2(T-t)^3}{6}\right]$. Placing these expressions into Equation (5.20) provides us with the relationship between the spot rate and short rate. In the Vasicek model, due to the nature of the probability distribution of a short rate, the probability of having a negative rate is positive and this may not be a desirable case when the interest rate level is expected to be positive. Parameters of the Vasicek model are obtained from historical data using an estimation method, such as a maximum likelihood estimation. For example, we can use the 1-month LIBOR or federal funds rate as a proxy for the short rate and find the maximum likelihood estimators for model parameters that best fit the historical rates.

Considering the normal distribution of the short rate in the Vasicek model, one way to simulate the short rate is to use an approximate discretized version of the Vasicek model as follows:

$$\Delta r(t) = k(\theta - r(s))\Delta t + \sigma \sqrt{\Delta t}\, \epsilon$$

This entails some discretization error. Given the short rate at time $s < t$ and setting $\Delta t = t - s$, the simulated short rate at time t is obtained as:

$$r(t) = r(s) + k(\theta - r(s))\Delta t + \sigma \sqrt{\Delta t}\, \epsilon \qquad (5.27)$$

By setting $r(0)$ equal to the current spot rate with a small term, we can simulate a path of the short rate as it evolves through time. In each step, ϵ is an independent instance from the standard normal distribution.

Example

Figure 5.4 presents three simulated paths of the short rate generated using the Vasicek model. Here the time step is assumed as one month $\Delta t = 1/12$, the initial short rate is 0.1762%, and the long-term level that the short rate is trending toward is set at 3%. K and σ parameters are assumed as 0.5 and 0.004, respectively. Each path is simulated for 10 years. The short rate in each path starts from the initial level of 0.1762% and moves higher toward the 3% long-term level while having a "noise" effect around the trend. For instance, the simulated short rate in path 1 at $t = 1/12$ year based on a random instance from the standard normal distribution of $\epsilon = 0.67475$ is calculated using Equation (5.27), as follows:

$$r(1/12) = 0.001762 + (0.5 \times (0.03 - 0.001762) \times (1/12)$$

$$+\, 0.004 \times \sqrt{1/12} \times 0.67475) = 0.003718$$

(continued)

(*continued*)

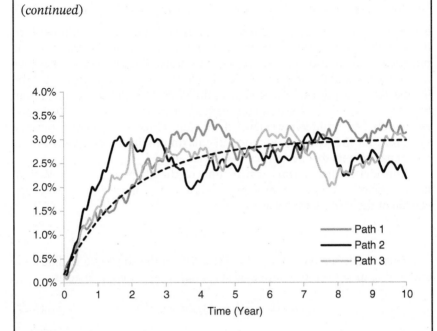

FIGURE 5.4 Three simulated paths using the Vasicek model ($r(0) = 0.1762\%$, $k = 0.5$, $\theta = 0.03$, and $\sigma = 0.004$)

The simulated short rate at $t = 2/12$ is then calculated using the short rate $r(1/12) = 0.3718\%$ obtained above and a random instance from the standard normal distribution of $\varepsilon = -0.08474$ as:

$$r(2/12) = 0.003718 + \left(0.5 \times (0.03 - 0.003718 \times (1/12) \right.$$

$$\left. + 0.004 \times \sqrt{1/12} \times (-0.08474) \right) = 0.004715$$

This recursive process is continued until $t = 10$, the end of the simulation horizon. Simulated rates for other paths are obtained similarly.

Using each simulated path of short rate $r(t)$ we can calculate simulated spot rates with different terms as of future dates using Equation (5.20). For example, consider path 1 in Figure 5.4 and assume that we are looking for the simulated 5-year spot rate as of $t = 1$ year. To calculate this rate, first using Equations (5.25) and (5.26), we have:

$$T - t = 5, r(0) = 0.1762\%, k = 0.5, \theta = 0.03, \text{ and } \sigma = 0.004$$

$$B(1,6) = \frac{1 - e^{-0.5 \times 5}}{0.5} = 1.835830$$

$$A(1,6) = \exp\left[(1.83583 - 5)\left(0.03 - \frac{0.004^2}{2 \times (0.5)^2}\right)\right.$$

$$\left. - \frac{0.004^2 \times 1.83583^2}{4 \times 0.5}\right] = 0.90950862$$

The simulated short rate at $t = 1$ year from path 1 of Figure 5.4 is $r(t) = 1.3102\%$. Using Equation (5.20), the simulated 5-year spot rate as of $t = 1$ year is obtained as:

$$r(1,6) = -\frac{1}{5} \times \ln 0.90950862 + \frac{1}{5} \times 1.835830 \times 0.013102 = 2.3781\%$$

Figure 5.5 presents simulated short rates $r(t)$ in path 1 of Figure 5.4 along with calculated 5-year spot rates $r(t, T)$ for a period of 10 years.

Spot rates with other terms can be calculated similarly. Figure 5.6 shows a simulated spot curve at $t = 1$ year based on a short rate of 1.3102% at that time.

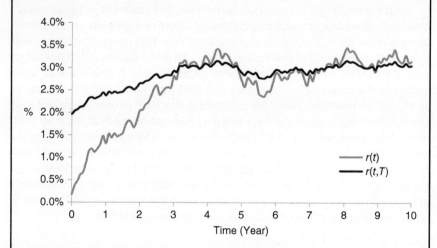

FIGURE 5.5 Simulated short rate $r(t)$ and simulated 5-year spot rate $r(t, T)$ using the Vasicek model ($r(0) = 0.1762\%$, $k = 0.5$, $\theta = 0.03$, and $\sigma = 0.004$)

(*continued*)

(*continued*)

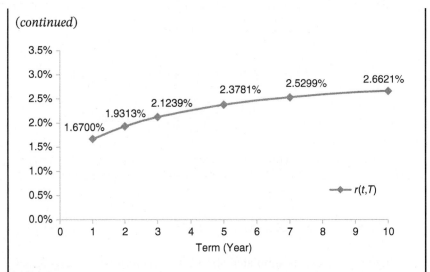

FIGURE 5.6 Simulated spot curve at $t = 1$ year using the Vasicek model based on a simulated short rate of 1.3102% ($r(0) = 0.1762\%$, $k = 0.5$, $\theta = 0.03$, and $\sigma = 0.004$)

In the preceding discussion we derived the spot curve at $t = 1$ year using a simulated short rate at that time. Following the same approach we can obtain the spot curve at $t = 0$ using the starting short rate. This means that the current spot curve is an output of the Vasicek model. To make the Vasicek model align with the current observable spot curve, parameters k, θ, and σ are selected such that the output spot curve for $t = 0$ conforms to the current spot curve as closely as possible. Thus, for calibrating the Vasicek model, parameters are obtained from historical data using an estimation method such as maximum likelihood, while trying to make the model arbitrage-free by forcing the model output for the current spot curve to be as close to the observed current spot curve as possible. This requires a trial-and-error approach and often the end result may not necessarily be a calibrated model that is completely arbitrage-free. This is one of the drawbacks of the Vasicek model, which is addressed in an extension model proposed by Hull and White.

HULL-WHITE MODEL

In their work published in 1990 Hull and White proposed a revised form of the Vasicek model. The original Vasicek model incorporates the mean reversion property where short rates generated by the stochastic model move toward a long-term level. However, due to the endogenous nature of the model, the initial term structure of the interest rate is an output of the model and not an input. Hence, one has to select the model parameters to produce the initial term structure of the interest rate as close as possible to the observed spot curve in the market. This usually results in a poor fit.

The *Hull-White one-factor* model can be considered to be an extension of the Vasicek model, where the initial term structure of interest rate is an input, along with other parameters, and hence the model fully incorporates and fits the current term structure of the interest rate. Due to this characteristic the Hull-White model is considered an arbitrage-free model. In this model the stochastic process for a short rate in a risk-neutral world is as follows:

$$dr(t) = (\theta(t) - k\, r(t))dt + \sigma\, dW(t) \tag{5.28}$$

Or, to put the stochastic process in the same form as the Vasicek model, we can write Equation (5.28) as:

$$dr(t) = k\left(\frac{\theta(t)}{k} - r(t)\right)dt + \sigma\, dW(t)$$

In this model the mean reversion level $\theta(t)/k$ is a function of time. The $\theta(t)$ variable is used to fit the initial term structure observed in the market. It defines the average slope of the short rate curve at time t. Here we assume that parameters k and σ are constant and not a function of time. In a more general form of the Hull-White model these two parameters can also be a function of time.

As discussed earlier, every spot curve can be represented by an instantaneous forward curve, and vice versa. We used the $f(t, T)$ notation to represent an instantaneous forward rate observed at time t for maturity T (meaning as seen at time t, where the forward starts at T) and with a very short term. With a slight change of notation, let $f(0, t)$ represents the instantaneous forward rate obtained from the current spot curve that is observed in the market for maturity t (meaning as seen at the current time, where the forward starts at t). It can be shown that $\theta(t)$ is calculated as follows (Brigo and Mercurio 2001):

$$\theta(t) = \frac{\partial f(0, t)}{\partial t} + kf(0, t) + \frac{\sigma^2}{2k}(1 - e^{-2kt}) \tag{5.29}$$

In Equation (5.11) we derived the following relationship between instantaneous forward rate and spot rate:

$$f(t, T) = r(t, T) + (T - t)\frac{\partial\, r(t, T)}{\partial T}$$

Using the notation change and by applying this to the spot rate and instantaneous forward rate at current time, we have:

$$f(0, t) = r(0, t) + t\frac{\partial\, r(0, t)}{\partial t} \tag{5.30}$$

where $f(0, t)$ is the instantaneous forward rate as seen at the current time with maturity t, and $r(0, t)$ is the current spot rate with maturity t. Using Equation (5.30) we can obtain instantaneous forward rates and hence $\theta(t)$ is fully defined for each t using current spot rates.

The Hull-White model has the same analytical tractability as the Vasicek model. By integrating Equation (5.28) for any $0 \leq s < t$, we have:

$$r(t) = r(s)e^{-k(t-s)} + \int_s^t e^{-k(t-\tau)}\theta(\tau)d\tau + \sigma \int_s^t e^{-k(t-\tau)}dW(\tau)$$

Using Equation (5.29), this equation can be written as:

$$r(t) = r(s)e^{-k(t-s)} + \left(f(0, t) + \frac{\sigma^2}{2k^2}(1 - e^{-kt})^2\right)$$
$$- \left(f(0, s) + \frac{\sigma^2}{2k^2}(1 - e^{-ks})^2\right)e^{-k(t-s)} + \sigma \int_s^t e^{-k(t-\tau)}dW(\tau) \quad (5.31)$$

To simplify the notation, we can define:

$$\alpha(t) = f(0, t) + \frac{\sigma^2}{2k^2}(1 - e^{-kt})^2 \quad (5.32)$$

So we have:

$$r(t) = r(s)e^{-k(t-s)} + \alpha(t) - \alpha(s)e^{-k(t-s)} + \sigma \int_s^t e^{-k(t-\tau)}dW(\tau) \quad (5.33)$$

In the Hull-White model the short rate $r(t)$ is normally distributed. For any $0 \leq s < t$ conditional mean and variance of the distribution, conditioned to all available information, until and including time s: $\mathcal{F}_s$, are:

$$E[r(t)|\mathcal{F}_s] = r(s)e^{-k(t-s)} + \alpha(t) - \alpha(s)e^{-k(t-s)} \quad (5.34)$$

$$Var[r(t)|\mathcal{F}_s] = \frac{\sigma^2}{2k}[1 - e^{-2k(t-s)}] \quad (5.35)$$

The Hull-White model, similar to Vasicek, is an affine term structure model, and the price of the zero-coupon bond can be presented as Equation (5.17), presented here. It can be shown that the expressions for $A(t, T)$ and $B(t, T)$ functions are (Brigo and Mercurio 2001):

$$P(t, T) = A(t, T)e^{-B(t,T)\,r(t)}$$

$$A(t, T) = \frac{P(0, T)}{P(0, t)}\exp\left[B(t, T)f(0, t) - \frac{\sigma^2}{4k}(1 - e^{-2kt})B(t, T^2)\right] \quad (5.36)$$

$$B(t, T) = \frac{1 - e^{-k(T-t)}}{k} \tag{5.37}$$

where $P(0, T)$ and $P(0, t)$ are price of the zero-coupon bonds currently observed in the market, paying \$1 at maturity of T and t, respectively. We discuss the case where $k = 0$ in the next section. Placing these expressions into Equation (5.20) provides us with the relationship between the spot rate and short rate.

Considering the normal distribution of short rates in the Hull-White model, one way to simulate the short rate is to use an approximate discretized version of the model, as follows:

$$\Delta r(t) = (\theta(t) - k\, r(t))\Delta t + \sigma \sqrt{\Delta t}\, \varepsilon \tag{5.38}$$

Simulation of short rates using the Hull-White model is done by following these steps:

- For small Δt, the approximate instantaneous forward rate using available spot rates is obtained as:

$$f(0, t) \cong r(0, t + \Delta t) + t\frac{r(0, t + \Delta t) - r(0, t)}{\Delta t} \tag{5.39}$$

- Given the instantaneous forward rate from the previous step and using Equation (5.29), we can calculate the approximate value for $\theta(t)$ as:

$$\theta(t) \cong \frac{f(0, t + \Delta t) - f(0, t)}{\Delta t} + kf(0, t) + \frac{\sigma^2}{2k}(1 - e^{-2kt}) \tag{5.40}$$

- After $\theta(t)$ is derived for every t during the simulation horizon, we can set $r(0)$ equal to the current spot rate with a small term. This is the starting point of a short rate path.
- Given $r(s)$, the short rate at any time $s < t$, and for $\Delta t = t - s$, the short rate at time t is calculated as:

$$r(t) = r(s) + (\theta(t) - k\, r(s))\Delta t + \sigma \sqrt{\Delta t}\, \varepsilon \tag{5.41}$$

This way we can recursively calculate the short rate for any t, given previous short rates. In each step ε is an independent instance from the standard normal distribution.

Example

To illustrate this procedure, assume that the spot curve at $t = 0$ is as shown in Figure 5.7. Assume that $\Delta t = 1/12$ year. Here we used a cubic spline

(*continued*)

(*continued*)

interpolation to obtain the spot rates at monthly intervals. The calculated instantaneous forward curves using Equation (5.39) are also shown in Figure 5.7.

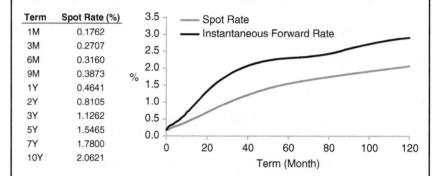

Term	Spot Rate (%)
1M	0.1762
3M	0.2707
6M	0.3160
9M	0.3873
1Y	0.4641
2Y	0.8105
3Y	1.1262
5Y	1.5465
7Y	1.7800
10Y	2.0621

FIGURE 5.7   Spot curve and instantaneous forward curve at $t = 0$ used in simulation of a short rate based on the Hull-White model

Assume that parameters k and σ are 0.5 and 0.004, respectively, obtained by calibrating the model to the observed market data. We discuss calibration of the Hull-White model later in this chapter. Having the instantaneous forward rates, we can obtain $\theta(t)$ using Equation (5.40). Figure 5.8 presents three simulated paths of short rates along with the instantaneous forward curve. Since $\Delta t = 1/12$ year, the initial short $r(0)$ is set equal to the one-month spot rate of 0.1762%. In practice, a shorter Δt is used.

Each path is simulated for 10 years with time intervals of 1/12 year. The short rate in each path starts from the initial level of 0.1762% and moves along an instantaneous forward curve. When a short rate deviates from that curve, it reverts back toward the curve at the rate of k while presenting a "noise" effect around the trend.

Consider path 1 of the short rates shown in Figure 5.8. From Figure 5.7 interpolated 1-month spot rates with terms of 1/12, 2/12, and 3/12 years are 0.1762%, 0.22%, and 0.25%, respectively, obtained using a cubic spline

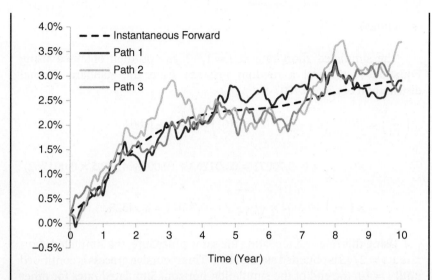

FIGURE 5.8 Three simulated paths using the Hull-White model ($r(0) = 0.1762\%$, $k = 0.5$, and $\sigma = 0.004$)

interpolation method. The approximate instantaneous forward rates at $t = 1/12$ and $t = 2/12$ are calculated using Equation (5.39) as:

$$f\left(0, \frac{1}{12}\right) = 0.0022 + \frac{1}{12} \times \frac{0.0022 - 0.001762}{1/12} = 0.2638\%$$

$$f\left(0, \frac{2}{12}\right) = 0.0025 + \frac{2}{12} \times \frac{0.0025 - 0.0022}{1/12} = 0.31\%$$

Having these instantaneous forward rates, we can use Equation (5.40) to find the value of θ at $t = 1/12$ as:

$$\theta\left(\frac{1}{12}\right) = \frac{f\left(0, \frac{2}{12}\right) - f\left(0, \frac{1}{12}\right)}{1/12} + 0.5$$

$$\times f\left(0, \frac{1}{12}\right) + \frac{0.004^2}{2 \times 0.5}\left(1 - e^{-2\times0.5\times\frac{1}{12}}\right) = \frac{0.0031 - 0.002638}{1/12} + 0.5$$

$$\times 0.002638 + \frac{0.004^2}{2 \times 0.5}\left(1 - e^{-2\times0.5\times\frac{1}{12}}\right) = 0.006864$$

(*continued*)

(*continued*)

The simulated short rate at $t = 1/12$ year is then obtained using Equation (5.41) and a random instance from the standard normal distribution of $\varepsilon = -0.7007$ as:

$$r\left(\frac{1}{12}\right) = r(0) + \left(\theta\left(\frac{1}{12}\right) - 0.5 \times r(0)\right) \times \left(\frac{1}{12}\right) + 0.004$$

$$\times \sqrt{\frac{1}{12}} \times (-0.7007) = 0.001762 + (0.006864 - 0.5 \times 0.001762)$$

$$\times \left(\frac{1}{12}\right) + 0.004 \times \sqrt{\frac{1}{12}} \times (-0.7007) = 0.1452\%$$

Using this rate and repeating the same procedure, the simulated short rate at $t = 2/12$ is obtained as -0.0713%. This recursive process is continued until $t = 10$, the end of the simulation horizon. Simulated rates for other paths are obtained similarly.

The simulated path of short rates can be used to calculate simulated spot rates with different terms for future dates. For example, consider path 1 of Figure 5.8 and assume we are looking for a simulated 5-year spot rate as of $t = 1$. From Figure 5.7, interpolated spot rates as of $t = 0$ with 1- and 6-year terms are $r(0, 1) = 0.4641\%$ and $r(0, 6) = 1.6760\%$, respectively. Similar to what is demonstrated previously, the instantaneous forward rate as of $t = 1$ years is calculated as $f(0, 1) = 0.8046\%$. Having these rates, we can use Equation (5.4) to calculate $P(0, 1)$ and $P(0, 6)$ as follows:

$$P(0, 1) = e^{-0.004641 \times 1} = 0.995370$$

$$P(0, 6) = e^{-0.016760 \times 6} = 0.904331$$

$A(1, 6)$ and $B(1, 6)$ are calculated using Equations (5.36) and (5.37):

$$T - t = 5, r(0) = 0.1762\%, k = 0.5, \text{ and } \sigma = 0.004$$

$$B(1, 6) = \frac{1 - e^{-0.5 \times 5}}{0.5} = 1.835830$$

$$A(1, 6) = \frac{0.904331}{0.995370} exp\left[1.83583 \times 0.008046\right.$$

$$\left. - \frac{0.004^2}{4 \times 0.5}\left(1 - e^{-2 \times 0.5 \times 1}\right) \times 1.83583^2\right] = 0.9220415$$

The simulated short rate at $t = 1$ in path 1 of Figure 5.8 is 0.5746%. Therefore, the simulated 5-year spot rate as of $t = 1$ is obtained using Equation (5.20) as:

$$r(1, 6) = -\frac{1}{5} \times \ln(0.9220415) + \frac{1}{5} \times 1.83583 \times 0.005746 = 1.8343\%$$

Figure 5.9 presents the simulated short rates in path 1 and the simulated 5-year spot rates based on this path for a period of 10 years.

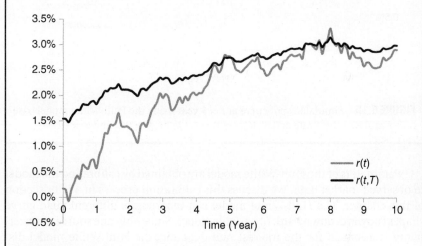

FIGURE 5.9 Simulated short rate $r(t)$ and simulated 5-year spot rate $r(t, T)$ using the Hull-White model ($r(0) = 0.1762\%$, $k = 0.5$, and $\sigma = 0.004$)

Spot rates with other terms are calculated similarly. Figure 5.10 shows a simulated spot curve at $t = 1$ year based on a short rate of 0.5746% at that time. Notably, if we calculate spot rates for different terms as of $t = 0$ we get a spot curve that is identical to the current spot curve in Figure 5.7. This is not surprising since we calibrated $\theta(t)$ such that it incorporates the current spot curve fully. Hence the output spot curve of the Hull-White model for $t = 0$ is the same as the current spot curve, observed in the market and used as an input in the model.

(continued)

(*continued*)

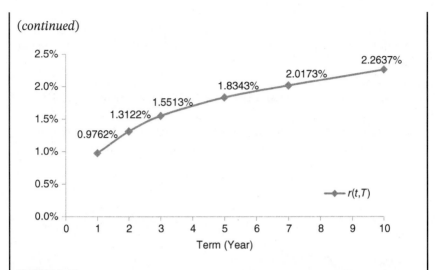

FIGURE 5.10   Simulated spot curve at $t = 1$ year using the Hull-White model base on a simulated short rate of 0.5746% ($r(0) = 0.1762\%$, $k = 0.5$, and $\sigma = 0.004$)

Parameters of the Hull-White model are obtained by calibrating the model to observed market data. We discuss this calibration process in a later section of this chapter. The Hull-White model can incorporate different yield curve shapes (upward, downward, or variable slope). Since only one source of uncertainty is assumed for the interest rate dynamic, the Hull-White model discussed here is a one-factor model. Hull and White also developed a two-factor model in which two stochastic variables are used in the modeling of the short rate (Hull and White 1994). Similar to the Vasicek model, short rates in the Hull-White model can become negative. For example, the simulated short rate at $t = 2/12$ of path 1 in Figure 5.8 is negative. This feature can be used to model a negative interest rate when warranted. If the modeled rate is expected to be always positive, the output of the Hull-White model is floored at zero.

HO-LEE MODEL

The short rate model developed by Ho and Lee (1986) is an arbitrage-free model. In its original form, the Ho-Lee model was first proposed before Hull and White extended the Vasicek model, but it can be considered to be a special case of the Hull-White model. In the Ho-Lee model the stochastic process for a short rate in a risk-neutral world is as follows:

$$dr(t) = \theta(t)\,dt + \sigma\,dW(t) \tag{5.42}$$

This model can be considered to be a special case of the Hull-White model where parameter k is zero. Similar to the Hull-White model $\theta(t)$ is used to fit the current term structure of the yield curve, but this model does not have the mean reversion property. It can be shown that $\theta(t)$ in this model is calculated as follows (Hull 1990):

$$\theta(t) = \frac{\partial f(0, t)}{\partial t} + \sigma^2 t \qquad (5.43)$$

where $f(0, t)$ is the instantaneous forward rate obtained from the current spot curve observed in the market for maturity t. The Ho-Lee model is an affine term structure model and the price of a zero-coupon bond can be presented as Equation (5.17). It can be shown that the expressions for $A(t, T)$ and $B(t, T)$ functions are as follows (Hull 1990):

$$A(t, T) = \frac{P(0, T)}{P(0, t)} exp \left[(T - t)f(0, t) - \frac{\sigma^2}{2} t (T - t)^2 \right] \qquad (5.44)$$

$$B(t, T) = T - t \qquad (5.45)$$

Simulation of short and spot rates based on the Ho-Lee model is performed using the same method explained for the Hull-White model, where parameter K is zero. Short rates produced by Ho-Lee model can be negative.

BLACK-KARASINSKI MODEL

In the three interest rate models we have studied so far, the short rate has a normal distribution and can take positive and negative values. In the *Black-Karasinski* model the short rate has a lognormal distribution and hence it is always positive. In this model the stochastic process for the short rate in a risk-neutral world is as follows:

$$d \ln r(t) = [\theta(t) - k \ln r(t)]dt + \sigma \, dW(t) \qquad (5.46)$$

Similar to the Hull-White and Ho-Lee models, $\theta(t)$ is a time-dependent variable used to fit the current term structure of the interest rate. However, unlike the three models studied before, Black-Karasinski is not an affine-term structure model and there is no closed-form solution for the price of a zero-coupon bond. Therefore there is no analytical way to associate the spot rate and short rate. When using this model, numerical methods, such as interest rate tree, are used to calculate bond and option prices. We discuss construction of interest rate tree based on the Black-Karasinski model in a later section of this chapter.

By setting $x(t) = \ln r(t)$ and applying Itô's lemma on $F(x, t) = e^x$, we have:

$$\frac{\partial F}{\partial x} = e^x \qquad \frac{\partial^2 F}{\partial x^2} = e^x \qquad \frac{\partial F}{\partial t} = 0$$

$$de^x = \left(e^x(\theta(t) - kx(t)) + 0 + \frac{1}{2}e^x\sigma^2\right)dt + e^x\sigma\,dW$$

And since $e^x = r(t)$:

$$dr(t) = r(t)\left(\theta(t) + \frac{\sigma^2}{2} - k\ln r(t)\right)dt + \sigma\,r(t)\,dW \qquad (5.47)$$

By integrating this equation for any $s < t$, we have:

$$r(t) = \exp\left[\ln r(s)e^{-k(t-s)} + \int_s^t e^{-k(t-\tau)}\theta(\tau)d\tau + \sigma\int_s^t e^{-k(t-\tau)}dW(\tau)\right] \qquad (5.48)$$

INTEREST RATE OPTIONS

An interest rate option is an option contract in which the underlying is an interest rate. In this section we introduce three types of interest rate options: swaption, interest rate cap, and interest rate floor contracts. Later in this chapter we use these instruments when describing the calibration process of interest rate models.

Swaption

A *European swaption* contract is a bilateral agreement in which the buyer, in exchange of a premium, receives the right, but not the obligation, to enter into a specific swap contract at a specified time in the future. Each European swaption contract is associated with two terms: time to the expiration of the option contract, and term of the underlying swap contract. For example, a 2 × 3 European swaption quoted now has two years to expiration of the option contract where the underlying swap contract, if the buyer decided to enter, starts two years from now with the term of three years. There are two types of European swaption: *payer swaption*, where the buyer of the contract has the option to enter into a swap as the fixed-rate payer, and *receiver swaption*, where the buyer has the option to enter into the swap as the fixed-rate receiver. A European swaption can be regarded as an option on a coupon-bearing bond where the strike price is equal to the bond principal. A payer swaption is equivalent to a put option and a receiver swaption is similar to a call option.

Consider a payer European swaption when a swap contract initiates at time T (option expiration date) and payment dates are $\{T_1, T_2, \cdots, T_n\}$. For ease of reference, assume that $T_0 = T$ and τ_i is the year fraction between two consecutive payment dates T_{i-1} and T_i, based on the contractual day count convention. We can find the current value of this swaption contract using the Black model as follows (Hull 1990; Brigo and Mercurio 2001):

$$V_{t=0} = N \left(\sum_{i=1}^{n} \tau_i \, P(0, T_i) \right) (S_0 \Phi(d_1) - X \, \Phi(d_2)) \tag{5.49}$$

$$d_1 = \frac{\ln(S_0/X) + \sigma^2 T/2}{\sigma \sqrt{T}} \tag{5.50}$$

$$d_2 = d_1 - \sigma \sqrt{T}$$

where

$N =$ Contract notional amount
$S_0 =$ Forward swap rate at time $t = 0$
$X =$ Strike rate
$\sigma =$ Volatility percentage per annum
$\Phi(.) =$ Cumulative probability distribution function of the standard normal distribution

The forward swap rate S_t is the fixed rate of the swap contract and at any time $t \leq T$ is obtained as:

$$S_t = \frac{P(t, T_0) - P(t, T_n)}{\sum_{i=1}^{n} \tau_i P(t, T_i)} \tag{5.51}$$

When $t = 0$, we have:

$$S_0 = \frac{P(0, T_0) - P(0, T_n)}{\sum_{i=1}^{n} \tau_i P(0, T_i)} \tag{5.52}$$

Similarly, the value of a receiver European swaption at $t = 0$ is obtained as:

$$V_{t=0} = N \left(\sum_{i=1}^{n} \tau_i \, P(0, T_i) \right) (X \, \Phi(-d_2) - S_0 \, \Phi(-d_1)) \tag{5.53}$$

The market convention for a European swaption contract is to quote at-the-money implied Black volatility, that is, the volatility that makes the price of an at-the-money swaption based on the Black model equal to its

TABLE 5.1   A typical market quotation convention for European swaption: mid-market volatility percentage per annum of at-the-money contracts

Expiry/ Term	1Y	2Y	3Y	4Y	5Y	6Y	7Y	8Y	9Y	10Y	15Y	20Y	25Y	30Y
1M	18.99	25.87	29.55	30.34	36.53	36.56	36.84	35.30	28.39	28.01	30.69	29.81	28.61	27.57
3M	25.81	35.48	37.10	37.46	36.56	34.20	33.80	34.80	34.47	30.58	31.52	29.75	28.63	27.65
6M	23.61	31.74	34.66	34.31	36.66	36.89	37.30	36.10	35.06	34.17	32.87	30.61	29.54	28.64
1Y	27.50	30.89	32.02	32.71	36.50	36.49	36.61	31.31	30.95	30.59	28.87	28.09	27.93	29.76
2Y	34.79	37.13	33.59	32.94	30.79	31.48	31.74	31.34	30.97	33.19	28.86	30.95	28.24	30.51
3Y	34.55	34.32	33.74	33.06	32.41	31.88	31.41	32.32	32.10	32.23	28.88	27.89	28.03	30.97
4Y	35.34	33.53	33.21	32.56	31.98	31.48	30.99	31.81	31.75	31.54	28.37	27.52	27.68	31.27
5Y	34.07	33.16	32.59	32.04	31.53	32.45	31.87	31.70	31.38	30.95	30.28	29.93	30.55	3149
7Y	31.23	31.03	30.31	29.99	29.37	29.31	29.31	29.50	29.48	29.30	29.01	28.91	30.17	31.42
10Y	28.77	27.09	27.36	27.15	26.38	27.78	26.44	27.55	27.27	26.82	27.09	27.26	29.24	30.55
15Y	27.27	26.56	26.43	24.87	24.52	24.69	24.77	24.63	24.43	24.08	24.85	26.02	27.58	29.85
20Y	25.70	25.53	25.90	24.33	23.72	23.94	23.87	23.55	23.45	23.09	24.01	25.37	27.91	29.94
25Y	25.39	24.83	24.38	23.97	23.25	23.99	24.18	24.23	23.47	23.47	25.13	27.61	30.15	32.40
30Y	28.02	27.08	26.58	26.21	25.87	25.46	24.99	24.54	24.09	23.57	26.89	29.12	31.64	34.43

market price. Table 5.1 shows a typical market quotation convention for a European swaption with various option expirations and swap terms. Since quotes are for swaption contracts that are at-the-money, strike rates are equal to forward swap rates.

Interest Rate Cap and Floor

Interest rate cap and *floor* are bilateral contracts where one side, in exchange of an upfront premium, agrees to pay the other side at specific times in the future if a reference rate (e.g., 3-month LIBOR) is different from a predetermined level. In an interest cap contract the seller pays the buyer if the reference rate exceeds a predetermined level, known as the *strike rate* or *cap rate*, and in an interest rate floor contract the seller pays the buyer if the reference rate falls below a predetermined level, known as the strike rate or *floor rate*. Interest rate cap and floor contracts are commonly used in finance to limit the impact of a change in the interest rate of a floating-rate note. For example, assume bank B sells an interest rate cap contract with the following specifications to customer C:

Notional: $1,000,000

Strike (cap) rate: 2%

Reference rate: 3-month LIBOR

Payment and reset frequency: quarterly

Life of contract: 2 years

Day count convention: 30/360

Based on this contract, every three months bank B pays customer C if the 3-month LIBOR exceeds 2%. The amount paid depends on the difference between the 3-month LIBOR at reset date and the cap rate of 2%. For example, assume that at three months from the contract initiation (i.e., at first reset date) the 3-month LIBOR is 1.95%. Since the reference is below the cap rate, bank B pays nothing to customer C. Now assume that another three months has passed and at six months from initiation (i.e., at second reset date) the 3-month LIBOR is 3.2%. In this case bank B pays customer C the amount of:

$$1{,}000{,}000 \times (3.2\% - 2\%) \times \frac{90}{360} = 3{,}000$$

This $3,000, however, will not be paid until the next payment date, at nine months from initiation. This continues until the last reset date at 21 months from initiation, when the last payment amount is determined. This last payment occurs at the maturity date (24 months from initiation), and the contract expires at that time. The interest rate floor works in a similar way, except the payment occurs if the reference rate is below the floor rate.

An interest rate cap contract can be considered to be a portfolio of call options on the reference interest rate. These interest rate options are called *caplets*. Therefore a cap is made up of several caplets. An interest rate cap can also be viewed as a portfolio of put options on zero-coupon bonds. Consider a cap contract with maturity date of T, reset dates of $t_0, t_1, \cdots, t_{n-1}$, and payment dates of $t_1, t_2, \cdots, t_n$, where the first reset is at t_0 and the last payment is at $t_n = T$. This contract consists of n caplets. Caplet i is an option where the reference interest rate is observed at reset date t_{i-1} and the payoff occurred at payment date t_i. τ_i is the year fraction between t_{i-1} and t_i based on the contractual day count convention. We can find the current value of this caplet using the Black model as follows:

$$V_{Caplet\ i_{t=0}} = N\ \tau_i\ P(0, t_i)\ (f_{i-1}\ \Phi(d_1) - X\ \Phi(d_2)) \tag{5.54}$$

$$d_1 = \frac{\ln(f_{i-1}/X) + \sigma_i^2 t_{i-1}/2}{\sigma_i \sqrt{t_{i-1}}} \tag{5.55}$$

$$d_2 = d_1 - \sigma_i \sqrt{t_{i-1}}$$

where

N = Contract notional amount
f_i = Forward rate between t_{i-1} and t_i
X = Cap rate (strike rate)
σ_i = Volatility percentage per annum

In this equation the cap rate and the forward rate have the same compounding frequency as the reset (or payment) frequency. The current value of the interest rate cap contract is the summation of current values of the corresponding caplets:

$$V_{Cap_{t=0}} = \sum_{i=1}^{n} V_{Caplet\ i_{t=0}} \tag{5.56}$$

Similarly, an interest rate floor contract can be characterized as a portfolio of put options on the reference interest rate. These put options are called *floorlets*. An interest rate floor contract can also be viewed as a portfolio of call options on zero-coupon bonds. The current value of such a caplet using the Black model is calculated as:

$$V_{Floorlet\ i_{t=0}} = N\ \tau_i\ P(0, t_i)\ (X\ \Phi(-d_2) - f_{i-1}\ \Phi(-d_1)) \tag{5.57}$$

Here X is the floor rate. The current value of the interest rate floor contract is the summation of the current values of corresponding floorlets:

$$V_{Floor_{t=0}} = \sum_{i=1}^{n} V_{Floorlet\ i_{t=0}} \tag{5.58}$$

An interest rate cap (floor) contract is at-the-money if the cap (floor) rate is equal to the swap rate of a swap contract with the same payment dates of the cap (floor). Therefore if S_0 is the swap rate calculated using Equation (5.52) based on the current spot curve, we have:

If cap rate < S_0: Cap is in-the-money

If cap rate = S_0: Cap is at-the-money

If cap rate > S_0: Cap is out-of-the-money

If floor rate < S_0: Floor is out-of-the-money

If floor rate = S_0: Floor is at-the-money

If floor rate > S_0: Floor is in-the-money

The market convention for a cap (floor) contract is to quote at-the-money implied Black volatility, that is, the volatility that makes the cap (floor) rate

TABLE 5.2 A typical market quotation convention for interest rate cap: mid-market volatility percentage per annum for at-the-money (ATM) contracts, and in/out-of-the-money contracts with various strike rates

Maturity	ATM	1.00%	2.00%	3.00%	4.00%	5.00%	6.00%	7.00%	8.00%	9.00%	10.00%
1Y	25.29	26.86	24.71	27.30	30.13	32.50	34.47	36.15	37.59	38.87	39.97
2Y	30.55	33.27	30.80	31.18	31.82	32.73	33.74	34.75	35.72	36.63	37.47
3Y	31.99	35.99	31.91	31.51	31.69	32.17	32.65	33.35	33.93	34.47	34.98
4Y	34.12	38.17	34.06	33.24	32.98	32.94	32.99	33.07	33.17	33.30	33.43
5Y	35.09	42.46	35.24	33.45	32.55	32.07	31.82	31.68	31.63	31.62	31.64
6Y	35.39	42.21	35.76	33.94	32.96	32.35	31.93	31.61	31.34	31.07	30.92
7Y	37.04	45.91	37.74	35.30	33.90	32.94	32.19	31.60	30.99	30.65	30.28
8Y	35.11	44.46	36.13	33.32	31.93	31.16	30.85	30.34	30.14	30.03	30.00
9Y	34.49	44.76	35.81	32.61	30.99	30.10	29.58	29.25	29.05	28.99	28.98
10Y	34.54	45.85	36.17	32.65	30.85	29.87	29.31	28.98	28.79	28.74	28.74
12Y	32.89	44.18	34.85	31.22	29.37	28.37	27.84	27.55	27.42	27.38	27.43
15Y	30.82	44.69	33.53	29.12	27.02	26.05	25.62	25.44	25.41	25.46	25.55
20Y	28.69	43.08	31.94	27.18	25.07	24.23	23.94	23.90	23.99	24.14	24.32
25Y	27.59	43.80	31.04	26.19	24.22	23.54	23.37	23.43	23.59	23.81	24.04
30Y	26.90	42.30	30.17	25.59	23.76	23.15	23.02	23.10	23.28	23.47	23.72

equal to the swap rate of the corresponding swap contract when the Black model is used for valuation. The quoted volatility is assumed the same for all caplets (floorlets) of the contract, but different for various maturities of the cap (floor).[3] Some market participants also quote implied Black volatility for in/out-of-the-money contracts with different strike rates. Table 5.2 presents a typical market quotation convention for cap implied volatilities for various maturities.

ANALYTICAL VALUATION OF BONDS AND OPTIONS

The assumption of the normal distribution of a short rate in the Hull-White model enables us to establish analytical valuation methods for bonds and interest rate option contracts.

Zero-Coupon Bond

Assume that $P(t, T)$ is the value of a \$1 notional zero-coupon bond at time t, maturing at time T. As discussed earlier in this chapter, based on the Hull-White model the value of this bond can be calculated from Equation (5.17), where $A(t, T)$ and $B(t, T)$ are according to Equations (5.36) and (5.37). These equations are reproduced here:

$$P(t, T) = A(t, T)e^{-B(t,T)\, r(t)}$$

$$A(t, T) = \frac{P(0, T)}{P(0, t)} \exp\left[B(t, T)f(0, t) - \frac{\sigma^2}{4k}(1 - e^{-2kt})B(t, T^2) \right]$$

$$B(t, T) = \frac{1 - e^{-k(T-t)}}{k}$$

If the notional value of the bond is N, the value of the zero-coupon bond is obtained as: $N \times P(t, T)$.

Option on a Zero-Coupon Bond

Assume that $V_{Call\, ZB}(t, T)$ is the value at time t of a European call option on a $1 notional zero-coupon bond, where the strike price is X, the option matures at time T, and the bond matures at time S $(S > T)$.[4] It can be shown that the value of this option is obtained as (Brigo and Mercurio 2001; Hull and White 1994):

$$V_{Call\, ZB}(t, T, S, X) = P(t, S)\, \Phi(h) - X\, P(t, T)\, \Phi(h - \sigma_P) \tag{5.59}$$

where

$$\sigma_P = \sigma\sqrt{\frac{1 - e^{-2k(T-t)}}{2k}}\, B(T, S) \tag{5.60}$$

$$h = \frac{1}{\sigma_P} \ln\frac{P(t, S)}{P(t, T)\, X} + \frac{\sigma_P}{2} \tag{5.61}$$

$B(T, S)$ is from Equation (5.37). Likewise, the value at time t of a European put option on a $1 notional zero-coupon bond is obtained as:

$$V_{Put\, ZB}(t, T, S, X) = X\, P(t, T)\, \Phi(-h + \sigma_P) - P(t, S)\, \Phi(-h) \tag{5.62}$$

If the notional value of the bond is N, the value of the call option is $N \times V_{Call\, ZB}(t, T, S, X)$ and the value of the put option is $N \times V_{Put\, ZB}(t, T, S, X)$. If in these equations we set $t = 0$, we obtain similar results as the Black model for pricing European zero-coupon bond options:

$$V_{Call\, ZB}(0, T, S, X) = P(0, S)\, \Phi(h) - X\, P(0, T)\, \Phi(h - \sigma_P) \tag{5.63}$$

$$V_{Put\, ZB}(0, T, S, X) = X\, P(0, T)\, \Phi(-h + \sigma_P) - P(0, S)\, \Phi(-h)$$

$$\sigma_P = \sigma\sqrt{\frac{1 - e^{-2k\, T}}{2k}}\, B(T, S)$$

$$h = \frac{1}{\sigma_P} \ln\frac{P(0, S)}{P(0, T)\, X} + \frac{\sigma_P}{2}$$

In these equations $P(0, S)$ and $P(0, T)$ are known values obtained from the current spot curve.

Interest Rate Cap and Floor

The interest rate cap or floor contracts can be regarded as a portfolio of options on zero-coupon bonds. Therefore we can use the equations presented earlier to obtain the value of an interest rate cap or floor. For an interest rate cap contract with notional value N and strike rate X, each individual caplet can be treated as a put option on a zero-coupon bond. For caplet i assume that the reset date is t_{i-1} and the payment date is t_i. τ_i is the year fraction between the reset and payment dates based on the contractual day count convention. It can be shown that the value of this caplet at time t is a multiple of the value at time t of a put option on a \$1 notional zero-coupon bond (Brigo and Mercurio 2001):

$$V_{Caplet_i}(t, t_{i-1}, t_i, \tau_i, N, X) = N(1 + X\tau_i) V_{Put\ ZB}\left(t, t_{i-1}, t_i, \frac{1}{1 + X\tau_i}\right) \quad (5.64)$$

In this equation $V_{Put\ ZB}\left(t, t_{i-1}, t_i, \frac{1}{1+X\tau_i}\right)$ is from Equation (5.62). The interest rate cap is a portfolio of individual caplets; hence the value at time t of an interest rate cap contract consisting of n caplets is:

$$V_{Cap}(t, \mathbb{T}, N, X) = \sum_{i=1}^{n} N(1 + X\tau_i) V_{Put\ ZB}\left(t, t_{i-1}, t_i, \frac{1}{1 + X\tau_i}\right) \quad (5.65)$$

where $\mathbb{T} = \{t_0, t_1, \cdots, t_n\}$ is the set of reset and payment dates and $t < t_0$. We can rewrite this equation using Equation (5.62) as:

$$V_{Cap}(t, \mathbb{T}, N, X) = N \sum_{i=1}^{n} (P(t, t_{i-1}) \Phi(-h_i + \sigma_{P_i}) - (1 + X\tau_i) P(t, t_i) \Phi(-h_i)) \quad (5.66)$$

where

$$\sigma_{P_i} = \sigma \sqrt{\frac{1 - e^{-2k(t_{i-1} - t)}}{2k}} B(t_{i-1}, t_i) \quad (5.67)$$

$$h_i = \frac{1}{\sigma_{P_i}} \ln \frac{P(t, t_i)(1 + X\tau_i)}{P(t, t_{i-1})} + \frac{\sigma_{P_i}}{2} \quad (5.68)$$

Similarly, each individual floorlet can be treated as a call option on a zero-coupon bond and the interest rate floor is a portfolio of such options. Therefore, the values of a floorlet and an interest rate floor contract at time t are obtained as:

$$V_{Floorlet_i}(t, t_{i-1}, t_i, \tau_i, N, X) = N(1 + X\tau_i) V_{Call\ ZB}\left(t, t_{i-1}, t_i, \frac{1}{1 + X\tau_i}\right) \quad (5.69)$$

$$V_{Floor}(t, \mathbb{T}, N, X) = \sum_{i=1}^{n} N(1 + X\tau_i) V_{Call\ ZB}\left(t, t_{i-1}, t_i, \frac{1}{1 + X\tau_i}\right) \quad (5.70)$$

or

$$V_{Floor}(t, \mathbb{T}, N, X) = N \sum_{i=1}^{n} ((1 + X\tau_i) \, P(t, t_i) \, \Phi(h_i) - P(t, t_{i-1}) \, \Phi(h_i - \sigma_{P_i}))$$

(5.71)

Option on a Coupon-Bearing Bond

Based on Jamshidian's decomposition (1989), the value of a European option on a coupon-bearing bond can be obtained from the value of a portfolio of options on zero-coupon bonds. Consider a European call option contract with a strike price of X and maturity of T on a bond that pays n coupons with the amounts $\mathbb{C} = \{C_1, C_2, \cdots, C_n\}$ at payment dates $\mathbb{T} = \{T_1, T_2, \cdots, T_n\}$, where $T_i > T$. Assume that r^* is the short rate at time T that makes the value of the coupon-bearing bond equal to strike price X. Therefore, r^* is the solution to:

$$\sum_{i=1}^{n} C_i \, A(T, T_i) \, e^{-B(T,T_i)r^*} = X$$

where $A(T, T_i)$ and $B(T, T_i)$ are from Equations (5.36) and (5.37). The value of r^* can be calculated using an iterative procedure such as the Newton-Raphson method. Also assume that X_i is the value at time T of a \$1 notional zero-coupon bond with maturity T_i when the short rate is r^*, obtained using Equation (5.17):

$$X_i = A(T, T_i) \, e^{-B(T,T_i)r^*}$$

Using this setup it can be shown that the value of the call option on a coupon-bearing bond at time $t < T$ is obtained as (Brigo and Mercurio 2001):

$$V_{Call\ CB}(t, T, \mathbb{T}, \mathbb{C}, X) = \sum_{i=1}^{n} C_i \, V_{Call\ ZB}(t, T, T_i, X_i) \qquad (5.72)$$

Similarly, the value of a put option on a coupon-bearing bond is calculated as:

$$V_{Put\ CB}(t, T, \mathbb{T}, \mathbb{C}, X) = \sum_{i=1}^{n} C_i V_{Put\ ZB}(t, T, T_i, X_i) \qquad (5.73)$$

In these equations $V_{Call\ ZB}(t, T, T_i, X_i)$ and $V_{Put\ ZB}(t, T, T_i, X_i)$ are from Equations (5.59) and (5.62), respectively.

Swaption

The method discussed earlier can also be used for valuation of European swaption contracts. A European swaption can be regarded as an option on a coupon-bearing bond where the strike price is equal to the bond principal. Consider a fixed-rate payer European swaption with notional value N and strike rate of X maturing at time T. The underlying swap contract of this swaption has payment dates of $\mathbb{T} = \{T_1, T_2, \cdots, T_n\}$, where $T_i > T$. The first rate setting happens at time T. For each reset date T_{i-1} and payment date T_i, τ_i is the year fraction between two dates based on the contractual day count convention. To use the method introduced earlier we need to set up a coupon-bearing bond. The principal of this bond is the par value of \$1 and the coupon rate is the strike rate X. Hence bond cash flows are $C_i = X\tau_i$ for $i = 1, \ldots, n - 1$, and $C_n = 1 + X\tau_n$ for last cash flow. Similar to what is discussed earlier, we need to find r^* as the short rate at time T that makes the value of this coupon-bearing bond equal to the strike price, which here is the par value of \$1. Thus r^* is the solution to:

$$\sum_{i=1}^{n} C_i \, A(T, T_i) \, e^{-B(T,T_i) r^*} = 1$$

Assume that X_i is the value at time T of a \$1 notional zero-coupon bond with maturity at T_i, when the short rate is r^*, obtained using Equation (5.17) as:

$$X_i = A(T, T_i) \, e^{-B(T,T_i) r^*}$$

Based on this setup the value of a fixed-rate payer European swaption at time $t < T$ can be obtained from the value of a portfolio of put options on zero-coupon bonds as:

$$V_{Swaption\ FP}(t, T, \mathbb{T}, \mathrm{N}, \mathrm{X}) = \mathrm{N}\sum_{i=1}^{n} C_i V_{Put\ ZB}(t, T, T_i, X_i) \qquad (5.74)$$

Similarly, the value of a fixed-rate receiver European swaption at time $t <$ T can be obtained from the value of a portfolio of call options on zero-coupon bonds:

$$V_{Swaption\ FR}(t, T, \mathbb{T}, \mathrm{N}, \mathrm{X}) = \mathrm{N}\sum_{i=1}^{n} C_i V_{Call\ ZB}(t, T, T_i, X_i) \qquad (5.75)$$

INTEREST RATE TREE

An *interest rate tree* is a discrete-time representation of a continuous-time interest rate model. An interest rate model represented in the form of an interest rate tree is sometimes referred to as a *lattice model*. An interest rate tree illustrates the evolution of an interest rate through time where time advances in discrete steps. An interest rate tree consists of one or more *nodes* at each time and *paths* that connect these nodes. Each node represents an interest rate at a given time. Since at each time there are one or more nodes,

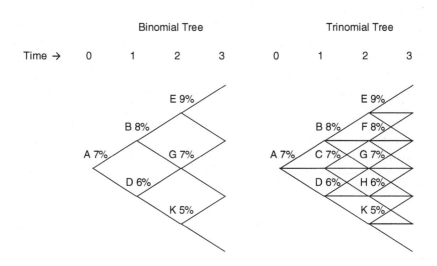

FIGURE 5.11 Binomial and trinomial interest rate trees

an interest rate tree represents the possibility of different interest rates at each given time. The value of interest rates and probabilities of moving from one node to another node in the next time step are defined by the interest rate model that the tree represents. If at each node there are two outgoing paths to two nodes at the next time step, the interest rate tree is called a *binomial tree*, and if there are three outgoing paths to three nodes at the next time step, the interest rate tree is a *trinomial tree*. Figure 5.11 presents examples of binomial and trinomial interest rate trees. Since a trinomial tree provides more flexibility to represent complex interest rate models, it is preferable to the binomial tree and is commonly used in practice. In this section we describe the process of building trinomial trees.

The interest rate at each node of a tree is the rate at the time the node is located and for a term of Δt period, where Δt is the time step between two consecutive discrete times of the tree. In the trinomial tree shown in Figure 5.11 the time step is assumed as one year ($\Delta t = 1$ year) so this tree shows the evolution of the interest rate for a three-year period and the interest rate at each node is for a term of one year. At node A (current time $t = 0$) the 1-year interest rate is 7%. There are three possible movements of the interest rate assumed in a trinomial tree. From node A the interest rate may:

1. Go up by taking the path AB and reaching to node B one year later, or
2. Stay at the same level and take straight path AC, reaching to node C one year later, or
3. Go down and taking path AD, reaching to node D one year later.

The interest rate at node B is at the 8% level. This is a 1-year interest rate one year from now. The magnitude of change in interest rate (here 1%) depends on the underlying interest rate model and we discuss it further on in more detail. If the interest rate takes path AB, it increases from 7% to 8% at the next discrete time $t = 1$. If the interest rate takes straight path AC, it remains at the current level 7%, and if it takes path AD, it goes down by 1%, reaching the 6% level at node D. This process is repeated at each node located at time $t = 1$. At node B the interest rate may go up by 1%, reaching node E at 9%, or staying at the same level and reaching node F at 8%, or going down and reaching node G at 7%. The same interest rate movement pattern can occur at nodes C and D. Similarly at every node at time $t = 2$ there are three possible outgoing paths available that lead to higher, equal, or lower interest rate levels, and so on.

The interest rate tree can be used in the valuation of floating-rate instruments, the valuation of derivative products such as options, or the valuation of financial instruments where cash flows depend on the path of interest rate movements, such as mortgage-backed securities. Before explaining how an interest rate tree is built, let's demonstrate its application using a simple example. Consider a European interest rate cap contract with a notional value of $1,000 maturing two years from now with the following payoff function at maturity:

$$Pay\ off = \begin{cases} 1000(r - 6\%) & if\ r > 6\% \\ 0 & otherwise \end{cases}$$

where r is the continuous compounding 1-year interest rate, set based on a reference index at maturity date in $t = 2$, while payoff occurs at $t = 3$. We can use the trinomial interest rate tree in Figure 5.11 for the valuation of this contract at $= 0$. Assume that the interest rates in this tree are stated with continuous compounding, and also assume at each node of the tree probabilities of outgoing up, straight, and down paths are $P_u = 0.17$, $P_m = 0.66$, and $P_d = 0.17$, respectively. Later in this section we discuss the derivation of these probabilities. We use the *backward induction* valuation method to value this contract at $t = 0$. In backward induction we start from nodes at the time when a contract matures and estimate the expectation of contract value at each node using path probabilities and going backward toward the current time one step at a time. The cash flow at maturity of the contract at $t = 2$ depends on the node where the evaluation is performed. At node E the 1-year interest rate is 9%, therefore payoff is $1000(9\% - 6\%) = 30$. The cash flow of this payoff occurs one period later, so the value of the contract at $t = 2$ is the discounted value of the payoff cash flow using the interest rate at node E: $30 \times e^{0.09 \times 1} = 27.42$. At node F the 1-year interest rate is 8% and hence the payoff is $1000(8\% - 6\%) = 20$. The value of the contract at that node is: $20 \times e^{0.08 \times 1} = 18.46$. Similarly, the

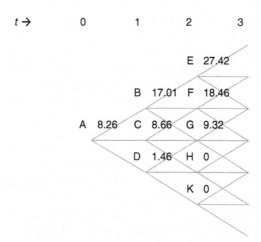

FIGURE 5.12 Valuation of an interest rate cap contract using a trinomial tree

payoff and value of the contract at node G are obtained as 10 and 9.32, respectively. At node H and K the 1-year interest rates are 6% and 5%. Therefore based on the payoff function the payoff and value of the contract is 0 at both of these nodes. Figure 5.12 shows the expected contract value at each node of the trinomial tree.

After the expected values of the contract at all terminal nodes at $t = 2$ are obtained, we can step back to time $t = 1$ and calculate the expected value of the contract at nodes B, C, and D. For each leading node at $t = 1$ there are three outgoing paths to three destination nodes at $t = 2$. The expected value of the contract at each leading node is the sum of the discounted value of contract at each destination node multiplied by the probability of the path, where the discount factor is obtained using the interest rate at the leading node. At node B, where the 1-year interest rate is 8%, three outgoing paths are to nodes E, F, and G; therefore the expected value of the contract at node B is obtained as:

$$(0.17 \times 27.42 + 0.66 \times 18.46 + 0.17 \times 9.32) \times e^{-0.08 \times 1} = 17.01$$

At node C, where the 1-year interest rate is 7% and destination nodes are F, G, and H, the expected value of the contract is:

$$(0.17 \times 18.46 + 0.66 \times 9.32 + 0.17 \times 0) \times e^{-0.07 \times 1} = 8.66$$

The expected value of the contract at node D is obtained similarly as 1.46. Stepping back to time $t = 0$, the expected value of the contract at node A, where the 1-year interest rate is 7%, is obtained using the contract values calculated in the previous step for nodes B, C, and D:

$$(0.17 \times 17.01 + 0.66 \times 8.66 + 0.17 \times 1.46) \times e^{-0.07 \times 1} = 8.26$$

Based on the trinomial tree used here, the current value of this option contract is $8.26.

If at each node of a trinomial tree three outgoing paths are always up, straight, and down, eventually at the top edge of the tree the interest rate increases to an unrealistically high level or at the bottom edge it grows to large negative levels. To avoid such issues and incorporate the mean reversion property of the interest rate model we can consider two other types of branching at the edges of the tree. Figure 5.13 presents three branching patterns. Branching (a) is the one we considered so far, where outgoing paths lead to nodes with the interest rate level up one level, at the same level, or down one level. Branching (b) is the pattern preventing the interest rate from increasing too much. In this branching method outgoing paths lead to nodes with the same level of interest rate, down one level or down two levels. Branching (c) prevents the interest rate from decreasing too much. In this branching method the outgoing paths lead to nodes with the same level of interest rate, up one level, or up two levels.

Figure 5.14 presents an extended version of the trinomial tree we introduced earlier. All nodes at time 0 to 4 have a branching pattern (a). Starting at $t = 4$ for nodes at the top edge of the tree, the branching pattern (b) is used. For example, at node T the outgoing paths lead to nodes with the same level of interest rate, down one level, or down two levels. Starting at $t = 4$ for nodes at the bottom edge of the tree, the branching pattern (c) is used. For example, at node U the outgoing paths are to nodes with the same level of interest rate, up one level, and up two levels. To change the branching pattern from (a) to (b) or (c), certain conditions must be satisfied to ensure that appropriate probabilities are assigned to outgoing paths. We will discuss this condition in the following section.

In the next section we describe a method to construct a trinomial tree that can be used for both the Hull-White and Ho-Lee interest rate models,

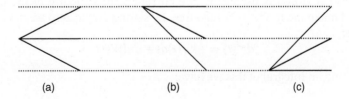

     (a)   (b)   (c)

FIGURE 5.13 Different branching patterns for a trinomial tree

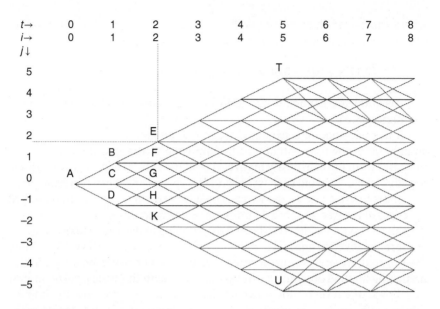

FIGURE 5.14   Trinomial interest rate tree with alternative branching at edge nodes

and in the following section we use a modified version of this method for the
Black-Krasinski model.

The Hull-White Tree

Hull and White (1994, 1996) developed a numerical procedure for building
a trinomial tree for the interest rate. Here we explain this method for the
Hull-White one-factor model that was introduced earlier in this chapter. Since
the Ho-Lee interest rate model is a special case of the Hull-White model, the
same procedure can be used for the Ho-Lee model. Consider the Hull-White
stochastic process:

$$dr(t) = (\theta(t) - k\, r(t))dt + \sigma\, dW(t)$$

Recall that $\theta(t)$ is used to fit the current term structure of the interest
rate and make the model arbitrage-free. By setting $\theta(t)$ to zero we have a new
process:

$$dr^*(t) = -k\, r(t)dt + \sigma\, dW(t)$$

Taking an integral of this we have:

$$r^*(t) = r^*(s)e^{-k(t-s)} + \sigma \int_s^t e^{-k(t-\tau)}dW(\tau)$$

By comparing this with Equation (5.33), we have:

$$r(t) = r^*(t) + \alpha(t)$$

where $\alpha(t)$ is defined in Equation (5.32) as:

$$\alpha(t) = f(0,t) + \frac{\sigma^2}{2k^2}(1 - e^{-kt})^2$$

Hull and White developed a two-stage procedure for building a trinomial interest rate tree that starts by building the tree based on the $r^*(t)$ process and then in the second stage shifting the constructed tree to represent the $r(t)$ process. In application of this two-stage process the explicit derivation of $\theta(t)$ using Equation (5.29) is not needed. This two-stage procedure is explained next.

First Stage: Construction of Tree Based on R*

For a selected time step Δt, $R(t)$ is the continuous compounding Δt-period interest rate at time t. We assume it has a similar stochastic process as $r(t)$:

$$dR = dt + \sigma \, dW(t) \qquad (5.76)$$

By setting $\theta(t)$ to zero we obtain a new process for $R^*(t)$:

$$dR^*(t) = -kr^*(t) \, dt + \sigma \, dW(t) \qquad (5.77)$$

where we have:

$$R(t) = R^*(t) + \alpha(t) \qquad (5.78)$$

Change in R^*, that is, $R^*(t + \Delta t) - R^*(t)$, has a normal distribution with mean $M \times R^*(t)$ and variance V where M and V are defined as[5]:

$$M = e^{-k\,\Delta t} - 1 \qquad (5.79)$$

$$V = \frac{\sigma^2(1 - e^{-2k\,\Delta t})}{2k} \qquad (5.80)$$

As explained earlier, in the first stage we build a trinomial tree for R^*. ΔR is the vertical distance between two adjacent nodes on the tree at a given time. For example, in trinomial trees in Figures 5.11 and 5.14 the vertical distance between nodes is $\Delta R = 1\%$. For the size of interest step ΔR, Hull and White chose $\Delta R = \sqrt{3\,V}$ and argued that this choice is appropriate for minimization of error. Note that ΔR and ΔR^* are the same.

$$\Delta R = \Delta R^* = \sqrt{3\,V} \qquad (5.81)$$

To build the R^* tree we define two indexes i and j to identify each node on the tree. Index i is a positive integer along the time horizon where $t = i\,\Delta t$ and index j is a positive or negative integer representing the vertical location of the node. For example, in Figure 5.14 node E has $i = +2$ and $j = +2$. Since in that tree $\Delta t = 1$ year, this node is located at time $t = i\Delta t = 2 \times 1 = 2$ year. Node A, where the tree starts, is always at $i = 0$ and $j = 0$. The R^* tree is symmetric around $i = 0$. Node E with $j = +2$ is at the vertical location, which is two steps above the central axis of tree. Since ΔR is the vertical distance between two adjacent nodes for a given time, we have $R^* = j\,\Delta R$. Using this identity we can calculate R^* at each node (i, j), where ΔR is from Equation (5.81).

We start building the tree by using the branching pattern (a) from Figure 5.13. When parameter k of the model is positive, the branching pattern (b) can be used at top edge nodes to avoid the tree reaching to a very high R^* level. Hull and White showed that the appropriate value of j to switch between branching pattern (a) to (b) is when j reaches the smallest integer greater than $0.184/(k\,\Delta t)$. Similarly for positive k, to avoid the tree reaching a very low R^* level we need to switch from branching pattern (a) to (c), when j reaches the smallest integer, less than $-0.184/(k\,\Delta t)$. These switching conditions ensure that the probabilities of outgoing paths at each node are always positive.[6] Probabilities of outgoing paths for each of the three branching patterns can be calculated by solving three equations simultaneously:

Equation (1): Setting the calculated expectation of change in R^* over time step Δt obtained using outgoing probabilities equal to the expectation of change in R^*: $MR^*(t)$

Equation (2): Setting the calculated variance of change in R^* over time step Δt obtained using outgoing probabilities equal to the variance of change in R^*: V

Equation (3): Setting the sum of the three probabilities equal to 1

If P_u, P_m and P_d are probabilities of up one level, straight, and down one level outgoing paths for the branching pattern (a), using the system of three equations we can calculate these probabilities as follows:

$$P_u = \frac{1}{6} + \frac{j^2 M^2 + jM}{2}$$

$$P_m = \frac{2}{3} - j^2 M^2 \qquad\qquad (5.82)$$

$$P_d = \frac{1}{6} + \frac{j^2 M^2 - jM}{2}$$

where M is defined in (5.79). Similarly, for branching pattern (b) if P_u, P_m, and P_d are probabilities of straight, one level down, and two levels down outgoing paths, they can be derived as follows:

$$P_u = \frac{7}{6} + \frac{j^2 M^2 + 3jM}{2}$$

$$P_m = -\frac{1}{3} - j^2 M^2 - 2jM \qquad (5.83)$$

$$P_d = \frac{1}{6} + \frac{j^2 M^2 + jM}{2}$$

And for branching pattern (c) if P_u, P_m, and P_d are probabilities of up two levels, up one level, and straight outgoing paths, they can be derived as follows:

$$P_u = \frac{1}{6} + \frac{j^2 M^2 - jM}{2}$$

$$P_m = -\frac{1}{3} - j^2 M^2 + 2jM \qquad (5.84)$$

$$P_d = \frac{7}{6} + \frac{j^2 M^2 - 3jM}{2}$$

To illustrate the first stage of the tree building process, consider a Hull-White short rate model with parameters $\sigma = 0.004$ and $k = 0.15$. Here we set the time step Δt for 1 year.[7] The first stage tree built based on these parameters is shown in Figure 5.15.

First we calculate the values of M and V using Equations (5.79) and (5.80):

$$M = e^{-k\,\Delta t} - 1 = e^{-0.15 \times 1} - 1 = -0.1393$$

$$V = \frac{\sigma^2(1 - e^{-2k\,\Delta t})}{2k} = \frac{(0.004^2)(1 - e^{-2 \times 0.15 \times 1})}{2 \times 0.15} = 0.000014$$

The vertical distance between two nodes is obtained as:

$$\Delta R = \sqrt{3\,V} = \sqrt{3 \times 0.000014} = 0.00644$$

We start at node A. This node is at $(i = 0, j = 0)$ and at time $t = 0$. For this node branching pattern (a) is used. Since probabilities of outgoing paths are a function of j, for all nodes with the same j the probabilities are the same. For node A and any node with $j = 0$ these probabilities are calculated using Equation (5.82) as $P_u = 0.1667$, $P_m = 0.6667$, and $P_d = 0.1667$, rounded to four

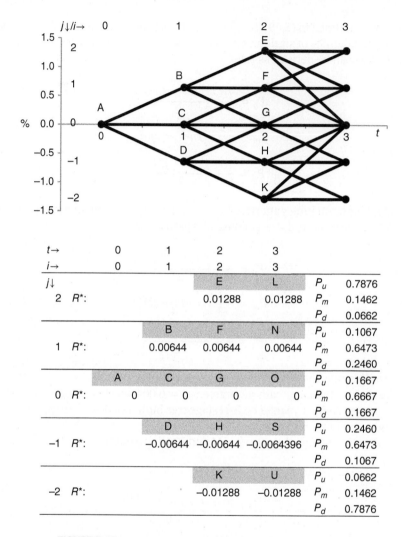

FIGURE 5.15 First stage of a Hull-White trinomial: R^* tree

decimals. The value of R^* at node A, and for all other nodes with $j = 0$, is zero: $R^* = j\,\Delta R = 0 \times 0.00644 = 0$.

The smallest integer greater than $0.184/(k\,\Delta t) = 0.184/(0.15 \times 1) = 1.2267$ is 2, so when $j = 2$ we need to switch from branching pattern (a) to (b), and when $j = -2$ we need to switch from branching pattern (a) to (c).

At $i = 1$, where $t = i\,\Delta t = 1 \times 1 = 1$ year, there are three nodes: B, C, and D. Since j values for these nodes are 1, 0, and –1, and they do not satisfy the condition to change the branching pattern, for these three nodes the branching pattern (a) is used. At node B where $(i = 1, j = 1)$, probabilities of outgoing paths are calculated using Equation (5.82) as $P_u = 0.1067$, $P_m = 0.6473$, and $P_d = 0.2460$. These probabilities are the same for any nodes with $j = 1$. The value of R^* at node B and for all other nodes with $j = 1$, is: $R^* = j\,\Delta R = 1 \times 0.00644 = 0.00644$. Probabilities of outgoing paths and the value of R^* at node C are similar to node A. For node D, where $(i = 1, j = -1)$, probabilities of outgoing paths are calculated using Equations (5.82) as $P_u = 0.2460$, $P_m = 0.6473$ and $P_d = 0.1067$. These probabilities are the same for any nodes with $j = -1$. The value of R^* at node D and for all other nodes with $j = -1$, is: $R^* = j\,\Delta R = -1 \times 0.00644 = -0.00644$.

We continue construction of the tree by moving to $i = 2$, where $t = i\,\Delta t = 2 \times 1 = 2$ years. At $i = 2$ there are five nodes E, F, G, H, and K. At node E, where $(i = 2, j = 2)$ we need to switch to branching pattern (b). Probabilities of outgoing paths at this node or any mode with $j = 2$ are calculated from Equation (5.83) as $P_u = 0.7876$, $P_m = 0.1462$, and $P_d = 0.0662$. The value of R^* at node E and for all other nodes with $j = 2$, is: $R^* = j\,\Delta R = 2 \times 0.00644 = 0.01288$. Values of j at nodes F, G, and H are –1, 0, and 1, respectively, and we use branching pattern (a) for them. Probabilities of outgoing paths and also the value of R^* for nodes F, G, and H are similar to nodes B, C, and D. At node K, where $(i = 2, j = -2)$, we need to use branching pattern (c). Probabilities of outgoing paths are calculated using Equations (5.84) as $P_u = 0.0662$, $P_m = 0.1462$ and $P_d = 0.7876$. These probabilities are the same for any nodes with $j = -2$. The value of R^* at node K and for all other nodes with $j = -2$, is: $R^* = j\,\Delta R = -2 \times 0.00644 = -0.01288$.

This process continues to any required time horizon by advancing i index. Index j advances until the condition for switching the branching pattern is satisfied. The first stage R^* tree shown in Figure 5.15 is constructed up to $i = 3$, $t = 3$, where at $j = 2$ the branching is changed from pattern (a) to (b) and at $j = -2$, the branching pattern is changed from (a) to (c).

Second Stage: Shifting R* Tree to R Tree

In the second stage of constructing a trinomial tree, the R^* tree built in the first stage is displaced so that it incorporates the current term structure of interest rate as it transforms into the R tree. Equation (5.78) is the basis of this transformation. In this process for each time t an additive displacement factor $\alpha(t)$ is obtained, such that when added to the R^* values of all nodes at time t, it produces the price of a zero-coupon bond that is in line with the current spot curve. The addition of $\alpha(t)$ to R^* values of all nodes at time t causes the R^* tree to shift up or down, turning it into an R tree while incorporating the current spot curve.

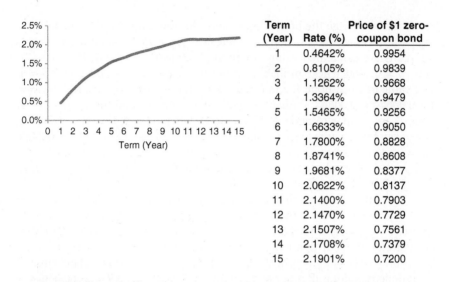

Term (Year)	Rate (%)	Price of $1 zero-coupon bond
1	0.4642%	0.9954
2	0.8105%	0.9839
3	1.1262%	0.9668
4	1.3364%	0.9479
5	1.5465%	0.9256
6	1.6633%	0.9050
7	1.7800%	0.8828
8	1.8741%	0.8608
9	1.9681%	0.8377
10	2.0622%	0.8137
11	2.1400%	0.7903
12	2.1470%	0.7729
13	2.1507%	0.7561
14	2.1708%	0.7379
15	2.1901%	0.7200

FIGURE 5.16 Current spot curve and associated prices of zero-coupon bonds

To illustrate the second stage, consider the current spot curve as shown in Figure 5.16. Rates are annualized with continuous compounding. The prices of zero-coupon bonds with $1 notional value maturing at term points are also included in the table. For example, the price of a zero-coupon bond that matures at $t = 2$ years and pays $1 at maturity is calculated as:

$$P = C\,e^{-r_c\,t} = 1 \times e^{-0.008105 \times 2} = 0.9839$$

When all displacement factors $\alpha(t)$ are calculated, the R tree shown in Figure 5.17 is obtained. To do this, we start from $t = 0$ and move forward in time. For $i = 0$ factor α_0 is set to the current spot rate with a term equal to Δt. Since in this example Δt is one year and the 1-year spot rate from Figure 5.16 is 0.00464, thus $\alpha_0 = 0.00464$. This is to be added to R^* at node A, hence the value of R at node A is $0 + 0.004642 = 0.4642\%$.

At $i = 1$ we need to find α_1, such that when it is added to R^* at nodes B, C, and D, and then resulting R interest rates are used to calculate current price (price at $t = 0$) of a zero-coupon bond maturing at $t = 2$, it would produce the same result as the one obtained from the current spot curve.

- The price of a zero-coupon bond as seen at node B: At node B the 1-year interest rate in R tree is $R^* + \alpha_1 = 0.00644 + \alpha_1$. To find the value of the zero-coupon bond maturing at $t = 2$, we discount the cash flow of this bond, that is, $1 occurring at $t = 2$, in two steps: first discounting it back one year to $t = 1$ using $R = 0.00644 + \alpha_1$ assumed for a 1-year interest rate at node B and then discounting it back one more year to $t = 0$ using an already-established 1-year interest rate of 0.4642% for node A:

$$1 \times e^{-0.004642 \times 1} \times e^{-[0.00644 + \alpha_1] \times 1}$$

▪ The price of a zero-coupon bond as seen at node C: At this node the 1-year interest rate in R tree is $R^* + \alpha_1 = 0 + \alpha_1 = \alpha_1$. To find the value of the zero-coupon bond maturing at $t = 2$, we discount the cash flow of this bond in two steps: first discounting it back one year to $t = 1$ using $R = 0 + \alpha_1$ assumed for the 1-year interest rate at node C, and then discounting it back one more year to $t = 0$ using the 1-year interest rate of 0.4642% for node A:

$$1 \times e^{-0.004642 \times 1} \times e^{-[\alpha_1] \times 1}$$

▪ The price of a zero-coupon bond as seen at node D: At node D the 1-year interest rate in R tree is $R^* + \alpha_1 = -0.00644 + \alpha_1$. To find the value of the zero-coupon bond maturing at $t = 2$, we discount the cash flow of this bond in two steps: first discounting it back one year to $t = 1$, using $R = -0.00644 + \alpha_1$ assumed for the 1-year interest rate at node D and then discounting it back one more year to $t = 0$ using the 1-year interest rate of 0.4642% for node A:

$$1 \times e^{-0.004642 \times 1} \times e^{-[-0.00644 + \alpha_1] \times 1}$$

Considering the probabilities of outgoing paths from node A at $t = 0$ to nodes B, C, and D, the expectation of the current price of the zero-coupon bond maturing at $t = 2$ is obtained as:

$$P_{u_A} \times (1 \times e^{-0.004642 \times 1} \times e^{-[0.00644 + \alpha_1] \times 1})$$

$$+ P_{m_A} \times (1 \times e^{-0.004642 \times 1} \times e^{-[\alpha_1] \times 1})$$

$$+ P_{d_A} \times (1 \times e^{-0.004642 \times 1} \times e^{-[-0.00644 + \alpha_1] \times 1})$$

Here P_{u_A}, P_{m_A}, and P_{d_A} are probabilities of up, straight, and down for outgoing paths from node A, and are obtained in the first stage in Figure 5.15. The price of a zero-coupon bond maturing at $t = 2$ based on the current spot curve is 0.9839 (from Figure 5.16). By setting the expectation of the zero-coupon bond price equal to its current value we have:

$$0.1667 \times (1 \times e^{-0.004642 \times 1} \times e^{-[0.00644 + \alpha_1] \times 1})$$

$$+ 0.6667 \times (1 \times e^{-0.004642 \times 1} \times e^{-[\alpha_1] \times 1})$$

$$+ 0.1667 \times (1 \times e^{-0.004642 \times 1} \times e^{-[-0.00644 + \alpha_1] \times 1})$$

$$= 0.9839$$

Solving this equation for α_1 provides us with $\alpha_1 = 0.01158$. When this value is added to R^* at nodes B, C, and D, the resulting R interest rates ensure that the current term structure of zero curve is incorporated in R tree up to $i = 1, t = 1$. The 1-year interest rates R at these nodes are:

B: $R = R^* + \alpha_1 = 0.00644 + 0.01158 = 1.802\%$

C: $R = R^* + \alpha_1 = 0 + 0.01158 = 1.158\%$

D: $R = R^* + \alpha_1 = -0.00644 + 0.01158 = 0.514\%$

To facilitate this calculation, Hull and White used an auxiliary variable $Q_{i,j}$, defined as the present value of \$1 if nodes (i,j) are reached and zero otherwise. For node A, $Q_{0,0}$ is always 1. To obtain the value of $Q_{1,1}$ at node B, we need to consider all paths and their probabilities that lead to node B. There is only one path AB by which node B can be reached. Therefore, using established R, the 1-year interest rate at node A, and based on the definition of Q variable, the value of $Q_{1,1}$ is calculated as:

$$Q_{1,1} = P_{u_A} \times 1 \times e^{-R_A \times \Delta t} = 0.1667\,e^{-0.004642 \times 1} = 0.16589$$

For $Q_{1,0}$ we need to consider all paths and their probabilities that lead to node C. There is only one path AC by which node C can be reached, and therefore the value of $Q_{1,0}$ is calculated as:

$$Q_{1,0} = P_{m_A} \times 1 \times e^{-R_A \times \Delta t} = 0.667\,e^{-0.004642 \times 1} = 0.66358$$

And there is only one path AD by which node D can be reached, so the value of $Q_{1,-1}$ is calculated as:

$$Q_{1,-1} = P_{d_A} \times 1 \times e^{-R_A \times \Delta t} = 0.1667\,e^{-0.004642 \times 1} = 0.16589$$

We can think of a Q value as a type of discount factor for a node, considering probabilities of all paths that lead to the node. Calculated Q values for nodes in R tree are summarized in Figure 5.17.

We can use Q values to calculate displacement factors. Let's use Q values for nodes B, C, and D to recalculate α_1. To do this we calculate the value of zero-coupon bond maturing at $t = 2$ at each node located at $t = 1$ using $R = R^* + \alpha_1$ interest rate and multiply the result by the Q value for that node. The summation of these quantities over all nodes at $t = 1$ provides us with the expected current value of zero-coupon bond maturing at $t = 2$. By setting this equal to current bond price, we have:

$$Q_{1,1} \times e^{-[0.00644 + \alpha_1] \times 1} + Q_{1,0} \times e^{-[0 + \alpha_1] \times 1} + Q_{1,-1} \times e^{-[-0.00644 + \alpha_1] \times 1} = 0.9839$$

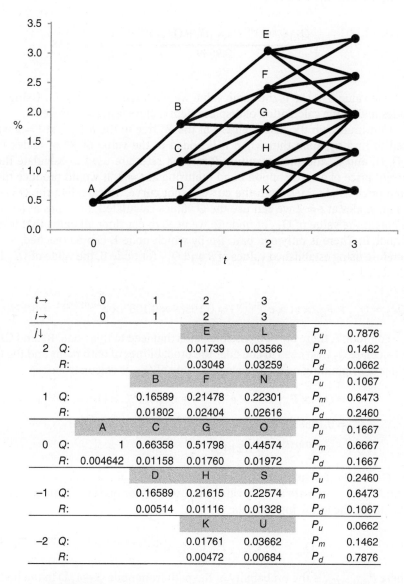

$t\rightarrow$		0	1	2	3		
$i\rightarrow$		0	1	2	3		
$j\downarrow$				E	L	P_u	0.7876
2	Q:			0.01739	0.03566	P_m	0.1462
	R:			0.03048	0.03259	P_d	0.0662
			B	F	N	P_u	0.1067
1	Q:		0.16589	0.21478	0.22301	P_m	0.6473
	R:		0.01802	0.02404	0.02616	P_d	0.2460
		A	C	G	O	P_u	0.1667
0	Q:	1	0.66358	0.51798	0.44574	P_m	0.6667
	R:	0.004642	0.01158	0.01760	0.01972	P_d	0.1667
			D	H	S	P_u	0.2460
−1	Q:		0.16589	0.21615	0.22574	P_m	0.6473
	R:		0.00514	0.01116	0.01328	P_d	0.1067
				K	U	P_u	0.0662
−2	Q:			0.01761	0.03662	P_m	0.1462
	R:			0.00472	0.00684	P_d	0.7876

FIGURE 5.17 Second stage of a Hull-White trinomial tree: R tree

Solving for α_1, we have:

$$\alpha_1 = ln\left(\frac{Q_{1,1}e^{-0.00644} + Q_{1,1}e^0 + Q_{1,-1}e^{0.00644}}{0.9839}\right) = 0.01158$$

The value 0.01158 is the same value we obtained for α_1 earlier. Using Q values makes the calculation of displacement factors faster and easier.

Continuing on the displacement of the R^* tree to the R tree, at $t = 2$ we need to find α_2, such that when it is added to the value of R^* of nodes E, F, G, H, and K, and then resulting R interest rates are used to calculate the current price of a zero-coupon bond maturing at $t = 3$, it would produce the same price as obtained from the current spot curve. To calculate the Q values for nodes at $t = 2$ we can use the Q values calculated for nodes at $t = 1$. To obtain the value of $Q_{2,2}$ at node E, we need to consider all paths that lead to node E. There is only one path BE by which node E can be reached, and therefore using established values of R and $Q_{1,1}$ for node B, the value of $Q_{2,2}$ is calculated as:

$$Q_{2,2} = Q_{1,1} \times P_{uB} \times (1 \times e^{-R_B \times \Delta t}) = 0.16589 \times 0.1067 \times e^{-0.01802 \times 1} = 0.1739$$

For node F, there are two possible paths that lead to this node: BF and CF. To calculate $Q_{2,1}$ we need to consider the probabilities of both paths and the Q values of originating nodes. Hence, the value of $Q_{2,1}$ is calculated as:

$$Q_{2,1} = Q_{1,1} \times P_{mB} \times (1 \times e^{-R_B \times \Delta t}) + Q_{1,0} \times P_{uC} \times (1 \times e^{-R_C \times \Delta t})$$

$$= 0.16589 \times 0.6473 \times e^{-0.01802 \times 1} + 0.66358 \times 0.1667$$

$$\times e^{-0.01158 \times 1} = 0.21478$$

Generally if displacement factors and Q values for all nodes up to and including $i - 1$ step are already calculated, then Q for node (i, j) can be calculated using the following formula:

$$Q_{i,j} = \sum_k Q_{i-1,k}\, P_{(i-1,k),(i,j)}\, e^{-[\alpha_{i-1} + k\,\Delta R]\,\Delta t} \tag{5.85}$$

where $P_{(i-1,k),(i,j)}$ is the probability of the path from node $(i - 1, k)$ to the node (i, j) for all paths for which this probability is non-zero, and α_{i-1} is the displacement factor at the $i - 1$ location obtained in the previous step. The summation is over all nodes with a path leading to node (i, j). Also note that $k\,\Delta R$ in the previous formula is the value of R^* for the leading node. For example, for node G, where leading nodes are B, C, and D, using Equation (5.85) $Q_{2,0}$ is calculated as:

$i = 2, j = 0, k \in \{-1, 0, 1\}, \Delta R = 0.00644, \Delta t = 1, \alpha_1 = 0.01158$

$Q_{2,0} = Q_{1,-1} \, P_{(1,-1),(2,0)} \, e^{-[\alpha_1 - 1 \times \Delta R] \times \Delta t}$

$\qquad + Q_{1,0} \, P_{(1,0),(2,0)} \, e^{-[\alpha_1 + 0 \times \Delta R] \times \Delta t} + Q_{1,1} \, P_{(1,1),(2,0)} \, e^{-[\alpha_1 + 1 \times \Delta R] \times \Delta t}$

$Q_{2,0} = 0.16589 \times 0.2460 \times e^{-[0.01158 - 0.00644] \times 1} + 0.66358 \times 0.6667$

$\qquad \times e^{-[0.01158] \times 1} + 0.16589 \times 0.2460 \times e^{-[0.01158 + 0.00644] \times 1} = 0.51798$

$Q_{2,-1} = 0.21615$ and $Q_{2,-2} = 0.01761$ are calculated similarly using Equation (5.85). To find the displacement factor at $t = 2$, we use the price of a zero-coupon bond maturing at $t = 3$, which from Figure 5.16 is 0.9668. Using Q values for nodes at $t = 2$, we can calculate the expected price of the bond based on the R tree and setting it equal to the current price:

$Q_{2,2} \times e^{-[0.01288 + \alpha_2] \times 1} + Q_{2,1} \times e^{-[0.00644 + \alpha_2] \times 1} + Q_{2,0} \times e^{-[0 + \alpha_2] \times 1}$

$\qquad + Q_{2,-1} \times e^{-[-0.00644 + \alpha_2] \times 1} + Q_{2,-2} \times e^{-[-0.01288 + \alpha_2] \times 1} = 0.9668$

Solving this for α_2 provides us with the displacement factor at $i = 2$: $\alpha_2 = 0.01760$. When this value is added to R^* at nodes E, F, G, H, and K, the resulting R interest rates ensure that the current term structure of zero curve is incorporated in the R tree up to $i = 2$, $t = 2$. The 1-year interest rates R at these nodes are:

E: $R = R^* + \alpha_2 = 0.00644 + 0.01760 = 3.048\%$

F: $R = R^* + \alpha_2 = 0.01288 + 0.01760 = 2.404\%$

G: $R = R^* + \alpha_2 = 0 + 0.01760 = 1.760\%$

H: $R = R^* + \alpha_2 = -0.00644 + 0.01760 = 1.116\%$

K: $R = R^* + \alpha_2 = -0.01288 + 0.01760 = 0.472\%$

For the Hull-White trinomial tree, the calculation of the displacement factor can be summarized in a formula. Assume for a given i, Q values for all nodes are already calculated and α_i is the displacement factor we need to find. If the price of a zero-coupon bond maturing at $i + 1$ based on the current spot curve is V_{i+1}, we have:

$$V_{i+1} = \sum_{j=-n_i}^{n_i} Q_{i,j} e^{-[\alpha_i + j \, \Delta R] \, \Delta t} \tag{5.86}$$

where n_i is the number of nodes at each side of central node. For example, in the R^* tree in Figure 5.15 or the R tree in Figure 5.17, n_i for $i = 1$ is 1, for $i = 2$ is 2, and for $i = 3$ is also 2. From this equation the displacement factor can be calculated as:

$$\alpha_i = \frac{\ln \sum_{j=-n_i}^{n_i} Q_{i,j} e^{-j \, \Delta R \, \Delta t} - \ln V_{i+1}}{\Delta t} \tag{5.87}$$

For example, for $i = 3$, first we calculated Q values using Equation (5.85) and the results are shown in Figure 5.17. The value of a zero-coupon bond maturing at $i = 4$ from Figure 5.16 is 0.9479. Using Equation (5.87) the displacement factor for $i = 3$ is calculated as:

$$\alpha_3 = \frac{1}{\Delta t} \left[\ln(Q_{3,2} \times e^{-2 \, \Delta R \, \Delta t} + Q_{3,1} \times e^{-1 \, \Delta R \, \Delta t} + Q_{3,0} \times e^{-0 \, \Delta R \, \Delta t} + Q_{3,-1} \right.$$
$$\left. \times e^{-(-1) \, \Delta R \, \Delta t} + Q_{3,-2} \times e^{-(-2) \, \Delta R \, \Delta t}) - \ln 0.9479 \right]$$

so:

$$\alpha_3 = \frac{1}{1} \left(\ln \left(0.03566 \times e^{-2 \times 0.00644 \times 1} + 0.22301 \times e^{-1 \times 0.00644 \times 1} + 0.44574 \right. \right.$$
$$\times e^{-0 \times 0.00644 \times 1} + 0.22574 \times e^{-(-1) \times 0.00644 \times 1} + 0.03662$$
$$\left. \left. \times e^{-(-2) \times 0.00644 \times 1} \right) - \ln 0.9479 \right) = 0.01972$$

We can continue this process for any number of time steps as needed. Figure 5.18 presents a longer version of the Hull-White trinomial tree we built

R^* tree:

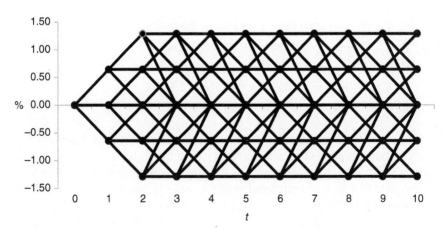

FIGURE 5.18 Two-stage construction of a Hull-White trinomial tree extended to 10 years ($\sigma = 0.004$, $k = 0.15$, $\Delta t = 1$ year)

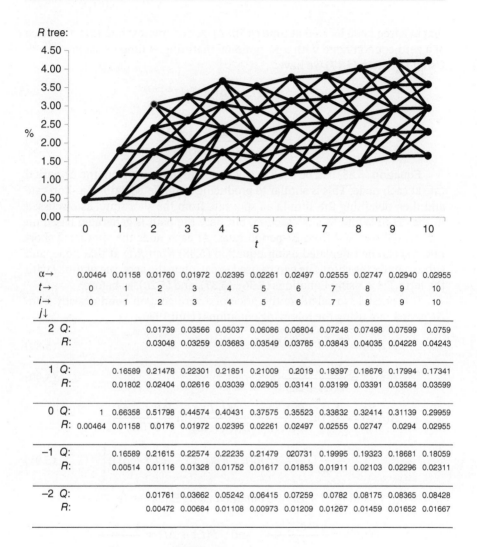

	0	1	2	3	4	5	6	7	8	9	10
α→	0.00464	0.01158	0.01760	0.01972	0.02395	0.02261	0.02497	0.02555	0.02747	0.02940	0.02955
t→	0	1	2	3	4	5	6	7	8	9	10
i→	0	1	2	3	4	5	6	7	8	9	10
j↓											
2 Q:			0.01739	0.03566	0.05037	0.06086	0.06804	0.07248	0.07498	0.07599	0.0759
R:			0.03048	0.03259	0.03683	0.03549	0.03785	0.03843	0.04035	0.04228	0.04243
1 Q:		0.16589	0.21478	0.22301	0.21851	0.21009	0.2019	0.19397	0.18676	0.17994	0.17341
R:		0.01802	0.02404	0.02616	0.03039	0.02905	0.03141	0.03199	0.03391	0.03584	0.03599
0 Q:	1	0.66358	0.51798	0.44574	0.40431	0.37575	0.35523	0.33832	0.32414	0.31139	0.29959
R:	0.00464	0.01158	0.0176	0.01972	0.02395	0.02261	0.02497	0.02555	0.02747	0.0294	0.02955
−1 Q:		0.16589	0.21615	0.22574	0.22235	0.21479	020731	0.19995	0.19323	0.18681	0.18059
R:		0.00514	0.01116	0.01328	0.01752	0.01617	0.01853	0.01911	0.02103	0.02296	0.02311
−2 Q:			0.01761	0.03662	0.05242	0.06415	0.07259	0.0782	0.08175	0.08365	0.08428
R:			0.00472	0.00684	0.01108	0.00973	0.01209	0.01267	0.01459	0.01652	0.01667

FIGURE 5.18 (*Continued*)

so far, where the tree is extended to 10 years. This R tree incorporates the current spot curve fully and hence is an arbitrage-free discrete-time representation of a Hull-White interest rate model with the given parameters.

Obtaining Short Rate and Spot Rate from Δt-Period Rate

The Δt-period interest rate $R(t)$ that is calculated at each node of the interest rate tree is not the same as the short rate $r(t)$. To obtain $r(t)$ from $R(t)$, first note that at a tree node located at time t with Δt-period interest rate $R(t)$, the price of a zero-coupon bond with a $1 notional maturing at time $t + \Delta t$ is $e^{-R(t)\,\Delta t}$. Using Equation (5.17) we have:

$$e^{-R(t)\,\Delta t} = A(t, t + \Delta t)e^{-B(t,t+\Delta t)\,r(t)}$$

or

$$r(t) = \frac{R(t)\Delta t + \ln A(t, t + \Delta t)}{B(t, t + \Delta t)} \tag{5.88}$$

Equation (5.88) can be used to calculate the short rate from the Δt-period rate at each node. This is similar to producing a simulated path of a short rate and then obtaining the simulated spot rate from the short rate, as discussed in the "Hull-White Model" section, but here the path is generated based on a trinomial tree and from Δt-period rates. At each node the simulated short rate $r(t)$ can be calculated using Equation (5.88) from $R(t)$ at that node, and subsequently the short rate can be used to calculate the spot rate at time t with the term $T - t$, using Equations (5.36), (5.37), and (5.20), as before.

It is possible to calculate the price of a zero-coupon bond directly from Δt-period rate using the following equations (Hull 1990):

$$P(t, T) = \hat{A}(t, T)e^{-\hat{B}(t,T)\,R(t)} \tag{5.89}$$

$$\hat{B}(t, T) = \frac{B(t, T)\,\Delta t}{B(t, t + \Delta t)} \tag{5.90}$$

$$\hat{A}(t, T) = exp\left[\ln\frac{P(0, T)}{P(0, t)} - \frac{B(t, T)}{B(t, t + \Delta t)}\ln\frac{P(0, t + \Delta t)}{P(0, t)}\right.$$
$$\left. - \frac{\sigma^2}{4k}(1 - e^{-2kt})B(t, T)[B(t, T) - B(t, t + \Delta t)]\right] \tag{5.91}$$

where $B(t, T)$ and $B(t, t + \Delta t)$ are obtained using Equation (5.37) as:

$$B(t, T) = \frac{1 - e^{-k(T-t)}}{k} \quad \text{and} \quad B(t, t + \Delta t) = \frac{1 - e^{-k\,\Delta t}}{k}$$

The derivation of $\hat{A}(t, T)$ and $\hat{B}(t, T)$ is presented in the Annex of this chapter. Finally, from Equation (5.5) we can calculate spot rate at time t with term $T - t$ as:

$$r(t, T) = -\frac{\ln P(t, T)}{T - t}$$

or

$$r(t, T) = -\frac{1}{T - t}\ln\hat{A}(t, T) + \frac{1}{T - t}\hat{B}(t, T)\,R(t) \tag{5.92}$$

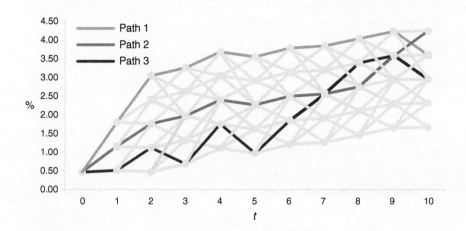

FIGURE 5.19   Simulated paths of a Δt-period rate based on the Hull-White trinomial tree

For example, Figure 5.19 highlights three simulated paths of Δt-period rate based on the Hull-White trinomial tree constructed in Figure 5.18, where $\Delta t = 1$ year. For each path of $R(t)$ we can obtain a simulated 5-year spot rate using Equations (5.90), (5.91), and (5.92), as shown in Figure 5.20. Table 5.3 ahead summarizes the calculation of a 5-year spot rate for path 1. To demonstrate this calculation consider $t = 1$. In path 1, $R(t)$ at this time is 1.802%. For

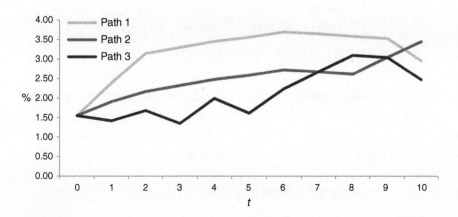

FIGURE 5.20   Simulated path of a 5-year spot rate obtained from the Hull-White trinomial tree

the 5-year spot rate $T - t = 5$, therefore:

$$t = 1, T = 6, \Delta t = 1, k = 0.15, \sigma = 0004$$

$$B(1, 6) = \frac{1 - e^{-0.15 \times 5}}{0.15} = 3.51756$$

$$B(1, 2) = \frac{1 - e^{-0.15 \times 1}}{0.15} = 0.92861$$

From Equation (5.90), we have:

$$\hat{B}(1, 6) = \frac{B(1, 6) \times 1}{B(1, 2)} = \frac{3.51753 \times 1}{0.92861} = 3.78797$$

From Figure 5.16 we have: $P(0, 1) = 0.9954$, $P(0, 2) = 0.9839$, and $P(0, 6) = 0.9050$. Using Equation (5.91), we can calculate $\hat{A}(1, 6)$ as:

$$\hat{A}(1, 6) = exp \left[\ln \frac{P(0, 6)}{P(0, 1)} - \frac{B(1, 6)}{B(1, 2)} \ln \frac{P(0, 2)}{P(0, 1)} \right.$$

$$\left. - \frac{\sigma^2}{4k}(1 - e^{-2kt})B(1, 6)[B(1, 6) - B(1, 2)] \right]$$

$$= exp \left[\ln \frac{0.9050}{0.9954} - \frac{3.51756}{0.92861} \times \ln \frac{0.9839}{0.9954} - \frac{0.004^2}{4 \times 0.15}(1 - e^{-2 \times 0.15 \times 0.004}) \right.$$

$$\left. \times 3.51756 \times [3.51756 - 0.92861] \right] = 0.94996$$

Finally, using Equation (5.92) we can calculate the simulated 5-year spot rate as:

$$r(1, 6) = -\frac{1}{5} \ln \hat{A}(1, 6) + \frac{1}{5} \hat{B}(1, 6) \times R(1)$$

$$= -\frac{1}{5} \times \ln 0.94996 + \frac{1}{5} \times 3.78797 \times 0.01802 = 0.02392$$

Thus the simulated 5-year spot rate is 2.392%. This is shown in the last row of Table 5.3 in the column for $t = 1$ year.

TABLE 5.3 Calculation of 5-year spot rate $r(t,T)$ for path 1 of $R(t)$ from Figure 5.19

t:	0	1	2	3	4	5	6	7	8	9	10
T:	5	6	7	8	9	10	11	12	13	14	15
$R(t)$:	0.00464	0.01802	0.03048	0.03259	0.03683	0.03549	0.03785	0.03843	0.04035	0.04228	0.03599
$B(t,T)$:	3.51756	3.51756	3.51756	3.51756	3.51756	3.51756	3.51756	3.51756	3.51756	3.51756	3.51756
$B(t,t+\Delta t)$:	0.92861	0.92861	0.92861	0.92861	0.92861	0.92861	0.92861	0.92861	0.92861	0.92861	0.92861
$\widehat{B}(t,T)$:	3.78797	3.78797	3.78797	3.78797	3.78797	3.78797	3.78797	3.78797	3.78797	3.78797	3.78797
$P(0,T)$:	0.92559	0.90502	0.88285	0.86077	0.83767	0.81366	0.79025	0.77287	0.75609	0.73793	0.71999
$P(0,t)$:	1.00000	0.99537	0.98392	0.96678	0.94795	0.92559	0.90502	0.88285	0.86077	0.83767	0.81366
$P(0,t+\Delta t)$:	0.99537	0.98392	0.96678	0.94795	0.92559	0.90502	0.88285	0.86077	0.83767	0.81366	0.79025
$\widehat{A}(t,T)$:	0.94200	0.94996	0.95905	0.95922	0.96729	0.95716	0.95920	0.96357	0.97374	0.98353	0.98831
$r(t,T)$:	0.01547	0.02392	0.03145	0.03302	0.03456	0.03565	0.03701	0.03654	0.03589	0.03535	0.02962

The Black-Karasinski Tree

As discussed before, there is no analytical solution for obtaining the price of zero-coupon bonds based on the Black-Karasinski short rate model, and numerical procedures, such as the interest rate tree, are the only way to use this model in the calculation of bond and option prices. With a slight modification we can use the same method explained in the previous section to build a trinomial tree based on the Black-Karasinski model. Consider the stochastic process for $R(t)$, the continuous compounding Δt-period interest rate at time t, presented in Equation (5.76):

$$dR(t) = (\theta(t) - k\,R(t))dt + \sigma\,dW(t)$$

We can generalize this process by introducing function f as:

$$df(R(t)) = (\theta(t) - k\,f(R(t)))dt + \sigma\,dW(t) \tag{5.93}$$

When function f has the form of $f(R(t)) = R(t)$, this process is the same as the Hull-White process and if $f(R(t)) = \ln R(t)$, this process is the Black-Karasinski process. To build a trinomial tree for the Black-Karasinski model we introduce a new process $X(t)$, where $X(t) = \ln R(t)$, build a trinomial tree for $X(t)$, and at the last step convert the tree to a tree for $R(t)$. The procedure for building a Black-Karasinski trinomial tree is as follows:

- Build a tree for $X(t)$: The process for $X(t)$ is as follows:

$$dX(t) = (\theta(t) - k\,X(t))dt + \sigma\,dW(t) \tag{5.94}$$

  This is done by using the same two-stage process discussed in previous section:

  - First Stage: Build a tree for $X^*(t)$: By setting $\theta(t)$ to zero, we obtain the process for $X^*(t)$:

$$dX^*(t) = -k\,X^*(t)\,dt + \sigma\,dW(t) \tag{5.95}$$

  - Second Stage: Shift $X^*(t)$ tree to fit the current term structure of the interest rate to obtain the $X(t)$ tree:

$$X(t) = X^*(t) + \alpha(t) \tag{5.96}$$

- Convert the $X(t)$ tree to the $R(t)$ tree: Since $X(t) = \ln R(t)$, we have:

$$R(t) = e^{X(t)} \tag{5.97}$$

To illustrate this procedure, consider a Black-Karasinski model with parameters $\sigma = 0.2$ and $k = 0.15$. Assume that time step Δt is one year. First we calculate the value of M and V using Equations (5.79) and (5.80):

$$M = e^{-k \, \Delta t} - 1 = e^{-0.15 \times 1} - 1 = -0.1393$$

$$V = \frac{\sigma^2(1 - e^{-2k \, \Delta t})}{2k} = \frac{(0.2^2)(1 - e^{-2 \times 0.15 \times 1})}{2 \times 0.15} = 0.034558$$

Note that the variance calculated is for $X(t)$ and not for $R(t)$. The vertical distance between the two nodes in $X(t)$ or $X^*(t)$ is obtained as:

$$\Delta X = \sqrt{3 \, V} = \sqrt{3 \times 0.034558} = 0.32198$$

The smallest integer greater than $0.184/(k \, \Delta t) = 0.184/(0.15 \times 1) = 1.2267$ is 2, so when $j = 2$ we need to switch from branching pattern (a) to (b), and when $j = -2$ we need to switch from branching pattern (a) to (c). The first stage tree for $X^*(t)$ up to $i = 3$, $t = 3$ is presented in Figure 5.21. Branching probabilities and values of X^* at each node are also included in this figure.

In the second stage we displace the $X(t)$ tree to obtain the $X^*(t)$ tree while fitting the current term structure of the interest rate. Assume the current spot curve as shown in Figure 5.16. Using Equations (5.96) and (5.97), and setting $X^* = j \, \Delta X$, Δt-period interest rate $R(t)$ can be expressed as:

$$R(t) = e^{X(t)} = e^{\alpha(t) + X^*(t)} = e^{\alpha(t) + j \, \Delta X}$$

Based on this, the equation of Q value for Black-Karasinski tree is modified as:

$$Q_{i,j} = \sum_k Q_{i-1,k} \, P_{(i-1,k),(i,j)} \, exp[-(e^{\alpha_{i-1} + k \, \Delta X}) \, \Delta t] \tag{5.98}$$

For example, assume that we are at $i = 2$ and the displacement factor and Q values for nodes at $i = 1$ are already calculated as: $Q_{1,1} = 0.16589$, $Q_{1,0} = 0.66358$, $Q_{1,-1} = 0.16589$, and $\alpha_1 = -4.4792$. We can use Equation (5.98) to calculate $Q_{2,0}$ for node G as follows:

$$i = 2, j = 0, k \in \{-1, 0, 1\}, \Delta X = 0.32198, \Delta t = 1, \alpha_1 = -4.4792$$

$$Q_{2,0} = Q_{1,-1} \, P_{(1,-1),(2,0)} \, exp[-(e^{\alpha_1 + (-1) \times \Delta X}) \, \Delta t]$$

$$+ \, Q_{1,0} \, P_{(1,0),(2,0)} \, exp[-(e^{\alpha_1 + 0 \times \Delta X}) \, \Delta t]$$

$$+ \, Q_{1,1} \, P_{(1,1),(2,0)} \, exp[-(e^{\alpha_1 + 1 \times \Delta X}) \, \Delta t]$$

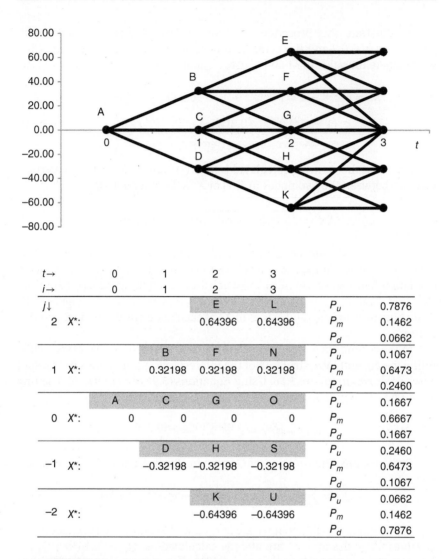

FIGURE 5.21 The first stage of a Black-Karasinski trinomial tree: X^* tree

$$Q_{2,0} = 0.16589 \times 0.2460 \times exp[-(e^{-4.4792+(-1)\times 0.32198}) \times 1]$$
$$+ 0.66358 \times 0.6667 \times exp[-(e^{-4.4792+0\times 0.32198}) \times 1] + 0.16589 \times 0.2460$$
$$\times exp[-(e^{-4.4792+1\times 0.32198}) \times 1] = 0.51805$$

For the Black-Karasinski tree, Equation (5.86) for the calculation of the price of a zero-coupon bond should be modified as follows:

$$V_{i+1} = \sum_{j=-n_i}^{n_i} Q_{i,j} \, exp[-(e^{\alpha_i+j\,\Delta X})\,\Delta t] \tag{5.99}$$

Having Q values for all nodes at a given i, we can solve the above equation for the displacement factor α_i. For example, assume Q values for five nodes at $i = 2$ are calculated as: $Q_{2,-2} = 0.01756$, $Q_{2,-1} = 0.21585$, $Q_{2,0} = 0.51805$, $Q_{2,1} = 0.21506$, and $Q_{2,2} = 0.01743$. From Figure 5.16, the current price of a zero-coupon bond maturing at $i = 3$ is 0.9668; therefore we have:

$$0.9668 = Q_{2,-2} \, exp[-(e^{\alpha_2+(-2)\times\Delta X})\,\Delta t] + Q_{2,-1} \, exp[-(e^{\alpha_2+(-1)\times\Delta X})\,\Delta t]$$
$$+ Q_{2,0} \, exp[-(e^{\alpha_2+0\times\Delta X})\,\Delta t] + Q_{2,1} \, exp[-(e^{\alpha_2+1\times\Delta X})\,\Delta t]$$
$$+ Q_{2,2} \, exp[-(e^{\alpha_2+2\times\Delta X})\,\Delta t]$$

$$0.9668 = 0.01756 \times exp[-(e^{\alpha_2+(-2)\times0.32198}) \times 1] + 0.21585$$
$$\times exp[-(e^{\alpha_2+(-1)\times0.32198}) \times 1] + 0.51805 \times exp[-(e^{\alpha_2+0\times0.32198}) \times 1]$$
$$+ 0.21506 \times exp[-(e^{\alpha_2+1\times0.32198}) \times 1] + 0.01743$$
$$\times exp[-(e^{\alpha_2+2\times0.32198}) \times 1]$$

This equation can be solved using a numerical method such as Newton-Raphson to obtain the value of the displacement factor $\alpha_2 = -4.07465$.[8]

The last step in building a Black-Karasinski trinomial tree is to transform an X tree into an R tree. This is done using Equations (5.96) and (5.97):

$$R(t) = e^{X(t)} = e^{\alpha(t)+X^*(t)}$$

For example, at node E the value of $X^* = j\,\Delta X = 2 \times 0.32198 = 0.64396$. Hence:

$$X = X^* + \alpha_2 = 0.64396 - 4.07465 = -3.43068$$

and

$$R = e^X = e^{-3.43068} = 3.236\%.$$

The X tree and R tree up to $i = 3$, $t = 3$ of the Black-Karasinski trinomial tree of our example are presented in Figure 5.22.

X Tree:

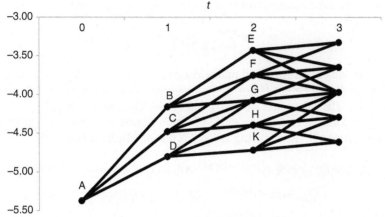

R Tree:

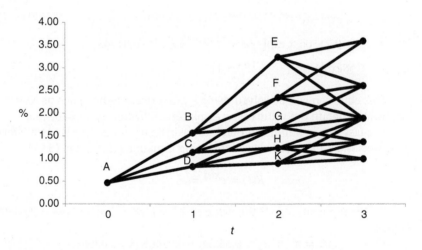

FIGURE 5.22   Second stage of a Black-Karasinski trinomial tree: *X* tree and *R* tree

α→		-5.37272	-4.47920	-4.07465	-3.97126		
t→		0	1	2	3		
i→		0	1	2	3		
j↓				E	L		
2	Q:			0.01743	0.03571	P_u	0.7876
	X:			-3.43068	-3.32729	P_m	0.1462
	R:			0.032365	0.03589	P_d	0.0662
			B	F	N		
1	Q:		0.16589	0.21506	0.22333	P_u	0.1067
	X:		-4.15722	-3.75267	-3.64928	P_m	0.6473
	R:		0.015651	0.023455	0.02601	P_d	0.2460
		A	C	G	O		
0	Q:	1	0.66358	0.51805	0.44595	P_u	0.1667
	X:	-5.37272	-4.47920	-4.07465	-3.97126	P_m	0.6667
	R:	0.004642	0.011342	0.016998	0.01885	P_d	0.1667
			D	H	S		
-1	Q:		0.16589	0.21585	0.22543	P_u	0.2460
	X:		-4.80118	-4.39663	-4.29324	P_m	0.6473
	R:		0.00822	0.012319	0.013661	P_d	0.1067
				K	U		
-2	Q:			0.01756	0.03646	P_u	0.0662
	X:			-4.71861	-4.61522	P_m	0.1462
	R:			0.008928	0.0099	P_d	0.7876

FIGURE 5.22   (*Continued*)

CALIBRATION

Calibration of an interest rate model refers to the process of obtaining the appropriate values for parameters of the model. With the exception of Ho-Lee, the interest rate models we studied in this chapter have two parameters: volatility parameter σ and mean reversion parameter k. The Ho-Lee model has only one volatility parameter. In our discussion so far we have assumed that values of the model parameters are known. In this section we discuss methods that can be used to obtain parameter values. As a general guideline, the method and data used in the calibration process should be in line with the purpose of the interest rate.

There are generally two approaches for calibration of interest rate models: using historical rates and using current market prices. In using historical rates to calibrate parameters of an interest rate model, the first step is to choose a proxy to a short rate. For instance, in the U.S. market, the 1-month LIBOR, effective federal funds rate, or secured overnight funding rate are sometimes used as proxies to the short rate. After selecting an appropriate proxy, the discretized version of the interest rate model is fitted to the historical values of the proxy rate. This is done by using a statistical estimation procedure, such as maximum likelihood method, to obtain parameter values. The advantage of this approach is the less frequent need for recalibration of the model. After initial calibration, the model recalibration is needed only when there is a major change in rate environment, such as material shift in the rate level or volatility. However, use of parameters estimated using this method may result in an unrealistic short rate and spot rates (e.g., very high or very low). Since the model is calibrated using historical rates, it also usually cannot reproduce the market value of interest rate–sensitive securities or derivative contracts traded in the market. Due to these shortcomings, this calibration method is not commonly used in practice.

The most common calibration method of interest rate models is the use of market prices of interest rate–sensitive securities or derivatives. In this approach the parameters of the model are selected such that when the model is used for the valuation of market-traded instruments, it produces the closest values to the current market values of the instruments. To find estimates of the parameters, usually several interest rate-sensitive instruments with different characteristics (e.g., different maturities) are used and the estimation process is based on optimization of a *merit function*. One common merit function is the sum of square differences between market values and model values. Assume that there are n interest rate–sensitive instruments used in calibration. For a model with two parameters k and σ, the calibration process can be summarized as:

Calibration Process (I):

$$\text{Find } \sigma \text{ and } k \text{ such that } \sum_{i=1}^{n}(V_{iModel} - V_{iMarket})^2 \text{ is minimized}$$

Here V_{iModel} is the value of instrument i using the interest rate model, and $V_{iMarket}$ is the market value of instrument i. Some practitioners prefer to define the merit function in the form of relative measurement, as the sum of square percentage differences between market values and model values. In that case the calibration process can be summarized as:

Calibration Process (II):

$$\text{Find } \sigma \text{ and } k \text{ such that } \sum_{i=1}^{n} \left(\frac{V_{iModel} - V_{iMarket}}{V_{iMarket}} \right)^2 \text{ is minimized}$$

Sometimes it is appropriate to have a different level of influence for the instruments used in the calibration. For example, if one instrument has less liquidity than others, it may be desirable to change the merit function such that less importance is given to that instrument with respect to its impact on estimated parameters. In such cases a weight can be applied to market and model values of each instrument and the calibration process can be summarized as:

Calibration Process (III):

$$\text{Find } \sigma \text{ and } k \text{ such that } \sum_{i=1}^{n} \omega_i \left(\frac{V_{iModel} - V_{iMarket}}{V_{iMarket}} \right)^2 \text{ is minimized}$$

where ω_i is the weight factor applied to instrument i and the sum of the weight factors is 1. Sometimes the merit function is enhanced by the addition of a penalty function that includes parameters to be estimated. Such a penalty function can be designed to penalize large changes in the values of parameters from one step of the calibration to the next. In practice, minimization of the merit function is an iterative approach. In each iteration of the calibration process:

1. A new set of model parameters is considered.
2. Using the interest rate mode, the values of market instruments are calculated.
3. The merit function is evaluated and compared with a predetermined threshold.

This repetitive process is continued until the value of the merit function reaches the target threshold.

When selecting the interest rate–sensitive financial instruments for using in the calibration process we need to consider the purpose of the model. Calibration instruments should cover a wide range of maturities and also should be highly liquid so their market values are reliable. Interest rate cap or floor and swaption derivative contracts are often used for the calibration of interest rate models, where European swaption contracts are the most used in practice since they are highly liquid. In the following sections we first discuss calibration of interest rate models introduced earlier using an analytical approach, and then explain how an interest rate tree can be used in the calibration process when there is no analytical solution available for bond and derivative pricing.

Calibration Using the Analytical Method

For the Vasicek, Hull-White, and Ho-Lee interest rate models there are analytical methods available to calculate values of zero-coupon bonds and options on zero-coupon bonds. We can use those analytical techniques in the calibration process. Here we demonstrate the use of the analytical method in the calibration of the Hull-White model.

Consider a 5×3 at-the-money payer European swaption contract with a quoted volatility of $\sigma = 32.59\%$. The underlying swap has a semi-annual payment frequency and for simplicity assume that the day count convention is 30/360. The notional value of the contract is \$100. If the market value of the swaption contract is available, it can be used in the calibration process. Here we calculate the market value of this swaption using the Black model and compare it with the contract value obtained using the Hull-White model based on some initial parameter values. Then we iteratively change the parameter values until the Hull-White model produces the same contract value as the market value from the Black model. As mentioned before, in practice a series of swaption contracts are used together and the calibration processes (i), (ii), or (iii) are used to find the optimum parameters that minimize the merit function. For demonstration purposes here we consider only one swaption contract. For this example we assume the LIBOR-swap spot curve with continuous compounding and corresponding values of zero-coupon bonds are as shown in Table 5.4.

Since the payment frequency of the underlying swap contract is semi-annual and the day count convention is 30/360, $\tau_i = 0.5$ for any i. For this contract, the forward swap rate can be calculated using the spot curve and Equation (5.52), as $S_0 = 2.43\%$. This rate is based on continuous compounding and since the swap contract has a semi-annual frequency we need to convert it to semi-annual compounding, as follows:

$$r = m(e^{(r_c/m)} - 1) = 2(e^{(0.0243/2)} - 1) = 2.45\%$$

If the strike rate is not included in the market quote, it can be obtained by noting that the contract is at-the-money, and hence the strike rate is equal to the forward swap rate, therefore $X = 2.45\%$ with semi-annual compounding. The value of this swaption at $t = 0$ can be calculated using Equations (5.49)

TABLE 5.4 LIBOR-swap spot rates and zero-coupon bond prices used in a Hull-White calibration example

Term	Term: t (month)	Term: t (year)	Rate (%)	P(0,t)
1M	1	0.083	0.1762%	0.99985
3M	3	0.25	0.2707%	0.99932
6M	6	0.5	0.3160%	0.99842
1Y	12	1	0.4642%	0.99537
1.5Y	18	1.5	0.6373%	0.99049
2Y	24	2	0.8105%	0.98392
2.5Y	30	2.5	0.9684%	0.97608
3Y	36	3	1.1262%	0.96678
3.5Y	42	3.5	1.2313%	0.95782
4Y	48	4	1.3364%	0.94795
4.5Y	54	4.5	1.4415%	0.93719
5Y	60	5	1.5465%	0.92559
5.5Y	66	5.5	1.6049%	0.91551
6Y	72	6	1.6633%	0.90502
6.5Y	78	6.5	1.7216%	0.89413
7Y	84	7	1.7800%	0.88285
7.5Y	90	7.5	1.8270%	0.87195
8Y	96	8	1.8741%	0.86077
8.5Y	102	8.5	1.9211%	0.84934
9Y	108	9	1.9681%	0.83767
9.5Y	114	9.5	2.0152%	0.82577
10Y	120	10	2.0622%	0.81366

and (5.50), as follows:

$$n = 6, \sigma = 0.3259, S_0 = 0.0245, X = 0.0245, \text{For any } i: \tau_i = 0.5, N = 100$$

$$T = T_0 = 5, T_1 = 5.5, T_2 = 6, T_3 = 6.5, T_4 = 7, T_5 = 7.5, T_6 = 8$$

$P(0, T_i)$ are from Table 5.4.

$$d_1 = \frac{\ln(S_0/X) + \sigma^2 T/2}{\sigma\sqrt{T}} = \frac{\ln(0.0245/0.0245) + (0.3259^2 \times 5)/2}{0.3259 \times \sqrt{5}} = 0.3643$$

$$d_2 = d_1 - \sigma\sqrt{T} = 0.3643 - 0.3259 \times \sqrt{5} = -0.3643$$

$$V_{t=0} = N \left(\sum_{i=1}^{n} \tau_i \, P(0, T_i) \right) (S_0 \Phi(d_1) - X \, \Phi(d_2)) = 100 \times 0.5$$

$$\times (0.91551 + 0.90502 + 0.89413 + 0.88285 + 0.87195 + 0.86077)$$

$$\times (0.0245 \times \Phi(0.3643) - 0.0245 \times \Phi(-0.3643)) = 1.85$$

The market value of this swaption at $t = 0$ using the Black model is $1.85.

To calculate the value of this swaption using the Hull-White model, we use the analytical method introduced earlier in the section "Analytical Valuation of Bonds and Options." This method is computationally more efficient compared to building the interest rate tree. We start by setting parameters of the Hull-White model to initial values of $\sigma = 0.004$ and $k = 0.15$ and selecting a time step of $\Delta t = 0.5$ year. A European swaption can be regarded as an option on a coupon-bearing bond, where the strike price is equal to the bond principal, and the value of the coupon-bearing bond can be obtained from the value of a portfolio of options on zero-coupon bonds.

The underlying swap contract of this swaption has payment dates at $T_1 = 5.5$, $T_2 = 6$, $T_3 = 6.5$, $T_4 = 7$, $T_5 = 7.5$, and $T_6 = 8$ years. To value this swaption, first we need to set up a coupon-bearing bond. The principal of this bond is par value of $1 and coupon rate is the strike rate $X = 2.45\%$. The cash flows of this bond are $C_i = X\tau_i = 0.0245 \times 0.5 = 0.0122$ for the first five payments ($i = 1$ to 5), occurring at T_1, T_2, T_3, T_4, and T_5. The last cash flow is $C_6 = 1 + 0.0245 \times 0.5 = 1.0122$ occurring at $T_6 = 8$ year. The option matures at $T = 5$ year.

We need to find r^* as the short rate at time T that sets the value of this coupon-bearing bond equal to the strike price, which here is the par value of $1 of the coupon-bearing bond. Therefore r^* is the solution to:

$$\sum_{i=1}^{n} C_i \, A(T, T_i) \, e^{-B(T,T_i)r^*} = 1$$

where $A(T, T_i)$ and $B(T, T_i)$ are from Equations (5.36) and (5.37) for the Hull-White model, reproduced here to reflect the change of notation:

$$A(T, T_i) = \frac{P(0, T_i)}{P(0, T)} exp\left[B(T, T_i)f(0, T) - \frac{\sigma^2}{4k}(1 - e^{-2kT})B(T, T_i)^2 \right]$$

$$B(T, T_i) = \frac{1 - e^{-k(T_i - T)}}{k}$$

To calculate $A(T, T_i)$, we need the instantaneous forward rate $f(0, T)$ for $T = 5$ years, which can be approximately calculated using Equation (5.39) and the spot curve in Table 5.4, as $f(0, 5) = 2.13\%$. In the previous equations, $P(0, T)$ and $P(0, T_i)$ are from Table 5.4. Using initial parameter values of $\sigma =$

0.004 and $k = 0.15$, for $T_1 = 5.5$ years, we have:

$$B(5, 5.5) = \frac{1 - e^{-0.15 \, (5.5-5)}}{0.15} = 0.48171$$

$$A(5, 5.5) = \frac{0.91551}{0.92559} exp \left[0.4817 \times 0.0213 - \frac{0.004^2}{4 \times 0.15} \right.$$

$$\left. \times (1 - e^{-2 \times 0.15 \times 5}) \times 0.4817^2 \right] = 0.99931$$

For other payment dates, $A(T, T_i)$ and $B(T, T_i)$ are calculated similarly. Next, using some initial value for r^* we need to calculate the value of $C_i \, A(T, T_i) \, e^{-B(T, T_i) r^*}$ for each cash flow C_i at time T_i and iteratively search for r^*, which makes the summation of these values for all cash flows equal to 1. The upper part of Table 5.5 summarizes the calculation needed to obtain r^*. We started with the initial value of 1% and found the final value of $r^* = 2.1434\%$.

TABLE 5.5 Calculation of value of payer European swaption using the Hull-White model, for $r^* = 2.1434\%$

T	T_i	τ_i	C_i	$f(0,T)$	$P(0,T)$	$P(0,T_i)$	$B(T,T_i)$	$A(T,T_i)$	$C_i \, A(T,T_i) \, e^{-B(T,T_i) \, r^*}$
5	5.5	0.5	0.0122	0.0213	0.92559	0.91551	0.48171	0.99931	0.01210
5	6	0.5	0.0122	0.0213	0.92559	0.90502	0.92861	0.99730	0.01196
5	6.5	0.5	0.0122	0.0213	0.92559	0.89413	1.34323	0.99401	0.01182
5	7	0.5	0.0122	0.0213	0.92559	0.88285	1.72788	0.98953	0.01167
5	7.5	0.5	0.0122	0.0213	0.92559	0.87195	2.08474	0.98474	0.01152
5	8	0.5	1.0122	0.0213	0.92559	0.86077	2.41581	0.97897	0.94094
									$\sum_i = 1.00000$

T_i	X_i	σ_{P_i}	h_i	$V_{Put \, ZB}(0, T, T_i, X_i)$	$C_i \, V_{Put \, ZB}$
5.5	0.98905	0.00310	0.02367	0.00110	0.00001
6	0.97764	0.00598	0.02655	0.00209	0.00003
6.5	0.96580	0.00865	0.02921	0.00299	0.00004
7	0.95355	0.01112	0.03169	0.00379	0.00005
7.5	0.94170	0.01342	0.03399	0.00451	0.00006
8	0.92956	0.01555	0.03612	0.00515	0.00521
					$\sum = 0.00539$

Once r^* is found, for each payment date T_i, we calculate X_i as the value at time T of a \$1 notional zero-coupon bond with maturity at T_i, when the short rate is $r^* = 2.1434\%$. For example, for $T_1 = 5.5$ years, we have:

$$X_1 = A(T, T_1)\, e^{-B(T, T_1)r^*} = 0.99931\, e^{-0.48171\times 0.021434} = 0.98905$$

X_i for other payment dates is calculated similarly. Based on this setup, the value of the payer European swaption at time $t = 0$ is obtained from the value of a portfolio of put options on zero-coupon bonds:

$$V_{t=0} = N \sum_{i=1}^{n} C_i V_{Put\ ZB}(0, T, T_i, X_i)$$

where

$$V_{Put\ ZB}(0, T, T_i, X_i) = X_i\, P(0, T)\, \Phi(-h_i + \sigma_{P_i}) - P(0, T_i)\, \Phi(-h_i)$$

$$\sigma_{P_i} = \sigma \sqrt{\frac{1 - e^{-2k\,T}}{2k}}\, B(T, T_i)$$

$$h_i = \frac{1}{\sigma_{P_i}} \ln \frac{P(0, T_i)}{P(0, T)\, X_i} + \frac{\sigma_{P_i}}{2}$$

$\Phi(.)$ is the cumulative probability distribution of standard normal distribution. For example, for $T_1 = 5.5$ years we have:

$$\sigma_{P_1} = 0.004 \times \sqrt{\frac{1 - e^{-2\times 0.15\times 5}}{2 \times 0.15}} \times 0.48171 = 0.0031$$

$$h_1 = \frac{1}{0.0031} \times \ln \frac{0.91551}{0.92559 \times 0.98905} + \frac{0.0031}{2}$$

$$= 0.02367$$

$$V_{Put\ ZB}(0, T, T_1, X_1) = 0.98905 \times 0.92559 \times \Phi(-0.0267 + 0.0031)$$

$$- 0.91551 \times \Phi(-0.02367) = 0.0011$$

$$C_1 \times V_{Put\ ZB}(0, T, T_1, X_1) = 0.0122 \times 0.0011 = 0.00001$$

The values of put options for zero-coupon bonds associated with other payment dates are calculated similarly. The lower part of Table 5.5 summarizes this calculation. Finally, the value of the swaption is the summation of values of the individual put options (the sum of the last column in the second part of Table 5.5), multiplied by the swaption notional amount:

$$V_{t=0} = 100 \times 0.00539 = 0.54$$

Therefore, based on initial parameters of $\sigma = 0.004$ and $k = 0.15$, the value of this payer European swaption at $t = 0$ using the Hull-White model is $0.54. Recall that the market value of the swaption was $1.85. Assume that we are using the calibration process (i) introduced earlier and the threshold is $0.001. Since we only used one market instrument in our example, the evaluated merit function is:

$$(V_{Model} - V_{Market})^2 = (0.54 - 1.85)^2 = 1.7240$$

As the evaluated merit function is above the threshold, we need to change the Hull-White model parameters and repeat the calculation explained earlier until the merit function threshold is reached. Using an interactive approach, we found that the Hull-White model with parameters $\sigma = 0.00945$ and $k = 0.05$ produces swaption values of $1.85, matching the Black model market value and satisfying the merit function threshold. We now have a Hull-White interest rate model with parameters $\sigma = 0.00945$ and $k = 0.05$ that is calibrated to the market based on the market value of the one payer European swaption contract we used. In practice, several swaptions with different option expirations and terms should be used in the calibration process to provide more reliable parameter values.

Calibration Using the Interest Rate Tree

Among the interest rate models we have discussed in this chapter, the Black-Karasinski model does not have closed-form analytical solutions for the price of a zero-coupon bond or an option on a zero-coupon bond. Consequently, the analytical approach explained in the previous section is not useable for this model. In order to calibrate this model we need to build an interest rate tree in each iteration of the calibration process.

We start the calibration process based on some initial parameters σ and k, and build the interest rate tree. Using this tree, market-traded instruments are valued and the merit function is evaluated and compared to the threshold. If the threshold is not reached, model parameters are changed incrementally and the process is repeated until the threshold is reached.

Here we demonstrate the calibration process of the Black-Karasinski model using an interest rate cap as the market instrument. For simplicity we consider only one caplet and calibrate the model based on the market value of this single option contract. However, in practice many rate-sensitive instruments with different characteristics (e.g., different terms) should be used in optimization of the collective merit function. Consider a caplet that caps the 3-month LIBOR. The option matures 1.25 year from now, and the term of the contract is three months. The strike or cap rate is 1% with quarterly compounding. For simplicity assume that the day count convention of this contract is 30/360. Market-quoted Black implied volatility is 23.2% and the notional amount of the contract is $10,000. Assume the spot curve is as presented in Table 5.4. We use linear interpolation to obtain spot rates that are not explicitly given in this table. The 3-month forward rate at $t = 1.25$ years is calculated as 1.0703% with continuous compounding, or 1.0717% with quarterly compounding. The current market value of this caplet based on quoted Black volatility is found using Equation (5.54), as follows:

$$t_{i-1} = 1.25, t_i = 1.5, \tau_i = 0.25, f_{i-1} = 1.0717\%, X = 1\%, \sigma_i = 0.232,$$

$$N = 10000, P(0, t_i) = 0.99049$$

$$d_1 = \frac{\ln(0.010717/0.01) + 0.232^2 \times 1.25/2}{0.232 \times \sqrt{1.25}} = 0.3968$$

$$d_2 = 0.3968 - 0.232 \times \sqrt{1.25} = 0.1374$$

$$V_{Caplet_{t=0}} = 10000 \times 0.25 \times 0.99049$$

$$\times (0.01717 \times \Phi(0.3968) - 0.01 \times \Phi(0.1374)) = 3.6282$$

The market value of this caplet at $t = 0$ using the Black model is $3.6282.

To calculate the value of this caplet using the Black-Karasinski model, we need to build an interest rate tree that extends at least until $t = 1.25$ years, with $\Delta t = 0.25$ year. Here we initialized volatility and mean reversion parameters as $\sigma = 0.2$ and $k = 0.4$. The smallest integer greater than $0.184/(k\,\Delta t) = 0.184/(0.4 \times 0.25) = 1.84$ is 2, so when $j = 2$, we need to switch from branching pattern (a) to (b) and when $j = -2$, we need to switch from branching pattern (a) to (c). Following the procedure explained in the "Black-Karasinski" section, we built the initial Black-Karasinski interest rate tree presented in Figure 5.23. The tree is fitted to the spot curve in Table 5.4.

Having the interest rate tree built, we can use the backward induction method, introduced at the beginning of this chapter, to value the caplet. The payoff of this option at the maturity at $t_{i-1} = 1.25$ years can be expressed as $Max[0, N\,\tau_i\,(r - X)]$, where r is the interest rate at a node of the tree (annual rate with quarterly compounding). Starting from nodes at 1.25 years, first consider node ($i = 5, j = 2$). From the tree, the continuous compounding annual rate at this node is 1.4654%. Converting this rate to quarterly compounding, we have:

$$r = 4(e^{(0.014654/4)} - 1) = 1.4680\%$$

The payoff at this node is:

$$Max[0, 10000 \times 0.25 \times (0.014680 - 0.01)] = 11.7011$$

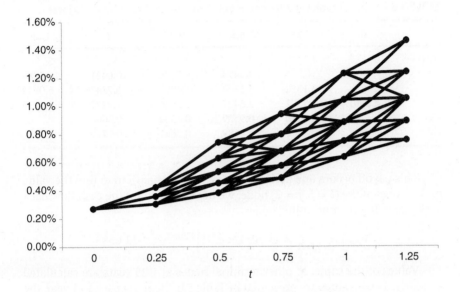

$t\rightarrow$	0	0.25	0.5	0.75	1	1.25		
$j\downarrow/i\rightarrow$	0	1	2	3	4	5		
2			0.7424%	0.9439%	1.2307%	1.4654%	P_u	0.8993
							P_m	0.0111
							P_d	0.0896
1		0.4241%	0.6295%	0.8004%	1.0436%	1.2426%	P_u	0.1236
							P_m	0.6576
							P_d	0.2188
0	0.2707%	0.3597%	0.5338%	0.6787%	0.8849%	1.0537%	P_u	0.1667
							P_m	0.6667
							P_d	0.1667
−1		0.3050%	0.4527%	0.5755%	0.7504%	0.8935%	P_u	0.2188
							P_m	0.6576
							P_d	0.1236
−2			0.3839%	0.4880%	0.6363%	0.7577%	P_u	0.0896
							P_m	0.0111
							P_d	0.8993

FIGURE 5.23 Initial Black-Karasinski tree constructed for valuation of a caplet

TABLE 5.6   Value of caplet at different nodes of the initial Black-Karasinski tree

$t\rightarrow$	0	0.25	0.5	0.75	1	1.25
$j\downarrow/i\rightarrow$	0	1	2	3	4	5
2			9.0474	9.7836	10.6421	11.6583
1		5.1652	5.3162	5.4971	5.7343	6.0943
0	2.8901	2.7372	2.5427	2.2866	1.9272	1.3736
−1		1.2386	0.9509	0.6332	0.3000	0
−2			0.4689	0.2862	0.1229	0

This payoff occurs one period later (i.e., at 1.5 years), so to find the value of the caplet at the $(i = 5, j = 2)$ node, we need to discount the cash flow back 0.25 year using the rate at this node:

$$V_{Caplet_{(i=5,j=2)}} = 11.7011 \times e^{-0.014654 \times 0.25} = 11.6583$$

Values of the caplet at other terminal nodes at 1.25 years are calculated similarly. These values are presented in Table 5.6. Stepping back to 1 year, the expected caplet value at each node is calculated using outgoing probabilities from the tree and the value of the caplet at destination nodes, discounted back 0.25 year. For example, consider node $(i = 4, j = 2)$. The upward, middle, and downward outgoing paths from this node are to nodes $(i = 5, j = 2)$, $(i = 5, j = 1)$, and $(i = 5, j = 0)$, respectively. Based on the value of the caplet at these destination nodes from Table 5.6, and using outgoing probabilities and the rate at node $(i = 4, j = 2)$ from the tree in Figure 5.23, we have:

$$V_{Caplet_{(i=4,j=2)}} = (0.8993 \times 11.6583 + 0.0111 \times 6.0943 + 0.0896 \times 1.3736)$$

$$\times e^{-0.012307 \times 0.25} = 10.6421$$

The expected values of the caplet in other nodes at $t = 1$ year are calculated similarly. This process is continued until the current value of the caplet at $t = 0$ is calculated as:

$$V_{Caplet_{(i=0,j=0)}} = (0.1667 \times 5.1652 + 0.6667 \times 2.7372 + 0.1667 \times 1.2386)$$

$$\times e^{-0.002707 \times 0.25} = 2.8901$$

where 5.1652, 2.7372, and 1.2386 are the expected values of the caplet at nodes $(i = 1, j = 1)$, $(i = 1, j = 0)$, and $(i = 1, j = -1)$, respectively, and outgoing probabilities and rates at node $(i = 0, j = 0)$ are from the tree in Figure 5.23.

Using the tree with initial parameters of $\sigma = 0.2$ and $k = 0.4$, the value of this caplet at $t = 0$ is $2.8901. Recall that the market value of the caplet was $3.6282. Assume we are using the calibration process (I) and the threshold is $0.001. Since we used only one market instrument in our example, evaluated merit function is:

$$(V_{Model} - V_{Market})^2 = (3.6282 - 2.8901)^2 = 0.5448$$

As the evaluated merit function is above the threshold, we need to change the model parameters, rebuild the interest rate tree, and repeat the valuation of the caplet using the tree until the merit function threshold is reached. We used an iterative process and found that the Black-Karasinski tree with parameters $\sigma = 0.25$ and $k = 0.1$ produces a value of $3.6290 for the caplet, where the merit function threshold is reached. This final Black-Karasinski tree is shown in Figure 5.24 and the value of the caplet at different nodes of this tree is shown in Table 5.7. Figure 5.25 presents a comparison of the initial and final Black-Karasinski trees used in the calibration process.

When calibrating an interest rate model to market instruments, it is possible to find more than one set of parameters that satisfy the threshold of the merit function. However, as the number and variety (with respect to term) of the market instruments used in calibration increase, the possibility of such a situation diminishes fast.

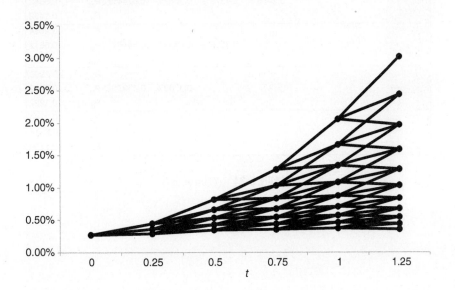

FIGURE 5.24 Final Black-Karasinski tree constructed for valuation of a caplet

$t\rightarrow$	0	0.25	0.5	0.75	1	1.25		
$j\downarrow/i\rightarrow$	0	1	2	3	4	5		
5						3.0128%	P_u	0.1126
							P_m	0.6514
							P_d	0.2360
4					2.0516%	2.4328%	P_u	0.1222
							P_m	0.6569
							P_d	0.2209
3				1.2757%	1.6566%	1.9644%	P_u	0.1324
							P_m	0.6612
							P_d	0.2064
2			0.8133%	1.0301%	1.3377%	1.5863%	P_u	0.1432
							P_m	0.6642
							P_d	0.1926
1		0.4440%	0.6567%	0.8318%	1.0802%	1.2809%	P_u	0.1546
							P_m	0.6661
							P_d	0.1793
0	0.2707%	0.3586%	0.5303%	0.6717%	0.8722%	1.0343%	P_u	0.1667
							P_m	0.6667
							P_d	0.1667
−1		0.2895%	0.4282%	0.5424%	0.7043%	0.8352%	P_u	0.1793
							P_m	0.6661
							P_d	0.1546
−2			0.3458%	0.4379%	0.5687%	0.6744%	P_u	0.1926
							P_m	0.6642
							P_d	0.1432
−3				0.3536%	0.4592%	0.5446%	P_u	0.2064
							P_m	0.6612
							P_d	0.1324
−4					0.3708%	0.4397%	P_u	0.2209
							P_m	0.6569
							P_d	0.1222
−5						0.3551%	P_u	0.2360
							P_m	0.6514
							P_d	0.1126

FIGURE 5.24   (*Continued*)

TABLE 5.7   Value of caplet at different nodes of the final Black-Karasinski tree

$t\rightarrow$	0	0.25	0.5	0.75	1	1.25
$j\downarrow/\,i\rightarrow$	0	1	2	3	4	5
5						50.2239
4					34.7923	35.7864
3				23.1393	23.6122	24.1129
2			14.2184	14.3510	14.5108	14.6768
1		7.6872	7.4813	7.2777	7.1057	7.0507
0	3.6290	3.2745	2.8678	2.3825	1.7636	0.8885
−1		1.0034	0.7120	0.4216	0.1590	0
−2			0.1014	0.0306	0	0
−3				0	0	0
−4					0	0
−5						0

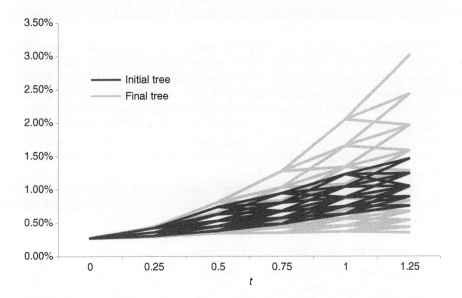

FIGURE 5.25   Comparison of initial and final Black-Karasinski interest rate trees used in the calibration process

LIBOR MARKET MODEL

The interest rate models we studied so far in this chapter were based on modeling the instantaneous spot interest rate (i.e., short rate). Short rates are not directly observable in the market. The *LIBOR market model* describes the behavior of forward rates that are directly observable in the market. These are the same LIBOR forward rates used in interest rate cap and floor contracts. Another desirable characteristic of the LIBOR market model is that the modeled forward rates have the same compounding frequency as the term of the rate (usually three months), which is the usual market convention.

The stochastic process underlying the interest rate models we have studied so far is a Markov process, where the future interest rate depends only on its current level, and the path the interest rate took in the past to get to the current level does not play a role in determination of the future rate. The LIBOR market model is a non-Markov model where the interest rate in the future depends on the path it followed in the past. The path dependency of an interest rate model is desirable when valuing financial instruments such as mortgage-backed securities, where the prepayment depends on the interest rate path. The short rate models discussed earlier in this chapter were all single-factor models, where only one source of uncertainty is assumed for the instantaneous spot interest rate. A few researchers, including Hull and White (1994), have studied two-factor models of short rate. On the other hand, the LIBOR market model in its general form is a multi-factor model where several sources of uncertainty can be incorporated in the model. The LIBOR Market model was developed by Brace, Gatarek, and Musiela (1997)[9] and Jamshidian (1997), among other researchers. Here we review a version of this model proposed by Hull and White (2000).

Assume that the reset dates of a cap contract are $t_1, t_2, t_3, \cdots, t_n$. The current time is $t_0 = 0$ and t_{n+1} is the date of the final payment. Consider the following notations:

τ_i = Year fraction between t_i and t_{i+1}: $\tau_i = t_{i+1} - t_i$.

$f_i(t)$ = Forward rate observed at time t for term τ_i between t_i and t_{i+1} with compounding period of τ_i.

$m(t)$ = Index of the next reset date from time t. For example, if t is between t_0 and t_1 then $m(t) = 1$, meaninig the next reset date is t_1.

N_q = Number of factors considered.

$\xi_{i,q}(t)$ = Component of volatility of $f_i(t)$ associated with factor q.

In this version of the LIBOR market model, it is assumed that components of volatility are independent and only functions of time. Hull and White showed the process of $f_i(t)$ is as follows:

$$df_i(t) = \sum_{j=m(t)}^{i} \frac{\tau_j f_j(t) \sum_{q=1}^{N_q} \xi_{j,q}(t)\xi_{i,q}(t)}{1 + \tau_j f_j(t)} f_i(t)dt + \sum_{q=1}^{N_q} \xi_{i,q}(t) f_i(t)\, dW_q(t)$$

(5.100)

where $dW_q(t)$ is an independent Wiener process for factor q. In the LIBOR market model, forward rates have a lognormal distribution. The forward rate that follows this process can be used to discount a cash flow from time t_{i+1} to t_i. As mentioned earlier the compounding frequency of the forward rates is the same as the term of the rate and we can discount expected cash flow one accrual period at a time using modeled forward rates. If we take the limit of Equation (5.100) when $\tau_i \to 0$, we have:

$$df(t, T) = \sum_{q=1}^{N_q} \xi_q(t, T) f(t, T) \int_{x=t}^{T} \xi_q(t,x) f(t,x)\, dx$$

$$+ \sum_{q=1}^{N_q} \xi_q(t, T) f(t, T)\, dW_q(t)$$

(5.101)

where $f(t, T)$ is the instantaneous forward rate at time t for maturity T, and $\xi_q(t, T)$ is the component of volatility of $f(t, T)$ associated with factor q. This is the *HJM model* which was originally developed by Heath, Jarrow, and Morton (1990). The HJM model is a special case of the LIBOR market model.

In this version of the LIBOR market model, Hull and White make a simplifying assumption that $\xi_{i,q}(t)$ is only a function of the number of accrual periods between the next reset date and time t_i. Assume $\lambda_{j,q}$ is the value of $\xi_{i,q}(t)$, when there are j accrual periods between the next reset date and t_i, hence:

$$\xi_{i,q}(t) = \lambda_{i-m(t),q}$$

(5.102)

Defining Λ_j as the total volatility of the forward rate $f_i(t)$ when there are j accrual periods until time t_i, we have:

$$\Lambda_j = \sqrt{\sum_{q=1}^{N_q} \lambda_{j,q}^2}$$

(5.103)

Λ_j are found from the market volatilities of traded contracts (e.g., caps and floors), and $\lambda_{j,q}$ are found such that Equation (5.103) holds. The LIBOR market model is implemented using Monte Carlo simulation. Using the $\lambda_{j,q}$ notation introduced previously and based on the assumption of a constant drift for $\ln f_i$

for time period t_k to t_{k+1}, Hull and White provided the following discretization of the model, which can be used in generating simulated interest rate paths:

$$
f_i(t_{k+1}) = f_i(t_k) \, Exp \left[\left(\sum_{j=k+1}^{i} \frac{\tau_j f_j(t_k) \sum_{q=1}^{N_q} \lambda_{j-k-1,q} \lambda_{i-k-1,q}}{1 + \tau_j f_j(t_k)} - \sum_{q=1}^{N_q} \frac{\lambda_{i-k-1,q}^2}{2} \right) \tau_k \right.
$$

$$
\left. + \sum_{q=1}^{N_q} \lambda_{i-k-1,q} \, \varepsilon_q \, \sqrt{\tau_k} \right] \tag{5.104}
$$

where ε_q are independent random draws from the standard normal distribution. In order to use the LIBOR market model, we first need to find values of Λ_j from volatilities observed in the market from traded cap and floor contracts. After that, each Λ_j needs to be split into $\lambda_{j,q}$. Hull and White used principal component analysis and historical data to derive $\lambda_{j,q}$ from Λ_j. This leads to the following relationship between $\lambda_{j,q}$ and Λ_j:

$$
\lambda_{j,q} = \frac{\Lambda_j \, s_q \, \alpha_{j,q}}{\sqrt{\sum_{q=1}^{N_q} s_q^2 \, \alpha_{i,q}^2}} \tag{5.105}
$$

where s_q is the standard deviation of the qth factor score and $\alpha_{j,q}$ is the factor loading for the qth factor and jth forward rate.[10] We can use a similar approach explained for calibration of short rate models to derive Λ_j from market volatilities. This based on minimization of a merit function, such as the sum of squared differences between market values of cap or floor contracts and values obtained from the model.

Example

To demonstrate the use of the LIBOR market model in generating a simulated interest rate path, consider that the current 3-month forward rates (i.e., as of $t_0 = 0$) with quarterly compounding for five quarters are as follows:

t:	t_0	t_1	t_2	t_3	t_4
$f_i(t_0)$:	0.29%	0.30%	0.35%	0.36%	0.37%

For simplicity assume that $\tau_i = \tau = 0.25$ year as terms of all rates. Here we consider one factor only (i.e., $N_q = 1$). The principal component analysis resulted in the following $\lambda_{i,q}$ values:

t:	t_0	t_1	t_2	t_3	t_4
$\lambda_{i,q}$:	0.35	0.34	0.36	0.33	0.32

Table 5.8 shows the current forward rate as of $t_0 = 0$ and the simulated forward rate as seen at times $t_1 = 0.25, t_2 = 0.5, t_3 = 0.75$, and $t_4 = 1$, for the first iteration of simulation. As we move through the times, the number of simulated forward rates is reduced by one, since the as-of date of the forward rate is advancing by one period. The first row of Table 5.8 is available from current forward rates and no simulation is needed. We start the calculation from the first rate of the second row, where $k + 1 = 1$ and $i = 1$, that is, $f_1(t_1)$. This is the forward rate as seen at time t_1, from time t_1 to t_2. Since here we consider only one factor ($N_q = 1$), from Equation (5.104) we have:

$$f_1(t_1) = f_1(t_0)\, Exp\left[\left(\frac{\tau f_1(t_0)\, \lambda_{0,q}\, \lambda_{0,q}}{1 + \tau f_1(t_0)} - \frac{\lambda_{0,q}^2}{2}\right)\tau_k + \lambda_{0,q}\, \varepsilon_q\, \sqrt{\tau}\right]$$

TABLE 5.8 Simulated forward rates using the LIBOR market model: iteration 1 (rates in %)

$k\downarrow$	$k+1\downarrow$	$i\rightarrow$	$t\rightarrow$ 0 t_0 0	0.25 t_1 1	0.5 t_2 2	0.75 t_3 3	1 t_4 4
	0	$f_i(t_0)$:	**0.29000**	0.30000	0.35000	0.36000	0.37000
0	1	$f_i(t_1)$:		**0.23697**	0.35496	0.37421	0.42410
1	2	$f_i(t_2)$:			**0.41809**	0.30533	0.60618
2	3	$f_i(t_3)$:				**0.29415**	0.50508
3	4	$f_i(t_4)$:					**0.72600**

Assume that an independent draw from the standard normal distribution resulted in $\varepsilon_q = -1.272418$. Using $\lambda_{0,q} = 0.35, \tau = 0.25$ and $f_1(t_0) =$

(continued)

(*continued*)

0.30% (current forward rate from time t_1 to t_2), we can calculate the simulated forward rate as seen at time t_1, from time t_1 to t_2 as:

$$f_1(t_1) = 0.0030 \times Exp\left[\left(\frac{0.25 \times 0.0030 \times 0.35 \times 0.35}{1 + 0.25 \times 0.0030} - \frac{0.35^2}{2}\right)\right.$$

$$\left. \times 0.25 + 0.35 \times (-1.272418) \times \sqrt{0.25}\right] = 0.002367$$

So $f_1(t_1) = 0.23697\%$. For the second rate of the second row in Table 5.8 we have $k + 1 = 1$ and $i = 2$, that is, $f_2(t_1)$. This is the forward rate as seen at time t_1 for time t_2 to t_3. Using Equation (5.104) we have:

$$f_2(t_1) = f_2(t_0)\, Exp\left[\left(\sum_{j=1}^{2} \frac{\tau\, f_j(t_0)\, \lambda_{j-1,q}\lambda_{1,q}}{1 + \tau\, f_j(t_0)} - \frac{\lambda_{1,q}^2}{2}\right)\tau + \lambda_{1,q}\, \varepsilon_q\, \sqrt{\tau}\right]$$

or

$$f_2(t_1)$$

$$= f_2(t_0)\, Exp\left[\left(\frac{\tau\, f_1(t_0)\, \lambda_{0,q}\, \lambda_{1,q}}{1 + \tau\, f_1(t_0)} + \frac{\tau\, f_2(t_0)\, \lambda_{1,q}\, \lambda_{1,q}}{1 + \tau\, f_2(t_0)} - \frac{\lambda_{1,q}^2}{2}\right)\tau + \lambda_{1,q}\, \varepsilon_q\, \sqrt{\tau}\right]$$

If an independent draw from the standard normal distribution is $\varepsilon_q = 0.141829$, using $\tau = 0.25$, $\lambda_{0,q} = 0.35$, $\lambda_{1,q} = 0.34$, $f_1(t_0) = 0.30\%$ and $f_2(t_0) = 0.35\%$, we can calculate the simulated forward rate as seen at time t_1, from time t_2 to t_3 as $f_2(t_1) = 0.35496\%$. Following the same method, $f_3(t_1)$ and $f_4(t_1)$ are calculated as 0.37421% and 0.42410%, respectively. Therefore the simulated forward rates as seen at time t_1 in the first iteration of the simulation are:

t:	t_1	t_2	t_3	t_4
$f_i(t_1)$:	0.23697%	0.35496%	0.37421%	0.42410%

Notice that since these simulated forward rates are as seen at time t_1 there is no rate for time t_0. After obtaining the simulated rate as of t_1 we can move to the third row of Table 5.8 to calculate simulated forward rates as seen at time t_2. Focusing on the first rate, we have $k + 1 = 2$ and $i = 2$, that is, $f_2(t_2)$. This is the simulated forward rate as seen at time t_2, from time t_2 to t_3. From Equation (5.104), we have:

$$f_2(t_2) = f_2(t_1) \, Exp \left[\left(\frac{\tau f_2(t_1) \, \lambda_{0,q} \lambda_{0,q}}{1 + \tau f_2(t_1)} - \frac{\lambda_{0,q}^2}{2} \right) \tau + \lambda_{0,q} \, \varepsilon_q \, \sqrt{\tau} \right]$$

Using $\tau = 0.25$, an independent draw from the standard normal distribution of $\varepsilon_q = 1.008727$, $\lambda_{0,q} = 0.35$, and $f_2(t_1) = 0.35496\%$ obtained in the previous step, we can calculate the simulated forward rate as seen at time t_2, from time t_2 to t_3 as $f_2(t_2) = 0.41809\%$. Simulated forward rates $f_3(t_2)$ and $f_4(t_2)$ for the first iteration of simulation are obtained similarly:

t:	t_2	t_3	t_4
$f_i(t_2)$:	0.41809%	0.30533%	0.60618%

Using a similar method we can obtain simulated forward rates as seen at time t_3 and t_4 to complete Table 5.8. This table provides one iteration of simulated forward rates based on the LIBOR market model. This process can be repeated for a large number of simulation iterations to produce many interest rate paths. Simulated interest rate paths generated from the LIBOR market model can be used for valuation of derivatives, mortgage-backed securities, and other financial instruments.

SUMMARY

- An interest rate model is a mathematical construct that characterizes the movement of an interest rate over a period of time.
- The instantaneous forward rate at a time t is the rate in the future with a very short term, as seen at time t. The instantaneous spot rate or short rate at time t is the spot rate at time t with a very short term. Equivalently it is the instantaneous forward rate at time t, prevailing at time t.
- An affine term structure model is a type of interest rate model where the spot rate is an affine function of a short rate.
- In quantitative finance, spot rates are often represented using prices of zero-coupon bonds.

- Mean reversion is a property of an interest rate model where short rates generated by the stochastic model move toward a long-term level.
- The Vasicek model is an affine term structure model with mean reversion property, but it is not necessarily an arbitrage-free model. It has two parameters: the speed that short rate approaches the long-term level and the volatility. In the Vasicek model, the short rate has normal distribution.
- Hull-White is an affine term structure model with mean reversion property and it is an arbitrage-free model. The Hull-White one-factor model can be considered as an extension of the Vasicek model, where the initial term structure of interest rate is an input. It has two parameters: the speed that the short rate approaches the long-term level and the volatility. In the Hull-White model the short rate has normal distribution.
- Ho-Lee interest rate model is an affine term structure model without mean reversion property, but it is an arbitrage-free model. It can be considered as a special case of the Hull-White model where the speed parameter is zero, so it has only one volatility parameter. In the Ho-Lee model the short rate has normal distribution.
- Short rates produced by the Vasicek, Hull-White, and Ho-Lee models can be negative.
- The Black-Karasinski interest rate model is not an affine term structure model but it has the mean reversion property and it is an arbitrage-free model. In Black-Karasinski model short rate has lognormal distribution; hence short rates produced by this model are positive.
- The Vasicek, Hull-White, and Ho-Lee models are affine term structure models, and there are analytical solutions for prices of zero-coupon bonds based on these models. The Black-Karasinski is not an affine term structure model, so there is no closed-form solution for prices of zero-coupon bonds based on that model.
- A discrete version of an interest rate model can be used in Monte-Carlo simulation approach in valuation of financial instruments.
- A European swaption contract is a bilateral agreement where the buyer, in exchange of a premium, receives the right, but not the obligation, to enter into a specific swap contract at a specific time in the future. The Black model can be used to find the value of a swaption contract.
- The market convention for a European swaption contract is to quote its at-the-money implied Black volatility.
- The interest rate cap is a bilateral contract where one side, in exchange of an upfront premium, agrees to pay the other side at specific times in the future if a reference rate exceeds a predetermined level, known as strike or cap rate.
- An interest rate floor is a bilateral contract where one side, in exchange of an upfront premium, agrees to pay the other side at specific times in

the future if a reference rate falls below a predetermined level, known as strike or floor rate.

- An interest rate cap contract can be considered as a portfolio of call options on the reference interest rate, known as caplets.
- An interest rate floor contract can be considered as a portfolio of put options on the reference interest rate, known as floorlets.
- The market convention for cap and floor contracts is to quote its at-the-money implied Black volatility.
- An interest rate tree or lattice model is a discrete-time representation of a continuous-time interest rate model. An interest rate tree consists of one or mode nodes at each discrete time and paths that connect nodes.
- Hull-White and Black-Karasinski trinomial trees are commonly used in the valuation of financial instruments with embedded optionality.
- The common method in construction of an arbitrage-free interest rate tree is to first create a tree that captures the stochastic nature of the interest rate movement and then in the second stage shift the tree to incorporate the current spot curve and become arbitrage-free.
- Calibration of an interest rate model is the process of obtaining appropriate values for parameters of the model. There are two approaches for the calibration of interest rate models: using historical rates and using current market prices of financial instruments.
- One way to estimate the parameters of an interest rate tree is to choose an observable interest rate index as the proxy for the short rate and then using a statistical estimation technique find parameter values that best fit the historical values of the selected interest rate index.
- In using current market prices in calibration process, parameters of the model are selected such that when the model is used for valuation of market-traded instruments, it produces the closest values to the current market values of the instruments.
- The LIBOR market model is a non-Markov model that can incorporate multiple sources of uncertainty. It captures the behavior of forward rates that are directly observable in the market.

ANNEX: DERIVATION OF ZERO-COUPON BOND PRICE USING A ΔT-PERIOD RATE FROM THE HULL-WHITE TREE

We derived the relations between short rate $r(t)$ and Δt-period interest rate $R(t)$ obtained from an interest rate tree as:

$$r(t) = \frac{R(t)\Delta t + \ln A(t, t + \Delta t)}{B(t, t + \Delta t)}$$

From Equation (5.17) we have:

$$P(t, T) = A(t, T)e^{-B(t,T)\ r(t)}$$

$$P(t, T) = A(t, T)e^{-B(t,T)\ \frac{R(t)\Delta t + \ln A(t,t+\Delta t)}{B(t,t+\Delta t)}} = A(t, T)e^{-\frac{B(t,T)\ln A(t,t+\Delta t)}{B(t,t+\Delta t)}}e^{-\frac{B(t,T)\ \Delta t\ R(t)}{B(t,t+\Delta t)}}$$

Therefore we can rewrite the equation for $P(t, T)$ as:

$$P(t, T) = \widehat{A}(t, T)e^{-\widehat{B}(t,T)\ R(t)}$$

where:

$$\widehat{B}(t, T) = \frac{B(t, T)\ \Delta t}{B(t, t + \Delta t)}$$

and

$$\widehat{A}(t, T) = A(t, T)e^{-\frac{B(t,T)\ln A(t,t+\Delta t)}{B(t,t+\Delta t)}}$$

By taking the natural logarithm from both sides of this equation, we have:

$$\ln \widehat{A}(t, T) = \ln A(t, T) - \frac{B(t, T)\ln A(t, t + \Delta t)}{B(t, t + \Delta t)}$$

Based on Equation (5.36) expression for $A(t, T)$ in the Hull-White model is:

$$A(t, T) = \frac{P(0, T)}{P(0, t)}exp\left[B(t, T)f(0, t) - \frac{\sigma^2}{4k}(1 - e^{-2kt})B(t, T^2)\right]$$

or

$$\ln A(t, T) = \ln \frac{P(0, T)}{P(0, t)} + B(t, T)f(0, t) - \frac{\sigma^2}{4k}(1 - e^{-2kt})B(t, T)^2$$

Therefore:

$$\ln \widehat{A}(t, T) = \ln \frac{P(0, T)}{P(0, t)} + B(t, T)f(0, t) - \frac{\sigma^2}{4k}(1 - e^{-2kt})B(t, T)^2$$
$$- \frac{B(t, T)}{B(t, t + \Delta t)}\left[\ln \frac{P(0, t + \Delta t)}{P(0, t)}\right.$$
$$\left. + B(t, t + \Delta t)f(0, t) - \frac{\sigma^2}{4k}(1 - e^{-2kt})B(t, t + \Delta t^2)\right]$$

$$\ln \hat{A}(t, T) = \ln \frac{P(0, T)}{P(0, t)} - \frac{B(t, T)}{B(t, t + \Delta t)} \ln \frac{P(0, t + \Delta t)}{P(0, t)} - \frac{\sigma^2}{4k}(1 - e^{-2kt})B(t, T)^2$$

$$+ B(t, T)\left(\frac{\sigma^2}{4k}\right)(1 - e^{-2kt})B(t, t + \Delta t)$$

$$\ln \hat{A}(t, T) = \ln \frac{P(0, T)}{P(0, t)} - \frac{B(t, T)}{B(t, t + \Delta t)} \ln \frac{P(0, t + \Delta t)}{P(0, t)}$$

$$- \frac{\sigma^2}{4k}(1 - e^{-2kt})B(t, T)[B(t, T) - B(t, t + \Delta t)]$$

or

$$\hat{A}(t, T) = exp\left[\ln \frac{P(0, T)}{P(0, t)} - \frac{B(t, T)}{B(t, t + \Delta t)} \ln \frac{P(0, t + \Delta t)}{P(0, t)}\right.$$

$$\left. - \frac{\sigma^2}{4k}(1 - e^{-2kt})B(t, T)[B(t, T) - B(t, t + \Delta t)]\right]$$

where:

$$B(t, T) = \frac{1 - e^{-k(T-t)}}{k}$$

$$B(t, t + \Delta t) = \frac{1 - e^{-k \, \Delta t}}{k}$$

Note that $\hat{A}(t, T)$ as derived above is independent of the instantaneous forward rate $f(0, t)$. This is a desirable case since the forward rate is sensitive to the shape of the spot curve and can vary significantly, depending on the interpolation method used to build the spot curve.

NOTES

1. If the term of the forward rates is not short, this curve is referred to as the *forward curve*.
2. Generally speaking, an affine function is a function comprised of a linear function and a constant.
3. Some market participants assume different volatilities for each caplet of a cap contract.
4. In this section we use the notations *ZB* for zero-coupon bond and *CB* for coupon-bearing bond.

5. If we ignore terms of a higher order than Δt, the approximate equations for M and V are: $M = -k\,\Delta t$ and $V = \sigma^2 \Delta t$.

6. When k is negative, the condition to switch is reversed: we switch from branching pattern (a) to (b) when j reaches the smallest integer less than $-0.184/(k\,\Delta t)$, and we switch from branching pattern (a) to (c) when j reaches the smallest integer greater than $0.184/(k\,\Delta t)$.

7. In practice, a shorter time step is selected, for example, one month. It is also possible to have a varying time step in a trinomial tree, with a shorter time step at the beginning of the tree and gradual increases in the length of the time step as the tree evolves over time.

8. Microsoft® Excel Solver can be used to solve this equation.

9. Sometimes the LIBOR market model is referred to as the BGM model.

10. The fundamentals of principal component analysis are explained in this book's Appendix.

BIBLIOGRAPHY

Black, Fischer, and Piotr Karasinski. "Bond and Option Pricing When Short Rates Are Lognormal." *Financial Analysis Journal* 47 (1991): 52–59.

Brace, Alan, Dariusz Gatarek, and Marek Musiela. "The Market Model of Interest Rate Dynamics." *Mathematical Finance* 2, no. 2 (1997): 127–147.

Brigo, Damiano, and Fabio Mercurio. *Interest Rate Models, Theory and Practice*. New York: Springer, 2001.

Cox, John C., Jonathan E. Ingersoll, Jr., and Stephen A. Ross. "A Theory of the Term Structure of Interest Rates." *Econometrica* 53, no. 2 (1985): 385–407.

Heath, David, Robert Jarrow, and Andrew Morton. "Bond Pricing and the Term Structure of Interest Rates: A Discrete Time Approximation." *Journal of Financial and Quantitative Analysis* 25, no. 4 (1990): 419–440.

Ho, Thomas S. Y., and Sang-Bin Lee. "Term Structure Movements and Pricing Interest Rate Contingent Claims. *Journal of Finance* 41 (1986): 1011–1029.

Hull, John C. *Options, Futures, and Other Derivatives*, 6th ed. Upper Saddle River, NJ: Prentice-Hall, 2005.

Hull, John C., and Alan D. White. "Forward Rate Volatilities, Swap Rate Volatilities, and Implementation of the LIBOR Market Model." *Journal of Fixed Income* 10, no. 2 (2000): 46–62.

Hull, John C., and Alan D. White. "The General Hull-White Model and Supercalibration." *Financial Analysts Journal* 57, no. 6 (2001): 34–43.

Hull, John C., and Alan D. White. "Numerical Procedures for Implementing Term Structure Models I: Single Factor Models." *Journal of Derivatives* 2, no. 1 (1994): 7–16.

Hull, John C., and Alan D. White. "Numerical Procedures for Implementing Term Structure Models II: Two-Factor Models." *Journal of Derivatives* 2, no. 2 (1994): 37–48.

Hull, John C., and A. White. "Pricing Interest Rate Derivative Securities." *Review of Financial Studies* 3, no. 4 (1990): 573–592.

Hull, John C., and Alan D. White. "Using Hull-White Interest Rate Trees." *Journal of Derivatives* 3, no. 3 (1996): 26–36.

Jamshidian, Farshid. "An Exact Bond Option Pricing Formula." *The Journal of Finance* 44, no. 1 (1989).

Jamshidian, Farshid. "LIBOR and Swap Market Models and Measures." *Finance and Stochastics* 1 (1997): 293–330.

Ross, Sheldon. *Introduction to Probability Models,* 7th ed. New York: Academic Press, 2000.

Vasicek, Oldrich. "An Equilibrium Characterization of the Term Structure. *Journal of Financial Economics* 5 (1977): 177–188.

CHAPTER 6

Valuation of Bonds with Embedded Options

I n Chapter 3 we introduced the discounted cash flow technique as the fundamental method for valuation of fixed-income securities. When cash flows of a bond at the valuation date are known, as is the case for a fixed-rate bond, the valuation is straightforward. For a floating-rate bond, future cash flows are not known at the present date but can be estimated using forecasted interest rates. Once the cash flows are estimated, the value of the bond can be obtained using the discounted cash flow method. An alternative approach in valuation of a floating-rate bond is to use the Monte Carlo simulation method, explained in a previous chapter. A callable or a putable bond has an embedded option that allows the issuer or the investor to terminate the bond earlier than its stated maturity, if certain conditions are met. Exercise of such an option can materially change the future cash flows and because of this the discounted cash flow method by itself is not a suitable valuation technique for bonds with embedded options. In this chapter we explain the use of the interest rate tree, introduced in the previous chapter, in valuation of callable and putable bonds.

CALLABLE BOND

A *callable bond* is a type of bond that is redeemable by the issuer prior to its maturity date. The issuer of a callable bond includes the call option in the structure of the note to protect against the risk of a fall in the interest rate. The issuer of a fixed-rate option-free bond is obligated to pay the contractual coupon rate even when the interest rate falls. In a declining interest rate environment, the embedded call option of the bond provides the issuer with the ability to call the bond, terminate it, and, if needed, issue a new bond with a lower coupon rate. Therefore, the ability to redeem a bond before its stated maturity date is an option held by the issuer and hence the value of this option is reflected in the bond value.

A callable bond has a *call price* and a *call date* in addition to all other contractual characteristics of a bond. Call date is the framework that defines the timing in which the issuer can call the bond. A call date could be in the form of a single date after which the issuer has the right, but not the obligation, to call the bond. For example, a callable bond is callable after one year from the issuance date. Call date can also be in the form of a schedule of several dates. Call price defines the other condition that makes a bond eligible to call. For example, based on the call date or call schedule, the issuer has the right, but not the obligation, to call the bond when its market price increases above the call price.

Due to the embedded call option, the future cash flows of a callable bond are uncertain and thus the simple discounted cash flow method is unsuitable for its valuation. One common method to value a callable bond is the use of an interest rate tree. In Chapter 5 we discussed interest rate trees based on Hull-White and Black-Karasinski models. In this section we use an interest rate tree to demonstrate the valuation of a callable bond. Aside from the interest rate environment, an issuer may consider other broad economic factors and idiosyncratic issues, including cost of new issuance and replacement of the bond, before calling a bond. Here we assume a simple call rule that the issuer exercises the call option when the bond price rises above the call price.

Consider a callable bond with a notional amount of \$1 million. To simplify the notation we use \$100 as the notional amount of this bond. The calculated value of the bond can then be multiplied by 10,000 to obtain the dollar value of the bond. The bond has a 6.5% coupon with quarterly payment frequency and a 30/360 day count convention. The original bond had a term of two years and at analysis date ($t = 0$) it has one year remaining to maturity. This bond is callable during the second year of its term and for simplicity here we assume that the bond is callable at payment dates of $t = 0.25, 0.5,$ and 0.75 year. $t = 1$ year is the maturity date of the bond and at that time the principal amount is repaid. In this example the call price is assumed as \$101.

The first step of valuation of this callable bond is to construct an interest tree with a horizon of at least one year. We use a Black-Karasinski interest rate tree with a quarterly time step to demonstrate the valuation of this bond. In practice a shorter time step, such as monthly or weekly, is preferred to obtain more accurate results. Table 6.1 presents the spot curve assumed in our example with continuous compounding and Figure 6.1 shows the Black-Karasinski interest rate tree constructed based on this spot curve using volatility and drift parameters of $\sigma = 0.35$ and $k = 0.1$. The tree has a 1.25-year horizon. Recall from Chapter 5 that rates produced by a Black-Karasinski model are always positive. Table 6.2 presents the branching probability of the tree in Figure 6.1, where j is the vertical index of tree nodes. See Chapter 5 for details on how to build and calibrate a Black-Karasinski interest rate tree.

For valuation of a bond with an embedded option using an interest rate tree we can use the *backward induction technique*. We introduced this method

TABLE 6.1 Assumed spot rate for examples of valuation of callable and putable bonds (annualized rates with continuous compounding)

Term	Rate
3M	2.37%
6M	2.82%
9M	*3.04%*
1Y	3.26%
1.25Y	*3.60%*
1.5Y	*3.74%*
1.75Y	*4.27%*
2Y	*4.61%*

in a previous chapter and used it to calculate the value of an option contract. In the backward induction method we start from the nodes at the end of the tree at the maturity date (in our example, $t = 1$ year) and calculate the expectation of discounted values of cash flows going backward one time step at a time toward the current time ($t = 0$). In our example, the time step is $\Delta t = 0.25$ year. In this process periodic discount factors are calculated using the Δt-period rates at each node of the tree and branching probabilities are used in calculating expected values. If the instrument has embedded optionality, the possibility of option exercise and its impact on the cash flows is evaluated at each node. Figure 6.2 presents the valuation of the callable bond in our example. Each box in this figure presents one node of the tree. Starting from $t = 1$ year, the valuation process is as follows:

$t = 1$ year:

The interest rate tree has nine nodes at this time: nodes 17 to 25. This is the maturity date of the bond so the principal cash flow of $100 is repaid at each node. Also the last coupon payment occurs at $t = 1$. The amount of every coupon payment of this bond based on a 30/360 accrual basis is calculated as:

$$100 \times \frac{6.5}{100} \times \frac{90}{360} = 1.625$$

Total cash flow at each terminating node is $100 + $1.625 = $101.625. Since $t = 1$ is the maturity date of the bond, no decision is needed regarding the call option.

$t = 0.75$ year:

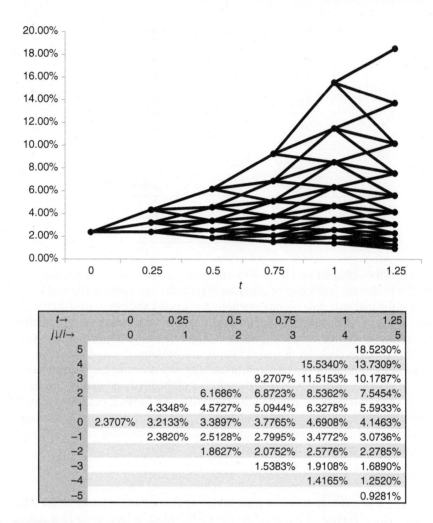

$t\rightarrow$	0	0.25	0.5	0.75	1	1.25
$j\downarrow/i\rightarrow$	0	1	2	3	4	5
5						18.5230%
4					15.5340%	13.7309%
3				9.2707%	11.5153%	10.1787%
2			6.1686%	6.8723%	8.5362%	7.5454%
1		4.3348%	4.5727%	5.0944%	6.3278%	5.5933%
0	2.3707%	3.2133%	3.3897%	3.7765%	4.6908%	4.1463%
−1		2.3820%	2.5128%	2.7995%	3.4772%	3.0736%
−2			1.8627%	2.0752%	2.5776%	2.2785%
−3				1.5383%	1.9108%	1.6890%
−4					1.4165%	1.2520%
−5						0.9281%

FIGURE 6.1   Black-Karasinski interest rate tree with a 1.25-year time horizon and 0.25-year time step, $\sigma = 0.35$ and $k = 0.1$

The interest rate tree has seven nodes at this time: nodes 10 to 16. At each node we need to evaluate three items:

i. Discounted value of expected future cash flows at following (destination) nodes
ii. The impact of the call option exercise
iii. The value of the bond at current node, including the coupon payment

TABLE 6.2 Probability of branching for the interest rate tree in Figure 6.1 (j is vertical index of each node)

$j\downarrow$		Prob.	$j\downarrow$		Prob.	$j\downarrow$		Prob.
5	P_u	0.112561	-1	P_u	0.179317	0	P_u	0.166667
	P_m	0.651427		P_m	0.666057		P_m	0.666667
	P_d	0.236012		P_d	0.154626		P_d	0.166667
4	P_u	0.122163	-2	P_u	0.192576			
	P_m	0.656913		P_m	0.664228			
	P_d	0.220924		P_d	0.143196			
3	P_u	0.132375	-3	P_u	0.206445			
	P_m	0.661180		P_m	0.66118			
	P_d	0.206445		P_d	0.132375			
2	P_u	0.143196	-4	P_u	0.220924			
	P_m	0.664228		P_m	0.656913			
	P_d	0.192576		P_d	0.122163			
1	P_u	0.154626	-5	P_u	0.236012			
	P_m	0.666057		P_m	0.651427			
	P_d	0.179317		P_d	0.112561			

Consider node 10. The following nodes that branched out from node 10 are nodes 17, 18, and 19. Total cash flow at each of these nodes is $101.625. To discount these cash flow back to node 10, we use the rate at the originating node. Node 10 is at the $i = 3$ and $j = 3$ position of our interest rate tree so $r_{Node\ 10} = 9.2707\%$. Hence the discount factor is calculated as: $DF_{Node\ 10} = e^{-0.092707\times0.25} = 0.977090$.

The expected cash flows at following (destination) nodes discounted back to the originating node is obtained by multiplying: (a) the outgoing branching probability from the originating node, (b) total cash flow at the destination node, and (c) the discount factor at the originating node, and summing the results over all destination nodes. Hence discounted expected future cash flows at node 10 are calculated as:

$$E[\text{discounted future cash flows}]_{Node\ 10}$$

$$= 0.132375 \times 0.977090 \times 101.625$$

$$+ 0.661180 \times 0.977090 \times 101.625$$

$$+ 0.206445 \times 0.977090 \times 101.625 = 99.2967$$

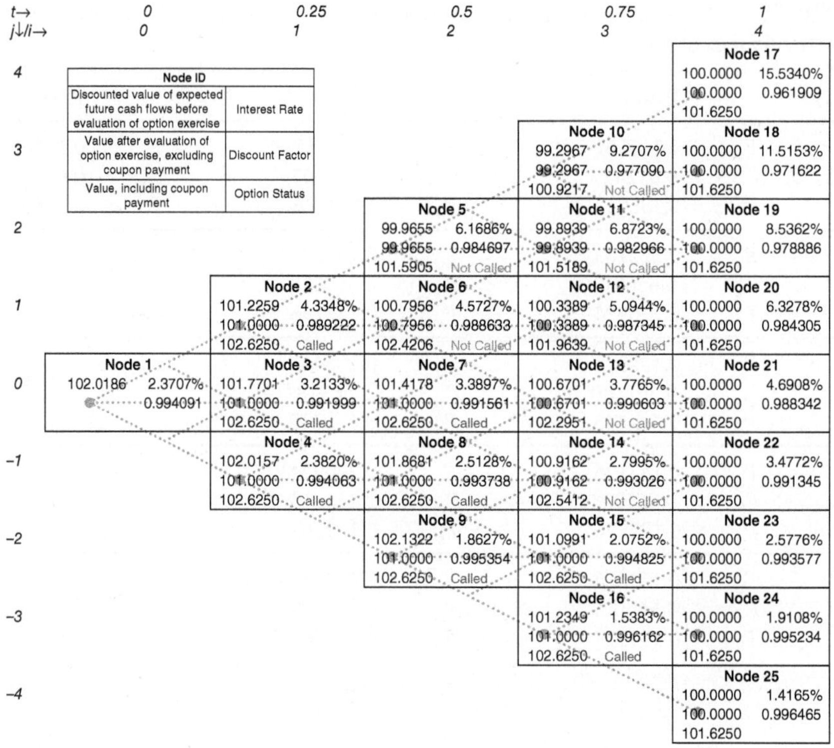

$t \rightarrow$	0	0.25	0.5	0.75	1
$j\downarrow/i \rightarrow$	0	1	2	3	4

Legend box:

Node ID	
Discounted value of expected future cash flows before evaluation of option exercise	Interest Rate
Value after evaluation of option exercise, excluding coupon payment	Discount Factor
Value, including coupon payment	Option Status

4

Node 17
100.0000 15.5340%
100.0000 0.961909
101.6250

3

Node 10
99.2967 9.2707%
99.2967 0.977090
100.9217 Not Called

Node 18
100.0000 11.5153%
100.0000 0.971622
101.6250

2

Node 5
99.9655 6.1686%
99.9655 0.984697
101.5905 Not Called

Node 11
99.8939 6.8723%
99.8939 0.982966
101.5189 Not Called

Node 19
100.0000 8.5362%
100.0000 0.978886
101.6250

1

Node 2
101.2259 4.3348%
101.0000 0.989222
102.6250 Called

Node 6
100.7956 4.5727%
100.7956 0.988633
102.4206 Not Called

Node 12
100.3389 5.0944%
100.3389 0.987345
101.9639 Not Called

Node 20
100.0000 6.3278%
100.0000 0.984305
101.6250

0

Node 1
102.0186 2.3707%
0.994091

Node 3
101.7701 3.2133%
101.0000 0.991999
102.6250 Called

Node 7
101.4178 3.3897%
101.0000 0.991561
102.6250 Called

Node 13
100.6701 3.7765%
100.6701 0.990603
102.2951 Not Called

Node 21
100.0000 4.6908%
100.0000 0.988342
101.6250

−1

Node 4
102.0157 2.3820%
101.0000 0.994063
102.6250 Called

Node 8
101.8681 2.5128%
101.0000 0.993738
102.6250 Called

Node 14
100.9162 2.7995%
100.9162 0.993026
102.5412 Not Called

Node 22
100.0000 3.4772%
100.0000 0.991345
101.6250

−2

Node 9
102.1322 1.8627%
101.0000 0.995354
102.6250 Called

Node 15
101.0991 2.0752%
101.0000 0.994825
102.6250 Called

Node 23
100.0000 2.5776%
100.0000 0.993577
101.6250

−3

Node 16
101.2349 1.5383%
101.0000 0.996162
102.6250 Called

Node 24
100.0000 1.9108%
100.0000 0.995234
101.6250

−4

Node 25
100.0000 1.4165%
100.0000 0.996465
101.6250

FIGURE 6.2 Valuation of a callable bond using an interest rate tree

where 0.132375, 0.661180, and 0.206445 are the outgoing branching probabilities for node 10 ($j = 3$) from Table 6.2.

Since this bond is callable at $t = 0.25$, $t = 0.5$, and $t = 0.75$, the exercise of the call option should be evaluated at each node located in these dates. To evaluate the call option exercise at node 10 we need to compare the discounted expected future cash flows obtained above (i.e., \$99.2967) with the bond's call price of \$101. Based on the call rule of this bond and since \$99.2967 is less than \$101, the bond is not called at this node.

The coupon payment at this node is \$1.625. Therefore, the value of the bond at node 10 is the summation of the discounted expected future cash flows from following nodes and the coupon payment at the current node: \$99.2967 + \$1.625 = \$100.9217. Each box in Figure 6.2 contains items (i), (ii), and (iii) explained earlier, along with the node interest rate, discount factor, and call option status. For node 10 these values are:

Node 10	
Discounted value of expected future cash flows *before* evaluation of option exercise: **99.2967**	Interest rate: **9.2707%**
Value *after* evaluation of option exercise, excluding coupon payment: **99.2967**	Discount factor: **0.977090**
Value, including coupon payment: **100.9217**	Option status: **Not Called**

The values of the bond at nodes 12, 13, and 14 are calculated similarly.

At nodes 15 and 16 the bond is called. Consider node 16. This node is followed by nodes 23, 24, and 25 with a cash flow of $101.625 at each. The rate at node 16 is 1.5383%. Therefore, the discount factor and expected future cash flows at this node are calculated as:

$$DF_{Node\ 16} = e^{-0.015383 \times 0.25} = 0.996162$$

$E[\text{discounted future cash flows}]_{Node\ 16}$

$$= 0.206445 \times 0.996162 \times 101.625$$

$$+ 0.661180 \times 0.996162 \times 101.625$$

$$+ 0.132375 \times 0.996162 \times 101.625 = 101.2349$$

where 0.206445, 0.661180, and 0.132375 are the outgoing branching probabilities for node 16 ($j = -3$) from Table 6.2. Since $101.2349 is more than the call price of $101 the call option is exercised at this node and the bond is redeemed at the call price of $101. To value the bond at node 16 we need to use the call price instead of the discounted expected future cash flows. Hence the value of the bond at this node is the summation of the call price and the coupon payment: $101 + $1.625 = $102.625. In Figure 6.2 the box for node 16 contains the following information:

Node 16	
Discounted value of expected future cash flows *before* evaluation of option exercise: **101.2349**	Interest rate: **1.5383%**
Value *after* evaluation of option exercise, excluding coupon payment: **101**	Discount factor: **0.996162**
Value, including coupon payment: **102.625**	Option status: **Called**

The valuation of the bond at node 15 is similar to what was explained earlier for node 16.

$t = 0.50, t = 0.25$, and $t = 0$ year:

The procedure for valuation of the bond at the nodes located at these times is the same as explained earlier. For a particular node n, first we need to find the discounted expected future cash flows at the following nodes as:

$$V_I = \sum_{Following\ Nodes} \begin{matrix} \text{Outgoing Branching Probability of Node } n \\ \times \text{Discount Factor Based on Node } n \text{ Rate} \\ \times \text{Cash Flow at Following Node} \end{matrix} \qquad (6.1)$$

Then the impact of the call option exercise on this value is to be evaluated:

$$V_{II} = Min(V_I, \text{Call Price}) \qquad (6.2)$$

And finally, if there is a coupon payment cash flow at node n, it needs to be incorporated in the value of the bond at that node:

$$V_{III} = V_{II} + \text{Coupon Payment at Node } n \qquad (6.3)$$

V_{III} is the estimated value of the bond at node n. The current value of the bond in our example is the value obtained at node 1 at $t = 0$ as:

$$E[\text{discounted future cash flows}]_{Node\ 1}$$

$$= 0.166667 \times 0.994091 \times 101.2259$$

$$+ 0.666667 \times 0.994091 \times 101.7701$$

$$+ 0.166667 \times 0.994091 \times 102.0157 = 102.0186$$

The embedded call option in a callable bond is an option held by the issuer, so the value of this option should be reflected in the bond price from the point of view of the investor, so:

Value of Callable Bond

$$= \text{Value of Option-Free Bond} - \text{Value of Call Option} \qquad (6.4)$$

To find the value of an option-free bond using the interest rate tree we can use the same procedure described earlier but without evaluating an option at nodes, that is, assuming that values V_I and V_{II} in Equations (6.1) and (6.2) are identical. If we repeat this process for the bond in our example while assuming that there is no embedded call option, the bond value is obtained as \$103.1674. Therefore, the value of the call option is:

Value of Call Option

$$= \text{Value of Option-Free Bond} - \text{Value of Callable Bond}$$

$$= \$103.1674 - \$102.0186 = \$1.1488$$

Option-Adjusted Spread

The value of a callable bond that is obtained using the interest rate tree is the *intrinsic* or *economic value* of the bond. This value is not necessarily equal to the market price of the bond. We can define a spread that when added to all rates of the tree makes the economic value of the bond equal to its market (traded) price. This spread is called the *option-adjusted spread (OAS)*. A *mark-to-market spread* is the spread added to all terms of the spot curve used in valuation of an option-free bond that makes the economic value of the security derived using the discounted cash flow method equal to its market value. If the spot curve used in valuation is the Treasury curve, the mark-to-market spread is referred to as a *zero-volatility spread* or *z-spread*. OAS adjusts (removes) the optionality effect from the callable bond and provides investors with a measurement to compare a callable bond with a comparable option-free bond with similar characteristics (rate, term, etc.). Since OAS is derived using an interest rate tree, it captures the volatility of the interest rate included in the construction of the tree, and in that sense it is a good measurement of return for securities with embedded options while considering the volatility.

To derive OAS using an interest rate tree, we start by adding an arbitrary spread to the rates of all nodes of the tree and revalue the callable bond using the modified tree. This spread is iteratively changed until the bond value obtained from the tree is equal to its market value. The final additional spread added to all rates of the tree is the OAS. Returning to our callable bond example, assume that the market value of this bond is $101.8052. We used an iterative process by adding a spread to the rates of the tree in Figure 6.1 and recalculated the callable bond value using the procedure described earlier. At the end, OAS was obtained as 69 bps, which made the value from the tree equal to the market price of $101.8052. The final valuation tree with inclusion of OAS is shown in Figure 6.3.

In a previous chapter we introduced the effective duration and effective convexity for instruments with a complex valuation structure, such as a callable bond. We can use the interest rate tree and valuation technique explained here to calculate the approximate measurements of the bond duration and convexity. To do so, we need to shift the spot curve upward by a small amount, say 25 bps, reconstruct the interest rate tree, and revalue the callable bond using the new tree while including the OAS in the tree. This is repeated for a downward small shift in the spot curve. In this approach we assume that the OAS is constant and does not change when the underlying spot curve is changed. The effective duration and the effective convexity are:

$$D_{Eff} = \frac{V_- - V_+}{2\,V\,\Delta r} \tag{6.5}$$

$$Conv_{Eff} = \frac{V_+ + V_- - 2V}{V\,(\Delta r)^2} \tag{6.6}$$

where V is the current value of the bond and V_+ and V_- are bond values using the interest rate tree when the spot curve is shifted upward and downward respectively by a small Δr. V, V_+, and V_- are derived with inclusion of the same OAS obtained using the market value of the bond. For the callable bond in our example, we applied an upward shift of +25 bps to the spot curve, reconstructed the Black-Karasinski interest rate tree while including the OAS of 69 bps, and obtained a bond value of $101.7031. We repeated this for a downward shift of –25 bps and obtained a bond value of $101.9059. Since the bond

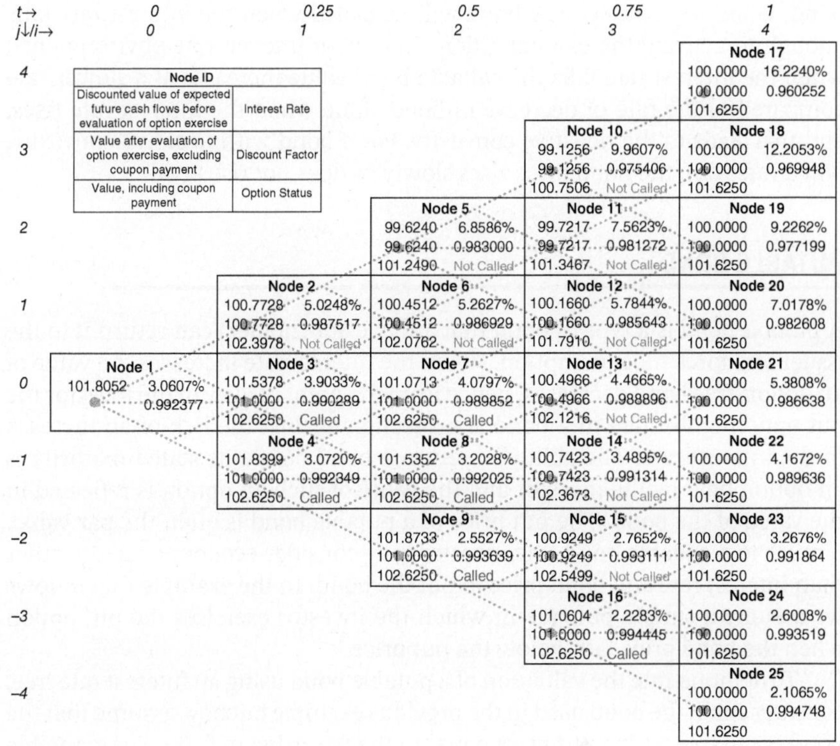

t→	0	0.25	0.5	0.75	1
j↓/i→	0	1	2	3	4

Legend box:

Node ID	
Discounted value of expected future cash flows before evaluation of option exercise	Interest Rate
Value after evaluation of option exercise, excluding coupon payment	Discount Factor
Value, including coupon payment	Option Status

Row 4 — Node 17 (t=1): 100.0000 16.2240%; 100.0000 0.960252; 101.6250

Row 3
- Node 10 (t=0.75): 99.1256 9.9607%; 99.1256 0.975406; 100.7506 Not Called
- Node 18 (t=1): 100.0000 12.2053%; 100.0000 0.969948; 101.6250

Row 2
- Node 5 (t=0.5): 99.6240 6.8586%; 99.6240 0.983000; 101.2490 Not Called
- Node 11 (t=0.75): 99.7217 7.5623%; 99.7217 0.981272; 101.3467 Not Called
- Node 19 (t=1): 100.0000 9.2262%; 100.0000 0.977199; 101.6250

Row 1
- Node 2 (t=0.25): 100.7728 5.0248%; 100.7728 0.987517; 102.3978 Not Called
- Node 6 (t=0.5): 100.4512 5.2627%; 100.4512 0.986929; 102.0762 Not Called
- Node 12 (t=0.75): 100.1660 5.7844%; 100.1660 0.985643; 101.7910 Not Called
- Node 20 (t=1): 100.0000 7.0178%; 100.0000 0.982608; 101.6250

Row 0
- Node 1 (t=0): 101.8052 3.0607%; 0.992377
- Node 3 (t=0.25): 101.5378 3.9033%; 101.0000 0.990289; 102.6250 Called
- Node 7 (t=0.5): 101.0713 4.0797%; 101.0000 0.989852; 102.6250 Called
- Node 13 (t=0.75): 100.4966 4.4665%; 100.4966 0.988896; 102.1216 Not Called
- Node 21 (t=1): 100.0000 5.3808%; 100.0000 0.986638; 101.6250

Row -1
- Node 4 (t=0.25): 101.8399 3.0720%; 101.0000 0.992349; 102.6250 Called
- Node 8 (t=0.5): 101.5352 3.2028%; 101.0000 0.992025; 102.6250 Called
- Node 14 (t=0.75): 100.7423 3.4895%; 100.7423 0.991314; 102.3673 Not Called
- Node 22 (t=1): 100.0000 4.1672%; 100.0000 0.989636; 101.6250

Row -2
- Node 9 (t=0.5): 101.8733 2.5527%; 101.0000 0.993639; 102.6250 Called
- Node 15 (t=0.75): 100.9249 2.7652%; 100.9249 0.993111; 102.5499 Not Called
- Node 23 (t=1): 100.0000 3.2676%; 100.0000 0.991864; 101.6250

Row -3
- Node 16 (t=0.75): 101.0604 2.2283%; 101.0000 0.994445; 102.6250 Called
- Node 24 (t=1): 100.0000 2.6008%; 100.0000 0.993519; 101.6250

Row -4 — Node 25 (t=1): 100.0000 2.1065%; 100.0000 0.994748; 101.6250

FIGURE 6.3 Derivation of an option-adjusted spread (OAS) for a callable bond using an interest rate tree

value with the inclusion of OAS was \$101.8082, the effective duration and the effective convexity are calculated as:

$$D_{Eff} = \frac{V_- - V_+}{2\,V\,\Delta r} = \frac{101.9059 - 101.7031}{2 \times 101.8052 \times 0.0025} = 0.3985$$

$$Conv_{Eff} = \frac{V_+ + V_- - 2V}{V\,(\Delta r)^2} = \frac{101.7031 + 101.9059 - 2 \times 101.8052}{101.8052 \times (0.0025)^2} = -2.0547$$

The convexity of this bond is negative. Negative convexity is often a characteristic of callable bonds. This is due to the uneven change in value of the callable bond when the interest rate rises or falls. In this example when the spot curve is shifted upward by +25 bps, the bond value decreased by an absolute value of \$0.1021 (from \$101.8052 to \$101.7031) but for a downward shift of −25 bps in the spot curve the bond value increased by a smaller absolute value of \$0.1007 (from \$101.8052 to \$101.9059). This is due to the call feature of the bond, when we assumed the bond will be called when the interest rate falls enough to activate the call condition. In certain interest rate environments, when the interest rate falls the callable bond value increases at a slower rate compared to the rate of decrease in bond value when the interest rate rises, and this leads to the negative convexity. For a bond with negative convexity, when rates fall, the bond price rises slowly or does not rise at all.

PUTABLE BOND

A *putable bond* is a type of bond that an investor (holder) can return it to the issuer and force the redemption. When the interest rate increases the value of an option-free bond decreases, hence from the point of view of the investor the put option embedded in a bond is protection against the risk of an increase in the interest rate. The ability to return a bond before its stated maturity is an option held by the investor and the value of such an option is reflected in the value of the bond. The put price of a putable bond is often the par value. Similar to a callable bond, the investor may consider economic factors other than interest rate and bond price to put the bond. In the example that follows we assume a simple put rule in which the investor exercises the put option when the bond price falls below the put price.[1]

To demonstrate the valuation of a putable bond using an interest rate tree, consider again the bond used in the previous example but now assume that the bond is putable with a put price equal to the par value of $100. For a putable bond, the backward induction valuation technique is the same as explained earlier for a callable bond but the evaluation of the put option exercise and its impact on the cash flow and bond value at each node is different. If the investor exercises the put option when the bond price falls below the put price, the impact of the put option on the value of the bond at a node can be stated as:

$$V_{II} = \text{Max}(V_I, \text{Put Price}) \tag{6.7}$$

Figure 6.4 presents the valuation of the putable bond in our example using the interest rate tree from Figure 6.1. Consider node 10 at $t = 0.75$ year. Nodes 17, 18, and 19 are following nodes from node 10 and the total cash flow at each of these nodes is $101.635, consisting of the principal and the last coupon payment at the maturity date. Using the discount factor obtained based on the rate at node 10 and the outgoing branching probabilities from this node, the discounted expected future cash flow at node 10 is obtained as $V_I = \$99.2967$. Since this value is less than the put price of $100, we assume that the bond is put and the bond value at this node, excluding the coupon payment, is the put price: $V_{II} = \text{Max}(\$99.2967, \$100) = \$100$. The final value at this node is

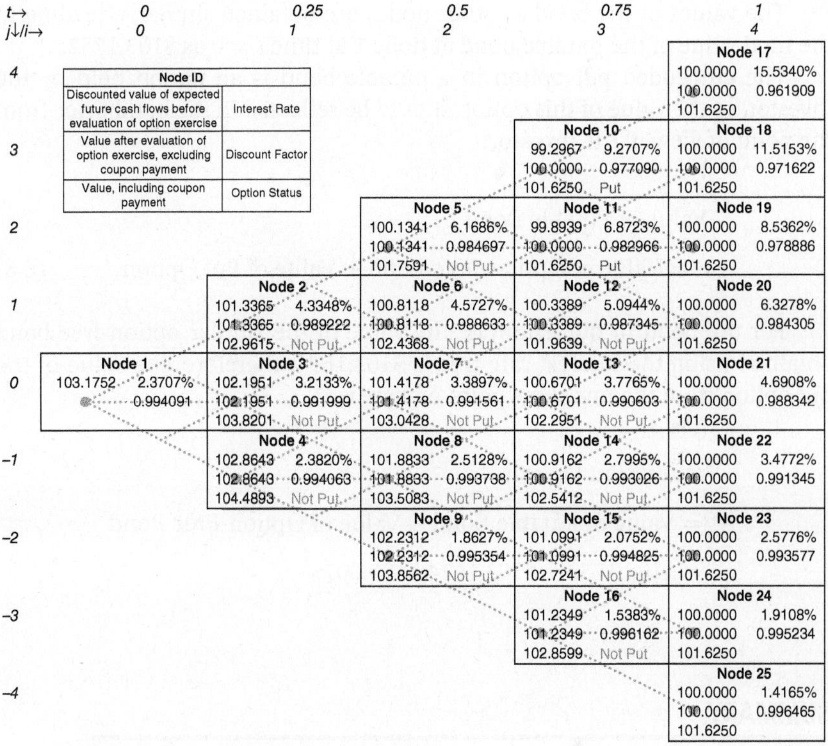

$t\rightarrow$	0	0.25	0.5	0.75	1
$j\downarrow/i\rightarrow$	0	1	2	3	4

Legend box:

Node ID	Interest Rate
Discounted value of expected future cash flows before evaluation of option exercise	Interest Rate
Value after evaluation of option exercise, excluding coupon payment	Discount Factor
Value, including coupon payment	Option Status

Interest rate tree (Figure 6.4):

	t = 0	t = 0.25	t = 0.5	t = 0.75	t = 1
j = 4					**Node 17** 100.0000 15.5340% / 100.0000 0.961909 / 101.6250
j = 3				**Node 10** 99.2967 9.2707% / 100.0000 0.977090 / 101.6250 Put	**Node 18** 100.0000 11.5153% / 100.0000 0.971622 / 101.6250
j = 2			**Node 5** 100.1341 6.1686% / 100.1341 0.984697 / 101.7591 Not Put	**Node 11** 99.8939 6.8723% / 100.0000 0.982966 / 101.6250 Put	**Node 19** 100.0000 8.5362% / 100.0000 0.978886 / 101.6250
j = 1		**Node 2** 101.3365 4.3348% / 101.3365 0.989222 / 102.9615 Not Put	**Node 6** 100.8118 4.5727% / 100.8118 0.988633 / 102.4368 Not Put	**Node 12** 100.3389 5.0944% / 100.3389 0.987345 / 101.9639 Not Put	**Node 20** 100.0000 6.3278% / 100.0000 0.984305 / 101.6250
j = 0	**Node 1** 103.1752 2.3707% / 0.994091	**Node 3** 102.1951 3.2133% / 102.1951 0.991999 / 103.8201 Not Put	**Node 7** 101.4178 3.3897% / 101.4178 0.991561 / 103.0428 Not Put	**Node 13** 100.6701 3.7765% / 100.6701 0.990603 / 102.2951 Not Put	**Node 21** 100.0000 4.6908% / 100.0000 0.988342 / 101.6250
j = -1		**Node 4** 102.8643 2.3820% / 102.8643 0.994063 / 104.4893 Not Put	**Node 8** 101.8833 2.5128% / 101.8833 0.993738 / 103.5083 Not Put	**Node 14** 100.9162 2.7995% / 100.9162 0.993026 / 102.5412 Not Put	**Node 22** 100.0000 3.4772% / 100.0000 0.991345 / 101.6250
j = -2			**Node 9** 102.2312 1.8627% / 102.2312 0.995354 / 103.8562 Not Put	**Node 15** 101.0991 2.0752% / 101.0991 0.994825 / 102.7241 Not Put	**Node 23** 100.0000 2.5776% / 100.0000 0.993577 / 101.6250
j = -3				**Node 16** 101.2349 1.5383% / 101.2349 0.996162 / 102.8599 Not Put	**Node 24** 100.0000 1.9108% / 100.0000 0.995234 / 101.6250
j = -4					**Node 25** 100.0000 1.4165% / 100.0000 0.996465 / 101.6250

FIGURE 6.4 Valuation of a putable bond using an interest rate tree

obtained by including the coupon payment: $100 + $1.625 = $101.625. The box for node 10 in Figure 6.4 contains the following information:

Node 10	
Discounted value of expected future cash flows *before* evaluation of option exercise: **99.2967**	Interest rate: **9.2707%**
Value *after* evaluation of option exercise, excluding coupon payment: **100**	Discount factor: **0.977090**
Value, including coupon payment: **101.625**	Option status: **Put**

The values of the bond at other nodes are obtained similarly, leading to the final value of the putable bond at node 1 at time $t = 0$ as \$103.1752.

The embedded put option in a putable bond is an option held by the investor, so the value of this option should be reflected in the bond price from the point of view of the investor:

Value of Putable Bond

= Value of Option-Free Bond + Value of Put Option   (6.8)

For the bond in our example, the value of the similar option-free bond obtained using the interest rate tree is \$103.1674; therefore, the value of the put option from the investor's point of view is:

Value of Put Option

= Value of Putable Bond − Value of Option-Free Bond

= \$103.1752 − \$103.1674 = \$0.0078

SUMMARY

- A callable bond is redeemable by the issuer prior to its maturity date. A call option protects the issuer against a rise in interest rate.
- An investor can return a putable bond to the issuer and force the redemption. A put option protects the investor against a rise in interest rate.
- Due to the embedded option, the future cash flows of callable or putable bonds are uncertain and thus the simple discounted cash flow method is not a suitable valuation method for these instruments. An interest rate tree is commonly used for valuation of callable and putable bonds. In this method the possibility of option exercise at each eligible note is evaluated and then the bond value at the node is determined.
- An option-adjusted spread is a spread that when added to the rates of all nodes of an interest rate tree, makes the value of a bond with embedded options obtained using the tree equal to its market value.

NOTE

1. Some bonds and CDs have death puts, where the bondholder's estate has the right, but not the obligation, to return the bond back to the issuer at the put price, often the par value, if the bondholder dies.

BIBLIOGRAPHY

Fabozzi, Frank J., and Steven V. Mann. *The Handbook of Fixed Income Securities*, 8th ed. McGraw-Hill Education, 2012.
Hull, John C. *Options, Futures, and Other Derivatives*, 6th ed. Prentice-Hall, 2005.

Valuation of Mortgage-Backed and Asset-Backed Securities

S *ecuritization* refers to the process of packaging financial instruments and creating new securities backed by the cash flows of the original instruments. The repackaging process distributes the risk of the original products where synthetic instruments created through the securitization process have various levels of risk and return. This provides investors with the option to select those *structured securities* that better fit their investment needs.

Mortgage loans constitute one of the largest sectors in financial markets all around the world, where many bank and non-bank institutions actively market, underwrite, and service them. To free up funding, mortgage issuers often package mortgages and sell them as new financial securities, backed by the cash flows of the pooled loans. These structured instruments, often referred to as *mortgage-backed securities (MBSs)*, have a very liquid market and institutional investors actively trade and include them in their investment portfolios. Other financial instruments, such as student loans or car loans, are also used in the securitization. Many financial and non-financial companies package different asset types and sell structured notes, generally referred to as *asset-backed securities (ABSs)*.

The complex structure of such synthetic instruments necessitates the use of more advanced valuation techniques than the simple discounted cash flow method. Uncertainty in contractual cash flows of such instruments is often augmented by the natural volatility of market factors, such as the interest rate, which makes their valuation even more difficult. For example, the existence of implicit or explicit optionality in an instrument, such as the possibility of prepayment, changes its cash flow structure, both in amount and timing, and an appropriate valuation technique should consider these uncertainties.

In this chapter we first introduce the mortgage mathematics required for cash flow determination of mortgage-backed securities. Then we explain how the Monte Carlo simulation method is used for valuation of MBSs. We then follow by introducing four ABS classes backed by student loans, credit card

449

receivables, car loans and leases, and home equity loans, and illustrate the use of Monte Carlo simulation in their valuation.

MORTGAGE-BACKED SECURITIES

In most developed countries, the housing sector is one of the main contributors to the country's economy. In the United States, housing is a cyclical deriver of GDP. According to the U.S. National Association of Home Builders, residential investment on average accounts for roughly 3% to 5% of GDP. This figure includes construction of new single-family and multi-family buildings, remodeling, manufactured housing, and brokers' fees.[1] Mortgage loans provided by banks and non-bank entities are the backbone of the housing sector. The Federal Reserve released data in the first quarter of 2018 indicating that there was more than $10.6 trillion of one- to four-family residential mortgage debt outstanding at the end of 2017.[2]

In the United States there are different types of mortgage loans originated by bank and non-bank institutions. The most common mortgage is the *conventional loan*. This type of mortgage is a secured loan collateralized by the real property being purchased with a fixed interest rate where the loan balance is amortized throughout the life of the mortgage. The monthly payment amount is constant and the term of the loan is usually 15 or 30 years. A conventional loan can be *conforming* or *non-conforming*. A conforming loan refers to a loan that has satisfied conditions set by the *Federal National Mortgage Association (Fannie Mae)* and the *Federal Home Loan Mortgage Corporation (Freddie Mac)*, including the maximum loan amount and the ratio of borrowers' income to loan amount. A mortgage loan that does not satisfy those conditions is a non-conforming loan. Credit score is often a major factor in the underwriting of a mortgage loan.

Fannie Mae and Freddie Mac are two *government-sponsored entities (GSEs)* created by U.S. Congress to facilitate housing financing and affordability.[3] They play a pivotal role by providing liquidity and stability to the housing finance market. They buy mortgage loans from originators and either hold them or package them into *mortgage-backed securities (MBSs)* and sell them in the secondary market. This in turn provides liquidity to lenders such as banks and mortgage companies, and enables them to use the funds for further lending. The selling of MBSs in the secondary market also provides other market participants that are not directly in the mortgage lending business with the opportunity to invest in the housing sector of the economy. Fannie Mae and Freddie Mac are privately owned companies that operate under congressional charter.

The *Government National Mortgage Association (Ginnie Mae)* is a U.S. government agency that provides guarantees to lenders for federally insured mortgage loans. Ginnie Mae does not originate mortgage loans or purchase them from other entities; however, institutions that are approved by Ginnie Mae originate eligible loans, pool them into securities, and issue Ginnie Mae MBSs.

Ginnie Mae MBS instruments, along with MBSs issued by Fannie Mae and Freddie Mac, are referred to as *agency MBSs*. *Pass-through certificates* are pools of mortgage loans that are used as collateral for the issuance of securities. They are the most common form of mortgage-backed securities, where the principal and interest of the underlying loans are proportionally passed through to investors (MBS buyers) minus a servicing cost. Figure 7.1 presents a schematic of a pass-through MBS and its relevant cash flows. Private entities, such as banks and other financial institutions, also issue mortgage-backed securities. These are referred to as *non-agency MBSs*. Since agency MBSs are issued by quasi-government entities, they are presumed to be high-quality securities with very low default risk, whereas non-agency MBSs are thought of as having default risk.

An *adjustable-rate mortgage (ARM)* is another mortgage type originated by banks and non-bank entities. Interest rates of such loans can change periodically. The most popular adjustable-rate mortgage is the 5/1 ARM, in which the introductory rate lasts for five years and after that the interest rate can change every year. These floating-rate mortgage loans are often indexed to constant maturity Treasury yield, the 11th District Cost of Funds Index (COFI), or LIBOR. MBSs can also be backed by adjustable-rate mortgage collaterals.

Mortgage-backed securities have a very active market. Banks, investment banks, pension funds, and other investment companies actively buy and sell MBSs and include them in their portfolio management activities. Agency and non-agency MBSs are often used as collateral for repurchase

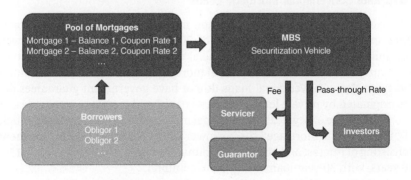

FIGURE 7.1   Schematic of a pass-through MBS

agreement contracts. Mortgage-backed securities are quoted similar to Treasury notes. For example, a quoted price of 102-31 for an MBS reflects a price of $102 + 31/32 = 102.969$.

Mortgage lenders often allow borrowers to pay back part or all of the borrowed amounts ahead of the scheduled amortization time. This is referred to as *prepayment*. Most mortgages in the United States do not have a prepayment penalty and this makes prepayment a valuable option for borrowers. During certain market and economic conditions, refinancing activity of mortgage borrowers increases, which leads to higher prepayments. Specifically, prepayment is highly dependent on the level of the prevailing mortgage rate (refinancing rate) in comparison with the current rate of a borrower's mortgage contract.

Prepayment creates uncertainty in cash flows of mortgages and subsequently in the value of mortgage-backed securities that are collateralized by such mortgage loans. This uncertainty in cash flows makes the valuation of MBSs not straightforward. The most common method used in practice for valuation of MBSs is the Monte Carlo simulation approach. In this method an interest rate model is used to produce a large number of simulated paths of interest rate in the future and a prepayment model is used to produce prepayment rates associated with those simulated interest rate paths. Then, based on the simulated interest and prepayment rates, the expected cash flows of each path are calculated and used for derivation of the expected value of the security.

In the following sections we first introduce the conventional mortgage and explain the basics of mortgage mathematics, first without consideration of the prepayment and then with the prepayment. We then continue our discussion by demonstrating how simulated interest rate paths can be used for valuation of MBSs.

Fixed-Rate Conventional Mortgage Loans

The fixed-rate loan is the most common mortgage type in the United States. Prior to the housing market crash of 2007, floating-rate mortgages were becoming popular but after the financial crisis that followed, they lost their popularity and fixed-rate conventional mortgages again became the dominant mortgage type. Conventional loans do not have government guarantees and are originated by private lenders, such as banks and mortgage companies.

The balance of a typical conventional mortgage loan is amortized throughout the life of the mortgage. The borrower pays a constant monthly payment, consisting of interest and principal amounts. The term of the loan is often 15 or 30 years, with 30-year loans being more common.

In a previous chapter we introduced the annuity contract. Fixed-rate conventional mortgages are annuity contracts with a predefined term. Consider a mortgage loan with a borrowed amount of N. The constant monthly payment paid by the borrower to the lender is calculated using the equation of the payment amount of an annuity as:

$$C_{si} = N \frac{r}{1 - \frac{1}{(1+r)^n}} \tag{7.1}$$

where

C_{si} = Scheduled periodic (monthly) payment amount for period i (constant for all periods)

N = Mortgage principal amount

r = Periodic (monthly) interest rate (i.e., the annual rate divided by 12)

n = Number of periods (months) of the original term of loan (e.g., for a 30-year mortgage, $n = 30 \times 12 = 360$)

For example, consider a 30-year fixed-rate mortgage loan with a notional amount of $135,000. This is the principal amount of the loan that the lender loans to the borrower. It is this amount that must be repaid by the borrower and is the base for calculation of the interest amount. This amount is not necessarily the money the borrower receives at the origination of the loan. Often other fees, such as lawyer and bank fees, are deducted from it and the net amount is used in the closing of the real estate transaction. However, the entire notional amount is used for principal repayment determination and interest calculation. Assume that the annual rate of this loan is 4.3750%. The monthly rate of this loan is $r = 4.375\%/12 = 0.364583\%$ and the constant payment amount, payable by the borrower each month to the lender, is calculated using Equation (7.1) as:

$$C_{si} = 135,000 \times \frac{0.364583/100}{1 - \frac{1}{(1 + 0.3646/100)^{360}}} = 674.04$$

If the borrower keeps the loan until its maturity date of 30 years from the origination date, at the end of each month he is supposed to pay $674.04 to the lender or its servicing agent. This payment amount is constant each month and does not change over the life of the mortgage. Since the loan is amortized over the life of 30 years, part of each monthly payment of $674.04 is the interest payment and part of it is the principal repayment, and the interest and principal amounts change over the life of the mortgage. For month 1 (period 1), the starting balance is equal to the notional amount of \$135,000. The interest amount for month 1 is calculated as:

$$I_{s1} = 135,000 \times \frac{0.364583}{100} = 492.19$$

where 0.364583 is the monthly (periodic) interest rate. Subscript s indicates that this is the scheduled interest amount and subscript 1 is the period indictor. The remaining portion of the total payment of \$674.04 goes toward the principal payment:

$$P_{s1} = 674.04 - 492.19 = 181.85$$

The outstanding balance at the end of month 1 is reduced by this principal payment and is obtained as:

$$B_{s1} = B_{s0} - P_{s1} = 135,000 - 181.85 = 134,818.15$$

The outstanding balance at the beginning of month 2 is the same as the balance at the end of month 1 and the scheduled interest and principal payments in month 2 and the outstanding balance at the end of month 2 are calculated as:

$$I_{s2} = 134,818.15 \times \frac{0.364583}{100} = 491.52$$

$$P_{s2} = 674.04 - 491.52 = 182.51$$

$$B_{s2} = B_{s1} - P_{s2} = 134,818.15 - 182.51 = 134,635.64$$

Scheduled interest and principal payments and outstanding balance for the remaining 358 months of the life of the loan are calculated similarly. The last principal payment in month 360 brings the outstanding balance to zero. At that month the principal amount is completely paid off and the loan is matured. Table 7.1 presents a partial view of the amortization schedule of the mortgage in our example, including scheduled outstanding balances and interest and principal amounts for each period. Entries in this table for each period are obtained based on the ending outstanding balance of the previous period, as demonstrated previously for months 1 and 2.

As can be seen in Table 7.1, as the age of the mortgage increases and the outstanding balance decreases, a smaller portion of each constant monthly payment is allocated to the interest payment and a larger portion to the principal payment. Figure 7.2 shows the monthly interest and principal payment amounts for this loan presented in a stacked format. While the total monthly payment is constant for the entire life of the loan, this graph clearly shows the gradual change of the composition of monthly payment. At the end of the

TABLE 7.1 A partial view of an amortization schedule of a conventional 30-year fixed-rate mortgage loan with a notional amount of $135,000 and an annual rate of 4.375%. No prepayment is assumed.

	Total:	$107,652.64	$135,000.00	$242,652.64		
						Principal
	Beginning	Interest	Principal	Total	Ending	Paid
	Balance	Payment	Payment	Payment	Balance	So Far
Period	($)	($)	($)	($)	($)	($)
0	135,000.00				135,000.00	
1	135,000.00	492.19	181.85	674.04	134,818.15	181.85
2	134,818.15	491.52	182.51	674.04	134,635.64	364.36
3	134,635.64	490.86	183.18	674.04	134,452.47	547.53
4	134,452.47	490.19	183.84	674.04	134,268.62	731.38
5	134,268.62	489.52	184.51	674.04	134,084.11	915.89
6	134,084.11	488.85	185.19	674.04	133,898.92	1,101.08
7	133,898.92	488.17	185.86	674.04	133,713.06	1,286.94
8	133,713.06	487.50	186.54	674.04	133,526.52	1,473.48
...	...	...	...	...	...	...
168	93,287.39	340.11	333.92	674.04	92,953.46	42,046.54
169	92,953.46	338.89	335.14	674.04	92,618.32	42,381.68
170	92,618.32	337.67	336.36	674.04	92,281.95	42,718.05
171	92,281.95	336.44	337.59	674.04	91,944.36	43,055.64
172	91,944.36	335.21	338.82	674.04	91,605.54	43,394.46
...	...	...	...	...	...	...
358	2,007.45	7.32	666.72	674.04	1,340.73	133,659.27
359	1,340.73	4.89	669.15	674.04	671.59	134,328.41
360	671.59	2.45	671.59	674.04	0	135,000.00

30-year life of the loan, the total principal payment is equal to the original borrowed amount of $135,000. During this period the borrower pays $107,652.64 interest, for a total payment of $135,000 + $107,652.64 = $242,652.64. This is for a case in which the borrower does not partially or fully prepay the borrowed amount.

We can derive formulas that provide us with the monthly scheduled interest and principal payment amounts and the scheduled outstanding balance at the end of a month without relying on the ending balance of the previous period. To do this, using the present value formula of an annuity we can obtain the outstanding balance at the end of month i as follows:

$$B_{s_i} = C_{s_i} \frac{1 - \frac{1}{(1+r)^{n-i}}}{r} \tag{7.2}$$

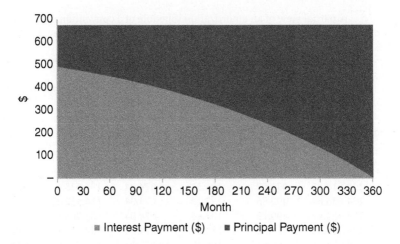

FIGURE 7.2 Monthly principal and interest payments of a 30-year fixed-rate mortgage loan with a notional amount of $135,000 and annual rate of 4.375%. No prepayment is assumed.

C_{si} is the scheduled payment amount, which is constant for all periods.[4] This equation is obtained by calculating the present value of the annuity at the end of period i instead of at time 0. $n - i$ is the remaining life of the loan, in months. If $i = 0$, Equation (7.2) provides the balance at period 0, which is the notional amount of the mortgage, so:

$$B_{s0} = N = C_{s0} \frac{1 - \dfrac{1}{(1 + r)^n}}{r}$$

By dividing both sides of this equation and Equation (7.2), and since payment amount C_{si} is constant and equal for all i, after simplification we have:

$$\frac{B_{si}}{N} = \frac{(1 + r)^n - (1 + r)^i}{(1 + r)^n - 1}$$

$\frac{B_{si}}{N}$ is the ratio of the outstanding balance of the loan at the end of period i to the mortgage notional amount. This ratio is known as *amortization factor*, A_i, and represents the scheduled balance at the end of a period i for $1 of the loan's notional amount. So:

$$A_i = \frac{B_{si}}{N} \tag{7.3}$$

or

$$A_i = \frac{(1+r)^n - (1+r)^i}{(1+r)^n - 1} \tag{7.4}$$

Or equivalently we can show the amortization factor as:

$$A_i = \frac{1 - (1+r)^{-(n-i)}}{1 - (1+r)^{-n}} \tag{7.5}$$

Based on this, the scheduled balance at the end of any period i can be obtained by simply multiplying the loan's notional amount by the amortization factor for that period, from either Equation (7.4) or (7.5):

$$B_{si} = A_i N \tag{7.6}$$

Since $B_{si-1} = A_{i-1} N$ or $N = \frac{B_{si-1}}{A_{i-1}}$ we have:

$$B_{si} = B_{si-1} \frac{A_i}{A_{i-1}} \tag{7.7}$$

Equation (7.7) states that to obtain the scheduled balance at the end of a period we can take the scheduled ending balance of the previous period and multiply it by the ratio of this period's amortization factor to the previous period's amortization factor. We use this property later in this section.

If P_{si} is the scheduled principal payment amount for period i, it is equal to the difference between the scheduled outstanding balances at the end of period $i - 1$ and i. So:

$$P_{si} = B_{si-1} - B_{si}$$

or

$$P_{si} = B_{si-1} - B_{si-1} \frac{A_i}{A_{i-1}}$$

Hence, the scheduled principal payment amount P_{si} can be derived as:

$$P_{si} = B_{si-1} \left(1 - \frac{A_i}{A_{i-1}}\right) \tag{7.8}$$

From this and using Equation (7.4), it is easy to show that:

$$P_{si} = B_{si-1} \frac{r}{(1+r)^{n-i+1} - 1} \tag{7.9}$$

We can derive P_{si} without the use of the previous period's scheduled ending balance as:

$$P_{si} = N(A_{i-1} - A_i) = N\left(\frac{(1+r)^n - (1+r)^{i-1}}{(1+r)^n - 1} - \frac{(1+r)^n - (1+r)^i}{(1+r)^n - 1}\right)$$

By simplifying this equation we have:

$$P_{si} = N\frac{r(1+r)^{i-1}}{(1+r)^n - 1} \tag{7.10}$$

I_{si} is the scheduled interest payment amount for period i, so:

$$I_{si} = B_{si-1}\, r \tag{7.11}$$

This can be written as:
$$I_{si} = N\, A_{i-1}\, r$$

By using Equation (7.4) and after simplification we have:

$$I_{si} = N\frac{r(1 - (1+r)^{-(n-i+1)})}{1 - (1+r)^{-n}} \tag{7.12}$$

Thus far we have shown that when there is no prepayment, the scheduled principal and interest payments and the scheduled outstanding balance for each month over the life of the mortgage loan can be derived either by using the previous month's ending balance or independent from it. The following table summarizes the equations we have developed so far for scheduled values.

Conventional Mortgage with No Prepayment (scheduled values)
Amortization Factor and Ending Balance:

$$A_i = \frac{(1+r)^n - (1+r)^i}{(1+r)^n - 1} \qquad\qquad B_{si} = A_i\, N$$

Monthly Payment:

$$C_{si} = N\frac{r}{1 - \dfrac{1}{(1+r)^n}} \qquad\qquad C_{si} = I_{si} + P_{si}$$

Using the previous month's scheduled ending balance:	Not using the previous month's scheduled ending balance:
Principal Payment:	Principal Payment:
$$P_{s_i} = B_{s_{i-1}} \left(1 - \frac{A_i}{A_{i-1}}\right)$$	$$P_{s_i} = N \frac{r(1+r)^{i-1}}{(1+r)^n - 1}$$
or	Interest Payment:
$$P_{s_i} = B_{s_{i-1}} \frac{r}{(1+r)^{n-i+1} - 1}$$	$$I_{s_i} = N \frac{r(1 - (1+r)^{-(n-i+1)})}{1 - (1+r)^{-n}}$$
Interest Payment:	
$$I_{s_i} = B_{s_{i-1}} r$$	Outstanding Balance (end of period):
Outstanding Balance (end of period):	$$B_{s_i} = C_{s_i} \frac{1 - \dfrac{1}{(1+r)^{n-i}}}{r}$$
$$B_{s_i} = B_{s_{i-1}} \frac{A_i}{A_{i-1}}$$	
or	
$$B_{s_i} = B_{s_{i-1}} - P_{s_i}$$	

C_{s_i} = Scheduled monthly payment; B_{s_i} = Scheduled end of month outstanding balance; P_{s_i} = Scheduled principal payment; I_{s_i} = Scheduled interest payment; N = Notional amount; r = Coupon rate; n = Term; A_i = Amortization factor

Deriving the scheduled outstanding balance and scheduled principal and interest payment amounts without the use of previous month ending balance becomes handy in valuation of MBSs. As an example, consider month 170 for the \$135,000 mortgage loan introduced earlier in this section. The scheduled ending balance and scheduled principal and interest payments of this month can be calculated directly as follows:

Using Equation (7.2):

$$B_{s170} = 674.04 \times \frac{1 - \dfrac{1}{(1 + 0.364583/100)^{360-170}}}{0.364583/100} = 92{,}281.95$$

Using Equation (7.10):

$$P_{s170} = 135{,}000 \times \frac{0.364583/100(1 + 0.364583/100)^{170-1}}{(1 + 0.364583/100)^{360} - 1} = 336.36$$

Using Equation (7.12):

$$I_{s170} = 135,000$$

$$\times \frac{0.364583/100 \times (1 - (1 + 0.364583/100)^{-(360-170+1)})}{1 - (1 + 0.364583/100)^{-360}} = 337.67$$

These results are the same as the corresponding values from Table 7.1 for month 170.[5]

Prepayment

The original borrowed amount of a mortgage loan can be repaid in several different ways:

- **Scheduled repayment:** When the borrower repays the original borrowed amount based on a predetermined schedule set at the initiation time of the mortgage loan. This schedule is the amortization schedule we discussed earlier in this section.
- **Curtailment:** When the borrower pays an additional principal amount in excess of the required monthly scheduled principal payment. This partial repayment reduces the outstanding principal of the loan.
- **Refinancing:** When the borrower engages another lending entity to obtain a new mortgage loan and with the proceeds from the new loan repays the existing loan. In this process, the borrower intends to either reduce his mortgage rate or cash out the difference between the notional amount of the second loan and the remaining balance of the first loan.
- **Housing turnover:** When the borrower sells the property used as collateral for the mortgage and repays the loan.
- **Default:** When the borrower is unable to make the monthly payments and forecloses the property. After appropriate legal procedures, this results in the lender (or its agent) taking over the property and recovering the loan amount, often by reselling the property.

Prepayment refers to a payment more than the required scheduled principal payment, either through curtailment, refinancing, or housing turnover. Therefore, prepayment can be for a portion of the remaining balance (curtailment) or for the entire remaining balance (refinancing or turnover). In the United States most conventional mortgages do not have a prepayment penalty and borrowers can repay any amount in excess of the scheduled principal at any time.

There are many incentives that may lead to mortgage prepayment. If the coupon rate of a mortgage is higher than the current mortgage refinancing rate in the market, the borrower may have enough of an incentive to refinance his current mortgage. The refinancing rate should be lower enough than the mortgage coupon rate to justify the refinancing process, which itself is costly and time consuming. Therefore, not every borrower refinances his mortgage when the refinancing rate falls below his current mortgage coupon rate, at least not immediately. A borrower may not even behave rationally, economically speaking, in making a refinancing decision. Economic conditions, especially in the housing sector, can also incentivize prepayment. In an expanding housing market, more properties are bought and sold, and this leads to more mortgage prepayments. Conversely, when the housing market slows down, there are fewer housing turnovers and mortgage prepayment decreases. Other macroeconomic conditions such as unemployment rate may also impact prepayment decisions.

Since prepayments alter the cash flows of underlying mortgages of mortgage-backed securities, it is necessary to model the prepayment rate in different interest rate and market conditions. Such a prepayment model then can be used for generating expected cash flows of MBSs in different scenarios. When mortgages are considered as a large pool of loans, their overall behavior can be studied using statistical methods. Such studies have revealed that there are a few main factors affecting the prepayment rate:

- **Refinancing rate:** As mentioned earlier, the spread between the prevailing market refinancing rate and the mortgage's coupon rate plays an important role in making prepayment decisions and hence impacts the prepayment rate.
- **Burnout effect:** Generally, it is expected that a decrease in the refinancing rate leads to an increase in the prepayment rate. However, in practice such a relationship does not always hold. When the refinancing rate decreases, those borrowers who can refinance do so when the rate falls sufficiently to justify initiating the refinancing process. Those who, for various reasons such as low credit score or low equity ownership in the property, cannot refinance would not refinance even though the mortgage rate is falling. If the refinancing rate drops further, since those who could refinance already have done it, the prepayment rate actually decreases. This phenomenon is known as the *burnout effect*. The burnout effect refers to a decrease in the prepayment rate even though the refinancing rate is decreasing.

Due to the burnout effect, valuation of mortgage-backed securities depends on the path that the interest rate takes to reach a point in time. For example, assume that the weighted average coupon of a mortgage pool is 5%. The current refinancing rate is 5.2% and it may follow these two paths over the next three years:

Path 1: Year 0: 5.2%	Year 1: 6%	Year 2: 6%	Year 3: 4%
Path 2: Year 0: 5.2%	Year 1: 4.4%	Year 2: 5.5%	Year 3: 4%

When the mortgage rate changes according to path 1, the impact of the refinancing rate on the prepayment rate in years 1 and 2 would be low since the prevailing market rate is materially above the mortgage's coupon rates. In year 3, however, the impact of the refinancing rate on the prepayment rate increases significantly as the market refinancing rate is well below the mortgage's coupon rate.

Now consider the case in which the mortgage rate follows path 2. Due to the relative spread between the mortgage's coupon rate and the market refinancing rate, the impact of the refinancing rate on the prepayment rate would be high in year 1 and then low in year 2. However, in year 3, even though the market refinancing rate is well below the mortgage's coupon rate the impact of the refinancing rate on the prepayment rate most probably would be low, since those who could refinance would have done so in year 1, and a decrease in the refinancing rate in year 3 would not lead to a major increase in the prepayment rate. This is the burnout effect and it highlights the path dependency of the valuation of MBSs (Fabozzi 2016).

- **Seasoning:** The mortgage prepayment rate often rises slowly at the beginning of the life of mortgage loans and as their ages increase, it approaches a steady level. This effect is known as *mortgage seasoning*.
- **Seasonality:** The month of the year also has an impact on prepayment, where the prepayment rate often decreases during the winter season and increases during the fall, possibly due to a lag from typical summer housing movement and its associated prepayment activity (Richard and Roll 1989).
- **Geographic and demographic influence:** The location of the properties collateralizing the mortgages and the demographic characteristics of those locations impact the prepayment rate.
- **Mortgage characteristics:** Aside from the mortgage coupon rate and its relative spread to the market refinancing rate, other characteristics of the mortgage loan, such as remaining balance, loan-to-value ratio, and credit score of the borrower may also impact the prepayment rate.
- **Economic factors and housing turnover:** General macroeconomic factors and specifically those that affect housing turnover have a direct impact on the prepayment rate.

Impact of Prepayment on Mortgage-Backed Securities

There are two alternatives in cash flow analysis and valuation of pass-through mortgage-backed securities considering prepayment. First is to perform an analysis of the individual loans that constitute the pool supporting an MBS and then aggregate the results. The second approach is to perform the analysis at the pool level. The second approach, particularly in prepayment analysis, is more common in practice.

In the previous section we introduced C_{si}, P_{si}, I_{si}, and B_{si} notations and used them to refer to scheduled monthly payment, principal payment, interest payment, and ending outstanding balance for month i for an individual loan. Subscript s in these notations is to emphasize that these are all scheduled values when no prepayment exists. We can use the same notations to refer to the corresponding pool level values. For a mortgage-backed security and when no prepayment is considered, we have:

r = Weighted average coupon rate (WAC) of the mortgages in the supporting pool, weighted by each mortgage's remaining balance.

n = Weighted average maturity (WAM) or remaining term of mortgages in the supporting pool, weighted by each mortgage's remaining balance.

B_{si} = Sum of scheduled outstanding balances of mortgages in the supporting pool at the end of month i.

P_{si} = Sum of scheduled principal payments of mortgages in the supporting pool in month i.

I_{si} = Sum of scheduled interest payments of mortgages in the supporting pool in month i, adjusted for servicing cost.

C_{si} = Sum of scheduled monthly payments of mortgages in the supporting pool in month i.

N = Sum of the notional amounts of mortgages in the supporting pool.

For the scheduled interest amount of an MBS we need to adjust the equation to incorporate the servicing cost by the servicing agent. This cost includes guarantee fees and charges for services such as payment collection, record keeping, tax document preparation, and initiation of a foreclosure process, if necessary. The servicing cost is incorporated in an MBS in the form of a spread s deducted from the weighted average coupon rate and $r - s$ is known as the *pass-through rate*. We can modify Equations (7.11) and (7.12) to reflect the impact of the servicing spread on the scheduled interest amount, as:

$$I_{si} = B_{si-1}\,(r - s) \tag{7.13}$$

or

$$I_{s_i} = N\frac{(r - s)(1 - (1 + r)^{-(n-i+1)})}{1 - (1 + r)^{-n}} \tag{7.14}$$

We now introduce C_i, P_i, I_i, and B_i notations to represent monthly payment, principal payment, interest payment, and ending outstanding balance when prepayment is considered. Also, we use PP_i to represent the prepayment amount in month i. Therefore, for a mortgage-backed security with prepayment we have:

P_i = Aggregated principal payment of the supporting pool in month i.

I_i = Aggregated interest payment of the supporting pool in month i, adjusted for servicing cost.

C_i = Aggregated monthly payment of the supporting pool in month i.

B_i = Aggregated outstanding balance of the supporting pool at the end of period i.

PP_i = Aggregated prepayment amount in month i.

The lack of subscript s in these notations indicates that they represent values considering prepayment and are different from scheduled values. Other relevant information of the mortgages in a pool, such as borrowers' credit scores and loan-to-value ratios, can be aggregated as well. In the remainder of this section any variable or measurement introduced or used in an equation is an aggregated value at the pool level, unless otherwise stated.

A *prepayment model* takes in factors mentioned in the previous section, specifically path of mortgage rate along with pool-level data, and produces prepayment rates for future months. Many commercially available prepayment models or those that are developed by research groups within large banks are based on a common assumption that a mortgage pool, which contains many actual mortgages, consists of a larger pool of many micro \$1 mortgage loans and when prepayment occurs the entire remaining balance of a micro loan is repaid. This assumption has an implication on the constant monthly payment. Although the pool-level scheduled monthly payment C_{s_i} is constant every month, the monthly payment considering prepayment C_i is not. When a micro \$1 loan is assumed to be prepaid, the monthly payment of that loan will be gone and this changes the aggregated monthly payment. Here we follow the same assumption when building the mathematical relationship between MBS measurements considering prepayment and their corresponding scheduled values.

The mortgage prepayment rate is usually expressed in the form of a monthly rate, known as *single monthly mortality (SMM)*. The single monthly mortality rate is defined as the ratio of the prepayment amount in a month to the available amount to prepay. Using the above notations, the single monthly mortality rate is stated as:

$$SMM_i = \frac{PP_i}{B_{i-1} - P_i} \qquad (7.15)$$

where SMM_i is the monthly prepayment rate in month i and B_{i-1} is the ending balance of the previous month $i - 1$, which is the same as the beginning balance of month i. The *conditional prepayment rate* or *constant prepayment rate (CPR)* is an annual measurement of prepayment and is related to SMM based on the following equation:

$$CPR_i = 1 - (1 - SMM_i)^{12} \qquad (7.16)$$

where CPR_i is the annualized prepayment rate for month i. When the CPR is known, it can be converted to SMM using:

$$SMM_i = 1 - (1 - CPR_i)^{\frac{1}{12}} \qquad (7.17)$$

In the 1980s, the *Public Securities Association (PSA)*, currently known as the *Securities Industry and Financial Markets Association (SIFMA)*, developed a standard prepayment scale for MBSs, commonly referred to as the *PSA prepayment standard*. The PSA provides a monthly series of CPRs. The standard 100 PSA benchmark prepayment scale assumes a 0.2% CPR at month 1 and increases by 0.2% each month until month 30, when it reaches 6% at that month. After that, the CPR is assumed constant at 6%. The relationship between CPR and PSA can be stated as follows:

$$CPR_i = PSA_i \times 0.06 \times \min\left(1, \frac{Age}{30}\right) \qquad (7.18)$$

$$PSA_i = CPR_i \times \frac{1}{0.06} \times \max\left(1, \frac{30}{Age}\right) \qquad (7.19)$$

In these equations PSA_i is expressed in a percentage, so, for example, for 100 PSA, 100% or 1 should be used and *Age*, expressed in months, refers to the weighted average age of mortgages included in the supporting pool from their corresponding initiation times, weighted by the remaining balances. Other prepayments are stated as multiples of the 100 PSA. For example, CPRs based on a 150 PSA scale are 1.5 times the CPRs from the 100 PSA. For a 150 PSA scale, the CPR at month 30 is 9%. For a 50 PSA scale, CPRs are half of the 100 PSA CPRs. For a 50 PSA scale, the CPR at month 30 is 3%. CPRs based on 50 PSA, 100 PSA, and 150 PSA scales are shown in Figure 7.3 for 360 months of mortgage age. For a pool of mortgages supporting an MBS, when a PSA is

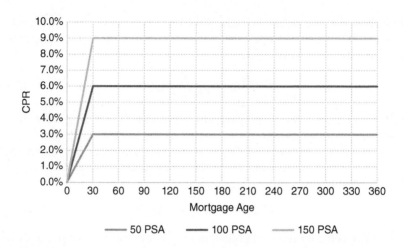

FIGURE 7.3   50 PSA, 100 PSA, and 150 PSA prepayment scales for 360-month mortgage age

assumed for a month it can be converted easily to CPR and then SMM using Equations (7.18) and (7.17).

For pass-through MBSs, the *pool factor* is the ratio of the outstanding balance at the end of a month to the notional amount of the pool:

$$Pool\ Factor_i = \frac{B_i}{N} \tag{7.20}$$

Earlier we introduced the amortization factor as the ratio of the scheduled outstanding balance at the end of a month to the notional amount. *Survival factor Q_i* is the ratio of the pool factor to the amortization factor:

$$Survival\ Factor = \frac{Pool\ Factor}{Amortization\ Factor} \tag{7.21}$$

By replacing the pool factor and amortization factor with their definition from Equations (7.3) and (7.20) we have:

$$Q_i = \frac{B_i}{B_{s_i}} \tag{7.22}$$

Survival factor is the key concept that associates scheduled measurements of MBSs without prepayment to the corresponding measurements with prepayment.

We can develop individual equations for monthly principal and interest payments and the ending outstanding balance of the mortgage pool when prepayment is considered. To start, note that if the outstanding balance of a pool at the beginning of month i is B_{i-1}, the scheduled principal payment alone reduces this balance at the end of month i to $B_{i-1}\dfrac{A_i}{A_{i-1}}$. Therefore, the principal payment for month i can be expressed as:

$$P_i = B_{i-1} - B_{i-1}\frac{A_i}{A_{i-1}}$$

or

$$P_i = B_{i-1}\left(1 - \frac{A_i}{A_{i-1}}\right) \tag{7.23}$$

Since $B_{i-1}\dfrac{A_i}{A_{i-1}}$ is the ending balance of month i without prepayment and B_i is the ending balance when prepayment is considered, the difference between these two values is the prepayment amount PP_i:

$$PP_i = B_{i-1}\frac{A_i}{A_{i-1}} - B_i$$

In Equation (7.15), where SMM is defined, if we replace PP_i and P_i with their equivalents from the above, we have:

$$SMM_i = \frac{PP_i}{B_{i-1} - P_i} = \frac{B_{i-1}\dfrac{A_i}{A_{i-1}} - B_i}{B_{i-1} - B_{i-1}\left(1 - \dfrac{A_i}{A_{i-1}}\right)}$$

After simplification and rearrangement, we have:

$$SMM_i = 1 - \frac{\dfrac{B_i}{A_i}}{\dfrac{B_{i-1}}{A_{i-1}}}$$

or

$$SMM_i = 1 - \frac{Q_i}{Q_{i-1}} \tag{7.24}$$

Equation (7.24) provides SMM as a function of two consecutive survival factors. To derive an equation for prepayment amount, using Equations (7.15) and (7.23) we have:

$$PP_i = (B_{i-1} - P_i)\,SMM_i = \left(B_{i-1} - B_{i-1}\left(1 - \frac{A_i}{A_{i-1}}\right)\right)SMM_i$$

or

$$PP_i = B_{i-1} \frac{A_i}{A_{i-1}} SMM_i \qquad (7.25)$$

The ending outstanding balance of month i with prepayment can be expressed as:

$$B_i = B_{i-1} - P_i - PP_i \qquad (7.26)$$

In Equation (7.26), by replacing P_i and PP_i with their equivalents from Equations (7.23) and (7.25) we have:

$$B_i = B_{i-1} - B_{i-1}\left(1 - \frac{A_i}{A_{i-1}}\right) - B_{i-1}\frac{A_i}{A_{i-1}} SMM_i$$

After simplifying this we obtain:

$$B_i = B_{i-1}\frac{A_i}{A_{i-1}}(1 - SMM_i) \qquad (7.27)$$

Finally, the interest payment and monthly payment in month i can be expressed as:

$$I_i = B_{i-1}(r - s) \qquad (7.28)$$

$$C_i = I_i + P_i \qquad (7.29)$$

where r is the weighted average coupon rate of the pool and s is the servicing spread. Equations (7.23), (7.25), (7.27), and (7.28) provide the principal and interest payments, prepayment amount and ending outstanding balance for a month based on the SMM of that month, amortization factors, and the previous month's ending balance. These equations can be used to obtain the cash flows to MBS holders that are needed for valuation of the note.

These equations rely on previous month ending balance. We can develop another set of equations that associates principal and interest payments, prepayment amount, and ending outstanding balance of a month with prepayment to the corresponding scheduled values without prepayment. This provides us with an easier way to produce the cash flows of an MBS for each month, since we have already developed equations for scheduled values that do not rely on the previous month's ending balance. To do this, consider Equation (7.27). By applying this equation to month $i - 1$ we have:

$$B_{i-1} = B_{i-2}\frac{A_{i-1}}{A_{i-2}}(1 - SMM_{i-1})$$

By placing B_{i-1} from this equation into Equation (7.27) and simplifying we have:

$$B_i = B_{i-2} \frac{A_i}{A_{i-2}} (1 - SMM_i)(1 - SMM_{i-1})$$

By repeating this process iteratively and noting that $B_0 = N$ and $A_0 = 1$ we obtain the following formula for B_i:

$$B_i = NA_i \prod_{j=1}^{i} (1 - SMM_j)$$

Since $B_{s_i} = NA_i$ we can write this equation as:

$$B_i = B_{s_i} \prod_{j=1}^{i} (1 - SMM_j) \tag{7.30}$$

This formula associates the ending balance of month i with prepayment, B_i, to the scheduled ending balance without prepayment, B_{s_i}. It can be shown that the second part of the right side of Equation (7.30) is equal to the survival factor Q_i:

$$Q_i = \prod_{j=1}^{i} (1 - SMM_j) \tag{7.31}$$

Proof of this is presented in the Annex of this chapter. So:

$$B_i = Q_i B_{s_i} \tag{7.32}$$

Similarly, the principal payment and the scheduled principal payment are associated as:

$$P_i = Q_{i-1} P_{s_i} \tag{7.33}$$

Proof of this is also presented in the Annex of this chapter. For the interest payment, combining Equations (7.28) and (7.32) provides us with:

$$I_i = Q_{i-1} I_{s_i} \tag{7.34}$$

The monthly payment consisting of principal and interest payments can then be written as:

$$C_i = Q_{i-1} C_{s_i} \tag{7.35}$$

Prepayment for period i is obtained as:

$$PP_i = (Q_{i-1} B_{s_{i-1}} - Q_{i-1} P_{s_i}) SMM_i \tag{7.36}$$

And finally, the total monthly cash flow of an MBS for month i is:

$$CF_i = P_i + PP_i + I_i \tag{7.37}$$

Since the interest payment is adjusted for the servicing cost, the total monthly cash flow obtained from Equation (7.37) is adjusted as well. Equations (7.32) to (7.36) provide us with principal and interest payments, prepayment amount, and ending outstanding balance of an MBS when prepayment is considered, as functions of the corresponding scheduled values and survival factor. The following table summarizes the formulas we developed for MBSs.

Mortgage-Backed Security

Without Prepayment (scheduled values)	**With Prepayment**	
Principal Payment: $$P_{s_i} = N\frac{r(1+r)^{i-1}}{(1+r)^n - 1}$$	Using previous period balance: Principal Payment: $$P_i = B_{i-1}\left(1 - \frac{A_i}{A_{i-1}}\right)$$	Using scheduled values: Principal Payment: $$P_i = Q_{i-1}P_{s_i}$$
Interest Payment: $$I_{s_i} = N\frac{(r - s)(1 - (1+r)^{-(n-i+1)})}{1 - (1+r)^{-n}}$$	Interest Payment: $$I_i = B_{i-1}(r - s)$$	Interest Payment: $$I_i = Q_{i-1}I_{s_i}$$
Monthly Payment: $$C_{s_i} = I_{s_i} + P_{s_i}$$	Monthly Payment: $$C_i = I_i + P_i$$	Monthly Payment: $$C_i = Q_{i-1}C_{s_i}$$
Outstanding Balance (end of period): $$B_{s_i} = C_{s_i}\frac{1 - \dfrac{1}{(1+r)^{n-i}}}{r}$$	Prepayment: $$PP_i = B_{i-1}\frac{A_i}{A_{i-1}}SMM_i$$	Prepayment: $$PP_i = (Q_{i-1}B_{s_{i-1}} - Q_{i-1}P_{s_i})SMM_i$$
	Outstanding Balance (end of period): $$B_i = B_{i-1}\frac{A_i}{A_{i-1}}(1 - SMM_i)$$	Outstanding Balance (end of period): $$B_i = Q_iB_{s_i}$$
		Survival Factor: $$Q_i = \prod_{j=1}^{i}(1 - SMM_j)$$

C_{s_i} = Scheduled monthly payment; C_i = Actual monthly payment; B_{s_i} = Scheduled end of month outstanding balance; B_i = Actual end of month outstanding balance; P_{s_i} = Scheduled principal payment; P_i = Actual principal payment; PP_i = Prepayment amount; I_{s_i} = Scheduled interest payment; I_i = Actual interest payment; N = Notional amount; r = Weighted average coupon rate; s = Servicing spread; Q_i = Survival factor; SMM_i = Single monthly mortality rate; n = Weighted average maturity; A_i = Amortization factor

To illustrate the use of equations developed in this section, assume that today is October 1, 2018, and an MBS is just issued with a notional amount of $2,004,247, supported by a pool of conventional fixed-rate mortgage loans with a weighted average coupon rate of 4.189% and pass-through rate of 3.5%, maturing on October 1, 2048. The weighted average remaining life is $n = 360$, the monthly coupon rate is $r = 4.189\%/12 = 0.349083\%$, and the monthly servicing spread is $s = 0.689\%/12 = 0.057417\%$.

To obtain the cash flows of this MBS for a given month, we need to make an assumption regarding prepayment speed. Assume that at initiation time of this security we believe that the MBS follows a 100 PSA prepayment speed. Since $B_0 = N = 2,004,247$, the interest amount of month 1 is obtained using Equation (7.28) as:[6]

$$I_1 = B_0(r - s) = 2,004,247 \times (0.00349083 - 0.00057417) = 5,845.72$$

Since $A_0 = 1$, the amortization factor for month 1, calculated using Equation (7.4), is used in Equation (7.23) to obtain the principal payment for month 1 as:

$$A_1 = \frac{(1 + r)^{360} - (1 + r)^1}{(1 + r)^{360} - 1} = \frac{(1 + 0.00349083)^{360} - (1 + 0.00349083)^1}{(1 + 0.00349083)^{360} - 1}$$

$$= 0.99860708$$

$$P_1 = B_0 \left(1 - \frac{A_1}{A_0}\right) = 2,004,247 \left(1 - \frac{0.99860708}{1}\right) = 2,791.76$$

For a prepayment speed of 100 PSA, the CPR of month 1 is 0.2% and SMM is calculated using Equation (7.17) as:

$$SMM_1 = 1 - (1 - CPR_1)^{\frac{1}{12}} = 1 - (1 - 0.002)^{\frac{1}{12}} = 0.016682\%$$

Using this SMM and Equation (7.25) we can calculate the prepayment amount for month 1 as:

$$PP_1 = B_0 \frac{A_1}{A_0} SMM_1 = 2,004,247 \times \frac{0.99860708}{1} \times 0.00016682 = 333.88$$

Based on these results, the total cash flow for month 1 is:

$$CF_1 = I_1 + P_1 + PP_1 = 5,845.72 + 2,791.76 + 333.88 = 8,971.36$$

The outstanding balance at the end of month 1 can be calculated using either Equation (7.26) or (7.27) as:

$$B_1 = B_0 - P_1 - PP_1 = 2,004,247 - 2,791.76 - 333.88 = 2,001,121.36$$

The ending balance of month 1 is the beginning balance of month 2, and this process can be repeated for month 2 through month 360 to obtain the cash flows and the ending balance of each month. We can summarize these results in a table similar to the amortization schedule demonstrated for a single conventional mortgage. Table 7.2 presents a partial view of this table for the MBS example discussed here. Figure 7.4 shows the total cash flows of this MBS for

TABLE 7.2 A partial view of a cash flow schedule of an MBS with a notional amount of $2,004,247, WAC of 4.189%, pass-through rate of 3.5%, and WAM of 360 months. Prepayments are based on 100 PSA scale.

Period	Total: Beginning Balance ($)	$761,343.61 Interest Payment ($)	$812,843.41 Principal Payment ($)	$1,191,403.59 Pre-payment ($)	$2,765,590.61 Total Cash Flow ($)	Ending Balance ($)
0	2,004,247.00					2,004,247.00
1	2,004,247.00	5,845.72	2,791.76	333.88	8,971.36	2,001,121.36
2	2,001,121.36	5,836.60	2,801.03	667.33	9,304.97	1,997,653.00
3	1,997,653.00	5,826.49	2,809.87	1,000.18	9,636.54	1,993,842.95
4	1,993,842.95	5,815.38	2,818.27	1,332.24	9,965.89	1,989,692.44
5	1,989,692.44	5,803.27	2,826.21	1,663.36	10,292.84	1,985,202.86
6	1,985,202.86	5,790.18	2,833.71	1,993.36	10,617.24	1,980,375.80
7	1,980,375.80	5,776.10	2,840.74	2,322.06	10,938.90	1,975,213.00
8	1,975,213.00	5,761.04	2,847.31	2,649.31	11,257.65	1,969,716.38
...	...	...	...	...	...	...
108	1,020,479.78	2,976.40	2,517.79	5,235.39	10,729.58	1,012,726.60
109	1,012,726.60	2,953.79	2,513.58	5,195.54	10,662.91	1,005,017.48
110	1,005,017.48	2,931.30	2,509.38	5,155.91	10,596.60	997,352.19
111	997,352.19	2,908.94	2,505.19	5,116.51	10,530.65	989,730.48
112	989,730.48	2,886.71	2,501.01	5,077.33	10,465.06	982,152.14
...	...	...	...	...	...	...
237	314,226.53	916.49	2,029.43	1,605.63	4,551.55	310,591.48
238	310,591.48	905.89	2,026.04	1,586.96	4,518.88	306,978.48
239	306,978.48	895.35	2,022.65	1,568.39	4,486.40	303,387.44
240	303,387.44	884.88	2,019.27	1,549.94	4,454.09	299,818.22
241	299,818.22	874.47	2,015.90	1,531.60	4,421.97	296,270.72
...	...	...	...	...	...	...
356	8,375.08	24.43	1,663.36	34.52	1,722.31	6,677.20
357	6,677.20	19.48	1,660.58	25.80	1,705.86	4,990.81
358	4,990.81	14.56	1,657.81	17.14	1,689.51	3,315.86
359	3,315.86	9.67	1,655.04	8.54	1,673.25	1,652.28
360	1,652.28	4.82	1,652.28	0.00	1,657.10	0

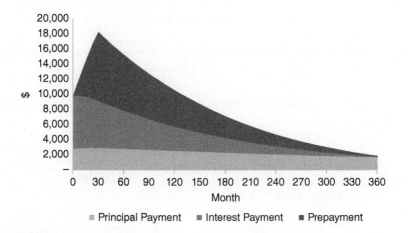

FIGURE 7.4 Total monthly cash flow and its components: principal, interest, and prepayment of an MBS with a notional amount of $2,004,247, WAC of 4.189%, pass-through rate of 3.5%, and WAM of 360 months, based on 100 PSA prepayment speed

each month and its three components: principal payment, interest payment, and prepayment, presented in a stacked format. It can be seen from this graph that as the prepayment rate increases the monthly prepayment amount also increases, peaking at month 30. After that the prepayment rate is constant as a CPR of 6% and as the outstanding balance decreases, the prepayment amount also decreases accordingly.

Using equations developed in this section, we can derive the cash flows of this MBS for any month without the need to have the ending balance of the previous month. To illustrate this approach, consider month 6. In order to obtain the cash flows and outstanding balance for this month we need to calculate the survival factors for month 5 and 6. Based on a 100 PSA prepayment assumption, the CPRs for months 1 to 6 are 0.2%, 0.4%, 0.6%, 0.8%, 1%, and 1.2%. SMM equivalents of these CPRs are 0.016682%, 0.033395%, 0.050138%, 0.066912%, 0.083718%, and 0.100554%. Using these SMMs and Equation (7.31), the survival factors for months 5 and 6 are calculated as:

$$Q_5 = \prod_{j=1}^{5}(1 - SMM_j)$$

$$= (1 - 0.016682\%) \times (1 - 0.033395\%) \times (1 - 0.050138\%)$$

$$\times (1 - 0.066912\%) \times (1 - 0.083718\%) = 0.99749393$$

$$Q_6 = 0.99749393 \times (1 - 0.100554\%) = 0.99649091$$

The scheduled monthly payment using Equation (7.1) is calculated as:

$$C_{s6} = N \frac{r}{1 - \dfrac{1}{(1+r)^{360}}} = 2,004,247 \times \frac{0.00349083}{1 - \dfrac{1}{(1+0.00349083)^{360}}} = 9,788.25$$

The scheduled ending balance of months 5 and 6 can then be calculated using Equation (7.2) as:

$$B_{s5} = C_{s5} \frac{1 - \dfrac{1}{(1+r)^{360-5}}}{r} = 9,788.25 \times \frac{1 - \dfrac{1}{(1+0.00349083)^{355}}}{0.00349083}$$

$$= 1,990,190.42$$

$$B_{s6} = C_{s6} \frac{1 - \dfrac{1}{(1+r)^{360-6}}}{r} = 9,788.25 \times \frac{1 - \dfrac{1}{(1+0.00349083)^{354}}}{0.00349083}$$

$$= 1,987,349.60$$

Having the scheduled ending balance and survival factor for month 6, the outstanding balance with prepayment is calculated using Equation (7.32) as:

$$B_6 = Q_6 B_{s6} = 0.99649091 \times 1,987,349.60 = 1,980,375.80$$

The scheduled principal payment and interest payment adjusted for the servicing cost for month 6 are calculated using Equations (7.10) and (7.14) as:

$$P_{s6} = N \frac{r(1+r)^{6-1}}{(1+r)^{360} - 1}$$

$$= 2,004,247 \times \frac{0.00349083 \times (1+0.00349083)^5}{(1+0.00349083)^{360} - 1} = 2,840.83$$

$$I_{s6} = N \frac{(r-s)(1 - (1+r)^{-(360-6+1)})}{1 - (1+r)^{-360}} = 2,004,247$$

$$\times \frac{(0.00349083 - 0.00057417) \times (1 - (1+0.00349083)^{-355})}{1 - (1+0.00349083)^{-360}} = 5,804.72$$

By using these scheduled amounts and the survival factors, we can calculate the principal and interest payments using Equations (7.33) and (7.34) as:

$$P_6 = Q_5 P_{s6} = 0.99749393 \times 2,840.83 = 2,833.71$$

$$I_6 = Q_5 I_{s6} = 0.99749393 \times 5,804.72 = 5,790.18$$

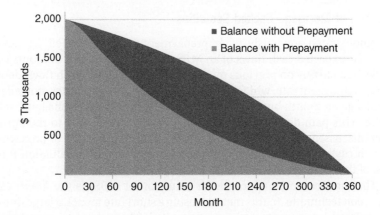

FIGURE 7.5 Outstanding balance without prepayment (scheduled) and with prepayment based on a 100 PSA speed, for an MBS with a notional amount of $2,004,247, WAC of 4.189%, pass-through rate of 3.5%, and WAM of 360 months

The prepayment amount for month 6 can be calculated using Equation (7.36) as:

$$PP_6 = (Q_5 B_{s_5} - Q_5 P_{s_6})\, SMM_6$$
$$= (0.99749393 \times 1,990,190.42 - 0.99749393 \times 2,833.71) \times 0.00100554$$
$$= 1,993.36$$

And finally, total cash flow for month 6 is:

$$CF_6 = I_6 + P_6 + PP_6 = 5,790.18 + 2,833.71 + 1,993.36 = 10,617.24$$

The results obtained here are the same as the ones shown in Table 7.2. This process can be repeated for any month to obtain expected cash flows of the MBS. Figure 7.5 shows the outstanding month-end balances of the MBS in our example for two cases when: (1) no prepayment assumed and (2) prepayment with a speed of 100 PSA is assumed. The difference between the shapes of the outstanding balance curves in this graph clearly demonstrates the importance of considering prepayment in MBS valuation.

Valuation of Mortgage-Backed Securities

As demonstrated previously, when prepayment rates are defined, we can calculate the expected cash flows of an MBS using the scheduled amounts without the need to rely on previous month-end balances. MBS cash flows depend on the prepayment rate, which in turn depends on mortgage rates, not only the rate at a given month but also the path the rate took to reach the level at that month. This path dependency of the prepayment rate is due to the burnout effect, discussed earlier. The impact of the path dependency of prepayment rates on cash flows of MBSs should be incorporated in the valuation framework of the security.

The most common approach for valuation of MBSs is the *Monte Carlo simulation* technique. In this method, using a short rate model, a large number of simulated interest rate paths are generated. These short rates are used to generate discount factors and simulated long-term rates. The long-term rates are then used in another model and converted into mortgage refinancing rates.

The mortgage rates, along with other inputs such as economic and housing turnover indicators, are used in a *prepayment model* to generate simulated prepayment rates. The prepayment rates, combined with characteristics of mortgages in the supporting pool, are used to produce the expected cash flow of an MBS for each month over the remaining term of the security, and for each interest rate path. These cash flows are then discounted using discount factors from the short rate model to obtain the present value for each path. The average of the present values over all simulation paths provides the expected security value.

The valuation framework of mortgage-backed securities based on the Monte Carlo simulation method consists of the following components:

1. Short rate model
2. Mortgage refinancing rate model
3. Prepayment model
4. Cash flow generator
5. Discounting and aggregation framework

Figure 7.6 presents a schematic view of these components and relationships to each other. In the following section we use the example mortgage-backed security studied earlier and demonstrate the use of these components in valuation of that security.

Short Rate Model

A short rate model is the starting point in MBS valuation. We discussed several short rate models in a previous chapter. We can use such models to generate

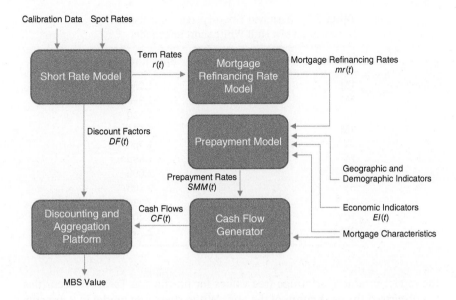

FIGURE 7.6 Schematic view of components required for valuation of mortgage-backed securities using the Monte Carlo simulation method

simulated paths of a short rate for the remaining term of an MBS. These simulated paths are needed for two purposes. First, the short rates are used to generate a simulated interest rate with a longer term, for example, 5-year or 10-year rates. These long-term interest rates are then used in another model, discussed next, to generate simulated mortgage refinancing rates. The second use of simulated short rates is to calculate simulated discount factors that are required for cash flow discounting in the last step of the valuation process.

One-factor and two-factor Hull-White models and the LIBOR market model are commonly used in practice for simulating short rates in MBS valuation. Here we use a single-factor Hull-White model to generate simulated short rates needed for our valuation example. Recall from a previous chapter that a one-factor Hull-White model has the following form:

$$dr(t) = (\theta(t) - k\,r(t))dt + \sigma\,dW(t) \tag{7.38}$$

In this model, $\theta(t)$ is calibrated to a Treasury spot curve as of the valuation date. The assumed spot curve is shown in Table 7.3. Rates in this table are quoted with continuous compounding. The time step of the model is monthly, hence $\Delta t = 1/12$ year. We used parameter values of $\sigma = 0.3$ and $k = 0.05$ in this example. These parameters should be calibrated such that

TABLE 7.3   Assumed Treasury spot curve used in construction of a Hull-White short rate model

Term	Spot Rate (%)
1M	1.280
3M	1.390
6M	1.530
9M	1.645
1Y	1.760
2Y	1.890
3Y	2.000
5Y	2.200
7Y	2.330
10Y	2.403
30Y	2.740

the model produces arbitrage-free values for on-the-run Treasury securities. We discussed the calibration of the Hull-White short rate model in a previous chapter. Figure 7.7 presents three simulated paths of a 1-month rate generated by this Hull-White model for 360 months in the future. In practice a large number of simulation paths (e.g., 1,000), are needed to obtain converging results. Here and for demonstration purposes, we consider only three paths in our example. The simulated 1-month rates are used for two purposes:

1. **Generating long-term rates:** The 1-month short rates can be used for calculating longer-term rates such as 5-year or 10-year rates. In a previous chapter we discussed the method of calculating a Δt-period rate from the short rate. These long-term rates are needed to generate a simulated mortgage refinancing rate, as explained in the next section. Here we use a model that converts 5-year Treasury rates to a mortgage refinancing rate; thus we need 5-year rates. Figure 7.8 shows three simulated paths of 5-year rates generated based on the corresponding 1-month rates from Figure 7.7.
2. **Generating discount factors:** In order to discount the expected cash flows of an MBS to the valuation date we need to calculate the discount factors for each month-end date and each interest rate path. The 1-month rates can be used to calculate one-period discount factors and then aggregate into cumulative discount factors. In our example, the 1-month rates

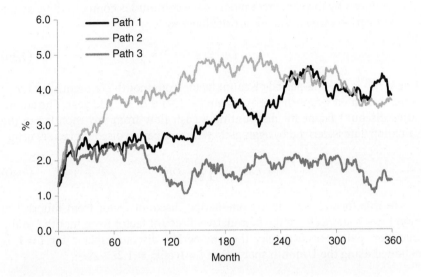

FIGURE 7.7 Three simulated paths of a 1-month rate produced by a Hull-White model

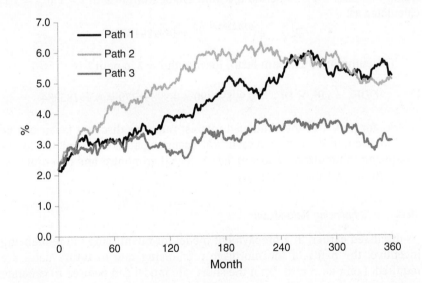

FIGURE 7.8 Three simulated paths of a 5-year rate produced by a Hull-White model

produced by the short rate model have continuous compounding, so the one-period discount factor is calculated as:

$$DF_i = e^{-r_{i-1}\,\Delta t} \tag{7.39}$$

where DF_i is the one-period discount factor from month i to month $i-1$, r_{i-1} is the simulated 1-month rate at month $i-1$, and $\Delta t = 1/12$ year. The cumulative discount factor for discounting a cash flow from any month i to the valuation date is derived by aggregating the one-period discount factors using:

$$CDF_i = \prod_{j=1}^{i} DF_j \tag{7.40}$$

In this formula DF_j is the one-period discount factor from month j to month $j-1$ and CDF_i is the cumulative discount factor from month i to the valuation date. For example, the one-period discount factor for $i=1$ is obtained using the 1-month spot rate at $i=0$ of $r_0 = 1.28\%$ as:

$$DF_1 = e^{-0.0128\times\left(\frac{1}{12}\right)} = 0.99893390$$

The simulated 1-month rate in path 1 of Figure 7.7 at $i=1$ is $r_1 = 1.2994\%$. Using this rate, the one-period discount factor from month $i=2$ to $i=1$ is calculated as:

$$DF_2 = e^{-0.012994\times\left(\frac{1}{12}\right)} = 0.99891779$$

The cumulative discount factor for month $i=2$ in path 1 is:

$$CDF_2 = DF_1 \times DF_2 = 0.99893390 \times 0.99891779 = 0.99785284$$

So, for path 1 of the simulated interest rate, this discount factor can be used to discount the expected cash flow occurring at month $i=2$ to the valuation date. Cumulative discount factors for other months and other interest rate paths are calculated similarly.

Mortgage Refinancing Rate Model

As discussed earlier, in a prepayment model for quantifying the refinancing incentive, the paths of the mortgage refinancing rate in future dates are required. Long-term rates from the short rate model can be used to generate simulated mortgage refinancing rates. Analysis of historical data in the United

FIGURE 7.9 Monthly average of 30-year mortgage rates and 5-year constant maturity Treasury rates
Data source: Treasury rate: Federal Reserve Bank of St. Louis; mortgage rate: Freddie Mac, retrieved from FRED (https://fred.stlouisfed.org/).

States shows that there is a strong relationship between Treasury and swap rates and the mortgage rate. Figure 7.9 presents the average of the U.S. 30-year mortgage rate and 5-year constant maturity Treasury rate from January 1980 to September 2018 on a monthly basis. The high correlation between the two rates is clear. Using historical data and regression or autoregressive modeling techniques, we can build models that convert simulated Treasury or swap rates to mortgage rates. Linear regression models that use interest rates as predictor variables often display autocorrelation in error terms and require modifications to remediate this issue. Here we use an autoregressive error correction model to convert simulated 5-year rates generated by the short rate model to 30-year mortgage refinancing rate. This model has the form:

$$mr_t = \beta_0 + \beta_1 \times 5Y\ Treasury_t + \delta_t$$
$$\delta_t = \varphi_1 \times \delta_{t-1} + \varepsilon_t$$

$$(7.41)$$

In this model, mr_t is the mortgage rate at month t and ε_t is the error term. β_0, β_1, and φ_1 are the parameters of the model, to be estimated. We fit this model to monthly data of 5-year Treasury and 30-year mortgage rates from Figure 7.9 and obtain estimated parameter values of $\beta_0 = 4.6564$,

$\beta_1 = 0.5835$, and $\varphi_1 = 0.9902$. While the result of this model presents a good fit, it should be emphasized that this autoregressive model is used in our example only to illustrate the valuation process of an MBS and is not necessarily an ideal framework for modeling mortgage rates. The Office of Thrift Supervision (OTS)[7] has a mortgage rate model based on Treasury rates. Similar to the model described here, the OTS model uses 5-year Treasury rates plus a spread to model the mortgage rate. The spread is the average of differences between 30-year mortgage rates and 5-year Treasury rates over the last 12 quarters (Office of Thrift Supervision 2000). There are alternative mortgage rate models proposed and used in practice. The *Fixed Income Clearing Corporation (FICC)*, a subsidiary of the *Depository Trust & Clearing Corporation (DTCC)*, is a major fixed-income clearing organization for mortgage-backed and government securities in the United States. In October 2012, FICC proposed a model that uses 2-year and 5-year swap rates as predictors while considering the cointegration of variables (DTCC 2012).

For the valuation example discussed in this section we use the model in Equation (7.41) with the calibrated coefficients stated above. The simulated 5-year rates from the Hull-White short rate model are inputs to this model and outputs are the simulated 30-year mortgage rates. Figure 7.10 presents three simulated paths of mortgage rates generated based on the corresponding 5-year rates from Figure 7.8.

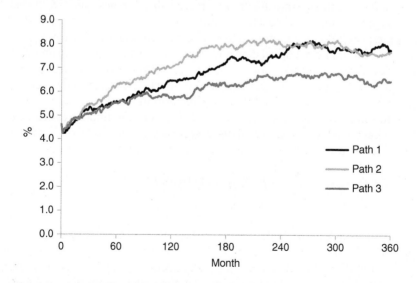

FIGURE 7.10 Three simulated paths of 30-year mortgage refinancing rates produced using an autoregressive error correction model based on simulated 5-year Treasury rates from a Hull-White model

Prepayment Model

The inputs of a typical prepayment model include forecasts of econometric variables, geographic and demographic information, simulated interest rate paths, and characteristics of mortgages in the supporting pool. The model then produces forecasted prepayment rates in the future. Future prepayment rates could be in the form of vectors of PSA, CPR, or SMM. Each of these metrics is easily converted to other forms using equations explained earlier. Richard and Roll (1989) proposed a prepayment model that produces CPRs for each month in the future and has four multiplicative factors, covering effects of refinancing incentive, seasoning, seasonality, and burnout:

$$CPR_t = (Refinancing\ Incentive\ Effect)_t \times (Seasoning\ Effect)_t$$
$$\times (Seasonality\ Effect)_t \times (Burnout\ Effect)_t \tag{7.42}$$

Richard and Roll provided details for each factor in Equation (7.42). Other academic and regulatory works developed different methodologies for these factors (for an example of such works, see Office of Thrift Supervision 2000). For valuation of an MBS using Monte Carlo simulation, the simulated mortgage refinancing rates are inputted into the prepayment model along with other econometric forecasts and housing turnover data. Using these, the prepayment model produces forecasted SMM for each month of a path, for the remaining term of the MBS.

Details of development of a prepayment model are beyond the scope of this book. For the purpose of demonstrating valuation of the MBS in our example, we make simple assumptions based on a PSA scale for the prepayment rates. Particularly, for paths 1, 2, and 3 of the simulated interest rates presented earlier, we assume 100 PSA, 120 PSA, and 80 PSA, respectively, and derive SMM for the remaining term of 360 months. It should be emphasized that typical prepayment models used in practice do not necessarily produce forecasted CPRs that match a PSA scale and the prepayment rates vary based on forecasted econometric variables and simulated interest rate paths. Here, for simplicity we assume that the prepayments for the sample interest rate paths follow three specific PSA scales. This assumption does not change the methodology of MBS valuation using the Monte Carlo simulation, and treatment of SMM for a given month, whether output of a prepayment model or based on an assumption of PSA scale, is the same.

Cash Flow Generator

After prepayment rates for each interest rate path are produced, we can calculate the expected cash flows of the security for the remaining months, either

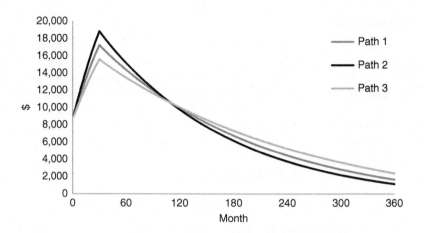

FIGURE 7.11 Expected cash flows of an MBS with a notional amount of $2,004,247, WAC of 4.189%, pass-through rate of 3.5%, and WAM of 360 months, for three simulated interest rate paths and assumed prepayment speeds of 100 PSA, 120 PSA, and 80 PSA for paths 1, 2, and 3, respectively

progressively using previous month-ending balances or using scheduled amounts and survival factors. We demonstrate both methods in the section "Impact of Prepayment on Mortgage-Backed Securities," where the expected cash flow based on a 100 PSA prepayment scale for month 1 was derived as $8,971.36 and $10,617.24 for month 6. Expected cash flows for any month and for any prepayment rate are obtained in a similar way. Each cash flow consists of three components: interest payment, principal payment, and prepayment. Figure 7.11 presents the expected total cash flows of the mortgage-backed security in our example for months 1 to 360 for three sample interest rate paths and the assumed prepayment rates.

Discounting and Aggregation Platform

The next step in valuation of the MBS is to discount the expected cash flows of each interest rate path to the valuation date. Each simulated interest rate path results in a series of expected cash flows occurring at month-ends of the remaining term of the MBS and the short rate model provides us with the cumulative discount factor for each month-end. The value of the MBS for a given interest rate path is the summation of the discounted expected cash flows at the valuation date:

$$V_k = \sum_{i=1}^{n} CF_{i,k} \times CDF_{i,k} \qquad (7.43)$$

TABLE 7.4   Value of an MBS with a notional amount of $2,004,247, WAC of 4.189%, pass-through rate of 3.5%, and WAM of 360 months, for three simulated interest rate paths

Interest Rate Path	Security Value ($)	Assumed Prepayment Speed (PSA)
1	2,175,495.45	100
2	2,028,957.25	120
3	2,310,405.77	80
Average:	2,171.619.49	

In this equation k represents an interest rate path, $CF_{i,k}$ is the expected cash flow occurring at month i for path k, and $CDF_{i,k}$ is the cumulative discount factor of month i for path k. This process is repeated for a sufficiently large number of interest rate paths. Finally, the value of the security is the average of the values of all interest rate paths:

$$V_{MBS} = \frac{1}{M}\sum_{k=1}^{M} V_k \tag{7.44}$$

In this equation M is the number of simulated interest rate paths. For the MBS in our example, we used the cash flows from Figure 7.11 and, using cumulative discount factors from the short rate model, we calculated the value of the MBS for each of the three interest rate paths in Figure 7.7. These values are presented in Table 7.4. The average of these three simulated values is $2,171.619.49. In practice, three interest rate paths are not enough and a much larger number of simulated paths (e.g., 1,000) is required to converge to a more reliable result.

For mortgage-backed securities, it is possible to perform the valuation at the individual loan level and obtain the value of an MBS by aggregating these results. However, this is not the common approach in practice and often the Monte Carlo simulation at the pool level is used. Payments of mortgages in the supporting pool are due on the first day of each month. It takes the mortgage servicer a few days to collect and send payments to MBS holders. This creates a delay between mortgage due dates and actual payment dates to MBS investors. For simplicity we did not consider this delay in our example, but a more accurate valuation should consider this delay. While here our focus is on the cash flow uncertainty due to prepayment, default of underlying mortgages can also create uncertainty in the cash flows of a pass-through MBS. Due to implicit and explicit guarantees, default and recovery rates are less relevant for agency MBSs but very important for non-agency MBSs. In a following section we discuss the impact of default on cash flows of MBSs.

Due to embedded prepayment options in mortgage-backed securities, investors often use the option-adjusted spread (OAS) to evaluate and compare these bonds. For an MBS, an OAS is the additional spread added to the rates from the short rate model used in calculation of cumulative discount factors, which makes the average of the path values (i.e., theoretical value) equal to the observed market price. Therefore, if rates from the short rate model have continuous compounding, OAS is the spread γ that satisfies the following equation:

$$MV_{MBS} = \frac{1}{M} \sum_{k=1}^{M} \sum_{i=1}^{n} \left[CF_{i,k} \times \prod_{j=1}^{i} e^{-(r_{j-1}+\gamma)\,\Delta t} \right] \tag{7.45}$$

where:

MV_{MBS} = Observed market value of MBS
$CF_{i,k}$ = Total cash flow at month i for path k
r_{j-1} = 1-month short rate for month $j-1$
M = Number of simulated interest rate paths

This equation is derived by combining Equations (7.39), (7.40), (7.43), and (7.44) while incorporating an OAS in one-period discount factors.

Number of Simulated Paths and Convergence

An important step in valuation of an MBS using Monte Carlo simulation is the decision about the number of simulated interest rate paths, or in other words, the sample size. As the number of simulated paths increases, the accuracy of the estimated value also increases. Since in Monte Carlo simulation the value of the MBS is derived as the average of simulated values over all interest rate paths, one way to decide the appropriate number of simulated paths is by creating a confidence interval around this average value and use the width of the confidence interval as the decision criterion. Assume that X is a continuous random variable representing the value of the security and $X_1, X_2, \cdots, X_n$ are simulated values of the security, forming a sample of size n. When sample size is large, sample mean has a normal distribution with mean μ and standard deviation of σ^2/n, where μ and σ are the mean and standard deviation of the population. Unknown population mean and standard deviation can be estimated by sample mean and sample standard deviation as:

$$\overline{X} = \frac{\sum_{i=1}^{n} X_i}{n} \tag{7.46}$$

$$S = \sqrt{\frac{\sum_{i=1}^{n}(X_i - \overline{X})^2}{n-1}} \tag{7.47}$$

The $(1 - \alpha)100\%$ confidence interval of the population mean is constructed as:

$$\overline{X} - Z_{\frac{\alpha}{2}} \frac{S}{\sqrt{n}} \leq \mu \leq \overline{X} + Z_{\frac{\alpha}{2}} \frac{S}{\sqrt{n}} \tag{7.48}$$

where $Z_{\frac{\alpha}{2}}$ is the inverse of the standard normal cumulative distribution function for probability $\frac{\alpha}{2}$.[8] Consider again the mortgage-backed security we studied in the example in the previous section. Figure 7.12 presents a 95% confidence interval around the average of simulated values for this MBS for different numbers of simulated interest rate paths. For example, if based on simulated values for sample size $n = 1,000$ the sample mean and sample standard deviation are \$2,498,763.84 and \$99,709.83, the 95% confidence interval around the mean of the population representing the security value is:

$$2,498,763.84 - 1.96 \times \frac{99,709.83}{\sqrt{1000}} \leq \mu \leq 2,498,763.84 + 1.96 \times \frac{99,709.83}{\sqrt{1000}}$$

or

$$2,492,583.93 \leq \mu \leq 2,504,943.74$$

where 1.96 is the Z-value from the standard normal table for $\alpha/2 = 0.025$. Therefore, based on this with 95% probability we are confident that the value

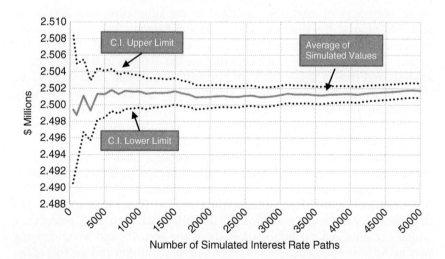

FIGURE 7.12 A 95% confidence interval around the mean of a random variable representing the value of an MBS with a notional amount of \$2,004,247, WAC of 4.189%, pass-through rate of 3.5%, and WAM of 360 months, for different numbers of simulated interest rate paths (sample size)

of the security is between \$2,492,583.93 and \$2,504,943.74. If this level of accuracy is acceptable, then 1,000 is an appropriate sample size. For a tighter confidence interval, we need to increase the number of simulated interest rate paths. In deciding the appropriate number of simulated interest rate paths we need to consider two issues. First, as can be seen from Figure 7.12, as the number of simulated paths increases the width of confidence interval decreases, but the increase has a diminishing impact in reducing the confidence interval width. For example, when sample size is increased from 1,000 to 2,000 the width of the confidence interval decreases rather significantly, resulting in a more accurate estimate for the value of the security. But an increase from 10,000 to 11,000 does not have a similar magnitude of impact in reducing the confidence interval width. At larger sample sizes, further increases do not materially change the width of the confidence interval. The second issue is the computational time and its associated cost. As the number of simulated interest rate paths increases computational time also increases and this creates a tradeoff between the increase in number of simulated paths and the cost of analysis. An ALM analyst should consider both the diminishing impact of increase in sample size and the cost of the analysis when deciding the number of simulated interest rate paths used in valuation of an MBS.

Impact of Default on Mortgage-Backed Securities

When borrowers of mortgages included in the supporting pool default on their obligations, the cash flows, outstanding balance, and overall performance of the MBS supported by the pool are also impacted. To study the impact of default, one approach is to include the defaults in the prepayment analysis and treat a default as a prepayment of the loan. Alternatively, we can study the impact of the default explicitly and separate from the voluntary prepayment. In this section we take the latter approach. However, as we will see shortly, the prepayment and default influence each other since they are both associated with outstanding loan balances in the pool.

To start our discussion, first we need to define what constitutes a loan default. Banks and lending companies use different conditions and definitions for default. For example, a bank may consider a loan in default when it is delinquent more than 90 days while another issuer may consider 120 days delinquency as the condition for default. Usually an MBS prospectus, which contains general information about the security and its underlying pool at the time of issuance, clarifies the default definition and the role of the mortgage servicer in case of default. *Servicer advances* are a customary feature of MBSs that plays an important role in default analysis of these securities. Servicer advances are funds paid by the mortgage servicer under the terms of agreement to MBS investors on behalf of borrowers who are late in principal or interest payments. When a mortgage borrower does not pay the expected monthly principal and interest in full, the servicer advances the monthly payment in full to investors. Once the borrower becomes current on his payment, or when losses are recovered through the foreclosure and subsequent sale of the collateral property, the servicer is repaid for advanced funds. Depending on the structure of the MBS, servicer advances may also be recovered from insurance proceeds. In the following analysis when we explain the MBS cash flows in the presence of defaults, we assume that servicer advances are made.

For mortgage-backed securities, similar to prepayment, defaults in future months are assumed as a percentage of the outstanding balance at the end of the previous month (beginning of the current month). It is also assumed that once a mortgage is defaulted it remains in default state until it is liquidated and partially recovered. For defaults, there are two rates that each play an important role in cash flow analysis of an MBS. *Monthly default rate (MDR)* is the percentage of the outstanding balance at the end of the previous month that defaults in the current month. The MDR defines the amount of new defaults in a month. Once a portion of the outstanding balance of the supporting pool is presumed defaulted, it is assumed that the loss is partially recovered after a period known as *month to liquidation (MTL)*. This is the expected period for foreclosure, property acquisition, and the eventual sale and liquidation of property used as the collateral of a defaulted mortgage loan. *Loss rate (LR)* is the percentage of the defaulted balance that is not recovered at the liquidation month.

For default analysis of an MBS, the outstanding loan balance of a supporting pool can be separated into two parts: a *performing balance* and a *non-performing balance*. A performing balance consists of the balance of loans that are not defaulted and are carrying on as expected, making principal and interest payments and voluntary prepayments. A non-performing balance consists of loans that are defaulted and in the foreclosure process but not liquidated yet. For cash flow analysis of an MBS, often the non-performing balance is still amortized. Usually when servicer advances are part of the structure of an MBS, the principal and interest payments of the non-performing loans are covered and paid by the servicer. Depending on the structure of the MBS, another possibility is that only principal payments are advanced while the non-performing balance is considered as non-accrual and hence interest payments are not advanced. Here and in the following discussions, we assume that both principal and interest of non-performing loans are advanced. Repayment of the funds used in principal and interest advances should be included in determining the loss rate, along with all other costs such as foreclosure and legal fees.

If D_i is the new default amount in month i and $B_{perf,i-1}$ is the performing loan balance of the supporting pool at the end of month $i-1$, the monthly default rate for month i is defined as:

$$MDR_i = \frac{D_i}{B_{Perf,i-1}} \qquad (7.49)$$

The MDR for default is analogous to SMM for prepayment but with one major difference: SMM is the ratio of prepayment to the outstanding balance at the beginning of month *after* the expected principal payment for the current month is deducted while the MDR is the ratio of the default to the outstanding performing balance at the beginning of the month *before* deducting the current month's expected principal payment. *Constant default rate (CDR)* is the annualized default rate, calculated as follows:

$$CDR_i = 1 - (1 - MDR_i)^{12} \qquad (7.50)$$

The CDR for default is analogous to the CPR for prepayment. The CDR can be converted to the MDR using:

$$MDR_i = 1 - (1 - CDR_i)^{\frac{1}{12}} \qquad (7.51)$$

Similar to prepayment rates, to calculate cash flow of an MBS monthly default rates can be either modeled directly or based on assumed standards. The *Standard Default Assumption (SDA)*, developed by the *Bond Market Association*, currently known as the Securities Industry and Financial Markets Association, is a standard method of indicating the constant default rate assumed at different months over the life of the mortgage pool. SDA provides a monthly series of CDR. The 100 SDA benchmark scale specifies that:

- CDR rises from 0% at month 0 to 0.60% at month 30, increasing by 0.02% per month.
- From month 31 to month 60, CDR remains at a peak of 0.60%.
- From month 61 to month 120, CDR declines from 0.60% to 0.03%, decreasing by 0.0095% per month.
- CDR remains at 0.03% level from month 121 until the end of pool term, with the exception that at the last few months corresponding to the month to liquidation (MTL), CDR drops to 0%. For example, if the term of the loans in the pool is 360 months and the assumed MTL is 12 months, CDR for months 349 to 360 is set to 0%.

This pattern for standard 100 SDA is often observed in practice where in the early months after the origination, the default rate increases steadily, reaching a peak level, and after a period of staying at the peak level, it starts to decline. The relationship between CDR and standard 100 SDA can be summarized as follows:

$$CDR_i = SDA_i$$

$$\times \begin{cases} 0.02\% \times Age & \text{if } Age \leq 30 \\ 0.60\% & \text{if } 30 < Age \leq 60 \\ 0.60\% - 0.0095\% \times (Age - 60) & \text{if } 61 < Age \leq 120 \\ 0.03\% & 120 < Age \leq Term - MTL \\ 0\% & Term - MTL < Age \end{cases}$$

$$(7.52)$$

In this equation SDA_i is expressed in percentage, so for example, for 100 SDA, 100% or 1 should be used; *Term* is the weighted average term of mortgages in the pool; and *Age*, expressed in months, is the weighted average age of mortgages included in the supporting pool from their corresponding initiation times, weighted by the remaining balance of each mortgage. Other default scales are stated as multiples of the 100 SDA. For example, CDRs based on a 150 SDA scale are 1.5 times the CDRs from the 100 SDA and for a 50 SDA scale, CDRs are half of the 100 SDA standard CDRs. CDRs based on 50 SDA, 100 SDA, and 150 SDA scales are shown in Figure 7.13 for 360 months of mortgage

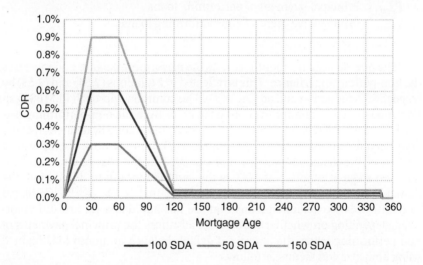

FIGURE 7.13 50 SDA, 100 SDA, and 150 SDA default scales for 360 months mortgage age and 12 months to liquidation

age and an MTL of 12 months. A CDR derived from an assumed SDA can be converted to an MDR using Equation (7.51).

Whether the MDR is modeled, or an SDA is assumed and converted to a CDR and MDR, it can be used to calculate the expected new default using:

$$D_i = B_{Perf,i-1} \times MDR_i \qquad (7.53)$$

As mentioned before, the outstanding loan balance of the supporting pool at the end of a month i can be separated into a performing balance and a non-performing balance, each calculated recursively as follows:

$$B_{Perf,i} = B_{Perf,i-1} - D_i - PP_i - P_{Perf,i} \qquad (7.54)$$

$$B_{Non\text{-}Perf,i} = B_{Non\text{-}Perf,i-1} + D_i - ADB_i - P_{Non\text{-}Perf,i} \qquad (7.55)$$

These equations are extensions of Equation (7.26) when default is considered, where:

$$B_{Perf,i} = \text{Performing balance at the end of month } i$$
$$B_{Non\text{-}Perf,i} = \text{Non-performing balance at the end of month } i$$
$$D_i = \text{New default in month } i$$
$$PP_i = \text{Voluntary prepayment in month } i$$
$$ADB_i = \text{Amortized default balance in month } i$$
$$P_{Perf,i} = \text{Principal payment of performing loans}$$
$$P_{Non\text{-}Perf,i} = \text{Principal payment of non-performing loans}$$

The new default in a month reduces the performing balance and increases the non-performing balance. This is reflected in Equations (7.54) and (7.55) by respectively deducting and adding of D_i. The common approach in MBS cash flow modeling is to remove the liquidated loans from the non-performing balance at the month when liquidation happens. This is done by deduction of the amortized default balance ADB_i in Equation (7.55) to remove the amortized portion of the defaulted balance that occurred in the past and reached liquidation stage in month i. If MTL is the assumed month to liquidation, the new default that occurred in month $i - MTL$, that is, D_{i-MTL}, is liquidated in month i. Since defaulted loans that are not liquidated yet are still amortized, depending on whether the servicer advances the principal payments of non-performing loans, the amortized default balance in month i is obtained using amortization factors as follows:

$$ADB_i = \begin{cases} D_{i-MTL}\left(\dfrac{A_{i-1}}{A_{i-1-MTL}}\right) & \textit{with servicer advance} \\[2ex] D_{i-MTL} & \textit{without servicer advance} \end{cases} \qquad (7.56)$$

Since the non-performing balance is still amortized, the principal payment in each month also has two parts: principal payment of the performing balance and principal payment of the non-performing balance. The principal payment of the performing balance is calculated as:

$$P_{Perf,i} = (B_{Perf,i-1} - D_i)\left(1 - \frac{A_i}{A_{i-1}}\right) \tag{7.57}$$

This is an extension of Equation (7.23) when default is considered. Depending on whether the servicer advances the principal payments of non-performing loans, principal payment of non-performing balance is calculated as:

$$P_{Non-Perf,i} =$$

$$
\begin{cases}
(B_{Non-Perf,i-1} + D_i - ADB_i)\left(1 - \frac{A_i}{A_{i-1}}\right) & \text{\textit{with servicer advance}} \\
0 & \text{\textit{without servicer advance}}
\end{cases}
\tag{7.58}
$$

The total principal payment is the summation of principal payments from the performing and non-performing balances:

$$P_i =$$

$$
\begin{cases}
(B_{Perf,i-1} + B_{Non-Perf,i} - ADB_i)\left(1 - \frac{A_i}{A_{i-1}}\right) & \text{\textit{with servicer advance}} \\
(B_{Perf,i-1} - D_i)\left(1 - \frac{A_i}{A_{i-1}}\right) & \text{\textit{without servicer advance}}
\end{cases}
\tag{7.59}
$$

Voluntary prepayment used in Equation (7.54) is calculated as before, using the monthly prepayment rate:

$$PP_i = B_{Perf,i-1}\left(\frac{A_i}{A_{i-1}}\right) SMM_i \tag{7.60}$$

New default D_{i-MTL} occurring at month $i - MTL$ is amortized until month i when liquidation occurs. At this month, part of the amortized default balance is recovered and part of it is considered a loss. The loss amount is determined using an assumed loss rate LR. If $D_{i-MTL} \times LR$ is less than the amortized default balance at month i, then $D_{i-MTL} \times LR$ is the amount of principal loss in month i and the difference between the amortized default balance and the principal loss is the principal recovery amount. Generally, we have:

$$P_{Loss,i} = min(D_{i-MTL} \times LR, ADB_i) \tag{7.61}$$

$$P_{Rcvr,i} = max(ADB_i - P_{Loss,i}, 0) \tag{7.62}$$

where:

$$P_{Loss,i} = \text{Principal loss in month } i$$
$$P_{Rcvr,i} = \text{Principal recovery in month } i$$
$$LR = \text{Loss rate } (\%)$$

Repayment of servicer advances, cost of foreclosure, legal fees, and property sales should be considered when estimating the loss rate. Similar to the principal payment, the interest payment also has two parts: interest payment from the performing balance and interest payment from the non-performing balance. The interest payment of the performing balance is calculated as:

$$I_{Perf,i} = (B_{Perf,i-1} - D_i)(r - s) \tag{7.63}$$

where r is the weighted average coupon rate of the performing loans and s is the servicing spread. Depending on whether the servicer advances the interest payment of non-performing loans, the interest payment of the non-performing balance is calculated as:

$$I_{Non-Perf,i} = \begin{cases} (B_{Non-Perf,i-1} + D_i)(r - s) & \text{\textit{with servicer advance}} \\ 0 & \text{\textit{without servicer advance}} \end{cases} \tag{7.64}$$

The total interest payment is the summation of interest payments from the performing and the non-performing balances:

$$I_i = \begin{cases} (B_{Perf,i-1} + B_{Non-Perf,i-1})(r - s) & \text{\textit{with servicer advance}} \\ (B_{Perf,i-1} - D_i)(r - s) & \text{\textit{without servicer advance}} \end{cases} \tag{7.65}$$

Finally, based on these components, the total monthly cash flow of an MBS in month i is obtained as:

$$CF_i = P_i + PP_i + I_i + P_{Rcvr,i} \tag{7.66}$$

This is an extension of Equation (7.37) when default is considered. The following table summarizes the formulas discussed here when both prepayment and default are considered in derivation of MBS cash flows.

Mortgage-Backed Security with Prepayment and Default

Using previous period balance:

Outstanding Balance (end of period):

$$B_{Perf,i} = B_{Perf,i-1} - D_i - PP_i - P_{Perf,i}$$

$$B_{Non\text{-}Perf,i} = B_{Non\text{-}Perf,i-1} + D_i - ADB_i - P_{Non\text{-}Perf,i}$$

Principal Payment:

$$P_{Perf,i} = (B_{Perf,i-1} - D_i)\left(1 - \frac{A_i}{A_{i-1}}\right)$$

$$P_{Non\text{-}Perf,i} = \begin{cases} (B_{Non\text{-}Perf,i-1} + D_i - ADB_i)\left(1 - \frac{A_i}{A_{i-1}}\right) & \text{\textit{with servicer advance}} \\ 0 & \text{\textit{without servicer advance}} \end{cases}$$

$$P_i = P_{Perf,i} + P_{Non\text{-}Perf,i}$$

Interest Payment:

$$I_{Perf,i} = (B_{Perf,i-1} - D_i)(r - s)$$

$$I_{Non\text{-}Perf,i} = \begin{cases} (B_{Non\text{-}Perf,i-1} + D_i)(r - s) & \text{\textit{with servicer advance}} \\ 0 & \text{\textit{without servicer advance}} \end{cases}$$

$$I_i = I_{Perf,i} + I_{Non\text{-}Perf,i}$$

Prepayment:

$$PP_i = B_{Perf,i-1}\left(\frac{A_i}{A_{i-1}}\right) SMM_i$$

Default:

$$D_i = B_{Perf,i-1} \times MDR_i$$

$$ADB_i = \begin{cases} D_{i-MTL}\left(\frac{A_{i-1}}{A_{i-1-MTL}}\right) & \text{\textit{with servicer advance}} \\ D_{i-MTL} & \text{\textit{without servicer advance}} \end{cases}$$

Loss and Recovery:

$$P_{Loss,i} = Min(D_{i-MTL} \times LR, ADB_i)$$
$$P_{Rcvr,i} = Max(ADB_i - P_{Loss,i}, 0)$$

Total cash flow:

$$CF_i = P_i + PP_i + I_i + P_{Rcvr,i}$$

$B_{Perf,i}$ = Performing balance; $B_{Non\text{-}Perf,i}$ = Non-performing balance; $P_{Perf,i}$ = Principal payment of performing balance; $P_{Non\text{-}Perf,i}$ = Principal payment of non-performing balance; P_i = Total principal payment; $I_{Perf,i}$ = Interest payment of performing balance; $I_{Non\text{-}Perf,i}$ = Interest payment of non-performing balance; I_i = Total interest payment; PP_i = Prepayment amount; r = Weighted average coupon rate; s = Servicing spread; SMM_i = Single monthly mortality rate; A_i = Amortization factor; D_i = Default amount; ADB_i = Amortized default balance; $P_{Loss,i}$ = Principal loss; $P_{Rcvr,i}$ = Principal recovery; CF_i = Total cash flow

To demonstrate the inclusion of default in cash flow estimation of an MBS, consider again the security discussed in the example in the previous section. Recall that the notional amount of this MBS is $2,004,247, supported by a pool of conventional fixed-rate mortgage loans with a weighted average coupon rate of 4.189% and a pass-through rate of 3.5%. The current date is October 1, 2018, and the MBS maturing date is October 1, 2048. The weighted average remaining life is $n = 360$, the monthly coupon rate is $r = 4.189\%/12 = 0.349083\%$, and the monthly servicing spread is $s = 0.689\%/12 = 0.057417\%$. Other assumptions used in our example are:

- Default rate in the next 360 months follows 100 SDA. This means that the CDR in each month is obtained using Equation (7.52) with $SDA_i = 1$.
- Prepayment rate is based on 100 PSA.
- Month to liquidation is 12 months.
- Loss rate is 30%.
- Servicer advances both principal and interest of non-performing balances.

Month 1

For month 1 the CDR is 0.02% and the MDR is calculated using Equation (7.51) as:

$$MDR_1 = 1 - (1 - 0.02\%)^{\frac{1}{12}} = 0.0017\%$$

The non-performing balance at the inception of the MBS is zero. The default in month 1 is obtained using Equation (7.53) based on the performing balance of $2,004,247 as:

$$D_1 = 2,004,247 \times MDR_1 = 2,004,247 \times 0.0017\% = 33.41$$

The amortized default balance for month 1 is zero as there is no past default liquidated in this month. The principal payments of the performing and non-performing balances are calculated using Equations (7.57) and (7.58) where amortization factors are calculated using Equations (7.4) or (7.5):

$$P_{Perf,1} = (2,004,247 - D_1)\left(1 - \frac{A_1}{A_0}\right)$$

$$= (2,004,247 - 33.41)\left(1 - \frac{0.99860708}{1}\right) = 2,791.71$$

$$P_{Non\text{-}Perf,1} = (0 + D_1 - ADB_1)\left(1 - \frac{A_1}{A_0}\right)$$

$$= (0 + 33.41 - 0)\left(1 - \frac{0.99860708}{1}\right) = 0.05$$

The total principal payment is:

$$P_1 = 2{,}791.71 + 0.05 = 2{,}791.76$$

The monthly prepayment rate based on 100 PSA is 0.016682%; therefore, prepayment for month 1 can be calculated using Equation (7.60) as:

$$PP_1 = 2{,}004{,}247 \times \left(\frac{0.99860708}{1}\right) \times 0.0167\% = 333.88$$

Having the values of default, amortized default balance, prepayment, and principal payments, we can calculate the performing and non-performing balances at the end of month 1 using Equations (7.54) and (7.55) as:

$$B_{Perf,1} = 2{,}004{,}247 - D_1 - PP_1 - P_{Perf,1}$$

$$= 2{,}004{,}247 - 33.41 - 333.88 - 2{,}791.71 = 2{,}001{,}088.00$$

$$B_{Non\text{-}Perf,1} = 0 + D_1 - ADB_1 - P_{Non\text{-}Perf,1} = 0 + 33.41 - 0 - 0.05$$

$$= 33.36$$

Interest payments for month 1 are obtained using Equations (7.63) and (7.64) as:

$$I_{Perf,1} = (2{,}004{,}247 - D_1)(r - s)$$

$$= (2{,}004{,}247 - 33.41) \times (0.349083\% - 0.057417\%) = 5{,}845.62$$

$$I_{Non\text{-}Perf,1} = (0 + D_1)(r - s)$$

$$= (0 + 33.41) \times (0.349083\% - 0.057417\%) = 0.10$$

The total interest payment is:

$$I_1 = 5{,}845.62 + 0.10 = 5{,}845.72$$

Principal loss and recovery for month 1 are both zero, as there was no past default liquidated in this month. Finally, total estimated cash flow for month 1 is obtained using Equation (7.66) as:

$$CF_1 = P_1 + PP_1 + I_1 + P_{Rcvr,1} = 2{,}791.76 + 333.88 + 5{,}845.72 + 0 = 8{,}971.36$$

Months 2 to 12

Cash flows in month 2 to month 12 are calculated similar to those in month 1. The only difference is that for each month the non-performing balance of the previous month is not zero. For example, for month 2 the previous month non-performing balance is $33.36 and the performing balance is $2,001,088.00, calculated for month 1. Similar to month 1 and since the assumed month to liquidation is 12 months, the amortized default balance, principal loss, and principal recovery for month 2 to month 12 are zero. Table 7.5 shows a partial view of different cash flows and balances for a few selected months for the MBS used in our example, when both prepayment and default are considered.

Month 13

Since month to liquidation is assumed as 12 months, month 13 is the first month with liquation and recovery. From Table 7.5 the performing and non-performing balances of the previous month (i.e., month 12) are $1,941,904.59 and $2,546.69 respectively. Based on assumed 100 SDA, the CDR for month 13 is 0.26% and the MDR is calculated as:

$$MDR_{13} = 1 - (1 - 0.26\%)^{\frac{1}{12}} = 0.0216925\%$$

The default in month 13 is calculated based on the performing balance of $1,941,904.59 as:

$$D_{13} = B_{Perf,12} \times MDR_{13} = 1,941,904.59 \times 0.0216925\% = 421.25$$

The default that occurred in month 1 reaches the liquidation stage in month 13. In month 1 the default amount was calculated as $33.41. This default balance is amortized in month 2 to month 12 and the amortized default balance in month 13 is calculated using Equation (7.56) where $MTL = 12$:

$$ADB_{13} = D_1 \left(\frac{A_{12}}{A_0}\right) = 33.41 \times \left(\frac{0.98296027}{1}\right) = 32.84$$

The difference between the original default amount of $33.41 in month 1 and the amortized default balance of $32.84 in month 13 is included in the principal payments of the non-performing balance of month 2 to month 12. This is due to the assumption that the servicer advances principal payments of non-performing balance. Principal payments of the performing and

TABLE 7.5 A partial view of cash flow schedule of an MBS with a notional amount of $2,004,247, WAC of 4.189%, pass-through rate of 3.5%, and WAM of 360 months. Defaults are based on 100 SDA and prepayments are based on 100 PSA.

Period	Date	Performing Balance ($)	Non-Performing Balance ($)	Amortized Default Balance ($)	Performing Principal Payment ($)	Non-Performing Principal Payment ($)	Default ($)	Prepayment ($)	Performing Interest Payment ($)	Non-Performing Interest Payment ($)	Principal Loss ($)	Principal Recovery ($)	Total Cash Flow ($)
						Total:	$786,494.32	$701,474.90	$59,210.64	$1,158,542.04	$742,359.72	$2,218.67	$17,762.89	$40,046.06	$2,731,062.49
0	11/1/2018	2,004,247.00	0.00	0.00									
1	12/1/2018	2,001,088.00	33.36	0.00	2,791.71	33.36	33.41	333.88	5,845.62	0.10	0.00	0.00	8,971.36
2	1/1/2019	1,997,553.07	99.94	0.00	2,800.89	99.94	66.72	667.32	5,836.31	0.29	0.00	0.00	9,304.96
3	2/1/2019	1,993,643.45	199.56	0.00	2,809.59	199.56	99.91	1,000.13	5,825.91	0.58	0.00	0.00	9,636.49
4	3/1/2019	1,989,360.58	332.05	0.00	2,817.80	332.05	132.96	1,332.11	5,814.41	0.97	0.00	0.00	9,965.75
⋮	⋮	⋮	⋮	⋮	⋮	⋮	⋮	⋮	⋮	⋮	⋮	⋮	⋮
11	9/1/2019	1,949,095.91	2,160.19	0.00	2,861.04	2,160.19	358.95	3,617.25	5,703.76	6.31	0.00	0.00	12,191.52
12	10/1/2019	1,941,904.59	2,546.69	0.00	2,865.13	2,546.69	390.25	3,935.95	5,683.72	7.44	0.00	0.00	12,495.99
13	11/1/2019	1,934,362.48	2,930.76	32.84	2,868.70	2,930.76	421.25	4,252.16	5,662.66	8.66	10.02	22.82	12,819.32
14	12/1/2019	1,926,473.12	3,312.19	65.57	2,871.73	3,312.19	451.93	4,565.70	5,640.57	9.87	20.01	45.56	13,138.35
15	1/1/2020	1,918,240.20	3,690.77	98.19	2,874.22	3,690.77	482.28	4,876.41	5,617.47	11.07	29.97	68.21	13,452.90
⋮	⋮	⋮	⋮	⋮	⋮	⋮	⋮	⋮	⋮	⋮	⋮	⋮	⋮
120	10/1/2028	888,161.53	761.58	114.46	2,374.49	761.58	22.38	4,591.56	2,610.79	2.56	35.41	79.05	9,660.47
121	11/1/2028	881,213.23	675.92	106.06	2,370.46	75.92	22.21	4,555.63	2,590.41	2.29	32.81	73.24	9,593.84
122	12/1/2028	874,304.83	598.56	97.78	2,366.45	598.56	22.03	4,519.92	2,570.14	2.04	30.26	67.52	9,527.68
⋮	⋮	⋮	⋮	⋮	⋮	⋮	⋮	⋮	⋮	⋮	⋮	⋮	⋮
358	8/1/2048	3,172.27	0.17	0.13	1,586.02	0.17	0.00	16.40	13.93	0.00	0.13	0.00	1,616.43
359	9/1/2048	1,580.73	0.04	0.08	1,583.37	0.04	0.00	8.17	9.25	0.00	0.08	0.00	1,600.84
360	10/1/2048	0.00	0.00	0.04	1,580.73	0.00	0.00	0.00	4.61	0.00	0.04	0.00	1,585.34

non-performing balances in month 13 are calculated using Equations (7.57) and (7.58) as:

$$P_{Perf,13} = (B_{Perf,12} - D_{13})\left(1 - \frac{A_{13}}{A_{12}}\right)$$

$$= (1,941,904.59 - 421.25)\left(1 - \frac{0.98150787}{0.98296027}\right) = 2,868.70$$

$$P_{Non\text{-}Perf,13} = (B_{Non\text{-}Perf,12} + D_{13} - ADB_{13})\left(1 - \frac{A_{13}}{A_{12}}\right)$$

$$= (2,546.69 + 421.25 - 32.84)\left(1 - \frac{0.98150787}{0.98296027}\right) = 4.34$$

The total principal payment is:

$$P_{13} = 2,868.70 + 4.34 = 2,873.04$$

Based on 100 PSA, the monthly prepayment rate in month 13 is 0.219292%, so the prepayment amount is calculated using Equation (7.60) as:

$$PP_{13} = B_{Perf,12}\left(\frac{A_{13}}{A_{12}}\right)SMM_{13}$$

$$= 1,941,904.59 \times \left(\frac{0.98150787}{0.98296027}\right) \times 0.219292\% = 4,252.16$$

The performing and non-performing balances at the end of month 13 are calculated using Equations (7.54) and (7.55) as:

$$B_{Perf,13} = B_{Perf,12} - D_{13} - PP_{13} - P_{Perf,13}$$

$$= 1,941,904.59 - 421.25 - 4,252.16 - 2,868.70 = 1,934,362.48$$

$$B_{Non\text{-}Perf,13} = B_{Non\text{-}Perf,12} + D_{13} - ADB_{13} - P_{Non\text{-}Perf,13}$$

$$= 2,546.69 + 421.25 - 32.84 - 4.34 = 2,930.76$$

Interest payments for month 13 are calculated using Equations (7.63) and (7.64) as:

$$I_{Perf,13} = (B_{Perf,12} - D_{13})(r - s)$$

$$= (1,941,904.59 - 421.25) \times (0.349083\% - 0.057417\%) = 5,662.66$$

$$I_{Non\text{-}Perf,13} = (B_{Non\text{-}Perf,12} + D_{13})(r - s)$$

$$= (2,546.69 + 421.25) \times (0.349083\% - 0.057417\%) = 8.66$$

The total interest payment is:

$$I_{13} = 5,662.66 + 8.66 = 5,671.32$$

The default that occurred in month 1, after amortization, reaches the liquidation stage in month 13. Based on an assumed loss rate of 30%, principal loss and recovery amounts in month 13 are calculated using Equations (7.61) and (7.62) as:

$$P_{Loss,13} = \text{Min}(D_1 \times 30\%, ADB_{13}) = \text{Min}(33.41 \times 30\%, 32.84) = 10.02$$

$$P_{Rcvr,13} = \text{Max}(ADB_{13} - P_{Loss,13}, 0) = \text{Max}(32.84 - 10.02, 0) = 22.82$$

Finally, the total estimated cash flow for month 13 is obtained, with some rounding error, as:

$$CF_{13} = P_{13} + PP_{13} + I_{13} + P_{Rcvr,13}$$
$$= 2,873.04 + 4,252.16 + 5,671.32 + 22.82 = 12819.32$$

Months 14 to 360

Estimated cash flows and balances for the months 14 to 360 are obtained similar to what was explained earlier. Table 7.5 presents cash flows and balances for a few selected months in this period. Figure 7.14 presents four components of the estimated cash flows of the MBS in our example: total principal payment, total interest payment, prepayment, and principal recovery for each month.

This methodology for estimating the cash flow of an MBS can be used for valuation purposes. Similar to the prepayment, banks use a quantitative technique to model default rates based on demographic and econometric data, specification of mortgages in the underlying pool (such as historical delinquencies), and their obligors' information (such as FICO® score[9]). Forecasted default rates, along with forecasted prepayment rates, are used to derive estimated future cash flows of the MBS. Figure 7.15 extends Figure 7.6 for components of MBS valuation while including the default model.

Default of *subprime* mortgages used in mortgage-backed securities issued prior to 2007 in the United States contributed significantly to the financial crisis of 2007–2009. Subprime mortgages generally refer to mortgages originated under lax lending practices that were dominant before 2007. Many of those loans were underwritten on properties that were worth less than the borrowed amounts and in many cases there was ample evidence indicating that borrowers were eventually not going to be able to repay their loans. Lack of

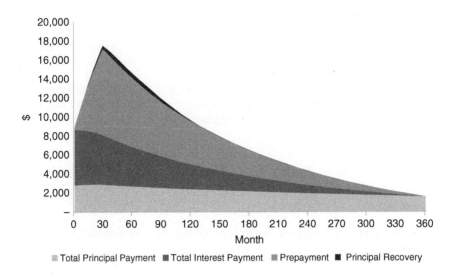

FIGURE 7.14 Total monthly cash flow and its components: principal, interest, prepayment, and principal recovery of an MBS with a notional amount of $2,004,247, WAC of 4.189%, pass-through rate of 3.5%, and WAM of 360 months based on 100 PSA prepayment and 100 SDA default

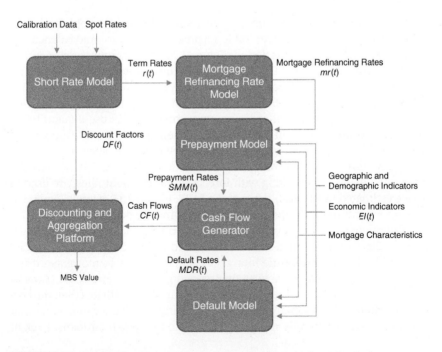

FIGURE 7.15 Schematic view of components required for valuation of mortgage-backed securities using Monte Carlo simulation, when both prepayment and default are considered

proper underwriting due diligence by lenders along with predatory practices by some brokers led to origination of a large number of subprime mortgages and many MBS issuers used those loans as the collateral in the supporting pools of the securities. Just before the financial crisis started the MBS market was saturated with securities that were supported by such *toxic* assets. To make the matter worse, many of these securities received a very high rating, often AAA, from various rating agencies, leaving investors oblivious to their high potential credit risk. When the underlying mortgages started to default, the MBS market took a hard hit and securities values dropped significantly, which led to a viral effect throughout the financial market. Investors generally avoided MBSs, even to the extent of not accepting them as collateral in repo contracts, which in turn pushed the price of MBSs further down. This downward pressure on MBSs continued throughout 2008 and 2009, until finally U.S. government interventions partially stabilized the market.

COLLATERALIZED MORTGAGE OBLIGATIONS

The uncertainty of cash flows of pass-through mortgage-backed securities creates several challenges in asset-liability management of portfolios that contain them. From an investor point of view, the prepayment risk embedded in pass-through MBSs have undesirable consequences both in increasing and decreasing rate environments. Similar to the callable bond studied in a previous chapter, a pass-through MBS often presents negative convexity characteristics. Consequently, when interest rate decreases, the increase in security value is not as large as the increase in value of a fixed-income security that does not have an embedded prepayment option. From an investor point of view this is another undesirable feature of a pass-through MBS.

A decrease in the market prevailing interest rate, when sufficiently large, leads to an increase in prepayments in underlying mortgages included in the supporting pool. This means that a larger proportion of principal amount is returned to the investor at the time that the market rate is low and reinvestment in that condition results in a lower yield. Since the increase in prepayment amounts effectively shortens the weighted average life of the MBS, the risk associated with this condition is known as *contraction risk*.

Conversely, when the interest rate rises, the value of a pass-through MBS declines as expected, but due to negative convexity, this decline is larger compared to a fixed-income security without the embedded prepayment option. At the same time, the increase in interest rate leads to a decrease in prepayment activity. Therefore, the return of principal slows down and the investor loses the opportunity to reinvest the principal at the higher market rate. Since the increase in interest rate effectively increases the weighted average life of the MBS, this condition is known as *extension risk*.

From an ALM point of view, both contraction and extension risks may result in a mismatch between assets and liabilities of a bank or an investment company. Portfolio managers that seek investment opportunities in the housing sector often look for *structured financial products* as a solution to this problem. A *collateralized mortgage obligation (CMO)* is a type of structured product that provides the opportunity to invest in the mortgage market while reducing the cash flow uncertainties. In a CMO, interest payments, principal payments, and prepayments of the mortgages in the supporting pool (*collaterals*) are distributed among different classes of the security, known as *tranches*. This distribution is based on predefined rules that specify how cash flows are allocated to each tranche. The allocation process significantly reduces the unpredictability of cash flows for tranches. Since different tranches of a CMO have different exposures to prepayment risk, investors can choose tranches that better fit with their ALM strategies and risk appetites. Each CMO tranche may have different schedules for the return of principal, coupon rates, allocation of prepayment amounts, and maturity dates. Often losses in the collaterals of a CMO are also distributed among tranches based on predefined allocation rules.

In valuation of a CMO, aside from the prepayment of underlying mortgages, we should also consider the structure of the note and the impact of tranches on each other in transferring prepayment and default risk. Due to the complexity of a CMO structure, the Monte Carlo simulation is the valuation method often used in practice.

To demonstrate the fundamentals of cash flow derivation and valuation of CMOs, here we consider a plain vanilla or *sequential pay* CMO. In this type of CMO tranches are amortized in a predetermined order. Holders of all tranches receive interest payments based on tranches' notional amounts and rates while the principal payments, scheduled and prepayment, are all allocated to the first tranche. When the first tranche is fully amortized and retired, the principal payments from the collaterals are then allocated to the second tranche, initiating its amortization. Tranches are amortized in this way and based on a specific order until the last tranche is retired and the security is terminated.

Consider a hypothetical sequential pay CMO with three tranches with notional amounts and coupon rates, shown in Table 7.6. Many CMOs are backed by pools of pass-through mortgage-backed securities. Here we assume the CMO is backed only by the pass-through security we studied in the example in the previous section without considering default. Recall that this security has a pass-through rate of 3.5%, a weighted average coupon rate of 4.189%, and a weighted average term of 360 months. For simplicity here we do not include the impact of default on the cash flows of the pool, but the general concept explained here can be extended to the case when default is

TABLE 7.6 Tranches of a hypothetical sequential pay CMO

Tranche	Notional Balance	Rate
Tranche A	$1,000,000	3.5%
Tranche B	$700,000	3.5%
Tranche C	$304,247	3.5%

also considered, as explained earlier. The payment rule of the CMO in our example indicates that the principal payments, scheduled or prepayment, are all allocated to tranche A until it is fully amortized and then they are used to amortize tranche B and finally tranche C. Each tranche receives interest payments based on their outstanding notional balance at the beginning of a month. A distribution scheme, such as the one described here, creates a *waterfall* structure for cash flows.

Assume that the underlying pass-through security has a 100 PSA prepayment speed. A partial view of the cash flows of the underlying pool based on this prepayment rate was presented in Table 7.2. Based on the payment rule of the CMO the scheduled principal payments and prepayments are all allocated to tranche A until the $1,000,000 balance of this tranche is amortized. A partial view of the cash flows and the outstanding balance of tranche A of the CMO in our example is presented in Table 7.7. For month 1 the beginning outstanding balance of tranche A is $1,000,000 and based on a 3.5% rate the interest amount is:

$$1,000,000 \times \frac{1}{12} \times \frac{3.5}{100} = 2,916.67$$

This interest is payable to the holders of tranche A. From Table 7.2, in month 1 the underlying pass-through security has a scheduled principal payment of $2,791.76 and prepayment of $333.88. These cash flows are payable to holders of tranche A. The principal cash flows are applied to the outstanding balance of tranche A and reduce it to $996,874.36 at the end of month 1.

The interest payment in month 2 is calculated based on the beginning balance of month 2, which is the same as the ending balance of month 1:

$$996,874.36 \times \frac{1}{12} \times \frac{3.5}{100} = 2,907.55$$

From Table 7.2, in month 2 the underlying pass-through security has a scheduled principal payment of $2,801.03 and prepayment of $667.33, based on a 100 PSA scale. These cash flows are applied to the outstanding

TABLE 7.7   A partial view of a cash flow schedule of tranche A of a hypothetical CMO. Tranche notional amount is $1,000,000 with a 3.5% rate. Prepayments of the underlying pass-through security are based on a 100 PSA scale.

| | Total: | $162,596.34 | $298,765.55 | $701,234.45 | $1,162,596.34 | |
Period	Beginning Balance ($)	Interest Payment ($)	Principal Payment ($)	Pre-payment ($)	Total Cash Flow ($)	Ending Balance ($)
0	1,000,000.00					1,000,000.00
1	1,000,000.00	2,916.67	2,791.76	333.88	6,042.31	996,874.36
2	996,874.36	2,907.55	2,801.03	667.33	6,375.92	993,406.00
3	993,406.00	2,897.43	2,809.87	1,000.18	6,707.48	989,595.95
4	989,595.95	2,886.32	2,818.27	1,332.24	7,036.83	985,445.44
5	985,445.44	2,874.22	2,826.21	1,663.36	7,363.79	980,955.86
6	980,955.86	2,861.12	2,833.71	1,993.36	7,688.18	976,128.80
7	976,128.80	2,847.04	2,840.74	2,322.06	8,009.84	970,966.00
8	970,966.00	2,831.98	2,847.31	2,649.31	8,328.60	965,469.38
...	...	...	...	...	...	...
108	16,232.78	47.35	2,517.79	5,235.39	7,800.52	8,479.60
109	8,479.60	24.73	2,513.58	5,195.54	7,733.85	770.48
110	770.48	2.25	770.48	0	772.73	0
111	0	0	0	0	0	0
112	0	0	0	0	0	0
...	...	...	...	...	...	...
237	0	0	0	0	0	0
238	0	0	0	0	0	0
239	0	0	0	0	0	0
240	0	0	0	0	0	0
241	0	0	0	0	0	0
...	...	...	...	...	...	...
356	0	0	0	0	0	0
357	0	0	0	0	0	0
358	0	0	0	0	0	0
359	0	0	0	0	0	0
360	0	0	0	0	0	0

Paydown Period (spanning periods 1–110)

principal of tranche A, reducing the balance at the end of month 2 to $996,874.36 − $2,801.03 − $667.33 = $993,406.00. Each month, holders of tranche A receive interest cash flow based on the amortized outstanding balance of the tranche and the entire principal cash flows, scheduled and pre-payment, of the underlying pass-through security. This process is continued until month 110 when the outstanding balance of tranche A is completely amortized and paid back. At this month tranche A is terminated and its holders do not receive any further cash flows. The period between month 1 when amortization started until month 110 when the tranche balance is fully paid is known as the *paydown period*.

In month 110, the scheduled principal payment and prepayment amounts from the underlying pass-through security are $2,509.38 and $5,155.91, respectively (from Table 7.2). Since the beginning balance of tranche A in month 110 is $770.48, only a portion of these principal cash flows is applied to the remaining balance of tranche A and the rest ($2,509.38 + $5,155.91 − $770.48 = $6,894.81) is applied to tranche B. Hence, at month 110 the amortization of tranche B starts. From month 1 to, and including, month 110, each month holders of tranche B receive an interest payment of:

$$700,000 \times \frac{1}{12} \times \frac{3.5}{100} = 2,041.67$$

At month 110 principal cash flows of $6,894.81 from the underlying pass-through security are applied to the outstanding balance of tranche B, reducing it from $700,000 to $693,105.19 at the end of month 110. In month 111 the holders of tranche B receive an interest payment of:

$$693,105.19 \times \frac{1}{12} \times \frac{3.5}{100} = 2,021.56$$

In this month the underlying pass-through security has a scheduled principal payment of $2,505.19 and a prepayment of $5,116.51. The entire amounts of these cash flows are applied to the outstanding balance of tranche B, reducing it to $693,105.19 − $2,505.19 − $5,116.51 = $685,483.48 at the end of month 111. This process is continued until month 239, when tranche B is fully amortized and terminated. After this month, holders of tranche B do not receive any further cash flow. Table 7.8 presents a partial view of cash flows and outstanding balances of tranche B of the CMO in our example, based on a 100 PSA prepayment speed of the underlying pass-through security. The paydown period of tranche B is from month 110 to month 239.

In month 239 the underlying pass-through security has a $2,022.65 scheduled principal payment and a $1,568.39 prepayment. Since the outstanding balance of tranche B at the beginning of month 239 is $2,731.48, only a portion of principal payment is applied to tranche B, reducing the outstanding balance to zero, and the rest ($2,022.65 + $1,568.39 − $2,731.48 = $859.56) is applied to tranche C, initiating its amortization. From month 1 to, and including, month 239, each month holders of tranche C receive interest cash flow of:

$$304,247 \times \frac{1}{12} \times \frac{3.5}{100} = 887.39$$

TABLE 7.8   A partial view of cash flow schedule of tranche B of a hypothetical CMO. The tranche notional amount is $700,000 with a 3.5% rate. Prepayments of the underlying pass-through security are based on a 100 PSA scale.

		Total: $339,516.14 Interest Payment	$292,684.55 Principal Payment	$407,315.45 Pre- payment	$1,039,516.14 Total Cash Flow	Ending
Period	Beginning Balance ($)	($)	($)	($)	($)	Balance ($)
0	700,000.00					700,000.00
1	700,000.00	2,041.67	0	0	2,041.67	700,000.00
2	700,000.00	2,041.67	0	0	2,041.67	700,000.00
3	700,000.00	2,041.67	0	0	2,041.67	700,000.00
4	700,000.00	2,041.67	0	0	2,041.67	700,000.00
5	700,000.00	2,041.67	0	0	2,041.67	700,000.00
6	700,000.00	2,041.67	0	0	2,041.67	700,000.00
7	700,000.00	2,041.67	0	0	2,041.67	700,000.00
8	700,000.00	2,041.67	0	0	2,041.67	700,000.00
...	...	...	...	...	...	...
108	700,000.00	2,041.67	0	0	2,041.67	700,000.00
109	700,000.00	2,041.67	0	0	2,041.67	700,000.00
110	700,000.00	2,041.67	1,738.90	5,155.91	8,936.48	693,105.19
111	693,105.19	2,021.56	2,505.19	5,116.51	9,643.26	685,483.48
112	685,483.48	1,999.33	2,501.01	5,077.33	9,577.67	677,905.14
...	...	...	...	...	...	...
237	9,979.53	29.11	2,029.43	1,605.63	3,664.17	6,344.48
238	6,344.48	18.50	2,026.04	1,586.96	3,631.50	2,731.48
239	2,731.48	7.97	2,022.65	708.83	2,739.45	0
240	0	0	0	0	0	0
241	0	0	0	0	0	0
...	...	...	...	...	...	...
356	0	0	0	0	0	0
357	0	0	0	0	0	0
358	0	0	0	0	0	0
359	0	0	0	0	0	0
360	0	0	0	0	0	0

(Paydown Period: periods 110–239)

At month 239 principal cash flow of $859.56 from the underlying pass-through security is applied to the outstanding balance of tranche C, reducing it from $304,247 to $303,387.44 at the end of that month. In month 240 and based on the beginning outstanding balance of $303,387.44, the holders of tranche C receive interest payments of:

$$303,387.44 \times \frac{1}{12} \times \frac{3.5}{100} = 884.88$$

From month 240 on, all principal payments, scheduled and prepayment, are applied to tranche C and gradually reduce its balance until its full amortization and termination in month 360. Table 7.9 presents a partial view of cash flows and outstanding balances of tranche C of the CMO in our example, based on a 100 PSA prepayment speed of the underlying pass-through security. The paydown period of tranche C is from month 239 to month 360.

TABLE 7.9 A partial view of a cash flow schedule of tranche C of a hypothetical CMO. The tranche notional amount is $304,247 with a 3.5% rate. Prepayments of the underlying pass-through security are based on 100 PSA.

Period	Beginning Balance ($)	*Total:* $259,231.13 Interest Payment ($)	$221,393.31 Principal Payment ($)	$82,853.69 Pre- payment ($)	$563,478.13 Total Cash Flow ($)	Ending Balance ($)
0	304,247.00					304,247.00
1	304,247.00	887.39	0	0	887.39	304,247.00
2	304,247.00	887.39	0	0	887.39	304,247.00
3	304,247.00	887.39	0	0	887.39	304,247.00
4	304,247.00	887.39	0	0	887.39	304,247.00
5	304,247.00	887.39	0	0	887.39	304,247.00
6	304,247.00	887.39	0	0	887.39	304,247.00
7	304,247.00	887.39	0	0	887.39	304,247.00
8	304,247.00	887.39	0	0	887.39	304,247.00
...	...	...	...	...	...	...
108	304,247.00	887.39	0	0	887.39	304,247.00
109	304,247.00	887.39	0	0	887.39	304,247.00
110	304,247.00	887.39	0	0	887.39	304,247.00
111	304,247.00	887.39	0	0	887.39	304,247.00
112	304,247.00	887.39	0	0	887.39	304,247.00
...	...	...	...	...	...	...
237	304,247.00	887.39	0	0	887.39	304,247.00
238	304,247.00	887.39	0	0	887.39	304,247.00
239	304,247.00	887.39	0	859.56	1,746.95	303,387.44
240	303,387.44	884.88	2,019.27	1,549.94	4,454.09	299,818.22
241	299,818.22	874.47	2,015.90	1,531.60	4,421.97	296,270.72
...	...	...	...	...	...	...
356	8,375.08	24.43	1,663.36	34.52	1,722.31	6,677.20
357	6,677.20	19.48	1,660.58	25.80	1,705.86	4,990.81
358	4,990.81	14.56	1,657.81	17.14	1,689.51	3,315.86
359	3,315.86	9.67	1,655.04	8.54	1,673.25	1,652.28
360	1,652.28	4.82	1,652.28	0	1,657.10	0

Paydown Period (covering periods 239 to 360)

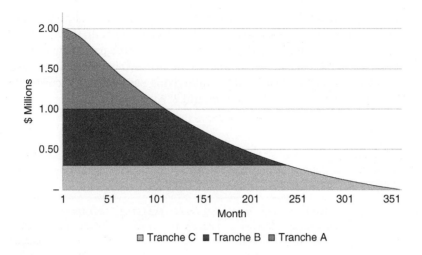

FIGURE 7.16   Balance profiles of hypothetical CMO tranches, assuming a 100 PSA prepayment speed

The payment rule of a CMO defines the allocation of principal payments and creates a different amortization schedule for each tranche. Figure 7.16 shows the balance profile of the CMO tranches considered in our example, when prepayment speed of 100 PSA is assumed. While the balance of tranche A starts decreasing at the first month, the balances of tranches B and C remain constant until their associated paydown periods start in months 110 and 239 respectively. For this CMO, Table 7.10 presents the weighted average life of each tranche and the underlying pass-through security based on a different prepayment speed assumption. Since tranche A is the first to receive the principal payments, it has a shorter weighted average life compared to the other tranches and the pass-through security, even for low prepayment speeds. Therefore, tranche A provides protection against the extension risk, whereas tranche C has a higher weighted average life, even for high prepayment speeds, providing protection against the contraction risk. This offers flexibility to investors by enabling them to choose from the available tranches based on their risk profiles and ALM matching requirements.

To further reduce the uncertainty of cash flows and stabilize the weighted average life of tranches, some CMOs have a special structure made up of one or more *planned amortization class (PAC) tranches* and one or more *support tranches*, also known as *sinking funds*. A PAC tranche has a predetermined principal payment schedule that is defined based on a pair of lower and

TABLE 7.10 Weighted average life (in years) of tranches of a hypothetical CMO, assuming a different prepayment speed for the underlying pass-through security

Prepayment Speed (PSA)	Tranche A	Tranche B	Tranche C	Pass-Through Security
0	6.88	11.90	14.36	10.96
25	5.32	10.69	14.03	10.17
50	4.21	9.44	13.57	9.42
75	3.46	8.28	13.00	8.71
100	2.94	7.27	12.34	8.05
125	2.56	6.42	11.63	7.44
150	2.28	5.73	10.92	6.88
175	2.06	5.16	10.23	6.36
200	1.89	4.68	9.57	5.90
225	1.75	4.29	8.95	5.48
250	1.64	3.95	8.38	5.10

upper prepayment scale bounds (e.g., 80 PSA and 200 PSA). As long as the actual prepayment of CMO collateral is within these two limits, the principal payments of the PAC tranche is known in advance. Principal payments from the collateral are allocated to the PAC tranches and any additional principal payments are allocated to the support tranches to keep the amortization of the PAC tranches according to the prespecified schedules. Even with such a mechanism, it is still possible that the principal payments of a PAC tranche deviate from its predetermined schedule, but this structure overall reduces the uncertainty of the cash flows and decreases the contraction and extension risks of the PAC tranche. This comes at the expense of the supporting tranches that absorb the uncertainty of cash flows and hence have higher prepayment risk.

Valuation of Collateralized Mortgage Obligations

Similar to a pass-through security, valuation of a CMO tranche depends on the path assumed for the interest rate in the future. As demonstrated previously, the estimated cash flows of each tranche depend on the prepayment speed of the underlying pass-through securities. Since different interest rate paths result in different prepayment patterns, the structure of the CMO creates an interdependency between tranches' cash flows, where both the timing and amount of cash flows of a tranche are impacted by the cash flows and paydown periods of other tranches. Due to these complications, using analytical methods in the valuation of CMO is not common in practice and the Monte Carlo simulation method is used instead. The general procedure for valuation of CMO tranches using Monte Carlo simulation is as follows:

1. A large number of simulated interest rate paths are produced using a short rate model for the maximum term of the underlying pass-through securities supporting the CMO. These rates are then used to generate simulated long-term rates and cumulative discount factors for each path.

2. Using a mortgage refinancing rate model, simulated long-term rates from the previous step are converted to simulated mortgage rates.

3. Simulated mortgage refinancing rates, along with forecasted macroeconomic factors and housing turnover, are used as inputs into a prepayment model. The output of this model is simulated prepayment rates for each interest rate path.

4. For each path and similar to what was explained for MBSs, the simulated prepayment rates and characteristics of underlying pass-through securities (e.g., rates, weighted average term, weighted average coupon rate, etc.) are used to generate principal payment and prepayment cash flows.

5. For each path, the principal payments from the previous step are distributed among tranches of the CMO based on the payment rules of the security, similar to what was demonstrated in the previous section, creating an amortization schedule for each tranche. Hence, for a given interest rate path and using the established amortization schedule, the principal and interest cash flows of each tranche are estimated.

6. Having estimated cash flows of tranches and their timings from step (5) and cumulative discount factors from step (1), the value of each tranche for a given interest rate path is obtained as the summation of discounted cash flows. Finally, the estimated value of a CMO tranche is obtained by averaging the tranche values over all simulated interest rate paths.

For the hypothetical CMO described in the example of this section, we used the three simulated interest rate paths from the Hull-White model presented in Figure 7.7 to value each tranche. Similar to the MBS example discussed earlier in this chapter, we assumed that paths 1, 2, and 3 result in prepayment speeds of 100 PSA, 120 PSA, and 80 PSA, respectively. As mentioned before, simulated prepayment rates from a prepayment model do not necessarily follow a PSA scale and here we used these assumed prepayment speeds only to demonstrate the valuation process of a CMO. For path 1, where the assumed prepayment speed is 100 PSA, the amortization and cash flow schedules of three tranches are as presented in Tables 7.7, 7.8, and 7.9, respectively. We built similar schedules when prepayment speeds are based on 120 PSA and 80 PSA for paths 2 and 3, and estimated cash flows of each tranche

TABLE 7.11 Values of three tranches of a hypothetical CMO for three simulated interest rate paths

Tranche	Path 1	Path 2	Path 3	Average ($)
Tranche A	1,054,999.40	1,030,601.99	1,065,672.43	1,050,424.61
Tranche B	782,189.23	707,554.37	843,356.27	777,699.96
Tranche C	338,306.81	290,800.89	401,377.07	343,494.92
Assumed Prepayment Speed (PSA):	*100*	*120*	*80*	

for each path. Then, using the cumulative discount factors calculated using the 1-month rates from Figure 7.7, we derived the value of each tranche for each path. These values are presented in Table 7.11 along with the average over three paths for tranches A, B, and C. Similar to MBS valuation, three simulated paths are not enough for valuation of CMO tranches and in practice a much larger number of paths (e.g., 1,000), is required to achieve convergence of results.

CMOs are not low-risk investment vehicles. In fact, investment in certain tranches of CMO can increase exposure to financial risks and lead to an increase in ALM mismatch. Certain tranches of CMOs can have higher prepayment risk while credit-supporting tranches carry a higher credit risk. Complexity of structuring rules can also result in higher modeling risk. During the financial crisis of 2007–2009 many CMOs backed by subprime mortgage collaterals suffered significant losses, even though they were often rated AAA by major rating agencies.

Similar to prepayment risk, default risk of underlying mortgages can also be partitioned in different tranches of collateralized mortgage obligations. In such CMOs new defaults are applied to designated lower tranches, creating a waterfall structure for losses and recoveries.

ASSET-BACKED SECURITIES

An *asset-backed security (ABS)* is a class of financial instruments created through the *securitization* process. Securitization broadly refers to the process of creating a legal and operational structure in which cash flows from an underlying pool of standardized and homogeneous assets support payments to investors. Different asset types are used in the underlying pool that supports an ABS. The most common ABSs are based on pools of auto loans, credit card receivables, student loans, home equity loans, and equipment loans and leases. Mortgage-backed securities can also be considered a special type of ABS, where underlying asset pools contain commercial or residential mortgages. The use of standardized instruments makes valuation and risk analysis of ABSs easier for investors and rating agencies. Securitization turns these illiquid assets into tradable and liquid securities. An ABS created through a securitization process can be *single-class* or *multi-class*. In a single-class ABS, all investors have a pro-rata claim on the supporting asset pool and its income while sharing the investment risk. In a multi-class ABS, investors in different classes (tranches) have different levels of claim on the supporting asset pool and its income while taking different levels of risk based on the structure of tranches they have invested.

Using an ABS, an originator of an illiquid asset can gain access to a broader base of investors. Figure 7.17 presents a schematic view of a generic ABS structure created through the securitization process. A typical securitization structure includes the following components:

- The *originator* or *sponsor* or *seller* is the company that originates loans, leases, or revolving products by marketing them to customers (*obligors*), evaluates their creditworthiness, and sells the products.
- A *special purpose entity (SPE)*, also sometimes called a *special purpose vehicle (SPV)*, is a legal entity separated from the originator, often established as a trust, that purchases the loans from the originator, packages them in

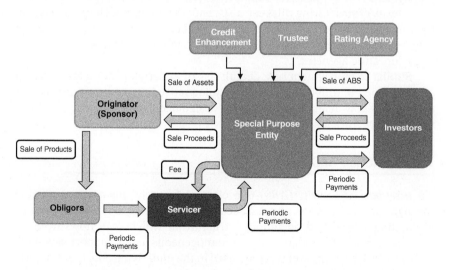

FIGURE 7.17 A generic securitization structure for ABS

the form of securities, and sells the ABS to investors. An SPE is the *issuer* of the ABS notes or bonds, also referred to as *investor certificates*. The legal structure of the SPE is customized depending on the type of instruments purchased from the originator and the laws of the country in which the trust is established. The main purpose of an SPE is to separate assets used to back the ABS from the originator and to protect them in case of originator bankruptcy.

■ The *servicer* is the company that provides loan servicing activities for the loans or leases included in the supporting pool of an ABS. These services include billing, collecting interest and principal payments from obligors, and recovering defaulted loans. The servicing fee is paid by the SPE to the servicer. Often, but not always, the servicer is a subsidiary of the originator.

■ The *trustee* is the entity that oversees the SPE and its relationship with the originator and the servicer, ensuring compliance by all parties. The trustee protects interests of the ABS investors. Trustees are usually other commercial banks that are not affiliated with the originator.

■ *Credit enhancements* that are often included in the structure of ABSs are facilities put in place to reduce the credit risk associated with the underlying assets in the supporting pool. ABS structures utilize a variety of internal and external credit enhancements to reduce the perceived credit risk of the underlying collaterals. *Overcollateralization*, creation of *senior-subordinate structure*, and *explicit guarantees* from the originator or third parties are some of the common forms of credit enhancement used in securitization vehicles of ABSs.

■ *Rating agencies* are companies that review the quality of the assets in the support pool, as well as the securitization structure, and perform stress testing to assign a rating to ABS notes. The three biggest rating agencies in the United States are *Moody's, Standard & Poor's (S&P)*, and *Fitch*. Many senior tranches of ABSs often receive AAA or AA ratings.

In addition to these components, a typical ABS structure has the following common features:

■ *Cleanup call*: An ABS structure usually includes a call provision that when the remaining pool balance falls below a certain percentage (usually 10%) of the original balance, the servicer has the right, but not the obligation, to call and repay the remaining notes. This is due to the fixed cost component of servicing an ABS that makes it uneconomical for the servicer if the pool balance falls below a certain limit.

■ *Reserve account*: To ensure that the special purpose entity (i.e., the trust) can satisfy its cash flow obligation to investors, an ABS structure often includes a reserve account that is funded at the issuance time and holds a cash balance equal to a percentage of the total notional of notes issued (e.g., 1% of total). This balance is kept until the last note is paid off and retired.

- *Excess spread*: ABS deals are often structured such that the collected interest from collaterals is higher than the interest and fees paid out. This produces an excess spread, which acts as another safety margin to ensure that the trust can meet its cash flow obligations. Excess spread can also perform as a tool to create and keep overcollateralization in the ABS structure, as higher inflows compared to outflows result in an increase in the pool balance. The level of excess balance created by the excess spread is related to the prepayment speed and loss rate of the underlying collaterals.

- *Available funds cap*: Some ABS structures may have a mechanism known as the available funds cap (AFC), which limits the amount of interest payable to note holders. The AFC is more common for floating-rate ABSs that are backed either by fixed-rate collaterals or floating-rate collaterals that have rate caps or are indexed to different reference rates than the one used in the ABS structure. This ensures that the interest received from collaterals is sufficient to pay interest to note holders.

- *Credit risk retention*: There are regulatory rules to ensure that ABS issuers' interests are aligned with those of investors. This feature has become more important after the financial crisis of 2007–2009. The *Dodd-Frank Wall Street Reform and Consumer Protection Act of 2010* amended a section of the *Securities Exchange Act of 1934* to impose the requirement of credit retention by ABS issuers. The final regulatory rule based on this law generally requires ABS issuers to retain an economic interest equal to at least 5% of the credit risk of issued securities and prohibits them from transferring or hedging this retained risk. There are some exceptions to this general rule, including for asset-backed securities that are collateralized exclusively by qualified residential mortgages (QRMs). The purpose of this requirement is to incentivize an issuer to monitor and control the underwriting of securitized assets and align issuers' interests with those of investors in securities. According to these regulatory rules, ABS issuers must retain risk in accordance with a standardized risk retention option or in accordance with a special risk retention option available for specific ABS types (Securities and Exchange Commission 2014). Broadly speaking, the risk retention requirement based on the standardized option is satisfied by holding interests in a single class or proportional interests in each class of ABS, or holding interest in a single or multiple classes that have the most subordinated claims to payment of principal and interest by the issuing entity, or a combination of these methods. Specifically, the rule does not consider overcollateralization to be a standard method of risk retention. For specific types of ABS structures, such as revolving pool securitization, that are commonly used for credit card receivable ABSs and asset-backed commercial papers, there are specific provisions included in the regulatory rules to satisfy the risk retention requirement. The issuer is required to disclose the risk retention method to investors at the time of issuance.

As mentioned earlier, ABSs are either single-class or multi-class. Multi-class ABSs are more common in practice and they usually have senior-subordinated as well as sequential pay structures. Subordinated tranches absorb losses incurred in the supporting pool before they are applied to senior tranches. Each senior or subordinate group of tranches also has a sequential pay structure, similar to what was discussed for CMOs in the previous section, where certain tranches have priority in receiving principal payments before other tranches, based on a prespecified order.

Issuers use a variety of loans in securitization structures to issue asset-backed securities. The most common ABSs are based on auto loans, student loans, home equity loans, and credit card receivables. In the following sections we briefly introduce each of these ABS types and highlight their features that impact cash flows and valuations.

Auto Loan ABSs

Collateral

Auto loan asset-backed securities are supported by pools of loans originated for the purpose of purchasing a new or used car. Auto lease contracts are occasionally used as the collaterals of an ABS. Next we briefly review cash flows of auto loan and auto lease contracts and then discuss the structure of the ABS backed by these instruments.

Auto Loan

An auto loan is a secured loan, collateralized by the new or used automobile being purchased. A consumer can obtain an auto loan directly from a lender or indirectly through the car dealer. Credit score is often a major factor in the underwriting of auto loans. Terms of auto loans are usually between 36 and 72 months and they can be either a fixed-rate or floating-rate type; fixed-rate is more common. Floating-rate auto loans are usually indexed to the prime rate. Generally, since balances of auto loans are relatively lower compared to mortgages, they have lower prepayment, as there is less incentive to prepay an auto loan when the interest rate drops. For auto loans, prepayment usually occurs when the car is sold and the loan is paid off with the proceeds from the sale, or when the car is damaged in an accident and declared as a total loss, in which case the loan is paid off by the insurance payment. The lender technically owns the car until the loan is fully paid off, at which point ownership is transferred to the consumer. Since the loan is collateralized by the vehicle, if the borrower fails to make payments during the term of the loan, the lender can repossess the vehicle and sell it to recover its loss. Banks, credit unions, and auto manufacturers are the biggest originators of auto loans.

An auto loan is amortized similar to a mortgage loan, as discussed earlier in this chapter. Particularly, the monthly payment of an auto loan is calculated as:

$$Monthly\ Payment = P_0 \frac{r}{1 - \frac{1}{(1+r)^n}} \tag{7.67}$$

where

P_0 = Loan amount
r = Monthly interest rate (i.e., annual rate divided by 12)
n = Loan term (in months)

Aside from the price of the car, some lenders allow applicable taxes and fees to be included in the loan amount. For example, consider a vehicle with a negotiated price of \$24,500. Assume that total taxes and fees are \$1,650 and the down payment is \$1,000. If inclusion of taxes and fees is requested by the borrower and allowed by the lender, the loan amount is \$24,500 + \$1,650 − \$1,000 = \$25,150. If the loan term is 36 months and the annual rate of the loan is 5.1%, the total monthly payment is calculated as:

$$Monthly\ Payment = 25,150 \times \frac{0.051/12}{1 - \frac{1}{(1 + 0.051/12)^{36}}} = 754.90$$

Part of this monthly payment is the interest and part of it is the principal repayment. An amortization schedule of an auto loan is constructed similar to that of a traditional mortgage loan, explained earlier in this chapter.

Auto Lease

In an auto lease contract, the lessor buys the vehicle from the dealer and leases it to the consumer, who pays the lessor a monthly payment for a specific term. Lease terms are usually between 24 and 60 months and the mileage usage is often limited (e.g., 10,000 miles per year). The lessor owns the vehicle. Auto manufacturers have their own finance leasing subsidiaries. Specialized leasing companies also participate in financing auto lease contracts. The *net capitalized cost* of the vehicle is the purchase price plus taxes and fees, less any down payment. The *residual value* is the expected resale value of the vehicle at the end of the lease term and is usually determined as a percentage of the *manufacturer's suggested retail price (MSRP)*. The lessee has an option to buy the car at the end of the lease term at a price equal to the residual value. The *money factor* or *lease factor* is the financial charge of the lease and is analogous to the interest rate of a loan. The *lease rate* is the money factor multiplied by 2,400. Unlike an auto loan, where the loan rate is applied to the amortized balance (a decreasing balance during the loan term), the money factor is applied to the net capitalized cost (a constant balance over the lease term).

The monthly lease payment consists of two components: the *finance charge* and *depreciation charge*, each calculated as follows:

$$Finance\ Charge = MF(P_0 + RV_n) \tag{7.68}$$

$$Depreciation\ Charge = \frac{(P_0 - RV_n)}{n} \tag{7.69}$$

$$Monthly\ Payment = Finance\ Charge + Depreciation\ Charge \tag{7.70}$$

where:

MF = Money factor
P_0 = Net capitalized cost
n = Lease term (in months)
RV_n = Residual value at month n at the end of lease term

For example, consider a vehicle with a $26,000 manufacturer's suggested retail price (MSRP) and a negotiated price of $24,500. If total taxes and fees are $1,650 and the down payment is $1,000, the net capitalized cost is $24,500 + $1,650 − $1,000 = $25,150. If the lease term is 36 months, the lease factor is 0.002125, and the residual value at the end of lease is estimated at $16,900 (65% of MSRP), the total monthly payment is calculated as:

$$Finance\ Charge = 0.002125 \times (25{,}150 + 16{,}900) = 89.36$$

$$Depreciation\ Charge = \frac{(25{,}150 - 16{,}900)}{36} = 229.17$$

$$Monthly\ Payment = 89.36 + 229.17 = 318.52$$

The approximate annual percentage rate for this contract is $0.002125 \times 2{,}400 = 5.10\%$.

Structure

Banks, auto manufacturers, and other specialized financial companies are the main issuers of securities backed by pools of auto loans or leases. The structure and components of an auto loan securitization entity generally are similar to the typical ABS discussed earlier in this section. When an auto loan is securitized, its outstanding balance at the cutoff time is included in the total balance of the supporting pool and when an auto lease is securitized, the present value of the lease cash flow is included in the pool balance. For ABSs that are based on auto leases, two issues are important:

1. The structure of the special purpose entity for auto lease ABSs is more involved compared to other ABS structures. Since final consumers are not owners of the collaterals (the vehicles), the leasing company, as the owner of the collaterals, first creates a *titling trust* as a bankruptcy-remote entity to hold titles of vehicles. The leasing company retains a beneficial interest in that trust and then a securitization trust is created to issue the ABS.

2. Since the present value of a lease contract depends on the residual value used at the contract initiation, auto lease ABSs are exposed to *residual value risk*. If the lessee does not exercise the option to purchase the vehicle at the end of the lease term, it will be returned to the dealer. If the dealer also chooses not to purchase the vehicle, the lessor takes possession of the vehicle and attempts to sell it and realize its residual value. In this case, if the actual retail resale value of the vehicle is below the residual value used in the contract, the lessor incurs a loss and if the lease contract is part of the supporting pool of an ABS, the loss is passed to the securitization entity and may impact ABS investors. To remediate this, companies that issue ABSs based on pools of auto leases use proprietary models and alternative sources to obtain a minimum residual value and use it in calculating the present value of the lease. For example, the *Automotive Lease Guide (ALG)* is an organization that provides vehicle residual value data in the United States and Canada. The issuer calculates the present value of a lease contract using contractual monthly payments of the lease and the lesser of (i) contractual residual value and (ii) modeled or ALG residual value. This present value is included in the supporting pool balance.

Collateral of auto loan ABSs often experiences large losses during a severe economic downturn. This often concurs with the drop in value of the vehicles used as collateral of the loans. Hence the use of appropriate assumptions or modeling of monthly default rates is crucial in valuation of the auto loan ABS. Similar to mortgage-backed securities, lax underwriting procedures and predatory practices by some dealers has led to an increase in subprime auto loans. According to a report by the Federal Reserve, as of February 2019 there are more subprime auto loan borrowers than ever (Haughwout, Lee, Scally, and der Klaauw 2019). ABSs that are supported by such loans carry higher credit risk and should be valued using higher monthly default rates.

Prepayment

Instead of using CPR, the prepayment of auto loans is measured using *absolute prepayment speed (APS)*,[10] which is a measurement of prepayment as a percentage of the original balance and not the current balance. So a 1% APS indicates that 1% of the original balance is prepaid each month. Since SMM is based on the current balance, for a constant APS as the age of the loan increases SMM also increases. APSs can be converted to SMM using (Fabozzi 1998):

$$SMM_i = \frac{APS}{1 - APS(Age_i - 1)} \tag{7.71}$$

where Age_i is the weighted average of the age of loans in the supporting pool at future month i. For example, assume a 1% APS for an ABS supported by loans with a weighted average age of three months. Then SMM at month 5 from now is calculated as:

$$SMM_5 = \frac{1\%}{1 - 1\% \times (8 - 1)} = 1.0753\%$$

The CPR equivalent of this SMM is obtained using Equation (7.16) as:

$$CPR_5 = 1 - (1 - 1.0753\%)^{12} = 12.1668\%$$

Figure 7.18 compares the absolute prepayment speed of 1% with the equivalent constant prepayment speed for a period of 60 months. Although prepayment as a percentage of the original balance is assumed constant, prepayment as a percentage of the current balance for each month is increasing. This may seem to contradict the general expectation of a low prepayment for auto loan ABSs. However, it should be noted that auto loans have relatively short terms and they do amortize fast. This means that in the distant future months the outstanding balances are relatively low, so a higher CPR then does not make much of an impact on valuation of notes.

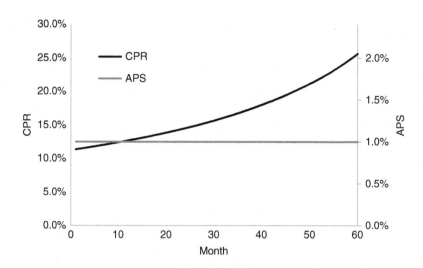

FIGURE 7.18 Absolute prepayment speed (APS) of 1% and the equivalent constant prepayment speed (CPR) for a period of 60 months

Home Equity Loan ABSs

Collateral

Home equity loan asset-backed securities are supported by pools of home equity loans. Collaterals used in supporting pools of home equity loan ABSs are diverse. Generally, they are secured loans collateralized by a real estate property, but typically exclude conventional first-lien mortgages that are used to back mortgage-backed securities. Home equity loans can be a fixed- or floating-rate type. The following loan types are often included in the supporting pools of home equity loan ABSs:

- Second-lien mortgage: This is a traditional mortgage that is subordinated to another mortgage. In case of default the first-lien mortgage is paid off first and then if enough of a balance remains the second-lien mortgage is paid off. Due to this, a second-lien mortgage has a higher credit risk compared to a conventional first-lien mortgage.
- Home improvement loan: This is a loan granted to cover a major home improvement project, such as an addition or remodeling.
- Interest-only mortgage: This type of loan allows the borrower to pay only interest for a fixed number of years. After that period ends, the loan converts to a conventional mortgage and the monthly payment, which includes both interest and principal, increases.

- Home equity line of credit (HELOC): A HELOC is a revolving credit line that is collateralized with a second lien on the property. It is usually a floating-rate type and is indexed to the prime rate. Similar to a credit card revolving line, utilization rate is an important characteristic for this type of loan.
- First-lien subprime mortgage: A conventional loan that is issued to a risky borrower with a low credit score is often referred to as a subprime mortgage. It has a higher credit risk compared to a conventional mortgage issued to a borrower with a high credit score (a prime mortgage). Subprime first-lien mortgages that are not eligible for inclusion in mortgage-backed securities are sometimes packaged in home equity loan ABSs.
- High loan-to-value (LTV) mortgage: This is a mortgage loan in which the ratio of loan amount to value of the property is higher than what is commonly used in underwriting a conventional mortgage. Due to this, this type of loan has a higher credit risk compared to a conventional mortgage.

Structure

Banks and specialized financial companies that are active in the home lending market are the main issuers of the home equity loan ABSs. Notes issued by home equity loan securitization entities can be either a fixed-rate or floating-rate type. Structures that issue floating-rate notes often include the available funds cap mechanism.

The structure of closed-end home equity loan securitization and their related cash flow analysis is very similar to CMO structures discussed earlier in this chapter. Home equity loan ABSs are usually multi-class notes with senior-subordination and sequential pay structure. They are often organized to have one or more PAC and support tranches with various, and sometimes complicated, payment rules. Their structure can include triggers that may result in the dedication of principal payments to PAC tranches only or other tests or triggers that may result in the prevention of principal payments to support tranches. Detailed analysis of these triggers and their impact on tranches is crucial in cash flow analysis and valuation of home equity loan ABSs.

Home equity loan ABSs have a lot in common with mortgage-backed securities, but due to the higher risk carried in typical collaterals used in home equity loan ABSs, credit risk analysis and default modeling is an important part of their valuation. For ABSs that are supported by subprime mortgages, even though they may have mortgage insurances paid by lenders or borrowers, the credit risk of the underlying collateral is still higher compared to MBSs or other ABS types. Due to this, use of multiple credit enhancement mechanisms such as senior-subordinate structure, excess spread, and overcollateralization are common in practice. Due to high delinquency and default rates of collaterals used in home equity loan ABSs, efficiency of delinquency management and recovery procedures of the servicer also play an important role in the value of ABSs.

In some home equity loan ABSs with a senior-subordinate structure, a *non-accelerated senior (NAS)* tranche is included that provides a greater protection against prepayment. In such a structure the NAS tranche receives a pro-rata share of principal cash flows based on a prespecified schedule (e.g., 0% for the first three years, 40% in years 4 and 5, etc.). This considerably reduces the uncertainty of principal cash flow timing for the tranche holders.

Prepayment

High interest rates of typical collaterals used in home equity loan ABSs increase the incentive for refinancing when interest rate falls. However, the refinancing also depends on the creditworthiness of the borrowers and the property values that may be impacted by the economic condition that led to the change in the interest rate level.

The repayment speed of home equity loan ABSs are usually indicated as a multiple of a deal-specific prepayment speed, known as *prospectus prepayment curve (PPC)*. A PPC is similar to a PSA in the sense that it indicates prepayment rates at different periods, but it is specific for each issuance and included in the prospectus of the deal. The PPC is often obtained based on historical data analysis. Usually, the deal is originally priced at 100 PPC (or 100% PPC) by using the exact prepayment rates indicated in the prospectus prepayment curve. Future valuation can be done using multiples of PPC if there are indications that prepayment is slower or faster than the speed originally indicated in the PPC.

Student Loan ABSs

Collateral

Student loan asset-backed securities (SLABS) are supported by pools of student loans. Student loan generally refers to an unsecured loan issued to a borrower to pay for post-secondary education.[11] There are different periods during the life of a student loan. The *in-school* period starts with the loan disbursement (payment to the school) and continues as long as the student is still in school on a full-time or at least half-time basis. The *grace* period starts when the student is finished with the school. Usually the grace period lasts for six months. Depending on the loan type, the borrower may or may not start repaying the principal of the loan during the aforementioned periods. Interest payments in these periods also depend on the type of the loan. For some loan types the federal government pays the interest in these two periods and for some other types the borrower is responsible for the interest payment. In the latter case, the borrower usually has the option to *capitalize* the interest, where the accrued interest is not paid on its due date and is added to the principal of the loan. The *repayment* period is when the borrower repays the principal of the loan; it is usually 10 years but could be shorter or longer, depending on the loan type and repayment plan. Upon meeting the eligibility requirement and when approved by the lending institution, the borrower may temporarily pay a reduced amount or completely stop payment for a specified period. Such a period is known as a *deferment* or *forbearance* period. Often when a borrower enters the repayment period and then returns to school or enters active military service, he or she can request a deferment from the lender. Depending on the loan, in deferment the borrower may not be responsible for the interest accrued in that period. If a borrower faces economic difficulty such as unemployment, he or she can apply for forbearance. In forbearance the borrower is still responsible for the accrued interest, which is often capitalized. Generally, there are two types of student loans: federal loans and private loans.

Federal Student Loan

In the past, most *federal student loans* were originated under the Federal Family Education Loan (FFEL) program. These loans were not funded by the federal government; rather, they were funded and originated by private banks and other financial companies but subsidized and reinsured by the U.S. federal government. This program ended in 2010 but there are still existing SLABS traded in the market that are based on pools that include loans issued under this program. There are several types of student loans issued under the FFEL program:

- *Subsidized Stafford*: In this type of loan the borrower is the student and eligibility is based on financial need. The federal government pays the interest during the in-school, grace, and forbearance or deferment periods. The borrower pays the interest over the repayment period. The repayment period starts after the in-school and grace periods and usually is 10 years.[12]
- *Unsubsidized Stafford*: In this type of loan the borrower is the student. Interest payments during the in-school, grace, forbearance or deferment, and repayment periods are all the borrower's responsibility, with the option for capitalization of the accrued interest. The repayment period starts after the in-school and grace periods and usually is 10 years.

- *PLUS (Parent Loan for Undergraduate Students):* In this type of loan the borrower is the parent of the student. Interest payments during the in-school, grace, forbearance or deferment, and repayment periods are all the borrower's responsibility. The repayment period usually starts a month or two after the loan is disbursed, unless a deferment is requested and approved, and often has a 10-year duration.
- *Consolidation*: This type of loan combines more than one federal loan into a single loan. Generally, the repayment period is between 10 and 30 years.

Subsidized and unsubsidized Stafford and PLUS loans issued before July 1, 2006, under the FFEL program were floating-rate loans based on the 91-day T-Bill reference rate plus a spread, with an annual reset date of July 1 and a cap on the total rate. Loans issued after July 1, 2006, are the fixed-rate type. Consolidation loans are also a fixed-rate type in which the rate is the weighted average of the interest rates on the loans being consolidated.

After the end of the FFEL program, the U.S. federal government started the Federal Direct Student Loan (FDSL) program, in which the government funds and issues student loans directly to students and parents. There are four types of student loans issued under the FDSL program that are very similar to loan types under the FFEL program:

- *Direct Subsidized*: In this type of loan the borrower is the undergraduate student and eligibility is based on financial need. The school determines the loan amount, subject to some limits and caps. The federal government pays the interest during the in-school, grace, and forbearance or deferment periods, and the borrower pays the interest over the repayment period. The repayment period starts after the in-school and grace periods and is usually 10 years.
- *Direct Unsubsidized*: In this type of loan the borrower is the undergraduate or graduate student and there is no eligibility requirement based on financial need. The school determines the loan amount, subject to some limits and caps. Interest payments during the in-school, grace, forbearance or deferment, and repayment periods are all the borrower's responsibility, with the option for capitalization of accrued interest. The payment period starts after the in-school and grace periods, and is usually 10 years.
- *Direct PLUS*: In this type of loan the borrower is the graduate or professional student or parents of an undergraduate student. For PLUS loans a credit check is required and the loan amount is based on the cost of attendance determined by the school. Interest payments during the in-school, grace, forbearance or deferment, and repayment periods are all the borrower's responsibility, with an option for capitalization of the accrued interest. When the borrower is a parent the repayment

period usually starts a month or two after the loan is disbursed (paid to the school), unless a deferment is requested and approved. When the borrower is graduate or professional student, the repayment period starts after the in-school and grace periods. The repayment period is usually 10 years.

- *Direct Consolidation*: This type of loan combines more than one federal student loan into a single loan. Interest payments are the borrower's responsibility. The repayment period starts 60 days after loan disbursement and is usually between 10 and 30 years.

Federal direct loans are the fixed-rate type. There is also a loan fee paid by the borrower that is deducted from the disbursement amount. The U.S. Department of Education, as the sponsor of federal student loans, offers a few repayment plans that a borrower can choose. Most notably, in income-based repayment (IBR) plans the payment amount is based on a percentage of borrower discretionary income (usually 10% to 15%), which may result in extension of the repayment period.

Private Student Loan

Private student loans are another major source of post-secondary education funding. These loans are originated and funded by private lenders such as banks, credit unions, and other financial institutions. Terms and conditions of private loans are set by individual lenders. Interest payments on the loan are the borrower's responsibility in any period. Various lenders offer different repayment plans, where in some plans principal repayment starts within a few months after loan disbursement and in other plans repayment starts after the in-school and grace periods. The length of the repayment period also varies, usually 10 years and above. The credit score of the borrower is an important factor considered at the time of underwriting and if the borrower is the student, the lender may also require co-signing by parents. Granting a deferment or forbearance period is at the discretion of the lending institution. Private loans can be a floating-rate or fixed-rate type, where floating-rate loans are often indexed to LIBOR or the prime reference rate.

The *SLM Corporation*[13] (commonly referred to as *Sallie Mae*) is one of the biggest originators of private student loans as well as a large issuer of SLABS. Sallie Mae originally was a shareholder-owned government-sponsored entity, originating federally reinsured student loans, servicing them, and providing a secondary market to student loans by purchasing student loans from other originators and securitizing them. Sallie Mae became fully private in 2004 and is now originating private student loans. In 2014 it spun off its servicing operation into *Navient*, which is now one of the largest student loan servicers. As of the beginning of 2019, Sallie Mae offers different loan types, where borrowers are student or parents, with different repayment options:

- Interest-only payments only during the in-school, grace, and deferment periods. Principal and interest payments in the repayment period.
- Fixed low payments during the in-school, grace, and deferment periods. Principal and interest payments in the repayment period. Unpaid interest during the in-school, grace, and deferment periods is capitalized.
- No payments (interest or principal) during the in-school and grace periods. Principal and interest payments in the repayment period. Interest during the in-school, grace, and deferment periods is capitalized.
- Principal and interest payments in all periods (typically when borrowers are parents of students).

Repayment terms of these loans varies between 5 and 20 years. Sallie Mae offers both fixed-rate loans and floating-rate loans that are indexed to LIBOR.

Structure

In the past, federal loans issued under the FFEL program were used in supporting pools of SLABS. Few of those securities are still traded in the market. Since the end of the FFEL program, most SLABS are supported by pools of private student loans. Large banks and non-bank financial institutions actively market and issue SLABS. The structure and components of student loan securitization vehicles generally are similar to the typical ABS discussed earlier in this section. Some of the characteristics of SLABS that are important for their cash flow analysis and valuation are as follows:

- Unlike federal loans issued under the FFEL program that were reinsured by the U.S. government,[14] private loans are not protected by such a guarantee. Federal and private student loans are generally not dischargeable in personal bankruptcy. Unlike mortgages, student loans are usually not collateralized. These factors should be considered in estimating collateral cash flows and recovery amounts.
- The portion of the outstanding balance of the supporting pool that is in delinquency, deferment, forbearance, or default impacts the underlying cash flows. Modeling or the use of explicit assumptions for balances in these states over the remaining life of a SLABS is an important step in valuation of the security.
- Direct prepayment, consolidation and refinancing, and cleanup call impact cash flows of the supporting pool and change the weighted average life of the SLABS.

- Sometimes a floating-rate SLABS is indexed to a reference rate that is different from the index used in loans included in the supporting pool. This can expose investors to *basis risk*.
- SLABS are usually overcollateralized. This is done at the time of issuance by ensuring that the total outstanding balances of student loans included in the supporting pool are higher than the total notional balances of all tranches of the issued notes. The percentage of overcollateralization varies in different securitization structures, usually around 10% to 15%.

Prepayment

Prepayment speed of SLABS is measured using CPR. Some issuers report another prepayment metric called *since-issued total CPR*, which measures voluntary and involuntary prepayment over the life of the supporting pool.

Credit Card Receivable ABSs

Collateral

This type of asset-backed security is supported by pools of accounts receivable generated from credit cards. Credit card exposure is created when a cardholder uses the card at a merchant location or online to purchase goods or services. The card issuer, which is usually a bank, pays the merchant on behalf of the cardholder, minus a charge often referred to as the *discount rate*. The discount rate is a negotiated rate between the card issuer and the merchant. The card issuer then charges the account of the cardholder for the transaction, creating an *account receivable (AR)* balance. The cardholder is billed on a monthly basis for the repayment of amounts charged on the card. Depending on the card type, the cardholder may choose to repay an amount between the minimum required payment (*min due*) and the total amount of charges. Any balance above the min due that is not paid is rolled over to the next month and starts to accrue interest (*finance charge*). Accounts that are used throughout a billing cycle and paid in full at the end of the cycle are usually referred to as *transactors* and the ones whose portion of balances are rolled to the next months are called *revolvers*. Transactor accounts generate fee income for the card issuer through the discount rate charged to merchants while revolver accounts generate both fee and interest incomes. The issuer effectively lends an amount equal to the purchase price to the cardholder from the time of the purchase until the upcoming due date of the cardholder's monthly payment. If the balance is paid in full at that due date, that is the end of the lending period, but if the cardholder rolls a portion of the balance to the following month, the lending period extends until the balance is fully paid. As the credit card account is a revolving line of credit, a cardholder who rolled some of the unpaid balance to future months may put additional charges in the following months on his card, resulting in an increase of the revolving balance that is incurring finance charges and if he pays down some of the revolving balance, the finance charge decreases accordingly.

Credit card loan is unsecured and since the repayment amount above the min due is the choice of the cardholder, the loan has an embedded option held by the cardholder. Due to this, cash flows of credit card loans are significantly impacted by the economic conditions that affect customers' behavior, both in their use of cards and their ability to repay outstanding balances. Credit card loans are usually a floating-rate type indexed to the prime rate, with high spreads.

Structure

ABS securitization vehicles that are backed by pools of credit card receivables share many components of the typical ABS structure discussed earlier in this section but there are some specific features that are unique to credit card ABSs. First, collaterals included in the pool do not have a schedule for principal repayment, since it is at the discretion of the customer to pay any amount above the min due. Second, the average life of credit card receivables in the supporting pool is much shorter than the term of the securities issued by the securitization vehicle. Third, sponsors of credit card receivable ABSs usually issue multiple series of notes through a *master trust* legal entity, instead of using a separate trust for each series issuance. Through the master trust, the issuer is able to sell multiple security series backed by a shared pool of collaterals. Each series has an undivided interest (claim) on the receivables in the shared collateral pool. Use of a master trust and shared collateral pool is a cost-effective securitization method and many card issuers use it as a low-cost and reliable source of funding.

In a typical credit card securitization, the card issuer sells receivable balances of designated accounts to the special purpose entity that is formed as a master trust. In this case the *seller*, *transferor*, and *sponsor* are the same as the card issuer. Only the receivable balance and associated cash flows of a designated account are sold to the master trust and not the account itself. Usually, but not always, the servicer of the master trust is the same as the card issuer.

The master trust issues one or more series of securities called *investor certificates* and sells them to investors that are usually asset management institutions and pension funds. The cash flows generated from collaterals in the pool are used to support obligations of the master trust, including interest and principal payments to the certificate holders and trust fees. If a series is not in the repayment period, principal payments from the cardholders are used to purchase new receivable balances from the seller to support long-term investor certificates. A *pooling and servicing agreement* is the legal document outlining the rules and responsibilities of different parties regarding the creation and maintenance of the collateral pool and the distribution method of cash flows. The mechanism of the recurring receivable purchase is discussed later in this section.

Each series issuance contains multiple classes with a senior-subordinated structure. Investor certificates can be fixed-rate or floating-rate types, where floating-rate certificates are often indexed to the LIBOR or SOFR. The certificates have a *final termination date*, which is the date by which all principal must be returned to investors. The most subordinated class of a series, often called *seller's interest*, is retained by the seller. The seller's interest is the portion of the collaterals in the pool that has not been pledged to support investor certificates. It acts as a buffer to absorb fluctuation in designated account receivable balances. If, due to the short average life of credit card receivables and seasonality effects, the pooled receivable balance is not enough to generate sufficient cash flows to support the investor certificates, the sellers' interest covers the shortfall. To ensure the availability of this protection, the seller's interest is required to be kept above a certain level during the life of the series. This level is usually set by a rating agency assigning a rating to the investor certificates. The mechanism of this coverage and how different series and different classes of a series, including the seller's interest, share the resources of the common pool is complicated. In the following section we describe one such allocation method.

The difference between the weighted average rate of collaterals and coupon rates of investor certificates and rates of servicer fees produces an *excess spread* in the structure. Due to the uncertainty of collateral cash flow, excess spread plays an important role in credit card receivable ABSs in ensuring that there is enough cash available each month to fulfill trust obligations.

Payments from a cardholder consist of two parts: the finance charge and principal payment. The finance charge includes interest on rolled balance, card fee, and cash advance fee. The remainder of the payment is considered principal payment. The distribution methods of finance charges and principal payments among different series and security classes are explained in the following section.

Cash Flow Distribution Method

Cash flow waterfall is the method of distribution of finance charges and principal payments in multi-series multi-class securitization structures. This distribution method varies among issuers and SPEs. Next we discuss one method that is more common in practice.

Finance Charge

The finance charge portion of cardholders' monthly payments is used to cover interest payments to investor certificates holders, trust and servicer fees, and charge-offs (credit losses). Generally:

1. Total collected finance charges are first distributed among all series in the master trust on a pro-rata basis, based on their total notional amounts, including notional amounts of the seller's interests. This way, the seller's interest receives its portion of finance charges and incurs charge-offs on a pro-rata basis. If the seller and servicer are different, it also contributes its portion of the servicing fees.
2. Allocated amounts to investor certificates of all series are pooled together and then distributed among different series in the master trust on a pro-rata basis, based on notional amounts of investor certificates.
3. Allocated amounts to a series are distributed among different classes within the series based on the specific priority indicated in the prospectus (e.g., class A notes are paid first, then class B notes, and so on). The allocated finance charge to a class covers the interest payments to certificate holders, allocated trust fees, and allocated charge-offs.
4. Excess finance charges allocated to a series are used to replenish the reserve account in case there is a shortfall in that account. In some structures there may be two separate accounts for coverage of future shortages: a reserve account to cover credit losses and an *excess account* to cover future finance charge needs.
5. If allowed by the pooling and servicing agreement, excess finance charges are shared among different series but after fulfillment of the series' own cash flow obligations. In this case, a finance charge shortage in one series is covered by a finance charge excess in other series.
6. Any remaining excess finance charge is released back to the seller.

Principal Payment

The principal portion of cardholders' monthly payments is used for repayment of the principal amount of investor certificates. In a typical credit card securitization structure there are two periods with respect to principal repayment:

- *Revolving period:* During this period no principal payment is made by the trust, and investor certificate holders only receive interest payments. The collected principal amount in this period is used to purchase additional receivables from the seller. Since the average life of credit card receivable exposures is much shorter than the term of the issued investor certificates, this continued purchase of new receivables ensures that there is a sufficient balance in the supporting pool to generate cash flow to fulfill trust obligations, including interest payments to certificate holders.

- *Controlled amortization or controlled accumulation period*: When the revolving period ends, either a controlled amortization period or a controlled accumulation period starts:
  - During the controlled amortization period, the collected principal amount is used to pay back the principal balances of investor certificates and to gradually reduce invested amounts. Collected principal payments are passed to investor certificate holders as they are received until the last note is retired. Investor certificates issued through securitizing structures that use a controlled amortization period have a variable amortization schedule.
  - During the controlled accumulation period, the collected principal amount is placed in a *principal funding account*. The balance of this account is invested in short-term instruments such as Treasury bills or money market products and the accumulated balance at the end of the period is used to repay principal balances of investor certificates in a single payment. Investor certificates issued through securitization structures that use controlled accumulation period have bullet amortization. In credit card securitization, use of a controlled accumulation period is more common compared to a controlled amortization period.

Similar to finance charges, different issuers use different methods for distribution of principal payments in multi-series multi-class securitization structures. Generally:

1. The total collected principal amount is first distributed among all series in the master trust on a pro-rata basis, based on their total notional amounts, including the notional amounts of the seller's interests.
2. If a given series is in a revolving period, the allocated principal amount is placed in the *shared principal collection pool*. If the series is in a controlled amortization period, the allocated principal amount is distributed among different classes within the series based on the specific priority indicated in the prospectus (e.g., class A notes are paid first, then class B notes, and so on). The seller's interest also receives its own share of principal payment. If the series is in a controlled accumulation period, the allocated principal amount is placed in a *principal funding account* to be used later for a bullet payment. Any excess principal amount is then placed in the shared principal collection pool.
3. If allowed by the pooling and servicing agreement, the shared principal collection pool is used to cover principal shortage in any outstanding series in the master trust.

4. Any remaining balance in the shared principal collection pool is used to purchase new receivables from the seller.

Sharing principal payments allows the sponsor to shorten the length of the accumulation period significantly, sometimes to just one month (Federal Deposit Insurance Corporation 2007).

Prepayment

Prepayment, as described earlier for other types of ABSs, is not applicable to credit card receivable ABSs. Since a cardholder has the option to pay any amount above the min due up to the total outstanding balance (including no additional payment at all), there is no scheduled principal payment other than the min due. The repayment performance of a credit card receivable ABS is usually measured using the *monthly payment rate (MPR)*. The monthly payment rate or *remittance rate* for a month is equal to total cardholders' payments, which include both interest and principal payments, as a percentage of the outstanding balance at the beginning of the month:

$$MPR_i = \frac{C_i}{B_{i-1}} \qquad (7.72)$$

where

MPR_i = Monthly payment rate in month i
  C_i = Cardholders' total payments
  B_{i-1} = Pool balance at the end of month $i-1$ (beginning of month i)

Early Amortization Event

To protect investors against deterioration of collateral quality, credit card securitization structures usually include one or more triggers that lead to an *early amortization* event. When one of these conditions are met, the securitization trust enters into an early amortization stage, where investors' principal amounts are repaid as soon as possible. If a series is in a revolving period, once the early amortization event is triggered, the revolving period ends immediately and all principal received is allocated for repayment of investor certificates of the affected series based on the priority specified in the prospectus (e.g., class A is repaid first, then class B, and so on). Some of the early amortization event triggers used in credit card securitization structures are:

- Occurrence of several consecutive and significant declines in the excess spread.

- ▪ Occurrence of several consecutive and significant declines in the monthly payment rate.
- ▪ Deterioration of credit quality of the collateral pool, when measured using credit scores of designated account holders or occurrence of several consecutive and significant charge-offs.
- ▪ Decline in seller's interest balance below a certain level.

Valuation of Asset-Backed Securities

Valuation of ABSs is based on the same principles discussed earlier in this chapter for MBSs and CMOs. Similar to MBSs, many, but not all, of ABS collaterals are amortized. Hence the methodology explained for MBSs, with and without defaults, can be used to obtain the collaterals' expected monthly balances and cash flows. Similar to CMOs, many ABS structures have multiple classes, where principal repayment and absorption of losses among tranches are subject to specific rules. The methodology explained for CMOs can be used to determine cash flow waterfalls and the impact of tranches on each other. Due to the complexity of ABS structures, which often include floating-rate type classes, the Monte Carlo simulation method is the most common approach used for valuation purposes. Generally, use of the Monte Carlo simulation in ABS valuation consists of the following steps:

- ▪ Using an interest rate model, a large number of simulated interest rate paths are generated that extend to the end of the expected life of the collaterals. These rates can be used for both coupon generation of the floating-rate notes as well as discount factor calculation.
- ▪ For a simulated interest rate path and using pool-level characteristics of collaterals, expected monthly cash flows and outstanding balances of the collateral are estimated. In practice and similar to MBS, pool-level cash flow estimation is more common than loan-level analysis. In cash flow and balance estimation, the relationship between different classes of an issuance, including principal waterfall and default allocation, should be considered.
- ▪ Using rates from the simulated path, periodic (i.e., 1-month) and cumulative discount factors are calculated. The cumulative discount factors are then used to calculate the present value of estimated cash flows of each class of the ABS structure. For each class, the summation of these discounted cash flows is the simulated value of the class for the given interest rate path.
- ▪ Repeating the previous two steps provides us with a large number of simulated values for each class. The expected value of the class is the average of these simulated values.

To demonstrate valuation of asset-backed securities using Monte Carlo simulation, consider a hypothetical SLABS with the following specifications:

- The collaterals are fixed-rate consolidation student loans, all in the repayment period. The total balance of collateral at cutoff time is $374,000,000 with a weighted average coupon rate of 6.15% and a weighted average remaining life of 120 months.
- The issuance has three classes: class A-1, class A-2, and class B. Class B is subordinate to classes A-1 and A-2. The structure is sequential pay, where class A-1 and A-2 notes are repaid first and then class B notes are repaid. During the paydown period of classes A-1 and A-2, principal received from collaterals are proportionally distributed between A-1 and A-2 based on their notional amounts at issuance time.
- Notional amounts and rates of the three classes are as follows:

Class	Notional ($)	Rate
Class A-1	220,000,000	LIBOR 1-month +0.85%
Class A-2	80,000,000	Fixed 4.25%
Class B	40,000,000	LIBOR 1-month +1.75%
	340,000,000	

- Since the total issuance amount is $340,000,000 and the collateral balance at cutoff time is $374,000,000, the issuance is 10% overcollateralized.
- Servicing spread is 0.80%.
- Current LIBOR 1-month rate as of the valuation date is 2.3%. Reset periodicity of the floating-rate notes is monthly and the rate is set at the beginning of each month.
- Length of deferment period is assumed to be a constant six months. Interest accrued during the deferment is capitalized at the end of this period.
- Monthly deferment rate is assumed constant at 0.25%.
- CPR is assumed constant at 7%, which results in a constant SMM of 0.60293081%.

In the following analysis we make a few simplifying assumptions:

- Although the USD LIBOR is quoted based on an Actual/360 convention, for simplicity here we assume a 30/360 accrual basis. Hence a simulated annual LIBOR is converted to a monthly rate by dividing it by 12.
- As mentioned before, ABS structures often have a cleanup call. Here we do not consider this call provision in our cash flow analysis. Exercise of this option shortens the life of the lowest class of the ABS (the class that

is repaid last) but the availability of cash in the trust also should be considered in evaluating the timing of this call.

■ We assume that the reserve account of this ABS structure is funded before repayment starts and its balance remains constant until all notes are retired, so no cash flow associated with the reserve account is considered in our analysis.

■ We do not consider default and its impact on the cash flow and instead focus on the deferment and the cash flow waterfall between classes.

■ Deferment rate for the last seven months is assumed to be zero. As will be clarified later, this is to avoid capitalized interest being generated at the last month (month 120).

Since two of the ABS classes are floating-rate based on the LIBOR, an interest rate model such as the Hull-White one-factor, Black-Karasinski, or LIBOR market model can be used to generate simulated LIBOR 1-month rates for a period of 120 months. The simulated rates are then used to determine the coupon rates of class A-1 and class B of the ABS in our example, as well as for discount factor calculation needed for valuation of all three classes. Figure 7.19 presents three simulated paths of LIBOR 1-month generated using an interest rate model for valuation of the ABS in our example. Here we value all three classes of this ABS for each simulated interest rate path and obtain the expected value as the average of three simulated values. In practice, a much larger number of simulated paths (e.g., 1,000), is required to obtain a stable and reliable estimated value for each class.

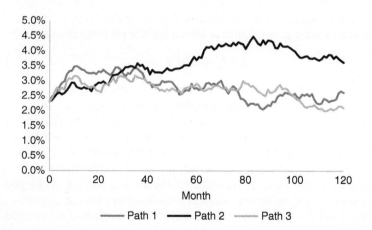

FIGURE 7.19 Three simulated paths of LIBOR 1-month generated using an interest rate model for 120 months

We start our cash flow analysis by focusing on the supporting pool. Recall that the method we used for MBS to model prepayment where the supporting pool was assumed to consist of a large pool of many $1 micro loans and a prepayment occurrence results in the entire remaining balance of one or more micro loans to be repaid. Here we take a similar approach for deferment and assume that the supporting pool of the ABS consisted of many $1 micro loans. Once a deferment is requested and approved, the entire macro loan balance is removed from the pool balance and added to the deferment balance. After the deferment period ends, the deferred amount is moved from the deferment balance back to the pool balance, with the additional capitalized interest during the deferment period. This procedure allows us to calculate the outstanding balance of the pool recursively using assumed or modeled prepayment and deferment rates. We have:

$$B_i = B_{i-1} - P_i - PP_i - DFR_i + DFR_{i-DP} + CI_i \qquad (7.73)$$

where

B_i = Pool balance at the end of month i
B_{i-1} = Pool balance at the end of month $i - 1$ (or at beginning of month i)
P_i = Principal payment in period i
PP_i = Prepayment amount in month i
DFR_i = New deferred amount in month i
DFR_{i-DP} = Deferred amount in month $i - DP$, where DP is the deferment period
CI_i = Capitalized interest in month i

The new deferred amount is calculated by multiplying a deferment rate by the outstanding pool balance at the end of the previous month:

$$DFR_i = MDFR_i \times B_{i-1} \qquad (7.74)$$

where $MDFR_i$ is the monthly deferment rate for month i. Similar to the prepayment rate, banks and other investors in ABSs use quantitative methods to model and forecast the deferment rate. In modeling the deferment rate, seasonality and seasoning of the loan should be considered. Here for simplicity we assume a constant deferment rate of 0.25% per month. Every month a portion of the pool balance is assumed to enter the deferment state. This is reflected in term $-DFR_i$ in Equation (7.73). Once a portion of the pool balance moves to the deferment stage it remains there for the duration of the deferment period, which we have assumed to be a constant six months here ($DP = 6$ months). The new deferred amount continues to accrue interest and after the six months, when the deferment period ends, the accrued interest is capitalized and added back to the outstanding pool balance. This is reflected in term $+CI_i$ in Equation (7.73). At a given month i, the deferred amount from six months ago is now assumed to be out of the deferment state and is added back to the pool balance. This is reflected in term $+DFR_{i-DP}$ in Equation (7.73). As was done for an MBS, in Equation (7.73) the term $-P_i$ is included to capture the impact of principal repayment and the term $-PP_i$ is for the prepayment. We can also calculate and track the deferment balance at each month recursively using:

$$DFRB_i = DFRB_{i-1} + DFR_i - DFR_{i-DP} \qquad (7.75)$$

where $DFRB_i$ is the deferment balance at month i. Table 7.12 presents a partial view of the outstanding balance of the supporting pool in our SLABS example, along with components affecting the balance.

Collateral, Months 1 to 6

Assuming a monthly deferment rate of 0.25% and a starting pool balance of $B_0 = 374,000,000$, the new deferred amount in month 1 is calculated as:

$$DFR_1 = 0.25\% \times 374,000,000 = 935,000$$

Scheduled principal repayment and prepayment for month 1 are calculated using Equations (7.23) and (7.25), based on the assumed constant SMM of 0.60293081%:

$$P_1 = B_0 \left(1 - \frac{A_1}{A_0} \right)$$

$$= 374,000,000 \times \left(1 - \frac{0.9939474737}{1} \right) = 2,263,644.84$$

$$PP_1 = B_0 \frac{A_1}{A_0} SMM_1$$

$$= 374,000,000 \times \left(\frac{0.9939474737}{1} \right) \times 0.60293081\% = 2241,313.00$$

As before, amortization factors used in this example are calculated using Equation (7.4) or (7.5). Since in month 1 there is no capitalized interest ($CI_1 = 0$) and no returning deferred amount from previous periods ($DFR_{1-DP} = 0$), the pool balance at the end of month 1 is calculated using Equation (7.73) as:[15]

$$B_1 = B_0 - P_1 - PP_1 - DFR_1 + DFR_{1-DP} + CI_1$$

$$= 374,000,000 - 2,263,644.84 - 2241,313.00 - 935,000 + 0 + 0$$

$$= 368,560,042.16$$

TABLE 7.12 A partial view of cash flows and balances of collaterals in a supporting pool of a hypothetical student loan ABS with prepayment and deferment. Default is not considered.

Period	Beginning Balance ($)	Principal ($)	Prepayment ($)	Deferment ($)	Interest ($)	Total Cash Flow ($)	Capitalized Interest ($)	Deferred Balance ($)	Ending Balance ($)
Total:	**$258,833,213.36**	**$116,471,893.06**	**$48,789,025.16**	**$87,278,362.02**	**$462,583,468.45**	**$1,305,106.42**			
0	374,000,000.00								374,000,000.00
1	374,000,000.00	2,263,644.84	2,241,313.00	935,000.00	1,667,416.67	6,172,374.51	0.00	935,000.00	368,560,042.16
2	368,560,042.16	2,255,805.11	2,208,561.09	921,400.11	1,643,163.52	6,107,529.72	0.00	1,856,400.11	363,174,275.85
3	363,174,275.85	2,247,992.14	2,176,135.75	907,935.69	1,619,151.98	6,043,279.87	0.00	2,764,335.80	357,842,212.27
4	357,842,212.27	2,240,205.83	2,144,034.05	894,605.53	1,595,379.86	5,979,619.74	0.00	3,658,941.33	352,563,366.86
5	352,563,366.86	2,232,446.09	2,112,253.05	881,408.42	1,571,845.01	5,916,544.15	0.00	4,540,349.74	347,337,259.31
6	347,337,259.31	2,224,712.82	2,080,789.86	868,343.15	1,548,545.28	5,854,047.97	0.00	5,408,692.89	342,163,413.48
7	342,163,413.48	2,217,005.93	2,049,641.62	855,408.53	1,525,478.55	5,792,126.10	25,011.25	5,329,101.42	338,001,368.65
8	338,001,368.65	2,215,618.25	2,024,555.73	845,003.42	1,506,922.77	5,747,096.75	24,647.45	5,252,704.74	333,862,238.80
⋮									
87	78,438,291.54	2,117,736.61	460,160.14	196,095.73	349,704.05	2,927,600.80	6,284.16	1,272,937.61	75,905,505.17
88	75,905,505.17	2,117,014.22	444,893.54	189,763.76	338,412.04	2,900,319.81	6,108.36	1,234,351.29	73,388,292.10
89	73,388,292.10	2,116,323.25	429,720.66	183,470.73	327,189.47	2,873,233.37	5,933.66	1,196,003.07	70,886,530.07
90	70,886,530.07	2,115,665.67	414,640.73	177,216.33	316,035.78	2,846,342.18	5,760.03	1,157,891.15	68,400,095.63
91	68,400,095.63	2,115,043.68	399,653.00	171,000.24	304,950.43	2,819,647.10	5,587.48	1,120,013.72	65,928,863.86
⋮									
104	37,411,217.16	2,111,816.30	212,830.96	93,528.04	166,791.68	2,491,438.94	3,438.28	648,078.70	35,125,013.87
105	35,125,013.87	2,112,153.05	199,044.71	87,812.53	156,599.02	2,467,796.77	3,279.89	613,278.70	32,851,896.00
106	32,851,896.00	2,112,626.57	185,336.53	82,129.74	146,464.70	2,444,427.80	3,122.44	578,681.83	30,591,652.22
⋮									
113	17,285,732.86	2,122,255.94	91,425.27	43,214.33	77,065.56	2,290,746.77	2,045.82	341,933.59	15,107,362.27
114	15,107,362.27	2,125,238.53	78,273.22	0.00	67,353.66	2,270,865.41	1,895.51	271,073.46	12,976,606.16
115	12,976,606.16	2,135,222.49	65,366.04	0.00	57,854.04	2,258,442.57	1,746.03	205,801.34	10,843,035.77
116	10,843,035.77	2,146,492.56	52,434.14	0.00	48,341.87	2,247,268.56	1,597.36	146,086.95	8,705,420.82
117	8,705,420.82	2,159,695.75	39,466.19	0.00	38,811.67	2,237,973.61	1,449.48	91,900.81	6,561,894.50
118	6,561,894.50	2,176,126.47	26,443.15	0.00	29,255.11	2,231,824.73	1,302.36	43,214.33	4,409,313.73
119	4,409,313.73	2,199,021.87	13,326.53	0.00	19,658.19	2,232,006.59	1,155.98	0.00	2,241,335.64
120	2,241,335.64	2,241,335.64	0.00	0.00	9,992.62	2,251,328.27	0.00	0.00	0.00

The interest payment in month 1 is calculated as:

$$I_1 = B_0 \left(\frac{r_1}{12} - \frac{s}{12} \right) = 374{,}000{,}000 \times \left(\frac{6.15\%}{12} - \frac{0.80\%}{12} \right) = 1{,}667{,}416.67$$

Cash flows and ending pool balances for months 2 to 6 are calculated similarly. These cash flows and balances are presented in Table 7.12. Month 7 is the first month that a capitalized interest is added to the pool balance and it is also the first month that a deferred amount from previous months is returned to the pool balance.

Collateral, Months 7 to 120

Since a deferment period of six months is assumed, the deferred amount of \$935,000 occurring in month 1 is assumed to be returning to the pool balance in month 7. The accrued interest of this deferred amount is also capitalized at the end of month 7. Since the deferred amount in month 1 was deducted from the pool balance at the end of that month, the deferment balance was increased at the beginning of month 2. Therefore, its capitalized interest, which is added to the pool balance at the end of month 7, is equal to the summation of accrued interest in month 2 to month 7 and is calculated using the weighted average coupon rate of 6.15% and servicing spread of 0.80% as:

$$CI_7 = \sum_{j=2}^{7} 935{,}000 \times \left(\frac{6.15\%}{12} - \frac{0.80\%}{12} \right)$$

$$= 935{,}000 \times 6 \times 0.004458333 = 25{,}011.25$$

This calculation can be generalized as:

$$CI_i = DFR_{i-DP} \sum_{j=i-DP+1}^{i} \left(\frac{r_j}{12} - \frac{s}{12} \right) \tag{7.76}$$

When loans in the supporting pool are all a fixed-rate type, as in our example, r_j is equal for all months, but it varies for floating-rate collaterals. Since the ending pool balance in month 6 is $B_6 = 342{,}163{,}413.48$, the pool balance at the end of month 7 is calculated as:

$$P_7 = B_6 \left(1 - \frac{A_7}{A_6} \right) = 342{,}163{,}413.48 \times \left(1 - \frac{0.9569753200}{0.9632163625} \right) = 2{,}217{,}005.93$$

$$PP_7 = B_6 \frac{A_7}{A_6} SMM_7 = 342{,}163{,}413.48 \times \left(\frac{0.9569753200}{0.9632163625} \right) \times 0.60293081\%$$

$$= 2{,}049{,}641.62$$

$$DFR_7 = MDFR_7 \times B_6 = 0.25\% \times 342{,}163{,}413.48 = 855{,}408.53$$

$$B_7 = B_6 - P_7 - PP_7 - DFR_7 + DFR_1 + CI_7$$

$$= 342{,}163{,}413.48 - 2{,}217{,}005.93 - 2{,}049{,}641.62 - 855{,}408.53$$

$$+ \ 935{,}000 + 25{,}011.25 = 338{,}001{,}368.65$$

In the last equation, the addition of $DFR_1 = 935{,}000$ is to capture the deferred amount occurring in month 1 that is returning to the pool balance in month 7, at the end of its six-month deferment period. The interest payment in month 7 is calculated as:

$$I_7 = B_6 \left(\frac{r_7}{12} - \frac{s}{12} \right) = 342{,}163{,}413.48 \times \left(\frac{6.15\%}{12} - \frac{0.80\%}{12} \right) = 1{,}525{,}478.55$$

Cash flows and ending pool balances for months 8 to 120 are calculated similarly as presented in Table 7.12. This table also shows the deferment balances that are recursively calculated using Equation (7.75). As mentioned earlier, here we assumed that the deferment rates for the last seven months are zero. This means that no new deferment amount is assumed for month 114 and, therefore, no capitalized interest is added to the pool balance in month 120.

Once the cash flows and outstanding balances of the supporting pool for the entire 120 months are estimated, we can determine the cash flows and balances of the three classes using the payment rule of the ABS. In the following section we use the LIBOR 1-month rate from the simulated path 1 in Figure 7.19.

Classes A-1 and A-2, Month 1

Since the SLABS in our example has a sequential pay structure, the principal payments from the collateral are first allocated proportionally to class A-1 and A-2 based on their original issuance notionals. Since the original notional balance of A-1 is \$220,000,000 and of A-2 is \$80,000,000, 73.333333% of principal received from collateral each month, including the scheduled principal payment and prepayment, is allocated to class A-1 and 26.666667% to class A-2. Class A-1 notes are a floating-rate type and receive LIBOR 1-month plus 0.85%. Since the rate of floating-rate notes of this SLABS is set at the beginning of each month, the effective rate of class A-1 notes in month 1 is obtained using the current LIBOR 1-month rate of 2.3%, as 2.3% + 0.85% = 3.15%. Class A-2 notes are a fixed-rate type with a constant effective rate of 4.25%.

In month 1 the total principal payment from collateral, as shown in Table 7.12, is:

$$P_1 + PP_1 = 2,263,644.84 + 2241,313.00 = 4,504,957.84$$

Based on this, the principal payments, interest payments, and ending outstanding balances for classes A-1 and A-2 in month 1 are calculated as:

Class A-1:

$$P_1 = 73.333333\% \times 4,504,957.84 = 3,303,635.75$$

$$B_1 = B_0 - P_1 = 220,000,000 - 3,303,635.75 = 216,696,364.25$$

$$I_1 = B_0 \times r_1 = 220,000,000 \times \left(\frac{2.3\% + 0.85\%}{12}\right) = 577,500.00$$

Class A-2:

$$P_1 = 26.666667\% \times 4,504,957.84 = 1,201,322.09$$

$$B_1 = B_0 - P_1 = 80,000,000 - 1,201,322.09 = 78,798,677.91$$

$$I_1 = B_0 \times r_1 = 80,000,000 \times \left(\frac{4.25\%}{12}\right) = 28,333.33$$

Classes A-1 and A-2, Months 2 to 88

Assuming that the simulated LIBOR 1-month rates in Figure 7.19 are as of month-ends, the effective rate of class A-1 notes in month 2 is calculated using the path 1 simulated rate of 2.47% at the end of month 1. Therefore the effective rate for class A-1 notes in month 2 is 2.47% + 0.85% = 3.32%. The effective rate of class A-2 notes is 4.25%. The total collateral principal payment in month 2 from Table 7.12 is:

$$P_2 + PP_2 = 2,255,805.11 + 2,208,561.09 = 4,464,366.20$$

Based on this, the principal payments, interest payments, and ending outstanding balances for classes A-1 and A-2 in month 2 are calculated as:

Class A-1:

$$P_2 = 73.333333\% \times 4,464,366.20 = 3,273,868.55$$

$$B_2 = B_1 - P_2 = 216,696,364.25 - 3,273,868.55 = 213,422,495.70$$

$$I_2 = B_1 \times r_2 = 216,696,364.25 \times \left(\frac{2.47\% + 0.85\%}{12}\right) = 599,526.61$$

Class A-2:

$$P_2 = 26.666667\% \times 4,464,366.20 = 1,190,497.65$$

$$B_2 = B_1 - P_2 = 78,798,677.91 - 1,190,497.65 = 77,608,180.26$$

$$I_2 = B_1 \times r_2 = 78,798,677.91 \times \left(\frac{4.25\%}{12}\right) = 279,078.65$$

Interest and principal cash flows and outstanding balances of classes A-1 and A-2 for month 3 and after are calculated recursively in a similar way as explained here. Tables 7.13 and 7.14 show a partial view of cash flows and outstanding balances of classes A-1 and A-2 for different months.

At the end of month 87 the outstanding balances of classes A-1 and A-2 are \$1,457,286.69 and \$529,922.43. The total principal payment from collateral in month 88 from Table 7.12 is:

$$P_{88} + PP_{88} = 2,117,014.22 + 444,893.54 = 2,561,907.76$$

From this total amount, \$1,457,286.69 is sent to class A-2 and \$529,922.43 is sent to class A-2. This brings the outstanding balances of these two classes to zero at the end of month 88. The remaining received principal amount of $2,561,907.76 - 1,457,286.69 - 529,922.43 = 574,698.64$ is sent to class B.

TABLE 7.13 A partial view of cash flows and outstanding balances of class A-1 of a hypothetical student loan ABS

Period	*Total:* $220,000,000.00 Beginning Balance ($)	Principal ($)	LIBOR 1-Month (%)	Interest Rate (%)	$28,952,479.40 Interest ($)	$248,952,479.40 Total Cash Flow ($)	Ending Balance ($)
0	220,000,000.00		2.30%				220,000,000.00
1	220,000,000.00	3,303,635.75	2.47%	3.15%	577,500.00	3,881,135.75	216,696,364.25
2	216,696,364.25	3,273,868.55	2.46%	3.32%	599,526.61	3,873,395.15	213,422,495.70
3	213,422,495.70	3,244,360.45	2.59%	3.31%	588,690.38	3,833,050.84	210,178,135.25
4	210,178,135.25	3,215,109.24	2.80%	3.44%	602,078.95	3,817,188.19	206,963,026.01
5	206,963,026.01	3,186,112.70	2.93%	3.65%	628,731.54	3,814,844.24	203,776,913.31
6	203,776,913.31	3,157,368.63	2.98%	3.78%	641,701.76	3,799,070.40	200,619,544.67
7	200,619,544.67	3,128,874.87	3.21%	3.83%	640,078.92	3,768,953.79	197,490,669.80
8	197,490,669.80	3,109,460.92	3.32%	4.06%	668,669.09	3,778,130.01	194,381,208.88
...	...	...	...	...	...	...	...
86	5,250,018.15	1,902,273.85	2.10%	3.08%	13,469.63	1,915,743.48	3,347,744.30
87	3,347,744.30	1,890,457.61	2.06%	2.95%	8,219.00	1,898,676.61	1,457,286.69
88	1,457,286.69	1,457,286.69	2.11%	2.91%	3,531.79	1,460,818.48	0.00

TABLE 7.14 A partial view of cash flows and outstanding balances of class A-2 of a hypothetical student loan ABS

Period	*Total:* Beginning Balance ($)	$80,000,000.00 Principal ($)	Interest Rate (%)	Interest ($)	$11,426,540.25 Total Cash Flow ($)	$91,426,540.25 Ending Balance ($)
0	80,000,000.00					80,000,000.00
1	80,000,000.00	1,201,322.09	4.25%	283,333.33	1,484,655.43	78,798,677.91
2	78,798,677.91	1,190,497.65	4.25%	279,078.65	1,469,576.30	77,608,180.26
3	77,608,180.26	1,179,767.44	4.25%	274,862.31	1,454,629.74	76,428,412.82
4	76,428,412.82	1,169,130.63	4.25%	270,683.96	1,439,814.60	75,259,282.18
5	75,259,282.18	1,158,586.44	4.25%	266,543.29	1,425,129.73	74,100,695.75
6	74,100,695.75	1,148,134.05	4.25%	262,439.96	1,410,574.01	72,952,561.70
7	72,952,561.70	1,137,772.68	4.25%	258,373.66	1,396,146.34	71,814,789.02
8	71,814,789.02	1,130,713.06	4.25%	254,344.04	1,385,057.11	70,684,075.96
...	...	...	...	...	...	...
86	1,909,097.51	691,735.94	4.25%	6,761.39	698,497.33	1,217,361.57
87	1,217,361.57	687,439.13	4.25%	4,311.49	691,750.62	529,922.43
88	529,922.43	529,922.43	4.25%	1,876.81	531,799.24	0.00

At the end of month 88 class A-1 and A-2 notes are retired while month 88 is the first month that class B notes receive a principal payment.

Class B, Months 1 to 87

Class B does not receive a principal payment until month 88, when classes A-1 and A-2 are fully repaid. The outstanding balance of class B remains at $40,000,000 until the end of month 87. Class B notes are floating-rate type, indexed to LIBOR 1-month plus a spread of 1.75%, so the effective interest rate in month 1 is 2.3% + 1.75% = 4.05%. Thus, the interest amount in month 1 is calculated as:

$$I_1 = B_0 \times r_1 = 40,000,00 \times \left(\frac{2.3\% + 1.75\%}{12} \right) = 135,000$$

Interest payments for month 2 to month 87 are calculated similarly, where the outstanding balance of $40,000,000 is unchanged and the effective rate for each month is obtained from the simulated LIBOR 1-month at the end of the previous month plus the constant spread of 1.75%. Table 7.15 presents a partial view of the cash flows and outstanding balances of class B for different months.

TABLE 7.15 A partial view of cash flows and outstanding balances of class B of a hypothetical student loan ABS

Period	Total: Beginning Balance ($)	Principal ($)	LIBOR 1-Month (%)	Interest Rate (%)	Interest ($)	Total Cash Flow ($)	Ending Balance ($)
	$40,000,000.00				$4,858,420.62	$54,858,420.62	
0	40,000,000.00		2.30%				40,000,000.00
1	40,000,000.00	0.00	2.47%	4.05%	135,000.00	135,000.00	40,000,000.00
2	40,000,000.00	0.00	2.46%	4.22%	140,666.67	140,666.67	40,000,000.00
3	40,000,000.00	0.00	2.59%	4.21%	140,333.33	140,333.33	40,000,000.00
4	40,000,000.00	0.00	2.80%	4.34%	144,584.51	144,584.51	40,000,000.00
5	40,000,000.00	0.00	2.93%	4.55%	151,515.72	151,515.72	40,000,000.00
6	40,000,000.00	0.00	2.98%	4.68%	155,961.62	155,961.62	40,000,000.00
7	40,000,000.00	0.00	3.21%	4.73%	157,620.45	157,620.45	40,000,000.00
8	40,000,000.00	0.00	3.32%	4.96%	165,433.05	165,433.05	40,000,000.00
...	...	...	...	...	...	...	...
86	40,000,000.00	0.00	2.10%	3.98%	132,625.41	132,625.41	40,000,000.00
87	40,000,000.00	0.00	2.06%	3.85%	128,203.40	128,203.40	40,000,000.00
88	40,000,000.00	574,698.64	2.11%	3.81%	126,941.46	701,640.10	39,425,301.36
89	39,425,301.36	2,546,043.90	2.20%	3.86%	126,877.69	2,672,921.59	36,879,257.46
90	36,879,257.46	2,530,306.40	2.17%	3.95%	121,376.96	2,651,683.36	34,348,951.06
91	34,348,951.06	2,514,696.67	2.31%	3.92%	112,250.30	2,626,946.98	31,834,254.39
...	...	...	...	...	...	...	...
104	2,825,708.01	2,324,647.27	2.53%	4.30%	10,132.14	2,334,779.41	501,060.75
105	501,060.75	501,060.75	2.57%	4.28%	1,785.87	502,846.62	0.00

Class B, Months 88 to 105

As discussed earlier, class B received its first principal payment of $574,698.64 from the collaterals in month 88. The ending balance in this month is calculated as:

$$B_{88} = B_{87} - P_{88} = 40,000,000 - 574,698.64 = 39,425,301.36$$

Using the path 1 simulated LIBOR 1-month rate at the end of month 87 of 2.0582%, class B's interest in month 88 is obtained as:

$$I_{88} = B_{87} \times r_{88} = 40,000,00 \times \left(\frac{2.0582\% + 1.75\%}{12} \right) = 126,941.46$$

At month 89 the entire principal payment received from collaterals is allocated to repayment of class B. At the beginning of month 105, the outstanding balance of class B is $501,060.75. In this month, this balance is repaid and class B notes are retired.

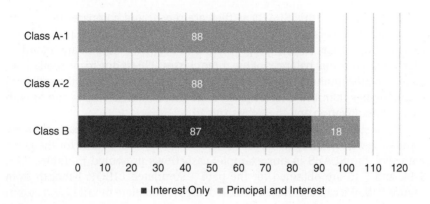

FIGURE 7.20 Comparison of principal and interest payment periods of different classes of a hypothetical student loan ABS

Figure 7.20 compares the principal and interest payment periods of the three classes of SLABS in our example. Based on our cash flow analysis, classes A-1 and A-2 receive principal and interest in periods 1 to 88 and are retired in month 88. Class B receives only interest from month 1 to month 87 and then receives both principal and interest from month 88 to month 105. It is retired in month 105. Figure 7.21 presents profiles of outstanding balances of

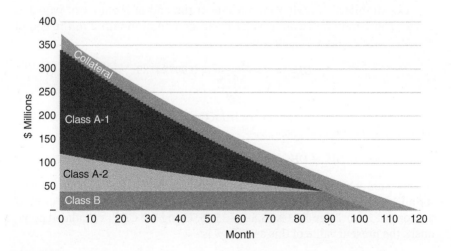

FIGURE 7.21 Balance profiles of classes of a hypothetical student loan ABS, assuming a 7% CPR and 0.25% monthly deferment rate with a deferment period length of six months

the three classes of this SLABS as they are repaid and compares them with the outstanding balance of the supporting pool. The supporting pool balance reflects the impacts of both prepayment and deferment and at any month is higher than the total balances of the three classes. This is due to overcollateralization at the initiation of the SLABS. The interest payment from the collateral is also higher than the interest paid to the three classes. This is due to both overcollateralization and the excess spread.

For a simulated interest rate path, once the cash flows of each class are estimated, we can discount them back to find the present value for the given path. For the SLABS in our example, cash flows presented in Tables 7.13, 7.14, and 7.15 are obtained for the path 1 simulated LIBOR 1-month from Figure 7.19. We can use those simulated rates to calculate monthly and cumulative discount factors and find the present value of estimated cash flows. We used the same approach for the MBS and CMO. Since the LIBOR is quoted as simple interest, the 1-month discount factor from the end of month 1 to $t = 0$ is calculated using the rate at $t = 0$ of 2.3% as:[16]

$$DF_1 = \frac{1}{1 + \dfrac{2.3\%}{12}} = 0.99808701$$

The cumulative discount factor from the end of month 1 to $t = 0$ is the same as DF_1:

$$CDF_1 = DF_1 = 0.99808701$$

The simulated LIBOR 1-month rate at the end of month 1 of path 1 is 2.47%. The 1-month discount factor from the end of month 2 to the end of month 1 is therefore calculated as:

$$DF_2 = \frac{1}{1 + \dfrac{2.47\%}{12}} = 0.99794589$$

The cumulative discount factor from the end of month 2 to $t = 0$ is calculated using DF_1 and DF_2 as:

$$CDF_2 = DF_1 \times DF_2 = 0.99808701 \times 0.99794589 = 0.99603682$$

We can continue this process to obtain the cumulative discount factors for all 120 months. Now consider class A-1. The total cash flow of this class at month 1 from Table 7.13 is $3,881,135.75. Using the CDF_1 calculated previously, the present value of this cash flow is:

$$3,881,135.75 \times 0.99808701 = 3,873,711.14$$

The total cash flow of class A-1 at month 2 from Table 7.13 is $3,873,395.15. Using CDF_2 calculated previously, the present value of the cash flow is calculated as:

$$3,873,395.15 \times 0.99603682 = 3,858,044.21$$

This is continued for monthly total cash flows of class A-1 until the end of month 88, when the class is fully repaid. The summation of all discounted cash flows provides us with the simulated value of class A-1 for path 1. We repeated this process for paths 2 and 3 from Figure 7.19, as well as for class A-2 and class B. Results are summarized in Table 7.16. The value of each class is the average of the simulated values over all interest rate paths. In practice, a large number of interest rate paths should be simulated and used in valuation to obtain stable and reliable results. Table 7.16 also shows the weighted average life of each class based on a 7% CPR and 0.25% monthly deferment rate, where weights are the outstanding balances at the end of each month over the life of a class.

In the cash flow analysis discussed earlier, we did not consider the cleanup call. If the SLABS structure has a provision to call the remaining notes once the pool balance drops below 10% of the original balance (i.e., at $37,400,000), the servicer has the right to call the remaining class B notes at month 90, when the balance in that month drops to $36,879,257.46. This shortens the life of class B and decreases its value. To evaluate the feasibility and timing of this call, the available cash in the trust should be estimated to assess whether repayment of outstanding notes in a future month is feasible. Trust cash at the end of a month is the accumulated cash from previous months plus cash received from collaterals in that month and after deduction of cash paid to note holders and fees to servicers.

TABLE 7.16 Values of three classes of a hypothetical student loan ABS for three simulated interest rate paths

Class	Notional ($)	W. Avg. Life (Year)	Path 1 Value ($)	Path 2 Value ($)	Path 3 Value ($)	Avg. Value ($)
Class A-1	220,000,000	2.29	225,848,538.94	225,867,642.24	225,880,578.80	225,865,586.66
Class A-2	80,000,000	2.29	82,955,378.21	82,948,877.47	83,519,241.41	83,141,165.69
Class B	40,000,000	3.98	44,981,610.11	44,954,064.09	45,018,261.66	44,984,645.29

SUMMARY

- Mortgage-backed securities are structured financial instruments backed by pools of mortgage loans. Pass-through certificates are the most common form of mortgage-backed securities, where the principal and interest of the underlying loans are proportionally passed through to investors minus a servicing cost. In the United States, the majority of mortgages are fixed-rate conventional loans.

- Prepayment refers to a principal payment more than the required scheduled amount. Prepayment can change the cash flows and future balances of the underlying pool of an MBS significantly. One main reason for prepayment is a decline in the prevailing interest rate, which incentivizes mortgage borrowers to refinance their loans.

- The burnout effect refers to a decrease in the prepayment rate even though the refinancing rate is decreasing. This happens when in the early stage of a rate decline eligible borrowers prepay and refinance their loans and in later stages there are not many eligible obligors remaining to prepay.

- Inclusion of prepayment and default in cash flow analysis of MBSs is generally done at the pool level when each supporting mortgage pool is assumed as a pool of many $1 micro loans. A default or prepayment event then removes the balance of an entire micro loan from the pool.

- The single monthly mortality rate is the ratio of prepayment amount in a month to the available amount to prepay. The conditional prepayment rate or constant prepayment rate is an annual measurement of prepayment.

- The pool factor is the ratio of the outstanding balance at the end of a month to the notional amount of the pool. The survival factor is the ratio of the pool factor to the amortization factor.

- Valuation of MBS is usually done using the Monte Carlo simulation technique. In this method the valuation framework consists of a short rate model, a mortgage refinancing rate model, a prepayment model, a cash flow generator, and a discounting and aggregation tool.

- A prepayment model considers various factors, including the refinancing incentive, seasoning, seasonality, and burnout effect.

- The prepayment rate, default rate, and recovery rate are three major inputs into the valuation framework of MBSs. For agency MBSs default and recovery rates are less important compared to non-agency MBSs.

- The monthly default rate is the percentage of the outstanding balance at the end of the previous month that defaults in the current month. The constant default rate is the annualized default rate.

- Month to liquidation is the expected period for a foreclosure procedure, property acquisition, and sale of property used as the collateral of a defaulted mortgage loan.

- The loss rate is the percentage of the defaulted balance that is not recovered at the liquidation month.
- Contraction risk refers to the possibility that the average life of an MBS can decrease due to an increase in prepayment. Extension risk refers to the possibility that the average life of an MBS can increase due to a decrease in prepayment.
- Collateralized mortgage obligations are structured financial instruments in which interest payments, principal payments, and prepayments from the mortgages in the supporting pools are distributed among different classes of the security, known as tranches, based on predetermined rules.
- Securitization refers to the process of creating a legal and operational structure in which cash flows from an underlying pool of standardized and homogeneous assets support payments to investors.
- Asset-backed securities are structured financial instruments backed by pools of homogeneous instruments. They are created through the securitization process. The most common ABSs are based on pools of auto loans, credit card receivables, student loans, home equity loans, and equipment loans and leases.
- Securitization can better identify, and in some cases reduce, the investment risk an ABS investor is facing, but it cannot eliminate the risk completely. Securitization is a data-intensive process and requires a significant amount of legal work.
- Overcollateralization, senior-subordinate structure, and explicit guarantees from the originator or third parties are some of the common forms of credit enhancement used in securitization vehicles of ABSs.
- Excess spread is the difference between interest collected from collaterals of an ABS structure and interest and fees paid out to investors and servicers. It creates a safety margin for the cash flow obligation of the issuing trust.
- The most common structure used in credit card receivable ABSs is a master trust for multiple series issuances while sharing a common collateral pool. Due to this, allocation of cash flows between series and among different classes of each series follows an allocation framework that is somewhat unique to credit card securitization.
- The credit quality of the collaterals in ABSs supported by credit card receivables changes considerably as general economic conditions change.
- Absolute prepayment speed is a measurement of prepayment as a percentage of the original loan balance.
- The money factor or lease factor is the financial charge of a lease contract analogous to the interest rate of a loan.

- While prepayment in auto loan ABSs exists, it is less of an issue compared to other types of securitized notes.
- For ABS structures that are backed by auto leases, residual value risk is significant. For valuation of such ABSs the methodology used by the issuer to derive the residual values should be carefully examined and tested for potential stress events.
- Credit risk analysis of ABSs backed by home equity loans is an important part of the evaluation of such notes.
- Newly issued student loan ABSs are backed by pools of private loans.

ANNEX: DERIVATION OF SURVIVAL FACTOR

Derivation of Equation (7.31): $Q_i = \prod_{j=1}^{i}(1 - SMM_j)$

From Equation (7.24) we have:

$$SMM_i = 1 - \frac{Q_i}{Q_{i-1}} \quad \Rightarrow \quad 1 - SMM_i = \frac{Q_i}{Q_{i-1}}$$

Based on this we have:

$$\prod_{j=1}^{i}(1 - SMM_j) = \frac{Q_1}{Q_0} \times \frac{Q_2}{Q_1} \times \frac{Q_3}{Q_2} \times \cdots \times \frac{Q_{i-1}}{Q_{i-2}} \times \frac{Q_i}{Q_{i-1}} = \frac{Q_i}{Q_0}$$

Since $Q_0 = 1$ we obtain:

$$Q_i = \prod_{j=1}^{i}(1 - SMM_j)$$

Derivation of Equation (7.33): $P_i = Q_{i-1}P_{si}$

When prepayment is considered, the difference between the ending balances of two consecutive months is the summation of principal and prepayment amounts:

$$B_{i-1} - B_i = P_i + PP_i$$

By replacing PP_i with its equivalent from Equation (7.25) and rearranging, we have:

$$P_i = B_{i-1} - B_i - B_{i-1}\frac{A_i}{A_{i-1}}SMM_i$$

or

$$P_i = B_{i-1}\left(1 - \frac{A_i}{A_{i-1}}SMM_i\right) - B_i$$

Using $B_i = Q_i B_{s_i}$ established earlier, we have:

$$P_i = Q_{i-1} B_{S_{i-1}} \left(1 - \frac{A_i}{A_{i-1}} SMM_i \right) - Q_i B_{s_i}$$

$$= Q_{i-1} \left(B_{S_{i-1}} - B_{S_{i-1}} \frac{A_i}{A_{i-1}} SMM_i - B_{s_i} \frac{Q_i}{Q_{i-1}} \right)$$

Since $\frac{Q_i}{Q_{i-1}} = 1 - SMM_i$, we have:

$$P_i = Q_{i-1} \left(B_{S_{i-1}} - B_{S_{i-1}} \frac{A_i}{A_{i-1}} SMM_i - B_{s_i} + B_{s_i} SMM_i \right)$$

From Equation (7.7), we have:

$$B_{S_{i-1}} \frac{A_i}{A_{i-1}} = B_{s_i}$$

Using this, we can simplify the previous equation for P_i as:

$$P_i = Q_{i-1} (B_{S_{i-1}} - B_{s_i} SMM_i - B_{s_i} + B_{s_i} SMM_i) = Q_{i-1} (B_{S_{i-1}} - B_{s_i})$$

Therefore:

$$P_i = Q_{i-1} P_{S_i}$$

NOTES

1. https://www.nahb.org/en/research/housing-economics/housings-economic-impact/.
2. https://www.federalreserve.gov/data/mortoutstand/.
3. https://www.fhfa.gov/SupervisionRegulation/FannieMaeandFreddieMac/.
4. Subscript i is not needed for C_{s_i} as the payment amount is constant for all i. We included it here as this notation is also used when there is prepayment and hence the payment amount is not constant for all periods.
5. Rounding errors may result in differences between results from direct calculation of scheduled values and the corresponding values obtained using previous month-end balances derived in an amortization schedule.
6. In this example due to rounding errors in the monthly coupon rate, amortization factors, and monthly servicing spread, the results from application of equations may be slightly different from results shown here.

7. In July 2011, the Office of Thrift Supervision (OTS) merged with the Office of the Comptroller of the Currency (OCC), which is part of the U.S. Department of Treasury (https://www.occ.treas.gov/about/who-we-are/occ-for-you/bankers/ots-integration.html).

8. Since the population variance is unknown, $\frac{\bar{X}-\mu}{\frac{s}{\sqrt{n}}}$ has a t-distribution with $n-1$ degree of freedom. Therefore, instead of $Z_{\frac{\alpha}{2}}$ we should use $t_{\frac{\alpha}{2},n-1}$ in building the confidence interval. However, when sample size is large ($n \geq 30$), t-distribution converges to the standard normal distribution and hence we can use $Z_{\frac{\alpha}{2}}$ and build the confidence interval as presented here.

9. A FICO score is a measure of consumer credit risk, originally developed by the Fair Isaac Corporation.

10. Some books and professional publications use the acronym *ABS* for absolute prepayment speed.

11. The description of student loans included in this section is for general discussion only and may not reflect the latest terms and conditions of loans offered by different entities.

12. Since for most student loan types there is no prepayment penalty, prepayment can reduce the repayment period.

13. Originally the Student Loan Marketing Association.

14. Not 100% of the losses were guaranteed. Coverage depended on the year the loan was disbursed; generally, up to 95% losses were covered.

15. Due to rounding errors, calculated results in this example may be slightly different from figures shown in corresponding tables.

16. As mentioned earlier, for simplicity here we assume that rates are quoted in a 30/360 basis.

BIBLIOGRAPHY

DTCC. "Proposed Changes to the MBSD Prepayment Model." Fixed Income Clearing Corporation, Mortgage-Backed Securities Division, October 2012 (www.dtcc.com/~/media/Files/pdf/2012/10/11/MBS142-12.pdf).

Fabozzi, Frank J., ed. *The Handbook of Mortgage-Backed Securities*, 7th ed. Oxford, UK: Oxford University Press, 2016.

Fabozzi, Frank J. *Handbook of Structured Financial Products*. Wiley, 1998.

Fabozzi, Frank J., and Steven V. Mann. *The Handbook of Fixed Income Securities*, 8th ed. McGraw-Hill Education, 2012.

Federal Deposit Insurance Corporation. *Credit Card Securitization Manual*. Division of Supervision and Consumer Protection, March 2007 (https://www.fdic.gov/regulations/examinations/credit_card_securitization).

Haughwout, Andrew, Donghoon Lee, Joelle Scally, and Wilbert van der Klaauw. "Just Released: Auto Loans in High Gear." Federal Reserve Bank of New York, February 2019.

Hayre, Lakhbir, ed. *Salomon Smith Barney Guide to Mortgage-Backed and Asset-Backed Securities*. John Wiley & Sons, 2001.

Lyuu, Yuh-Dauh. *Financial Engineering and Computation: Principles, Mathematics, Algorithms*. Cambridge University Press, 2001.

Office of Thrift Supervision. *The OTS Net Portfolio Value Model Manual*. March 2000.

Richard, Scott F., and Richard Roll. "Prepayments on Fixed-Rate Mortgage-Backed Securities." *Journal of Portfolio Management* 15, no. 3 (Spring 1989): 73–82. Securities and Exchange Commission (www.sec.gov), Credit Risk Retention Rule, 34-73407, October 2014 (*Federal Register* 79, no. 247 (December 2014); Joint Rule, Agencies: Office of the Comptroller of the Currency of Treasury Department; Board of Governors of the Federal Reserve System; Federal Deposit Insurance Corporation; U.S. Securities and Exchange Commission; Federal Housing Finance Agency; and Department of Housing and Urban Development).

CHAPTER 8

Economic Value of Equity

The ultimate goal of a balance sheet management team is to increase shareholders' *return on equity (ROE)*. Since values of a firm's assets and liabilities fluctuate by changes in market conditions, the value of the firm's equity also changes accordingly. The structure of assets and liabilities with respect to type, term, and mixture directly affects the real value of firm's equity, and hence it is crucial for equity holders to monitor and evaluate the firm's approach in asset-liability management. In particular, it is important for shareholders to have a measurement of a potential change in equity value if market conditions, such as interest rates or cross-currency exchange rates, change.

In this chapter we introduce the concept of *economic value of equity (EVE)* and explain various methods to study the impact of changes in market conditions on the EVE of a financial company. Derivation of the EVE involves the use of various valuation techniques and many assumptions, many of them introduced in earlier chapters. To reduce the effect of assumptions and calculation methods, firms usually focus on *change in economic value of equity (ΔEVE)* for different scenarios while keeping the underlying assumptions and calculation methods the same in all scenarios. This way they can concentrate on the impact of changes in market conditions on equity.

For an EVE analysis we need to make decisions on two important topics beforehand. First, we need to decide how to treat assets and liabilities that currently do not exist on the balance sheet but are planned or forecasted for future dates. The second decision is related to the treatment of the firm's own equity that is booked on the current balance sheet.

Regarding the treatment of planned or forecasted future assets and liabilities, the most common approach is to exclude them from EVE analysis and assume that the balance sheet is in a runoff mode. This approach enables us to focus on existing assets and liabilities at a snapshot in time and to avoid EVE scenario analysis results being distorted by potential new volumes of assets and liabilities that may or may not be on the balance sheet in future dates. In this approach only positions that contractually exist on the balance sheet as of the analysis date are valued and included in EVE analysis. At the end of this chapter we discuss how new volumes of assets and liabilities can be incorporated in EVE analysis and used for forecasting EVE.

Regarding the treatment of a firm's own equity, there are two general approaches. In the first method, the equity of the firm is ignored and removed from the analysis. In the second approach the portion of assets that is presumed to be financed by the firm's own equity are identified and an average duration is derived for that portion. Subsequently either the firm's own equity is included in economic value analysis with the same duration as the assets it financed, or both equity and assets financed by the equity are removed from the analysis. In practice, it is not easy to identify the exact portion of assets financed by firm's own equity and hence obtaining the average duration is not practical. Therefore, the first approach, where the firm's own equity is excluded from the analysis, is preferred and commonly used in practice. This is the approach we follow in this book.

Before we dive into EVE analysis, we should clarify a few concepts and terminologies used in this chapter:

- *Financial instrument* refers to a contractual agreement between two entities to deliver cash or other financial instruments. Stocks, bonds, mortgage loans, and interest rate swaps are examples of financial instruments.
- We use the term *position* to reflect a firm's holding in a certain financial instrument. For example, consider a bank that in the past invested in a bond issued by a local municipality by purchasing 2,000 bonds, each with a face value of $1,000. The bank paid $950 for each bond. This bank now has a position in this bond. A position can have a notional value, book value, market value, and economic value.
- *Notional value* is the amount that the interest calculation is based on. For the bank in our example, since it has purchased 2,000 bonds and each bond has a face value of $1,000, the notional value of this position is $2,000 \times 1,000 = \$2,000,000$.
- *Book value* is the original cost of a position. If applicable, the book value of a position can be the depreciated or amortized cost amount. In our example, the bank position in a Muni bond has a book value of $2,000 \times 950 = \$1,900,000$, obtained using the original cost of the bond purchase.
- The *market value* of a position is the value obtained based on the market price of the underlying financial instrument. Assume that the Muni bond in our example is currently being traded at 97.5, so the market value of the bank position in this Muni bond is $2,000 \times 1,000 \times 0.975 = \$1,950,000$. To have a meaningful market price, the underlying instrument needs to be

traded in an active and relatively liquid market, and for this reason not all positions on a bank balance sheet have market values.

- The *economic value* or *intrinsic value* of a position is the value that is supported by the cash flows of the underlying instrument and market conditions. To obtain the economic value of a position we utilize valuation models and methodologies. We discussed many of these valuation techniques in previous chapters. In an efficient market, these valuation models, when calibrated to the current market conditions, produce economic values that are equal or very close to the market values. However, sometimes market values can significantly deviate from the intrinsic or economic values due to supply and demand forces, and overreaction to news.
- In EVE analysis, intangible assets such as goodwill, intellectual property, brands and trademarks, and copyrights are often kept at their book values and assumed insensitive to market risk factors such as interest rate or cross-currency rate, unless there is a clear way to quantify the dependency of such assets to risk factors.
- We use the term *analysis date* to refer to the date that the valuation of the balance sheet is performed and results are obtained.
- In EVE analysis, where the balance sheet is assumed to be in a runoff mode, valuation of non-maturing products is done based on either *no new business*, *no new account*, or *constant balance with termination date* treatments, discussed in Chapter 2.
- In subsequent sections, we focus on balance sheets of banks, but the concepts introduced here are applicable to other firms, especially other financial companies.

ECONOMIC VALUE OF EQUITY: BASICS

The balance sheet of a bank reflects what the bank owns (assets) and what it owes (liabilities) at a snapshot in time. Generally, positions on the balance sheet are presented with their book values. Depending on the accounting convention used, book value is the original cost of the position less accumulated depreciation. Since the balance sheet reflects the book value of positions, both on the asset and liability sides, the book value of the equity might be far from its true economic value. Economic value of equity, or net worth, is the net present value of all assets, liabilities, and off-balance-sheet items of a company. Since the effect of off-balance-sheet items can be transformed into a combination of on-balance-sheet assets and liabilities, generally the economic value of equity is defined as the difference between the economic value of the bank's assets and the economic value of its liabilities:[1]

$$Economic\ Value\ of\ Equity = Economic\ Value\ of\ Assets$$

$$- Economic\ Value\ of\ Liabilities \qquad (8.1)$$

One way to obtain the economic value of assets and liabilities is to use the market values of positions (if available) and apply them in Equation (8.1) to calculate the EVE. This method of deriving the EVE is a *mark-to-market* approach. When the market value of a position is not available, a quantitative approach or a *model* can be used to value the position. We learned many of these valuation models and methods in previous chapters. If we derive the values of assets and liabilities using models, the EVE calculated from Equation (8.1) is derived using a *mark-to-model* approach.

As mentioned earlier, one of the main goals of asset-liability management is to study the impact of changes in market conditions on the net worth of a bank and its capital. Current market values of positions, if available, reflect only current market conditions. Thus, the mark-to-market approach has limited use in EVE scenario analysis. However, since market conditions are inputs to valuation models, their outputs are sensitive to market conditions and this makes them suitable for EVE scenario analysis. In the use of the mark-to-model approach, valuation models are first calibrated such that their outputs are in line with the available market values. This ensures that the arbitrage-free principle in the valuation of the balance sheet is satisfied and at the same time enables us to perform scenario and what-if analysis for different market conditions using those models.

To demonstrate the concept of economic value of equity, consider a regional bank with the balance sheet as of March 31, 2015, shown in Table 8.1.

Aside from $2.3 million available cash, the bank's assets include fixed- and floating-rate loans, and investment in government securities. The physical assets of the bank have a current book value of $1.5 million. The total book value of assets is $18 million. The bank's liabilities are fixed- and floating-rate debt notes and checking and savings deposits. The total book value of debts and deposits is $14.5 million and therefore the book value of equity is $3.5 million. These figures are all book values and do not reflect current market conditions or the creditworthiness of positions. Assume, using valuation techniques discussed in previous chapters, that the economic values of assets and liabilities of this regional bank are calculated as shown in Table 8.2. This table also shows portfolio-level durations. We will use these figures in the next section.

The total economic value of assets is $24.35 million and the total economic value of debts and deposits is $16.80 million. Therefore, the economic value of

TABLE 8.1 Balance sheet of a hypothetical regional bank – book values (in $ million)

Assets	Book Value ($MM)	Liabilities	Book Value ($MM)
Cash (incl. Deposit with Central Bank)	2.30	Fixed-Rate Short-Term Debt	3.20
Fixed-Rate Loan	8.50	Floating-Rate Long-Term Debt	5.50
Floating-Rate Loan	4.50	Deposit (Checking)	2.80
Investment in Fixed-Rate Government Debt Securities	1.20	Deposit (Savings)	3.00
Physical Assets	1.50	Equity	3.50
	18.00		**18.00**

TABLE 8.2 Balance sheet of a hypothetical regional bank – economic value (in $ million)

Assets	Economic Value ($MM)	Duration (years)	Liabilities	Economic Value ($MM)	Duration (years)
Cash (incl. Deposit with Central Bank)	2.30	0	Fixed-Rate Short-Term Debt	4.65	0.6
Fixed-Rate Loan	13.25	2.5	Floating-Rate Long-Term Debt	6.35	7.7
Floating-Rate Loan	4.65	1.8	Deposit (Checking)	2.80	0.1
Investment in Fixed-Rate Government Debt Securities	1.58	3.6	Deposit (Savings)	3.00	1.1
Physical Assets	2.57	0	Equity	7.55	
	24.35			**24.35**	

equity is: $24.35 million − $16.80 million = $7.55 million. A bank's economic value of equity is occasionally different from its market value. Market value of equity is what investors are willing to pay to own the bank. Assume that the bank in this example has 300,000 shares outstanding and that each share is currently traded for $28.50 in the market. Since the economic value of a share is $7.55 million/300,000 = $25.17, each share is traded at a premium of $28.50 − $25.17 = $3.33 compared to its economic value. The market value of equity of this bank is $28.50 × 300,000 = $8.55 million. The investors collectively are paying a premium of $1 million for the entire equity of the bank. One of the main reasons for the difference between the market and economic values of equity is the information disparity and market participants' lack of insight into the economic value of the bank's assets and liabilities. Derivation of economic value of equity requires access to the most-detailed information of the bank, including position-level data, that typically are not available to investors. In the absence of information on the EVE, investors use other indicators such as published financial reports to obtain an estimate of the true value of the equity, which may or may not be close to the EVE.

Generally, both investors and the bank's management team are interested in having an estimate of the impact of changes in market conditions on the economic value of equity. In the following sections we discuss different methods to obtain such an estimate, by first focusing on the interest rate risk factor and then considering the cross-currency exchange rate risk factor.

DURATION GAP

One of the basic methods of measuring the sensitivity of the economic value of equity to a change in interest rate is using the concept of duration that was introduced in a previous chapter. Recall that the modified duration (D_{Mod}) captures the approximate sensitivity of the value of a position to small changes in yield:

$$D_{Mod} = -\frac{1}{V}\frac{\Delta V}{\Delta y}$$

where V is the value of the position and y is the annual yield. We can rewrite this equation as:

$$\%\Delta V = -D_{Mod}\,\Delta y$$

The relationship between the modified duration (D_{Mod}) and Macaulay duration (D_{Mac}) is:

$$D_{Mod} = \frac{1}{1+\dfrac{y}{m}}D_{Mac}$$

We have:

$$\%\Delta V = -\frac{\Delta y}{1+\dfrac{y}{m}}D_{Mac}$$

where

$$D_{Mac} = \sum_{\substack{t \text{ for all} \\ \text{cash flows}}} t \, \frac{\frac{C_t}{\left(1+\frac{y}{m}\right)^{mt}}}{V}$$

In these equations, m is the compounding frequency of the yield and C_t is the cash flow of the position at time t. Assuming yield is expressed with annual compounding ($m = 1$), we have:

$$\%\Delta V = -\frac{\Delta y}{1+y} D_{Mac} \tag{8.2}$$

Equation (8.2) provides an approximate method to estimate the change in the value of a position due to a small change in the yield. Duration is additive and for a portfolio of assets or liabilities it is the weighted average of the durations of individual positions, where each weight is the proportion of the position in the portfolio.

We can use this approach in EVE analysis. Assume that the weighted average of duration of all assets of a bank is D_{MacA} and the weighted average of duration of all liabilities is D_{MacL}. A change in yield of Δy (i.e., a parallel shift in the yield curve) changes the economic value of assets and liabilities, so the change in the economic value of equity is derived as:

$$\Delta V_E = \Delta V_A - \Delta V_L \tag{8.3}$$

where:

V_A = Economic value of assets $\qquad \Delta V_A$ = Change in economic value of assets

V_L = Economic value of liabilities $\qquad \Delta V_L$ = Change in economic value of liabilities

V_E = Economic value of equity $\qquad \Delta V_E$ = Change in economic value of equity

Using Equation (8.2) we have:

$$\Delta V_E = \left(-\frac{\Delta y}{1+y} D_{MacA}\right) V_A - \left(-\frac{\Delta y}{1+y} D_{MacL}\right) V_L$$

$$= \left(-\frac{\Delta y}{1+y}\right) (D_{MacA} V_A - D_{MacL} V_L)$$

Dividing both sides of this identity by total value of assets V_A, we have:

$$\frac{\Delta V_E}{V_A} = \left(-\frac{\Delta y}{1+y}\right)\left(D_{MacA} - D_{MacL}\frac{V_L}{V_A}\right)$$

Thus, we can define duration gap as:

$$Duration\ Gap = D_{MacA} - D_{MacL}\frac{V_L}{V_A} \qquad (8.4)$$

so

$$\frac{\Delta V_E}{V_A} = -\frac{\Delta y}{1+y} \times Duration\ Gap \qquad (8.5)$$

Equivalently we can define duration gap as the change in economic value of equity as a percentage of total value of liabilities:

$$\frac{\Delta V_E}{V_L} = \left(-\frac{\Delta y}{1+y}\right)\left(D_{MacA}\frac{V_A}{V_L} - D_{MacL}\right)$$

$$Duration\ Gap = D_{MacA}\frac{V_A}{V_L} - D_{MacL} \qquad (8.6)$$

$$\frac{\Delta V_E}{V_L} = \left(-\frac{\Delta y}{1+y}\right) \times Duration\ Gap \qquad (8.7)$$

Duration gap as defined here provides an approximate method to obtain the change in economic value of equity as a percentage of the total value of assets or the total value of liabilities, due to a Δy change in the yield.

Example

Consider again the regional bank discussed in the previous section. The economic values of items on the balance sheet of the bank are presented in Table 8.2, and the current EVE of the bank is $7.55 million. We can use the duration gap to estimate the approximate impact of a 1% increase in the yield, from 5% to 6%, on the EVE of the bank. The first step is to calculate the Macaulay duration of each position and obtain the aggregated duration at portfolio levels. Assuming that the portfolio-level durations are as presented in Table 8.2, the Macaulay durations of total assets and total liabilities are calculated as the weighted average of corresponding durations, as:

$$V_A = \$24.35MM, \quad V_L = \$16.80MM$$

$$D_{MacA} = \left(\frac{2.3MM}{24.35MM}\right) \times 0 + \left(\frac{13.25MM}{24.35MM}\right) \times 2.5 + \left(\frac{4.65MM}{24.35MM}\right) \times 1.8$$

$$+ \left(\frac{1.58MM}{24.35MM}\right) \times 3.6 + \left(\frac{2.57MM}{24.35MM}\right) \times 0 = 1.93 \text{ year}$$

$$D_{MacL} = \left(\frac{4.65MM}{16.80MM}\right) \times 0.6 + \left(\frac{6.35MM}{16.80MM}\right) \times 7.7 + \left(\frac{2.80MM}{16.80MM}\right) \times 0.1$$

$$+ \left(\frac{3.00MM}{16.80MM}\right) \times 1.1 = 3.29 \text{ year}$$

Duration gap is then calculated as:

$$\text{Duration Gap} = D_{MacA} - D_{MacL} \times \frac{V_L}{V_A} = 1.93 - 3.29 \times \frac{16.80MM}{24.35MM} = -0.34$$

Hence, the approximate change in the EVE as a percentage of asset value due to an increase of 1% in the yield is calculated as:

$$\frac{\Delta V_E}{V_A} = -\frac{0.01}{1 + 0.05} \times (-0.34) = 0.33\%$$

$$\Delta V_E = 0.33\% \times 24.35 \text{ million} \cong \$0.080 \text{ million}$$

Overall, assets of this bank have lower durations compared to its liabilities and therefore have lower sensitivity to interest rate change. This is reflected in the negative duration gap. An increase in interest rate decreases the value of both assets and liabilities but the values of the liabilities decrease more. Hence, the economic value of equity increases in a rising interest rate environment. This is reflected in the positive ΔV_E obtained above. Therefore, from an economic value of equity point of view, there is no major concern for the bank equity owners if the interest rate rises in the future. However, due to the negative duration gap, a declining interest rate would decrease the economic value of equity of the bank and could deplete its capital.

TABLE 8.3 Change in EVE and its relationship to sign of duration gap and direction of interest rate movement

Change in EVE		Interest Rate	
		Rising	Falling
Duration Gap	Positive	Decrease ↘	Increase ↗
	Negative	Increase ↗	Decrease ↘

When the duration gap of a bank is positive, an increase in interest rate would decrease its EVE and a decrease in interest rate would increase its EVE. The relationship between a change in EVE with the sign of duration gap and direction of interest rate movement is summarized in Table 8.3.

Decreasing duration gap is the key to decreasing the sensitivity of a bank's EVE to change in interest rate. When durations of assets and liabilities of a bank are close, a change in interest rate affects both sides of the balance sheet almost equally, hence protecting the current value of the EVE. For example, for the regional bank in our example, which has a negative duration gap, to decrease the sensitivity of overall EVE to interest rate (especially for a possible declining interest rate environment) bank managers can increase the duration of their assets by investing in longer-term securities, underwriting longer-term loans, or converting some floating-rate loans to fixed-rate ones with higher duration. Alternatively, they can shorten the duration of their liabilities by issuing shorter-term debt notes. While a bank's interest rate risk with respect to its EVE can be decreased by the aforementioned adjustments, such fundamental changes in the bank's balance sheet can be costly and may not be in line with the bank's overall strategy and business plan. So instead of changing the balance sheet, the bank can use derivative products, such as swaps and forwards, to hedge its assets and liabilities to movement of interest rate to preserve the bank's net worth and capital position.

Duration gap analysis is a first step in analyzing EVE and its sensitivity to interest rate risk. The method, however, has some drawbacks. First, as you recall from a previous chapter, the use of duration for determining the change in value of a position due to a change in interest rate results in an approximation. The approximation deteriorates for positions with high convexity, embedded options, or prepayments. Second, the approximation is relatively good only for small changes in the yield and for higher magnitudes of change the approximation does not perform well. Third, since the method is based on change in position yield, it assumes a flat yield curve, where rates with different terms are equal. This is not the case in practice. Finally, the method only considers a parallel shift in the yield curve, as reflected by an increase or decrease in the yield. Changes in interest rate are rarely a pure parallel shift to the current yield curve. Due to these issues, duration gap analysis is often used as a first assessment of EVE sensitivity to interest rate, and banks regularly rely on full valuation of balance sheet positions to obtain a more accurate estimation of changes in net worth in different market condition scenarios.

RISK-ADJUSTED YIELD CURVE

Fundamentally, valuation of a financial instrument is based on discounting the actual or expected cash flows associated with a position on that instrument using appropriate discount factors that are calculated using interest rates that reflect the risk level of the position. For example, to value a position on a medium-term floating-rate note with rate indexed to 1-month LIBOR, the use of a LIBOR-swap yield curve as the base curve seems appropriate. This base curve is considered a risk-free curve for this position;[2] however, it should be adjusted to reflect the current riskiness of the position. This adjustment is done by adding a *risk spread* to the base yield curve and hence creating a *risk-adjusted yield curve*. The choice of base yield curve largely depends on the type of position and its risk exposure. Treasury, LIBOR-swap, and overnight index swap (OIS) curves are commonly used in practice as base curves in ALM analysis. The size of risk spread for each position depends on the base curve used. For example, if a Treasury yield curve is used as the base curve, the risk spreads are higher than if a LIBOR-swap curve is the base curve.

In EVE analysis, the first step in the valuation of a balance sheet is to determine the risk spread for different positions and setting up the appropriate risk-adjusted yield curves. When a financial instrument has an active and liquid market the risk spread can be obtained by determining the *mark-to-market spread*. The mark-to-market spread is the spread added to the base yield curve to make the value obtained from the valuation method equal to the available market value. Setting the risk spread equal to the mark-to-market spread to obtain the risk-adjusted curve is based on the assumption of an *efficient market*. This assumption implies that market participants who actively bid and ask on the price of an instrument have all available information pertinent to the instrument, including its associated risks. Hence the mark-to-market spread reflects the riskiness of the instrument from the point of view of market participants. Many financial instruments carried on the balance sheet of a bank have active and liquid markets. On the liability side of the balance sheet, the debt securities issued by a bank usually are actively traded by investment firms, broker-dealers, hedge funds, and other banks. Thus, current market prices for those securities are available. On the asset side, if a bank has investments in debt or equity securities, current market prices for those positions are obtained from the secondary markets in which they are traded. Market prices may be available for some other asset types as well. In the United States there is an active market for syndicated loans issued by banks and non-bank firms to small to medium-size corporates where market values of those loans can be obtained.

A mark-to-market spread is used to adjust the base yield curve such that the calculated present value of the position using discounted factors based on the adjusted curve produces the same value as the observed market value. At first, this may seem an unnecessary step: Since the market value of the position is available, why do we need to recalculate it again and find the spread that forces the discounted cash flow method to produce the same known market value? For valuation of the balance sheet in current market conditions, this is an unnecessary step; however, it should be noted that for ALM purposes, the bank performs scenario analysis for different market conditions and studies their impacts on position value. Current market value cannot be used for such analysis. For example, if the bank is interested to find the impact of a +100 bps change in interest rate on the economic value of equity, it needs to use a valuation model to study this scenario. Current market values are not valid in a +100 bps shock scenario. The correct approach here is to first use current market values to calibrate the valuation model by adding the mark-to-market spread to the base yield curve such that it produces the same economic values as the available market values. After this step is done and the risk-adjusted yield curve is established, then the valuation model can be used to value the balance sheet for a + 100 bps shock scenario and study the impact of the shock on the EVE of the bank.

Following is the procedure to obtain the risk-adjusted yield curve using mark-to-market spread as the risk spread:

1. Select the appropriate base yield curve (e.g., risk-free U.S. Treasury curve or LIBOR-swap curve) and construct the base spot curve. We discussed the bootstrapping technique for derivation of spot curve in Chapter 1.
2. Select the valuation model or methodology to be used for the specific position being valued (e.g., discounted cash flow or Monte Carlo simulation using an interest rate tree).

3. Add an arbitrary spread (e.g., 0.01%) to rates at all terms of the base spot curve to obtain a work-in-progress curve.

4. Using this work-in-progress spot curve and the selected valuation model, find the economic value of the position.

5. Compare the economic value obtained in the previous step with the available market value. If they are different, iteratively change the arbitrary spread, create a new work-in-progress spot curve, and solve for the economic value until the valuation model using the work-in-progress curve produces the same economic value as the available market value. The spread obtained at the end of this iterative approach is the mark-to-market spread for the position.

6. Set the risk spread equal to the mark-to-market spread. The base spot curve plus the risk spread is the risk-adjusted curve. Note that depending on the current rates and market value, the mark-to-market spread, and hence the risk spread, can be positive or negative.

$$Risk\text{-}Adjusted\ Spot\ Curve = Base\ Spot\ Curve + Risk\ Spread \qquad (8.8)$$

To illustrate this procedure, consider a bank that has a position in an instrument with the following specifications:

Instrument P1	
Type	**Fixed-Rate Note**
Currency	USD
Principal balance (notional amount)	100,000.00
Rate	3.525%
Maturity date	9/30/2017
Amortization type	Bullet at maturity date
Payment frequency	Semi-annual
Compounding frequency	Semi-annual
Accrual basis	30/360
Market price	103.45

For EVE analysis this bank has selected a LIBOR-swap yield curve as its base curve for valuation of instrument P1. Table 8.4 presents the spot rates of this curve. The analysis date is March 31, 2015.

The current market price of this instrument is $103.45. Considering the notional amount of $100,000, the current market value is $103,450.

TABLE 8.4 Assumed spot rates of a base curve

Term	Spot Rate (%)
1D	0.1140
1W	0.1407
1M	0.1763
3M	0.2708
6M	0.3160
9M	0.3873
1Y	0.4642
2Y	0.8105
3Y	1.1262
5Y	1.5465
7Y	1.7800
10Y	2.0622
30Y	2.4515

Discounted cash flow is the appropriate valuation method. Table 8.5 shows the valuation of this instrument using the base spot curve without any risk spread. Particularly, discount factors in this table are calculated using linearly interpolated spot rates without adding any risk spread. Since the instrument is fixed-rate, all interest cash flows are equal and calculated as:

$$\frac{3.525}{100} \times 100,000 \times \frac{180}{360} = 1,762.50$$

The value of instrument P1 without consideration of risk spread is $106,329.91, which is different than the market value of $103,450. Iteratively, we add a spread to the base spot curve, recalculating discount factors and determining the value of P1, until that value is equal to the available market value. When the additional spread is 1.146% the value obtained using the discounted cash flow is $103,450, as shown in Table 8.6. Therefore, the mark-to-market spread is 1.146%.

The risk-adjusted spot curve for this instrument is obtained by setting the risk spread equal to the mark-to-market spread. Figure 8.1 shows the base and risk-adjusted curves for the instrument in our example. After the risk-adjusted curve for the instrument is established it can be used for other analysis, for example for EVE scenario analysis when the base spot curve is shocked by +100 bps or −200 bps.

Many commercial ALM software packages provide functionality for derivation of mark-to-market spread. When market price and base spot curve are loaded as inputs, the software calculates the mark-to-market spread using

TABLE 8.5 Discounted cash flow valuation of instrument P1 using a base spot curve without risk spread (amounts in $)

Date	t (Day)	Day Count	Outstanding Principal	Principal Cash Flow	Interest Rate (%)	Interest Cash Flow	Total Cash Flow	Obtained using base spot curve DF	Discounted Value
3/31/2015									
9/30/2015	183	180	100,000.00		3.525%	1,762.50	1,762.50	0.998396	1,759.67
3/31/2016	366	180	100,000.00		3.525%	1,762.50	1,762.50	0.995375	1,754.35
9/30/2016	549	180	100,000.00		3.525%	1,762.50	1,762.50	0.990511	1,745.78
3/31/2017	731	180	100,000.00		3.525%	1,762.50	1,762.50	0.983953	1,734.22
9/30/2017	914	180	100,000.00	100,000.00	3.525%	1,762.50	101,762.50	0.976154	99,335.90
									106,329.91

TABLE 8.6 Discounted cash flow valuation of instrument P1 using a base spot curve and an additional risk spread of 1.146% (amounts in $)

Date	t (Day)	Day Count	Outstanding Principal	Principal Cash Flow	Interest Rate (%)	Interest Cash Flow	Total Cash Flow	Obtained using base spot curve + 1.146% DF	Discounted Value
3/31/2015									
9/30/2015	183	180	100,000.00		3.525%	1,762.50	1,762.50	0.992623	1,749.50
3/31/2016	366	180	100,000.00		3.525%	1,762.50	1,762.50	0.984091	1,734.46
9/30/2016	549	180	100,000.00		3.525%	1,762.50	1,762.50	0.973762	1,716.26
3/31/2017	731	180	100,000.00		3.525%	1,762.50	1,762.50	0.961809	1,695.19
9/30/2017	914	180	100,000.00	100,000.00	3.525%	1,762.50	101,762.50	0.948823	96,554.60
									103,450.00

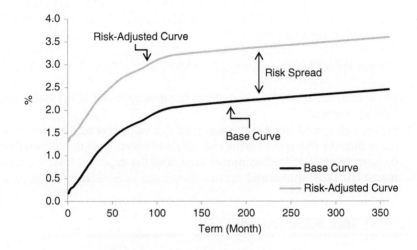

FIGURE 8.1 Base and risk-adjusted spot curves

the iterative approach explained earlier and stores it in a table, along with other position specifications. The spread is then used in scenario analysis, where for each position the spread is added to the base spot curve to create a position-specific risk-adjusted curve and used for discount factor calculation.

When market values are not available, we can consider a portfolio-wide risk-adjusted curve and use it for all positions in a specific portfolio. One way to do this is by using the portfolio fair value and its expected loss. Banks utilize various qualitative and quantitative methods to estimate the fair value and the expected loss of a portfolio and use these estimates for risk management or accounting purposes. Following is the procedure to obtain a portfolio-wide risk-adjusted curve using the fair value and the expected loss:

1. Select the appropriate base yield curve for the portfolio and obtain the associated spot curve.
2. Select the appropriate valuation model or methodology for the portfolio being valued.
3. Use the valuation model to find the present value of the portfolio using the base spot curve.
4. Use an appropriate qualitative or quantitative method to find the present value of the expected loss of the portfolio using the base spot curve.
5. Calculate the fair value of the portfolio as follows:

Fair Value = Present Value of Portfolio Using Base Spot Curve

$$- \textit{Present Value of Expected Loss Using Base Spot Curve} \quad (8.9)$$

6. Using the valuation model and an iterative approach, solve for a spread that satisfies the following equation:

Present Value of Portfolio Using [Base Spot Curve + Spread] = Fair Value

7. The spread obtained at the end of this iterative approach is the estimated fair value spread.

8. Set the risk spread equal to the estimated fair value spread. The base spot curve plus the risk spread is the risk-adjusted curve. Note that depending on current rates, valuation model used, and the expected loss, the estimated fair value spread and the risk spread can be positive or negative.

INTEREST RATE SCENARIO ANALYSIS

One of the main topics in ALM analysis is the study of the impact of change in interest rate on EVE. Consider the following questions:

- What is the impact on EVE if the yield curve is higher by 2% throughout all term points?
- What is the impact on EVE if the yield curve is lower by 1% throughout all term points?
- What is the impact on EVE if short-term rates are unchanged but mid- and long-term rates, starting from a 3-year term point, are higher by 0.5%?

The duration gap method explained earlier in this chapter is one way to estimate the impact of change in interest rate on the EVE. However, that approach has several deficiencies. Specifically, the duration gap method cannot be used to estimate the impact of a non-parallel shift in the yield curve. The appropriate method for such impact analysis is to apply the assumed changes (shocks) to the current yield curve and estimate the EVE based on the shocked curve. The difference between the EVE obtained using the current curve and the one obtained using the shocked curve is the estimated impact on the EVE due to the assumed shock.

An *interest rate shock scenario* is a rate change applied to the current yield curve to obtain a shocked yield curve. The rate change can be absolute (e.g., a 1% increase in all spot rates, meaning that 1% is added to each spot rate of the curve) or relative (e.g., a 5% relative increase, meaning that all spot rates of the curve are multiplied by 1.05). Since using absolute shock in designing a scenario for ALM analysis purposes is more common, we focus on absolute interest rate shocks in this chapter. To study the sensitivity of the EVE to change in interest rate, banks consider a variety of interest rate shocks including parallel, non-parallel, and butterfly shocks to the yield curve. We introduced these shocks in Chapter 1. In this section, we first study the impact of interest rate shocks on the value of financial instruments with different interest rate types (fixed vs. floating), and then study the impact on the EVE at the balance sheet level.

Product Type and Value Sensitivity

We start our discussion on interest rate scenario analysis by focusing on a single position first. Our goal here is to study how a product coupon rate type (fixed vs. floating) affects the sensitivity of its value to interest rate level. Consider an instrument P2, with the following specifications:

Instrument P2	
Type	**Fixed-Rate Loan**
Currency	USD
Principal balance	100,000.00
Maturity date	9/30/2019
Amortization type	Bullet at maturity date
Payment frequency	Semi-annual
Compounding frequency	Semi-annual
Accrual basis	Act/360

Assume that the valuation date is March 31, 2017. A position on instrument P2 has five payment dates and five payment periods, as listed in Table 8.7. For simplicity here we assume that, in the case of a floating-rate loan, rate setting dates fall on payment dates.

TABLE 8.7 Payment periods of position P2

Payment Date	Time (Day)	Payment Period	Period Limits	Period Length (Day)
3/31/2017		0		
9/30/2017	183	1	Apr. 1, 2017–Sep. 30, 2017	183
3/31/2018	365	2	Oct. 1, 2017–Mar. 31, 2018	182
9/30/2018	548	3	Apr. 1, 2018–Sep. 30, 2018	183
3/31/2019	730	4	Oct. 1, 2018–Mar. 31, 2019	182
9/30/2019	913	5	Apr. 1, 2019–Sep. 30, 2019	183

To study the interest rate sensitivity, we consider four cases for the coupon rate of position P2:

Case (I): The product is floating-rate with a coupon rate of 6-month LIBOR with no additional spread, and the first coupon rate is not set yet.

Case (II): The product is floating-rate with a coupon rate of 6-month LIBOR with no additional spread, and the first coupon rate is set and fixed at 1.6540%.

Case (III): The product is floating-rate with a coupon rate of 6-month LIBOR with an additional spread of 60 bps, and the first coupon is not set yet.

Case (IV): The product is fixed-rate with a coupon rate of 2.75%.

Consider the following five interest rate scenarios:

1. A base case scenario, when the spot curve as of the valuation date (current spot curve) is used to compute the discount factors and implied forward rates.
2. A +100 bps scenario, when the current spot curve is instantaneously shocked upward by 1%.
3. A +200 bps scenario, when the current spot curve is instantaneously shocked upward by 2%.
4. A −100 bps scenario, when the current spot curve is instantaneously shocked downward by 1%.
5. A −200 bps scenario, when the current spot curve is instantaneously shocked downward by 2%.

In case (I), since the coupon rate is 6-month LIBOR with no additional spread and the first period coupon rate is not set yet, the effective interest rate for all five payment periods would change when the spot curve is shocked. In case (II), the first coupon rate is set at the valuation date and hence it is fixed and only the effective rates of payment periods 2 to 5 are affected by a shock in the spot curve. In case (III), the first coupon rate is not set yet (similar to the first case); however, the coupon rate has a fixed component in the form of an additional spread added to 6-month LIBOR. And finally, in case (IV), the coupon rate is fixed and not impacted by a shock in the spot curve.

Assume that current spot rates associated with payment dates of P2 are as listed in Table 8.8 in the "Base Case" column. These rates are quoted with continuous compounding and an Act/365 convention. Discount factors are obtained from these spot rates. For example, the discount factor as of September 30, 2017, the first payment date, is calculated as:

$$DF_{Sep.30,2017} = e^{-0.0167\left(\frac{183}{365}\right)} = 0.99166208$$

183 is the actual number of days between March 31, 2017, and September 30, 2017. Discount factors as of other payment dates are calculated similarly and presented in Table 8.9 in the "Base Case" column. Assume that the 6-month LIBOR as of March 31, 2017, is 1.6540%, quoted in simple interest and an Act/360 convention.[3] The 6-month LIBOR implied forward rate as of September 30, 2017, is calculated using available discount factors as:[4]

$$r_{Sep.30,2017,6M} = \frac{360}{182}\left(\left(\frac{DF_{Mar.31,2018}}{DF_{Sep.30,2017}}\right)^{-1} - 1\right)$$

$$= \frac{360}{182}\left(\left(\frac{0.98284879}{0.99166208}\right)^{-1} - 1\right) = 1.7737\%$$

182 is the actual number of days between September 30, 2017, and March 31, 2018. The 6-month LIBOR implied forward rates as of other payment dates are obtained similarly and presented in Table 8.10 in the "Base Case" column. These rates are quoted in simple interest and an Act/360 convention.

When interest rate shocks of +100 bps, +200 bps, −100 bps, and −200 bps are applied to the spot curve, discount factors and implied forward rates are calculated in a similar way as explained earlier. Tables 8.8, 8.9, and 8.10 present

TABLE 8.8 Assumed base case and shocked spot curves associated with payment dates of position P2 (rates stated with continuous compounding and Act/365; VD: valuation date of March 31, 2017)

	Scenario				
Date	**+200 bps**	**+100 bps**	**Base Case**	**−100 bps**	**−200 bps**
9/30/2017 (VD + 6M)	3.6700%	2.6700%	1.6700%	0.6700%	0%
3/31/2018 (VD + 12M)	3.7300%	2.7300%	1.7300%	0.7300%	0%
9/30/2018 (VD + 18M)	3.8400%	2.8400%	1.8400%	0.8400%	0%
3/31/2019 (VD + 24M)	4.0100%	3.0100%	2.0100%	1.0100%	0.0100%
9/30/2019 (VD + 30M)	4.1300%	3.1300%	2.1300%	1.1300%	0.1300%

TABLE 8.9 Discount factors for base case and shock scenarios as of payment dates of position P2 (VD: valuation date of March 31, 2017)

	Scenario				
Date	+200 bps	+100 bps	Base Case	−100 bps	−200 bps
3/31/2017 (VD)	1	1	1	1	1
9/30/2017 (VD + 6M)	0.98176798	0.98670263	0.99166208	0.99664646	1
3/31/2018 (VD + 12M)	0.96338708	0.97306928	0.98284879	0.99272658	1
9/30/2018 (VD + 18M)	0.94397783	0.95825735	0.97275288	0.98746768	1
3/31/2019 (VD + 24M)	0.92293174	0.94157620	0.96059730	0.98000265	0.99980002
9/30/2019 (VD + 30M)	0.90185045	0.92469357	0.94811528	0.97213025	0.99675350

TABLE 8.10 6-month LIBOR implied forward rates for base case and shock scenarios as of payment dates of position P2, excluding last payment date (rates stated in simple interest and Act/360; VD: valuation date of March 31, 2017)

	Scenario				
Date	+200 bps	+100 bps	Base Case	−100 bps	−200 bps
3/31/2017 (VD)	3.6532%	2.6511%	1.6540%	0.6619%	0%
9/30/2017 (VD + 6M)	3.7740%	2.7713%	1.7737%	0.7810%	0 %
3/31/2018 (VD + 12M)	4.0448%	3.0408%	2.0417%	1.0477%	0 %
9/30/2018 (VD + 18M)	4.5106%	3.5043%	2.5030%	1.5067%	0.0396%
3/31/2019 (VD + 24M)	4.5985%	3.5916%	2.5899%	1.5931%	0.6013%

shocked spot curves for the aforementioned scenarios, along with computed discount factors and 6-month LIBOR implied forward rates. In calculating the implied forward rates for shock scenarios, the spot rates are first shocked and then the implied forward rates are calculated from the shocked spot rates. For a −200 bps scenario, spot rates as of first three payment dates became negative and hence floored to zero, leading to a discount factor of 1 for these dates. The difference between a spot rate with a 6-month term in Table 8.8 and 6-month LIBOR as of the valuation date in Table 8.10 for each scenario is due to different compounding frequency and day count convention used in quoted rates, where spot rates are stated with continuous compounding and an Act/365 convention, whereas 6-month LIBOR are stated in simple interest and an Act/360 convention.

Having the discount factors and implied forward rates, we can find the value of position P2 for each coupon rate case and for each interest rate scenario. Consider case (I) and the base case scenario. Using results from Tables 8.7, 8.9, and 8.10, the value of position P2 is obtained as:

$$V_{Case\ (I),Base\ Case} = 0.01654 \times \left(\frac{183}{360}\right) \times 100{,}000 \times 0.99166208$$

$$+ 0.017737 \times \left(\frac{182}{360}\right) \times 100{,}000 \times 0.98284879$$

$$+ 0.020417 \times \left(\frac{183}{360}\right) \times 100{,}000 \times 0.97275288$$

$$+ 0.02503 \times \left(\frac{182}{360}\right) \times 100{,}000 \times 0.96059730$$

$$+ \left(0.025899 \times \left(\frac{183}{360}\right) \times 100{,}000 + 100{,}000\right) \times 0.94811528$$

$$= 100{,}000.00$$

Since this valuation is for case (I), the effective interest rate (coupon rate) for each payment period is equal to the 6-month LIBOR implied forward rate without any additional spread. As seen here, the value of the product is \$100,000, equal to its notional amount. This is not surprising, since when discount factors and implied forward rates used in coupon rates are derived using the same spot curve, a floating-rate instrument with no additional spread in its coupon is at par at each payment date. We studied this property of floating-rate instruments in Chapter 2. Now consider a +100 bps interest rate scenario. The increase in spot curve affects the value of position P2 in case (I) in two ways. First, higher spot rates result in lower discount factors, which in turn decreases the value of the position. Second, higher spot rates result in higher implied forward rates and higher coupon rates, which increases the value of the position. Thus, an increase in spot rates has two opposite impacts on the value of this floating-rate instrument. The net result on the value of the position depends on various factors, including the timing of cash flows, timing of rate settings, and magnitude of shock to the spot curve. For our position P2, the value in case (I) for a +100 bps interest rate shock scenario is obtained as:

$$V_{Case\ (I),+100\ bps} = 0.026511 \times \left(\frac{183}{360}\right) \times 100{,}000 \times 0.98670263$$

$$+ 0.027713 \times \left(\frac{182}{360}\right) \times 100{,}000 \times 0.97306928$$

$$+\ 0.030408 \times \left(\frac{183}{360}\right) \times 100{,}000 \times 0.95825735$$

$$+\ 0.035043 \times \left(\frac{182}{360}\right) \times 100{,}000 \times 0.94157620$$

$$+\ \left(0.035916 \times \left(\frac{183}{360}\right) \times 100{,}000 + 100{,}000\right)$$

$$\times\ 0.92469357 = 100{,}000.00$$

Position P2 remains at par even when the spot curve is shocked upward by 1%. Again, this is due to the fact that at each payment date, a floating-rate product with no additional spread in its coupon is always at par, irrespective of the levels of spot rates. Repeating this calculation for +200 bps, −100 bps, and −200 bps interest rates produces the same result, where position P2 remains at par. Table 8.11 provides the value of position P2 for each coupon rate case and for each interest rate scenario introduced here. It also shows the change in value (Δvalue) of the position, which is the difference between the value in an interest rate shock scenario and the value in the base case scenario. As demonstrated earlier, for case (I), the value of position P2 is always at par and hence the change in value is zero for any shock scenario.

Now consider case (II), where there is no additional spread in coupon rate but the first coupon rate is set and hence it won't change when the spot curve is shocked. When the rate setting date is before, or immediately prior to, the

TABLE 8.11 Value and change in value of position P2 for different coupon rate cases and different interest rate scenarios

					Scenario		
Case	Coupon Rate		+200 bps	+100 bps	Base Case	−100 bps	−200 bps
I	LIBOR 6M	Value:	100,000.00	100,000.00	100,000.00	100,000.00	100,000.00
		ΔValue:	0.00	0.00		0.00	0.00
II	LIBOR 6M,	Value:	99,002.27	99,499.88	100,000.00	100,502.63	100,840.80
	First Coupon	ΔValue:	−997.73	−500.12		502.63	840.80
	Fixed: 1.6540%						
III	LIBOR 6M +	Value:	101,434.60	101,456.02	101,477.83	101,500.05	101,520.62
	Spread: 60 bps	ΔValue:	−43.23	−21.81		22.22	42.78
IV	Fixed 2.75%	Value:	96,760.30	99,142.78	101,584.93	104,088.25	106,644.84
		ΔValue:	−4,824.64	−2,442.15		2,503.32	5,059.91

valuation date, the coupon rate of the first payment period is fixed and any change in the spot rate won't impact the effective rate of the first period. Here the first coupon rate is 1.6540%. The value of position P2 in case (II) for the base case scenario remains the same at $100,000. However, for shock scenarios the position values would not remain at par. In this case a change in the spot curve affects the discount factor at the first payment date while the coupon rate of the first payment period remains unchanged. For example, the value of position P2 in case (II) for the +100 bps interest rate scenario is obtained as:

$$
\begin{aligned}
V_{Case\ (II),+100\ bps} = {} & 0.016540 \times \left(\frac{183}{360}\right) \times 100{,}000 \times 0.98670263 \\
& + 0.027713 \times \left(\frac{182}{360}\right) \times 100{,}000 \times 0.97306928 \\
& + 0.030408 \times \left(\frac{183}{360}\right) \times 100{,}000 \times 0.95825735 \\
& + 0.035043 \times \left(\frac{182}{360}\right) \times 100{,}000 \times 0.94157620 \\
& + \left(0.035916 \times \left(\frac{183}{360}\right) \times 100{,}000 + 100{,}000\right) \\
& \times 0.92469357 = 99{,}499.88
\end{aligned}
$$

The only difference between $V_{Case\ (I),+100\ bps}$ and $V_{Case\ (II),+100\ bps}$ is in the first coupon rate, where for $V_{Case\ (I),+100\ bps}$ the shocked rate of 2.6511% is used and for $V_{Case\ (II),+100\ bps}$ the unshocked rate of 1.6540% is used for the coupon rate of the first period. The value of position P2 along with the change in value for each interest rate scenario is presented in Table 8.11. From this table and for case (II) we observe that:

- The change in value of position P2 is no longer zero for interest rate shock scenarios. Having the first coupon rate fixed led to sensitivity of the position value to the interest rate level.
- Upward shocks to the spot curve decreased the value of position P2 while downward shocks increased its value. This is due to the effect of interest rate shocks on discount factors.

Let's now move to case (III), where the coupon rate has an additional spread of 60 bps added to the 6-month LIBOR while the first coupon is not set as of the valuation date. For case (III), the value of position P2 in the base case scenario is obtained as:

$$
\begin{aligned}
V_{Case\ (III),Base\ Case} = {} & (0.01654 + 0.0060) \times \left(\frac{183}{360}\right) \times 100{,}000 \times 0.99166208 \\
& + (0.017737 + 0.0060) \times \left(\frac{182}{360}\right) \times 100{,}000 \times 0.98284879 \\
& + (0.020417 + 0.0060) \times \left(\frac{183}{360}\right) \times 100{,}000 \times 0.97275288 \\
& + (0.02503 + 0.0060) \times \left(\frac{182}{360}\right) \times 100{,}000 \times 0.96059730 \\
& + \left((0.025899 + 0.0060) \times \left(\frac{183}{360}\right) \times 100{,}000 + 100{,}000\right) \\
& \times 0.94811528 \\
= {} & 101{,}477.83
\end{aligned}
$$

As seen here, floating-rate instrument P2 is no longer at par at a payment date. Similarly, for shock scenarios the position values would not remain at par. For example, for the +100 bps shock scenario the value of position P2 in case (III) is obtained as:

$$
\begin{aligned}
V_{Case\ (III),+100\ bps} = {} & (0.026511 + 0.0060) \times \left(\frac{183}{360}\right) \times 100{,}000 \times 0.98670263 \\
& + (0.027713 + 0.0060) \times \left(\frac{182}{360}\right) \times 100{,}000 \times 0.97306928 \\
& + (0.030408 + 0.0060) \times \left(\frac{183}{360}\right) \times 100{,}000 \times 0.95825735 \\
& + (0.035043 + 0.0060) \times \left(\frac{182}{360}\right) \times 100{,}000 \times 0.94157620 \\
& + \left((0.035916 + 0.0060) \times \left(\frac{183}{360}\right) \times 100{,}000 + 100{,}000\right) \\
& \times 0.92469357 = 101{,}456.02
\end{aligned}
$$

Here, the effective rate of each payment period is obtained by first shocking the spot curve, calculating the implied forward rate and then adding 0.60% to the result. Values and changes in value for position P2 for case (III) for different interest rate shock scenarios are presented in Table 8.11. Since the additional spread added to the coupon rate of this product is constant and does not change when the spot curve is shocked, there is some value sensitivity to interest rate level, as indicated by changes in value of case (III) in Table 8.11.

Finally, consider case (IV), where position P2 has a fixed rate of 2.75%. The value of P2 in the base case interest rate scenario in case (IV) is calculated as:

$$
\begin{aligned}
V_{Case\ (IV),Base\ Case} = {} & 0.0275 \times \left(\frac{183}{360}\right) \times 100{,}000 \times 0.99166208 \\
& + 0.0275 \times \left(\frac{182}{360}\right) \times 100{,}000 \times 0.98284879 \\
& + 0.0275 \times \left(\frac{183}{360}\right) \times 100{,}000 \times 0.97275288 \\
& + 0.0275 \times \left(\frac{182}{360}\right) \times 100{,}000 \times 0.96059730 \\
& + \left(0.0275 \times \left(\frac{183}{360}\right) \times 100{,}000 + 100{,}000\right) \times 0.94811528 \\
= {} & 101{,}584.93
\end{aligned}
$$

As indicated earlier, fixed-rate instrument P2 is not at par at a payment date. Similarly, in shock scenarios, the value of P2 changes and is different from its value at the base case. For example, in the +100 bps scenario, the value of P2 in case (IV) is calculated as:

$$
\begin{aligned}
V_{Case\ (IV),+100\ bps} = {} & 0.0275 \times \left(\frac{183}{360}\right) \times 100{,}000 \times 0.98670263 \\
& + 0.0275 \times \left(\frac{182}{360}\right) \times 100{,}000 \times 0.97306928 \\
& + 0.0275 \times \left(\frac{183}{360}\right) \times 100{,}000 \times 0.95825735 \\
& + 0.0275 \times \left(\frac{182}{360}\right) \times 100{,}000 \times 0.94157620 \\
& + \left(0.0275 \times \left(\frac{183}{360}\right) \times 100{,}000 + 100{,}000\right) \\
& \times 0.92469357 = 99{,}142.78
\end{aligned}
$$

Values and changes in value of position P2 in case (IV) for different interest rate shock scenarios are presented in Table 8.11. Upward shocks in the spot curve result in decreases in discount factors and a subsequent decrease in P2 value, whereas downward shocks had an opposite effect.

From this discussion we can deduce the following: if (A) a financial instrument is valued immediately after a payment date, and (B) discount factors and implied forward rates are based on the same spot curve, we have:

- If the position is a floating-rate instrument with a coupon rate that does not include a constant spread, and the first period coupon rate is not set yet, the position remains at par and its value is insensitive to the change in spot rates.
- If the position is a floating-rate instrument with a coupon rate that does not include a constant spread while the first period coupon rate is set and fixed, the position value using the current spot curve (base case) is equal to the par value. This is based on the assumption that the valuation date is immediately after the rate setting. However, the position won't remain at par when the spot curve is shocked. This means that its value is sensitive to the change in spot rates.
- If the position is a floating-rate instrument with a coupon rate that includes a constant spread, and the first period coupon rate is not set yet, the position may or may not be at par, but its value is sensitive to the change in spot rates.[5]
- If the position is a fixed-rate instrument, it may or may not be at par, but its value is highly sensitive to the change in spot rates.[6]

It should be also noted that if the valuation date is not immediately after a payment date, the case is similar to case (II), where the first period coupon rate is set and fixed. Hence, the position value is sensitive to the change in spot rates. To summarize, from a valuation point of view, fixed-rate instruments are very sensitive to changes in interest rate while floating-rate instruments are less sensitive. For a floating-rate instrument, the sensitivity of its value to the interest rate level depends on the valuation date and the magnitude of the constant spread, if any, added to the coupon rate.

Impact of Interest Rate Shocks on EVE

In the next step in interest rate scenario analysis we broaden our view to the balance sheet level and study the impact of interest rate shocks on the EVE. In the following discussions we assume that both base and shocked curves are risk-adjusted. The general procedure for performing interest rate shock analysis for the EVE is as follows:

1. Derive the risk spread and risk-adjusted curve based on the current spot curve. We refer to this risk-adjusted curve as the base spot curve.
2. Value the balance sheet using the base spot curve to obtain the base EVE: V_{E0} (index 0 refers to the base case).

3. Apply the interest rate shock (e.g., +100 bps parallel shock) to the current spot curve to obtain the shocked spot curve and then, using the same risk spreads obtained in step (1), construct the risk-adjusted shocked spot curve. In using the same risk spreads for constructing the risk-adjusted base and shocked curves we implicitly assume that factors that affect the risk spreads (e.g., credit risk, counterparty risk, etc.) are unchanged from the base to the shock scenarios. More sophisticated interest rate scenario analysis may consider the risk spreads that are a function of the shock amount (i.e., risk spreads are changing from scenario to scenario).

4. Value the balance sheet using the risk-adjusted shocked spot curve to obtain the shocked EVE: V_{E_s} (index s refers to a shock scenario).

5. The difference between the shocked EVE and base EVE is the *change in economic value of equity* due to the interest rate shock:

$$\Delta V_E = V_{E_s} - V_{E_0} \tag{8.10}$$

In this analysis we assume that an interest rate shock to the current spot curve is instantaneous. This means that for a shock scenario, the spot curve as of the analysis date is replaced by the shocked curve and all other calculations, including derivation of implied forward rates, are based on the shocked curve. Using a shocked spot curve has several implications in derivation of the EVE. For a shock scenario:

- Discount factors calculated based on the shocked curve assumed for the analysis date are different from the ones obtained from the base (current) curve. An upward shock decreases discount factors and a downward shock increases them.
- Implied forward rates calculated based on a shocked curve are different from rates obtained from the base curve. If the implied forward method is used for estimation of future interest payments of floating-rate instruments, this affects their values.
- Interest rate trees and simulated interest rate paths created based on a shocked curve are different from the ones obtained using the base curve and this affects the positions' values if these valuation methods are used.

Assume the spot curve as of March 31, 2015 (base curve) is as shown in Figure 8.2. This graph also includes four shock scenarios:

1. A parallel +100 bps shock where all terms of the spot curve are increased by 1%. This shock preserves the shape of the base curve.

2. A –100 bps shock where all terms of the spot curve are decreased by 1%. Here we applied a floor of 0% so shocked rates cannot become negative. Due to this floor the shocked curve is no longer parallel to the base curve and the shape of the curve is changed.

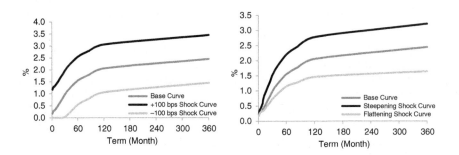

FIGURE 8.2   Base, parallel, and non-parallel shocked spot curves

3. A steepening shock where rates at different terms increased by different amounts, changing the shape and level of the curve. Here the shock
   started at the 1-month term point for an increase of 5 bps and gradually
   increased, reaching a 77 bps increase at the 30-year term point.
4. A flattening shock where rates at different terms decreased by different
   amounts, changing the shape and level of the curve. Here the shock
   started at the 9-month term point for a decrease of –5 bps and gradually
   changed, reaching a –80 bps decrease at the 30-year term point.

There are many ways to construct interest rate shocks for EVE analysis.
Banks usually consider several parallel shocks (e.g. ±100 bps or ±200 bps)
and several non-parallel shocks (e.g. steepening or flattening) in their ALM
analysis. An expectation of change in interest rate in the future, regulatory
requirements, and types of financial instruments on the balance sheet are a
few factors to consider when designing an interest rate shock scenario for EVE
analysis.

To illustrate interest rate scenario analysis for the EVE, consider a regional
bank with the balance sheet presented in Table 8.12 in the "Book Value" column. The "Duration" column in that table provides a descriptive indication of
whether a portfolio has a long duration (more sensitive to interest rate change)
or short duration (less sensitive to interest rate change). The non-maturing
deposits are valued using runoff profiles constructed for each portfolio.

The analysis date is March 31, 2015. Using the base spot curve of Figure 8.2
and the procedure explained in the previous section, risk-adjusted base spot
curve is constructed and the values of all portfolios are obtained. The economic values of portfolios are shown in the second column of Table 8.12, in
the "Base Case" column. The economic value of equity in the base case is
V_{E0} = \$7.04 million.

To estimate the impact of each shock scenario, we apply the same risk
spread used for the base case to obtain the risk-adjusted shocked curves. After
obtaining the risk-adjusted spot curves for each shock scenario, we revalue the

TABLE 8.12 Economic value of the balance sheet of a hypothetical regional bank in different scenarios – example of an asset-sensitive balance sheet

		Duration	Book Value	Economic Value				
				Base Case	+100 bps Shock	–100 bps Shock	Steepening Shock	Flattening Shock
Assets	Cash	–	5.00	5.00	5.00	5.00	5.00	5.00
	Fixed-Rate Loans	Long	12.50	14.30	12.54	15.98	12.46	16.07
	Floating-Rate Loans	Short	9.50	10.20	9.67	10.33	9.56	10.45
	Investment in Fixed-Rate Securities	Long	6.00	8.24	6.54	9.55	6.43	9.68
	Investment in Floating-Rate Securities	Short	2.20	2.95	2.65	3.01	2.59	3.05
	Physical Assets		3.50	3.50	3.50	3.50	3.50	3.50
			38.70	**44.19**	**39.90**	**47.37**	**39.54**	**47.75**
Liability	Fixed-Rate Debts	Short	11.20	12.45	11.99	13.85	11.87	13.92
	Floating-Rate Debts	Short	7.80	8.22	7.90	8.40	7.88	8.50
	Deposits (CD)	Short	3.20	3.70	3.22	4.21	3.15	4.27
	Deposits (Checking)	Short	8.00	8.10	7.88	8.25	7.53	8.27
	Deposits (Savings)	Short	4.50	4.68	4.40	4.80	4.34	4.81
	Equity	Short	4.00	7.04	4.51	7.86	4.77	7.98
			38.70	**44.19**	**39.90**	**47.37**	**39.54**	**47.75**

entire balance sheet and calculate the economic values of portfolios. They are shown in Table 8.12 in the "+100 bps Shock," "−100 bps Shock," "Steepening Shock," and "Flattening Shock" columns.

Consider the +100 bps shock. This change in interest rate decreases the value of fixed-rate positions as discount factors decrease. Since the fixed-rate asset portfolios in the balance sheet presented in Table 8.12 have long durations the impact is rather large and the portfolios' values dropped significantly. On the other hand, the fixed-rate liabilities on the balance sheet have short durations and their values declined less compared to the fixed-rate assets. The impact of this upward shock on a floating-rate position is twofold. On the one hand, the increase in interest rate leads to a decrease in discount factors, which results in a decrease in position value. On the other hand, the upward shift in interest rate increases the expected future interest payment cash flows of the floating-rate position. This results in an increase in position value. Hence an upward shift in interest rate has two opposing effects on the value of a floating-rate position. An increase or decrease in position value depends on the magnitude of the shock, the time to first rate reset, and the method of valuation of the floating-rate position. In our example, as shown in Table 8.12, the values of floating-rate asset and liability portfolios decreased due to a +100 parallel shock to the spot curve, but this is not always the case. The value of deposit portfolios also declined due to relatively short runoff profiles and hence short durations. Based on the recalculated economic values of asset and liability portfolios, the EVE of the bank for a +100 bps shock is obtained as $V_{E+100\ bps} = \$4.51$ million. Therefore, the change in EVE from the base case to this shock scenario is:

$$\Delta V_{E+100\ bps} = V_{E+100\ bps} - V_{E0} = \$4.51 \text{ million} - \$7.04 \text{ million}$$

$$= -\$2.53 \text{ million}$$

Focusing on the asset side, the increase in interest rate decreased the economic value of assets by $4.29 million (from $44.19 million to $39.90 million). On the other hand, on the liability side (excluding equity), the drop is $1.76 million (from $37.15 million to $35.39 million). The upward shock decreased the values of both the asset and liability sides of the balance sheet but the magnitude of the decrease in the asset side was larger than the magnitude of the decrease in the liability side. This was due to higher durations of assets compared to liabilities, especially for fixed-rate portfolios. The balance sheet presented in Table 8.12 is an example of an *asset-sensitive* balance sheet, where a change in interest rate has a higher impact on assets compared to liabilities.

This analysis highlights the risk of significant loss in this bank's equity and capital position for a modest 1% increase in interest rate. The portfolio composition, duration mismatch, and large percentage of fixed-rate positions on the balance sheet make this bank vulnerable to an increase in interest rate with respect to its EVE.

Now consider the –100 bps shock. As mentioned before, this shock is designed to be a parallel shock to the current (base) spot curve but due to flooring at 0%, the shape of the curve on the short end is changed. A downward shock in interest rate results in an increase in discount factors and this leads to an increase in the values of fixed-rate positions. For the bank in our example, the longer durations of fixed-rate assets result in a higher magnitude of increase in their values compared to fixed-rate liabilities. The downward shock in interest rate has a double effect on the value of floating-rate portfolios, where an increase in discount factors increases their values while a decline in expected future interest payment cash flows decreases their values. Therefore, the values of floating-rate positions may increase or decrease when the interest rate declines. The direction of the value change depends on the magnitude of the interest rate change, whether interest rates are floored or not, the valuation methodology, and rate reset times. For the bank in our example, in the –100 bps shock scenario, the value of floating-rate assets and liabilities increased compared to the base case, but this is not always the case. The value of deposit portfolios also increased. Based on the recalculated economic values of asset and liability portfolios, the EVE of the bank for a –100 bps shock is obtained as $V_{E-100\ bps} = \$7.86$ million. Therefore the change in the EVE from the base case to this shock scenario is:

$$\Delta V_{E-100\ bps} = V_{E-100\ bps} - V_{E0} = \$7.86 \text{ million} - \$7.04 \text{ million}$$
$$= \$0.82 \text{ million}$$

Focusing on the asset side, the decrease in interest rate increased the economic value of assets by $3.18 million (from $44.19 million to $47.37 million). On the other hand, on the liability side (excluding equity), the increase is $2.39 million (from $37.15 million to $39.51 million). The downward shock increased the values of both the asset and liability sides of the balance sheet but the magnitude of the increase in the asset side was larger than the magnitude of the increase in the liability side and this led to an increase in the EVE of $0.82 million. This result is expected, since the bank of our example is asset-sensitive, where assets have higher durations compared to liabilities, especially for fixed-rate portfolios. Changes in EVE for the steepening and flattening shock scenarios are obtained similarly. From Table 8.12 we have:

$$V_{E\,Steepening} = \$4.77 \text{ million}$$

$$\Delta V_{E\,Steepening} = V_{E\,Steepening} - V_{E0} = \$4.77 \text{ million} - \$7.04 \text{ million}$$

$$= -\$2.27 \text{ million}$$

$$V_{E\,Flattening} = \$7.98 \text{ million}$$

$$\Delta V_{E\,Flattening} = V_{E\,Flattening} - V_{E0} = \$7.98 \text{ million} - \$7.04 \text{ million}$$

$$= \$0.94 \text{ million}$$

Many banks have asset-sensitive balance sheets, where long-term assets are funded by short-term liabilities. There are some banks and non-bank finance companies that have *liability-sensitive* balance sheets. As an example, consider another regional bank with the balance sheet presented in Table 8.13. The analysis date is March 31, 2015. Economic values of the balance sheet items for the base case and for the same interest rate shock scenarios in Figure 8.2 are shown in Table 8.13. These economic values are obtained using risk-adjusted spot curves for the base and shock scenarios. Fixed-rate assets of this bank have shorter durations compared to its fixed-rate liabilities, therefore the liability side of the balance sheet has a higher sensitivity to a change in interest rate compared to the asset side. The economic value of equity of this bank in the base case is calculated as $V_{E0} = \$7.09$ million.

In a +100 bps shock, the values of floating-rate asset and liabilities as well as deposit portfolios dropped. The values of fixed-rate asset and liability portfolios also dropped but due to higher durations the values of liabilities decreased more than the values of assets. Based on the recalculated economic values of asset and liability portfolios, the EVE of the bank for a +100 bps shock is obtained as $V_{E+100\,bps} = \$8.07$ million. Thus, the change in EVE for this shock scenario is:

$$\Delta V_{E+100\,bps} = V_{E+100\,bps} - V_{E0} = \$8.07 \text{ million} - \$7.09 \text{ million}$$

$$= \$0.98 \text{ million}$$

At first it may seem counterintuitive that an interest rate shock that resulted in a decrease in values of all portfolios (asset and liability) led to an increase in the value of equity. Focusing on the asset side, the increase in interest rate decreased the economic value of assets by \$2.94 million (from \$50.69 million to \$47.75 million). On the liability side (excluding

TABLE 8.13 Economic value of the balance sheet of a hypothetical regional bank in different scenarios – example of a liability-sensitive balance sheet

		Duration	Book Value	Economic Value				
				Base Case	+100 bps Shock	−100 bps Shock	Steepening Shock	Flattening Shock
Assets	Cash	–	5.50	5.50	5.50	5.50	5.50	5.50
	Fixed-Rate Loans	Short	13.84	15.62	14.61	16.02	14.52	16.15
	Floating-Rate Loans	Short	10.82	11.52	10.99	11.65	10.88	11.77
	Investment in Fixed-Rate Securities	Short	7.32	9.56	8.46	10.11	8.32	10.33
	Investment in Floating-Rate Securities	Short	3.52	4.27	3.97	4.33	3.91	4.37
	Physical Assets	–	4.22	4.22	4.22	4.22	4.22	4.22
			45.22	50.69	47.75	51.83	47.35	52.34
Liability	Fixed-Rate Debts	Long	12.50	13.75	11.41	15.42	11.20	15.51
	Floating-Rate Debts	Short	9.10	9.52	9.20	9.70	9.28	9.80
	Deposits (CD)	Long	4.50	4.95	4.19	5.98	4.02	6.25
	Deposits (Checking)	Short	9.20	9.40	9.18	9.51	8.83	9.56
	Deposits (Savings)	Short	5.80	5.98	5.70	6.10	5.54	6.11
	Equity	Short	4.12	7.09	8.07	5.12	8.48	5.11
			45.22	50.69	47.75	51.83	47.35	52.34

equity), the decrease in value is $3.92 million (from $43.60 million to $39.68 million). Thus, the upward shock decreased the values of both the asset and liability sides of the balance sheet but the overall magnitude of the decrease in liabilities was larger than the decrease in assets. This was due to higher durations of liabilities compared to assets, especially for fixed-rate portfolios. This led to an increase in the bank's economic value of equity of $0.98 million.

In a −100 bps shock, the values of floating-rate assets and liabilities as well as deposit portfolios increased. The values of fixed-rate asset and liability portfolios also increased but due to higher durations the values of liabilities increased more than the values of assets. Based on the recalculated economic values of asset and liability portfolios, the EVE of the bank for a −100 bps shock is $V_{E-100\ bps}$ = $5.12 million. Therefore, the change in EVE for this shock scenario is calculated as:

$$\Delta V_{E-100\ bps} = V_{E-100\ bps} - V_{E0} = \$5.12 \text{ million} - \$7.09 \text{ million}$$
$$= -\$1.97 \text{ million}$$

On the asset side, the decrease in interest rate increased the economic value of assets by $1.14 million (from $50.69 million to $51.83 million). On the liability side (excluding equity), the increase in value is $3.11 million (from $43.60 million to $46.71 million). The downward shock increased the values of both the asset and liability sides of the balance sheet but, due to higher liability durations, the magnitude of increase in the liability side overall was larger than the increase in the asset side. This led to a decline in the bank's economic value of equity of $1.97 million.

The balance sheet presented in Table 8.13 is an example of a liability-sensitive balance sheet where changes in interest rate have a higher impact on liabilities compared to assets. For this bank, changes in EVE for the steepening and flattening shock scenarios are obtained similarly. From Table 8.13 we have:

$$V_{E\,Steepening} = \$8.48 \text{ million}$$
$$\Delta V_{E\,Steepening} = V_{E\,Steepening} - V_{E0} = \$8.48 \text{ million} - \$7.09 \text{ million}$$
$$= \$1.39 \text{ million}$$
$$V_{E\,Flattening} = \$5.11 \text{ million}$$
$$\Delta V_{E\,Flattening} = V_{E\,Flattening} - V_{E0} = \$5.11 \text{ million} - \$7.09 \text{ million}$$
$$= -\$1.98 \text{ million}$$

Balance Sheet Type and EVE Sensitivity

As illustrated in the previous section, the balance sheet of a bank can be categorized as asset-sensitive or liability-sensitive. In an asset-sensitive balance sheet, the values of asset portfolios overall have a higher sensitivity to changes in interest rate compared to liabilities. The impact of an upward or downward shock to interest rate is not always the same for an asset-sensitive balance sheet. This is due to the fact that values of floating-rate positions do not always move in the opposite direction of the change in interest rate. For floating-rate positions, an upward shock to interest rate decreases the discount factors but at the same time increases the expected future interest payment cash flows. Depending on which effect prevails, values of floating-rate positions may increase or decrease in an upward interest rate shock. A downward shock also has two opposing effects on the values of floating-rate positions, where on the one hand it increases discount factors and on the other hand it decreases the expected future interest payment cash flows. Again, depending on the dominant effect, values of floating-rate positions may increase or decrease in a downward interest rate shock. For an asset-sensitive balance sheet, if overall values of asset and liability portfolios are decreased due to an upward shock to interest rate, the economic value of equity decreases. This was the case for the bank presented in Table 8.12 for +100 bps and steepening shocks. Also, for an asset-sensitive balance sheet, if overall values of asset and liability portfolios are increased due to a downward shock to interest rate, the economic value of equity increases. This was the case for the bank presented in Table 8.12 for −100 bps and flattening shocks.

In a liability-sensitive balance sheet, values of liability portfolios overall have a higher sensitivity to changes in interest rate compare to assets, and similar to an asset-sensitive balance sheet, the impact of an upward or downward shock to interest rate is not always the same. For a liability-sensitive balance sheet, if overall values of asset and liability portfolios are decreased due to an upward shock to interest rate, the economic value of equity increases. This was the case for the bank presented in Table 8.13 for +100 bps and steepening shocks. For a liability-sensitive balance sheet, if overall values of asset and liability portfolios are increased due to a downward shock to interest rate, the economic value of equity decreases. This was the case for the bank presented in Table 8.13 for −100 bps and flattening shocks. These results are summarized in Table 8.14. To reiterate, the relationship between balance sheet type, direction of change in EVE, and direction of change in interest rate as presented in this table is only valid if the values of asset and liability portfolios, overall, move in the opposite direction of interest rate change.

TABLE 8.14   Change in EVE and its relationship to balance sheet type and direction of change in interest rate (if overall values of assets and liabilities move in the opposite direction of interest rate change)

Interest Rate	Asset-Sensitive	Liability-Sensitive
Rising (if overall values of asset and liability portfolios decrease)	$\Delta EVE < 0$	$\Delta EVE > 0$
Falling (if overall values of asset and liability portfolios increase)	$\Delta EVE > 0$	$\Delta EVE < 0$

CURRENCY EXCHANGE RATE SCENARIO ANALYSIS

For a bank with a multi-currency balance sheet, changes in cross-currency exchange rates (FX rates) can affect the economic value of equity. Similar to interest rate shock scenarios, FX rates can also be shocked to study their impact on EVE. An *FX rate shock scenario* is a rate change applied to a currency exchange rate to obtain a *shocked conversion rate*. The rate shock for an FX rate shock scenario is usually defined in a relative term (e.g., 5% appreciation in USD-EUR exchange rate).

To illustrate EVE analysis for FX rate shocks, consider a bank that has exposures in three currencies: U.S. Dollar (USD), British Pound (GBP), and Japanese Yen (JPY). Assume that the analysis date is August 31, 2015. The current aggregated economic values of items on this bank's balance sheet in local currencies are shown in Table 8.15.

Functional currency refers to the main currency used by a bank and it is often the domestic currency of the country where the bank is incorporated. The functional currency is often used in a bank's financial reporting. The functional currency of this bank is USD; hence to obtain the economic value of the equity we need to convert the exposures in GBP and JPY to USD using the spot FX rates as of August 31, 2015. This bank has USD-denominated assets with a current economic value of 10,000,000 USD. The bank also has assets denominated in JPY and GBP with current values of 1,200,000,000 JPY and 3,000,000 GBP respectively. Assume that the spot rates for these currencies as of August 31, 2015, are USD-JPY: 121.23 and GBP-USD: 1.5345. Thus, the values of these assets in USD are:

$$1,200,000,000 \; JPY \times \frac{1}{121.23} = 9,898,540 \; USD$$

$$3,000,000 \; GBP \times 1.5345 = 4,603,500 \; USD$$

TABLE 8.15 Economic value of a bank's balance sheet with exposures in USD, GBP, and JPY

Asset		Liability	
Currency	Economic Value	Currency	Economic Value
USD	10,000,000	USD	22,000,000
JPY	1,200,000,000		
GBP	3,000,000		

To convert JPY exposure to USD, the inverse of the quoted rate is used. The liabilities of the bank are all in USD with a current value of 22,000,000 USD. Having the *USD-equivalent* of the values of all assets and liabilities, the current economic value of the equity (base case) is then obtained as:

Total Asset Value − Total Liability Value

$$= 10,000,000 + 9,898,540 + 4,603,500 - 22,000,000$$

$$= 2,502,040 \; USD$$

To study the impact of a change in FX rates on EVE we assume that an instantaneous shock is applied to the spot FX rates as of the analysis date. Such a shock changes the conversion rates used to convert balance sheet items to the functional currency and hence impacts the EVE of the bank. The general procedure for performing FX rate shock analysis for EVE is as follows:

1. Derive the risk spreads and risk-adjusted curves based on the current spot curves for exposures in each local currency.
2. Value the balance sheet in local currencies using the relevant risk-adjusted spot curves.
3. Convert all economic values to the functional currency using current FX spot rates to obtain the base EVE in the functional currency: V_{E_0}.
4. Apply the FX rate shock (e.g., +5% appreciation of the functional currency) to the current spot FX rates to obtain shocked spot FX rates.
5. Convert all economic values in local currencies obtained in step (2) to the functional currency using the shocked spot FX rates from step (4) to obtain the shocked EVE in the functional currency: V_{E_S}. This implicitly assumes that the shock to spot FX rates does not alter the local currency interest rate spot curves.

6. The difference between the shocked EVE and base EVE, both in the functional currency, is the change in the economic value of equity due to the assumed FX rate shock.

In this analysis we assume that an FX rate shock to the current spot rates is instantaneous. This means that for a shock scenario, the spot FX rates as of the analysis date are replaced by the shocked spot FX rates and all other calculations, including derivation of forward FX rates, are based on the shocked spot FX rates. We also assume that the shock to the spot FX rate of a currency does not materially change the interest rate in that currency. This is a simplifying assumption to keep the analysis focused on the FX rate. A more comprehensive study should consider the impact of an instantaneous shock to the spot FX rate on interest rate and therefore the impact on the EVE would be due to changes in FX rates and interest rates.

As an example, consider again the bank with the balance sheet in Table 8.15 and assume that we are evaluating the impact of an instantaneous shock on EVE where the functional currency is appreciated by 5%. Current spot FX rates are USD-JPY: 121.23 and GBP-USD: 1.5345. A 5% appreciation in USD results in shocked spot FX rates of USD-JPY: 127.29 and GBP-USD: 1.4578 and the converted values of JPY and GBP exposures using these rates are:

$$1,200,000,000 \; JPY \times \frac{1}{127.29} = 9,427,181 \; USD$$

$$3,000,000 \; GBP \times 1.4578 = 4,373,325 \; USD$$

Using these shocked USD-equivalent values, the economic value of the equity in the functional currency for this scenario is obtained as:

$$Total \; Asset \; Value - Total \; Liability \; Value$$

$$= 10,000,000 + 9,427,181 + 4,373,325 - 22,000,000$$

$$= 1,800,506 \; USD$$

Thus, the change in the EVE due to a 5% appreciation of USD is:

$$\Delta V_{E \, 5\%USD \; Appreciation} = V_{E \, 5\%USD \; Appreciation} - V_{E0}$$

$$= 1,800,506 \; USD - 2,502,040 \; USD = -701,534 \; USD$$

So a 5% appreciation in USD would result in a reduction in this bank's EVE of approximately 28%. Since the impact of exchange rate on interest rate is not incorporated in the analysis, this result is approximate but it provides an insight into the significant cross-currency exchange rate risk the bank is carrying on its balance sheet with respect to the economic value of equity.

ECONOMIC VALUE OF EQUITY RISK LIMITS

Banks regularly perform scenario analysis similar to what we discussed in previous sections and compare the impacts on the EVE with predefined limits. These limits represent the risk appetite of the bank with respect to the risk factor considered (e.g., interest rate or FX rate risk factors). For example, consider again the bank with the balance sheet presented in Table 8.12. This bank has an asset-sensitive balance sheet and downward shocks to the spot curve reduce its EVE. Assume that the bank has a $1.5 million risk limit for any shock that results in a decline in EVE. From the analysis presented in the "Interest Rate Scenario Analysis" section, the –100 bps parallel shock and flattening non-parallel shock reduce the bank's EVE by $1.97 million and $1.98 million, respectively. The changes in EVE from these shocks breach the risk limit of $1.5 million. Since the risk limits represent the maximum tolerable risk, this bank carries excessive interest rate risk on its balance sheet with regard to the EVE. By using derivative products such as interest rate swaps, or making changes in assets and liabilities (e.g., changing terms and durations, or changing the percentage of fixed-rate products), the bank can remediate this risk.

The EVE risk limits for each scenario should be set based on the overall risk appetite of the bank. Some of the factors that are usually considered in setting risk limits are:

- The bank's risk appetite and tolerance level for change in the value of equity and capital level
- Regulatory requirements and the maximum allowable loss of capital defined by supervisory bodies
- Products offered on the asset side of the balance sheet
- Funding mechanisms and liability types
- An expectation of changes in risk factors in the future
- Plans for change in existing products or for a new product offering

BALANCE SHEET PLANNING AND EVE FORECASTING

Banks often develop short-, medium-, and long-range plans to guide the overall business strategy while considering economic forecasts for participating markets. Such plans usually include guidance for new volumes of the existing product to replace matured or amortized assets and a funding plan to replace future maturing debts or withdrawn deposits. In net interest income (NII) analysis, discussed in the next chapter, it is a common practice to consider the impact of these new volumes of assets and liabilities. For example, if the bank is planning to issue a new debt security one quarter from the analysis date, the interest expense of the new note should be considered in NII analysis starting from the next quarter. However, in economic value of equity analysis, the planned new volumes of assets and liabilities usually are not considered when EVE as of analysis date is calculated. Since in EVE analysis the balance sheet is considered to be a snapshot in time, only assets and liabilities that exist as of that date are used in calculating EVE.

Any planned new volumes of assets and liabilities can be used in the determination of forecasted EVE in future dates. To demonstrate this, consider a bank whose economic value of its total assets at current date $(t = 0)$ is $V_{At=0} =$ $120 million and economic value of its total liabilities, excluding equity, is $V_{Lt=0} = \$90$ million. These economic values are obtained using a risk-adjusted spot curve at $t = 0$.

Assume that at $t = 0$ we have forecasted spot curves at one and two periods in the future, at time $t = 1$ and $t = 2$. Such a forecast could have been obtained using implied forward rates or based on economic forecasts. Based on the current business plan, and to replace matured positions, the bank is planning to have the following new volumes of assets and liabilities at time $t = 1$ and $t = 2$:

Book Value ($ Million)	$t = 1$	$t = 2$
New Assets	15	8
New Liabilities	8	9

Since planned new volumes do not exist on the balance sheet at $t = 0$ they are not included in the calculation of EVE for that date. So the EVE at the current date is calculated as:

$$V_{Et=0} = V_{At=0} - V_{Lt=0} = \$120 \text{ million} - \$90 \text{ million} = \$30 \text{ million}$$

This is summarized in Figure 8.3 in the $t = 0$ column. The new volumes can be incorporated into EVE analysis as part of forecasting the EVE at future periods. Consider the case that at current date $t = 0$ we need to obtain a forecast of the EVE at future dates $t = 1$ and $t = 2$. Focusing on $t = 1$ first, from $t = 0$ to $t = 1$, and due to maturity, amortization, runoff, withdrawal, and prepayment, outstanding balances of existing assets and liabilities (A and L) decrease. Using the risk-adjusted forecasted spot curve for $t = 1$ and after taking into account the effect of maturities and runoffs, the economic values of existing assets and liabilities at $t = 1$ are obtained as $V_{At=1} = \$105$ million and $V_{Lt=1} = \$75$ million. The decrease in the values of assets and liabilities can be attributed to the decrease in outstanding balances, or the impact

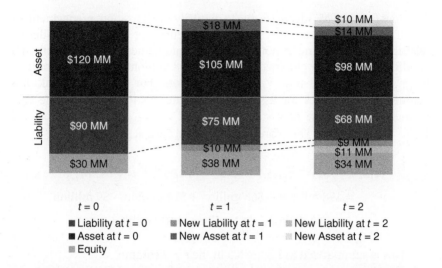

FIGURE 8.3 Incorporation of new asset and liability volumes in EVE analysis

of a forecasted spot curve at $t = 1$ that is different from the current spot curve at $t = 0$. At $t = 1$ the bank has planned new volumes for addition to the balance sheet. Using the risk-adjusted forecasted spot curve for $t = 1$ and using the relevant maturity and runoff schedules, the market values of these new volumes of assets and liabilities (NA and NL) are obtained as $V_{NA_{t=1}} = \$18$ million and $V_{NL_{t=1}} = \$10$ million respectively. Note that in this example, at $t = 1$ book values of new assets and new liabilities are \$15 million and \$8 million respectively while \$18 million and \$10 million are their corresponding economic values. These economic values are calculated by discounting cash flows of the new volumes back to $t = 1$ and not to $t = 0$, using the risk-adjusted forecasted spot curve for $t = 1$. This bank also has planned new volumes at $t = 2$ but those are not on the balance sheet at $t = 1$ so they are not included in the forecasted EVE at $t = 1$. Therefore the forecasted economic value of equity at time $t = 1$ is calculated as:

$$V_{E_{t=1}} = V_{A_{t=1}} - V_{L_{t=1}} + V_{NA_{t=1}} - V_{NL_{t=1}}$$

$$= \$105 \text{ million} - \$75 \text{ million} + \$18 \text{ million} - \$10 \text{ million}$$

$$= \$38 \text{ million}$$

This is summarized in Figure 8.3 in the $t = 1$ column. To forecast the EVE at $t = 2$ we note that from $t = 1$ to $t = 2$ the outstanding balances of existing assets and liabilities (A and L) and also new volumes of assets and liabilities (NA and NL) decrease due to maturity, amortization, prepayment, or runoff. Using a risk-adjusted forecasted spot curve for $t = 2$ and considering relevant maturities and runoffs, the economic values of these assets and liabilities at $t = 2$ are obtained as $V_{A_{t=2}} = \$98$ million, $V_{L_{t=2}} = \$68$ million, $V_{NA_{t=2}} = \$14$ million, and $V_{NL_{t=2}} = \$9$ million. For $t = 2$ the bank has planned new volumes for assets and liabilities (NA' and NL'). The economic values of these new volumes at $t = 2$ are $V_{NA'_{t=2}} = \$10$ million and $V_{NL'_{t=2}} = \$11$ million. Therefore, the forecasted EVE at $t = 2$ is:

$$V_{E_{t=2}} = V_{A_{t=2}} - V_{L_{t=2}} + V_{NA_{t=2}} - V_{NL_{t=2}} + V_{NA'_{t=2}} - V_{NL'_{t=2}}$$

$$= \$98 \text{ million} - \$68 \text{ million} + \$14 \text{ million} - \$9 \text{ million}$$

$$+ \$10 \text{ million} - \$11 \text{ million} = \$34 \text{ million}$$

This is summarized in Figure 8.3 in the $t = 2$ column.

This process can be repeated to obtain the forecasted EVE in subsequent future periods. As the existing balances mature, new volumes based on the business plan are added to the balance sheet. The new volumes themselves amortize at the succeeding periods. At each period only positions that are on the balance sheet, whether coming over from previous periods or planned for addition for that date, are considered in EVE calculation while positions that are planned to be added at later periods are not included.

BASEL ACCORD GUIDANCE ON EVE ANALYSIS

The *Basel Committee on Banking Supervision (BCBS)*, part of the *Bank for International Settlements (BIS)*, in 2004 introduced a series of principles for the management of interest rate risk (BCBS 2004). Most of the guidelines were broad and applicable to both trading and banking books while a few of them were specific to the banking book. These principles provided direction for the development of strategies and policies for identification, measurement, monitoring, and control of the interest rate risk. In 2016 the Basel Committee released an update to these guidelines by focusing on *interest rate risk in the banking book (IRRBB)*, as part of the pillar 2 supervisory review process of the capital adequacy framework (BCBS 2016).

The updated standard included 12 principles for managing interest rate risk in the banking book as well as measurement and reporting methods that are based on two ALM metrics: economic value of equity and net interest income. These principles are set to protect banks against potential adverse effects of change in interest rate on earnings and capital position. In this section we briefly review the principles outlined in the updated Basel standard and discuss the guidance provided for scenario construction and analysis of the economic value of equity. In the following chapter we discuss the standard's guidance for analysis of net interest income.[7]

Principles of Managing Interest Rate Risk in the Banking Book

Each of the 12 principles included in the Basel standard covers certain aspects of managing the interest rate risk in the banking book. A summary of these principles is as follows:[8]

Principle 1 – Identify, Measure, Monitor, and Control: This principle indicates the importance of the management of interest rate risk in the banking book. It emphasizes the need for efficient policies and procedures for identifying and measuring IRRBB, as well as monitoring and controlling the risk. The principle also highlights the need for the review of risk-taking initiatives, hedging activities, and new products prior to rollout to ensure compliance with the bank's overall IRRBB management framework.

Principle 2 – Governance: This principle describes the governance body of IRRBB and the importance of active oversight of a bank's management of interest rate risk. The governing unit is responsible for ensuring the effectiveness of the procedures for the identification, measurement, monitoring, and control of IRRBB. This is primarily done by setting standards of the measurements, the reporting and review process, internal controls, and periodic review of key assumptions. Setting appropriate limits, including guidance for exceptions, as well as controlling those limits is another aspect of effective governance.

Principle 3 – Risk Appetite: This principle indicates that IRRBB risk appetite must be clearly defined and integrated with the overall risk appetite of the bank and the IRRBB limits set by the governance body should be part of the bank's aggregate risk limits.

Principle 4 – Measurement: This principle indicates that the measurement of IRRBB should be based on both economic value and earnings (net interest income) as complementary assessment tools. The principle also provides guidance on the interest rate scenarios that banks should consider. These scenarios can be categorized as:
1. Any scenario required based on the Internal Capital Adequacy Assessment Process (ICAAP) of the bank
2. Historical or hypothetical stress scenarios
3. Six prescribed interest rate shock scenarios (these scenarios will be introduced later in this section)

4. Any scenario required by regulatory supervisors

5. Forward-looking scenarios based on change in portfolio composition such as merger and acquisition activities

The principle provides the following guidelines for the development of interest rate scenarios:

- Scenarios should be appropriate to the size of the bank, the complexity of its products, and the riskiness of its positions.
- Scenario development should be a collaborative task, including participation from subject matter experts from various groups, including treasury, risk management, and controllership departments.
- In developing scenarios for different currencies, the current term structure of the interest rate, historical and implied volatilities, and correlation between rates in different currencies should be considered.
- A wide range of scenarios (parallel and non-parallel shocks) should be studied to enable the bank to identify interest rate gap risk, basis risk, and option risk, if applicable.
- If a bank has a concentration in a specific financial instrument or sector, specific scenarios should be developed to stress those concentration areas.
- Interactions of interest rate risk with other areas such as liquidity risk and credit risk should be considered in scenario development.
- In cases of significant option risk, scenarios that result in the exercise of options should be included. Change in the interest rate volatility should also be included in scenario design.
- In designing scenarios, banks should clearly specify the term structure of the yield curve and the basis relationship between indices, and document all assumptions related to interest rates that are decided by the bank (e.g., the rate paid by the bank for its savings product) as opposed to market-driven interest rates (e.g., fed funds, LIBOR, or SOFR).
- Reverse stress tests should be performed to identify scenarios that adversely impact a bank's economic value of equity, its earnings, and eventually its capital position.

Principle 5 – Behavioral Modeling and Assumptions: This principle emphasizes the importance of sound behavioral modeling and assumptions in managing IRRBB. Such assumptions and modeling approaches should be clearly documented and reviewed. Banks should conduct sensitivity analysis on these assumptions and behavioral models to understand their potential impact on IRRBB. Some of these assumptions are:

- Option exercise assumptions
- Behavioral assumptions of non-maturing deposits with respect to the timing of cash flows and repricing

- Prepayment assumptions and the effect of interest rate on prepayment speed
- Assumptions related to the drawdown of commitment facilities for retail and commercial customers
- Assumptions related to the early redemption of term deposits

Principle 6 – Data Quality and Model Validation: This principle sets the expectation about the quality of the data and validation of models used for measuring IRRBB. Accuracy of the data is important in effectively managing IRRBB. Mapping rules from the data sources to models should be documented and reviewed for accuracy. Banks should have a policy for model validation that clearly defines the responsibilities of model owners and validation groups. An independent group within a bank should perform validation of the models used in the measurement of IRRBB for conceptual soundness. Ongoing monitoring, outcome analysis, and back-testing of those models should be performed periodically to evaluate their performance. Such validation and monitoring should also include any third-party vendor models used in the measurement of IRRBB.

Principle 7 – Reporting: This principle outlines key characteristics of regular reporting to the governing unit that oversees IRRBB. Such reports should include a summary of exposures and key assumptions, results of scenario and stress test analysis, the status of compliance with policies and limits, and findings by internal or external auditors and validators.

Principle 8 – Public Disclosure: This principle outlines the public disclosure requirement of the IRRBB. Banks are required to disclose changes in both economic value of equity (ΔEVE) and net interest income (ΔNII) for the prescribed scenarios, along with qualitative discussion and high-level description of the key assumptions, modeling approaches, aggregation techniques, and methods of the management and hedging of IRRBB. This principle requires banks to, in particular, disclose their assumptions regarding the average and the maximum of the repricing term of the non-maturity deposits. For the prescribed scenarios, banks should disclose the quantitative measurements for the current and previous periods.

Principle 9 – Capital Adequacy: According to this principle, the capital required for IRRBB should be considered in a bank internal capital adequacy assessment process. The capital requirement of IRRBB should be in line with a bank's risk appetite and must be based on the economic value metrics while earning metrics should be used in the determination of capital buffers.

Principle 10 – Supervisory Expectation: Collection of Information: This principle outlines the expectation from bank supervisors regarding the collection of information that enables them to effectively evaluate banks' procedures for management of IRRBB. This includes the need for regular information collection, and comparability and consistency of data collected from the banks they supervise.

Principle 11 – Supervisory Expectation: Assessment: This principle provides an overview of the characteristics of an effective supervisory assessment of banks' IRRBB management. This includes the assessment of policies, key assumptions and models, internal oversight and governance, and results of banks' IRRBB measurements. This principle also emphasizes the importance of sharing knowledge among different supervisory entities.

Principle 12 – Supervisory Expectation: Identification of Outlier: This principle indicates the need for supervisors to establish and publish their criteria for identifying a bank as an outlier regarding its management of IRRBB. One such criterion should be based on a comparison of a maximum ΔEVE of six prescribed shock scenarios with 15% of the tier 1 capital of a bank.[9] Supervisors may also have criteria that are based on earnings instead of economic value. Banks identified as outliers may be required to use a standardized method to compute their ΔEVE related to IRRBB (this method will be discussed later in this section), to take corrective actions, or to hold additional capital.

Scenario Construction and EVE Analysis

As mentioned earlier, the Basel standard considers the change in economic value of equity as one of the metrics suitable for measurement of IRRBB. The EVE analysis required by the standard is based on a series of prescribed interest rate shock scenarios to capture various types of risk, including interest rate gap, basis, and option risks. The standard sets the following guidelines for the calculation of ΔEVE:

- Cash flow from all interest rate-sensitive assets, liabilities, and off-balance-sheet items in the banking book should be included in the analysis but banks' own equity should be excluded.
- Banks should disclose whether commercial margins and spreads are included or excluded in the determination of cash flows.
- For cash flow discounting, banks can use a risk-free yield curve or a risk-adjusted yield curve (only if margins and spreads are included in the determination of cash flows). They need to disclose the type of yield curve used in the analysis.

- EVE analysis should be based on the existing balance sheet and in a runoff mode.
- There are six prescribed interest rate shock scenarios to be analyzed. They are:
  1. Parallel shock up
  2. Parallel shock down
  3. Steepening shock (short rates down and long rates up)
  4. Flattening shock (short rates up and long rates down)
  5. Short rates shock up
  6. Short rates shock down

To set up these scenarios, the standard first provides shock amounts for three general shock types – parallel, short, and long – for each currency. Table 8.16 presents the shock amounts provided in the Basel standard published in 2016. These shock amounts are calculated using historical interest rate data and are subject to periodic recalibration and change.

If the shock amounts in Table 8.16 for three general shock types and for each currency c are represented by $\bar{r}_{parallel,c}$, $\bar{r}_{short,c}$, and $\bar{r}_{long,c}$, interest rate shock scenarios are constructed as follows:

- Parallel shock up and down: Rates at all term points of the current yield curve are shocked by:

$$\Delta r_{parallel,c}(t) = \pm \bar{r}_{parallel,c}$$

where + is for the upward shock and – is for the downward shock.

TABLE 8.16　Interest rate shock amounts per currency for three general shock types

	ARS	AUD	BRL	CAD	CHF	CNY	EUR	GBP	HKD	IDR	INR
Parallel	400	300	400	200	100	250	200	250	200	400	400
Short	500	450	500	300	150	300	250	300	250	500	500
Long	300	200	300	150	100	150	100	150	100	350	300

	JPY	KRW	MXN	RUB	SAR	SEK	SGD	TRY	USD	ZAR
Parallel	100	300	400	400	200	200	150	400	200	400
Short	100	400	500	500	300	300	200	500	300	500
Long	100	200	300	300	150	150	100	300	150	300

Source: "Interest Rate Risk in the Banking Book," Basel Committee on Banking Supervision, April 2016, https://www.bis.org.

- Short rates shock up and down: Rates at each term point t of the yield curve are shocked by:

$$\Delta r_{short,c}(t) = \pm \bar{r}_{short,c} \, e^{-\frac{t}{4}}$$

where t is in years. $e^{-\frac{t}{4}}$ represents a decay factor resulting in a lower shock amount for longer term points.

  - Long rates shock up and down (these shocks by themselves are not part of the six prescribed shocks, but they are used for the construction of steepening and flattening shocks): Rates at each term point t of the yield curve are shocked by:

$$\Delta r_{long,c}(t) = \pm \bar{r}_{long,c} \left(1 - e^{-\frac{t}{4}}\right)$$

$1 - e^{-\frac{t}{4}}$ represents a decay factor resulting in a lower shock amount for shorter term points.

  - Flattening shock: Rates at each term point t of the yield curve are shocked by:

$$0.8 \times |\Delta r_{short,c}(t)| - 0.6 \times |\Delta r_{long,c}(t)|$$

  - Steepening shock: Rates at each term point t of the yield curve are shocked by:

$$-0.65 \times |\Delta r_{short,c}(t)| + 0.9 \times |\Delta r_{long,c}(t)|$$

If approved by regulatory supervisors, for downward shock scenarios a floor that is not greater than zero can be applied. For example, the USD shock amounts for parallel, short, and long shock types from Table 8.16 are 200, 300, and 150 basis points. The six prescribed shock scenarios are then constructed as follows:

  - Parallel shock up: Rates at all term points of the yield curve are shocked by +200 bps.
  - Parallel shock down: Rates at all term points of the yield curve are shocked by −200 bps.
  - Short rates shock up: Rates at each term point of the yield curve are shocked by $+300 \text{ bps} \times e^{-\frac{t}{4}}$.
  - Short rates shock down: Rates at each term point of the yield curve are shocked by $-300 \text{ bps} \times e^{-\frac{t}{4}}$.

- Flattening shock: Rates at each term point of the yield curve are shocked by:

$$+0.8 \times \left|+300 \text{ } bps \times e^{-\frac{t}{4}}\right| - 0.6 \times \left|+150 \text{ } bps \times \left(1 - e^{-\frac{t}{4}}\right)\right|$$

- Steepening shock: Rates at each term point of the yield curve are shocked by:

$$-0.65 \times \left|+300 \text{ } bps \times e^{-\frac{t}{4}}\right| + 0.9 \times \left|+150 \text{ } bps \times \left(1 - e^{-\frac{t}{4}}\right)\right|$$

Standardized Framework

Similar to other components of the Basel framework, the measurement of IRRBB has a standardized method, which either a bank chooses to adopt, or the supervisors mandate its adoption. The standardized method is based on the economic value of equity, where an approximate method is used to obtain estimates of ΔEVE for the six prescribed scenarios. A summary of this approach is discussed here (BCBS 2016).

The standardized method is based on *notional repricing cash flows*, which include principal payments, principal amounts that are to be repriced (i.e., principal amounts whose effective rates are to be changed), and interest payments that have not been paid or repriced yet. Notional repricing cash flows of interest rate-sensitive positions on- and off-balance-sheet are placed in 19 different time buckets based on their repricing times. The time buckets range from overnight to greater than 20 years and each bucket is assigned a midpoint (in years). These time buckets are presented in Table 8.17. The principal amounts of floating-rate instruments are placed in the time buckets in which their first rate reset dates are located.

For those products for whose exact timings of their notional repricing cash flows are not available (e.g., non-maturity deposits, loans subject to prepayment, or term deposits subject to early redemption), the standard provides certain guidelines for placement of relevant cash flows in the appropriate time buckets. For options or positions with embedded optionality, placement of cash flows in time buckets is done without consideration of optionality and later an add-on amount is applied to ΔEVE for inclusion of the options' effect.

For each currency c, the notional repricing cash flows in each time bucket are netted to obtain a single positive or negative cash flow for each bucket. Then for each scenario these cash flows (one per each time bucket) are discounted using the continuous compounded discount factors based on the risk-free spot rates:[10]

$$DF_{i,c}(t) = e^{-r_{i,c}(t) \times t} \tag{8.11}$$

TABLE 8.17   Time bucket scheme for standardized method of IRRBB measurement
(t: bucket midpoint in year)

Short-Term	Medium-Term	Long-Term
O/N (Overnight) ($t = 0.0028$ year)	2Y–3Y ($t = 2.5$ years)	7Y–8Y ($t = 7.5$ years)
O/N–1M ($t = 0.0417$ year)	3Y–4Y ($t = 3.5$ years)	8Y–9Y ($t = 8.5$ years)
1M–3M ($t = 0.1667$ year)	4Y–5Y ($t = 4.5$ years)	9Y–10Y ($t = 9.5$ years)
3M–6M ($t = 0.375$ year)	5Y–6Y ($t = 5.5$ years)	10Y–15Y ($t = 12.5$ years)
6M–9M ($t = 0.625$ year)	6Y–7Y ($t = 6.5$ years)	15Y–20Y ($t = 17.5$ years)
9M–1Y ($t = 0.875$ year)		> 20Y ($t = 25$ years)
1Y– 1.5Y ($t = 1.25$ years)		
1.5Y–2Y ($t = 1.75$ years)		

Source: Basel Committee on Banking Supervision, "Interest Rate Risk in the Banking Book," April 2016, https://www.bis.org.

where t is the midpoint of each time bucket from Table 8.17, and $r_{i,c}(t)$ is the risk-free spot rate for scenario i and currency c at time t. For the base scenario, the current spot curve is used (scenario $i = 0$), and for the six prescribed scenarios, the shocked spot curves constructed based on the method described in the previous section are used (scenarios $i = 1$ to 6).

The summation of discounted notional repricing cash flows provides an estimation of EVE for each scenario–currency combination. ΔEVE for each scenario–currency combination is obtained as the difference between the shock scenario EVE and base scenario EVE, plus an add-on amount for the consideration of options. Next, for each scenario i, ΔEVE is obtained by aggregating ΔEVEs across currencies for those cases when ΔEVE for the scenario–currency combination is representing a loss. Finally, ΔEVE based on the standardized method is obtained as the maximum of the worst aggregated decrease in EVE across six prescribed scenarios.

SUMMARY

- The economic value of equity is the difference between the economic value of assets and the economic value of liabilities on the balance sheet.
- The most common approach in EVE analysis is to exclude planned or forecasted new volumes and assume that the balance sheet is in a runoff mode.
- Planned new volumes of assets and liabilities can be used in forecasting EVE in future dates.

- A firm's own equity is usually excluded from EVE analysis.
- An interest rate shock scenario is a rate change applied to the current yield curve to obtain a shocked yield curve. An FX rate shock scenario is a rate change applied to a current currency exchange rate to obtain a shocked conversion rate. More complex scenario analysis for EVE includes simultaneous shocks to multiple risk factors.
- In the mark-to-market approach the economic value of a position is obtained based on its market price. In the mark-to-model approach the economic value of the position is obtained using a valuation model.
- When the equity of a firm is traded in the market, a market value of equity is available. That value is often different from the economic value of equity obtained using valuation models, even though the models are calibrated to ensure the arbitrage-free principle. One reason for this is the lack of market values for all positions on the firm's balance sheet.
- The market value of equity is obtained using share prices while the economic value of equity is obtained using valuation models and techniques. Prices of traded shares are derived based on supply and demand forces and can fluctuate substantially with daily news and economic conditions.
- Duration gap is a measurement that quantifies the difference between durations of assets and liabilities of a balance sheet and can be used for interest rate shock scenario analysis for EVE.
- When a duration gap is positive, an upward (downward) shock in interest rate results in a decrease (increase) in EVE. When a duration gap is negative, an upward (downward) shock in interest rate results in an increase (decrease) in EVE.
- The use of a duration gap in interest rate scenario analysis has several limitations.
- In the valuation of a financial instrument using the discounted cash flow method, risk spread is the spread added to the base yield curve to reflect the riskiness of the position being valued.
- A mark-to-market spread is the spread added to the base yield curve to make the value obtained from the valuation model equal to the available market value.
- An upward shock to an interest rate has two opposite impacts on the value of a floating-rate instrument. It decreases the discount factors, resulting in a decrease in position value, while it increases coupon rates, resulting in an increase in position value.
- With respect to interest rate risk factor, a balance sheet can be asset-sensitive or liability-sensitive.

▪ The Basel framework for banking supervision provides guidelines for managing interest rate risk in the banking book that are based on change in both the economic value of equity and the net interest income. It also provides a standardized method that banks can adopt, or its use may be mandated by regulatory supervisors, which is based on an approximate estimate for change in EVE.

NOTES

1. Liabilities here refer to all positions on the liability side of the balance sheet, excluding shareholders' equity.
2. As discussed in an earlier chapter, many practitioners no longer consider the LIBOR-swap curve as risk-free and use alternative curves, such as OIS or SOFR, as risk-free rates.
3. This rate is in line with an assumed 6-month spot rate of 1.67%. Since the spot rate is quoted with continuous compounding and an Act/365 convention, we can convert it to simple interest and an Act/360 convention using the following formula, developed in Chapter 1:

$$r_s = \frac{1}{t}(e^{r_c t} - 1) = \left(\frac{360}{183}\right)\left[e^{0.0167\left(\frac{183}{365}\right)} - 1\right] = 1.6540\%$$

4. Here we used a combination of the following formulas, developed in Chapter 1. Implied forward $r_{t,T}$ obtained this way is in simple interest: $DF_{t,T} = \frac{DF_{T_2}}{DF_{T_1}}$ and $r_{t,T} = \frac{1}{T} \times (DF_{t,T}^{-1} - 1)$.
5. If at the initiation time the spread is set such that the position was at par and if the current spot rates are similar to the rates at the initiation time, the position will be at par.
6. If at the initiation time the fixed rate is set such that the position was at par and if the current spot rates are similar to the rates at the initiation time, the position will be at par.
7. Materials and data provided in this section should be used for educational purposes only and may not reflect the latest rules or interpretation of various regulatory bodies of those rules. Practitioners should contact their relevant regulatory entities for rules, requirements, and implementation guidelines of Basel Committee standards.
8. Discussions in this section are a summary of the original materials published by the Basel Committee on Banking Supervision, Bank for International Settlements, "Interest Rate Risk in the Banking Book," April 2016.

9. Broadly speaking, tier 1 capital is a bank's core capital, primarily consisting of common equity and qualifying non-cumulative perpetual preferred stock.
10. The standard allows the use of a risk-adjusted yield curve if banks included commercial margins and other spreads in the determination of cash flows.

BIBLIOGRAPHY

Basel Committee on Banking Supervision. "Principles for the Management and Supervision of Interest Rate Risk." Bank for International Settlements, July 2004. https://www.bis.org.

Basel Committee on Banking Supervision. "Interest Rate Risk in the Banking Book." Bank for International Settlements, April 2016. https://www.bis.org.

CHAPTER 9

Net Interest Income

In traditional banking, interest income plays the most prominent role in banks' revenues. On the liability side, banks use different borrowing channels to fund their lending and trading activities, and the interest expense associated with these borrowings constitutes a major portion of banks' costs. *Net interest income (NII)* is the net value of interest income and interest expense during a specific time horizon. One of the main objectives in asset-liability management is to set and maintain a balance sheet that ensures that the net interest income is within certain limits, either implied by the target return on equity or specifically set by the bank's management team. Using net interest income scenario analysis the bank can assess its ability to continue a profitable operation under different market conditions. Stable earnings help the bank to pay a relatively constant level of dividends and keep a stable capital position. Analyzing the contribution of net interest income to the net income of the bank and studying the impact of potential changes in market conditions on net interest income are integral parts of asset-liability management.

Generally, there are three approaches for net interest income analysis:

1. In the first approach, a *runoff view* of the balance sheet is considered where positions are matured and amortized based on their maturity dates or amortization schedules as of the analysis date and new positions are assumed only to the extent needed for funding of the balance sheet as-is (i.e., assuming a runoff balance sheet).
2. In the second approach, a *static* or *constant view* of the balance sheet is assumed, where positions that mature during the analysis time horizon are replaced by similar positions with regard to their characteristics, specifically rates and spreads, to keep the balance sheet during the analysis time horizon similar to the balance sheet as of the analysis date (i.e., assuming a constant balance sheet).

3. In the third approach, a *dynamic view* of the balance sheet is considered when new volumes and new contracts are incorporated into the balance sheet, replenishing the maturing positions during the analysis time horizon, and also reflecting the business plan for growth (i.e., assuming a dynamic balance sheet).

In this chapter we discuss net interest income analysis based on these three views. We start by reviewing the basic calculations required to derive the net interest income, and then continue our discussion on net interest income scenario analysis, considering interest rate and exchange rate risk factors.

INTEREST INCOME AND EXPENSE: BASICS

The general approach in NII analysis is to first obtain the forecasted net interest income during a future time horizon. After the baseline forecast is established, different scenario analyses are performed to study the impact of change in risk factors on the forecasted net interest income. The analysis time horizon in NII analysis is typically short- to medium-term, often one to three years, and the focus is on interest-sensitive assets and liabilities. Fixed assets such as real estate, or intangible assets such as trademarks, as well as equity of the bank itself are excluded from the analysis.

To start our discussion of interest income and expense, consider a hypothetical bank with two positions: asset A1 and liability L1, with the following specifications:

Position A1	
Classification	Asset
Type	Fixed-rate loan
Currency	USD
Outstanding balance	$5,000.00
Rate	5%
Maturity date	6/15/2017
Payment frequency	Monthly
Compounding frequency	Monthly
Accrual basis	Act/365
Most recent payment date	12/15/2014

Position L1

Classification	Liability
Type	Fixed-rate debt
Currency	USD
Outstanding balance	$4,000.00
Rate	3.5%
Maturity date	11/30/2017
Payment frequency	Quarterly
Compounding frequency	Quarterly
Accrual basis	Act/365
Most recent payment date	11/30/2014

In this example we employ a runoff view of the balance sheet where positions are matured at their original maturity dates and not replaced with new positions. The *analysis date* is the date on which balance sheet positions and their specifications are taken and the forecasted net interest income is produced as of that date. Assume that the analysis date is December 31, 2014. The *analysis time horizon* is the period of time in the future where forecasted interest incomes and expenses are calculated. Here we assume a time horizon of three years. For simplicity, we assume the exact day payment, and no business day adjustment convention is considered. It is a common practice to report net interest income for time buckets with different time spans, for example, monthly, quarterly, or yearly. Here we consider the following time bucket scheme and calculate the interest income and expense for each time bucket:

Time Bucket	Description
0M–1M	Month 1
1M–2M	Month 2
2M–3M	Month 3
1Q–2Q	Months 4, 5, and 6
2Q–3Q	Months 7, 8, and 9
3Q–4Q	Months 10, 11, and 12
1Y–2Y	Months 13 to 24
2Y–3Y	Months 25 to 36

The assumed time buckets can be extended if positions have interest income or expense cash flows beyond three years. Since our analysis date is December 31, 2014, the begin and end dates of the time buckets in our example are as follows:

Time Bucket	Start Date	End Date
0M–1M	1/1/2015	1/31/2015
1M–2M	2/1/2015	2/28/2015
2M–3M	3/1/2015	3/31/2015
1Q–2Q	4/1/2015	6/30/2015
2Q–3Q	7/1/2015	9/30/2015
3Q–4Q	10/1/2015	12/31/2015
1Y–2Y	1/1/2016	12/31/2016
2Y–3Y	1/1/2017	12/31/2017

Analysis of Position A1

The accrued interest of position A1 from the last payment date of December 15, 2014, to the analysis date is calculated as:

$$5{,}000 \times \left(\frac{16}{365}\right) \times 0.05 = 10.96$$

where 16 is the number of actual days between and including December 16, 2014, and December 31, 2014. Since this interest amount is accrued before the analysis date, the common practice is to not include it in the interest income during the analysis time horizon. In general the interest income or expense amount during a period is calculated using:

$$I_j = B_j \, \tau_j \, r_j \tag{9.1}$$

where

I_j = Interest income or expense accrued during period j
τ_j = Accrual period j (e.g., actual days in period j divided by 365, etc.)
r_j = Effective annual interest rate for period j
B_j = Outstanding balance at the beginning of period j

For a fixed-rate instrument, r_j is constant and does not change from one period to another. Using Equation (9.1) we can calculate the interest income for position A1 for each of the time buckets, as shown in Table 9.1.

TABLE 9.1 Interest income for fixed-rate asset position A1

Time Bucket	From Date	To Date	Section	Day Count	Interest ($)
0M–1M	1/1/2015	1/31/2015		31	21.23
1M–2M	2/1/2015	2/28/2015		28	19.18
2M–3M	3/1/2015	3/31/2015		31	21.23
1Q–2Q	4/1/2015	6/30/2015		91	62.33
2Q–3Q	7/1/2015	9/30/2015		92	63.01
3Q–4Q	10/1/2015	12/31/2015		92	63.01
1Y–2Y	1/1/2016	12/31/2016		366	250.68
2Y–3Y	1/1/2017	6/15/2017	I	166	113.70
	6/16/2017	12/31/2017	II	199	0.00

For example, the interest income for time bucket 3Q–4Q, which contains 92 days, is calculated as:

$$5{,}000 \times \left(\frac{92}{365} \right) \times 0.05 = 63.01$$

The interest incomes for other time buckets in Table 9.1 are calculated similarly. Since the maturity date of the position A1 is June 15, 2017, we need to divide the 2Y–3Y time bucket (where the maturity date falls) into two separate sections, one from the bucket's start date up to the maturity date and one from day after maturity date to the end date of the bucket. During the first section, which contains 166 days (from January 1, 2017, to June 15, 2017), the interest income is calculated as follows:

$$5{,}000 \times \left(\frac{166}{365} \right) \times 0.05 = 113.70$$

During the second section of this time bucket (from June 16, 2017, to December 31, 2017) no interest income is generated, since the position is already expired at the start of that period.

Note that although the payment dates for position A1 are at the 15th of each month it is not required to separate other time buckets to more granular ones, since the rate is always constant at 5% and doesn't change at mid-month. Also, rates are the same for all time buckets. In the next section and in the discussion of floating-rate instruments, we will consider situations when it is necessary to divide time buckets into more granular sections to accommodate a change of interest rate within a time bucket.

TABLE 9.2   Interest expense for fixed-rate liability position L1

Time Bucket	From Date	To Date	Section	Day Count	Interest ($)
0M–1M	1/1/2015	1/31/2015		31	11.89
1M–2M	2/1/2015	2/28/2015		28	10.74
2M–3M	3/1/2015	3/31/2015		31	11.89
1Q–2Q	4/1/2015	6/30/2015		91	34.90
2Q–3Q	7/1/2015	9/30/2015		92	35.29
3Q–4Q	10/1/2015	12/31/2015		92	35.29
1Y–2Y	1/1/2016	12/31/2016		366	140.38
2Y–3Y	1/1/2017	11/30/2017	I	334	128.11
	12/1/2017	12/31/2017	II	31	0.00

Analysis of Position L1

The accrued interest of position L1 from the most recent payment date of November 30, 2014, to the analysis date is calculated as:

$$4{,}000 \times \left(\frac{31}{365} \right) \times 0.035 = 11.89$$

where 31 is the number of actual days between and including December 1, 2014, and December 31, 2014. This interest amount is accrued before the analysis date and hence is not included in the accrued interest expense during the analysis time horizon. Equation (9.1) can be used to calculate the interest expense of this liability position for each time bucket, as shown in Table 9.2.

For example, the interest expense for time bucket 2Q–3Q, which contains 92 days, is calculated as:

$$4{,}000 \times \left(\frac{92}{365} \right) \times 0.035 = 35.29$$

The interest expenses for other time buckets are calculated similarly. Since the L2 position matures on November 30, 2017, we need to separate the last time bucket 2Y–3Y, which contains this maturity date, into two sections, one before and including the maturity date and one after that date. The interest expense of the first section of this time bucket is calculated as:

$$4{,}000 \times \left(\frac{334}{365} \right) \times 0.035 = 128.11$$

There is no interest expense in the second section as the position is already expired at the beginning of that period.

The net interest income for each time bucket is calculated as:

$$Net\ Interest\ Income\ (NII) = Interest\ Income - Interest\ Expense \qquad (9.2)$$

Considering only two positions in our example, A1 and L1, the net interest income for each time bucket is calculated using Equation (9.2) and tabulated in Table 9.3. For example, in the 0M–1M bucket the interest income is $21.23 and the interest expense is $11.89, making the net interest income $21.23 − $11.89 = $9.34.

The main purpose of a simple *earning gap* analysis is to identify time buckets with low or negative net interest income. For the simple balance sheet in our example, Figure 9.1 compares the interest income and the interest expense for each time bucket. In this graph, interest expense is shown with a negative sign. A graph such as this helps in identifying the time bucket when the bank may face a potential earning gap issue in the future. In our simple balance sheet example it can be seen from Figure 9.1 that the net interest income is positive for all time buckets, except for 2Y–3Y, where the aggregated interest expense during that period exceeds the interest income. If needed, the year-long time bucket 2Y–3Y can be broken into monthly buckets to identify the month or months when the negative earning occurs.

TABLE 9.3 Net interest income for balance sheet comprised of positions A1 and L1

Time Bucket	Interest Income (A)	Interest Expense (B)	NII (C) = (A) – (B)
0M–1M	21.23	11.89	9.34
1M–2M	19.18	10.74	8.44
2M–3M	21.23	11.89	9.34
1Q–2Q	62.33	34.90	27.42
2Q–3Q	63.01	35.29	27.73
3Q–4Q	63.01	35.29	27.73
1Y–2Y	250.68	140.38	110.30
2Y–3Y	113.70	128.11	−14.41

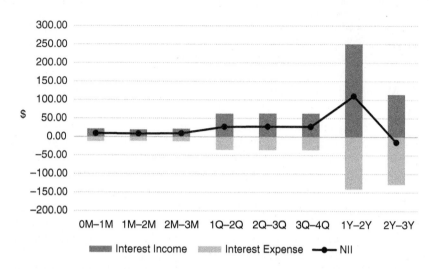

FIGURE 9.1 Net interest income of a simple balance sheet with fixed-rate asset and liability positions

INTEREST INCOME AND EXPENSE FOR FLOATING-RATE INSTRUMENTS

Calculation of interest income and expense for a floating-rate position requires determination of the effective rate for future periods. Unlike the fixed-rate positions discussed in previous section, where the effective rate was known at the analysis date, for floating-rate instruments future rates need to be estimated. Consider a floating-rate loan with a rate based on a 1-month LIBOR index with a contractual additional 30 bps spread. At the analysis date the effective (current) interest rate for this loan is known. Assuming that a pre-period-initiation rate setting is used, the 1-month LIBOR is determined at the previous reset date and the 30 bps is added to it. At the next reset date, which is in the future, the 1-month LIBOR is unknown and hence the effective rate of the loan cannot be determined unless an estimate of the 1-month LIBOR is obtained first. Generally, for net interest income analysis, there are three ways to obtain an estimate of the rate index: (1) using implied forward rates that are obtained using the spot curve as of analysis date, (2) using forecasted rates obtained from a model or survey, and (3) using simulated rate paths generated by a model. In this section we discuss the first two approaches in determining the net interest income when underlying positions are of the floating-rate type. The Monte Carlo simulation method will be discussed in the next chapter when we introduce earnings at risk.

For floating-rate instruments, rate setting is done either using a pre-period-initiation method (where the rate is set at the reset date before and closest to the beginning day of the accrual period) or a post-period-initiation method (where the rate is set at the reset date that is during the accrual period and closest to the ending day of the period). Since pre-period-initiation rate setting is more common in practice, in the remainder of this chapter we assume that all rate settings follow this rule. Similar to fixed-rate instruments, calculation of accrued interest income or expense for a period is done using Equation (9.1); however, for a floating-rate instrument the effective rate varies in different periods.

Using the Implied Forward Rate

As discussed in Chapter 1, the implied forward is the future rate with a given term determined using the current spot rates. Assume that the spot curve as of March 31, 2015, is as shown in Figure 9.2 (all rates are annualized).

Using this spot curve we calculated the annualized implied 1-month and 3-month forward rates for a few future dates from the analysis date of March 31, 2015. These rates are shown in Tables 9.4 and 9.5. Calculation of the implied

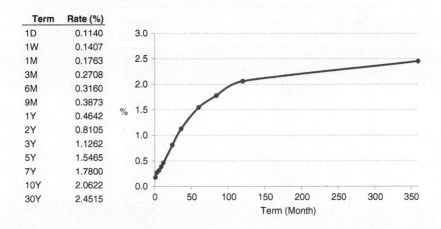

Term	Rate (%)
1D	0.1140
1W	0.1407
1M	0.1763
3M	0.2708
6M	0.3160
9M	0.3873
1Y	0.4642
2Y	0.8105
3Y	1.1262
5Y	1.5465
7Y	1.7800
10Y	2.0622
30Y	2.4515

FIGURE 9.2   Spot curve as of March 31, 2015

forward rates from the spot rates is discussed in Chapter 1. The rates in these tables are simple interest with an Act/360 day count convention. We will use these rates in our discussions throughout this chapter.

TABLE 9.4   Implied 1-month forward rate

Date	1-Month Rate (%)
3/15/2015	0.1760
6/15/2015	0.3555
9/15/2015	0.4335
12/15/2015	0.6077
3/15/2016	0.6880
6/15/2016	0.9751
9/15/2016	1.1472
12/15/2016	1.2955
3/15/2017	1.4330
6/15/2017	1.5849
9/15/2017	1.7415
12/15/2017	1.8639
3/15/2018	1.8633

TABLE 9.5   Implied 3-month forward rate

Date	3-Month Rate (%)
1/17/2015	0.2700
4/17/2015	0.3021
7/17/2015	0.3877
10/17/2015	0.5582
1/17/2016	0.6959
4/17/2016	0.9166
7/17/2016	1.0810
10/17/2016	1.2516
1/17/2017	1.4265
4/17/2017	1.5288
7/17/2017	1.6744
10/17/2017	1.8297
1/17/2018	1.9480

To discuss the use of the implied forward rate in NII calculation, consider a hypothetical bank with the following two positions on its balance sheet:

Position A2

Classification	Asset
Type	Floating-rate loan
Currency	USD
Outstanding balance	$7,000.00
Rate base index	1-month LIBOR
Spread (bps)	250
Maturity date	3/15/2018
Payment frequency	Quarterly
Compounding frequency	Quarterly
Reset frequency	Quarterly
Accrual basis	Act/360
Most recent payment date	3/15/2015
Most recent reset date	3/15/2015

Position L2

Classification	Liability
Type	Floating-rate debt
Currency	USD
Outstanding balance	$8,200.00
Rate base index	3-month LIBOR
Spread (bps)	30
Maturity date	1/17/2018
Payment frequency	Quarterly
Compounding frequency	Quarterly
Reset frequency	Quarterly
Accrual basis	Act/360
Most recent payment date	1/17/2015
Most recent reset date	1/17/2015

In this example we take a runoff view of the balance sheet where maturing positions are not replaced by new positions.

Analysis of Position A2

The analysis date is March 31, 2015. Assume that the 1-month LIBOR at the most recent reset date of March 15, 2015, was 0.1760%. The accrued interest of position A2 from the last payment date of March 15, 2015, to the analysis date is calculated as follows:

$$7{,}000 \times \left(\frac{16}{360}\right) \times \left(\frac{0.1760 + 2.5}{100}\right) = 8.33$$

where 16 is the actual number of days between and including March 16, 2015, and March 31, 2015, and 0.1760% + 2.5% = 2.6760% is the effective rate for the loan derived based on the 1-month LIBOR at the most recent reset date plus a 2.5% contractual spread. This interest is accrued before the analysis date and hence is not included in the interest income during the analysis time horizon. Considering the same time bucket scheme used in the previous example, the start and end dates of each bucket for this NII analysis are as follows:

Time Bucket	Description	Start Date	End Date
0M–1M	Month 1	4/1/2015	4/30/2015
1M–2M	Month 2	5/1/2015	5/31/2015
2M–3M	Month 3	6/1/2015	6/30/2015
1Q–2Q	Months 4, 5, and 6	7/1/2015	9/30/2015
2Q–3Q	Months 7, 8, and 9	10/1/2015	12/31/2015
3Q–4Q	Months 10, 11, and 12	1/1/2016	3/31/2016
1Y–2Y	Months 13 to 24	4/1/2016	3/31/2017
2Y–3Y	Months 24 to 36	4/1/2017	3/31/2018

Table 9.6 shows the calculation of the interest income for position A2 for each time bucket using Equation (9.1). Consider the time bucket 0M–1M. Since the reset frequency of this loan is quarterly, the next reset date is June 15, 2015. The effective rate during the 0M–1M time bucket is 0.1760% + 2.5% = 2.6760%, where 0.1760% is the 1-month LIBOR at the previous reset date of March 15, 2015, and 2.5% is the contractual spread. Thus, the accrued interest income for this time bucket is calculated as:

$$7{,}000 \times \left(\frac{30}{360}\right) \times \left(\frac{0.1760 + 2.5}{100}\right) = 15.61$$

where 30 is the number of actual days between and including April 1 and April 30. The interest income for the 1M–2M time bucket is calculated with the same

TABLE 9.6 Interest income for floating-rate asset position A2, using implied forward rates

Time Bucket	From Date	To Date	Section	Day Count	1-Month LIBOR (%)	Total Rate (%)	Interest ($)
0M–1M	4/1/2015	4/30/2015		30	0.1760	2.6760	15.61
1M–2M	5/1/2015	5/31/2015		31	0.1760	2.6760	16.13
2M–3M	6/1/2015	6/15/2015	I	15	0.1760	2.6760	7.81
	6/16/2015	6/30/2015	II	15	0.3555	2.8555	8.33
1Q–2Q	7/1/2015	9/15/2015	I	77	0.3555	2.8555	42.75
	9/16/2015	9/30/2015	II	15	0.4335	2.9335	8.56
2Q–3Q	10/1/2015	12/15/2015	I	76	0.4335	2.9335	43.35
	12/16/2015	12/31/2015	II	16	0.6077	3.1077	9.67
3Q–4Q	1/1/2016	3/15/2016	I	75	0.6077	3.1077	45.32
	3/16/2016	3/31/2016	II	16	0.6880	3.1880	9.92
1Y–2Y	4/1/2016	6/15/2016	I	76	0.6880	3.1880	47.11
	6/16/2016	9/15/2016	II	92	0.9751	3.4751	62.16
	9/16/2016	12/15/2016	III	91	1.1472	3.6472	64.54
	12/16/2016	3/15/2017	IV	90	1.2955	3.7955	66.42
	3/16/2017	3/31/2017	V	16	1.4330	3.9330	12.24
2Y–3Y	4/1/2017	6/15/2017	I	76	1.4330	3.9330	58.12
	6/16/2017	9/15/2017	II	92	1.5849	4.0849	73.07
	9/16/2017	12/15/2017	III	91	1.7415	4.2415	75.05
	12/16/2017	3/15/2018	IV	90	1.8639	4.3639	76.37
	3/16/2018	3/31/2018	V	16	0.0000	0.0000	0.00

effective rate of 2.6760%, since the rate has not reset yet:

$$7{,}000 \times \left(\frac{31}{365}\right) \times \left(\frac{0.1760 + 2.5}{100}\right) = 16.13$$

where 31 is the number of actual days between and including May 1 and May 31.

The 2M–3M time bucket, which has a starting date of June 1 and an ending date of June 30, contains the next reset date of June 15. Since on this date a new effective rate is set, we need to divide this time bucket into two sections: the first section is from June 1 to June 15 (15 days) and the second section is from June 16 to June 30 (15 days). During the first section the effective rate is the same as the rate used for two previous time buckets: 0.1760% + 2.5% = 2.6760%. On June 15 the rate is reset and the estimated effective rate for the second section is calculated using the implied 1-month LIBOR on this date.

From Table 9.4, the implied forward 1-month LIBOR on June 15, 2015, is 0.3555%; therefore, the effective rate for the second section of this time bucket is 0.3555% + 2.5% = 2.8555%. Note that this is a projected rate for a future period, estimated as of the analysis date, and it may be different from the actual rate. Using these effective rates, the interest income for each section of 2M–3M time bucket is calculated as follows:

Time bucket 2M–3M, section I:

$$7{,}000 \times \left(\frac{15}{360}\right) \times \left(\frac{0.1760 + 2.5}{100}\right) = 7.81$$

Time bucket 2M–3M, section II:

$$7{,}000 \times \left(\frac{15}{360}\right) \times \left(\frac{0.3555 + 2.5}{100}\right) = 8.33$$

Similarly, the next time bucket of 1Q–2Q should be divided into two sections, as the following reset date of September 15, 2015, falls within this period. The first section is from July 1, 2015, to September 15, 2015 (77 days) and the second section is from September 16, 2015, to September 30, 2015 (15 days). The effective rate in the first section is calculated as 0.3555% + 2.5% = 2.8555%, using the implied 1-month LIBOR as of previous reset date of June 15, 2015. On September 15, 2015, the rate is reset to a new rate where the implied 1-month LIBOR is 0.4335% (from Table 9.4), so the effective rate for this section is calculated as 0.4335% + 2.5% = 2.9335%. Using these effective rates, the interest income for each section of 1Q–2Q time bucket is calculated as follows:

Time bucket 1Q–2Q, section I:

$$7{,}000 \times \left(\frac{77}{360}\right) \times \left(\frac{0.3555 + 2.5}{100}\right) = 42.75$$

Time bucket 1Q–2Q, section II:

$$7{,}000 \times \left(\frac{15}{360}\right) \times \left(\frac{0.4335 + 2.5}{100}\right) = 8.56$$

The interest incomes for 2Q–3Q and 3Q–4Q time buckets are calculated similarly, where each bucket is divided into two sections to accommodate for the change of the effective rate at the reset dates of December 15, 2015, and March 15, 2016.

Since the 1Y–2Y and 2Y–3Y time buckets each include four reset dates, they should be divided into five sections and the interest income for each section is calculated using the effective rate that is determined using the implied 1-month LIBOR index at the previous reset date. Consider the 1Y–2Y time bucket. The start and end dates of this bucket are April 1, 2016, and March 31, 2017. Since this period includes four reset dates of June 15, 2016, September 15, 2016, December 15, 2016, and March 15, 2017, we need to divide this time bucket into five sections as shown in Table 9.6. For each section the effective rate is calculated as the implied 1-month LIBOR at the previous reset date plus 250 bps. For example, the effective rate for the first section of 1Y–2Y is 0.6880% + 2.5% = 3.1880%, where 0.6880% is the implied 1-month LIBOR on the previous reset date of March 15, 2016. Effective rates for other sections of 1Y–2Y and 2Y–3Y time buckets are determined in a similar way and Equation (9.1) is used afterward to calculate the interest income as shown in Table 9.6. Note that for the fifth section of the 2Y–3Y bucket, no interest income is considered as the position is expiring on March 15, 2018.

Analysis of Position L2

Assume that the 3-month LIBOR at the most recent reset date of January 17, 2015, was 0.2700%. The accrued interest of position L2 from the last payment date of January 17, 2015, to the analysis date of March 31, 2015, is calculated as:

$$8,200 \times \left(\frac{73}{360}\right) \times \left(\frac{0.2700 + 0.30}{100}\right) = 9.48$$

where 73 is the actual number of days between and including January 18, 2015, and March 31, 2015, and 0.2700% + 0.30% = 0.5700% is the effective rate for the note derived based on the 3-month LIBOR at the most recent reset date plus a 0.30% contractual spread. Since this interest is accrued before the analysis date it is not included in the accrued interest expense during the analysis time horizon. The interest expenses for all time buckets are calculated in Table 9.7.

Consider the 0M–1M time bucket. Position L2 has a quarterly reset frequency and the next reset date of April 17, 2015, falls within this time bucket. Therefore, we need to divide this time bucket into two sections. The first section is from April 1 to April 17 (17 days) and the second section is from April 18 to April 30 (13 days). The effective rate for the first section is 0.2700% + 0.30% = 0.5700%, where 0.2700% is the 3-month LIBOR on the previous reset date of January 17, 2015, and 0.30% is the contractual spread. On April 17 the note rate resets to a new rate based on the 3-month

TABLE 9.7 Interest expense for floating-rate liability position L2, using implied forward rates

Time Bucket	From Date	To Date	Section	Day Count	3-Month LIBOR (%)	Total Rate (%)	Interest ($)
0M–1M	4/1/2015	4/17/2015	I	17	0.2700	0.5700	2.21
	4/18/2015	4/30/2015	II	13	0.3021	0.6021	1.78
1M–2M	5/1/2015	5/31/2015		31	0.3021	0.6021	4.25
2M–3M	6/1/2015	6/30/2015		30	0.3021	0.6021	4.11
1Q–2Q	7/1/2015	7/17/2015	I	17	0.3021	0.6021	2.33
	7/18/2015	9/30/2015	II	75	0.3877	0.6877	11.75
2Q–3Q	10/1/2015	10/17/2015	I	17	0.3877	0.6877	2.66
	10/18/2015	12/31/2015	II	75	0.5582	0.8582	14.66
3Q–4Q	1/1/2016	1/17/2016	I	17	0.5582	0.8582	3.32
	1/18/2016	3/31/2016	II	74	0.6959	0.9959	16.79
1Y–2Y	4/1/2016	4/17/2016	I	17	0.6959	0.9959	3.86
	4/18/2016	7/17/2016	II	91	0.9166	1.2166	25.22
	7/18/2016	10/17/2016	III	92	1.0810	1.3810	28.94
	10/18/2016	1/17/2017	IV	92	1.2516	1.5516	32.51
	1/18/2017	3/31/2017	V	73	1.4265	1.7265	28.71
2Y–3Y	4/1/2017	4/17/2017	I	17	1.4265	1.7265	6.69
	4/18/2017	7/17/2017	II	91	1.5288	1.8288	37.91
	7/18/2017	10/17/2017	III	92	1.6744	1.9744	41.37
	10/18/2017	1/17/2018	IV	92	1.8297	2.1297	44.63
	1/18/2018	3/31/2018	V	73	0.0000	0.0000	0.00

LIBOR at that date. Therefore, the effective rate for the second section is 0.3021% + 0.30% = 06021%, where 0.3021% is the implied 3-month LIBOR at the reset date of April 17, 2015 (from Table 9.5) and 0.30% is the contractual spread. Using Equation (9.1) and these effective rates, the interest expenses for each section of the 0M–1M bucket are calculated as follows:

Time bucket 0M–1M, section I:

$$8{,}200 \times \left(\frac{17}{360}\right) \times \left(\frac{0.2700 + 0.30}{100}\right) = 2.21$$

Time bucket 0M–1M, section II:

$$8{,}200 \times \left(\frac{13}{360}\right) \times \left(\frac{0.3021 + 0.30}{100}\right) = 1.78$$

The interest expenses for other time buckets shown in Table 9.7 are calculated similarly by dividing time buckets to separate sections based on the number of reset days that fall within each bucket, and using the implied 3-month LIBOR to determine the effective rate. For example, consider time bucket 1Y–2Y. The interest expenses for five sections of this time bucket are calculated as follows:

Time bucket 1Y–2Y, section I (implied 3-month LIBOR at 1/17/2016 = 0.6959%):

$$8{,}200 \times \left(\frac{17}{360}\right) \times \left(\frac{0.6959 + 0.30}{100}\right) = 3.86$$

Time bucket 1Y–2Y, section II (implied 3-month LIBOR at 4/17/2016 = 0.9166%):

$$8{,}200 \times \left(\frac{91}{360}\right) \times \left(\frac{0.9166 + 0.30}{100}\right) = 25.22$$

Time bucket 1Y–2Y, section III (implied 3-month LIBOR at 7/17/2016 = 1.0810%):

$$8{,}200 \times \left(\frac{92}{360}\right) \times \left(\frac{1.0810 + 0.30}{100}\right) = 28.94$$

Time bucket 1Y–2Y, section IV (implied 3-month LIBOR at 10/17/2016 = 1.2516%):

$$8{,}200 \times \left(\frac{92}{360}\right) \times \left(\frac{1.2516 + 0.30}{100}\right) = 32.51$$

Time bucket 1Y–2Y, section V (implied 3-month LIBOR at 1/17/2017 = 1.4265%):

$$8{,}200 \times \left(\frac{73}{360}\right) \times \left(\frac{1.4265 + 0.30}{100}\right) = 28.71$$

Note that no interest expense is considered for the last section of 2Y–3Y since the L2 position matures on January 17, 2018.

Considering only two positions in our example, A2 and L2, the net interest income for each time bucket is calculated in Table 9.8 using Equation (9.2). For example, in the 1Y–2Y time bucket the total interest income (sum of interest incomes for all five sections in this bucket) from Table 9.6 is $252.47, and the total interest expense from Table 9.7 is $119.23. The net interest income for this time bucket is then calculated as $252.47 − $119.23 = $133.23. Figure 9.3 compares the interest income and the interest expense for each time bucket. In this graph, the interest expense is shown with a negative sign.

TABLE 9.8 Net interest income for balance sheet comprised of positions A2 and L2, using implied forward rates

Time Bucket	Interest Income (A)	Interest Expense (B)	NII (C) = (A) – (B)
0M–1M	15.61	3.99	11.62
1M–2M	16.13	4.25	11.88
2M–3M	16.13	4.11	12.02
1Q–2Q	51.31	14.08	37.23
2Q–3Q	53.02	17.32	35.69
3Q–4Q	55.24	20.11	35.13
1Y–2Y	252.47	119.23	133.23
2Y–3Y	282.62	130.59	152.02

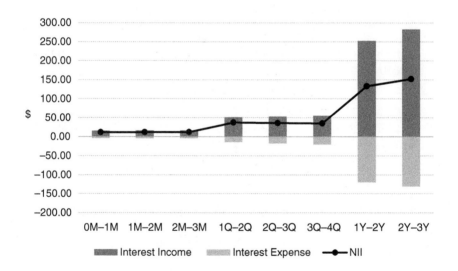

FIGURE 9.3 Net interest income of a simple balance sheet with floating-rate positions, using implied forward rates

For our example and from Figure 9.3 we can see that the forecasted NII is positive in all time buckets. When analysis similar to what is discussed here is extended to include all interest-sensitive positions on the balance sheet of a bank, it can be used to forecast the net interest income over a time horizon and estimate its contribution on total earnings.

Using the Forecasted Rate

Another approach in the estimation of the interest income or expense of floating-rate positions is to use forecasted rates for future periods. Forecasted rates are obtained either from quantitative forecasting models or through surveys of market participants. Banks utilize internally developed or externally procured models to forecast movement of interest rates in the future, and those forecasts can be used in estimating NII. To demonstrate the use of forecasted rates in NII calculation, assume that the actual 1-month LIBOR and prime index rate as of March 31, 2015, and forecasted rates for 36 months in the future, are as shown in Tables 9.9 and 9.10. Rates in these tables are simple interest, the LIBOR is based on Act/360, and the prime rate is based on an Act/365 convention.

Here we have assumed that the 1-month LIBOR and the prime rate have an upward trend during the next 36 months from the analysis date of March 31, 2015. Rates in Tables 9.9 and 9.10 are provided on a monthly basis with

TABLE 9.9   Forecasted 1-month LIBOR (annualized rate in %)

	Date	Rate (%)	Date	Rate (%)
Actual	3/31/2015	0.1763		
Forecast	4/30/2015	0.2161	10/31/2016	0.7563
	5/31/2015	0.2463	11/30/2016	0.7763
	6/30/2015	0.2828	12/31/2016	0.8261
	7/31/2015	0.3061	1/31/2017	0.8659
	8/31/2015	0.3489	2/28/2017	0.8943
	9/30/2015	0.3826	3/31/2017	0.9163
	10/31/2015	0.4040	4/30/2017	0.9615
	11/30/2015	0.4214	5/31/2017	0.9762
	12/31/2015	0.4563	6/30/2017	0.9960
	1/31/2016	0.5062	7/31/2017	1.0462
	2/29/2016	0.5261	8/31/2017	1.0563
	3/31/2016	0.5623	9/30/2017	1.0621
	4/30/2016	0.6054	10/31/2017	1.0860
	5/31/2016	0.6155	11/30/2017	1.1263
	6/30/2016	0.6466	12/31/2017	1.1769
	7/31/2016	0.6961	1/31/2018	1.1978
	8/31/2016	0.7245	2/28/2018	1.2223
	9/30/2016	0.7367	3/31/2018	1.2787

TABLE 9.10   Forecasted prime rate (annualized rate in %)

	Date	Rate (%)	Date	Rate (%)
Actual	3/31/2015	3.2500		
Forecast	4/30/2015	3.2500	10/31/2016	3.7500
	5/31/2015	3.2500	11/30/2016	3.7500
	6/30/2015	3.2500	12/31/2016	3.7500
	7/31/2015	3.2500	1/31/2017	4.2500
	8/31/2015	3.2500	2/28/2017	4.2500
	9/30/2015	3.2500	3/31/2017	4.3500
	10/31/2015	3.5000	4/30/2017	4.3500
	11/30/2015	3.5000	5/31/2017	4.3500
	12/31/2015	3.5000	6/30/2017	4.3500
	1/31/2016	3.5000	7/31/2017	4.3500
	2/29/2016	3.5000	8/31/2017	4.8500
	3/31/2016	3.5000	9/30/2017	4.8500
	4/30/2016	3.5000	10/31/2017	4.8500
	5/31/2016	3.6500	11/30/2017	4.8500
	6/30/2016	3.6500	12/31/2017	4.8500
	7/31/2016	3.7500	1/31/2018	4.8500
	8/31/2016	3.7500	2/28/2018	5.0000
	9/30/2016	3.7500	3/31/2018	5.0000

as-of dates that are future month-ends. When a forecasted rate is presented this way, it is important to know if it is representing the average rate during the future month or the forecasted rate for the exact future month-end date. The forecasting method used to derive the rate clarifies which of these two cases is pertinent. This information is needed for determining a reset rate when the reset date falls between two consecutive month-ends:

- If the forecasted rate for a future month is the average rate during that month, we can use the same average rate for any reset date falling within that month.
- If the forecasted rates are for the exact future month-end dates, we can interpolate the rates of two consecutive month-ends around the reset date to obtain the reset rate.

To illustrate the use of forecasted rates in the net interest income calculation, assume that the rates in Tables 9.9 and 9.10 are forecasted for the exact month-end dates and we use a linear interpolation to obtain the required rates at future reset dates. Consider a simple balance sheet that includes only the following two positions:

Position A3

Classification	Asset
Type	Floating-rate loan
Currency	USD
Outstanding balance	$7,000.00
Rate base index	Prime
Spread (bps)	200
Maturity date	3/15/2018
Payment frequency	Quarterly
Compounding frequency	Quarterly
Reset frequency	Quarterly
Accrual basis	Act/365
Most recent payment date	3/15/2015
Most recent reset date	3/15/2015

Position L3

Classification	Liability
Type	Floating-rate debt
Currency	USD
Outstanding balance	$6,800.00
Rate base index	1-month LIBOR
Spread (bps)	100
Maturity date	1/15/2018
Payment frequency	Quarterly
Compounding frequency	Quarterly
Reset frequency	Quarterly
Accrual basis	Act/360
Most recent payment date	1/15/2015
Most recent reset date	1/15/2015

In this example we employ a runoff view of the balance sheet where a matured position is not replaced by a new position. To obtain reset rates, we can use a linear interpolation as follows:

$$r = r_i + \frac{(t - t_i)}{(t_{i+1} - t_i)} \times (r_{i+1} - r_i) \tag{9.3}$$

where:

r = interpolated rate
t = interpolation date
t_i = date of previous month-end
r_i = rate at previous month-end
t_{i+1} = date of next month-end
r_{i+1} = rate at next month-end

Analysis of Position A3

The interest incomes of position A3 for different time buckets are shown in Table 9.11.

The prime rate at the most recent reset date of March 15, 2015, is assumed to be 3.25%. At each of the following reset dates the forecasted prime rate is

TABLE 9.11   Interest income for floating-rate asset position A3, using interpolated forecasted rates

Time Bucket	From Date	To Date	Section	Day Count	Prime Rate (%)	Total Rate (%)	Interest ($)
0M–1M	4/1/2015	4/30/2015		30	3.2500	5.2500	30.21
1M–2M	5/1/2015	5/31/2015		31	3.2500	5.2500	31.21
2M–3M	6/1/2015	6/15/2015	I	15	3.2500	5.2500	15.10
	6/16/2015	6/30/2015	II	15	3.2500	5.2500	15.10
1Q–2Q	7/1/2015	9/15/2015	I	77	3.2500	5.2500	77.53
	9/16/2015	9/30/2015	II	15	3.2500	5.2500	15.10
2Q–3Q	10/1/2015	12/15/2015	I	76	3.2500	5.2500	76.52
	12/16/2015	12/31/2015	II	16	3.5000	5.5000	16.88
3Q–4Q	1/1/2016	3/15/2016	I	75	3.5000	5.5000	79.11
	3/16/2016	3/31/2016	II	16	3.5000	5.5000	16.88
1Y–2Y	4/1/2016	6/15/2016	I	76	3.5000	5.5000	80.16
	6/16/2016	9/15/2016	II	92	3.6500	5.6500	99.69
	9/16/2016	12/15/2016	III	91	3.7500	5.7500	100.35
	12/16/2016	3/15/2017	IV	90	3.7500	5.7500	99.25
	3/16/2017	3/31/2017	V	16	4.2984	6.2984	19.33
2Y–3Y	4/1/2017	6/15/2017	I	76	4.2984	6.2984	91.80
	6/16/2017	9/15/2017	II	92	4.3500	6.3500	112.04
	9/16/2017	12/15/2017	III	91	4.8500	6.8500	119.55
	12/16/2017	3/15/2018	IV	90	4.8500	6.8500	118.23
	3/16/2018	3/31/2018	V	16	0.0000	0.0000	0.00

calculated as the interpolated value between rates at the previous month-end and the next month-end using Equation (9.3). For example, for section V of the 1Y–2Y bucket, the rate is reset on March 15, 2017. To find the forecasted prime rate at this date, forecasted rates for February 28, 2017, and March 31, 2017, from Table 9.10 are interpolated:

$$D_i = \text{Mar. } 15, 2017$$

$$D_1 = \text{Feb. } 28, 2017 \quad R_1 = 4.25\%$$

$$D_2 = \text{Mar. } 31, 2017 \quad R_2 = 4.35\%$$

$$R_i = \frac{15}{31} \times (4.35 - 4.25) + 4.25 = 4.2984\%$$

The interest income for this section is then calculated as:[1]

$$7,000 \times \left(\frac{16}{365}\right) \times \left(\frac{4.2984 + 2.00}{100}\right) = 19.33$$

The effective rates and interest incomes for other time buckets are obtained similarly.

Analysis of Position L3

The interest expenses for position L3 for different time buckets are shown in Table 9.12.

Here the 1-month LIBOR at the most recent reset date of January 15, 2015, is 0.1660%. At each of the following reset dates the forecasted 1-month LIBOR is calculated as the interpolated value between rates at the previous month-end and the next month-end using Equation (9.3). For example, for section II of the 0M–1M bucket, the rate is reset on April 15, 2015. To find the forecasted 1-month LIBOR at this date, rates as of March 31, 2015, and April 30, 2015, from Table 9.10 are interpolated as shown below:

$$D_i = \text{Apr. } 15, 2015$$

$$D_1 = \text{Mar. } 31, 2015 \quad R_1 = 0.1763\%$$

$$D_2 = \text{Apr. } 30, 2015 \quad R_2 = 0.2161\%$$

$$R_i = \frac{15}{30} \times (0.2161 - 0.1763) + 0.1763 = 0.1962\%$$

The interest income for this section is then calculated as:

$$6,800 \times \left(\frac{15}{360}\right) \times \left(\frac{0.1962 + 1.00}{100}\right) = 3.39$$

TABLE 9.12　Interest expense for floating-rate liability position L3, using interpolated forecasted rates

Time Bucket	From Date	To Date	Section	Day Count	1-Month LIBOR (%)	Total Rate (%)	Interest ($)
0M–1M	4/1/2015	4/15/2015	I	15	0.1660	1.1660	3.30
	4/16/2015	4/30/2015	II	15	0.1962	1.1962	3.39
1M–2M	5/1/2015	5/31/2015		31	0.1962	1.1962	7.00
2M–3M	6/1/2015	6/30/2015		30	0.1962	1.1962	6.78
1Q–2Q	7/1/2015	7/15/2015	I	15	0.1962	1.1962	3.39
	7/16/2015	9/30/2015	II	77	0.2941	1.2941	18.82
2Q–3Q	10/1/2015	10/15/2015	I	15	0.2941	1.2941	3.67
	10/16/2015	12/31/2015	II	77	0.3930	1.3930	20.26
3Q–4Q	1/1/2016	1/15/2016	I	15	0.3930	1.3930	3.95
	1/16/2016	3/31/2016	II	76	0.4804	1.4804	21.25
1Y–2Y	4/1/2016	4/15/2016	I	15	0.4804	1.4804	4.19
	4/16/2016	7/15/2016	II	91	0.5839	1.5839	27.22
	7/16/2016	10/15/2016	III	92	0.6706	1.6706	29.03
	10/16/2016	1/15/2017	IV	92	0.7462	1.7462	30.34
	1/16/2017	3/31/2017	V	75	0.8454	1.8454	26.14
2Y–3Y	4/1/2017	4/15/2017	I	15	0.8454	1.8454	5.23
	4/16/2017	7/15/2017	II	91	0.9389	1.9389	33.33
	7/16/2017	10/15/2017	III	92	1.0203	2.0203	35.11
	10/16/2017	1/15/2018	IV	92	1.0737	2.0737	36.04
	1/16/2018	3/31/2018	V	75	0.0000	0.0000	0.00

As another example, consider section II of the 3Q–4Q time bucket. The rate is reset on January 15, 2016. To obtain the forecasted 1–month LIBOR for this date, the forecasted rates for December 31, 2015, and January 31, 2016, are interpolated as shown below:

$$D_i = \text{Jan. }15, 2016$$

$$D_1 = \text{Dec. }31, 2015 \quad R_1 = 0.4563\%$$

$$D_2 = \text{Jan. }31, 2016 \quad R_2 = 0.5062\%$$

$$R_i = \frac{15}{31} \times (0.5062 - 0.4563) + 0.4563 = 0.4804\%$$

The interest income for this section is calculated as:

$$6,800 \times \left(\frac{76}{360}\right) \times \left(\frac{0.4804 + 1.00}{100}\right) = 21.25$$

The effective rates and interest expenses for other time buckets are obtained similarly. Considering only two positions in our example, A3 and L3, the net interest income for each time bucket is calculated using Equation (9.2) as shown in Table 9.13. Figure 9.4 compares the interest income, the interest expense (with negative sign), and the net interest income of the balance sheet consisting of two positions, A3 and L3. In our example, the NII is positive for all time buckets during the analysis time horizon.

TABLE 9.13 Net interest income for balance sheet comprised of positions A3 and L3, using interpolated forecasted rates

Time Bucket	Interest Income (A)	Interest Expense (B)	NII (C) = (A) – (B)
0M–1M	30.21	6.69	23.51
1M–2M	31.21	7.00	24.21
2M–3M	30.21	6.78	23.43
1Q–2Q	92.63	22.21	70.42
2Q–3Q	93.40	23.93	69.47
3Q–4Q	95.99	25.20	70.79
1Y–2Y	398.77	116.94	281.84
2Y–3Y	441.62	109.70	331.92

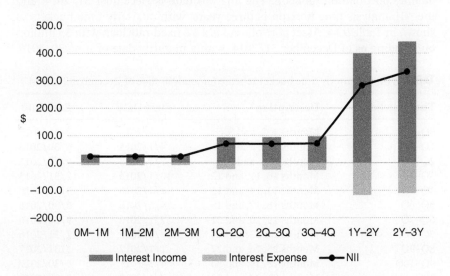

FIGURE 9.4 Net interest income of a simple balance sheet with floating-rate positions, using interpolated forecasted rates

INCORPORATING BALANCE SHEET CHANGE IN NII ANALYSIS

In the examples discussed in previous sections we used the runoff view of the balance sheet where maturing positions are not replaced by new positions and the balance sheet is assumed to be in a runoff mode. Net interest income analysis, however, is more practical when changes in the balance sheet and business plan are incorporated in the analysis. When expected changes in the balance sheet during the analysis time horizon are incorporated into the NII analysis, results not only reflect a forecast of the net interest income in various scenarios, but also include the impact of the business plan regarding the volume of new assets and liabilities. In this section we study several cases in which the forecasted changes in the balance sheet are included in the NII analysis.

Runoff View: No New Volume

Let's start our discussion by revising the runoff view where no balance sheet change is incorporated in the NII analysis. In this type of NII analysis only positions that exist on the balance sheet as of the analysis date are considered and the balance sheet is in a runoff mode, meaning that when a position is matured it is not replaced. New positions are assumed only to the extent needed for funding and balancing the balance sheet.

As an example, consider a bank with only one asset portfolio and one liability portfolio on its book. The analysis date is December 31, 2014, and the NII analysis time horizon is three years, with quarterly time buckets as shown in Table 9.14. Asset portfolio A4 is a 5% fixed-rate loan with $5 million outstanding as of December 31, 2014, with a maturity date of June 30, 2016.

TABLE 9.14 Quarterly time bucket scheme for analysis date of December 31, 2014

Time Bucket	Description	Start Date	End Date
0Q–1Q	Months 1, 2, and 3	1/1/2015	3/31/2015
1Q–2Q	Months 4, 5, and 6	4/1/2015	6/30/2015
2Q–3Q	Months 7, 8, and 9	7/1/2015	9/30/2015
3Q–4Q	Months 10, 11, and 12	10/1/2015	12/31/2015
4Q–5Q	Months 13, 14, and 15	1/1/2016	3/31/2016
5Q–6Q	Months 16, 17, and 18	4/1/2016	6/30/2016
6Q–7Q	Months 19, 20, and 21	7/1/2016	9/30/2016
7Q–8Q	Months 22, 23, and 24	10/1/2016	12/31/2016
8Q–9Q	Months 25, 26, and 27	1/1/2017	3/31/2017
9Q–10Q	Months 28, 29, and 30	4/1/2017	6/30/2017
10Q–11Q	Months 31, 32, and 33	7/1/2017	9/30/2017
11Q–12Q	Months 34, 35, and 36	10/1/2017	12/31/2017

Liability portfolio L4 is a 3% fixed-rate debt with a $3 million notional balance as of the analysis date and with a maturity date of March 31, 2017. This bank holds a cash account C4 with a national bank with a balance of $1 million as of December 31, 2014, earning a rate based on the fed funds index plus 50 bps. It is a common practice to incorporate such a cash account in an ALM analysis, where matured or amortized balances are placed in this account and required funds for repayment of maturing liabilities are sourced from this account. Considering the cash balance, the total assets of this bank are $6 million; hence, the book value of equity is $2 million. Assume that the fed funds rate as of December 31, 2014, is 0.25% with forecasted rates as shown in Table 9.15. For simplicity, here we assume (i) accrual basis of all accounts is 30/360, (ii) the floating-rate cash account has a monthly reset frequency with month-end reset dates, and (iii) the accrued interest of cash account is not compounded and rather paid out.

Based on a runoff view of the balance sheet, asset A4 earns interest income until its maturity date of June 30, 2016. At the maturity date the balance of the asset is returned to the bank and is added to the balance of cash account. Cash account C4 earns interest income based on the fed funds index plus

TABLE 9.15 Forecasted fed funds rate as of December 31, 2014

	Date	Rate (%)	Date	Rate (%)
Actual	12/31/2014	0.2500		
Forecast	1/31/2015	0.2500	7/31/2016	0.7500
	2/28/2015	0.2500	8/31/2016	0.7500
	3/31/2015	0.2500	9/30/2016	0.7500
	4/30/2015	0.2500	10/31/2016	0.7500
	5/31/2015	0.2500	11/30/2016	0.7500
	6/30/2015	0.2500	12/31/2016	0.7500
	7/31/2015	0.2500	1/31/2017	1.2500
	8/31/2015	0.2500	2/28/2017	1.2500
	9/30/2015	0.2500	3/31/2017	1.3500
	10/31/2015	0.5000	4/30/2017	1.3500
	11/30/2015	0.5000	5/31/2017	1.3500
	12/31/2015	0.5000	6/30/2017	1.3500
	1/31/2016	0.5000	7/31/2017	1.3500
	2/29/2016	0.5000	8/31/2017	1.8500
	3/31/2016	0.5000	9/30/2017	1.8500
	4/30/2016	0.5000	10/31/2017	1.8500
	5/31/2016	0.6500	11/30/2017	1.8500
	6/30/2016	0.6500	12/31/2017	1.8500

50 bps. From January 1, 2015, until June 30, 2016, the interest is earned on the balance of $1 million held in C4. Starting July 1, 2016, the balance of cash account C4 is increased by $5 million due to the returning balance of maturing asset A4.

Liability L4 incurs interest expense until its maturity date of March 31, 2017. At the maturity date the funds needed for repayment of the balance are sourced from the cash account. The balance of cash account C4 from July 1, 2017, to March 31, 2017, is $6 million, consisting of the original $1 million balance and $5 million from maturing asset A4. After repayment of maturing liability L4, the balance on April 1, 2017, falls to $2 million and remains at that level until the end of the analysis time horizon of December 31, 2017. The composition of assets and liabilities of this bank during the period from December 31, 2014, to December 31, 2017, is shown in Figure 9.5. In this runoff view of the balance sheet, the cash account acts as a buffer by absorbing the balance of maturing asset positions and providing funds for repayment of maturing liability positions. The book value of equity remains constant at $2 million throughout the analysis time horizon, but the balance sheet size changes during this period.

Figure 9.6 presents the interest income, the interest expense, and the net interest income in our example, with a runoff view of the balance sheet. Consider the first quarterly time bucket 0Q–1Q. Asset A4 earns 5% interest on a balance of $5 million. Based on a 30/360 accrual basis, the interest income for the first quarterly bucket is calculated as:

$$3 \times \left(5,000,000 \times \frac{5}{100} \times \frac{30}{360}\right) = 62,500$$

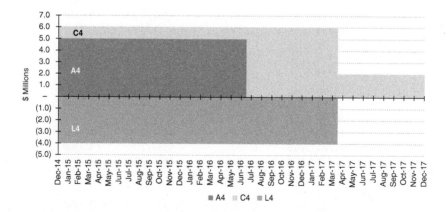

FIGURE 9.5 Composition of assets and liabilities of a hypothetical bank based on a runoff view of balance sheet

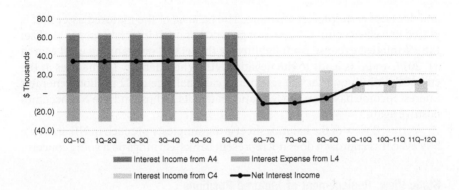

FIGURE 9.6 Interest income, expense, and NII in an example with a runoff view of a balance sheet

Cash account C4 earns interest income based on the fed funds rate plus 50 bps on a balance of $1 million in this time bucket. Since this account has a monthly reset frequency, we need to break the quarterly time bucket into three monthly sections. The fed funds rate for the first month is the actual rate as of December 31, 2014, of 0.25%. For the second and third monthly sections the forecasted fed funds rates as of January 31 and February 28, 2015, are 0.25% and 0.25% from Table 9.15. The interest income for the first quarterly bucket is therefore calculated as:

$$3 \times \left(1,000,000 \times \frac{0.25 + 0.50}{100} \times \frac{30}{360}\right) = 1,875$$

The interest expense from liability L4 based on a 3% rate on a balance of $4 million during the first quarterly bucket is calculated as:

$$3 \times \left(4,000,000 \times \frac{3}{100} \times \frac{30}{360}\right) = 30,000$$

In Figure 9.6 interest expenses are shown with a negative sign. The net interest income for the first quarterly bucket of 0Q–1Q is therefore:

$$\$62,500 + \$1,875 - \$30,000 = \$34,375$$

The interest income and expense for other quarterly time buckets are calculated similarly, using the outstanding balance of each account from Figure 9.5. In this example the net interest income becomes negative in time buckets 6Q–7Q, 7Q–8Q, and 8Q–9Q. In these periods asset A4 is matured and does not earn interest anymore. The balance of the matured asset that is placed in cash account C4 does not generate enough interest income to offset the 3% interest expense from liability L4 that is still outstanding until March 31, 2017, and this leads to the negative NII. When liability L4 matures at the end of the ninth quarter the remaining cash balance of $2 million generates interest income based on the fed funds rate plus 50 bps, and the NII becomes positive again.

A runoff view of the balance sheet is the simplest approach in NII analysis; however, this approach does not represent banks' earnings on a going concern.

Static View: Replacement of Matured Positions

In a static or constant view approach, positions in maturing products, such as term loans, are replaced at maturity dates by similar positions with equivalent balances, and positions in non-maturing products, such as deposits, are held with constant balances equal to balances as of the analysis date. In this approach, the balance sheet size is kept constant throughout the analysis time horizon. To illustrate the static view approach in NII analysis, consider the hypothetical bank in the example of the previous section. At the analysis date of December 31, 2014, this bank has an asset A4 with a $5 million balance, a cash account C4 with a $1 million balance, and a liability L4 with a $4 million balance. In the static view approach, when asset A4 matures on June 30, 2016, instead of placing the balance into cash account C4, we assume that a new asset is originated with a $5 million balance, starting July 1, 2016. The rate and term of new volume are based on the prevailing conditions of the market at the time of origination. In this example we assume that the rate of the newly originated fixed-rate loan portfolio A5 is 5.5% with a 2-year term, expiring on June 30, 2018, beyond the analysis time horizon of December 31, 2017.

Liability position L4 matures on March 31, 2017. At this maturity date, instead of sourcing the required funds from the cash account, we assume that the bank can immediately replace the maturing liability portfolio with new debt with an equivalent balance, but with a term and rate that are prevailing at the time of the new issuance. In this example we assume that the new debt L5 is issued on April 1, 2017, with a fixed rate of 3.45% and a 3-year term.

Replacing the maturing assets and liabilities with new positions with similar balances effectively keeps the balance sheet size constant over the analysis time horizon. The composition of assets and liabilities of the bank in our example during the 3-year period is shown in Figure 9.7. In this static view of the balance sheet, expiration of a position does not impact the balance of the cash account; hence, C4 has a constant balance during the analysis time horizon.[2] Also, sizes of total assets, total liabilities, and book value of equity of

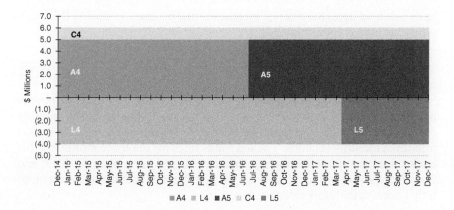

FIGURE 9.7 Composition of assets and liabilities of a hypothetical bank based on a static view of a balance sheet

the bank remain constant throughout the analysis time horizon, at $6 million, $4 million, and $2 million levels respectively.

Figure 9.8 presents the interest income, the interest expense, and the net interest income of the above example with the static view of the balance sheet. The interest amounts in this graph are calculated in the same way as explained in the previous example. For instance, consider the last quarterly time bucket during the analysis time horizon: 11Q–12Q. This time bucket is from October 1 to December 31, 2017. Asset A4 and liability L4 are already expired before this bucket and replaced by asset A5 and liability L5. Based on the 30/360 accrual

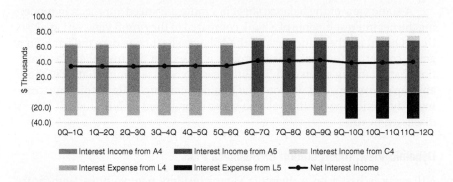

FIGURE 9.8 Interest income, expense, and NII in an example with a static view of a balance sheet

basis assumed here, the interest income earned by asset A5 during this quarterly time bucket is calculated as:

$$3 \times \left(5{,}000{,}000 \times \frac{5.5}{100} \times \frac{30}{360} \right) = 68{,}750$$

Cash account C4 earns interest income based on the fed funds rate plus 50 bps on a balance of $1 million in this time bucket. Considering the monthly reset frequency of this account, we need to break the quarterly time bucket into three monthly sections. The fed funds rates for the three months in this bucket are reset on September 30, October 31, and November 30, 2017, and from Table 9.15 all three rates are 1.85%. The interest income for the last quarterly bucket is therefore calculated as:

$$3 \times \left(1{,}000{,}000 \times \frac{1.85 + 0.50}{100} \times \frac{30}{360} \right) = 5{,}875$$

The interest expense from liability L5 is based on a 3.45% rate, and the balance of the $4 million during the last quarterly time bucket is calculated as:

$$3 \times \left(4{,}000{,}000 \times \frac{3.45}{100} \times \frac{30}{360} \right) = 34{,}500$$

Finally, the net interest income for bucket 11Q–12Q is:

$$\$68{,}750 + \$5{,}875 - \$34{,}500 = \$40{,}125$$

The interest income and expense for other quarterly time buckets are calculated similarly, using the outstanding balance of each account from Figure 9.7.

A static view of the balance sheet is a more advanced approach in modeling the net interest income of a bank compared to the runoff view. NII analysis that is based on the static view of the balance sheet considers the bank on a going concern. However, this approach is based on the unrealistic assumption that maturing assets and liabilities can be replaced immediately without any gap or overlap, and without any liquidity concern. Due to this shortcoming a dynamic view of the balance sheet is preferred in NII studies. This is discussed next.

Dynamic View: Incorporation of Business Plan

NII analysis based on a dynamic view considers new volumes and future changes in the balance sheet. In this approach the net interest income in different scenarios includes the impact of forecasted changes in the balance sheet, and hence the results are more practical and informative compared to the previous two approaches. Banks' corporate planning units often develop short- to medium-term strategies that reflect a business plan for new asset volumes, new liability issuances, portfolio acquisition, and other similar activities that impact the balance sheet. When these forecasted changes in the balance sheet are incorporated in NII analysis, the results are far more useful and informative to banks' management teams and other stakeholders.

To illustrate the dynamic view approach in NII analysis, consider again the same bank discussed in the previous two sections. Recall that at the analysis date of December 31, 2014, this bank has an asset A4 with a $5 million balance, a cash account C4 with a $1 million balance, and a liability L4 with a $4 million balance. The analysis time horizon is three years. The bank has an expansion plan to add an equivalent of a $1 million position at the beginning of October 2015 to its asset portfolio. The corporate planning of the bank forecasts that the rate of the new loan portfolio A6 issued at that time is 6% with a 5-year term. The bank also expects to be able to use the funds from the maturing A4 position plus an extra $1 million from the cash account to fund a new loan portfolio of $6 million starting July 2016. The forecasted rate of this new loan portfolio A7 is 5.5% with a 4-year term.

To fund the new assets A6 and A7 and keep enough liquidity throughout the three-year horizon, the bank's treasury department is planning to issue two sets of new debt securities: liability L6 is a $2 million, 3-year, 3.2% fixed-rate bond, to be issued at the beginning of July 2015, and liability L7 is a $3.5 million, 2-year, 3.45% fixed-rate bond, to be issued at the beginning of January 2017. The bank has selected the issuance dates of July 2015 and January 2017 to cover the funds needed for asset expansion and also to create an overlapping period for the maturing debt L4 that is set to expire at the end of March 2017. Such an overlapping period ensures the existence of enough liquidity for the bank in a time close to the maturity date of a large liability position. Figure 9.9 shows the composition of assets and liabilities of this bank during the three-year analysis time horizon. When liability L6 is issued on July 1, 2015, the acquired funds are placed in cash account C4 and the balance is increased from $1 million to $3 million. On October 1, 2015, the needed funding for origination of the new loan A6 is sourced from the cash account, which reduces its balance from $3 million to $2 million. The origination of the new loan A7 ($6 million) on July 1, 2016, is funded partially from maturing asset A4 ($5 million) and from cash account C4 ($1 million). Therefore, the balance of cash account C4 falls from $2 million to $1 million on July 1, 2016. In anticipation of the upcoming maturity of the L4 debt, the bank issues a new debt of $3.5 million on January 1, 2017, and proceeds are placed in the cash account, which brings the balance from $1 million to $4.5 million. When liability L4 matures, the repayment of the debt is funded from the cash account, which

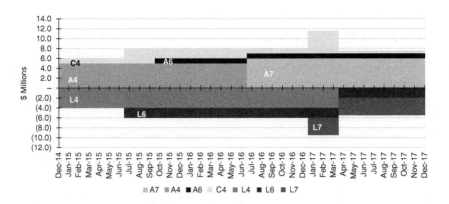

FIGURE 9.9   Composition of assets and liabilities of a hypothetical bank based on a dynamic view of a balance sheet

subsequently brings the balance of C4 to $0.5 million on April 1, 2017, and this balance is kept until the end of the 3-year horizon on December 31, 2017.

As can be seen from Figure 9.9, unlike the static view approach, in the dynamic view the size of the balance sheet is not constant and changes are based on the business plan and forecasted new volumes and issuances. The bank in our example has $6 million in assets and $4 million in liabilities until June 30, 2015. Then the new debt issuance increases the balance sheet size to $8 million in assets and $6 million in liabilities from July 1, 2015, to December 31, 2016. On January 1, 2017, the new debt issuance increases the balance sheet size again to $11.5 million in assets and $9.5 million in liabilities. The retiring of L4 liability on March 31, 2017, reduces the balance sheet size to $7.5 million in assets and $5.5 million in liabilities from April 1, 2017, to the end of the analysis time horizon on December 31, 2017. The book value of bank equity is constant at $2 million during this period.

Figure 9.10 presents the interest income, the interest expense, and the net interest income of the preceding example with the dynamic view of the balance sheet. The interest amounts in this graph are calculated in the same way as explained in the previous two examples. For instance, consider the quarterly time bucket 5Q–6Q. This time bucket is from April 1 to June 30, 2016. In this period the bank has assets A4 and A6 and cash account C4, which generate interest income, while liabilities L4 and L6 incur interest expenses. The interest income and expense of each of these positions in the 5Q–6Q time bucket are calculated as follows:

Asset A4:
$$3 \times \left(5,000,000 \times \frac{5}{100} \times \frac{30}{360} \right) = 62,500$$

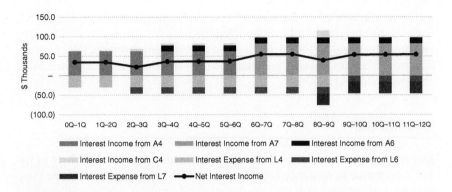

FIGURE 9.10 Interest income, expense, and NII in an example with a dynamic view of a balance sheet

Asset A6:

$$3 \times \left(1,000,000 \times \frac{6}{100} \times \frac{30}{360} \right) = 15,000$$

Cash account C4: From Table 9.15 forecasted fed funds rates as of March 31 and April 30, 2016, are both 0.50% and is 0.65% as of May 30, 2016. So:

$$2 \times \left(1,000,000 \times \frac{0.50 + 0.50}{100} \times \frac{30}{360} \right)$$
$$+ \left(1,000,000 \times \frac{0.65 + 0.50}{100} \times \frac{30}{360} \right) = 5,250$$

Liability L4:

$$3 \times \left(4,000,000 \times \frac{3}{100} \times \frac{30}{360} \right) = 30,000$$

Liability L6:

$$3 \times \left(2,000,000 \times \frac{3.2}{100} \times \frac{30}{360} \right) = 16,000$$

The net interest income in this time bucket is:

$$\$62,500 + \$15,000 + \$5,250 - \$30,000 - \$16,000 = \$36,750$$

Using the outstanding balance of each account from Figure 9.7, the interest income and expense for other quarterly time buckets are calculated similarly.

Dynamic view of the balance sheet is the most common approach in NII analysis. Application of this methodology requires relatively detailed funding and business plans for the duration of the analysis time horizon, which reflect forecasted changes in assets and planned debt issuances, as well as forecasted changes in deposit products.

EARNING GAP

Earning gap is one of the basic methods for measuring the sensitivity of net interest income to a change in interest rate. The earning gap is a static measurement of interest rate risk. In this method, interest rate–sensitive assets and liabilities are compared and the impact of a change in interest rate on the NII is estimated. For a bank with total rate-sensitive assets of *RSA* and total rate-sensitive liabilities of *RSL*, the earning gap is defined as:

$$Earning\ Gap = RSA - RSL \qquad (9.4)$$

Using the earning gap, an approximate estimate of change in the NII can be derived as:

$$\Delta NII \cong Earning\ Gap \times \Delta r \qquad (9.5)$$

where

Δr = Change in interest rate
ΔNII = Change in net interest income

In practice, those banks that use this method for measuring NII sensitivity calculate the earning gap for different time buckets and obtain periodic and cumulative earning gaps throughout the analysis time horizon. In each bucket the principal amounts of the rate-sensitive assets and liabilities that are expected to be repriced, matured, or amortized during that period are included. To illustrate this methodology, consider the balance sheet of a hypothetical bank as illustrated in Table 9.16. The bank has a total of $18 million assets of which $16.5 million are rate-sensitive. Total rate-sensitive liabilities of the bank are $15.5 million.

For earning gap analysis, this bank uses a quarterly time bucket scheme for the first year and one single time bucket for all positions that reprice beyond one year. An earning gap schedule for this bank is also shown in Table 9.16. In this schedule the portion of the outstanding asset or liability balances that are repriced, matured, or amortized are placed in the time buckets when repricing or maturity occur. For example, all of the $8.5 million

TABLE 9.16 Balance sheet and earning gap schedule of a hypothetical bank

Balance Sheet			Earning Gap Schedule				
	Balance	0Q–1Q	1Q–2Q	2Q–3Q	3Q–4Q	>1Y	Non-Rate-Sensitive
Cash	2,300,000						2,300,000
Fixed-Rate Loan	8,500,000	1,000,000	2,250,000	1,250,000	1,500,000	2,500,000	
Floating-Rate Loan	4,500,000	1,500,000	3,000,000				
Fixed-Rate Government Debt	1,200,000	200,000	200,000	200,000	200,000	400,000	
Non-Interest-Bearing Asset	1,500,000						1,500,000
Total Asset	**18,000,000** RSA:	**2,700,000**	**5,450,000**	**1,450,000**	**1,700,000**	**2,900,000**	**–**
Fixed-Rate CD	4,200,000	600,000	500,000	1,600,000	1,000,000	500,000	
Floating-Rate MTN Debt	5,500,000	2,375,000	3,125,000				
Floating-Rate ABS Debt	3,000,000	300,000	2,700,000				
Savings Deposit	2,800,000	2,800,000					
Non-Interest-Bearing Liability	500,000						500,000
Equity	2,000,000						2,000,000
Total Liability	**18,000,000** RSL:	**6,075,000**	**6,325,000**	**1,600,000**	**1,000,000**	**500,000**	**–**
Periodic Earning Gap:		(3,375,000)	(875,000)	(150,000)	700,000	2,400,000	
Cumulative Earning Gap:		(3,375,000)	(4,250,000)	(4,400,000)	(3,700,000)	(1,300,000)	

649

floating-rate asset-backed security (ABS) and medium-term note (MTN) debt of the bank and also its $4.5 million floating-rate loan portfolio are either repriced or matured during the first two quarters and hence placed in those two time buckets. The fixed-rate assets and liabilities of the bank are placed in the relevant time buckets based on their maturity dates and amortization schedules, assuming that when a fixed-rate position is matured it will be replaced with a new rate, that is, it will be repriced. Here the savings deposit balance is placed in the first quarterly time bucket, assuming rate of the entire portfolio is reset during this period.

Based on the earning gap schedule in Table 9.16 total rate-sensitive assets and rate-sensitive liabilities for the first quarterly time bucket are calculated as:

RSA = $1 million fixed-rate loan + $1.5 million floating-rate loan

+ $0.2 investment in fixed-rate government bond = $2.7 million

RSL = $0.6 million fixed-rate CD + $2.375 million floating-rate MTN

+ $0.3 million floating-rate ABS

+ $2.8 million savings deposit = $6.075 million

Thus, the earning gap for the first quarterly time bucket is:

$Earning\ Gap$ = $RSA - RSL$ = $2.7 million − $6.075 million

= −$3.375 million

Assuming all rate-sensitive assets and liabilities considered here have similar rate sensitivities, the impact of a 1% increase in interest rate on the NII of the bank for the first quarterly time bucket is approximately obtained as:

$$\Delta NII \cong -\$3.375 \text{ million} \times 0.01 = -\$33,750$$

This bank has more rate-sensitive liabilities repricing in the first quarter compared to rate-sensitive assets that are repriced in the same period. This is reflected in the negative periodic earning gap. The cumulative earning gap can be used to measure the aggregate interest rate sensitivity of the bank over several time buckets. For example, the cumulative earning gap of the bank in our example at the end of the first year is –$3.7 million as shown in Table 9.16. The negative cumulative gap for the entire year indicates that the bank has more rate-sensitive liabilities that are repricing during the first year compared to rate-sensitive assets repricing in the same period. An increase in the interest rate in this period increases the interest expense since there are more liability positions that are repriced in this period with higher interest rates. This leads to a lower net interest income. Therefore, from a net interest income point of view, there is concern for the bank if the bank managers believe that the interest rate will rise in the future. Conversely, due to the negative cumulative earning gap, the decline in interest rate increases the net interest income of the bank as more liabilities are repriced in this period with lower interest rates.

On the other hand, when the cumulative earning gap of a bank is positive, an increase in interest rate would increase its NII, and a decline in interest rate would decrease the NII. The relationship between a change in NII with the sign of the earning gap and the direction of interest rate movement is summarized in Table 9.17.

A decrease in the earning gap is the key to decreasing the sensitivity of a bank's overall NII to a change in interest rate. When the amount of rate-sensitive assets and liabilities of a bank are close, and their repricing times are aligned, a change in interest rate affects both sides of the balance sheet almost equally, keeping the NII relatively stable. For example, for the hypothetical bank in our example, a large portion of the assets are fixed-rate with maturity dates (repricing times) distributed throughout the 1-year horizon, with more concentration at the third quarterly time bucket and afterward, while a large portion of liabilities are of the floating-rate type that is repriced in the first two quarterly time buckets. To reduce the rate sensitivity of its NII, the bank can either change its funding practice and issue more fixed-rate debt, or originate more floating-rate loans that are repriced more frequently, aligned with the rate resetting pattern of the liabilities. Such fundamental changes in a bank's balance sheet, however, can be costly and may not be in line with the bank's overall strategy and business plan. Instead

TABLE 9.17 Change in NII and its relationship with the sign of an earning gap and the direction of interest rate movement

Change in NII		Interest Rate	
		Rising	**Falling**
Earning Gap	Positive	Increase ↗	Decrease ↘
	Negative	Decrease ↘	Increase ↗

of such major changes in the balance sheet, the bank can use derivative products, such as an interest rate swap, to hedge the net interest income against changes in the interest rate. In a later section of this chapter we review how swap contracts can be used to hedge the net interest income.

Earning gap analysis is a first step in analyzing the sensitivity of NII to the interest rate risk factor. The method, however, has some weaknesses. First, terms (time to maturity) of rate-sensitive assets or liabilities are not fully taken into account when calculating the impact on NII. Although in the earning gap method maturing positions are placed in the appropriate time bucket, the lack of consideration of the exact maturity dates can still introduce significant inaccuracy into the results, since the remaining life of a position plays a major role in its rate sensitivity. Second, the method only provides an approximate estimate for a change in the NII for a given change in interest rate level. Not considering the accrual period, compounding frequency, business day count, and other specifications of a position in calculation of its interest income or expense can alter the end result considerably. Third, the method assumes that rates at all term points of a yield curve are changing equally (i.e., a parallel shift in the curve). However, in practice rates at different term points may change by different amounts and this should be considered in the sensitivity analysis. Fourth, the earning gap method does not consider optionality of a position (if it exists) and its potential impact on NII. Fifth, and probably the most notable weakness, is that the earning gap assumes that all product types have the same sensitivity to interest rate. For example, it assumes that a 1% change in interest rate impacts the interest expenses of floating-rate debts and savings deposit similarly. There is historical evidence that shows that banks do not change their deposit rates in the same magnitude as the change in the overall market rate. For example, if the fed funds rate increases by 1%, a bank may increase its deposit rate by only 0.60%, or when the fed funds rate decreases by 1% the bank may decrease its deposit rate by only 0.40%. This ratio of change in the deposit rate to the change in the overall market rate is usually called the *beta* of the deposit product. Hence, this bank has a beta of 0.6 for the upward rate case and a beta of 0.4 for the downward rate case. The earning gap does not consider such patterns and differences in the rate sensitivity of different products.

Due to these issues, results obtained through the earning gap analysis are highly approximate. Hence, the method is often used as a first assessment of NII sensitivity to interest rate. Banks regularly rely on scenario analysis based on a full calculation of interest incomes and expenses of all rate-sensitive positions, along with forecasted interest rates, to obtain a more accurate estimate of changes in earning in different market conditions. The earning gap method can be used to perform a reasonability check on the results obtained through the full calculation method.

INTEREST RATE SCENARIO ANALYSIS

One of the core ALM analyses is the study of change in the interest rate environment on the net interest income of the bank. Often these change scenarios are assumed as instantaneous shocks to the yield curve. Such analysis focuses on the interest rate risk factor and evaluates its potential impact on the net interest income of the bank. The general procedure to perform interest rate shock analysis for the NII is as follows:

1. For the selected time bucket scheme, determine the interest income, interest expense, and net interest income using the current spot curve, and either implied forward or forecasted rates for future reset dates during the analysis time horizon. This is the NII of the base scenario (NII_0).
2. Apply the intended shock (e.g., +100 bps parallel shock) to the current spot curve. If the implied forward rate method is used, recalculate the implied forward rates based on the shocked curve. If the forecasted rate method is used, evaluate the impact of the shock on the spot curve on the forecasted rates and obtain new forecasted rates for the analysis time horizon.
3. Determine the interest income, interest expense, and net interest income for the given time bucket scheme using the shocked spot rates, shocked implied forward rates, or shocked forecasted rates. This is the NII of shock scenario (NII_S).
4. For each time bucket, the difference between the shocked NII and base NII is the *change in net interest income* due to assumed interest rate shock:

$$\Delta NII = NII_S - NII_0 \qquad (9.6)$$

In this analysis we assume that an interest rate shock to the current spot curve is instantaneous. This means that for a shock scenario, the spot curve as of the analysis date is replaced by the shocked curve and all other calculations, including derivation of implied forward or forecasted rates, are based on the shocked curve. Some banks and ALM software vendors use the term *earnings-at-risk* to refer to the *change in net interest income*, that is, ΔNII in Equation (9.1). However, since earnings-at-risk is also used to refer to a simulation-based NII metric, in this chapter we use "change in net interest income" to refer to the ΔNII metric. Simulation-based earnings-at-risk is discussed in the next chapter.

Since the coupon rate of a fixed-rate instrument does not change, it has no impact on the ΔNII, as long as its maturity date is beyond the analysis time horizon, or when its maturity date is within the horizon but upon maturity it is not replaced, for example, if a runoff view of the balance sheet is assumed.[3] When a fixed-rate instrument is matured within the analysis time horizon and is replaced with a new fixed-rate instrument, the coupon rate of the replacement is different from the matured position and the new rate is impacted by the shock scenario. Hence, in such a case the fixed-rate instrument contributes to the ΔNII. A floating-rate instrument also impacts ΔNII, as its coupon rate varies in different interest rate scenarios. In the following discussions we focus on floating-rate instruments and study the impact of different interest rate shocks on the NII based on the implied forward rate method.

Parallel Shocks

To study parallel shocks and their impacts on NII we return to the simple balance sheet with positions A2 and L2 introduced earlier in the section "Using Implied Forward Rate," where we determined the NII using the implied forward rates. For simplicity, we use the runoff view of the balance sheet in examples of this section but the concept can be extended to static or dynamic view approaches in a similar fashion. Figure 9.11 and Table 9.18 present the original LIBOR-swap spot curve we used in an example earlier in this chapter along with two parallel shocks of −100 bps and +100 bps to this curve. Here we floored the rates in a −100 bps scenario at zero.

Recall from the section "Using Implied Forward Rate" that positions A2 and L2 are floating-rate positions with rate indexes of 1-month LIBOR and 3-month LIBOR respectively. In order to analyze the impact of the parallel shocks we need to obtain the implied forward rates of 1-month and 3-month LIBOR based on +100 bps and −100 bps shocked spot curves. We can use the same methodology discussed in Chapter 1 to calculate these rates.

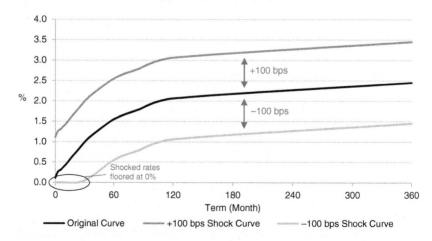

FIGURE 9.11   Original LIBOR-swap spot curve with −100 bps and +100 bps parallel shocks

TABLE 9.18 Original LIBOR-swap spot curve and two shocked curves: +100 bps and −100 bps

Term	Original Rate (%)	+100 bps Shock Rate (%)	−100 bps Shock Rate (%)
1D	0.1140	1.1140	0.0000
1W	0.1407	1.1407	0.0000
1M	0.1763	1.1763	0.0000
3M	0.2708	1.2708	0.0000
6M	0.3160	1.3160	0.0000
9M	0.3873	1.3873	0.0000
1Y	0.4642	1.4642	0.0000
2Y	0.8105	1.8105	0.0000
3Y	1.1262	2.1262	0.1262
5Y	1.5465	2.5465	0.5465
7Y	1.7800	2.7800	0.7800
10Y	2.0622	3.0622	1.0622
30Y	2.4515	3.4515	1.4515

The calculated 1-month LIBOR and 3-month LIBOR implied rates for the relevant reset dates of positions A2 and L2, based on two shocked curves, are shown in Tables 9.19 and 9.20.

TABLE 9.19 Implied 1-month rate for +100 bps and −100 bps shocked curves

	+100 bps Shock		−100 bps Shock
Date	1-Month Rate (%)	Date	1-Month Rate (%)
3/15/2015	0.1760	3/15/2015	0.1760
6/15/2015	1.3521	6/15/2015	0.0000
9/15/2015	1.4254	9/15/2015	0.0000
12/15/2015	1.5936	12/15/2015	0.0000
3/15/2016	1.5076	3/15/2016	0.0000
6/15/2016	1.9689	6/15/2016	0.0000
9/15/2016	2.1404	9/15/2016	0.0000
12/15/2016	2.2558	12/15/2016	0.0000
3/15/2017	2.3928	3/15/2017	0.1228
6/15/2017	2.5763	6/15/2017	0.3112
9/15/2017	2.7322	9/15/2017	0.3741
12/15/2017	2.8219	12/15/2017	0.4337
3/15/2018	2.8213	3/15/2018	0.6162

TABLE 9.20   Implied 3-month rate for +100 bps and −100 bps shocked curves

Date	+100 bps Shock 3-Month Rate (%)	Date	−100 bps Shock 3-Month Rate (%)
1/17/2015	0.2700	1/17/2015	0.2700
4/17/2015	1.3014	4/17/2015	0.0000
7/17/2015	1.3827	7/17/2015	0.0000
10/17/2015	1.5478	10/17/2015	0.0000
1/17/2016	1.6248	1/17/2016	0.0000
4/17/2016	1.9021	4/17/2016	0.0000
7/17/2016	2.0554	7/17/2016	0.0000
10/17/2016	2.2255	10/17/2016	0.0000
1/17/2017	2.4217	1/17/2017	0.0481
4/17/2017	2.5127	4/17/2017	0.2915
7/17/2017	2.6473	7/17/2017	0.3533
10/17/2017	2.8022	10/17/2017	0.4156
1/17/2018	2.9420	1/17/2018	0.5275

As before, the analysis date is March 31, 2015. Note that the 1-month LIBOR as of March 15, 2015 (0.1760%) and the 3-month LIBOR as of January 17, 2015 (0.2700%) are not shocked. Those are actual rates that are set before the analysis date while scenarios are assumed as instantaneous shocks to the curve as of March 31, 2015. Also note that, while the rates of the shocked spot curves are exactly 1% higher or lower than the rates of the original curve (with consideration of flooring to zero for downward shock), the implied forward rates for the parallel shocks are not exactly 1% higher or lower than the original implied forward rates. This is due to the day count convention and compounding frequency of spot rates and the interpolation method used.

Using the shocked implied forward rates from Tables 9.19 and 9.20 we can recalculate the interest income and expense of positions A2 and L2, and determine the NII in each shock scenario.

+100 bps Shock Scenario

Tables 9.21 and 9.22 show calculation details for the interest income and expense of positions A2 and L2 when rates are based on +100 bps shock scenario.

The interest income and expense of positions A2 and L2 in a +100 bps shock scenario are calculated in a similar way explained earlier in the section

TABLE 9.21   Interest income of floating-rate asset position A2 for a +100 bps shock scenario

Time Bucket	From Date	To Date	Section	Day Count	1-Month LIBOR (%)	Total Rate (%)	Interest ($)
0M–1M	4/1/2015	4/30/2015		30	0.1760	2.6760	15.61
1M–2M	5/1/2015	5/31/2015		31	0.1760	2.6760	16.13
2M–3M	6/1/2015	6/15/2015	I	15	0.1760	2.6760	7.81
	6/16/2015	6/30/2015	II	15	1.3521	3.8521	11.24
1Q–2Q	7/1/2015	9/15/2015	I	77	1.3521	3.8521	57.68
	9/16/2015	9/30/2015	II	15	1.4254	3.9254	11.45
2Q–3Q	10/1/2015	12/15/2015	I	76	1.4254	3.9254	58.01
	12/16/2015	12/31/2015	II	16	1.5936	4.0936	12.74
3Q–4Q	1/1/2016	3/15/2016	I	75	1.5936	4.0936	59.70
	3/16/2016	3/31/2016	II	16	1.5076	4.0076	12.47
1Y–2Y	4/1/2016	6/15/2016	I	76	1.5076	4.0076	59.22
	6/16/2016	9/15/2016	II	92	1.9689	4.4689	79.94
	9/16/2016	12/15/2016	III	91	2.1404	4.6404	82.11
	12/16/2016	3/15/2017	IV	90	2.2558	4.7558	83.23
	3/16/2017	3/31/2017	V	16	2.3928	4.8928	15.22
2Y–3Y	4/1/2017	6/15/2017	I	76	2.3928	4.8928	72.31
	6/16/2017	9/15/2017	II	92	2.5763	5.0763	90.81
	9/16/2017	12/15/2017	III	91	2.7322	5.2322	92.58
	12/16/2017	3/15/2018	IV	90	2.8219	5.3219	93.13
	3/16/2018	3/31/2018	V	16	0.0000	0.0000	0.00

"Using the Implied Forward Rate." For example, consider position A2 and time bucket 3Q–4Q, section I. The effective 1-month LIBOR is set at the previous reset date of December 15, 2015. The shocked implied forward rate for that date from Table 9.19 is 1.5936%. Considering the 250 bps contractual spread, the effective rate is 1.5936% + 2.50% = 4.0936%. Therefore, the interest income is calculated as:

$$7,000 \times \left(\frac{75}{360}\right) \times \left(\frac{1.5936 + 2.5}{100}\right) = 59.70$$

As another example, consider position L2 and time bucket 2Y–3Y, section IV. The effective 3-month LIBOR is set at the most recent reset date of October 17, 2017. The shocked implied forward rate for that date from Table 9.20 is 2.8022%. Considering the 30 bps contractual spread, the effective rate is

TABLE 9.22   Interest expense of floating-rate liability position L2 for a +100 bps shock scenario

Time Bucket	From Date	To Date	Section	Day Count	3-Month LIBOR (%)	Total Rate (%)	Interest ($)
0M–1M	4/1/2015	4/17/2015	I	17	0.2700	0.5700	2.21
	4/18/2015	4/30/2015	II	13	1.3014	1.6014	4.74
1M–2M	5/1/2015	5/31/2015		31	1.3014	1.6014	11.31
2M–3M	6/1/2015	6/30/2015		30	1.3014	1.6014	10.94
1Q–2Q	7/1/2015	7/17/2015	I	17	1.3014	1.6014	6.20
	7/18/2015	9/30/2015	II	75	1.3827	1.6827	28.75
2Q–3Q	10/1/2015	10/17/2015	I	17	1.3827	1.6827	6.52
	10/18/2015	12/31/2015	II	75	1.5478	1.8478	31.57
3Q–4Q	1/1/2016	1/17/2016	I	17	1.5478	1.8478	7.16
	1/18/2016	3/31/2016	II	74	1.6248	1.9248	32.44
1Y–2Y	4/1/2016	4/17/2016	I	17	1.6248	1.9248	7.45
	4/18/2016	7/17/2016	II	91	1.9021	2.2021	45.64
	7/18/2016	10/17/2016	III	92	2.0554	2.3554	49.36
	10/18/2016	1/17/2017	IV	92	2.2255	2.5255	52.92
	1/18/2017	3/31/2017	V	73	2.4217	2.7217	45.26
2Y–3Y	4/1/2017	4/17/2017	I	17	2.4217	2.7217	10.54
	4/18/2017	7/17/2017	II	91	2.5127	2.8127	58.30
	7/18/2017	10/17/2017	III	92	2.6473	2.9473	61.76
	10/18/2017	1/17/2018	IV	92	2.8022	3.1022	65.01
	1/18/2018	3/31/2018	V	73	0.0000	0.0000	0.00

2.8022% + 0.30% = 3.1022%. Therefore, the interest expense is calculated as:

$$8,200 \times \left(\frac{92}{360}\right) \times \left(\frac{2.8022 + 0.30}{100}\right) = 65.01$$

The net interest income for this simple balance sheet consisting of only positions A2 and L2 for the +100 bps shock scenario is calculated using Equation (9.2) and presented in Table 9.23.

To better understand the impact of the +100 bps shock, it is helpful to compare the NII for the shock scenario to the NII obtained using the original curve. The result using the original curve is referred to as the base scenario or base case. Figure 9.12 presents this comparison. From this graph we can see that the +100 bps instantaneous shock to the spot curve decreased the NII for all time buckets except for the 2Y–3Y bucket. The decrease in NII is due to the fact that shock to the spot curve increased both the interest income and

TABLE 9.23 Net interest income for a balance sheet comprised of positions A2 and L2 for +100 bps shock scenario

Time Bucket	After-Shock Interest Income	After-Shock Interest Expense	After-Shock NII
0M–1M	15.61	6.95	8.66
1M–2M	16.13	11.31	4.82
2M–3M	19.04	10.94	8.10
1Q–2Q	69.12	34.95	34.18
2Q–3Q	70.74	38.08	32.66
3Q–4Q	72.17	39.60	32.57
1Y–2Y	319.73	200.63	119.09
2Y–3Y	348.83	195.61	153.22

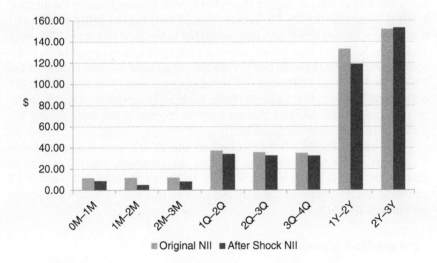

FIGURE 9.12 Comparison of NII in base and +100 bps shock scenarios

expense but the interest expense, which is based on 3-month LIBOR, increased more compared to the interest income, which is based on 1-month LIBOR, as balance of liability L2 is higher than balance of asset A2. Table 9.24 shows the impact of the +100 bps shock to the spot curve on the interest income, interest expense, and NII. In this table, changes are calculated by taking the difference between the interest income, interest expense, and NII derived using the original curve (from Table 9.8) and the corresponding values of the +100 bps shocked curve (from Table 9.23).

TABLE 9.24 Change in interest income, interest expense, and NII for a +100 bps shock to spot curve

Time Bucket	Δ Interest Income	Δ Interest Expense	Δ NII
0M–1M	0.00	2.96	−2.96
1M–2M	0.00	7.06	−7.06
2M–3M	2.91	6.83	−3.92
1Q–2Q	17.81	20.87	−3.05
2Q–3Q	17.73	20.76	−3.03
3Q–4Q	16.93	19.49	−2.56
1Y–2Y	67.26	81.40	−14.14
2Y–3Y	66.21	65.02	1.20

From Table 9.24 we can see that changes in the interest expense due to the +100 bps shock are higher than changes in interest income for all time buckets except for the 2Y–3Y bucket. This in turn led to having a lower NII under the +100 bps shock scenario compared to the base scenario ($\Delta NII < 0$). Therefore, for this simple balance sheet a +100 bps instantaneous shock to the spot curve has a negative impact on the NII for all time buckets except for the 2Y–3Y bucket. Total ΔNII from this shock (i.e., the sum of all ΔNII in the last column of Table 9.24) is −$35.53. Thus, such an instantaneous shock to the interest rate would decrease the net interest income of the bank during the 3-year time horizon by around $35.

The reason the NII has increased in the 2Y–3Y time bucket ($\Delta NII = \$1.20 > 0$) is due to the fact that position A2 generates interest income in this bucket for 349 days before it matures on March 15, 2018, but position L2 generates interest expense for only 292 days in this bucket before it matures on January 17, 2018.

−100 bps Shock Scenario

Tables 9.25 and 9.26 show details of calculation of the interest income and expense for positions A2 and L2, for the same time buckets considered previously, and when rates are based on −100 bps shock scenario.

The interest income and expense of positions A2 and L2 under the −100 bps shock scenario are calculated in a similar way as explained earlier. For example, consider position A2 and time bucket 1Y–2Y section I. The effective 1-month LIBOR is set at the previous reset date of March 15, 2016. The shocked implied forward rate for that date from Table 9.19 is 0%. Unless we specifically intend to study the impact of negative rates, it is a common

TABLE 9.25 Interest income of floating-rate asset position A2 for −100 bps shock scenario

Time Bucket	From Date	To Date	Section	Day Count	1-Month LIBOR (%)	Total Rate (%)	Interest ($)
0M–1M	4/1/2015	4/30/2015		30	0.1760	2.6760	15.61
1M–2M	5/1/2015	5/31/2015		31	0.1760	2.6760	16.13
2M–3M	6/1/2015	6/15/2015	I	15	0.1760	2.6760	7.81
	6/16/2015	6/30/2015	II	15	0.0000	2.5000	7.29
1Q–2Q	7/1/2015	9/15/2015	I	77	0.0000	2.5000	37.43
	9/16/2015	9/30/2015	II	15	0.0000	2.5000	7.29
2Q–3Q	10/1/2015	12/15/2015	I	76	0.0000	2.5000	36.94
	12/16/2015	12/31/2015	II	16	0.0000	2.5000	7.78
3Q–4Q	1/1/2016	3/15/2016	I	75	0.0000	2.5000	36.46
	3/16/2016	3/31/2016	II	16	0.0000	2.5000	7.78
1Y–2Y	4/1/2016	6/15/2016	I	76	0.0000	2.5000	36.94
	6/16/2016	9/15/2016	II	92	0.0000	2.5000	44.72
	9/16/2016	12/15/2016	III	91	0.0000	2.5000	44.24
	12/16/2016	3/15/2017	IV	90	0.0000	2.5000	43.75
	3/16/2017	3/31/2017	V	16	0.1228	2.6228	8.16
2Y–3Y	4/1/2017	6/15/2017	I	76	0.1228	2.6228	38.76
	6/16/2017	9/15/2017	II	92	0.3112	2.8112	50.29
	9/16/2017	12/15/2017	III	91	0.3741	2.8741	50.86
	12/16/2017	3/15/2018	IV	90	0.4337	2.9337	51.34
	3/16/2018	3/31/2018	V	16	0.0000	0.0000	0.00

practice to floor interest rates at zero and avoid negative rates. The −100 bps shock to the original spot curve would result in negative rates for some terms, and this in turn would lead to negative implied forward rates. Here we have floored the shocked rates at zero and hence the implied forward rate is zero for some reset dates of position A2. Considering the 250 bps contractual spread, the effective rate is 0.00% + 2.50% = 2.50%. Thus, the interest income is calculated as:

$$7,000 \times \left(\frac{76}{360} \right) \times \left(\frac{0.00 + 2.50}{100} \right) = 36.94$$

As another example, consider position L2 and time bucket 2M–3M. The effective 3-month LIBOR is set at the most recent reset date of April 17, 2015. The shocked implied forward rate for that date from Table 9.20 is 0.00%.

TABLE 9.26   Interest expense of floating-rate liability position L2 for a −100 bps shock scenario

Time Bucket	From Date	To Date	Section	Day Count	3-Month LIBOR (%)	Total Rate (%)	Interest ($)
0M–1M	4/1/2015	4/17/2015	I	17	0.2700	0.5700	2.21
	4/18/2015	4/30/2015	II	13	0.0000	0.3000	0.89
1M–2M	5/1/2015	5/31/2015		31	0.0000	0.3000	2.12
2M–3M	6/1/2015	6/30/2015		30	0.0000	0.3000	2.05
1Q–2Q	7/1/2015	7/17/2015	I	17	0.0000	0.3000	1.16
	7/18/2015	9/30/2015	II	75	0.0000	0.3000	5.13
2Q–3Q	10/1/2015	10/17/2015	I	17	0.0000	0.3000	1.16
	10/18/2015	12/31/2015	II	75	0.0000	0.3000	5.13
3Q–4Q	1/1/2016	1/17/2016	I	17	0.0000	0.3000	1.16
	1/18/2016	3/31/2016	II	74	0.0000	0.3000	5.06
1Y–2Y	4/1/2016	4/17/2016	I	17	0.0000	0.3000	1.16
	4/18/2016	7/17/2016	II	91	0.0000	0.3000	6.22
	7/18/2016	10/17/2016	III	92	0.0000	0.3000	6.29
	10/18/2016	1/17/2017	IV	92	0.0000	0.3000	6.29
	1/18/2017	3/31/2017	V	73	0.0481	0.3481	5.79
2Y–3Y	4/1/2017	4/17/2017	I	17	0.0481	0.3481	1.35
	4/18/2017	7/17/2017	II	91	0.2915	0.5915	12.26
	7/18/2017	10/17/2017	III	92	0.3533	0.6533	13.69
	10/18/2017	1/17/2018	IV	92	0.4156	0.7156	15.00
	1/18/2018	3/31/2018	V	73	0.0000	0.0000	0.00

Considering the 30 bps contractual spread, the effective rate is 0.00% + 0.30% = 0.30%. Therefore, the interest expense is calculated as:

$$8{,}200 \times \left(\frac{30}{360}\right) \times \left(\frac{0.00 + 0.30}{100}\right) = 2.05$$

The net interest income for this simple balance sheet consisting of only positions A2 and L2 for the −100 bps shock scenario is presented in Table 9.27, calculated using Equation (9.2).

Figure 9.13 presents a comparison of the NII obtained in a −100 bps shock to the spot curve and the base scenario results. In this figure we can see that the −100 bps shock led to an increase in the NII for all time buckets except for the 2Y–3Y bucket. This can be explained when changes in the interest income and the interest expense are analyzed separately. Table 9.28 provides changes

TABLE 9.27 Net interest income for balance sheet comprised of positions A2 and L2 for −100 bps shock scenario

Time Bucket	After-Shock Interest Income	After-Shock Interest Expense	After-Shock NII
0M–1M	15.61	3.10	12.51
1M–2M	16.13	2.12	14.01
2M–3M	15.10	2.05	13.05
1Q–2Q	44.72	6.29	38.44
2Q–3Q	44.72	6.29	38.44
3Q–4Q	44.24	6.22	38.02
1Y–2Y	177.81	25.74	152.07
2Y–3Y	191.24	42.29	148.95

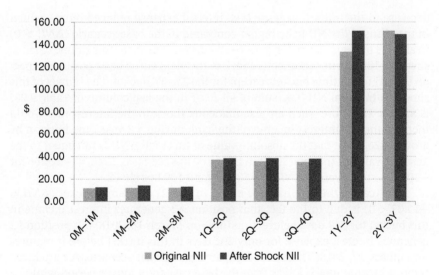

FIGURE 9.13 Comparison of NII in base scenario and −100 bps shock scenario

in the interest income, interest expense, and NII that result from the −100 bps shock to the spot curve. Results in Table 9.28 are obtained by taking the difference between the interest income, interest expense, and NII derived using the original curve (from Table 9.8) and the corresponding values in the −100 bps shocked curve (from Table 9.27). From this table it can be seen that while both the interest income and expense decreased as a result of the downward shock to the interest rate, the decrease in the interest income is smaller than the

TABLE 9.28 Change in interest income, interest expense, and NII for a −100 bps shock to spot curve

Time Bucket	Δ Interest Income	Δ Interest Expense	Δ NII
0M–1M	0.00	−0.89	0.89
1M–2M	0.00	−2.13	2.13
2M–3M	−1.04	−2.06	1.03
1Q–2Q	−6.59	−7.79	1.21
2Q–3Q	−8.30	−11.04	2.74
3Q–4Q	−11.00	−13.89	2.89
1Y–2Y	−74.66	−93.49	18.84
2Y–3Y	−91.37	−88.30	−3.07

decrease in the interest expense (i.e., interest expense reduced more), which in turn caused the NII to be higher compared to the base scenario ($\Delta NII > 0$) in all time buckets except for the 2Y–3Y bucket. Hence, for this simple balance sheet a −100 bps instantaneous shock to the yield curve has a positive impact on the NII for all time buckets except for the 2Y–3Y bucket. The impact of this shock on the total NII (i.e., sum of all ΔNII in the last column of Table 9.28) is $26.66. Therefore, such an instantaneous shock to the interest rate would increase the net interest income of the bank during a 3-year time horizon by around $26. Note that the absolute value of this total ΔNII is not equal to the absolute value of the total ΔNII in the +100 bps scenario: $\Delta NII = +\$26.66$ for −100 bps shock versus $\Delta NII = -\$35.53$ for +100 bps shock.

The reason the NII has decreased in the 2Y–3Y time bucket ($\Delta NII = -\$3.07 < 0$) is due to the fact that position A2 generates interest income in this bucket for 349 days before it matures on March 15, 2018, but position L2 generates interest expense for only 292 days in this bucket before it matures on January 17, 2018. Therefore, compared to the base scenario, A2 produced interest income that is lower than the base case for a longer period while L2 produced an interest expense that is lower than the base case for a shorter period.

Non-Parallel Shocks

To study the non-parallel shocks we consider a steepening shock to the LIBOR-swap curve used in the previous example and study its impact on a simple balance sheet consisting of the positions A2 and L2 introduced earlier. Figure 9.14 and Table 9.29 present the original spot curve along with a steepening shocked curve.

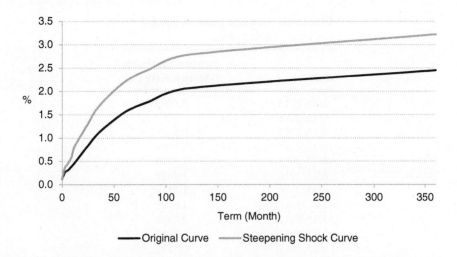

FIGURE 9.14   Original LIBOR-swap spot curve and a steepening shock

TABLE 9.29   Original LIBOR-swap curve and a steepening shock curve

Term	Original Rate (%)	Steepening Shock Rate (%)
1D	0.1140	0.1140
1W	0.1407	0.1407
1M	0.1763	0.2263
3M	0.2708	0.3708
6M	0.3160	0.4660
9M	0.3873	0.5873
1Y	0.4642	0.8142
2Y	0.8105	1.2705
3Y	1.1262	1.6962
5Y	1.5465	2.1965
7Y	1.7800	2.4700
10Y	2.0622	2.7822
30Y	2.4515	3.2215

The implied forward rates for 1-month and 3-month LIBOR based on the steepening shock curve are presented in Tables 9.30 and 9.31.

Tables 9.32 and 9.33 show details of calculation of the interest income and expense of positions A2 and L2, for the same time buckets considered before and when rates are from the steepening shock scenario.

TABLE 9.30   Implied 1-month forward rate for steepening shock

Date	Steepening Shock 1-Month Rate (%)
3/15/2015	0.1760
6/15/2015	0.5153
9/15/2015	0.6821
12/15/2015	1.1088
3/15/2016	1.3195
6/15/2016	1.4855
9/15/2016	1.7119
12/15/2016	1.9003
3/15/2017	2.0906
6/15/2017	2.3112
9/15/2017	2.5219
12/15/2017	2.6807
3/15/2018	2.6319

TABLE 9.31   Implied 3-month forward rate for steepening shock

Date	Steepening Shock 3-Month Rate (%)
1/17/2015	0.2700
4/17/2015	0.4276
7/17/2015	0.6052
10/17/2015	0.9343
1/17/2016	1.4317
4/17/2016	1.4071
7/17/2016	1.6214
10/17/2016	1.8459
1/17/2017	2.0842
4/17/2017	2.2353
7/17/2017	2.4295
10/17/2017	2.6386
1/17/2018	2.7830

Calculation of the interest income and expense for each time bucket in Tables 9.32 and 9.33 is as explained before. For example, consider position A2 and time bucket 2Q–3Q, section II. The effective 1-month LIBOR is set at the most recent reset date of December 15, 2015. The shocked implied forward 1-month LIBOR from Table 9.30 as of this date is 1.1088%. Considering the

TABLE 9.32 Interest income of floating-rate asset position A2 for a steepening shock scenario

Time Bucket	From Date	To Date	Section	Day Count	1-Month LIBOR (%)	Total Rate (%)	Interest ($)
0M–1M	4/1/2015	4/30/2015		30	0.1760	2.6760	15.61
1M–2M	5/1/2015	5/31/2015		31	0.1760	2.6760	16.13
2M–3M	6/1/2015	6/15/2015	I	15	0.1760	2.6760	7.81
	6/16/2015	6/30/2015	II	15	0.5153	3.0153	8.79
1Q–2Q	7/1/2015	9/15/2015	I	77	0.5153	3.0153	45.15
	9/16/2015	9/30/2015	II	15	0.6821	3.1821	9.28
2Q–3Q	10/1/2015	12/15/2015	I	76	0.6821	3.1821	47.02
	12/16/2015	12/31/2015	II	16	1.1088	3.6088	11.23
3Q–4Q	1/1/2016	3/15/2016	I	75	1.1088	3.6088	52.63
	3/16/2016	3/31/2016	II	16	1.3195	3.8195	11.88
1Y–2Y	4/1/2016	6/15/2016	I	76	1.3195	3.8195	56.44
	6/16/2016	9/15/2016	II	92	1.4855	3.9855	71.30
	9/16/2016	12/15/2016	III	91	1.7119	4.2119	74.53
	12/16/2016	3/15/2017	IV	90	1.9003	4.4003	77.01
	3/16/2017	3/31/2017	V	16	2.0906	4.5906	14.28
2Y–3Y	4/1/2017	6/15/2017	I	76	2.0906	4.5906	67.84
	6/16/2017	9/15/2017	II	92	2.3112	4.8112	86.07
	9/16/2017	12/15/2017	III	91	2.5219	5.0219	88.86
	12/16/2017	3/15/2018	IV	90	2.6807	5.1807	90.66
	3/16/2018	3/31/2018	V	16	0.0000	0.0000	0.00

contractual spread of 2.5%, the effective rate is $1.1088\% + 2.50\% = 3.6088\%$. So, the interest income is calculated as:

$$7,000 \times \left(\frac{16}{360}\right) \times \left(\frac{1.1088 + 2.50}{100}\right) = 11.23$$

As another example, consider position L2 and time bucket 1M–2M. The effective 3-month LIBOR is set at the most recent reset date of April 17, 2015. The shocked implied forward rate for that date from Table 9.31 is 0.4276%. Considering the 30 bps contractual spread, the effective rate is $0.4276\% + 0.30\% = 0.7276\%$. Therefore, the interest expense is calculated as:

$$8,200 \times \left(\frac{31}{360}\right) \times \left(\frac{0.4276 + 0.30}{100}\right) = 5.14$$

The net interest income for the steepening shock scenario is presented in Table 9.34, and comparison of the NII results from the steepening shock

TABLE 9.33   Interest expense of floating-rate liability position L2 for a steepening shock scenario

Time Bucket	From Date	To Date	Section	Day Count	3-Month LIBOR (%)	Total Rate (%)	Interest ($)
0M–1M	4/1/2015	4/17/2015	I	17	0.2700	0.5700	2.21
	4/18/2015	4/30/2015	II	13	0.4276	0.7276	2.15
1M–2M	5/1/2015	5/31/2015		31	0.4276	0.7276	5.14
2M–3M	6/1/2015	6/30/2015		30	0.4276	0.7276	4.97
1Q–2Q	7/1/2015	7/17/2015	I	17	0.4276	0.7276	2.82
	7/18/2015	9/30/2015	II	75	0.6052	0.9052	15.46
2Q–3Q	10/1/2015	10/17/2015	I	17	0.6052	0.9052	3.51
	10/18/2015	12/31/2015	II	75	0.9343	1.2343	21.09
3Q–4Q	1/1/2016	1/17/2016	I	17	0.9343	1.2343	4.78
	1/18/2016	3/31/2016	II	74	1.4317	1.7317	29.19
1Y–2Y	4/1/2016	4/17/2016	I	17	1.4317	1.7317	6.71
	4/18/2016	7/17/2016	II	91	1.4071	1.7071	35.38
	7/18/2016	10/17/2016	III	92	1.6214	1.9214	40.26
	10/18/2016	1/17/2017	IV	92	1.8459	2.1459	44.97
	1/18/2017	3/31/2017	V	73	2.0842	2.3842	39.64
2Y–3Y	4/1/2017	4/17/2017	I	17	2.0842	2.3842	9.23
	4/18/2017	7/17/2017	II	91	2.2353	2.5353	52.55
	7/18/2017	10/17/2017	III	92	2.4295	2.7295	57.20
	10/18/2017	1/17/2018	IV	92	2.6386	2.9386	61.58
	1/18/2018	3/31/2018	V	73	0.0000	0.0000	0.00

TABLE 9.34   Net interest income for a balance sheet comprised of positions A2 and L2 for a steepening shock scenario

Time Bucket	After-Shock Interest Income	After-Shock Interest Expense	After-Shock NII
0M–1M	15.61	4.36	11.25
1M–2M	16.13	5.14	10.99
2M–3M	16.60	4.97	11.63
1Q–2Q	54.43	18.28	36.14
2Q–3Q	58.25	24.59	33.66
3Q–4Q	64.51	33.97	30.54
1Y–2Y	293.55	166.96	126.59
2Y–3Y	333.43	180.56	152.87

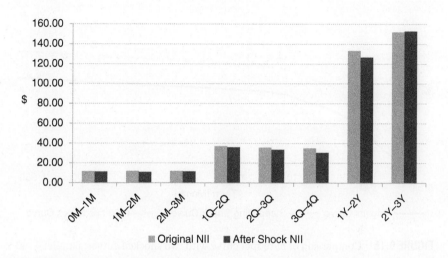

FIGURE 9.15 Comparison of NII in base scenario and steepening shock scenario

scenario and the base scenario is presented in Figure 9.15. From this graph we can see that the steepening shock applied to the spot curve caused the NII to decrease in all time buckets except for the 2Y–3Y bucket. The change in NII, calculated using Equation (9.6), is presented in Table 9.35. Total ΔNII from this shock is –$15.16 (the sum of the last column of Table 9.35).

The effect of this steepening shock on the NII is in the same direction as what we observed for the +100 bps parallel shock but it has a less adverse impact. This can be explained by a comparison of the two shocked spot curves. Figure 9.16 shows the original spot curve and two shocked curves: the +100

TABLE 9.35 Change in interest income, interest expense, and NII for steepening shock to spot curve

Time Bucket	Δ Interest Income	Δ Interest Expense	Δ NII
0M–1M	0.00	0.37	−0.37
1M–2M	0.00	0.89	−0.89
2M–3M	0.47	0.86	−0.39
1Q–2Q	3.12	4.20	−1.09
2Q–3Q	5.23	7.27	−2.03
3Q–4Q	9.27	13.86	−4.59
1Y–2Y	41.09	47.73	−6.64
2Y–3Y	50.81	49.97	0.84

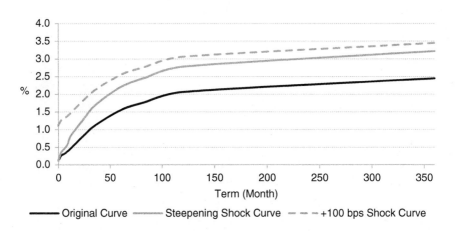

FIGURE 9.16 Comparison of base spot curve with two shocked curves: parallel +100 bps and steepening scenarios

bps parallel scenario and the steepening non-parallel scenario, where the latter is positioned between the original curve and the +100 bps shocked curve. From our earlier discussions we learned that the simple balance sheet consisting of positions A2 and L2 is adversely sensitive to the upward shocks (i.e., upward shocks result in negative ΔNII). A higher upward shock to the spot curve leads to a higher increase in the interest expense compared to the increase in the interest income, resulting in a lower NII. The parallel +100 bps shock shown in Figure 9.16 is a higher upward shock compared to the steepening shock; therefore it resulted in a larger decrease in ΔNII.

The study of the impact of other types of non-parallel interest rate shocks, such as flattening or butterfly, on the NII is done in a way similar to the method explained here for the steepening shock.

Balance Sheet Type and NII Sensitivity

The structure of the balance sheet of a bank and the relationship between its assets and liabilities with regard to their types, terms, and rate settings define how upward or downward shocks to the interest rate impact the net interest income. Generally, with respect to NII sensitivity, a balance sheet is either *asset-sensitive* or *liability-sensitive*. Consider a balance sheet in which a +100 bps upward shock in the interest rate would produce an increase of $10 million in the interest income generated from assets and an increase of $12 million in the interest expense from liabilities. ΔNII from this shock is –$2 million, calculated as follows:

(in $ million)

$$II : Interest\ Income$$

$$IE : Interest\ Expense$$

$$\Delta II = +10 \;\rightarrow\; II_{Shock} = II_{Base} + 10$$

$$\Delta IE = +12 \;\rightarrow\; IE_{Shock} = IE_{Base} + 12$$

$$NII_{Shock} = II_{Shock} - IE_{Shock} = (II_{Base} + 10) - (IE_{Base} + 12)$$

$$= (II_{Base} - IE_{Base}) - 2 = NII_{Base} - 2$$

$$\Delta NII = -2$$

A balance sheet similar to what is described here is liability-sensitive, since the upward shock to the interest rate produced a higher magnitude increase in the interest expense (+$12 million) compared to the magnitude of the increase in the interest income (+$10 million). This caused an undesirable impact on the NII, that is, a negative ΔNII (–$2 million).

Consider another balance sheet in which a -100 bps downward shock to the interest rate would cause the interest income to decrease by $15 million while the interest expense decreases by $20 million. The change in the NII is therefore +$5 million, calculated as follows:

(in $ million)

$$\Delta II = -15 \;\rightarrow\; II_{Shock} = II_{Base} - 15$$

$$\Delta IE = -20 \;\rightarrow\; IE_{Shock} = IE_{Base} - 20$$

$$NII_{Shock} = II_{Shock} - IE_{Shock} = (II_{Base} - 15) - (IE_{Base} - 20)$$

$$= (II_{Base} - IE_{Base}) + 5 = NII_{Base} + 5$$

$$\Delta NII = +5$$

Such a balance sheet is again considered liability-sensitive, since a downward shock to the interest rate caused the magnitude of decrease in the interest expense to be larger than the magnitude of decrease in the interest income. This had a desirable impact on the NII and a positive ΔNII (+$5 million). Therefore, a liability-sensitive balance sheet can be characterized such that, for any upward or downward shock: $|\Delta\ Interest\ Expense| > |\Delta\ Interest\ Income|$.

When a balance sheet is liability-sensitive, an upward shock to the interest rate produces an unfavorable impact on the NII ($\Delta NII < 0$) while a downward shock results in a favorable impact on the NII (($\Delta NII > 0$). The simple balance sheet consisting of positions A2 and L2, considered earlier is an example of a liability-sensitive balance sheet. There we noticed that the upward +100 bps shock produced a negative ΔNII of –\$35.04 while the downward shock of -100 bps produced a positive ΔNII of +\$26.29.

Now consider a balance sheet in which a +100 bps upward shock would result in an increase of \$10 million in the interest income and an increase of \$8 million in the interest expense. The impact on the NII is therefore an increase of \$2 million, calculated as follows:

(in \$ million)

$$\Delta II = +10 \;\rightarrow\; II_{Shock} = II_{Base} + 10$$
$$\Delta IE = +8 \;\rightarrow\; IE_{Shock} = IE_{Base} + 8$$
$$NII_{Shock} = II_{Shock} - IE_{Shock} = (II_{Base} + 10) - (IE_{Base} + 8)$$
$$= (II_{Base} - IE_{Base}) + 2 = NII_{Base} + 2$$
$$\Delta NII = +2$$

This balance sheet is asset-sensitive, since an upward shock to the interest rate caused a higher magnitude increase in the interest income compared to the magnitude of increase in the interest expense. This produced a favorable outcome with respect to the NII (i.e., a positive ΔNII of +\$2 million).

Finally, consider another balance sheet in which a -100 bps downward shock to the interest rate would result in a decrease in the interest income by \$15 million and a decrease in the interest expense by \$10 million. The impact on the NII is therefore a decrease of \$5 million, calculated as follows:

(in \$ million)

$$\Delta II = -15 \;\rightarrow\; II_{Shock} = II_{Base} - 15$$
$$\Delta IE = -10 \;\rightarrow\; IE_{Shock} = IE_{Base} - 10$$
$$NII_{Shock} = II_{Shock} - IE_{Shock} = (II_{Base} - 15) - (IE_{Base} - 10)$$
$$= (II_{Base} - IE_{Base}) - 5 = NII_{Base} - 5$$
$$\Delta NII = -5$$

This balance sheet is also asset-sensitive, since a downward shock to the interest rate caused a higher magnitude decline in the interest income compared to the magnitude of decline in the interest expense. This produced an unfavorable outcome with respect to NII (i.e., a negative ΔNII of –\$5 million). Generally, an asset-sensitive balance sheet can be characterized such that, for any upward or downward shock: $|\Delta\, Interest\ Expense| < |\Delta\, Interest\ Income|$.

TABLE 9.36 Change in NII for different balance sheet type and interest rate shock

	Asset-Sensitive	Liability-Sensitive
Upward Shock	$\Delta NII > 0$	$\Delta NII < 0$
Downward Shock	$\Delta NII < 0$	$\Delta NII > 0$

When a balance sheet is asset-sensitive, an upward shock to the interest rate produces a favorable impact on NII ($\Delta NII > 0$) while a downward shock results in an unfavorable impact on NII ($\Delta NII < 0$). Table 9.36 summarizes the relationship between the balance sheet type and sign of the ΔNII for different interest rate shocks.

Consider a bank where most assets are either fixed-rate loans (e.g., personal loans) or fee-based charge credit cards (consumer credit cards that do not allow holders to revolve the balance and must be paid in full at the end of the period, and hence produce no interest income), and most liabilities are floating-rate notes or deposits based on floating-rate indexes. The balance sheet of such a bank would be classified as a liability-sensitive type. Due to non-sensitivity on the interest rate of assets, a decrease in interest rate would decrease the interest expense while having no significant impact on the interest income (a favorable outcome). However, an increase in interest rate would increase the interest expense of the bank more severely than an increase in the interest income, causing an unfavorable impact on the net interest income of the bank. This bank has risk exposure to an upward movement of the interest rate, which could negatively impact the net income and bottom line numbers. Such a bank can utilize interest rate derivatives to hedge the balance sheet to movements of interest rate. In a later section of this chapter we discuss the use of interest rate swaps for the hedging of the net interest income.

IMPACT OF INTEREST RATE OPTIONS ON NII

Implicit and explicit options can impact the net interest income and ΔNII in different interest rate scenarios. Interest rate cap and floor contracts are two derivative types that are widely used by banks and their clients to hedge interest rate risk exposure. Recall from Chapter 5 that an interest rate cap is a derivative contract based on an interest rate index, such as 1-month LIBOR. The buyer of the cap receives payment at each contractually defined period when the index exceeds an agreed level, known as the strike rate or cap rate.

The payments are based on a contractual notional amount. The buyer pays a premium at the contract inception time to acquire the option. An interest rate cap contract can be considered as a series of European call options known as caplets. Each caplet is an option on the interest rate index for a given period. The option is exercised if the level of the index for that period exceeds the strike rate.

A cap contract can be used to hedge a floating-rate position against the risk of increase in the interest rate. An interest rate cap can be bought or sold as a standalone contract or embedded in the floating-rate contract itself. Payoff of each caplet in period i is based on the underlying index observed at the end of the previous period $i - 1$ and paid at the end of period i. The amount of the payoff is:

$$Payoff_i = N \times \tau_{i-1,i} \times Max(r_{i-1} - k, 0) \tag{9.7}$$

where $i = 1, 2, 3, \ldots, T$ and:

T = Term of contract
N = Notional amount
$\tau_{i-1,i}$ = Length of period i based on contract day count convention
r_{i-1} = Level of underlying interest rate index observed at the end of period $i - 1$ (beginning of period i)
k = Strike rate

Similarly, an interest rate floor is a derivative contract where the buyer receives a payment at each period of the contract when the interest rate index falls below the strike rate. An interest rate floor consists of a series of European put options, known as floorlets, each for a given period during the life of the floor contract. The interest rate floor can be used to hedge a floating-rate position against the risk of decline in the interest rate. Payoff of a floorlet for period i is:

$$Payoff_i = N \times \tau_{i-1,i} \times Max(k - r_{i-1}, 0) \tag{9.8}$$

An *interest rate collar* is the combination of buying a cap contract and selling a floor contract, simultaneously. Purchase of the cap protects the buyer against the rise of the interest rate above the strike rate while selling of the floor generates a premium that fully or partially covers the premium needed to purchase the cap.

To demonstrate the impact of interest rate options on NII and ΔNII, consider a simple balance sheet consisting of two floating-rate positions A4 and L4 with the following specifications:[4]

Position A4

Classification	Asset
Type	Floating-rate debt
Currency	USD
Outstanding balance	10,000.00
Rate base index	1-month LIBOR
Spread (bps)	350
Maturity date	12/31/2018
Payment frequency	Quarterly
Compounding frequency	Quarterly
Reset frequency	Quarterly
Accrual basis	30/360
First payment date	3/31/2017
First reset date	3/31/2017

Position L4

Classification	Liability
Type	Floating-rate debt
Currency	USD
Outstanding balance	10,000.00
Rate base index	1-month LIBOR
Spread (bps)	50
Maturity date	12/31/2018
Payment frequency	Quarterly
Compounding frequency	Quarterly
Reset frequency	Quarterly
Accrual basis	30/360
First payment date	3/31/2017
First reset date	3/31/2017

Assume that the analysis date is December 31, 2016 (end of day), and the inception dates, and hence the first accrual days, of both positions are January 1, 2017. A balance sheet consisting of positions A4 and L4 has a natural hedge against the change in interest rate with respect to NII. Since both positions are floating-rate type and based on a 1-month LIBOR, any change in the reference rate affects asset and liability positions equally. Specifically, the balance sheet is immune to basis risk. The interest rate basis risk arises when the interest rate indexes of floating-rate asset and liability positions are different; therefore, unequal changes in those indexes can result in an unexpected change in NII. We discuss the basis risk and its hedging method in more detail in a later section of this chapter.

To perform NII calculation and scenario analysis, the bank in our example uses a quarterly time bucket scheme with a 2-year horizon and forecasted 1-month LIBOR for eight quarters in the future, as listed in Table 9.37. The current spot 1-month LIBOR is assumed 1.8%. The bank regularly performs two interest rate scenario analyses where the forecasted 1-month LIBOR including current spot rate, are shocked by +100 bps and +200 bps. The shocked rates for these two scenarios are also listed in Table 9.37. For simplicity, rates for base and shocked scenarios in this table are quoted on a 30/360 day count convention.

Table 9.38 presents the interest income of asset A4 using spot and forecasted 1-month LIBOR for eight quarterly time buckets, and Table 9.39 presents the interest expense for liability L4 for the same time buckets. Both tables present the results for the base scenario and two shock scenarios where spot and forecasted rates are shocked by +100 bps and +200 bps.

As before, the interest income or expense for each time bucket is calculated by multiplying the effective rate by the outstanding balance at the beginning of the period and by the accrual period based on the 30/360 contractual accrual basis. In this example, reset and payment frequencies of both positions are quarterly and aligned with the time buckets, so the effective interest rate of each position is constant throughout a time bucket and therefore there is no need to break a time bucket into different sections. The effective rate column in Tables 9.38 and 9.39 consists of the 1-month LIBOR (spot and forecast),

TABLE 9.37   Sample 1-month LIBOR spot (period 0) and forecasts (periods 1 to 8), for base and two shock scenarios

Period (Quarterly)	1-Month LIBOR (%)	1-Month LIBOR +1%	1-Month LIBOR + 2%
0	1.80	2.80	3.80
1	1.85	2.85	3.85
2	1.92	2.92	3.92
3	1.99	2.99	3.99
4	2.05	3.05	4.05
5	2.11	3.11	4.11
6	2.12	3.12	4.12
7	2.20	3.20	4.20
8	2.40	3.40	4.40

TABLE 9.38 Interest income of asset A4 for base and two shock scenarios using forecasted 1-month LIBOR without any interest rate cap

Time Bucket	Base Case		+100 bps		+200 bps	
	Effective Rate (%)	Interest ($)	Effective Rate (%)	Interest ($)	Effective Rate (%)	Interest ($)
0Q–1Q	5.30	132.50	6.30	157.50	7.30	182.50
1Q–2Q	5.35	133.75	6.35	158.75	7.35	183.75
2Q–3Q	5.42	135.50	6.42	160.50	7.42	185.50
3Q–4Q	5.49	137.25	6.49	162.25	7.49	187.25
4Q–5Q	5.55	138.75	6.55	163.75	7.55	188.75
5Q–6Q	5.61	140.25	6.61	165.25	7.61	190.25
6Q–7Q	5.62	140.50	6.62	165.50	7.62	190.50
7Q–8Q	5.70	142.50	6.70	167.50	7.70	192.50

TABLE 9.39 Interest expense of liability L4 for base and two shock scenarios using forecasted 1-month LIBOR

Time Bucket	Base Case		+100 bps		+200 bps	
	Effective Rate (%)	Interest ($)	Effective Rate (%)	Interest ($)	Effective Rate (%)	Interest ($)
0Q–1Q	2.30	57.50	3.30	82.50	4.30	107.50
1Q–2Q	2.35	58.75	3.35	83.75	4.35	108.75
2Q–3Q	2.42	60.50	3.42	85.50	4.42	110.50
3Q–4Q	2.49	62.25	3.49	87.25	4.49	112.25
4Q–5Q	2.55	63.75	3.55	88.75	4.55	113.75
5Q–6Q	2.61	65.25	3.61	90.25	4.61	115.25
6Q–7Q	2.62	65.50	3.62	90.50	4.62	115.50
7Q–8Q	2.70	67.50	3.70	92.50	4.70	117.50

shock amount (0% for base case, +1% or +2% for two shock scenarios), and contractual spread. For example, the interest income for asset A4 in the base scenario for time bucket 0Q–1Q is calculated using the spot rate at period 0 of 1.8% as:

$$10,000 \times \frac{1.8 + 3.5}{100} \times \frac{90}{360} = 132.50$$

where 3.5% is the contractual spread of asset A4, hence the effective rate is 1.8% + 3.5% = 5.3%. For shock scenarios, the shocked 1-month LIBOR is used for calculation of the interest income. For example, for +100 bps scenario the interest income for time bucket 7Q–8Q is calculated by using the forecasted

1-month LIBOR as of period 7 (beginning of the time bucket) of 2.2%, shocked by adding 1%:

$$10,000 \times \frac{(2.2 + 1) + 3.5}{100} \times \frac{90}{360} = 167.50$$

The effective rate is: 2.2% + 1% + 3.5% = 6.7%. The interest expenses of position L4 for base and shock scenarios are calculated similarly. For example, the interest expense for time bucket 7Q–8Q in +100 shock scenario is calculated using forecasted 1-month LBIOR as of period 7 of 2.2%, shocked by adding 1%:

$$10,000 \times \frac{(2.2 + 1) + 0.5}{100} \times \frac{90}{360} = 92.50$$

where 0.5% is the contractual spread of liability L4; hence, the effective rate is 2.2% + 1% + 0.5% = 3.7%. The effective rates and interest incomes and expenses for other time buckets in each scenario are calculated similarly.

The net interest income for three scenarios is presented in Table 9.40. As mentioned earlier, since both positions are based on the same reference rate and their reset timings are also aligned, the net interest income for all scenarios and all buckets is the same. For example, the net interest income in time bucket 7Q–8Q for +100 bps shock scenario is calculated by taking the difference between the interest income of asset A4 and the interest expense of liability L4:

$$NII = \$167.50 - \$92.50 = \$75.00$$

As forecasted 1-month LIBOR changes, it impacts the interest income of A4 and the interest expense of L4 equally and hence the net interest income in all three scenarios and for all time buckets remains the same. Therefore, ΔNII in +100 bps and +200 bps shock scenarios are $0 in all buckets. Considering only these two positions, the bank's NII is hedged against movement of the interest rate.

To see the impact of an interest rate option, now consider the case when asset A4 is originated with an embedded interest rate cap with the following specifications:[5]

Interest Rate Cap	
Classification	Off-balance sheet
Currency	USD
Notional	10,000.00
Rate base index	1-month LIBOR
Maturity date	12/31/2018
Payment frequency	Quarterly
Accrual basis	30/360
Strike rate	2.0%

TABLE 9.40 Net interest income for base and two shock scenarios without any interest rate cap option

Time Bucket	Base Case			+100 bps Shock				+200 bps Shock			
	Interest Income	Interest Expense	NII	Interest Income	Interest Expense	NII	ΔNII	Interest Income	Interest Expense	NII	ΔNII
0Q–1Q	132.50	57.50	75.00	157.50	82.50	75.00	0.00	182.50	107.50	75.00	0.00
1Q–2Q	133.75	58.75	75.00	158.75	83.75	75.00	0.00	183.75	108.75	75.00	0.00
2Q–3Q	135.50	60.50	75.00	160.50	85.50	75.00	0.00	185.50	110.50	75.00	0.00
3Q–4Q	137.25	62.25	75.00	162.25	87.25	75.00	0.00	187.25	112.25	75.00	0.00
4Q–5Q	138.75	63.75	75.00	163.75	88.75	75.00	0.00	188.75	113.75	75.00	0.00
5Q–6Q	140.25	65.25	75.00	165.25	90.25	75.00	0.00	190.25	115.25	75.00	0.00
6Q–7Q	140.50	65.50	75.00	165.50	90.50	75.00	0.00	190.50	115.50	75.00	0.00
7Q–8Q	142.50	67.50	75.00	167.50	92.50	75.00	0.00	192.50	117.50	75.00	0.00

TABLE 9.41   Interest income of asset A4 for base and two shock scenarios using forecasted rates with an interest rate cap on 1-month LIBOR

Time Bucket	Base Case		+100 bps		+200 bps	
	Effective Rate (%)	Interest ($)	Effective Rate (%)	Interest ($)	Effective Rate (%)	Interest ($)
0Q–1Q	5.30	132.50	5.50	137.50	5.50	137.50
1Q–2Q	5.35	133.75	5.50	137.50	5.50	137.50
2Q–3Q	5.42	135.50	5.50	137.50	5.50	137.50
3Q–4Q	5.49	137.25	5.50	137.50	5.50	137.50
4Q–5Q	5.50	137.50	5.50	137.50	5.50	137.50
5Q–6Q	5.50	137.50	5.50	137.50	5.50	137.50
6Q–7Q	5.50	137.50	5.50	137.50	5.50	137.50
7Q–8Q	5.50	137.50	5.50	137.50	5.50	137.50

In this case the bank has sold the option. The client has purchased this cap to protect herself against the upward movement of the interest rate. At each period that 1-month LIBOR exceeds 2%, the bank pays the client based on the difference between the 1-month LIBOR at the beginning of the period and the 2% cap rate. By netting against the interest payment from the client to the bank, effectively the client payments are capped based on the interest rate of 2% + 3.5% = 5.5%, so at no period does the client's interest rate exceed 5.5%. The maximum quarterly interest income for the bank from the asset A4 is calculated as:

$$10,000 \times \frac{2 + 3.5}{100} \times \frac{90}{360} = 137.50$$

Table 9.41 presents the interest income for asset A4, including the impact of the embedded interest rate cap option. In the base scenario, since the spot and forecasted 1-month LIBOR for periods 0, 1, 2, and 3 from Table 9.37 are below 2%, the interest rate cap does not become effective in the 0Q–1Q, 1Q–2Q, 2Q–3Q, and 3Q–4Q time buckets and the effective total interest rate and interest income amounts are the same as the case without interest rate cap. Starting from period 4 the forecasted 1-month LIBOR exceeds the strike rate of 2%; hence, the client effective rate and interest amount are capped at 5.5% and $137.50 in time buckets 4Q–5Q, 5Q–6Q, 6Q–7Q, and 7Q–8Q. Figure 9.17 compares the quarterly interest income amount for asset A4 with and without the embedded interest rate cap option in the base case.

Table 9.41 also presents the interest income of asset A4 with the embedded interest rate cap option for two shock scenarios. In these scenarios, since the 1-month LIBOR are assumed to be 1% and 2% higher compared to

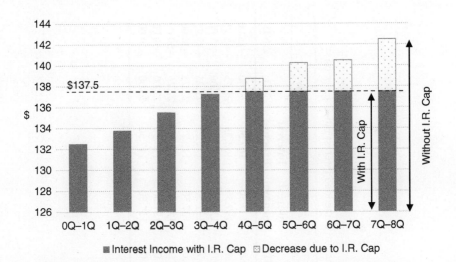

FIGURE 9.17 Effect of interest rate cap on base case interest income from asset A4

the original forecasted rates, the shocked 1-month LIBOR are higher than the 2% strike rate and hence the interest rate cap is applicable in all quarterly buckets. The effective interest rate and interest income of asset A4 for both +100 and +200 shock scenarios in all time buckets are capped at 5.5% and $137.50. For example, for the +100 bps shock scenario the interest income in 7Q–8Q time bucket is calculated as:

$$10{,}000 \times \frac{Min(2, 2.2 + 1) + 3.5}{100} \times \frac{90}{360} = 137.50$$

Assuming the liability L4 is as before, we can obtain the net interest income of the bank considering the interest incomes from asset A4 with the embedded cap option and the interest expenses from the liability L4. Table 9.42 presents the NII for the base and shock scenarios and the ΔNII for +100 bps and + 200 bps shock scenarios. For example, the net interest income in time bucket 7Q-8Q for +100 bps shock scenario is calculated by taking the difference between the interest income of asset A4 with the embedded cap option and the interest expense of liability L4 as:

$$NII = \$137.50 - \$92.50 = \$45.00$$

In Table 9.42, unlike the case without the embedded cap option, for a given scenario the net interest incomes are different across time buckets and also different among scenarios. This is due to the impact of the embedded cap

TABLE 9.42 Net interest income for base and two shock scenarios when asset A4 has an embedded interest rate cap option

Time Bucket	Base Case			+100 bps Shock				+200 bps Shock			
	Interest Income	Interest Expense	NII	Interest Income	Interest Expense	NII	ΔNII	Interest Income	Interest Expense	NII	ΔNII
0Q–1Q	132.50	57.50	75.00	137.50	82.50	55.00	−20.00	137.50	107.50	30.00	−45.00
1Q–2Q	133.75	58.75	75.00	137.50	83.75	53.75	−21.25	137.50	108.75	28.75	−46.25
2Q–3Q	135.50	60.50	75.00	137.50	85.50	52.00	−23.00	137.50	110.50	27.00	−48.00
3Q–4Q	137.25	62.25	75.00	137.50	87.25	50.25	−24.75	137.50	112.25	25.25	−49.75
4Q–5Q	137.50	63.75	73.75	137.50	88.75	48.75	−25.00	137.50	113.75	23.75	−50.00
5Q–6Q	137.50	65.25	72.25	137.50	90.25	47.25	−25.00	137.50	115.25	22.25	−50.00
6Q–7Q	137.50	65.50	72.00	137.50	90.50	47.00	−25.00	137.50	115.50	22.00	−50.00
7Q–8Q	137.50	67.50	70.00	137.50	92.50	45.00	−25.00	137.50	117.50	20.00	−50.00

option. As the forecasted interest rate has an upward trend, the increase in the 1-month LIBOR increases the interest expense; however, the interest income is capped at $137.50 in any time bucket. This leads to a decrease in the NII in later time buckets. The effect of the interest rate cap is even more noticeable in +100 bps and +200 bps shock scenarios, as higher interest expense and capped interest income lead to a lower NII and therefore negative ΔNII in all time buckets for both shock scenarios.

The optionality of a position can have a significant impact on its interest income or expense, and its sensitivity to the change in interest rate level. The earning gap method cannot capture the impact of such optionality and detailed scenario analysis, similar to what has been explained here, is required to estimate the impact of options on *NII* and ΔNII.

CURRENCY EXCHANGE RATE SCENARIO ANALYSIS

A cross-currency exchange rate is another principal risk factor that can affect the earnings of a bank with a multi-currency balance sheet. The study of the impact of change in cross-currency exchange rates (FX rates) on the earnings in general, and on the net interest income in particular, is a typical component of ALM analysis of multi-currency banks. A *currency exchange rate scenario* or *exchange rate shock* is a change applied to one or more currency conversion rates to obtain *shocked conversion rates*. In practice, there are several methods to design exchange rate shocks in NII analysis. To explain these methods, we first need to learn about currency forward rates. In the following section we introduce the currency forward contract and interest rate parity. Then we use these concepts to introduce a few methods to design currency exchange rate shocks. After that we demonstrate the use of shocked exchange rates in NII analysis.

Currency Forward and Interest Rate Parity

A currency exchange forward contract (FX forward) is a derivative product that locks in the currency exchange rate for a pair of currencies at a specific time in the future, hence removing the uncertainty of the exchange rate volatility at the target future date. Consider a case when a bank expects to receive €10 million in income from a subsidiary 90 days from now. Since in 90 days the bank is supposed to exchange the euros to dollars, it enters into a currency forward contract offered by a brokerage firm, to sell euros and buy dollars, with a 90-day maturity date for a €10 million amount. Assume the contractual rate of the forward contract is EUR-USD 1.1723, that is, €1 will be exchanged for $1.1723 at the maturity date of the contract. By entering into this contract, the bank hedged its exposure to the EUR-USD exchange rate risk factor, since no matter what the spot exchange rate is at the maturity of the contract, it converts the €10 million at the 1.1723 contractual rate. At the maturity of the contract the bank pays the brokerage firm €10,000,000 and receives €10,000,000 × 1.1723 = $11,723,000. Currency forward contracts often have a cash settlement option, where only the net amount is transferred from one side to the other. Assume at the maturity date of the above forward contract the spot EUR-USD exchange rate is 1.1678. In this case and if cash settlement is chosen, the brokerage firm pays the bank $(1.1723 - 1.1678) \times$ €10,000,000 = $45,000. The bank can convert the €10 million at the spot rate of 1.1678 receiving €10,000,000 × 1.1678 = $11,678,000, and considering the $45,000 received from the brokerage firm, the total amount is $11,678,000 + $45,000 = $11,723,000. This is the same amount the bank would receive if delivery settlement option was chosen.

Each currency forward contract can be decomposed into two components (*legs*). For example, the above currency forward contract from point of view of the bank can be characterized as follows:

	Notional	Currency	Term
Pay	10,000,000.00	EUR	90 days
Receive	11,723,000.00	USD	

To value a currency forward contract at any time between contract initiation and its maturity, we need to consider both cash flows in their original currencies occurring at the maturity date, discount them from the maturity date to the valuation date using the relevant interest rates, and then convert the discounted cash flow in one currency to the other currency, using the spot exchange rate at the time of valuation. For example, assume that 30 days have passed from the inception of the above currency forward contract and that the EUR-USD spot exchange rate at this time is 1.1700. Assume that the USD risk-free rate at this time is 1.4% and the EUR risk-free rate is 1.3%, both annualized rates compounded annually, with an Act/365 accrual basis. The value of the currency forward contract in USD at this time is obtained as:

$$V_{USD} = \textit{Value of Receive Leg in USD} - \textit{Value of Pay Leg in USD}$$

$$= \frac{11,723,000 \; USD}{(1 + 0.014)^{\frac{60}{365}}} - \frac{10,000,000 \; EUR \times 1.1700}{(1 + 0.013)^{\frac{60}{365}}}$$

$$= \$21,054.00$$

This can be generalized as follows:

$$V_{Rec_t} = \frac{N_{Rec}}{(1 + r_{Rec})^{T-t}} - \frac{N_{Pay} \times S_t}{(1 + r_{Pay})^{T-t}} \qquad (9.9)$$

where:

V_{Rec_t} = Value of currency forward contract in receive currency at time t
N_{Rec} = Notional amount of receive currency
r_{Rec} = Risk-free interest rate in receive currency (annualized rate with annual compounding)
N_{Pay} = Notional amount of pay currency
r_{Pay} = Risk-free interest rate in pay currency (annualized rate with annual compounding)
S_t = Spot exchange rate at valuation time t in receive currency per unit of pay currency
$T - t$ = Time to maturity of contract based on applicable accrual basis

Or equivalently we have:

$$V_{Rec_t} = \frac{N_{Pay} \times F_{0,T}}{(1 + r_{Rec})^{T-t}} - \frac{N_{Pay} \times S_t}{(1 + r_{Pay})^{T-t}} \qquad (9.10)$$

where:

$F_{0,T}$ = contractual forward exchange rate at inception of contract at time 0 and for term T in receive currency per unit of pay currency

The method we used to derive the valuation of currency forward contract highlights the relationship between interest rates in two currencies and their exchange rate. A currency forward contract at its inception ($t = 0$) should have zero value to either party; therefore using Equation (9.10) and assuming one unit of notional amount of pay currency, we have:

$$\frac{F_{0,T}}{(1 + r_{Rec})^T} = \frac{S_0}{(1 + r_{Pay})^T}$$

or

$$F_{0,T} = \frac{(1 + r_{Rec})^T}{(1 + r_{Pay})^T} \times S_0 \qquad (9.11)$$

where both spot and forward exchange rates are in receive currency per unit of pay currency. Equation (9.11) is known as *covered interest rate parity*.

This equation indicates that, in the absence of transaction cost and tax complication, for a currency pair, forward and spot exchange rates are associated with each other through the risk-free interest rates in those currencies.

Interest rate parity is a market state achieved when investors have no preference in investing in bank deposit products offered in two different currencies. This condition is based on an arbitrage-free pricing principle, where return of investment in bank deposits in one currency for a given period of time is equivalent to the return of investment in the second currency, considering the exchange rate. Interest rate parity condition is based on assumption that two bank deposit products, with respect to risk and liquidity, are complete substitutes of each other and there is no restriction on movement of capital from one currency to the other.

If the interest rate parity condition does not hold, an investor can (i) borrow in lower interest rate currency, (ii) exchange the principal to the second currency at spot rate, (iii) invest in a deposit product of the second currency with the higher interest rate, (iv) exchange back to the first currency at the end of the investment period, (v) repay the borrowed amount and earn a profit in the process. If such an arbitrage opportunity exists, market participants take advantage of it and erode the opportunity quickly, leading to the interest rate parity state again.

In *uncovered interest rate parity*, the arbitrage-free state explained above is achieved without the use of currency forward contracts. Using notation of domestic and foreign currencies, uncovered interest rate parity can be formulated as:

$$E[S_T] = \frac{(1 + r_{DC})^T}{(1 + r_{FC})^T} \times S_0 \tag{9.12}$$

where:

S_0 = Spot exchange rate in domestic currency per unit of foreign currency
$E[S_T]$ = Expectation of spot rate at time T in domestic currency per unit of foreign currency
r_{DC} = Risk-free rate in domestic currency (annualized rate with annual compounding)
r_{FC} = Risk-free rate in foreign currency (annualized rate with annual compounding)

When the arbitrage-free state is achieved with the use of currency forward contracts, the condition is known as covered interest rate parity, which is discussed when Equation (9.11) is derived. Using notation of domestic and foreign currencies, covered interest rate parity can be stated as:

$$F_{0,T} = \frac{(1 + r_{DC})^T}{(1 + r_{FC})^T} \times S_0 \tag{9.13}$$

where:

$F_{0,T}$ = Forward exchange rate in domestic currency per unit of foreign currency as of time $t = 0$ and for term T

By comparing Equations (9.11), (9.12), and (9.13) it can be deduced that when the no-arbitrage state is achieved the forward exchange rate is an unbiased estimator of the future spot exchange rate. In practice, the uncovered interest rate party more or less holds for major currencies where capital can flow easily between countries. The covered interest rate parity is affected by the transaction costs and tax issues, resulting in deviation from the no-arbitrage state. This allows for the arbitrage trading activities. There was a significant deviation from the covered interest rate parity during the financial crisis of 2007–2009 due to market uncertainty and counterparty risk. Most currencies have a very active and liquid forward market, where for each currency pair many market participants provide quotes for forward exchange rates with different terms. Banks sometimes use forward exchange rates as a forecast of spot exchange rates in the future periods for NII analysis.

Exchange Rate Shock Scenarios

In the following discussions we assume that all exchange rates are in the domestic currency per unit of a foreign currency and the domestic currency is the functional currency of the bank. Banks with currency trading desks often utilize quantitative and econometric models for forecasting currency exchange rates and utilize these forecasts in their trading activities and hedging their trading books. While market-quoted forward exchange rates are not always the best estimations of future spot rates, in the lack of better forecasting methods, they can be used in ALM scenario analysis. Particularly in NII analysis, we can use forward rates to convert the expected net interest income earned in future time buckets from a local currency to the functional currency of the bank. This method is often used to obtain the base NII for a multi-currency balance sheet. There are a few methods available for creating shocked currency exchange rates for NII analysis:

1. This method is based on assuming appreciation (or depreciation) of domestic currency in all forward exchange rates by a certain percentage. Hence the forward exchange rates used as forecasted rates for all time buckets of NII analysis are shocked and decreased (or increased) accordingly.
2. In this method we assume that the spot exchange rate is increased (or decreased) by a certain percentage but risk-free rates in domestic and foreign currencies are unchanged. Then using covered interest rate parity we

can calculate the shocked forward exchange rates and use them as fore-casted rates for NII time buckets.

3. In this method we assume that the spot exchange rate is unchanged but risk-free rates in domestic and foreign currencies are shocked (i.e., by applying either a parallel or non-parallel shock to the currency spot curve). Then using covered interest rate parity we can calculate the shocked forward exchange rates and use them as forecasted rates for NII time buckets.

4. In this method we assume that the spot exchange rate is increased (or decreased) by a certain percentage and also risk-free rates in domestic and foreign currencies are shocked. Then using covered interest rate parity we can calculate shocked forward exchange rates and use them as forecasted rates for NII time buckets.

While there are other ways to create shocked exchange rate scenarios, analysis based on the above four methods should provide plenty of information to the bank managers about the currency exchange rate risk factor and its implication on the net interest income.

The general procedure to perform exchange rate shock analysis for NII is as follows:

1. Obtaining forecasts of the interest income and the interest expense in the local currencies for all time buckets during the NII time horizon.

2. Obtaining forecasted spot exchange rates when the interest income or expense in the local currencies are to be converted to the functional currency. For simplicity, sometimes it is assumed that the conversion happens at the end of each time bucket.

3. Calculating the base net interest income (NII_0) for each time bucket by converting the interest income and expense in the bucket from the local currency to the functional currency using forecasted spot exchange rates from the previous step.

4. Using one of the methods described above, obtaining shocked forecasted spot exchange rates for all time buckets during the NII time horizon.

5. Calculating the shocked net interest income (NII_s) for each time bucket by converting the interest income and expense in the bucket from the local currency to the functional currency using shocked forecasted spot exchange rates from the previous step.

6. Difference between the shocked NII and the base NII, which are both con-verted to the functional currency, is the change in the net interest income due to the assumed exchange rate shock.

To demonstrate the use of shocked currency exchange rates in NII anal-ysis, assume a bank has interest-earning assets in USD and EUR while all

TABLE 9.43 Expected interest income and expense of a hypothetical bank for the next four quarters in local currencies

		Q1	Q2	Q3	Q4
Income	EUR	500,000	525,000	480,000	645,000
	USD	680,000	565,000	340,000	730,000
Expense	USD	220,000	210,000	285,000	390,000

liabilities of this bank are in USD. The functional currency of the bank is USD. Table 9.43 provides the expected interest income and interest expense of this bank for the next four quarters in their associated currencies. Assume that the current spot EUR-USD rate is $S_0 = 1.1850$ and forward exchange rates with terms at the end of each four quarters in the future are $F_{0,1Q} = 1.1855$, $F_{0,2Q} = 1.1865$, $F_{0,3Q} = 1.1874$, and $F_{0,4Q} = 1.1862$. These exchange rates are all in U.S. dollars for one unit of euro.

For the base scenario, here we use the forward exchange rates as the forecasted spot exchange rates to convert EUR-based interest income, and then by adding USD-based interest income we can obtain the total interest income in each time bucket. Since the interest expenses are all in USD, NII can be calculated by taking the difference between USD-equivalent total interest income and USD-based interest expense in each quarterly time bucket. Table 9.44 summarizes this calculation. The last row in this table provides the base scenario net interest income of the bank in its functional currency U.S. dollar in a quarterly time bucket scheme.

Assume that the annually compounded risk-free rates with 3-, 6-, 9-, and 12-month terms for USD and EUR are as presented in Table 9.45. To create

TABLE 9.44 Calculation of net interest income for a base scenario using forward exchange rates as forecasts of spot exchange rates

		Q1	Q2	Q3	Q4
EUR-based	EUR	500,000	525,000	480,000	645,000
interest	× [USD per 1 EUR]	1.1855	1.1865	1.1874	1.1862
Income	= USD (I)	592,750	622,913	569,952	765,099
USD-based interest income (II)		680,000	565,000	340,000	730,000
Total interest income (USD) (III) = (I) + (II)		1,272,750	1,187,913	909,952	1,495,099
Interest expense (USD) (IV)		220,000	210,000	285,000	390,000
NII_0 (USD) (IIII) – (IV)		1,052,750	977,913	624,952	1,105,099

TABLE 9.45 USD and EUR risk-free rates with 3-, 6-, 9-, and 12-month terms

Term:	3M	6M	9M	12M
r_{USD}	1.00%	1.20%	1.22%	1.31%
r_{EUR}	0.83%	0.94%	0.95%	1.21%

a shocked currency exchange rate scenario, here we consider the case where EUR-USD spot exchange rate is shocked when USD is appreciated by 5%, and then using risk-free rates listed in Table 9.45 we recalculate forward exchange rates using covered interest rate parity. The spot exchange rate after appreciation of USD by 5% is 1.1286, so shocked forward exchange rate with term ending Q1 using Equation (9.13) is calculated as:

$$F_{0,1Q_s} = \frac{(1 + 0.0100)^{0.25}}{(1 + 0.0083)^{0.25}} \times 1.1286 = 1.1290$$

Subscript s is used here to indicate a shocked value. Shocked forward exchange rates with 6-, 9-, and 12-month terms are obtained similarly as $F_{0,2Q_s} = 1.1300$, $F_{0,3Q_s} = 1.1308$, and $F_{0,4Q_s} = 1.1297$.[6] Part I of Table 9.46

TABLE 9.46 Part I: Calculation of net interest income for shock scenario using shocked forward exchange rates as forecasts of spot exchange rates. Part II: Change in net interest income for exchange rate shock scenario.

		Part I:			
		Q1	Q2	Q3	Q4
EUR-based	EUR	500,000	525,000	480,000	645,000
interest income	× [USD per 1 EUR]	1.1290	1.1300	1.1308	1.1297
(USD)	= USD (I)	564,524	593,250	542,801	728,666
USD-based interest income (II)		680,000	565,000	340,000	730,000
Total interest income (USD) (III) = (I) + (II)		1,244,524	1,158,250	882,801	1,458,666
Interest expense (USD) (IV)		220,000	210,000	285,000	390,000
NII_s (USD) (IIII) – (IV)		1,024,524	948,250	597,801	1,068,666

	Part II:			
	Q1	Q2	Q3	Q4
ΔNII (USD)	(28,226)	(29,663)	(27,151)	(36,433)

presents the calculation of the net interest income using these shocked forward exchange rates as forecasts of spot exchange rates and part II of this table shows the change in the net interest income in USD, calculated as the NII of the shock scenario minus NII of the base scenario. Here the negative ΔNII figures indicate the potential adverse effect of U.S. dollar appreciation on the net interest income of this bank.

NET INTEREST INCOME HEDGING

Changes in interest and exchange rates can adversely impact the net interest income of a bank. The scenario analysis discussed in the previous sections enables banks to identify the potential risks related to such changes, to quantify the impact of them on the net interest income, and to plan accordingly. Broadly speaking, a decrease in the earning gap in a balance sheet is the key in decreasing the interest rate risk of the net interest income. Generally, this can be accomplished by *matched maturity funding* (i.e., funding short-term assets with short-term liabilities and long-term assets with long-term liabilities) and *matched rate funding* (i.e., funding fixed-rate assets with fixed-rate liabilities and floating-rate assets with floating-rate liabilities). In every bank, treasury department, and in particular ALM unit, coordinate activities of various business units with the funding plans to decrease the earning gap to a manageable level within the risk tolerance of the bank. Coordination and planning on asset origination, new product approval, funding plan development, contingency liquidity planning, and new debt issuance are important factors in managing the earning gap.

Typically, the ALM unit of a bank's treasury department is tasked with managing two types of risk: interest rate gap risk and basis risk. Interest rate gap risk arises when asset and liability positions have different setups and timing with respect to change in the interest rate level. For example, if a bank has floating-rate liability positions that reset on a semi-annual frequency, but its asset positions reset quarterly, this bank faces interest rate gap risk. Another case that leads to the rise of interest rate gap risk is when the liabilities of a bank are mostly the fixed-rate type but its assets are mostly the floating-rate type. In both cases a decrease in interest rate level leads to a decrease in the net interest income. Interest rate basis risk arises when floating-rate asset and liability positions are based on different interest rate indexes; for example, assets are based on the prime index rate and liabilities are based on 1-month LIBOR. In this case, non-parallel movement of the underlying indexes may lead to a decrease in the net interest income.

Banks often use derivative products, such as interest rate swap contracts, to hedge the interest rate gap risk. To demonstrate the use of interest rate swaps in NII hedging, consider a hypothetical bank with the following asset and liability positions, both initiated at the current date:

> Asset: Principal amount of $1,000, interest rate of 1-month LIBOR + 5%, term of five years, semi-annual payment and reset frequencies, Act/360 accrual basis.

> Liability: Principal amount of $1,000, interest rate of 3% fixed, term of five years, semi-annual payment frequency, Act/360 accrual basis.

Net interest margin (NIM) is the difference between interest rates of the asset and liability positions, in percentage. Assume that the current 1-month LIBOR is 1.8%. The net interest margin of two positions on the balance sheet of this bank is:

$$NIM = 1.8\% + 5\% - 3\% = 3.8\%$$

This net interest margin of 3.8% is calculated at the inception date of the positions based on the 1-month LIBOR at that date but due to the floating-rate nature of asset, this net interest margin is not constant and can change as the level of 1-month LIBOR changes. The net interest margin remains at the 3.8% level until the next reset date of the asset position. Assume that at that date the 1-month LIBOR increases to 2.8%. Then the net interest margin also increases to 4.8%. However, conversely, a decrease in 1-month LIBOR to 0.8% decreases the net interest margin to 2.8%. Focusing only on these two positions, the bank in our example is asset-sensitive, and a decrease in interest rate leads to a decrease of its net interest income. To hedge this risk, the bank can use a fixed-float interest rate swap contract. We introduced this derivative contract in a previous chapter. Assume the bank enters into an interest rate swap with notional amount of $1,000 and 5-year term. The bank is the floating-rate payer with 1-month LIBOR + 2% rate and the counterparty is the fixed-rate payer with 3% rate. The notional amount of the swap contract is equal to the principals of the asset and liability positions and payment frequency and day count convention are also the same. Fixed-rate payments based on 3% rate received by the bank from the swap counterparty are the same as payments made to the investor of the liability position with the same rate. Floating-rate payments received by the bank from the asset position are based on 1-month LIBOR + 5% while floating-rate payments made to the swap counterparty are based on 1-month LIBOR + 3%. Therefore, by entering into this plain-vanilla swap contract, the bank effectively locked in a net interest margin of 2%, the difference between spread on the floating leg of the swap and the spread of the asset position. This net interest margin remains constant throughout the 5-year term of all contracts. While this action removes the potential of a windfall from a possible increase in interest rate, it hedges the net interest income of

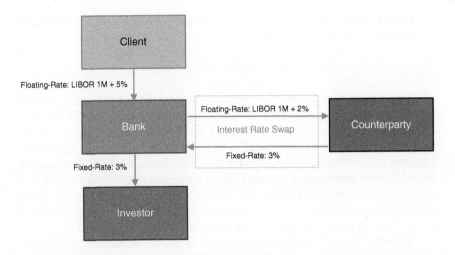

FIGURE 9.18 Using interest rate swap contract to hedge interest rate gap risk

the bank against the risk of decrease in 1-month LIBOR. Figure 9.18 presents a schematic view of the cash flows and their rates between the bank, the swap counterparty, the investor, and the client. Note that, if the day count conventions, payment frequencies, or reset frequencies of the asset and liability positions, and the swap contract are not the same, the cash flows will not perfectly match, and the hedge is not completely effective.

Interest rate basis swap contracts can be used to hedge a bank's exposure to basis risk. These contracts are similar to the interest rate swap contract discussed before but both legs of basis swap are floating-rate type but based on different indexes. For example, one leg of the contract can be based on 1-month LIBOR and the other based on the prime rate. The 1-month LIBOR, 3-month LIBOR, 6-month LIBOR, prime rate, SOFR, and fed funds rate are the most common indexes used in basis swap contracts. To demonstrate the use of a basis swap in hedging the interest rate basis risk of the NII, consider a hypothetical bank with the following two positions, both initiated at the current date:

Asset: Principal amount of $1,000, interest rate of 6-month LIBOR + 2%, term of five years, semi-annual payment and reset frequencies, Act/360 accrual basis.

Liability: Principal amount of $1,000, interest rate of 1-month LIBOR + 0.30%, term of five years, semi-annual payment and reset frequencies, Act/360 accrual basis.

Assume that the current 1-month and 6-month LIBOR are 1.8% and 2.2% respectively. The current net interest margin of these two positions is:

$$NIM = (2.2\% + 2\%) + (1.8\% + 0.3\%) = 2.1\%$$

This margin remains intact until the next reset date of positions. Assume that at the next reset date both the 1-month and 6-month LIBOR increase by 30 bps. Since the change of both asset and liability rates is equal, the net interest margin remains unchanged at 2.1%. However, assume the case where 1-month LIBOR increases by 20 bps while the 6-month LIBOR increases by 30 bps. In this case the net interest margin decreases to 2%. Focusing only on these two positions, due to different interest rate indexes, the decrease of the spread between 6-month LIBOR and 1-month LIBOR at upcoming reset dates would have an adverse impact on the net interest income of the bank.

To hedge this risk, the bank can use an interest rate basis swap contract. Assume it enters into a swap contract with a $1,000 notional amount, where the bank pays based on the 6-month LIBOR and the counterparty pays based on 1-month LIBOR + 0.30%. Since the notional amount of the swap contract is equal to the principals of the asset and liability positions, and payment frequency and day count convention are the same, floating-rate cash flows based on the 1-month LIBOR + 0.30% rate received by the bank from the swap counterparty are the same as payments made to the investor of the liability position with the same rate. Floating-rate cash flows received by the bank from the asset position are based on 6-month LIBOR + 2% while floating-rate payments made to the swap counterparty are based on 6-month LIBOR. By using this basis swap contract, the bank effectively locked in a net interest margin of 2%, the difference between spread on the pay leg of the swap (from the point of view of the bank) and the spread of the asset position. Change in the interest rate, whether affecting 1-month and 6-month LIBOR equally or not, would not have any impact on this margin (assuming day count conventions, and payment and reset frequencies of the positions and the swap contract match). This net interest margin remains constant throughout the 5-year term of all contracts. While this action removes the potential of a windfall from a possible widening of spread between 6-month and 1-month LIBOR indexes, which is beneficial to the bank, it hedges the net interest income against the risk of a narrowing of this spread in the future. Figure 9.19 presents a schematic view of the cash flows and their rates between the bank, the swap counterparty, the investor, and the client, in the example discussed here.

Banks also use derivative products to hedge the net interest income against the exchange rate risk. A currency exchange forward contract, introduced earlier in this chapter, is often used to hedge exchange rate risk for a future cash flow that is known or can be estimated with good precision.

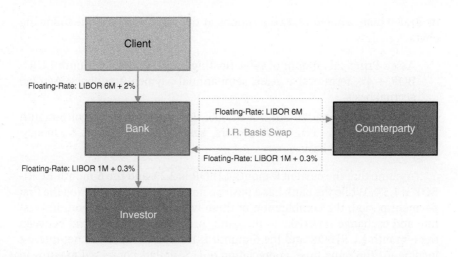

FIGURE 9.19 Using interest rate basis swap contract to hedge basis risk

A *cross-currency interest rate swap* is another derivative product that is widely used by banks and other firms to hedge the exchange rate risk. This type of swap contract is similar to the interest rate swap discussed earlier but two legs of the contract are denominated in different currencies. Another difference between these contracts is the exchange of notional or principal amounts. In interest rate swap two sides of the contract do not exchange the notional amount, but in a cross-currency interest rate swap, the notional amounts that are in two different currencies are usually exchanged at the inception and returned at the maturity of the contract. Since interest rate of each leg of a cross currency swap can be fixed or floating, the contract can be used to hedge both interest and exchange rate risks.

To demonstrate the use of the cross-currency interest rate swap, here we use an example that involves conversion of cash flows between euros and U.S. dollars. Assume a bank has a better presence in the U.S. capital market and can borrow with a more favorable term in U.S. dollars. At the same time, the bank has a euro-based lending opportunity. The bank is planning to borrow $1,000 for five years at a 6-month LIBOR + 0.5% rate, exchange the proceeds at the current spot exchange rate of 1.1111 EUR-USD to €900, and lend out this amount for five years with a 6-month EURIBOR + 4% rate. The bank is planning to convert the interest income at each payment date back to U.S. dollars to cover the interest expense payable for the liability position, and when the loan is matured, convert the €900 back to U.S. dollars and repay its $1,000 debt. Therefore, two positions at the inception have the following characteristics:

> Asset: Principal amount of €900, floating interest rate of 6-month EURIBOR + 4%, term of five years, semi-annual payment frequency, Act/360 accrual basis.

> Liability: Principal amount of $1,000, floating interest rate of 6-month LIBOR + 0.5%, term of five years, semi-annual payment frequency, Act/360 accrual basis.

Assume that the current 6-month LIBOR is 2.2% and the 6-month EURIBOR is 1.5%. While the bank has a positive net interest margin during the first payment period, the combination of these two positions poses both interest rate and exchange rate risks to the bank. A decrease of the spread between the 6-month EURIBOR and the 6-month LIBOR can reduce the net interest income. At the same time, appreciation of U.S. dollars compared to euros in the future can also have an adverse impact on the net interest income. To hedge these risks, the bank enters into a 5-year cross-currency interest rate swap where it is the payer of €900 with a 6-month EURIBOR + 4% rate and receiver of $1,000 with a 6-month LIBOR + 2.5% rate. The payment and reset frequencies of the swap are assumed as semi-annual and day count convention is Act/360.

At the inception of the contract, the bank converts $1,000 that it has borrowed to €900 through the exchange of notional of the swap contract and uses it to originate the loan. At each payment date, it receives interest income based on €900 and the rate of 6-month EURIBOR + 4% from the client and passes it to the swap counterparty and receives 6-month LIBOR + 2.5% rate based on $1,000. It uses this cash inflow to pay the interest expense on the $1,000 liability. This, irrelevant of the level of the 6-month EURIBOR and 6-month LIBOR locks in a net interest margin of 2% for the bank on $1,000. At the maturity date the bank receives €900 from the client, passes it to the swap counterparty, receives $1,000, and uses it to close the liability position. Using the cross-currency interest rate swap, the bank has effectively hedged both exchange rate and interest rate risks while locking in a constant net interest margin throughout the entire life of the positions. This comes at the expense of relinquishing the potential of windfall from a favorable movement of interest rate and exchange rate in the future that could increase the net interest margin. As before, for this hedge to work effectively, payment frequency, reset frequency, and day count convention of loan, debt, and swap positions should be aligned. Figure 9.20 presents a schematic view of the cash flows and their rates at each payment date of this example.

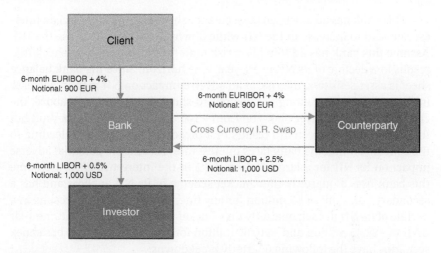

FIGURE 9.20 Using cross-currency interest rate swap contract to hedge interest rate and currency exchange rate risks. Shown cash flows and rates are for each interest payment date.

NET INTEREST INCOME RISK LIMITS

Banks usually use commercial ALM software that can handle a large number of positions and different product types to calculate the NII for the base case and various shock scenarios. Results from such a scenario analysis are often compared to predetermined limits to assess the potential risk on the net interest income and total earnings of the bank. These limits represent the risk appetite of the bank with respect to the interest rate and exchange rate risk factors. The tolerance limits related to net interest income are either established based on the maximum allowable change in NII for the entire time horizon or for a given time bucket during the horizon. For example, assume that for a bank five interest rate shock scenarios resulted in the following changes in the expected net interest income during a 1-year time horizon:

1. Parallel +100 bps shock on current spot curve: $\Delta NII = +\$13,500,000$
2. Parallel +200 bps shock on current spot curve: $\Delta NII = +\$15,500,000$
3. Parallel -100 bps shock on current spot curve: $\Delta NII = -\$8,450,000$
4. Parallel −200 bps shock on current spot curve: $\Delta NII = -\$10,650,000$
5. A steepening shock on current spot curve that increases rates at all term points but with different amounts: $\Delta NII = +\$8,350,000$

This bank has an asset-sensitive balance sheet as upward shocks on interest rate lead to increase in the NII while downward shocks decrease the NII. Assume this bank has a $10 million risk limit for any interest rate shock that results in a decline of its NII in a 1-year time horizon. Since the bank balance sheet is asset-sensitive, the risk of an adverse impact on NII is from decrease in the interest rate. Among the downward shock scenarios listed above, the change in NII for a 1-year horizon from −100 bps is within the risk limit but the −200 bps shock scenario results in a breach of the risk limit, leading to the conclusion that the bank faces interest rate risk and the potential adverse impact on its NII for a large decline of 2% in the interest rate. Now assume this bank uses a quarterly time bucket scheme in its NII analysis and has a secondary risk limit of $5 million for any interest rate shock that results in a decline of its NII in each quarterly time bucket. Also assume that the one-year ΔNII of −$8.45 million and −$10.65 million for −100 bps and −200 bps shock scenarios have the following quarterly breakdowns:

(in $million) Scenario	Q1 ΔNII	Q2 ΔNII	Q3 ΔNII	Q4 ΔNII	Total 1-Year ΔNII
−100 bps parallel shock	−$3.10	1.20	−5.40	−1.15	−8.45
−200 bps parallel shock	−3.90	1.60	−6.50	−1.85	−10.65

For a −100 bps shock scenario, although the total 1-year ΔNII is within the $10 million risk limit, the third quarter ΔNII of −$5.4 million has breached the $5 million permissible limit. The third quarter ΔNII in −200 bps parallel shock scenario also exceeded this limit, indicating the mismatch between the interest income and expense is more severe in that quarter. The purpose of NII risk limits that are specific to a time bucket is to ensure the bank's ALM and interest rate risk management is focused on more granular time periods than just annual performances.

Another risk limit applicable to the net interest income is based on restricting the earning gap. Recall from an earlier section that the earning gap is the difference between rate-sensitive assets and rate-sensitive liabilities. When the absolute value of the earning gap is high, the bank faces the interest rate risk with respect to its NII. When the earning gap is positive, decrease in interest rate results in decline in the NII, and when earning gap is negative, increase in interest rate results in a decline in the NII. Therefore, banks may place limits on the maximum positive level of the earning gap to manage the NII risk for downward changes in the interest rate and set limits on the minimum negative level of the earning gap for upward changes.

The NII risk limits are usually set based on the overall risk appetite of the bank. However, regulatory requirements are often incorporated in the limit settings. Banks usually perform NII analysis based on parallel shocks (e.g., +100 bps, +200 bps, +300 bps, −100 bps, −200 bps, or −300 bps) and non-parallel shocks (steepening, flattening, and butterfly) and for each scenario have a different risk limit, either for the entire time horizon or for each time bucket. Some of the factors that are usually considered in setting NII risk limits are as follows:

- The bank's risk appetite and tolerance level for changes in earnings
- Regulatory requirements and the maximum allowable loss in NII that impacts the capital level of the bank
- Products offered on the asset side of the balance sheet
- Funding channels and liability type
- Planned changes to the balance sheet or new product offering
- The expectation of changes in risk factors in the future

REQUIRED DATA AND OTHER CONSIDERATIONS IN NII ANALYSIS

The complexity of the NII analysis depends on the diversity of a bank's assets and liabilities, and types of financial instruments that exist on the balance sheet or on the off-balance-sheet books. In calculating the expected interest income or expense, characteristics of each financial instrument should be considered in the analysis. For example, financial instruments with explicit or implicit optionality may behave differently in different interest rate environments, and this can impact the generated interest income or expense. As illustrated throughout this chapter, positions' characteristics and market data are required data in an NII analysis. In this section we summarize some of the key inputs and other points that should be considered in an NII analysis.

- **Forecast of Risk Factors:** Forecasted interest rates, exchange rates, and other risk factors for the duration of the analysis time horizon are required inputs in the NII analysis. For the interest rate risk factor, while the implied forward rates based on the current spot curve reflect overall market expectation of future interest rates, in practice the implied forward rates often perform poorly as forecasts of future rates for medium-term analysis time horizon (e.g., three to five years).
- **Forecast of Changes in Balance Sheet:** As discussed earlier, in a dynamic view of the balance sheet, planned and expected changes in the balance sheet are incorporated in an NII analysis. A bank's *corporate planning* unit develops short- to medium-term business plans that outline strategic changes in portfolios, including acquisitions and sales

intentions. These business plans are crucial inputs in the NII analysis when a dynamic view of the balance sheet is assumed.

- **Funding Plan:** A bank's treasury and corporate planning units develop funding plans that reflect the funds needed for medium to long-term horizon, along with the availability of funding sources and timing of future debt issuances. Such funding plans are designed and developed not only to address business needs but also to satisfy the internal liquidity requirements and external regulatory rules (e.g., LCR ratio, discussed in a later chapter). When a dynamic view of the balance sheet is assumed, the funding plan is a required input in the NII analysis, which along with existing liability structure determines the interest expense part of the NII during the analysis time horizon.

- **Behavioral Assumptions and Models:** Forecasting of balances and characteristics of some financial products require the use of quantitative models and application of certain assumptions. For deposit products, forecasting of future account balances at an aggregated level requires various assumptions regarding customers' behaviors on future deposits and withdrawals based on different market conditions and the competitive nature of the bank's deposit offerings. For credit card receivable portfolios assumptions of future volume of cards usage, paydown rates at due dates, and percentage of account balances that are revolving are required to model the interest income for those portfolios. For line-of-credit product types (e.g., personal line of credit and HELOC) assumptions related to future drawdowns and repayments are needed to obtain forecasted balances. These assumptions are often derived using quantitative models that are developed based on historical portfolio data and expectations of future econometric variables, such as GDP and the unemployment rate.

- **Delinquencies, Non-Accruals, and Defaults:** Delinquent accounts may or may not contribute to the interest income of the bank. Non-accrual or non-performing loans, while still on books of the bank, do not generate interest income. The existence of delinquent and non-performing positions on current balance sheet of the bank and the potential of change in their numbers and balances during the analysis time horizon should be incorporated in the NII analysis. Banks often use quantitative models to forecast the occurrence of new defaults in their portfolios during a specific future period. Since such positions no longer contribute to the NII, the impact of new loan defaults during the analysis time horizon should also be incorporated in the NII analysis. Delinquencies, non-accruals, and defaults are all crucial inputs that can have material impact on the NII in base and shock scenarios.

- **Interest Rate Path Dependency:** For some products, such as mortgage loans or mortgage-backed securities, the forecasted interest amounts earned or incurred depend not only on the level of the forecasted interest rate but also on the path the rate takes during the analysis time horizon. When the level of the forecasted interest rate changes, depending on the path of the interest rate during the analysis time horizon, prepayment and refinancing result in changes in the mortgage portfolios and their outstanding balances. These changes impact interest earnings on existing positions while providing the opportunity for new originations with new effective rates. Interest earnings from investment in mortgage-backed securities are also affected by prepayment of underlying loans. The possibility and timing of such changes in the structure of a portfolio should be considered when forecasting its interest income or expense.

- **Options:** Many financial products include implicit or explicit options that impact their interest cash flows. For the NII analysis we need to incorporate the impact of such options on the interest income or expense calculations. For example, the interest income from a floating-rate loan with a contractual cap on the coupon rate is limited by the cap. When the forecasted interest rate increases to a level that the cap becomes effective, the exercise of the cap option limits the interest income earned from the loan. Similarly, for a floating-rate debt with a contractual floor on the coupon rate, when the forecasted interest rate decreases to a level that the floor becomes effective, the exercise of the floor option should be considered when calculating the interest expense of the debt. Many banks issue callable debt securities to be able to manage their interest expense in the case of a sizable change in the interest rate level. Depending on the forecasted interest rate during the analysis time horizon, the possibility and timing of a call on an existing debt note and potential for issuance of replacement debt with a new rate should be considered in the NII analysis. Alternatively, if a bank carries a callable security in its investment portfolio, a call by the issuer impacts the portfolio composition and its interest income, and this should be considered in the analysis.

BASEL ACCORD GUIDANCE ON NII ANALYSIS

In the previous chapter we introduced the Basel standard released in 2016, which provides directions for EVE analysis. That standard also considers the net interest income as one of the metrics suitable for the measurement of interest rate risk in the banking book. The NII analysis required by the standard is based on two prescribed interest rate shock scenarios. The standard sets the following guideline for calculation of ΔNII (Basel Committee on Banking Supervision 2016):

- Banks should include expected cash flows, with inclusion of margins and spreads, of all interest rate-sensitive assets, liabilities, and off-balance-sheet items in the banking book.

- NII analysis should be based on a constant balance sheet where maturing positions are replaced by identical positions with regard to the characteristics, rates, and spreads. Repricing of new volumes required to hold the balance sheet constant should be considered.
- ΔNII should be reported for a rolling 12-month period.
- There are two prescribed interest rate shock scenarios to be analyzed. They are:
  1. Parallel shock up
  2. Parallel shock down

Construction of these shocks for different currencies are done in a similar way explained in the previous chapter for EVE analysis.

SUMMARY

- Net interest income is the difference between the interest income earned and the interest expense incurred during a specific time horizon.
- In a runoff view of the balance sheet when positions are matured or amortized during the analysis time horizon, they are not replaced, and new positions of maturing products or new volumes of non-maturing products are assumed only to the extent needed for funding and balancing the balance sheet.
- In static or constant view of the balance sheet when positions are matured or amortized during the analysis time horizon they are replaced by similar positions to keep the forecasted balance sheet constant and comparable to the balance sheet as of the analysis date.
- In a dynamic view of the balance sheet, new positions of maturing products and new volumes of non-maturing products are incorporated into the forecasted balance sheet to reflect the future business and funding plans.
- In the net interest income analysis, focus is on interest-sensitive assets and liabilities while fixed assets, intangible assets, and equity of the bank are not included in the analysis.
- The effective rate of a fixed-rate instrument does not change during the NII analysis time horizon.
- The effective rate of a floating-rate instrument changes during the NII analysis time horizon. There are three ways to obtain an estimate of the rate index used in a floating-rate instrument: using implied forward rate, using forecasted rate, or using simulated rate.
- In NII analysis, when rate setting dates of floating-rate positions fall within time buckets, it may be necessary to separate each time bucket into two or more sections defined by rate setting dates.

- Interest rate gap risk arises when asset and liability positions have different setup and timing for change in the interest rate level.
- Interest rate basis risk arises when floating-rate asset and liability positions are based on different interest rate indexes.
- The basic earning gap analysis is based on the net value of the total principal amounts of rate-sensitive assets and liabilities that are expected to be repriced, matured, amortized, or run-off during a period in the future.
- Decrease of the earning gap is the key to managing the interest rate gap risk. Matched maturity funding and matched rate funding are two methods to decrease the earning gap. The matched maturity funding approach is based on funding short-term assets with short-term liabilities and long-term assets with long-term liabilities. The matched rate funding approach is based on funding fixed-rate assets with fixed-rate liabilities and floating-rate assets with comparable floating-rate liabilities.
- In an interest rate scenario analysis, a parallel or non-parallel instantaneous shock is applied to the current spot curve and the resulting NII is compared with the NII in the base case.
- An upward shock to the interest rate increases the NII of an asset-sensitive balance sheet while a downward shock decreases the NII.
- An upward shock to the interest rate decreases the NII of a liability-sensitive balance sheet while a downward shock increases the NII.
- A position's implicit or explicit option can impact its interest income or expense.
- In a multi-currency balance sheet, we can use forward exchange rates to convert future interest incomes or expenses in the base case of the NII analysis.
- For NII analysis of a multi-currency balance sheet, an exchange rate shock scenario can be created by a shock to the forward rates, or a combination of shock to the spot rates and to the risk-free interest rates of a currency pair. Then the resulting NII is compared with the base NII to estimate the impact of the shock scenario.
- Covered interest rate parity defines the relationship between spot and forward exchange rates of a currency pair.
- Interest rate parity is a market state achieved when investors have no preference in investing in bank deposit products offered in two different currencies. This is based on arbitrage-free pricing principle.
- In uncovered interest rate parity, the arbitrage-free state of interest rate parity is achieved without the use of currency forward contracts.
- Plain-vanilla interest rate swap, basis swap, and cross-currency swap contracts can be used to hedge the net interest income of a bank.
- Net interest margin is the difference between the interest rates of the asset and liability positions.

- NII risk limits are set based on a bank's risk appetite and regulatory requirements.
- Forecasted interest rates and exchange rates, expected changes in the balance sheet, funding plans, and behavioral assumptions are main inputs of the NII analysis.

NOTES

1. It should be noted that, since the prime rate usually moves in discrete intervals, such as 10 or 25 basis points, here the 4.2984% level is an approximation to facilitate the calculation of forecasted interest income in a future time bucket.
2. For simplicity, here we do not consider other cash flows such as operating expenses that can impact the cash account balance.
3. Even in a runoff view of the balance sheet, a matured fixed-rate debt position may need to be replaced to provide funding for the outstanding assets and balancing the balance sheet.
4. Floating-rate positions based on LIBOR reference rate often have an Act/360 accrual basis. For simplicity, here we assumed a 30/360 basis.
5. Interest rate cap or floor contracts based on LIBOR reference rate often have an Act/360 accrual basis. For simplicity, here we assumed a 30/360 basis to be aligned with the assumption for underlying asset A4.
6. For simplicity, here we assumed that the ending times of the next four quarters are 0.25, 0.50, 0.75, and 1 year.

BIBLIOGRAPHY

Basel Committee on Banking Supervision. "Interest Rate Risk in the Banking Book." Bank for International Settlements, April 2016. https://www.bis.org.

Basel Committee on Banking Supervision. "Principles for the Management and Supervision of Interest Rate Risk." Bank for International Settlements, July 2004. https://www.bis.org.

CHAPTER 10

Equity and Earnings at Risk

I n previous chapters we discussed how the economic value of equity (EVE) and net interest income (NII) are obtained. We then followed with a study of the impact of change in different risk factors on those metrics. We focused on one scenario at a time when a risk factor, such as interest rate, was shocked, and the impact on ALM metrics was analyzed. Scenario analysis is a very useful tool in ALM analysis; however, its use is limited only to those scenarios considered. For example, what we learn from the results of a +100 bps parallel shock to the spot curve is applicable only to that scenario. The management team of a bank is often interested in gaining insight on scenarios that would produce extremely adverse conditions for the bank, both from a balance sheet management point of view as well as the earnings. However, identifying those extreme scenarios may not be possible and, even when identified once, they may change as economic and market conditions change or as the balance sheet and products of the bank evolve.

A common approach in the analysis of extreme scenarios is to use simulation to construct probability distribution of an ALM metric and use that distribution to obtain information on likelihoods of extreme cases and their potential impacts on the bank balance sheet and earnings. This approach is based on a very popular risk management technique known as value-at-risk (VaR). VaR methodology was first introduced by the risk management group at J.P. Morgan in 1994. It was later commercialized when RiskMetrics™ was spun off from J.P. Morgan in 1998 and then acquired by MSCI in 2010.[1] One of the common uses of VaR is in trading desks' limits setting, based on risk assessments obtained from daily VaR analysis.

In this chapter we first introduce the concept of value-at-risk and then extend its application to EVE and NII. In doing so we focus on two general methods of scenario generation: historical sampling and Monte Carlo simulation methods, and our discussion will be focused on two important risk factors of interest rate and currency exchange rate. The generation of simulated scenarios for these two risk factors based on the Monte Carlo method requires the use of stochastic models. We introduce a few of these models in this chapter and discuss how they can be used to generate the simulated values of risk factors.

INTRODUCTION TO VALUE-AT-RISK

Value-at-risk (VaR) is a measurement of the maximum potential loss in value of a financial instrument or a portfolio of instruments over a given period of time with a probabilistic confidence level. The period of time that is used for estimation of potential loss is known as the VaR *time horizon*. Consider a financial instrument, for instance, a corporate bond. The price of this bond changes during a trading day and also from one day to another. A natural and necessary question for an investor is "If I invest in this bond, what is the maximum amount of loss that I may have in my investment in a period of time, say one month?" Here, the 1-month period is the investment horizon. The worst-case scenario in this situation is obviously a loss equal to the entire investment. For example, if the investor purchased a $1,000 face value corporate bond at a price of 98, the worst-case loss for him is to lose the entire $980 he paid for the bond (assuming no commission, fee, or tax). While a loss of total investment is possible (e.g., a default event with no prospect of recovery), the likelihood of the complete loss of the investment is small. Considering this probability, the investor may refine his question to "What is the maximum amount of loss that I may have in my investment in one month, with a confidence level of, say 95%?" In other words, the investor is asking for the maximum loss possible in his investment in a 1-month horizon, assuming there is a 5% chance that the maximum loss exceeds the measurement he is looking for. In this case, VaR is the measurement that the investor is seeking.

Assume that the current value of the bond is V_0, its value at the horizon is V_h, and return on this investment is R. One way to define R is as follows:

$$R = \frac{V_h - V_0}{V_0} \tag{10.1}$$

There are other ways to define the return on an investment, and we will discuss one of them later in this chapter, but for now the definition of return given here suffices for introduction of VaR. Based on this, a negative return over the investment horizon indicates a loss, a positive return represents a gain, and a return of zero means the value of the bond is not changed over the horizon. Now assume you were able to determine the probability distribution of the bond return, as shown in Figure 10.1. Later in this chapter we discuss how this is done. Point A in this graph represents a zero return, so current bond value can be indicated by R_A, which is zero. If point B in the graph denotes the return that represents the fifth percentile of the distribution (data sorted from lowest to highest), we can state that with 95% probability any return is equal to or above the return represented by point B:

$$P(R \geq R_B) = 95\%$$

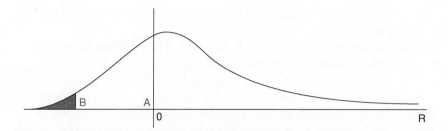

FIGURE 10.1 Probability distribution of return of a corporate bond

Thus, with a 95% probability the maximum negative return or maximum loss is the return represented at point B. Return R_B, when converted to a dollar value, is 1-month VaR with a 95% confidence limit. It is important to notice that VaR provides a probabilistic representation of maximum loss, not a deterministic one. In this example there is still a 5% chance that the maximum negative return exceeds R_B. Also note that VaR is measured using a one-sided confidence interval.

Formally a T-period, C% confidence limit of VaR in the form of a return is defined as:

$$VaR_{C\%} = \{r \mid P(R \geq r) = C\%\} \tag{10.2}$$

where R is the random variable representing the T-period return of the financial instrument. Once VaR in return form is derived it can be converted to a dollar value. For example, if returns are defined as in Equation (10.1), VaR can be converted to a dollar value by multiplying it by the current value of the bond. To calculate VaR for a given confidence limit of C% we must determine the $100(1 - C)$th percentile of return over the required time horizon. For example, for determining VaR with a 90% confidence limit, we need to sort the return data from the lowest to the highest and find the 10th percentile value.

In the preceding example we focused on only one instrument. To find VaR for a portfolio of instruments we need to consider the portfolio's total return and therefore the correlation of returns of individual instruments within the portfolio must be taken into account.

From this discussion two characteristics of VaR are clear:

1. VaR is determined for a given time horizon. For trading securities, such as stocks and bonds, it is common to calculate daily VaR. Daily VaR can be scaled for other time horizons using the approximation in Equation (10.3):

$$T - Day\ VaR \cong \sqrt{T} \times 1\text{-}Day\ VaR \tag{10.3}$$

For example, to determine the 10-day VaR we can multiply daily VaR by $\sqrt{10} = 3.162$ as an approximation.

2. VaR is associated with a confidence limit. The existence of such confidence limit highlights the probabilistic nature of the VaR.

Generally, there are three methods for measuring value-at-risk, although there are many variations of these methods used in practice. In the following sections we introduce each of these methods briefly and later in this chapter we explain their applications in ALM.

Variance-Covariance Method

According to this method the first step in measuring VaR is to determine the probability distribution of the return. Consider a financial instrument where its 1-day return has a normal distribution with mean μ and standard deviation σ, where volatility of the return is stationary and independent of time. Since the probability distribution is fully determined, finding the percentile and hence VaR for a given confidence limit is straightforward. For instance in this case the 95% confidence limit 1-day VaR is -1.645σ. Note that, since VaR is expressed using a one-sided confidence limit here, we used a 1.645 multiplier for a 95% one-sided confidence limit.[2] So $P(R \geq -1.645\sigma) = 95\%$.

Now consider a portfolio consisting of two instruments, with T-period returns that are normally distributed with means μ_1 and μ_2, standard deviations σ_1 and σ_2, and covariance σ_{12}. If weights of instruments in the portfolio are ω_1 and ω_2, the portfolio return is normally distributed with mean μ_p and variance σ_p^2 obtained as:

$$\mu_P = \omega_1\mu_1 + \omega_2\mu_2 \tag{10.4}$$

$$\sigma_P^2 = \omega_1^2\sigma_1^2 + \omega_2^2\sigma_2^2 + 2\omega_1\omega_2\sigma_{12} \tag{10.5}$$

Since the portfolio return is normally distributed, determining portfolio VaR is similar to the single instrument case. For this example, assuming that the returns and standard deviations in the previous equations are for a 1-day time horizon, the 99% confidence limit for a 1-day portfolio VaR is $-2.326\sigma_P$, where 2.326 is the Z-score for a 99% one-sided confidence interval.

Extension of this method to a portfolio of n instruments is straightforward. If we assume that the return of instrument i is normally distributed with mean μ_i and standard deviation σ_i, the portfolio return has a multivariate normal distribution. Multivariate normal distribution is discussed in the Appendix to this book. Assume weights, means, and variance-covariance of T-period returns of n instruments are summarized in matrix notation as follows:[3]

$$
\mu = \begin{bmatrix} \mu_1 \\ \mu_2 \\ \vdots \\ \mu_n \end{bmatrix} \qquad \omega = \begin{bmatrix} \omega_1 \\ \omega_2 \\ \vdots \\ \omega_n \end{bmatrix} \qquad \Sigma = \begin{bmatrix} \sigma_{11} & \sigma_{12} & \cdots & \sigma_{1n} \\ \sigma_{21} & \sigma_{22} & \cdots & \sigma_{2n} \\ \vdots & \vdots & \ddots & \vdots \\ \sigma_{n1} & \sigma_{n2} & \cdots & \sigma_{nn} \end{bmatrix} \tag{10.6}
$$

where σ_{ii} is the variance of return i and σ_{ij} is the covariance of returns i and j. The portfolio mean and variance are obtained as:

$$
\mu_p = \omega'\mu = [\omega_1 \ \omega_2 \ \cdots \ \omega_n] \begin{bmatrix} \mu_1 \\ \mu_2 \\ \vdots \\ \mu_n \end{bmatrix} = \sum_{i=1}^{n} \omega_i \mu_i \tag{10.7}
$$

$$
\sigma_p^2 = \omega'\Sigma\omega = [\omega_1 \ \omega_2 \ \cdots \ \omega_n] \begin{bmatrix} \sigma_{11} & \sigma_{12} & \cdots & \sigma_{1n} \\ \sigma_{21} & \sigma_{22} & \cdots & \sigma_{2n} \\ \vdots & \vdots & \ddots & \vdots \\ \sigma_{n1} & \sigma_{n2} & \cdots & \sigma_{nn} \end{bmatrix} \begin{bmatrix} \omega_1 \\ \omega_2 \\ \vdots \\ \omega_n \end{bmatrix} = \sum_{i=1}^{n}\sum_{j=1}^{n} \omega_i \omega_j \sigma_{ij} \tag{10.8}
$$

The variance-covariance matrix can be obtained using the historical return data. After the variance of a portfolio return is calculated, the VaR for a given confidence limit and time horizon can be determined as before. Derivation of variance-covariance matrix using the historical data of instruments' returns is often computationally preventive. The historical return data for certain instruments may not be readily available and as the number of instruments in the portfolio increases, the number of variance and covariance elements increases rapidly. Also, for actively managed funds, every time the portfolio is adjusted by removing some instruments and adding new ones, the variance-covariance matrix needs to be recomputed.

An alternative method to this approach is to segregate and map each instrument in the portfolio to one or more standard instruments, each representing a specific risk factor. Selected standard instruments are liquid and have sufficient historical data for volatility calculation. For example, a zero-coupon 3-month T-bill can be a standard instrument representing the interest rate risk factor for a 3-month term. We can then determine variance-covariance matrix for the set of all standard instruments and use it to calculate the standard deviation and VaR of the original portfolio (Damodaran 2007).

In this approach, we first segregate and map the original instruments into standard instruments, where each original instrument is represented by an equivalent set of positions in standard instruments. For example, an amortized loan with four remaining payments can be mapped to four zero-coupon Treasury instruments with the same terms and amounts of loan cash flows. After this we deal only with a replacement portfolio consisting of standard instruments, which is equivalent to the original portfolio. Once the variance-covariance matrix of the standard instruments is determined, we can calculate the standard deviation of the return for the replacement portfolio using Equation (10.8) and obtain the standard deviation of the return for the original portfolio.

The variance-covariance method is intuitive and easy to implement but the clear limitation of this approach is the need for probability distribution of return. An inaccurate assumption for the probability distribution of return may result in imprecise measurement of VaR. For example, if the true distribution of the return has a long tail, the assumption of normal distribution may result in underestimating the true VaR. Another issue to consider is the possibility of a non-stationary volatility structure. In more sophisticated approaches the volatility of the return is changing over time.

Historical Sampling Method

In this method historical data of return of an instrument or a portfolio of instruments is used to determine the VaR. Unlike the variance-covariance method, in this approach no explicit assumption about the distribution of the return is required, but there is an implicit assumption that historical changes in instruments values are reasonable representations of future changes.

To determine the VaR according to this method, the time series of return data are used to obtain the percentile for the desirable confidence limit. To demonstrate this method, assume that we have daily returns for the past 250 trading days of an equity asset. Figure 10.2 shows the time series of daily returns in percentage for this security. The time index represents the day that

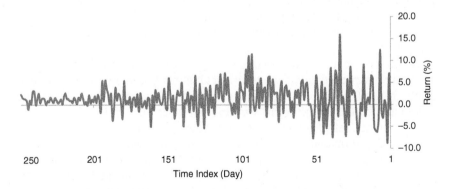

FIGURE 10.2 Time series of daily returns in percentage

each return is associated with, where index 1 is used to designate the most recent return, index 2 is for one day before the most recent day, and so on. The oldest data is designated by a time index of 250.

We can use the historical returns to find the VaR. For example, to find the 95% VaR we need to find the 5th percentile of the return data distribution. To do this, first we assume each daily return has an equal probability of reoccurrence. In other words, we consider that each daily return, irrespective of how recent or old it is, has equal chance of happening again. Since there are 250 daily returns available each has a probability of 1/250 or 0.004. Table 10.1 shows a partial view of the daily return data in our example, reordered based on an increasing size of return. This table also shows the probability and cumulative probability of each return. For example, the day with index 3 has the lowest historically observed return of –8.664% in the past 250 days. Since our target is the 5th percentile, we need to interpolate the return values for

TABLE 10.1   Finding 95% VaR using historical daily returns

Time Index	Return (%)	Probability	Cumulative Probability
3	–8.664	0.004	0.004
53	–7.707	0.004	0.008
40	–7.233	0.004	0.012
31	–7.018	0.004	0.016
23	–6.700	0.004	0.020
46	–6.632	0.004	0.024
10	–6.232	0.004	0.028
11	–6.039	0.004	0.032
126	–5.323	0.004	0.036
44	–5.301	0.004	0.040
12	–5.073	0.004	0.044
162	–5.046	0.004	0.048
140	–4.884	0.004	0.052
22	–4.834	0.004	0.056
130	–4.628	0.004	0.060
29	–4.575	0.004	0.064
...	...	...	...
19	9.056	0.004	0.984
96	10.998	0.004	0.988
94	11.449	0.004	0.992
8	12.396	0.004	0.996
35	15.955	0.004	1.000

the rows with a cumulative probability of 0.048 and 0.052. To do this, we can use a linear interpolation as follows:

$$R = R_l + (p - p_l)\frac{R_h - R_l}{p_h - p_l} \tag{10.9}$$

Using $\rho = 0.05$, $p_l = 0.048$, $p_h = 0.052$, $R_l = -5.046\%$, and $R_h = -4.884\%$ in Equation (10.9) provides us with $R = -4.965\%$. Therefore the 95% daily VaR in percentage is 4.965%. Aside from the linear interpolation used here, there are other methods available to obtain percentile of a discrete distribution. A few of them are presented in the Appendix to this book.

While considering an equal probability for each historical daily return is acceptable, there are cases that may require applying different weights to different observed data. For example, sometimes it may be more appropriate to consider recent data as more relevant in determining VaR compared to older data. This is even more important if there has been a shift in the volatility of the return. In our example we can see from Figure 10.2 that the volatility of the return is significantly higher in recent days (closer to time index 1) compared to older dates (toward time index 250). This could be the result of a change in market condition or an idiosyncratic event related to this stock. If we assign equal probabilities to all historical data, the obtained VaR may be understated. To address this issue, we can adjust the probabilities assigned to historical returns. The most common way to do this is to consider an *exponential weighting* scheme with a *decay factor* λ. In this method each data point is weighted by $(1 - \lambda)\lambda^{t-1}/(1 - \lambda^N)$ where t for the most recent day is 1 and increases for older data, and N is total number of data points available. Division by $1 - \lambda^N$ is to make the weights add up to 1. The decay factor is a number between 0 and 1. A lower decay factor results in higher weights assigned to the more recent data and vice versa. For example, with a decay factor $\lambda = 0.95$ and $N = 250$, the weight of the most recent day ($t = 1$) is 0.05, for the day before that ($t = 2$) is 0.0475, and so on. If we use this weighting scheme with a decay factor of 0.95 in our example, the 95% daily VaR is determined to be around 7.609%, which is significantly higher than the 4.965% we obtained with equal weights. The reason for this is obvious from Figure 10.2. Since during the past 250 days a noticeable increase in volatility has occurred, considering all historical data with equal weights results in a lower VaR compared to the case where higher weights are assigned to more recent data when volatility was higher.

Using a low decay factor results in assigning higher weights to more recent data while a higher decay factor has the opposite effect. The use of a high decay factor is suitable when volatility is stable. Figure 10.3 presents

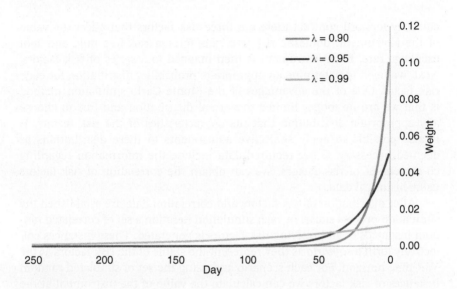

FIGURE 10.3 Exponential weights for three different decay factors. Day $t = 1$ is the most recent date and $t = 250$ is the oldest date.

exponential weights for 250 historical data points for three different decay factors of 0.99, 0.95, and 0.90.

Bootstrapping is an alternative approach in the historical sampling method where the available historical return data are first resampled using a random scheme and then used for construction of the probability distribution of the return. The advantage of historical sampling in obtaining VaR is the absence of a need to make an explicit assumption on the probability distribution of returns. However, there are disadvantages to this method. First and foremost, this approach makes an explicit assumption that the history is a good representation of the future. That may not be a valid assumption in some cases. Another drawback of this approach is that historical data may not be available for different instruments, especially for new products with insufficient past performance data.

Monte Carlo Simulation Method

Another method in obtaining value-at-risk is Monte Carlo simulation. In this approach and at the first step we need to identify all risk factors that affect the value of the instrument or a portfolio of instruments. For example, for a currency forward contract there are three risk factors that affect the value of the instrument: domestic risk-free rate, foreign risk-free rate, and spot exchange rate. Each instrument is then mapped to a series of risk factors. Next, we need to determine an appropriate probability distribution for each risk factor. One of the advantages of the Monte Carlo simulation method is that we are no longer limited to normal distribution and free to choose any appropriate distribution that fits characteristics of the risk factors. It is also possible to apply subjective adjustments to these distributions as deemed necessary. Other required data include the information regarding co-movement of risk factors. We can obtain the correlation of risk factors using historical data.

After distribution of risk factors and correlation data are established the simulation process starts. In each simulation iteration a set of correlated random instances of all involving risk factors is generated. These instances collectively form a *scenario* as they represent the status of the risk factors at the VaR time horizon. For each scenario and using the set of simulated random instances of risk factors we can calculate the value of the instrument at the time horizon. Return for the given scenario is then obtained as the difference between the current value of an instrument and the calculated value at the time horizon using simulated risk factors, in percentage form. By repeating these steps many times we can generate enough instances of the instrument return to construct its discrete probability distribution. Having this empirical probability distribution, and similar to the historical sampling method, we can determine the VaR at the desired percentile.

Example

Consider a portfolio that consists of two fixed-rate bonds as follows:

> Asset A: $1,000,000 notional value 6% semi-annual corporate bond, 18 months to maturity, non-callable, non-putable, 30/360 day count convention
>
> Asset B: $2,000,000 notional value 8% semi-annual corporate bond, 12 months to maturity, non-callable, non-putable, 30/360 day count convention

Assume that the latest coupons of two bonds are just paid. A schematic view of the remaining cash flows of these two bonds is shown in Figure 10.4.

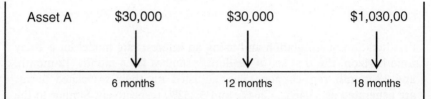

FIGURE 10.4 Assets A and B cash flows used in an example for the use of a Monte Carlo simulation in VaR calculation

Cash flows consist of coupon payments (three for asset A and two for asset B) and return of face values at the maturity. For simplicity assume the interest rate is the only risk factor considered and no credit spread is included in the valuation of securities. The first step is to map assets A and B into a set of risk factors. Since here the cash flows occur at 6-month, 12-month, and 18-month intervals, the appropriate risk factors are zero-coupon rates for these terms. Assume that current zero-coupon rates with 6-month, 12-month, and 18-month terms are 2%, 2.5%, and 3.5%, respectively, adjusted for their associated terms. Hence, the current values of individual assets and the portfolio are calculated as:

$$V_{A0} = \frac{30,000}{1+0.02} + \frac{30,000}{1+0.025} + \frac{1,030,000}{1+0.035} = \$1,053,849$$

$$V_{B0} = \frac{80,000}{1+0.02} + \frac{2,080,000}{1+0.025} = \$2,107,700$$

$$V_{P0} = V_A + V_B = \$3,161,549$$

Index 0 is used to represent current value. Note that here we calculated the current value of the portfolio using a discounted cash flow method. If market prices are available, it may be more appropriate to use those to determine the current portfolio value. To find VaR, in the

(continued)

(*continued*)

first iteration of simulation and using an interest rate model for a 1-day time horizon, the first set of random instances for 6-month, 12-month, and 18-month zero-coupon rates, adjusted for their associated terms, are generated as 3.046%, 4.264%, and 5.252%, respectively. Similar to the preceding calculation and using these rates, the values of assets A and B and portfolio P for scenario 1 are calculated as $1,036,487, $2,072,570, and $3,109,056, respectively. To obtain VaR we can either construct the distribution of return and then convert the return at the target percentile to a dollar amount, or directly construct the distribution of change-in-value in a dollar amount. Here we use the latter approach. The difference between instruments and portfolio values in scenario 1 and their current values is:

$$\Delta V_{A1} = V_{A1} - V_{A0} = -\$17,363$$

$$\Delta V_{B1} = V_{B1} - V_{B0} = -\$35,130$$

$$\Delta V_{P1} = V_{P1} - V_{P0} = -\$52,493$$

Repeating this process many times produces enough instances to build the empirical probability distribution and to determine the VaR. For example, we repeated the process 10,000 times and ranked the calculated change-in-values from the lowest to the highest. The 95% VaR is the 500th lowest value, and 99.5% VaR is the 50th lowest value. The following table shows the dollar value of 95% and 99.5% VaR that we obtained for our example using 10,000 simulated scenarios:

	99.5% VaR ($)	95% VaR ($)
Asset A:	30,720	21,177
Asset B:	63,439	49,911
Portfolio P:	76,779	58,843

As noted in the previous example the summation of VaR of asset A and VaR of asset B is not equal to VaR of portfolio P in either 95% or 99.5% confidence limit cases. The reason for this is the correlation between change-in-values (or returns) of asset A and asset B. Generally, for a portfolio with n asset, we have:

$$VaR_P \leq \sum_{i=1}^{n} VaR_i \tag{10.10}$$

The equality in Equation (10.10) is for the case when returns of assets in the portfolio are not correlated. This result highlights the effect of *diversification* in a portfolio in reducing its market risk.

As mentioned before, one of the advantages of the Monte Carlo simulation method in determining VaR is the flexibility in the use of different probability distributions for different risk factors. While this is an advantage in the sense that we are no longer limited to the normal distribution, it may also appear as a limitation for this method. Defining a probability distribution for a risk factor may not be always feasible or accurate. In practice, instead of assuming a particular probability distribution, stochastic models that simulate the evolution of the risk factor through time are developed and used. In upcoming sections of this chapter we discuss a few of such stochastic models.

Another issue to consider in using the Monte Carlo simulation is its computational time and the complexity of its calculations. As the number of relevant risk factor increases, the number of iterations required to obtain a good estimate for the desirable percentile also increases accordingly. One approach to address this issue is the use of a variance reduction techniques such as *importance sampling*, which focuses the sampling around the area of interest and hence reduces the need for a large number of iterations.

Conditional Value-at-Risk

From our discussion so far it should be clear that VaR does not represent extreme losses. When you determine the value of 90% VaR, it is implied that there is a 10% probability that loss may exceed that value, but VaR by itself provides no information about the loss beyond this value. When an extreme loss has occurred the actual loss can be much higher than VaR. *Conditional value-at-risk (CVaR)*, also known as *expected shortfall*, is a measurement that attempts to provide further information about the loss beyond a VaR point. CvaR is the conditional expectation of the return subject to the return being below the VaR. Formally CvaR is defined as follows:

$$CVaR_{C\%} = E[R \mid R \leq VaR_{C\%}] \tag{10.11}$$

where R is the random variable representing the return. You may find this definition in different forms in other references and books. Here we are following a return notation in the sense that a negative return represents a loss; thus, if the return is less than the VaR, it means the loss exceeded the VaR.

Value-at-risk can be used as a measurement of potential loss in a portfolio of financial instruments. The flexibility in measurement methods has led to popularity of VaR as a risk measurement tool for different risk factors. Use of VaR as a risk measurement has increased significantly since the 1990s when it was first introduced. Risk managers throughout the finance industry and their regulatory counterparts depend on VaR measurements to quantify underlying risks of different portfolios.

Selection of the method of calculation of VaR depends on its use and the availability of the data. For a short time horizon, the variance-covariance method provides a reasonable estimate of the VaR with low standard errors. When there are substantial historical data available for different risk factors, a historical sampling method can be used. Monte Carlo simulation is the method of choice when assets in the portfolio have non-linear payoff structures (e.g., options).

VaR is highly sensitive to the inputs used in its derivation. If returns do not follow a normal distribution, VaR calculated using variance-covariance method, the way introduced earlier here, is unreliable and requires revision. In the historical sampling method it is explicitly assumed that historical data is a good representative of future events. This may not be always true and in fact can lead to misjudgment about the riskiness of a portfolio. Incorrect assumptions of probability distributions used in the Monte Carlo simulation method also may render the VaR results inaccurate and biased.

VaR is not an exact representation of loss in the value of an asset or a portfolio of assets and should not be considered as such. The very probabilistic nature of VaR indicates that considering VaR as the only measurement of loss is not prudent and such a supposition could be catastrophic. Many academicians and practitioners blame the heavy reliance on VaR in financial risk management as one of the catalysts to overconfidence that led to the global financial crisis of 2007–2009.

It is important to note that VaR does not quantify extreme losses. When you calculate a 95% 1-day VaR of $1,000,000, there is a 5% probability that the loss may exceed the $1,000,000 but the measurement is indifferent to the magnitude of such a loss (is the extreme loss $5,000,000 or $10,000,000? VaR would not answer that).

Many banks, investment banks, and broker-dealers use VaR as a risk control tool. Risk management departments of those financial firms usually establish a daily VaR limit for their portfolio managers and monitor their positions accordingly. Heavy reliance on VaR as a risk control tool can be dangerous.

First, VaR does not consider extreme cases. While the VaR of a portfolio may well be within the acceptable range, the extreme scenario such as a sudden movement in market or heavy concentration on certain assets within the portfolio may result in large losses that are well beyond the VaR. Second, VaR can be gamed. Portfolio managers that understand the nature and method of calculation of VaR can take advantage of it by taking excessive risks while staying within the required VaR limits.

While VaR is a useful method that provides insight into risk and potential future losses, it should be used as a supplement to prudent risk management practices, supplemented with a robust and intelligent regulatory oversight.

APPLICATION OF VAR METHODOLOGY IN ALM

The concept of VaR can be extended and used in ALM analysis. In previous chapters we discussed assessment of the impact of interest rate changes on economic value of equity and net interest income and in each case we considered various instantaneous shock scenarios and studied their impacts. Consider a bank where a scenario analysis revealed that a +100 bps instantaneous parallel shock in spot curve decreases bank's economic value of equity by $22 million. Also for the same bank another scenario analysis revealed a steepening shock where the spot curve is shocked +100 bps at a 2-year term, and after, decreases the net interest income by $110 million. While these two scenarios are useful and informative to the bank management, they have limited scope and cannot provide insight into a potential decrease in EVE and NII due to other possible changes in interest rate. By extending the concept of VaR to EVE and NII we can obtain a probabilistic view into potential changes that can impact the earnings and capital of the bank.

Equity-at-risk determines the maximum potential decrease in the economic value of equity of the bank due to changes in different risk factors, such as interest rate, for a specific time horizon and a specific confidence level. *Net interest income-at-risk* determines the maximum potential decrease in the net interest income of the bank due to changes in risk factors, during a specific time horizon and for a specific confidence level. While our emphasis in this chapter is on the net interest income, by inclusion of non-interest income, such as fees and other revenues, we can define *earnings-at-risk* (EaR) as the maximum potential decrease in estimated earnings of the bank due to changes in risk factors, during a specific time horizon and for a specific confidence level.

Before we start our discussion on equity- and earnings-at-risk, we need to clarify a few terms, including analysis date, time horizon, time step, and horizon date. The *analysis date* is the as-of date of the analysis, often chosen as the most recent month-end date. For example, for an analysis performed during the month of January 2019, the selected analysis date can be December 31, 2018. The *time horizon* is the period during which the changes in EVE or NII are considered. For example, a time horizon can be one year. A time horizon is divided into several *time steps* and risk factors evolve through these time steps. For example, a 1-year time horizon can be divided into 12 monthly time steps. Each simulated path of a risk factor evolves through these 12 time steps where the value of the risk factor changes from one month to the next. The *horizon date* is the future date at the end of the time horizon, specified as the analysis date plus the time horizon. For example, if the analysis date is December 31, 2018, and the time horizon is one year, then the horizon date is December 31, 2019. Figure 10.5 provides a schematic view of these terms.

Equity-at-risk is derived using distribution of EVE at the horizon date. For example, if the analysis time horizon is one year, the probability distribution of EVE at the horizon date of "analysis date + 1 year" is constructed and used in equity-at-risk derivation. Earnings-at-risk is derived using the distribution of earnings during the time horizon. For example, if the time horizon is one year, the probability distribution of earnings during the 1-year period, starting from the analysis date and ending at the horizon date of "analysis date + 1 year" is constructed and used for derivation of earnings-at-risk.

Conceptually, derivations of equity- and earnings-at-risk analysis are very similar to the derivation of VaR discussed earlier. Scenario generation is the first step in both analyses. For each risk factor a large number of scenarios are generated where in each scenario the evolution of a risk factor from the analysis date to the horizon date is simulated. In earnings-at-risk analysis the simulated paths of different risk factors during the time horizon are used to calculate simulated earrings and constructing the probability distribution of change-in-earnings during that period. In equity-at-risk analysis, for each simulated path, values of risk factors at the horizon date are used to calculate simulated EVE and construct the probability distribution of change-in-EVE

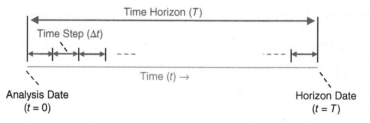

FIGURE 10.5 Analysis date, time horizon, time step, and horizon date terms used in equity- and earnings-at-risk

at that date. In the following sections we discuss how the simulated scenarios are generated and used in derivation of equity-at-risk and earnings-at-risk metrics.

SCENARIO GENERATION

The first step in equity- or earnings-at-risk analysis is to generate scenarios of risk factors that can be used in the construction of the probability distribution of EVE or NII. In practice, both historical sampling and Monte Carlo simulation methods are used for scenario generation. In this section we revisit these two methods for several risk factors while focusing on their applications in equity-at-risk and earnings-at-risk.

Historical Sampling

In the historical sampling method a risk factor's past data is used to construct the simulated paths in the future. This approach is usually used for longer time horizon (e.g., one year or longer), divided into smaller time steps (e.g., daily or monthly). In this method each simulated path of the risk factor is constructed by first randomly selecting a sample period from the historical data of the risk factor, where the length of the sample period is equal to the analysis time horizon. Then, changes of the risk factor values within a sampled period are calculated based on the selected time step. For example, if time horizon is one year and time step is monthly, a sample historical period contains one year of risk factor data and change-in-values is calculated based on risk factor values in the sample that are one month apart. A change-in-value can be calculated using either absolute method or relative method as explained later. Once a sample set of change-in-values is obtained, it is progressively applied to the risk factor values starting from the analysis date to create a simulated path from the analysis date to the horizon date.

The same approach can be used when there are multiple risk factors involved. First a historical period is sampled and then changes in value of all risk factors are calculated based on the data in the sample period. This way the correlations between risk factors are preserved, and when the obtained changes-in-value are used to create simulated paths of risk factors, they present the same correlations among themselves. This is one of the main advantages of the historical sampling method.

Here we illustrate the historical sampling method by focusing on the interest rate risk factor. The application of this technique to other risk factors is similar. Assume that for EVE and NII analysis of a floating-rate instrument with daily reset frequency, a bank uses a spot curve with overnight, 1-month,

3-month, 6-month, and 1-year term points. Historical data for indexes of this curve are available for business days from January 1, 2000, to April 30, 2015. The analysis date is April 30, 2015, the time horizon is $T = 5$ days, and the time step is one day ($\Delta t = 1$ day). This means, since May 2 and 3 are weekend days, that the equity-at-risk is performed based on simulated interest rate curves on May 7 (i.e., five business days after the analysis date) and earnings-at-risk is performed using simulated interest rate paths that change each day between May 1 and May 7 (i.e., during a period of five business days with one business day time step).

The simulation starts by random selection of a start date from the available historical dates to select a five-business-day sample period. Selection of the starting date is done by either assigning equal probabilities to all available historical dates or using an exponential weighting scheme as demonstrated earlier in this chapter. Assume the first randomly selected start date is January 4, 2006. Since we need five daily rate changes, a sample period should include six business days. Assume that the rates for this sample period are as shown in Table 10.2. Based on the time step of one day, this table also shows daily rate changes for each rate index obtained using the *absolute method*. In the absolute method a change-in-rate is calculated as the difference between rates at two dates within the sample period that are Δt days apart. For example, on January 4 the overnight rate was 4.31% and on January 5 it was 4.27%. Therefore, the first 1-day change-in-rate for this index is 4.27% − 4.31% = −0.04%. Or since the overnight rate on January 6 was 4.29%, the second 1-day change-in-rate (January 5th to 6th) is 4.29% − 4.27% = 0.02%. The remaining 1-day rate changes for overnight rate index and other indexes are obtained similarly, as shown in Table 10.2. Since

TABLE 10.2 Historical sampling using absolute method: sample 1 with starting date of January 4, 2016

| | | Rate (%) | | | | | Change-in-Rate (%) – Absolute | | | | |
| | | Term | | | | | Term | | | | |
	Date	O/N	1M	3M	6M	1Y	O/N	1M	3M	6M	1Y
	1/4/2006	4.31	4.40	4.53	4.66	4.77					
	1/5/2006	4.27	4.42	4.55	4.67	4.78	−0.04	0.02	0.02	0.01	0.01
Sample 1	1/6/2006	4.29	4.42	4.51	4.68	4.80	0.02	0.00	−0.04	0.01	0.02
	1/9/2006	4.30	4.44	4.35	4.68	4.65	0.01	0.02	−0.16	0.00	−0.15
	1/10/2006	4.34	4.37	4.56	4.79	4.79	0.04	−0.07	0.21	0.11	0.14
	1/11/2006	4.29	4.44	4.57	4.72	4.86	−0.05	0.07	0.01	−0.07	0.07

rate changes for different indexes are all based on the same sample period of January 4 to January 10, their correlations are preserved.

In the next step, each set of rate changes is used to generate a simulated path for each index. Assume that overnight, 1-month, 3-month, 6-month, and 1-year rates as of the analysis date of April 30, 2015, are 0.12%, 0.19%, 0.28%, 0.34%, and 0.49%, respectively. Rate changes from Table 10.2 can be applied to these indexes progressively to generate daily-changing simulated paths over a time horizon of five business days. Consider the overnight index. The starting rate as of April 30, 2015 (D) is 0.12% and the first 1-day rate change is –0.04%, so the simulated overnight rate as of May 1 (D + 1) is 0.12% − 0.04% = 0.08%. The second 1-day rate change is 0.02%, and since May 2 and 3 are weekend days, the simulated overnight rate as of May 4 (D + 2) is 0.08% + 0.02% = 0.10%. The third 1-day charge for overnight rate from Table 10.2 is 0.01%, hence the simulated overnight rate as of May 5 (D + 3) is 0.10% + 0.01% = 0.11%. Similarly, since the fourth and fifth 1-day rate changes from Table 10.2 are 0.04% and –0.05%, the simulated overnight rate for May 6 (D + 4) and May 7 (D + 5) are obtained as: 0.11% + 0.04% = 0.15% and 0.15% − 0.05% = 0.10%, respectively. Calculated rates of 0.08%, 0.10%, 0.11%, 0.15%, and 0.10% create a simulated path for the overnight rate from the analysis date of April 30, 2015, to the horizon date of May 7, 2015. The simulated paths for rates with other terms are obtained similarly, by starting from the actual rate as of the analysis date and progressively applying the associated rate changes. At the end of this process we have one simulated path for each rate index over a five-day time horizon as presented in Table 10.3. Collectively, these simulated paths create rates for the first scenario of the simulation. This procedure can be repeated to produce a large number of rate scenarios that can be used in equity-at-risk and earnings-at-risk analyses.

TABLE 10.3 Historical sampling using the absolute method: simulated rates (%) of scenario 1 for different indexes of a spot curve

↓Date/Term→	Date	O/N	1M	3M	6M	1Y	
D (Analysis Date)	4/30/2015	0.12	0.19	0.28	0.34	0.49	*Actual*
D+1	5/1/2015	0.08	0.21	0.30	0.35	0.50	*Simulated*
D+2	5/4/2015	0.10	0.21	0.26	0.36	0.52	*Simulated*
D+3	5/5/2015	0.11	0.23	0.10	0.36	0.37	*Simulated*
D+4	5/6/2015	0.15	0.16	0.31	0.47	0.51	*Simulated*
D+5 (Horizon Date)	5/7/2015	0.10	0.23	0.32	0.40	0.58	*Simulated*

Path 1 of overnight rate

Path 1 of 3-month rate

Scenario 1

In the preceding discussion we used the absolute method to calculate a change-in-rate. Alternatively, we can use the *relative method* for this purpose. In the relative method a change-in-rate is calculated as the ratio of rates at two dates within the sample period that are Δt days apart. Subsequently, to create a simulated interest rate from the rate ratios, we start from the actual rate as of the analysis date and progressively multiply the rates by the rate ratios. To demonstrate the relative method, consider the preceding example again and assume another randomly selected sample period has the starting date of May 27, 2011. Assume that historical rates from May 27 to June 3, 2011 (a period of six business days, since May 28 and 29 are weekend days) are as presented in Table 10.4. On May 27 the overnight rate was 0.13% and on May 30 it was 0.14%. Thus, the 1-day rate ratio is 0.14%/0.13% = 1.0769. Or since the overnight rate as of May 31 was 0.12%, the 1-day rate ratio is 0.12%/0.14% = 0.8571. Other 1-day rate ratios are calculated similarly, as shown in Table 10.4. To create simulated rate paths using the rate ratios, we start from the actual rates as of the analysis date and progressively multiply the rates by the 1-day rate ratios. For example, since the actual overnight rate as of the analysis date of April 30, 2015 (D) is 0.12%, and the first 1-day rate ratio for the overnight rate is 1.0769, the simulated overnight rate as of May 1, 2015 (D + 1) is obtained as 0.12% × 1.0769 = 0.1292%. Also, since the second 1-day rate ratio for overnight rate is 0.8571, the simulated overnight rate as of May 4, 2015 (D + 2) is 0.1292% × 0.8571 = 0.1108%, and so on. Simulated rates based on the second sample and relative method are presented in Table 10.5.

A simulated scenario includes a rate path for each term point of the spot curve. Thus, based on the time step of the analysis, at some dates between analysis date and horizon date a simulated spot curve is available. In the preceding example, since the time step is one day, at each business day between the analysis date of April 30, 2015, and the horizon date of May 7, 2015, there is a simulated spot curve available. Therefore, for a given scenario, rates of these

TABLE 10.4   Historical sampling using relative method: sample 2 with starting date of May 27, 2011

		Rate (%)				Change-in-Rate (%) – Relative				
	Date	O/N	1M	3M	6M	1Y	O/N	1M	3M	6M	1Y
Sample 2	5/27/2011	0.13	0.19	0.25	0.29	0.36					
	5/30/2011	0.14	0.22	0.29	0.27	0.36	1.0769	1.1579	1.1600	0.9310	1.0000
	5/31/2011	0.12	0.12	0.27	0.29	0.35	0.8571	0.5455	0.9310	1.0741	0.9722
	6/1/2011	0.14	0.19	0.25	0.33	0.31	1.1667	1.5833	0.9259	1.1379	0.8857
	6/2/2011	0.11	0.19	0.25	0.29	0.42	0.7857	1.0000	1.0000	0.8788	1.3548
	6/3/2011	0.09	0.25	0.25	0.37	0.39	0.8182	1.3158	1.0000	1.2759	0.9286

TABLE 10.5 Historical sampling using relative method: simulated rates (%) of scenario 2 for different indexes of a spot curve

	Date	Date	O/N	1M	3M	6M	1Y	
	D (Analysis Date)	4/30/2015	0.12	0.19	0.28	0.34	0.49	*Actual*
	D + 1	5/1/2015	0.1292	0.2200	0.3248	0.3166	0.4900	*Simulated*
	D + 2	5/4/2015	0.1108	0.1200	0.3024	0.3400	0.4764	*Simulated*
	D + 3	5/5/2015	0.1292	0.1900	0.2800	0.3869	0.4219	*Simulated*
	D + 4	5/6/2015	0.1015	0.1900	0.2800	0.3400	0.5717	*Simulated*
	D + 5 (Horizon Date)	5/7/2015	0.0831	0.2500	0.2800	0.4338	0.5308	*Simulated*

The first unlabeled column above reads "Term" as a spanning header over O/N, 1M, 3M, 6M, 1Y. A vertical label "Scenario 2" runs alongside the data rows.

curves during the horizon time can be used for NII calculation and spot curve at the horizon date can be used for EVE calculation.

As seen in the preceding example, a change-in-rate (also called *shock amount*) obtained using the absolute method can be negative. This in turn may cause the simulated rate (also called *shocked rate*) to become negative. This can happen more often when the actual rate as of the analysis date is sufficiently low. This is one of the drawbacks of using the absolute method in historical sampling. To avoid having negative simulated rates, they can be floored at a predetermined level (e.g., flooring to zero). The relative method does not have this problem, since when a rate as of the analysis date is positive, the simulated rates are also positive. Even with the possibility of producing negative simulated rates, the absolute method provides a more intuitive way for scenario generation, and therefore it is often used for simulating the interest rate risk factor. Generally, the use of the absolute method is recommended when the volatility of the risk factor is low. When the risk factor historical data presents a high volatility, use of the relative method is more appropriate.

For an asset price risk factor (e.g., stock price or commodity price), use of the relative method is more common in practice. However, instead of calculating the ratio of two prices the natural logarithm of the ratio is used. This is to assume a continuous compounding rate of return for the price movement over the time step. If Δt is the time step, P_t, and $P_{t+\Delta t}$ are historical prices of an asset at time t and $t + \Delta t$, and r is the periodic continuous compounding rate of return for this asset from time t to $t + \Delta t$, we have:

$$P_{t+\Delta t} = P_t e^{r\Delta t} \qquad (10.12)$$

Thus, the sampled periodic continuous compounding rate of return for time step Δt is:

$$r = \frac{1}{\Delta t} \ln \frac{P_{t+\Delta t}}{P_t} \qquad (10.13)$$

This sampled rate can then be used for generation of a simulated price. Note that in Equation (10.13) r is the periodic rate of return over period Δt and not an annualized rate. The relative method is also commonly used for the currency exchange rate risk factor. For the calculation of shock ratios, some practitioners use the ratio of two exchange rates (similar to the interest rate risk factor discussed earlier) and some treat the exchange rate as the price of an asset in foreign currency and use the natural logarithm of the ratio of two exchange rates.

Monte Carlo Simulation

In the Monte Carlo simulation method the evolution of paths of all involved risk factors is produced over the time horizon. The evolution paths are created based on either probability distributions assumed for factors or by using stochastic models. In each iteration of the simulation a set of correlated random instances of all involved risk factors is generated, which collectively form a scenario. In a previous chapter we introduced interest rate models and discussed how simulated interest rates are generated. In this section we introduce a few general methods for the simulation of different risk factors, including stock price, commodity price, and exchange rate.

Standard and Generalized Brownian Motion

Recall from an earlier chapter that a standard *Brownian motion* or Wiener process $W(t)$ is a stochastic process where the change in a random variable over a small period of time Δt is $\sqrt{\Delta t}\,\varepsilon$, where ε is a random variable with the standard normal distribution. Assuming that $W(0) = 0$, then $W(t) \sim N(0, t)$, that is, $W(t)$ has normal distribution with mean zero and variance t. Also for $0 \leq s < t$ increments of this random variable are independent and identically distributed as $W(t) - W(s) \sim N(0, t - s)$. In a limiting case when $\Delta t \to 0$ we use notation $dW(t)$ to represent a change in this variable, where $dW(t) = \sqrt{dt}\,\varepsilon$. To generalize this process, we can add a drift rate μ and volatility rate σ to the standard Brownian motion process to obtain:

$$X(t) = \mu\,t + \sigma\,W(t) \tag{10.14}$$

This model indicates that the variable $X(t)$ changes with time at the rate of μ and the standard Brownian motion $W(t)$ adds a randomness or noise to this change with the rate of σ. Random variable $X(t)$ also has a normal distribution as $X(t) \sim N(\mu\, t, \sigma^2\, t)$. In a limiting case this process can be presented in the form of a stochastic differential equation as:

$$dX(t) = \mu\, dt + \sigma\, dW(t) \tag{10.15}$$

$dX(t)$ has a normal distribution as $dX(t) \sim N(\mu\, dt, \sigma^2\, dt)$. To further generalize this process, we can assume that drift and volatility rates vary by time as:

$$dX(t) = \mu(t)\, dt + \sigma(t)\, dW(t) \tag{10.16}$$

The solution of this stochastic differential equation is in the form of:

$$X(t) = X(0) + \int_0^t \mu(\tau)d\tau + \int_0^t \sigma(\tau)dW(\tau)$$

For $0 \le s < t$ increments of the random variable are independent and identically distributed as $X(t) - X(s) \sim N\left(\int_s^t \mu(\tau)d\tau, \int_s^t \sigma^2(\tau)d(\tau)\right)$. This property allows us to generate random instances of the increment as the variable evolves through time. A stochastic process in the form of Equation (10.15) or (10.16) is a generalized Brownian motion model.

If we assume that a risk factor follows the generalized Brownian motion introduced in the preceding discussion, we can simulate its evolution through the analysis time horizon and produce simulated paths of the risk factor. Consider that we need to generate a random path of the risk factor at discrete times $0 < t_1 < t_1 < \cdots < t_n$, where t_n is the equity-at-risk or earnings-at-risk time horizon. If the risk factor follows the process defined in Equation (10.15), the path can be recursively generated using:

$$X(t_{i+1}) = X(t_i) + \mu \times (t_{i+1} - t_i) + \sigma \sqrt{t_{i+1} - t_i}\, \varepsilon_{i+1} \tag{10.17}$$

where $i = 0, 1, \cdots, n-1$ and ε_{i+1} is an independent random instance generated from the standard normal distribution. In this recursion the value of the risk factor at each discrete time is obtained from the value at the previous time considering the drift of the risk factor while the volatility is incorporated using the volatility rate and the independent draw from the standard normal distribution. If the risk factor follows the stochastic process defined in Equation (10.16), the recursive equation is as follows:

$$X(t_{i+1}) = X(t_i) + \int_{t_i}^{t_{i+1}} \mu(\tau)d\tau + \sqrt{N\left(\int_{t_i}^{t_{i+1}} \sigma^2(\tau)d(\tau)\right)}\, \varepsilon_{i+1} \tag{10.18}$$

Using the Euler scheme the approximate discretized version of this equation is:

$$X(t_{i+1}) = X(t_i) + \mu(t_i) \times (t_{i+1} - t_i) + \sigma(t_i) \sqrt{t_{i+1} - t_i}\, \varepsilon_{i+1} \tag{10.19}$$

where $\mu(t_i)$ and $\sigma(t_i)$ are drift and volatility rates at time t_i. This recursive process is not exact and contains some discretization error (Glasserman 2003).

Example

Assume that an asset price risk factor follows the diffusion process in Equation (10.15). The time horizon is 10 days and we intend to generate random paths with a daily time step. The current value of the risk factor is 10.3 and the daily drift and volatility rates are $\mu = 0.7$ and $\sigma = 0.65$. For the first simulated value of the risk factor we start from the current value of the risk factor at $t = 0$ and using Equation (10.17) calculate the simulated value at $t = 1$ as:

$$X(t = 1) = X(t = 0) + \mu \times (1 - 0) + \sigma \times \sqrt{1 - 0}\, \varepsilon_{i+1}$$

or

$$X(t = 1) = 10.3 + 0.7 \times (1) + 0.65 \times \sqrt{1} \times (-0.3249) = 10.7888$$

where –0.3249 is a random draw from the standard normal distribution. The simulated value of the risk factor at $t = 2$ is subsequently obtained using the simulated value at $t = 1$ calculated previously, as:

$$X(t = 2) = 10.7888 + 0.7 \times (1) + 0.65 \times \sqrt{1} \times (-1.0016) = 10.8378$$

where –1.0016 is an independent random draw from the standard normal distribution. The simulated values at time $t = 3$ to $t = 10$ days for this path are obtained similarly and shown in Table 10.6. The entries in the last column of this table represent one simulated path for the risk factor for a time horizon of 10 days. Each simulated path starts from the value of the risk factor at the current time ($t = 0$) and progresses through the time horizon on a daily time step. The random instances ε are independently generated for each time step of a path and independently generated from one path to another. Figure 10.6 presents three simulated paths for this risk factor generated as explained here, where path 1 is the same as shown in Table 10.6.

TABLE 10.6 Simulated path of a risk factor using a generalized Brownian motion stochastic process with constant drift and volatility rates of $\mu = 0.7$ and $\sigma = 0.65$

t	ε	$X(t)$(Path 1)
0		10.3
1	−0.3249	10.7888
2	−1.0016	10.8378
3	0.8210	12.0714
4	0.5256	13.1131
5	−1.4037	12.9007
6	−0.0991	13.5362
7	0.1546	14.3367
8	1.5380	16.0364
9	0.8098	17.2628
10	−1.2980	17.1191

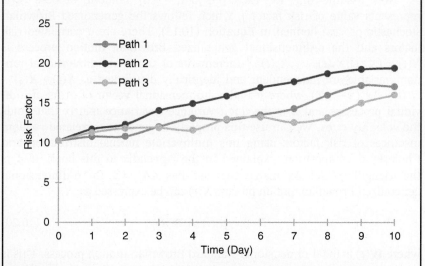

FIGURE 10.6 Three random paths generated using a generalized Brownian motion stochastic process with constant drift and volatility rates of $\mu = 0.7$ and $\sigma = 0.65$

To use Brownian motion stochastic process to simulate the evolution of a risk factor through time, we first need to estimate drift and volatility rate parameters. We can use historical values of the risk factor and an estimation technique, such as maximum likelihood or least square methods, both explained in the Appendix to this book, to estimate these parameters.

Multi-dimensional Brownian Motion

The extension of the model described previously to a multi-dimensional version is done using a known probability outcome that a linear combination of independent random variables with normal distributions has a multivariate normal distribution. Multivariate normal distribution is introduced in the Appendix to this book.

Consider a d-dimensional Brownian motion process $W(t) = (W_1(t), W_2(t), \cdots, W_d(t))T.$[4] Since increments of each $W_j(t)$, $j \in \{0, 1, \cdots, d\}$ are independent and identically distributed with normal distribution, increments of the multi-dimensional random variable W are independent and identically distributed as $W(t) - W(s) \sim N(\mathbf{0}, (t-s)I)$, where $\mathbf{0}$ and I are the d-dimensional zero and identity matrices, respectively, and $0 \leq s < t$.

Now assume that for each $j \in \{0, 1, \cdots, d\}$ random variable $X_j(t)$ represents value of risk factor j, which follows the generalized Brownian stochastic process defined in Equation (10.15). There are d correlated risk factors and the d-dimensional generalized Brownian motion process is $X(t) = (X_1(t), X_2(t), \cdots, X_d(t)).^T$ Increments of this multi-dimensional random variable are independent and identically distributed as $X(t) - X(s) \sim N((t-s)\mu, (t-s)\Sigma)$, where μ is the d-dimensional vector of drifts of individual processes and Σ is the $d \times d$ variance-covariance matrix that holds the volatility rates. We can use this property to generate correlated random instances of risk factors using this multivariate normal distribution and Cholesky decomposition, explained in the Appendix to this book. If A is the triangular Cholesky matrix that satisfies $AA^T = \Sigma$, the d-dimensional generalized Brownian motion process $X(t)$ can be expressed as:

$$X(t) = \mu t + A W(t) \tag{10.20}$$

where $W(t)$ is the d-dimensional standard Brownian motion process. This is an extension of the process introduced in (10.14) to a multi-dimensional case. In the limiting case this model can be presented in the form of a stochastic differential equation as:

$$dX(t) = \mu dt + A dW(t) \tag{10.21}$$

To simulate evolution of d correlated risk factors at discrete times $0 < t_1 < t_1 < \cdots < t_n$, where t_n is the equity-at-risk or earnings-at-risk time horizon, we can use the following recursive formula:

$$X(t_{i+1}) = X(t_i) + \mu \times (t_{i+1} - t_i) + \sqrt{t_{i+1} - t_i} \, A \, \varepsilon_{i+1} \tag{10.22}$$

where $i = 0, 1, \cdots, n - 1$ and ε_{i+1} is a vector of independent random instances generated from the standard normal distribution. This is an extension of recursive equation in Equation (10.17) to a multi-dimensional case. Similar to a one-dimensional model, the drift and variance-covariance matrices can be time dependent, and in that case the stochastic process in the limiting case is presented as:

$$dX(t) = \mu(t) \, dt + A(t) \, dW(t) \tag{10.23}$$

where $A(t) \, A(t)^T = \Sigma(t)$.

Geometric Brownian Motion

The *geometric Brownian motion* stochastic process is often used to model stock prices. The generalized Brownian motion stochastic process introduced in Equation (10.15) represents the change-in-value of a risk factor in a short period of time. In the geometric Brownian motion stochastic process the percentage change of the risk factor in a short period of time is modeled. This process in the form of a stochastic differential equation is presented as:

$$\frac{dX(t)}{X(t)} = \mu \, dt + \sigma \, dW(t) \tag{10.24}$$

If $X(t)$ characterizes an asset price risk factor, $\frac{dX(t)}{X(t)}$ represents the rate of return of that asset over a short period of time. This random variable has a normal distribution as $\frac{dX(t)}{X(t)} \sim N(\mu \, dt, \sigma^2 \, dt)$. Similarly we can write:

$$dX(t) = \mu \, X(t) \, dt + \sigma \, X(t) \, dW(t) \tag{10.25}$$

Consider a new variable: $Y(t) = \ln X(t)$. If F is the natural logarithm function, by using Itô's lemma,[5] we have:

$$dF = \left(\frac{\partial F}{\partial X} \mu \, X(t) + \frac{\partial F}{\partial t} + \frac{1}{2} \frac{\partial^2 F}{\partial X^2} \sigma^2 X(t)^2 \right) dt + \frac{\partial F}{\partial X} \sigma \, X(t) \, dW(t)$$

$$\frac{\partial F}{\partial x} = \frac{1}{X(t)} \qquad \frac{\partial F}{\partial t} = 0 \qquad \frac{\partial^2 F}{\partial X^2} = -\frac{1}{X(t)^2}$$

This leads to:

$$d \ln X(t) = \left(\mu - \frac{\sigma^2}{2} \right) dt + \sigma \, dW(t) \tag{10.26}$$

From Equation (10.26) we can see that $\ln X(t)$ has a generalized Brownian motion process similar to what we introduced in Equation (10.15), where μ is replaced by $\mu - \frac{\sigma^2}{2}$ and $X(t)$ by $\ln X(t)$. Thus, $d \ln X(t)$ has a normal distribution as $d \ln X(t) \sim N \left(\left(\mu - \frac{\sigma^2}{2} \right) dt, \sigma^2 \, dt \right)$. If the value of X at time zero, X_0, is positive, and dt is the time interval between time zero and t, we have:

$$\ln X(t) - \ln X_0 = \left(\mu - \frac{\sigma^2}{2} \right) dt + \sigma \, dW(t)$$

or

$$\ln X(t) = \ln X_0 + \left(\mu - \frac{\sigma^2}{2} \right) dt + \sigma \, dW(t)$$

Therefore $\ln X(t)$ has a normal distribution as $\ln X(t) \sim N \left(\ln X_0 + \left(\mu - \frac{\sigma^2}{2} \right) dt, \sigma^2 \, dt \right)$. When natural logarithm of a random variable has normal distribution the random variable itself has lognormal distribution. Lognormal distribution is introduced in the Appendix to this book. Hence $X(t)$ random variable has a lognormal distribution and is always positive. It can be shown that mean and variance of $X(t)$ are given by Hull (2005):

$$E[X(t)] = X_0 e^{\mu t} \tag{10.27}$$

$$Var[X(t)] = X_0^2 e^{2\mu t}(e^{\sigma^2 t} - 1) \tag{10.28}$$

The stochastic process in (10.26) is a simple modeling approach for simulation of stock price risk factor. We can use a recursive procedure to simulate the evaluation of the risk factor $X(t)$ that follows a geometric Brownian motion process through time. For discrete times $0 < t_1 < t_1 < \cdots < t_n$, where t_n is the equity-at-risk or earnings-at-risk time horizon, and from Equation (10.26), we have:

$$X(t_{i+1}) = X(t_i) \exp \left[\left(\mu - \frac{\sigma^2}{2} \right) \times (t_{i+1} - t_i) + \sigma \sqrt{t_{i+1} - t_i} \, \varepsilon_{i+1} \right] \tag{10.29}$$

where $i = 0, 1, \cdots, n - 1$ and ε_{i+1} is an independent random instance generated from the standard normal distribution.

Example

Assume that a stock price risk factor follows diffusion process presented in Equation (10.26). We need to generate random paths for this risk factor for 10 days with a daily time step. The current stock price is \$98.9. Using historical prices daily drift and volatility rates are estimated as $\mu = 0.008$ and $\sigma = 0.12$. Using Equation (10.29) we can calculate the first simulated value at $t = 1$ as:

$$X(t = 1) = X(t = 0) \times \exp\left[\left(\mu - \frac{\sigma^2}{2}\right) \times (1 - 0) + \sigma\sqrt{1 - 0}\ \varepsilon_{i+1}\right]$$

or

$$X(t = 1) = 98.9 \times \exp\left[\left(0.008 - \frac{0.12^2}{2}\right)(1) + 0.12 \times \sqrt{1} \times (-0.8176)\right]$$

$$= 89.7294$$

where −0.8176 is a random draw from the standard normal distribution. The simulated value of stock price at $t = 2$ is subsequently obtained using Equation (10.29) and the simulated value at $t = 1$ calculated earlier, as:

$$X(t = 2) = 89.7294$$

$$\times \exp\left[\left(0.008 - \frac{0.12^2}{2}\right) \times (2 - 1) + 0.12 \times \sqrt{2 - 1} \times (1.8224)\right]$$

$$= 111.752$$

where 1.8224 is an independent random draw from the standard normal distribution. The simulated values at time $t = 3$ to $t = 10$ days for this path are obtained similarly and shown in Table 10.7. The last column in this table provides one simulated path for this stock price. We can repeat this process to generate more paths. These simulated paths can be used in valuation of options on this asset. The geometric Brownian motion stochastic process is one of the fundamental models used in simulation of stock prices.

(continued)

(*continued*)

TABLE 10.7 Simulated path of a risk factor using a geometric Brownian motion stochastic process with constant drift and volatility rates $\mu = 0.008$ and $\sigma = 0.12$

t	ε	X(t)(Path 1)
0		98.9
1	−0.8176	89.7294
2	1.8224	111.7520
3	0.7334	122.1309
4	−0.2392	118.7697
5	1.3114	139.1222
6	−0.0929	137.6899
7	−1.3700	116.9106
8	−0.7595	106.8120
9	−0.9060	95.8846
10	1.3038	112.2137

Mean-Reverting Brownian Motion

Some risk factors, such as interest rate, commodity price, and exchange rate, tend to drift over time toward their long-term means. A stochastic process that models this behavior is referred to as a *mean-reverting* model. Such a stochastic process is also known as the *Ornstein–Uhlenbeck* process, named after the two physicists who initially proposed the model. In a mean-reverting stochastic process the evolution of the random variable representing a risk factor follows a drift toward the long-term mean level while the stochastic part of the process creates noise around this drift. When the current level of the risk factor is lower than the mean reversion level, the drift is positive and when the current level is higher than the mean reversion level, the drift is negative. The mean-reverting stochastic process is presented as:

$$dX(t) = k\,(\mu - X(t))\,dt + \sigma\,dW(t) \qquad (10.30)$$

where μ is the mean reversion level and k is the speed of reversion. By integrating this equation for any $0 \le s < t$ we have:

$$X(t) = X(s)\,e^{-k(t-s)} + \mu \times (1 - e^{-k(t-s)}) + \sigma \int_s^t e^{-k(t-\tau)}dW(\tau) \qquad (10.31)$$

$X(t)$ has a normal distribution. For any $0 \leq s < t$ conditional mean and variance of the distribution, conditional to all available information until time s (I_s), are:

$$E[X(t)|I_s] = X(s)\, e^{-k(t-s)} + \mu \times (1 - e^{-k(t-s)}) \tag{10.32}$$

$$Var[X(t)|I_s] = \frac{\sigma^2}{2k}[1 - e^{-2k(t-s)}] \tag{10.33}$$

To generate a random path for a risk factor that follows the mean-reverting process in Equation (10.30) at discrete times $0 < t_1 < t_1 < \cdots < t_n$, we can use the following approximate discretized version of the process obtained using the Euler scheme:

$$X(t_{i+1}) = X(t_i) + k\,(\mu - X(t_i))\,(t_{i+1} - t_i) + \sigma\,\sqrt{t_{i+1} - t_i}\,\varepsilon_{i+1} \tag{10.34}$$

where $i = 0, 1, \cdots, n-1$ and ε_{i+1} is an independent random instance generated from the standard normal distribution. In Equation (10.34), the value of the risk factor at each discrete time is obtained from the value at the previous time, considering the drift of the risk factor that tends toward the long-run mean, while the volatility is incorporated using the volatility rate and an independent draw from the standard normal distribution.

Example

Assume that a commodity price risk factor follows the mean-reverting process in Equation (10.30). The current value of the asset is \$100. The mean reversion level at 365 days from now is assumed to be \$190. We want to simulate the evolution of this process at a daily step for 365 days. Using historical data the daily reversion speed and volatility parameters are estimated as $k = 0.01$ and $\sigma = 1.1$. We can use recursive Equation (10.34) to simulate daily evolution of this risk factor. For the first path, the simulated value at $t = 1$ day is obtained as:

$$X(t = 1) = X(t = 0) + k \times (\mu - X(t = 0)) \times (1 - 0) + \sigma \sqrt{1 - 0}\,\varepsilon_{i+1}$$

or

$$X(t = 1) = 100 + 0.01 \times (190 - 100) \times (1) + 1.1 \times \sqrt{1} \times 1.1563 = 102.172$$

(*continued*)

(*continued*)

where 1.1563 is a random draw from the standard normal distribution. The simulated value at $t = 2$ for this path is calculated from the simulated value at $t = 1$ obtained previously, as:

$$X(t = 2) = 102.172 + 0.01 \times (190 - 102.172) \times (2 - 1) + 1.1 \times \sqrt{2 - 1}$$

$$\times 0.3530 = 103.4386$$

In this formula 0.3530 is a random draw from the standard normal distribution. Simulated values for $t = 3$ to $t = 365$ of this random path are calculated similarly in a recursive fashion. Figure 10.7 presents one random path from day 0 to day 365, generated using the mean-reverting Brownian motion process. Since the starting value of the risk factor is lower than the mean reversion level the process has a positive drift and the simulated values trend upward. At the beginning time steps, since the simulated values of the risk factor are significantly lower than the mean reversion level of $190, the drift part of the stochastic process (the first part in Equation (10.30)) produces larger positive values and pushes the simulated values faster toward the mean reversion level. In later time steps of the simulation and as the simulated values of risk factor approach the mean reversion level, the impact of the drift part of the process diminishes. When the noise part of the stochastic process (the second part in Equation (10.30)) causes the total simulated value at a time step to deviate from the mean reversion level, the drift part in the next time step pushes the simulated value back toward the mean reversion level. Part (a) of Figure 10.7 shows the magnitude of the drift part of the simulated values in our example and part (b) shows the magnitude of the noise part from day 1 to day 365. Part (c) of this graph shows the total simulated value which is trending upward toward the mean reversion level.

When the starting value of the risk factor is higher than the mean reversion level the process has a negative drift and the simulated values trend downward. Figure 10.8 shows one simulated path generated using the same drift speed and volatility parameters as used previously but with mean reversion level of $10. At the beginning time steps of the simulation process, since the values of the risk factor are significantly higher than the mean reversion level of $10, the drift part of the process produces larger negative values and pushes the simulated values faster toward the mean reversion level. In later time steps, as the simulated values of the risk factor approach the mean reversion level, the absolute value of the drift part decreases and its effect diminishes.

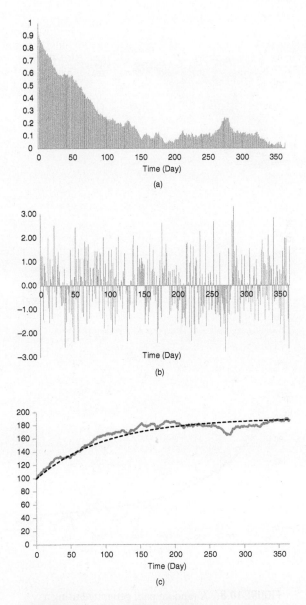

FIGURE 10.7 A random path generated using a mean-reverting Brownian motion stochastic process with a starting value of \$100 and parameters: $\mu = 190$, $\sigma = 1.1$, and $k = 0.01$: (a) drift part, (b) noise part, (c) total simulated value

(continued)

(continued)

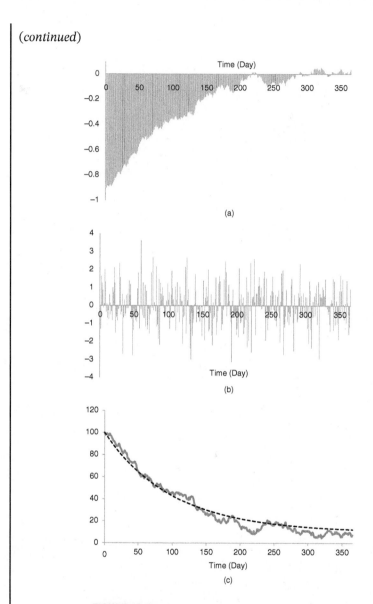

FIGURE 10.8 A random path generated using a mean-reverting Brownian motion stochastic process with starting value of $100 and parameters: $\mu = 10$, $\sigma = 1.1$, and $k = 0.01$: (a) drift part, (b) noise part, (c) total simulated value

In an earlier chapter we introduced several stochastic processes to model the evolution of interest rate through time. The Vasicek model is a mean-reverting Brownian motion model. In the form of a stochastic differential equation this model is presented as:

$$dr(t) = k\,(\mu - r(t))\,dt + \sigma\,dW(t) \tag{10.35}$$

The Hull-White model is an extension of the Vasicek model where the mean reversion level μ varies by time to incorporate the current term structure of the interest rate and hence is an arbitrage-free model. This model is presented as:

$$dr(t) = k\left(\frac{\mu(t)}{k} - r(t)\right)dt + \sigma\,dW(t) \tag{10.36}$$

The Black-Karasinski model is also a mean-reverting process where the rate variable is replaced by the natural logarithm of the rate. This model is presented as:

$$d\ln r(t) = k\left[\frac{\theta(t)}{k} - \ln r(t)\right]dt + \sigma\,dW(t) \tag{10.37}$$

Ho-Lee is a special case of Hull-White where there is no mean reversion assumed and hence the model is a generalized Brownian motion process. This model is presented as:

$$dr(t) = \mu(t)\,dt + \sigma\,dW(t) \tag{10.38}$$

Simulation of the interest rate based on these models is explained in Chapter 5.

Geometric Mean-Reverting Brownian Motion

In a *geometric mean-reversing Brownian motion* or *geometric Ornstein–Uhlenbeck* process, the percentage change of a risk factor in a short period of time evolves through time while trending toward a long-term mean level. This process is popular in simulation of exchange rate and commodity price risk factors. Dixit and Pindyck (1994) proposed one of the original versions of the geometric mean-reverting Brownian motion process, as follows:

$$\frac{dX(t)}{X(t)} = k\,[\mu - X(t)]\,dt + \sigma\,dW(t) \tag{10.39}$$

or equivalently:

$$dX(t) = k\,[\mu - X(t)]\,X(t)\,dt + \sigma\,X(t)\,dW(t) \tag{10.40}$$

Similar to geometric Brownian motion, $\frac{dX(t)}{X(t)}$ in this model is the instantaneous rate of return for the risk factor that is represented by (t). Schwartz

(1997) proposed a variation of the above model that eases the estimation of the parameters. The Schwartz model is presented as:

$$\frac{dX(t)}{X(t)} = k\,[\mu - \ln X(t)]\,dt + \sigma\,dW(t) \tag{10.41}$$

or equivalently:

$$dX(t) = k\,[\mu - \ln X(t)]\,X(t)\,dt + \sigma\,X(t)\,dW(t) \tag{10.42}$$

If $Y(t) = \ln X(t)$, by applying Itô's lemma we have (F is the natural logarithm function):

$$dF = \left(\frac{\partial F}{\partial X}\,k\,[\mu - \ln X(t)]\,X(t) + \frac{\partial F}{\partial t} + \frac{1}{2}\frac{\partial^2 F}{\partial X^2}\,\sigma^2 X(t)^2\right)dt$$

$$+ \frac{\partial F}{\partial X}\,\sigma\,X(t)\,dW(t)$$

$$\frac{\partial F}{\partial x} = \frac{1}{X(t)} \qquad \frac{\partial F}{\partial t} = 0 \qquad \frac{\partial^2 F}{\partial X^2} = -\frac{1}{X(t)^2}$$

This leads to:

$$d\ln X(t) = k\left(\mu - \frac{\sigma^2}{2k} - \ln X(t)\right)dt + \sigma\,dW(t) \tag{10.43}$$

In this version of the geometric mean-reverting model, the natural logarithm of the variable tends toward the mean reversion level. While this process is less intuitive, estimation of parameters of the model is easier. From Equation (10.43) we can see that $\ln X(t)$ has a mean-reverting process that is similar to what is introduced in Equation (10.30), where μ is replaced by $\mu - \frac{\sigma^2}{2k}$ and $X(t)$ by $\ln X(t)$. Therefore, $\ln X(t)$ has a normal distribution. By integrating this equation for any $0 \le s < t$, we have:

$$\ln X(t) = \ln X(s)e^{-k(t-s)} + \left(\mu - \frac{\sigma^2}{2k}\right)(1 - e^{-k(t-s)}) + \sigma\int_s^t e^{-k(t-\tau)}dW(\tau)$$

$$\tag{10.44}$$

For any $0 \le s < t$, the conditional mean and variance of the distribution of $\ln X(t)$ conditional to all available information until time s are:

$$E[\ln X(t)|I_s] = (\ln X(s))e^{-k(t-s)} + \left(\mu - \frac{\sigma^2}{2k}\right)(1 - e^{-k(t-s)}) \tag{10.45}$$

$$Var[\ln X(t)|I_s] = \frac{\sigma^2}{2k}[1 - e^{-2k(t-s)}] \tag{10.46}$$

Since $\ln X(t)$ has a normal distribution, $X(t)$ has a lognormal distribution. We can use the Euler scheme to obtain the following approximate discrete version of the above process and simulate the evolution of $X(t)$ at discrete times $0 < t_1 < t_1 < \cdots < t_n$:

$$X(t_{i+1}) = X(t_i) \, \exp\left[k\left(\left(\mu - \frac{\sigma^2}{2k}\right) - \ln X(t_i)\right) \times (t_{i+1} - t_i) + \sigma\sqrt{t_{i+1} - t_i}\, \varepsilon_{i+1} \right]$$

(10.47)

where $i = 0, 1, \cdots, n-1$, and ε_{i+1} is an independent random instance generated from the standard normal distribution.

Example

Assume that the EUR-USD exchange rate follows the geometric mean-reverting Brownian motion process presented in Equation (10.43). We are interested to simulate the exchange rate for a 90-day time horizon on a daily time step. The current exchange rate is 1.22. Using daily historical data, the parameters of the process are estimated as $= 0.25$, $k = 0.02$, and $\sigma = 0.01$. In Equation (10.43) $\ln X(t)$ tends toward $\mu - \frac{\sigma^2}{2k} = 0.2475$; therefore, the exchange rate $X(t)$ trends toward $e^{0.2475} = 1.2808$. In the first path of the simulation, the simulated value of the risk factor at $t = 1$ is calculated using Equation (10.47) as:

$$X(t = 1) = X(t = 0)$$

$$\times \exp\left[k\left(\left(\mu - \frac{\sigma^2}{2k}\right) - \ln X(t = 0)\right) \times (1 - 0) + \sigma\sqrt{1 - 0}\, \varepsilon_{i+1} \right]$$

or

$$X(t = 1) = 1.22$$

$$\times \exp\left[0.02 \times \left(\left(0.25 - \frac{0.01^2}{2 \times 0.02}\right) - \ln(1.22)\right) \times (1) + 0.01 \times \sqrt{1} \right.$$

$$\times 1.3003] = 1.2372$$

(continued)

(*continued*)

where 1.3003 is a random draw from the standard normal distribution. The simulated value of the risk factor at $t = 2$ is recursively calculated as:

$$X(t = 2) = 1.2372$$

$$\times exp\left[0.02 \times \left(\left(0.25 - \frac{0.01^2}{2 \times 0.02}\right) - \ln(1.2372)\right) \times (1)\right.$$

$$\left. + 0.01 \times \sqrt{1} \times 0.5449\right] = 1.2448$$

where 0.5449 is a random draw from the standard normal distribution. The simulated values of the exchange rate for $t = 3$ to $t = 90$ day of this path are obtained similarly. Figure 10.9 presents three simulated paths for EUR-USD exchange rate generated using the geometric mean-reverting Brownian motion model with the aforementioned parameter values. In this graph the simulated exchange rate trends toward 1.2808 while the stochastic part of the model produces random variations around this trend.

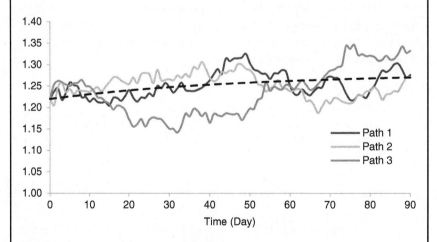

FIGURE 10.9 Three simulated paths of EUR-USD exchange rate generated using geometric mean-reverting Brownian motion model based on parameters $\mu = 0.25$, $k = 0.02$, and $\sigma = 0.01$

The simulated path of interest and exchange rate risk factors are particularly useful in valuation of financial products and derivatives with path-dependent cash flows and payouts.

Calibration

Parameters of the Brownian motion models discussed in this chapter can be estimated using least squares error or maximum likelihood methods, both explained in the Appendix to this book. Consider the mean-reverting Brownian motion (Ornstein–Uhlenbeck) model introduced in Equation (10.30). Following Equation (10.31) an approximate discrete-time version of this continuous-time stochastic differential equation is:

$$X(t_{i+1}) = X(t_i)e^{-k\Delta t} + \mu \times (1 - e^{-k\Delta t}) + \xi_t$$

where ξ_t has a normal distribution with mean zero and variance of $\sigma_{\xi_t}^2 = \frac{\sigma^2}{2k}[1 - e^{-2k\Delta t}]$. This is a first-order autoregressive model and can be re-parameterized as:

$$X(t_{i+1}) = \beta_0 + \beta_1 X(t_i) + \xi_t$$

Assuming a constant Δt and by using the least squares error method we can estimate β_0, β_1, and σ_{ξ_t} from historical data of $X(t)$. Subsequently, the original parameters of k, μ, and σ are obtained from estimated β_0, β_1, and σ_{ξ_t} as:

$$k = -\frac{\ln \beta_1}{\Delta t} \tag{10.48}$$

$$\mu = \frac{\beta_0}{1 - \beta_1} \tag{10.49}$$

$$\sigma = \sigma_{\xi_t} \sqrt{\frac{2 \ln \beta_1}{\Delta t(\beta_1^2 - 1)}} \tag{10.50}$$

EQUITY-AT-RISK

The EVE scenario analysis discussed in an earlier chapter is usually performed for a limited number of scenarios (e.g., +100 bps or –100 bps shocks in interest rate or 10% depreciation of base currency exchange rate, etc.). This leaves the firm exposed to potential cases that were not considered. Consider a bank that performs the following interest rate scenario analyses and studies the impact of each on its EVE:

- +100 bps and –100 bps parallel shocks
- –200 bps and –200 bps parallel shocks
- Steepening shock with a +50 bps increase at 1-year term, +200 bps increase at 30-year term, and interpolated rates between these two term points

While analysis of these variations of yield curve is useful, there are many different cases that yield curve can change which are not included in the preceding set of scenarios. For example, the following are some possible cases that are not considered by the bank:

- +5 bps change at 3-month term, –30 bps change at 6-month term
- +50 bps change at 5-year term, +150 bps change at 10-year term, and interpolated rates between these two term points

Each of these scenarios would result in different discount factors and implied forward rates, which in turn could result in different ΔEVE. Another shortfall of scenario analysis is the instantaneous nature of the shocks considered. If the value of the portfolio held by a bank depends on the path that risk factors take, such instantaneous shock scenarios do not capture the potential change in value of the portfolio accurately.

Due to these shortcomings of scenario analysis, many banks enhance their ALM studies by performing equity-at-risk analysis. As discussed earlier, equity-at-risk is the maximum potential decrease in the economic value of equity of the bank due to changes in risk factors for a given time horizon and with a certain confidence level. Simulated paths of risk factors can be used to obtain a probabilistic estimation of potential decrease in the economic value of equity in the future. By simulating a large number of evolution paths of risk factors from the analysis date to the horizon date and performing EVE analysis at the horizon date for each path, we can construct the probability distribution of ΔEVE at the horizon date and obtain statistical metrics, such as standard deviation and percentiles of ΔEVE. This helps us to gain a better understanding of possibilities of change in EVE of the bank over the time horizon in the future. In the following sections we discuss equity-at-risk, focusing on interest rate and currency exchange rate risk factors.

Interest Rate Risk Factor

To demonstrate the equity-at-risk concept, first assume that the interest rate is the only risk factor and that the current spot curve is as shown in Figure 10.10

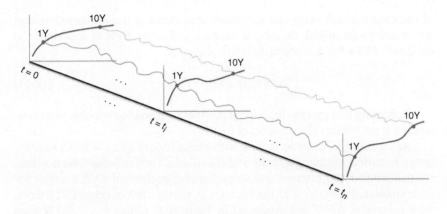

FIGURE 10.10   Simulated spot curves from analysis date $t = 0$ to horizon date $t = t_n$

at time $t = 0$. To obtain the ΔEVE at time horizon t_n we can simulate the evolution of rates at different terms of the curve by using either the historical sampling or the Monte Carlo simulation methods introduced earlier. In each simulation iteration and at each time step t_i a simulated spot curve can be constructed using the simulated rates of different terms of the curve. Figure 10.10 shows one path of a simulated 1-year rate and one path of a simulated 10-year rate from the current time to the horizon date t_n. At the horizon date the simulated spot curve can be used to obtain the EVE of the balance sheet at t_n. Also, simulated paths of interest rates for different terms at transition times $t = 0, t_1, \cdots, t_{n-1}, t_n$ can be used for valuation of path-dependent instruments, such as mortgage-backed securities. The value of a path-dependent financial instrument at horizon date t_n depends on the path the interest rate took from time $t = 0$ to t_n.

To obtain the EVE at the horizon date, a forecasted balance sheet at that time is needed. One option is to assume the balance sheet at the horizon is the same as the current balance sheet while the alternative is to incorporate the bank's business plan along with maturity and runoff profiles to construct an estimated balance sheet at the horizon. In the latter case the matured positions are replaced with the new positions with specifications (rate, accrual basis, day count convention, term, etc.) and balances that are expected at the horizon date.

Assume that the economic value of equity of the current balance sheet and using the current spot curve is EVE_0. This is usually referred to as the base scenario. For simulated scenario i the economic value of equity for the forecasted balance sheet and simulated spot curve at the horizon date is EVE_i. EVE_i is obtained by valuation of forecasted assets and liabilities at the end of the time horizon using the simulated spot curve at the horizon date and simulated paths of risk factors, if needed. Once the EVE of a scenario is obtained, ΔEVE for that scenario is calculated as:

$$\Delta EVE_i = EVE_i - EVE_0 \qquad (10.51)$$

Repeating this process for a large number of scenarios enables us to construct the probability distribution of ΔEVE.

As an example, consider a bank with a base EVE of $EVE_0 = \$19.5$ million. Using historical sampling and the absolute method with a 1-day time horizon, we generated 1,000 interest rate scenarios and performed EVE analysis for each simulated spot curve at the horizon. A partial view of these EVEs along with calculated ΔEVE are presented in Table 10.8. Equation (10.51) is used to calculate ΔEVE for each scenario. For example, $\Delta EVE_1 = \$19,526,917 - \$19,500,000 = \$26,917$.

To determine the change in EVE for a given confidence level, we need to rank the obtained ΔEVE in an ascending order (excluding scenario 0), as shown in Table 10.9. Assume we are considering a one-sided confidence level

TABLE 10.8 A partial view of EVE and ΔEVE (\$) for 1,000 scenarios generated using historical sampling of interest rate risk factor and absolute method

Scenario	EVE (\$)	ΔEVE (\$)
0	19,500,000	
1	19,526,917	26,917
2	19,136,366	(363,634)
3	18,205,588	(1,294,412)
4	18,235,467	(1,264,533)
5	19,789,568	289,568
6	20,803,829	1,303,829
7	18,971,009	(528,991)
8	19,898,988	398,988
9	18,531,025	(968,975)
10	19,458,246	(41,754)
11	20,379,177	879,177
12	20,908,119	1,408,119
...	...	...
996	18,820,627	(679,373)
997	19,062,479	(437,521)
998	20,010,871	510,871
999	18,121,224	(1,378,776)
1000	19,849,018	349,018

TABLE 10.9 Ranked ΔEVE ($) for 1,000 scenarios using historical sampling of interest rate risk factor and absolute method

Scenario	EVE	ΔEVE	Rank	Ordinal Rank
841	17,373,131	(2,126,869)	1000	1
893	17,442,147	(2,057,853)	999	0.999
287	17,473,067	(2,026,933)	998	0.998
170	17,519,253	(1,980,747)	997	0.997
406	17,549,027	(1,950,973)	996	0.996
535	17,586,725	(1,913,275)	995	0.995
423	17,593,604	(1,906,396)	994	0.994
643	17,632,935	(1,867,065)	993	0.993
153	17,665,307	(1,834,693)	992	0.992
34	17,670,260	(1,829,740)	991	0.991
562	17,674,840	(1,825,160)	990	0.990
917	17,702,179	(1,797,821)	989	0.989
375	17,704,595	(1,795,405)	988	0.988
...	...	...	...	...
259	21,534,412	2,034,412	5	0.005
97	21,662,769	2,162,769	4	0.004
379	21,862,217	2,362,217	3	0.003
79	21,973,855	2,473,855	2	0.002
183	22,427,234	2,927,234	1	0.001

of 0.01. In Table 10.9 the 99th percentile is the ΔEVE at rank 990, which is −$1,825,160 and is associated with scenario 562.[6] Since the time horizon used is one day, based on this analysis, with 99% probability the EVE of this bank can decrease by $1,825,160 or less in one day (there is still a 1% chance the decrease can exceed the $1,825,160). Empirical distribution of ΔEVE for this example is shown in Figure 10.11.

It should be noted that the number of scenarios considered in our example is barely sufficient, and for a robust equity-at-risk analysis a larger sample size (i.e., more simulated scenarios) is needed. Depending on the sample size, the number of positions on the balance sheet, and the products' complexity, the process discussed here can be computationally challenging and, hence, increase of the sample size may be prohibitive. To overcome this issue, some commercial ALM software packages incorporate variance reduction techniques such as *importance sampling* to focus the sampling on a specific area of ΔEVE distribution to alleviate the need for very large sample sizes.

While for banks with large trading books it is common to consider a short time horizon (e.g., one, three, or five days), for equity-at-risk analysis, and especially for banks with material banking books a longer horizon (e.g., one year) is often used in practice.

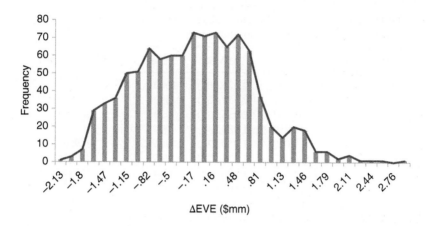

ΔEVE ($mm)

FIGURE 10.11   Distribution of ΔEVE ($ million) using simulated spot curves at 1-day time horizon for 1,000 scenarios

Component Contribution

We can quantify the contribution of a portfolio or an individual position toward ΔEVE of an equity-at-risk analysis. Let's assume that i represents an individual portfolio or position on the asset side and j represents an individual portfolio or position on the liability side of the balance sheet. Also assume that b is the scenario number that corresponds to the required percentile at which ΔEVE is derived. In the example demonstrated in the previous section, the 99th percentile ΔEVE was at scenario 562; therefore $b = 562$. ΔEVE for scenario b is calculated using Equation (10.51) as:

$$\Delta EVE_b = EVE_b - EVE_0$$

Using notation EV to represent the economic value, this equation can be expanded as follows:

$$\Delta EVE_b = EVE_b - EVE_0$$

$$= \left(\sum_{i}^{\text{All Asset}} EV_{ib} - \sum_{j}^{\text{All Liab.}} EV_{jb} \right)$$

$$- \left(\sum_{i}^{\text{All Asset}} EV_{i0} - \sum_{j}^{\text{All Liab.}} EV_{j0} \right)$$

or equivalently

$$\Delta EVE_b = \overset{All\ Asset}{\underset{i}{\sum}} (EV_{i_b} - EV_{i_0}) - \overset{All\ Liab.}{\underset{j}{\sum}} (EV_{j_b} - EV_{j_0}) \qquad (10.52)$$

In Equation (10.52) $EV_{i_b} - EV_{i_0}$ is the contribution of asset i and $-(EV_{j_b} - EV_{j_0})$ is the contribution of liability j in the total ΔEVE_b obtained in this equity-at-risk analysis.

Approximation Techniques

One challenge in an equity-at-risk analysis is its computational intensity and the need for significant computation resources and considerable analysis time. Depending on the number of simulated scenarios, full revaluation of the entire balance sheet for each simulation iteration can be very time consuming and usually requires dedicated software and hardware resources. For this reason, many banks choose a bare minimum sample size for their equity-at-risk analysis, which can adversely impact the accuracy of the percentile measurements at the tail of ΔEVE distribution.

To reduce the computation intensity, instead of full revaluation of the balance sheet positions for each simulated scenario, we can use an approximate method to obtain positions' change-in-values. These approximate changes-in-value then can be used to construct the distribution of ΔEVE. Here, we discuss an approximation method used for this purpose.

In the *delta approximation* technique we find the sensitivity of a position value to an underlying risk factor and then use that sensitivity measure to obtain an approximate value of the position in each simulated scenario of that risk factor. *Delta* is a sensitivity measurement defined as the rate of value change to the change in a relevant risk factor:

$$Delta = \frac{\Delta V}{\Delta X} \qquad (10.53)$$

where V is the position value, X is the underlying risk factor that is relevant to the financial instrument of the position, and Δ in Equation (10.53) represents the change. This measurement is commonly used for option contracts when the risk factor is the underlying asset price, but the concept can be extended to other financial instruments with relevant underlying risk factors. Equation (10.53) is approximate since it captures only the linear relationship between the change of the position value and the change in the underlying risk factor. Considering value of a position as a function of the underlying risk factor, delta is the first derivative of this function with respect to the risk factor.

When delta of a position is determined, the approximate change-in-value for a given change in the underlying risk factor is obtained as:

$$\Delta V \cong Delta \times \Delta X \tag{10.54}$$

To improve the accuracy of this approximation, we can incorporate the *gamma* measurement to capture the potential non-linear relation between a position value and the underlying risk factor. Gamma is the rate of change of delta to the change in the underlying risk factor. It is the second derivative of the value function with respect to the underlying risk factor. Using the Taylor series, a better approximation of a position change-in-value using both delta and gamma is obtained as:

$$\Delta V \cong Delta \times \Delta X + \frac{1}{2} \times Gamma \times (\Delta X)^2 \tag{10.55}$$

This approach is known as the *delta-gamma approximation* technique. When risk factor is the interest rate, equivalent of delta and gamma are dollar duration and dollar convexity, defined in Chapter 2. Recall from that chapter that modified duration and convexity are:

$$D_{Mod} = -\frac{1}{V}\frac{\Delta V}{\Delta y}$$

$$Conv = \frac{1}{V}\frac{\Delta^2 V}{\Delta y^2}$$

where y is the yield. A change in the value of the position due to a change of Δy in the yield is approximately obtained as:

$$V(y + \Delta y) - V(y) \cong -D_{Mod} \times V(y) \times \Delta y + \frac{1}{2}Conv \times V(y) \times (\Delta y)^2$$

The negative sign in front of the modified duration indicates the opposite relationship that exists between movement in yield and the change in position value. Rearranging the preceding equations provides us with dollar duration and dollar convexity as:

$$D_{Dollar} = D_{Mod} \times V = -\frac{\Delta V}{\Delta y}$$

$$Conv_{Dollar} = Conv \times V = \frac{\Delta^2 V}{\Delta y^2}$$

and

$$\Delta V \cong -D_{Dollar} \times \Delta y + \frac{1}{2} \times Conv_{Dollar} \times (\Delta y)^2$$

This relationship is comparable to Equation (10.55). It should be noted that while using this equation generally provides a reasonably good approximation, it is only applicable when a parallel shock to the spot curve is considered (i.e., a change in position yield). As we saw in previous sections, simulated scenarios of interest rate, whether from historical sampling or the Monte Carlo method, are not necessarily parallel shifts of the current spot curve. For an approximation of changes in value for interest rate scenarios the use of *key rate duration (KRD)* is more appropriate. A key rate duration is the sensitivity of position value to change in rate at one term point of the spot curve. To use key rate duration in equity-at-risk analysis first we need to derive the effective key rate duration of each position or portfolio for each term point of the spot curve. This can be done by applying upward and downward shocks of a specified amount, say $\Delta r = 10$ *bps*, one at a time to each term point and revalue the position or the portfolio. The effective key rate duration for a given term point t is then derived as:

$$KRD_{t\ Eff} = \frac{V(r - \Delta r_t) - V(r + \Delta r_t)}{2\ V_0\ \Delta r} \tag{10.56}$$

where

$$r = (r_1, r_2, \cdots, r_t, \cdots, r_n) = \text{Vector of spot rates for all key terms in base scenario}$$

$$V_0 = V(r) = \text{Value of position using base spot curve of } r, \text{ i.e., current value}$$

$$r + \Delta r_t = (r_1, r_2, \cdots, r_t + \Delta r, \cdots, r_n) = \text{Vector of spot rates when only rate at term point } t \text{ is shifted upward by } \Delta r:$$
$$r + \Delta r_t = (r_1, r_2, \cdots, r_t, \cdots, r_n) + (0, 0, \cdots, \Delta r, \cdots, 0)$$

$$V(r + \Delta r_t) = \text{Value of position when only rate at term point } t \text{ is shifted upward by } \Delta r$$

$$r - \Delta r_t = (r_1, r_2, \cdots, r_t - \Delta r, \cdots, r_n) = \text{Vector of spot rates when only rate at term point } t \text{ is shifted downward by } \Delta r:$$
$$r - \Delta r_t = (r_1, r_2, \cdots, r_t, \cdots, r_n) - (0, 0, \cdots, \Delta r, \cdots, 0)$$

$$V(r - \Delta r_t) = \text{Value of position when only rate at term point } t \text{ is shifted downward by } \Delta r$$

After the key rate durations of a position are obtained, the change-in-value for a simulated scenario is obtained by multiplying the simulated shock amount for each term point by the KRD of that term point and by the base value of the position, then summing up over all key term points:

$$\Delta V \cong \sum_{\substack{\text{All key term} \\ \text{points } t}} -KRD_t \, V_0 \, \Delta r_{s_t} \qquad (10.57)$$

In Equation (10.57) Δr_{s_t} is the shock amount to the interest rate at term point t in a simulated scenario, for example, if the spot curve is defined with term points 1-year, 3-year, 5-year, and 10-year and the vector representing current spot curve is $r_0 = (r_{1-year}, r_{3-year}, r_{5-year}, r_{10-year}) = (1.22\%, 2.21\%, 2.35\%, 3.74\%)$. If the simulated interest rate curve for a scenario is $r_s = (0.97\%, 0\%, 2.75\%, 3.03\%)$, then $\Delta r_s = (-0.25\%, -2.21\%, +0.40\%, -0.71\%)$ obtained by finding differences between the base scenario spot curve and the simulated spot curve. In Chapter 2 we discussed calculation of key rate duration in more detail and provided an example of how it can be used to approximately obtain the change-in-value for non-parallel shocks to the spot curve.

Currency Exchange Rate Risk Factor

For banks with multi-currency balance sheets, foreign currency exchange rates (FX rates) can be simulated to study the impact of potential change in the FX rates on the economic value of equity over a specific time horizon. Both historical sampling and the Monte Carlo simulation methods can be used to produce simulated scenarios for currency exchange rate risk factor. To demonstrate equity-at-risk analysis for the currency exchange rate risk factor, consider a bank that has positions in three currencies: U.S. dollar (USD), British pound (GBP), and Japanese yen (JPY). Current economic values of elements of the bank's balance sheet in local currencies are shown in Table 10.10.

The analysis date is August 31, 2015. The functional currency of this bank is USD; hence, to obtain the economic value of equity we need to convert assets in GBP and JPY to USD using the spot rates on August 31, 2015. As shown in Table 10.10 this bank has USD-denominated assets with current value of 10,000,000 USD. The bank also has assets denominated in JPY and GBP with

TABLE 10.10 Economic value of a hypothetical bank balance sheet with positions in USD, GBP, and JPY (values shown are economic values and not book values)

Asset		Liability	
10,000,000	USD	22,000,000	USD
1,200,000,000	JPY		
3,000,000	GBP		

current values of 1,200,000,000 JPY and 3,000,000 GBP, respectively. Using the spot rates of USD-JPY: 121.23 and GBP-USD: 1.5345, the values of these assets in USD are:

$$1,200,000,000 \; JPY \times \frac{1}{121.23} = 9,898,540 \; USD$$

$$3,000,000 \; GBP \times 1.5345 = 4,603,500 \; USD$$

To convert JPY to USD the reciprocal of the quoted rate is used. The liabilities of the bank are all in USD with a current value of $22,000,000. Having the USD-equivalent values of all assets and liabilities, the current economic value of the equity (base scenario) is then obtained as:

$$Total \; Asset \; Value - Total \; Liability \; Value$$

$$= 10,000,000 + 9,898,540 + 4,603,500 - 22,000,000$$

$$= 2,502,040 \; USD$$

These calculations are summarized in Table 10.11.

For this equity-at-risk analysis example, assume that the time horizon is three days and the time step is one day. We can use the historical sampling method to produce simulated scenarios for USD-JPY and GBP-USD. Here we use the relative method for shock calculation and selection of the starting point of each random draw is done by using equal weights for available historical data. Table 10.12 presents a partial view of the assumed historical exchange rates for these two currency pairs, from January 1, 2002, to August 31, 2015.

Since we are assigning equal weights to all available historical data, each date has an equal probability to be selected as the starting point of a historical path. Assume a random draw from the available historical dates resulted in selection of January 2, 2002, as the starting day of scenario 1. Since

TABLE 10.11 Determination of EVE in USD for base scenario for a multi-currency balance sheet

Balance Sheet Type	Economic Value	Currency	FX Rate	USD Equivalent
Asset	10,000,000	USD	1.0000	10,000,000
Asset	1,200,000,000	JPY	0.0082	9,898,540
Asset	3,000,000	GBP	1.5345	4,603,500
		Total Assets:		24,502,040
Liability	22,000,000	USD	1.0000	22,000,000
	Total Liabilities:			22,000,000
EVE (USD) = Total Assets – Total Liabilities:				2,502,040

TABLE 10.12   A partial view of assumed historical FX rate for USD-JPY and GBP-USD pairs

Date	USD-JPY	GBP-USD
1/1/2002	131.6500	1.4534
1/2/2002	132.1300	1.4468
1/3/2002	131.8000	1.4385
1/4/2002	131.0400	1.4473
1/7/2002	131.0900	1.4404
1/8/2002	132.8600	1.4394
...	...	...
10/27/2011	75.9500	1.6099
10/28/2011	75.8200	1.6130
10/31/2011	78.1700	1.6087
11/1/2011	78.3700	1.5949
11/2/2011	78.0500	1.5949
11/3/2011	78.0600	1.6041
...	...	...
8/21/2015	122.0400	1.5694
8/24/2015	118.4100	1.5776
8/25/2015	118.8300	1.5687
8/26/2015	119.9200	1.5463
8/27/2015	121.0300	1.5403
8/28/2015	121.7100	1.5391
8/31/2015	121.2300	1.5345

the time horizon is three days, FX rates at four days are needed for generating a scenario. For scenario 1 these days are January 2, January 3, January 4, and January 7, 2002 (January 5 and January 6 are weekend days). Using historical exchange rates at these four days, we can calculate three 1-day change ratios and compute the 3-day change ratio, as shown in Table 10.13. In this table each 1-day shock is obtained by dividing two consecutive FX rates. For example, the 1-day shock between January 2 and January 3 for JPY is obtained by dividing the FX rate on January 3 by the FX rate on January 2: $131.8000/132.1300 = 0.9975$. The 3-day shock is then calculated by multiplying three 1-day shocks. For example, for JPY the 3-day shock for this scenario is: $0.9975 \times 0.9942 \times 1.0004 = 0.9921$. The shocked FX rate for scenario 1 is eventually calculated by multiplying the 3-day shock and the current spot rate (FX rate as of August 31, 2015). For USD-JPY the shocked FX rate for scenario 1 is calculated as: $121.2300 \times 0.9921 = 120.2758$. The shocked rate for GBP-USD is calculated similarly as 1.5277, as shown in Table 10.13.

Having the shocked FX rates for scenario 1, we can revalue the balance sheet by converting the foreign currency values to USD using the shocked rates. Here we assume the balance sheet at the time horizon of three days is the same as the current balance sheet. The calculation of the EVE for scenario

TABLE 10.13 Scenario 1 of historical sampling of exchange rate risk factor

	Historical Path	**USD-JPY**	**1-Day Shock**	**GBP-USD**	**1-Day Shock**
$t-3$	1/2/2002	132.1300		1.4468	
$t-2$	1/3/2002	131.8000	0.9975	1.4385	0.9943
$t-1$	1/4/2002	131.0400	0.9942	1.4473	1.0061
t	1/7/2002	131.0900	1.0004	1.4404	0.9952
		×	0.9921	×	0.9956
	Shocked FX Rate:		120.2758		1.5277

1 using shocked FX rates is shown in Table 10.14. In this table the shocked USD-JPY of 120.2758 is used to convert the JPY value to USD by multiplying the JPY exposure by $1/120.2758 = 0.0083$. Also, the shocked GBP-USD FX rate of 1.5277 from Table 10.13 is used to convert GBP exposure to USD. The EVE for the first scenario is then calculated as:

$$\text{Total Asset Value} - \text{Total Liability Value} = 2{,}560{,}206 \text{ USD}$$

The difference between this EVE and EVE for the base scenario provides us with the change in EVE for the first scenario as: $\Delta EVE_1 = 58{,}166\ USD$.

Assume now the randomly selected starting day for another historical path is November 2, 2011. The four days in the path are October 28, October 31, November 1, and November 2, 2011 (October 29 and October 30 are weekend days). The 1-day shocks for JPY and GBP FX rates and the calculated 3-day shocks for this scenario are presented in Table 10.15, calculated in a similar way as explained for the first scenario.

TABLE 10.14 Revalued balance sheet at horizon date for scenario 1 of exchange rate risk factor

Balance Sheet Type	Economic Value	Currency	FX Rate	USD Equivalent
Asset	10,000,000	USD	1.0000	10,000,000
Asset	1,200,000,000	JPY	0.0083	9,977,070
Asset	3,000,000	GBP	1.5277	4,583,136
	Total Assets:			24,560,206
Liability	22,000,000	USD	1.0000	22,000,000
		Total Liabilities:		22,000,000
EVE (USD) = Total Assets – Total Liabilities:				2,560,206

The shocked USD-JPY and GBP-USD FX rates for scenario 2 are calculated by multiplying the FX rates as of August 31, 2015, by the 3-day shocks. The shocked GBP-USD for scenario 2 is therefore $1.5345 \times 0.9888 = 1.5173$ and the shocked USD-JPY FX rate is $121.2300 \times 1.0294 = 124.7956$. Revaluing the balance sheet at the horizon date of September 3, 2015, using the shocked rates for scenario 2 is presented in Table 10.16, where JPY and GBP exposures are converted to USD using the shocked FX rates for scenario 2. The economic value of equity for this scenario is obtained as:

$$Total\ Asset\ Value - Total\ Liability\ Value = 2,167,567\ USD$$

The change in economic value of equity for the second scenario is obtained as: $\Delta EVE_2 = EVE_2 - EVE_0 = 2,167,567 - 2,502,040 = -334,473\ USD$.

Repeating this process for a large number of scenarios provides us with the distribution of ΔEVE. Table 10.17 shows a partial view of the calculated

TABLE 10.15 Scenario 2 of historical sampling of exchange rate risk factor

	Historical Path	**USD-JPY**	**1-Day Shock**	**GBP-USD**	**1-Day Shock**
$t-3$	10/28/2011	75.8200		1.6130	
$t-2$	10/31/2011	78.1700	1.0310	1.6087	0.9973
$t-1$	11/1/2011	78.3700	1.0026	1.5949	0.9914
t	11/2/2011	78.0500	0.9959	1.5949	1.0000
		$\times$	1.0294	$\times$	0.9888
	Shocked FX Rate:		124.7956		1.5173

TABLE 10.16 Revalued balance sheet at horizon date for scenario 2 of exchange rate risk factor

Balance Sheet Type	Economic Value	Currency	FX Rate	USD Equivalent
Asset	10,000,000	USD	1.0000	10,000,000
Asset	1,200,000,000	JPY	0.0080	9,615,725
Asset	3,000,000	GBP	1.5173	4,551,843
		Total Assets:		24,167,567
Liability	22,000,000	USD	1.0000	22,000,000
		Total Liabilities:		22,000,000
EVE (USD) = Total Assets – Total Liabilities:				2,167,567

TABLE 10.17 A partial view of changes in the economic value of equity for 10,000 scenarios using historical sampling of exchange rate risk factor

(a) Before Reordering

Scenario	EVE	ΔEVE
0	2,502,040	
1	2,560,206	58,166
2	2,167,567	(334,473)
3	2,178,918	(323,122)
4	2,373,132	(128,908)
5	2,527,653	25,613
6	2,569,362	67,322
7	2,461,360	(40,679)
8	2,734,973	232,933
9	2,580,008	77,968
10	2,594,205	92,165
11	2,600,898	98,858
12	2,711,352	209,312
...		
9996	2,527,921	25,881
9997	2,519,667	17,627
9998	2,595,680	93,640
9999	2,528,100	26,060
10000	2,480,613	(21,427)

(b) After Reordering

Scenario	EVE	ΔEVE	Rank	Ordinal Rank
2769	2,105,277	(396,763)	10000	1.0000
9959	2,133,496	(368,544)	9999	0.9999
2163	2,143,197	(358,843)	9998	0.9998
4976	2,152,637	(349,403)	9997	0.9997
...	...	...	...	...
8612	2,270,018	(232,022)	9906	0.9906
7528	2,272,140	(229,900)	9905	0.9905
4937	2,272,600	(229,440)	9904	0.9904
8320	2,272,877	(229,163)	9903	0.9903
9877	2,273,578	(228,462)	9902	0.9902
5375	2,273,663	(228,377)	9901	0.9901
438	2,273,824	(228,216)	9900	0.9900
5219	2,274,066	(227,974)	9899	0.9899
...	...	...	...	...
9505	2,840,826	338,786	5	0.0005
6974	2,857,172	355,132	4	0.0004
8790	2,868,622	366,582	3	0.0003
3816	2,876,643	374,603	2	0.0002
1708	2,878,578	376,538	1	0.0001

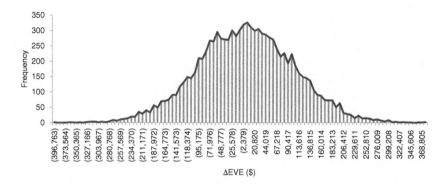

FIGURE 10.12 Distribution of ΔEVE using historical sampling of FX rates for 10,000 scenarios

Δ*EVE* for 10,000 scenarios. Panel (a) of this table contains changes in EVE before sorting and panel (b) presents the results after sorting on ascending order of Δ*EVE*. The 99th percentile is the value of Δ*EVE* at ordinal rank of 0.9900, a change in EVE of –$228,216. Based on this analysis, with 99% probability the EVE of this bank can decrease by $228,216 or less in three days due to a change in exchange rates (there is still a 1% chance the decrease can exceed $228,216). Empirical distribution of Δ*EVE* for this example is shown in Figure 10.12.

SAMPLE SIZE AND CONVERGENCE

Decisions about the number of simulation iterations, or sample size, is the first step in equity-at-risk analysis. An appropriate sample size should provide a stable estimation of the target percentile. Considering ΔEVE as a random variable and treating a percentile point of its distribution as a parameter, as sample size increases, the estimated value of the percentile converges to the population parameter. The question is at what sample size we are confident about the accuracy and stability of the estimated value. One way to answer this is by constructing a confidence interval around the percentile point estimate. As width of this confidence interval depends on the sample size, we can choose the sample size that provides the stable confidence interval at the desirable accuracy level. To build the needed confidence interval, a nonparametric approach is required where we do not make any assumption about the distribution of the percentile point estimator.

Assume that X is a continuous random variable representing ΔEVE and $X_1, X_2, \cdots, X_n$ are members of a sample of size n. Assume π_p is the percentile point when the probability of ΔEVE to be less than π_p is p:

$$p = P(X < \pi_p)$$

If $X_{(1)}, X_{(2)}, \cdots, X_{(n)}$ is the sample sorted in an ascending order, π_p is derived by finding the member of this order statistic where $p\%$ of the members are below π_p. To construct a $(1 - \alpha)100\%$ confidence interval around π_p we need to find two values $X_{(r)}$ and $X_{(s)}$, such that:

$$P(X_{(r)} < \pi_p < X_{(s)}) = 1 - \alpha$$

Gibbons and Chakraborti (2010) showed:

$$P(X_{(r)} < \pi_p < X_{(s)}) = \sum_{j=r}^{s-1} \binom{n}{j} p^j (1-p)^{n-j} = P(r \le K \le s-1) \qquad (10.58)$$

where K is a random variable with binomial distribution with parameters n and p. r and s are selected such that $s - r$ is minimum for a given α. Due to the discrete nature of binomial distribution the resulting probability in Equation (10.58) may not be exactly $1 - \alpha$, so a conservative approach is to find r and s, when $s - r$ is minimum and the probability is at least $1 - \alpha$, i.e.:

$$P(X_{(r)} < \pi_p < X_{(s)}) = \sum_{j=r}^{s-1} \binom{n}{j} p^j (1-p)^{n-j} \ge 1 - \alpha \qquad (10.59)$$

Since it is possible to find more than one pair of r and s that satisfies Equation (10.59), to find a unique solution, one approach is to assume equal probabilities of $\alpha/2$ on two sides of the confidence interval. Therefore we seek to find r and s as the largest and smallest integers, such that $1 \le r < s \le n$ and:

$$\sum_{j=0}^{r-1} \binom{n}{j} p^j (1-p)^{n-j} \le \frac{\alpha}{2}$$

and $\qquad\qquad\qquad\qquad\qquad\qquad\qquad\qquad\qquad\qquad\qquad (10.60)$

$$\sum_{j=0}^{s-1} \binom{n}{j} p^j (1-p)^{n-j} \ge 1 - \frac{\alpha}{2}$$

If the sample size is large, we can use normal approximation to binomial distribution to obtain r and s using the following equations:

$$r = np + 0.5 - Z_{\frac{\alpha}{2}}\sqrt{np(1-p)}$$

$$s = np + 0.5 + Z_{\frac{\alpha}{2}}\sqrt{np(1-p)}$$

(10.61)

where $Z_{\frac{\alpha}{2}}$ is the value of inverse of cumulative standard normal distribution for probability $\frac{\alpha}{2}$. We need to round down r and round up s to the nearest integers.

To demonstrate this method, consider again the equity-at-risk analysis discussed earlier when we focused on the exchange rate risk factor. Recall in that example, based on a sample size of $n = 10,000$, the 99th percentile of ΔEVE was –\$228,216. This value was selected at the rank 100 from the 10,000 simulated ΔEVEs ordered ascendingly (i.e., at ordinal rank of 0.9900). For a sample size of 10,000, to build a 95% nonparametric confidence interval ($\alpha = 0.05$) around the 99th percentile of ΔEVE ($p = 0.01$), we can search for rank r and s that satisfy Equation (10.60). Particularly, for $r = 81$ and $s = 121$ we have:[7]

$$\sum_{j=0}^{81-1} \binom{10,000}{j} 0.01^j \times 0.99^{10,000-j} = 0.0221 < 0.025$$

$$\sum_{j=0}^{121-1} \binom{10,000}{j} 0.01^j \times 0.99^{10,000-j} = 0.9779 > 0.975$$

Therefore, choosing ΔEVEs at rank 81 and 121 provides us with a confidence interval around the point estimator of equity-at-risk with the probability of $0.9779 - 0.0221 = 0.9558$. As noted previously, using this method may not result in an exact 95% confidence interval, rather in a confidence interval with probability that is at least 95% (here 95.58%). Searching through the sorted values of ΔEVEs we found ΔEVE at rank 81 is –\$237,194 and the one at rank 121 is –\$223,954. This results in a confidence interval with the absolute width of \$13,239. Therefore, with 95.58% probability we are confident the equity-at-risk is between is –\$237,194 and –\$223,954. If this is an acceptable level of accuracy, then the sample size of 10,000 is appropriate, otherwise we can increase the sample size to reduce the confidence interval width. Table 10.18 presents several at-least 95% confidence intervals based on different sample sizes built around the 99th percentile of ΔEVE for the exchange rate risk factor example. As expected, the increase in sample size decreases the width of the confidence

TABLE 10.18 At-least 95% confidence interval of equity-at-risk based on the 99th percentile of ΔEVE for different sample sizes

n	r	s	99th Percentile Rank	Exact C.I. (Prob.)	C.I. Width ($)
1,000	4	18	10	0.9761	69,937
2,000	10	30	20	0.9739	36,096
3,000	18	42	30	0.9714	33,586
4,000	28	54	40	0.9616	25,044
5,000	37	65	50	0.9537	23,559
6,000	45	77	60	0.9624	23,390
7,000	54	88	70	0.9591	17,542
8,000	63	99	80	0.9571	14,510
9,000	72	110	90	0.9561	13,805
10,000	81	121	100	0.9558	13,239
20,000	172	229	200	0.9573	11,496
30,000	266	335	300	0.9548	8,731
40,000	361	440	400	0.9529	7,238
50,000	456	545	500	0.9546	7,022

interval. Analysis such as this provides a method to choose the sample size that satisfies the required level of accuracy.

When selecting the sample size two issues should be considered. The first is the incremental impact of increase in the sample size. While increasing the sample size decreases the confidence interval width around the point estimator of equity-at-risk, this impact, however, diminishes as sample size increases. Figure 10.13 shows the 99th percentile of ΔEVE for our example with an at-least 95% confidence interval around it when the sample size is increased from 1,000 to 50,000 with an increment of 1,000. From this graph the diminishing impact of increase in sample size on decreasing the confidence interval width is clear. For example, the increase of sample size by doubling it from 2,000 to 4,000 had a larger impact in reducing the confidence interval width (both from a dollar or percentage point of view) compared to when the sample size is doubled from 10,000 to 20,000. Also from this graph we can see for a sample size above 35,000 the width of the confidence interval does not change materially. Hence, if a narrower confidence interval is required, the sample size should be increased but the diminishing effect of this increase should also be considered in choosing the appropriate sample size.

The second issue in selecting the appropriate sample size is the computational cost of the analysis. An increase in the number of simulation iterations leads to a larger computation time and resource requirement. There is a trade-off between the increase in the sample size for higher accuracy and

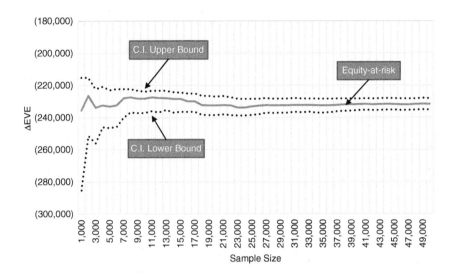

FIGURE 10.13 Increase of sample size has a diminishing impact in decreasing the confidence interval width (C.I.: confidence interval)

the computational time and its associated cost (e.g., cost of computer servers, memory, storage, etc.). This trade-off should be considered in choosing the appropriate sample size in simulation-based analysis.

EARNINGS-AT-RISK

Similar to the economic value of equity, a limited number of scenarios considered in the net interest income analysis exposes a financial firm to the potential adverse impact of cases that were not analyzed. Earnings-at-risk (EaR) is a measurement that helps a bank's management team to better understand the potential changes in earnings and to plan for them accordingly. Earnings-at-risk is the maximum potential decrease in estimated earnings of the bank due to changes in risk factors for a given time horizon and for a given confidence level. Derivation of earnings-at-risk requires calculation of earnings over the time horizon using simulated paths of involved risk factors.

In earnings-at-risk analysis, simulated paths of risk factors from the current date to the horizon date are used to obtain a probabilistic estimation of potential change in earnings of the bank over the time horizon. By simulating a large number of evolution paths of risk factors from the analysis date to the horizon date and performing NII analysis for each path, we can construct the probability distribution of ΔNII and obtain statistical metrics, such as standard deviation and percentiles of ΔNII. To explain the concept of earnings-at-risk, in the following section we use interest rate and exchange rate risk factors and demonstrate how earnings-at-risk is calculated and used.

Interest Rate Risk Factor

We start our discussion on earnings-at-risk by assuming interest rate is the only major risk factor impacting the earnings of a bank. Assume that the bank has a simple balance sheet including a $1,200 million floating-rate asset with an interest rate of 1-year LIBOR plus 200 bps spread, and a $250 million fixed-rate asset with a 5.25% rate. Liabilities of this bank consist of a $1,000 million debt with an interest rate of 1-month LIBOR plus 20 bps spread and $120 million of fixed-rate debt with 3.3% rate. This bank uses a 1-year time horizon for net interest income analysis and the time step is one month. Here we focus on only net interest income and omit other components of earnings in the analysis. The reset frequency of floating-rate assets and liabilities is monthly, and here we assume the balance of all positions (fixed or floating) to remain constant during the 1-year horizon. For simplicity we assume all assets and liabilities have a 30/360 accrual basis and no business day adjustment convention is applied. Also for floating-rate positions we assume the rate resets occur at month-ends without any business day adjustments and effective rates for each month are derived using the previous month-end rate of the corresponding index.

For net interest income analysis, this bank uses implied forward rates for the base scenario. The 1-month and 1-year LIBOR implied forwards assumed here are presented in the first two columns of Table 10.19 for the current date ($t = 0$) and 12 month-ends in the future until the horizon date. These forward rates are calculated from the LIBOR-Swap spot curve as of the analysis date.

To create simulated paths of interest rate, we used a Vasicek model.[8] Since the time step of the analysis is one month and the time horizon is one year, each simulated path of the short rate contains 12 rates at each month-end between the analysis date and the horizon date. These short rates are then used to calculate simulated 1-month and 1-year rates at each month-end. For details of the Vasicek model and the method of calculation of term rates from the short rate, refer to Chapter 5. Table 10.19 presents the first three simulated interest rate paths of 1-month and 1-year rates generated by this model. These term rates are needed for calculation of the net interest income of the bank in our example. Using this model we generated 10,000 simulated paths of 1-month and 1-year rates.

Next, we need to calculate the net interest income for 12 monthly time buckets from the analysis date until the horizon date to obtain one year of net interest income for the base scenario and each simulated scenario.

TABLE 10.19 Implied forward and three simulated paths of 1-month and 1-year LIBOR (all rates are annualized and in %)*

	Implied Forward		Path 1		Path 2		Path 3	
t (Month)	r(t,1M)	r(t,1Y)	r(t,1M)	r(t,1Y)	r(t,1M)	r(t,1Y)	r(t,1M)	r(t,1Y)
0	0.6808	0.9048	0.6808	0.9048	0.6808	0.9048	0.6808	0.9048
1	0.6907	0.9152	0.7632	0.9827	0.8048	1.0220	0.8045	1.0218
2	0.7040	0.9208	0.7666	0.9859	0.8428	1.0580	0.8260	1.0421
3	0.7156	0.9392	0.7888	1.0069	0.9661	1.1746	0.9241	1.1349
4	0.7909	0.9408	0.8449	1.0600	0.9748	1.1829	1.0015	1.2081
5	0.8124	0.9507	0.8950	1.1074	1.0186	1.2243	0.9409	1.1508
6	0.8383	0.9704	0.9336	1.1439	1.1328	1.3324	1.0398	1.2444
7	0.8394	0.9908	0.9916	1.1988	1.1641	1.3620	0.9043	1.1162
8	0.8430	1.0202	1.0445	1.2489	1.0794	1.2819	0.9690	1.1774
9	0.9245	1.0502	1.1352	1.3347	1.0268	1.2321	0.9515	1.1609
10	0.9345	1.0634	1.1037	1.3049	1.0968	1.2983	0.9965	1.2035
11	0.9456	1.1637	1.2453	1.4388	1.1850	1.3817	0.9390	1.1490
12	0.9505	1.2721	1.3314	1.5203	1.2489	1.4422	0.9383	1.1484

*Rates at $t = 0$ are spot rates.

Base Scenario

Interest income of the fixed-rate $250 million asset portfolio for each of the 12 monthly time buckets is the same and assuming a 30/360 accrual basis it is calculated as:

$$250,000,000 \times \frac{30}{360} \times \frac{5.25}{100} = \$1,093,750$$

The effective rate of the floating-rate $1,200 million asset portfolio for the first monthly time bucket is spot 1-year LIBOR plus 200 bps or 0.9048% + 2% = 2.9048%. Therefore, the interest income of the first monthly time bucket is calculated as:

$$1,200,000,000 \times \frac{30}{360} \times \frac{2.9048}{100} = \$2,904,778.03$$

For the second monthly time bucket the effective rate is derived using the implied forward of 1-year LIBOR at the end of month one and is calculated as 0.9152% + 2% = 2.9152%. So the interest income for this period is calculated as:

$$1,200,000,000 \times \frac{30}{360} \times \frac{2.9152}{100} = \$2,915,200$$

Interest income for monthly time buckets of 3 to 12 is calculated similarly using the implied forward 1-year LIBOR at each previous month-end.

TABLE 10.20 Interest income from fixed and floating-rate assets in base case (implied forward)

Period (Month)	Floating-Rate Asset			Fixed-Rate Asset		Total Interest Income ($)
	1-Year LIBOR (%)	Effective Rate (%)	Interest Income ($)	Effective Rate (%)	Interest Income ($)	
0	0.9048					
1	0.9152	2.9048	2,904,778.03	5.25	1,093,750.00	3,998,528.03
2	0.9208	2.9152	2,915,200.00	5.25	1,093,750.00	4,008,950.00
3	0.9392	2.9208	2,920,800.00	5.25	1,093,750.00	4,014,550.00
4	0.9408	2.9392	2,939,200.00	5.25	1,093,750.00	4,032,950.00
5	0.9507	2.9408	2,940,800.00	5.25	1,093,750.00	4,034,550.00
6	0.9704	2.9507	2,950,700.00	5.25	1,093,750.00	4,044,450.00
7	0.9908	2.9704	2,970,400.00	5.25	1,093,750.00	4,064,150.00
8	1.0202	2.9908	2,990,800.00	5.25	1,093,750.00	4,084,550.00
9	1.0502	3.0202	3,020,200.00	5.25	1,093,750.00	4,113,950.00
10	1.0634	3.0502	3,050,200.00	5.25	1,093,750.00	4,143,950.00
11	1.1637	3.0634	3,063,400.00	5.25	1,093,750.00	4,157,150.00
12	1.2721	3.1637	3,163,700.00	5.25	1,093,750.00	4,257,450.00
			Total 1-Year Interest Income:			**48,955,178.03**

The results of these calculations are summarized in Table 10.20 where total 1-year interest income (including income from both fixed and floating-rate positions) for the base scenario is obtained as $48,955,178.03.

Interest expense of the fixed and floating-rate liabilities is calculated similarly, where a constant 3.3% rate is used for the fixed-rate $120 million debt portfolio and implied forward 1-month LIBOR plus 20 bps is used for derivation of the effective rate for the $1,000 million floating-rate debt portfolio. Calculated interest expense for 12 monthly time buckets for the base scenario is presented in Table 10.21 where total 1-year interest expense (including expense from both fixed and floating-rate positions) is $14,059,787.75. Hence the net interest income of the base scenario is obtained as:

$$\$48,955,178.03 - \$14,059,787.75 = \$34,895,390.28$$

Simulated Scenarios

The interest income and expense during the 1-year time horizon for each simulated interest rate path is calculated in a similar way explained previously, where instead of implied forward rates simulated 1-month and 1-year LIBOR

TABLE 10.21 Interest expense from fixed and floating-rate liabilities in base case (implied forward)

| Period (Month) | 1-Month LIBOR (%) | Floating-Rate Liability | | Fixed-Rate Liability | | Total Interest Expense ($) |
		Effective Rate (%)	Interest Expense ($)	Effective Rate (%)	Interest Expense ($)	
0	0.6808					
1	0.6907	0.8808	734,037.75	3.3	330,000.00	1,064,037.75
2	0.7040	0.8907	742,250.00	3.3	330,000.00	1,072,250.00
3	0.7156	0.9040	753,333.33	3.3	330,000.00	1,083,333.33
4	0.7909	0.9156	763,000.00	3.3	330,000.00	1,093,000.00
5	0.8124	0.9909	825,750.00	3.3	330,000.00	1,155,750.00
6	0.8383	1.0124	843,666.67	3.3	330,000.00	1,173,666.67
7	0.8394	1.0383	865,250.00	3.3	330,000.00	1,195,250.00
8	0.8430	1.0394	866,166.67	3.3	330,000.00	1,196,166.67
9	0.9245	1.0430	869,166.67	3.3	330,000.00	1,199,166.67
10	0.9345	1.1245	937,083.33	3.3	330,000.00	1,267,083.33
11	0.9456	1.1345	945,416.67	3.3	330,000.00	1,275,416.67
12	0.9505	1.1456	954,666.67	3.3	330,000.00	1,284,666.67
	Total 1-Year Interest Expense:					**14,059,787.75**

are used. For example, from Table 10.19 the simulated 1-year LIBOR at the end of month 1 of path 1 is 0.9827. Therefore the interest income of the floating-rate $1,200 million asset portfolio for the second monthly time bucket is calculated as:

$$1,200,000,000 \times \frac{30}{360} \times \frac{0.9827 + 2}{100} = \$2,982,683.56$$

Rates and interest income and expense of the fixed-rate asset and liability portfolios are the same as the base scenario. Interest income and expense for monthly time buckets based on rates from simulated path 1 are presented in Tables 10.22 and 10.23 where net interest income for a 1-year time horizon is calculated as:

$$\$50,842,628.46 - \$15,287,733.83 = \$35,554,894.63$$

Based on the results in the previous tables, the change in the net interest income for scenario 1 is calculated as:

$$\Delta NII = NII_1 - NII_0 = \$35,554,894.63 - \$34,895,390.28 = \$659,504.35$$

TABLE 10.22 Interest income from fixed and floating-rate assets for simulated path 1 scenario

| Period (Month) | Floating-Rate Asset | | | Fixed-Rate Asset | | Total |
	1-Year LIBOR (%)	Effective Rate (%)	Interest Income ($)	Effective Rate (%)	Interest Income ($)	Interest Income ($)
0	0.9048					
1	0.9827	2.9048	2,904,778.03	5.25	1,093,750.00	3,998,528.03
2	0.9859	2.9827	2,982,683.56	5.25	1,093,750.00	4,076,433.56
3	1.0069	2.9859	2,985,907.11	5.25	1,093,750.00	4,079,657.11
4	1.0600	3.0069	3,006,937.28	5.25	1,093,750.00	4,100,687.28
5	1.1074	3.0600	3,059,998.87	5.25	1,093,750.00	4,153,748.87
6	1.1439	3.1074	3,107,383.19	5.25	1,093,750.00	4,201,133.19
7	1.1988	3.1439	3,143,896.46	5.25	1,093,750.00	4,237,646.46
8	1.2489	3.1988	3,198,814.60	5.25	1,093,750.00	4,292,564.60
9	1.3347	3.2489	3,248,872.27	5.25	1,093,750.00	4,342,622.27
10	1.3049	3.3347	3,334,687.74	5.25	1,093,750.00	4,428,437.74
11	1.4388	3.3049	3,304,868.62	5.25	1,093,750.00	4,398,618.62
12	1.5203	3.4388	3,438,800.73	5.25	1,093,750.00	4,532,550.73
			Total 1-Year Interest Income:			**50,842,628.46**

TABLE 10.23 Interest expense from fixed and floating-rate liabilities for simulated path 1 scenario

| Period (Month) | Floating-Rate Liability | | | Fixed-Rate Liability | | Total |
	1-Month LIBOR (%)	Effective Rate (%)	Interest Expense ($)	Effective Rate (%)	Interest Expense ($)	Interest Expense ($)
0	0.6808					
1	0.7632	0.8808	734,037.75	3.3	330,000.00	1,064,037.75
2	0.7666	0.9632	802,655.18	3.3	330,000.00	1,132,655.18
3	0.7888	0.9666	805,494.42	3.3	330,000.00	1,135,494.42
4	0.8449	0.9888	824,017.32	3.3	330,000.00	1,154,017.32
5	0.8950	1.0449	870,752.77	3.3	330,000.00	1,200,752.77
6	0.9336	1.0950	912,487.81	3.3	330,000.00	1,242,487.81
7	0.9916	1.1336	944,647.88	3.3	330,000.00	1,274,647.88
8	1.0445	1.1916	993,018.53	3.3	330,000.00	1,323,018.53
9	1.1352	1.2445	1,037,108.20	3.3	330,000.00	1,367,108.20
10	1.1037	1.3352	1,112,692.53	3.3	330,000.00	1,442,692.53
11	1.2453	1.3037	1,086,428.53	3.3	330,000.00	1,416,428.53
12	1.3314	1.4453	1,204,392.91	3.3	330,000.00	1,534,392.91
			Total 1-Year Interest Expense:			**15,287,733.83**

TABLE 10.24 A partial view of changes in net interest income for 1-year time horizon using 10,000 simulated interest rate paths

a) Before Reordering

Scenario	NII ($)	ΔNII ($)
0	34,895,390	
1	35,554,895	659,504
2	35,642,814	747,423
3	35,530,615	635,224
4	35,675,804	780,413
5	35,604,247	708,857
6	35,263,375	367,985
7	35,553,483	658,093
8	35,553,176	657,786
9	35,525,901	630,511
10	35,711,414	816,023
11	35,706,455	811,065
12	35,413,726	518,336
...		
9996	35,483,607	588,216
9997	35,779,793	884,403
9998	35,931,404	1,036,013
9999	35,702,174	806,784
10000	35,508,812	613,421

b) After Reordering

Scenario	NII ($)	ΔNII ($)	Rank	Ordinal Rank
9560	34,846,251	(49,139)	10000	1.0000
396	34,968,747	73,357	9999	0.9999
2363	34,986,631	91,241	9998	0.9998
2929	35,009,993	114,602	9997	0.9997
9104	35,021,451	126,061	9996	0.9996
641	35,024,732	129,342	9995	0.9995
5825	35,030,182	134,792	9994	0.9994
9083	35,049,834	154,444	9993	0.9993
8600	35,051,588	156,197	9992	0.9992
5139	35,072,613	177,223	9991	0.9991
3652	35,076,490	181,100	9990	0.9990
8797	35,080,518	185,128	9989	0.9989
1553	35,082,305	186,914	9988	0.9988
...			...	
1243	36,146,703	1,251,313	5	0.0005
6275	36,149,758	1,254,367	4	0.0004
4810	36,162,122	1,266,732	3	0.0003
2949	36,165,472	1,270,081	2	0.0002
9151	36,293,994	1,398,603	1	0.0001

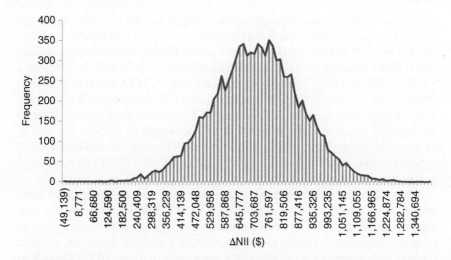

FIGURE 10.14 Distribution of ΔNII for a 1-year time horizon using 10,000 simulated interest rate paths

Repeating this process for a large number of simulated interest rate paths provides us with the distribution of ΔNII. Table 10.24 provides a partial view of the net interest income for 10,000 simulated scenarios. To obtain the 99.9th percentile of ΔNII, we sort the ΔNII values in an ascending order and the required percentile is at the ordinal rank of 0.9990, with a value of $181,100, rounded to the nearest dollar. Therefore, based on this analysis with 99.9% probability, the change in net interest income of this bank due to a change in interest rate, for a 1-year time horizon, is an increase of $181,100 or higher (there is still a 0.1% chance that the change in net interest income is lower than $181,100 or that NII may even decrease). Figure 10.14 shows the empirical distribution of ΔNII for our example.

Currency Exchange Rate Risk Factor

Changes in currency exchange rates impact the net interest income and earnings of banks with multi-currency balance sheets. Similar to interest rate risk, earnings-at-risk analysis for a currency exchange rate risk factor is performed by building the distribution of changes in the net interest income at the horizon date by simulating paths of exchange rates from the analysis date to the horizon date. The simulated paths of exchange rates can be produced using the historical sampling or the Monte Carlo simulation method.

To demonstrate the earnings-at-risk analysis for the currency exchange rate risk factor, consider a bank that has interest income and expense in three currencies: U.S. dollar (USD), Swedish krona (SEK), and European Union Euro (EUR). Assume a current spot exchange rate for EUR-USD is 1.1850 and for SEK-USD is 0.1100, where both rates are quoted as an amount of foreign currency for 1 unit of USD. This bank performs NII analysis based on a 1-year time horizon with a 3-month time step and quarterly time bucket. Interest income and expense in EUR and SEK are converted to USD at the end of each quarter in the future. Table 10.25 provides expected interest income and expense in four quarters in the future in USD, SEK, and EUR. The functional currency of the bank is U.S. dollar.

To obtain NII for the base scenario, we use the forward exchange rates presented in Table 10.26 to convert EUR and SEK-based interest income and expense to USD. As explained in a previous chapter, use of forward exchange rates as estimates of future exchange rates is a practice based on covered interest rate parity. This calculation is presented in Table 10.27. Rows 1 to 6 show conversion of EUR and SEK-based interest income to USD using forward exchange rates from Table 10.26. Row 7 contains USD-based interest income that doesn't require conversion and row 8 is the total interest income in the base scenario for each quarterly bucket. The "Total" column provides the total amount in each row for the entire 1 year of the time horizon.

TABLE 10.25   Expected four quarters interest income and expense of a hypothetical bank in USD, EUR, and SEK

		Q1	Q2	Q3	Q4	Total
Income	EUR	600,000	505,000	485,000	450,000	2,040,000
	SEK	1,000,000	1,500,000	2,350,000	1,450,000	6,300,000
	USD	770,000	545,000	265,000	850,000	2,430,000
Expense	EUR	100,000	180,000	200,000	235,000	715,000
	SEK	450,000	745,000	1,200,000	900,000	3,295,000
	USD	250,000	300,000	185,000	260,000	995,000

TABLE 10.26   Spot and forward EUR-USD and SEK-USD exchange rates

Currency Pair	s_0	$f_{0,3M}$	$f_{0,6M}$	$f_{0,9M}$	$f_{0,12M}$
EUR-USD	1.1850	1.1855	1.1865	1.1874	1.1862
SEK-USD	0.1100	0.1118	0.1154	0.1161	0.1205

TABLE 10.27 Calculation of base scenario NII using forward EUR-USD and SEK-USD exchange rates

		Q1	Q2	Q3	Q4	Total	Row #
EUR-based	EUR	600,000	505,000	485,000	450,000		1
Interest Income	× [USD per 1 EUR]	1.1855	1.1865	1.1874	1.1862		2
	= USD	711,300	599,183	575,889	533,790	2,420,162	3
SEK-based	SEK	1,000,000	1,500,000	2,350,000	1,450,000		4
Interest Income	× [USD per 1 SEK]	0.1118	0.1154	0.1161	0.1205		5
	= USD	111,800	173,100	272,835	174,725	732,460	6
USD-based Interest Income		770,000	545,000	265,000	850,000	2,430,000	7
Total Interest Income (USD)		**1,593,100**	**1,317,283**	**1,113,724**	**1,558,515**	**5,582,622**	8
EUR-based	EUR	100,000	180,000	200,000	235,000		9
Interest Expense	× [USD per 1 EUR]	1.1855	1.1865	1.1874	1.1862		10
	= USD	118,550	213,570	237,480	278,757	848,357	11
SEK-based	SEK	450,000	745,000	1,200,000	900,000		12
Interest Expense	× [USD per 1 SEK]	0.1118	0.1154	0.1161	0.1205		13
	=USD	50,310	85,973	139,320	108,450	384,053	14
USD-based Interest Expense		250,000	300,000	185,000	260,000	995,000	15
Interest Expense (USD)		**418,860**	**599,543**	**561,800**	**647,207**	**2,227,410**	16
NII (USD)		**1,174,240**	**717,740**	**551,924**	**911,308**	**3,355,212**	17

Rows 9 to 16 of this table perform the same conversion for interest expense, and row 17 is the net interest income calculated as row 8 amounts minus row 16 amounts. Total expected NII for 1-year time horizon in the base scenario using forward exchange rates is $3,355,212.

To create simulated path of EUR-USD and SEK-USD exchange rates during 1-year time horizon, we can use either historical sampling or Monte Carlo simulation methods. Figure 10.15 presents three simulated paths of EUR-USD and SEK-USD exchange rates produced using the Monte Carlo simulation method.[9]

Consider path 1 of EUR-USD and SEK-USD exchange rates from Figure 10.15. We can use these simulated rates to calculate scenario 1 net

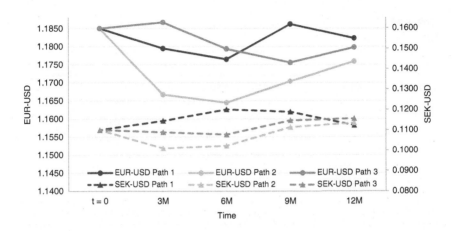

FIGURE 10.15   Three simulated paths of EUR-USD and SEK-USD exchange rates for four quarters in the future. EUR-USD exchange rate scale is shown on the left vertical axis and the SEK-USD scale is on the right vertical axis.

interest income in USD for each quarterly time bucket over the 1-year time horizon. Table 10.28 presents this calculation. Similar to what is explained for the base scenario, rows 1 to 8 convert EUR and SEK-based interest incomes using simulated exchange rates of path 1 and add them to USD-based interest income to obtain the total interest income in USD in row 8. Rows 9 to 16 do the same for the interest expenses and row 17 provides the net interest income as the total interest incomes in row 8 minus the total interest expense in row 16.

Total simulated expected NII for the 1-year horizon in scenario 1 is $3,322,696. Finally, row 18 provides the change in interest income for scenario 1, obtained as the difference between the net interest income of scenario 1 and the base scenario, for a total 1 year ΔNII of –$32,516.

We produced 10,000 simulated paths of EUR-USD and SEK-USD exchange rates and calculated ΔNII for each scenario for a 1-year time horizon. Table 10.29 presents a partial view of these simulated ΔNII. To obtain the 99.9th percentile of ΔNII, we sort the ΔNII values in an ascending order and the required percentile is at the ordinal rank of 0.9990, with a value of –$157,663, rounded to the nearest dollar. Therefore, based on this analysis, with 99.9% probability the change in the net interest income of this bank for a 1-year time horizon and due to the change in EUR-USD and SEK-USD exchange rates is a decrease of $157,663 or lower (there is still a 0.1% chance that the decrease in net interest income is higher in magnitude than $157,663). Figure 10.16 shows the empirical distribution of ΔNII for our example.

TABLE 10.28 Calculation of NII for shock scenario 1 using simulated EUR-USD and SEK-USD exchange rates

		Q1	Q2	Q3	Q4	Total	Row #
EUR-based	EUR	600,000	505,000	485,000	450,000		1
Interest	× [USD per 1	1.1795	1.1765	1.1862	1.1823		2
Income	EUR]						
	= USD	707,700	594,133	575,307	532,035	2,409,175	3
SEK-based	SEK	1,000,000	1,500,000	2,350,000	1,450,000		4
Interest	× [USD per 1	0.1010	0.1023	0.1114	0.1135		5
Income	SEK]						
	= USD	101,000	153,450	261,790	164,575	680,815	6
USD-based Interest Income		770,000	545,000	265,000	850,000	2,430,000	7
Total Interest Income (USD)		**1,578,700**	**1,292,583**	**1,102,097**	**1,546,610**	**5,519,990**	8
EUR-based	EUR	100,000	180,000	200,000	235,000		9
Interest	× [USD per 1	1.1795	1.1765	1.1862	1.1823		10
Expense	EUR]						
	= USD	117,950	211,770	237,240	277,841	844,801	11
SEK-based	SEK	450,000	745,000	1,200,000	900,000		12
Interest	× [USD per 1	0.1010	0.1023	0.1114	0.1135		13
Expense	SEK]						
	= USD	45,450	76,214	133,680	102,150	357,494	14
USD-based Interest Expense		250,000	300,000	185,000	260,000	995,000	15
Interest Expense (USD)		**413,400**	**587,984**	**555,920**	**639,991**	**2,197,294**	16
NII (USD)		**1,165,300**	**704,599**	**546,177**	**906,620**	**3,322,696**	17
ΔNII (USD)		**(8,940)**	**(13,141)**	**(5,747)**	**(4,689)**	**(32,516)**	18

TABLE 10.29 A partial view of changes in net interest income for a 1-year time horizon using 10,000 simulated currency exchange rate paths

a) Before Reordering

Scenario	NII ($)	ΔNII ($)
0	3,355,212	
1	3,322,696	(32,516)
2	3,329,690	(25,522)
3	3,353,534	(1,678)
4	3,347,290	(7,922)
5	3,212,567	(142,645)
6	3,240,867	(114,345)
7	3,400,158	44,946
8	3,425,493	70,282
9	3,247,776	(107,436)
10	3,375,008	19,796
11	3,341,585	(13,627)
12	3,310,834	(44,377)
...		
9997	3,370,234	15,023
9998	3,393,058	37,847
9999	3,289,638	(65,574)
10000	3,321,591	(33,621)

b) After Reordering

Scenario	NII ($)	ΔNII ($)	Rank	Ordinal Rank
6552	3,180,625	(174,587)	10000	1.0000
190	3,186,291	(168,921)	9999	0.9999
6086	3,191,196	(164,015)	9998	0.9998
1618	3,193,405	(161,807)	9997	0.9997
1027	3,193,636	(161,576)	9996	0.9996
1801	3,194,363	(160,849)	9995	0.9995
3042	3,195,529	(159,683)	9994	0.9994
3913	3,196,604	(158,608)	9993	0.9993
9108	3,196,641	(158,571)	9992	0.9992
4801	3,196,968	(158,244)	9991	0.9991
3648	3,197,549	(157,663)	9990	0.9990
8633	3,199,862	(155,349)	9989	0.9989
8809	3,200,361	(154,851)	9988	0.9988
...			...	...
7857	3,482,485	127,274	4	0.0004
1821	3,488,285	133,073	3	0.0003
3964	3,492,411	137,200	2	0.0002
4753	3,514,730	159,519	1	0.0001

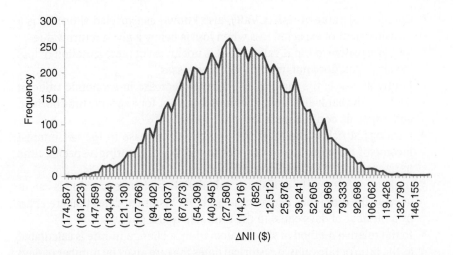

FIGURE 10.16 Distribution of ΔNII for a 1-year time horizon using 10,000 simulated currency exchange rate paths

SUMMARY

- The limited number of cases considered in EVE or NII scenario analysis is considered a drawback of those studies.
- One approach to extend the EVE and NII scenario analysis is to use simulation to construct probability distribution of these ALM metrics and use that distribution to obtain information on potential impacts on the bank balance sheet and earnings.
- Value-at-risk (VaR) is a measurement of maximum potential loss in the value of a financial instrument or a portfolio of instruments over a given time horizon with a specific confidence level.
- To find the VaR of a portfolio of instruments the correlation of returns of individual instruments within the portfolio must be taken into account.
- Generally, there are three methods to obtain VaR:
  1. In the variance-covariance method, VaR is derived based on an assumed probability distribution of return.
  2. In the historical sampling method, historical return data are used to determine VaR.
  3. In the Monte-Carlo simulation method, stochastic models are used to create simulated paths of risk factors over a time horizon. The simulated paths are then used to obtain VaR.
- In the historical sampling method an exponential weighting scheme can be used to put higher weight on data from more recent dates.

■ Conditional value-at-risk (CVaR), also known as expected shortfall, is a measurement of expected loss when loss is below a given return value.

■ VaR is sensitive to input values. VaR is not an exact representation of loss in value. VaR does not quantify extreme losses.

■ Equity-at-risk is the maximum potential decrease in economic value of equity of the bank due to changes in risk factors, for a specific time horizon and a specific confidence level.

■ Earnings-at-risk is the maximum potential decrease in the net interest income of the bank due to changes in risk factors, during a specific time horizon, and for a specific confidence level.

■ In the absolute method of shock calculation, a change-in-value is calculated as the difference between rates at two historical dates that are apart by a number of days equal to the time step of the analysis.

■ In the relative method of shock calculation, a change-in-rate is calculated as the ratio of rates at two historical dates that are apart by number of days equal to the time step of the analysis.

■ The generalized Brownian motion stochastic process models the change-in-value of a risk factor in a short period of time. In geometric Brownian motion stochastic process the percentage change of the risk factor in a short period of time is modeled. In a mean-reverting Brownian motion model, also known as Ornstein–Uhlenbeck process, risk factor trends toward its long-term mean.

■ In equity-at-risk analysis, the simulated spot rate and forecasted balance sheet at the horizon date is used to build the probability distribution of EVE at the horizon date. Paths of risk factors from the analysis date to the horizon date can be used for valuation of path-dependent positions at the horizon date.

■ In earnings-at-risk analysis simulated paths of risk factors are used to build distribution of NII (or more generally earnings) over the time horizon.

■ Delta and delta-gamma are two approximation methods to obtain changes-in-values for different simulated scenarios and often used as ways to decrease the computational burden of equity-at-risk analysis.

NOTES

1. www.MSCI.com.
2. In Microsoft Excel a Z-score of 1.645 is obtained using the NORM.INV(0.95,0,1) function.
3. Here we use **bold** notation to represent a matrix or vector.

4. Here we use **bold** letters to represent vectors or matrices. A^T indicates the transposition of matrix A.

5. Itô's lemma is discussed in the Appendix to this book.

6. Here we used $(k/100) \times n$ (k is the rank and n is the sample size) to calculate the ordinal ranks of the data, which in turn are used to find the value corresponding to 99th percentile. Other methods of the calculation of ordinal rank may lead to a different value for the 99th percentile. If the required percentile does not correspond exactly with an ordinal rank of the data, an interpolation method can be used to derive the percentile value from the values of the nearest ordinal ranks. The Appendix to this book presents a few different methods of calculating percentiles.

7. The summations in Equation 10.60 are the cumulative probability of binomial distribution and can be found from a binomial probability table or by using Excel's BINOM.DIST function.

8. Parameters of the Vasicek model used here are: $K = 0.15$, $\theta = 5$, $dt = 1/12$ year, and $\sigma = 0.25$. The current short rate is assumed as 0.6%. See a previous chapter for more details on the generation of simulated interest rate paths using the Vasicek model.

9. The simulated paths in our example are created using a model with a monthly time step but since the earnings-at-risk time step is three months, only the exchange rates at 3, 6, 9, and 12 months coinciding with four quarter-ends are used.

BIBLIOGRAPHY

Damodaran, Aswath. *Strategic Risk Taking: A Framework for Risk Management.* Upper Saddle River, NJ: Pearson Prentice Hall, 2007.

Dixit, Avinash, and Robert Pindyck. *Investment under Uncertainty.* Princeton, NJ: Princeton University Press, 1994.

Gibbons, Jean Dickinson, and Subhabrata Chakraborti. *Nonparametric Statistical Inference*, 5th ed. London: Chapman and Hall, 2010.

Glasserman, Paul. *Monte Carlo Methods in Financial Engineering.* New York: Springer, 2003.

Hull, John C. *Options, Futures, and Other Derivatives,* 6th ed. Upper Saddle River, NJ: Prentice-Hall, 2005.

Huynh, Huu Tue, Van Son Lai, and Issouf Soumare. *Stochastic Simulation and Applications in Finance with MATLAB Programs.* Hoboken, NJ: John Wiley & Sons, 2008.

Mil'shtejn, G. N. "Approximate Integration of Stochastic Differential Equations." *Theory of Probability & Its Applications* 19, no. 3 (1975): 557–562.

Samuelson, Paul A. "Mathematics of Speculative Price." *SIAM Review* 15, no. 1 (January 1973) 1–42.

Schwartz, Eduardo S. "The Stochastic Behavior of Commodity Prices: Implication for Valuation and Hedging." *Journal of Finance* 52, no. 3 (July 1997): 923–973.

CHAPTER 11

Liquidity Risk

In previous chapters we discussed how a bank manages its sources and uses of funds by analyzing the impact of raised funds (liabilities) and used funds (assets) on its net interest income and the economic value of equity. An imbalance between incomes earned and expenses paid, or a mismatch between economic values of assets and liabilities, can expose the bank to *market risk*. Another aspect of efficient bank management is with regard to the timing of when principal or interest of funds borrowed are due and funds lent are returned. A mismatch in the timing of these cash flows can expose the bank to *liquidity risk*. Liquidity risk is the risk arising from a firm's inability to meet its obligations when they come due without incurring excessive losses or unacceptable costs.

Prior to 2007, financial companies generally treated liquidity risk management as an isolated task and often part of their cash management activities. Traditionally, teams that oversaw a firm's assets had freedom to market and sell their products or make relevant investments, with some restrictions, but often regardless of the impact of their activities on overall liquidity of the firm. This was not causing issues particularly for banks and investment banks during the 1990s and early 2000s due to ease of raising funds. In that period, innovation such as *securitization* and short-term borrowing through *repurchase agreement (repo)* contracts made it easy for many financial firms to borrow, and allowed them to change the size of their balance sheets as dictated by the activities on the asset side.

The financial crisis of 2007–2009 revealed that lack of coordination between the asset managers and teams that are in charge of ALM and liquidity risk can be costly. While credit events, such as counterparty bankruptcy, or market events, such as change in interest rate level, can adversely impact assets' values or overall earnings of a firm, usually their impacts are limited and not catastrophic. On the other hand, a liquidity event, such as the inability to pay back the principal of a matured bond, can make a firm completely insolvent, leading to eventual bankruptcy.

After the financial crisis of 2007–2009 the importance of liquidity risk management significantly increased, and nowadays it has become an integral part of risk management in the banking industry. Banks and investment banks now have large dedicated teams tasked to liquidity risk assessment and mitigation. Often those teams either are part of the banks' asset-liability management organizations or work closely with ALM teams.

In previous chapters we demonstrated how an effective asset-liability management approach relies on detailed cash flows analysis. Many banks use ALM software, either internally developed or procured from software vendors, to produce expected future cash flows of their assets and liabilities that are needed for earnings and equity-at-risk analysis. As we discuss in this chapter, one of the fundamental tools in liquidity risk management is cash flow gap analysis, which also requires estimation of future cash flows. Due to this common requirement, many banks integrate their ALM and liquidity risk management systems to take advantage of the cost efficiency of having a single system developed and maintained for both purposes, as well as creating a holistic approach to the balance sheet risk management.

Use of short-term funding mechanisms, particularly through the repo contract, is considered to be one of the catalysts that made the global financial crisis of 2007–2009 especially severe for many banks and investment banks that were involved in the repo market. Many researchers and academicians consider the repo market as part of *shadow banking*, characterized by significantly fewer regulations and government oversights compared to the traditional banking system.

In this chapter we first introduce a few funding mechanisms commonly used by financial institutions and explain the liquidity risk associated with each. We then discuss the repo contract and demonstrate how unmitigated use of it can lead to a liquidity risk event. Cash flow gap analysis and liquidity stress testing are explained in later sections. We then follow up by introducing a few methods used by regulators for assessment of the liquidity risk.

FUNDING SOURCE AND LIQUIDITY RISK

Companies fund their assets using a combination of debts and equities while for banks and other financial companies the portion of debt is significantly higher than for non-financial companies. Banks utilize the capital market to issue debt securities to finance their lending activities and investments. To issue debt securities at a relatively low cost, it is important for banks to receive a high rating from rating agencies on their issued debts. Debt securities can be classified based on their terms (short-, medium-, or long-term), seniority (senior or subordinated), collateral guarantee (secured or unsecured), or embedded option (callable or non-callable). Deposits are another major liability class for depository institutions. Not all financial firms are eligible to take deposits. Commercial and savings banks, credit unions, and savings and loans associations are examples of entities that are legally allowed to accept money as a deposit. Short-term secured funding is another major funding source, especially for firms that are active in the capital market and security trading.

The funding source mixture used by a bank depends on many factors, including asset types and their maturity profiles, interest rate environment, economic condition, and regulatory atmosphere. In this section we review the most common funding sources used by banks and discuss the conditions that may lead to a liquidity event for each of these funding sources.

Deposits

Deposits are the main source of funding for banks. Based on data published by the Federal Reserve, as of March 2017, 81% of total liabilities of commercial banks in the United States were in the form of deposits.[1] Historically, while this percentage has changed, the deposit remained the most dominant funding source for U.S. banks. *Demand deposit* refers to deposit products that can be withdrawn by depositors without any notice. Checking and savings accounts are examples of demand deposits. *Money market deposit accounts (MMDA)* and *negotiable order of withdrawal (NOW)* products, although they have restrictions on the number of withdrawals per month, from an ALM point of view are usually considered to be demand deposits. These products generally are the cheapest sources of funding but since they do not have contractual maturity, they can expose banks to liquidity risk.

Term deposits are bank products that have specific maturity dates and usually there are penalties for early withdrawal, but the interest rates are relatively higher than non-term deposits. The *certificate of deposit (CD)* is the most common term deposit in the United States. The term of a CD available to consumers is generally from one month to five years and usually a minimum deposit amount is required to open an account. At the maturity date the depositor has the option to withdraw the fund or rollover the CD for a new term. Corporations also use CD products to hold some of their cash in interest-bearing accounts. Many banks provide commercial CDs specifically designed for corporations.

From a liquidity risk management point of view, the fixed maturity of term deposit products is a favorable feature, as the timings of cash flows are known. Also, the existence of an early withdrawal penalty usually discourages a depositor from withdrawing the funds before the maturity date. Although the interest paid on term deposits is usually higher than the demand deposits, it is still one of the most important and widely used funding sources for banks in the United States.

Banks, as financial intermediaries, use non-maturing demand deposits or term deposits that have relatively short terms to fund their longer-term lending in the form of consumer and commercial loans, residential and commercial mortgages, car loans, and so on. Such assets cannot be recalled until their contractual maturity dates while depositors have the option to withdraw their demand deposits at any time or not to roll their term deposits at the maturity dates. This mismatch exposes a bank to significant liquidity risk should it face an unexpected withdrawal by its depositors. A *bank run* or *run on deposit* refers to the case when a large number of bank customers withdraw their deposits since they believe the bank may fail. Central banks, as the lenders of last resort, provide facilities to the banking systems of their corresponding countries to remediate such situation. Also, deposit insurance providers, such as the *Federal Deposit Insurance Corporation (FDIC)* in the United States, help to reduce the necessity of a run on deposits from the depositors' point of view.

There were several cases of bank run during the financial crisis of 2007–2009. In August 2007 Countrywide Financial, one of the biggest residential mortgage originators in the United States, faced a bank run when customers started withdrawing money from their accounts. At that time significant losses that stemmed from subprime lending in early 2007 led to rumors about the bank's liquidity problem, which eventually forced the company to announce plans to draw $11.5 billion from an existing line of credit provided by a consortium of banks.[2] Countrywide Financial eventually was sold to Bank of America in 2008.

The California-based bank IndyMac, also a large mortgage originator, faced a significant run on its deposits in June 2008 and eventually was seized by the FDIC in July 2008. The failure of IndyMac was one of the largest bank failures in United States, and was also mainly due to the collapse of the subprime mortgage market in 2007.

In September 2008 the *Office of Thrift Supervision (OTS)* placed the Washington Mutual under the receivership of FDIC, after the bank faced a massive run on its deposits for several days, leading to the seizure. The Washington Mutual collapse is considered the largest bank failure in the United States to date.

Immediately after the collapse and seizure of Washington Mutual, the Wachovia bank faced a run on its deposits when companies and businesses withdrew their funds, to bring their deposits below the FDIC insurance limit, which was $100,000 at the time. While technically the bank did not fail and was not placed under receivership of the FDIC, federal regulators pressured Wachovia to put itself up for sale and the bank eventually was sold to Wells Fargo.

When analyzing the liquidity risk related to deposit products, risk managers should consider the following:

1. The impact of deposit products on the overall liquidity of a bank depends on the type of stress the bank is facing. When a bank is experiencing an idiosyncratic stress event, the likelihood of a run on its deposits is high. In such a situation depositors may prefer to pull their deposits from the bank and transfer them to other banks that are not facing any specific problem. However, the existence of government-sponsored deposit insurance to some extent alleviates the need for such transfers. In contrast, during a market-wide stress period, the insured deposit products are generally considered safer places to hold cash compared to other investment alternatives. Therefore bank deposits may even increase during a market-wide stress period.

2. Deposit insurance program limits should be considered in analyzing the impact of a deposit product on the liquidity position of a bank during a stress period. As of August 2019, the FDIC coverage limit is $250,000 per depositor, per member bank, and per ownership category. If a bank has a large portion of its deposits concentrated with accounts that have significantly higher balances than the limit, it should consider the possibility of rapid withdrawal from those accounts if it faces an idiosyncratic stress event and incorporate this scenario in its liquidity risk management analysis. In the case of a bank-specific event, depositors with high balances most likely withdraw all, or at least their excess deposits above the insurance limit, and transfer them to other banks.

3. While the penalty for term deposit early withdrawal may discourage depositors from withdrawing their funds during normal times, it may not dissuade depositors from withdrawal when the bank faces an idiosyncratic stress event.

Short-Term Debt

Borrowing through repurchase agreement (repo) transactions and issuance of commercial paper are the most common forms of short-term funding. We discuss funding through repo and its associated liquidity risk in more detail in a later section when we review secured funding. Here we focus on commercial paper.

Commercial paper (CP) is short-term unsecured promissory notes issued by financial and non-financial companies. They are usually sold at a discount from the face value and have a term of less than 270 days.[3] The common terms of CP are 1, 7, 15, 30, 60, and 90 days. The unsecured nature of CP requires an issuer to maintain high credit rating to be able to participate in CP market. Companies generally use CP to cover short-term funding needs, for example, to cover seasonality in their accounts receivable.

Similar to Treasury bills, commercial papers are quoted on a discount basis. The discount rate for a commercial paper is defined as:

$$d = \frac{F - P}{F} \times \frac{360}{t} \qquad (11.1)$$

where d is the discount rate, t is the term of CP in days, F is the face value, and P is the price. Commercial papers issued in the United States are based on Act/360 accrual basis, similar to other money market instruments. The bond equivalent yield (y) for the CP is calculated as:

$$y = \frac{F - P}{P} \times \frac{365}{t} \qquad (11.2)$$

For example, if a 30-day CP with \$1 million face value is sold at \$999,888, the discount rate and bond equivalent yield are as follows:

$$d = \frac{1{,}000{,}000 - 999{,}888}{1{,}000{,}000} \times \frac{360}{30} = 0.134\%$$

$$y = \frac{1{,}000{,}000 - 999{,}888}{999{,}888} \times \frac{365}{30} = 0.136\%$$

Asset-backed commercial papers (ABCPs) are CPs that are backed by assets such as pools of credit card account receivables, auto loans, and equipment leases. Some ABCPs are backed by structured securities such as MBSs, ABSs, and CDOs. Repayment of an ABCP is dependent on the cash flow of the under-lying assets. Similar to the ABS discussed in an earlier chapter, the heart of an ABCP program is a bankruptcy-remote special purpose vehicle (SPV), com-monly referred to as "conduit," which is usually minimally capitalized and is designed to purchase the assets and issue ABCPs to fund them.

ABCP programs are often sponsored by financial firms to finance their own assets or to provide financing to their clients, but large non-financial corporations also sponsor their own ABCP programs. A program sponsor initiates the ABCP program and usually retains a financial stake in the program by providing credit enhancement and liquidity facilities. If the program is set up to fund assets originated by a single firm, the program is called a *single-seller*, whereas a *multi-seller* program purchases assets from more than one company. Another type of ABCP program is the *structured investment vehicle (SIV)*, where proceeds from CP issuances are used to invest

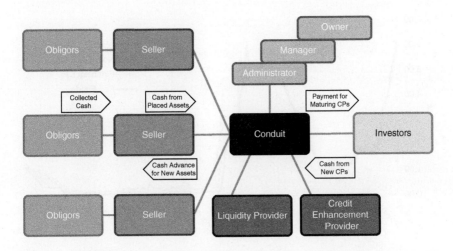

FIGURE 11.1 Schematic view of a multi-seller ABCP program

in high rated securities. Figure 11.1 presents a schematic view of a multi-seller ABCP program. A conduit has an administrator that manages the operation of the conduit and employs agents to manage the issuance and repayment of CPs, referral, accounting, and recordkeeping. The administrator often is an affiliate or a subsidiary of the sponsor but can be an independent company. A conduit also has a manager that oversees the administrator, and an owner that provides the minimal equity; both are usually unaffiliated with the sponsor.

To remediate liquidity risk due to a potential mismatch between cash flows from assets and liabilities, ABCP conduits are usually structured to include liquidity facilities that are used to support the cash outflow obligations. It is also common to include credit enhancement facilities in the structure of the conduit to hedge against losses occurring in the asset portfolios.

Due to the short-term and relative ease of issuance, CP is generally considered a cost-effective funding source. Figure 11.2 presents the monthly average annual rate of AA-rated 90-day CP from January 2001 to June 2017, collected and published by the Federal Reserve System. The rates are categorized into three groups: (1) CP issued by financial firms excluding ABCP, (2) CP issued by non-financial firms excluding ABCP, and (3) all ABCP. CP rates generally follow the fed funds rate; however, during the financial crisis of 2007–2009, CP rates, especially for ABCP and financial CP, had large deviations from the fed funds rate. Figure 11.3 shows the month-end outstanding balances of commercial papers for the three categories mentioned above, from January 2001 to June 2017. The graph also shows overall CP balances. At the peak of its

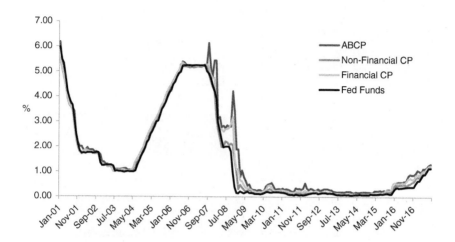

FIGURE 11.2   Commercial paper rates (%) not seasonally adjusted: (1) CP issued by financial firms excluding ABCP, (2) CP issued by non-financial firms excluding ABCP, (3) all ABCP
Source: Federal Reserve Economic Data (FRED), Federal Reserve Bank of St. Louis (https://fred.stlouisfed.org).

use in mid-2007 there was more than $2.1 trillion outstanding CP. After the collapse of the CP market during the financial crisis, market size shrank and by mid-2017 it was roughly half of its peak size, mainly due to the decrease in ABCP.

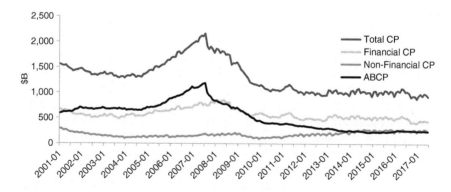

FIGURE 11.3   Outstanding commercial paper balance (in $ billion) not seasonally adjusted: (1) CP issued by financial firms excluding ABCP, (2) CP issued by non-financial firms excluding ABCP, (3) all ABCP
Source: Federal Reserve Economic Data (FRED), Federal Reserve Bank of St. Louis (https://fred.stlouisfed.org).

Commercial paper played a major role in the global financial crisis of 2007–2009. The most notable feature of an ABCP conduit is its use in funding long-term assets by issuing short-term liabilities. While from a cost point of view this is an effective method of funding, it exposes the conduit to potential shortfall in repayment if there is a mismatch between cash inflows from assets or new CPs and cash outflows from maturing CP. The liquidity facilities included in the structure of ABCP programs are meant to remediate this risk. However, during the financial crisis the extent of CP market collapse was so severe that it made the liquidity facilities ineffective. Toward the end of 2008 the problem of the CP market rapidly spread among ABCP as well, forcing many sponsors to unwind the programs, which in turn put pressure on their own liquidity positions.

Prior to the financial crisis of 2007–2009, many financial firms set up off-balance-sheet special purpose vehicles to circumvent the capital requirements of the Basel accords by moving their risky assets to these entities. These risky assets were funded by issuing ABCPs through conduits. To entice investors and particularly to be able to sell ABCP to money market funds, which are required by law to invest only in high-rated securities, sponsoring firms were providing guarantees for the ABCP programs in the form of liquidity and credit enhancement facilities. These guarantees effectively put the risk of assets back to sponsoring entities, but that risk was not evident on their balance sheets, nor was it adequately capitalized. Prior to Lehman Brothers' bankruptcy, money market funds were generally assumed to be a safe investment type, and as the mortgage crisis was severely impacting the banking sector, many institutional investors decided to place their cash in money market funds. Traditionally money market funds had large investments in commercial paper, as they were deemed to be a safe asset class. The problem in the ABCP market first surfaced when BNP Paribas suspended redemption of three special purpose vehicles in August 2007. These were bankruptcy-remote entities that were investing in subprime lending and financing the investment through the issuance of asset-backed commercial papers. The significant blow to the CP market came after the bankruptcy of Lehman Brothers on September 2008, when the Reserve Primary Fund, one of the largest money market funds, revealed that it had a major investment in Lehman's commercial papers, and consequently it lowered its share price to below $1. This resulted in a run on money market funds, and subsequently a freeze in the commercial paper market. The money market stabilized only after intervention by the Federal Reserve through establishment of multiple programs to inject liquidity into the commercial paper and money markets.

However, loss of confidence in the CP market and credit problems in assets backing ABCPs continued to plague the issuers. Without investors that are willing to buy commercial papers, many sponsors of CP programs found it difficult and more expensive to roll their short-term CPs. The increase in the rate of ABCP and drop in balances in this period are evident in Figures 11.2 and 11.3. Sponsors had to pull the risky assets placed on off-balance-sheet vehicles back into their balance sheets. This in turn resulted in significant financial losses for sponsors. Acharya, Schnabl, and Suarez (2013) found evidences that when the CP market collapsed the financial losses were mostly transferred back to the sponsoring entities through the guarantees provided.

Use of short-term commercial papers to fund long-term assets can potentially create a significant liquidity gap and, as evident during the global financial crisis, may lead to a systematic problem in the entire money market.

Medium-Term Notes

A *medium-term note (MTN)* is a class of debt instrument that is usually issued to fill the gap between short-term debts, such as CP, and long-term bonds. MTNs are issued through agents of issuers and are continuously offered based on a shelf registration.[4] MTNs usually have a term between 3 and 10 years, but shorter or longer terms are also possible. *Euro medium-term notes (EMTNs)* are MTNs that are issued outside of the United States, particularly in Europe. The MTN market typically is very liquid and its popularity among both issuers and investors is increasing. The continuous offering nature of MTN provides investors with a large pool of securities to select those that fit their portfolios the best to achieve a desirable risk–return balance. From the issuer's point of view, flexibility in the timing of issuance and customization of notes are some of the important features of MTNs. The flexibility in issuance time provides banks and other financial firms options to better tailor new issuances to their liquidity profiles.

The high underwriting cost of long-term bonds makes customized offerings impractical; thus, long-term bond issuances are usually based on long-range business and funding plans. In contrast, the flexibility in MTNs enables the issuer to customize the offering based on short- to medium-term liquidity requirements. However, relying on MTNs as an on-demand source of funding can expose the issuer to liquidity gap, should it fail to issue as expected. Prior to the global financial crisis of 2007–2009 many structured investment vehicles were issuing MTNs to fund investment in long-term risky assets, such as MBS and CDO securities. When the subprime mortgage crisis hit the values of these securities hard, investors became hesitant to invest in MTNs issued by those SIVs. Unable to roll maturing MTNs, many SIVs were forced to sell their assets at deep discounts. Such fire sales put further downward pressure on security prices, triggering trouble for many other SIVs, hedge funds, and investment firms.

The MTN market, similar to other financial markets, is subject to change, and during an economic slowdown even issuers of well-established MTN programs may not find investors. During the Eurozone debt crisis that started in 2009, some European banks found it more difficult and materially more expensive to issue MTNs, especially in unsecured form (Allen and Moessner 2013). While an appropriately timed MTN issuance helps the issuer to create a more efficient debt structure, over-customization can also expose the issuer to liquidity risk, should part of the expected issuance fail to materialize.

Long-Term Debt

Traditionally, long-term debt is considered to be a stable and reliable source of funds for banks and other financial institutions. The extended term of long-term debt allows the issuer to use the acquired funds to invest in long-term assets that are usually more profitable. To issue debt securities at a relatively low rate, firms need to maintain a high credit rating. Long-term debt securities can be classified based on their seniority (senior, subordinated), collateral guarantee (secured, unsecured), or embedded option (callable, non-callable). Senior debt has priority in repayment to other bonds in the case of an issuer's bankruptcy and secured debt is collateralized by some assets. Callable bonds provide the issuer with the right to redeem the bond prior to its maturity. Some bonds have put options, in which the investor has the right to return the bonds to the issuer prior to maturity for the redemption value.

From a liquidity risk point of view a portion of long-term debts that have maturity dates beyond a 1-year horizon from the analysis date is usually considered to be a stable funding source. This period allows the treasury department of the firm to plan ahead and arrange for replacement of maturing debts. This is usually done by issuance of new debt securities where the proceeds from the new notes are used to pay maturing notes.

Similar to other funding sources discussed in this section so far, the maturing long-term debt can lead to a liquidity event if it cannot be replaced in a timely manner or at the right cost. During the financial crisis of 2007–2009 many companies found it difficult to issue new debt securities. This was particularly more problematic for banks and other financial companies because they rely on constant rolling of the maturing debt by issuing new securities to fund their activities. The uncertainty in the market and failures of several large banks and investment banks drove the investors away from debt securities issued by financial companies toward safer assets such as U.S. Treasury bonds. In 2009 CIT Group, a New York–based lender to small and medium-size companies, found itself in a situation where it was unable to replace a large portion of its debt that was due to mature in that year. Unable to issue new debt securities at a reasonable cost and without a government bailout, CIT

Group entered into negotiation with its debtholders and eventually filed for a prepackaged bankruptcy on November 2009 to restructure its massive debt.

Securitization

As discussed in an earlier chapter, securitization is the process of packaging illiquid financial assets and underwriting marketable debt securities that are backed by the assets pool. Asset-backed securities (ABSs) are backed by pools of assets such as credit card receivables, student loans, car loans, or equipment leases. The generated cash flows from these assets support the security cash outflows. Mortgage-backed securities (MBSs) are backed by pools of mortgages. Loans included in the supporting pool of an MBS are either residential mortgages or commercial mortgages. *Collateralized debt obligations (CDOs)* are securitized debt where the underlying pooled assets are other debt securities, such as corporate bonds and asset-backed and mortgage-backed securities. In the United States, major issuers of mortgage-backed securities are the Government National Mortgage Association (GNMA, or Ginnie Mae), and two government-sponsored entities, the Federal National Mortgage Association (FNMA, or Fannie Mae) and the Federal Home Loan Mortgage Corporation (FHLMC, or Freddie Mac). MBSs issued by these entities are generally referred to as *agency MBSs. Non-agency MBSs* are mainly issued by banks with large home-lending portfolios. ABSs are issued by banks, credit card companies, and other financial firms with specialized lending portfolios such as student lending, auto lending, or equipment lease financing. Securitization vehicles are often structured in the form of trust companies. Debt securities that are created and sold through securitization comprise a significant portion of the capital market around the world.

The individual loans and leases used in the supporting pools of securitization vehicles are generally not marketable by themselves. Through securitization, banks and other financial firms move those illiquid assets off their balance sheets while obtaining alternative funding sources for underwriting more of those asset types. For banks, securitization has the additional benefit of reducing their regulatory capital requirements when risky assets are moved from their balance sheets to off-balance-sheet entities.

In a typical securitization process, the originator of assets (e.g., a bank that underwrites loans and mortgages) sells assets to a special purpose vehicle (SPV). The SPV then sells the debt securities to investors where cash inflows from the underlying assets support cash outflows of the debt securities. Typically, the securities issued are categorized into different tranches based on repayment priority and credit risk. The originator usually retains some of the lower-rated tranches as part of the credit enhancement it offers to the securitized notes. SPVs can have external credit and liquidity enhancement facilities supporting the debt securities. Securitization has several benefits to the originator:

- It generally reduces borrowing costs.
- It diversifies the funding sources and provides additional liquidity that can be used for further investment or lending.
- It transfers some of risk of underlying assets to investors and limits the originator's exposure to the portion that it retains as a credit enhancement.
- For originators that are regulated banks, it has the additional benefit of lowering regulatory minimum capital requirements.

Securitization activities grew in the 1990s and 2000s, and the amount of outstanding ABSs and MBSs peaked at 2007. Figures 11.4 and 11.5 present outstanding balances for agency and non-agency MBSs from 1985 to 2016. In this period, overall agency MBS balances increased steadily while non-agency MBS balances peaked in 2007 and then declined afterward. Figure 11.6 shows outstanding balances for ABS for the same period and for different underlying asset types. Similar to non-agency MBSs, overall ABS balances peaked in 2007 and declined afterward, with a slight upward trend after 2013.

Securitization is largely blamed for the financial crisis of 2007–2009. The mortgage crisis that started in 2006 affected MBS and CDO securities that were collateralized by subprime mortgages, resulting in significant

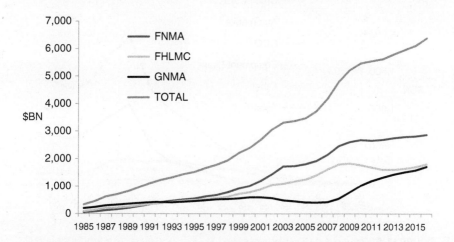

FIGURE 11.4 Outstanding balances of agency mortgage-backed securities (in $ billion)
Source: Securities Industry and Financial Markets Association (SIFMA) (https://www.sifma.org).

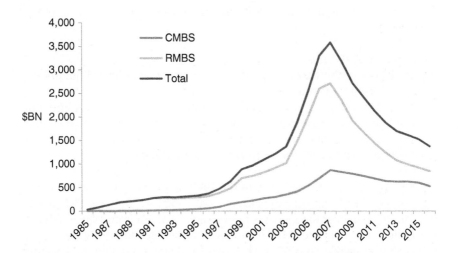

FIGURE 11.5   Outstanding balances of non-agency residential mortgage-backed securities (RMBS) and commercial mortgage-backed securities (CMBS) (in $ billion)
Source: Securities Industry and Financial Markets Association (SIFMA) (https://www .sifma.org).

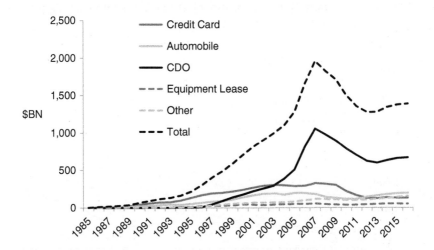

FIGURE 11.6   Outstanding balances of asset-backed securities (in $ billion), for different underlying asset types
Source: Securities Industry and Financial Markets Association (SIFMA) (https://www .sifma.org).

losses for holders. The problem later reached the ABS market and spread throughout the United States and international financial markets. Many banks and mortgage companies failed during the crisis due to their exposures to subprime loans and securitized debts that were backed by those assets. Even government-sponsored entities, Fannie Mae and Freddie Mac, were not immune from the problem. After suffering major losses, in September 2008 they were both placed into conservatorship by the U.S. government to prevent their total collapse.

Excessive reliance on securitization as a funding source exposes the originator to the liquidity risk. Many securitization vehicles, especially the ones backed by revolving credit products, have an early amortization mechanism that when triggered requires payback of principal amounts, effectively forcing the originator to bring the assets back to its balance sheet and fund them internally. This can have a significant negative impact on the liquidity of the originator. Since many conditions that lead to an early amortization are likely to be triggered during a market downturn, when the originator's liquidity already is under pressure, the effect of early amortization can be quite severe to the originator's liquidity.

Similar to other funding sources discussed in this section, trouble in the general market may prevent the originator from using the securitization as a funding mechanism. During a market downturn risk-averse investors prefer to invest in safer assets such as U.S. Treasury bonds and the appetite to invest in securitized assets may be significantly reduced. Not having investors to purchase the asset-backed securities, the originator ends up with keeping the illiquid assets on the balance sheet and funds them internally.

Credit and Liquidity Facilities

Many banks and larger financial institutions provide credit and liquidity facilities to corporate clients or other banks. A *credit facility* is a committed line of credit where the client can draw funds up to a limit. Credit facilities are often used for general working capital needs. A *liquidity facility* is a committed undrawn line provided to a client specifically for the purpose of supplying liquidity when needed, for example, when the client cannot roll its maturing debt. The term, interest rate, and repayment schedule of both types of facilities are expressed in the contracts. The client pays a commitment fee to keep the facility open and often the provider of the fund is a syndication of several banks.

Many financial firms and smaller banks use such facilities regularly to cover short-term cash needs, particularly the ones that have seasonal demands. However, unexpected use of credit or liquidity facilities may be regarded as a liquidity problem and this in turn may impact a firm's other liquidity sources. For example, upon drawing from a liquidity facility the firm may face difficulty in selling short-term debt, as risk-averse investors become reluctant to take a position in its debt.

For a facility to be considered a reliable source of liquidity, it must be contractually binding and irrevocable. A facility that can be canceled at the discretion of the fund provider cannot be relied on as an available source of funds at the time of distress. Also, the undrawn portion of the facility should be large enough to cover a potential cash shortage in case of a liquidity event.

In many countries central banks, as lenders of last resort, provide liquidity facilities to their banking systems. In the United States, the Federal Reserve System provides *discount window* facility to its member banks. Member banks can borrow for a short term (usually overnight) from this facility at a rate known as *discount rate*. The facility is intended to work as a backup funding source for member banks. Borrowing through the discount window is collateralized by posting sufficient amount of acceptable securities. There are three types of discount window facilities:

1. *Primary credit* facility is available to any depository institutions that are in good condition. The lending through this facility is done with fewer restrictions, usually overnight, and at a rate that is 50 basis points above the fed funds target rate.
2. *Secondary credit* facility is available to troubled depository institutions. The lending is usually done overnight, its use is restricted, and at a rate that is 50 basis points higher than the primary credit facility rate.
3. *Seasonal credit* facility provides funding for member banks that regularly face a seasonal pattern in their funding needs. The rate for the facility is a floating rate based on prevailing market rates.[5]

For example, based on data published by the Federal Reserve, during the fourth quarter of 2014 there were close to $897 million loans with terms between 1 and 7 days provided to banks through the primary credit facility while the amount of lending through the secondary credit facility was only $142,000, with terms between 1 and 3 days. During the same period there were $1,292 million loans through the seasonal credit facility, with terms between 1 and 33 days.

The discount window as a source of liquidity is available only to banks. Borrowing through the discount window may be perceived by the market as a sign that the bank is facing a liquidity shortage, which could lead to further troubles down the road. Thus, the discount window is used only as a last option. Generally, bank holding companies (BHC) have more stringent capital requirements and are under extra regulations compared to non-bank financial firms. Due to this, prior to the financial crisis of 2007–2009, non-depository firms such as investment banks and specialized financing companies avoided becoming bank holding companies. This practice changed during and after the financial crisis as several investment banks and specialized financing firms applied and became bank holding companies, to be eligible for the discount window borrowing. For example, on September 2008 and in the midst of the crisis, Goldman Sachs and Morgan Stanley, two of the largest investment banks in the United States, announced that they had become bank holding companies, regulated by the Federal Reserve.

Eurodollar Deposit and Federal Funds Market

Eurodollar deposits are unsecured U.S. dollar-denominated deposits at foreign banks, or branches of U.S. banks, outside of the United States. The U.S.-based banks can also take eurodollar deposits domestically through an *international banking facility (IBF)*. Despite the name, the deposit location is not limited to European countries and there are such deposits in many other regions, such as Canada, Hong Kong, Japan, or Caribbean islands. There is a very active market for these deposits and banks often use it as a funding source.

In the United States all depository institutions, including banks, credit unions, and savings and loan associations are required to keep funds in reserve with the Federal Reserve based on the amount of deposits they are holding. The portion of this reserve that is required by the Fed is known as *required reserve* and any additional amount is known as *excess reserve*. To maintain the reserve requirement, banks with deficits in their reserves can borrow from other banks that have excess reserves. This lending or borrowing between banks to satisfy the reserve requirement is commonly known as the *fed funds market*. The term of lending is usually overnight and unsecured. The *effective fed funds* rate is the volume-weighted average of the rates of reported fed funds lending, published by the New York Federal Reserve Bank for each business day. The fed funds market is an important pillar of the money market in the United States and is widely used by banks as a funding source to obtain funds needed to satisfy the reserve requirement.

Usually U.S. banks consider funding through the fed funds market and eurodollars market to be close substitutes. However, the fed funds market is only accessible to depository institutions and some government-sponsored entities, whereas a broader set of institutions participate in the eurodollar market. Extensive reliance on these two markets as funding sources may expose a bank to liquidity risk. While both markets are accessible to banks, when a bank is perceived as a high credit risk it may not be able to borrow through either market, and this can have an adverse impact on the bank's operations and its liquidity position.

Other Sources of Funding

Services offered by commercial and investment banks often require cash withholding at clients' accounts with the banks. Cash management, security clearing and custody, prime brokerage, and payroll services are examples of such activities that often result in clients' cash being withheld at the bank for a period of time. Clients' cash is usually held at separate accounts from the firm's own cash accounts. Depending on the number and type of clients and time of the year, the amount of a client's cash with the bank can be substantial. Reliance on clients' operational cash as a source of funding, however, can expose the servicing bank to liquidity risk. The operational nature of clients' cash means it can be gone very fast, either by the clients' withdrawal of excess funds or by use in activities that cash is originally collected for. Drainage of operational cash can happen quickly during a stress period and its impact can be more damaging to the holding bank's liquidity position during such a period.

Financial firms and smaller banks often use term loans from other banks or large corporations as funding source. These loans usually have a higher cost for borrowers compared to other funding sources discussed in this section and failure to roll a maturing loan when needed exposes the borrowing firm to a liquidity risk similar to medium- and long-term debt funding sources.

SHORT-TERM SECURED FUNDING: REPURCHASE AGREEMENTS

Repo Basics

One of the most common forms of short-term lending or borrowing is through the use of *repurchase agreement (repo)* market. The repo market is widely used by hedge funds, investment banks, mutual funds, pension funds, and money market funds, among others. In the United States, the Federal Reserve bank also participates in the repo market through its Open Market operation to implement the monetary policies. The reason for involvement in the repo market is also very diverse. Participants may use the repo market to fund the purchase of bonds, to increase leverage, to lend cash, to lend securities, or even for risk management purposes.

A *repurchase agreement*, commonly known as *repo*, is a contract when a seller (or repo side) sells a security to a buyer (or *reverse repo* side) with the commitment to buy the security back at a specific time in the future and with a price that is agreed on in advance. The repo side is effectively borrowing cash by placing the security as collateral (hence a secured borrowing deal) and the reverse repo side is lending while receiving the security as collateral

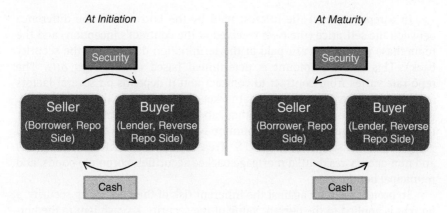

FIGURE 11.7 Schematic of a repurchase agreement contract

(hence a secured lending deal). Figure 11.7 presents a schematic view of a repo contract at its initiation time and at its termination. Whether a transaction is considered repo or reverse repo depends on the side of contract from which the transaction is viewed. The market convention is to call the transaction repo if the contract participant is borrowing cash and providing security as collateral. The transaction is called a reverse repo if the contract participant is lending cash and receiving security as collateral.

The repo market generally is very liquid and at any moment there are many participants that are willing to enter into a repo or reverse repo contract. Market liquidity and the low borrowing cost of a repo contract are attractive features from a borrower's point of view. From the lender side, liquidity of the market, flexibility of the lending term, and low risk due to the secured nature of lending are desirable characteristics.

An *overnight repo* is a repo contract whose term, from initiation to termination, is one trading day. When the repo term is longer than one day it is called a *term repo*. An *open repo* is a contract that does not have a predetermined termination date, and it can be ended by either side at any date in the future after a notice is given.

The borrower or repo side remains the beneficial owner of the security used as collateral and any coupon or dividend paid during the term of the repo is returned to the borrower. In U.S. bankruptcy law, an automatic stay refers to an automatic ruling that halts actions by creditors to collect debts from a debtor who has declared bankruptcy. Repo contracts on most securities, however, are exempt from this rule and in the case of bankruptcy of the borrower, the lender can exercise its right to take possession and liquidate the collateral.

In a repo contract the interest paid by the borrower is the difference between the sell price (the cash received at the contract's inception) and the repurchase price (the cash paid at the termination date to buy the security back). This interest amount is determined based on the *repo rate*. The repo rate varies from contract to contract and it depends on several factors including the prevailing short-term market rate, the term of the repo contract, the collateral type and delivery method, and if there is any special demand for the collateral security. The most common types of securities used as collateral are government securities (e.g., U.S. Treasury notes or U.K. Gilts), agency and non-agency residential mortgage backed securities, corporate bonds, and municipal bonds.

To protect a lender against the inherent risk of the underlying security, a *haircut* is applied to the current value of the security, so cash lent to the borrower is less than the security value. The amount of this discount in value is known as the *initial margin*. A haircut depends on the collateral type and generally for Treasury notes and agency mortgage-backed securities, haircuts are lower than non-agency mortgage-backed securities and corporate bonds. One way to present the haircut is to consider it as the difference between security value and loan amount as a percentage of loan. If L is the loan amount, V is the collateral value (including accrued interest), and h is the haircut percentage, we have:

$$h = \left(\frac{V - L}{L}\right) \times 100 \tag{11.3}$$

Hence the loan amount borrowed at contract initiation is calculated as follows:

$$L = \frac{V}{(100 + h)/100} \tag{11.4}$$

Assume that a bank owns 5-year U.S. Treasury notes with current value of \$1,000,600 (including accrued interest). To cover some short-term funding requirement, the bank enters into an overnight repo contract with a counterparty using Treasury notes as collateral. Assume the repo rate is 0.90% (annual rate, simple interest, Act/360 day count convention) and the haircut agreed to in the contract for Treasury notes is 1%. Using Equation (11.4), the loan amount is:

$$L = \frac{1,000,600}{(100 + 1)/100} = 990,693.07$$

The repo interest amount is calculated as follows:

$$I = L \times \frac{r}{100} \times \frac{d}{360} \tag{11.5}$$

where I is the interest amount, r is the repo rate, and d is the actual number of days in repo term. Considering the 0.90% repo rate for this overnight repo contract we have:

$$I = 990,693.07 \times \frac{0.90}{100} \times \frac{1}{360} = 24.77$$

The amount to be paid at the termination of the contract by the bank to the counterparty is the initial loan amount plus the interest: \$990,693.07 + \$24.77 = \$990,717.84.

An alternative convention for the haircut is to calculate it as the difference between the security value and loan amount as a percentage of security value:

$$h' = \left(\frac{V - L}{V}\right) \times 100 \qquad (11.6)$$

Hence the loan amount is calculated as:

$$L = V \times \frac{(100 - h')}{100} \qquad (11.7)$$

The denominators in formulas in Equations (11.3) and (11.6) are different. Obviously h and h' are not equal. The relationship between h and h' (when considered as percentages) is derived as:

$$h' = \frac{h}{100 + h} \qquad (11.8)$$

The Bloomberg terminal, which is widely used for repo calculation, uses the h convention described in Equation (11.3) for the haircut. The haircut convention used in *Global Master Repurchase Agreements (GMRAs)* by the *International Capital Market Association (ICMA)* is based on the h' method in Equation (11.6). Equation (11.8) can be used to transfer one haircut convention to the other. For example, for the overnight repo described here where haircut $h = 1\%$ we can calculate the equivalent haircut based on GMRA as $h' = \frac{h}{100+h} = \frac{1}{100+1} = 0.9901\%$ and the loan amount is calculated using Equation (11.7) as:

$$L = 1,000,600 \times \frac{(100 - 0.9901)}{100} = 990.693.07$$

which is the same loan amount calculated before. The repo market is deep and many financial and non-financial firms are actively involved in borrowing or lending through this market. In a staff report by the Federal Reserve Bank of

New York (FRBNY) in 2015, the size of the repo contracts by primary dealers was estimated to be $2.2 trillion, and on the reverse repo side it was slightly below $2 trillion.[6] These figures reflected only repo activity of primary dealers and not the total repo market.

Repo Margin

Aside from the initial margin that protects the lender, repo contracts are marked-to-market during the term of the contract, usually on a daily basis (trading days). The *variation margin* is the amount sent from a party on one side of a repo contract to the other side to cover the change in value of the collateral. If the market value of the collateral increases, the lender sends collateral to the borrower; and if the collateral value decreases, the borrower sends extra collateral to the lender. This ensures that the value of the collateral held by the lender is always enough to cover the loan amount, since the collateral value at any given day during the term of repo consists of the current market value of the security and the extra margin posted by the borrower to compensate for any decrease in collateral value. Marking-to-market also ensures that the value of collateral posted by the borrower does not exceed the initial value considered at the contract inception. In practice, repo participants usually have a bilateral netting agreement that enables them to exchange margin at the aggregated level and after netting opposite cash flows.

Consider again the example we discussed earlier where a bank enters into a repo contract using $1,000,600 Treasury notes as collateral, but instead of overnight assume this is a 5-day term repo. Assume that the repo rate is 0.90% and the haircut is 1% as before. The loan amount as calculated before is $990,693.07. Assume that on the second day of the repo term the value of the Treasury collateral (principal and accrued interest in total) dropped to $1,000,500. To maintain the initial 1% margin, the bank needs to post additional collateral with the counterparty. The amount of this variation margin is calculated as:

$$M = \frac{(100 + h)}{100} \times (L + I_c) - V_c \qquad (11.9)$$

where V_c is the current value of collateral, I_c is the repo interest charged to date, L is the original loan amount, h is the original haircut, and M is the variation margin. The repo interest amount for one day since the inception of the contract is:

$$I_C = 990,693.07 \times \frac{0.90}{100} \times \frac{1}{360} = 24.77$$

Therefore:

$$M = \frac{(100 + 1)}{100} \times (990,693.07 + 24.77) - 1,000,500 = 125.01$$

This is the variation margin to be posted by the bank. This effectively keeps the initial margin at the 1% level, as originally intended in the contract.

Collateral Delivery Methods and Triparty Repo

One of the delivery methods used in bilateral repo contract is "delivery versus payment" (DVP). In this method the security used as collateral is delivered via a settlement service offered by clearing agencies and placed at the lender security account. At the termination of the contract the security is sent back and received at the borrower's security account. This method provides plenty of protection to the lender as it actually takes custody of the underlying security during the terms of repo. However, this method of delivery is expensive due to settlement and other operational costs. This cost is reflected in the contract repo rate. For a contract with this delivery method, the repo rate paid by the borrower is usually lower than in the case when delivery is not required.

Another method to provide collateral of a repo contract is "hold-in-custody" (HIC). In this method the security is not actually delivered to the lender but is held in a segregated custody account on the borrower side. This method has less protection for the lender, since it is possible that the borrower uses the security as collateral elsewhere, even though this is not permitted. If this method of settlement is used, to compensate for the risk the lender faces, the repo rate paid by the borrower is usually higher.

Triparty repo is the type of repo contract that significantly reduces the risk the lender faces in the hold-in-custody method. In triparty repo, as the name implies, a third party acts as an agent for both the borrower and the lender, providing security custody, valuation, and settlement services. Figure 11.8 presents a schematic view of triparty repo. In the United States the *Bank of New York Mellon* and in Europe *Clearstream* are two main triparty clearing organizations.[7] For participating in triparty repo both borrower and lender first need to establish custody accounts with the clearing organization. When a repo contract is executed, the security provided by the borrower as collateral is placed into a segregated custody account and held there until the termination of the contract. On a daily basis the clearing organization, on behalf of the lender, ensures there is enough collateral in the custody account to cover the loan amount. It also provides cash management services related to margin calls. The clearing organizations perform these services for a fee. Triparty repo is one of the main funding sources for primary dealers in the United States.[8] Collateral used in triparty repos is mainly in Treasury and agency RMBS securities.

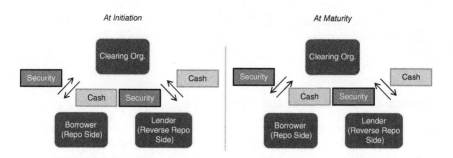

FIGURE 11.8 Schematic view of triparty repurchase agreement

Use of Repo

Funding: One of the common uses of repo is to fund the purchase of bonds. Consider that a dealer in an investment bank fixed-income desk is planning to take a long position in a bond for 30 days. The dealer believes that the price of the bond will increase and, including the accrued interest, the total yield provided in this period through investment in this bond is high. Since the dealer is buying this bond for the inventory of the investment bank itself and not for a customer, the position is booked in a "house" account. To fund this purchase the dealer has two options. One is to use the investment bank's current available cash. For this investment to be economically sound, the cost of funding the purchase and holding the bond for 30 days should be lower than the total yield from the investment. The overall cost of funding for the bank includes the costs of medium- and long-term debts, which are usually high compared to short-term money market rates. This can make the investment economically unjustified. Alternatively the dealer can fund the investment through the repo market by purchasing the bond and simultaneously using it as collateral in a repo contract to borrow the cash needed to fund the purchase. This way the total yield from the investment in the security for 30 days should be higher that the repo interest paid in this period, to make the investment economically justified.[9] A broker can perform the same service for a customer, where cash and securities are booked in segregated "customer" accounts.

Leverage: Often, hedge funds and investment banks use repo to increase their leverage when investing in fixed-income securities. To demonstrate this, consider a hypothetical hedge fund with the following simple balance sheet:

Assets		Liabilities	
Cash	$10,000,000	Long-term debt	$9,000,000
		Equity	$1,000,000
	$10,000,000		**$10,000,000**

Currently the hedge fund has $10 million cash as asset. The cash is funded by $9 million long-term debt and $1 million equity. The debt-to-equity ratio is 9-to-1 and the equity-to-asset ratio is 10%. For simplicity we ignore repo interest and assume the repo haircut is 2% for all contracts. Using its cash the hedge fund purchases fixed-income security A of $8 million value and simultaneously enters into a repo contract using this bond as collateral. The loan amount from this repo is $8,000,000/1.02 = $7,843,137 (rounded down to nearest integer). The simple balance sheet of the hedge fund before and after repo is shown below:

Before repo of security A:

Assets		Liabilities	
Security A: Unencumbered	$8,000,000	Long-term debt	$9,000,000
Cash	$2,000,000	Equity	$1,000,000
	$10,000,000		**$10,000,000**

After repo of security A:

Assets		Liabilities	
Security A: Encumbered	$8,000,000	Long-term debt	$9,000,000
		Short-term debt (from security A repo)	$7,843,137
Cash	$9,843,137	Equity	$1,000,000
	$17,843,137		**$17,843,137**

Security A, although encumbered in a repo contract, remains on the balance sheet of the hedge fund as the beneficial owner of the security. The debt-to-equity and equity-to-asset ratios after initiation of the repo contract are:

$$D/E = \frac{9,000,000 + 7,843,137}{1,000,000} = 16.8$$

$$E/A = \frac{1,000,000}{17,843,137} = 5.6\%$$

As noted in these ratios the hedge fund balance sheet leverage has increased significantly. Now assume that the hedge fund uses $8.5 million of its available cash to take a long position in another security, fixed-income security B, and simultaneously enters into another repo contract using this bond as collateral. Considering the 2% haircut, the loan amount from this second repo is $8,500,000/1.02 = $8,333,333 (rounded down to nearest integer). The simple balance sheet of the hedge fund before and after this second repo contract is shown below:

Before repo of security B:

Assets		Liabilities	
Security A: Encumbered	$8,000,000	Long-term debt	$9,000,000
Security B: Unencumbered	$8,500,000	Short-term debt (from security A repo)	$7,843,137
Cash	$1,343,137	Equity	$1,000,000
	$17,843,137		$17,843,137

After repo of security B:

Assets		Liabilities	
Security A: Encumbered	$8,000,000	Long-term debt	$9,000,000
Security B: Encumbered	$8,500,000	Short-term debt (from repo of security A)	$7,843,137
		Short-term debt (from repo of security B)	$8,333,333
Cash	$9,676,471	Equity	$1,000,000
	$26,176,471		$26,176,471

Both securities A and B are now encumbered in repo contracts but remain on the balance sheet of the hedge fund. The debt-to-equity and equity-to-asset ratios after initiation of the second repo contract are:

$$D/E = \frac{9{,}000{,}000 + 7{,}843{,}137 + 8{,}333{,}333}{1{,}000{,}000} = 25.2$$

$$E/A = \frac{1{,}000{,}000}{26{,}176{,}471} = 3.8\%$$

In this example the rapid increase in leverage and balance sheet size is noticeable. Many hedge funds and investment banks use repurchase agreements to leverage up their balance in a short period of time. The leverage can be decreased by unwinding the repo contracts and closing the long positions. The use of repo as a leveraging tool sometimes has been exploited when demonstrating the extent of balance sheet leverage. A firm can increase its leverage significantly and relatively quickly during a quarter using repo transactions, and close to the quarter-end, when financial reports are issued, it can decrease the leverage by systematically unwinding the repo positions, hence concealing the amount of risk it takes between quarterly reports. Prior to its bankruptcy Lehman Brothers used a loophole in Financial Accounting Standards Board (FASB) rule 140 to book its repo transactions as an outright sale by removing the securities from its asset side of the balance sheet and using the cash received to pay some of its debts, hence improving its leverage ratios temporarily and presenting a balance sheet that looked less risky.

Matched Book: Another common practice in the repo market is for a broker-dealer or fund manager to take opposite sides in repo and reverse repo contracts based on the same collateral. Generally the rate offered on a repo contract for a given collateral is lower than the rate asked for the reverse repo contract with the same security. This spread provides a way for some market participants to create a "matched book" by simultaneously entering into repo and reverse contracts with the same term and based on the same underlying security, and earn the spread. For example, consider an agency RMBS with a current value of $1,000,780. Assume that the current offer rate for an overnight repo of this collateral is 0.90% and the current ask overnight reverse repo rate for the same security is 0.93%. Assume that the haircut is 2%. A broker-dealer firm enters into an overnight repo contract. The cash received in this contract is:

$$\frac{1{,}000{,}780}{1.02} = 981{,}156.86$$

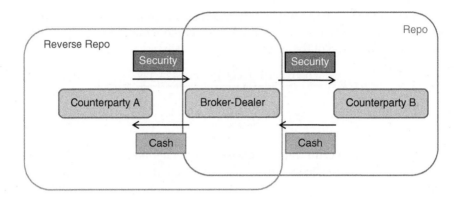

FIGURE 11.9 Schematic of a matched book deal at initiation (repo and reverse repo are from the point of view of broker-dealer)

The repo interest for one day is:

$$981{,}156.86 \times \frac{0.90}{100} \times \frac{1}{360} = 24.43$$

The broker-dealer simultaneously enters into an overnight reverse repo contract with a different counterparty based on the same security as collateral and lends out the cash received from the repo contract. The interest earned from the reverse repo is:

$$981{,}156.86 \times \frac{0.93}{100} \times \frac{1}{360} = 25.31$$

The schematic of transactions at inception for this matched book deal is shown in Figure 11.9. While the cash and security inflow and outflow cancel each other, the broker-dealer earned $0.82, the difference between the repo interest cost and the reverse repo interest earning. The spreads between repo and reverse repo rates for different terms are usually very small and, considering the operating costs, the volume of the matched book should be high enough to make it economically justified. Occasionally and on purpose, trades create a mismatch in their matched book to speculate on the movement of the short-term interest rate and demand on securities.

Security Borrowing: Another use of a repo contract is for borrowing of a security for a specific time. Security borrowing and lending is more common for equity securities. This is explained in more detail in the next section. However, borrowing fixed-income securities through a repo contract is also common. There are several reasons for the need to borrow a security. One reason is to cover a short position that was opened in the past. At the time of closing the short seller needs to deliver the security. If it does not own the security in its inventory, it may buy it from the market outright, or it may borrow it through a reverse repo contract and deliver to the short buyer. Another reason to borrow a security is to cover *failed transactions*. Consider a bank that is expecting to receive a security through a transaction. It is planning to deliver the same security to a third party in another transaction. When the first transaction fails, the bank doesn't receive the security, but it is still required to deliver the security to the third party. In this case the bank may borrow the security through a reverse repo contract to cover the fail.

Arbitrage: In the repo market when there is a high demand for a security, it is referred to as "on special." "General collateral" is a security that is not on special. Due to higher demand the repo rates for on special securities are generally lower than the general collaterals. The owner of special collaterals can use them to generate earnings through arbitrage. Consider a bank owns $5,000,000 of a special security. The repo rate for this security is 0.70% for a term of five days and the haircut is 1%. Also assume the current money market rate for an unsecured investment is 0.80% for a term of five days (annual rate, simple interest, Act/360 day count convention). The bank enters into a repo contract using this security as collateral. The cash received is:

$$\frac{5,000,000}{1.01} = 4,950,495.05$$

The repo interest for five days is:

$$4,950,495.05 \times \frac{0.70}{100} \times \frac{5}{360} = 481.3$$

The bank immediately invests the proceeds from the repo into a money market account. The payoff for five days is:

$$4,950,495.05 \times \frac{0.80}{100} \times \frac{5}{360} = 550.06$$

The difference between the interest paid for repo and the interest earned through the money market is an arbitrage gain of $68.76 earned by the bank in a five-day period.

Security Lending

Security lending is a financial contract between two parties where one side lends a security (or a basket of securities) to the other side for a given period of time and for a fee, payable at termination. The security borrower places either cash or another security (or a basket of securities) as collateral with the security lender. If cash collateral is used, the lender is required to invest the cash and rebate an agreed proportion of the return back to the borrower. Usually this rebate and the fee are netted into one payment and the fee is quoted net of rebate.

There are many similarities between a security lending contract and a repurchase agreement. Similar to repo, the security lending contract can be overnight, term, or open. Also similar to repo, the lender remains the beneficial owner of the security, and any coupon or dividend paid during the term of contract is returned to the lender of security. There are some differences between these two types of contracts. Unlike a repo, a securing lending contract does not involve selling and buying back a security and is based on the temporary transfer of the security from one party to the other side. Underlying securities of repo contracts are usually fixed-income securities, such as government-issued bonds, mortgage-backed securities, or corporate and municipal bonds, while security lending contracts are mainly based on equities and convertible bonds. A security lending contract often has a recall option providing the security lender with the opportunity to participate in corporate actions or exercise its voting rights by recalling the security. Repo contracts usually do not have such a recall option.

Generally, security lending is not used as a funding source. The main purpose of borrowing a security is to take a short position or to settle a short position established before. It is also used to cover transactions that are failed to deliver a needed security. Banks, investment banks, hedge funds, and retirement funds are the main participants in the security lending market.

For example, consider a hedge fund that is planning to take a $2 million short position on an equity security for four days. The current price of the equity is $20 per share. The fee for this borrowing is 15 bps (net of rebate due to the borrower) for borrowing 100,000 shares of the equity for four days. The margin for this security is 5% and the hedge fund is planning to use cash collateral in this transaction. The amount of cash collateral needed is:

$$2,000,000 \times 1.05 = 2,100,000$$

The fee payable to the equity lender at the end of four days is:

$$2,000,000 \times \frac{0.15}{100} \times \frac{4}{365} = 32.88$$

One trading strategy for the hedge fund is to borrow the security and sell it immediately in the market for the current price. If the equity price drops after four days, it can buy back the equity at the market outright for the lower price and deliver it back to the equity lender. The return for the hedge fund is the earnings from selling the security at a high price and buying it back at a lower price, net of the borrowing fee and funding cost of $2.1 million collateral. Of course if the security price actually increases, by taking this short position the hedge fund ends up with a loss.

REPO AND LIQUIDITY RISK

In normal conditions the repo market functions smoothly and many financial firms use it to finance their investments or to lend their excess cash. The liquidity of the market, the short term of the contract, and the securitized nature of lending are all desirable features for participants in the repo market. The growth in repo market size is evidence of its popularity among participants both as borrowers and lenders.

While repo as a secured borrowing mechanism is a cheap and flexible method of funding, especially for investment portfolios in government, mortgage-backed, and corporate securities, the short term of the funding and even the secured nature of the repo can adversely impact a borrower during a stress period and create a liquidity shortage event. In a repo contract the main concern of the lender is the credit risk of the underlying security used as collateral. The initial haircut and variation margin are mechanisms put in place to limit this risk. Since the lending is secured with collateral, and partially due to an exemption from an automatic stay in the case of bankruptcy of borrower, the exposure to the credit risk of the borrower is a lesser concern for the lender. However, the exposure to the credit risk of collateral securities is, indeed, one of the reasons that a firm may face difficulty in using repo during a stress period.

Consider a firm that is using repo as a funding source for its investment portfolio. A *run on repo* for this firm is the case when the lending side of repo contracts (i.e., parties on the reverse repo side) either refuse to roll open, overnight, or maturing term repos, or they increase the required haircut significantly. Either action may put significant pressure on the liquidity of the borrowing firm:

> **Refusal to roll maturing contracts:** Since the firm uses repo to fund its investments, it relies on lending counterparties to roll the maturing repos. If for any reason, lenders refuse to roll the repo contracts, the firm either has to find an alternative funding source, and find it very fast, or sell its investments in the market and return the cash borrowed through repo contracts.

Higher haircut: When the lender counterparties have concerns about the credit risk of the collateral securities, they may increase the haircut requirement before rolling repo contracts. This forces the firm to find alternative funding source for the portion of cash it didn't receive due to the higher haircut.

During the global financial crisis of 2007–2009 several large security firms found themselves in a liquidity crunch due to a run on their repo portfolios. There was a significant repo run on two Bear Stearns hedge funds in 2007, which led to their failure and eventually to the total collapse of the firm in 2008. Prior to their collapse, these two hedge funds were using repo heavily to fund their investments in the subprime mortgage sector through MBS and CDO securities that were backed by subprime mortgages. The mortgage crisis that materialized in the first quarter of 2007 highlighted the credit risk of securities used as collateral for the hedge funds repos. In June 2017 creditors, led by Merrill Lynch, asked for more collateral from these two hedge funds. When lenders eventually refused to roll repos, it led to the collapse of these two funds in July 2007.

Systematic risk inherited in repo market makes the participants vulnerable during a stress period. When the financial market is facing a stress event and when values of collaterals drop, lenders increase the haircut requirement before rolling the matured repos. Borrowers may need recourse to fire sales of securities at heavy discount to pay back the borrowed cash. This in turn creates more downward pressure on the prices of those securities, leading to further increases in the repo haircut requirement, which can circle back to force more fire sales by borrowers. An increase in required margins also depletes the liquidity of borrowers. A decrease in the value of a security and an increase in its haircut impacts all participants in the repo market that are using that particular security as collateral; hence, the problem soon spreads throughout the repo market and affects more participants. The decrease in value of securities not only puts further pressure on the liquidity of repo market participants, it also results in financial losses for investors that hold those securities. Effectively, the problem that begins in the repo market spreads throughout the financial markets and overall economy.

This indeed happened during the global financial crisis of 2007–2009. During this period the market for CDO and MBS was under significant stress, and either there was no liquidity in the market for these securities or they were being traded at heavy discounts. Fire sales of MBS and CDO securities during this period resulted in a higher repo haircut requirement, which put even more pressure on repo market participant. Gorton and Metrick (2012) presented the evidence of significant increase in the repo haircut during the financial crisis period. The problem snowballed throughout the repo market and on several occasions during the 2007–2009 crisis period the repo market came close to a freeze. After the bankruptcy of Lehman Brothers, the repo market came to a near halt even for U.S. Treasury notes and settlement fails increased significantly. Only intervention by the Federal Reserve as the lender-of-last-resort opened up the repo market and prevented a catastrophic failure.

Managing Liquidity Risk of Repo

While managing the inherent systematic risk in repo market is difficult, there are several ways that repo participants can control this risk.

Stress testing: A periodic stress test analysis on the liquidity of a firm provides management with an understanding of the potential pitfalls in funding policies and liquidity management practices. In stress test analysis the liquidity of the firm during a given period is analyzed while assuming it is facing a stress event that lasts for a while and impacts its businesses and funding sources. Cash flow gap analysis is the common tool used for such stress testing. We discuss cash flow gap analysis for different scenarios in more detail in an upcoming section of this chapter. When developing cash flow gaps for market-wide and idiosyncratic stress scenarios, the possibility of a freeze in the repo market should be included in the design of scenarios. For an idiosyncratic stress scenario one common practice is to assume that repo counterparties refuse to roll maturing repos during the stress period. In such cases the firm cannot roll its bilateral repos and the only possible option would be the utilization of triparty repo and only for collaterals that are clearing-eligible. All repos with collaterals that are not clearing-eligible should be assumed to be unwound, which results in cash outflows at the maturity dates of current repos. In a market-wide stress scenario it may be assumed not only that bilateral repos are not rolling but that triparty repos for most collateral are no longer available (except maybe for government bonds that are assumed to be the safest). While this may seem as an extreme case, the partial shutdown of the repo market during the 2007–2009 financial crisis justifies consideration of such a conservative assumption. After the financial crisis many banks and investment firms included the above assumptions in their stress testing analysis to study the impact of a repo run on their liquidity and funding position. We discuss liquidity stress tests for idiosyncratic and market-wide scenarios in more detail in the next section.

Use of high-quality collateral: By virtue of being secured, lending through a repo contract is considered safe as long as the collateral is of high quality. For funding planning purposes, when collateral used in a repo contract is a high-quality asset such as a government bond, the assumption that the repo contract will be rolled in the future when needed is a relatively safe bet. Even if the current counterparty decided not to roll the repo, one can assume that there are other lenders that are willing to take the reverse repo side when collateral is a high-quality security.

This is not the case for risky collaterals. For repos that are collateralized with high-risk assets such as non-agency MBSs or CDOs, current or replacement lenders may decide not to roll or increase the required haircut in the future. Funding investment in risky assets through short-term repos increases the risk of a run on the repo portfolio of the firm. Such an investment should be funded using more stable and longer-term funding sources, so a short-term stress period in the market doesn't create a major liquidity crunch for the firm.

Assessment and tracking of secured funding and unencumbered assets: Effective tracking of assets used in short-term secured funding (or lending) transactions is instrumental in managing liquidity risk of repo. The short-term nature of the repo transaction requires daily tracking of assets that are encumbered (i.e., used as collateral in repo) versus those that are unencumbered. Unencumbered assets are the ones that are free of legal, contractual, regulatory, or any other restrictions on the bank's ability to sell, transfer, or allocate the asset. For example, consider a broker-dealer firm that uses repo and reverse repo contracts on a daily basis. The firm uses repo contracts to fund its own inventory of investment securities or to fund customer positions on their behalf. It also manages a matched book through repo and reverse repo transactions with its customers or other counterparties. Currently the firm has $2,358 million in encumbered assets (cash value) and $1,400 million in unencumbered assets, as listed in Table 11.1.[10] A daily update of an asset summary like the one presented in Table 11.1(a) provides firm management with an up-to-date view of the asset status with respect to encumbrance. A safe practice from a liquidity risk point of view is to keep an appropriate portion of assets unencumbered. This way if the firm is faced with a liquidity shortage, it can rely on cash generated from either outright sale of these assets or borrowing against them in the repo market. As shown in the example in Table 11.1(a) the report for encumbered and unencumbered assets should be broken down with respect to asset type to provide a better picture of overall assets status. The granularity of the breakdown depends on the business structure and can be based on security type, trading desk, legal entity, or a combination of these factors. House assets and customer collaterals that can be re-pledged should be separately reported.

Another helpful daily update to the firm management is the breakdown of the repo and reverse repo positions that are placed for matched book versus the ones that are used for financing of the firm (house) inventory or lending excess cash. Table 11.1(b) provides this breakdown for the broker-dealer in our example. Here the firm's matched book is actually unmatched as part of its speculation strategy in rate movement.

TABLE 11.1 Example of (a) encumbered and unencumbered asset reporting for a hypothetical broker-dealer firm, and (b) breakdown of matched book versus house inventory financing (in $ million)

(a)

Asset Type	Unencumbered	Encumbered	Total
Treasury	267	670	937
Agency debt	167	859	1026
Agency MBS	245	244	489
Non-agency MBS	367	236	603
Non-agency ABS	50	80	130
Corporate debt	213	125	338
Municipal debt	23	61	84
Equity	45	60	105
Convertible bond	23	23	46
	1,400	2,358	3,758

(b)

	Repo	Reverse Repo
Matched book	529	580
House financing	1829	738
	2,358	1,318

A typical exercise in liquidity risk management is to study cash flow or maturity gap on assets and liabilities. A maturity gap schedule for repo portfolio can be created by placing repo and reverse positions based on their maturity in a time bucket scheme. Comparison of cash inflows (when reverse positions are matured and not rolled) versus cash outflows (when repo positions are matured and not rolled) is helpful in analyzing the potential liquidity shortage if the firm is unable to roll its repos. For example, consider the broker-dealer in our example, which currently has a total of $2,358 million repo positions and $1,318 million reverse repos (cash value). Table 11.2 presents a breakdown of repo and reverse positions grouped together based on term and collateral

TABLE 11.2 Example of repo and reverse repo reporting for a hypothetical broker-dealer firm (in $ million)

Repo:

Asset Type	Amount	Encumbrance Term Distribution					
		OvN	2D–1W	1W–1M	1M–3M	3M–6M	6M–12M
Treasury	670	374	80	90	12	47	67
Agency debt	859	230	351	124	77	77	0
Agency MBS	244	30	50	33	120	6	5
Non-agency MBS	236	100	24	20	17	75	0
Non-agency ABS	80	10	0	33	37	0	0
Corporate debt	125	0	0	100	25	0	0
Municipal debt	61	26	0	0	0	35	0
Equity	60	55	5	0	0	0	0
Convertible bond	23	20	3	0	0	0	0
	2,358	845	513	400	288	240	72

Reverse Repo:

Asset Type	Amount	Encumbrance Term Distribution					
		OvN	2D–1W	1W–1M	1M–3M	3M–6M	6M–12M
Treasury	490	300	100	57	13	0	20
Agency debt	236	36	0	170	20	5	5
Agency MBS	145	45	0	100	0	0	0
Non-agency MBS	67	0	24	5	38	0	0
Non-agency ABS	68	10	0	33	25	0	0
Corporate debt	212	0	50	12	100	50	0
Municipal debt	55	5	25	0	0	25	0
Equity	27	27	0	0	0	0	0
Convertible bond	18	18	0	0	0	0	0
	1,318	441	199	377	196	80	25

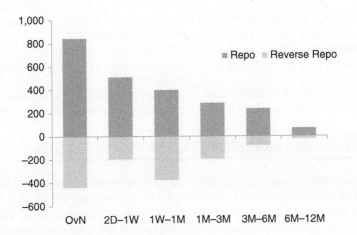

FIGURE 11.10 Example of maturity gap for repo and reverse repo positions of a hypothetical broker-dealer firm (in $ million)

type, placed into several time buckets, from "overnight" to "6 to 12 months." Figure 11.10 shows a comparison between these repo and reverse positions, where reverses are shown as negative numbers. From this graph it is obvious that the firm has large gaps between its repo liabilities and reverse repo assets for all time buckets. The gap is particularly large between overnight borrowing and lending. This implies that, if for any reason the firm cannot roll its overnight repos, not rolling its overnight reverses is not enough to cover its funding needs ($845 million overnight repo versus $441 million overnight reverse repo). This shows the potential for an adverse liquidity event.

Diversification of repo counterparties: Repo participants diversify their repo portfolio among many lenders. This is to avoid losing a major portion of funding when a limited number of repo counterparties do not roll maturing contracts. This way the exit of a few counterparties from repo deals does not result in a significant liquidity shock to the borrower. However, it should be noted that due to the systematic risk inherent in the repo market, when one repo counterparty refuses to roll repos, this decision may spread to others quickly and the borrower may face a run on its entire repo portfolio.

Maintaining a liquidity pool: A liquidity pool is a selection of high-quality unencumbered assets that can be converted into cash quickly, either through outright sales or by borrowing against them in the repo market. An asset type that is considered for a liquidity pool should have the following characteristics:

- It should have a very liquid trading market.
- It is considered a low-risk investment.

- Historical evidence shows that it holds its value during a stress period.
- It is actively used in the repo market as collateral.
- Historically it has low repo haircut.
- Preferably it is eligible for triparty repo through a clearing organization.

Maintaining a liquidity pool is a common practice among banks and investment firms, especially after the global financial crisis of 2007–2009.

CASH FLOW GAP ANALYSIS AND LIQUIDITY STRESS TESTS

One fundamental tool in liquidity risk management is the comparison of expected cash inflows and cash outflows for a given period of time in the future. Such gap analysis provides insight into expected liquidity position of the firm. This analysis should include cash flows from trading activities, lending products, funding sources, and derivative contracts.[11]

One general categorization of cash flows for gap analysis is to separate contractual cash flows from those that are based on either behavioral assumption or business planning. Usually the amount and timing of contractual cash flows are known at the time of analysis and hence they should be included in the gap analysis accordingly. A bank should include its own contractual and obligated cash outflows in the analysis. Contractual cash inflows from the bank's counterparties that are expected in the future, when there is no reason to doubt the occurrence or timing of such cash flows, should also be included in the analysis. Impacts from uncertainty of these cash inflows, such as the effect of defaults or deferments, can be included in the part of gap analysis that represents behavioral assumptions.

Behavioral assumptions are important parts of cash flow gap analysis. For example, when we assume current repo contracts will be rolled in the future with the same terms and haircuts, implicitly we are assuming that there are counterparties that are willing to participate in such contracts in the future, hence making a behavioral assumption. The assumption of deposit runoff rate is another example of behavioral assumption. Behavioral assumptions are often outputs of quantitative models and the uncertain nature of such assumptions should be considered when interpreting the results of gap analysis.

Cash flows that are the results of future business plans, for example, the launch of new products, merger and acquisition activities, or new volume of lending products, can be included in the gap analysis when there is high certainty for the occurrence and timing of those cash flows. It is recommended to separate cash flows of future business plans from the contractual cash flows so the gap can be determined with and without future plans.

In the following section we first demonstrate construction of a sample cash flow gap schedule for a business-as-usual (BAU) scenario, incorporating both contractual cash flows and cash flows based on behavioral assumptions or forecasts. After this baseline case is established, we then move to constructing cash flow gaps for two stress scenarios: an idiosyncratic stress scenario specific to the bank, and a market-wide stress scenario.

It should be noted that the sample cash flow gap schedules demonstrated in this chapter are used to discuss the gap analysis concept, and they do not include all possible cash flows that a bank may experience during the normal course of business or during a stress period. Specifically, for simplicity, interest cash flows are not included in our examples and the focus is on only principal cash flows. A robust cash flow gap should include both principal and interest. Also, in our examples we assume that certain cash flows are obtained based on behavioral assumptions or forecasting techniques. Modeling of those assumption-dependent or forecasted cash flows is not the focus of this chapter and we assume those cash flows are inputs into our gap schedules.

Cash flow gap schedules are often reported at aggregated time periods with varying lengths, where estimated daily cash flows are aggregated into predetermined time buckets. For example, Table 11.3 shows a common time bucket scheme used for reporting cash flow gap. Time buckets in this table are constructed from the analysis date of May 31, 2017. The first bucket includes only the first day after the analysis date. All cash flows in that date are aggregated in the "Day 1" bucket. The second bucket is from the second day from the analysis date to the end of the first week and all cash flows in these six days are aggregated into the "Week 1" bucket. The third bucket of "Month 1" is from the start of the second week to the end of the first month from the analysis date. The fourth bucket of "Quarter 1" is from the start of the second month to the end of the third month from the analysis date. The "Quarter 2" bucket includes cash flows occurring in months 4, 5, and 6 from the analysis date. Similarly, the "Quarter 3" bucket includes cash flows occurring in months 7, 8, and 9 from the analysis date. Finally the "Year 1" bucket includes cash flows occurring in months 10, 11, and 12 from the analysis date. Cash flows placed in these buckets are not cumulative. For example, cash flows in the "Week 1" bucket do not include cash flows in the "Day 1" bucket. The effect of accumulation of the cash flows is incorporated in the gap schedule when available cash balances are calculated.

TABLE 11.3 Cash flow gap time buckets—analysis date: May 31, 2017

Bucket Name:	Day 1	Week 1	Month 1	Quarter 1	Quarter 2	Quarter 3	Year 1
Period:	[Day 1]	(Day 1– Week 1]	(Week 1– Month 1]	(Month 1– Quarter 1]	(Quarter 1– Quarter 2]	(Quarter 2– Quarter 3]	(Quarter 3– Year 1]
From:	–	6/2/2017	6/8/2017	7/1/2017	9/1/2017	12/1/2017	3/1/2018
To:	6/1/2017	6/7/2017	6/30/2017	8/31/2017	11/30/2017	2/28/2018	5/31/2018

Here we illustrate the cash flow gap analysis for a hypothetical bank. Consider a regional bank with assets, liabilities, off-balance-sheet items, and equity as listed in Tables 11.4, 11.5, 11.6, and 11.7. Figures in these tables are in millions of dollars and as of May 31, 2017. This bank has $34.50 million cash, including an $8 million required deposit with the central bank and $4.5 million operational cash deposited with a custodian bank that is used for repo and margin settlement. The bank has investment in a variety of securities, with a total current value of $66.5 million. The invested securities include U.S. Treasury notes, agency and non-agency residential mortgage-backed securities, and corporate bonds with different ratings; $37.5 million of the invested securities are used as collateral in repo contracts and $29 million are unencumbered. All invested securities have a maturity date beyond one year from the analysis date of May 31, 2017. The bank has reverse repo positions with collateral of U.S. Treasury notes, agency RMBSs, and corporate bonds with a cash disbursed amount of $10.63 million. Reverse repo contracts have terms between overnight to 60 days. The lending portfolio of this bank includes $57.38 million loans to financial and non-financial firms and also small business customers. These loans do not have any prepayment or put option. Among the outstanding loans $1.38 million is considered as non-performing. The total line of credit provided to customers is $17 million where $7.6 million of it is drawn. Among the drawn portion $0.3 million is considered as non-performing. The total monthly minimum due payment to the bank from the credit facilities extended to customers is $0.07 million.

On the liability side, this bank has a $54.25 million debt, consisting of long-term bonds, short-term notes, and commercial papers. The bank has deposits from financial firms, non-financial firms, and small business customers for a total of $60.6 million, where $1 million of it is the operational deposit for cash management purposes. The bank has used $37.5 million of its invested securities in repo contracts and received $35.41 million cash.

This regional bank uses an interest rate swap to hedge its net interest income. The current market value of its swaps is presented in two separate lines in Table 11.6: assets of $3.2 million (i.e., swaps with positive value for the bank) and liabilities of $1 million (i.e., swaps with negative value for the bank). The total posted initial margin is $0.35 million and the current variation margin posted with counterparties is $0.8 million. Counterparties currently have not posted any margin, initial or variation, with the bank.

This regional bank has a liquidity facility provided by a national bank with a total line of $25 million. Currently the regional bank has not drawn from this facility. The bank has a published dividend payment guideline of $0.3 million per quarter. No dividend payment is declared.

In the following sections we use the data of this regional bank as stated earlier to construct the cash flow gap schedules in different scenarios.

TABLE 11.4 Assets of regional bank assumed for cash flow gap analysis (in $ million)

(a) Cash

ID	Category	Type	Counterparty	Amount
A1	Cash	Operational deposit	Custodian bank	4.50
A2	Cash	Deposit	National bank	18.00
A3	Cash	Required deposit	Central bank	8.00
A4	Cash	Excess deposit	Central bank	4.00
				34.50

(b) Investment Asset

ID	Category	Type	Current Market Value	Encumbered Amount	Unencumbered Amount	Repo Haircut
A5	Investment	U.S. Treasury	23.00	19.00	4.00	1%
A6	Investment	Agency RMBS AAA-rated securities	16.00	12.00	4.00	5%
A7	Investment	Non-agency RMBS A-rated securities	8.00	3.00	5.00	20%
A8	Investment	Corporate Bond AA-rated securities	10.50	3.50	7.00	20%
A9	Investment	Corporate Bond A-rated securities	4.70	0.00	4.70	25%
A10	Investment	Corporate Bond BBB-rated securities	2.30	0.00	2.30	40%
A11	Investment	Corporate Bond B-rated securities	2.00	0.00	2.00	50%
			66.50	37.50	29.00	

(continued)

TABLE 11.4 (Continued)

Residual Maturity of Securities

ID	1 Day	1 Day–1 Week	1 Week–1 Month	1 Month–3 Month	3 Month–6 Month	6 Month–9 Month	9 Month–12 Month	> 1 Year
A5	0.00	0.00	0.00	0.00	0.00	0.00	0.00	23.00
A6	0.00	0.00	0.00	0.00	0.00	0.00	0.00	16.00
A7	0.00	0.00	0.00	0.00	0.00	0.00	0.00	8.00
A8	0.00	0.00	0.00	0.00	0.00	0.00	0.00	10.50
A9	0.00	0.00	0.00	0.00	0.00	0.00	0.00	4.70
A10	0.00	0.00	0.00	0.00	0.00	0.00	0.00	2.30
A11	0.00	0.00	0.00	0.00	0.00	0.00	0.00	2.00
	0.00	**0.00**	**0.00**	**0.00**	**0.00**	**0.00**	**0.00**	**66.50**

(c) Reverse Repo

ID	Category	Collateral Type	Counterparty	Term	Current Market Value	Haircut (%)	Cash Disbursed
A12	Reverse repo	U.S. Treasury	Financial firm	Open	5.00	1%	4.95
A13	Reverse repo	Agency RMBS AAA-rated securities	Financial firm	Overnight	1.00	5%	0.95
A14	Reverse repo	Agency RMBS AAA-rated securities	Financial firm	15 Days	3.00	5%	2.85
A15	Reverse repo	Corporate Bond A-rated securities	Non-financial firm	60 Days	2.50	25%	1.88
					11.50		**10.63**

(d) Lending Asset

ID	Category	Counterparty	Amount	Non-Performing	Performing
A16	Term loan	Small business	42.20	1.20	41.00
A17	Term loan	Non-financial firm	12.18	0.18	12.00
A18	Term loan	Financial firm	3.00	0.00	3.00
			57.38	1.38	56.00

Residual Maturity of Performing

ID	1 Day	1 Day–1 Week	1 Week–1 Month	1 Month–3 Month	3 Month–6 Month	6 Month–9 Month	9 Month–12 Month	> 1 Year
A16	0.00	0.00	1.00	4.00	4.50	3.00	2.00	26.50
A17	0.00	0.00	1.50	3.45	0.80	2.05	0.00	4.20
A18	0.00	0.00	0.00	0.00	0.00	2.00	0.00	1.00
	0.00	0.00	2.50	7.45	5.30	7.05	2.00	31.70

(e) Revolving Credit Facility to Customers

ID	Category	Counterparty	Total Line	Undrawn	Drawn	Drawn Breakdown		Monthly Min. Due
						Non-Performing	Performing	
A19	Credit facility	Small business	10.00	5.50	4.50	0.10	4.40	0.04
A20	Credit facility	Non-financial firm	5.00	2.00	3.00	0.20	2.80	0.03
A21	Credit facility	Financial firm	2.00	1.90	0.10	0.00	0.10	0.00
			17.00	9.40	7.60	0.30	7.30	0.07

TABLE 11.5 Liabilities of regional bank assumed for cash flow gap analysis (in $ million)

(a) Short-Term and Long-Term Debt

ID	Category	Type	Amount
L1	Debt	Unsecured long-term	32.70
L2	Debt	Unsecured short-term	14.55
L3	Debt	Commercial paper	7.00
			54.25

Residual Maturity

ID	1 Day	1 Day–1 Week	1 Week–1 Month	1 Month–3 Month	3 Month–6 Month	6 Month–9 Month	9 Month–12 Month	> 1 Year
L1	0.00	0.00	6.00	4.20	4.00	3.00	0.00	15.50
L2	0.00	0.00	11.30	2.75	0.50	0.00	0.00	0.00
L3	0.00	0.00	3.00	4.00	0.00	0.00	0.00	0.00
	0.00	**0.00**	**20.30**	**10.95**	**4.50**	**3.00**	**0.00**	**15.50**

(b) Deposit

ID	Category	Type	Counterparty	Amount
L4	Deposit	Demand deposit	Small business	34.50
L5	Deposit	Demand deposit	Non-financial firm	23.20
L6	Deposit	Demand deposit	Financial firm	1.90
L7	Deposit	Operational deposit	Financial firm	1.00
				60.60

(c) Repo

ID	Category	Collateral Type	Counterparty	Term	Current Market Value	Haircut (%)	Cash Received
L8	Repo	U.S. Treasury	Financial firm	Open	19.00	1%	18.81
L9	Repo	Agency RMBS AAA-rated securities	Financial firm	45 days	12.00	5%	11.40
L10	Repo	Non-agency RMBS A-rated securities	Financial firm	3 days	3.00	20%	2.40
L11	Repo	Corporate Bond AA-rated securities	Financial firm	20 days	3.50	20%	2.80
					37.50		**35.41**

TABLE 11.6 Off-balance-sheet items of regional bank assumed for cash flow gap analysis (in $ million)

(a) Derivatives

ID	Category	Type	Counterparty	Current Market Value	Initial Margin Posted	Variation Margin Posted
D1	Derivative	Interest rate swap	Financial firm	3.20	0.15	0.00
D2	Derivative	Interest rate swap	Financial firm	−1.00	0.20	0.80
				2.20	0.35	0.80

(b) Liquidity Facility from a National Bank

ID	Category	Counterparty	Total Line	Undrawn	Drawn
LQ1	Liquidity facility	Financial firm	25.00	25.00	0.00

TABLE 11.7 Equity of regional bank assumed for cash flow gap analysis (in $ million)

ID	Category	Type	Book Value
E1	Equity	Common share	12.00

Dividend Payment (Guideline)

ID	1 Day	1 Day– 1 Week	1 Week– 1 Month	1 Month– 3 Month	3 Month– 6 Month	6 Month– 9 Month	9 Month– 12 Month
E1	0.00	0.00	0.30	0.00	0.30	0.30	0.30

Cash Flow Gap: Business-as-Usual

We start our cash flow gap analysis by constructing the gap schedule for the business-as-usual scenario. Our gap schedule is constructed as of May 31, 2017, using the time bucket scheme in Table 11.3. In this schedule contractual cash inflows and outflows are included, and then the schedule is enhanced by inclusion of forecasted cash flows based on business plan and behavioral assumptions that are relevant to each item. Table 11.8 presents the cash flow gap schedule for the business-as-usual scenario for the regional bank in our example. Here cash inflows are shown as positive numbers and cash outflows are negative. This schedule is partitioned based on the nature of cash flows or balances. The categories are:

- **Cash:** Figures in this category of the gap schedule are balances and not cash flows. The starting point of the schedule is the available cash at the beginning of the "Day 1" bucket. The bank has $34.5 million cash available in its accounts but $4.5 million of it is operational cash deposited with a custodian bank. Generally such cash is not considered as readily available and therefore from the regional bank point of view this cash is restricted and should be excluded from the available cash. Aside from the cash at its accounts the bank does not have any other liquidity pool and hence the starting cash is $30 million. This is shown in row 3 of the gap schedule at the start of bucket "Day 1." Here we are assuming the remaining $30 million is all operational cash. Any part of that cash that is non-operational should also be removed from the starting cash balance.

- **Investment:** In this category of the schedule the expected cash flows associated with the investment portfolio of the bank are shown. As mentioned earlier, here we are only considering principal cash flows and, for simplicity, ignoring interest payments. *Maturity* line item (cash inflow) shows contractual cash flows resulting from maturity of securities when the principal is returned to the bank. Based on Table 11.4(b) no invested security is matured within one year from the analysis date and hence no cash inflow is expected. *New Purchase* (cash outflow) and *Sales* (cash inflow) line items are to include cash flows associated with any planned new investment or sale of current investment. The bank currently does not have any such action on its business-as-usual plan. Based on this no cash inflow or outflow is expected related to the investment portfolio.

- **Repo:** In this category cash flows associated with repo contracts are included. The *Maturity* line item (cash outflow) includes contractual return of borrowed amount to counterparties at the maturity of repo contracts. One common practice is to treat open repo contracts as an overnight. This is a conservative assumption from the liquidity risk point of view. From Table 11.5(c) there is $18.81 million (cash value) of open repo collateralized with U.S. Treasury notes. Here we assume this repo contract to be maturing in "Day 1" bucket; hence, a cash outflow equal to this amount is added to row 7 of this bucket. A repo contract collateralized with non-agency RMBS and cash value of $2.4 million is maturing three days from the analysis date and hence a cash outflow equal to this amount is considered in the "Week 1" bucket. Similarly $2.8 million and $11.4 million cash outflows are included in the "Month 1" and "Quarter 1" buckets, based on repo contracts maturing 20 days and 45 days from the analysis date. The *New and Rollover* line item (cash inflow) represents the bank's plan to roll over existing repo contracts or to enter into new contracts. As part of the business-as-usual plan this bank has plans to roll over all existing repo contracts when they mature, with no new repo contract planned. Therefore in row 8 of the gap schedule we include cash inflows that are equal to but with the opposite sign of cash outflows in row 7. Based on this, there is no cash flow impact expected from the repo contracts for the business-as-usual scenario.

■ **Reverse Repo:** In this category cash flows associated with reverse repo contracts are included. The *Maturity* line item (cash inflow) includes contractual return of lent amount from counterparties at the maturity of reverse repo contracts. Here we assume the open reverse repo contracts are matured overnight. Based on Table 11.4(c) the bank has lent $5.9 million through reverse repo contracts that are open or overnight. So a combined cash inflow equal to this amount is included in row 9 of the "Day 1" bucket representing maturity of these contracts and return of the loan amount. Similarly $2.85 million and $1.88 million cash inflows are assumed in "Month 1" and "Quarter 1" for reverse repo contracts maturing 15 and 60 days from the analysis dates. The *New and Rollover* line item (cash outflow) represents the bank's plan to roll over existing reverse repo contracts or to enter into new contracts. As part of the business-as-usual plan this bank has a plan to roll over all existing reverse repo contracts when they mature, and no new reverse repo contract is planned. Therefore, in row 10 of the gap schedule we include cash outflows that are equal to but with the opposite sign of cash inflows in row 9. Based on this there is no cash flow impact expected from the reverse repo contracts for the business-as-usual scenario.

■ **Debt:** This category represents cash flows related to the debt securities issued by the bank. The *Maturity* line item (cash outflow) includes the contractual obligation to repay holder when those debt securities are matured. Based on Table 11.5(b) $38.75 million of the bank debt are to mature during the 1-year horizon from the analysis date. Cash outflows representing repayment of principal amounts to the debt holders are included in row 11 of the gap schedule, based on maturity dates from Table 11.5(b). The *New Issuance* line item (cash inflow) represents the bank plan to issue new debt securities. As part of business-as-usual this bank is planning to roll over all maturing dates by issuing new securities with comparable terms. The bank believes the capital market condition during the upcoming year allows for the issuance of new debt securities and there is no impediment to this. Therefore in row 12 of the gap schedule we include cash inflows that are equal to but with the opposite sign of cash outflows in row 11 to reflect the bank plan to roll over maturing debt. The *Repurchase* line item (cash outflow) shows the bank's plan to call or buy back its own debt. The bank currently has no plan for this action; therefore no cash outflow is included in row 13 of the gap schedule. Based on this no cash flow impact is expected from the debt for the business-as-usual scenario.

- **Deposit:** This category represents cash flows associated with deposit products the bank offers to its customers. Generally for cash flow gap analysis, no contractual cash flow is considered for demand deposit products. This is due to uncertainty around the timing and size of cash inflows or outflows. Depositors can withdraw or add to their funds at any time with minimal or no notice. For term deposits, while there is some level of information available about timing of cash flows, nevertheless the sizes of cash flows are unknown. Cash flows related to deposit products are usually the output of quantitative models that incorporate social and macroeconomic variables, along with information about the competitiveness of the bank's interest rate.

  The regional bank in our example has $60.6 million in deposits from financial, non-financial, and small business customers, where all but $1 million of it is demand deposits. The *New Volume* line item (cash inflow) represents the bank's forecast of new deposits. For the business-as-usual scenario the regional bank forecasts increase of 3% of current outstanding deposit, or $1.82 million additional deposits, distributed equally throughout the year, starting at week 2 from the analysis date. This cash inflow is included in row 14 of the cash flow gap.

  The *Runoff* line item (cash outflow) represents the bank's forecast of withdrawal of fund by depositors. The deposit runoff may occur for different reasons, including uncompetitive interest rate offered or a reputational event that impacts the bank directly. The regional bank in our example does not expect any runoff to occur to the portfolio; hence no cash outflow is included in the gap schedule at row 15. We can combine *New Volume* and *Runoff* into a single line item representing the net cash flow of the deposit products.

- **Term Loan:** In this category cash flows associated with the loan portfolio of the bank are included. As mentioned earlier, for simplicity here we only consider principal cash flows. A more comprehensive gap schedule would include both principal and interest cash flows. The *Maturity* line item (cash inflow) represents contractual cash flows for the return of principal amounts from the amortized or matured loans. The current outstanding loan portfolio of the regional bank in our example is $57.38 million, where $56 million of it is performing. As a conservative measure, here we do not include cash inflows from non-performing loans in our gap schedule. Such cash inflows can be derived using assumed or modeled recovery rates. Based on Table 11.4(d) $24.3 million of the bank's term loans will be maturing during the 1-year horizon from the analysis date. The principal returns of these maturing loans are considered as cash inflows and included in row 16 of the gap schedule based on maturity time from Table 11.4(d). The *New Volume* line item (cash outflow) represents the bank's plans for new loan volume. In its annual business-as-usual plan the bank is considering rollover or replacement of all maturing loans with comparable new term loans, meaning a new volume of $24.3 million. It also expects an increase of 3% in outstanding loan balance, that is, an additional new volume of $1.72 million, distributed equally throughout the year, starting at week 2 from the analysis date. Therefore total cash outflow of $26.02 million is added to row 17 of the gap schedule, based on maturity time from Table 11.4(d) and equal distribution of the growth portion throughout the year.

- **Credit Facility:** This category represents cash flows related to credit facilities the bank provides to its customers. Similar to deposit products, cash flows associated with credit facilities are hard to predict. Many factors, including economic conditions and availability of credit from competitors, can affect drawdown or repayment amounts. Expected cash flows of credit facilities are often outputs of quantitative models that forecast customers' behaviors based on econometric variables and overall availability of credit in the market. The *Minimum Due Payment* line item (cash inflow) is the contractual minimum amount due by the customers. The regional bank in our example currently has $17 million credit lines extended to its customers, where $7.6 million of it is drawn; $0.3 million of the drawn portion are currently non-performing. In Table 11.4(e) the total monthly minimum due payment for the performing drawn portion is $0.07 million, for a total of $0.84 million a year. This is included as cash inflows in row 18 of the gap schedule. The *Repayment* line item (cash inflow) represents any expected return of principal from customers. The bank predicts $0.46 million (or 6% of currently drawn portion) will be returned during the next year, distributed equally throughout the year, starting at week 2 from the analysis date. This forecast is included in the business-as-usual gap schedule in row 19. The *New Drawdown* line item (cash outflow) represents any expected draw from credit facilities extended to customers. The bank predicts $0.47 million (or 5% of currently undrawn portion) additional drawdowns during the next year, distributed equally throughout the year, starting at week 2 from the analysis date. This forecast is included in the gap schedule in row 20. We can combine *Repayment* and *New Drawdown* into a single line item representing the net forecasted cash flow of the credit facility products. However, it is not recommended to combine the *Minimum Due Payment* line as that item is contractual, whereas *Repayment* and *New Drawdown* are forecasts.
- **Derivative:** This category represents cash flows associated with the derivative contracts. The dependency of derivative contracts on market conditions and embedded leverage in most derivatives make their future cash flows very volatile. In the gap schedule of the regional bank we

have two *Net Margin Call/Return* line items (net cash inflows and outflows), one for cash flows related to margin calls or returns that are contractually required and one for cash flows that are forecasted. Since most banks nowadays enter into netting agreements with their derivative counterparties, the margin calls or return of collaterals are usually netted on a daily basis; hence, we did not separate cash inflows and outflows in the gap schedule of the regional bank. But, as mentioned before, it is recommended to separate contractual cash flows from forecasts. As of May 31, 2017, the regional bank is required to send a net amount of $0.02 million additional collateral in one day to its counterparties. This is included as cash outflow in the gap schedule in the "1 Day" bucket at row 21. The bank does not expect any additional collateral exchange and hence no cash flow is included in row 22 of the schedule.

- **Equity:** This category represents cash flows associated with equity of the bank. In *Dividend* line item (cash outflow) the future dividend payments to shareholder based on announced guideline are included. While dividend before declaration is not a liability and contractually not payable, skipping dividend payments that are previously announced as part of an annual plan would be considered as a sign of stress and hence generally avoided. The regional bank in its annual plan has included guidelines for a quarterly dividend payment of $0.30 million (total to all shareholders), payable at the end of each quarter for the upcoming year. These cash outflows are included in the gap schedule in row 23 for a total of $1.2 million per year. *New Offering* line item (cash inflow) represents any cash raised through the issuance of new equity and the *Repurchase* line item (cash outflow) represents any payment for buying back the equity of the bank from current holders. The regional bank currently has no plan to issue new equity or repurchase its own equity during the upcoming one year and hence no cash flow is included in rows 24 and 25 of the schedule.

- **Liquidity Facility:** This category represents cash flow associated with off-balance-sheet liquidity facilities. Financial institutions and small to medium-size banks usually have several backup liquidity facilities from larger banks, to be used when they face liquidity shortage. Since use of the liquidity facility is generally perceived as a sign of significant liquidity stress, it is usually considered as a last option. The *Drawdown* line item (cash inflow) represents cash flows when the bank draws from its liquidity facilities, and the *Repayment* line item (cash outflow) represents cash flows associated with repayment of a drawn line. The regional bank in our example currently has no plan to draw from its liquidity facility, and since the line is not drawn from before, no future repayment is expected. Therefore, no cash flow is included in rows 26 and 27 of the gap schedule.

■ **Other:** This category is intended to include any other major cash flows that are not included in the categories discussed above. Examples of such cash flows are compensations and operating expenses. For clarity we can separate cash inflows from outflows. As before it is recommended to separate contractual cash flows from the planned or forecasted cash flows. The regional bank has $3.99 million contractual cash outflow in the upcoming one year. These are included in row 30 of the gap schedule.

After all contractual and forecasted cash flows are placed in their corresponding time buckets, the ending cash balance for each bucket is calculated using:

$$Ending\ Cash = Starting\ Cash + Cash\ Inflows - Cash\ Outflows \qquad (11.10)$$

Consider the "Day 1" bucket in cash flow gap of the regional bank in Table 11.8. The starting cash is $30 million (after exclusion of $4.5 million restricted operational cash). Total cash inflow in this bucket is $24.71 million and total cash outflow is $24.78 million, for a net cash outflow of $0.07 million. Therefore the available cash at the end of the "Day 1" bucket is $30 − $0.07 = $29.93 million. The ending cash balance for each time bucket is shown in row 36 of the gap schedule. The ending cash balance for one bucket is the starting cash balance for the next bucket. For the "Week 1" bucket the starting cash balance is $29.93 million, which is the ending cash balance for the "Day 1" bucket. There is a net cash outflow of $0.01 million in the "Week 1" bucket, hence the ending cash balance of this bucket is calculated as: $29.93 − $0.01 = $29.92 million. This calculation is continued until the ending cash balance for the bucket "Year 1" is obtained as $25.71. Row 35 of the gap schedule in Table 11.8 shows cumulative cash flows, that is, cash flows in a given bucket and all preceding buckets combined.

In the cash flow gap in Table 11.8 we have assumed the operational cash of $4.5 million is needed throughout the year, and hence the amount is kept constant in row 2. The *Cash and Liquidity Pool* line item in row 1 for the "Week 1" to "Year 1" buckets is the summation of the *Starting Cash* line item in row 3, and the absolute value of the *Restricted Operational Cash* line item in row 2, representing total cash available to the bank, including its deposit with the custodian bank that is needed for cash management and settlement support purposes.

Figure 11.11 presents total cash inflows, outflows, and ending balances for each time bucket of the cash flow gap schedule for the regional bank in our example for the business-as-usual scenario. As can be seen from this figure and Table 11.8 net cash flows at each bucket are relatively low in this scenario, especially in the first half of the upcoming year. Expected total cumulative

TABLE 11.8 Cash flow gap schedule for a regional bank—business-as-usual scenario (in $ million)

Row	Category	Item	Description	Day 1	Week 1	Month 1	Quarter 1	Quarter 2	Quarter 3	Year 1
1	Cash	Cash and Liquidity Pool		34.50	34.43	34.42	34.08	33.57	32.55	31.48
2		Restricted Operational Cash		−4.50	−4.50	−4.50	−4.50	−4.50	−4.50	−4.50
3		**Starting Cash Balance**		**30.00**	**29.93**	**29.92**	**29.58**	**29.07**	**28.05**	**26.98**
4	Investment	Maturity	Contractual	0.00	0.00	0.00	0.00	0.00	0.00	0.00
5		New Purchase	Plan/Forecast	0.00	0.00	0.00	0.00	0.00	0.00	0.00
6		Sale	Plan/Forecast	0.00	0.00	0.00	0.00	0.00	0.00	0.00
7	Repo	Maturity	Contractual	−18.81	−2.40	−2.80	−11.40	0.00	0.00	0.00
8		New and Rollover	Plan/Forecast	18.81	2.40	2.80	11.40	0.00	0.00	0.00
9	Reverse Repo	Maturity	Contractual	5.90	0.00	2.85	1.88	0.00	0.00	0.00
10		New and Rollover	Plan/Forecast	−5.90	0.00	−2.85	−1.88	0.00	0.00	0.00
11	Debt	Maturity	Contractual	0.00	0.00	−20.30	−10.95	−4.50	−3.00	0.00
12		New Issuance	Plan/Forecast	0.00	0.00	20.30	10.95	4.50	3.00	0.00
13		Repurchase	Plan/Forecast	0.00	0.00	0.00	0.00	0.00	0.00	0.00
14	Deposit	New Volume	Plan/Forecast	0.00	0.00	0.15	0.30	0.45	0.45	0.45
15		Runoff	Plan/Forecast	0.00	0.00	0.00	0.00	0.00	0.00	0.00
16	Term Loan	Maturity	Contractual	0.00	0.00	2.50	7.45	5.30	7.05	2.00
17		New Volume	Plan/Forecast	0.00	0.00	−2.64	−7.74	−5.73	−7.48	−2.43
18	Credit	Min. Due Payment	Contractual	0.00	0.00	0.07	0.14	0.21	0.21	0.21

No.	Category	Item	Basis							
19	Facility	Repayment	Plan/Forecast	0.00	0.00	0.04	0.08	0.11	0.11	0.11
20		New Drawdown	Plan/Forecast	0.00	0.00	-0.04	-0.08	-0.12	-0.12	-0.12
21	Derivative	Net Margin Call/Return	Contractual	-0.02	0.00	0.00	0.00	0.00	0.00	0.00
22		Net Margin Call/Return	Plan/Forecast	0.00	0.00	0.00	0.00	0.00	0.00	0.00
23	Equity	Dividend	Guideline	0.00	0.00	-0.30	0.00	-0.30	-0.30	-0.30
24		New Offering	Plan/Forecast	0.00	0.00	0.00	0.00	0.00	0.00	0.00
25		Repurchase	Plan/Forecast	0.00	0.00	0.00	0.00	0.00	0.00	0.00
26	Liquidity Facility	Drawdown	Plan/Forecast	0.00	0.00	0.00	0.00	0.00	0.00	0.00
27		Repayment	Plan/Forecast	0.00	0.00	0.00	0.00	0.00	0.00	0.00
28	Other	Other Inflow	Contractual	0.00	0.00	0.00	0.00	0.00	0.00	0.00
29			Plan/Forecast	0.00	0.00	0.00	0.00	0.00	0.00	0.00
30		Other Outflow	Contractual	-0.05	-0.01	-0.12	-0.66	-0.95	-1.00	-1.20
31			Plan/Forecast	0.00	0.00	0.00	0.00	0.00	0.00	0.00
32		***Total Cash Inflow***		*24.71*	*2.40*	*28.71*	*32.19*	*10.58*	*10.83*	*2.78*
33		***Total Cash Outflow***		*-24.78*	*-2.41*	*-29.05*	*-32.70*	*-11.60*	*-11.90*	*-4.05*
34		***Total Net Cash Flow***		*-0.07*	*-0.01*	*-0.34*	*-0.51*	*-1.02*	*-1.07*	*-1.27*
35		***Cumulative Cash Flow***		*-0.07*	*-0.08*	*-0.42*	*-0.93*	*-1.95*	*-3.02*	*-4.29*
36		***Ending Cash Balance***		*29.93*	*29.92*	*29.58*	*29.07*	*28.05*	*26.98*	*25.71*

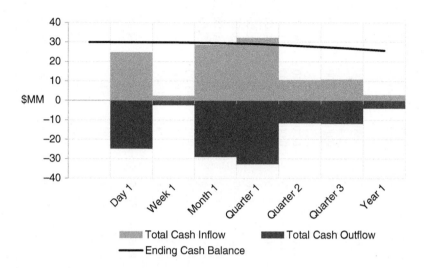

FIGURE 11.11   Cash Inflow, outflow, and ending balance for cash flow gap analysis of a regional bank—business-as-usual scenario (in $ million)

cash flow six months from the analysis date is $1.95 million outflow. The outflows grow in the second half of the 1-year horizon to a cumulative amount of $4.29 million. Based on this analysis the bank expects its readily available cash of $30 million to be reduced for about 14% to $25.71 million in a 1-year period. Such a decrease in available liquidity should signal the bank management to take corrective action, for example, by either revising their plan for new business volumes or to consider issuance of new debt securities, other than the ones already included in the plan. It should be noted the ending cash balance derived in this gap schedule is based on both contractual and forecasted cash flows. While there is a high level of confidence in the occurrence of contractual cash flows, the uncertainty of line items that are based on plan or forecast should be considered when results of the gap analysis are interpreted.

Past experience, particularly during the global financial crisis of 2007–2009, showed that market-wide or firm-specific stress events adversely impact the liquidity positions of banks. Preparation for such scenarios should be an integral part of liquidity risk management of a bank. For this reason, banks regularly conduct stress testing on their liquidity positions under different conditions and study the results. In the following sections we extend the cash flow gap analysis of the hypothetical regional bank in our example for two stress scenarios: one when a firm-specific event has occurred and one when a market-wide stress condition is present.

Cash Flow Gap: Idiosyncratic Stress

A business-as-usual cash flow gap can be used for evaluation of future liquidity needs but it does not address the necessity for quantification of liquidity risk during a stress period. In the cash flow gap schedule we developed in the previous section, many line items were based on a business plan or depend on behavioral assumptions. During a stress period a business plan may not go as intended and the behavioral assumptions may no longer be valid or relevant. To assess their readiness, it is important for banks to test their liquidity positions under different stress conditions regularly and reexamine their liquidity positions, plans, and policies accordingly.

Occurrence of an idiosyncratic stress event is one of the scenarios which is commonly examined in liquidity stress testing. Such an event is a firm-specific incident that affects only the bank itself and has very little or no impact on overall market. Incidents that lead to major losses, large-scale fraud cases, and reputational events such as management scandals are examples of idiosyncratic events that may push the bank into a stress condition. An idiosyncratic event can impact the liquidity position of a bank in several ways:

- The bank may not be able to actively participate in the capital market for issuance of new debt or equity. When a bank is experiencing an idiosyncratic stress event, investors may consider the bank such a high risk that they are not willing to invest in its debt or equity, even if the potential yield is significant.
- Repo counterparties may not be willing to enter into new contracts with the bank or roll over the existing open contracts.
- Drawdown on credit facilities may increase significantly. An idiosyncratic stress event for the bank may increase concern about the availability of the credit lines extended to customers, and in turn this may lead to an increase in drawdowns, particularly by corporate clients.
- The bank may experience a partial run on its deposits. A deposit insurance program such as FDIC insurance in the United States can reduce this risk but often such programs do not cover all deposit amounts and aside from this, customers still may prefer to pull their deposits from a bank that is experiencing problems and transfer to another bank that currently has no issue.
- Many bilateral derivative contracts have margin requirements that are related to the credit rating of the bank. When a bank suffers from an idiosyncratic stress event it may be downgraded by rating agencies and this downgrade itself may result in an increase of margin requirement, draining further the bank's liquidity.

Depending on the type of products offered by the bank, market condition and severity, an idiosyncratic stress event may impact the liquidity of the bank in many other ways. Here we study the impact of the above conditions when the hypothetical regional bank we used in the previous section faces an idiosyncratic stress event. We assume that the stress event lasts throughout the analysis horizon, which is one year in our example. Table 11.9 presents the cash flow gap schedule for this analysis. The schedule is constructed as follows:

- **Cash:** The starting cash for the "Day 1" bucket, after removal of restricted operational cash, is $30 million.
- **Investment:** During the 1-year horizon of the schedule none of the currently invested securities mature and the bank does not plan to invest in any new securities, so the *Maturity* and *New Purchase* line items do not contain any cash flow. However, unlike the business-as-usual scenario, due to potential liquidity shortage, the bank is considering the sale of $4 million Treasury securities at a 1% discount during the second quarter from the analysis date and sales of $4 million agency RMBS AAA-rated securities at a 5% discount during the third quarter from the analysis date. Due to this plan $3.96 million and $3.8 million cash inflows are included in row 6 of the gap schedule for the *Sales* line item in "Quarter 2" and "Quarter 3" time buckets. It should be noted that, since the bank currently does not facing any adverse conditions and this stress testing is rather a *what-if* analysis, the bank is neither making any actual commitment to sell those securities in the future nor having such sales in its annual plan, as explained in the business-as-usual scenario. These cash flows are included in the gap analysis as a potential source of liquidity to offset liquidity usage if such a stress event is to happen. Since this is a firm-specific event which has affected only the bank itself, it is safe to assume the bank can sell the securities close to their market values with a marginal discount. However, the value of the securities in the future may be significantly different from their current values. Market condition and security-specific characteristics may cause the value of a security to change materially in six or nine months. This should be considered in estimating the cash amount that can be generated from the sale of a security. Here we have assumed that the values of securities considered for sale remain relatively unchanged during the 1-year stress horizon while applying the 1% and 5% discounts to capture any potential change in values. If it is believed the security could lose more of its value, then the applicable discount should be higher. It is also important to consider only the sale of securities that are unencumbered at the time of sale as a source of liquidity. The sale of encumbered assets cannot be viewed as a source of liquidity.
- **Repo:** Due to the idiosyncratic nature of the stress scenario we assume bilateral repo counterparties do not roll current contracts or enter into

new repo contracts with the regional bank. Therefore it is assumed that the bank is required to repay total cash of $35.41 million raised through repo contracts. These cash outflows are included at the time buckets that correspond to maturity of current contracts in row 7 of the gap schedule in the *Maturity* line item.

Since this is a firm-specific stress event it is safe to assume that the overall repo market is still functioning and repo contracts through clearing organizations in triparty format are still available to the regional bank. Not all security types are eligible as collateral for repos through clearing organizations. Here we assume only Treasury and agency MBS AAA-rated securities are clearing-eligible. Since in this stress scenario it is assumed that maturing bilateral repos are not rolled, the regional bank is considering the alternative option of rolling a portion of those repo contracts that are collateralized by clearing-eligible securities through a clearing organization.[12] Based on this assumption cash inflows of $18.81 million and $11.4 million are assumed in the "Day 1" and "Quarter 1" of row 8 in the *New and Rollover* line item. This is based on the assumption that repo contracts maturing in those buckets are rolled as needed throughout the one-year horizon and through a clearing organization. The repo contracts that are matured in the "Week 1" and "Month 1" are collateralized by non-clearing-eligible securities and hence cannot be rolled through a clearing organization. This results in an overall $5.2 million cash outflow in the 1-year horizon, related to repo contracts.

- **Reverse Repo:** In this stress scenario we assume the regional bank does not roll maturing reverse repo contracts to preserve cash. This leads to inclusion of total cash inflow of $10.63 million in row 9 of the gap schedule in the *Maturity* line item, placed in buckets that correspond to maturity dates of reverse repo contracts. The bank does not plan to enter into any new reverse repo, so no cash outflow is assumed in the *New and Rollover* line item.
- **Debt:** The regional bank has $38.75 million debt notes that are maturing during the 1-year horizon. Due to the firm-specific stress event we are assuming the bank cannot issue any new security to roll the maturing debt and hence the total $38.75 million is assumed to be a cash outflow in row 11 of the gap schedule in the *Maturity* line item. This cash outflow is distributed to time buckets based on the maturity dates of debt notes. Based on the same assumption no cash flow is assumed in the *New Issuance* line item. The bank also does not have any plan to repurchase back its own debt, hence no cash flow is assumed in the *Repurchase* line item.
- **Deposit:** Due to the idiosyncratic nature of the stress test scenario it is assumed the regional bank is experiencing a partial run on its deposits. In our example the assumption is that 10% of the total deposits of the bank

will be withdrawn during the 1-year horizon, distributed equally throughout the year, starting at week 2 from the analysis date. Therefore no cash inflow considered in row 14 of the gap schedule for the *New Volume* line item and total $6.06 million cash outflow is assumed for row 15 in the *Runoff* line item placed in the "Month 1" to "Year 1" buckets.

- **Term Loan:** Maturing term loans provide total cash inflow of $24.3 million during the 1-year horizon, placed in row 16 of the schedule in the *Maturity* line item. Unlike business as usual, in this stress scenario and to preserve cash, the bank plans to replace only 50% of the maturing loans with new comparable loans. This leads to $12.15 million cash outflow placed in row 17 in the *New Volume* line item, distributed according to dates that existing loans are maturing. While from a liquidity management point of view, it makes more sense not to issue any new loans during a stress period, it is generally believed that a total stoppage of new loan issuance may damage a bank's market share and reputation in the long term.

- **Credit Facility:** In this scenario $0.84 million is considered as a cash inflow in the *Minimum Due Payment* line item. Compared to the business-as-usual scenario, here we assume that repayment slows from 6% of the drawn amount expected in the business-as-usual plan to only 3%, distributed throughout the year equally, starting at week 2 from the analysis date. This leads to a cash inflow of $0.23 million in row 19 of the gap schedule. On the other hand we assume a significant increase in drawdown from the credit facilities due to the idiosyncratic nature of the stress scenario. Customers' concern about availability of their credit lines may result in an increase of their drawdowns to improve their own liquidity positions, despite the incremental cost of additional borrowings. In a business-as-usual scenario we assume 5% of undrawn portion to be drawn during the 1-year horizon. In this idiosyncratic stress scenario we assume 15% of the undrawn portion or $1.41 million additional drawdown to occur during the 1-year horizon, distributed equally throughout the year, starting at week 2 from the analysis date. This cash outflow is included in row 20 of the gap schedule in the *New Drawdown* line item. As mentioned earlier we have assumed cash inflows from the minimum due payments to remain at the same level assumed for the business-as-usual scenario. An increase in drawn amounts leads to an increase in minimum due payments. Here we do not include that incremental increase in contractual cash inflows. This is a conservative assumption from the liquidity risk point of view.

- **Derivative:** The bank has a margin payment due in "Day 1" of $0.02 million, included in row 21 of the gap schedule. Aside from this contractual cash flow, due to the idiosyncratic stress condition the bank expects additional margin calls of $0.2 million in each quarter during the 1-year horizon, for a total of $0.8 million cash outflow, as shown in row 22 of the gap schedule in Table 11.9.

- **Equity:** For the dividend we assume the bank keeps the payments to shareholders in line with the published guideline of $0.3 million each quarter. Since a sudden termination of the dividend payment may be considered as a clear signal for significant problems, it is considered only as a last resort option for preservation of the liquidity. Here we assume that the dividend payments continue similar to the business-as-usual scenario for a total of $1.2 million during the 1-year horizon, as shown in row 23 of the gap schedule. The bank has no plan to issue new equity so no cash flow is shown in row 24 of the schedule.

    When a bank experiences an idiosyncratic stress event, the price of its market-traded equity may decline significantly. To support the equity price a bank can repurchase its own equity back. In our example we assume the regional bank spends $1 million during the second and third months from the analysis date in buying back its own equity to support the price. This cash outflow is included in row 25 of the gap schedule in the *Repurchase* line item.

- **Liquidity Facility:** As mentioned in the business-as-usual scenario the regional bank in our example has access to a $25 million liquidity facility provided by a national bank. Use of a liquidity facility is generally considered as a sign of significant stress and considered only as a last resort action. Aside from that, since the purpose of this gap analysis is to study the resilience of the bank to endure an idiosyncratic stress event, it is not appropriate to include the potential drawdown from the liquidity facility as a source of liquidity in our analysis. Hence here we assume the regional bank does not draw from the line in this scenario and so no cash flow is assumed in rows 26 and 27 of the gap schedule.

- **Other:** In this scenario we assume a total of $3.99 million contractual net cash outflow for any other major items that are not considered in other parts of the gap schedule, as shown in row 30.

After contractual and estimated cash flows for each category and line item are placed in the appropriate time bucket, the ending cash balances are derived using Equation (11.10). For the "Day 1" bucket the starting (available) cash balance is $30 million. The total cash inflow is $24.71 million and the total cash outflow is $18.9 million. Therefore the ending cash balance for the "Day 1" bucket is: $30 + $24.71 − $18.9 = $35.81 million. Ending cash balances for other time buckets are derived similarly. Row 35 of the gap schedule in Table 11.9 shows the cumulative cash flows throughout the time buckets and row 36 includes the ending cash balances.

TABLE 11.9 Cash flow gap schedule for a regional bank—idiosyncratic stress scenario (in $ million)

Row	Category	Item	Description	Day 1	Week 1	Month 1	Quarter 1	Quarter 2	Quarter 3	Year 1
1	Cash	Cash and Liquidity Pool		34.50	40.31	37.85	17.87	9.69	8.75	9.97
2		Restricted Operational Cash		-4.50	-4.50	-4.50	-4.50	-4.50	-4.50	-4.50
3		*Starting Cash Balance*		*30.00*	*35.81*	*33.35*	*13.37*	*5.19*	*4.25*	*5.47*
4	Investment	Maturity	Contractual	0.00	0.00	0.00	0.00	0.00	0.00	0.00
5		New Purchase	Plan/Forecast	0.00	0.00	0.00	0.00	0.00	0.00	0.00
6		Sale	Plan/Forecast	0.00	0.00	0.00	0.00	3.96	3.80	0.00
7	Repo	Maturity	Contractual	-18.81	-2.40	-2.80	-11.40	0.00	0.00	0.00
8		New and Rollover	Plan/Forecast	18.81	0.00	0.00	11.40	0.00	0.00	0.00
9	Reverse Repo	Maturity	Contractual	5.90	0.00	2.85	1.88	0.00	0.00	0.00
10		New and Rollover	Plan/Forecast	0.00	0.00	0.00	0.00	0.00	0.00	0.00
11	Debt	Maturity	Contractual	0.00	0.00	-20.30	-10.95	-4.50	-3.00	0.00
12		New Issuance	Plan/Forecast	0.00	0.00	0.00	0.00	0.00	0.00	0.00
13		Repurchase	Plan/Forecast	0.00	0.00	0.00	0.00	0.00	0.00	0.00
14	Deposit	New Volume	Plan/Forecast	0.00	0.00	0.00	0.00	0.00	0.00	0.00
15		Runoff	Plan/Forecast	0.00	0.00	-0.51	-1.01	-1.52	-1.52	-1.52
16	Term Loan	Maturity	Contractual	0.00	0.00	2.50	7.45	5.30	7.05	2.00
17		New Volume	Plan/Forecast	0.00	0.00	-1.25	-3.73	-2.65	-3.53	-1.00
18	Credit	Minimum Due Payment	Contractual	0.00	0.00	0.07	0.14	0.21	0.21	0.21

#		Item	Type							
19	Facility	Repayment	Plan/Forecast	0.00	0.00	0.02	0.04	0.06	0.06	0.06
20		New Drawdown	Plan/Forecast	0.00	0.00	-0.12	-0.24	-0.35	-0.35	-0.35
21	Derivative	Net Margin Call/Return	Contractual	-0.02	0.00	0.00	0.00	0.00	0.00	0.00
22		Net Margin Call/Return	Plan/Forecast	-0.02	-0.05	-0.03	-0.10	-0.20	-0.20	-0.20
23	Equity	Dividend	Guideline	0.00	0.00	-0.30	0.00	-0.30	-0.30	-0.30
24		New Offering	Plan/Forecast	0.00	0.00	0.00	0.00	0.00	0.00	0.00
25		Repurchase	Plan/Forecast	0.00	0.00	0.00	-1.00	0.00	0.00	0.00
26	Liquidity Facility	Drawdown	Plan/Forecast	0.00	0.00	0.00	0.00	0.00	0.00	0.00
27		Repayment	Plan/Forecast	0.00	0.00	0.00	0.00	0.00	0.00	0.00
28	Other	Other Inflow	Contractual	0.00	0.00	0.00	0.00	0.00	0.00	0.00
29		Other Inflow	Plan/Forecast	0.00	0.00	0.00	0.00	0.00	0.00	0.00
30		Other Outflow	Contractual	-0.05	-0.01	-0.12	-0.66	-0.95	-1.00	-1.20
31		Other Outflow	Plan/Forecast	0.00	0.00	0.00	0.00	0.00	0.00	0.00
32	*Total Cash Inflow*			*24.71*	*0.00*	*5.44*	*20.90*	*9.53*	*11.12*	*2.27*
33	*Total Cash Outflow*			*-18.90*	*-2.46*	*-25.42*	*-29.08*	*-10.47*	*-9.89*	*-4.57*
34	*Total Net Cash Flow*			*5.81*	*-2.46*	*-19.98*	*-8.18*	*-0.94*	*1.22*	*-2.30*
35	*Cumulative Cash Flow*			*5.81*	*3.35*	*-16.63*	*-24.81*	*-25.75*	*-24.53*	*-26.83*
36	*Ending Cash Balance*			*35.81*	*33.35*	*13.37*	*5.19*	*4.25*	*5.47*	*3.17*

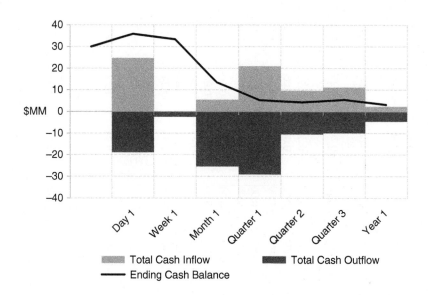

FIGURE 11.12 Cash Inflow, outflow, and ending balance for cash flow gap analysis of a regional bank—idiosyncratic stress scenario (in $ million)

Figure 11.12 presents total cash inflows, outflows, and ending balances for the idiosyncratic stress scenario of the regional bank. The initial increase in cash balance is due to the bank's decision to not roll open and overnight reverse repo contracts and subsequent return of lent amounts. However, as major cash outflows, such as the ones related to maturing debts, are materialized, the liquidity position of the bank deteriorates fast, where the cash balance at the end of the first month from the analysis date drops to only $13.37 million. This decline of cash balance is continued through the second, third, and fourth quarters from the analysis date. Asset sales planned in the second and third quarters slightly help with undoing some of the cash drainage. The ending cash balance at the end of the 1-year horizon reaches to lowest level of only $3.7 million.

We can use the cash flow gap schedule constructed here to study the sensitivity of the estimated liquidity to assumptions that are used in derivation of cash flows. For example, consider the assumption for deposit runoff used in cash flow gap in Table 11.9, where a 10% runoff is assumed under an idiosyncratic stress scenario. It is helpful to the bank management to understand the impact on liquidity if the deposit runoff is higher or lower than this assumed rate. To do so we can use the current gap schedule in Table 11.9, adjust the deposit runoff in row 15 incrementally higher or lower while keeping all other inputs and assumptions unchanged, and record the

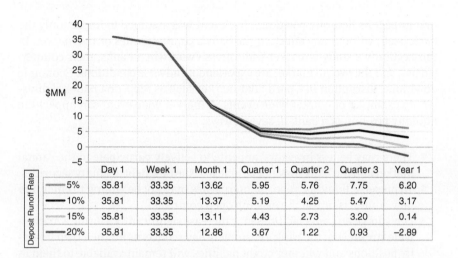

Deposit Runoff Rate		Day 1	Week 1	Month 1	Quarter 1	Quarter 2	Quarter 3	Year 1
	5%	35.81	33.35	13.62	5.95	5.76	7.75	6.20
	10%	35.81	33.35	13.37	5.19	4.25	5.47	3.17
	15%	35.81	33.35	13.11	4.43	2.73	3.20	0.14
	20%	35.81	33.35	12.86	3.67	1.22	0.93	-2.89

FIGURE 11.13 Sensitivity analysis of a regional bank liquidity under idiosyncratic stress scenario to deposit runoff rate assumption. Figures in the graph are ending cash balance for each time bucket (in $ million).

results. Figure 11.13 presents the results of this sensitivity analysis. Here we considered four cases where deposit runoff is 5%, 10%, 15%, and 20% of the current balance, distributed equally throughout the year, starting at the second week from the analysis date. For each case we recorded the ending cash balances as shown in Figure 11.13. Naturally as assumed deposits runoff increases the ending cash balance decreases. Particularly for the case where 20% of current deposits are assumed to be withdrawn in one year, the ending cash balance at the end stress horizon becomes negative, an indication of a catastrophic scenario for the bank. A similar sensitivity analysis can be performed for other cash flow items that are based on behavioral assumptions.

The stress analysis and supplementary sensitivity tests described in this section provide bank management with the necessary information to prepare for a potential liquidity shortage if an idiosyncratic stress event occurred. This preparation may include creations of liquidity pools consisting of highly liquid investment securities or contingency planning for asset sales at the right time during an idiosyncratic stress event.

Cash Flow Gap: Market-Wide Stress

The stress scenario assumed in the previous section was the occurrence of a firm-specific event that adversely impacts the bank and leads to conditions that impact its liquidity position. That event was assumed to impact only the bank itself, without any effect on the bank's counterparties or the market. In this section we study a market-wide stress event when banks, their counterparties, and the overall market are experiencing adverse conditions. Economic downturn, disruption in a particular market such as repo, or a national disaster are examples of market-wide events. A market-wide event can impact the liquidity position of a bank in several ways:

- There may be less investors' appetite to actively participate in the capital market and the bank may not be able to issue new debt or equity securities.
- To preserve liquidity, repo counterparties may not be willing to enter into new contracts or roll the existing open contracts.
- Drawdown on credit facilities may increase significantly. During a market-wide stress event the bank's customers have concerns for their own liquidity positions and whether credit facilities will remain available to them in the near future. This may result in customers increasing drawdowns from credit facilities to build up a liquidity cushion for themselves, putting pressure on the bank's liquidity in turn.
- If bank deposit products are insured, they are usually considered as safer vehicles to keep cash during a market-wide stress period, and this may lead to an increase in deposit balances. Even with an insurance program, however, it is still possible that the bank may experience a runoff on its deposits. An insurance program, such as FDIC insurance in the United States, only partially covers customer deposits, so the uncovered portion may be drawn. Deposits from corporate clients also may decrease significantly during a market-wide stress event, as those firms are similarly facing the same adverse conditions.
- During a market-wide stress period as market condition changes, margin requirements for derivative contracts may fluctuate significantly, resulting in large cash outflows from the bank to its counterparties.

Depending on the type of products offered by the bank and the severity of the market-wide stress condition, such an event may impact the liquidity of the bank in many other ways. Here we study the impact of the aforementioned conditions when the hypothetical regional bank we used in previous sections faces a market-wide stress event. We assume that the stress event lasts throughout the analysis horizon of one year. Table 11.10 presents the cash flow gap schedule for this analysis. The schedule is constructed as follows:

- **Cash:** The starting cash for the "Day 1" bucket, after the removal of restricted operational cash, is $30 million.

- **Investment:** During the 1-year horizon of the schedule none of the currently invested securities matures and the bank does not plan to invest in any new securities, so the *Maturity* and *New Purchase* line items do not contain any cash flow. Similar to the idiosyncratic scenario and due to a potential liquidity shortage, the bank is considering asset sales to raise cash. The plan is to sell $4 million U.S. Treasury notes in the first quarter from the analysis date, and to sell $4 million agency RMBS AAA-rated securities and $7 million corporate bond AA-rated securities at the second quarter. However, due to a market-wide stress the bank cannot assume securities would sell close to their current market values and has to consider the possibility of fire sales. Here we assume that Treasuries are sold at a 10% discount, and agency RMBS and corporate bonds are sold at a 50% discount. This leads to cash inflows of $3.6 million in the "Quarter 1" time bucket and $5.5 million in the "Quarter 2" bucket, as shown in row 6 of the gap schedule in the *Sale* line item. The securities considered for sale are unencumbered at the time of trade.
- **Repo:** In this market-wide stress scenario we assume bilateral repo contracts cannot be rolled and the bank cannot enter into new repo contracts with new counterparties. We assume this condition lasts throughout the 1-year horizon. While this may seem an extreme assumption it is meant to reproduce the condition that many investment banks faced during the global financial crisis of 2007–2009, when the repo market seized up for a period of time. Hence we assume $35.41 million cash outflow due to maturity of repo contracts to occur during the 1-year horizon, placed in appropriate time buckets based on repo maturity dates. On the other hand we assume repo contracts are made through clearing organizations and in triparty form are still available to the bank but only with U.S. Treasury note collaterals. The regional bank has raised $18.81 million cash through open repo contracts that are collateralized with U.S. Treasury notes. In row 7 of the gap schedule a cash outflow of $18.81 million is assumed in the "Day 1" bucket to represent maturity of these repo contracts which are not rolled by bilateral counterparties. In row 8 of the schedule and in the *New and Rollover* line item we include $18.81 million cash inflow to represent rolling these contracts through a clearing organization with the same haircut. It is also assumed these repos will be continuously rolled through the clearing organization throughout the 1-year horizon; hence, no subsequent cash outflow is considered. This results in an overall $16.6 million cash outflow within the 1-year horizon, related to repo contracts.
- **Reverse Repo:** In this stress scenario we assume the regional bank does not roll maturing reverse repos to preserve its cash. This leads to total cash inflow of $10.63 million in row 9 of the gap schedule in the *Maturity* line item, placed in buckets that correspond to maturity dates of reverse repos.

The bank does not plan to enter into any new reverse repo so no cash outflow is assumed in the *New and Rollover* line item.

- **Debt:** The regional bank has $38.75 million debt notes that are maturing during the 1-year horizon. Due to a market-wide stress event we are assuming the bank cannot issue any new security to roll the maturing debt and hence the total $38.75 million is assumed as a cash outflow in row 11 of the gap schedule in *Maturity* line item, distributed to time buckets based on the maturity dates of debt notes. No cash flow is assumed in the *New Issuance* line item. Also the bank does not have any plan to repurchase back its own debt; hence, no cash flow is assumed in the *Repurchase* line item.

- **Deposit:** Considering the main customers of the regional bank in our example are corporates, for this market-wide stress scenario we assume a decrease in deposits equal to 2% of the current $60.6 million balance. This results in total cash outflow of $1.21 million, distributed equally throughout the year, starting at the second week after the analysis date, as shown in row 15 in the *Runoff* line item of the gap schedule. No cash inflow is assumed for the *New Volume* line item in row 14.

- **Term Loan:** Maturing term loans provide total cash inflow of $24.3 million during the 1-year horizon, placed in row 16 of the gap schedule in the *Maturity* line item. In this stress scenario we assume the bank plans to replace only 25% of the maturing loans with new comparable loans. This leads to $6.08 million cash outflow placed in row 17 in the *New Volume* line item, distributed according to the dates when existing loans are maturing. Reduction of lending is a typical reaction by banks during a market-wide stress period to preserve cash. However, this decline in credits offered to businesses may lead to the extension of the downturn period.

- **Credit Facility:** During a market-wide stress scenario usually drawdowns from the credit facilities extended by a bank to its customers increase while optional repayments decrease, as customers try to improve their own liquidity positions. Here we assume 25% of the currently undrawn portion of outstaying credit facilities to be drawn during the 1-year horizon, distributed equally throughout the year, starting at week 2 from the analysis date. This is reflected as total cash outflow of $2.35 million in row 20 of the gap schedule in the *New Volume* line item. Also we assume that due to market condition repayments of already drawn amounts will stop during the 1-year horizon, so no cash inflow is included in row 19 in the *Repayment* line item. We assume minimum due payments to remain as the contractually expected amount of $0.84 in one year. This is included as cash inflow in row 18 of the schedule in *Minimum Due Payment* line item.

- **Derivative:** The regional bank has an upcoming margin payment of $0.02 million in 1 day from the analysis date and this is reflected in row 21 as contractual portion of the *Net Margin Call/Return* line item. Aside from this contractual cash flow, due to the market-wide stress condition the bank forecasts additional margin calls of $0.25 million in each quarter during the 1-year horizon for a total of $1 million total cash outflow, as shown in row 22 of the gap schedule.
- **Equity:** We assume the bank keeps the dividend payment in line with the published guideline of $0.3 million for the first quarter from the analysis date and it stops dividend payments after that. This assumption is reflected as $0.3 million cash outflow in the "Month 1" bucket where the first dividend payment is expected, and after that no cash outflow is included in row 23 of the gap schedule. While termination of dividend payments may be considered as a sign of stress for the bank, during a market-wide stress period many financial firms may reduce or stop dividend payments. The expected nature of this action and its wide practice reduces the negative message of the dividend cut. We also assume the regional bank spends $1 million during the second and third months from the analysis date in buying back its own equity to support its price. This cash outflow is included in row 25 of the gap schedule in the *Repurchase* line item. No new equity offering is planned in this scenario so no cash flow is included in row 24 of the schedule in the *New Offering* line item.
- **Liquidity Facility:** Since the purpose of this gap analysis is to study the resilience of the bank to withstand a prolonged market-wide stress, it is not appropriate to include the potential drawdown from the liquidity facility, a last resort action, in our analysis. Similar to the previous scenarios, in a market-wide stress scenario we assume that the regional bank does not have any plan to draw from its liquidity facility, hence no cash flow is assumed in rows 26 and 27 of the gap schedule.
- **Other:** In this scenario we assume a total of $3.99 million contractual net cash outflow for any other major items that are not considered in other parts of the gap schedule, as shown in row 30.

As in the previous two scenarios, after contractual and estimated cash flows for each category and line item are placed in the appropriate time buckets, the ending cash balances are calculated using Equation (11.10). For the "Day 1" bucket the starting (available) cash balance is $30 million. Total cash inflow is $24.71 million and total cash outflow is $18.9 million. Therefore the ending cash balance for the "Day 1" bucket is: $30 + $24.71 − $18.9 = $35.81 million. Ending cash balances for other time buckets are obtained similarly. Row 35 of the gap schedule in Table 11.10 contains the cumulative cash flows throughout the time buckets and row 36 includes the ending cash balances.

TABLE 11.10 Cash flow gap schedule for a regional bank—market-wide stress scenario (in $ million)

Row	Category	Item	Description	Day 1	Week 1	Month 1	Quarter 1	Quarter 2	Quarter 3	Year 1
1	Cash	Cash and Liquidity Pool		34.50	40.31	37.85	18.80	5.25	8.34	8.70
2		Restricted Operational Cash		-4.50	-4.50	-4.50	-4.50	-4.50	-4.50	-4.50
3		*Starting Cash Balance*		*30.00*	*35.81*	*33.35*	*14.30*	*0.75*	*3.84*	*4.20*
4		Maturity	Contractual	0.00	0.00	0.00	0.00	0.00	0.00	0.00
5	Investment	New Purchase	Plan/Forecast	0.00	0.00	0.00	0.00	0.00	0.00	0.00
6		Sale	Plan/Forecast	0.00	0.00	0.00	3.60	5.50	0.00	0.00
7	Repo	Maturity	Contractual	-18.81	-2.40	-2.80	-11.40	0.00	0.00	0.00
8		New and Rollover	Plan/Forecast	18.81	0.00	0.00	0.00	0.00	0.00	0.00
9	Reverse	Maturity	Contractual	5.90	0.00	2.85	1.88	0.00	0.00	0.00
10	Repo	New and Rollover	Plan/Forecast	0.00	0.00	0.00	0.00	0.00	0.00	0.00
11	Debt	Maturity	Contractual	0.00	0.00	-20.30	-10.95	-4.50	-3.00	0.00
12		New Issuance	Plan/Forecast	0.00	0.00	0.00	0.00	0.00	0.00	0.00
13		Repurchase	Plan/Forecast	0.00	0.00	0.00	0.00	0.00	0.00	0.00
14	Deposit	New Volume	Plan/Forecast	0.00	0.00	0.00	0.00	0.00	0.00	0.00
15		Runoff	Plan/Forecast	0.00	0.00	-0.10	-0.20	-0.30	-0.30	-0.30
16	Term Loan	Maturity	Contractual	0.00	0.00	2.50	7.45	5.30	7.05	2.00
17		New Volume	Plan/Forecast	0.00	0.00	-0.63	-1.86	-1.33	-1.76	-0.50
18	Credit	Minimum Due Payment	Contractual	0.00	0.00	0.07	0.14	0.21	0.21	0.21

19	Facility	Repayment	Plan/Forecast	0.00	0.00	0.00	0.00	0.00	0.00	0.00
20		New Drawdown	Plan/Forecast	0.00	0.00	−0.20	−0.39	−0.59	−0.59	−0.59
21	Derivative	Net Margin Call/Return	Contractual	−0.02	0.00	0.00	0.00	0.00	0.00	0.00
22		Net Margin Call/Return	Plan/Forecast	−0.02	−0.05	−0.03	−0.15	−0.25	−0.25	−0.25
23	Equity	Dividend	Guideline	0.00	0.00	−0.30	0.00	0.00	0.00	0.00
24		New Offering	Plan/Forecast	0.00	0.00	0.00	0.00	0.00	0.00	0.00
25		Repurchase	Plan/Forecast	0.00	0.00	0.00	−1.00	0.00	0.00	0.00
26	Liquidity Facility	Drawdown	Plan/Forecast	0.00	0.00	0.00	0.00	0.00	0.00	0.00
27		Repayment	Plan/Forecast	0.00	0.00	0.00	0.00	0.00	0.00	0.00
28		Other Inflow	Contractual	0.00	0.00	0.00	0.00	0.00	0.00	0.00
29	Other		Plan/Forecast	0.00	0.00	0.00	0.00	0.00	0.00	0.00
30		Other Outflow	Contractual	−0.05	−0.01	−0.12	−0.66	−0.95	−1.00	−1.20
31			Plan/Forecast	0.00	0.00	0.00	0.00	0.00	0.00	0.00
32		*Total Cash Inflow*		*24.71*	*0.00*	*5.42*	*13.07*	*11.01*	*7.26*	*2.21*
33		*Total Cash Outflow*		*−18.90*	*−2.46*	*−24.47*	*−26.62*	*−7.92*	*−6.90*	*−2.84*
34		*Total Net Cash Flow*		*5.81*	*−2.46*	*−19.05*	*−13.55*	*3.09*	*0.36*	*−0.63*
35		*Cumulative Cash Flow*		*5.81*	*3.35*	*−15.70*	*−29.25*	*−26.16*	*−25.80*	*−26.43*
36		*Ending Cash Balance*		*35.81*	*33.35*	*14.30*	*0.75*	*3.84*	*4.20*	*3.57*

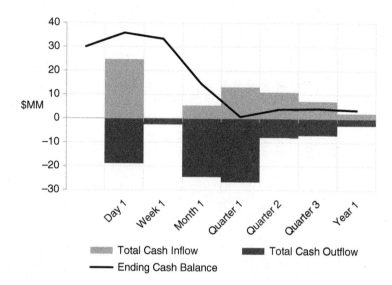

FIGURE 11.14   Cash Inflow, outflow, and ending balance for cash flow gap analysis of a hypothetical regional bank—market-wide stress scenario (in $ million)

Figure 11.14 presents total cash inflows, outflows and ending balances for market-wide stress scenario of the regional bank. Similar to the idiosyncratic scenario, the initial increase in cash balance is due to return of lent amounts through the open reverse repos when they are not rolled. As major cash outflows, such as the ones related to maturing debts and expiring repos, are materialized, the liquidity position of the bank declines, where the cash balance at the end of the first month from the analysis date drops to only $14.3 million. This decline in cash is continued during the second and third months from the analysis date, where cash balance at the end of the "Quarter 1" bucket reaches to the lowest level of only $0.75 million. Asset sales and principal returns from maturing term loans slightly improve the cash balance during the second and third quarters from the analysis. The ending cash balance at the end of the 1-year horizon reaches to the $3.57 million level. The extremely low liquidity only one quarter from the analysis date should be a wakeup call to the bank management. The regional bank clearly is exposed to high liquidity risk during a market-wide stress scenario, as predicted in the cash flow gap analysis performed here, and this risk should be mitigated. Creation of liquidity pools that are comprised of highly liquid unencumbered assets, issuance of new debt securities, decrease in activities that use the available cash, and establishment of liquidity contingency plans are a few ways to

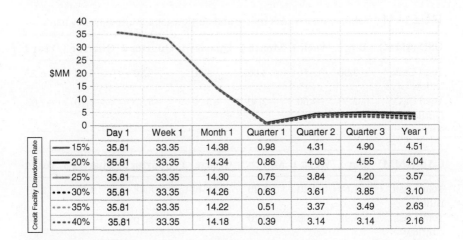

Credit Facility Drawdown Rate	Day 1	Week 1	Month 1	Quarter 1	Quarter 2	Quarter 3	Year 1
15%	35.81	33.35	14.38	0.98	4.31	4.90	4.51
20%	35.81	33.35	14.34	0.86	4.08	4.55	4.04
25%	35.81	33.35	14.30	0.75	3.84	4.20	3.57
30%	35.81	33.35	14.26	0.63	3.61	3.85	3.10
35%	35.81	33.35	14.22	0.51	3.37	3.49	2.63
40%	35.81	33.35	14.18	0.39	3.14	3.14	2.16

FIGURE 11.15 Sensitivity analysis of a regional bank liquidity under a market-wide stress scenario to credit facility drawdown rate assumption. Figures in the graph are the ending cash balances for each bucket (in $ million).

address the liquidity risk the bank is facing if a market-wide stress scenario were to occur.

In the cash flow gap constructed in Table 11.10 it was assumed that 25% of the currently undrawn portion of outstaying credit facilities would be drawn during the 1-year horizon. Using this cash flow gap schedule we can study the sensitivity of ending cash balances in a market-wide stress scenario to this assumption. Figure 11.15 shows results of this sensitivity analysis where the ending cash balances for different drawdown rates are presented. As can be seen from this figure, the drawdown rate assumption does not have material impact on the ending cash balances. Such an analysis can help the bank management in preparation of liquidity risk mitigation actions and contingency planning.

Cash Flow Gap: Multi-Currency

Banks with foreign subsidiaries and financial firms that serve international clients have exposures in multiple currencies. The primary currency that bank businesses are based on is known as the functional currency and usually is the national currency of the bank's incorporation location. For banks that have significant activity in multiple currencies, one way to analyze the cash flow gap while taking into account the possible currency mismatch is to construct the cash flow gap in each major currency and incorporate the transfers between currencies, when needed. In doing so, the ability to transfer a liquidity surplus from one currency to another, potential barrier in such a transfer, and the

TABLE 11.11   Estimated total cash inflow and outflow for a multi-currency bank

USD ($MM)	Day 1	Week 1	Month 1	Quarter 1	Quarter 2	Quarter 3	Year 1
Total Cash Inflow	3.00	5.50	3.00	4.00	3.90	5.00	6.25
Total Cash Outflow	−2.30	−4.50	−2.30	−5.00	−4.30	−5.10	−7.00

CAD ($MM)	Day 1	Week 1	Month 1	Quarter 1	Quarter 2	Quarter 3	Year 1
Total Cash Inflow	1.63	4.20	1.40	11.40	8.88	4.00	2.30
Total Cash Outflow	−5.98	−8.90	−9.10	−5.60	−6.70	−6.00	−2.00

impact of exchange rate should be considered in the construction of the cash flow gap. To demonstrate the cash flow gap analysis for a multi-currency bank, consider a bank that has major activities in two currencies: the U.S. dollar and the Canadian dollar.

The bank's main liquidity pool is in USD, with a current balance of $20 million cash. It also has C$5 million cash balance. For a business-as-usual scenario, estimated total cash inflows and outflows in each currency for a period of one year are shown in Table 11.11, where cash flows are aggregated into seven buckets, similar to gap schedules analyzed earlier in this chapter. To cover the potential cash flow gap in CAD, the bank relies on exchange of excess USD liquidity to CAD and vice versa. To estimate the impact of the exchange rate on the bank's liquidity position, estimates of exchange rates for different buckets are needed. Market-traded cross-currency forward contracts are often used to obtain an estimate of the future exchange rates. For our example we assume that approximate bucket-wide estimates for USD-CAD exchange rates are available as listed in Table 11.12. We also assume there is no restriction on the bank to exchange USD and CAD currencies at any denomination.

TABLE 11.12   USD-CAD average exchange rate for each bucket, estimated for cash flow gap analysis of a multi-currency bank

Exchange Rate	Day 1	Week 1	Month 1	Quarter 1	Quarter 2	Quarter 3	Year 1
1 USD = X CAD	1.20	1.22	1.23	1.24	1.30	1.32	1.34

Since this bank has exposures in two major currencies we need to construct a cash flow gap schedule for each currency, including possible cross-currency flows. These schedules for the business-as-usual scenario are shown in Figure 11.16 for USD, and Figure 11.17 for CAD. For simplicity we included only the aggregated cash in- and outflows in these gap schedules.

USD ($MM)	Day 1	Week 1	Month 1	Quarter 1	Quarter 2	Quarter 3	Year 1
Starting USD Cash Balance	20.00	20.70	18.38	12.82	11.82	11.42	11.32
Total Cash Inflow	3.00	5.50	3.00	4.00	3.90	5.00	6.25
Total Cash Outflow	−2.30	−4.50	−2.30	−5.00	−4.30	−5.10	−7.00
Ending Cash Before Cross-Currency Transfer	20.70	21.70	19.08	11.82	11.42	11.32	10.57
Cross-Currency Transfer	0.00	−3.32	−6.26	0.00	0.00	0.00	0.00
Ending Cash Balance	20.70	18.38	12.82	11.82	11.42	11.32	10.57

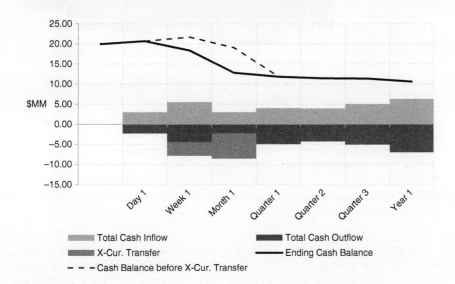

FIGURE 11.16 Cash flow gap schedule for a multi-currency bank—business-as-usual scenario—USD (in million)

CAD ($MM)	Day 1	Week 1	Month 1	Quarter 1	Quarter 2	Quarter 3	Year 1
Starting Cash Balance	5.00	0.65	0.00	0.00	5.80	7.98	5.98
Total Cash Inflow	1.63	4.20	1.40	11.40	8.88	4.00	2.30
Total Cash Outflow	−5.98	−8.90	−9.10	−5.60	−6.70	−6.00	−2.00
Ending Cash Before Cross-Currency Transfer	0.65	−4.05	−7.70	5.80	7.98	5.98	6.28
Cross-Currency Transfer	0.00	4.05	7.70	0.00	0.00	0.00	0.00
Ending Cash Balance	0.65	0.00	0.00	5.80	7.98	5.98	6.28

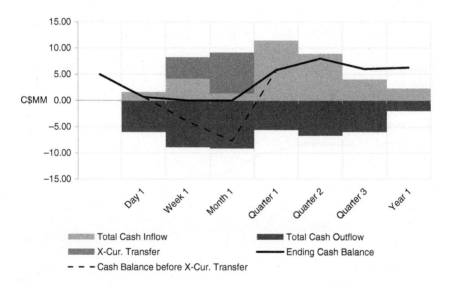

FIGURE 11.17 Cash flow gap schedule for a multi-currency bank—business-as-usual scenario—CAD (in million)

Starting from the "Day 1" bucket, the available balance in each currency is large enough to cover potential cash outflows without the need for any cross-currency flows. The net USD cash flow in "Day 1" bucket is $3 − $2.3 = $0.7 million and, considering the starting cash of $20 million, the ending USD cash for this bucket is $20.7 million. The net CAD cash flow in the "Day 1" bucket is C\$1.63 − C\$5.98 = −C\$4.35 million and considering the starting cash of C\$5 million, the ending CAD cash for this bucket is C\$0.65 million. Since the ending cash balance in each currency is positive, no cross-currency cash flow is needed.

For the "Week 1" bucket, the starting USD and CAD cash balances are \$20.7 million and C\$0.65 million, respectively. The net USD cash flow is \$5.5 − \$4.5 = \$1 million. Therefore USD cash balance before cross-currency transfer is \$20.7 + \$1 = \$21.7 million. On the CAD side the net cash flow is C\$4.2 − C\$8.9 = −C\$4.7 million. Therefore CAD cash balance before cross-currency transfer is C\$0.65 − C\$4.7 = −C\$4.05 million. To cover the CAD shortage the bank needs to send a cross-currency cash flow and use its USD cash position to cover the CAD deficiency. Assuming an estimated average exchange rate of 1.22 CAD/USD from Table 11.12 for the "Week 1" period, to cover the C\$4.05 million shortage, the bank converts \$3.32 million to \$3.32 × 1.22 = C\$4.05 million. Therefore the ending USD and CAD cash after cross-currency transfer are \$21.7 − \$3.32 = \$18.38 million and −C\$4.05 + C\$4.05 = C\$0 million, respectively.

The starting USD and CAD cash balances in the "Month 1" bucket are \$18.38 million and C\$0, respectively. The net USD cash flow is \$3 − \$2.3 = +\$0.7 million. The USD cash before cross-currency transfer is therefore \$18.38 + \$0.7 = +\$19.08 million. The net cash flow in CAD is C\$1.4 − C\$9.1 = −C\$7.7 million, so CAD cash before cross-currency transfer is C\$0 − C\$7.7 = −C\$7.7 million. Similar to previous bucket, a cross-currency cash flow from USD to CAD is needed to cover the CAD shortage. Assuming an estimated average exchange rate of 1.23 CAD/USD from Table 11.12 for the "Month 1" bucket, to cover the C\$7.7 million shortage, the bank converts \$6.26 million to \$6.26 × 1.23 = C\$7.7 million. Therefore the ending USD and CAD cash after the cross-currency transfer are \$19.08 − \$6.26 = \$12.82 million and −C\$7.7 + C\$7.7 = C\$0 million, respectively.

This calculation is repeated for remaining buckets where due to higher CAD cash inflows versus outflows no cross-currency flow is needed. In gap analysis of a multi-currency balance sheet, it should be noted that the assumption of an average exchange rate for the entire time bucket introduces some approximation into the cash flow gap schedule, and high exchange rate volatility increases the level of approximation. Also, any restriction for exchange between currencies, among legal entities and across jurisdictions, should be carefully assessed and cross-currency logistical restrictions, such as lack of counterparty or lack of account with an exchange house, should be included in idiosyncratic or market-wide stress scenarios.

In the aggregation of gap schedules that are developed separately for different currencies, the timing of conversion of cash flow is important. If cash flows are converted at each bucket, aggregated to a single functional currency and then rolled from one bucket to the next, the result would be different from when each currency gap schedule separately rolled and then the ending cash balances are converted into a single functional currency. This is due to different estimated exchange rates from one time bucket to another.

FUNDING CONCENTRATION RISK

As we discuss in the section "Funding Source and Liquidity Risk," banks have a variety of funding sources to raise the cash needed for their daily operations and lending activities. Traditionally commercial banks depend on deposits and debt issuances to fund their balance sheet while investment banks rely more on short-term funding methods, such as repos, to fund their investment. While short-term funding sources are usually cheaper compared to more stable long-term mechanisms, funding long-term assets with short-term liabilities increases the maturity gap of the balance sheet and worsens the liquidity risk. In determination of the funding mix a broad risk–return view should include the following considerations:

■ **Term:** A good balance between the term of the assets and liabilities ensures the bank is protected against the potential maturity gap risk. Funding long-term assets with short-term liabilities increases this risk. Cash flow gap analysis, explained in the previous section, is a good tool to provide insight into this risk and to help to determine the appropriate amount of long-term liabilities.
■ **Stability:** Funding sources that are stable and reliable reduce the chance for the occurrence of a liquidity event.
■ **Cost:** While the reduction in the cost of the funds is a goal for the treasury department of any bank, this reduction should not come with the added risk of instability in funding sources.

Diversification of funding sources plays an important role in a bank's overall business strategy and its financial health. Excessive concentration on one funding mechanism or reliance on a limited number of counterparties can lead to elevated levels of liquidity risk. To manage this risk banks monitor concentrations in these areas:

Source Concentration: Having a diversified set of funding channels safeguards the bank against the potential adverse effect of a liquidity event that may result from unavailability of one or a few sources. Consider again the regional bank example used in our discussions on cash flow gap schedules. Table 11.13 summarizes different funding sources utilized by the bank, as of May 31, 2017; 38% of the bank's funding is

TABLE 11.13 Concentration of funding methods for a regional bank (in $ million)

Long-Term Debt	Short-Term Debt, incl. CP	Repo	Deposit from Financial Firms	Deposit from Non-Financial Firms and Small Businesses
32.70	21.55	35.41	2.90	57.70
22%	14%	24%	2%	38%

from deposits by non-financial firms and small businesses. Such deposits are usually considered as more stable sources compared to deposits from financial firms. On the other hand, short-term debt and repo combined covers 38% of the bank's funding. Short-term funding, particularly repo, exposes the bank to higher liquidity risk.

Counterparty Concentration: Within each funding source, diversification of counterparties reduces the risk of a large adverse impact on the liquidity position should one or a few counterparties retract their funds. For retail deposit products banks can control their concentration risk by limiting the maximum amount in individual or joint accounts. For corporate deposit products, banks diversify their clientele among different industries, sectors, or geographic locations. When using repo as a funding tool, banks manage the concentration risk by increasing their repo counterparties as well as using clearinghouses. While diversification of funding counterparties is a good practice, it should be noted that since during a market-wide stress all funding counterparties may face the same liquidity problem, diversification may not be enough to prevent the occurrence of a liquidity event.

Maturity Concentration: When maturity dates of a large portion of term liabilities are concentrated in a short period of time, a bank may face difficulty in replacing the maturing debts. A well-defined funding plan distributes the maturity dates so termination dates of maturing securities issued by the bank are spaced out based on the ability of the bank to roll and replace them.

BASEL ACCORD LIQUIDITY RISK MONITORING TOOLS

In order to quantify and measure liquidity risk in the banking industry, in 2010 the Basel Committee on Banking Supervision (BCBS), part of the Bank for International Settlements (BIS), introduced the Liquidity Coverage Ratio and

Net Stable Funding Ratio as part of the Basel III framework for liquidity risk measurement (BCBS 2010). Revised versions of standards for both ratios were issued in 2013 (BCBS 2013) and in 2014 (BCBS 2014). Liquidity coverage ratio is a measurement of a bank's resilience to liquidity stress in a short period of one month while the net stable funding ratio is to capture the bank's use of stable funding, and hence a measurement of its liquidity risk in a longer period of one year. These two ratios are designed to be complementary and overall provide a view of the bank liquidity risk status. The Basel committee recommended a gradual implementation of the minimum required levels for these ratios. Considering the importance of intraday liquidity and the risk associated with it, in 2013 the committee introduced tools for management of intraday liquidity (BCBS 2013). In this section we review these tools and explain the calculations related to each.[13]

Liquidity Coverage Ratio

The purpose of the *liquidity coverage ratio (LCR)* is to capture the short-term resilience of a bank to liquidity stress scenarios. The measurement considers the amount of a bank's unencumbered *high-quality liquid assets (HQLAs)* that can be converted easily into cash to meet the liquidity needs for a 30-calendar-day period. The LCR is defined as:

$$LCR = \frac{Stock\ of\ High\text{-}Quality\ Liquid\ Assets}{Total\ Net\ Cash\ Outflow\ Over\ Next\ 30\ Calendar\ Days} \qquad (11.11)$$

This ratio must be at least 100% to ensure the bank has enough high-quality liquid assets to survive a severe liquidity stress event.[14] This means that on an ongoing basis, the stock of HQLA should at least equal the net cash outflows in a period of 30 days. This ratio is an assessment of sources and uses of liquidity under assumed combined idiosyncratic and market-wide stress scenarios. In this stress scenario it is assumed that wholesale funding is limited and the bank is experiencing a partial runoff on the retail deposits. It is also assumed that secured short-term funding, such as the repo market, is under stress and partially unavailable while the bank is experiencing unexpected cash outflow due to various conditions such as draws of committed lines, collateral calls due to deterioration of credit rating, or the potential need to buy back debt. Components of LCR are: high-quality liquid assets and net cash outflow over 30 days period. The LCR should be used as an ongoing monitoring tool for liquidity risk. The frequency of reporting LCR to regulatory supervisors is initially set to be monthly, with eventual move toward a daily reporting.

High-Quality Liquid Asset

The numerator of the LCR is the value of a bank's high-quality liquid assets under the stress scenario at the first day of the stress period (*reporting date*). Generally, to be eligible as an HQLA an asset must be liquid during the stress period and easily convertible into cash without significant loss of the value. One general guideline for an asset to be considered as an HQLA is to be eligible as collateral for the central bank's liquidity facilities. The Basel standard introduces the following characteristics of an HQLA:

- Low risk (e.g., low credit and interest rate risk)
- Certainty in the value and ease of valuation method
- Low correlation with risky assets
- Having an active market (e.g., being listed in an exchange, high trading volume, high number of market participants, existence of multiple market makers, and low bid–ask spread)
- Low volatility
- Historical evidence of being safe-haven asset

Aside from these characteristics, there are certain operational requirements for HQLA to ensure that during a stress period a bank can convert it into cash in order to generate liquidity in a timely manner without restriction or significant loss of value. This can be done through an outright sale or repo transaction. The standard requires banks to periodically test the operational aspect of monetization of part of their HQLA portfolio to assess their readiness and study the impact of such actions on banks and also on overall market. One of the main operational requirements of HQLA is for the asset to be unencumbered. Assets that are pre-pledged to the central bank as collateral for liquidity facilities but not used for liquidity generation from those facilities can also be used as HQLA. The asset considered to be HQLA also should have no internal restriction within the bank, for example, no restriction on asset transfer with respect to legal, regulatory, location, tax, or accounting considerations. Also HQLA should not have restrictions from a risk management point of view, for example, not being used to hedge a risky asset that is not part of an HQLA portfolio. Assets received in reverse repo-style transactions that are not re-pledged as collateral and legally and contractually available to the bank may be included in HQLA. Any surplus of HQLA at a subsidiary can only be rolled up to the consolidated level (parent) if those assets are freely available to the consolidated entity at all times. The Basel standard categorizes HQLA into two groups:

Level 1 Asset: This group of assets can be included in the total stock of HQLA (numerator of LCR) without limit. Generally level 1 assets are not subject to haircut, unless required by regulatory supervisors. Following are eligible level 1 asset types:

- Cash
- Reserves held at the central bank
- Government or governmental agencies' issued securities that have a 0% risk-weight based on Basel II standardized approach[15] (e.g., U.S. Treasury notes)

Level 2 Asset: This group of assets can only be included in stock of HQLA up to 40% of the total stock, after applying the haircut percentage. This group has two subgroups: 2A and 2B. Total 2A and 2B assets cannot exceed 40% of the total stock of HQLA while 2B assets cannot exceed 15% of the total stock of HQLA, after applying the appropriate haircut.

When including a level 2A asset in HQLA in the numerator of LCR, a 15% haircut is to be applied to the current market value of the asset (market value as of the reporting date). Following are eligible level 2A asset types:

- Securities issued by the government or government-sponsored entities that have a 20% risk-weight based on Basel II standardized approach have an active and liquid cash or repo market, and were reliable sources of liquidity during previous stress periods.
- Corporate debt securities that are not issued by a financial institution have at least a AA credit rating, have an active and liquid cash or repo market, and were reliable sources of liquidity during previous stress periods.

The applicable haircut for level 2B assets depends on the type of asset. Following are eligible level 2B asset types:

- Residential mortgage-backed securities (RMBSs) that are not issued by the bank itself (also underlying assets not originated by the bank), have at least a AA credit rating, have an active and liquid cash or repo market, and were reliable sources of liquidity during previous stress periods. Structured products other than RMBS are not included in this category. This class of level 2B assets receives a 25% haircut.
- Corporate debt securities that are not issued by a financial institution, have a credit rating between A+ and BBB–, have an active and liquid cash or repo market, and were reliable sources of liquidity during previous stress periods. This class of level 2B assets receives a 50% haircut.
- Common equity shares that are not issued by a financial institution, exchange traded and centrally cleared, part of a major stock index, denominated in the major currency of the bank's home jurisdiction, have an active and liquid market, and were reliable sources of liquidity during previous stress periods. This class of level 2B assets receives a 50% haircut.

For jurisdictions that there is proven shortage of acceptable HQLA, the standard provides alternative options for inclusion as HQLA in the numerator of LCR, conditional to regulatory approval. These alternative options are:

- Use of fee-based contractually committed liquidity facilities from central banks.
- Use of foreign currency HQLA to cover domestic currency liquidity needs (additional haircut is applied).
- Use of level 2 assets in a higher percentage than originally allowed by the standard (additional haircut is applied).

Level 1 and level 2 securities maturing within 30 days may be included in the stock of HQLA providing all the conditions discussed previously are satisfied and haircuts are considered. Table 11.14 summarizes HQLA types and applicable haircuts. The stock of HQLA in the numerator of the LCR is the summation of level 1, level 2A, and level 2B assets that meet the described requirements.[16]

Total Net Cash Outflows in Next 30 Days

The denominator of the LCR is the total expected cash outflows minus total expected cash inflows under the stress scenario for the next 30 calendar days

TABLE 11.14   HQLA categories, applicable haircuts, and asset types

Group	Max. % of HQLA Stock	Sub-Group	Max. % of HQLA Stock	Applicable Haircut %	Asset Type
Level 1	100%			0%	Cash, government securities (with risk-weight of 0%), reserves at central banks
Level 2	40%	**2A**	40%	15%	Government securities (with risk-weight of 20%), corporate bonds (with AA– or better rating)
		2B	15%	25%	RMBS (with AA or better rating)
				50%	Corporate bonds (with rating between A+ and BBB–), common equities

from the reporting date while the total expected cash inflow is capped at 75% of the total expected cash outflows:

$$Total\ Net\ Cash\ Outflow\ in\ Next\ 30\ Days$$

$$= Total\ Expected\ Cash\ Outflows$$

$$- \min(Total\ Expected\ Cash\ Inflows, 0.75$$

$$\times Total\ Expected\ Cash\ Outflows) \qquad (11.12)$$

Generally, cash inflows and outflows are determined by multiplying the outstanding balance of an asset or expected cash flow of a contract by a pre-scribed rate (between 0% and 100%) to determine the cash inflows or outflows that should be included in the denominator of the LCR. For cash inflows and to prevent double counting, if an asset is included in HQLA in the numerator of the LCR, the standard does not allow the cash inflows of that asset to be included in the denominator of the LCR.

The Basel standard provides details of how to treat different funding sources, asset types, and cash flows when calculating the denominator of the LCR. They are summarized in Tables 11.15 and 11.16, for expected cash outflows and expected cash inflows separately.[17] If there is any restriction on asset or liquidity transfers between a legal entity and the parent, the excess liquidity in the legal entity cannot be recognized at the consolidated level LCR.

To illustrate the calculation of LCR consider again the hypotheti-cal regional bank we used in examples of cash flow gap analysis earlier. Assets, liabilities, and off-balance-sheet items of this bank are listed in Tables 11.4, 11.5, and 11.6. The analysis date (reporting date) of this LCR calculation is May 31, 2017.

HQLA

Among the bank assets, cash and some of invested securities are qualified as HQLA, as presented in Table 11.17. Removing $4.5 million of operational cash deposited with a custodian bank, the regional bank has $30 million cash, which received a haircut of 0%. Only unencumbered securities can be consid-ered as HQLA. The bank has $29 million encumbered securities of different types. It has $4 million unencumbered U.S. Treasury notes that are considered level 1, which receive a 0% haircut. AA-rated corporate bonds are considered as a level 2A asset while agency RMBS AAA-rated securities, corporate bond A-rated securities, and corporate bond BBB-rated securities are considered as level 2B assets. Haircuts for these assets are determined based on Table 11.14.

TABLE 11.15 Expected cash outflows for LCR

Funding, Product, or Contract Type	Treatment
Retail Deposit: Deposits by individuals	
Term retail deposits with residual maturity greater than 30 days	0% of balance as of reporting date considered as cash outflow
Stable retail deposits	5% of balance as of reporting date considered as cash outflow
Stable retail deposits that are fully insured and depositors have established relationships with the bank or deposits are done through transactions (e.g., direct deposit of salaries)[1]	3% of balance as of reporting date considered as cash outflow
Less-stable retail deposits, e.g., deposits not fully covered by insurance, deposits from wealthy individuals, deposits that can be withdrawn quickly such as internet deposits	10% of balance as of reporting date considered as cash outflow
Unsecured Wholesale Funding: Deposits or funding provided by proprietorships and partnerships, and unsecured debt notes issued	
Term deposits or term lending with contractual call date beyond 30 days	0% of balance as of reporting date considered as cash outflow
Stable deposits by small business customers	5% of balance as of reporting date considered as cash outflow
Less-stable deposits by small business customers	10% of balance as of reporting date considered as cash outflow
Operational deposits generated by custody, cash management, or clearing activities, where the fund is placed with the bank only for fulfillment of operational requirement of such activities based on a legally binding contract[2]	25% of balance as of reporting date considered as cash outflow
Portion of operational deposits that is fully insured	5% of balance as of reporting date considered as cash outflow
Required deposits of cooperative bank in an institutional network with the central institution	25% of balance as of reporting date considered as cash outflow
Deposits by non-financial institutions or corporates, sovereigns, or central banks	40% of balance as of reporting date considered as cash outflow

(continued)

TABLE 11.15 *(Continued)*

Funding, Product, or Contract Type	Treatment
Deposits by non-financial institutions or corporates, sovereigns, or central banks, if entire deposit is fully insured	20% of balance as of reporting date considered as cash outflow
Deposits by other legal entities not included above, including banks, other financial institutions, and insurance companies	100% of balance as of reporting date considered as cash outflow
Unsecured notes and bonds issued by the bank with contractual maturity within 30 days	100% of balance as of reporting date considered as cash outflow[4]

Secured Borrowing: Funding raised through collateralized agreements, including repo-style transactions, and secured debt notes issued

Secured funding transactions with contractual maturity beyond 30 days	0% of fund raised through transaction considered as cash outflow

When contractual maturity is within 30 days of open contracts:

Secured funding transactions (e.g., repo-style transactions) with central banks as counterparty	0% of fund raised through transaction considered as cash outflow[3]
Secured funding transactions with any counterparty that are collateralized by level 1 assets	0% of fund raised through transaction considered as cash outflow
Secured funding transactions with any counterparty that are collateralized by level 2A assets	15% of fund raised through transaction considered as cash outflow
Secured funding transactions with domestic government or government-sponsored entities counterparties that are collateralized by assets that are not level 1 or level 2A assets	25% of fund raised through transaction considered as cash outflow
Secured funding transitions with any non-domestic government counterparties that are collateralized with level 2B RMBS assets	25% of fund raised through transaction considered as cash outflow
Secured funding transitions with any non-domestic government counterparties that are collateralized with level 2B assets other than RMBS	50% of fund raised through transaction considered as cash outflow

TABLE 11.15 *(Continued)*

Funding, Product, or Contract Type	Treatment
Secured funding transitions with any non-domestic government counterparties that are collateralized by non-HQLA	100% of fund raised through transaction considered as cash outflow
All other secured funding transactions not included above	100% of fund raised through transaction considered as cash outflow
Asset-backed securities issued by the bank with contractual maturity within 30-day horizon	100% of balance as of reporting date considered as cash outflow[4]
Commercial papers issued by the bank with contractual maturity within 30-day horizon	100% of balance as of reporting date considered as cash outflow
Derivative[5]	
Required derivative collaterals that are not posted yet	100% of collaterals are considered as cash outflow[6]
Expected additional collateral for derivative contracts in case of three-notch downgrade in credit rating of the bank	100% of expected additional collaterals considered as cash outflow
Expected additional liquidity needs for potential changes in values of posted collaterals of derivative contracts	For collaterals that are level 1 assets, 0%, and for other asset types, 20% of values of posted collaterals considered as cash outflow
Expected additional liquidity needs for potential changes in values of derivative contracts	Largest absolute net 30-day collateral outflow related to market value changes realized during the preceding 24 months from the reporting date is considered as cash outflow[7]
Excess collaterals held by the bank for derivative contracts	100% of excess collaterals considered as cash outflow
Expected additional liquidity needs for derivative contracts that allow collateral substitution to non-HQLA	100% of HQLA collateral that can be substituted for non-HQLA is considered as cash outflow
Structure Financing: Funding raised through special purpose vehicles, conduits, or securities investment vehicles	
Supported debts maturing within 30-day horizon	100% of maturing amount is considered as cash outflow

(continued)

TABLE 11.15 *(Continued)*

Funding, Product, or Contract Type	Treatment
If there are embedded options in the financing contracts that allow for the return of assets	100% of assets that can be returned is considered as cash outflow

Committed Credit Facilities: Credit and liquidity facilities are contractual commitments to provide funds at future dates to customers or companies. The standard uses *credit facility* as the general term referring to such facilities (e.g., general working capital facility provided to a company or retail credit card) while the term *liquidity facility* refers to commitments by the bank to provide funds to a company for refinancing or rolling over maturing debts (e.g., facility provided to a hedge fund). For liquidity facility the undrawn amount is assumed as the current outstanding debt issued by the counterparty that is supported by the facility and maturing within the 30-day period. Any additional capacity of the facility is treated as a credit facility.

Credit facilities to retail consumers (e.g., credit cards), and to small business customers	5% of undrawn amount of credit facility is considered as cash outflow[8]
Credit and liquidity facilities to non-financial companies, governments, and government-sponsored entities and central banks	10% of undrawn amount of credit facility and 30% of undrawn amount of liquidity facility is considered as cash outflow
Credit and liquidity facilities to banks subject to prudential supervision	40% of undrawn amount of credit or liquidity facility is considered as cash outflow
Credit and liquidity facilities to other financial institutions and insurance companies	40% of undrawn amount of credit facility and 100% of undrawn amount of liquidity facility is considered as cash outflow
Credit and liquidity facilities to other legal entities, including special purpose vehicles and conduits	100% of undrawn amount of credit or liquidity facility is considered as cash outflow
Any contractual commitments to extend fund to financial institutions within 30 days that are not included above	100% of the commitment is considered as cash outflow
Trade finance agreements	0% to 5% of the committed amount is considered as cash outflow (based on regulatory supervisors discretion)

TABLE 11.15 (*Continued*)

Funding, Product, or Contract Type	Treatment
Any other contingent funding obligations not included above	Drawdown rate is at regulatory supervisor's discretion
Broker-Dealer and Trading Activities:	
When the bank covers customers' short positions using other customers' collaterals, when collaterals are not level 1 or 2	50% of value of position as of reporting date is considered as cash outflow
Bank's uncovered short positions that are expected to be closed within 30 days	100% of value of position as of reporting date is considered as cash outflow
Bank's unsecured collateral borrowings that expected to be returned within 30 days	100% of value of position as of reporting date is considered as cash outflow
Others:	
Dividends and contractual interest payments	100% of expected cash flow is considered as cash outflow
Operating costs	0% of expected cash flow is considered as cash outflow[9]
Any other contractual cash flow within 30 days not included above	100% of expected cash flow is considered as cash outflow

Notes:

[1] If only a portion of a deposit is insured, the deposit up to the insurance limit can be treated as a stable deposit and the remainder would be treated as less stable.

[2] Any excess fund beyond the operational requirement is not considered in this category.

[3] Cash outflow is calculated based on the amount of funds raised through the transaction, and not the value of underlying collateral.

[4] This is equivalent to assuming no refinancing is possible.

[5] Option contracts are assumed exercised when they are in-the-money to the option buyer.

[6] If a contract is collateralized by HQLA, this is net of any corresponding cash inflows.

[7] Netting is per counterparty when legal master netting agreement exists.

[8] Undrawn portion of committed facility is calculated net of any HQLA collateral posted. Such HQLA cannot be counted toward the numerator of LCR.

[9] Outflows related to operating costs are not included in the standard.

TABLE 11.16 Expected cash inflows for LCR

Funding, Product, Transaction or Contract Type	Treatment
Secured Lending: Reverse repo-style contracts and margin loans	
Secured lending transactions with contractual maturity beyond 30 days	0% of fund distributed through transaction considered as cash inflow

When contractual maturity is within 30 days and collateral is not used to cover short positions:

Secured lending transactions collateralized by level 1 assets	0% of fund distributed through transaction considered as cash inflow (i.e., full rollover)
Secured lending transactions collateralized by level 2A assets	15% of fund distributed through transaction considered as cash inflow (i.e., partial rollover)
Secured lending transactions collateralized by level 2B RMBS assets	25% of fund distributed through transaction considered as cash inflow (i.e., partial rollover)
Secured lending transactions collateralized by level 2B non-RMBS assets	50% of fund distributed through transaction considered as cash inflow (i.e., partial rollover)
Secured lending transactions collateralized by non-HQLA	100% of fund distributed through transaction considered as cash inflow (i.e., no rollover)
Margin loans collateralized by non-HQLA	50% of fund distributed through transaction considered as cash inflow

When contractual maturity is within 30 days and collateral is used to cover short positions:

Secured lending transactions collateralized by any asset type	0% of fund distributed through transaction considered as cash inflow (i.e., full rollover)
Committed Credit Facilities	
Credit or liquidity facilities available to the bank	0% of undrawn amount of credit or liquidity facilities is considered as cash inflow (i.e., lines cannot be drawn)
Loans and Other Lending Products	
Interest and scheduled principal payments within 30 days from exposures to retails and small business customers[1]	50% of contractual cash inflows is considered[2]

TABLE 11.16 *(Continued)*

Funding, Product, Transaction or Contract Type	Treatment
Interest and scheduled principal payments within 30 days from exposures to non-financial companies[1]	50% of contractual cash inflows is considered[2]
Interest and scheduled principal payments within 30 days from exposures to financial companies, governments or government-sponsored entities, or central banks	100% of contractual cash inflows is considered
Securities held as asset maturing within 30 days and not included in the stock of HQLA in the numerator of LCR	100% of contractual cash inflows is considered
Non-maturing products with no minimum payment requirements	No cash inflow is considered
Non-maturing products with contractual minimum payment due within 30 days	50% (for retail, small business, or non-financial wholesale counterparties) or 100% (for financial and sovereign counterparties) of the contractual minimum due payment is considered as cash inflow
Derivatives	
Derivative contracts	100% of net of cash inflows is considered
Others	
Operational deposits held with another financial institution for support of activities such as custody, clearing, and cash management	0% of balance is considered as cash inflow (i.e., no cash inflow)
Required deposits of cooperative bank in an institutional network with the central institution	0% of balance is considered as cash inflow (i.e., no cash inflow)
Other contracts	Rate of contractual cash inflows is at regulatory supervisor's discretion
Cash inflows related to non-financial revenues	No cash inflow is considered

[1] Only contractual cash inflows from outstanding exposures as of the reporting date that are performing and not expected to default within next 30 days are included.

[2] The assumption is that 100% of expected cash inflows occur and at the same time the bank continues to issue new loans at the rate of 50% of inflows; hence the end result is 50% cash inflows.

TABLE 11.17   HQLA for a hypothetical regional bank (in $ million)

Category	Item	Description	Available Amount	Haircut	Factor	HQLA = Amount × Factor
Cash	Cash Deposit	Level 1 asset	30.00	0%	100%	30.00
	U.S. Treasury	Level 1 asset	4.00	0%	100%	4.00
	Agency RMBS AAA-rated securities	Level 2B asset	4.00	25%	75%	3.00
	Non-agency RMBS A-rated securities	Non-HQLA	5.00	100%	0%	0.00
Investment	Corporate bond AA-rated securities	Level 2A asset	7.00	15%	85%	5.95
	Corporate bond A-rated securities	Level 2B asset	4.70	50%	50%	2.35
	Corporate bond BBB-rated securities	Level 2B asset	2.30	50%	50%	1.15
	Corporate bond B-rated securities	Non-HQLA	2.00	100%	0%	0.00
					Total HQLA:	**46.45**

Non-agency RMBS A-rated securities and corporate bond B-rated securities are not considered as HQLA, and hence receive a 100% haircut.

Based on Table 11.17 the regional bank currently has $46.45 million HQLA, for the purpose of calculating LCR. Also note that only 27% of HQLA is level 2 and only 14% of HQLA is level 2B; hence, the maximum allowable limits of 40% level 2 and 15% level 2B assets are satisfied.

Based on the assets, liabilities, and off-balance-sheet items listed in Tables 11.4, 11.5, and 11.6 we can calculate cash outflows and inflows as follows.

Cash Outflow

For calculation of cash outflow of the regional bank we need to consider term loan, credit facility, repo, deposit, maturing debt, derivative, and equity categories. Based on the treatments explained in Table 11.15 we can calculate cash outflows as shown in Table 11.18.

TABLE 11.18 Cash outflows of a hypothetical regional bank for LCR calculation (in $ million)

Category	Item	Description	Amount	Factor	Cash Outflow = Amount × Factor
Deposit	By small business	Stable	20.00	5%	1.00
	By small business	Less-stable	14.50	10%	1.45
	By non-financial firm		23.20	40%	9.28
	By financial firm		1.90	100%	1.90
	Operational deposit		1.00	25%	0.25
Debt	Unsecured long-term	Maturity ≤ 30 days	6.00	100%	6.00
	Unsecured short-term	Maturity ≤ 30 days	11.30	100%	11.30
	Unsecured commercial paper	Maturity ≤ 30 days	3.00	100%	3.00
Repo	U.S. Treasury	Level 1 asset – Repo maturity ≤ 30 days	18.81	0%	0.00
	Agency RMBS AAA-rated securities	Level 2B asset – Repo maturity ≤ 30 days	0.00	25%	0.00
	Non-agency RMBS A-rated securities	Non-HQLA – Repo maturity ≤ 30 days	2.40	100%	2.40
	Corporate bond AA-rated securities	Level 2A asset – Repo maturity ≤ 30 days	2.80	15%	0.42
Derivative	Additional collateral if three-notch downgrade		1.40	100%	1.40
Credit Facility	To small business	Undrawn balance	5.50	5%	0.28
	To non-financial firm	Undrawn balance	2.00	10%	0.20
	To financial firm	Undrawn balance	1.90	40%	0.76
Debt	Obligatory payment	Interest payment – within 30 days	0.60	100%	0.60
Equity	Obligatory payment	Dividend – within 30 days	0.30	100%	0.30
				Total Cash Outflow:	**40.54**

- **Deposit:** Based on customer data and deposit insurance limits, the bank is able to categorize its deposits of $34.50 million from small businesses into a stable portion of $20 million and a less-stable portion of $14.5 million. These two subgroups of deposits have runoff rates of 5% and 10% from Table 11.15, respectively. Deposits from financial and non-financial firms and operational deposits are considered as wholesale funding and assigned 40%, 100%, and 25% runoff rates, respectively.
- **Debt:** From the $54.25 million debts issued by this bank, $20.3 million matures within the 30-day period and 100% of this amount is considered as cash outflow. Based on debt coupon payment schedules the bank is obligated to pay $0.6 million interest in the upcoming 30 days from the analysis date. This cash outflow is included in Table 11.15 with 100% outflow rate.
- **Repo:** The bank has used part of its investment in U.S. Treasury notes as collateral in repo contracts and raised $18.81 million cash. These are open repos so should be considered in the cash outflow, assuming repos would not be rolled. However, since the collateral is a level 1 asset the cash outflow rate is 0%. The bank also has used part of its AA-rated corporate bonds as collateral in 20 days repo contracts and raised $2.8 million cash. Since collateral is level 2A the appropriate outflow rate is 15%. No cash outflow is considered for repo contracts based on agency RMBS AAA-rated securities since the maturity of the repo contract is 45 days, beyond the 30-day horizon. Repos collateralized with non-agency RMBS A-rated securities that are maturing in three days are assigned 100% cash outflow rate, since the collateral is non-HQLA.
- **Derivative:** For its interest rate swap portfolio the bank currently has posted $1.15 million collateral with its counterparties, including the $0.02 million to be sent in one day from the analysis date. Based on a *potential future exposure (PFE)* analysis, the bank expects posting an additional $1.4 million collateral in case of a three-notch downgrade of its long-term credit rating. This amount in its entirety is considered as cash outflow.
- **Credit and Liquidity Facility:** This bank provides no liquidity facility to any of its customers. It has provided credit facilities to small business, non-financial, and financial customers and the undrawn portions of these facilities are assigned outflow rates of 5%, 10%, and 40%, respectively, as shown in Table 11.18.
- **Equity:** We include the dividend payment of $0.3 million that is expected at the end of June 2017 in the cash outflow schedule.

Based on the items listed here, the total expected cash outflow in a 30-day period is $40.54 million.

Cash Inflow

For calculation of cash inflows of the regional bank we need to consider the reverse repo, term loan, and credit facility categories. Based on the treatments explained in Table 11.16 we can calculate cash inflows as shown in Table 11.19.

TABLE 11.19 Cash inflows of a hypothetical regional bank for LCR calculation (in $ million)

Category	Item	Description	Amount	Factor	Cash Inflow = Amount × Factor
Reverse Repo	U.S. Treasury	Level 1 asset – Reverse repo maturity ≤ 30 days	4.95	0%	0.00
	Agency RMBS AAA-rated securities	Level 2B asset – Reverse repo maturity ≤ 30 days	3.80	25%	0.95
	Corporate bond A-rated securities	Level 2B asset – Reverse repo maturity ≤ 30 days	0.00	50%	0.00
Term Loan	To small business	Interest and principal payment – within 30 days	1.15	50%	0.58
	To non-financial firm	Interest and principal payment – within 30 days	1.60	50%	0.80
	To financial firm	Interest and principal payment – within 30 days	0.04	100%	0.04
Credit Facility	To small business	Minimum-due payment – within 30 days	0.04	50%	0.02
	To non-financial firm	Minimum-due payment – within 30 days	0.03	50%	0.015
	To financial firm	Minimum-due payment – within 30 days	0.00	100%	0.00
			Total Cash Inflow:		**2.40**

- **Reverse Repo:** The bank has reverse repo contracts with different collateral types; $4.95 of the lent amount through reverse repo is collateralized by U.S. Treasury notes, which are a level 1 asset, and hence receives a 0% inflow rate; $3.8 million is loaned through reverse repos that are collateralized by agency RMBS AAA-rated securities, which are a type 2B asset with a 25% inflow rate. The reverse repos collateralized by corporate bond A-rated securities would receive a 50% inflow rate, but those contracts mature in 60 days, beyond the 30-day LCR horizon.
- **Term Loan:** The bank has term loans to small business and non-financial and financial firms. The contractual cash inflows (interest and scheduled principal payments) from the performing portion of these loans within the next 30 days are expected to be $1.15 million, $1.6 million, and $0.04 million, and corresponding inflow rates are 50%, 50%, and 100%, respectively, as shown in Table 11.19.
- **Credit and Liquidity Facility:** The contractual minimum due payments from credit facilities provided to small business and non-financial counterparties within the next 30 days are $0.04 million and $0.03 million, with associated inflow rates of 50% for each. The contractual minimum due payments from credit facilities provided to financial counterparties within the next 30 days is negligible.

Based on the items listed here, the total expected cash inflow in a 30-day period is $2.4 million.

Using these results, the LCR as of the reporting date of May 31, 2017, is calculated as follows:

(in $ million)

$$Total\ Net\ Cash\ Outflow = Total\ Cash\ Outflows$$
$$- min(Total\ Cash\ Inflows, 0.75$$
$$\times Total\ Cash\ Outflows)$$
$$= \$40.54 - min(\$2.4, 0.75 \times \$40.54) = \$38.14$$

$$LCR = \frac{Stock\ of\ HQLA}{Total\ Net\ Cash\ Outflow} = \frac{\$46.45}{\$38.14} = 121.8\%$$

Based on the Basel III standard, the LCR ratio of 121.8% is an indication that this bank has enough liquid and high-quality assets that can be used as sources of liquidity during a stress scenario that combines market-wide and firm-specific stress events.

A decrease in LCR may occur due to any of the following reasons:

- Unanticipated decrease in expected cash inflow
- Unanticipated increase in expected cash outflow
- Decline in HQLA
- An idiosyncratic or market-wide stress event that adversely impacts one or more of above items

Banks are required to monitor the LCR on an ongoing basis, analyze the reason for decrease in the LCR, and report to regulatory supervisors accordingly. While the LCR is a step toward the right direction in readiness of banks for short-term liquidity stress scenarios, it suffers from a few drawbacks:

- Meeting the 100% requirement of the ratio by itself doesn't mean there is a full coverage of the cash outflow in the 30-day stress period, since there is a possibility that cash outflows and monetization of HQLA are not completely synchronized. This means that even though the LCR is above 100% it is possible that during a few days in the 30-day stress period the bank may face a liquidity shortage.
- LCR does not cover intraday liquidity needs. Hence a bank may still face an intraday liquidity shortage while having an LCR above 100%.
- During a stress period a bank is supposed to use HQLA to cover its liquidity needs; therefore, the LCR may fall below the indicated 100% threshold. This may have unexpected consequences when a bank doesn't use its HQLA as source of liquidity, in order to avoid failing the LCR requirement from a regulatory point of view. To counter such a situation the standard recommends when evaluating a reported LCR below 100% by a bank, regulatory supervisors should consider the extent to which the reported decline in the LCR is due to a firm-specific or market-wide stress event.

Net Stable Funding Ratio

While the main purpose of liquidity coverage ratio is to capture resilience of banks to stress events in short-term, the *net stable funding ratio (NSFR)* is focused on longer term funding sources with the intention of limiting excess reliance of banks on short-term funding. While borrowing in the short term and lending in the long term is one of the fundamental business strategies of financial intermediaries such as banks, past experience, particularly during the most recent global financial crisis of 2007–2009, showed that short-term funding sources can disappear very fast, leading to major disruptions in banking operations and the overall health of the economy. To address this concern the Basel Committee on Banking Supervision introduced the net stable funding ratio as part of the Basel III framework for liquidity risk measurement (BCBS 2014).

NSFR is based on *stable funding*, which is the capital and liabilities that are perceived as reliable over a long time horizon. The time horizon of NSFR is one year and the ratio is defined as:

$$NSFR = \frac{Available\ Amount\ of\ Stable\ Funding}{Required\ Amount\ of\ Stable\ Funding} \tag{11.13}$$

This ratio must be at least 100% to ensure the bank has stable and established funding sources for its operations on an ongoing basis and in a relatively long time horizon. NSFR has two components: available stable funding and required stable funding. Depending on the term, type, and the counterparty of the funding, in calculation of the NSFR the funding amounts are calibrated by applying factors provided by the Basel standard. This is done to better reflect the stability of the funding sources. The NSFR is set to be reported at least quarterly to the regulatory supervisors.

Available Stable Funding

Determination of available stable funding for NSFR is based on general assumptions that (i) long-term liabilities are more stable than short-term liabilities, and (ii) funding from retail and small business customers is more stable than wholesale funding. To obtain the available stable funding, various liabilities of the bank are first categorized into five different groups, and then funding amounts (carrying values) are multiplied by weight factors of each group. The sum of these weighted amounts is the available stable funding used in the numerator of NSFR. The weight factors are determined based on the expectation of stability of funding channels or the possibility of withdrawal of funding by counterparties. Table 11.20 presents a summary of the five groups of funding sources and the related weight factors as provided by the standard. For complete details of these groups see the Basel Committee on Banking Supervision (2014).

Required Stable Funding

Determination of required stable funding for NSFR is based on general assumptions that (i) banks prefer to roll over a proportion of maturing loans to preserve business and customer relationship, and (ii) high-quality unencumbered assets can be used to raise funds (either through outright sale or repo) and hence require less stable funding.

TABLE 11.20 Available stable funding groups and associated weight factors

Group	Liability (Funding) Type[1]	Weight Factor
Group 1	Regulatory capital as defined in the Basel III standard (most notably common equity), excluding the portion of Tier 2 capital that matures within one year Secured or unsecured liabilities, and term deposits with residual maturities beyond one year	100%
Group 2	Non-maturing stable deposits, or term deposits with residual maturity less than one year, by small business and retail customers	95%
Group 3	Non-maturing less-stable deposits, or term deposits with residual maturity less than one year, by small business and retail customers	90%
Group 4	Secured or unsecured funding with residual maturity less than one year, provided by non-financial counterparties Operational deposits generated by custody, cash management, or clearing activities Funding from government or government-sponsored entities with residual maturity less than one year Secured or unsecured funding not included above with residual maturity between six months and one year, and funding from central banks and financial firms	50%
Group 5	Other liabilities not included above, and other funding with residual maturity of less than six months from central banks and financial firms Other liabilities without a stated maturity or open liabilities[2] Trade date payables from purchase of financial instruments, commodities, or foreign currencies Derivative liability net of derivative assets, if derivative liabilities are greater than derivative assets[3]	0%

[1] For callable funding, investors are assumed to redeem the call option at the earliest possible date.
[2] With the exception of deferred tax liabilities and minority interest, which are assigned a weight factor depending on the nearest possible date which these liabilities could be realized. If this date is beyond one year, the weight factor is 100%, and if it is between six months and one year, the weight factor is 50%.
[3] NSFR Derivative liabilities = (Derivative liabilities when contract has negative value) – (Cash collateral posted as variation margin)
NSFR Derivative assets = (Derivative assets when contract has positive value) – (Cash collateral received as variation margin)

To obtain the required stable funding for the purpose of NSFR, various assets and off-balance-sheet items of the bank are first categorized into eight different groups, and then carrying values are multiplied by weight factors of each group. The sum of these weighted amounts is the required stable funding used in the denominator of NSFR. The weight factors are determined based on assets rollover expectation or level of difficulty in selling assets or using them as collaterals in secured funding transactions. Table 11.21 presents a summary of these eight groups and the related weight factors as provided by the standard. For complete details of these groups see the Basel Committee on Banking Supervision (2014).

TABLE 11.21 Required stable funding groups and associated weight factors

Group	Asset Type[1]	Weight Factor
Group 1	Cash and reserves with central banks (required and excess) Trade date receivables from sales of financial instruments, commodities, or foreign currencies	0%
Group 2	Unencumbered level 1 asset, as defined for LCR, excluding those that are already included in group 1 above Undrawn portion of credit and liquidity facilities provided to customers that cannot be revoked	5%
Group 3	Unencumbered loans to financial firms with residual maturities of less than six months, where: (i) the loan is collateralized with level 1 assets, and (ii) the bank has the ability to repledge the received collateral	10%
Group 4	Unencumbered level 2A assets Unencumbered loans to financial companies with residual maturities of less than six months and not included in group 3 above	15%
Group 5	Unencumbered level 2B assets Encumbered HQLA with residual encumbrance term between six months and one year Loans to financial firms or central banks with residual maturity between six months and one year Operational deposits held at other financial firms Non-HQLA with residual maturity less than one year, that are not included in groups above, including loans to non-financial firms, retail businesses, and small business customers	50%

TABLE 11.21 *(Continued)*

Group	Asset Type[1]	Weight Factor
Group 6	Unencumbered residential mortgages with residual maturity one year or more, that have 35% or less risk-weight based on the Basel II standard	65%
	Unencumbered loans not included in above groups, excluding loans to financial firms, with a residual maturity one year or more that would have 35% or lower risk-weight based on the Basel II standard	
	Cash and securities posted as initial margin for derivative contracts	85%
Group 7	Unencumbered loans that are performing and not included in above groups, excluding loans to financial firms, with a residual maturity one year or more that would have higher than 35% risk-weight based on the Basel II standard	
	Unencumbered non-HQLA securities with residual maturity of one year or more, and exchange-traded equities	
	Physically traded commodities	
	Encumbered assets with residual encumbrance term of one year or more	100%
Group 8	Other assets not included in groups above, including non-performing loans, fixed assets, non-exchange-traded equities, retained interest, defaulted securities, and insurance assets	
	Derivative assets net of derivative liabilities, if derivative assets are greater than derivative liabilities[2]	
	20% of derivative liabilities before deduction of posted variation margin	
	Loans to financial firms with a residual maturity of one year or more	

[1] For assets with options it should be assumed that any option that extends the maturity is exercised.
[2] NSFR Derivative liabilities = (Derivative liabilities when contract has negative value) − (Cash collateral posted as variation margin)
NSFR Derivative assets = (Derivative assets when contract has positive value) − (Cash collateral received as variation margin)

TABLE 11.22   Adjustment of weight factor for encumbered assets

Less than six months	Between six months and one year		Greater than one year
Same weight factor as unencumbered	**If unencumbered weight factor is ≤ 50%**	**If unencumbered weight factor is > 50%**	100%
	50%	Same weight factor as unencumbered	

Assets that are borrowed through reverse repo-style transactions, where the bank does not have beneficial ownership of the underlying assets, may be excluded from the calculation of the required stable funding. On the other hand, the bank should include assets that are lent through repo-style transactions where it holds the beneficial ownership of the underlying assets. When a bilateral netting contract exists, secured transactions with a counterparty may be netted when included in the calculation of NSFR. For encumbered assets risk factors should be adjusted to reflect the time remaining until assets are unencumbered. The required adjustment based on residual encumbrance term is shown in Table 11.22.

To illustrate calculation of NSFR consider again the regional bank from the earlier examples of this chapter. This bank utilizes a variety of funding sources inducing short-term and long-term debts, repos, and deposits.

Available Stable Funding

Using data from Tables 11.4, 11.5, and 11.6, five groups of available stable funding for the bank are presented in Table 11.23:

> **Group 1:** Common equity of $12 million and $15.5 million long-term debt with maturity greater than one year are in this group and receive a 100% weight factor.
>
> **Group 2:** $20 million stable portion of deposits by small business customers is in this group and receives a 95% weight factor.
>
> **Group 3:** The remaining $14.5 million deposits by small business customers that are considered as less stable are in group 3, which receives a 90% weight factor.
>
> **Group 4:** $1 million operational deposits from financial firm customers and $3 million unsecured debt with residual maturity between six months and one year are included in this group and receive a 50% weight factor.

Group 5: Other funding sources, including $35.41 million repos with residual maturity less than six months, $25.1 million deposits by financial and non-financial firms, $35.75 debt securities with residual maturity less than six months, and net derivative liability are part of this group. They all receive a 0% weight factor. They are listed in Table 11.23. Using data from Table 11.6(a), and considering derivative counterparties currently have no margin posted with the regional bank, the net derivative liability is calculated as follows:

$$NSFR\ derivative\ assets = (derivative\ assets)$$
$$- (cash\ collateral\ received\ as\ variation\ margin$$
$$on\ derivative\ assets) = \$3.2 - 0 = \$3.2\ million$$
$$NSFR\ derivative\ liabilities = (derivative\ liabilities)$$
$$- (total\ collateral\ posted\ as\ variation\ margin$$
$$on\ derivative\ liabilities) = \$1 - \$0.8$$
$$= \$0.2\ million$$
$$Net\ derivative\ liabilities = Max\ ((NSFR\ derivative\ liabilities$$
$$- NSFR\ derivative\ assets), 0)$$
$$= Max(\$0.2 - \$3.2, 0) = 0$$

Considering the above items, the available stable funding of the regional bank is $61.55 million as shown in Table 11.23.

Required Stable Funding

Using data from Tables 11.4, 11.5, and 11.6, eight groups of required stable funding for the bank are shown in Table 11.24:

- **Group 1:** $30 million cash of the bank is in this group, which receives a 0% weight factor.
- **Group 2:** $4 million unencumbered U.S. Treasury notes and $9.4 million undrawn portion of the credit facilities are in this group, which receives a 5% weight factor.
- **Group 3:** Term loans to financial firms are not collateralized by level 1 asset, so no asset is included in this group.
- **Group 4:** $7 million unencumbered corporate bond AA-rated securities are included in this group, which receives a 15% weight factor. There are

TABLE 11.23 Available stable funding for a hypothetical regional bank (in $ million)

Group	Category	Item	Description	Amount	Weight Factor	Available Stable Funding = Amount × Weight Factor
Group 1	Equity	Common share		12.00	100%	12.00
	Debt	Unsecured long-term	Maturity ≥ 1 year	15.50	100%	15.50
Group 2	Deposit	By small business	Stable	20.00	95%	19.00
Group 3	Deposit	By small business	Less-stable	14.50	90%	13.05
Group 4	Deposit	Operational deposit		1.00	50%	0.50
	Debt	Unsecured long- and short-term	Maturity between 6 months and 1 year	3.00	50%	1.50
Group 5	Repo	Treasury, agency, and non-agency RMBS and corporate bond	Repo maturity < 6 months	35.41	0%	0.00
	Deposit	By non-financial firm		23.20	0%	0.00
	Deposit	By financial firm		1.90	0%	0.00
	Debt	Unsecured long- and short-term, commercial paper	Maturity < 6 months	35.75	0%	0.00
	Derivative	Derivative liability net of derivative asset		0.00	0%	0.00
					Available Stable Funding:	61.55

TABLE 11.24 Required stable funding for a hypothetical regional bank (in $ million) – part (I)

Group	Category	Item	Description	Amount	Weight Factor	Required Stable Funding = Amount × Weight Factor
Group 1	Cash	Cash Deposit		30.00	0%	0.00
Group 2	Investment	U.S. Treasury	Unencumbered – level 1	4.00	5%	0.20
	Credit facility	Irrevocable line of credit to customers	Undrawn portion	9.40	5%	0.47
Group 3	Term loan	To financial firm	Maturity < 6 month – Collateralized by level 1 asset	0.00	10%	0.00
Group 4	Investment	Corporate bond AA-rated securities	Unencumbered – Level 2A	7.00	15%	1.05
Group 5	Term loan	To financial firm	Maturity < 6 month	0.00	15%	0.00
	Investment	Agency RMBS AAA-rated securities	Unencumbered – Level 2B	4.00	50%	2.00
	Investment	Corporate bond A-rated securities	Unencumbered – Level 2B	4.70	50%	2.35
	Investment	Corporate bond BBB-rated securities	Unencumbered – Level 2B	2.30	50%	1.15
	Investment (used in repo)	HQLA	Encumbered - Repo maturity between 6 months and 1 year	0.00	50%	0.00

(continued)

TABLE 11.24 (*Continued*)

Group	Category	Item	Description	Amount	Weight Factor	Required Stable Funding = Amount × Weight Factor
	Term loan	To financial firm	Maturity between 6 months and 1 year	2.00	50%	1.00
	Term loan	To small business	Maturity < 1 year	14.50	50%	7.25
	Term loan	To non-financial firm	Maturity < 1 year	7.80	50%	3.90
	Deposit	Operational deposit		4.5	50%	2.25
Group 6	Term loan	To small business	Maturity ≥ 1 year	26.50	65%	17.23
	Term loan	To non-financial firm	Maturity ≥ 1 year	4.20	65%	2.73
Group 7	Derivative	Initial margin posted		0.35	85%	0.30
Group 8	Investment	Non-HQLA	Maturity ≥ 1 year	7.00	85%	5.95
	Investment (used in repo)	HQLA and non-HQLA	Encumbered – repo maturity ≥ 1 year	0.00	100%	0.00
	Term loan	To financial firm	Maturity ≥ 1 year	1.00	100%	1.00
	Derivative	Derivative asset net of derivative liability		3.00	100%	3.00
	Derivative	20% of derivative liabilities before deduction of posted variation margin		0.20	100%	0.20
	Credit facility	Non-performing		0.30	100%	0.30
	Term loan	Non-performing		1.38	100%	1.38
			Part (I) of Required Stable Funding:			53.70

no term loans to financial firms with residual maturity in fewer than six months, so no entry is considered for this item in group 4.

■ **Group 5:** $11 million unencumbered level 2B assets including agency RMBS AAA-rated securities, corporate bond A-rated securities, and corporate bond BBB-rated securities are included in this group. There is no encumbered HQLA with a residual encumbrance term between six months and one year, so no entry is considered in group 5 for this item. There are $2 million term loans to financial firms with residual maturity between six months and one year and this is included in group 5. Also, there are $22.3 million term loans to small business customers and non-financial firms where residual maturity is less than one year. They are included in group 5. Finally the operational cash of $4.5 million that the regional bank has with a custodian bank is also included in this group. All these items receive a 50% weight factor.

■ **Group 6:** There are $30.7 million term loans to small business customers and non-financial firms with residual maturity greater than one year. This amount is placed in group 6, which receives a 65% weight factor.

■ **Group 7:** There is $0.35 million initial margin posted for the derivative contracts. Also there is $5 million in unencumbered non-HQLA assets related to investment in non-agency RMBS A-rated securities. These are placed in group 7, which receives a 85% weight factor.

■ **Group 8:** The bank does not have any encumbered asset that residual encumbrance term is greater than 1 year, hence no required funding is included for this item in group 8. There are $1 million term loans to financial firms with residual maturity greater than one year and this is included in this group. Amount of derivative liabilities before deduction of posted variation margin is $1 million. The NSFR rule requires inclusion of 20% of this amount in group 8 (i.e., $0.2 million). Also, using NSFR derivative assets and liabilities calculated in available stable funding section of this example, the net derivative asset is calculated as:

$$Max\,((NSFR\ derivative\ assets - NSFR\ derivative\ liabilities), 0)$$

$$= Max(\$3.2 - \$0.2, 0) = \$3\ million$$

This amount is included in group 8. Finally, $1.68 million in a non-performing portion of term loans and credit facilities are included in group 8. All items in group 8 receive 100% weight factor.

The regional bank has encumbered assets with maturity less than six months that are not included in calculation of required stable funding in Table 11.24. These assets should be included in this calculation after adjustment of the weight factors based on the residual encumbrance term, using the method outlined in Table 11.22. Calculation of this additional required stable funding is presented in Table 11.25, where:

- $19 million encumbered U.S. Treasury notes, which are level 1 assets, have residual encumbrance term of less than six months. Hence they receive a 5% weight factor, the same as being unencumbered, in line with group 2.
- $12 million encumbered agency RMBS AAA-rated securities, which are considered as level 2B asset, have a residual encumbrance term of less than six months. Hence they receive a 50% weight factor, the same as being unencumbered, in line with group 5.
- $3 million encumbered non-agency RMBS A-rated securities, which are considered as non-HQLA, have a residual encumbrance term of less than six months. Hence they receive a 85% weight factor, the same as being unencumbered, in line with group 7.
- $3.5 million encumbered corporate bond A-rated securities, which are considered as level 2A asset, have a residual encumbrance term of less than six months. Hence they receive a 15% weight factor, the same as being unencumbered, in line with group 4.

Total required stable funding from Tables 11.24 and 11.25 is $53.7 million and $10.03 million, for a grand total of $63.73 million. Therefore the net stable funding ratio is calculated as:

(in $ million)

$$NSFR = \frac{Available\ Amount\ of\ Stable\ Funding}{Required\ Amount\ of\ Stable\ Funding} = \frac{\$61.55}{\$63.73} = 96.58\%$$

The NSFR for this regional bank as of May 31, 2017, is below the required level of 100%. This is an indication of a lack of stable and established funding sources for the bank's operations on an ongoing basis and in a relatively long time horizon. This finding is in line with what was observed in cash flow gap analysis of idiosyncratic and market-wide stress scenarios, where the liquidity position of the bank during a 1-year horizon was estimated to be at dangerously low levels. The low NSFR calculated here is another wake-up call for the bank management to shore up its liquidity risk management practices.

Intraday Liquidity

Intraday liquidity refers to funds that are available during a business day to make required payments. Intraday liquidity management is the set of policies, monitoring, and measurement that focuses on the ability of a bank to meet its payment obligation during a day on a timely basis. Banks as intermediary

TABLE 11.25 Required stable funding for a hypothetical regional bank (in $ million) – part (II): encumbered assets

Group	Category	Item	Description	Amount	Weight Factor	Required Stable Funding = Amount × Weight Factor
Group 2	Investment (used in repo)	U.S. Treasury	Encumbered – Level 1 – Repo maturity < 6 months	19.00	5%	0.95
Group 5	Investment (used in repo)	Agency RMBS AAA-rated securities	Encumbered – Level 2B – Repo maturity < 6 months	12.00	50%	6.00
Group 7	Investment (used in repo)	Non-agency RMBS A-rated securities	Encumbered – Non-HQLA – Repo maturity < 6 months	3.00	85%	2.55
Group 4	Investment (used in repo)	Corporate bond AA-rated securities	Encumbered – Level 2A – Repo maturity < 6 months	3.50	15%	0.53
			Part (II) of Required Stable Funding:			10.03

institutions have cash inflows and obligatory cash outflows during the day that can swing the intraday liquidity position significantly, and managing this risk should be an integral part of a bank's liquidity risk controls.

The Basel committee outlines the operational requirement of sound intraday liquidity risk management, signifying a bank should be able to (BCBS 2013):

- Measure expected daily gross inflows and outflows and their estimated timing.
- Monitor intraday liquidity against the expected activities.
- Acquire sufficient intraday funding.
- Manage collaterals required for intraday funding.
- Manage timing of cash outflows in line with its intraday liquidity plan.
- Develop contingency plan for unexpected intraday outflows.

The LCR and NSFR measurements are not designed to monitor intraday liquidity. In 2013 the committee introduced a different set of measurements and monitoring tools specifically for intraday liquidity. To define these measurements, the Basel standard considers the following as sources and usages of intraday liquidity:

Sources

- Reserve at central bank
- Collateral posted with central banks that can be freely converted to intraday liquidity
- Unencumbered assets that can be freely converted into intraday liquidity
- Credit lines that are available for intraday use
- Cash balances with other banks that can be used for intraday payments
- Payments received from payment systems and correspondent banks

Usages

- Payments to payment systems and correspondent banks
- Credit lines offered for intraday use
- Contingency payments for failed transactions

The Basel standard introduced the following seven intraday liquidity measurements and monitoring tools. The initial frequency of reporting of these metrics to regulatory supervisors is monthly.

1. Daily Maximum Intraday Liquidity Usage

This measurement is based on net balance of all payments made and received in all accounts with a central bank and correspondent banks throughout a business day in a normal condition. The largest negative net cumulative balance shows the maximum daily intraday liquidity usage. At any point of time a negative net cumulative balance indicates that up to that point of the day the bank had more outflow payments than inflows. For example, consider a regional bank which had daily transactions through its accounts with central bank or correspondent banks as listed in Table 11.26. The bank has a $12 million deposit with the central bank and an $18 million deposit with a correspondent bank that can be freely used as intraday liquidity. The bank has $15 million (value after haircut) of unencumbered assets, which are eligible collateral for liquidity facility of the central bank, if needed. Also, the bank has $25 million in an undrawn liquidity facility provided by a syndication of national banks that can be used as a source of intraday liquidity.

Figure 11.18 shows the net cumulative balance of payments throughout the day. At 12:45 p.m. the bank had the maximum negative net cumulative balance of –$12.6 million, indicating it relies on its intraday liquidity to cover this amount for the day. The maximum positive net cumulative balance of $35.5 million occurs at 9:45 a.m.

Those banks that are required to report this measurement to their regulatory supervisors report the three largest daily negative cumulative balances and daily average of negative cumulative balances for a given reporting period (e.g., a month). They also need to report the largest positive cumulative balance and daily average positive cumulative balance over the reporting period.

2. Available Intraday Liquidity at Start of Day

This measurement is the available intraday liquidity balance, based on sources listed earlier, at the start of each business day in normal conditions. The required banks report the three lowest starting balances and also average starting balances during a given period. The low level of available intraday liquidity at the start of a business day may lead to a liquidity shortage during the day. For the regional bank in our example, the start of the day available intraday liquidity is:

$12 million deposit with central bank

+ $18 million deposit with correspondent bank

+ $15 million eligible unencumbered assets

+ $25 million facility = $70 million

TABLE 11.26 Transactions of a bank with central bank and its correspondent banks, for a given day (in $ million)

Time	Payment Received	Payment Sent	Description	Cumulative Cash Flow
7:00:00 a.m.				0.00
7:34:00 a.m.	30.30			30.30
8:01:00 a.m.		7.00		23.30
8:24:00 a.m.		13.00	Time sensitive	10.30
8:58:00 a.m.	20.00			30.30
9:45:00 a.m.	5.20			35.50
10:10:00 a.m.		28.00		7.50
11:23:00 a.m.		20.00		−12.50
12:45:00 p.m.		0.10	On behalf of counterparty using some of $2 MM credit line provided by bank	−12.60
1:34:00 p.m.	30.00			17.40

Time	Payment Received	Payment Sent	Description	Cumulative Cash Flow
2:06:00 p.m.	10.00			27.40
2:26:00 p.m.	2.50			29.90
3:36:00 p.m.		2.30		27.60
3:42:00 p.m.	5.60			33.20
3:46:00 p.m.		10.00		23.20
3:54:00 p.m.		4.00		19.20
4:09:00 p.m.		1.20		18.00
4:15:00 p.m.	2.20			20.20
4:47:00 p.m.	7.00			27.20
5:00:00 p.m.		27.20		0.00

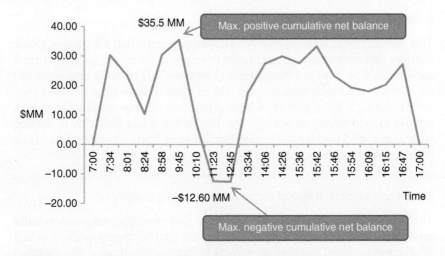

FIGURE 11.18 Daily net cumulative balance of payments to/from accounts of a regional bank with central bank and its correspondent banks (in $ million)

This starting intraday liquidity is sufficient to cover the maximum cumulative outflow of $12.6 million occurring during the day.

3. Total Payments

This measurement is the bank's total gross payments sent and received through its accounts with the central bank and correspondent banks in normal conditions. The required banks report the three largest total daily gross payments sent and received, and also averages of these total payments, during a given period. For the regional bank in our example the daily total gross payments sent and received are:

$$\text{Total Gross Payment Sent} = \$(30.3 + 20 + 5.2 + 30 + 10 + 2.5$$
$$+ 5.6 + 2.2 + 7) \text{ million}$$
$$= \$112.80 \text{ million}$$

$$\text{Total Gross Payment Received} = \$(7 + 13 + 28 + 20 + 0.1 + 2.3$$
$$+ 10 + 4 + 1.2 + 27.2) \text{ million}$$
$$= \$112.80 \text{ million}$$

4. Time-Sensitive Obligations

This measurement is based on a bank's total payments that are time-sensitive during a day, such as margin payments or return of overnight loans in normal conditions. The required banks report the three largest total time-sensitive payments settled each day, and also the average of total time-sensitive payments, during a given period. A high proportion of time-sensitive payments relative to total payments is a sign that the bank has less flexibility in dealing with unexpected payments. For the regional bank in our example there is one time-sensitive payment of $13 million.

5. Payments Made on Behalf of Correspondent Banking Customers

This measurement is specific to those banks that provide correspondent bank services to other monetary institutions. It is the total payments made on behalf of all correspondent banking customers in normal conditions. The required banks report the three largest daily total such payments, and also the average of these total payments, during a given period. For the regional bank in our example the total payment on behalf of counterparties is $0.1 million.

6. Intraday Credit Lines Extended to Customers

This measurement is also specific to those banks that provide correspondent bank services to other monetary institutions. It is the total intraday credit lines extended to a bank's customers in normal conditions. The required bank reports the three largest of such credit lines in a given period, and the peak usage of them by their customers, including details such as whether the lines are committed or not and whether they are secured or unsecured. For the regional bank in our example the total credit line extended for intraday liquidity is $2 million with $0.1 million drawn.

7. Intraday Throughput

This measurement is specific to those banks that directly interact with the payment systems without the need for another intermediary. For a given period and in normal conditions, this metric is the percentages of outflow payments to total payments, within each hour of a business day. Banks report the averages of this daily percentage profile over the reporting period. Using data from Table 11.26, intraday throughput for the regional bank in our example is shown in Table 11.27.

These seven intraday liquidity measurements are calculated assuming that banks are operating in normal conditions. To emphasize the importance

TABLE 11.27 Intraday throughput of a regional bank for a given day (in $ million)

Time	Cumulative Payment Sent	% Sent
7:00	0.00	0%
8:00	0.00	0%
9:00	20.00	18%
10:00	20.00	18%
11:00	48.00	43%
12:00	68.00	60%
13:00	68.10	60%
14:00	68.10	60%
15:00	68.10	60%
16:00	84.40	75%
17:00	112.80	100%
18:00	112.80	100%

of measuring the effects of stress conditions on intraday liquidity, the standard recommends four stress scenarios. These scenarios are:

- A firm-specific event where counterparties defer their payments or draw on intraday credit lines.
- A major counterparty is facing an intraday stress event and unable to make payments to the bank, reducing available intraday liquidity of the bank.
- A customer bank of a correspondent bank is facing a stress event, resulting in deferred payments to the customer bank, which in turn results in adverse impact on intraday liquidity of the correspondent bank.
- A market-wide stress event that impacts sources of intraday liquidity, specifically reducing values of collaterals that can be used as sources of intraday liquidity.

In analyzing the intraday liquidity position of a bank the following restrictions should be carefully examined:

- Restrictions on transfers between payment systems
- Restrictions on cross-currency and cross-border transfers
- Restrictions on transfers among legal entities of the bank
- Timing differences and other logistical constraints on the movement of cash and collateral

EARLY WARNING INDICATORS

Early warning indicators (EWIs) are a set of quantitative and qualitative metrics that help bank management in detecting the emergence of liquidity events. Monitoring these indicators provides the bank management with insight into a forthcoming event that could adversely impact the liquidity position of the bank. The indicators and their efficiencies in predicting a liquidity event depend on bank products and its funding structure. Some of the common market-wide early warning indicators used by banks are:

- Increase in credit spread indexes such as the CDX index
- Declining trend in mortgage credit quality indicators such as the ABX index
- Declining trend over a significant period of time in equity indexes such as the S&P 500 index or Dow Jones Industrial Average index
- Increase in spread between 3-month LIBOR and 3-month overnight index swap (OIS) rates, as an indication of repo market distress

Some of the firm-specific early warning indicators commonly used in practice are:

- Declining trend in equity price
- Increase in debt spread compared to peer group
- Increase in credit default swap (CDS) spread compared to peer group
- Decrease in weighted average maturity of term liabilities
- Difficulty in issuance of short-term or long-term securities
- Increase in haircuts demanded by repo counterparties
- Increase in currency mismatches
- First occurrence of an early amortization trigger event (early amortization usually occurs after a trigger event, such as negative cash flow, occurs several times successively)
- Increase in redemptions of CDs before maturity
- A credit rating downgrade by a rating agency
- Decrease or closure of uncommitted lines of credit by counterparties
- Rising delinquencies or increase in default rates in products offered by the bank
- A negative reputational event, such as a management or accounting scandal
- Significant deterioration in bank's financials and earnings
- Increase in wholesale or retail funding costs compared to peer group

LIQUIDITY CONTINGENCY PLAN

A *contingency funding plan (CFP)* is a framework for identifying liquidity events that a bank may face and outlining the action plans for each event. A liquidity contingency plan is essentially a liquidity crisis management plan. Depending on the type of product offered and level of exposures, events that lead to a liquidity shortage can be unique to a bank. Identifying such events and planning for them should be an integral part of a sound liquidity risk management practice. At a high level, a liquidity contingency plan should cover the following areas:

- **Identifying Event:** The bank should perform a thorough analysis to identify under what circumstances it would face a liquidity shortage. This analysis should include correlation between different conditions that may affect liquidity and estimating their potential impacts.
- **Action Plan:** For each potential liquidity event identified in the previous step, the bank should have an action plan and identify the remediation arrangements as well as the roles and responsibilities of personnel and departments. The action plan should include:
  - Potential replacement funding sources
  - Steps for managing the existing liquidity, including line of businesses actions

The plan should also consider side effects of actions prepared for each event, including recognizing the impact on a bank's reputation that can affect other funding channels and operational concerns of each action.

SUMMARY

- Liquidity risk is the risk associated with a firm's inability to meet its financial obligations when they come due without incurring excessive losses or unacceptable costs.
- Prior to the financial crisis of 2007–2009 liquidity risk management was usually treated as a subtask of cash management and funding planning but nowadays it plays a major role in overall risk management frameworks.
- Deposits, short-term debts, medium-term notes, long-term debts, securitization vehicles, and credit facilities are some of the common funding sources used by banks.
- Excessive use of short-term funding mechanisms without proper liquidity risk management is considered as one of the main contributors to the financial crisis of 2007–2009.

- Deposits are the main source of funding for banks. Deposits can be categorized as maturing (term deposits such as CDs) and non-maturing (such as checking and savings accounts).
- A run on a bank's deposits can occur if a large number of depositors withdraw their funds during a short period of time. This can create an adverse liquidity event for the bank.
- Traditionally, deposits and long-term debts are considered to be more stable and reliable source of funds for banks.
- When, due to either a firm-specific event or a market-wide adverse condition, a bank cannot roll its maturing debt at the required time and within a reasonable pricing range, it can create an adverse liquidity event for the bank.
- Securitization is the process of packaging illiquid financial assets and underwriting marketable debt securities that are backed by asset pools. Unmitigated risk in securitization process can create an adverse liquidity event for the sponsoring entities, whether it is a bank or a non-bank financial institution.
- A credit facility is a committed line of credit where clients can draw funds up to a limit. Liquidity facility is a committed line provided to a client specifically for the purpose of supplying liquidity when needed. For a facility to be considered a reliable source of liquidity, it must be contractually binding and irrevocable.
- A repurchase agreement (repo) is a contract in which a seller (repo side) sells a security to a buyer (reverse repo side) with the commitment to buy it back at a specific time in the future and at a specific price. The term of a repo contract can be overnight or longer. An open repo does not have a termination date and can be ended by either side at any date in the future after a notice is given.
- A repo haircut is the discount applied to the value of the security used as collateral in a repo contract. This discount makes up the initial margin. The variation margin is the amount exchanged by repo counterparties to cover the change in value of the collateral after contract initiation.
- In the delivery versus payment method the security used as collateral in a repo contract is delivered via a settlement service offered by clearinghouses and placed at the lender security account. In the hold-in-custody method the security is not delivered to the lender and is held in a segregated custody account of the borrower. In a triparty repo contract a clearinghouse acts as agent of both borrower and lender, providing security custody, valuation, and settlement services for both.
- Banks, investment banks, and hedge funds often use repo as a short-term funding mechanism. It is also used as an arbitrage tool.

- Security lending is a financial contract where one side lends a security to the other side for a given period of time and for a fee, payable at termination.
- A repo run is the case where repo lenders choose not to roll the contracts or significantly increase the haircuts required for the collaterals.
- There is systematic risk inherent in repo market: when a borrower cannot roll a repo collateralized by a security it may be forced to sell the security in the market. A fire sale in an illiquid market pushes the security price further down, causing financial loss for any holder of that security (whether participating in the repo market or not), as well as increasing the repo haircut further. Therefore any participant in the repo market who uses that security as collateral now needs to post more margin and faces the same problem when it's time to roll its repos. This spiral effect deteriorates the repo market liquidity further.
- Cash flow gap analysis is a useful tool for liquidity stress testing. Using the cash flow gap, banks can assess their readiness for different scenarios that may adversely impact their liquidity positions.
- In cash flow gap analysis, contractual cash flows are usually separated from cash flows that are estimated based on behavioral assumptions or business plans.
- In a business-as-usual cash flow gap schedule, contractual cash inflows and outflows along with forecasted cash flows based on business plans and behavioral assumptions are included.
- Liquidity stress testing using cash flow gap analysis for occurrences of an idiosyncratic event and a market-wide adverse condition provide valuable information to banks' management teams about their liquidity risk under each scenario.
- Diversification of funding mechanisms is an important factor in liquidity risk management.
- The liquidity coverage ratio (LCR) assesses the short-term resilience of a bank to liquidity stress scenarios. It is calculated as the ratio of stock of high-quality liquid assets to total net cash outflow over the next 30 calendar days. This ratio must be at least 100%.
- The net stable funding ratio (NSFR) assesses the long-term funding structure of a bank with the intention of limiting excess reliance on short-term funding. It is calculated as the ratio of available amount of stable funding to required amount of stable funding. This ratio must be at least 100%.
- Intraday liquidity refers to funds that are available during a business day to cover the required payments.
- Early warning indicators are a set of quantitative and qualitative metrics that help bank management to monitor and detect signs of a possible adverse liquidity event.

■ Contingency funding plan is a framework for identifying liquidity events that a bank may face and outlining the action plans for such events.

NOTES

1. Source: https://www.federalreserve.gov/releases/h8/current/.
2. Source: *Los Angeles Times*, August 17, 2007.
3. With a term of less than 270 days the issuer does not need to file registration statement with the SEC, which makes the issuance easier and cheaper.
4. Shelf registration is a type of offering allowed by the SEC where an issuer can register an offering that is expected to happen in the next two years and sell securities during this period.
5. Source: Federal Reserve System website: https://www.federalreserve.gov/regreform/discount-window.htm.
6. Repo transactions between primary dealers themselves are double counted in these figures.
7. *JPMorgan Chase* was also a clearing organization for triparty repos in the United States but in 2016 it announced its plan to exit this business.
8. Primary dealers are banks, investment banks, and broker-dealer firms that trade in U.S. government securities through the Federal Reserve Bank of New York. The Federal Reserve uses its Open Market desk to engage in trades in order to implement monetary policy.
9. In practice, the yield should be higher than a threshold above the repo interest cost to make the trade economically justified for the bank. The threshold is to consider operating and lost opportunity costs.
10. For ease of reference here we consider security lending/borrowing transactions as repo/reverse repo deals.
11. Since traditionally the main cash outflows of a bank are related to the maturity of its debts, and the main cash inflows are related to return of principal from maturing lending products, sometimes this analysis is referred to as "maturity gap analysis."
12. This is assuming that the regional bank has an established account with a triparty clearing organization.
13. Materials, ratios, and tables presented in this section should be used for educational purposes only and may not reflect the latest rules or interpretation of various regulatory bodies of those rules. Practitioners should contact their relevant regulatory entities for rules, requirements, and implementation guidelines of Basel Committee standards.
14. During a stress event, when a bank uses its HQLA to support its liquidity position the ratio may fall below 100%. Hence during a crisis period the bank is not required to keep the LCR at 100% at all costs and, rather, it should use its liquidity sources as needed.
15. The Basel II standard categorizes different financial assets based on their riskiness and assigns a risk-weight to each asset type. Generally the higher the risk-weight the riskier the asset is. Assignment of the risk-weight is based on the type of asset, nature of the counterparty, and the associated risk. The standard

provides two options for derivation of risk-weights: the standardized approach, where risk-weights are prescribed by the standard, and the internal rating-based approach, where the bank's internal models are utilized to estimate the riskiness of assets and assign risk-weights.

16. In order to ensure that the conditions for allowable limits of level 2 and level 2B assets are satisfied, the standard provides the following alternative formula for calculation of HQLA:

$$Stock\ of\ HQLA = Level\ 1 + Level\ 2A + Level\ 2B$$

$$- Max\ ((Level\ 2A + Level\ 2B)$$

$$- 2/3 \times Level\ 1, Level\ 2B - 15/85$$

$$\times (Level\ 1 + Level\ 2A), 0)$$

17. For complete details of cash inflows and outflows, see Basel Committee on Banking Supervision (2013).

BIBLIOGRAPHY

Acharya, Viral V., Philipp Schnabl, and Gustavo Suarez. "Securitization without Risk Transfer." *Journal of Financial Economics* 107 (2013): 515–536.

Allen, William A., and Richhild Moessner. *"The Liquidity Consequences of the Euro Area Sovereign Debt Crisis."* Bank for International Settlements Working Papers no. 390, October 2012, revised March 2013.

Baklanova, Viktoria, Adam Copeland, and Rebecca McCaughrin. "Reference Guide to U.S. Repo and Securities Lending Markets." Federal Reserve Bank of New York. Staff Report No. 740, 2015.

Basel Committee on Banking Supervision. "Basel III: International Framework for Liquidity Risk Measurement, Standards and Monitoring." Bank for International Settlements, December 2010.

Basel Committee on Banking Supervision. "Basel III: The Liquidity Coverage Ratio and Liquidity Risk Monitoring Tools." Bank for International Settlements, January 2013.

Basel Committee on Banking Supervision. "Basel III: The Net Stable Funding Ratio." Bank for International Settlements, October 2014.

Basel Committee on Banking Supervision. "Monitoring Tools for Intraday Liquidity Management." Bank for International Settlements, April 2013.

Choudhry, Moorad. *The Repo Handbook*, 2nd ed. Oxford: Butterworth-Heinemann, 2010.

Fabozzi, Frank J., and Steven V. Mann (eds.). *Securities Finance*. Hoboken, NJ: John Wiley & Sons, 2005.

Gorton, Gary, and Andrew Metrick. "Securitized Banking and the Run on Repo." *Journal of Financial Economics*, no. 104 (2012): 424–451.

Mishkin, Frederic, Stanley Eakins. *Financial Markets and Institutions*, 7th ed. Prentice Hall, 2012.

CHAPTER 12

Funds Transfer Pricing

F *unds transfer pricing (FTP)* is an internal process to assign funding rates to interest-earning assets and earning rates to fund-generating liabilities of a bank. The FTP process is a useful tool in measuring the ex-ante risk-adjusted performance of the business units of a bank, especially for banking books consisting of products such as commercial loans, home mortgages, and deposits. Three main purposes of funds transfer pricing are:

1. Internal allocation of the net interest margin among different business units
2. Centralization of interest rate and liquidity risk management
3. Internal allocation of the cost of managing interest rate and liquidity risks to each business unit based on riskiness of positions

   Traditionally, the treasury department of a bank manages the liability side of the balance sheet and along with the deposit units incurs the liability cost for the entire bank. This cost is mainly in the form of interest expense. On the other hand, business units manage the asset side of the balance sheet, including loan and lease portfolios that generate income, mainly in the form of interest income and fees. An FTP system treats each part of the bank as a value-adding entity. This is done by assigning earnings to the treasury and deposit units for their fund-generating activities and costs to business units for their use of funds and risk-taking activities. This turns each entity into a standalone *profit center* that contributes to the bank's overall return and profitability. A properly developed FTP system performs this allocation on a risk-adjusted basis.

   FTP as an allocation system requires position-level data and market rates and spreads. Due to this, FTP is often integrated with an ALM system. Commercially available ALM software packages usually have an FTP module that shares the implementation platform and data with the ALM module. In this chapter we review the basics of funds transfer pricing and discuss a few methods used in practice in the implementation of FTP systems.

FUNDS TRANSFER PRICING: BASICS

To demonstrate the concept and mechanism of funds transfer pricing, we first need to define the net interest margin. *Net interest margin (NIM)* is the difference between the interest income from an asset (or group of assets) and the interest expense from a liability (or group of liabilities). Net interest margin is often expressed in percentage as the interest rate earned from assets minus the interest rate paid on liabilities:

Net Interest Margin (%) = Asset Interest Rate (%) − Liability Interest Rate (%)

$$(12.1)$$

Consider a bank with two entities: business unit 1 and business unit 2. Each business unit engages in collection of funds and origination of assets. Assume that business unit 1 has issued a 2-year certificate of deposit with $1,000 principal and a 2.5% annual rate (deposit L1). It has also originated a 2-year loan with $1,000 principal and a 4% annual rate (loan A1). Business unit 2 has a 1-year certificate of deposit liability with $1,000 principal and a 2% annual rate (deposit L2), and a 3-year loan asset with $1,000 principal and a 5% annual rate (loan A2). Figure 12.1 presents the schematic of the principal cash flows of assets and liabilities of business units 1 and 2 as outlined above.

Considering each business unit as a standalone entity, the asset and liability positions of business unit 1 match each other, both in size and term of

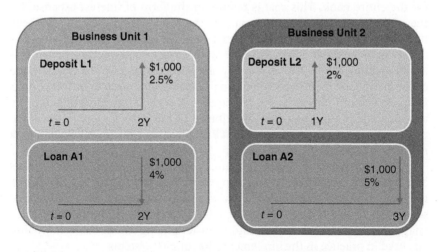

FIGURE 12.1   Schematic of principal cash flows of assets and liabilities of business units 1 and 2

exposures. When default risk is ignored, due to offsetting asset and liability positions, business unit 1 does not face any interest rate or liquidity risk. Since the term of the liability matches the term of the asset, there is no require-ment to roll the liability position at the end of its term to continue funding the asset position, and hence there is no liquidity risk. Also, since the term of the liability matches the term of the asset and the rates of both are fixed, there is no need for refinancing the liability position during its 2-year term at a potentially different rate. Therefore, in the absence of default risk, the net interest margin is maintained and hence there is no interest rate risk with regard to the net interest income.[1] Based on the annual rates of these two posi-tions, the net interest margin of business unit 1 is calculated as *NIM* = 4% − 2.5% = 1.5%.

On the other hand, business unit 2, due to maturity mismatch of its asset and liability positions, is exposed to both liquidity and interest rate risk. This entity has funded a 3-year loan with a 1-year deposit. While a 1-year deposit is cheaper compared to longer-term liabilities of a similar type and structure, at the end of the 1-year term, business unit 2 needs to roll this position, as the generated funds from the deposit are used and locked in the 3-year loan. At the end of one year, business unit 2 can either roll the deposit for another two years or attempt to roll it twice, for two 1-year terms. Either way, if it cannot roll the liability position, it faces a liquidity shortage. Hence entering into these mismatched asset and liability positions generated liquidity risk for business unit 2. Also, since the rate of the liability is only locked for the 1-year term of the deposit, if the interest rate increases during this year, business unit 2 needs to roll the deposit at a higher interest rate, leading to an erosion in the net interest margin. Therefore, the mismatched asset and liability positions also created interest rate risk for business unit 2. Based on the annual rates of these two positions, the net interest margin of business unit 2 is calculated as *NIM* = 5% − 2% = 3%.

Funding a longer-term asset with a cheaper short-term liability provided business unit 2 with a higher net interest margin of 3% compared to business unit 1's net interest margin of 1.5%, although this is achieved by taking liquid-ity and interest rate risks.

Funds transfer pricing is an internal mechanism to distribute the net inter-est margin of the bank among different business units based on the types, characteristics, and riskiness of the asset and liability positions they originate. In a traditional funds transfer pricing system, a central *funding center*, which is usually the treasury department of the bank, books all the asset and liabil-ity positions in an FTP book and assigns funding rates to assets and earning rates to liabilities based on their features and risk levels. Funds transfer pricing effectively is equivalent to interest rate swap agreements between the funding center and the business units.

Based on the funding sources currently used and availability of alternative channels, the bank's treasury creates a *cost of funds curve* for use in the FTP system. This curve, which is also known as the *FTP curve,* represents current rates for raising funds through the capital market using established funding channels. Rates at different terms of this curve are often based on wholesale cash market rates. Some banks create specific cost of funds curves for their FTP systems while others use market curves such as LIBOR-swap or OIS as the base of the FTP curve and adjust it according to their own marginal cost of funds (e.g., based on their credit ratings) and term liquidity. Occasionally, banks consider multiple cost of funds curves for their FTP systems, using separate curves for different types of assets and liabilities. This practice, however, has its critics and it has been argued that it leads to undesirable consequences in the funds transfer pricing system (Shih 2004). Figure 12.2 presents a sample cost of funds curve.

In a typical FTP system, the central funding center itself is considered to be a business unit and a profit center. The funding center assigns a funding rate to a newly originated asset position and an earning rate to a newly raised funding position. These transactions are booked as liabilities and assets of the funding center and offsetting transactions are created on the books of the business units that originated the asset or raised the fund. The funding and earning rates are assigned based on rates from the cost of funds curve used in the FTP system. Assume the bank in our example uses the cost of funds curve in Figure 12.2. Consider the positions of business unit 1 first. Deposit L1 has a 2-year term with a client rate of 2.5%. Based on the cost of funds curve in Figure 12.2 the bank can raise 2-year funds from the capital

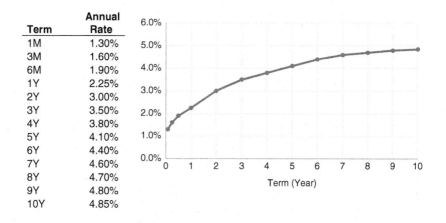

Term	Annual Rate
1M	1.30%
3M	1.60%
6M	1.90%
1Y	2.25%
2Y	3.00%
3Y	3.50%
4Y	3.80%
5Y	4.10%
6Y	4.40%
7Y	4.60%
8Y	4.70%
9Y	4.80%
10Y	4.85%

FIGURE 12.2   A sample cost of funds curve

market at the rate of 3%. The funding center assigns an FTP rate (earning rate) of 3% to this deposit and records two offsetting transactions, one for business unit 1 and one for the funding center. An asset balance is booked for business unit 1 with a notional amount of $1,000 earning 3% annually and a liability balance is booked for the funding center with a notional amount of $1,000 and a 3% rate. While these transactions are all internal to the bank, they do impact the net interest margin of the business unit and the funding center. This way, the funding center effectively has borrowed the $1,000 deposit from business unit 1 at the FTP rate of 3% while the business unit pays 2.5% to the client, so the net interest margin of this position for business unit 1 is: $NIM_{L1} = 3\% - 2.5\% = 0.5\%$. Therefore, a positive net interest margin is assigned to this deposit, reflecting the value of the deposit raised for business unit 1 and the entire bank.

Now consider loan A1 originated by business unit 1. This loan has a 2-year term and a client rate of 4%, with a $1,000 notional amount. Based on the cost of funds curve from Figure 12.2, the funding center assigns an FTP rate (funding rate) of 3% to this loan and books two internal offsetting transactions. A liability balance is booked for business unit 1 with a notional amount of $1,000 and a rate of 3% and an asset balance is booked for the funding center with the same notional amount and rate. In doing this, the funding center has effectively lent $1,000 to business unit 1 to fund the A1 loan at the FTP rate of 3% while the business unit receives 4% from the client. The net interest margin of this loan for business unit 1 is therefore calculated as: $NIM_{A1} = 4\% - 3\% = 1\%$.

Figure 12.3 presents the FTP rate assignments from the funding center to business unit 1 as explained previously. Based on client rates of 2.5% and 4% for deposit L1 and loan A1, the total net interest margin from these two

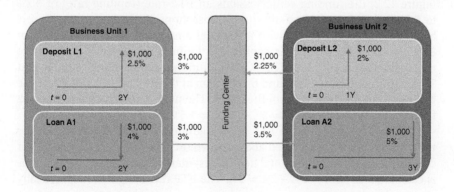

FIGURE 12.3 FTP rate assignment using a funding center

positions is calculated as $NIM = 4\% - 2.5\% = 1.5\%$. FTP rate assignments practically separated this net interest margin into three parts and allocated them as follows:

1. Net interest margin from deposit L1, booked at business unit 1: $NIM_{BU1:L1} = 3\% - 2.5\% = 0.5\%$
2. Net interest margin from loan A1, booked at business unit 1: $NIM_{BU1:A1} = 4\% - 3\% = 1\%$
3. Net interest margin from FTP book, booked at funding center: $NIM_{FC} = 3\% - 3\% = 0\%$

As mentioned earlier, since the terms of deposit L1 and loan A1 are the same, the combination of the two positions does not produce any liquidity or interest rate risk, and hence no margin is allocated to the funding center to manage these risks.

Now consider business unit 2 and positions L2 and A2. Deposit L2 has a term of one year and a client rate of 2%. The FTP rate for a 1-year term from the cost of funds curve of Figure 12.2 is 2.25%, so the funding center assigns an FTP rate (earning rate) of 2.25% to this deposit and books two offsetting transactions, one for business unit 2 and one for the funding center. An asset transaction is booked for business unit 2 with a notional amount of $1,000 earning 2.25% annually and a liability transaction is booked for the funding center with the same notional amount and rate. Therefore, the funding center effectively has borrowed the $1,000 deposit from business unit 2 at the FTP rate of 2.25% while the business unit pays 2% to the client. The net interest margin of this position for business unit 2 is $NIM_{L2} = 2.25\% - 2\% = 0.25\%$.

Loan A2 originated by business unit 2 has a 3-year term and a client rate of 5%, with a $1,000 notional amount. From the cost of funds curve in Figure 12.2, the funding center assigns an FTP rate (funding rate) of 3.5% to this loan and books two offsetting transactions. A liability transaction is booked for business unit 2 with a notional amount of $1,000 and a rate of 3.5% and an asset position is booked for the funding center with the same notional amount and rate. This way, the funding center effectively has lent $1,000 to business unit 2 to fund the A2 loan at the FTP rate of 3.5% while the business unit receives 5% from the client. The net interest margin of loan A2 for business unit 2 is $NIM_{A2} = 5\% - 3.5\% = 1.5\%$.

Figure 12.3 presents the FTP rate assignments from the funding center to business unit 2 as explained above. Based on client rates of 2% and 5% for deposit L2 and loan A2, the total net interest margin from these two positions is calculated as $NIM = 5\% - 2\% = 3\%$. The FTP rate assignments practically separated this net interest margin into three parts and allocated them as follows:

1. Net interest margin from deposit L2, booked at business unit 2: $NIM_{BU2:L2} = 2.25\% - 2\% = 0.25\%$
2. Net interest margin from loan A2, booked at business unit 2: $NIM_{BU2:A2} = 5\% - 3.5\% = 1.5\%$
3. Net interest margin from FTP book, booked at funding center: $NIM_{FC} = 3.5\% - 2.25\% = 1.25\%$

As explained earlier, due to the mismatch of deposit L2 and loan A2 terms, the combination of the two positions created both liquidity and interest rate risks. The funds transfer pricing transfers those risks to the funding center while allocating 1.25% of the total 3% net interest margin to the funding center.

By using funds transfer pricing, the bank effectively achieved two objectives:

1. It allocated the net interest margin among the asset and liability positions based on their contribution in generating liquidity and interest rate risks. Figure 12.4 shows the net interest margin of each position in our example and the relationship of client rates to FTP rates and the cost of funds curve.

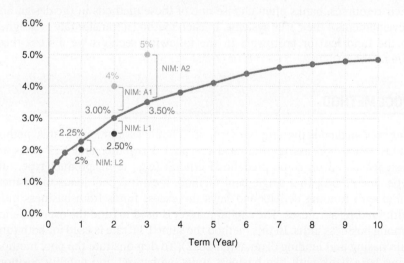

FIGURE 12.4 Allocation of net interest margin (NIM) to asset and liability positions

2. Using the FTP rate assignment and double-entry booking, it has effectively transferred the interest rate and liquidity risks of its business units to the funding center. Having a centralized system helps the bank manage these risks more efficiently.

The method we used here to determine funds transfer pricing rates is known as the *matched maturity* method where FTP rates are assigned based on the term of the positions. We discuss this method in more detail in a later section of this chapter. The cost of funds curve used in derivation of the FTP rate is often the prevailing curve at the time of asset origination or raising the fund (i.e., historical cost of funds curve). This way, when an FTP rate is assigned to a position, it remains the same throughout the life of the position. The alternative to this approach is to use a current cost of funds curve at each analysis date, causing the FTP rate to change over the life of the position. This means that each position may receive a new FTP rate assignment at each analysis date. Generally, the use of a historical cost of funds curve is preferable as it enables the bank to evaluate the performance of business unit management decisions in the origination and pricing of their products (Wyle and Tsaig 2011).

While there is no industry-wide agreement on the funds transfer pricing implementation method, there are two broad approaches that are commonly used in practice: the pool method and matched maturity. Depending on their resources, banks often choose one of these methods in the design and development of their FTP systems. In each method a transfer rate is assigned to the fund lent or borrowed. In the following sections we discuss these two methods.

POOL METHOD

The *pool method* is the simplest form of FTP rate assignment. In this method funds raised and assets originated are pooled together and FTP rates are assigned based on some predefined criteria (e.g., term, product type, rate type, and so on). In a single-pool method, a central pool lends to business units with funding deficits and buys the excess funds from business units with funding surpluses. The capital market is used to fund the overall deficit among business units. In this method the same FTP rate is used for both fund purchasing and lending (Tumasyan 2012). To demonstrate the pool method, consider a bank with two business units, with asset and liability positions originated at the current date as shown below.

List 1: Fixed-rate assets and liabilities originated by two business units of a bank

Business Unit 1:

Asset A1: $1,000 loan, 3-year term, 5% annual rate

Liability L1: $700 deposit, 2-year term, 2.5% annual rate

Business Unit 2:

Asset A2: $1,000 loan, 4-year term, 5.5% annual rate

Liability L2: $1,100 deposit, 1-year term, 2% annual rate

First assume the case where the bank does not have an FTP system in place. Considering both assets A1 and A2, and both liabilities L1 and L2, the bank has a deficit of $200. Assume that the funding center borrows this amount through the capital market at the prevailing market rate of 2.25% with a 1-year term. For the first year, the annual interest income of each unit is calculated as follows:[2]

Business Unit 1:	*Net Interest Income* $= 1,000 \times 5\% - 700 \times 2.5\% = \$32.5$
Business Unit 2:	*Net Interest Income* $= 1,000 \times 5.5\% - 1,100 \times 2\% = \$33$
Funding Center:	*Net Interest Income* $= -200 \times 2.25\% = -\$4.5$
Bank:	*Net Interest Income* $= 32.5 + 33 - 4.5 = \$61$

The funding center, acting as the borrower of the deficit amount, has a negative net interest income. Also, business unit 2, which provides excess funds of $100 used in the other unit, is charged with the cost of that excess borrowing. On the other hand, business unit 1, which has a funding deficit, is rewarded with lower interest expense. Without an FTP system, the distribution of the overall net interest income of the bank among business units is neither based on a risk-adjusted method nor based on the contribution of the lines of business in the funding structure of the overall bank.

In the pool method of funds transfer pricing, the funding center collects deficit and excess funds from business units into a pool and balances the funding requirement there. This results in an allocation of the net interest income based on the contribution of each unit in the funding structure of the bank. Assume that the cost of funds of this bank is as presented in Figure 12.2. At the origination time of the asset and liability positions, business unit 1 has a funding deficit of $300 while business unit 2 has a surplus of $100. The funding center gathers this surplus by purchasing $100 excess funds from business unit 2 at the FTP rate of 2.25% based on a 1-year term. This creates an internal asset balance on the book of business unit 2 for the amount of $100 with a 2.25% rate and an internal liability position on the FTP book of the funding center with the same amount and rate.

Since business unit 1 is short $300, the funding center borrows the remaining $200 from the capital market at the current prevailing market rate of 2.25% based on a 1-year term. This external liability balance is recorded on the funding center book. The funding center then lends $300 to business unit 1 at the FTP rate of 2.25% for a 1-year term. This creates an internal liability balance on the book of business unit 1 for the amount of $300 with a 2.25% rate and an internal asset position on the FTP book of the funding center with the same amount and rate.

Using this FTP system, the funding center collects the excess funds from one business unit into the pool and funds the deficit of the other unit from this pool while borrowing through the capital market to cover the shortage of the pool. Figure 12.5 presents the FTP rate assignments based on the pool method for business units 1 and 2.

The single pool method is the simplest approach for FTP implementation. A natural extension of this method is to consider multiple pools that collect positions with similar characteristics into one collection and assign the FTP rates. Each pool has its own FTP rate and the criteria that define a pool may be based on the product type, term, optionality, geographic location, or market features.

The main advantage of the pool method is the ease of implementation. Some smaller banks choose to use this method as they start developing their

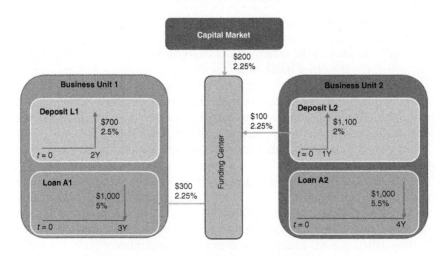

FIGURE 12.5   FTP rate assignment using the pool method

FTP systems. However, this method has some deficiencies that make it less suitable as a permanent and practical FTP system solution. First, in the pool method the funding center does not have the full information on the funding and lending activities of business units, so it cannot effectively decide on the funding actions, alternatives, or timing. In the example, business unit 2 produced $100 excess funding, but there is a term mismatch in the asset and liability positions of the unit, where in one year and after maturity of the deposit L2, it needs to raise funds again to support its own internal balance sheet. This information was not readily available to the funding center when it decided to use that excess to fund the deficit of business unit 1.

The second problem with the pool method is the uncertainty and inefficiency of funding activities through the capital market. Again, due to incomplete information, the funding center does not have clear insight into the terms of the funding requirements. In the preceding example, the funding center raised the deficit of $200 needed to fund business unit 1 for a 1-year term. But this may not be the most efficient way to raise funds, since business unit 1 has a longer-term asset that requires funding beyond one year.

Maybe the biggest weakness of the pool method is the lack of a centralized risk management system. In the pool method the interest rate and liquidity risks remain at business units. This may create incentives for each line of business to take on additional risk without proper mitigating actions, to boost their own performance measures. Such unchecked risk-taking activities can lead to significant problems later on for the entire bank.

In the pool method, calculation of the net interest income for each business unit is straightforward. For our example and for the first year, the annual interest income of each unit is calculated as follows:

Business Unit 1:	*Net Interest Income* $= 1{,}000 \times 5\% - 700 \times 2.5\% - 300 \times 2.25\% = \$25.75$
Business Unit 2:	*Net Interest Income* $= 1{,}000 \times 5.5\% - 1{,}100 \times 2\% + 100 \times 2.25\% = \$35.25$
Funding Center:	*Net Interest Income* $= 300 \times 2.25\% - 100 \times 2.25\% - 200 \times 2.25\% = \$0$
Bank:	*Net Interest Income* $= 25.75 + 35.25 + 0 = \$61$

Compared to the case of no FTP system, the allocated net interest income of business unit 2 is increased, reflecting the contribution it has in funding the overall bank, and allocation to business unit 1 is decreased due to incorporation of the interest expense for the entire fund it uses. Also, the funding center no longer has a negative net interest income.

MATCHED MATURITY METHOD

As discussed earlier in this chapter, in the matched maturity method FTP rates are assigned based on terms of positions. The matched maturity rate assignment is generally considered the preferred method and banks often use this approach in the implementation of their FTP system. In this method, each originated asset or liability position is assigned an FTP rate from the cost of funds curve that matches the maturity of position. If the term of the position does not exactly match a term point of the cost of funds curve, an interpolation method is used to obtain the matching FTP rate. In this section we first discuss the matched maturity method for fixed-rate maturing products and then explain its application for floating-rate maturing products. This is followed by a discussion on how this method can be extended and used for non-maturing products.

FTP Rate for Fixed-Rate Maturing Products

In the matched maturity method, the FTP rate for a fixed-rate maturing product is the rate with the same term as the cost of funds curve. If the term of the position does not exactly match a term point of the cost of funds curve, we can use an interpolation method, such as a linear or cubic spline method, to obtain the appropriate rate from the cost of funds curve.

To demonstrate the matched maturity method for fixed-rate maturing products, consider again the bank introduced in the previous section's example. Starting from business unit 1 and assuming that the cost of funds curve is as presented in Figure 12.2, deposit L1 with a 2-year term and client rate of 2.5% receives an FTP rate of 3%. Based on the double-entry booking, this creates an internal asset balance on the book of business unit 1 for the amount of $700 with a 3% rate and an internal liability position on the FTP book of the funding center with the same amount and rate. The net interest margin of this position for business unit 1 is: $NIM_{L1} = 3\% - 2.5\% = 0.5\%$. Asset A1 with a 3-year term and client rate of 5% receives an FTP rate of 3.5% obtained from the cost of funds curve, based on the term of the loan. This creates an internal liability balance on the book of business unit 1 for the amount of $1,000 with a 3.5% rate and an internal asset position on the FTP book of the funding center with the same amount and rate. The net interest margin of this position for business unit 1 is: $NIM_{A1} = 5\% - 3.5\% = 1.5\%$.

For business unit 2, deposit L2 with a 1-year term and client rate of 2% is assigned an FTP rate of 2.25% based on the 1-year rate from the cost of funds curve. This creates an internal asset balance on the book of business unit 2 for the amount of $1,100 with a 2.25% rate and an internal liability position on the FTP book of the funding center with the same amount and rate. The net interest margin of this position for business unit 2 is $NIM_{L2} = 2.25\% - 2\% = 0.25\%$. Asset A2 with a 4-year term and client rate of 5.5% is assigned an FTP rate of 3.8% obtained from the cost of funds curve. This creates an internal liability balance on the book of business unit 2 for the amount of $1,000 with a 3.8% rate and an internal asset position on the FTP book of the funding center with the same amount and rate. The net interest margin of this position for business unit 2 is $NIM_{A2} = 5.5\% - 3.8\% = 1.7\%$.

To cover the funding shortage of $200, the funding center can borrow this amount from the capital market at the prevailing market rate. To keep our example comparable with the one in the previous section, here we assume the funding center borrows $200 for a 1-year term with a 2.25% rate. Figure 12.6 presents the FTP rate assignments based on the matched maturity method as explained earlier.

The first-year net interest income for business units 1 and 2 and the funding center are calculated as follows:

Business Unit 1:	*Net Interest Income* $= 1,000 \times (5\% - 3.5\%) + 700 \times (3\% - 2.5\%) = \$18.5$
Business Unit 2:	*Net Interest Income* $= 1,000 \times (5.5\% - 3.8\%) + 1,100 \times (2.25\% - 2\%) = \$19.75$
Funding Center:	*Net Interest Income* $= 1,000 \times 3.5\% - 700 \times 3\% + 1,000 \times 3.8\% - 1,100 \times 2.25\% - 200 \times 2.25\% = \$22.75$
Bank:	*Net Interest Income* $= 18.5 + 19.75 + 22.75 = \$61$

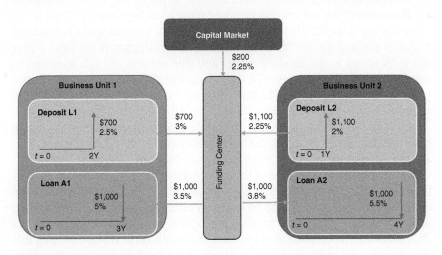

FIGURE 12.6 FTP rate assignment for fixed-rate maturing products using the matched maturity method

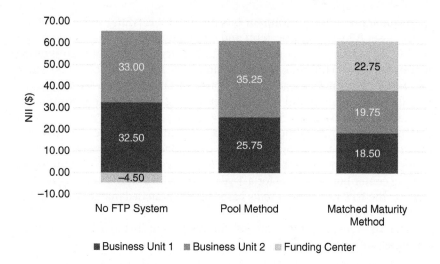

FIGURE 12.7   Comparison of net interest income for three cases: (1) no FTP system, (2) pool method, and (3) matched maturity method, for a hypothetical bank with two business units

In this example, while the total net interest income calculated using the matched maturity is the same as the one obtained using the pool method in the previous section, the distribution of the NII is different. Figure 12.7 compares the allocation of the net interest income for the bank in our example for three cases discussed so far: (1) no FTP system, (2) pool method, and (3) matched maturity method. In the matched maturity method, part of the total 1-year NII is allocated to the funding center and this reduces the NII allocated to two business units compared to the pool method. This allocation reflects the interest rate and liquidity risks that business units generated by originating mismatched asset and liability positions. The matched maturity method transferred these risks to the funding center while allocating part of the net interest income to the center, based on the level of risk embedded in each position. The allocated NII to the funding center can be used for risk mitigation actions.

As mentioned earlier, one of the drawbacks of the pool method is that the funding center does not have complete information regarding the terms of the assets and liabilities originated by business units. In contrast, in the matched maturity method, since each position is properly priced and transferred to the funding center, a complete view of assets and liabilities is available. Using this information, the bank treasury can decide about funding requirements more efficiently and optimize its short- and long-term funding plans. For example, if it believes that the interest rate will increase in the future, having complete information of positions' maturities, the treasury may decide to borrow the $200 fund shortage for a longer term than the one year assumed here. The treasury may even borrow more than $200 to mitigate some of the liquidity risk created by the mismatched asset and liability positions. Transferring liquidity and interest rate risks to the funding center along with the availability of exposures information enables the treasury to better manage these risks.

For a fixed-rate maturing product where principal cash flow occurs at the maturity date of the position, the FTP rate is the rate from the cost of funds curve whose term matches the principal cash flow time (i.e., the maturity date of the position). For fixed-rate maturing products with multiple principal cash flows there are a few different approaches available and used in practice. Some banks use all the cash flows of a position in deriving its transfer pricing rate and some only use principal cash flows. Next we review a few of these methods and provide an example for each. Since these methods may result in different FTP rates, when a method is selected the same approach should be applied consistently to similar products throughout all business units.

Weighted Average Method

The simplest method of deriving the FTP rate of a position with multiple principal cash flows is to use the weighted average of funding rates associated with the principal cash flow terms where weights are the principal amount at each term:

$$r_{FTP} = \frac{\sum_{i=1}^{T} N_i \times r_i}{\sum_{i=1}^{T} N_i} \tag{12.2}$$

Here T is the maturity date, N_i is the principal cash flow where $i = 1, \ldots, T$, and r_i is the funding rate from the cost of funds curve with the term corresponding to period i. For example, consider a 6% fixed-rate loan with a $10,000 notional amount and annual interest payment schedule, originated at the current time and maturing four years from now with a straight-line amortization schedule. There are four $2,500 principal cash flows occurring at 1, 2, 3, and 4 years. Using the cost of funds curve from Figure 12.2, the funding rates are 2.25%, 3%, 3.5%, and 3.8% respectively, and the FTP rate of the loan is calculated as:

$$r_{FTP} = \frac{\begin{array}{c} 2,500 \times 2.25\% + 2,500 \times 3\% \\ + 2,500 \times 3.5\% + 2,500 \times 3.8\% \end{array}}{10,000} = 3.1375\%$$

An extension of this method is to use all cash flows in the FTP rate calculation and also include the terms of the cash flows in weights:

$$r_{FTP} = \frac{\sum_{i=1}^{T} CF_i \times t_i \times r_i}{\sum_{i=1}^{T} CF_i \times t_i} \tag{12.3}$$

where CF_i is the cash flow for period i, both principal and interest payments, and t_i is the term of this cash flow, in years. Assuming an Actual/365 accrual basis, the interest payments of the loan in this example are: at the end of year 1: $10,000 \times 6\% = \$600$, at the end of year 2: $7,500 \times 6\% = \$450$, at the end of year 3: $5,000 \times 6\% = \$300$, and at the end of year 4: $2,500 \times 6\% = \$150$.[3] Applying the extended method, the FTP rate is calculated as:

$$r_{FTP} = \frac{\begin{array}{c}(2,500 + 600) \times 1 \times 2.25\% + (2,500 + 450) \times 2 \times 3\% \\ +(2,500 + 300) \times 3 \times 3.5\% + (2,500 + 150) \times 4 \times 3.8\%\end{array}}{\begin{array}{c}(2,500 + 600) \times 1 + (2,500 + 450) \times 2 \\ +(2,500 + 300) \times 3 + (2,500 + 150) \times 4\end{array}} = 3.3698\%$$

An alternative approach in setting weights is to use present values of cash flows:

$$r_{FTP} = \frac{\sum_{i=1}^{T} CF_i \times df_i \times t_i \times r_i}{\sum_{i=1}^{T} CF_i \times df_i \times t_i} \tag{12.4}$$

where df_i is the discount factor for period i. For our example, assume that the discount factors at the end of years 1 to 4 are $df_1 = 0.999799$, $df_2 = 0.999437$, $df_3 = 0.998991$, and $df_4 = 0.998522$. Using Equation (12.4), the FTP rate for this loan is calculated as:

$$r_{FTP}$$

$$= \frac{\begin{array}{c}(2,500 + 600) \times 0.999799 \times 1 \times 2.25\% + (2,500 + 450) \\ \times 0.999437 \times 2 \times 3\% + (2,500 + 300) \times 0.998991 \times 3 \times 3.5\% \\ +(2,500 + 150) \times 0.998522 \times 4 \times 3.8\%\end{array}}{\begin{array}{c}(2,500 + 600) \times 0.999799 \times 1 + (2,500 + 450) \times 0.999437 \times 2 \\ +(2,500 + 300) \times 0.998991 \times 3 + (2,500 + 150) \times 0.998522 \times 4\end{array}}$$

$$= 3.3696\%$$

Duration Method

Another method for calculating the FTP rate for fixed-rate maturing products is to use the duration of the position. Recall from Chapter 2 that the duration of a maturing product is the weighted average of cash flow terms, where weights are present value of cash flows:

$$D = \frac{\sum_{i=1}^{T} CF_i \times df_i \times t_i}{\sum_{i=i}^{T} CF_i \times df_i} \qquad (12.5)$$

After the duration of the position is obtained we can use it to assign the appropriate transfer rate to the position. This is done by selecting the rate from the cost of funds curve that has the same term as the duration. If there is no rate on the cost of funds curve whose term exactly matches the calculated duration, we can use an interpolation method to obtain the FTP rate. To demonstrate, consider the 4-year loan introduced earlier. The duration of this position is calculated as:

$$D = \frac{\begin{array}{l}(2{,}500 + 600) \times 0.999799 \times 1 + (2{,}500 + 450) \times 0.999437 \times 2 \\ +(2{,}500 + 300) \times 0.998991 \times 3 + (2{,}500 + 150) \times 0.998522 \times 4\end{array}}{\begin{array}{l}(2{,}500 + 600) \times 0.999799 + (2{,}500 + 450) \times 0.999437 \\ +(2{,}500 + 300) \times 0.998991 + (2{,}500 + 150) \times 0.998522\end{array}} = 2.4343$$

From the cost of funds curve in Figure 12.2, the two adjacent terms to the calculated duration of 2.4343 are 2-year and 3-year, with funding rates of 3% and 3.5%. Using a linear interpolation, the FTP rate for this position is calculated as:

$$r_{FTP} = r_i + \frac{(D - t_i)}{(t_{i+1} - t_i)} \times (r_{i+1} - r_i) = 3\% + \left[\frac{(2.4343 - 2)}{(3 - 2)} \times (3.5\% - 3\%)\right]$$

$$= 3.2171\%$$

Refinancing Method

This method is based on the assumption that the outstanding balance of a position at each payment date is refinanced. The refinancing rate is the implied forward rate at each payment date derived based on the current cost of funds curve and with the term equal to each payment period length. Consider a position with client rate c. Assume for a given period i that B_{i-1} is the outstanding balance at the previous period and τ_i is the length of period i, stated in years and based on the accrual basis of the position. The current value of this position considering all interest and principal cash flows is:

$$V = \sum_{i=1}^{T} B_{i-1} \times \tau_i \times c \times df_i + \sum_{i=1}^{T} N_i \times df_i$$

where N_i is the principal payment at period i. Assume that the outstanding balance is refinanced at each payment date and the client rate is replaced by the implied forward rate at that date. We have:

$$V' = \sum_{i=1}^{T} B_{i-1} \times \tau_i \times r_{i-1,i} \times df_i + \sum_{i=1}^{T} N_i \times df_i$$

where $r_{i-1,i}$ is the implied forward rate at period $i-1$ with the term equal to the period length from $i-1$ to i. The value of the internal position to be created by the FTP system to allocate the net interest margin is calculated using the FTP rate, as follows:

$$V'' = \sum_{i=1}^{T} B_{i-1} \times \tau_i \times r_{FTP} \times df_i + \sum_{i=1}^{T} N_i \times df_i$$

In the refinancing method we assume that the transfer rate is the one that makes the value of the refinanced position (V') and the value of the internal position created by the FTP system (V'') equal. So:

$$\sum_{i=1}^{T} B_{i-1} \times \tau_i \times r_{FTP} \times df_i + \sum_{i=1}^{T} N_i \times df_i$$

$$= \sum_{i=1}^{T} B_{i-1} \times \tau_i \times r_{i-1,i} \times df_i + \sum_{i=1}^{T} N_i \times df_i$$

Therefore:

$$r_{FTP} = \frac{\sum_{i=1}^{T} B_{i-1} \times \tau_i \times r_{i-1,i} \times df_i}{\sum_{i=1}^{T} B_{i-1} \times \tau_i \times df_i} \tag{12.6}$$

Consider again the 4-year \$10,000 loan we used in previous examples. The 1-year implied forward rates at the end of years 1, 2, and 3 based on the curve in Figure 12.2 are: $r_{1,2} = 3.6226\%$, $r_{2,3} = 4.4671\%$, and $r_{3,4} = 4.6992\%$. See Chapter 1 for details on the calculation of implied forward rates. Also, the 1-year funding rate from Figure 12.2 is $r_{0,1} = 2.25\%$. Using Equation (12.6) and since $\tau_i = 1$ year for any i, we can calculate the FTP rate as follows:

$$r_{FTP} = \frac{\begin{array}{l} 10,000 \times 1 \times 2.25\% \times 0.999799 + 7,500 \times 1 \times 3.6226\% \times 0.999437 \\ +5,000 \times 1 \times 4.4671\% \times 0.998991 + 2,500 \times 1 \times 4.6992\% \times 0.998522 \end{array}}{\begin{array}{l} 10,000 \times 1 \times 0.999799 + 7,500 \times 1 \times 0.999437 \\ +5,000 \times 1 \times 0.998991 + 2,500 \times 1 \times 0.998522 \end{array}}$$

$$= 3.3497\%$$

FTP Rate for Floating-Rate Maturing Products

Funds transfer pricing for a floating-rate maturing product is performed by associating the FTP rate to the interest rate index that the client rate is based on. The interest rate of floating-rate products often is based on an interest rate index such as LIBOR, SOFR, or overnight index swap. When the rate index changes, the client interest rate also changes accordingly. The timing of the client rate change and the time that it remains effective, however, depend on the contractual reset frequency. For example, consider a loan based on a 3-month LIBOR index with a 6-month reset frequency. The rate of this loan is set every six months based on the level of 3-month LIBOR at the reset dates and the rate remains constant during each 6-month period. The client rate often has an additional spread added to the rate index that reflects various risks perceived in the contract. For example, a loan may have a client rate of 1-month LIBOR plus 50 bps. The 50 bps additional spread remains constant over the life of the contract while the 1-month LIBOR changes and the rate is set at each reset date based on the 1-month LIBOR at that date plus 50 bps.

Banks use floating-rate maturing products, such as medium-term notes or asset-backed securities, to fund their balance sheets. Such funding instruments often have an additional spread added to the reference interest rate index. This *funding spread*, also known as a *liquidity premium*, reflects the additional percentage points a potential investor requires to invest in the floating-rate note issued by the bank for a specific term. Similar to the cost of funds curve and for funds transfer pricing purposes, the treasury of a bank creates a funding spread curve for each underlying interest rate index. Figure 12.8 presents a sample funding spread curve over the 1-month LIBOR.

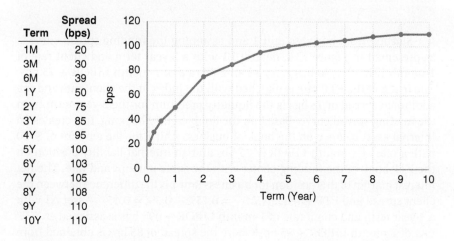

Term	Spread (bps)
1M	20
3M	30
6M	39
1Y	50
2Y	75
3Y	85
4Y	95
5Y	100
6Y	103
7Y	105
8Y	108
9Y	110
10Y	110

FIGURE 12.8 A sample funding spread curve over 1-month LIBOR (in basis points)

For each given term, the spread from this curve represents the additional basis points to be added to the 1-month LIBOR index to obtain the appropriate floating-rate funding cost for the bank. For example, in Figure 12.8 the 50 bps spread for a 1-year term indicates that the bank can raise 1-year debt from the capital market at a rate of 1-month LIBOR plus 50 bps. Banks often construct several such funding spread curves based on different indexes they use as the reference in their floating-rate borrowing (e.g., one for 1-month LIBOR and another one for SOFR, and so on).

To demonstrate the FTP rate assignment for floating-rate maturing positions, consider again the bank we used in the examples in the previous sections. We now assume the asset and liability positions of two business units have floating rates as shown below.

List 2: Floating-rate assets and liabilities originated by two business units of a bank

Business Unit 1:

> Asset A1: $1,000 loan, 3-year term, rate of 1-month LIBOR + 490 bps
>
> Liability L1: $700 deposit, 2-year term, rate of 1-month LIBOR + 30 bps

Business Unit 2:

> Asset A2: $1,000 loan, 4-year term, rate of 1-month LIBOR + 510 bps
>
> Liability L2: $1,100 deposit, 1-year term, rate of 1-month LIBOR + 27 bps

Starting from business unit 1 and assuming the funding spread curve is as presented in Figure 12.8, deposit L1 with a 2-year term and client rate of 1-month LIBOR + 30 bps receives an FTP rate of 1-month LIBOR + 75 bps. The index of the FTP rate is matched with the index of the client rate and the additional spread of 75 bps is the liquidity premium for the 2-year term from the funding spread curve. Based on the double-entry booking, this creates an internal asset balance on the book of business unit 1 for the amount of $700 with a rate of 1-month LIBOR + 75 bps and an internal liability position on the FTP book of the funding center with the same amount and rate. The net interest margin of this position for business unit 1 is the difference between the client spread and FTP spread: $NIM_{L1} = 0.75\% - 0.3\% = 0.45\%$. Asset A1 with a 3-year term and client rate of 1-month LIBOR + 490 bps is assigned an FTP rate of 1-month LIBOR + 85 bps where the spread of 85 bps is obtained from the funding spread curve for a 3-year term. This creates an internal liability balance on the book of business unit 1 for the amount of $1,000 and a rate of 1-month LIBOR + 85 bps and an internal asset position on the FTP book of the funding center with the same amount and rate. The net interest margin of this position for business unit 1 is: $NIM_{A1} = 4.9\% - 0.85\% = 4.05\%$, derived as the difference between the client spread and FTP spread.

Focusing on business unit 2, deposit L2 with a 1-year term and client rate of 1-month LIBOR + 27 bps is assigned an FTP rate of 1-month LIBOR + 50 bps based on the 1-year term of the funding spread curve in Figure 12.8. This creates an internal asset balance on the book of business unit 2 for the amount of $1,100 and a rate of 1-month LIBOR + 50 bps and an internal liability position on the FTP book of the funding center with the same amount and rate. The net interest margin of this position for business unit 2 is calculated as $NIM_{L2} = 0.50\% - 0.27\% = 0.23\%$. Asset A2 with a 4-year term and a client rate of 1-month LIBOR + 510 bps is assigned an FTP rate of 1-month LIBOR + 95 bps. This creates an internal liability balance on the book of business unit 2 for the amount of $1,000 and a rate of 1-month LIBOR + 95 bps and an internal asset position on the FTP book of the funding center with the same amount and rate. The net interest margin of this position for business unit 2 is $NIM_{A2} = 5.1\% - 0.95\% = 4.15\%$. Figure 12.9 presents the FTP rate assignment for floating-rate positions of the bank in our example.

To cover the shortage of $200, the funding center borrows from the capital market. The bank treasury, as the sponsoring entity of the funding center, now has several options in funding this deficit. Having the liquidity and interest

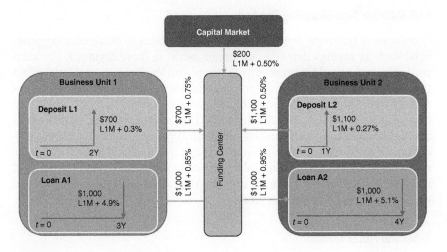

FIGURE 12.9 FTP rate assignment for floating-rate maturing products using the matched maturity method (L1M: 1-month LIBOR)

rate risks transferred to the funding center, and with the availability of full information on terms, rates, and other characteristics of positions originated by the business units, the treasury can execute different funding strategies. It can borrow the $200 amount from the capital market at a 1-month LIBOR + 50 bps rate with a 1-year term, where a 50 bps spread is the current liquidity premium specific to the bank. This is the option shown in Figure 12.9. If the treasury forecasts that the interest rate will rise in the future, it may decide to borrow at a fixed rate to lock in the current lower rate. This, however, creates interest rate risk, as a floating-rate asset is funded by a fixed-rate liability. It may borrow based on a different interest rate index if it has a lower liquidity premium compared to 1-month LIBOR. This creates basis risk for the bank. If the treasury believes that the liquidity premium will increase in the future, it may borrow for a longer term to lock in the current lower funding spread. The treasury may even borrow more than the $200 minimum required to mitigate some of the liquidity risk created by the mismatched asset and liability positions. Each of these options has different impacts on the bank's overall net interest income and risk level. Having the full information of exposures and their risks enables the treasury to choose the most appropriate funding strategy for the bank.

To calculate the net interest income of the business units and the funding center, we need to either obtain forecasted 1-month LIBOR at reset dates or use implied forward rates. For more details on calculating interest income or expense for floating-rate instruments, see Chapter 9.

FTP Rate for Non-Maturing Products

Compared to maturing products, assigning FTP rates to non-maturing products, such as savings deposits and credit cards, is more involved. For such products, not only do economic conditions and the interest rate level affect the duration, but the bank's own policies and practice in setting the client rates and the customers' behavior in using, repaying, or withdrawing the funds also have a significant impact on the duration. Due to the uncertain nature of the amount and timing of cash flows of non-maturing products, the straight application of the matched maturity method is not readily feasible. While there is no industry-wide consensus on the appropriate method of transfer pricing of non-maturing products, there are a few methods that are used in practice and we discuss two of them in this section.

Behavioral Model Method

Behavioral modeling generally refers to the methodologies used in quantitative finance to model consumer activities for retail financial products, such as credit cards, mortgages, and deposits. Broadly speaking, behavior models utilize statistical techniques to predict consumers' actions in different economic conditions as an overall mass, rather than attempting to predict the idiosyncratic effect of individual accounts. Regression modeling, time series analysis, and machine learning techniques such as clustering and decision trees are some of the common methods used in behavioral modeling. A *prepayment model* is an example of a behavioral model for mortgage contracts that predicts the pattern of prepayment of borrowed amounts by customers in different economic and interest rate environments.

Another class of the behavior models commonly used in finance are *runoff models*. These models are used for products such as deposits and credit cards where customer cash flows are not deterministic. We discussed the use of runoff profiles in valuation of non-maturing products in Chapter 2. A runoff profile represents the repayment of the outstanding balance of a non-maturing product over time for a group of accounts or the entire portfolio, usually by incorporating assumptions such as "no new business" or "no new account." We can think of a runoff profile as a synthetic amortization schedule for the group of accounts of a non-maturing product. This characterization can be used in the FTP rate assignment. In using a runoff profile in transfer pricing, the common practice is to first separate the accounts of the non-maturing product into several homogeneous groups. This is done on a cohort basis and the classification could be based on past behaviors in product use (such as number of transactions for deposits), perceived risk (such as credit score of account holders for credit cards), or other account characteristics.

Here we demonstrate the use of a runoff profile in funds transfer pricing using an example for a deposit product. The first step in this process is to separate the balance into core and non-core portions. The core is the stable portion of the balance and the non-core is the volatile part. The criteria that define the stable versus non-stable part can be based on a volatility measurement derived using historical data of portfolio balances. The non-core part of the deposit balance is often assigned a short-term FTP rate from the cost of funds curve (e.g., a rate with a 1-day or 1-month term). Some banks treat the non-core part of the deposit balance as a floating-rate product and use an interest rate index, such as fed funds, SOFR, or overnight index swap, as their FTP rate.

For the core part of the deposit balance the runoff profile can be used for transfer pricing. This is done by using the runoff profile to determine the amount and timing of cash flows related to repayment of the outstanding balance and then applying the matched maturity method to calculate the FTP rate. As an example, consider a deposit product with month-end balances from December 2016 to April 2017 as listed in Figure 12.10. In this example we consider a general case where the actual deposit balance from one month-end to the next may increase or decrease.

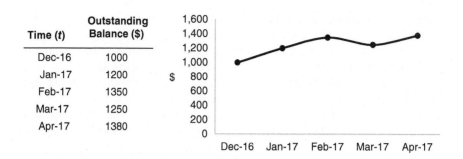

Time (*t*)	Outstanding Balance ($)
Dec-16	1000
Jan-17	1200
Feb-17	1350
Mar-17	1250
Apr-17	1380

FIGURE 12.10   Outstanding balances of a sample deposit product from December 2016 to April 2017

Period	Cumulative Runoff	Periodic Runoff
t	100%	
t + 1M	50%	50%
t + 2M	20%	30%
t + 3M	5%	15%
t + 4M	0%	5%

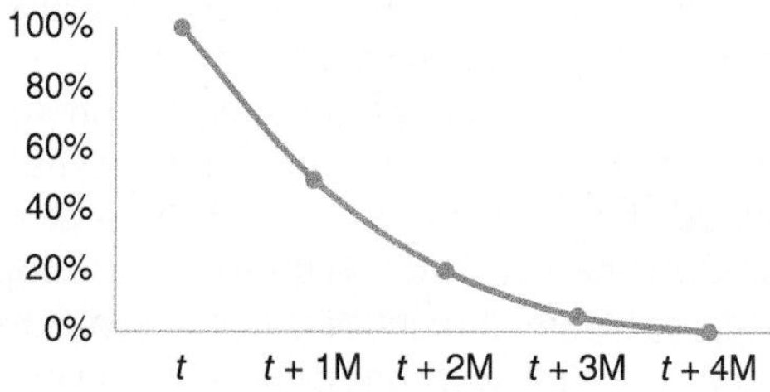

FIGURE 12.11   A sample runoff profile for a deposit product

To be able to determine the FTP rate we need the runoff profile for this deposit product. Assume that the runoff profile is as shown in Figure 12.11. To simplify the calculations in our example, here we assumed a short runoff profile where the balance at each month-end is depleted in the next four months. In practice, the runoff profile of a deposit product, especially for the core part, is much longer.

December 2016's month-end is the first date that FTP rate assignment begins. Our goal here is to derive an FTP rate as of each month-end from December 2016 to April 2017, using the actual balances, runoff profile, and cost of funds curves. Assumed cost of funds curves for these month-ends are as shown in Table 12.1. Since based on the runoff profile we assume that an outstanding balance runs off in four months, we only need a funding rate with 1-month, 2-month, 3-month, and 4-month terms.

In using the runoff profile in FTP rate determination there are two approaches available. In the first approach the runoff profile is applied to the outstanding balance at a period and in the second approach it is applied only to the new volume in a period. The second method is preferred as it retains the historical FTP rate assigned to the runoff cash flows in previous periods.

TABLE 12.1 Cost of funds curves for five month-ends from December 2016 to April 2017. Each curve shows rates with 1-month, 2-month, 3-month, and 4-month terms.

Time	Term			
	1M	**2M**	**3M**	**4M**
Dec-16	1.30%	1.40%	1.60%	1.70%
Jan-17	1.36%	1.46%	1.66%	1.77%
Feb-17	1.43%	1.53%	1.73%	1.84%
Mar-17	1.47%	1.57%	1.78%	1.89%
Apr-17	1.50%	1.60%	1.82%	1.92%

Below we start by reviewing the first method and then extend our discussion to the second method.

Method 1: Using Runoff Profile with Outstanding Balance

In this method a runoff profile is applied to the outstanding balance of the deposit at each month and there is no need to keep track of how much of the change in balance from one month to the next is due to the new volume and how much of it is the replacement of the assumed runoff amounts from previous months.

FTP Rate for December 2016

Starting from December 2016 and by applying the periodic runoff rates of 50%, 30%, 15%, and 5% to the outstanding balance of $1,000, the runoff cash flows assumed for January, February, March, and April 2017 are $500, $300, $150, and $50 respectively. These runoff cash flows are shown in the first row of the upper section of Table 12.2. Based on the weighted average matched maturity method, with principal cash flows as weights, and using the funding rate as of December 2016 from Table 12.1, the FTP rate is calculated as:

$$r_{FTP\,Dec\text{-}16} = \frac{500 \times 1.30\% + 300 \times 1.40\% + 150 \times 1.60\% + 50 \times 1.70\%}{500 + 300 + 150 + 50} = 1.40\%$$

FTP Rate for January 2017

The FTP rate as of January 2017 is calculated similarly by first applying the periodic runoff rates to the outstanding balance of $1,200, resulting in runoff

TABLE 12.2 FTP rate calculation of a sample deposit product using runoff profile applied to outstanding balances

← Runoff Cash Flow →

Time (t)	Balance	Jan-17	Feb-17	Mar-17	Apr-17	May-17	Jun-17	Jul-17	Aug-17
Dec-16	1,000	500	300	150	50				
Jan-17	1,200		600	360	180	60			
Feb-17	1,350			675	405	203	68		
Mar-17	1,250				625	375	188	63	
Apr-17	1,380					690	414	207	69

← Funding Rate →

Time (t)	Jan-17	Feb-17	Mar-17	Apr-17	May-17	Jun-17	Jul-17	Aug-17		FTP Rate
Dec-16	1.30%	1.40%	1.60%	1.70%	1.77%					1.40%
Jan-17		1.36%	1.46%	1.66%	1.73%	1.84%				1.46%
Feb-17			1.43%	1.53%	1.57%	1.78%	1.89%			1.53%
Mar-17				1.47%	1.57%	1.60%	1.82%			1.57%
Apr-17					1.50%	1.60%	1.82%	1.92%	✕ →	1.60%

cash flows of $600, $360, $180, and $60 in the next four following months. Using the funding rate as of January 2017 from Table 12.1 we have:

$$r_{FTP\,Jan\text{-}17} = \frac{600 \times 1.36\% + 360 \times 1.46\% + 180 \times 1.66\% + 60 \times 1.77\%}{600 + 360 + 180 + 60} = 1.46\%$$

FTP rates as of February, March, and April 2017 are calculated similarly as 1.53%, 1.57%, and 1.60% respectively. These calculations are summarized in Table 12.2. We can generalize this method using the following formula:

$$r_{FTP_t} = \frac{\sum_{j=t+1}^{t+h} RCF_j \times r_j}{\sum_{j=t+1}^{t+h} RCF_j} \tag{12.7}$$

where RCF_j is the runoff cash flow for period j, h is the length of the runoff profile, and r_j is the matched maturity funding rate. In our example $h = 4$ months. As mentioned earlier the runoff cash flows in this approach are derived by applying the runoff profile to the outstanding balance at each month.

While the implementation of this method is simple, it does not capture the effect of the FTP rate assignments of previous periods. In this approach the FTP rate at each period is derived solely based on the outstanding balance at that period and the runoff profile, irrespective of the rate assigned to the runoff cash flows from previous periods.

Method 2: Using Runoff Profile with New Volume

In the second method of using a runoff profile in FTP rate determination, the runoff profile is applied to the portion of the balance that is considered as new volume for the period. The new volume amount is derived using the runoff cash flows in previous periods and the change in actual balances from one period to the next.

FTP Rate for December 2016

Starting from December 2016, since this is the first month that an FTP rate calculation is performed, the entire balance of $1,000 is assumed as new volume and by applying the periodic runoff rates, the runoff cash flows for months of January, February, March, and April 2017 are obtained as $500, $300, $150, and $50 respectively. We can then calculate the FTP rate as:

$$r_{FTP\,Dec\text{-}16} = \frac{500 \times 1.30\% + 300 \times 1.40\% + 150 \times 1.60\% + 50 \times 1.70\%}{500 + 300 + 150 + 50} = 1.40\%$$

This is the same FTP rate for December 2016 that was obtained using the first method.

FTP Rate for January 2017

The outstanding deposit balance as of January 2017 is $1,200. Compared to December 2016 the balance has increased by $200. At the same time since the $500 of runoff cash flows from December 2016 had a term of one month we assume that the amount is run off in January 2017. Hence the new volume in January 2017 has two parts: $500 to replenish the runoff amount and an additional $200 that resulted in an increase in the actual outstanding balance. So, the new volume for the month of January 2017 is $200 + $500 = $700.

To calculate the FTP rate as of January 2017 we need to consider two sets of cash flows:

1. Runoff cash flows carried over from December 2016: The $500 cash flow is matured in January 2017 but $300, $150, and $50 cash flows have not run off yet. These cash flows received FTP rates of 1.40%, 1.60%, and 1.70%, respectively, in the previous step.
2. Runoff cash flows related to the new volume: These cash flows are obtained by applying the periodic runoff rates to the new volume of $700, resulting in $350, $210, $105, and $35 cash flows maturing in February, March, April, and May 2017. These cash flows receive matched maturity funding rates of 1.36%, 1.46%, 1.66%, and 1.77% from the cost of funds curve as of January 2017.

The FTP rate is then calculated as:

$$r_{FTP\,Jan\text{-}17} = \frac{\begin{array}{c}(300 \times 1.40\% + 150 \times 1.60\% + 50 \times 1.70\%) + \\ (350 \times 1.36\% + 210 \times 1.46\% + 105 \times 1.66\% + 35 \times 1.77\%)\end{array}}{(300 + 150 + 50) + (350 + 210 + 105 + 35)}$$

$$= 1.47\%$$

Notice that the first set of cash flows captured $500 of the deposit balance as of January 2017 and the second set captured $700 of it, so the entire outstanding balance of $1,200 is transfer priced but the FTP rate assignments from December 2016 are incorporated in calculation of the FTP rate as of January 2017.

FTP Rate for February 2017

The deposit balance as of February 2017 is $1,350, $150 higher than the outstanding balance of the previous month. Cash flows that are assumed to mature by February 2017 are $300 from December 2016, which had an original term of 2 months, and $350 from January 2017, which had a 1-month term.

Therefore, the new volume for February 2017 is $150 + $300 + $350 = $800. To calculate the FTP rate as of February 2017 we need to consider three sets of cash flows:

1. Runoff cash flows carried over from December 2016: $500 and $300 cash flows are matured but $150 and $50 cash flows are still not matured and received FTP rates of 1.60% and 1.70% respectively.
2. Runoff cash flows carried over from January 2017: The $350 cash flow is matured by February 2017 but the $210, $105, and $35 cash flows have not matured yet. These cash flows received FTP rates of 1.46%, 1.66%, and 1.77% respectively.
3. Runoff cash flows of the new volume: These cash flows are obtained by applying the periodic runoff rates to the new volume of $800, resulting in $400, $240, $120, and $40 cash flows maturing in March, April, May, and June 2017. These cash flows received matched maturity funding rates of 1.43%, 1.53%, 1.73%, and 1.84% from the cost of funds curve as of February 2017.

The FTP rate is then calculated as:

$$r_{FTP\,Feb\text{-}17} = \frac{\begin{array}{c}(150 \times 1.60\% + 50 \times 1.70\%) + \\ (210 \times 1.46\% + 105 \times 1.66\% + 35 \times 1.77\%) + \\ (400 \times 1.43\% + 240 \times 1.53\% + 120 \times 1.73\% + 40 \times 1.84\%)\end{array}}{(150 + 50) + (210 + 105 + 35) + (400 + 240 + 120 + 40)}$$

$$= 1.55\%$$

The first set of cash flows captured $200 of the deposit balance as of February 2017, the second set captured $350, and the third set captured $800. Therefore, the total outstanding balance of $1,350 as of February 2017 is transfer priced.

FTP rates for March and April 2017 are calculated similarly as 1.60% and 1.64% respectively. Table 12.3 summarizes these calculations for all five month-ends. To generalize this method, notice that for a given month-end we need to include the runoff cash flows from previous month-ends that are not matured yet. For example, for March 2017 since the $50 runoff cash flow from December 2016 is not matured yet, it needs to be included in the FTP rate calculation, but for April 2017 no runoff cash flow from December 2016 remains to be included. Therefore, the FTP rate calculation based on the second method can be generalized as:

$$r_{FTP_t} = \frac{\sum_{i=t-h+1}^{t} \sum_{j=t+1}^{t+h} RCF_{i,j} \times r_{i,j}}{\sum_{i=t-h+1}^{t} \sum_{j=t+1}^{t+h} RCF_{i,j}} \tag{12.8}$$

TABLE 12.3 FTP rate calculation of a sample deposit product using runoff profile applied to new volumes

← Runoff →

Time (t)	Previous Period(s) Runoff	New Volume	Balance	Jan-17	Feb-17	Mar-17	Apr-17	May-17	Jun-17	Jul-17	Aug-17
Dec-16	0	1,000	1,000	500	300	150	50				
Jan-17	500	700	1,200		350	210	105	35			
Feb-17	650	800	1,350			400	240	120	40		
Mar-17	760	660	1,250				330	198	99	33	
Apr-17	725	855	1,380					428	257	128	43

×

← Funding Rate →

Time (t)	Jan-17	Feb-17	Mar-17	Apr-17	May-17	Jun-17	Jul-17	Aug-17	FTP Rate
Dec-16	1.30%	1.40%	1.60%	1.70%	1.77%				1.40%
Jan-17		1.36%	1.46%	1.66%	1.73%	1.84%			1.47%
Feb-17			1.43%	1.53%	1.57%	1.78%	1.89%		1.55%
Mar-17				1.47%	1.50%	1.60%	1.82%	1.92%	1.60%
Apr-17									1.64%

where i represents period (month-end time), j represents maturity date, $RCF_{i,j}$ is the runoff cash flow of new volume, h is the length of the runoff profile, and $r_{i,j}$ is the matched maturity funding rate. For some i and j combinations runoff cash flows are zero. For example, Equation (12.8) can be used for derivation of the FTP rate as of April 2017 as follows:

Since $h = 4$ months and $t = Apr$-17, we have:

$$t - h + 1 = t - 3 \text{ month} = Jan\text{-}17$$

$$t + 1 = May\text{-}17$$

$$t + h = t + 4 \text{ months} = Aug\text{-}17$$

$$r_{FTP_{Apr-17}} = \frac{\sum_{i=Jan\text{-}17}^{Apr\text{-}17} \sum_{j=May\text{-}17}^{Aug\text{-}17} RCF_{i,j} \times r_{i,j}}{\sum_{i=Jan\text{-}17}^{Apr\text{-}17} \sum_{j=May\text{-}17}^{Aug\text{-}17} RCF_{i,j}} =$$

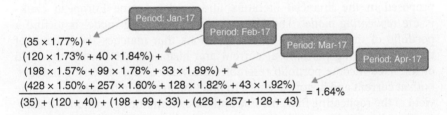

The runoff profile is often used for derivation of the FTP rate only for the core part of the deposit balance. The core portion itself is broken down into multiple segments and a runoff profile is developed for each segment. Subsequently the FTP rate of each segment is derived using the methodology described earlier and the total FTP rate is the aggregated FTP rates of all segments. The method of aggregation depends on how the core part is segregated in the first place.

The method discussed here can be used for FTP rate determination of other non-maturing product types. For example, for a credit card accounts receivable portfolio, the balance can be divided into two sections: a *minimum-due* part and a *discretionary* part. The minimum-due part is the portion of the credit card balances that customers are contractually obligated to repay each month. This part receives a short-term FTP rate, such as a 1-month rate from the cost of funds curve. The discretionary section is the portion of the balances that customers decide to roll to the next month, partially repay, or fully repay. The discretionary section itself can be divided into subsections: a *revolving* part, consisting of balances customers roll to the next month, and a *non-revolving* part for balances customers pay in the current month above the minimum-due amount. The FTP rate for the non-revolving subsection is also assigned a short-term funding rate. FTP rates for the revolving subsection can be derived using the runoff profile as demonstrated previously for deposits.

An alternative method of using a runoff profile in determining an FTP rate of a non-maturing product is to use the curve in the valuation of the product and then calculating the portfolio's effective duration. In this method, by treating the runoff profile as a synthetic amortization schedule we can calculate the value of the portfolio in different interest rate scenarios and calculate the effective duration using those values. The FTP rate associated with the term equal to the effective duration is then used in transfer pricing of the non-maturing product.

Replicating Model Method

Another approach for derivation of the FTP rate of no-maturing products proposed in the financial literature and used by some European banks is the *replicating model*. The idea behind a replicating model is to find a portfolio of maturing fixed-income positions that matches the balance of the non-maturing portfolio at current and historical dates while the yield of the fixed-income portfolio resembles the yield of non-maturing product, both at current and historical dates. In practice, instead of trying to match the yield of the replicating fixed-income and the non-maturing portfolios exactly, an objective criterion that relates the two yields is optimized. The yield of a constructed replicating portfolio represents the potential return if the balance of the non-maturing product is invested in the fixed-income instruments included in the replicating portfolio. This can be considered the appropriate FTP rate for the non-maturing portfolio. The portfolio of the fixed-income positions can be built either using existing market-traded instruments (e.g., Treasury notes, bonds, strips) or synthetic instruments (e.g., products with yields equal to LIBOR or swap rates).

Maes and Timmermans (2005) suggested two objective criteria for the determination of a replicating portfolio for a deposit product:

1. Most stable margin: In this method the standard deviation of the deposit margin is minimized, where the margin is defined as the difference between the replicating portfolio yield and the deposit yield. The

composition of the replicating model is defined by the weight of each fixed-income instrument included in the portfolio. These weights can be found by solving the following optimization problem:

Minimize Standard Deviation $(y_P - r_D)$

Subject to:

(i) $\sum_{i=1}^{n} w_i = 1$ (12.9)

(ii) $w_i \geq 0 \quad i = 1, \ldots, n$

(iii) $V_{P_t} = B_{D_t}$

where:

n = Number of fixed-income instruments considered in replicating portfolio

w_i = Weight of instrument i in replicating portfolio

$y_P = (y_{P_h} \cdots, y_{P_t}, \cdots, y_{P_0})$ = Vector of replicating portfolio yields from historical date h to current date, where y_{P_0} is the current yield

$r_D = (r_{D_h} \cdots, r_{D_t}, \cdots, r_{D_0})$ = Vector of deposit portfolio yields from historical date h to current date, where r_{D_0} is the current yield

y_{P_t} = Yield of replicating portfolio at time t where $y_{P_t} = \sum_{i=1}^{n} w_i y_{i_t}$ and y_{i_t} is yield of instrument i at time t

V_{P_t} = Value of replicating portfolio at time t

B_{D_t} = Balance of deposit portfolio at time t

The replicating portfolio is constructed by solving this optimization problem, which aims to minimize the volatility of differences between the replicating portfolio yield and the deposit yield throughout the historical period. The first condition ensures that the sum of the weights adds up to 1 while the second condition restricts the short selling in the replicating portfolio. The third condition ensures that at each historical date the value of the replicating portfolio is the same as the balance of the deposit. The instruments that are included in the replicating portfolio are assumed to be held to maturity and rolled over at their maturity dates.

2. Maximizing risk-adjusted margin: In this method the ratio of the average deposit to its standard deviation is maximized. Weights applied to the

fixed-income instruments in the replicating portfolio can be found by solving the following optimization problem:

$$Maximize \ \frac{Average \ (\mathbf{y}_P - \mathbf{r}_D)}{Standard \ Deviation \ (\mathbf{y}_P - \mathbf{r}_D)}$$

Subject to:

(i) $\sum_{i=1}^{n} w_i = 1$ (12.10)

(ii) $w_i \geq 0 \quad i = 1, \ldots, n$

(iii) $V_{P_t} = B_{D_t}$

Maes and Timmermans suggested first dividing the deposit portfolio into three sections: a core part that is relatively insensitive to the interest rate changes, a volatile part that is sensitive to the interest rate changes, and the remaining portion. The core part can be assigned a long-term FTP rate while a short-term FTP rate assignment is more appropriate for the sensitive part. The replicating model then can be used for the remaining part where the yield of the replicating portfolio can be used as the FTP rate.

One of the drawbacks of the replicating model approach is an inherited inconsistency in the duration of the fixed-income portfolio, which in turn results in irregularity in FTP rate assignment. This inconsistency is rooted in the dependency of the constructed portfolio to assumptions such as the historical period considered for data and the optimization criterion used to obtain instrument weights.

These methods can be modified and used for other non-maturing products. A more advanced form of the replicating model uses dynamic instrument selection and allows for different weight sets at each historical date. For an example of such a model see Frauendorfer and Schurle (2003).

COMPONENTS OF FTP RATE

The difference between the client rate and the FTP rate assigned to a position reflects the prospect of its economic benefit to the originating bank. To quantify this benefit, different costs associated with the position, such as the funding charge, as well as its benefits, such as interest earnings, should be included in the FTP rate. The bank also needs to choose which components of risks associated with the position are transferred to the funding center. The cost of managing those risks by the funding center should be included in the FTP rate. The combination of these costs and benefits constitutes the FTP rate, which impacts the ex-ante economic benefit of the position. By using an FTP system that transfers several risk types, a bank can obtain risk-adjusted performance measurements for different positions originated by its business units and is able to compare exposures with respect to their individual performance and their contributions to the bank's overall return.

The main component of an FTP rate is the *funding rate*, also referred to as the *refinancing rate*. Our discussion so far has been focused on finding this funding rate component. By using the matched maturity method for obtaining the funding rate, the interest rate and liquidity risks of a position are transferred to the funding center and hence the funding rate component reflects these risks.

While FTP is often used for centralizing interest rate and liquidity risks, other risks can also be transferred through the FTP system. It is recommended that the cost of contingency liquidity be included in the FTP rate and this cost be allocated to business units. Contingency liquidity is the standby cash, cash equivalent, and unencumbered high-quality liquid assets (e.g., U.S. Treasury notes) held for the purpose of liquidity risk management. After the global financial crisis of 2007–2009, as regulators require more banks to hold larger contingency liquidity portfolios, inclusion of an additional spread in the FTP rate for contingency liquidity has become a common practice. Internalizing the cost of holding this portfolio to business units is considered a sound risk management practice. This ensures that the business units are considering the impact of their activities and new origination decisions on the bank's liquidity requirements, as their own profitability measurements are impacted through the cost internalization by the FTP system.

A contingency liquidity cost is added as an extra spread to the FTP rate. Assignment of contingency liquidity cost through the FTP system can be based on the potential and probability of need for the use of such liquidity sources during a stress period. For example, for contracts with committed lines of credit to customers, or for trading positions that have potential collateral calls or an increase in haircuts, a higher spread for the contingency liquidity component should be included in the FTP rate.

Credit and operational risks of a position can also be transferred to the funding center through the FTP system. Transferring these risks, however, may desensitize business units to them. This can create disincentives in actively managing these risks and lead to a potential increase in financial losses due to credit or operational events, both at the unit level and at the bank.

If a bank decides to include the credit risk in transfer pricing, this is done by adding a credit spread component to the FTP rate. For a non-trading position, the credit spread is often derived using the expected loss rate of the position, which is calculated using a probability of default (PD) and loss given default (LGD) rate. For example, if a position's PD is 2% and its LGD is 30%, then the extra spread for credit risk added to the FTP rate is associated with the expected loss level of $EL = 2\% \times 30\% = 0.60\%$. In some implementations this entire 60 bps is added to the FTP rate while in others the expected loss level is used as a guideline to determine the credit spread component. For example, a bank may have a policy to add a 25 bps credit spread to the FTP rate of any position with an expected loss of less than 0.50% and 40 bps for any positions with an expected loss greater than or equal to 0.50%. In a more sophisticated FTP implementation the expected loss rate can also be term-dependent, similar to the cost of funds curve, so the credit spread component of the FTP rate depends on the term of the position (or its duration). For a trading position, such as a fixed-income security, if there exists a credit default swap associated with the security or the issuer, the CDS spread can be used as the credit spread component of the FTP rate.

The cost of optionality of a product is often included in the FTP rate. For example, products with explicit interest rate caps or floors have embedded options that affect the client rates and hence such impacts should be considered in their transfer pricing. Other examples of embedded options are customers' right to withdraw funds in a demand deposit product, or a mortgage prepayment option. To incorporate an option cost in transfer pricing, the common practice is to add the *option-adjusted spread (OAS)* of the position to the FTP rate (Skoglund 2010). For a position with an embedded option, the option-adjusted spread is the additional spread added to the spot curve used in valuation that makes the value of the position comparable to a similar position without the optionality. For a callable bond, since the market price of the bond reflects both the value of an equivalent non-callable bond and the value of the option contact embedded in the callable bond, the OAS is the spread added to the spot curve that makes the present value of the bond's cash flows equal to its market price.

To summarize, the following equation shows various components that are often considered and included in an FTP rate:

$$r_{FTP} = Funding\ Rate + Contingency\ Liquidity\ Spread + Credit\ Risk\ Spread$$

$$+ Operational\ Risk\ Spread + Option\text{-}Adjusted\ Spread \qquad (12.11)$$

CHARACTERISTICS OF A GOOD FTP SYSTEM

Funds transfer pricing is a critical element of risk decomposition and internal measurement of profitability of a bank's business units. Through the FTP system banks are able to allocate net interest margin and net interest income to various positions and business units based on a uniform risk-adjusted basis. A well-defined and properly implemented FTP system can help banks in business planning, performance measurement, budgeting, and risk management. At the same time, a weak implementation of an FTP system can cause confusions in a bank's internal profitability measurement efforts, as it improperly distributes profits and costs among business units and may lead to internal controversy and disagreement. More importantly, a poorly designed FTP system may not properly reflect risks of products, and may even mask and hide some of them, leading to unexpected losses at both business unit and bank levels.

The variation of funds transfer pricing methodologies used by banks and the importance of the FTP system in risk management practices, especially related to interest rate and liquidity risks, have caught the attention of various regulatory agencies around the world. In March 2016, three main regulatory bodies of banking and finance industries in the United States, namely the Federal Reserve System, the Federal Deposit Insurance Corporation, and the Office of the Comptroller of the Currency, jointly issued a guidance on funds transfer pricing ("Interagency Guidance" 2016). This guidance outlines some of the best practices for a well-established FTP system, with emphasis on interest rate, liquidity, and contingent liquidity risks. While in practice there is no industry-wide consensus on the best approach in implementation of an FTP system, following are some of the features of a good FTP system:

- The complexity and scope of a bank's FTP system should be aligned with its balance sheet size, complexity of its activities and products, and its risk appetite. This alignment is important to ensure that the right amount of resources and expertise are allocated to the development and maintenance of the FTP system.
- The FTP rate assigned to a position is in line with the economics of the position and its inherent risks. If this is done appropriately, it leads to better risk management, both at the originating unit and at the overall bank. Business units should remain immune to interest rate risk since by locking a transferred rate they pass the risk to the funding center. Bringing the cost of liquidity risk to business units is one of the features of a good FTP system. To properly transfer these risks, different characteristics of the position and particularly the timing of principal cash flows and its duration should be taken into account. For this reason, the matched maturity method is preferred to the pool method in FTP rate determination.
- The FTP system should be designed such that transfer pricing is done at an appropriate granularity level. Transfer pricing that is done at the contract or position level can better fulfill risk-adjusted performance measurement and risk transference. If transfer pricing at the contract or account level

is not feasible, the aggregation of positions should be done such that the created groups are homogeneous with respect to their risks and other relevant characteristics. The appropriateness of the granularity of the FTP system should be examined both at the product type and business unit levels.

- When transfer pricing is done at a contract or position initiation period, and the assigned rate is held in the subsequent periods, it can be used for the assessment of pricing decisions by business unit management.
- A well-designed FTP system should have an appropriate governance structure, including oversight by bank's senior managers.
- An appropriate amount of resources should be allocated to maintain the FTP system. The cost of funds and funding spread curves should be updated frequently and built based on reliable and readily available data.
- The FTP system should be implemented consistently among business units and product types. This enables banks to assess the profitability of products, positions, and business units on a comparable basis and make informed decisions on refinement of those activities and origination decisions.
- Since there are several transfer pricing methodologies available for maturing and non-maturing products, and there is no industry-wide consensus on the best approach, the impact of these options in FTP implementation should be studied. For example, as mentioned in a previous section of this chapter, if a bank decided to use the weighted average method to calculate the FTP rate for fixed-rate maturing products, it should also decide whether to use only principal cash flows as the weights, or all cash flows. There is even an option to use the present value of cash flows as the weights. The bank should study the impact of these methods on its FTP system and select the implementation method based on such analysis.
- For trading positions, days the security is intended to be held should be considered in assigning the FTP rate.
- Proper documentation of fund transfer pricing methods, assumptions, and data provides the funding center and business unit personnel with a clear understanding of how FTP works and its associated costs and benefits. A well-designed FTP system is transparent and traceable.

SUMMARY

- FTP is a tool for measuring risk-adjusted performance and profitability. By allocating net interest margin on a risk-adjusted basis, the FTP promotes sound originations and pricing practices and aligns activities of business units with a bank's overall risk appetite.

- Mispriced funding cost allocations to business unit activities can be an incentive for a unit to take excessive risk to improve its own performance measures while such activities may not be aligned with a bank's policies and risk limits. A properly implemented FTP system helps align risk-taking activities in business units with the bank's overall strategy, business plan, and risk tolerance.
- FTP is also a tool for centralizing the management of various risks, especially interest rate and liquidity risks. FTP provides a method to aggregate these risks in a centralized unit within the bank and provides a wider view of all exposures and their inherited risks for better hedging and mitigation planning.
- Having information on all exposures in a centralized repository provides the bank with a better understanding of its funding needs and required contingency liquidity.
- Net interest margin is the difference between the interest rate earned on an asset (or group of assets) and the interest rate paid on a liability (or group of liabilities). A common practice in banking is to fund long-term assets with short-term liabilities. While this often leads to better net interest margins, it can create liquidity and interest rate risks.
- A cost of funds or FTP curve represents current rates for raising funds through the capital market.
- In a typical FTP system, the central funding center itself is a profit center.
- In the pool method of FTP implementation, funds raised and assets originated are pooled together and FTP rates are assigned based on positions' characteristics such as their types or terms.
- In the matched maturity method of FTP implementation, each originated asset or liability position is assigned an FTP rate from the cost of funds curve that matches the position's term.
- In the matched maturity method, the FTP rate of a fixed-rate maturing product is the rate with the same term as the cost of funds curve. If a position has multiple principal cash flows with different timings, a weighted average method is used to obtain the FTP rate.
- In the matched maturity method, the FTP rate of a floating-rate maturing product is obtained as the funding spread associated with the client rate index.
- When using a runoff profile in FTP rate assignment of a non-maturing product, the profile is treated as a synthetic amortization curve to establish the principal payment cash flow schedule, which in turn is used to obtain the FTP rate.
- The replicating portfolio method is based on finding a portfolio of maturing fixed-income positions that matches the balance of a non-maturing product at current and historical dates while the yield of the fixed-income

portfolio resembles the yield of a non-maturing product. The yield of the replicating portfolio can be used as the FTP rate of the non-maturing product.

■ Funding rate and contingency liquidity spread are two main components of the FTP rate. Some banks also transfer credit and operational risks to the funding center and hence add a spread for each to the FTP rate. For positions with optionality, the option-adjusted spread is also added to the FTP rate.

NOTES

1. With regard to valuation, business unit 1 is still exposed to interest rate risk as a change in yield curve can change the values of asset and liability positions differently as rates and timings of interest cash flows are different.
2. For simplicity in this chapter we assume that all positions have an Actual/Actual accrual basis; therefore, the interest income or expense for one full year is simply calculated as the balance multiplied by the annual interest rate.
3. For simplicity here we did not consider the effect of a leap year.

BIBLIOGRAPHY

Maes, Konstantijn, and Thierry Timmermans. "Measuring the Interest Rate Risk of Belgian Regulated Savings Deposits." *Financial Stability Review, National Bank of Belgium* 3, no. 1 (June 2005): 137–151.

Frauendorfer, Karl, and Michael Schürle. "Management of Non-Maturing Deposits by Multistage Stochastic Programming." *European Journal of Operation Research* 151, no. 3 (December 2003): 602–616.

"Interagency Guidance on Funds Transfer Pricing Related to Funding and Contingent Liquidity Risks." SR 16-3. Board of Governors of the Federal Reserve System, Federal Depository Insurance Corporation, and Office of the Comptroller of the Currency, March 2016 (https://www.federalreserve.gov/supervisionreg/srletters/sr1603.htm).

Shih, Andre, David Crandon, and Steven Wofford. "Transfer Pricing: Pitfalls in Using Multiple Benchmark Yield Curves." *Journal of Performance Management* 17, no. 2 (2004): 33–46.

Skoglund, Jimmy. "Funds Transfer Pricing and Risk-Adjusted Performance Measurement." SAS Institute White Paper, May 30, 2010.

Tumasyan, Hovik. "Revisiting Funds Transfer Pricing." PricewaterhouseCoopers LLP, February 2012.

Wyle, Robert J., and Yaakov Tsaig. "Implementing High Value Funds Transfer Pricing Systems." Moody's Analytics, September 2011.

Appendix: Elements of Probability and Statistics

I n this Appendix we provide a brief overview of some statistical concepts that are needed for a better understanding of the materials discussed in the body of the text.

RANDOM VARIABLES

The set of all possible outcomes of an experiment is called the *sample space* of that experiment. For example, in rolling a fair six-sided die, the sample space is $S = \{1, 2, 3, 4, 5, 6\}$. A *random variable* is a real-valued function defined on the sample space that associates each outcome of an experiment to a real number. The *state space* is all possible real values that a random variable can assume. Therefore, random variable X is a function from sample space S to state space T where members of the sample space are all possible outcomes of the experiment and members of state space T are all possible values that the random variable can assume. For example, in an experiment in which a fair die is rolled four times, the sample space consists of all possible sequences of numbers that may be obtained; 3-4-1-6 is one possible outcome and 3-4-1-1 is another. There are many more possible outcomes that exist in this sample space. Assume that random variable X represents the sum of the numbers in each sequence obtained in this experiment. Then for a 3-4-1-6 outcome $X = 14$ and for a 3-4-1-1 outcome $X = 9$. The state space of random variable X is any integer between, and including, 4 and 24.

If s is a particular outcome of an experiment ($s \in S$), a specific value of random variable $X(s) = x$ is often called a *realization* of that variable ($x \in T$). Random variables are usually shown with capital letters (e.g., X) and a realization with a lowercase letter (e.g., x). For example, if random variable Y

represents the value of a fixed-income security in percentage form, $y = 99.9345$ is a realization of this random variable.

If the state space of a random variable contains countable values (i.e., a finite number of different values), the random variable is called a *discrete* random variable, whereas the state space of a *continuous* random variable contains uncountable values (i.e., any values in an interval). For example, the status of a personal loan (current, past due, default) can be modeled using a discrete random variable while the time to default of the loan can be represented using a continuous random variable.

DISTRIBUTION FUNCTION

A probability distribution function assigns a probability to each value in the state space of a random variable. For a discrete random variable X, *probability mass function (pmf)* is defined as function f_X such that:

$$f_X(x) = P(X = x) \tag{A.1}$$

where x is a realization of random variable X. This function takes in any possible values of the random variable and associates a probability, including 0, to that value. For example, if random variable X represents the value obtained from rolling a fair die, then:

$$f_X(x) = \frac{1}{6} \quad x \in \{1, 2, 3, 4, 5, 6\}$$

For a discrete random variable X with a probability mass function f_X, the probability of X belonging to a subset A is obtained as:

$$P(X \in A) = \sum_{x_i \in A} f_X(x_i) \tag{A.2}$$

For example, in rolling a fair die experiment, the probability of getting any value in subset $\{2, 5\}$ is $\frac{1}{6} + \frac{1}{6} = \frac{1}{3}$. For a continuous random variable X and for any subset A of its state space, *probability density function (pdf)* is defined as a non-negative function f_X such that:

$$P(X \in A) = \int_A f_X(x) \, dx \tag{A.3}$$

Figure A.1 presents an example of a probability density function of a continuous random variable. For a continuous random variable X with probability density function f_X, the probability of X to be between real numbers a and b is obtained as:

$$P(a \leq X \leq b) = \int_a^b f_X(x)\, dx \tag{A.4}$$

In Figure A.1 this probability is the shaded area under the probability density function curve, between a and b. For a continuous random variable X with probability density function f_X we have:

- $P(X = x) = 0$ for any specific x in the state space of X
- $f_X(x) \geq 0$
- $\int_{-\infty}^{+\infty} f_X(x)\, dx = 1$

Cumulative distribution function (cdf) is defined as a nondecreasing function F_X such that:

$$F_X(x) = P(X \leq x) \tag{A.5}$$

For any $-\infty < x < +\infty$. If X is a discrete random variable with probability mass function f_X, we have:

$$F_X(x) = \sum_{x_i \leq x} f_X(x_i) \tag{A.6}$$

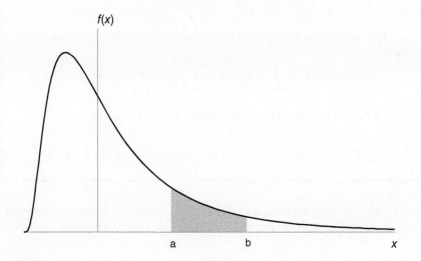

FIGURE A.1 Example of a probability density function. Shaded area is $P(a \leq X \leq b)$.

Equivalently, if X is a continuous random variable with probability density function f_X, we have:

$$F_X(x) = \int_{-\infty}^{x} f_X(\tau)\,d\tau \tag{A.7}$$

Moreover, for a continuous random variable X:

$$F'_X(x) = \frac{dF_X(x)}{dx} = f_X(x) \tag{A.8}$$

A few properties of the cumulative distribution function are as follows:

- If $x_1 < x_2$, then $F_X(x_1) \le F_X(x_2)$
- $\lim_{x \to -\infty} F_X(x) = 0$ and $\lim_{x \to +\infty} F_X(x) = 1$
- $P(X > x) = 1 - F_X(x)$
- $P(x_1 < X < x_2) = F_X(x_2) - F_X(x_1)$

Example

Assume that the probability density function of a continuous random variable is as follows:

$$f_X(x) = \begin{cases} \dfrac{2}{25}x & \text{If } 0 < x < 5 \\ 0 & \text{Otherwise} \end{cases} \tag{A.9}$$

The cumulative distribution function of this variable is obtained as follows:

$$F_X(x) = \int_0^x f_X(\tau)\,d\tau = \int_0^x \frac{2}{25}\tau\,d\tau = \frac{1}{25}x^2$$

Using this we can find the probability $P(1 < X < 3)$ as:

$$P(1 < X < 3) = F_X(3) - F_X(1) = \frac{1}{25}(9) - \frac{1}{25}(1) = \frac{8}{25}$$

In the following sections we discuss a few important discrete and continuous distributions that are commonly used in quantitative finance.

Joint Probability Distribution

A *joint probability distribution* involves the relationship between two or more random variables simultaneously and it provides the probability of an event involving two or more variables. For example, for credit risk analysis we may be interested in the probability of a customer default on his credit card loan and a default on his home mortgage loan, together. The joint probability distribution of two random variables is called a *bivariate distribution* and if the number of random variables is more than two, it is called a *multivariate distribution*.

Assume that X and Y are two discrete random variables. For a given pair of (x, y) from all possible pair values that X and Y together can take, the joint probability mass function of these two random variables is defined as:

$$f_{X,Y}(x, y) = P(X = x \text{ and } Y = y) \tag{A.10}$$

If X and Y are two continuous random variables, for any subset A of an x-y plane, their joint probability density function is a non-negative function $f_{X,Y}$ such that:

$$P((X, Y) \in A) = \iint_A f_{X,Y}(x, y) \, dx \, dy \tag{A.11}$$

Based on this definition, we have:

- $f_{X,Y}(x, y) \geq 0$
- $\int_{-\infty}^{+\infty} \int_{-\infty}^{+\infty} f_{X,Y}(x, y) \, dx \, dy = 1$

If $-\infty < x < +\infty$ and $-\infty < y < +\infty$, the joint cumulative distribution function of two discrete random variables X and Y is defined as:

$$F_{X,Y}(x, y) = P(X \leq x \text{ and } Y \leq y) \tag{A.12}$$

And if continuous random variables X and Y have a joint probability density function $f_{X,Y}$, their joint cumulative distribution function is defined as:

$$F_{X,Y}(x, y) = \int_{-\infty}^{y} \int_{-\infty}^{x} f_{X,Y}(\tau, v) \, d\tau \, dv \tag{A.13}$$

Similar to the case of distribution for one random variable, the relationship between the joint probability density function and the joint cumulative distribution function for two continuous random variables X and Y can be expressed as:

$$\frac{\partial^2 F_{X,Y}(x,y)}{\partial x\, \partial y} = f_{X,Y}(x,y) \tag{A.14}$$

Given the joint distribution of two random variables, we can remove the influence of one variable and obtain the *marginal distribution* of the other variable. If X and Y are two discrete random variables with joint probability mass function $f_{X,Y}$, the marginal distribution of X is obtained as:

$$g_X(x) = \sum\nolimits_{All\ y} f_{X,Y}(x,y) \tag{A.15}$$

And the marginal distribution of Y is:

$$h_Y(y) = \sum\nolimits_{All\ x} f_{X,Y}(x,y) \tag{A.16}$$

Equivalently, if X and Y are two continuous random variables with a joint probability density function $f_{X,Y}$, the marginal distribution of X is obtained as:

$$g_X(x) = \int_{-\infty}^{+\infty} f_{X,Y}(x,y)\, dy \tag{A.17}$$

And the marginal distribution of Y is:

$$h_Y(y) = \int_{-\infty}^{+\infty} f_{X,Y}(x,y)\, dx \tag{A.18}$$

Two random variables are *independent* if they have no impact on each other. In other words, two independent random variables provide no information about each other. If $f_{X,Y}$ is the joint distribution function (either mass or density) of two random variables X and Y (either discrete or continuous) and the marginal distributions of these two random variables are g_X and h_Y, then X and Y are independent if and only if:

$$f_{X,Y}(x,y) = g_X(x)\, h_Y(y) \tag{A.19}$$

EXPECTATION AND VARIANCE

The *expectation* of a random variable represents the central tendency point of its distribution. If X is a discrete random variable with a probability mass function of f_X, its expectation is defined as:

$$E[X] = \sum_{all\ x} x f_X(x) \qquad (A.20)$$

The expectation of a random variable, also called *mean*, is a real number and often is shown by μ notation. For a discrete random variable with an equal probability for each member of its state space, the mean or expectation is equivalent to the arithmetic *average* of all members of the state space of the random variable. Equivalently, for a continuous random variable X with a probability density function f_X, the expectation is defined as:

$$E[X] = \int_{-\infty}^{+\infty} x\ f_X(x)dx \qquad (A.21)$$

Example

Consider again the random variable X with a probability density function as given in (A.9). The expectation of this random variable is calculated as:

$$E[X] = \int_{-\infty}^{+\infty} x\left(\frac{2}{25}x\right)dx = \int_{0}^{5}\frac{2}{25}x^2\ dx = \frac{2}{25}\frac{x^3}{3}\bigg|_{0}^{5} = \frac{10}{3}$$

The expectation of a function of a random variable $g(X)$ for a discrete random variable is obtained as:

$$E[g(X)] = \sum_{all\ x} g(x) f_X(x) \qquad (A.22)$$

And for a continuous random variable we have:

$$E[g(X)] = \int_{-\infty}^{+\infty} g(x) f_X(x)\ dx \qquad (A.23)$$

Two important properties of the expectation are:

- If $X_1, X_2, \ldots, X_n$ are n random variables, the expectation of a linear combination of them is equal to the linear combination of their expectations. If $a_1, a_2, \ldots, a_n$ and b are constant real numbers and expectations of all n random variables exist, we have:

$$E[a_1 X_1 + a_2 X_2 + \cdots + a_n X_n + b]$$
$$= a_1 E[X_1] + a_2 E[X_2] + \cdots + a_n E[X_n] + b \tag{A.24}$$

- If $X_1, X_2, \ldots, X_n$ are n independent random variables, the expectation of their product is equal to the product of their expectations:

$$E\left[\prod_{i=1}^{n} X_i\right] = \prod_{i=1}^{n} E[X_i] \tag{A.25}$$

Variance of a random variable is a measurement of its dispersion around its central tendency point. The variance of random variable X is defined as:

$$\text{Var}[X] = E[(X - E[X])^2] \tag{A.26}$$

The notation σ^2 is often used to show the variance and the square root of the variance σ is known as the standard deviation. Alternatively, it can be shown that the variance of random variable X can be obtained using the following equation:

$$\text{Var}[X] = E[X^2] - (E[X])^2 \tag{A.27}$$

An important property of the variance is as follows:

- If $X_1, X_2, \ldots, X_n$ are n independent random variables, $a_1, a_2, \ldots, a_n$ and b are constant real numbers and variances of all n random variables exist, we have:

$$\text{Var}[a_1 X_1 + a_2 X_2 + \cdots + a_n X_n + b]$$
$$= a_1^2 \text{Var}[X_1] + a_2^2 \text{Var}[X_2] + \cdots + a_n^2 \text{Var}[X_n] \tag{A.28}$$

The moment of a random variable generalizes these concepts. Consider a random variable X and positive integer number k. $E[X^k]$ is called the kth moment. In particular, the mean of a random variable is its first moment ($k = 1$). If $E[X] = \mu$, then for any positive integer k, $E[(X - \mu)^k]$ is called the kth central moment of random variable X. By this definition, the first central moment of X is zero and the second central moment is its variance.

Example

Assume that random variable X represents the value of an option contract that can take any values in set $\{1010, 1150, 1304, 1402\}$ with an equal probability of 0.25. The mean, variance, and standard deviation of this random variable are calculated as follows:

$$E[X] = \mu = 0.25 \times 1010 + 0.25 \times 1150 + 0.25 \times 1304 + 0.25 \times 1402$$

$$= 1216.5$$

$$E[X^2] = 0.25 \times (1010)^2 + 0.25 \times (1150)^2 + 0.25 \times (1304)^2 + 0.25$$

$$\times (1402)^2 = 1502155$$

$$\text{Var}[X] = \sigma^2 = E[X^2] - (E[X])^2 = 1502155 - (1216.5)^2 = 22282.75$$

$$\sigma = \sqrt{22282.75} = 149.2741$$

MEDIAN AND MODE

Aside from the mean, there are two other important central tendency measurements: *median* and *mode*. The mode of a random variable is the real number at which its probability distribution function attains its maximum value. The median is a real number that separates the probability distribution of a random variable into two equal parts. Formally, if X is a discrete random variable, median is a real number m such that:

$$P(X \le m) \ge \frac{1}{2} \qquad and \qquad P(X \ge m) \ge \frac{1}{2} \qquad (A.29)$$

Based on this definition, for a discrete probability distribution it is possible that the median does not exactly cut the probability into two equal parts. It is also possible to have more than one median. For a continuous random variable, the median of a probability distribution is the value where the cumulative distribution function is 0.5. Formally, if X is a continuous random variable, the median is a real number m such that:

$$P(X \le m) = P(X \ge m) = \int_{-\infty}^{m} f_X(x)\, dx = \frac{1}{2} \qquad (A.30)$$

Mean, median, and mode are all measurements of the central tendency of a random variable, but they do not necessarily have equal values or the same applications. For a random variable that represents *nominal* data that has distinct categories (e.g., gender) or *ordinal* data with distinct categories that have a natural order (e.g., level of preference of a product), mode is a more appropriate measurement of central tendency. For *interval* data where the distance of values is meaningful and important, and there is no natural zero for the variable (e.g., temperature), or *ratio* data where both the distance and ratio of values are meaningful and important, and there is a natural zero for the variable (e.g., weight), all three measurements of mode, mean, and median are often used.

Example

Consider discrete random variable X representing the number of withdrawals made by 20 customers with savings accounts over the past 30 days, as listed in Table A.1.

TABLE A.1 Number of withdrawals of 20 customers with savings account over past 30 days

Customer ID	Number of Withdrawals	Customer ID	Number of Withdrawals
1	1	11	3
2	2	12	4
3	0	13	2
4	3	14	1
5	5	15	0
6	2	16	1
7	2	17	2
8	0	18	3
9	0	19	1
10	1	20	2

Based on the data in this table, X can be a member of set $\{0, 1, 2, 3, 4, 5\}$. The probability mass function of this random variable is constructed using the observed frequency of each possible value. Table A.2 shows the frequencies of possible values of this random variable, along with the corresponding $f_X(x)$ and $F_X(x)$, presented in an ascending order of x.

TABLE A.2 Frequencies and probabilities of possible values of random variable X, representing number of withdrawals from a savings account product over past 30 days

x	Frequency	$f_X(x)$	$F_X(x)$
0	4	0.2	0.2
1	5	0.25	0.45
2	6	0.3	0.75
3	3	0.15	0.9
4	1	0.05	0.95
5	1	0.05	1

For example, since there are four customers who had zero withdrawals over the past 30 days and the total number of customers is 20, we have: $f_X(0) = \frac{4}{20} = 0.2$. The probabilities of other possible values of the random variable are obtained similarly. Since in this table x values are shown in an ascending order, the last column of the table, $F_X(x)$, is simply a running total of the $f_X(x)$ column. Figure A.2 shows a frequency plot, also known

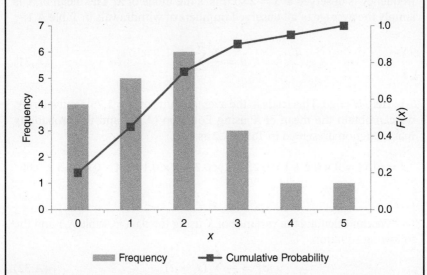

FIGURE A.2 Frequency plot of a random variable representing number of withdrawals of 20 customers over the past 30 days, along with the corresponding cumulative probabilities

(*continued*)

(*continued*)

as a histogram, of this random variable. Here each possible value of X is presented in a separate bin. In a frequency plot when the number of possible values of a random variable is large, we can group several of them in separate bins. Then each bar indicates the frequency of all possible values that are grouped in a specific bin. Figure A.2 also presents the cumulative probability of each possible value of the random variable X.

Having the probability mass function of the random variable defined, we can obtain the median of X using the definition presented in Equation (A.29). From Table A.2 we can verify that:

$$P(X \leq 2) = 0.2 + 0.25 + 0.3 = 0.75 \geq \frac{1}{2}$$

and

$$P(X \geq 2) = 0.05 + 0.05 + 0.15 + 0.3 = 0.55 \geq \frac{1}{2}$$

Therefore $m = 2$ is the median of X. Also, from Table A.2 the highest frequency is observed at $x = 2$ so this is the mode of X. The mean of X is simply the average of all observed numbers of withdrawals in Table A.1:

$$\mu = \frac{1}{N} \sum_{i=1}^{N} x_i \tag{A.31}$$

Here $N = 20$. This leads to the average value of $\mu = 1.75$. Equivalently, we can obtain the mean of X using Equation (A.20) and the probability mass function presented in Table A.2 as:

$$\mu = E[X] = 0 \times 0.2 + 1 \times 0.25 + 2 \times 0.3 + 3 \times 0.15 + 4 \times 0.05 + 5 \times 0.05$$

$$= 1.75$$

We can calculate the variance of X using the data in Table A.1 and the following equation:

$$\sigma^2 = \frac{1}{N} \sum_{i=1}^{N} (x_i - \mu)^2 \tag{A.32}$$

This is equivalent to the definition of variance provided in Equation (A.26). Using $\mu = 1.75$ calculated previously, this leads to the variance of $\sigma^2 = 1.7875$. Equivalently, we can obtain the variance of

X using Equation (A.26) and the probability mass function presented in Table A.2 as:

$$\sigma^2 = E[(X - \mu)^2]$$

$$= (0 - 1.75)^2 \times 0.2 + (1 - 1.75)^2 \times 0.25 + (2 - 1.75)^2 \times 0.3$$

$$+ (3 - 1.75)^2 \times 0.15 + (4 - 1.75)^2 \times 0.05 + (5 - 1.75)^2 \times 0.05$$

$$= 1.7875$$

As noted, for this random variable the median and mode are equal, but the value of the mean is different.

Example

Consider continuous random variable X with the following probability density function:

$$f_X(x) = \begin{cases} \frac{3}{2}x - \frac{3}{4}x^2 & \text{If } 0 \le x \le 2 \\ 0 & \text{Otherwise} \end{cases}$$

The mean of this random variable is calculated using Equation (A.21) as:

$$E[X] = \int_0^2 x\left(\frac{3}{2}x - \frac{3}{4}x^2\right) dx = \int_0^2 \left(\frac{3}{2}x^2 - \frac{3}{4}x^3\right) dx$$

$$= \left(\frac{1}{2}x^3 - \frac{3}{16}x^4\right)\Bigg|_0^2 = 4 - 3 = 1 \longleftarrow mean$$

The median of X is obtained using Equation (A.30) as:

$$\int_0^m \left(\frac{3}{2}x - \frac{3}{4}x^2\right) dx = \frac{1}{2}$$

(continued)

(*continued*)

or

$$\left(\frac{3}{4}x^2 - \frac{1}{4}x^3\right)\Bigg|_0^m = \frac{1}{2}$$

$$\frac{3}{4}m^2 - \frac{1}{4}m^3 = \frac{1}{2} \qquad \Longrightarrow \qquad m = 1 \longleftarrow median$$

To find the mode of X we need to find the value of x that maximizes the probability density function of the random variable. We can find that point by taking the first derivative of f_X and setting it equal to zero as:

$$\frac{d}{dx}\left(\frac{3}{2}x - \frac{3}{4}x^2\right) = 0 \quad \Rightarrow \quad \frac{3}{2} - \frac{3}{2}x = 0 \quad \Rightarrow \quad x = 1 \longleftarrow mode$$

For this random variable mean, median, and mode are all equal to 1. This is not always the case and these three central tendency measurements are not always equal. The distribution of the random variable in our example is symmetric, which resulted in the mean, mode, and median being equal. We can use Equation (A.27) to calculate the variance of X. To do this, first we need to obtain $E[X^2]$ using Equation (A.23) as:

$$E[X^2] = \int_0^2 x^2\left(\frac{3}{2}x - \frac{3}{4}x^2\right)dx = \int_0^2 \left(\frac{3}{2}x^3 - \frac{3}{4}x^4\right)dx$$

$$= \left(\frac{3}{8}x^4 - \frac{3}{20}x^5\right)\Bigg|_0^2 = 6 - \frac{24}{5} = \frac{6}{5}$$

$$\mathrm{Var}[X] = E[X^2] - (E[X])^2 = \frac{6}{5} - 1^2 = \frac{1}{5}$$

PERCENTILE

The p*th percentile* of a continuous probability distribution divides the distribution such that $100p\%$ of the probability is below that value and $100(1-p)\%$ is higher than that value. Based on the definition of median, the 50th percentile is the median. The 25th and 75th percentiles are known as lower and upper *quartiles*.

For a discrete probability distribution, percentile is defined similarly. Assume that $x_1, x_2, \ldots, x_n$ are n members of a dataset. Such a dataset could be the state space of a discrete random variable or a sample from it. Assume that $x_{(1)}, x_{(2)}, \ldots, x_{(n)}$ is that dataset ordered in an ascending fashion. This ordered dataset is known as the *order statistic* of the original set. Percentile $x_{(p)}$ is a value from this order statistic where at most $100p\%$ of the original data are less than $x_{(p)}$ and at most $100(1 - p)\%$ are greater than $x_{(p)}$. There is no unique method for the computation of a percentile for a discrete dataset. Hyndman and Fan (1996) provided a comprehensive review of different methods used in common statistical packages. In the following we review a few of such methods. Here we use the notation $\lceil x \rceil$ to indicate the smallest integer not less than x and $\lfloor x \rfloor$ to indicate the largest integer not greater than x.

Method 1

The simplest method to obtain the percentile $x_{(p)}$ is to choose the value from the ordered dataset with the rank nearest to np, or more precisely the value $x_{(k)}$ from the order statistics at rank $k = \lceil np \rceil$, where $0 \leq p \leq 1$. For cases of $k = 0$ and $k = n$ we choose the smallest and largest member of the dataset as the target percentile, respectively. When a dataset is large this method provides a fast and easy way to obtain a percentile.

Method 2

In this method we first compute $(n + 1)p$ and break it into two parts: an integer part k and a fraction part f:

$$K + f = (n + 1)p \tag{A.33}$$

where $0 < p < 1$. The target percentile is obtained using an interpolation method as:[1]

$$\text{For } 0 < k < n: \ X_{(p)} = X_{(k)} + f \times (X_{(k+1)} - X_{(k)}) \tag{A.34}$$

$$\text{For } = 0: \ X_{(p)} = X_{(1)}$$

$$\text{For } k \geq n: \ X_{(p)} = X_{(n)}$$

Method 3

In this method we first compute $(n-1)p+1$ and break it into two parts: an integer part k and a fraction part f:

$$K + f = (n-1)p + 1 \tag{A.35}$$

where $0 \leq p \leq 1$. The target percentile is then obtained using the following interpolation:[2]

$$X_{(p)} = X_{(k)} + f \times (X_{(k+1)} - X_{(k)}) \tag{A.36}$$

Example

Consider the following ordered dataset:

Rank	Value
1	45
2	50
3	67
4	77
5	78
6	89
7	100
8	125
9	134
10	135

We can use the three methods described earlier to obtain the 25th and 50th percentiles as follows:

Method 1

Since for the 25th percentile $p = 0.25$ and here $n = 10$, the percentile is the value at rank $\lceil 10 \times 0.25 \rceil = \lceil 2.5 \rceil = 3$. So the 25th percentile is 67. The rank of the 50th percentile, which is the median, is $\lceil 10 \times 0.50 \rceil = \lceil 5 \rceil = 5$. From the preceding table, the 50th percentile is 78.

Method 2

For the 25th percentile we have $(n + 1)p = (10 + 1) \times 0.25 = 2.75$. Therefore $k = 2$ and $f = 0.75$. So:

$$25\text{th percentile} = X_{(2)} + 0.75 \times (X_{(3)} - X_{(2)})$$

$$= 50 + 0.75 \times (67 - 50) = 62.75$$

For the 50th percentile we have: $(n + 1)p = (10 + 1) \times 0.5 = 5.5$. So $k = 5$ and $f = 0.5$ and the percentile value is obtained as:

$$50\text{th percentile} = X_{(5)} + 0.5 \times (X_{(6)} - X_{(5)}) = 78 + 0.5 \times (89 - 78) = 83.5$$

Method 3

For the 25th percentile we have: $(n - 1)p + 1 = (10 - 1) \times 0.25 + 1 = 3.25$. Therefore $k = 3, f = 0.25$, and we have:

$$25\text{th percentile} = X_{(3)} + 0.25 \times (X_{(4)} - X_{(3)})$$

$$= 67 + 0.25 \times (77 - 67) = 69.5$$

For the 50th percentile we have: $(n - 1)p + 1 = (10 - 1) \times 0.5 + 1 = 5.5$. So $k = 5, f = 0.5$, and the percentile value is:

$$50th\ percentile = X_{(5)} + 0.5 \times (X_{(6)} - X_{(5)}) = 78 + 0.5 \times (89 - 78) = 83.5$$

As noted above, these methods can lead to different results for a target percentile. As the number of members in the dataset increases, the obtained percentile values from different methods converge to similar results.

COVARIANCE AND CORRELATION

Variance is a measurement of the variability of one random variable. *Covariance* extends that concept to two or more random variables and captures how those variables vary together. It is a measurement of the association between two random variables. The covariance of two random variables X and Y is defined as:

$$Cov[X, Y] = E[(X - E[X])(Y - E[Y])] \qquad (A.37)$$

The value of a covariance can be positive, zero, or negative. When the covariance of two random variables is positive, if the value of one variable increases, the value of the other one also increases, and when the value of one variable decreases, the value of the other one decreases as well. However, the magnitude of the change between the two variables does not necessarily need to be the same. A negative covariance is an indication that two random variables do not change in the same direction. If two random variables are independent, their covariance is zero, but the converse is not always true. It can be shown that the covariance of X and Y can also be obtained using:

$$Cov[X, Y] = E[XY] - E[X]E[Y] \qquad (A.38)$$

A few important properties of covariance are as follows:

- $Cov[X, Y] = Cov[Y, X]$
- $Cov[X, X] = Var[X]$
- $Var[X + Y] = Var[X] + Var[Y] + 2Cov[X, Y]$
- $Cov[aX + b, cY + d] = ac\, Cov[X, Y]$
- $Cov[X_1 + X_2, Y] = Cov[X_1, Y] + Cov[X_2, Y]$

The variance and covariance of several random variables are often summarized in a *variance-covariance matrix*. This is a square matrix in which the diagonal elements of the matrix are the variances of individual random variables and the off-diagonal elements are the covariances between pairs of variables.

Correlation between two random variables is the covariance of them normalized by their variances. It is a measurement of the linear relationship between two variables. The correlation of random variables X and Y is defined as:

$$Corr[X, Y] = \frac{Cov[X, Y]}{\sqrt{Var[X]Var[Y]}} \qquad (A.39)$$

A ρ notation is often used to show the correlation. ρ is a real number between -1 and 1. The correlation of two independent random variables is zero but the converse is not always true.

CONDITIONAL EXPECTATION AND CONDITIONAL VARIANCE

In order to define conditional expectation and conditional variance, first we need to define the concept of conditional probability and conditional probability distribution. *Conditional probability* is the probability of an event given that another event has occurred. Assume that X and Y are two discrete random variables. The probability of random variable X having value x condition to random variable Y having value y, that is, $P(X = x|Y = y)$, is given as:

$$P(X = x|Y = y) = \frac{P(X = x \text{ and } Y = y)}{P(Y = y)} \tag{A.40}$$

Based on the conditional probability defined in Equation (A.40) and assuming X and Y have joint probability mass function $f_{X,Y}$ and marginal distributions of g_X and h_Y, the *conditional probability mass function* of random variable X given that $Y = y$ when $h_Y(y) > 0$ is defined as:

$$w_{X|Y}(x|y) = \frac{f_{X,Y}(x,y)}{h_Y(y)} \tag{A.41}$$

Similarly, the conditional probability mass function of random variable Y given $X = x$ when $g_X(x) > 0$ is defined as:

$$\omega_{Y|X}(y|x) = \frac{f_{X,Y}(x,y)}{g_X(x)} \tag{A.42}$$

In Equations (A.41) and (A.42) we used two distinct notations of $w_{X|Y}$ and $\omega_{Y|X}$ to emphasize that the conditional distribution of X given $Y = y$ and the conditional distribution of Y given $X = x$ are two different functions. Using the analogy between probability mass function and probability density function, the definitions given in (A.41) and (A.42) are also applicable if X and Y are two continuous random variables, with a joint probability density function of $f_{X,Y}$ and marginal distributions of g_X and h_Y.

If two random variables X and Y are independent, using Equation (A.19) we can show:

$$w_{X|Y}(x|y) = g_X(x) \tag{A.43}$$

$$\omega_{Y|X}(y|x) = h_Y(y) \tag{A.44}$$

The *conditional expectation* of X given $Y = y$ is the mean of the conditional distribution of X given $Y = y$, that is, $w_{X|Y}(x|y)$, and if X and Y are discrete random variables, it is defined as:

$$E[X|y] = \sum_x x\, w_{X|Y}(x|y) \qquad (A.45)$$

If X and Y are continuous random variables, the conditional expectation of X given $Y = y$ is defined as:

$$E[X|y] = \int_{-\infty}^{+\infty} x\, w_{X|Y}(x|y)\, dx \qquad (A.46)$$

It should be noted that since $w_{X|Y}(x|y)$ is a function of both x and y, $E[X|y]$, which is the summation or integral over all x values, itself is a function of y. To generalize, we can define the conditional expectation of X given Y, $E[X|Y]$, as a random variable that is a function of random variable Y, with its own probability distribution function. In other words, $E[X|Y]$ is a random variable whose value is equal to $E[X|y]$ as defined in Equations (A.45) and (A.46) when $Y = y$.

Similarly, for two discrete random variables X and Y the conditional expectation of Y given $X = x$ is defined as:

$$E[Y|x] = \sum_y y\, \omega_{Y|X}(y|x) \qquad (A.47)$$

And for two continuous random variables X and Y, the conditional expectation of Y given $X = x$ is defined as:

$$E[Y|x] = \int_{-\infty}^{+\infty} y\, \omega_{Y|X}(y|x)\, dy \qquad (A.48)$$

Since $E[X|Y]$ is a random variable, it can be shown that its expectation is equal to the expectation of X (DeGroot 1989):

$$E[E[X|Y]\,] = E[X] \qquad (A.49)$$

Following the same approach, the *conditional variance* of X given $Y = y$ is defined as:

$$\mathrm{Var}[X|y] = E[(X - E[X/y])^2|y] \qquad (A.50)$$

This is the variance of random variable X when we know that random variable Y has a value of y. $\mathrm{Var}[X|y]$ is a function of y. It can be shown that $\mathrm{Var}[X|y]$ is also given as:

$$\mathrm{Var}[X|y] = E[X^2|y] - (E[X|y])^2 \qquad (A.51)$$

Similar to our discussion of conditional expectation, we can define $\text{Var}[X|Y]$ as a random variable that is a function of random variable Y. That is, $\text{Var}[X|Y]$ is a random variable whose value is equal to $\text{Var}[X|y]$ as defined in Equations (A.50) and (A.51) when $Y = y$.

BINOMIAL DISTRIBUTION

Binomial distribution is a discrete distribution representing the number of successes in a series of independent trials when each trial is either a success or failure. In finance, binomial distribution is often used in credit risk modeling. If X is a random variable with a binomial distribution representing the number of successes in total n trials and the probability of success in each trial is p, the probability of getting exactly x success, that is, $P(X = x)$, is obtained using the probability density function of the binomial distribution:

$$f_X(x) = \binom{n}{x} p^x (1-p)^{n-x} \tag{A.52}$$

where $= 0, 1, \ldots, n$, $0 < p < 1$ and

$$\binom{n}{x} = \frac{n!}{x!(n-x)!} \tag{A.53}$$

The binomial distribution has two parameters, n: total number of trials and p: probability of success in a trial. The notation $X \sim B(n, p)$ is often used to indicate that random variable X has a binomial distribution with parameters n and p. The mean and variance of the binomial distribution are:

$$E[X] = np \tag{A.54}$$

$$\text{Var}[X] = np(1-p) \tag{A.55}$$

The cumulative distribution function of the binomial distribution is expressed as:

$$F_X(k) = P(X \le k) = \sum_{i=0}^{\lfloor k \rfloor} \binom{n}{i} p^i (1-p)^{n-i} \tag{A.56}$$

where $\lfloor k \rfloor$ denotes the largest integer less than or equal to k. Figure A.3 presents the probability density function and cumulative distribution function of the binomial distribution for three different sets of parameter values. For p values close to 0.5 the distribution becomes more symmetric.

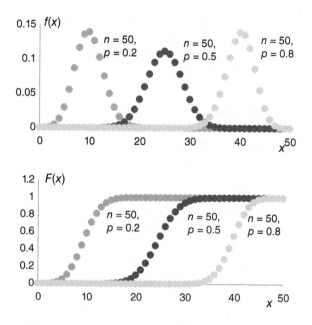

FIGURE A.3 Probability density function and cumulative distribution function of binomial distribution with different parameter values

NORMAL DISTRIBUTION

A random variable that has a *normal distribution* can assume any values between $-\infty$ and $+\infty$ while concentrated around a certain value. Normal distribution is a continuous distribution widely used in science, engineering, and finance, where many analyses are based on the assumption of normal distribution for the underlying random variable. For example, return on investment in an equity security (stock) is often assumed to have a normal distribution. Normal distribution has two parameters: a location parameter μ and a scale parameter σ. The location parameter is the mean of the variable, which is the value of the central tendency point; the scale parameter is the standard deviation of the variable, which is the measurement of the dispersion around the central tendency point. Hence, the expectation and variance of a random variable with a normal distribution with parameters μ and σ are:

$$E[X] = \mu \tag{A.57}$$

$$\text{Var}[X] = \sigma^2 \tag{A.58}$$

The notation $X \sim N(\mu, \sigma^2)$ is often used to indicate that random variable X has a normal distribution with mean μ and variance σ^2. The median and mode of a normal distribution are equal to its mean μ. The probability density function of the normal distribution is as follows:

$$f_X(x) = \frac{1}{\sigma\sqrt{2\pi}} exp\left(-\frac{(x-\mu)^2}{2\sigma^2}\right) \qquad (A.59)$$

where $-\infty < x < +\infty$. There is no closed form for the cumulative distribution function of the normal distribution and it is evaluated numerically. The probability density and cumulative distribution functions of a normally distributed random variable with a mean of 0 and variance of 1 are presented in Figure A.4.

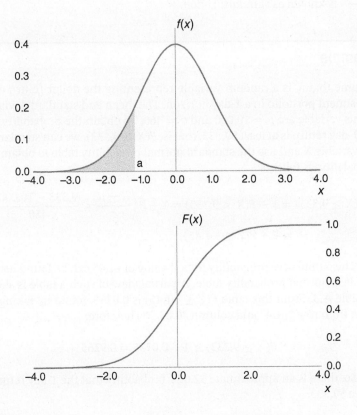

FIGURE A.4 Probability density function and cumulative distribution function of normal distribution with $\mu = 0$ and $\sigma = 1$. The shaded area in the graph is $P(X \leq a)$.

It can be shown that if $X \sim N(\mu, \sigma^2)$, random variable $Z = \frac{X-\mu}{\sigma}$ has a normal distribution with mean 0 and variance 1. This distribution is known as the *standard normal distribution*, hence: $Z \sim N(0, 1)$. The cumulative probability of the standard normal distribution is tabulated and can be used to obtain the cumulative probability of a random variable that has a normal distribution with any mean and variance. If $X \sim N(\mu, \sigma^2)$ we have:

$$F_X(x) = P(X \le x) = P\left(\frac{X-\mu}{\sigma} \le \frac{x-\mu}{\sigma}\right) = P\left(Z \le \frac{x-\mu}{\sigma}\right) = \Phi\left(\frac{x-\mu}{\sigma}\right)$$

$$(A.60)$$

where $\Phi(.)$ is the cumulative distribution function of the standard normal distribution. The process of changing random variable X to random variable $Z = \frac{X-\mu}{\sigma}$ is known as *standardization*.

Example

Assume that X is a random variable representing the dollar return of an investment portfolio in a 1-day horizon. The mean and standard deviation of this variable are $\mu = 10,000$ and $\sigma = 460$. To obtain the probability that the 1-day return is at least \$9,333, that is, $P(X \ge 9,333)$, we can standardize the variable X and use the standard normal probability table to obtain this probability, as follows:

$$P(X \ge 9,333) = 1 - P(X < 9,333) = 1 - P\left(\frac{X-\mu}{\sigma} < \frac{9,333 - 10,000}{460}\right)$$

$$= 1 - P(Z \le -1.45)$$

The cumulative probability for a Z-value of -1.45 can be found using a standard normal probability table. A partial view of such a table is shown in Table A.3. From this table $P(Z \le -1.45)$ is 0.0735, found by taking the value from row "-1.4" and column "0.05."[3] Therefore:

$$P(X \ge 9,333) \cong 1 - 0.0735 = 0.9265$$

So, there is an approximate 92.65% probability that the 1-day return is above \$9,333.

TABLE A.3 Partial view of the standard normal probability table

	0	0.01	0.02	0.03	0.04	0.05	0.06	0.07	0.08	0.09
...	...	...	...	...	...	...	...	...	...	...
−1.5	0.0668	0.0655	0.0643	0.0630	0.0618	0.0606	0.0594	0.0582	0.0571	0.0559
−1.4	0.0808	0.0793	0.0778	0.0764	0.0749	**0.0735**	0.0721	0.0708	0.0694	0.0681
−1.3	0.0968	0.0951	0.0934	0.0918	0.0901	0.0885	0.0869	0.0853	0.0838	0.0823
...	...	...	...	...	...	...	...	...	...	...
1.3	0.9032	0.9049	0.9066	0.9082	0.9099	0.9115	0.9131	0.9147	0.9162	0.9177
1.4	0.9192	0.9207	0.9222	0.9236	0.9251	0.9265	0.9279	0.9292	0.9306	0.9319
1.5	0.9332	0.9345	0.9357	0.9370	0.9382	0.9394	0.9406	0.9418	0.9429	0.9441
...	...	...	...	...	...	...	...	...	...	...

It can be shown that if $X_1, X_2, \ldots, X_n$ are n independent random variables normally distributed with means $\mu_1, \mu_2, \ldots, \mu_n$ and variances $\sigma_1^2, \sigma_2^2, \ldots, \sigma_n^2$, a linear combination of these variables in the form of $a_1 X_1 + a_2 X_2 + \cdots + a_n X_n$ where $a_1, a_2, \ldots, a_n$ are real numbers, also has a normal distribution with a mean of $a_1 \mu_1 + a_2 \mu_2 + \cdots + a_n \mu_n$ and a variance of $a_1^2 \sigma_1^2 + a_2^2 \sigma_2^2 + \cdots + a_n^2 \sigma_n^2$. Moreover, the *central limit theorem* states that if $X_1, X_2, \ldots, X_n$ are n independent random variables with an arbitrary distribution with means $\mu_1, \mu_2, \ldots, \mu_n$ and variances $\sigma_1^2, \sigma_2^2, \ldots, \sigma_n^2$, then the random variable

$$\frac{\sum_{i=1}^{n} X_i - \sum_{i=1}^{n} \mu_i}{\sqrt{\sum_{i=1}^{n} \sigma_i^2}}$$

has the standard normal distribution as n approaches infinity. This theory implies that, for large n and regardless of the distribution of individual independent variables, their sum is approximately normally distributed. This is an important result when the distribution of the mean of a sample is studied.

LOGNORMAL DISTRIBUTION

A random variable that has a *lognormal distribution* can assume any values between 0 and $+\infty$. Lognormal distribution is a continuous distribution often used in finance to model variables that are naturally positive, such as commodity prices. When a random variable has a lognormal distribution the logarithm of that variable has a normal distribution. So, if X is a random variable with a lognormal distribution, then $ln(X) \sim N(\mu, \sigma^2)$. Lognormal distribution has two parameters, μ and σ; however, these are not the location and scale parameters of the distribution. The probability density function of a lognormal distribution is:

$$f_X(x) = \frac{1}{x\,\sigma\sqrt{2\pi}} exp\left(-\frac{(\ln x - \mu)^2}{2\sigma^2}\right) \tag{A.61}$$

The mean and variance of the random variable X with a lognormal distribution are:

$$E[X] = exp\left(\mu + \frac{\sigma^2}{2}\right) \tag{A.62}$$

$$Var[X] = [exp(\sigma^2) - 1]\,exp(2\mu + \sigma^2) \tag{A.63}$$

It can be shown that the cumulative distribution function of the random variable X with a lognormal distribution can be expressed based on the parameters of the random variable $ln(X) \sim N(\mu, \sigma^2)$ as follows:

$$F_X(x) = P(X \leq x) = \Phi\left(\frac{\ln x - \mu}{\sigma}\right) \tag{A.64}$$

Figure A.5 presents the density function and cumulative distribution function of the lognormal distribution for a few different parameter values.

MULTIVARIATE NORMAL DISTRIBUTION

A multivariate normal distribution is a generalization of a univariate normal distribution. In a d-dimensional space the probability density function of a multivariate normal distribution is:

$$f(\boldsymbol{x}) = \frac{1}{(2\pi)^{d/2}|\boldsymbol{\Sigma}|^{1/2}} exp\left(-\frac{1}{2}(\boldsymbol{x} - \boldsymbol{\mu})^T\boldsymbol{\Sigma}^{-1}(\boldsymbol{x} - \boldsymbol{\mu})\right) \tag{A.65}$$

where $\boldsymbol{x} \in \mathbb{R}^d$, $\boldsymbol{\mu}$ is the mean vector $(1 \times d)$, and $\boldsymbol{\Sigma}$ is the symmetric and positive definite[4] variance-covariance matrix $(d \times d)$. Here we use bold characters to represent vectors or matrixes. We use $\boldsymbol{X} \sim N_d(\boldsymbol{\mu}, \boldsymbol{\Sigma})$ to indicate that random vector $\boldsymbol{X}$ has a d-dimensional multivariate normal distribution with mean $\boldsymbol{\mu}$

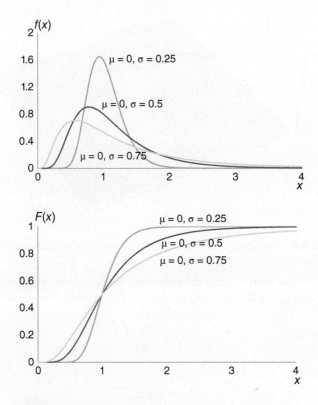

FIGURE A.5 Probability density function and cumulative distribution function of lognormal distribution with different parameter values

and variance Σ. Figure A.6 presents a graph of the probability density function of a bivariate normal distribution with $\boldsymbol{\mu} = \{0, 0\}$ and $\boldsymbol{\Sigma} = \begin{Bmatrix} 1 & 0 \\ 0 & 1 \end{Bmatrix}$.

If $\boldsymbol{X}$ has a multivariate normal distribution $\boldsymbol{X} \sim N_d(\boldsymbol{\mu}, \boldsymbol{\Sigma})$, any linear transformation $\boldsymbol{Y} = \boldsymbol{A}\boldsymbol{X} + \boldsymbol{C}$ ($\boldsymbol{A} : q \times d$, $\boldsymbol{C} : d \times 1$) also has a multivariate normal distribution as $\boldsymbol{Y} \sim N_q(\boldsymbol{A}\boldsymbol{\mu} + \boldsymbol{C}, \boldsymbol{A}\boldsymbol{\Sigma}\boldsymbol{A}^T)$. If random vector $\boldsymbol{X}$ has a multivariate normal distribution with mean $\boldsymbol{\mu}$ and variance $\boldsymbol{\Sigma}$, then the ith component X_i has a normal distribution with mean μ_i and variance σ_i^2 where μ_i is the ith member of the mean vector and σ_i^2 is the diagonal member of $\boldsymbol{\Sigma}$ at row i and column i. We have:

$$\text{Cov}[X_i, X_j] = E[(X_i - \mu_i)(X_j - \mu_j)] = \sigma_{ij} \qquad (A.66)$$

$$\text{Var}[X_i] = E[(X_i - \mu_i)^2] = \sigma_{ii} = \sigma_i^2 \qquad (A.67)$$

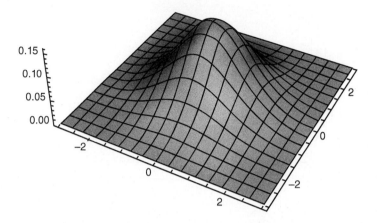

FIGURE A.6   Probability density function of a bivariate normal distribution

Here we use both σ_{ii} and σ_i^2 notations to denote the variance of component X_i and σ_i for its standard deviation. The correlation between X_i and X_j is:

$$\rho_{ij} = \frac{\sigma_{ij}}{\sigma_i \sigma_j} \tag{A.68}$$

Or equivalently:

$$\sigma_{ij} = \sigma_i \sigma_j \rho_{ij}$$

Using these notations, the variance-covariance matrix Σ can be presented as:

$$\Sigma = \begin{bmatrix} \sigma_{11} & \sigma_{12} & \cdots & \sigma_{1d} \\ \sigma_{21} & \sigma_{22} & \cdots & \sigma_{2d} \\ \vdots & \vdots & \ddots & \vdots \\ \sigma_{d1} & \sigma_{d2} & \cdots & \sigma_{dd} \end{bmatrix}$$

This matrix can be also presented using correlation and variance matrixes separately as:

$$\Sigma = \begin{bmatrix} \sigma_1 & & & \\ & \sigma_2 & & \\ & & \ddots & \\ & & & \sigma_d \end{bmatrix} \begin{bmatrix} \rho_{11} & \rho_{12} & \cdots & \rho_{1d} \\ \rho_{21} & \rho_{22} & \cdots & \rho_{2d} \\ \vdots & \vdots & \ddots & \vdots \\ \rho_{d1} & d_{d2} & \cdots & \rho_{dd} \end{bmatrix} \begin{bmatrix} \sigma_1 & & & \\ & \sigma_2 & & \\ & & \ddots & \\ & & & \sigma_d \end{bmatrix} \tag{A.69}$$

Note that in Equation (A.69) $\sigma_i = \sqrt{\sigma_{ii}}$ is the standard deviation of component X_i and $\rho_{ij} = \rho_{ji}$.

Consider a vector of standard normal variables $Z \sim N_d(\mathbf{0}, I)$ where $\mathbf{0}$ is the zero vector and I is the identity matrix. From the linear transformation property discussed earlier, random vector $X = \mu + AZ$ has a multivariate normal distribution $X \sim N_d(\mu, AA^T)$. This can be used to generate correlated random instances from the $N_d(\mu, \Sigma)$ distribution. To do this we can generate independent random instance vector Z where components have the standard normal distribution and then transform that vector to random instance vector X using $X = \mu + AZ$ condition to $A^T = \Sigma$. This requires us to find matrix A such that it satisfies this condition. Cholesky decomposition, explained next, is a technique to find such a matrix.

Cholesky Decomposition

Cholesky decomposition is a method for the factorization of a positive definite matrix, such as a variance-covariance matrix, into a triangular matrix A and its transpose A^T such that $AA^T = \Sigma$. Assume that matrix A is defined as:

$$A = \begin{bmatrix} A_{11} & & & \\ A_{21} & A_{22} & & \\ \vdots & \vdots & \ddots & \\ A_{d1} & A_{d2} & \cdots & A_{dd} \end{bmatrix}$$

Then for identity $AA^T = \Sigma$ to hold we have:

$$\begin{bmatrix} A_{11} & & & \\ A_{21} & A_{22} & & \\ \vdots & \vdots & \ddots & \\ A_{d1} & A_{d2} & \cdots & A_{dd} \end{bmatrix} \begin{bmatrix} A_{11} & A_{21} & \cdots & A_{d1} \\ & A_{22} & \cdots & A_{d2} \\ & & \ddots & \vdots \\ & & & A_{dd} \end{bmatrix} = \begin{bmatrix} \sigma_{11} & \sigma_{12} & \cdots & \sigma_{1d} \\ \sigma_{21} & \sigma_{22} & \cdots & \sigma_{2d} \\ \vdots & \vdots & \ddots & \vdots \\ \sigma_{d1} & \sigma_{d2} & \cdots & \sigma_{dd} \end{bmatrix}$$

From this, the following equations are obtained:

$$A_{11}^2 = \sigma_{11}$$
$$A_{21} A_{11} = \sigma_{21}$$
$$\vdots$$
$$A_{d1}^2 + A_{d2}^2 + \cdots + A_{dd}^2 = \sigma_{dd}$$

Having members of matrix Σ available, this set of equations can be solved recursively to obtain members of matrix A. This calculation can be summarized as:

$$A_{ii} = \left(\sigma_{ii} - \sum_{k=1}^{i-1} A_{ik}^2 \right)^{1/2} \tag{A.70}$$

$$A_{ij} = \frac{1}{A_{jj}} \left(\sigma_{ij} - \sum_{k=1}^{j-1} A_{ik} A_{jk} \right) \quad \text{for } j < i \qquad (A.71)$$

The pseudocode in List A.1 provides an implementation of this calculation.

LIST 1: Pseudocode to obtain Cholesky decomposition lower triangular matrix

```
S: Square matrix to be factorized
d: Size of S
A: Cholesky lower triangular matrix
For i = 1 To d
    For j = 1 To d
        Sum = S(i, j)

        For k = 1 To i - 1
            Sum = Sum - A(i, k) * A(j, k)
        Next k

        If i = j Then
            A(i, i) = Sqr(Sum)
        ElseIf i < j Then
            A(j, i) = Sum / A(i, i)
        End If
    Next j
Next i
```

Example

Consider the following variance-covariance matrix:

$$\Sigma = \begin{bmatrix} 4.5 & 1.2 & 0.7 \\ 1.2 & 2.3 & 1.6 \\ 0.7 & 1.6 & 2.8 \end{bmatrix}$$

To obtain the lower triangular Cholesky matrix A that factorizes Σ, using Equations (A.70) and (A.71) we have:

$$A_{11} = \sqrt{\sigma_{11}} = 2.1213$$

$$A_{21} = \frac{1}{A_{11}} (\sigma_{21}) = \frac{1}{2.1213} (1.2) = 0.5675$$

$$A_{22} = \sqrt{\sigma_{22} - (A_{21}{}^2)} = \sqrt{2.3 - (0.5675^2)} = 1.4071$$

$$A_{31} = \frac{1}{A_{11}}(\sigma_{31}) = \frac{1}{2.1213}(0.7) = 0.3300$$

$$A_{32} = \frac{1}{A_{22}}(\sigma_{32} - (A_{31}A_{21})) = \frac{1}{1.4071}(1.6 - (0.3300 \times 0.5675)) = 1.0044$$

$$A_{33} = \sqrt{\sigma_{33} - (A_{31}{}^2 + A_{32}{}^2)} = \sqrt{2.8 - (0.3300^2 + 1.0044^2)} = 1.2970$$

$$A = \begin{bmatrix} 2.1213 & & \\ 0.5657 & 1.4071 & \\ 0.3300 & 1.0044 & 1.2970 \end{bmatrix}$$

It is easy to verify that matrix A as defined here satisfies: $AA^T = \Sigma$.

The triangularity of matrix A reduces the number of calculation steps needed for the factorization of Σ. When A is obtained it can be used in $X = \mu + AZ$ to transform independent random vector $Z \sim N_d(0, I)$ to correlated random vector $X \sim N_d(\mu, AA^T)$. This is helpful in the Monte Carlo simulation when a set of correlated random instances from normal distribution is needed. We can create uncorrelated random instances from $N_d(0, I)$ and transform them into corrected random instances from $N_d(\mu, \Sigma)$ using the transformation explained here.

Example

To demonstrate the use of Cholesky decomposition in generating correlated random instances, consider a multivariate normal distribution with the following mean and variance-covariance matrixes:

$$\mu = \begin{bmatrix} 12.8 \\ 13.5 \\ 11.3 \end{bmatrix} \quad \Sigma = \begin{bmatrix} 4.5 & 1.2 & 0.7 \\ 1.2 & 2.3 & 1.6 \\ 0.7 & 1.6 & 2.8 \end{bmatrix}$$

In the previous example the A matrix that satisfies $AA^T = \Sigma$ is obtained as:

$$A = \begin{bmatrix} 2.1213 & & \\ 0.5657 & 1.4071 & \\ 0.3300 & 1.0044 & 1.2970 \end{bmatrix}$$

(continued)

(*continued*)

Now consider a random vector Z_1, whose components are generated randomly and independently from the standard normal distribution:

$$Z_1 = \begin{bmatrix} -0.8 \\ 1.3 \\ 0.55 \end{bmatrix}$$

To generate a random instance X_1 from a multivariate normal distribution with the preceding mean and variance-covariance matrixes we can transform random vector Z_1 to X_1 using $X_1 = \mu + AZ_1$, as follows:

$$X_1 = \mu + AZ_1 = \begin{bmatrix} 12.8 \\ 13.5 \\ 11.3 \end{bmatrix} + \begin{bmatrix} 2.1213 & & \\ 0.5657 & 1.4071 & \\ 0.3300 & 1.0044 & 1.2970 \end{bmatrix} \begin{bmatrix} -0.8 \\ 1.3 \\ 0.55 \end{bmatrix} = \begin{bmatrix} 11.1030 \\ 14.8767 \\ 13.0551 \end{bmatrix}$$

While components of random vector Z_1 are uncorrelated, components of random vector X_1 are correlated based on correlations embedded in variance-covariance matrix Σ.

SAMPLING

In statistics, the term *population* is often used to denote a large group of elements having some common features. For example, all accounts in a credit card portfolio can be considered as a population. A *sample* is a subset of the population that is selected to represent the entire group. Statistical analysis based on a sample has several advantages. First, it is often cheaper and less time consuming to perform the analysis based on a subset of the population rather than on the entire group. Second, sometimes an analysis using the entire population is not feasible. For example, consider a quality control test that is destructive. Performing such a test on the entire population is simply not feasible and such a test can only be applied to a sample. Third, sometimes an analysis performed on a properly selected sample provides more accurate results than performing that analysis on the entire population, if a larger analysis increases the chance of human or computational errors.

In a *non-probabilistic sampling*, a subset of the population members is selected without utilizing any probabilistic method in the selection process. For example, consider a case where a market research analyst living in New York City talks to a few of his neighbors to understand the general market awareness of a new product. He has not selected the households based on any probabilistic method; his selection is only based on the convenience of data collection. In a *probabilistic sampling* a subset of members of the population is selected randomly following a probabilistic process. Such a sample is called a *random sample*. Data from a non-probabilistic sample cannot be used for any statistical analysis that assumes a random sample. Random selection of members of a population can be done using a random number generator computer program or using a table of random numbers.

In *simple random sampling* each member of the population has an equal probability of being selected into the sample. This is the most common sampling method. Assume that a population has N members. When we select a sample of n members from this population, every combination of n members from the population has the same chance of being selected as the random sample; n is known as *sample size*. In *statistical inference* a conclusion is drawn for a population based on the analysis performed on a probabilistic sample from that population.

The mean μ and variance σ^2 of the population are calculated using Equations (A.31) and (A.32). For a sample $\{x_1, x_2, \cdots, x_n\}$ sample mean $\bar{x}$ and sample variance s^2 are obtained as follows:

$$\bar{x} = \frac{1}{n}\sum_{i=1}^{n} x_i \tag{A.72}$$

$$s^2 = \frac{1}{n-1}\sum_{i=1}^{n} (x_i - \bar{x})^2 \tag{A.73}$$

Here, n is the sample size and $n - 1$ is referred to as the *degree of freedom*. $\bar{x}$ and s^2 represent the central tendency point and the dispersion measurement of the sample. A consequence of the central limit theorem indicates that, regardless of the distribution of the population, the sample mean as a random variable has an approximately normal distribution with a mean of μ (i.e., equal to the population mean) and a variance of $\frac{\sigma^2}{n}$ (i.e., equal to the population variance divided by the sample size), so $\overline{X} \sim N\left(\mu, \frac{\sigma^2}{n}\right)$.[5]

t-distribution is a probability distribution that is often used in conjunction with sampling.[6] The probability density function of t-distribution is as follows:

$$f(t) = \frac{\Gamma\left(\frac{v+1}{2}\right)}{\sqrt{v\pi}\,\Gamma\left(\frac{v}{2}\right)}\left(1 + \frac{t^2}{v}\right)^{-\frac{v+1}{2}} \qquad -\infty < t < +\infty \tag{A.74}$$

v is the degree of freedom and $\Gamma(.)$ is the gamma function.[7] Similar to the standard normal probability table, probabilities based on t-distribution for different degrees of freedom are tabulated. The mean of t-distribution is 0 and its variance is $\frac{\nu}{\nu-2}$ when $\nu > 2$. As the degree of freedom increases the t-distribution approaches the standard normal distribution. At a limiting case of $\nu \to \infty$, the t-distribution is the same as the standard normal distribution.

One important application of the t-distribution is in determining the distribution of the sample mean when the population variance is unknown. Specifically, for a sample of size n, statistic

$$\frac{\overline{X} - \mu}{\frac{S}{\sqrt{n}}}$$

has a t-distribution with an $n - 1$ degree of freedom. This property can be used in building a confidence interval around a population mean where the population variance is unknown and the sample size is small.

In estimating a parameter, a *confidence interval* is an interval between two values that includes the true value of the parameter, with some probability. When using the sample mean as an estimate of the population mean and when the population variance σ^2 is known, an approximate $100(1 - \alpha)\%$ two-sided confidence interval for the population mean is defined as:

$$\overline{x} - Z_{\frac{\alpha}{2}} \frac{\sigma}{\sqrt{n}} \leq \mu \leq \overline{x} + Z_{\frac{\alpha}{2}} \frac{\sigma}{\sqrt{n}} \tag{A.75}$$

where α is known as *significant level*. For example, for a 95% two-sided confidence interval $\alpha = 0.05$. $Z_{\frac{\alpha}{2}}$ is the Z-value corresponding to probability $\frac{\alpha}{2}$, that is, the inverse of the standard normal cumulative probability distribution function where $P\left(Z \geq Z_{\frac{\alpha}{2}}\right) = \frac{\alpha}{2}$.[8] An interpretation of the confidence interval is that if we resample the population a large number of times and build a $100(1 - \alpha)\%$ confidence interval based on data from each sample, then $100(1 - \alpha)\%$ of those intervals contain the true value of μ (Montgomery 2001). Loosely speaking, when two limits in Equation (A.75) are obtained, we can state that we are $100(1 - \alpha)\%$ confident that the true population mean is between those two limits. Similarly, we can build a one-sided confidence interval for the population mean. An upper $100(1 - \alpha)\%$ confidence interval for μ is:

$$\mu \leq \overline{x} + Z_{\alpha} \frac{\sigma}{\sqrt{n}} \tag{A.76}$$

And a lower $100(1 - \alpha)\%$ confidence interval for μ is:

$$\overline{x} - Z_{\alpha} \frac{\sigma}{\sqrt{n}} \leq \mu \tag{A.77}$$

Note that in one-sided confidence intervals we use Z_{α} and not $Z_{\frac{\alpha}{2}}$.

When the population variance is unknown it can be estimated using s^2 computed from sample data and using Equation (A.73). If the sample size is large ($n \geq 30$), the confidence interval defined in Equation (A.75) can still be used by replacing σ with s. For small sample sizes, assuming the population has a normal distribution, the $100(1 - \alpha)\%$ two-sided confidence interval for the population mean when the population variance is unknown is defined as:

$$\bar{x} - t_{\frac{\alpha}{2},n-1}\frac{s}{\sqrt{n}} \leq \mu \leq \bar{x} + t_{\frac{\alpha}{2},n-1}\frac{s}{\sqrt{n}} \tag{A.78}$$

where $t_{\frac{\alpha}{2},n-1}$ is the inverse of the t-distribution cumulative distribution function with an $n - 1$ degree of freedom such that $P\left(t \geq t_{\frac{\alpha}{2},n-1}\right) = \frac{\alpha}{2}$.[9] An upper $100(1 - \alpha)\%$ confidence interval for μ is:

$$\mu \leq \bar{x} + t_{\alpha,n-1}\frac{s}{\sqrt{n}} \tag{A.79}$$

whereas a lower $100(1 - \alpha)\%$ confidence interval for μ is:

$$\bar{x} - t_{\alpha,n-1}\frac{s}{\sqrt{n}} \leq \mu \tag{A.80}$$

Example

Assume that the following table contains information about the ages of a sample of 20 customers who have home equity line of credit (HELOC) accounts with a bank:

Customer ID	Age	Customer ID	Age
1	45	11	28
2	44	12	33
3	34	13	49
4	23	14	67
5	45	15	66
6	78	16	56
7	34	17	78
8	23	18	22
9	19	19	38
10	25	20	59

(*continued*)

(*continued*)

To build a two-sided 95% confidence interval for the age of the entire population of HELOC account holders, we can use Equation (A.78). If x_i represents the age of account holder i in the sample, the sample mean and sample standard deviation are calculated as:

$$\bar{x} = \frac{1}{20} \sum_{i=1}^{20} x_i = 43.3$$

$$s = \sqrt{\frac{1}{19} \sum_{i=1}^{20} (x_i - 43.3)^2} = 18.7451$$

Since $\alpha = 0.05$ and $n - 1 = 19$, the absolute value of $t_{0.025,19}$ is 2.093, obtained from a t-distribution table or using Microsoft Excel. So assuming that the random variable representing the ages of account holders is approximately normally distributed, a two-sided 95% confidence interval for population age using Equation (A.78) is:

$$43.3 - 2.093 \times \frac{18.7451}{\sqrt{20}} \leq \mu \leq 43.3 + 2.093 \times \frac{18.7451}{\sqrt{20}}$$

or

$$34.52 \leq \mu \leq 52.07$$

Stratified sampling is another probabilistic sampling method in which the selection process is done in two steps. In the first step the population is divided into mutually exclusive and exhaustive subsets, called *strata*. Then in the second step a random set of members is selected from each subset. Stratified sampling can be cost effective, lead to smaller sampling error, and provide statistical information about each subset. To build a confidence interval for population mean when stratified sampling is used and population variance is unknown, we can use Equation (A.78), but sample mean and sample standard deviation are calculated by aggregating the means and standard deviations of samples from subsets by applying the appropriate weights. Assume that population size is N and it is divided into L mutually exclusive and exhaustive subsets with sizes $N_1, N_2, \ldots, N_L$, where $N = N_1 + N_2 + \cdots + N_L$. The sizes of samples selected from these subsets are $n_1, n_2, \ldots, n_L$. If $\bar{x}_1, \bar{x}_2, \ldots, \bar{x}_L$ are sample means calculated using Equation (A.72) and $s_1^2, s_2^2, \ldots, s_L^2$ are sample variances calculated using Equation (A.73), the aggregated sample mean and sample variance are:

$$\bar{x} = \sum_{i=1}^{L} \frac{N_i}{N} \bar{x}_i \tag{A.81}$$

$$s^2 = \sum_{i=1}^{L} \left(\frac{N_i}{N}\right)^2 s_i^2 \tag{A.82}$$

Now consider a proportion of a class or group within a population, for example, the proportion of a bank's customers with checking accounts who also have savings accounts with the same bank. Population proportion is usually shown by π. Consider a sample of n customers with checking accounts who are randomly selected and we noted that x of them also have a savings account with the bank. The sample proportion is $p = x/n$. This is an unbiased estimator of the population proportion. Sample proportion P, as a random variable, has a binomial distribution. When sample size is large and population proportion is not too close to 0 or 1, this distribution can be approximated by a normal distribution: $P \sim N\left(\pi, \frac{\pi(1-\pi)}{n}\right)$. Thus, the two-sided $100(1 - \alpha)\%$ confidence interval for the population proportion is obtained as:

$$p - Z_{\frac{\alpha}{2}} \sqrt{\frac{p(1-p)}{n}} \leq \pi \leq p + Z_{\frac{\alpha}{2}} \sqrt{\frac{p(1-p)}{n}} \tag{A.83}$$

And the upper and lower $100(1 - \alpha)\%$ confidence intervals for π are:

$$\pi \leq p + Z_{\alpha} \sqrt{\frac{p(1-p)}{n}} \tag{A.84}$$

$$p - Z_{\alpha} \sqrt{\frac{p(1-p)}{n}} \leq \pi \tag{A.85}$$

PARAMETER ESTIMATION

Parameter estimation is the process of obtaining an estimated value of a model or distribution parameters using observed data. Financial models often assume that there are structural relationships between two or more variables and such structures usually involve several parameters that should be estimated to properly capture the assumed relationships. Parameter estimation is also used to find estimates of unknown parameters of a random variable's probability distribution. Assume random variables $\{X_1, X_2, \cdots, X_n\}$ are n independent random variables from a probability distribution with m parameters $\theta_1, \theta_2, \cdots, \theta_m$. Also assume that $\{x_1, x_2, \cdots, x_n\}$ is one instance or realization of this random sample. Then $\widehat{\Theta}_i = g_i(X_1, X_2, \cdots, X_n)$ is an *estimator* or *point estimator* for parameter θ_i and $\widehat{\theta}_i = g_i(x_1, x_2, \cdots, x_n)$ is the *estimate* of this parameter based on observed data. Since $X_1, X_2, \cdots, X_n$ are random variables, estimator $\widehat{\Theta}_i$ is a random variable as well but the estimate $\widehat{\theta}_i$ is a fixed number that is obtained from the empirical data. The hat in $\widehat{\Theta}_i$ or $\widehat{\theta}_i$ indicates that it is estimated and not the true value of the parameter.

At a very high level, the statistical estimation method can be classified into two broad methods: Bayesian and classical (frequentist). In this section we review a few classical estimation methods that are commonly used in financial modeling.

Maximum Likelihood Method

The *maximum likelihood estimator (MLE)* is a popular and intuitive approach in the estimation of population distribution parameters. Consider a random sample $\{X_1, X_2, \cdots, X_n\}$ from a probability distribution that has one parameter θ and set $\{x_1, x_2, \cdots, x_n\}$ is an instance of this random sample. The maximum likelihood method is based on finding an estimator $g(x_1, x_2, \cdots, x_n)$ for the parameter of the distribution that maximizes the likelihood of observing $\{x_1, x_2, \cdots, x_n\}$. If $f(x_i; \theta)$ is the probability distribution function of X_i, and since $X_1, X_2, \cdots, X_n$ are independent, the joint probability density (or mass) function of sample observation $X_1, X_2, \cdots, X_n$ is:

$$P(X_1 = x_1, X_2 = x_2, \cdots X_n = x_n) = f(x_1; \theta)f(x_2; \theta) \cdots f(x_n; \theta)$$

In maximum likelihood estimation, this joint probability distribution function is called *likelihood function* $L(\theta)$ and the objective is to find θ such that it maximizes $L(\theta)$. This is done by taking the derivative of $L(\theta)$ with respect to θ, setting it equal to zero, and solving for the parameter:

$$\text{Find } \theta \text{ such that } L(\theta) \text{ is maximized} \tag{A.86}$$

To demonstrate the use of the maximum likelihood method, consider a random variable that can take a value of 1 with probability p and value 0 with probability $1 - p$. This simple discrete distribution with a binary outcome of $\{0, 1\}$ is known as *Bernoulli distribution*. Thus if X has a Bernoulli distribution, its probability mass function has one parameter p:

$$f(x) = \begin{cases} p & if\, x = 1 \\ 1 - p & if\, x = 0 \end{cases}$$

Or equivalently $f(x) = p^x(1-p)^{1-x}$. Expectation of a random variable with a Bernoulli distribution is p and its variance is $p(1-p)$. Bernoulli distribution is a special case of binomial distribution with $n = 1$ (i.e., one trial) where p is the probability of success. To find an estimator for parameter p, assume that random sample $\{X_1, X_2, \cdots, X_n\}$ is from a Bernoulli distribution and $\{x_1, x_2, \cdots, x_n\}$ is an instance of this random sample. The likelihood function is:

$$L(p) = f(x_1; p)f(x_2; p) \cdots f(x_n; p)$$
$$= (p^{x_1}(1-p)^{1-x_1})(p^{x_2}(1-p)^{1-x_2}) \cdots (p^{x_n}(1-p)^{1-x_n})$$

or

$$L(p) = p^{\sum_{i=1}^{n} x_i} (1-p)^{n-\sum_{i=1}^{n} x_i}$$

The value of p that maximizes $L(p)$ is the same value that maximizes its natural logarithm. Therefore, to simplify the calculation we first take the natural logarithm of $L(p)$ as:

$$\ln L(p) = \left(\sum_{i=1}^{n} x_i\right) \ln p + \left(n - \sum_{i=1}^{n} x_i\right) \ln(1-p)$$

By taking the derivative of $\ln L(p)$ with respect to p and setting it equal to zero we have:

$$\frac{\partial \ln L(p)}{\partial p} = \frac{1}{p}\left(\sum_{i=1}^{n} x_i\right) - \frac{1}{1-p}\left(n - \sum_{i=1}^{n} x_i\right) = 0$$

By solving for p we obtain:

$$\hat{p} = \frac{1}{n}\sum_{i=1}^{n} x_i$$

The hat in $\hat{p}$ indicates that this is an estimate and not the true value of the parameter. It is easy to check that this is indeed the value that maximizes the likelihood function by taking the second derivative of the log likelihood function and confirming that it is negative. Therefore, the maximum likelihood estimator of parameter p is the sample mean. To be more specific, the maximum likelihood estimator of the parameter of the Bernoulli distribution is:

$$\hat{P} = \frac{1}{n}\sum_{i=1}^{n} X_i \tag{A.87}$$

To generalize the maximum likelihood estimation method for a distribution with multiple parameters, assume that random sample $\{X_1, X_2, \cdots, X_n\}$ is from a distribution with a probability density (or mass) function that has m parameters: $f(x_i; \theta_1, \theta_2, \cdots, \theta_m)$, and $\{x_1, x_2, \cdots, x_n\}$ is an instance of this random sample. In this case, the likelihood function is:

$$L(\theta_1, \theta_2, \cdots, \theta_m) = \prod_{i=1}^{n} f(x_i; \theta_1, \theta_2, \cdots, \theta_m) \qquad \text{(A.88)}$$

$\widehat{\theta}_j = g_j(x_1, x_2, \cdots, x_n)$ for $j = 1, 2, \cdots, m$ that maximizes $L(\theta_1, \theta_2, \cdots, \theta_m)$ is the maximum likelihood estimator of parameter θ_j. As explained before, to find the value that maximizes $L(\theta_1, \theta_2, \cdots, \theta_m)$ the log likelihood function $\ln L(\theta_1, \theta_2, \cdots, \theta_m)$ is often used.

Consider a random sample $\{X_1, X_2, \cdots, X_n\}$ from the normal distribution that has two parameters: mean μ and variance σ^2. To simplify the notation when taking the derivative of the log likelihood function we use ϑ to show the variance: $\vartheta = \sigma^2$. Assume that $\{x_1, x_2, \cdots, x_n\}$ is an instance of this random sample. Recall that the probability density function of a normal distribution is:

$$f(x_i; \mu, \vartheta) = \frac{1}{\sqrt{2\pi\vartheta}} exp\left(-\frac{(x_i - \mu)^2}{2\vartheta}\right)$$

when $i = 1, 2, \cdots, n, -\infty < x_i < +\infty, -\infty < \mu < +\infty$ and $0 < \vartheta < +\infty$. Based on this, the likelihood function is:

$$L(\mu, \vartheta) = \prod_{i=1}^{n} f(x_i; \mu, \vartheta) = (2\pi)^{-\frac{n}{2}} \vartheta^{-\frac{n}{2}} exp\left(\frac{-\sum_{i=1}^{n}(x_i - \mu)^2}{2\vartheta}\right)$$

and the log likelihood function is:

$$\ln L(\mu, \vartheta) = -\frac{n}{2} \ln 2\pi - \frac{n}{2} \ln \vartheta - \frac{\sum_{i=1}^{n}(x_i - \mu)^2}{2\vartheta} \qquad \text{(A.89)}$$

By taking a partial derivative of this log likelihood function with respect to μ and setting it equal to zero we have:

$$\frac{\partial \ln L(\mu, \vartheta)}{\partial \mu} = -\frac{-2\sum_{i=1}^{n}(x_i - \mu)}{2\vartheta} = 0$$

So:

$$\sum_{i=1}^{n}(x_i - \mu) = \left(\sum_{i=1}^{n} x_i\right) - n\mu = 0$$

Hence:

$$\hat{\mu} = \frac{1}{n} \sum_{i=1}^{n} x_i$$

Hence the maximum likelihood estimator of the normal distribution mean is the sample mean. To obtain the estimator for variance we take a partial derivative of the log likelihood function in Equation (A.89) with respect to ϑ and set it equal to zero:

$$\frac{\partial \ln L(\mu, \vartheta)}{\partial \vartheta} = \left(-\frac{n}{2}\right)(\vartheta^{-1}) - \left(\frac{\sum_{i=1}^{n}(x_i - \mu)^2}{2}\right)(-\vartheta^{-2}) = 0$$

By multiplying both sides of this equation by $2\vartheta^{-2}$ we have:

$$-n\vartheta + \sum_{i=1}^{n}(x_i - \mu)^2 = 0$$

or

$$\vartheta = \frac{1}{n} \sum_{i=1}^{n}(x_i - \mu)^2$$

Therefore, the maximum likelihood estimators of the mean and variance of a normal distribution are obtained as:

$$\hat{\mu} = \overline{X} = \frac{1}{n} \sum_{i=1}^{n} X_i \tag{A.90}$$

$$\hat{\sigma}^2 = \frac{1}{n} \sum_{i=1}^{n} (X_i - \overline{X})^2 \tag{A.91}$$

Recall that sample variance S^2 introduced in Equation (A.73) has $n - 1$ in the denominator but in Equation (A.91) the denominator is n. Thus, while the maximum likelihood estimator of the mean of a normal distribution is the sample mean, the estimator for variance based on the maximum likelihood method is not the sample variance.

A statistical estimator is called *unbiased* if its expectation is equal to the parameter being estimated. For example, the sample mean is an unbiased estimator of the mean of normal distribution, since:

$$E[\overline{X}] = E\left[\frac{1}{n} \sum_{i=1}^{n} X_i\right] = \frac{1}{n} \sum_{i=1}^{n} E[X_i] = \frac{1}{n} \times n\mu = \mu$$

It can be shown that the expectation of the maximum likelihood estimator for the variance of the normal distribution in Equation (A.91) is $\frac{n-1}{n}\sigma^2$, which is not equal to the parameter being estimated, that is, σ^2.[10] Hence the estimator in Equation (A.91) is biased. While generally an unbiased estimator is preferred to a biased estimator, in practice and when an unbiased estimator of a parameter is not available a biased estimator, if exists, is used.

Example

Assume that the daily return of investing in an asset is normally distributed. Table A.4 provides a random sample of 10 daily returns for this asset. Based on this random sample, the maximum likelihood estimates for the mean and variance of the distribution are:

$$\hat{\mu} = \frac{1}{10}(3\% + 2.2\% - 0.4\% - 3\% + 1.5\% + 2.3\% + 1.95\% - 1\%$$

$$(+2.67\% + 1.05\% = 1.03\%$$

$$\hat{\sigma}^2 = \frac{1}{10}((3\% - 1.03\%)^2 + (2.2\% - 1.03\%)^2 + \cdots + (1.67\% - 1.03\%)^2$$

$$+ (1.05\% - 1.03\%)^2) = 0.033\%$$

TABLE A.4 A random sample of daily return of an asset

Observation	Daily Return
1	3.00%
2	2.20%
3	−0.40%
4	−3.00%
5	1.50%
6	2.30%
7	1.95%
8	−1.00%
9	2.67%
10	1.05%

We can estimate the parameters of a multivariate normal distribution using the maximum likelihood estimator following the same approach discussed previously. Recall that a d-dimensional multivariate normal distribution has two parameters in matrix form: μ is the mean vector $(1 \times d)$ and Σ is the variance-covariance matrix $(d \times d)$. Assume that $\{X_1, X_2, \cdots, X_n\}$ is a random sample from a d-dimensional multivariate normal distribution where each variable is a $d \times 1$ vector, and $\{x_1, x_2, \cdots, x_n\}$ is an instance of this random sample. It can be shown that the log likelihood function and estimator of μ and Σ are:

$$\ln L(\mu, \Sigma) = -\frac{nd}{2} \ln(2\pi) - \frac{n}{2} \ln|\Sigma| - \frac{1}{2} \sum_{i=1}^{n} [(x_i - \mu)^T \Sigma^{-1} (x_i - \mu)] \quad \text{(A.92)}$$

$$\hat{\mu} = \overline{X} = \frac{1}{n} \sum_{i=1}^{n} X_i \quad \text{(A.93)}$$

$$\hat{\Sigma} = \frac{1}{n} \sum_{i=1}^{n} (X_i - \overline{X})(X_i - \overline{X})^T \quad \text{(A.94)}$$

where $|\Sigma|$ is the determinant of Σ. For derivation of these equations see Johnson and Wichern (2007) or Flury (1997).

Method of Moments

We introduced the moment of a random variable earlier. For a random variable X and any positive integer k, $E[X^k]$ is the k*th moment of X about zero*, also known as the *raw moment*. The expectation of a random variable is the first raw moment of that random variable. If $E[X] = \mu$, then $E[(X - \mu)^k]$ is the k*th moment of X about mean*, also known as the *central moment*. The variance of a random variable is the second central moment of that random variable. Hence:

$$k\text{th theoretical raw moment} = E[X^k] \quad \text{(A.95)}$$

$$k\text{th theoretical central moment} = E[(X - \mu)^k] \quad \text{(A.96)}$$

Based on the definitions of moments, the kth sample raw and central moments are:

$$k\text{th sample raw moment} = \frac{1}{n} \sum_{i=1}^{n} X_i^k \quad \text{(A.97)}$$

$$k\text{th sample central moment} = \frac{1}{n} \sum_{i=1}^{n} (X_i - \overline{X})^k \quad \text{(A.98)}$$

In parameter estimation based on the *method of moments*, theoretical moments, either raw or central, are derived using the assumed distribution of the random variable and are set equal to the sample moments calculated from the observations. To estimate m parameters, m moments are required to have an adequate number of independent equations.

To demonstrate the use of the method of moments consider random variable X with a normal distribution. Since this distribution has two parameters, we need to consider two moments. The first and second theoretical moments of X around zero are:

$$\text{First theoretical moment} = E[X] = \mu$$

$$\text{Second theoretical moment} = E[X^2] = \sigma^2 + \mu^2$$

where the second moment is obtained using Equation (A.27). If random sample $\{X_1, X_2, \cdots, X_n\}$ is from the same normal distribution, the first and second sample moments around zero are:

$$\text{First sample moment} = \frac{1}{n} \sum_{i=1}^{n} X_i$$

$$\text{Second sample moment} = \frac{1}{n} \sum_{i=1}^{n} X_i^2$$

By setting the theoretical first and second moments equal to their corresponding sample moments we have:

$$\hat{\mu} = \frac{1}{n} \sum_{i=1}^{n} X_i$$

$$\sigma^2 + \mu^2 = \frac{1}{n} \sum_{i=1}^{n} X_i^2$$

The second equation above can be written as:

$$\sigma^2 = \frac{1}{n} \sum_{i=1}^{n} X_i^2 - \overline{X}^2 = \frac{1}{n} \sum_{i=1}^{n} X_i^2 - 2\,\overline{X}\,\overline{X} + \overline{X}^2$$

$$= \frac{1}{n} \sum_{i=1}^{n} X_i^2 - \frac{2}{n} \left(\sum_{i=1}^{n} X_i \right) \overline{X} + \frac{1}{n} n\overline{X}^2 = \frac{1}{n} \sum_{i=1}^{n} (X_i^2 - 2X_i\overline{X} + \overline{X}^2)$$

$$= \frac{1}{n} \sum_{i=1}^{n} (X_i - \overline{X})^2$$

therefore:

$$\hat{\sigma}^2 = \frac{1}{n} \sum_{i=1}^{n} (X_i - \overline{X})^2$$

As shown here, estimators of the mean and variance of the normal distribution based on the method of moments are the same as the ones derived using the maximum likelihood method.

In application of the method of moments, sometimes it is easier to use central moments instead of raw moments. The method of moments is a straightforward parameter estimation tool that is particularly useful when finding a closed-form solution for the maximum likelihood estimator is not possible or is very difficult. However, this approach often produces biased estimators.

Least Squares Method

The *least squares method* is the most popular statistical estimation technique. This method can be used when a structural relationship is assumed between two or more variables and that relationship is parameterized. The relationship between variables or between parameters to be estimated can be linear or nonlinear. Here we discuss the least squares method in the context of a *linear regression model* where the relationship between variables and between parameters is linear. In a simple linear regression model the relationship between two variables is stated as:

$$Y_i = \beta_0 + \beta_1 X_i + \epsilon_i \text{ for } i = 1, 2, \cdots, n \tag{A.99}$$

X_i is called the *predictor* or *independent variable* and Y_i is the *response* or *dependent variable*. This model is first-order since the X_i and Y_i variables are only in their first power. Regression models are often used for forecasting dependent variables based on observations of independent variables. ϵ_i is called an *error term* or *residual term*. It is a random variable with mean 0 and constant variance σ^2, where ϵ_i and ϵ_j for $i \neq j$ are not correlated. To be able to make an inference about parameters and study the appropriateness of the regression model, it is a common practice to assume a normal distribution $N(0, \sigma^2)$ for the error term. Since $E[\epsilon_i] = 0$, $E[Y_i] = \beta_0 + \beta_1 X_i$. This means that for an observed pair (X_i, Y_i) the model prediction or *fitted value* for Y_i is $E[Y_i] = \beta_0 + \beta_1 X_i$. The difference between fitted value $E[Y_i]$ and observed value Y_i is the error term ϵ_i. In the least squares estimation method we intend to find estimates for β_0 and β_1 that minimize the sum of the squares of these errors:

$$\text{Find } \beta_0 \text{ and } \beta_1 \text{ such that } \sum_{i=1}^{n} (Y_i - (\beta_0 + \beta_1 X_i))^2 \text{ is minimized} \tag{A.100}$$

where n as before is the sample size. We can find estimators $\hat{\beta}_0$ and $\hat{\beta}_1$ either by using a numerical search algorithm or by taking a partial derivative of the expression in Equation (A.100) with respect to β_0 and β_1, setting the results equal to zero, and solving for the estimators:

$$\frac{\partial \sum_{i=1}^{n}(Y_i - (\beta_0 + \beta_1 X_i))^2}{\partial \beta_0} = -2\sum_{i=1}^{n}(Y_i - \beta_0 - \beta_1 X_i) = 0$$

$$\frac{\partial \sum_{i=1}^{n}(Y_i - (\beta_0 + \beta_1 X_i))^2}{\partial \beta_1} = -2\sum_{i=1}^{n}X_i(Y_i - \beta_0 - \beta_1 X_i) = 0$$

So we have:

$$\sum_{i=1}^{n} Y_i - n\beta_0 - \beta_1 \sum_{i=1}^{n} X_i = 0$$

$$\sum_{i=1}^{n} X_i Y_i - \beta_0 \sum_{i=1}^{n} X_i - \beta_1 \sum_{i=1}^{n} X_i^2 = 0$$

These two equations are called *normal equations* and by solving them simultaneously for β_0 and β_1 we have:

$$\hat{\beta}_1 = \frac{n\sum_{i=1}^{n} X_i Y_i - \sum_{i=1}^{n} X_i \sum_{i=1}^{n} Y_i}{n\sum_{i=1}^{n} X_i^2 - \left(\sum_{i=1}^{n} X_i\right)^2} \qquad (A.101)$$

$$\hat{\beta}_0 = \frac{\sum_{i=1}^{n} Y_i - \beta_1 \sum_{i=1}^{n} X_i}{n} = \overline{Y} - \hat{\beta}_1 \overline{X} \qquad (A.102)$$

It can be shown that $\hat{\beta}_1$ in Equation (A.101) can also be written as:[11]

$$\hat{\beta}_1 = \frac{\sum_{i=1}^{n}(X_i - \overline{X})(Y_i - \overline{Y})}{\sum_{i=1}^{n}(X_i - \overline{X})^2} \qquad (A.103)$$

Estimators $\hat{\beta}_0$ and $\hat{\beta}_1$ obtained in the preceding equations are unbiased estimators of the parameters of the regression model in Equation (A.99).

Example

Table A.5 presents sales of financial products (Y) and the promotion budget (X) for a sample of 12 branches of a hypothetical bank for a period of one year. A bank analyst believes that the relationship between sales and promotion budget is of the form presented in Equation (A.99). We can use Equations (A.102) and (A.103) to obtain estimates of the parameters of this relationship. Calculation of components of these equations is shown in Table A.5. Using results from Table A.5 we have:

$$\hat{\beta}_1 = \frac{\sum_{i=1}^{12}(X_i - \overline{X})(Y_i - \overline{Y})}{\sum_{i=1}^{12}(X_i - \overline{X})^2} = \frac{1,677,176,375}{417,568,691.67} = 4.016528$$

$$\hat{\beta}_0 = \overline{Y} - \beta_1\overline{X} = 2,588,495.50 - 4.016528 \times 18,085.83 = 2,515,853.26$$

TABLE A.5 Financial products sales and promotion budgets for a sample of 12 branches of a hypothetical bank

Branch	X_i: Promotional Budget ($)	Y_i: Sales ($)	$(X_i - \overline{X})$	$(Y_i - \overline{Y})$	$(X_i - \overline{X})(Y_i - \overline{Y})$	$(X_i - \overline{X})^2$
1	14,030.00	2,574,389.00	−4,055.83	−14,106.50	57,213,612.92	16,449,784.03
2	12,060.00	2,549,446.00	−6,025.83	−39,049.50	235,305,778.75	36,310,667.36
3	26,290.00	2,626,378.00	8,204.17	37,882.50	310,794,343.75	67,308,350.69
4	18,490.00	2,582,421.00	404.17	−6,074.50	−2455110.42	163,350.69
5	20,430.00	2,613,672.00	2,344.17	25,176.50	59,017,912.08	5,495,117.36
6	24,570.00	2,613,797.00	6,484.17	25,301.50	164,059,142.92	42,044,417.36
7	16,340.00	2,599,386.00	−1,745.83	10,890.50	−19,012,997.92	3,047,934.03
8	28,240.00	2,611,430.00	10,154.17	22,934.50	232,880,735.42	103,107,100.69
9	10,100.00	2,560,206.00	−7,985.83	−28,289.50	225,915,232.08	63,773,534.03
10	21,730.00	2,611,472.00	3,644.17	22,976.50	83,730,195.42	13,279,950.69
11	11,550.00	2,559,345.00	−6,535.83	−29,150.50	190,522,809.58	42,717,117.36
12	13,200.00	2,560,004.00	−4,885.83	−28,491.50	139,204,720.42	23,871,367.36
Average:	18,085.83	2,588,495.50			Sum: 1,677,176,375.00	417,568,691.67

Hence the estimated relationship between sales and promotional budget is:

Expected Sales = 2,515,853.26 + 4.016528 × *Promotional Budget* (A.104)

Figure A.7 shows the 12 observations of (promotional budget, sales) pairs along with the fitted line in Equation (A.104). As can be seen from this graph, the fitted line does not necessarily go through all observations; however, by design it minimizes the squares of differences between fitted values $\hat{Y}_i$ and observed values Y_i over all observations. For example, for

(continued)

(*continued*)

branch 7 with the (promotional budget, sales) pair of ($16,340, $2,599,386) the fitted value of sales based on the obtained regression model is:

$$2{,}515{,}853.26 + 4.016528 \times 16{,}340 = 2{,}581{,}483.31$$

And the residual or error for this observation is:

$$2{,}599{,}386 - 2{,}581{,}483.31 = 17{,}902.69$$

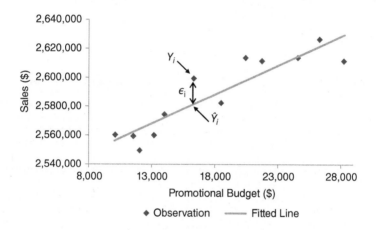

FIGURE A.7 Estimated linear relationship between financial product sales and promotional budget of branches of a bank

It is also helpful to have an estimator for σ^2, the variance of ϵ_i that is also the variance of $\widehat{Y}_i$. This estimator is:

$$s^2 = \frac{\sum_{i=1}^{n}(Y_i - \widehat{Y}_i)^2}{n-2} \tag{A.105}$$

$\sum_{i=1}^{n}(Y_i - \widehat{Y}_i)^2$ in the numerator of Equation (A.105) is called the *error sum of squares*, and since $Y_i - \widehat{Y}_i = \epsilon_i$, it is equal to $\sum_{i=1}^{n}\epsilon_i^2$ and the denominator is the degree of freedom. Estimator s^2 is called the *mean squared error (MSE)* and is an unbiased estimator of σ^2 for the regression model presented in Equation (A.99).

A common way to quantify the linear relationship between the dependent and independent variables in a regression model is to calculate the *coefficient of determination* R^2, defined as:

$$R^2 = \frac{\sum_{i=1}^{n} (\widehat{Y}_i - \overline{Y})^2}{\sum_{i=1}^{n} (Y_i - \overline{Y})^2} = 1 - \frac{\sum_{i=1}^{n} (Y_i - \widehat{Y}_i)^2}{\sum_{i=1}^{n} (Y_i - \overline{Y})^2} \qquad \text{(A.106)}$$

In this equation $\sum_{i=1}^{n} (\widehat{Y}_i - \overline{Y})^2$ is called the *regression sum of squares* and $\sum_{i=1}^{n} (Y_i - \overline{Y})^2$ is called the *total sum of squares*. R^2 is a measurement between zero and one. A larger value for R^2 is an indication that a larger proportion of variation in a dependent variable is explained by the variation of the independent variable, suggesting the existence of a stronger linear relationship between the two. For the sales versus promotional budget example discussed earlier, R^2 is 0.83, supporting the assumption of a linear relationship between the two variables.

We can extend the least squares estimation method to a model with more than two parameters by considering a multiple linear regression model as:

$$Y_i = \beta_0 X_0 + \beta_1 X_{1i} + \beta_2 X_{2i} + \cdots + \beta_m X_{mi} + \epsilon_i \text{ for } i = 1, 2, \cdots, n \quad \text{(A.107)}$$

To make the simple linear regression model in Equation (A.99) a special case of the multiple linear regression model in Equation (A.107), we set $X_0 \equiv 1$, so for $m = 1$ two models are equivalent. In Equation (A.107) there are m independent variables and $m + 1$ parameters to be estimated. Considering a sample size n and using matrix notation, the model implies:

$$\begin{bmatrix} Y_1 \\ Y_2 \\ \vdots \\ Y_n \end{bmatrix} = \begin{bmatrix} 1 & X_{11} & X_{21} & \cdots & X_{m1} \\ 1 & X_{12} & X_{22} & \cdots & X_{m2} \\ \vdots & \vdots & \vdots & \ddots & \vdots \\ 1 & X_{1n} & X_{2n} & \cdots & X_{mn} \end{bmatrix} \begin{bmatrix} \beta_0 \\ \beta_1 \\ \vdots \\ \beta_m \end{bmatrix} + \begin{bmatrix} \epsilon_1 \\ \epsilon_2 \\ \vdots \\ \epsilon_n \end{bmatrix}$$

This can be expressed in a short notation as:

$$Y = X\beta + \epsilon \qquad \text{(A.108)}$$

where:

- Y is an $n \times 1$ vector of observations of the dependent variable:

$$Y = \begin{bmatrix} Y_1 \\ Y_2 \\ \vdots \\ Y_n \end{bmatrix}$$

- X is an $n \times (m+1)$ matrix of observations of independent variables, where X_{ij} refers to observation j of the independent variable i:

$$X = \begin{bmatrix} 1 & X_{11} & X_{21} & \cdots & X_{m1} \\ 1 & X_{12} & X_{22} & \cdots & X_{m2} \\ \vdots & \vdots & \vdots & \ddots & \vdots \\ 1 & X_{1n} & X_{2n} & \cdots & X_{mn} \end{bmatrix}$$

- β is an $(m+1) \times 1$ vector of parameters:

$$\beta = \begin{bmatrix} \beta_0 \\ \beta_1 \\ \beta_2 \\ \vdots \\ \beta_m \end{bmatrix}$$

- ϵ is an $n \times 1$ vector of error terms:

$$\epsilon = \begin{bmatrix} \epsilon_1 \\ \epsilon_2 \\ \vdots \\ \epsilon_n \end{bmatrix}$$

Similar to the simple regression model, the error terms have mean of zero and consonant variance of σ^2, so using matrix notation we have:

$$E[\epsilon] = \begin{bmatrix} 0 \\ 0 \\ \vdots \\ 0 \end{bmatrix} = \mathbf{0}$$

$$\text{Var}[\epsilon] = \begin{bmatrix} \sigma^2 & 0 & \cdots & 0 \\ 0 & \sigma^2 & \cdots & 0 \\ \vdots & \vdots & \ddots & \vdots \\ 0 & 0 & \cdots & \sigma^2 \end{bmatrix} = \sigma^2 I$$

Using a similar approach as explained previously and matrix algebra, the normal equation for the multiple regression model in Equation (A.108) is derived as:

$$X^T X \beta = X^T Y \tag{A.109}$$

This leads to the following solution for parameter estimators:

$$\beta = (X^T X)^{-1} X^T Y \tag{A.110}$$

Example

Assume that six observations of dependent variable Y and two independent variables X_1 and X_2 are as follows:

Y	X₁	X₂
1,060	0.040	5
470	0.052	9.5
680	0.045	7
950	0.070	8.3
895	0.029	9
580	0.038	11

We assume a linear relationship between these variables as:

$$Y_i = \beta_0 X_0 + \beta_1 X_{1_i} + \beta_2 X_{2_i} + \epsilon_i$$

where $X_0 \equiv 1$. To find estimates of parameters β_0, β_1 and β_2 we can define the following matrices:

$$Y = \begin{bmatrix} 1,060 \\ 470 \\ 680 \\ 950 \\ 895 \\ 580 \end{bmatrix} \quad X = \begin{bmatrix} 1 & 0.040 & 5 \\ 1 & 0.052 & 9.5 \\ 1 & 0.045 & 7 \\ 1 & 0.070 & 8.3 \\ 1 & 0.029 & 9 \\ 1 & 0.038 & 11 \end{bmatrix} \quad \beta = \begin{bmatrix} \beta_0 \\ \beta_1 \\ \beta_2 \end{bmatrix}$$

Using matrix algebra X^T, $X^T X$, and $(X^T X)^{-1}$ are derived as:

$$X^T = \begin{bmatrix} 1 & 1 & 1 & 1 & 1 & 1 \\ 0.040 & 0.052 & 0.045 & 0.070 & 0.029 & 0.038 \\ 5 & 9.5 & 7 & 8.3 & 9 & 11 \end{bmatrix}$$

$$X^T X = \begin{bmatrix} 6.0000 & 0.2740 & 49.8000 \\ 0.2740 & 0.0135 & 2.2690 \\ 49.8000 & 2.2690 & 435.1400 \end{bmatrix}$$

$$(X^T X)^{-1} = \begin{bmatrix} 5.5967 & -47.6421 & -0.3921 \\ -47.6421 & 999.9070 & 0.2385 \\ -0.3921 & 0.2385 & 0.0459 \end{bmatrix}$$

(*continued*)

(continued)

Finally, using Equation (A.110) we have:

$$\beta = (X^T X)^{-1} X^T Y = \begin{bmatrix} 1{,}396.9921 \\ -117.7230 \\ -74.5923 \end{bmatrix}$$

Hence based on this sample, the least squares estimates of β_0, β_1, and β_2 are 1,396.9921, –117.7230, and –74.5923 respectively. In practice, the sample size should be large enough to obtain reasonable estimates of parameters. For large sample sizes the calculation demonstrated here becomes computationally challenging and often statistical software packages such as SAS® or SPSS® are used for parameter estimation. Microsoft Excel also has regression analysis functionality that can be used for this purpose.

PRINCIPAL COMPONENT ANALYSIS

Principal component analysis (PCA) is a statistical method to transform observations from a set of random variables into a set of constructed variables that capture most of the variability in the original variables. In applied statistics, principal component analysis is widely used as a variable reduction technique. In such applications the original variables are replaced by a few newly constructed variables and although the number of new variables is less than the original variables, they represent a large portion of the variability in the original variables. Assume that we have a series of observed values for 20 variables and we are planning to use them in a regression model to predict values of an independent variable. If it is believed that some of these variables are redundant and do not contain new information, instead of using the original 20 variables as predictors we can perform a principal component analysis and choose a subset of the principal components to use in the model.

Principal components are linear combinations of the original variables that are constructed in a particular way. Assume that we have n variables $X_1, X_2, \cdots, X_n$. The ith principal component of this set is defined as:

$$P_i = c_{i1} X_1 + c_{i2} X_2 + \cdots + c_{in} X_n \quad i = 1, \cdots, n \qquad (A.111)$$

For n original variables, n principal components can be constructed. However, usually only the first few principal components are kept and used. The coefficients c_i in the Equation (A.111) are elements of the eigenvectors of the covariance matrix of the original variables.

Eigenvalue and Eigenvector

Consider $n \times n$ square matrix A. If I is the $n \times n$ identity matrix, $\lambda_1, \lambda_2, \cdots, \lambda_n$ are eigenvalues of A if they satisfy $|A - \lambda I| = 0$. For each eigenvalue λ, if a non-zero vector v satisfies $Av = \lambda v$, then v is an eigenvector of A associated with eigenvalue λ (Johnson and Wichern 2007).

Assume that the variance-covariance matrix of the original variables is Σ and $\lambda_1, \lambda_2, \cdots, \lambda_n$ are eigenvalues of Σ where $\lambda_1 \geq \lambda_2 \geq \cdots, \lambda_n \geq 0$. If $v_1, v_2, \cdots, v_n$ are the associated eigenvectors to $\lambda_1, \lambda_2, \cdots, \lambda_n$ respectively, elements of v_1 are the coefficients of the first principal component, and so on. We have:

$$P_1 = c_{11}X_1 + c_{12}X_2 + \cdots + c_{1n}X_n$$
$$P_2 = c_{21}X_1 + c_{22}X_2 + \cdots + c_{2n}X_n$$
$$\vdots$$
$$P_n = c_{n1}X_1 + c_{n2}X_2 + \cdots + c_{nn}X_n$$

(A.112)

When principal components are constructed as shown here, the variance of the principal component i is equal to the eigenvalue λ_i and the portion of variability of the original variables that principal component i explains is:

$$\frac{\lambda_i}{\lambda_1 + \lambda_2 + \cdots + \lambda_n}$$

The first principal component is associated with the largest eigenvalue λ_1. It explains the largest amount of variability in the original variables. The second principal component that is associated with the second largest eigenvalue λ_2 explains the largest amount of variability in the original variables that is not explained by the first principal component, and so on. Each subsequent principal component contributes less in explanation of variability in the original variables and for this reason usually only the first few principal components are kept and used, and the rest are ignored.

One important characteristic of the *orthogonal* principal components that are derived in this way is that they are not correlated. Each principal component is uncorrelated with all preceding principal components. This is a desirable feature when using principal components as predictors in a regression model. Geometrically, the principal component analysis finds a new coordinate system that is obtained from rotating the original axes so that the new axes represent the direction of the maximum variability (Figure A.8).

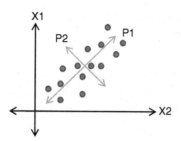

FIGURE A.8 Principal components

Once the principal components are constructed, the observed original variables are used to compute new principal component observations, which are called *scores*. If out of n principal components m are kept, the principal component scores for observation j are calculated as:

$$p_{1j} = c_{11}x_{1j} + c_{12}x_{2j} + \cdots + c_{1n}x_{nj}$$

$$p_{2j} = c_{21}x_{1j} + c_{22}x_{2j} + \cdots + c_{2n}x_{nj}$$

$$\vdots$$

$$p_{mj} = c_{m1}x_{1j} + c_{m2}x_{2j} + \cdots + c_{mn}x_{nj}$$

$$(A.113)$$

To avoid dealing with differences in scale of the original variables, it is a common practice to standardize them (zero mean and unit variance). Therefore the total variance of the original variables is simply equal to the number of variables and the covariance matrix of those variables becomes the correlation matrix. In this case the summation of all eigenvalues, which is equal to the total variance, is also equal to the number of the original variables.

Many statistical software packages, such as SAS, have built-in procedures that can calculate eigenvalues and eigenvectors and perform principal component analysis. To demonstrate the concept discussed earlier, here we use SAS to perform a principal component analysis on the U.S. Treasury yield curve and explain outputs produced by the software. Assume that we are planning to use historical U.S. Treasury yields in a predictive model to forecast risk spreads for some other financial products. Instead of using Treasury yields with differ-ent terms we can perform a PCA and find the principal components of the curve to use in the model. Table A.6 shows a partial view of the U.S. Trea-sury yields we used as the original variables. There are eight original variables considered. They are yields with 6-month, 1-year, 2-year, 3-year, 5-year, 7-year,

TABLE A.6   A partial view of U.S. Treasury yields used in PCA analysis

Date	Tsy6M	Tsy1Y	Tsy2Y	Tsy3Y	Tsy5Y	Tsy7Y	Tsy10Y	Tsy30Y
3/2/2009	0.45	0.67	0.89	1.28	1.86	2.54	2.91	3.64
3/3/2009	0.44	0.68	0.91	1.31	1.87	2.58	2.93	3.67
3/4/2009	0.44	0.71	0.97	1.4	1.97	2.67	3.01	3.69
3/5/2009	0.4	0.66	0.9	1.3	1.82	2.49	2.83	3.51
3/6/2009	0.39	0.67	0.91	1.34	1.83	2.49	2.83	3.5
3/9/2009	0.47	0.69	0.96	1.38	1.9	2.53	2.89	3.59
...	...	...	...	...	...	...	...	...
5/26/2015	0.09	0.24	0.64	0.99	1.54	1.9	2.14	2.89
5/27/2015	0.09	0.27	0.64	1	1.53	1.9	2.14	2.88
5/28/2015	0.08	0.26	0.62	0.97	1.51	1.89	2.13	2.89
5/29/2015	0.06	0.26	0.61	0.94	1.49	1.86	2.12	2.88

Source: U.S. Department of Treasury website (https://www.treasury.gov/resource-center/data-chart-center/interest-rates).

10-year, and 30-year terms. These yields are collected daily from March 2009 to May 2015.

In SAS we can use PRINCOMP or FACTOR procedures to perform a principal component analysis. List A.2 presents a sample SAS code using PRINCOMP procedure to extract principal components of the Treasury yield curve.

LIST 2:   **A sample SAS code to extract principal components of the Treasury yields**

```
proc princomp data=tsy_y out=tsyprinc outstat=tsypcstat;
        var Tsy6M Tsy1Y Tsy2Y Tsy3Y Tsy5Y Tsy7Y Tsy10Y Tsy30Y;
run;
```

In this code:

- *tsy_y* is the name of the input SAS dataset that holds the Treasury yields data.
- *tsypcstat* is the name of the output SAS dataset that contains basic statistics (mean and standard deviation) of the original variables, number of observations, correlation matrix, eigenvalues, and eigenvectors.
- *tsyprinc* is the name of the output SAS dataset that contains the original variables and also the computed principal component scores for all observations.
- The *var* statement indicates which variables from the input dataset are to be used for the principal component analysis.

■ Option *std* (not used in the code) can be used to indicate that scores produced in the output file are to be standardized.

■ Option *N* (not used in the code) can be used to indicate how many principal components are to be computed.

Output of this SAS code includes the correlation matrix of the original variables as presented in Table A.7. From this table it is clear that there is a significant correlation between yields at the short end of the curve (e.g., the correlation coefficient between the 6-month Treasury and 1-year Treasury is 0.9279). Similarly, yields at the long end of the curve are also significantly correlated (e.g., the correlation coefficient between the 30-year Treasury and 10-year Treasury is 0.9553).

Output of the SAS PRINCOMP procedure also includes principal components (eigenvectors), the associated eigenvalues, and the proportion of the variability each principal component explains. These are shown in Tables A.8

TABLE A.7 Correlation of Treasury yields

	Tsy6M	Tsy1Y	Tsy2Y	Tsy3Y	Tsy5Y	Tsy7Y	Tsy10Y	Tsy30Y
Tsy6M	1	0.9279	0.6898	0.5611	0.4579	0.4714	0.4765	0.4703
Tsy1Y	0.9279	1	0.8644	0.7572	0.649	0.6413	0.6099	0.5414
Tsy2Y	0.6898	0.8644	1	0.9747	0.9097	0.8751	0.8045	0.6594
Tsy3Y	0.5611	0.7572	0.9747	1	0.9671	0.9302	0.8529	0.6874
Tsy5Y	0.4579	0.649	0.9097	0.9671	1	0.9887	0.9411	0.8063
Tsy7Y	0.4714	0.6413	0.8751	0.9302	0.9887	1	0.9796	0.8798
Tsy10Y	0.4765	0.6099	0.8045	0.8529	0.9411	0.9796	1	0.9553
Tsy30Y	0.4703	0.5414	0.6594	0.6874	0.8063	0.8798	0.9553	1

TABLE A.8 Principal components of Treasury yields (eigenvectors)

	Prin1	Prin2	Prin3	Prin4	Prin5	Prin6	Prin7	Prin8
Tsy6M	0.2708	0.6497	0.3421	0.6050	0.1402	−0.0413	0.0074	−0.0045
Tsy1Y	0.3261	0.5246	0.0158	−0.5957	−0.4936	0.1240	0.0530	0.0390
Tsy2Y	0.3767	0.1395	−0.3723	−0.2807	0.5943	−0.5176	−0.0062	0.0109
Tsy3Y	0.3767	−0.0361	−0.4446	0.1335	0.1667	0.7036	−0.3058	−0.1582
Tsy5Y	0.3778	−0.2298	−0.2397	0.2576	−0.2026	0.0163	0.6186	0.5066
Tsy7Y	0.3799	−0.2579	−0.0308	0.1839	−0.3769	−0.3192	0.0523	−0.7126
Tsy10Y	0.3709	−0.2863	0.2549	0.0375	−0.1846	−0.2057	−0.6658	0.4409
Tsy30Y	0.3346	−0.2839	0.6504	−0.2843	0.3722	0.2750	0.2737	−0.1203

TABLE A.9 Proportion of variation explained by each principal component of Treasury yields

#	Eigenvalue	Difference	Proportion	Cumulative
1	6.3918	5.2901	0.7990	0.799
2	1.1016	0.6529	0.1377	0.9367
3	0.4488	0.4120	0.0561	0.9928
4	0.0368	0.0208	0.0046	0.9974
5	0.0160	0.0128	0.0020	0.9994
6	0.0032	0.0019	0.0004	0.9998
7	0.0014	0.0009	0.0002	0.9999
8	0.0004		0.0001	1

and A.9. Since there are 8 original variables, 8 principal components are constructed and total variance is equal to 8. As mentioned earlier, after standardizing the original variables, total variance is equal to the number of original variables. The first principal component's eigenvalue is 6.3918, that is, it explains 6.3918 of the total variance of 8, hence it represents 79.90% of the total variability in the original variables. The second principal component explains a much lower portion of the variability: 1.1016 out of 8, which is about 13.77% of the total variance. The first two principal components together explain about 93.67% of the total variance in the original variables. Since these two components together contain a significant portion of the variability in the original variables, we can keep these two principal components and discard the rest. While the interpretation of the principal components is subjective and no exact interpretation method is available, broadly speaking, the first principal component of the Treasury yield curve developed here seems to represent the level of the curve in general and the second component appears to represent the slope of the curve. Eigenvectors produced by the SAS PRINCOMP procedure have unit length. The members of these eigenvectors are coefficients c_{ij} in Equations (A.112) and (A.113) that are used to compute the principal component scores.

To understand how principal component scores are calculated, consider the scoring of the first two principal components for a date with the following yields (observation j):

Tsy6M	Tsy1Y	Tsy2Y	Tsy3Y	Tsy5Y	Tsy7Y	Tsy10Y	Tsy30Y
0.4114	0.6417	0.8671	1.2399	1.8158	2.4952	2.8624	3.6106

Since we did not include the *std* option in SAS code, the produced scores have a variance equal to the eigenvalue of each component and are not standardized in the output dataset. We can standardize these scores. From Table A.8, coefficients c_{ij} for the first principal component are:

$$c_{11} = 0.2708 \quad c_{12} = 0.3261 \quad c_{13} = 0.3767 \quad c_{14} = 0.3767$$

$$c_{15} = 0.3778 \quad c_{16} = 0.3799 \quad c_{17} = 0.3709 \quad c_{18} = 0.3346$$

To standardize observations of an original variable we can deduct the mean of the variable from each observation value and divide the result by the standard deviation of the variable. For example, the mean and the standard deviation of the first variable (Tsy6M) from the SAS output are 0.1244 and 0.0772, respectively. Therefore, the standardized value of Tsy6M for observation j selected above is calculated as:

$$\frac{0.4114 - 0.1244}{0.0772} = 3.7190$$

Standardized values for the other seven variables for observation j are obtained similarly as 3.5928, 1.3762, 1.0057, 0.5238, 0.6242, 0.4029, and 0.0241. From Equation (A.113) the first principal component standardized score for observation j is computed as:

$$p_{1j} = c_{11}x_{1j} + c_{12}x_{2j} + c_{13}x_{3j} + c_{14}x_{4j} + c_{15}x_{5j} + c_{16}x_{6j} + c_{17}x_{7j} + c_{18}x_{8j}$$

$$= 0.2708 \times 3.7190 + 0.3261 \times 3.5928 + 0.3767 \times 1.3762$$

$$+ 0.3767 \times 1.0057 + 0.3778 \times 0.5238 + 0.3799 \times 0.6242$$

$$+ 0.3709 \times 0.4029 + 0.3346 \times 0.0241 = 3.6685$$

The score for the second principal component is calculated similarly, using members of the eigenvector for that component. From Table A.8 we have:

$$c_{21} = 0.6497 \quad c_{22} = 0.5246 \quad c_{23} = 0.1395 \quad c_{24} = -0.0361$$

$$c_{25} = -0.2298 \quad c_{26} = -0.2579 \quad c_{27} = -0.2863 \quad c_{28} = -0.2839$$

Using these eigenvector members and the standardized values of observation j, the standardized score for the second component is calculated as 4.0533. Scores for other observations and other components are calculated similarly.

Inclusion of the *std* option in SAS code of the PRINCOMP procedure would result in standardization of the produced scores in the *tsyprinc* output dataset. We can also use the FACTOR procedure in SAS to perform a principal component analysis. The FACTOR procedure by default produces scores that are standardized.

STOCHASTIC PROCESS

A *stochastic process* specifies the evolution of a process with a probabilistic nature through time. Since the state of the variable at different times is random, a stochastic process can be defined as a collection of random variables. Set $\{X(t), t \in A\}$ is a stochastic process where for each $t \in A$, $X(t)$ is a random variable representing the state of the process at time t. If set A is countable, stochastic process $X(t)$ is a *discrete-time process* and if A is an interval of continuous time, $X(t)$ is a *continuous-time process*. For example, interest rate can be presented as a stochastic process as the rate changes over time and at any time it can be represented by a random variable. The set of possible values that a random variable in a stochastic process can take is its state space. For example, consider a discrete-time stochastic process representing the default status of a bond issuer at the beginning of each trading day. Each day, that status can be represented by a random variable that can have either "defaulted" or "not defaulted" values. This set is the state space of the process.

A *Markov stochastic process* is a special type of stochastic process where only the current state of the variable is important in determining its future states and the path the variable took in the past to get to the current state is irrelevant in determining its future states. Stock price is usually assumed to follow a Markov process. A *Wiener process* or *Brownian motion*[12] $W(t)$ is a Markov stochastic process where the change in the variable's value over a short period of time Δt is $\sqrt{\Delta t}\,\epsilon$ where ϵ is a random variable with the standard normal distribution:

$$\Delta W = \sqrt{\Delta t}\,\epsilon$$

The ΔW for any short intervals of time Δt are independent. ΔW is also normally distributed with a mean of zero and a standard deviation of $\sqrt{\Delta t}$. For a limiting case when $\Delta t \to 0$ we use dW to represent a Wiener process:

$$dW(t) = \sqrt{dt}\,\epsilon \tag{A.114}$$

where (t) in $dW(t)$ is an indication that dW is a function of time. Since the mean of dW is zero, the expected change in the value of variable in a short interval of time dt is zero. To generalize the Wiener process we can add a drift rate μ and variance rate σ^2 (or standard deviation rate σ) to obtain a generalized Wiener process as follows:

$$dX(t) = \mu\, dt + \sigma\, dW(t) = \mu\, dt + \sigma\sqrt{dt}\,\epsilon \tag{A.115}$$

where μ and σ are constants. The generalized Wiener process dX has a normal distribution with mean $\mu\, dt$ and a standard deviation of $\sigma\sqrt{dt}$. In a short interval of time dt the value of a variable that follows the generalized Wiener process changes by $\mu\, dt$ plus a noise with a value equal to $\sigma\sqrt{dt}\,\epsilon$ where ϵ is a random variable with the standard normal distribution.

In a generalized Wiener process if drift rate and standard deviation rate are functions of X and t, then the stochastic process is known as an *Itô process*, defined as follows:

$$dX(t) = g(X, t)\, dt + h(X, t)\, dW(t) \tag{A.116}$$

A useful tool in stochastic calculus, known as *Itô's lemma*, first introduced by mathematician Itô (1951), states that when X follows the Itô process as defined in Equation (A.116), any function F of X and t, follows an Itô process as:

$$dF = \left(\frac{\partial F}{\partial X} g + \frac{\partial F}{\partial t} + \frac{1}{2} \frac{\partial^2 F}{\partial X^2} h^2 \right) dt + \frac{\partial F}{\partial X} h\, dW(t) \tag{A.117}$$

We can use Itô's lemma to determine the stochastic process of a function of another process.

To demonstrate the use of Itô's lemma consider the stock price of a market-traded company presented by random variable S. The common approach in modeling the stochastic process of a stock price is to assume that the percentage of change in stock price in a short period of time, that is, $\frac{dS(t)}{S}$, follows a generalized Wiener process similar to Equation (A.115). So:

$$\frac{dS(t)}{S} = \mu\, dt + \sigma\, dW(t) \tag{A.118}$$

A generalized Wiener process with this form is known as geometric Brownian motion. Equivalently we can write this process as:

$$dS(t) = \mu S\, dt + \sigma S\, dW(t) \tag{A.119}$$

By comparing Equations (A.119) and (A.116) it is clear that this is an Itô process where the drift rate is $g(S, t) = \mu S$ and the standard deviation rate is $h(S, t) = \sigma S$.

Consider another process defined as natural logarithm of stock price. Using Itô's lemma the process for $F = \ln S$ is obtained as follows:

$$\frac{\partial F}{\partial S} = \frac{1}{S} \qquad \frac{\partial F}{\partial t} = 0 \qquad \frac{\partial^2 F}{\partial S^2} = -\frac{1}{S^2}$$

By placing these in Equation (A.117) we have:

$$dF = \left(\frac{1}{S}(\mu S) + 0 + \frac{1}{2} \left(-\frac{1}{S^2} \right)(\sigma S)^2 \right) dt + \frac{1}{S}(\sigma S) \, dW(t)$$

or

$$d \ln S(t) = \left(\mu - \frac{1}{2}\sigma^2 \right) dt + \sigma \, dW(t) \qquad \text{(A.120)}$$

Since μ and σ are constant, this process is also a generalized Wiener process. Hence $d \ln S(t)$ has a normal distribution with mean $\left(\mu - \frac{1}{2}\sigma^2 \right) dt$, and a standard deviation of $\sigma\sqrt{dt}$. We have used this result in the valuation of option contracts in Chapter 4.

NOTES

1. Microsoft Excel function PERCENTILE.EXC uses this method.
2. Microsoft Excel function PERCENTILE.INC uses this method.
3. We can obtain a probability of $Z \leq -1.45$ using the Microsoft Excel normal probability function: NORM.DIST(–1.45,0,1,TRUE).
4. A matrix A is positive definite when for any non-zero $x \in \mathbb{R}^d$ we have $xA \, x^T > 0$. A is positive semidefinite when $xA \, x^T \geq 0$.
5. Here we used capital notation $\overline{X}$ to indicate that the sample mean itself is a random variable.
6. Also known as *student's t*-distribution.
7. Gamma function for a number with a positive real part is defined as:

$$\Gamma(x) = \int_0^\infty y^{x-1} e^{-y} dy$$

For a positive integer number, gamma function is a variation of the factorial:

$$\Gamma(x) = (x - 1)!$$

Specifically, we have: $\Gamma(1/2) = \sqrt{\pi}, \Gamma(1) = 1, \Gamma(x + 1) = x\Gamma(x) \quad x > 0$

8. We can use Microsoft Excel function ABS(NORM.S.INV($\frac{\alpha}{2}$)) to obtain an absolute value of $Z_{\frac{\alpha}{2}}$.
9. We can use Microsoft Excel function ABS(T.INV($\frac{\alpha}{2}$, $n - 1$)) to obtain an absolute value of $t_{\frac{\alpha}{2},n-1}$.

10. The expectation of the maximum likelihood estimator for the variance of a normal distribution is:

$$E[\hat{\sigma}^2] = E\left[\frac{1}{n}\sum_{i=1}^{n}(X_i - \overline{X})^2\right] = E\left[\frac{1}{n}\sum_{i=1}^{n}(X_i^2 - 2X_i\overline{X} + \overline{X}^2)\right]$$

$$= E\left[\frac{1}{n}\sum_{i=1}^{n}X_i^2 - \frac{2}{n}\left(\sum_{i=1}^{n}X_i\right)\overline{X} + \frac{1}{n}n\overline{X}^2\right] = E\left[\frac{1}{n}\sum_{i=1}^{n}X_i^2 - 2\overline{X}\,\overline{X} + \overline{X}^2\right]$$

$$= E\left[\frac{1}{n}\sum_{i=1}^{n}X_i^2 - \overline{X}^2\right] = \frac{1}{n}\left(\sum_{i=1}^{n}E[X_i^2]\right) - E[\overline{X}^2]$$

In this expression we can replace $E[\overline{X}^2]$ and $E[X_i^2]$ with their equivalents as follows:

- From an earlier discussion we know that the distribution of a sample mean is normal with mean μ and variance $\frac{\sigma^2}{n}$, so $\mathrm{Var}[\overline{X}] = \frac{\sigma^2}{n}$. From Equation (A.27) we have: $\mathrm{Var}[\overline{X}] = E[\overline{X}^2] - (E[\overline{X}])^2$. So $E[\overline{X}^2] - (E[\overline{X}])^2 = \frac{\sigma^2}{n}$ or $E[\overline{X}^2] = \frac{\sigma^2}{n} + \mu^2$.
- From Equation (A.27) we have: $\mathrm{Var}[X_i] = E[X_i^2] - (E[X_i])^2$ or $E[X_i^2] = \sigma^2 + \mu^2$.

$$E[\hat{\sigma}^2] = \frac{1}{n}\sum_{i=1}^{n}(\sigma^2 + \mu^2) - \left(\frac{\sigma^2}{n} + \mu^2\right) = \frac{1}{n}(n\sigma^2 + n\mu^2) - \left(\frac{\sigma^2}{n} + \mu^2\right) = \frac{(n-1)}{n}\sigma^2$$

11. The numerator of Equation (A.101) can be written as:

$$n\left[\sum_{i=1}^{n}X_iY_i - \frac{\sum_{i=1}^{n}X_i\sum_{i=1}^{n}Y_i}{n}\right]$$

$$= n\left[\sum_{i=1}^{n}X_iY_i - \frac{\sum_{i=1}^{n}X_i\sum_{i=1}^{n}Y_i}{n} - \frac{\sum_{i=1}^{n}X_i\sum_{i=1}^{n}Y_i}{n} + \frac{n\left(\sum_{i=1}^{n}X_i\sum_{i=1}^{n}Y_i\right)}{n^2}\right]$$

$$= n\left[\sum_{i=1}^{n}X_iY_i - \overline{X}\sum_{i=1}^{n}Y_i - \overline{Y}\sum_{i=1}^{n}X_i + n\overline{XY}\right]$$

$$= n\sum_{i=1}^{n}(X_i - \overline{X})(Y_i - \overline{Y})$$

Similarly, the denominator of Equation (A.101) can be written as:

$$n\sum_{i=1}^{n} X_i^2 - 2\left(\sum_{i=1}^{n} X_i\right)^2 + \left(\sum_{i=1}^{n} X_i\right)^2$$

$$= n\left[\sum_{i=1}^{n} X_i^2 - 2\frac{\sum_{i=1}^{n} X_i \times \sum_{i=1}^{n} X_i}{n} + n\frac{\sum_{i=1}^{n} X_i \times \sum_{i=1}^{n} X_i}{n \times n}\right]$$

$$= n\left[\sum_{i=1}^{n} X_i^2 - 2\overline{X}\sum_{i=1}^{n} X_i + n\overline{X}^2\right] = n\sum_{i=1}^{n} (X_i - \overline{X})^2$$

From these two equations, the result in Equation (A.103) is obtained.
12. After English scientist Robert Brown.

BIBLIOGRAPHY

DeGroot, Morris H. *Probability and Statistics*, 2nd ed. Addison-Wesley, 1989.

Flury, Bernard. *A First Course in Multivariate Statistics*. Springer, 1997.

Golub, Gene H., and Charles F. Van Loan. *Matrix Computations*, 3rd ed. Johns Hopkins University Press, 1996.

Hyndman, Rob J., and Yanan Fan. "Sample Quantiles in Statistical Packages." *The American Statistician* 50, no. 4 (1996): 361–365.

Johnson, Richard A., and Dean W. Wichern. *Applied Multivariate Statistical Analysis*, 6th ed. Pearson Education, 2007.

Montgomery, Douglas C. *Introduction to Statistical Quality Control*, 4th ed. John Wiley & Sons, 2001.

Ross, Sheldon M. *Introduction to Probability Models*, 7th ed. Academic Press, 2000.

Index

1003